Cover Image:
North American, Northwest Coast Indians, A Beaver Dancing Apron (detail), Tlingit, Chilkat Technique.

Catalogue No. 224417, Department of Anthropology, Smithsonian Institution

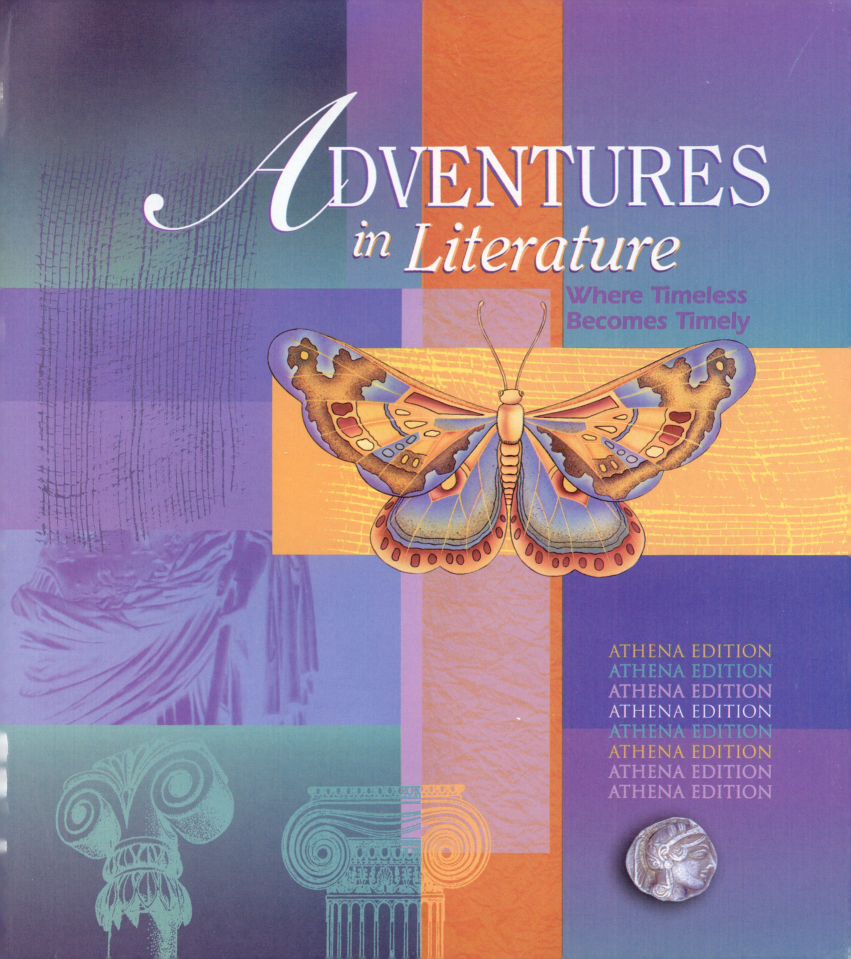

Adventures in Literature

Where Timeless Becomes Timely

ATHENA EDITION
ATHENA EDITION
ATHENA EDITION
ATHENA EDITION
ATHENA EDITION
ATHENA EDITION
ATHENA EDITION
ATHENA EDITION

CLASSIC TALES AND

Classic literature is timeless and timely—
forever lifting time-bound travelers
beyond the boundaries of their ages
with supreme grace and beauty.

For nearly 70 years,
Adventures in Literature
has helped teachers to bring about
this transformation in their classrooms.

LITERATURE SOARS TO NEW HEIGHTS

Our Athena Edition ©1996, for grades 6 through 12,
expands upon the traditional flight of the imagination
and travels along some new and exciting paths.

You'll find

- Time-honored classics you love to teach and new
  selections to further enlighten and engage students

- Cross-cultural connections to elevate student
  awareness of literature's global reach

- Interdisciplinary bridges that make selections
  more relevant to students

- Stimulating activities to develop and improve
  students' writing skills

- Special critical-reading and thinking features to
  enhance students' literary insight

DVE

NEW ADVENTURES

*T*hese well-organized support materials not only meet your students' needs, but also will save you valuable lesson planning time by enhancing students' learning experiences, integrating language arts skills, and offering multiple assessment options.

TIMELY MATERIALS FOR TODAY'S CLASSROOM

Pupil's Edition

Annotated Teacher's Edition

Teaching Resources with Organizer

- Teaching Resources Booklets
  - Teacher's Notes and Answer Keys
  - Reading Checks
  - Reading Focus Worksheets (Grade 6)
  - Study Guides
  - Language Skills Worksheets
  - Building Vocabulary Worksheets
  - Selection Vocabulary Tests
  - Selection Tests
  - Mastery Tests
  - Analogy Lessons
  - Analogy Tests
  - Revision Worksheets (Grade 6); Composition Tests (Grades 7-12)
- Portfolio Assessment and Professional Support Materials
- Teaching Resource Organizer

Test Generator

- IBM® PC and Compatibles
- Macintosh® Computers

Audiovisual Resources Binder

- Fine Art and Instructional Transparencies with Teacher's Notes and Blackline Masters
- Many Voices: Selection Audiocassettes with Teacher's Notes

ANNOTATED TEACHER'S EDITION

Adventures
for Readers
BOOK TWO

A T H E N A   E D I T I O N

HOLT, RINEHART AND WINSTON
Harcourt Brace & Company

Austin • **New York** • Orlando • Atlanta • San Francisco • Boston • Dallas • Toronto • London

For permission to reprint copyrighted material, grateful acknowledgment is made to the following sources:

Estate of Gerald Carson: From abridgement of "The Glorious Bird" by Gerald Carson from *Natural History,* vol. 88, no. 6, June-July 1979.

Arthur Gordon: From "The Sea Devil" by Arthur Gordon. Copyright © 1983 by Arthur Gordon.

Little, Brown and Company: From "The Panther" and from "The Rhinoceros" from *Verses from 1929 On* by Ogden Nash. Copyright 1933, 1940, 1942 by Ogden Nash. "The Panther" first appeared in *The New Yorker.* "The Rhinoceros" first appeared in *The Saturday Evening Post.*

Liveright Publishing Corporation: From "old age sticks" from *Complete Poems, 1904-1962* by E. E. Cummings, edited by George J. Firmage. Copyright © 1958, 1986, 1991 by the Trustees for the E. E. Cummings Trust.

Harold Matson Company, Inc.: From "Top Man" by James Ramsey Ullman. Copyright © 1940 and renewed © 1968 by James Ramsey Ullman.

Ian Serraillier: From *Beowulf the Warrior* by Ian Serraillier. Copyright © by Ian Serraillier and Oxford University Press, England.

The Literary Estate of May Swenson: From "Southbound on the Freeway" by May Swenson. Copyright © 1963 by May Swenson; copyright renewed © 1991 by the Estate of May Swenson. First appeared in *The New Yorker.*

University of Notre Dame Press: From *Barrio Boy* by Ernesto Galarza. Copyright © 1971 by the University of Notre Dame Press.

Printed in the United States of America

ISBN 0-03-098631-1

1 2 3 4 5   041   97 96 95 94

Critical Readers AND Contributors

H. Edward Deluzain
A. Crawford Mosley High School
Panama City, Florida

Bob Emerson
Westwood Middle School
Blaine, Minnesota

Beverly Grossman
Austin, Texas

Annie Hartnett
Austin, Texas

Theresa Holloway
George Washington Intermediate
School
Honolulu, Hawaii

Carolee Lanier
Rockville, Maryland

Emily Licate
West Junior High School
Ashtabula, Ohio

Suzanne R. Montgomery
Sycamore Junior High School
Cincinnati, Ohio

Nancy Nowlin
Austin, Texas

Barbara Scroggie
Austin, Texas

Kathy Thompson
Kepner Middle School
Denver, Colorado

Donna Townsend
Austin, Texas

Trudy Williams
Austin, Texas

Contents

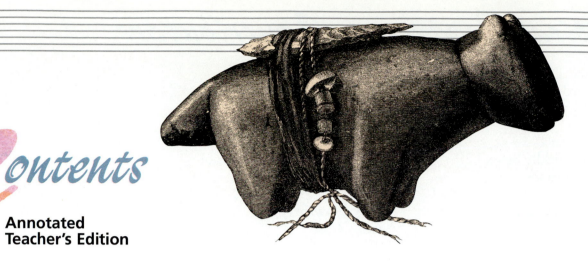

**Annotated
Teacher's Edition**

Unit 1

CHALLENGES

Unit 2

GENERATIONS

Unit 3

AMERICAN
HERITAGE

Part Two Forms of Literature

Unit 4

SHORT STORIES

Unit 5

Unit 6

NONFICTION

Unit 7

POETRY

Language and Meaning

Sound and Meaning

Types of Poetry

Unit 8

THE NOVEL

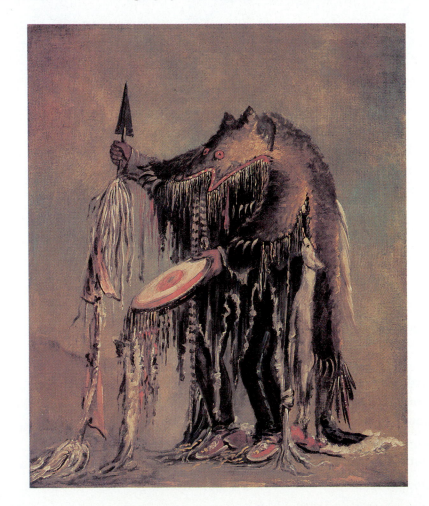

Part Three Literary Heritage

Unit 9

THE EPIC

WRITING ABOUT
LITERATURE

Index of Titles by Themes

Note to Teachers

EXCERPTED LITERARY WORKS USED IN THIS TEXT

The following selections are excerpts from larger works. Excerpts were chosen on the basis of key literary or thematic elements as well as cultural and historical characteristics.

FROM *An American Childhood*

FROM *The Story of a Shipwrecked Sailor*

FROM *Black Boy*

FROM *The Aye-Aye and I*

FROM *My Family and Other Animals*

FROM *Cimarron*

FROM *Barrio Boy*

FROM *The Journal of* Walt Whitman

FROM *A Midsummer Night's Dream*

FROM *Anne Frank Remembered*

FROM *Harriet Tubman: Conductor on the Underground Railroad*

FROM *Life on the Mississippi*

FROM *I Know Why the Caged Bird Sings*

FROM the *Iliad*

FROM *Beowulf*

FROM *Sundiata: An Epic of Old Mali*

Adventures
for Readers
BOOK TWO

A T H E N A   E D I T I O N

HOLT, RINEHART AND WINSTON

Harcourt Brace & Company

Austin • **New York** • Orlando • Atlanta • San Francisco • Boston • Dallas • Toronto • London

CHALLENGES

OVERVIEW OF THE UNIT

Since adolescence presents one challenge after another, eighth-graders should identify readily with the theme explored in this introductory unit. Each selection recounts an ordeal that tests the mettle of the protagonist. Some stories concern young people, and others are about adult characters who also struggle and grow. Thus, the unit explores issues of identity relevant to both adolescence and adulthood.

The seven selections also offer windows on different times, places, and cultures. Kurt Vonnegut's "The No-Talent Kid" could have taken place last week in any suburban high school. In this short story, the band room becomes the proving ground for a boy whose grit outstrips his talent. Likewise, Toni Cade Bambara's "Raymond's Run" is set in today's world; this time, the perspective is that of a young girl living in Harlem. Bright and competitive, she bases her identity upon her ability to run. In Arthur Gordon's "The Sea Devil," a fisherman learns great respect for nature when he is engaged in a life-and-death struggle with a giant manta ray, while in Gabriel García Márquez' story "Fighting Off the Sharks for a Fish" a shipwrecked sailor, his fear temporarily subdued by hunger, battles a shark. Similarly, the perilous aspects of nature play an important role in "Top Man" by James Ramsey Ullman. In this story, however, the conflicting desires and personalities of a group of mountain climbers create greater danger than the mountain itself. In contrast, the excerpt from Richard Wright's autobiography, *Black Boy,* tells the story of a young boy who overcomes fear and faces up to a street gang, and the last selection, "Chanclas" by Sandra Cisneros, describes a young girl's triumph over her own feelings of embarrassment.

Throughout the unit, questions and exercises help students to explore significant elements of plot, character, and theme and encourage readers to relate literary selections to their own lives by responding emotionally and imaginatively as well as analytically. The unit also offers opportunities for vocabulary building and for oral and written expression. Writing activities focus on descriptive writing, building skills such as using specific sensory details. These skills should be regarded as cumulative. Thus, the **Focus on Writing** section at the end of the unit synthesizes the skills that students have been developing, guiding students through the process of writing and critically evaluating their own descriptions.

OBJECTIVES OF THE UNIT

The aims of the unit are for the student:
◆ To identify characteristics such as courage, honesty, strength, and intelligence in the protagonists of short stories
◆ To demonstrate the ability to read critically by identifying the main idea, the sequence of events, cause-and-effect relationships, and the writer's purpose
◆ To analyze how the elements of plot, setting, characterization, and conflict contribute to the overall meaning of a short story
◆ To determine the meanings of selected words, prefixes, and suffixes by using a dictionary and context clues
◆ To develop reading and critical thinking skills
◆ To make connections between literature and mathematics, science, and cultures
◆ To write a description

CONCEPTS AND SKILLS

The following concepts and skills are treated in this unit:

CLOSE READING OF A SELECTION

LITERARY ELEMENTS/TERMS AND TECHNIQUES

LANGUAGE AND VOCABULARY SKILLS

OPPORTUNITIES FOR WRITING

Focus on Descriptive Writing

CONNECTIONS

READING AND CRITICAL THINKING

FOCUS ON WRITING

PLANNING GUIDE

FOR UNIT PLANNING

- Transparencies 1–5: *Audiovisual Resources Binder*
- *Portfolio Assessment: Professional Support Materials*
- Test Generator

- Mastery Tests: Teaching Resources A, pp. 134, 136
- Analogy Lessons: Teaching Resources A, pp. 139–150
- Analogy Test: Teaching Resources A, p. 151
- Composition Test: Teaching Resources A, p. 152

SELECTION (Pupil's Page)	TEACHING RESOURCES A (page numbers shown below)							AV BINDER
	Teacher's Notes	Reading Check	Study Guide	Language Skills	Building Vocabulary	Selection Vocab. Test	Selection Test	Audio-cassette
CHALLENGES *Introduction* (p. 1)	1							
Annie Dillard from *An American Childhood* (p. 2)	2							
Kurt Vonnegut *The No-Talent Kid* (p. 10)	3	7	9	13, 16	20		22	
Toni Cade Bambara *Raymond's Run* (p. 21)	24	28	9	34, 37	40	42	44	
Arthur Gordon *The Sea Devil* (p. 30)	47	51	52	56	60	62	64	
Gabriel García Márquez *Fighting Off the Sharks for a Fish* (p. 40)	67	70	71	74	77		78	
Richard Wright from *Black Boy* (p. 47)	80	83	85	89, 92	96	98	99	
James Ramsey Ullman *Top Man* (p. 51)	101	105	106	111	115, 116		117	
Sandra Cisneros *Chanclas* (p. 68)	119	120	123	126			130	

The following unit support materials with specific correlations to literature selections are available in the **Fine Art and Instructional Transparencies with Teacher's Notes and Blackline Masters** section of your *Audiovisual Resources Binder*.

FINE ART TRANSPARENCIES

Theme: Those Who Dare
1 *Zapata*, David Alfaro Siqueiros
2 *Japanese Ports,* Anonymous

READER RESPONSE
3 Award a Medal

LITERARY ELEMENTS
4 Character

WRITING PROCESS
5 Writing a Description

INTRODUCING THE UNIT

You might begin with activities that will heighten interest and involvement in the theme of proving oneself. Students daily face various "tests" that force them to prove themselves to peers, to parents, and to teachers. Allow two or three minutes for each student to jot down as many kinds of tests as he or she can think of. Make a composite list on the board, perhaps by category. Discuss why such tests might be necessary. Ask how people might feel when they are being tested in various ways—for example, being clocked during a qualifying race, trying out for a varsity team, or taking a mathematics quiz. Elicit examples of less formal tests that might evoke similar feelings. Relate this discussion to the introductory comments on p. 9.

Explain to students that tests continue throughout life and may be responded to in inspiring ways. A day or two before the unit is to be introduced, ask each student to clip a news item about a person who has shown great courage, honesty, strength, or alertness during a time of crisis. Students, perhaps in small groups, may then discuss the test posed by each situation, the choices that had to be made, and the qualities that allowed each person to triumph. Cluster related news stories on a bulletin board. Then invite students to note parallels as they read the stories in the unit.

Ask students to think back over their lives and to consider what tests they have faced. Each student might write and share a brief account of the most challenging incident in his or her life thus far. You might provide poster boards, magazines, scissors, and other supplies for individuals, partners, or small groups to use in making collages representing such challenges. After students have completed these activities, relate the kinds of challenges depicted in collages or reflected in written accounts to specific stories in the unit. Link this preview to the introductory comments on p. 9.

Sometimes people react to challenges in unexpected ways; occasionally they overreact. Read aloud William Saroyan's humorous short story "One of Our Future Poets, You Might Say" (*My Name is Aram,* Harcourt Brace Jovanovich). Encourage students to speculate on why the boy made such a farce of the physical examination. What, if anything, did his behavior have to do with his being a future poet? Ask whether anyone in the class has ever been tempted to overreact to a test or challenge of some kind. Why? Introduce **Challenges** as a collection of stories about people who are tested in various ways. After calling attention to the introductory comments on p. 9, observe that the first story approaches this theme humorously.

You may want to include additional activities before individual selections. For example, before reading "The No-Talent Kid," students might interview their parents to determine what activities parents were involved in during their teen years. What commitments did their parents make to those activities?

"Raymond's Run" provides students with an excellent opportunity to discuss the importance of competition. Before assigning the story, initiate a class discussion about both the positive and negative aspects of competition. You may want to expand the discussion to include students' ideas on the importance of paying attention to the needs of others. How might others' needs prove to be a challenge to students?

To prepare students to read "The Sea Devil" and "Fighting off the Sharks for a Fish," you might ask them to discuss their experiences with nature. Few students, if any, will have had the kind of experience that the main characters in these selections have, but many of them will have been challenged by nature in small ways—by thunderstorms when walking to school, by ants at a picnic, by squirrels that steal grain from the bird feeder, and so forth.

Before reading the excerpt from *Black Boy,* lead students in a discussion of the types of conflict that arise in urban settings. Consider giving students an overview of Wright's life and reading aloud other selected passages from Wright's autobiography.

Before students read "Top Man," you might initiate a discussion of rivalry and conflict between individuals. Some students may have experienced rivalry with siblings, and others may have been in conflict with friends. They may have been frustrated by what they perceived to be the shortcomings of others. Some students might be willing to share these experiences.

To introduce "Chanclas" to students, have them discuss various types of internal conflicts. Ask students to consider how embarrassment can be seen as a conflict within the individual.

While teaching this unit, you will want to provide students ample opportunity for further reading. Your school librarian might be able to supply titles of works that involve the theme of challenges.

You also might ask students who have read books involving characters who face challenges to share what they have read with the class. Students might enjoy creating their own annotated bibliographies of books they consider appropriate companion pieces to the selections in **Challenges.**

PORTFOLIO ASSESSMENT

Suggestions for use of portfolios as support for this unit are described in the *Portfolio Assessment and Professional Support Materials* booklet accompanying this program. Specific suggestions are provided for a variety of student projects that may be suitable for inclusion in a portfolio. In addition, copying masters are provided for guides that may be used for evaluation and assessment of student projects.

CHALLENGES

1. Creating a Time Line

Ask students to make time lines that show challenges they have faced in their lives. Students might include challenges such as learning to ride a bike, resolving a problem, getting over an illness, entering a contest, or playing in a championship game. Suggest that students include challenges they were unable to overcome, too. Stress that wisdom comes through experience and not all challenges can be met successfully. After students have finished, ask them to present their time lines to the class. Students should explain each challenge and how they tried to deal with it.

2. Drawing an Advertisement

Advertisements often tell us that a particular product will help us meet a challenge. For example, an advertisement for a computer might suggest that the computer will bring its owner success in school or business. Have students find advertisements in newspapers and magazines that use this tactic. Then ask students to draw a magazine advertisement—for a made-up product—that makes this type of promise directly or implicitly.

3. Examining the Challenges of Disability

People with disabilities are sometimes referred to as "challenged." Ask students to discuss why they think this term is used and what challenges persons with specific disabilities might face. Then invite a teacher from your school who has a disability to come and talk to your class about the challenges he or she faces every day. Afterward, invite students to discuss whether or not these challenges are fundamentally different from the ones they face.

4. Making a Challenges Collage

Eighth-grade students are about to make the transition to high school. Ask students to create collages to represent the challenges they face in this or other areas of their lives. Challenges might exist in the areas of academic performance, friendship, sports, family, hobbies, and dating. Students might also enjoy creating collages to represent their lives after they have successfully faced these challenges.

5. Creating an Explorer's Journal

Explorers often keep journals to record daily events. Have students write a journal from the point of view of the narrator in "Top Man." Journals might include accounts of events not included in the story, measurements of altitude, weather conditions, survival techniques, and other information related to the progress of the climbing team in "Top Man." Students might also enjoy reading the biographies or autobiographies of other famous explorers and creating similar journal entries. For example, students could create journal entries for Roald Amundsen's exploration of the Northwest Passage and the South Pole, or Robert F. Scott's long journey from Cape Evans to the South Pole.

6. Making Movie Posters

Discuss how attitudes toward wild animals are shaped, distorted, or created by television programs and movies. Have students work in small groups to create made-up movie posters. Each group should choose one animal and create two posters—one in which the animal is portrayed as being friendly or benevolent and one in which the animal is portrayed as being unfriendly or evil. Groups can then give short reports on each poster, pointing out elements that will make the public see the animal as either frightening or friendly.

7. Making an Oral Presentation

Explain to students that a rite of passage is an event that marks a passing from one stage of life into another, such as when the boy in the excerpt from *Black Boy* stands up to the street gang and thus passes from adolescence into adulthood. Ask students to think of and list rites of passage in their own culture, such as getting a driver's license or graduating from high school. Then have each student find out about a rite of passage in another culture and give an oral presentation about it to the class.

8. Creating a Cartoon

Sandra Cisneros shows us in "Chanclas" how appealing characters with human frailties can be—especially characters who suffer from embarrassment. Have each student create a cartoon from a real or imagined embarrassing moment. End frames should show the characters accepting their embarrassment positively.

9. Agreeing on a Challenging Dilemma

Assign groups of three students to work together to create lists of items one might need to survive a shipwreck. Ask each group to make a list of twenty-five items. Then ask students to discuss the merits of each item and have each group decide on only one. Groups can present their choices to the class. Each group should be able to justify its choice.

TRANSPARENCIES 1 & 2

Fine Art
Theme: *Those Who Dare* – invites students to explore artworks that examine the idea of perseverance despite difficult situations.

VISUAL CONNECTIONS

Exploring the Subject

The sport of sky diving, jumping from an airplane and executing free-fall maneuvers before opening the parachute, is a relatively new addition to the list of athletic challenges. The first successful parachute jump was made by a Frenchman in 1797. Jacques Garnerin made his daring jump from a balloon that floated 3,000 feet aloft. It was not until World War I that the possibility of using sky divers, or paratroopers, to jump into enemy territory was considered. The war, however, ended before the United States could actually employ the tactic. Consequently, Russia was first to conduct major parachute maneuvers, in 1931. Later, the German army used paratroopers when invading the Netherlands. By the time of World War II, parachutes were used both as a means of slipping quietly behind enemy lines and as a means of escaping a doomed aircraft. Today, however, it takes neither war nor necessity to prompt sky divers to take their leaps; they simply enjoy the challenge of learning the skill, the excitement of soaring through blue skies, and the beauty of a "bird's-eye" view.

Ideas for Writing

You may want to have students imagine they are among the sky divers pictured and write brief essays or short poems in which they describe their thoughts about the free fall. Before beginning their writings, students could interview friends or relatives who have sky-dived.

CHALLENGES

Challenge.

What does the word make you think of? The photographer who took this picture of skydivers in midair has caught the sense of a daring and exciting test of physical courage.

If you wanted to illustrate your idea of challenge, what would you choose? Would it be a test of strength or skill? Would it be a test of courage, honesty, or intelligence? Share your ideas with others in the class.

The challenges in this unit take many forms. In one story a character wages a life-and-death battle with a gigantic sea monster. In another story a girl decides to protect and teach her handicapped brother. In still another story, a young boy faces a gang of bullies and wins pride and self-respect. All of the people in this unit are "tested" and prove themselves to be winners. You might find that some of their tests are ones that you yourself have already faced.

TEACHING RESOURCES A
Teacher's Notes, p. 1

Challenges

Ask students to give their own definitions of the word *challenge.* Then engage them in a discussion centering around the questions asked in the text. Now have students look at the titles listed under **Challenges** in the Table of Contents and speculate about the kinds of challenges the protagonist in each of the stories might face. Ask them to decide whether the titles suggest a conflict between a person and another person, a person and the environment (either social or natural), or a person and himself or herself. Although students may find later that some of their conjectures prove inaccurate, such an exercise will help to establish an atmosphere of inquiry. Tell them to keep in mind the speculations as they read the stories in the unit.

You might also ask students to give their opinions about why **Challenges** is the first of the three thematic units in this part. Thematically, the units move outward from the individual reader. **Challenges** deals with individual choices and conflicts; **Generations** specifically concerns the individual in relationship to the family; **American Heritage** considers the individual in relationship to society and his or her sense of nationalism.

After the class has completed all three units, students will see that basic issues and feelings overlap from one unit to another because life is a series of individual "challenges."

The overall aim is for students to analyze the main character's actions and attitudes in Kurt Vonnegut's "The No-Talent Kid." For a complete list of objectives, see the **Teacher's Notes.**

The underlined words are in the Glossary. The **Language and Vocabulary** exercise on pp. 19–20 gives students practice in using footnotes, the Glossary, and a dictionary to find pronunciations and meanings of specific words.

Ask students to name traditional awards for outstanding achievement in school activities (band and athletic letters, club pins, etc.). What kind of commitment is required? Can everyone excel in every activity? Why or why not?

PREREADING FOCUS

The headnote prepares the students for the **tone** of the story. Ask students what the comparison of Plummer's nonmusical ear to that of a boiled cabbage suggests about Vonnegut's treatment of Plummer's desires and problems.

VISUAL CONNECTIONS

About the Artist

Georges Schreiber was born in Brussels, Belgium, and grew up there during the German occupation of World War I. Before coming to the United States in 1928, he studied art in West Germany, London, Florence, Paris, and Rome. He became a naturalized United States citizen in 1938. During World War II, he worked for the government as a war correspondent and created three official war-loan posters for the Treasury Department. Schreiber worked in oils, watercolors, and graphics. He contributed to many magazines, illustrated several books, and exhibited in major museums and galleries throughout the world.

Exploring the Subject

You may invite students to discuss the techniques Schreiber uses to capture the vitality and action of a violin concerto. Notice that there are only two human figures (the conductor is shown in three poses) in the painting but that Schreiber suggests many more in his tilted, scattered placement of violin bows, music stands, and musical instruments. Varied colors suggest a blending of musical sounds.

The No-Talent Kid

KURT VONNEGUT

Plummer was as tone-deaf as boiled cabbage. But he was determined to win a place with the A Band. All it finally took was a smart business deal—and an eight-foot bass drum.

Walter Plummer desperately wants to play in the A Band, but he has no musical talent. Mr. Helmholtz, the band director, attempts to handle the **conflict** with patience, but he has absolutely no intention of giving in to Plummer. Helmholtz seems destined for many years of explaining to Plummer why he cannot be in the A Band. Then Plummer acquires the eight-foot bass drum Helmholtz desires for the band. Helmholtz wants the drum, but he does not want Plummer. Who will prevail? Plummer, Helmholtz, or both?

This story is straightforward enough for most eighth-graders to read silently. However, you may want to read part of it aloud—perhaps to the end of the third paragraph on p. 14. This oral reading will allow students to share the humor

---

1 It was autumn, and the leaves outside Lincoln High School were turning the same rusty color as the bare brick walls in the band-rehearsal room. George M. Helmholtz, head of the music department and director of the band, was ringed by folding chairs and instrument cases; and on each chair sat a very young man, nervously prepared to blow through something, or, in the case of the percussion section, to hit something, the instant Mr. Helmholtz lowered his white baton.

2 Mr. Helmholtz, a man of forty, who believed that his great belly was a sign of health, strength and dignity, smiled angelically, as though he were about to release the most exquisite sounds ever heard by men. Down came his baton.

3 "Blooooomp!" went the big sousaphones.

"Blat! Blat!" echoed the French horns, and the plodding, shrieking, querulous[1] waltz was begun.

4 Mr. Helmholtz's expression did not change as the brasses lost their places, as the woodwinds' nerve failed and they became inaudible rather than have their mistakes heard, as the percussion section shifted into a rhythm pattern belonging to a march they knew and liked better.

"A-a-a-a-ta-ta, a-a-a-a-a-a, ta-ta-ta-ta!" sang Mr. Helmholtz in a loud tenor, singing the first-cornet part when the first cornetist, florid and perspiring, gave up and slouched in his chair, his instrument in his lap.

5 "Saxophones, let me hear you," called Mr. Helmholtz. "Good!"

6 This was the C Band, and, for the C Band, the performance was good; it couldn't have been more polished for the fifth session of the school year. Most of the youngsters were just starting out as bandsmen, and in the years ahead of them they would acquire artistry enough to move into the B Band, which met in the next hour. And finally the best of them would gain positions in the pride of the city, the Lincoln High School Ten Square Band.

---

1. **querulous** (kwĕr′ə-ləs): fretful; complaining. In other words, it wasn't much like a waltz.

Violin Concerto (1971) by George Schreiber (1904–1971). Watercolor.
Courtesy of Kennedy Galleries, Inc., New York

1
Setting. The time is early in school year; place for most of action is band hall of Lincoln High School.

2
Characterization. Mr. Helmholtz takes pride in himself (even his "great belly") and his band.

3
Sousaphone: instrument named for its inventor, John Phillip Sousa, who composed band marches.

4
Brasses are horns: trumpets, trombones etc.; *woodwinds* are saxophones, clarinets, and other reed instruments.

5
Description. Vonnegut's crisp, compressed description creates vivid picture of first cornetist's condition and position.

6 Making Generalizations
What does this exposition reveal about the process for achieving a place in the A Band? Process is gradual, and only the few most talented make the A Band.

The focus on **characterization** and **plot** in the **For Study and Discussion** questions will provide opportunity for reinforcing these two important literary elements.

MEETING INDIVIDUAL NEEDS

ESL/LEP • This story contains idiomatic expressions that may prove confusing to some students. As students read the story, encourage them to make lists of words and phrases whose meanings are unclear to them. Here are a few examples of potentially confusing expressions.

. . . would have had the gall . . . (p. 13)
(would have been daring enough)
That's the ticket! (p. 15)
(That's exactly right!)
Rub it in! . . . (p. 18)

---

7 Analyzing
What does this list of achievements suggest about Mr. Helmholtz's ability as a teacher? He is resourceful, supplementing skills of students with showy maneuvers and devices. Some readers may feel he emphasizes "show" too much.

8
Irony. Helmholtz is not the only one who relies on "glitz" instead of talent; contest judges also are impressed by showy gadgets.

9
Snare drum: small, double-headed drum with one or more cords extended across bottom head to magnify reverberation.

10
Helmholtz thinks his only hope of winning is to acquire a bass drum bigger than Johnstown band's.

11
Characterization. Plummer works very hard, not only in band but also in swimming. He awaits a "challenge."

12
Simile. Statement that Plummer is "as tone-deaf as boiled cabbage" creates humor through exaggeration.

The football team lost half its games and the basketball team lost two thirds of its, but the band, in the ten years Mr. Helmholtz had been running it, had been second to none until last June. It had been first in the state to use flag twirlers, the first to use choral as well as instrumental numbers, the first to use triple-tonguing extensively, the first to march in breathtaking double time, the first to put a **7** light in its bass drum. Lincoln High School awarded letter sweaters to the members of the A Band, and the sweaters were deeply respected—and properly so. The band had won every statewide high school band competition in the last ten years—every one save the one in June.

As the members of the C Band dropped out of the waltz, one by one, as though mustard gas[2] were coming out of the ventilators, Mr. Helmholtz continued to smile and wave his baton for the survivors, and to brood inwardly over the defeat his band had sustained in June, when Johnstown High School had won with a secret weapon, a bass drum seven feet in **8** diameter. The judges, who were not musicians but politicians, had had eyes and ears for nothing but this eighth wonder of the world, and since then Mr. Helmholtz had thought of little else. But the school budget was already lopsided with band expenses. When the school board had given him the last special appropriation he'd begged so desperately—money to **12** wire the plumes of the bandsmen's hats with flashlight bulbs and batteries for night games—the board had made him swear that this was the last time.

Only two members of the C Band were play- **9** ing now, a clarinetist and a snare drummer, both playing loudly, proudly, confidently, and all wrong. Mr. Helmholtz, coming out of his **10** wistful dream of a bass drum bigger than the

one that had beaten him, administered the *coup de grâce*[3] to the waltz by clattering his stick against his music stand. "All righty, all righty," he said cheerily, and he nodded his congratulations to the two who had persevered to the bitter end.

11 Walter Plummer, the clarinetist, nodded back soberly, like a concert soloist receiving an ovation led by the director of a symphony orchestra. He was small, but with a thick chest developed in summers spent at the bottom of swimming pools, and he could hold a note longer than anyone in the A Band, much longer, but that was all he could do. He drew back his tired, reddened lips, showing the two large front teeth that gave him the look of a squirrel, adjusted his reed, limbered his fingers, and awaited the next challenge to his virtuosity.

This would be Plummer's third year in the C Band, Mr. Helmholtz thought, with a mixture of pity and fear. Nothing, apparently, could shake Plummer's determination to earn the right to wear one of the sacred letters of the A Band, so far, terribly far away.

Mr. Helmholtz had tried to tell Plummer how misplaced his ambitions were, to recommend other fields for his great lungs and enthusiasm, where pitch would be unimportant. But Plummer was blindly in love, not with music, but with the letter sweaters, and, being **12** as tone-deaf as boiled cabbage, he could detect nothing in his own playing to be discouraged about.

"Remember, now," said Mr. Helmholtz to the C Band, "Friday is challenge day, so be on your toes. The chairs you have now were assigned arbitrarily.[4] On challenge day it'll be up to you to prove which chair you deserve." He avoided

---

2. **mustard gas:** a poisonous gas.

3. ***coup de grâce*** (kōō′də gräs′): finishing stroke (strictly speaking, the blow that ends suffering).
4. **arbitrarily** (är′bə-trĕr′ə-lē): without any rules or standards.

After students have completed their lists, suggest that they seek help in understanding the expressions from you or from one of their classmates.

MUSIC LINK
To help students appreciate individual instrument sounds, play parts of Prokofiev's *Peter and the Wolf*. Extend this activity by inviting students who play an instrument to perform for the class, or by visiting a practice of your school's band.

You might ask the band director to have band members demonstrate the sound of each instrument and to show both the instrument and its case.

the narrowed, confident eyes of Plummer, who had taken the first clarinetist's chair without consulting the seating plan posted on the bulletin board. Challenge day occurred every two weeks, and on that day any bandsman could challenge anyone ahead of him to a contest for his position, with Mr. Helmholtz as utterly dispassionate judge.

Plummer's hand was raised, its fingers snapping urgently.

"Yes, Plummer?" said Mr. Helmholtz, smiling bleakly. He had come to dread challenge days because of Plummer, and had come to think of it as Plummer's day. Plummer never challenged anybody in the C Band or even in the B Band, but stormed the organization at the very top, challenging, as was unfortunately the privilege of all, only members of the A Band. The waste of the A Band's time was troubling enough, but infinitely more painful for Mr. Helmholtz were Plummer's looks of stunned disbelief when he heard Mr. Helmholtz's decision that he hadn't outplayed the men he'd challenged. And Mr. Helmholtz was thus rebuked not just on challenge days, but every day, just before supper, when Plummer delivered the evening paper. "Something about challenge day, Plummer?" said Mr. Helmholtz uneasily.

"Mr. Helmholtz," said Plummer coolly, "I'd like to come to A Band session that day."

"All right—if you feel up to it." Plummer always felt up to it, and it would have been more of a surprise if Plummer had announced that he wouldn't be at the A Band session.

"I'd like to challenge Flammer."

The rustling of sheet music and clicking of instrument-case latches stopped. Flammer was the first clarinetist in the A Band, a genius that not even members of the A Band would have had the gall to challenge.

Mr. Helmholtz cleared his throat. "I admire your spirit, Plummer, but isn't that rather

ambitious for the first of the year? Perhaps you should start out with, say, challenging Ed Delaney." Delaney held down the last chair in the B Band.

"You don't understand," said Plummer patiently. "You haven't noticed I have a new clarinet."

"H'm'm? Oh—well, so you do."

Plummer stroked the satin-black barrel of the instrument as though it were like King Arthur's sword, giving magical powers to whoever possessed it. "It's as good as Flammer's," said Plummer. "Better, even."

There was a warning in his voice, telling Mr. Helmholtz that the days of discrimination were over, that nobody in his right mind would dare to hold back a man with an instrument like this.

VISUAL CONNECTIONS
Exploring the Subject
Many high school music programs feature concert bands and marching bands. Concert bands usually have fifty to eighty musicians, and marching bands often have seventy-two to ninety-six (may have fewer or even several hundred).

13
Theme. Challenge day emphasizes main idea of story—importance of meeting inward challenge to keep striving to achieve ambitions.

14 Drawing Conclusions
What do Plummer's looks of "stunned disbelief" reveal?
That he does not know that he is tone-deaf, has no talent, and therefore cannot succeed in his ambition.

15
That Plummer is Helmholtz's newsboy shows that Plummer is independent (earns his own money) and has opportunity to let Helmholtz know his disappointment daily.

16
Characterization. Plummer is straightforward, still believing in himself despite his many disappointments.

17
Plummer mistakenly feels that because he has a new instrument, he cannot lose.

18
Allusion. The legendary King Arthur, leader of the Knights of the Round Table, had a magic sword called Excalibur.

32

Characterization. Helmholtz's thoughts reveal both dreamer and planner aspects of his character: dreams that he will get drum for low price and plans how he will be reimbursed by school.

33

Helmholtz is now confident that he will soon have the drum; he thinks his problem is solved.

34

Foreshadowing. "Undelivered newspapers" indicates Plummer is involved in something very important to him because it is unlike him to leave a job undone.

35 Summarizing
Making Inferences

What does Mr. Helmholtz assume Plummer has in mind when the boy leaves the band director's house? What is Plummer really doing? Assumes Plummer has gone to find his papers. Actually going to buy drum.

36

Irony. Helmholtz misinterprets news that Plummer is selling his clarinet; Plummer now intends to play bass drum.

37

Helmholtz, frustrated because he has not yet purchased drum, lets his anger show.

38

Plummer has occupied last chair for so long that the chair has come to represent Plummer himself; even though Plummer's playing is uniquely *bad,* still it is unique.

---

32 drum, he told himself, and he could name his own price. If he offered fifty dollars for it, he could probably have it! He'd put up his own money, and get the school to pay him back in three years, when the plumes with the electric lights in them were paid for in full.

33 He lit a cigarette, and laughed like a department-store Santa Claus at this magnificent stroke of fortune. As he exhaled happily, his gaze dropped from heaven to his lawn, and he **34** saw Plummer's undelivered newspapers lying beneath the shrubbery.

He went inside and called the Sublime Chamberlain again, with the same results. To make the time go, and to do a Christian good turn, he called Plummer's home to let him know where the papers were mislaid. But the Plummers' line was busy too.

He dialed alternately the Plummers' number and the Sublime Chamberlain's number for fifteen minutes before getting a ringing signal.

"Yes?" said Mrs. Plummer.

"This is Mr. Helmholtz, Mrs. Plummer. Is Walter there?"

"He was here a minute ago, telephoning, but he just went out of here like a shot."

35 "Looking for his papers? He left them under my spiraea."[8]

"He did? Heavens, I have no idea where he was going. He didn't say anything about his papers, but I thought I overheard something about selling his clarinet." She sighed and then laughed nervously. "Having money of their own makes them awfully independent. He never tells me anything."

"Well, you tell him I think maybe it's for the best, his selling his clarinet. And tell him where his papers are."

36 It was unexpected good news that Plummer had at last seen the light about his musical career, and Mr. Helmholtz now called the Sub-

---

8. **spiraea** (spī-rē′ə): a shrub in the rose family.

---

lime Chamberlain's home again for more good news. He got through this time, but was momentarily disappointed to learn that the man had just left on some sort of lodge business.

For years Mr. Helmholtz had managed to smile and keep his wits about him in C Band practice sessions. But on the day after his fruitless efforts to find out anything about the Knights of Kandahar's bass drum, his defenses were down, and the poisonous music penetrated to the roots of his soul.

37 "No, no, no!" he cried in pain, and he threw his white baton against the brick wall. The springy stick bounded off the bricks and fell into an empty folding chair at the rear of the clarinet section—Plummer's empty chair.

As Mr. Helmholtz, red-faced and apologetic, retrieved the baton, he found himself unex- **38** pectedly moved by the symbol of the empty chair. No one else, he realized, no matter how untalented, could ever fill the last chair in the organization as well as Plummer had. He looked up to find many of the bandsmen contemplating the chair with him, as though they, too, sensed that something great, in a fantastic way, had disappeared, and that life would be a good bit duller on account of it.

During the ten minutes between the C Band and B Band sessions, Mr. Helmholtz hurried to his office and again tried to get in touch with the Sublime Chamberlain of the Knights of Kandahar, and was again told what he'd been told substantially several times during the night before and again in the morning.

"Lord knows where he's off to now. He was in for just a second, but went right out again. I gave him your name, so I expect he'll call you when he gets a minute. You're the drum gentleman, aren't you?"

"That's right—the drum gentleman."

The buzzers in the hall were sounding, marking the beginning of another class

---

period. Mr. Helmholtz wanted to stay by the phone until he'd caught the Sublime Chamberlain and closed the deal, but the B Band was waiting—and after that it would be the A Band.

An inspiration came to him. He called Western Union, and sent a telegram to the man, offering fifty dollars for the drum, and requesting a reply collect.

But no reply came during B Band practice. Nor had one come by the halfway point of the A Band session. The bandsmen, a sensitive, high-strung lot, knew immediately that their director was on edge about something, and the rehearsal went badly. Mr. Helmholtz was growing so nervous about the drum that he stopped a march in the middle because of a small noise coming from the large double doors at one end of the room, where someone out-of-doors was apparently working on the lock.

"All right, all right, let's wait until the racket dies down so we can hear ourselves," he said.

At that moment, a student messenger **39** handed him a telegram. Mr. Helmholtz beamed, tore open the envelope, and read:

DRUM SOLD STOP COULD YOU USE A STUFFED CAMEL ON WHEELS STOP.

The wooden doors opened with a shriek of rusty hinges, and a snappy autumn gust showered the band with leaves. Plummer stood in **40** the great opening, winded and perspiring, harnessed to a drum on wheels that could have contained a dozen youngsters his size.

"I know this isn't challenge day," said Plummer, "but I thought you might make an exception in my case."

He walked in with splendid dignity, the huge apparatus grumbling along behind him.

Mr. Helmholtz rushed to meet him, and crushed Plummer's right hand between both of his. "Plummer, boy! You got it for us! Good **41** boy! I'll pay you whatever you paid for it," he cried, and in his joy he added rashly, "and a nice little profit besides. Good boy!"

Plummer laughed modestly. "Sell it?" he said. "Heck fire, I'll give it to you when I graduate," he said grandly. "All I want to do is play it in the A Band while I'm here."

"But, Plummer," said Mr. Helmholtz uneasily, "you don't know anything about drums."

"I'll practice hard," said Plummer reassuringly. He started to back his instrument into an aisle between the tubas and the trombones— **42** like a man backing a trailer truck into a narrow alley—backing it toward the percussion section, where the amazed musicians were hastily making room.

"Now, just a minute," said Mr. Helmholtz, **43** chuckling as though Plummer were joking, and knowing full well he wasn't. "There's more to drum playing than just lambasting[9] the thing whenever you take a notion to, you know. It takes years to be a drummer."

"Well," said Plummer cheerfully, "the quicker I get at it, the quicker I'll get good."

"What I meant was that I'm afraid you won't be quite ready for the A Band for a little while."

Plummer stopped his backing. "How long?" he asked suspiciously.

"Oh, sometime in your senior year, perhaps. Meanwhile, you could let the band have your drum to use until you're ready."

Mr. Helmholtz's skin began to itch all over as Plummer stared at him coldly, appraisingly. **45** "Until hell freezes over?" Plummer said at last.

Mr. Helmholtz sighed resignedly. "I'm afraid that's about right." He shook his head sadly. "It's what I tried to tell you yesterday afternoon: nobody can do everything well, and we've all got to face up to our limitations. You're a fine boy, Plummer, but you'll never be

9. **lambasting** (lăm-bāst′ĭng): beating or pounding.

The No-Talent Kid **17**

39
Irony. Helmholtz is excited because he is sure the telegram will bring good news; reader suspects, and soon learns, otherwise.

40
Even here, Plummer is working to his fullest, "winded and perspiring."

41 Summarizing
Making Inferences
What does Helmholtz assume when he offers Plummer money for the drum? Does it seem consistent with Plummer's character that he would easily give up the drum? Helmholtz assumes that Plummer will sell him the drum. That Plummer would easily give up drum seems inconsistent with his character. Plummer is determined to play in A Band; he sees his possession of drum as a means to that end.

42
Simile. Comparison creates image of Plummer carefully maneuvering among instruments and stands.

43
Another dimension has been added to **conflict** between Helmholtz and Plummer: now Plummer has something Helmholtz wants.

44
Helmholtz is trying to pacify Plummer with vague promise that he can play drum someday; in meantime, he wants Plummer to give up drum.

45
Plummer is too wary to fall for Helmholtz's trick.

VISUAL CONNECTIONS
Exploring the Subject
Bass drums, like the one in this photograph and the one Plummer acquires, are among the most prominent, expected features of marching bands. Percussion instruments, such as drums, brass, and woodwind instruments, dominate in marching bands.

46
Plummer is unable to completely hide his pain, but he quickly checks his tears and retaliates.

47
Plummer turns Helmholtz's words around to apply them to band director's dream of having drum.

48
Helmholtz, in desperation, again assumes incorrectly that Plummer will sell drum.

49
Use to answer **study question 4a,** p. 19.

50
Connotation. "Unscarred" cases indicate that new members are not as experienced in life as Plummer.

Finding Details
51 Synthesizing
What does Plummer say the new kids need? What does he mean? Plummer says they need "seasoning." By this, he means they need challenges to face with determination and optimism.

a musician—not in a million years. The only thing to do is what we all have to do now and then: smile, shrug, and say, 'Well, that's just one of those things that's not for me.'"

46 Tears formed on the rims of Plummer's eyes, but went no farther. He walked slowly toward the doorway, with the drum tagging after him. He paused on the doorsill for one more wistful look at the A Band that would never have a chair for him. He smiled feebly and shrugged. **47** "Some people have eight-foot drums," he said kindly, "and others don't, and that's just the way life is. You're a fine man, Mr. Helmholtz, but you'll never get this drum in a million years, because I'm going to give it to my **51** mother for a coffee table."

"Plummer!" cried Mr. Helmholtz. His plaintive voice was drowned out by the rumble and

rattle of the big drum as it followed its small master down the school's concrete driveway.

Mr. Helmholtz ran after him with a <u>floundering</u>, foot-slapping gait. Plummer and his drum had stopped at an intersection to wait for a light to change, and Mr. Helmholtz caught him there, and seized his arm. "We've **48** got to have that drum," he panted. "How much do you want?"

"Smile," said Plummer. "Shrug! That's what I did." Plummer did it again. "See? So I can't get into the A Band, so you can't have the drum. Who cares? All part of the growing-up process."

"The situations aren't the same!" said Mr. Helmholtz furiously. "Not at all the same!"

"You're right," said Plummer, without a smile. "I'm growing up, and you're not."

The light changed, and Plummer left Mr. Helmholtz on the corner, stunned.

Mr. Helmholtz had to run after him again. "Plummer," he said sweetly, "you'll never be able to play it well."

"Rub it in," said Plummer, bitterly.

49 "But you're doing a beautiful job of pulling it, and if we got it, I don't think we'd ever be able to find anybody who could do it as well."

Plummer stopped, backed and turned the instrument on the narrow sidewalk with speed and hair-breadth precision, and headed back for Lincoln High School, skipping once to get in step with Mr. Helmholtz.

As they approached the school they both loved, they met and passed a group of young- **50** sters from the C Band, who carried unscarred instrument cases and spoke self-consciously of music.

"Got a good bunch of kids coming up this year," said Plummer judiciously.[10] "All they **51** need's a little seasoning."

10. **judiciously** (jo͞o-dĭsh′əs-lē): wisely and carefully, like a judge.

Reading Check

1. What do the members of the A band receive?
2. Before the last competition, how many years in a row had the band won all the state contests?
3. What does Mr. Helmholtz think the band needs in order to win the next contest?
4. Why doesn't Mr. Helmholtz buy the drum that the Knights of Kandahar are selling?
5. What does Plummer say he will do with the drum if Mr. Helmholtz will not let him use it in the band?

For Study and Discussion

Analyzing and Interpreting the Story

1. In this humorous story, Mr. Helmholtz has a problem: he wants to beat Johnstown High School in the next statewide band competition. What does he think he needs in order to accomplish this?

2. Walter Plummer has a problem, too. Why does he want so much to be a member of the A Band?

3. How does Plummer plan to solve both problems?

4. Like all other comedies, this one ends with everyone happy and all problems solved. **a.** What compromise does Mr. Helmholtz finally propose? **b.** By accepting this offer, what will Plummer get?

5. Plummer may be "as tone-deaf as boiled cabbage," but he is certainly *not* a "no-talent kid." Tell what you think Plummer's talents are.

Language and Vocabulary

Using Footnotes, Glossary, and Dictionary

There are several methods you can use to find the meaning of an unfamiliar word in this book. You can check to see whether it is footnoted, as the word *querulous* is on page 11.

If an unfamiliar word isn't footnoted, it may be in the glossary in the back of this book. For example, you might not have known the meaning of the word *florid*, used on page 11 to describe the cornetist. The glossary defines *florid* in this way:

florid (flôr′ĭd) *adj.* Red-faced; ruddy.

The abbreviation *adj.* tells you that the word is an adjective. You will find a key to the pronunciations in the glossary at the back of this book.

A dictionary contains more information than either the footnotes or the glossary. A dictionary not only cites all the meanings a word has, but also tells something about the history of the word. For example, here is a complete dictionary entry for the word *florid* from *Webster's New World Dictionary of American English*. (Like all dictionaries, this one uses its own symbols to indicate pronunciation.)

flor|id (flôr′id, flär′-) *adj.* [[L *floridus,* flowery <*flos,* a FLOWER]] **1** flushed with red or pink; rosy; ruddy: said of the complexion **2** highly decorated; gaudy; showy; ornate [a *florid* musical passage] **3** [Obs.] decorated with flowers; flowery —**flo·rid·i|ty** (flō rid′ə tē, flô-, flə-) or **flor′id·ness** *n.*—**flor′id|ly** *adv.*

1 What does the information in brackets tell you about the origin of the word *florid*? The third meaning that is given appears with the **2** abbreviation *Obs.* What does that information **3** tell you? What other parts of speech are related to the adjective form?

READING CHECK
1. Letter sweaters (p. 12).
2. Ten years (p. 12).
3. A bass drum (p. 12).
4. Plummer has already bought it (p. 17).
5. He will let his mother use it as a coffee table (p. 18).

FOR STUDY AND DISCUSSION
1. He longs for secret weapon, a bass drum bigger than one that beat him in June.
2. Members of A Band are awarded letter sweaters, which are deeply respected. Unaware of his lack of musical talent and undaunted by Mr. Helmholtz's lack of encouragement, Plummer dreams of earning sacred letter.
3. Plummer hopes that purchasing a huge drum from Knights of Kandahar will get him into A Band and help Mr. Helmholtz win next competition.
4a. Though Plummer will never learn to play drum, Mr. Helmholtz proposes that he pull it for A Band. 4b. Plummer will get into A Band and will receive long-awaited letter sweater.
5. Responses will vary. He is hard-working, independent, determined, and enterprising, with a particular talent for persevering and getting what he wants.

LANGUAGE AND VOCABULARY
1. It comes from Latin.
2. This meaning is obsolete (no longer in common use).
3. Noun and adverb.

Students might write a report on the story in which they explain their reactions to the characters and the **plot**. Have them state clearly whether they find the characters of Mr. Helmholtz and Plummer believable and whether they think the ending is logical and convincing.

Since characters in this story lend themselves to caricature, students might like to draw cartoons or comic strips of favorite scenes.

Individuals or small groups might like to write sequels to "The No-Talent Kid" in which Plum-mer and his drum go with the Lincoln High School band to the state band contest. Students will have to decide whether the great drum helps Lincoln to win.

LANGUAGE AND VOCABULARY

1a. *Percussion:* (pər-kush´ən) n. class of musical instrument played by striking.

1b. *Sustain:* (sə-stān) v. to keep up; to keep in effect; to experience; to undergo.

1c. *Discrimination:* (dis-krim´ə-nā´shən) n. prejudice.

FOCUS ON DESCRIPTIVE WRITING

Students might start a journal especially designed to keep their writing ideas and notes from **Focus** sections. Students can date and title their notes.

For this activity, encourage students to extend their lists to areas of their lives other than home and school, such as places in their communities where they go to participate in activities—sports, hobbies, and so on.

ABOUT THE AUTHOR

Other Vonnegut books include *Galapagos* (1985), a science fiction novel about the devastating effect on the world of humankind's "big brains"; *Palm Sunday: An Autobiographical Collage* (1981); and *Sun Moon Star,* a children's Christmas story (1980).

---

1 Use the glossary to find the pronunciations and meanings of the italicized words in the following quotations from "The No-Talent Kid." Compare these definitions with what a dictionary tells you.

a …or, in the case of the *percussion* section, to hit something….

b …to brood inwardly over the defeat his band had *sustained* in June….

c …the days of *discrimination* were over….

Focus on Descriptive Writing

Finding a Focus

In the first paragraph Vonnegut puts the reader inside the band room at Lincoln High School. This paragraph is an example of **descriptive writing.**

In descriptive writing you use details and precise words to help your reader form clear images of a person, place, thing, or event. When you choose a subject for description, look for a specific focus. Make a focusing diagram like the one below:

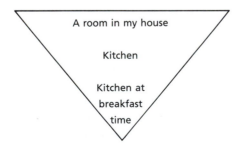

A room in my house

Kitchen

Kitchen at breakfast time

Make a list of familiar places at school or at home. Pick one or two that you would like to describe in an essay. Make a focusing diagram to limit your subject. Save your notes.

About the Author

Kurt Vonnegut (1922–)

Kurt Vonnegut tried many jobs before finally becoming a writer. He studied biochemistry and anthropology in college, and worked as a police reporter, public-relations person, and teacher. During World War II, when he served in the infantry, he was captured by the Germans and kept underground in a slaughterhouse in Dresden. He was in Dresden when the city was firebombed by the Allied forces. Vonnegut based *Slaughterhouse-Five* (1969), one of his best-known novels, on his war experiences.

Vonnegut is known for his science fiction and humorous social criticism. His science fiction includes *Player Piano* (1952), his first novel, and *Cat's Cradle* (1963). In the novels *Breakfast of Champions* (1973), *Slapstick* (1976), and *Jailbird* (1979), he offers distinctive perspectives on the Nixon years and life in general. His recent works include *Fates Worse Than Death* (1985) and *Hocus Pocus* (1991).

Vonnegut's writing has won him a strong following among college students. He has written another story about Mr. Helmholtz, called "The Kid Nobody Could Handle." He has also written many science-fiction stories, including "EPICAC," which is about a computer that falls in love with a mathematician.

Raymond's Run

TONI CADE BAMBARA

Squeaky had a roomful of ribbons and medals and awards. But what did her brother Raymond have to call his own?

21

MOTIVATIONAL SUMMARY

Squeaky works hard to train for a big race. When she arrives at the park to run, she thinks only of winning. By the end of the race, however, she feels that her own performance is unimportant. What causes her change of heart?

PRESENTATION

Although little more than a child herself, Squeaky is responsible enough to care for her older brother, whom she describes as "not quite right." She is loyal, forthright, and courageous. She prides herself on her honesty and her practicality, and she never pretends to be what she is not. What she is, she believes, is a runner. Only after she sees her mentally disabled brother as "a great runner in the family tradition" and envisions other possibilities for herself does she come to a true respect for herself and others.

Raymond's Run

1

Exposition. Squeaky begins her story by mentioning members of her family and telling about her own responsibility in family.

2

First-person narrator tells her story in conversational style.

3

Squeaky later identifies George as another brother.

4

Characterization. Squeaky describes herself as straightforward, tough, and fast.

5 Making Inferences
What can you infer about the setting from "two-fire-hydrant head start"? It is a city.

6

Conflict. Track-meet competition established between Squeaky and fellow student.

7

Squeaky uses present tense to tell about past incident.

8

Squeaky is completely responsible for what Raymond does. She gets in trouble if Raymond does something wrong.

---

1 I don't have much work to do around the house like some girls. My mother does that. And I don't have to earn my pocket money. George runs errands for the big boys and sells Christmas cards. And anything else that's got to get done, my father does. All I have to do in life is mind my brother Raymond, which is enough.

2 Sometimes I slip and say my little brother Raymond. But as any fool can see, he's much bigger and he's older too. But a lot of people call him my little brother cause he needs looking after cause he's not quite right. And a lot of smart mouths got lots to say about that too, **3** especially when George was minding him. But now, if anybody has anything to say to Raymond, anything to say about his big head, they **4** have to come by me. And I don't play the dozens[1] or believe in standing around with somebody in my face doing a lot of talking. I much rather just knock you down and take my chances even if I am a little girl with skinny arms and a squeaky voice, which is how I got the name Squeaky. And if things get too rough, I run. And as anybody can tell you, I'm the fastest thing on two feet.

There is no track meet that I don't win the first-place medal. I used to win the twenty-yard dash when I was a little kid in kindergarten. Nowadays, it's the fifty-yard dash. And tomorrow I'm subject to run the quarter-meter relay all by myself and come in first, second, and third. The big kids call me Mercury[2] cause I'm the swiftest thing in the neighborhood. Everybody knows that—except two people who know better, my father and me. He can beat me to Amsterdam Avenue with me having a **5** two-fire-hydrant head start and him running with his hands in his pockets and whistling. But that's private information. Cause can you imagine some thirty-five-year-old man stuffing **6** himself into PAL[3] shorts to race little kids? So as far as everyone's concerned, I'm the fastest and that goes for Gretchen, too, who has put out the tale that she is going to win the first-place medal this year. Ridiculous. In the second place, she's got short legs. In the third place, she's got freckles. In the first place, no one can beat me and that's all there is to it.

7 I'm standing on the corner admiring the weather and about to take a stroll down Broadway so I can practice my breathing exercises, and I've got Raymond walking on the inside close to the buildings, cause he's subject to fits of fantasy and starts thinking he's a circus performer and that the curb is a tightrope strung high in the air. And sometimes after a rain he likes to step down off his tightrope right into the gutter and slosh around getting his shoes **8** and cuffs wet. Then I get hit when I get home. Or sometimes if you don't watch him he'll dash across traffic to the island in the middle of Broadway and give the pigeons a fit. Then I have to go behind him apologizing to all the old people sitting around trying to get some sun and getting all upset with the pigeons fluttering around them, scattering their newspapers and upsetting the wax-paper lunches in their laps. So I keep Raymond on the inside of me, and he plays like he's driving a stagecoach, which is OK by me so long as he doesn't run me over or interrupt my breathing exercises, which I have to do on account of I'm serious about my running, and I don't care who knows it.

Now some people like to act like things come easy to them, won't let on that they practice. Not me. I'll high-prance down 34th Street like a rodeo pony to keep my knees strong even if it does get my mother uptight so that she walks ahead like she's not with me, don't know me, is

---

1. **the dozens:** a game in which players trade insults. The first person who shows anger is the loser.
2. **Mercury:** the ancient Roman messenger god, known for his speed.
3. **PAL:** Police Athletic League.

22 CHALLENGES

all by herself on a shopping trip, and I am somebody else's crazy child. Now you take Cynthia Procter for instance. She's just the opposite. If there's a test tomorrow, she'll say something like, "Oh, I guess I'll play handball this afternoon and watch television tonight," just to let you know she ain't thinking about the test. Or like last week when she won the spelling bee for the millionth time, "A good thing you got *receive,* Squeaky, cause I would have got it wrong. I completely forgot about the spelling bee." And she'll clutch the lace on her blouse like it was a narrow escape. Oh, brother. But of course when I pass her house on my early morning trots around the block, she is practicing the scales on her piano over and over and over and over. Then in music class she always lets herself get bumped around so she falls accidentally on purpose onto the piano stool and is so surprised to find herself sitting there that she decides just for fun to try out the ole keys. And what do you know—Chopin's[4] waltzes just spring out of her fingertips and she's the most surprised thing in the world. A regular <u>prodigy.</u> I could kill people like that. I stay up all night studying the words for the spelling bee. And you can see me any time of day practicing running. I never walk if I can trot, and shame on Raymond if he can't keep up. But of course he does, cause if he hangs back someone's liable to walk up to him and get smart, or take his allowance from him, or ask him where he got that great big pumpkin head. People are so stupid sometimes.

So I'm strolling down Broadway breathing out and breathing in on counts of seven, which is my lucky number, and here comes Gretchen and her sidekicks: Mary Louise, who used to be a friend of mine when she first moved to Harlem from Baltimore and got beat up by everybody till I took up for her on account of her mother and my mother used to sing in the same choir when they were young girls, but people ain't grateful, so now she hangs out with the new girl Gretchen and talks about me like a dog; and Rosie, who is as fat as I am skinny and has a big mouth where Raymond is concerned and is too stupid to know that there is not a big deal of difference between herself and Raymond and that she can't afford to throw stones. So they are steady coming up Broadway and I see right away that it's going to be one of those Dodge City[5] scenes cause the street ain't that big and they're close to the buildings just as we are. First I think I'll just step into the candy store and look over the new comics and let them pass. But that's chicken and I've got a reputation to consider. So then I think I'll just walk straight on through them or even over them if necessary. But as they get to me, they slow down. I'm ready to fight, cause like I said I don't feature a whole lot of chitchat, I much prefer to just knock you down right from the jump and save everybody a lotta precious time.

"You signing up for the May Day races?" smiles Mary Louise, only it's not a smile at all. A dumb question like that doesn't deserve an answer. Besides, there's just me and Gretchen standing there really, so no use wasting my breath talking to shadows.

"I don't think you're going to win this time," says Rosie, trying to signify with her hands on her hips all salty, completely forgetting that I have whupped her many times for less salt than that.

"I always win cause I'm the best," I say straight at Gretchen, who is, as far as I'm concerned, the only one talking in this ventriloquist-dummy routine. Gretchen smiles, but it's

---

4. **Chopin** (shō′păn′): Frédéric François Chopin (1810–1849), a Polish composer and pianist.

5. **Dodge City:** the setting of the old television series "Gunsmoke," which often featured a showdown between the marshal and a gunfighter.

9
Squeaky exaggerates to show her extreme dislike for pretentious people. Squeaky is straightforward and thinks everyone should be.

10
Raymond depends on Squeaky to protect him from cruel remarks and actions of others.

11
Setting. Although Squeaky has mentioned Amsterdam Avenue and 34th street, this is first positive identification of setting as Harlem.

12 Drawing Conclusions
What does Squeaky mean when she says that Rosie "has a big mouth where Raymond is concerned"? Rosie makes fun of him.

13
Allusion. Squeaky's allusion to television series popular in 1950s and 1960s gives reader image of confrontation Squeaky expects.

14
Characterization. Squeaky's thoughts show that she does not like confrontations but will not back down from one.

15 Finding Details / Drawing Conclusions
To whom does Squeaky refer as "shadows"? What does she mean by the word? Mary Louise and Rosie. They are merely "sidekicks" of Gretchen. As far as Squeaky is concerned, Mary Louise and Rosie do not exist.

story interpreted dramatically.

16
Squeaky implies that women, like girls, are so competitive that they do not really smile at one another.

Finding Details
Analyzing
17
What does Squeaky say she will be if anyone says anything more about Raymond? What does she mean? She says she will be their mother too. She will "whip" them.

18
Dancers go around Maypole while holding streamers radiating from pole.

19
Squeaky is practical. She cannot understand why people want to pretend to be something they are not.

20
Characterization. Squeaky is comfortable with herself as a person and associates herself with running.

21
Parkees: those who regularly attend the park.

22
Squeaky has uncanny insight into thoughts and feelings of others. She quickly judges every situation she faces.

not a smile, and I'm thinking that girls never really smile at each other because they don't know how and don't want to know how and there's probably no one to teach us how, cause **16** grown-up girls don't know either. Then they all look at Raymond, who has just brought his mule team to a standstill. And they're about to see what trouble they can get into through him.

"What grade you in now, Raymond?"

"You got anything to say to my brother, you say it to me, Mary Louise Williams of Raggedy Town, Baltimore."

"What are you, his mother?" sasses Rosie.

"That's right, Fatso. And the next word out **17** of anybody and I'll be *their* mother too." So they just stand there and Gretchen shifts from one leg to the other and so do they. Then Gretchen puts her hands on her hips and is about to say something with her freckle-face self but doesn't. Then she walks around me looking me up and down but keeps walking up Broadway, and her sidekicks follow her. So me and Raymond smile at each other and he says, "Gidyap" to his team and I continue with my breathing exercises, strolling down Broadway toward the ice man on 145th with not a care in the world cause I am Miss Quicksilver herself.

I take my time getting to the park on May Day because the track meet is the last thing on the program. The biggest thing on the pro-**18** gram is the Maypole dancing, which I can do without, thank you, even if my mother thinks it's a shame I don't take part and act like a girl for a change. You'd think my mother'd be grateful not to have to make me a white organdy dress with a big satin sash and buy me new white baby-doll shoes that can't be taken out of the box till the big day. You'd think she'd be glad her daughter ain't out there prancing around a Maypole getting the new clothes all dirty and sweaty and trying to act like a fairy or a flower or whatever you're supposed to be

when you should be trying to be yourself, whatever that is, which is, as far as I am con-**19** cerned, a poor black girl who really can't afford to buy shoes and a new dress you only wear once a lifetime cause it won't fit next year.

I was once a strawberry in a Hansel and Gretel pageant when I was in nursery school and didn't have no better sense than to dance on tiptoe with my arms in a circle over my head doing umbrella steps and being a perfect fool just so my mother and father could come dressed up and clap. You'd think they'd know better than to encourage that kind of non-**20** sense. I am not a strawberry. I do not dance on my toes. I run. That is what I am all about. So I always come late to the May Day program, just in time to get my number pinned on and lay in the grass till they announce the fifty-yard dash.

I put Raymond in the little swings, which is a tight squeeze this year and will be impossible next year. Then I look around for Mr. Pearson, who pins the numbers on. I'm really looking for Gretchen if you want to know the truth, but she's not around. The park is jam-packed. Parents in hats and corsages and breast-pocket handkerchiefs peeking up. Kids in white **21** dresses and light-blue suits. The parkees unfolding chairs and chasing the rowdy kids from Lenox as if they had no right to be there. The big guys with their caps on backwards, leaning against the fence swirling the basket-**22** balls on the tips of their fingers, waiting for all these crazy people to clear out the park so they can play. Most of the kids in my class are carrying bass drums and glockenspiels[6] and flutes. You'd think they'd put in a few bongos or something for real like that.

Then here comes Mr. Pearson with his clipboard and his cards and pencils and whistles and safety pins and fifty million other things

6. **glockenspiels** (glŏk′ən-spēlz′): musical instruments, something like xylophones, often used in marching bands.

SPORTS LINK
Encourage interested students to find out about the fastest women in the world. Students could research the winners of the women's track-and-field events at the most recent Olympic Games. Have students give informal oral reports to the

class on their findings.

COOPERATIVE LEARNING
Encourage small groups of students to research Harlem to learn more about the inner-city lifestyle that Squeaky describes in the story. Have a spokesperson for each group report findings to the class.

he's always dropping all over the place with his clumsy self. He sticks out in a crowd because 23 he's on stilts. We used to call him Jack and the Beanstalk to get him mad. But I'm the only one that can outrun him and get away, and I'm too grown for that silliness now.

"Well, Squeaky," he says, checking my name off the list and handing me number seven and two pins. And I'm thinking he's got no right to call me Squeaky, if I can't call him Beanstalk.

24 "Hazel Elizabeth Deborah Parker," I correct him and tell him to write it down on his board.

"Well, Hazel Elizabeth Deborah Parker, going to give someone else a break this year?" I squint at him real hard to see if he is seriously thinking I should lose the race on purpose just to give someone else a break. "Only six girls running this time," he continues, shaking his head sadly like it's my fault all of New York didn't turn out in sneakers. "That new girl 25 should give you a run for your money." He looks around the park for Gretchen like a periscope in a submarine movie. "Wouldn't it 28 be a nice gesture if you were . . . to ahhh . . ."

I give him such a look he couldn't finish putting that idea into words. Grown-ups got a lot of nerve sometimes. I pin number seven to 26 myself and stomp away, I'm so burnt. And I go straight for the track and stretch out on the grass while the band winds up with "Oh, the Monkey Wrapped His Tail Around the Flagpole," which my teacher calls by some other name. The man on the loudspeaker is calling everyone over to the track and I'm on my back looking at the sky, trying to pretend I'm in the 27 country, but I can't, because even the grass in the city feels as hard as sidewalk, and there's just no pretending you are anywhere but in a "concrete jungle" as my grandfather says.

The twenty-yard dash takes all of two minutes cause most of the little kids don't know no better than to run off the track or run the wrong way or run smack into the fence and fall

down and cry. One little kid, though, has got the good sense to run straight for the white ribbon up ahead so he wins. Then the second-graders line up for the thirty-yard dash and I don't even bother to turn my head to watch cause Raphael Perez always wins. He wins before he even begins by psyching the runners, telling them they're going to trip on their shoelaces and fall on their faces or lose their shorts or something, which he doesn't really have to do since he is very fast, almost as fast as I am. After that is the forty-yard dash, which I used to run when I was in first grade. Raymond is hollering from the swings cause he knows I'm about to do my thing cause the man on the loudspeaker has just announced the fifty-yard dash, although he might just as well be giving a recipe for angel food cake cause you can hardly make out what he's saying for the static. I get up and slip off my sweat pants and then I see Gretchen standing at the starting line, kicking her legs out like a pro. Then 28 as I get into place I see that ole Raymond is on line on the other side of the fence, bending down with his fingers on the ground just like he knew what he was doing. I was going to yell at him but then I didn't. It burns up your energy to holler.

Every time, just before I take off in a race, I always feel like I'm in a dream, the kind of dream you have when you're sick with fever 29 and feel all hot and weightless. I dream I'm flying over a sandy beach in the early morning sun, kissing the leaves of the trees as I fly by. And there's always the smell of apples, just like in the country when I was little and used to think I was a choo-choo train, running through the fields of corn and chugging up the hill to the orchard. And all the time I'm dreaming this, I get lighter and lighter until I'm flying over the beach again, getting blown through the sky like a feather that weighs nothing at all. But once I spread my fingers in

23
Squeaky describes Mr. Pearson as being on stilts, indicating that he is very tall. She shows that she is now too mature to make fun of a person because of physical attributes.

24
Squeaky is feeling grown-up and superior. She demands that Mr. Pearson show his respect by calling her by her real name.

25
Simile. Comparison emphasizes Mr. Pearson's height.

26 Analyzing
Why is Squeaky angry? How is this response to Mr. Pearson's suggestion consistent with Squeaky's character? Squeaky is angry because Mr. Pearson suggests she deliberately lose the race. Squeaky does not like anything that is fake or dishonest.

27
Simile. Comparison of feel of grass to that of sidewalk emphasizes harshness (hardness) of inner-city life.

28
Even though Squeaky is about to run an important race, Raymond is never out of her mind. She is constantly aware of her responsibility to him.

29
Squeaky "psyches herself up" as she prepares to run.

TRANSPARENCIES 1 & 2

Fine Art
Theme: *Those Who Dare* – invites students to explore artworks that examine the idea of perseverance despite difficult situations.

VISUAL CONNECTIONS

Ideas for Writing

Taking a cue from the enthusiasm of the runner in this photograph, students might write about races or other athletic or scholastic competitions in which they have felt the exhilaration of meeting challenges. Writings might be in the form of short stories, essays, or poems.

30

Her mental preparation for race includes building her confidence. Closest Squeaky comes to lying is that she tells herself she can beat her father.

31

Realization that Raymond can run almost makes Squeaky forget about her own race.

32 Finding Details / Analyzing

Who does Squeaky say can "walk tall for another year"? What does she mean? "Everybody on 151st Street" probably refers to her family and friends. Squeaky means that they can be proud that someone from their family (or neighborhood) has won race.

33

Squeaky begins to respect Gretchen because she, too, is a skilled athlete.

34

Simile. Squeaky at first thinks of Raymond as clumsy, but as he starts to climb fence, she begins to realize his movements are graceful.

the dirt and crouch over the Get on Your Mark, the dream goes and I am solid again and am telling myself, Squeaky you must win, you must **30** win, you are the fastest thing in the world, you can even beat your father up Amsterdam if you really try. And then I feel my weight coming back just behind my knees then down to my feet then into the earth and the pistol shot explodes in my blood and I am off and weightless again, flying past the other runners, my arms pumping up and down and the whole world is quiet except for the crunch as I zoom over the gravel in the track. I glance to my left and there is no one. To the right, a blurred Gretchen, who's got her chin jutting out as if it would win the race all by itself. And on the other side of the fence is Raymond with his arms down to his side and the palms tucked up behind him, running in his very own style, and **31** it's the first time I ever saw that and I almost stop to watch my brother Raymond on his first run. But the white ribbon is bouncing toward me and I tear past it, racing into the distance till my feet with a mind of their own start digging up footfuls of dirt and brake me short. Then all the kids standing on the side pile on me, banging me on the back and slapping my head with their May Day programs, for I have **32** won again and everybody on 151st Street can walk tall for another year.

"In first place . . ." the man on the loudspeaker is clear as a bell now. But then he pauses and the loudspeaker starts to whine. Then static. And I lean down to catch my breath and here comes Gretchen walking back, for she's overshot the finish line too, huffing and puffing with her hands on her hips taking **33** it slow, breathing in steady time like a real pro and I sort of like her a little for the first time. "In first place . . ." and then three or four voices **34** get all mixed up on the loudspeaker and I dig my sneaker into the grass and stare at Gretchen, who's staring back, we both wonder-

ing just who did win. I can hear old Beanstalk arguing with the man on the loudspeaker and then a few others running their mouths about what the stopwatches say. Then I hear Raymond yanking at the fence to call me and I wave to shush him, but he keeps rattling the fence like a gorilla in a cage like in them gorilla movies, but then like a dancer or something he starts climbing up nice and easy but very fast.

And it occurs to me, watching how smoothly he climbs hand over hand and remembering how **40** he looked running with his arms down to his side and with the wind pulling his mouth back and his teeth showing and all, it occurred to **35** me that Raymond would make a very fine runner. Doesn't he always keep up with me on my trots? And he surely knows how to breathe in counts of seven cause he's always doing it at the dinner table, which drives my brother George up the wall. And I'm smiling to beat the band cause if I've lost this race, or if me and Gretchen tied, or even if I've won, I can always retire as a runner and begin a whole new **36** career as a coach with Raymond as my champion. After all, with a little more study I can beat Cynthia and her phony self at the spelling bee. And if I bugged my mother, I could get **37** piano lessons and become a star. And I have a big rep as the baddest thing around. And I've got a roomful of ribbons and medals and **38** awards. But what has Raymond got to call his own?

So I stand there with my new plans, laughing out loud by this time as Raymond jumps down from the fence and runs over with his teeth showing and his arms down to the side, which no one before him has quite mastered as a running style. And by the time he comes over I'm jumping up and down so glad to see him— my brother Raymond, a great runner in the family tradition. But of course everyone thinks I'm jumping up and down because the men on the loudspeaker have finally gotten themselves together and compared notes and are **39** announcing "In first place—Miss Hazel Elizabeth Deborah Parker." (Dig that.) "In second place—Miss Gretchen P. Lewis." And I look over at Gretchen wondering what the *P* stands for. And I smile. Cause she's good, no doubt about it. Maybe she'd like to help me coach Raymond; she obviously is serious about running, as any fool can see. And she nods to congratulate me and she smiles. And I smile. We **40** stand there with this big smile of respect between us. It's about as real a smile as girls can do for each other, considering we don't practice real smiling every day, you know, **41** cause maybe we too busy being flowers or fairies or strawberries instead of something honest and worthy of respect . . . you know . . . like being people.

TRANSPARENCY 4

Literary Elements
Character – explores the ways that an author can reveal characterization.

CLOSURE
Ask students to explain how Squeaky responds to the realization that Raymond can run and that Gretchen is, like Squeaky, a "real" person and a skilled athlete.

READING CHECK
1. Taking care of her brother Raymond (p. 22).
2. Raymond is mentally and physically handicapped (p. 22).
3. Harlem (p. 23).
4. Practices breathing and leg exercises (p. 22).
5. Squeaky (p. 27).

FOR STUDY AND DISCUSSION
1. She is fastest thing on two feet and can do anything well if she works at it.
2. Cynthia pretends that everything she does comes easily, when actually she practices hard to achieve her triumphs.
3a. To take part in the Maypole dancing and to be more ladylike; she would also like Squeaky to stop high-prancing down street when she is with her. 3b. To lose race for a change and give someone else a "break."
4. Retire from running and train Raymond to be a runner.
5. Squeaky realizes that Gretchen is serious about running, too. They respect each other.
6. Responses will vary. Perhaps because an important moment in story occurs as result of Raymond's run. Squeaky realizes that Raymond would make fine runner and would have something "to call his own."

LITERARY ELEMENTS
1. Defends him and refuses to let other youngsters ridicule him; puts him on swings. Decision to "give" Raymond something of which he can be proud also shows loyalty and kindness.
2a. She is honest and has realistic view of herself.
2b. She is brave and willing to face problems.
2c. She is generous and appreciates excellence in anyone.

Reading Check

1. What is Squeaky's only chore at home?
2. Why does Squeaky have to take care of Raymond, who is older and bigger?
3. Where does Squeaky live?
4. What does she do while she walks with Raymond?
5. Who wins the fifty-yard dash?

For Study and Discussion

Analyzing and Interpreting the Story

1. In "Raymond's Run," a girl who believes in herself discovers the joy of believing in other people as well. What does Squeaky believe about her own abilities?

2. Squeaky believes in being honest. What actions of Cynthia Procter's irritate her?

3. Some people in the story think Squeaky should be a different kind of person. **a.** What would Squeaky's mother like her to do? **b.** What would Mr. Pearson like her to do?

4. Squeaky knows that she can win medals and "become a star." But she asks herself, "What has Raymond got to call his own?" After Raymond's run, what does Squeaky plan to do for her brother?

5. Squeaky also discovers something about her rival, Gretchen. Why do she and Gretchen smile at each other after the race?

6. Why do you think the author called this story "Raymond's Run"?

Literary Elements

Drawing Conclusions About a Character

In some stories, the writer may tell you directly that a character is loyal, or courageous, or mean, or dishonest. But in most stories, the writer lets you draw your own conclusions about a character's personal qualities.

In "Raymond's Run," for example, you learn a great deal about Squeaky from what she says and does, and even from what she thinks. But you are not told directly what her personal qualities are.

One way to learn about Squeaky's personal qualities is to notice how she acts toward Raymond. It would be easy to be cruel to Raymond, as some of the characters are. Name at least two of Squeaky's actions that reveal that she is loyal and kind to Raymond.

2. What personal qualities does Squeaky reveal by each of the following actions?

a. Squeaky admits that she needs to practice her running and her spelling.

b. Squeaky does not hide from the girls she meets on the street.

c. Squeaky smiles at Gretchen and admits that her rival is a good runner.

Language and Vocabulary

Recognizing Informal Language

Since Squeaky is the narrator in "Raymond's Run," the story is told from her point of view. To make Squeaky seem real, the author has her speak the same kind of informal language and slang that a tough, streetwise girl might use.

On page 27 Squeaky says:

And I have a big rep as the baddest thing around.

This sentence sounds like Squeaky speaking.

Individual students or small groups might like to write a short sequel to this story, in which Raymond enters his first official race. If possible, the sequels should be written from Squeaky's **point of view.**

Students who are particularly interested in running might collect information from magazine articles or from popular how-to books and report on the sport. Alternatively, they might do research on a favorite Olympic runner.

After reviewing Squeaky's tirade about May-pole dancing and playing the strawberry in a nursery school pageant, students might like to write or draw accounts of their own experiences in such school programs.

In slang, the word *bad* means "very good." Someone writing more formally might put the idea this way:

> I have a well-deserved reputation in the neighborhood for accomplishing anything I set out to do and, when I choose, for winning any contest I enter.

1 Some other slang and informal expressions from the story are italicized below. What does each italicized word mean?

> …run *smack* into the fence…
> …and *stomp* away so *burnt.*
> But that's *chicken…*
> …I don't *feature* a whole lot of chitchat.

2 Rewrite these quotations substituting more formal words for the italicized ones. Do they still sound like Squeaky talking?

Focus on Descriptive Writing

Identifying Your Purpose

Your **purpose** or goal in a description is related to the kind of description you write. If you want to inform, you will usually write an **objective description,** or a factual, realistic picture of the subject. If your purpose is to be creative, you will usually write a **subjective description,** which combines details about the subject with your thoughts and feelings. In "Raymond's Run," for example, Squeaky gives a subjective description of the May Day races.

Choose two subjects, one for an objective description and one for a subjective description. Each subject should be a familiar person, place, or thing. Here are some possible subjects:

a snowstorm	a parade	a tree
a basketball	a bird	a beach

Freewrite for five minutes about each subject. Save your writing.

About the Author

Toni Cade Bambara   (1939–   )

Toni Cade Bambara (bäm-bä′rä) took her last name from a signature on a sketchbook she found in her great-grandmother's trunk. (Bambara is the name of a people in northwest Africa who are noted for their delicate wood carvings.) Like her character Squeaky, Cade Bambara grew up in New York City. After receiving a college degree from New York City's Queens College, she studied in Italy and France.

In the 1960s and 1970s, she became active in civil rights issues. She has lectured extensively and been involved in many community programs and art groups. She has also worked as a social worker. In addition, Cade Bambara has taught African American studies and English and been a writer-in-residence at many universities.

In her fiction Cade Bambara focuses on the unique experiences of African Americans. Poet Lucille Clifton has said of the stories in *Gorilla, My Love* (1972): "She has captured it all, how we really talk, how we really are; and done it with love and respect." In her novel *Salt Eaters* (1980), which won the 1981 American Book Award, Cade Bambara uses several dialects to tell the story of a depressed woman who seeks help from a healer.

The overall aim is for students to analyze the man's actions important to the **crisis** in "The Sea Devil" and to identify the story's main idea. For a complete list of objectives, see the **Teacher's Notes.**

The underlined words are in the Glossary. The **Language and Vocabulary** exercise on pp. 38–39 will give students practice in finding the meanings of prefixes and suffixes.

Discuss with students how people today challenge nature—for example, shooting the rapids of a swift river, climbing mountains, and surfing. Why do people forego comfort and risk danger to confront nature in these ways?

PREREADING FOCUS

The headnote mentions nature's propensity for producing challenges. Ask students to discuss situations in which they have faced challenges of nature.

The Sea Devil

1

Setting. Southern Florida coast. The man leaves security of lighted house to face a foreboding darkness.

2

Personification. Image is one of persistent, harsh presence of summer weather.

3

Sea wall: a wall or embankment made to break force of waves and to protect shore from erosion; humans' fortress against nature, symbolizing edge of civilization.

4

The man is described as intellectually and physically strong.

5

Use to answer **study question 1**, p. 38.

6 Making Inferences
To what does the phrase "in the beginning" refer? A time of innocent, unspoiled life, when humans lived in harmony with nature and survived by hunting for their food.

The Sea Devil

ARTHUR GORDON

Nature can provide sudden, unexpected challenges that demand intelligence rather than strength for survival. As you read this story, think about how you would react in a similar situation.

The man came out of the house and stood quite still, listening. Behind him, the lights glowed in the cheerful room, the books were neat and orderly in their cases, the radio **1** talked importantly to itself. In front of him, the bay stretched dark and silent, one of the countless lagoons that border the coast where Florida thrusts its green thumb deep into the tropics.

It was late in September. The night was **2** breathless; summer's dead hand still lay heavy on the land. The man moved forward six paces **3** and stood on the sea wall. He dropped his cigarette and noted where the tiny spark hissed and went out. The tide was beginning to ebb.

Somewhere out in the blackness a mullet jumped and fell back with a sullen splash. Heavy with roe,[1] they were jumping less often, now. They would not take a hook, but a practiced eye could see the swirls they made in the glassy water. In the dark of the moon, a skilled man with a cast net might take half a dozen in an hour's work. And a big mullet makes a meal for a family.

The man turned abruptly and went into the garage, where his cast net hung. He was in his late twenties, wide-shouldered and strong. He **4** did not have to fish for a living, or even for food. He was a man who worked with his head, not with his hands. But he liked to go casting alone at night.

He liked the loneliness and the labor of it. **5** He liked the clean taste of salt when he gripped the edge of the net with his teeth as a cast netter must. He liked the arching flight of sixteen pounds of lead and linen against the starlight, and the weltering crash[2] of the net into the unsuspecting water. He liked the harsh tug of the retrieving rope around his wrist, and the way the net came alive when the cast was true, and the thud of captured fish on the floorboards of the skiff.

He liked all that because he found in it a reality that seemed to be missing from his twentieth-century job and from his daily life. He liked being the hunter, skilled and solitary and elemental. There was no conscious cruelty in the way he felt. It was the way things had **6** been in the beginning.

The man lifted the net down carefully and lowered it into a bucket. He put a paddle beside the bucket. Then he went into the house. When

1. **roe:** fish eggs.

2. **weltering crash:** a crash that causes a great disturbance in the water.

MOTIVATIONAL SUMMARY
A young man sets out on one of his fishing excursions alone at night in a lagoon in Florida. Feeling powerful and competent, he thinks of himself as returning to an elemental state in which he is the hunter in contest with nature. At first, all goes well. He catches a mullet and an angelfish. The next time he casts, however, he nets a giant ray by mistake. The powerful ray, nine feet from one wing tip to the other, swims away and pulls the man out of the boat by the net rope attached to his wrist. The man is pulled underwater and comes closer and closer to drowning. His intelligence and determination to live seem no match for the ray's strength.

©1986 James H. Carmichael, Jr./The Image Bank

he came out, he was wearing swimming trunks and a pair of old tennis shoes. Nothing else.

7 The skiff, flat-bottomed, was moored off the sea wall. He would not go far, he told himself. Just to the tumbledown dock half a mile away. Mullet had a way of feeding around old pilings after dark. If he moved quietly, he might pick up two or three in one cast close to the dock. And maybe a couple of others on the way down or back.

He shoved off and stood motionless for a moment, letting his eyes grow accustomed to the dark. Somewhere out in the channel a porpoise blew with a sound like steam escaping.
8 The man smiled a little; porpoises were his friends. Once, fishing in the Gulf, he had seen the charter-boat captain reach overside and gaff[3] a baby porpoise through the sinewy part of the tail. He had hoisted it aboard, had dropped it into the bait well, where it thrashed around, puzzled and unhappy. And the mother had swum alongside the boat and under the boat and around the boat, nudging the stout planking with her back, slapping it **9** with her tail, until the man felt sorry for her and made the captain let the baby porpoise go.

He took the net from the bucket, slipped the noose in the retrieving rope over his wrist, pulled the slipknot tight. It was an old net, but still serviceable; he had rewoven the rents[4] made by underwater snags. He coiled the

3. **gaff:** spear.
4. **rents:** holes.

7 Analyzing
What decision indicates that the man is cautious? His vow not to journey far beyond sea wall into unknown open water.

8
Use to answer **study question 4a,** p. 38.

9
Characterization. Although he is a hunter, the man is sympathetic toward at least one species—the porpoise.

This story is simple and compelling enough for independent reading, either in class or as homework. After students have had a chance to talk informally about their responses to the story, you might lead a discussion of questions 1–5 in the

For Study and Discussion feature. Reserve questions 6 and 7, which require students to draw inferences and imagine the character's thoughts, for individual responses in writing. You might then have students compare their responses and discuss interpretations.

MATH LINK

Challenge students who enjoy mathematics to determine, using the diameter measurement given in the story, the actual circumference of the circular net. Then, ask students to measure and mark the actual size and circular shape of

---

10

Ancient design of net recalls the man's reason for fishing—to take him away from modern world and back to a more natural, primitive time.

11

Simile. "Black as a witch's cat" reinforces gloominess and darkness of ocean **setting**.

12

Description of hazards to left and to right lets reader know that the man's venture is not a completely safe one.

13

That fish is both gleaming (bright) and dull (dark) is paradox.

14 Comparing/Contrasting

How would the hunt of primitive humans be different from the man's hunt? Primitive humans hunted mainly for food and survival; the man hunts for sport.

15

Simile. Movements of net compared to closing of giant fist around trapped prey.

---

thirty-foot rope carefully, making sure there were no kinks. A tangled rope, he knew, would spoil any cast.

10 The basic design of the net had not changed in three thousand years. It was a mesh circle with a diameter of fourteen feet. It measured close to fifteen yards around the circumference and could, if thrown perfectly, blanket a hundred fifty square feet of sea water. In the center of this radial trap[5] was a small iron collar where the retrieving rope met the twenty-three separate drawstrings leading to the outer rim of the net. Along this rim, spaced an inch and a half apart, were the heavy lead sinkers.

The man raised the iron collar until it was a foot above his head. The net hung soft and pliant and deadly. He shook it gently, making sure that the drawstrings were not tangled, that the sinkers were hanging true. Then he eased it down and picked up the paddle.

11 The night was black as a witch's cat; the stars looked fuzzy and dim. Down to the southward, the lights of a causeway made a yellow necklace **12** across the sky. To the man's left were the tangled roots of a mangrove swamp; to his right, the open waters of the bay. Most of it was fairly shallow, but there were channels eight feet deep. The man could not see the old dock, but he knew where it was. He pulled the paddle quietly through the water, and the phosphorescence[6] glowed and died.

For five minutes he paddled. Then, twenty feet ahead of the skiff, a mullet jumped. A big fish, close to three pounds. For a moment it **13** hung in the still air, gleaming dully. Then it vanished. But the ripples marked the spot, and where there was one there were often others.

The man stood up quickly. He picked up the coiled rope, and with the same hand grasped

---

5. **radial** (rā′dē-əl) **trap:** The drawstrings of the net lead out from a small iron collar, like spokes from the center of a wheel.
6. **phosphorescence** (fŏs′fə-rĕs′əns): glowing light.

---

the net at a point four feet below the iron collar. He raised the skirt to his mouth, gripped it strongly with his teeth. He slid his free hand as far as it would go down the circumference of the net, so that he had three points of contact with the mass of cordage and metal. He made sure his feet were planted solidly. Then he waited, feeling the tension that is older than the human race, the fierce exhilaration of the hunter at the moment of ambush, the atavistic **14** desire[7] to capture and kill and ultimately consume.

A mullet swirled, ahead and to the left. The man swung the heavy net back, twisting his body and bending his knees so as to get more upward thrust. He shot it forward, letting go simultaneously with rope hand and with teeth, holding a fraction of a second longer with the other hand so as to give the net the necessary spin, impart the centrifugal force[8] that would make it flare into a circle. The skiff ducked sideways, but he kept his balance. The net fell with a splash.

The man waited for five seconds. Then he began to retrieve it, pulling in a series of sharp jerks so that the drawstrings would gather the **15** net inward, like a giant fist closing on this segment of the teeming sea. He felt the net quiver, and he knew it was not empty. He swung it, dripping, over the gunwale,[9] saw the broad silver side of the mullet quivering, saw too the gleam of a smaller fish. He looked closely to make sure no stingray[10] was hidden in the mesh, then raised the iron collar and shook the net out. The mullet fell with a thud and flapped wildly. The other victim was an

---

7. **atavistic** (ăt′ə-vĭs′tĭk) **desire:** a desire that his earliest ancestors would have had.
8. **centrifugal** (sĕn-trĭf′yə-gəl) **force:** the force that makes an object moving in a circle (here, the net) move away from the center of the circle (here, the man).
9. **gunwale** (gŭn′əl): the upper edge of the side of the boat.
10. **stingray:** a fish with a long, whiplike tail, which has one or more dangerous spines.

---

angelfish, beautifully marked, but too small to keep. The man picked it up gently and dropped it overboard. He coiled the rope, took up the paddle. He would cast no more until he came to the dock.

The skiff moved on. At last, ten feet apart, a pair of stakes rose up gauntly out of the night. **16** Barnacle-encrusted, they once had marked the approach from the main channel. The man guided the skiff between them, then put the paddle down softly. He stood up, reached for the net, tightened the noose around his wrist. From here he could drift down upon the dock. He could see it now, a ruined skeleton in the starshine. Beyond it a mullet jumped and fell back with a flat, liquid sound. The man raised the edge of the net, put it between his teeth. He would not cast at a single swirl, he decided; he would wait until he saw two or three close together. The skiff was barely moving. He felt **17** his muscles tense themselves, awaiting the signal from the brain.

Behind him in the channel he heard the porpoise blow again, nearer now. He frowned in the darkness. If the porpoise chose to fish this area, the mullet would scatter and vanish. There was no time to lose.

18 A school of sardines surfaced suddenly, skittering along like drops of mercury. Something, perhaps the shadow of the skiff, had frightened them. The old dock loomed very close. A mullet broke water just too far away; then another, nearer. The man marked[11] the spreading ripples and decided to wait no longer.

He swung back the net, heavier now that it **23** was wet. He had to turn his head, but out of the corner of his eye he saw two swirls in the black water just off the starboard bow.[12] They were about eight feet apart, and they had the sluggish oily look that marks the presence of

11. **marked:** here, noticed.
12. **starboard bow:** the right-hand side of the front of the boat.

something big just below the surface. His conscious mind had no time to function, but instinct told him that the net was wide enough to cover both swirls if he could alter the direction of his cast. He could not halt the swing, but he shifted his feet slightly and made the cast off balance. He saw the net shoot forward, flare into an oval, and drop just where he wanted it.

Then the sea exploded in his face. In a **19** frenzy of spray, a great horned thing shot like a huge bat out of the water. The man saw the mesh of his net etched against the mottled blackness of its body and he knew, in the split second in which thought was still possible, that those twin swirls had been made not by two mullet, but by the wing tips of the giant ray of the Gulf Coast, *Manta birostris*, also known as clam cracker, devil ray, sea devil.

The man gave a hoarse cry. He tried to claw the slipknot off his wrist, but there was no time. The quarter-inch line snapped taut. He **20** shot over the side of the skiff as if he had roped a runaway locomotive. He hit the water head first and seemed to bounce once. He plowed a blinding furrow for perhaps ten yards. Then the line went slack as the sea devil jumped again. It was not the full-grown manta of the deep Gulf, but it was close to nine feet from tip to tip and it weighed over a thousand pounds. **21** Up into the air it went, pearl-colored underbelly gleaming as it twisted in a frantic effort to dislodge the clinging thing that had fallen upon it. Up into the starlight, a monstrous sur- **22** vival from the dawn of time.

The water was less than four feet deep. Sobbing and choking, the man struggled for a foothold on the slimy bottom. Sucking in great gulps of air, he fought to free himself from the rope. But the slipknot was jammed deep into his wrist; he might as well have tried to loosen a circle of steel.

The ray came down with a thunderous splash and drove forward again. The flexible

16
Barnacle: type of shellfish that attaches itself to wood, rock, and large sea mammals.

17
While fishing, the man uses both physical and mental skills; on his job, he uses mental skills only.

18
Foreshadowing. Frightened agitation of sardines hints at impending danger.

19
Simile. Comparison makes creature seem evil, thus supporting name "sea devil."

20
Sea devil, a powerful natural force, is compared to locomotive, a powerful human-made force.

21
Irony. Sea devil is threat to the man only because the man has netted and threatened it.

22 Drawing Conclusions
What does "survival from the dawn of time" suggest about the ray? Suggests idea of creature so in command of its environment that it has survived from beginning of time; furthers **theme** of human against nature.

23
Irony. The forceful pull of the ray causes the man to be snared by the rope he uses to catch fish.

Invite interested students to research mangroves and the animals and birds that live in and around them. Ask students to determine what role mangroves play in protecting shorelines. Extend this activity by having students create a mural showing the marine food chain in a mangrove forest. The mural should illustrate the plant- and meat-eating sea animals at the top of the chain all the way down to the scavengers and decomposing matter at the bottom of the chain.

24

The ray weighs about six times more than the man does.

25

The man feels totally powerless against awesome force of sea devil.

26

The man understands how it feels to be a struggling fish as roles of hunter (fisherman) and hunted (fish) are reversed.

27 Finding Details
Drawing Conclusions
What is flashing through the man's mind? What do these pictures suggest? Scenes of his life flash through his mind. The pictures suggest the man is near death.

28

Symbol. The man, too, is "gasping [his] life away" in an alien environment.

29 Making Inferences
How might the man's body fight for its "existence"? His muscles might tense, as a reflexive action, against pull of sea devil.

VISUAL CONNECTIONS
Exploring the Subject
The ray in this photograph is a member of one of from 300 to 350 different species of rays. Rays are closely related to sharks although rays have gill openings on the underside of their bodies and pectoral fins attached to the sides of their heads. Rays spend much of their time lying on the ocean bottom partly covered by mud or sand. They usually eat plankton, small fish, and shellfish.

net followed every movement, <u>impeding</u> it hardly at all. The man weighed a hundred seventy-five pounds, and he was braced for the shock, and he had the desperate strength that comes from looking into the blank eyes of death. It was useless. His arm straightened out with a jerk that seemed to dislocate his shoulder; his feet shot out from under him; his head went under again. Now at last he knew how the fish must feel when the line tightens and drags him toward the <u>alien</u> element that is his doom. Now he knew.

Desperately he dug the fingers of his free hand into the ooze, felt them dredge a futile channel through broken shells and the ribbon-like sea grasses. He tried to raise his head, but could not get it clear. Torrents of spray choked him as the ray plunged toward deep water.

His eyes were of no use to him in the foam-streaked blackness. He closed them tight, and at once an insane sequence of pictures flashed through his mind. He saw his wife sitting in their living room, reading, waiting calmly for his return. He saw the mullet he had just caught, gasping its life away on the floorboards of the skiff. He saw the cigarette he had flung from the sea wall touch the water and <u>expire</u> with a tiny hiss. He saw all these things and many others simultaneously in his mind as his body fought silently and <u>tenaciously</u> for its existence. His hand touched something hard and closed on it in a death grip, but it was only

the sharp-edged helmet of a horseshoe crab, and after an instant he let it go.

He had been underwater perhaps fifteen seconds now, and something in his brain told him quite calmly that he could last another **30** forty or fifty and then the red flashes behind his eyes would merge into darkness, and the water would pour into his lungs in one sharp painful shock, and he would be finished.

This thought spurred him to a desperate effort. He reached up and caught his <u>pinioned</u> wrist with his free hand. He doubled up his knees to create more drag. He thrashed his **31** body madly, like a fighting fish, from side to side. This did not disturb the ray, but now one of the great wings tore through the mesh, and the net slipped lower over the fins projecting like horns from below the nightmare head, and the sea devil jumped again.

And once more the man was able to get his feet on the bottom and his head above water, and he saw ahead of him the pair of ancient stakes that marked the approach to the channel. He knew that if he was dragged much beyond those stakes he would be in eight feet **32** of water, and the ray would go down to hug the bottom as rays always do, and then no power on earth could save him. So in the moment of respite[13] that was granted him, he flung himself toward them.

For a moment he thought his <u>captor</u> yielded a bit. Then the ray moved off again, but more slowly now, and for a few yards the man was able to keep his feet on the bottom. Twice he hurled himself back against the rope with all his strength, hoping that something would **33** break. But nothing broke. The mesh of the net was ripped and torn, but the draw lines were strong, and the stout perimeter cord threaded through the sinkers was even stronger.

The man could feel nothing now in his **34** trapped hand, it was numb; but the ray could feel the powerful lunges of the unknown thing that was trying to restrain it. It drove its great wings against the unyielding water and forged ahead, dragging the man and pushing a sullen wave in front of it.

The man had swung as far as he could toward the stakes. He plunged toward one and missed it by inches. His feet slipped and he went down on his knees. Then the ray swerved sharply and the second stake came right at him. He reached out with his free hand and caught it.

He caught it just above the surface, six or eight inches below high-water mark. He felt the razor-sharp barnacles bite into his hand, collapse under the pressure, drive their tiny slime-covered shell splinters deep into his **35** flesh. He felt the pain, and he welcomed it, and **36** he made his fingers into an iron claw that would hold until the tendons were severed or the skin was shredded from the bone. The ray felt the pressure increase with a jerk that stopped it dead in the water. For a moment all was still as the tremendous forces came into equilibrium.[14]

Then the net slipped again, and the <u>perimeter cord</u> came down over the sea devil's eyes, blinding it momentarily. The great ray settled to the bottom and braced its wings against the mud and hurled itself forward and upward.

The stake was only a four-by-four of creosoted[15] pine, and it was old. Ten thousand tides had swirled around it. Worms had bored; parasites had clung. Under the crust of barnacles it still had some heart left, but not enough. The man's grip was five feet above the floor of the bay; the leverage was too great. The stake snapped off at its base.

The ray lunged upward, dragging the man

14. **equilibrium** (ē′kwə-lĭb′rē-əm): balance.
15. **creosoted** (krē′ə-sōt′ĭd): treated with creosote, a preservative.

13. **respite** (rĕs′pĭt): relief.

30
The man perceives what he thinks will be physical sensations of drowning.

31
The man, because of his struggle with his own prey, is able to empathize with struggling fish.

32
The man bases his prediction on knowledge of the ray's behavior, a knowledge that gives people an advantage over lower animals.

33
Irony. Human-made net has caught the man instead of the fish for which it was intended.

34
Point of view. Omniscient narrator tells how the ray feels and reacts.

35   Drawing Conclusions
Why does the man welcome a feeling of pain as he attempts to cling to a barnacle-covered stake? Any kind of sensation, including that of pain, reassures the man that he is alive; he savors pain because he hopes the sharp barnacle shells will do to the perimeter cord what they are doing to his hand.

36
Description of hand as "iron claw" implies that the man's grip is unbreakable and impervious to pain.

The underlined passage may be used to give students practice in the reading skill of drawing logical conclusions. Ask students to read the passage carefully and choose the answer that best states what can be concluded about the porpoise's motive in striking the ray.

A. The porpoise knew the man needed help and struck the ray to help the man get away. (Unsupported. The man is not mentioned.)
B. The porpoise was hungry and thought the ray would make a good meal. (Contradicted. Porpoise is described as having "fed well.") C. The porpoise is defending itself against what appears to be an offensive act by the ray. (Correct.)
D. The porpoise was startled by the shadow and smell of the ray. (Irrelevant. Selection does not mention the smell of the ray.)

37
In despair, the man thinks of ending his torturous struggle quickly.

38
Use to answer **study question 4b**, p. 38.

39
Simile. "Like a pistol shot" creates sound image that emphasizes force of porpoise's blow.

40 Summarizing
How has the battle affected the man? Has sapped the man's physical strength but not his will to live.

41
Theme. Absence of fear frees the man's mind to plan; emphasizes idea that rational thought can overcome superior physical power.

42
"Five seconds" shows the man's calculating, rational thought.

---

and the useless timber. The man had his lungs full of air, but when the stake snapped he thought of expelling the air and inhaling the water so as to have it finished quickly. He **37** thought of this, but he did not do it. And then, just at the channel's edge, the ray met the porpoise, coming in.

► The porpoise had fed well this night and was in no hurry, but it was a methodical creature and it intended to make a sweep around the old dock before the tide dropped too low. It had no quarrel with any ray, but it feared no fish in the sea, and when the great black shadow came rushing blindly and unavoidably, **38** it rolled fast and struck once with its massive horizontal tail. ◄

39 The blow descended on the ray's flat body with a sound like a pistol shot. It would have broken a buffalo's back, and even the sea devil was half stunned. It veered wildly and turned back toward shallow water. It passed within ten feet of the man, face down in the water. It slowed and almost stopped, wing tips moving faintly, gathering strength for another rush.

The man had heard the tremendous slap of the great mammal's tail and the snorting gasp as it plunged away. He felt the line go slack again, and he raised his dripping face, and he reached for the bottom with his feet. He found it, but now the water was up to his neck. He plucked at the noose once more with his lacer-**40** ated hand, but there was no strength in his fingers. He felt the tension come back into the line as the ray began to move again, and for half a second he was tempted to throw himself backward and fight as he had been doing, pitting his strength against the vastly superior strength of the brute.

But the acceptance of imminent death had **42** done something to his brain. It had driven out the fear, and with the fear had gone the panic. He could think now, and he knew with absolute certainty that if he was to make any use of this last chance that had been given him, it would have to be based on the one faculty that had carried man to his preeminence above all **41** beasts, the faculty of reason. Only by using his brain could he possibly survive, and he called on his brain for a solution, and his brain responded. It offered him one.

He did not know whether his body still had the strength to carry out the brain's commands, but he began to swim forward, toward the ray that was still moving hesitantly away from the channel. He swam forward, feeling the rope go slack as he gained on the creature.

Ahead of him he saw the one remaining stake, and he made himself swim faster until he was parallel with the ray and the rope trailed behind both of them in a deep U. He swam with a surge of desperate energy that came from nowhere, so that he was slightly in the lead as they came to the stake. He passed on one side of it; the ray was on the other.

Then the man took one last deep breath, and he went down under the black water until he was sitting on the bottom of the bay. He put one foot over the line so that it passed under his bent knee. He drove both his heels into the mud, and he clutched the slimy grass with his bleeding hand, and he waited for the tension to come again.

The ray passed on the other side of the stake, moving faster now. The rope grew taut again, and it began to drag the man back toward the stake. He held his prisoned wrist close to the bottom, under his knee, and he prayed that the stake would not break. He felt the rope vibrate as the barnacles bit into it. He did not know whether the rope would crush the barnacles, or whether the barnacles would cut the rope. All he knew was that in five seconds or less he would be dragged into the stake and cut to ribbons if he tried to hold on, or drowned if he didn't.

He felt himself sliding slowly, and then

► Reading Skills Objective: Drawing Logical Conclusions

VISUAL CONNECTIONS
Exploring the Subject
The sea devil is described as "a great horned thing" that "shot like a huge bat out of the water." The resemblance of the sea devil to a bat and its "horns" make the sea devil appear threatening and evil.

43
Conflict. The man's plan has worked—barnacles have cut rope, ending struggle. He has used superior intellect to overcome sea devil's great physical force.

44
Use to answer **study question 6a,** p. 38.

45
"Nightly plane" reinforces idea that humans can, at times, master nature.

46   Making Inferences
What might the man be feeling? Responses will vary. Possibly relief, thankfulness, gladness, exhaustion, humility, triumph.

47
Characterization. The man's actions show empathy for mullet's plight.

48
The man's mind is blank except for realization that he does not want to chance such an experience again.

faster, and suddenly the ray made a great leap forward, and the rope burned around the base *43* of the stake, and the man's foot hit it hard. He kicked himself backward with his remaining strength, and the rope parted, and he was free.

He came slowly to the surface. Thirty feet away the sea devil made one tremendous leap and disappeared into the darkness. The man raised his wrist and looked at the frayed length of rope dangling from it. Twenty inches, perhaps. He lifted his other hand and felt the hot blood start instantly, but he didn't care. He put his hand on the stake above the barnacles and held on to the good, rough, honest wood. He heard a strange noise, and realized that it was *44* himself, sobbing.

High above, there was a droning sound, and *45* looking up he saw the nightly plane from New Orleans inbound for Tampa. Calm and serene, it sailed, symbol of man's proud mastery over nature. Its lights winked red and green for a moment; then it was gone.

Slowly, painfully, the man began to move *46* through the placid water. He came to the skiff at last and climbed into it. The mullet, still *47* alive, slapped convulsively with its tail. The man reached down with his torn hand, picked up the mullet, let it go.

He began to work on the slipknot doggedly *48* with his teeth. His mind was almost a blank, but not quite. He knew one thing. He knew he would do no more casting alone at night. Not in the dark of the moon. No, not he.

OBJECTIVES

The overall aim is for students to analyze the main character's actions in relation to his struggle with the forces of nature and to evaluate sensory details. For a complete list of objectives, see the **Teacher's Notes.**

VOCABULARY

Call students' attention to the vocabulary footnotes in their textbooks. Encourage students to list and define other unfamiliar words.

FOCUS / MOTIVATION

Ask students to relate any true stories they know about survival—for example, people lost in the wilderness, people trapped in rubble of earthquakes or tornadoes, people in airplane crashes. What traits would a person need to sur-

PREREADING FOCUS

The headnote introduces the protagonist of the story and his conflict with the forces of nature. Ask students to identify the personality traits they think a person needs to survive being lost and alone at sea.

Fighting Off the Sharks for a Fish

1
Style. Narrator shifts from first person to second person as a way of making his experiences universal.

2
Setting. Sea and sun described as friendly and gentle toward sailor. Setting is in direct contrast to terrible events that occur in story.

3 Drawing Conclusions
Why does sailor compare sea to aquarium? Colorful fish seem more like those kept in aquariums for entertainment than like fish in ocean.

4
Sailor's long days at sea have caused him to lose perspective on his situation. It is as though he loses touch with reality.

Fighting Off the Sharks for a Fish

GABRIEL GARCÍA MÁRQUEZ°

In February 1955, eight members of the destroyer Caldos, *of the Colombian Navy, were washed overboard and disappeared in the Caribbean Sea. Ten days later, one of the seamen, Luis Alejandro Velasco, turned up on a beach in northern Colombia. He later told his story to Gabriel García Márquez, who reconstructed the events in* The Story of a Shipwrecked Sailor.

Imagine yourself drifting on a raft at sea for more than a week without food or water. Read ahead and ask yourself if you would be able to live through such an ordeal with the odds against your survival.

1 The thought that for seven days I had been drifting farther out to sea rather than nearing land crushed my <u>resolve</u> to keep on struggling. But when you feel close to death, your instinct for self-preservation grows stronger. For several reasons, that day was very different from the previous days: the sea was dark and calm; the sun, warm and tranquil, hugged my body; a gentle breeze guided the raft along; even my sunburn felt a bit better.

The fish were different, too. From very early on they had <u>escorted</u> the raft, swimming near the surface. And I could see them clearly: blue fish, gray-brown ones, red ones. There were fish of every color, all shapes and sizes. It seemed as if the raft were floating in an aquarium.

I don't know whether, after seven days without food and adrift at sea, one becomes accustomed to living that way. I think so. The hopelessness of the previous day was replaced by a mellow <u>res-</u>

°**Gabriel García Márquez** (gär-sē′ä mär′kĕs).

Jeffrey L. Rotman

vive such catastrophes? What other elements, such as the availability of basic tools for survival, are important?

MOTIVATIONAL SUMMARY
The narrator has been drifting alone for seven days on a raft at sea. After struggling with harsh winds, waves, starvation, and thirst, he has finally resigned himself to the hopelessness of his situation. When he tries to appease his hunger by catching one of the many fish that have surrounded the raft, the blood from small fish bites on his fingers attracts sharks. Then he discovers he must also battle the shark, not only for the food, but also for his life on the precarious raft.

ignation devoid of emotion. I was sure that everything was different, that the sea and the sky were no longer hostile, and that the fish accom-

5 panying me on my journey were my friends. My old acquaintances of seven days.

That morning I wasn't thinking about reaching any destination. I was certain that the raft had arrived in a region where there were no ships, where even sea gulls could go astray.

I thought, however, that after seven days adrift I would become accustomed to the sea, to my anxious way of life, without having to spur my imagination in order to survive. After all, I had endured a week of harsh winds and waves. Why wouldn't it be possible to live on the raft indefinitely? The fish swam near the surface; the

6 sea was clear and calm. There were so many lovely, tempting fish around the raft it looked as if I could grab them with my hands. Not a shark was in sight. Confidently I put my hand in the water and tried to seize a round fish, a bright blue one about twenty centimeters[1] long. It was

7 as if I had flung a stone: all the fish fled instantly, momentarily churning up the water. Then slowly they came back to the surface.

You have to be crafty to fish with your hand, I thought. Underwater, the hand didn't have as much strength or agility. I chose one fish from the bunch. I tried to grab it. And in fact I did. But I felt it slip through my fingers with discon-

8 certing speed and nimbleness. I waited patiently, not pressuring myself, just trying to catch a fish. I wasn't thinking about the shark which might be out there, waiting until I put my arm in up to the elbow so he could make off with it in one sure bite. I kept busy trying to catch fish until a little after ten o'clock. But it was useless. They nibbled at my fingers, gently at first, as when they nibble at bait. Then a little harder. A smooth silver fish about a foot and a half long, with minute, sharp

9 teeth, tore the skin off my thumb. Then I realized that the nibbles of the other fish hadn't been harmless: all my fingers had small bleeding cuts.

Shark in the raft!

I don't know if it was the blood from my
10 fingers, but in an instant there was a riot of sharks around the raft. I had never seen so many. I had never seen them so voracious. They leaped like dolphins, chasing the fish and devouring them. Terrified, I sat in the middle of the raft and watched the massacre.

The next thing happened so quickly that I didn't realize just when it was that the shark leaped out of the water, thrashing its tail vio-
11 lently, and the raft, tottering, sank beneath the gleaming foam. In the midst of the huge, glittering wave that crashed over the side there was
12 a metallic flash. Instinctively I grabbed an oar and prepared to strike a deathblow. But then I saw the enormous fin, and I realized what had happened. Chased by the shark, a brilliant green fish, almost half a meter[2] long, had leaped into the raft. With all my strength I walloped it on the head with my oar.

Killing a fish inside a raft isn't easy. The vessel tottered with each blow; it might have turned over. It was a perilous moment. I needed all my strength and all my wits about me. If I struck out blindly, the raft would turn over and I would plunge into a sea full of hungry sharks. If I didn't aim carefully, my quarry
13 would escape. I stood between life and death. I would either end up in the gullet of a shark or get four pounds of fresh fish to appease the hunger of seven days.

I braced myself on the gunwale[3] and struck the second blow. I felt the wooden oar drive into

---

1. **twenty centimeters:** about eight inches. One inch is equal to 2.54 centimeters.

2. **meter:** the fundamental unit of length in the metric system, equal to 39.37 inches.
3. **gunwale** (gŭn′əl): the upper edge of a ship or raft's side.

5
Irony. Seven-day period seems like a long time to the sailor, but it really is not long enough for the fish to be considered "old acquaintances."

6 Making Inferences
Why are fish drawn to raft? Answers will vary. Students may point out that raft creates disturbance on surface of water, and disturbance attracts fish out of curiosity.

7
Fish disappear as though someone had scared them by throwing a stone at them.

8
Sailor tries not to put pressure on himself by thinking he has to catch a fish quickly.

9 Analyzing
Why does sailor not feel cuts on his hands? Answers will vary. Some students may point out that the water is cold, and cold water tends to numb skin. Since the cuts are tiny, they may not be deep enough to penetrate the numbness. Others may say sailor's full concentration is on catching fish, so he does not notice tiny cuts.

10
Metaphor. Movement of sharks in water creates as much disturbance as a riot would.

11
Wave washes over raft, and it appears to sink. Raft pops to surface again when wave passes.

12 Drawing Conclusions
What causes the metallic flash? Sun reflecting on fish's scales.

13
Conflict. Sailor caught in conflict: satisfying his hunger or avoiding being eaten by sharks.

Introduce "Fighting Off the Sharks for a Fish" as a story based on the actual experiences of a man who single-handedly survives a hazardous ordeal at sea. After students have had a chance to discuss any real-life survival stories they know, explain that this story features a man who battles death and wins. This story is similar to "The Sea Devil" in pitting the protagonist against nature. Like "The Sea Devil," Márquez' story draws the reader in with suspense. Like all the stories in this unit, "Fighting Off the Sharks for a Fish" reinforces the **theme** of challenge. The narrator must use his wits not only to satisfy his hunger and thirst but also to overcome the physical threat of the sharks. This story provides an opportunity to point out how the instinct for survival often requires people to do things they

14

Exaggeration. Author uses exaggeration to emphasize that sailor would do anything to capture fish.

15

Metaphor. Shark's teeth are as hard and strong as steel, not made of steel.

16   Making Generalizations

Why does sailor associate color green with poison? Answers will vary. Some students might think most poison comes from green plants or reptiles. Others might be familiar with connotation of green as "sickly" or "bilious."

17   Making Inferences

What does section title suggest that section will deal with? Title suggests section will deal with effects of ordeal on sailor's body. Title is ambiguous and can also apply to carcass of fish that sharks eat.

18

Irony. Statement is ironic because the opposite would seem to be true: when food is in sight, hunger is bearable because it will soon be satisfied.

19

Prospect of eating after seven days of hunger enables sailor to overcome enormous obstacles to preparing food.

20

Sailor's frustration with sharks and with fish almost makes him reckless.

the fish's skull. The raft bounced. The sharks shuddered below. I pressed myself firmly against the side. When the raft stabilized, the fish was still alive.

In agony, a fish can jump higher and farther than it otherwise can. I knew the third blow had to be a sure one or I would lose my prey forever.

After a lunge at the fish, I found myself sitting on the floor, where I thought I had a better **14** chance of grabbing it. If necessary, I would have captured it with my feet, between my knees, or in my teeth. I anchored myself to the floor. Trying not to make a mistake and convinced that my life depended on my next blow, I swung the oar with all my strength. The fish stopped moving and a thread of dark blood tinted the water inside the raft.

I could smell the blood, and the sharks sensed it, too. Suddenly, with four pounds of fish within my grasp, I felt uncontrollable terror: driven wild by the scent of blood, the sharks hurled themselves with all their strength against the bottom of the raft. The raft shook. I realized that it could turn over in an instant. **15** I could be torn to pieces by the three rows of steel teeth in the jaws of each shark.

But the pressure of hunger was greater than anything else. I squeezed the fish between my legs and, staggering, began the difficult job of balancing the raft each time it suffered another assault by the sharks. That went on for several minutes. Whenever the raft stabilized, I threw the bloody water overboard. Little by little the water cleared and the beasts calmed down. But I had to be careful: a terrifyingly huge shark fin—the biggest I had ever seen—protruded more than a meter above the water's surface. The shark was swimming peacefully, but I knew that if it caught the scent of blood it would give a shudder that could capsize the raft. With extreme caution I began to try to pull my fish apart.

A creature that's half a meter long is protected by a hard crust of scales: if you try to pull them off, you find that they adhere to the flesh like armor plating. I had no sharp instruments. I tried to shave off the scales with my keys, but they wouldn't budge. Meanwhile, it occurred to me that I had never seen a fish like this one: it was deep green and thickly scaled. **16** From when I was little, I had associated the color green with poison. Incredibly, although my stomach was throbbing painfully at the prospect of even a mouthful of fresh fish, I had trouble deciding whether or not that strange creature might be poisonous.

My poor body

18 Hunger is bearable when you have no hope of food. But it was never so insistent as when I was trying to slash that shiny green flesh with my keys.

After a few minutes, I realized I would have to use more violent methods if I wanted to eat **19** my victim. I stood up, stepped hard on its tail, and stuck the oar handle into one of its gills. I saw that the fish wasn't dead yet. I hit it on the head again. Then I tried to tear off the hard protective plates that covered the gills. I couldn't tell whether the blood streaming over my fingers was from the fish or from me; my hands were covered with wounds and my fingertips were raw.

The scent of blood once again stirred the sharks' hunger. It seems unbelievable but, furi-**20** ous at the hungry beasts and disgusted by the sight of the bloody fish, I was on the point of throwing it to the sharks, as I had done with the sea gull. I felt utterly frustrated and helpless at the sight of the solid, impenetrable body of the fish.

I examined it meticulously[4] for soft spots.

4. **meticulously** (mə-tĭk′yə-ləs′lē): very carefully; precisely.

For students to appreciate what the narrator experiences, you may want to have a few volunteers read this selection orally. Between readers, you can answer questions and engage students in discussion of **characterization**, **setting**, and **conflict**.

MEETING INDIVIDUAL NEEDS

ESL/LEP • As students read the story, ask them to look for words with *–tion* endings. Remind them that when the *–tion* suffix is added to a verb, the word becomes a noun. Examples include *resignation, imagination,* and *frustration.*

Have students brainstorm other verbs that become nouns in this way.

Finally I found a slit between the gills and with my finger I began to pull out the entrails. The innards of a fish are soft and without substance. It is said that if you strike a hard blow to a shark's tail the stomach and intestines fall out of **21** its mouth. In Cartagena,[5] I had seen sharks hanging by their tails, with huge thick masses of dark innards oozing from their mouths.

Luckily the entrails of my fish were as soft as those of the sharks. It didn't take long to remove them with my finger. It was a female: among the entrails I found a string of eggs. When it was completely gutted I took the first bite. I couldn't break through the crust of scales. But on the second try, with renewed strength, I bit down desperately, until my jaw ached. Then I managed to tear off the first mouthful and began to chew the cold, tough flesh.

22 I chewed with disgust. I had always found the odor of raw fish repulsive, but the flavor is even more repugnant. It tastes vaguely like raw palm, but oilier and less palatable. I couldn't imagine that anyone had ever eaten a live fish, but as I chewed the first food that had reached my lips in seven days, I had the awful certainty that I was in fact eating one.

After the first piece, I felt better immediately. I took a second bite and chewed again. A moment before, I had thought I could eat a **23** whole shark. But now I felt full after the second mouthful. The terrible hunger of seven days was appeased in an instant. I was strong again, as on the first day.

I now know that raw fish slakes your thirst. I hadn't known it before, but I realized that the fish had appeased not only my hunger but my **24** thirst as well. I was sated and optimistic. I still had food for a long time, since I had taken only two small bites of a creature half a meter long.

5. **Cartagena** (kär′tä-hē′nä, kär′tə-jē′nə): a large port in northwestern Colombia, on the Caribbean coast.

I decided to wrap the fish in my shirt and store it in the bottom of the raft to keep it fresh. **25** But first I had to wash it. Absentmindedly I held it by the tail and dunked it once over the side. But blood had coagulated[6] between the scales. It would have to be scrubbed. Naively I submerged it again. And that was when I felt the charge of the violent thrust of the shark's jaws. I hung on to the tail of the fish with all the strength I had. The beast's lunge upset my balance. I was thrown against the side of the raft but I held on to my food supply; I clung to it like a savage. In that fraction of a second, it didn't occur to me that with another bite the shark could have ripped my arm off at the shoulder. I kept pulling with all my strength, **26** but now there was nothing in my hands. The shark had made off with my prey. Infuriated, rabid[7] with frustration, I grabbed an oar and delivered a tremendous blow to the shark's head when it passed by the side of the raft. The beast leaped; it twisted furiously and with one clean, savage bite splintered the oar and swallowed half of it.

6. **coagulated** (kō-ăg′yə-lāt′əd): clotted, as the blood dries into a soft or semisolid mass.
7. **rabid** (răb′ĭd): here, raging; violent.

Reading Check

1. After he is adrift at sea for seven days, how does the narrator's mood change?
2. Why does he consider the fish alongside the raft "old acquaintances"?
3. How does the narrator finally get a fish?
4. Why is he unable to pull the fish apart?
5. How does he lose the fish?

21
As a seaport on Caribbean coast, Cartagena is home to many fishermen who catch sharks and bring them to shore.

22
Sailor's intense hunger enables him to overcome bad taste of fish.

23 Making Generalizations
Why is sailor full after only two bites? Answers will vary. Some students might point out that person's stomach shrinks when deprived of food, as sailor has been for seven days. Others might say hard exertion of sailor in struggle with sharks and fish makes him unable to eat much.

24 Drawing Conclusions
Why is sailor optimistic? Sailor's hunger and thirst are satisfied for first time in days. Having remains of large fish makes him think things will go well in future.

25
Sailor forgets sharks may still be near raft when he dunks fish in sea.

26
Irony. Sailor's struggle in shark attack and in killing fish for food ends with his feeding sharks without intending to do so.

READING CHECK
1. He becomes resigned to his situation.
2. The fish have surrounded the raft for seven days and seem to escort the narrator on his journey out to sea.
3. Sharks chase the fish onto the raft.
4. The protective scales are too hard.
5. He tries to wash the fish to prepare it for storage, and the blood again attracts the shark who takes the food.

FOR STUDY AND DISCUSSION

1. Responses will vary; however, the events seem to prove the narrator's claim. After having no food or water and enduring harsh weather, the narrator seems close to death, but finds strength and determination to find food, battle sharks, and eat raw fish.

2. By letting the fish nibble his fingers, the narrator receives small, bleeding cuts. The blood attracts the sharks.

3. Responses will vary. Students might point out the taste and the texture of the raw fish, as well as the narrator's feeling of fullness and replenishment.

4. Answers will vary. Students should mention the descriptive details and how the narrator is forced to balance himself on the unstable raft.

5. Responses will vary. Students might experience empathy with the narrator's plight, fear for the narrator's battle with the sharks, or horror at what the narrator has to endure to satisfy his hunger and thirst.

FOCUS ON READING

After students have completed their charts, you might write the five senses as columns on the chalkboard. Ask students to write their examples under the appropriate heading, being careful about repetitious examples. Students can then evaluate which sensory details tend to dominate the story, why the author chose those kinds of details, and how the story would change if there were a different focus of images.

FOCUS ON DESCRIPTIVE WRITING

After students have selected their subjects, encourage them to list at least five sensory details in each column. Then group the pairs with other pairs who have chosen the same subject and let them compare their lists.

For Study and Discussion

Analyzing and Interpreting the Selection

1. The narrator says that the instinct for self-preservation grows stronger when one feels close to death. Do the events of the narrative prove this to be true? Explain.

2. How do the narrator's attempts to catch a fish attract sharks to the raft?

3. What does the narrator discover when he finally eats some of the raw fish?

4. How does the narrative capture the excitement and terror of the struggle against the sharks? Find and read aloud the passages you found most gripping.

5. Describe your own response to this narrative. Did you predict what would happen to the narrator's food supply? Were you eager to know what would happen when the sharks appeared? Do you want to know what will happen next?

Focus on Reading

Responding to Sensory Details

The narrator describes his encounter with sharks in vivid detail. **Sensory details** are words or phrases that describe one or more of the five senses—sight, sound, smell, taste, and touch. Create a chart that lists the different types of sensory details and find examples from the selection to illustrate each type. Compare your examples with those chosen by other students.

Sensory Details	Examples
Sight	
Sound	
Smell	
Taste	
Touch	

Focus on Descriptive Writing

Using Sensory Details

In the first paragraph of his narrative, García Márquez uses details that appeal to sight and touch in a subjective description of the sea, the sun, and the wind. Sensory details help you describe a subject vividly and clearly.

Get together with a partner and choose one of the following four subjects. See how many sensory details you can collect to describe the subject you have chosen. Write your details on an **observation chart** like the one below. Save your notes.

an apple	seaweed
a computer	a crowded bus

Observation Chart

Subject: _____

Sight	Sound	Smell	Taste	Touch
___	___	___	___	___
___	___	___	___	___
___	___	___	___	___
___	___	___	___	___

About the Author

Gabriel García Márquez (1928–)

Gabriel García Márquez was born in Aracataca, Colombia, where he was raised in his maternal grandparents' home. He attended universities in Bogota and Cartagena. He studied law

CLOSURE
Ask students to trace the narrator's difficulties and explain how the author uses these events to create **suspense** in the story.

EXTENSION AND ENRICHMENT
Students might write essays responding to the narrator's comment that the instinct for self-preservation grows stronger when one feels close to death. Students might look in magazines and newspapers for articles about survival that

they could develop into stories, or they can create their own survival stories.

Pairs of students might act out the interview between the author and the narrator, especially focusing on the events that happened before the story's action.

until 1950 when he switched to journalism. In 1955 he published his first short story, "Leaf Storm" ("La Hojarasca").

In the mid-1950s he worked as a newspaper reporter in Europe but returned to Colombia to marry. He eventually settled in Mexico, where he became a screenwriter and worked with the famous Mexican novelist Carlos Fuentes. While in Mexico, García Márquez wrote *One Hundred Years of Solitude* (1970) (*Cien Años de Soledad*), which established him as one of this century's greatest authors. Many of his stories and novels have been translated into English, including his most recent works: *Innocent Erendira and Other Stories* (1978) (*La Candida Erendira*); *Love in the Time of Cholera* (1988) (*El Amor en Los Tiempos del Cólera*); *The General in His Labyrinth* (1990) (*El General en Su Laberinto*); and *Strange Pilgrims* (1993) (*Doce Cuentos Peregrinos*), a collection of short stories. In 1982 he won the Nobel Prize for literature.

Literature and Mathematics

Measurement Systems

The metric system is a decimal system of measurement, in which the basic unit of length is the *meter* and the basic unit of mass is the *kilogram*. The international system of measurement is based largely on the metric system. Some dictionaries now contain a conversion table, which tells you how to convert the United States Customary System to the metric system and vice versa.

Making Connections: Activities

Consult a math book or a dictionary with a measurement table and familiarize yourself with the relationship between the U.S. Customary System and the metric system of measurement. Create a chart for your own use that will allow

you to convert units of length (such as the inch, the foot, the mile) into metric equivalents (such as the centimeter and the kilometer) and vice versa; units of volume or capacity (such as the ounce, the pint, the gallon) into metric equivalents (such as the milliliter and liter) and vice versa; and units of weight (such as the ounce, the pound, the ton) into metric equivalents (such as the kilogram) and vice versa. Check your work with a partner.

Literature and Science

Sharks: Fact and Fiction

Shark fossil remains show that sharks are much older than the dinosaurs. According to one estimate, sharks have been around for 415 million years. Apart from the fear associated with sharks, most people know little about the characteristics of sharks, how they use their senses, and how they adapt to their environment.

Making Connections: Activities

1. Read "Shark Close-ups" in *The Silent World*, by Jacques-Ives Cousteau, an eminent environmentalist and explorer. How does the information in this article compare with what you know or have believed about sharks?

2. Dr. Eugenie Clark has been investigating the mystery of the "sleeping sharks" found in caves off the Yucatan Peninsula in Mexico. Read *The Desert Beneath the Sea* to find out what she has discovered about sharks by swimming alongside them.

3. John Singleton Copley, an American portrait painter of colonial America, painted a work called *Watson and the Shark* (1778), which was based on a true incident. Some artists have specialized in depicting sharks and other sea creatures. See if you can find art reproductions in your school or local library and share these illustrations with the class.

LITERATURE AND MATHEMATICS
Students can work in pairs to develop their charts. Suggest that students be creative with their charts and make them different from the ones found in dictionaries and math books. Caution students to keep their charts practical and readable. Their math teachers might then check the charts, which can be displayed in either the math or language arts class.

LITERATURE AND SCIENCE
Students might use these activities as stimuli for oral presentations, or students might find other sources for facts and fiction about sharks to share with the class.

About the Artwork

Black-and-white photography has qualities that many photographers prefer. In this picture, the lighter area within the dark edges draws the viewer's attention to the boy's face, nearly obscured by the dirt on the window. The texture of the wood is very distinct as is the graininess of the dirt on the glass. Photographs taken with a telephoto lens have this quality of a specific in-focus image with foreground and background blurred, such as the bricks are in this picture. The black-and-white format gives a stark, gritty quality to this picture with the haunting image of the child in the center.

Ideas for Writing

The child in the window is looking out from the protection and shelter of the building. Before students read the story, ask them to speculate on what the child is looking at and interpret the expression on the child's face. Have students write paragraphs describing what they think the child is feeling. You might start by having them list possible objects or people visible to the child.

OBJECTIVES
The overall aim is for students to analyze and interpret the underlying **theme** of the selection. For a complete list of objectives, see the **Teacher's Notes.**

VOCABULARY
The underlined words are in the Glossary. The **Literary Elements** exercise on p. 50 deals with Wright's creative use of the word "hunger" in describing his childhood feelings.

FOCUS / MOTIVATION
Ask students to define the word *dilemma* and to give examples of common dilemmas. Invite volunteers to share childhood experiences in which they were frightened by both of two opposing courses of action.

FROM
Black Boy

RICHARD WRIGHT

The boy was so full of fear he could hardly breathe. But he had an adult's responsibility now. He had to make the journey down those streets.

1 Hunger stole upon me so slowly that at first I was not aware of what hunger really meant. Hunger had always been more or less at my elbow when I played, but now I began to wake up at night to find hunger standing at my bedside, staring at me gauntly. The hunger I had known before this had been no grim, hostile stranger; it had been a normal hunger that had made me beg constantly for bread, and when I ate a crust or two I was satisfied. But **2** this new hunger baffled me, scared me, made me angry and insistent. Whenever I begged for food now my mother would pour me a cup of tea which would still the clamor[1] in my stomach for a moment or two; but a little later I would feel hunger nudging my ribs, twisting **3** my empty guts until they ached. I would grow dizzy and my vision would dim. I became less active in my play, and for the first time in my **4** life I had to pause and think of what was happening to me.

"Mama, I'm hungry," I complained one afternoon.

"Jump up and catch a kungry," she said, trying to make me laugh and forget.

"What's a *kungry?*"

"It's what little boys eat when they get hungry," she said.

"What does it taste like?"

"I don't know."

"Then why do you tell me to catch one?"

"Because you said that you were hungry," she said, smiling.

I sensed that she was teasing me and it made me angry.

"But I'm hungry. I want to eat."

"You'll have to wait."

"But I want to eat now."

"But there's nothing to eat," she told me.

"Why?"

"Just because there's none," she explained.

"But I want to eat," I said, beginning to cry.

"You'll just have to wait," she said again.

"But why?"

5 "For God to send some food."

"When is He going to send it?"

"I don't know."

"But I'm hungry!"

She was ironing and she paused and looked at me with tears in her eyes.

"Where's your father?" she asked me.

I stared in bewilderment. Yes, it was true that my father had not come home to sleep for many days now and I could make as much noise as I wanted. Though I had not known why he was absent, I had been glad that he was not there to shout his restrictions at me. But it **6** had never occurred to me that his absence would mean that there would be no food.

"I don't know," I said.

"Who brings food into the house?" my mother asked me.

1. **clamor:** noise.

TEACHING RESOURCES A
Teacher's Notes, p. 80
Reading Check, p. 83
Study Guide, p. 85
Language Skills, pp. 89, 92
Building Vocabulary, p. 96
Selection Vocabulary Test, p. 98
Selection Test, p. 99

AV RESOURCES BINDER
Audiocassette 1, Side A

PREREADING FOCUS
The headnote emphasizes internal and external conflicts the boy confronts and overcomes. Ask students to share their experiences with fear and adversity. How did they deal with these situations? How did the outcomes affect them?

Black Boy

1
Personification. Hunger is given human qualities, making condition even more sinister. Hunger presented as both physical and spiritual.

2 Finding Details
What emotions does the author show can be caused by hunger? Both fear and anger.

3
Use to answer **study question 1b,** p. 50.

4
Self-awareness is important stage in maturation process. That this is "first time" emphasizes importance of this experience in author's life.

5
The mother has no one to whom she can turn for help, but she maintains her strong faith.

6
The father's absence allows freedom but also results in hunger.

The boy fights hunger when his father leaves the family without money or food. When his mother brings home her pay from her new job, she sends him to the store to buy food. On his way to the store, older boys take his money. When he comes crying home, his mother gives him more money and tells him to go back to the store. As he creeps down the stairs, he sees the same gang of boys.

Introduce this selection as a true story about a child who later became one of America's major writers. This story is a short excerpt from Richard Wright's critically acclaimed autobiography *Black Boy,* published in 1945. This story is

---

7 Analyzing
Why is it ironic that the mother works as a cook? She cannot afford food to cook for her family.

8
Children must take on responsibility of caring for themselves—a disturbing idea since the children are pre-school age.

9
The boy takes on more responsibility, an especially important experience that will change him.

10
Conflict. The boy is confronted by a gang of boys; here, conflict is physical.

11 Summarizing
Expressing an Opinion
What emotion is the boy feeling? Is the child's emotional state justified? The boy is feeling fear. Responses to the second question will vary. Some students will be familiar with intimidation by groups of older children and bullies.

12
Connotation. Use of "deadly tone" indicates seriousness of situation and mother's determination.

13
Among other responsibilities, the boy must be responsible for defending himself.

"Papa," I said. "He always brought food."

"Well, your father isn't here now," she said.

"Where is he?"

"I don't know," she said.

"But I'm hungry," I whimpered, stomping my feet.

"You'll have to wait until I get a job and buy food," she said.

As the days slid past, the image of my father became associated with my pangs of hunger, and whenever I felt hunger I thought of him with a deep biological bitterness.

7 My mother finally went to work as a cook and left me and my brother alone in the flat[2] each day with a loaf of bread and a pot of tea. When she returned at evening she would be tired and dispirited and would cry a lot. Sometimes, when she was in despair, she would call us to her and talk to us for hours, telling us that we now had no father, that our lives would **8** be different from those of other children, that we must learn as soon as possible to take care of ourselves, to dress ourselves, to prepare our own food; that we must take upon ourselves the responsibility of the flat while she worked. Half frightened, we would promise solemnly. We did not understand what had happened between our father and our mother and the most that these long talks did to us was to make us feel a vague dread. Whenever we asked why Father had left, she would tell us that we were too young to know.

One evening my mother told me that there-**9** after I would have to do the shopping for food. She took me to the corner store to show me the way. I was proud; I felt like a grown-up. The next afternoon I looped the basket over my arm and went down the pavement toward the **10** store. When I reached the corner, a gang of boys grabbed me, knocked me down, snatched the basket, took the money, and sent me run-

2. **flat:** an apartment.

ning home in panic. That evening I told my mother what had happened, but she made no comment; she sat down at once, wrote another note, gave me more money, and sent me out to the grocery again. I crept down the steps and saw the same gang of boys playing down the street. I ran back into the house.

"What's the matter?" my mother asked.

"It's those same boys," I said. "They'll beat me."

"You've got to get over that," she said. "Now, go on."

11 "I'm scared," I said.

"Go on and don't pay any attention to them," she said.

I went out of the door and walked briskly down the sidewalk, praying that the gang would not molest me. But when I came abreast of them someone shouted.

"There he is!"

They came toward me and I broke into a wild run toward home. They overtook me and flung me to the pavement. I yelled, pleaded, kicked, but they wrenched the money out of my hand. They yanked me to my feet, gave me a few slaps, and sent me home sobbing. My mother met me at the door.

"They b-beat m-me," I gasped. "They t-t-took the m-money."

I started up the steps, seeking the shelter of the house.

"Don't you come in here," my mother warned me.

I froze in my tracks and stared at her.

"But they're coming after me," I said.

"You just stay right where you are," she said **12** in a deadly tone. "I'm going to teach you this **13** night to stand up and fight for yourself."

She went into the house and I waited, terrified, wondering what she was about. Presently, she returned with more money and another note; she also had a long heavy stick.

"Take this money, this note, and this stick,"

set in Memphis, Tennessee, but the experience of a child forced to assume adult responsibility could happen anywhere. This selection provides students insight into a major literary **theme:** human conflict—both with one's self and between people.

In this excerpt from *Black Boy,* Wright describes the transition he makes from having only the responsibilities of a boy to taking on those of a man. This process culminates in a kind of initiation during which Wright proves his ability to defend himself and after which he has gained a new status.

Invite students to learn about initiation rituals performed in various cultures and to present their findings to the class.

she said. "Go to the store and buy those groceries. If those boys bother you, then fight."

14   I was baffled. My mother was telling me to fight, a thing that she had never done before.

"But I'm scared," I said.

"Don't you come into this house until you've gotten those groceries," she said.

"They'll beat me; they'll beat me," I said.

15   "Then stay in the streets; don't come back here!"

I ran up the steps and tried to force my way past her into the house. A stinging slap came on my jaw. I stood on the sidewalk, crying.

"Please, let me wait until tomorrow," I begged.

"No," she said. "Go now! If you come back into this house without those groceries, I'll whip you!"

She slammed the door and I heard the key turn in the lock. I shook with fright. I was alone upon the dark, hostile streets and gangs

16 were after me, I had the choice of being beaten at home or away from home. I clutched the stick, crying, trying to reason. If I were beaten at home, there was absolutely nothing that I could do about it; but if I were beaten in the streets, I had a chance to fight and defend myself. I walked slowly down the sidewalk, coming closer to the gang of boys, holding the stick tightly. I was so full of fear that I could scarcely breathe. I was almost upon them now.

"There he is again!" the cry went up.

They surrounded me quickly and began to grab for my hand.

"I'll kill you!" I threatened.

They closed in. In blind fear I let the stick fly, feeling it crack against a boy's skull. I swung again, lamming another skull, then

17 another. Realizing that they would retaliate if I let up for but a second, I fought to lay them low, to knock them cold, to kill them so that they could not strike back at me. I flayed with tears in my eyes, teeth clenched, stark fear making

me throw every ounce of my strength behind each blow. I hit again and again, dropping the money and the grocery list. The boys scattered, yelling, nursing their heads, staring at me in utter disbelief. They had never seen such frenzy. I stood panting, egging them on, taunting them to come on and fight. When they refused, I ran after them and they tore out for their homes, screaming. The parents of the boys rushed into the streets and threatened me, and for the first time in my life I shouted at grown-ups, telling them that I would give them the same if they bothered me. I finally found my grocery list and the money and went to the store. On my way back I kept my stick

18 poised for instant use, but there was not a single boy in sight. That night I won the right to the streets of Memphis.

VISUAL CONNECTIONS
Relating Expression Skills
The street in the picture looks forbidding and might seem terrifying to a young boy. In improvised monologues, students might dramatize how the mother must have felt as she forced her young son to face the dangers of the street.

14   Analyzing
Why is the boy "baffled" by his mother's orders to fight if necessary? Her orders are not what he had expected. He may even have been told in past not to fight.

15
Characterization. Mother's refusal to give in to her child shows her strength and courage. She is not acting out of cruelty but out of necessity when she forces the boy to prove himself.

16
Conflict. The boy must choose between two undesirable alternatives—being beaten at home or in streets.

17
The boy fights for his own survival: strength and fighting skills probably are enhanced by adrenal reaction to fear.

18
The boy's victory has greater implications than winning "the right to the streets of Memphis"; it becomes foundation on which he will build his place in world and basis for his growth to manhood.

TRANSPARENCY 3
Reader Response
Award a Medal – invites students to celebrate one of a notable character's outstanding characteristics.

TRANSPARENCY 4
Literary Elements
Character – explores the ways that an author can reveal characterization.

READING CHECK
1. Father left; family had no money (pp. 47–48).
2. Job as a cook (p. 48).
3. Groceries (p. 48).
4. Street gang (p. 48).
5. Stick (p. 48).

FOR STUDY AND DISCUSSION
1a. Hunger. 1b. Boy became dizzy, and his vision dimmed; became less active in his play; grew angry and insistent; his stomach ached.
2. Responses will vary. Mother knew he had to become tough to survive, that sooner or later he would have to have his first fight.
3. Responses will vary. Proved that he was brave, though fearful, and that he was strong enough to survive and even thrive.

LITERARY ELEMENTS
1. At night, he finds hunger staring at him gauntly at his bedside.
2. Hunger looks like a grim, gaunt, hostile stranger.
3. Responses will vary. Perhaps description of hunger helped students understand how hunger can be a real presence, something terrifying that *hurts.*

ABOUT THE AUTHOR
After winning a prize in 1938 for a collection of stories titled *Uncle Tom's Children,* Wright was on his way to becoming a major writer. His most popular work *Native Son* (1940) established him as one of the leading black authors in America.

Reading Check

1. Why didn't the family have food at the beginning of the story?
2. What job did the mother find?
3. What did she send the boy to buy?
4. Who took the boy's money?
5. After the boy had been robbed twice, what did his mother give him in addition to money and a note?

For Study and Discussion

Analyzing and Interpreting the Selection

1. In this true story, a boy battled a street gang. But the boy's family faced another "enemy" at home. Look back at the opening paragraph. **a.** What enemy did the family face? **b.** How did this enemy hurt the boy?

2. When a hero in a story has to fight, it is usually for some purpose that we understand and sympathize with. Sometimes a hero is unwilling to fight. Why do you think the mother forced the boy to face the gang in the street?

3. What do you think the boy proved, to his mother and to himself, by winning the street battle?

Literary Elements

Responding to Figurative Language

Wright wants to impress upon the reader how hunger haunted his family. To do this, he describes hunger as if it were a person: "Hunger had always been more or less at my **1** elbow when I played." Where does he find **2** hunger at night? What does hunger look like to him?

Wright is using **figurative language** here. He is comparing hunger to a person. Figurative language is not literally, or factually, true. Hunger does not really have eyes, and it can't actually stand or move. But figurative language **3** helps you see things in sharp, new ways. How did Wright's unusual description of hunger affect you?

About the Author

Richard Wright (1908–1960)

The Granger Collection, New York

This selection is taken from *Black Boy,* the autobiography of Richard Wright. Wright's childhood was full of heartbreak. It was disrupted by family problems and by his mother's long illness. When he was very young, Wright learned to escape through listening to stories. With his mother's help, he learned to read before he entered school. His formal schooling didn't last long. Wright was only fifteen years old when he left home and set off on his own. Later in his life he said that it had been only through books that he had managed to keep himself alive. Whenever his environment failed to support or nourish him, he clutched at books. Wright is now recognized as one of the important American writers of the twentieth century.

OBJECTIVES
The overall aim is for students to analyze **conflict** and **characterization** in James Ramsey Ullman's "Top Man." For a complete list of objectives, see the **Teacher's Notes.**

VOCABULARY
The underlined words are in the Glossary. The **Language and Vocabulary** exercise on p. 67 will give students practice in using context clues to find the meanings of unfamiliar words.

FOCUS / MOTIVATION
Ask several students in advance to prepare brief oral reports on topics such as famous mountain climbers, equipment used in mountain climbing, safety measures for mountain climbing, and highest mountains in the world.

Top Man

JAMES RAMSEY ULLMAN

"The mountain, to all of us, was no longer a mere giant of rock and ice; it had become a living thing, an enemy, watching us, waiting for us, hostile, relentless, and aware."

1 The gorge bent. The walk fell suddenly away, and we came out on the edge of a bleak, boulder-strewn valley. . . . *And there it was.*

Osborn saw it first. He had been leading the column, threading his way slowly among the huge rock masses of the gorge's mouth. Then he came to the first flat bare place and stopped. He neither pointed nor cried out, but every man behind him knew instantly what it was. **2** The long file sprang taut, like a jerked rope. As **3** swiftly as we could, but in complete silence, we came out one by one into the open space where Osborn stood, and we raised our eyes with his.

In the records of the Indian Topographical Survey it says: "Kalpurtha: altitude 27,930 feet. The highest peak in the Garhwal Himalayas and probably fourth highest in the world. Also known as K3. A Tertiary formation of sedimentary limestone. . . ."

There were men among us who had spent

TEACHING RESOURCES A
Teacher's Notes, p. 101
Reading Check, p. 105
Study Guide, p. 106
Language Skills, p. 111
Building Vocabulary, pp. 115, 116
Selection Test, p. 117

PREREADING FOCUS
The headnote, which is a quotation from "Top Man," suggests a bitter struggle between the mountain climbers and the mountain. That the mountain is personified, described as a "living . . . enemy," implies both the mountain's affinity with and antagonism toward the climbers. Ask students to give other examples of this dual relationship between humans and nature.

Top Man

1 Finding Details
Analyzing
To what does the word "it" refer? How does the use of the pronoun add to the story?
Refers to Kalpurtha (K3). Reader is left to wonder about reference, adding **suspense.**

2
Simile. "Like a jerked rope" suggests sudden stop because of tremendous force: the men are stopped by magnificence of mountain.

3
Point of view. Pronoun "we" indicates that the story has first-person narrator.

VISUAL CONNECTIONS
Exploring the Subject
Toward the end of the nineteenth century, Europeans interested in mountain climbing turned their attention to the Himalayas and other challenging peaks outside Europe. By 1870, all the Alpine peaks had been scaled, and mountaineers attempted higher mountains on other continents.

Eight mountain climbers set off on an expedition to reach the summit of one of the world's highest peaks—Kalpurtha, or K3. Among the group are Nace, a cautious, experienced climber, and Osborn, a relatively impulsive but skilled climber.

Along the way, the group faces obstacles—the mountain itself and a blinding snowstorm. More threatening, however, is the **conflict** between Nace and Osborn. The two men have very different ideas about how to accomplish their goal.

The **theme** of challenges is prominent in "Top Man," a tale of mountaineering in the Himalayas. The climbers are challenged by the rigors of the weather, the altitude, and the mountain itself. The **conflict** between the two main char-

---

4

"Single electric perception" suggests that men are so emotionally stirred by awe-inspiring mountain that nothing else is in their thoughts.

5

Optical illusion makes valley appear to narrow and rise.

6

Simile. Description of sight of mountain peak as "stupendous crash of music" enhances idea of men's emotional and spiritual exhilaration.

7 Finding Details
Analyzing

Which words in this sentence create a stark contrast with "a stupendous crash of music"? What effect do the words create? "Sudden silent moment" suggests that men now see mountain as formidable antagonist.

8

Personification. Reference to mountain as crouching "white-hooded giant" creates visual image of mountain as vigilant, living being.

9

Characterization. Description of Osborn at moment of first sight of mountain helps establish his character. He is young, impulsive, and confident that he can conquer mountain.

10

Nace's reaction to mountain contrasts with Osborn's. Nace already "knows" mountain; his "almost shut" eyes suggest that he is calculating, cautiously planning assault on mountain.

---

months of their lives—in some cases years—reading, thinking, planning about what now lay before us; but at that moment statistics and geology, knowledge, thought, and plans, were as remote and forgotten as the faraway western cities from which we had come. We were men bereft of everything but eyes, everything but **4** the single electric perception: *there it was!*

Before us the valley stretched into miles of rocky desolation. To right and left it was bounded by low ridges, which, as the eye followed them, slowly mounted and drew closer **5** together, until the valley was no longer a valley at all, but a narrowing, rising corridor between **6** the cliffs. What happened then I can describe only as a stupendous crash of music. At the end of the corridor and above it—so far above it that it shut out half the sky—hung the blinding white mass of K3.

It was like the many pictures I had seen, and at the same time utterly unlike them. The shape was there, and the familiar distinguishing features: the sweeping skirt of glaciers; the monstrous vertical precipices of the face and the jagged ice-line of the east ridge; finally, the symmetrical summit pyramid that transfixed the sky. But whereas in the pictures the mountain had always seemed unreal—a dream-image of cloud, snow, and crystal—it was now no longer an image at all. It was a mass: solid, **7** immanent, appalling. We were still too far away to see the windy whipping of its snow plumes or to hear the cannonading of its avalanches, but in that sudden silent moment every man of us was for the first time aware of it not as a picture in his mind, but as a thing, an **8** antagonist. For all its twenty-eight thousand feet of lofty grandeur it seemed, somehow, less to tower than to crouch—a white-hooded giant, secret and remote, but living. Living and on guard.

I turned my eyes from the dazzling glare and looked at my companions. Osborn still

9 stood a little in front of the others. He was absolutely motionless, his young face tense and shining, his eyes devouring the mountain as a lover's might devour the form of his beloved. One could feel in the very set of his body the overwhelming desire that swelled in him to act, to come to grips, to conquer. A little behind him were ranged the other white men of the expedition: Randolph, our leader, Wittmer and Johns, Dr. Schlapp and Bixler. All were still, their eyes cast upward. Off to one side a little stood Nace, the Englishman, the only one among us who was not staring at K3 for the first time. He had been the last to come up out of the gorge and stood now with arms folded on his chest, squinting at the great peak he had known so long and fought so tirelessly and fiercely. His lean British face, under its mask of stubble and windburn, was expressionless. His lips were a thin line, and his eyes **10** seemed almost shut. Behind the sahibs[1] ranged the porters, bent forward over their staffs, their brown seamed faces straining upward from beneath their loads.

For a long while no one spoke or moved. The only sounds between earth and sky were the soft hiss of our breathing and the pounding of our hearts.

Through the long afternoon we wound slowly between the great boulders of the valley and at sundown pitched camp in the bed of a dried-up stream. The porters ate their rations in silence, wrapped themselves in their blankets, and fell asleep under the stars. The rest of us, as was our custom, sat close about the fire that blazed in the circle of tents, discussing the events of the day and the plans for the next. It was a flawlessly clear Himalayan night, and K3 tiered[2] up into the blackness like a monstrous beacon lighted from within. There was no

---

1. **sahibs** (sä′ĭbz): *Sahib* is a title of respect used in India.
2. **tiered** (tērd) **up:** rose upward in rows or *tiers.*

acters is central to the story. Both men are skilled climbers, but Nace is characterized by cautious experience while Osborn is characterized by the impulsiveness of youth. The story explores the consequences of each man's personality within the context of the story's **setting.** The author also uses sensory details to add to the story's **suspense.**

VISUAL CONNECTIONS
Exploring the Subject
Hiking at the lower altitudes may not provide the spectacular views seen while rock climbing near the peaks, but it is fundamental to climbing. Hiking can require great persistence, particularly when carrying heavy loads for long periods of time over rough terrain.

Ideas for Writing
Careful observation is one of the critical climbing skills. Ask students to study the photograph carefully and to write a list of at least five adjectives that would describe elements of the picture.

You may also wish to have students imagine that the photograph is an illustration for a story they are writing. Then have them write a paragraph describing the picture in the context of the story.

11 wind, but a great tide of cold air crept down the valley from the ice fields above, penetrating our clothing, pressing gently against the canvas of the tents.

"Another night or two and we'll be needing the sleeping bags," commented Randolph.

Osborn nodded. "We could use them tonight would be my guess."

Randolph turned to Nace. "What do you say, Martin?"

The Englishman puffed at his pipe a moment. "Rather think it might be better to wait," he said at last.

12 "Wait? Why?" Osborn jerked his head up.

"Well, it gets pretty nippy high up, you know. I've seen it thirty below at twenty-five thousand on the east ridge. Longer we wait for the bags, better acclimated we'll get."

Osborn snorted. "A lot of good being acclimated will do, if we have frozen feet."

"Easy, Paul, easy," cautioned Randolph. "It seems to me Martin's right."

Osborn bit his lip, but said nothing. The other men entered the conversation, and soon it had veered to other matters: the weather, the porters and pack animals, routes, camps, and strategy, the inevitable, inexhaustible topics of the climber's world.

There were all kinds of men among the eight of us, men with a great diversity of back-**13** ground and interest. Sayre Randolph, whom the Alpine Club had named leader of our expedition, had for years been a well-known explorer and lecturer. Now in his middle fifties, he was no longer equal to the grueling physical demands of high climbing, but served as planner and organizer of the enterprise. Wittmer was a Seattle lawyer, who had recently made a name for himself by a series of difficult ascents in the Coast Range of British Colum-

11

Imagery. Sea imagery used to describe air suggests that weather, like great wave, is a powerful natural force.

12

Conflict. This first suggestion of conflict between Osborn and Nace reinforces idea that Osborn is impulsive and Nace is a careful planner.

13 Analyzing
Does Randolph, the leader of the expedition, always seem to be in complete command? Some students may point out that he often looks to Nace before making decisions.

14 Summarizing
Drawing Conclusions

What are some of the men's occupations? What conclusion can be drawn from the descriptions of them? Explorer, lawyer, ranger, law enforcer, physician, meteorologist, professor of geology. Men are from a variety of backgrounds and levels of experience.

15

A more detailed description of Osborn and Nace suggests that they will be main characters in story.

16 Finding Main Ideas
Making Inferences

Whom does the narrator most want to reach summit? Why? Nace. Answers might include that narrator thinks Nace is most deserving because he has tried several times to reach summit and has come closer to it than anyone else; also narrator's **tone** suggests his sympathy for Nace's loss of lifelong friend during last attempt.

17

Foreshadowing. Narrator suspects "friction" between Osborn and Nace will increase and hints **conflict** may lead to trouble, perhaps disaster.

18

Metaphor. "Monster" furthers idea of mountain as antagonistic and dangerous force.

19

"Fever" contrasts with actual cold; men are warmed by their desires to conquer mountain.

20

In 1924, George Mallory and Andrew Irvine vanished while making unsuccessful bid for summit of Mt. Everest, world's highest mountain.

bia. Johns was an Alaskan, fantastically strong, able sourdough,[3] who had been a ranger in the U.S. Forestry Service and had accompanied many famous Alaskan expeditions. Schlapp was a practicing physician from Milwaukee, Bixler a government meteorologist with a talent for photography. I, at the time, was an **14** assistant professor of geology at an eastern university.

Finally, and preeminently, there were Osborn and Nace. I say "preeminently" because, even at this time, when we had been together as a party for little more than a month, I believe all of us realized that these were the two key men of our venture. None, to my knowledge, ever expressed it in words, but the conviction was none the less there that if any of us were eventually to stand on the summit of K3, it would be one of them, or both. **15** They were utterly dissimilar men. Osborn was twenty-three and a year out of college, a compact, buoyant mass of energy and high spirits, He seemed to be wholly unaffected by either the physical or mental hazards of mountaineering and had already, by virtue of many spectacular ascents in the Alps and Rockies, won a reputation as the most skilled and audacious of younger American climbers. Nace was in his forties—lean, taciturn,[4] introspective. An official in the Indian Civil Service, he had explored and climbed in the Himalayas for twenty years. He had been a member of all five of the unsuccessful British expeditions to K3, and in his last attempt had attained to within **20** five hundred feet of the summit, the highest point which any man had reached on the unconquered giant. This had been the famous, tragic attempt in which his fellow climber and lifelong friend, Captain Furness, had slipped and fallen ten thousand feet to his death. Nace

rarely mentioned his name, but on the steel head of his ice ax were engraved the words: TO MARTIN FROM JOHN. If fate were to grant that the ax of any one of us should be planted upon **16** the summit of K3, I hoped it would be this one.

Such were the men who huddled about the fire in the deep, still cold of a Himalayan night. There were many differences among us, in temperament as well as in background. In one **17** or two cases, notably that of Osborn and Nace, there had already been a certain amount of friction, and as the venture continued and the struggles and hardships of the actual ascent began, it would, I knew, increase. But differences were unimportant. What mattered—all that mattered—was that our purpose was one: **18** to conquer the monster of rock and ice that now loomed above us in the night; to stand for a moment where no man, no living thing, had ever stood before. To that end we had come from half a world away, across oceans and continents to the fastnesses[5] of inner Asia. To that end we were prepared to endure cold, exhaustion, and danger, even to the very last extremity of human endurance. . . . Why? There is no answer, and at the same time every man among us knew the answer; every man who has ever looked upon a great mountain and felt the **19** fever in his blood to climb and conquer knows the answer. George Leigh Mallory, greatest of mountaineers, expressed it once and for all when he was asked why he wanted to climb unconquered Everest.

20 "I want to climb it," said Mallory, "because it is there."

Day after day we crept on and upward. Sometimes the mountain was brilliant above us, as it had been when we first saw it; sometimes it was

3. **sourdough:** a slang word meaning "pioneer" or "prospector."
4. **taciturn** (tăs'ə-tûrn): reserved, quiet.

5. **fastnesses:** fortresses or strongholds. Here, the author is comparing the mountains to fortresses.

partially or wholly obscured by tiers of clouds. The naked desolation of the valley was unrelieved by any motion, color, or sound; and as we progressed, the great rock walls that enclosed it grew so high and steep that its floor received the sun for less than two hours each day. The rest of the time it lay in ashen half-light, its gloom intensified by the dazzling brilliance of the ice slopes above. As long as we remained there we had the sensation of **21** imprisonment; it was like being trapped at the bottom of a deep well or in a sealed court between great skyscrapers. Soon we were thinking of the ascent of the shining mountain not only as an end in itself, but as an escape.

In our nightly discussions around the fire our conversation narrowed more and more to the immediate problems confronting us, and during them I began to realize that the tension **25** between Osborn and Nace went deeper than I **22** had at first surmised. There was rarely any outright argument between them—they were **26** both far too able mountain men to disagree on fundamentals—but I saw that at almost every turn they were rubbing each other the wrong way. It was a matter of personalities, chiefly. Osborn was talkative, enthusiastic, optimistic, always chafing to be up and at it, always wanting to take the short straight line to the given point. Nace, on the other hand, was matter-of-fact, cautious, slow. He was the apostle of trial-and-error and watchful waiting. Because of his far greater experience and intimate knowl- **27** edge of K3, Randolph almost invariably followed his advice, rather than Osborn's, when a difference of opinion arose. The younger man usually capitulated with good grace, but I could tell that he was irked.

During the days in the valley I had few occasions to talk privately with either of them, and only once did either mention the other in any **23** but the most casual manner. Even then, the remarks they made seemed unimportant and I remember them only in view of what happened later.

My conversation with Osborn occurred first. It was while we were on the march, and Osborn, who was directly behind me, came up suddenly to my side. "You're a geologist, **24** Frank," he began without preamble. "What do you think of Nace's theory about the ridge?"

"What theory?" I asked.

"He believes we should traverse[6] under it from the glacier up. Says the ridge itself is too exposed."

"It looks pretty mean through the telescope."

"But it's been done before. He's done it himself. All right, it's tough—I'll admit that. But a decent climber could make it in half the time the traverse will take."

"Nace knows the traverse is longer," I said. **25** "But he seems certain it will be much easier for us."

"Easier for *him* is what he means." Osborn **26** paused, looking moodily at the ground. "He was a great climber in his day. It's a shame a man can't be honest enough with himself to know when he's through." He fell silent and a moment later dropped back into his place in line.

It was that same night, I think, that I awoke to find Nace sitting up in his blanket and staring at the mountain.

"How clear it is!" I whispered.

The Englishman pointed. "See the ridge?"

27 I nodded, my eyes fixed on the great, twisting spine of ice that limbed into the sky. I could see now, more clearly than in the blinding sunlight, its huge indentations and jagged, windswept pitches. "It looks impossible," I said.

"No, it can be done. Trouble is, when you've made it you're too done in for the summit."

"Osborn seems to think its shortness would make up for its difficulty."

6. **traverse** (trăv′ərs, trə-vûrs′): To traverse a mountain is to crisscross it instead of climbing straight up.

21
Men feel caged, further adding to anxiety to "escape" and climb.

22
Conflict. Tension between Osborn and Nace is deeper than mere conflict of ideas; the men seem to contrast in almost every way except their desire to climb mountain.

23
Suspense. Narrator hints at important event that will be related in some way to clash between Osborn and Nace.

24 Expressing an Opinion
Why do you think Osborn questions the narrator? Responses will vary. Perhaps he hopes to use expert's opinion as support for his side of an argument with Nace.

25
Narrator indicates his faith in Nace's opinions.

26
Osborn thinks that Nace is too old to climb and that he is overly cautious because of age.

27
Personification. Image supports earlier description of mountain as dreadful giant.

TRANSPARENCIES 1 & 2

Fine Art
Theme: *Those Who Dare* – invites students to explore artworks that examine the idea of perseverance despite difficult situations.

VISUAL CONNECTIONS
Exploring the Subject
In this photograph, two climbers are dwarfed by the snow masses on either side. It is particularly important to have a knowledge of snow and how it is affected by the sun and other weather conditions. Snow cornices, which resemble crests of waves, are caused by wind. From the windward side, they are difficult to see, but they must be avoided because the weight of a climber will cause them to break.

Relating Expression Skills
The photograph suggests the painstaking, tedious procedure of mapping routes and of establishing multiple camps from which to coordinate and supply a mountain-climbing expedition. Divide the class into groups and ask each group to list reasons why they think so much preparation is necessary. What sorts of things require that so much care and caution be exercised before the final assault on a mountain peak?

28 Summarizing
What is Nace suggesting? That Osborn's route might result in disaster. Nace's friend Furness had died because he thought that route was best.

29
Tongue: narrow extension from leading edge of glacier.

30
Climbers want to know as much as possible about terrain before they actually climb. Suggests preparation time may exceed time it takes to make climb.

31
Although Randolph is official leader, Nace appears to be real authority on expedition.

Nace was silent a long moment before answering. Then for the first and only time I heard him speak the name of his dead companion. "That's what Furness thought," he said quietly. Then he lay down and wrapped himself in his blanket.

For the next two weeks the uppermost point of the valley was our home and workshop. We established our base camp as close to the

mountain as we could, less than half a mile from the tongue of its lowest glacier, and plunged into the arduous tasks of preparation for the ascent. Our food and equipment were unpacked, inspected and sorted, and finally repacked in lighter loads for transportation to more advanced camps. Hours were spent poring over maps and charts and studying the monstrous heights above us through telescope and binoculars. Under Nace's supervision, a thorough reconnaissance of the glacier was made and the route across it laid out; then began the backbreaking labor of moving up supplies and establishing the chain of camps.

Camps I and II were set up on the glacier itself, in the most sheltered sites we could find. Camp III we built at its upper end, as near as possible to the point where the great rock spine of K3 thrust itself free of ice and began its precipitous ascent. According to our plans, this would be the advance base of operations during the climb. The camps to be established higher up, on the mountain proper, would be too small and too exposed to serve as anything more than one or two nights' shelter. The total distance between the base camp and Camp III was only fifteen miles, but the utmost daily progress of our porters was five miles, and it was essential that we should never be more than twelve hours' march from food and shelter. Hour after hour, day after day, the long file of men wound up and down among the hummocks[7] and crevasses of the glacier, and finally the time arrived when we were ready to advance.

Leaving Dr. Schlapp in charge of eight porters at the base camp, we proceeded easily and on schedule, reaching Camp I the first night, Camp II the second, and the advance base the third. No men were left at Camps I and II, inasmuch as they were designed simply

---

7 **hummocks:** here, mounds of ice.

as caches for food and equipment; and furthermore we knew we would need all the manpower available for the establishment of the higher camps on the mountain proper.

32 For more than three weeks now the weather had held perfectly, but on our first night at the advance base, as if by malignant prearrangement of nature, we had our first taste of the fury of a high Himalayan storm. It began with great streamers of lightning that flashed about **33** the mountain like a halo; then heavily through **34** the weird glare, snow began to fall. The wind rose. At first it was only sound—a remote, desolate moaning in the night high above us—but soon it descended, sucked down the deep valley as if into a gigantic funnel. Hour after hour it howled about the tents with hurricane frenzy, and the wild flapping of the canvas dinned in our ears like machine-gun fire.

There was no sleep for us that night or the next. For thirty-six hours the storm raged without lull, while we huddled in the icy gloom of the tents, exerting our last ounce of strength to keep from being buried alive or blown into eternity. At last, on the third morning, it was over, and we came out into a world transformed by a twelve-foot cloak of snow. No single landmark remained as it had been before, and our supplies and equipment were in the wildest confusion. Fortunately there had not **38** been a single serious injury, but it was another three days before we had regained our strength and put the camp in order.

Then we waited. The storm did not return, and the sky beyond the ridges gleamed flaw- **39** lessly clear; but night and day we could hear the roaring thunder of avalanches on the mountain above us. To have ventured so much as one step into that savage vertical wilderness before the new-fallen snow froze tight would **35** have been suicidal. We chafed or waited patiently, according to our individual temperaments, while the days dragged by.

It was late one afternoon that Osborn returned from a short reconnaissance up the ridge. His eyes were shining and his voice jubilant.

"It's tight!" he cried. "Tight as a drum. We can go!" All of us stopped whatever we were doing. His excitement leaped like an electric spark from one to another. "I went about a thousand feet, and it's sound all the way. What do you say, Sayre? Tomorrow?"

Randolph hesitated, then looked at Nace.

"Better give it another day or two," said the Englishman.

Osborn glared at him. "Why?" he challenged.

"It's usually safer to wait till——"

"Wait! Wait!" Osborn exploded. "Don't you ever think of anything but waiting? My God, man, the snow's firm, I tell you!"

"It's firm down here," Nace replied quietly, "because the sun hits it only two hours a day. Up above it gets the sun twelve hours. It may not have frozen yet."

"The avalanches have stopped."

"That doesn't necessarily mean it will hold a man's weight."

"It seems to me Martin's point——" Randolph began.

Osborn wheeled on him. "Sure," he snapped. "I know. Martin's right. The cautious bloody English are always right. Let him have his way, and we'll be sitting here chewing our nails until the mountain falls down on us." His eyes flashed to Nace. "Maybe with a little less of that bloody cautiousness you English wouldn't have made such a mess of Everest. Maybe your pals Mallory and Furness wouldn't be dead."

"Osborn!" commanded Randolph sharply.

The youngster stared at Nace for another moment, breathing heavily. Then abruptly he turned away.

The next two days were clear and windless, but we still waited, following Nace's advice. There were no further brushes between him

40
Like the weather, clear and windless, emotional climate between Osborn and Nace is relatively calm but subject to violent eruptions.

41
Analyzing
Drawing Conclusions
What is meant by "paling of the sky"? Why do the men now continue to climb? "Paling of the sky" refers to dawn. Men continue climb because snow has hardened enough to support weight of men and supplies they carry.

42
Osborn and Nace are in separate groups—a separation perhaps intended to lessen tension between them.

43
Conflict. In addition to obstacles they face in climbing K3, they are assaulted by an even more unpredictable enemy—weather.

44
Climbers are spared attack of new snow, which would have delayed their progress by making terrain soft and more hazardous.

45
Although Osborn's and Nace's temperaments are very different, they share traits of strength and skill.

46
Characterization. Osborn is at his best during climb; he proves himself to be superior climber.

and Osborn, but an unpleasant air of restlessness and tension hung over the camp. I found myself chafing almost as impatiently as Osborn himself for the moment when we would break out of that maddening inactivity and begin the assault.

At last the day came. With the first paling of the sky a roped file of men, bent almost double beneath heavy loads, began slowly to climb the ice slope, just beneath the jagged line of the great east ridge. In accordance with prearranged plan, we proceeded in relays, this first group consisting of Nace, Johns, myself, and eight porters. It was our job to ascend approximately two thousand feet in a day's climbing and establish Camp IV at the most level and sheltered site we could find. We would spend the night there and return to the advance base next day, while the second relay, consisting of Osborn, Wittmer, and eight more porters, went up with their loads. This process was to continue until all necessary supplies were at Camp IV, and then the whole thing would be repeated between Camps IV and V and V and VI. From VI, at an altitude of about twenty-six thousand feet, the ablest and fittest men—presumably Nace and Osborn—would make the direct assault on the summit. Randolph and Bixler were to remain at the advance base throughout the operations, acting as directors and co-ordinators. We were under the strictest orders that any man—sahib or porter—who suffered illness or injury should be brought down immediately.

How shall I describe those next two weeks beneath the great ice ridge of K3? In a sense there was no occurrence of importance, and at the same time everything happened that could possibly happen, short of actual disaster. We established Camp IV, came down again, went up again, came down again. Then we crept laboriously higher. With our axes we hacked uncountable thousands of steps in the gleaming walls of ice. Among the rocky outcroppings of the cliffs we clung to holds and strained at ropes until we thought our arms would spring from their sockets. Storms swooped down on us, battered us, and passed. The wind increased, and the air grew steadily colder and more difficult to breathe. One morning two of the porters awoke with their feet frozen black; they had to be sent down. A short while later Johns developed an uncontrollable nosebleed and was forced to descend to a lower camp. Wittmer was suffering from racking headaches and I from a continually dry throat. But providentially, the one enemy we feared the most in that icy gale-lashed hell did not again attack us. No snow fell. And day by day, foot by foot, we ascended.

It is during ordeals like this that the surface trappings of a man are shed and his secret mettle[8] laid bare. There were no shirkers or quitters among us—I had known that from the beginning—but now, with each passing day, it became more manifest which were the strongest and ablest among us. Beyond all argument, these were Osborn and Nace.

Osborn was magnificent. All the boyish impatience and moodiness which he had exhibited earlier were gone, and, now that he was at last at work in his natural element, he emerged as the peerless mountaineer he was. His energy was inexhaustible, his speed, both on rock and ice, almost twice that of any other man in the party. He was always discovering new routes and shortcuts. Often he ascended by the ridge itself, instead of using the traverse beneath it, as had been officially prescribed; but his craftsmanship was so sure and his performance so brilliant that no one ever thought of taking him to task. Indeed, there was such vigor, buoyancy, and youth in everything he did that it gave heart to all the rest of us.

8. **mettle** (mĕt'l): courage, spirit.

58 CHALLENGES

47 In contrast, Nace was slow, methodical, unspectacular. Since he and I worked in the same relay, I was with him almost constantly, and to this day I carry in my mind the clear image of the man: his tall body bent almost double against endless shimmering slopes of ice; his lean brown face bent in utter concentration on the problem in hand, then raised searchingly to the next; the bright prong of his ax rising, falling, rising, falling, with tireless rhythm, until the steps in the glassy incline were so wide and deep that the most clumsy of the porters could not have slipped from them had he tried. Osborn attacked the mountain head-on. Nace studied it, sparred with it, wore it down. His spirit did not flap from his sleeve like a pennon;[9] it was deep inside him— **49** patient, indomitable.

The day soon came when I learned from him what it is to be a great mountaineer. We

9. **pennon** (pĕn'ən): flag.

were making the ascent from Camp IV to V, and an almost perpendicular ice wall had made it necessary for us to come out for a few yards on the exposed crest of the ridge. There were six of us in the party, roped together, with Nace leading, myself second, and four porters **48** bringing up the rear. The ridge at this particular point was free of snow, but razor-thin, and the rocks were covered with a smooth glaze of ice. On either side the mountain dropped away in sheer precipices of five thousand feet.

Suddenly the last porter slipped. I heard the ominous scraping of boot nails behind me and, turning, saw a gesticulating figure plunge sideways into the abyss. There was a scream as the next porter was jerked off too. I remember trying frantically to dig into the ridge with my ax, realizing at the same time it would no more hold against the weight of the falling men than a pin stuck in a wall. Then I heard Nace shout, "Jump!" As he said it, the rope went tight about my waist, and I went hurtling after him into

47 Comparing/Contrasting
What are the differences between Nace's and Osborn's climbing styles? Nace's caution, rationality, and concern stand in stark contrast to Osborn's speed, energy, and rashness.

48
Suspense. "Razor-thin" ridge and ice-covered rocks increase tension; the men are in an intensely dangerous situation.

49
Ax, a manufactured instrument, proves useless against nature.

VISUAL CONNECTIONS
Exploring the Subject
The man in this photograph appears to be climbing a glacier, a prominent feature of the Himalayas (*himal* means "snowfield"). Glaciers are important features, not only for the way they shape the landscape but also for water to form mountain rivers. Glaciers are the drainage system of mountains; those in the Great Himalayan Range feed rivers that eventually empty into the Indus River.

space on the opposite side of the ridge. After me came the nearest porter. . . .

What happened then must have happened in five yards and a fifth of a second. I heard myself cry out, and the glacier, a mile below, rushed up at me, spinning. Then both were blotted out in a violent spasm, as the rope **50** jerked taut. I hung for a moment, an inert mass, feeling that my body had been cut in two; then I swung in slowly to the side of the **55** mountain. Above me the rope lay tight and motionless across the crest of the ridge, our weight exactly counterbalancing that of the men who had fallen on the far slope.

Nace's voice came up from below. "You chaps on the other side!" he shouted. "Start climbing slowly. We're climbing too."

In five minutes we had all regained the ridge. The porters and I crouched panting on **51** the jagged rocks, our eyes closed, the sweat beading our faces in frozen drops. Nace carefully examined the rope that again hung loosely between us.

52   "All right, men," he said presently. "Let's get on to camp for a cup of tea."

Above Camp V the whole aspect of the ascent changed. The angle of the ridge eased off, and the ice, which lower down had covered the mountain like a sheath, lay only in scattered **53** patches between the rocks. Fresh enemies, however, instantly appeared to take the place of the old. We were now laboring at an altitude of more than twenty-five thousand feet—well above the summits of the highest surrounding peaks—and day and night, without protection or respite, we were buffeted by the fury of the **54** wind. Worse than this was that the atmosphere had become so rarefied it could scarcely support life. Breathing itself was a major physical effort, and our progress upward consisted of two or three painful steps followed by a long period of rest in which our hearts pounded

wildly and our burning lungs gasped for air. Each of us carried a small cylinder of oxygen in his pack, but we used it only in emergencies and found that, while its immediate effect was salutary, it left us later even worse off than before. My throat dried and contracted until it felt as if it were lined with brass. The faces of all of us, under our beards and windburn, grew haggard and strained.

But the great struggle was now mental as much as physical. The lack of air induced a lethargy of mind and spirit; confidence and the powers of thought and decision waned, and dark foreboding crept out from the secret recesses of the subconscious. The wind seemed to carry strange sounds, and we kept imagining we saw things which we knew were not there. The mountain, to all of us, was no longer a mere giant of rock and ice; it had become a living thing, an enemy, watching us, waiting for us, hostile, relentless, and aware. Inch by inch we crept upward through that empty forgotten world above the world, and only one last thing remained to us of human **56** consciousness and human will: to go on. To go on.

On the fifteenth day after we had first left the advance base we pitched Camp VI at an altitude of almost twenty-six thousand feet. It was located near the uppermost extremity of the great east ridge, directly beneath the so-called shoulder of the mountain. On the far side of the shoulder the monstrous north face of K3 fell sheer to the glaciers, two miles below. And above it and to the left rose the symmetrical bulk of the summit pyramid. The topmost rocks of its highest pinnacle were clearly visible from the shoulder, and the intervening two thousand feet seemed to offer no insuperable obstacles.

Camp VI, which was in reality no camp at all, but a single tent, was large enough to accommodate only three men. Osborn established it with the aid of Wittmer and one another, the end had come. Our meager food supply was running out; even with careful rationing there was enough left for only two more days.

porter; then, the following morning, Wittmer and the porter descended to Camp V, and Nace and I went up. It was our plan that Osborn and Nace should launch the final assault—the next day, if the weather held—with myself in support, following their progress through binoculars and going to their aid or summoning help from below if anything went wrong. As the three of us lay in the tent that night, the summit seemed already within arm's reach, victory

57 securely in our grasp.

58 And then the blow fell. With malignant timing, which no power on earth could have made us believe was a simple accident of nature, the mountain hurled at us its last line of defense. It snowed.

For a day and a night the great flakes drove down on us, swirling and swooping in the wind, blotting out the summit, the shoulder, everything beyond the tiny white-walled radius of our tents. Hour after hour we lay in our sleeping bags, stirring only to eat or to secure the straining rope and canvas. Our feet froze under their thick layers of wool and rawhide. Our heads and bodies throbbed with a dull

59 nameless aching, and time crept over our numbed minds like a glacier. At last, during the morning of the following day, it cleared.

62 The sun came out in a thin blue sky, and the summit pyramid again appeared above us, now whitely robed in fresh snow. But still we waited. Until the snow either froze or was blown away by the wind it would have been the rashest courting of destruction for us to have ascended a foot beyond the camp. Another day

63 passed. And another.

By the third nightfall our nerves were at the breaking point. For hours on end we had scarcely moved or spoken, and the only sounds in all the world were the endless moaning of the wind outside and the harsh sucking noise of our breathing. I knew that, one way or

60 another, the end had come. Our meager food supply was running out; even with careful rationing there was enough left for only two more days.

Presently Nace stirred in his sleeping bag

61 and sat up. "We'll have to go down tomorrow," he said quietly.

For a moment there was silence in the tent. Then Osborn struggled to a sitting position and faced him.

"No," he said.

"There's still too much loose snow above. We can't make it,"

"But it's clear. As long as we can see——"

Nace shook his head. "Too dangerous. We'll go down tomorrow and lay in a fresh supply. Then we'll try again."

"Once we go down we're licked. You know it."

Nace shrugged. "Better to be licked than . . ." The strain of speech was suddenly too much for him and he fell into a violent paroxysm of coughing. When it had passed there was a long silence.

Then suddenly Osborn spoke again. "Look, Nace," he said, "I'm going up tomorrow."

The Englishman shook his head.

"I'm going—understand?"

For the first time since I had known him I

62 saw Nace's eyes flash in anger. "I'm the senior member of this group," he said, "I forbid you to go!"

Osborn jerked himself to his knees, almost upsetting the tiny tent. "You forbid me? This may be your sixth time on this mountain, and all that, but you don't *own* it! I know what

63 you're up to. You haven't got it in you to make the top yourself, so you don't want anyone else to make it. That's it, isn't it? Isn't it?" He sat down again suddenly, gasping for breath.

Nace looked at him with level eyes. "This mountain has beaten me five times," he said softly. "It killed my best friend. It means more to me to climb it than anything else in the

57
Even though only Nace and Osborn are to make actual climb to summit, other members of group have been partly responsible for anticipated success and will share victory.

58
Personification. Mountain is attributed with having malicious intent to keep men from reaching its peak.

59
Time is now an enemy. Before, only their impatience pushed them against time; now, frigid weather threatens their survival.

60
"The end had come" shows men's desperation and suggests possible disaster.

61
Nace knows that they cannot attempt summit because of conditions; he calmly faces reality of defeat.

62 Analyzing Expressing an Opinion
Why does Nace use his position of authority against Osborn? What do you think is Nace's motive? Nace uses position because rational arguments have failed. He wants to save Osborn from results of Osborn's own impulsive nature; probably remembers friend he lost.

63
Osborn thinks only of his desire to conquer mountain; he sees Nace's interference as selfishly motivated.

Have students locate Asia and the Himalayas on a world map and then use the map and reference sources to find out about this part of the world. Encourage students to record what they learn in learning logs or journals, or to give informal oral reports to the class. You might ask students the following questions to get them started. What are the names of the countries through which this mountain range extends? What are the names and elevations of some of its highest peaks? How do these elevations compare to those in other mountain ranges such as the Alps and the Rocky Mountains?

VISUAL CONNECTIONS

Exploring the Subject

Ask students to examine the photograph carefully. Is it possible for a mountain to be both beautiful and terrifying at the same time? Can a mountain display an attitude, a personality, an active rather than passive presence? Ullman seems to think it can, often referring to Kalpurtha as if it had a will to resist being climbed. Ask students what personality traits or attitudes they would assign to the mountain in the photograph.

Ideas for Writing

Mountain climbing requires not only considerable physical strength and conditioning but great mental discipline as well. Above all, it requires an intense desire to reach a goal. Ask students to write a paragraph in which they discuss what sort of person climbs mountains. What character traits and attributes might such a person have? You might direct students' attention to the narrator's description of the climbers in "Top Man" and to the quotation by George Mallory on p. 54: "I want to climb it because it is there."

You might also choose to have students write a paragraph from either Nace's or Osborn's point of view. Each student could present an argument, supported with logical reasons, contending that the climbers should either go on to the summit or retreat to the lower base camp.

64 world. Maybe I'll make it and maybe I won't.
65 But if I do, it will be as a <u>rational</u> intelligent human being—not as a fool throwing my life away. . . ."

66 He collapsed into another fit of coughing and fell back in his sleeping bag. Osborn, too, was still. They lay there <u>inert</u>, panting, too exhausted for speech.

It was hours later that I awoke from dull, uneasy sleep. In the faint light I saw Nace fumbling with the flap of the tent.

"What is it?" I asked.

"Osborn. He's gone."

67 The words cut like a blade through my lethargy. I struggled to my feet and followed Nace from the tent.

Outside, the dawn was seeping up the eastern sky. It was very cold, but the wind had fallen and the mountain seemed to hang suspended in a vast stillness. Above us the summit pyramid climbed bleakly into space, like the
68 last outpost of a spent and lifeless planet. Raising my binoculars, I swept them over the gray waste. At first I saw nothing but rock and ice; then, suddenly, something moved.

"I've got him," I whispered.

As I spoke, the figure of Osborn sprang into clear focus against a patch of ice. He took three or four slow upward steps, stopped, went on again. I handed the glasses to Nace.

The Englishman squinted through them, returned them to me, and reentered the tent. When I followed, he had already laced his boots and was pulling on his outer gloves.

"He's not far," he said. "Can't have been gone more than half an hour." He seized his ice ax and started out again.

"Wait," I said. "I'm going with you."

69 Nace shook his head. "Better stay here."

"I'm going with you," I said.

He said nothing further, but waited while I made ready. In a few moments we left the tent, roped up, and started off.

64
Nace's conquest of mountain would, in a way, avenge death of his best friend, yet he accepts possibility that he might not achieve that goal.

65 Finding Main Ideas
What is the essence of Nace's character that he conveys here? He is too intelligent to give up his life in reckless pursuit of conquest.

66
Nace has used precious energy to convince Osborn that an attempt at this time would be foolishly tragic.

67
Simile. "Words cut like a blade" suggests narrator senses that Osborn is in grave danger.

68
Imagery. "Spent and lifeless planet" creates foreboding image of isolation from humanity and of hostility of mountainside.

69
Nace does not want to risk yet another life, but narrator is determined to go with him to find Osborn.

TRANSPARENCY 4

Literary Elements
Character – explores the ways that an
author can reveal characterization.

70

Personification. Time seems to move slowly forward; "crawling" minutes suggest men's slow movements.

71

Climbers become mentally distanced from physical surroundings as they devote full attention to each careful step.

72

Again, as climbers remain intent on their task, their perception of time is distorted.

73

The usually agile and swift Osborn, even after head start, is overtaken by Nace and narrator.

74

Nace's concern for Osborn's safety causes him to move at pace that jeopardizes his own safety.

75 Summarizing
Finding Cause and Effect

How does the narrator describe his realization that Osborn is supported only by melting ice? Why would this realization affect him in such a way? Describes realization as "sudden" and "sickening." He knows that Osborn might at any moment fall to his death.

Almost immediately we were on the shoulder and confronted with the paralyzing two-mile drop of the north face; but we negotiated the short exposed stretch without mishap, and in ten minutes were working up the base of the summit pyramid. The going here was easier, in a purely climbing sense: the angle of ascent was not steep, and there was firm rock for hand- and foot-holds between the patches of snow and ice. Our progress, however, was creepingly slow. There seemed to be literally no air at all to breathe, and after almost every step we were forced to rest, panting and gasping as we leaned forward against our axes. My heart swelled and throbbed with every movement until I thought it would explode.

70 The minutes crawled into hours and still we climbed. Presently the sun came up. Its level rays streamed across the clouds, far below, and glinted from the summits of distant peaks. But, although the pinnacle of K3 soared a full three thousand feet above anything in the surrounding world, we had scarcely any sense of height. The wilderness of mountain valley and glacier that spread beneath us to the horizon

71 was flattened and remote, an unreal, insubstantial landscape seen in a dream. We had no connection with it, or it with us. All living, all awareness, purpose, and will, was concentrated in the last step and the next: to put one foot before the other; to breathe; to ascend. We struggled on in silence.

72 I do not know how long it was since we had left the camp—it might have been two hours, it might have been six—when we suddenly sighted Osborn. We had not been able to find him again since our first glimpse through the binoculars; but now, unexpectedly and

73 abruptly, as we came up over a jagged outcropping of rock, there he was. He was at a point, only a few yards above us, where the mountain steepened into an almost vertical wall. The smooth surface directly in front of him was

obviously unclimbable, but two alternate routes were presented. To the left, a chimney[10] cut obliquely across the wall, forbiddingly steep, but seeming to offer adequate holds. To the right was a gentle slope of snow that curved upward and out of sight behind the rocks. As we watched, Osborn ascended to the edge of the snow, stopped, and probed it with his ax. Then, apparently satisfied that it would bear his weight he stepped out on the slope.

I felt Nace's body tense. "Paul!" he cried out.

His voice was too weak and hoarse to carry. Osborn continued his ascent.

Nace cupped his hands and called his name again, and this time Osborn turned. "Wait!" cried the Englishman.

Osborn stood still, watching us, as we struggled up the few yards to the edge of the snow slope. Nace's breath came in shuddering gasps,
74 but he climbed faster than I had ever seen him climb before.

"Come back!" he called. "Come off the snow!"

"It's all right. The crust is firm," Osborn called back.

"But it's melting. There's . . ." Nace paused, fighting for air. "There's nothing underneath!"

75 In a sudden sickening flash I saw what he meant. Looked at from directly below, at the point where Osborn had come to it, the slope on which he stood appeared as a harmless covering of snow over the rocks. From where we were now, however, a little to one side, it could be seen that it was in reality no covering at all, but merely a cornice or unsupported platform clinging to the side of the mountain. Below it was not rock, but ten thousand feet of blue air.

"Come back!" I cried. "Come back!"

Osborn hesitated, then took a downward step. But he never took the next. For in that same instant the snow directly in front of him

10. **chimney:** formation of rock resembling a chimney.

disappeared. It did not seem to fall or to break **76** away. It was just soundlessly and magically no longer there. In the spot where Osborn had been about to set his foot there was now revealed the abysmal drop of the north face of K3.

I shut my eyes, but only for a second, and when I reopened them Osborn was still, miraculously, there. Nace was shouting, "Don't move! Don't move an inch!"

"The rope—" I heard myself saying.

The Englishman shook his head. "We'd have to throw it, and the impact would be too much. Brace yourself and play it out." As he **77** spoke, his eyes were traveling over the rocks that bordered the snow bridge. Then he moved forward.

I wedged myself into a cleft in the wall and let out the rope which extended between us. A few yards away Osborn stood in the snow, transfixed, one foot a little in front of the other. But my eyes now were on Nace. Cautiously, but with astonishing rapidity, he edged along the rocks beside the cornice. There was a moment when his only support was an inch-wide ledge beneath his feet, another where there was nothing under his feet at all, and he supported himself wholly by his elbows and hands. But he advanced steadily and at last reached a shelf wide enough for him to turn around on. At this point he was perhaps six feet away from Osborn.

"It's wide enough here to hold both of us," he **78** said in a quiet voice. "I'm going to reach out my ax. Don't move until you're sure you have a grip on it. When I pull, jump."

He searched the wall behind him and found **82** a hold for his left hand. Then he slowly extended his ice ax, head foremost, until it was within two feet of Osborn's shoulder. "Grip it!" he cried suddenly. Osborn's hands shot out and seized the ax. "Jump!"

There was a flash of steel in the sunlight and **79** a hunched figure hurtled inward from the snow to the ledge. Simultaneously another figure hurtled out. The haft[11] of the ax jerked suddenly from Nace's hand, and he lurched forward and downward. A violent spasm convulsed his body as the rope went taut. Then it was gone. Nace did not seem to hit the snow; he simply disappeared through it, soundlessly. In the same instant the snow itself was gone. The frayed, yellow end of broken rope spun lazily in space. . . .

Somehow my eyes went to Osborn. He was **80** crouched on the ledge where Nace had been a moment before, staring dully at the ax he held in his hands. Beyond his head, not two hundred feet above, the white untrodden pinnacle of K3 stabbed the sky.

Perhaps ten minutes passed, perhaps a half hour. I closed my eyes and leaned forward motionless against the rock, my face against **81** my arm. I neither thought nor felt; my body and mind alike were enveloped in a suffocating numbness. Through it at last came the sound of Osborn moving. Looking up, I saw he was standing beside me.

"I'm going to try for the top," he said tonelessly.

I merely stared at him.

"Will you come?"

"No," I said.

Osborn hesitated; then turned and began slowly climbing the steep chimney above us. Halfway up he paused, struggling for breath. Then he resumed his laborious upward progress and presently disappeared beyond the crest.

I stayed where I was, and the hours passed. The sun reached its zenith above the peak and sloped away behind it. And at last I heard above me the sound of Osborn returning. As I looked up, his figure appeared at the top of the

11. **haft:** handle.

76
Imagery. "Soundlessly and magically" creates dreamlike image; reinforces idea that security of snow is illusionary.

77
Again, Nace assesses situation before taking action.

78
Nace's quiet voice is probably meant to calm Osborn and also to prevent vibration from sound that might cause snow ledge to give way.

79
Climax. In this climactic moment, Osborn is pulled to safety by Nace, and Nace falls to his death.

80
Irony. That more experienced, cautious Nace dies and impetuous Osborn survives is unexpected, creating **irony of situation.**

81 Finding Details
Analyzing
What phrase does the narrator use to describe his reaction to Nace's death? What do you think he means by the words? His reaction is one of "suffocating numbness." These words suggest he is physically and emotionally paralyzed.

82
Narrator waits for Osborn; the two men have a better chance of successfully going down mountain together.

83
Narrator suggests that there is more to the story, something unknown to him when he and others left mountain.

84 Synthesizing
What does the discovery of the ax reveal about Osborn's character? He has been changed by Nace's sacrifice. He reaches top and does not boast of it in order to give honor to Nace.

READING CHECK
1. Kalpurtha, or K3 (p. 51).
2. It has never been climbed successfully (p. 54).
3. Fear of avalanches and insecure footing (p. 57).
4. Lack of oxygen (p. 60).
5. Osborn leaves Nace's ax (p. 66).

FOR STUDY AND DISCUSSION
1a. Nace is cautious; Osborn, more impulsive and aggressive. Men's goal of reaching summit is threatened by storms, by steepness and icy condition of mountain. 1b. Responses will vary. For those interested in climbing, conflict with nature might be more important. Conflict between Nace and Osborn generates suspense.
2a. Nace is experienced, cautious; Osborn, overly confident, impulsive. 2b. Third full paragraph on p. 52, starting "I turned . . . ," and passage on pp. 61–63, starting "Presently Nace . . . ."
3. Nace dies while rescuing Osborn, and Osborn gives Nace credit for reaching summit. In conflict between men and nature, Nace loses, Osborn wins.

chimney and began the descent. His clothing was in tatters, and I could tell from his movements that only the thin flame of his will stood between him and collapse. In another few minutes he was standing beside me.

"Did you get there?" I asked dully.

He shook his head. "I couldn't make it," he answered. "I didn't have what it takes."

We roped together silently and began the descent to the camp.

There is nothing more to be told of the sixth assault on K3—at least not from the experiences of the men who made it. Osborn and I reached Camp V in safety, and three days later the entire expedition gathered at the advance base. It was decided, in view of the tragedy that had occurred, to make no further attempt on the summit, and by the end of the week we had begun the evacuation of the mountain.

83 It remained for another year and other men to reveal the epilogue.

The summer following our attempt a combined English-Swiss expedition stormed the peak successfully. After weeks of hardship and struggle they attained the topmost pinnacle of the giant, only to find that what should have been their great moment of triumph was, instead, a moment of the bitterest disappointment. For when they came out at last upon the summit they saw that they were *not* the first. An ax stood there. Its haft was embedded in rock and ice and on its steel head were the

84 engraved words: TO MARTIN FROM JOHN.

They were sporting men. On their return to civilization they told their story, and the name of the conqueror of K3 was made known to the world.

For Study and Discussion

Analyzing and Interpreting the Story

1a. Describe the two conflicts in this story: the conflict between Nace and Osborn and the conflict between the exploring party and the natural obstacles they faced. **b.** In which conflict were you more interested? Why?

2a. In what ways are Nace and Osborn different? **b.** Refer to paragraphs in the story that bring out these differences.

3. The two conflicts are resolved at the end of the story. How do they turn out?

4a. What do you think the ax symbolizes or means in the story? **b.** Why does Osborn place it on top of the mountain?

5. In what ways does K3 function as a character in this story?

66

Both Nace and Osborn can be described as heroes of ''Top Man.'' Ask students to write essays that compare and contrast the characteristics of these heroes, citing specific details from the story.

Students could be asked to write essays, stories, or poems about one thing they personally would like to conquer.

To give students practice in interviewing techniques, you might request that they contact someone who enjoys mountaineering and ask about that person's interest in the sport. Why does he or she participate? What are the dangers? What are the rewards? What advice would this person give to someone interested in mountaineering?

Language and Vocabulary

Using Context Clues

You can often find the meaning of an unfamiliar word by using clues provided by the word's **context,** the rest of the words in the sentence or passage. In the following sentence from the story, you can use context clues to find the meaning of *accommodate:*

> Camp VI, which was in reality no camp at all, but a single tent, was large enough to *accommodate* only three men.

1 What clues tell you that the word *accommodate* means "to supply room for"?

2 Use context clues to determine the meanings of the italicized words in the following passages from the story. Check your answers in the glossary or in a dictionary.

a The naked *desolation* of the valley was unrelieved by any motion, color, or sound…

b …with each passing day, it became more *manifest* which were the strongest and ablest among us.

c …while its immediate effect was *salutary,* it left us later even worse off than before.

Focus on Descriptive Writing

▶ Organizing Descriptive Details

You will help your readers understand and appreciate your description if you organize it clearly. To make a description easy to follow, use one of the following techniques:

Spatial Order: Arrange details in the way you see them: for example, from top to bottom, from left to right, from outside to inside, from far to near.

Order of Importance: Put the most important details either first or last.

Chronological (Time) Order: Arrange details in the order that you notice them. For example, in the first paragraph on page 57, Ullman uses time order to describe the storm. Notice the **transitional words and phrases** that help make the order clear in this paragraph: *began, then, at first, soon, hour after hour.*

Review the chart of details for the assignment on page 39 or make a new chart on a different subject. Use one of the methods above to arrange your details in a logical order. Save your notes.

About the Author

James Ramsey Ullman (1907-1971)

James Ramsey Ullman was born in New York City and attended Andover and Princeton. After his senior thesis won a prize, he decided on a writing career. He worked as a reporter and as a producer of plays before settling down to full-time writing.

Ullman is best known for his books on mountains and mountain climbing. *High Conquest* is a history of mountaineering. His novel *The White Tower* is a dramatic story about mountain climbing in the Alps.

4a. Ax symbolizes Nace's love for lost friend and his effort to rescue Osborn. In larger sense, it might symbolize remembrance, heroic effort. **4b.** He owes his life to Nace and comes to understand that one does not reach summit without benefit of others' experiences.

5. Storms and difficult terrain appear to stem from mountain's personal desire to defeat climbers and remain unconquered.

LANGUAGE AND VOCABULARY

1. *Tent* provides a clear context clue. One normally speaks of tent size in terms of how many people it can hold, in this case three; thus, **accommodate** means ''to supply room for.''

2a. *Desolation* is condition of loneliness and abandonment, suggested here by lack of ''motion, color, or sound.''

2b. Clarity of an appearance increases with time; thus, *manifest* means something ''clear to the eye.''

2c. *Even worse off* suggests opposite of *salutary;* therefore, *salutary* means ''beneficial'' or ''positive.''

FOCUS ON DESCRIPTIVE WRITING

You may want to help students find examples of each organizational pattern from the stories they have read in this unit. Students can work in small groups to find passages that use these techniques and then share with the class how their examples fit the patterns. After students have seen some good models of each type of organization, they can use one method to arrange details about their chosen subjects.

▶ Before students begin this writing assignment, you may want to refer them to the **Focus on Writing** section on p. 73.

OBJECTIVES

The overall aim is for students to analyze the main character's feelings and how they affect her attitude about herself and her relationships with other characters. For a complete list of objectives, see the **Teacher's Notes.**

TEACHING RESOURCES A

Teacher's Notes, p. 119
Reading Check, p. 120
Study Guide, p. 123
Language Skills, p. 126
Selection Test, p. 130

AV RESOURCES BINDER

Audiocassette 1, Side A

PREREADING FOCUS

The headnote points out that this story is one of several about the central character, Esperanza, as she remembers her adolescent years. Ask students to speculate about what Esperanza will experience based on the title "Chanclas."

VOCABULARY

Call students' attention to the vocabulary footnotes in their textbook. The **Focus on Descriptive Writing** activity deals with using precise words.

FOCUS / MOTIVATION

Ask students to do some freewriting about personal experiences that were awkward at first but turned out well. Invite students to share these times with the class. Discuss what a person can gain from such experiences.

© The Cleveland Museum of Art, Gift of the Hanna Fund, 47.69

Woman Reaching for the Moon (1946) by Rufino Tamayo, Mexican (1899-1991). Oil on canvas 91.5 x 66 cm.

Esperanza prepares to attend her little cousin's baptism. Her mother has bought her new clothes, but she has forgotten to get appropriate shoes. Esperanza must wear her old, worn school shoes. At the baptism party, she sits by the wall, feeling embarrassed because the shoes are scuffed and make her feet look big. She imagines that everyone notices her ugly feet and refuses to participate in the activities. Finally, her uncle pulls her onto the dance floor, and she really becomes the center of attention.

Chanclas°

SANDRA CISNEROS°

This story is from The House on Mango Street, *a collection of stories that the author has described as a "cross between poetry and fiction." The main character in these narratives is Esperanza, a young Hispanic American girl. In this selection, she shares her feelings of both pride and embarrassment when family members pay special attention to her in public. As you read, note how the narrator talks about these feelings and ask yourself if you have had similar experiences that were awkward and nice at the same time.*

1 It's me—Mama, Mama said. I open up and she's there with bags and big boxes, the new clothes and, yes, she's got the socks and a new slip with a little rose on it and a pink and white striped dress. What about the shoes? I forgot. Too late now. I'm tired. Whew!

Six-thirty already and my little cousin's baptism is over. All day waiting, the door locked, don't open up for nobody, and I don't till Mama gets back and buys everything except the shoes.

Now Uncle Nacho is coming in his car, and we have to hurry to get to Precious Blood Church quick because that's where the baptism party is, in the basement rented for today for dancing 2 and tamales and everyone's kids running all over the place.

Mama dances, laughs, dances. All of a sudden, Mama is sick. I fan her hot face with a paper plate. Too many tamales, but Uncle 3 Nacho says too many this and tilts his thumb to his lips.

4 Everybody laughing except me, because I'm wearing the new dress, pink and white with stripes, and new underclothes and new socks and the old saddle shoes I wear to school, brown and white, the kind I get every Septem-5 ber because they last long and they do. My feet scuffed and round, and the heels all crooked that look dumb with this dress, so I just sit.

Meanwhile that boy who is my cousin by first communion or something, asks me to dance and I can't. Just stuff my feet under the metal folding chair stamped Precious Blood and pick on a wad of brown gum that's stuck beneath the 6 seat. I shake my head no. My feet growing bigger and bigger.

7 Then Uncle Nacho is pulling and pulling my arm and it doesn't matter how new the dress Mama bought is because my feet are ugly until my uncle who is a liar says, You are the prettiest girl here, will you dance, but I believe him, and yes, we are dancing, my Uncle Nacho and me, only I don't want to at first. My feet swell big and heavy like plungers, but I drag them across the linoleum floor straight center where Uncle wants to show off the new dance we learned.

°**Chanclas** (chän'kläs): old, down-at-heel shoes.
°**Cisneros** (sēs-nä'rōs).

Esperanza might have learned about herself and her family after her experience. Before discussing the **For Study and Discussion** section, allow students a few minutes to jot down individual responses, and then have students share their ideas with the class.

8

Description. Calling her arms "skinny" further emphasizes how awkward she feels.

9

Style. Nonstandard pronoun usage emphasizes informality of story and reinforces fact that story is memory of a young teenager.

10

Repetition and shift to past tense reinforces importance of this fact to Esperanza.

FOR STUDY AND DISCUSSION

1. Answers may vary. Students will probably mention that Esperanza feels embarrassed about her shoes and her ability to perform the new dance.

2. He tells her she is the prettiest girl there, and by dancing with her, he allows Esperanza to demonstrate that she is a good dancer.

3. She feels pride.

4. They laugh, poke gentle fun, and compliment each other.

5. Responses will vary.

a. Students might point out how Esperanza overcomes her self-consciousness and resolves her internal conflict about how she looks to others.

b. Students will probably relate to Esperanza's experience since young teenagers often worry about their appearance and what others think of them.

FOCUS ON READING

Since this story is relatively short, you might copy it onto a transparency. Then ask students to help you identify the **dialogue** so that you can put quotation marks around it. You might talk about how standard punctuation and paragraphing of dialogue changes the appearance of the story. Ask students how they feel about the changes.

---

8 And Uncle spins me, and my skinny arms bend the way he taught me, and my mother watches, and my little cousins watch, and the boy who is my cousin by first communion watches, and everyone says, wow, who are those two who dance like in the movies, until I forget that I am wearing only ordinary shoes, brown and white, the kind my mother buys each year for school.

And all I hear is the clapping when the music **9** stops. My uncle and me bow and he walks me back in my thick shoes to my mother who is proud to be my mother. All night the boy who **10** is a man watches me dance. He watched me dance.

For Study and Discussion

Analyzing and Interpreting the Story

1. Why does Esperanza feel self-conscious about dancing?

2. How does her uncle help her overcome her embarrassment?

3. What is Esperanza's mood at the end of the story?

4. How do you know that the people in this family are close and affectionate?

5a. How would you describe the "challenge" in this story? **b.** Have you faced similar challenges?

Focus on Reading

Identifying Dialogue

In a short story or novel the **dialogue** of characters is usually enclosed in quotation marks. In Cisneros' story, however, the dialogue is run into the text without quotation marks.

Go through the story and identify the passages that represent actual conversations between characters. If you wish, read the story aloud to determine what the characters actually say. Also identify the passages that are conversations reported by the narrator.

Focus on Descriptive Writing

Choosing Precise Words

Precise words—nouns, verbs, adjectives, and adverbs—will help you write a sharp, vivid description. Here are some examples of precise words and phrases from the next-to-last paragraph of "Chanclas":

Precise Words	
Noun	big and heavy like *plungers*
Verb	I *drag* them Uncle *spins* me
Modifier	across the *linoleum* floor my *skinny* arms bend

Study the messages on some greeting cards. Choose one of the messages and rewrite it, using precise words to express the same or similar thoughts. You might want to rewrite the message in the form of a short poem. Save your writing.

Ask students to list all the feelings that Esperanza experiences as the story unfolds and then to answer the following question: What has Esperanza learned by the end of the story?

Students might write personal narratives about self-conscious moments and what they learned from their experiences. Some students might enjoy rewriting "Chanclas" from another character's point of view.

Encourage students to find stories about other ethnic groups, perhaps their own, to share with the class. They might also enjoy reading more about Esperanza in *The House on Mango Street*.

About the Author

Sandra Cisneros (1954–   )

Many of Sandra Cisneros' ideas for her fiction and poetry come from her childhood experiences. She often felt homeless and displaced because her family frequently moved back and forth between the United States and Mexico. She found comfort, however, in reading. She also wrote poems and stories throughout her childhood. Later, in graduate school, she realized that as a Latina, her experiences were different from those of her classmates. In her best-known work, *The House on Mango Street* (1983), from which the selection "Chanclas" comes, Cisneros reflects on what it means to be a young Hispanic girl in America. The book explores the hopes, disappointments, and awkward adolescence of Esperanza. Cisneros has written another collection of stories, *Women Hollering Creek* (1991), and several collections of poetry, including *Bad Boys* (1980).

Connecting Cultures

Foods of Hispanic Origin

Many foods now popular throughout the United States have come from different parts of Latin America. In "Chanclas" the narrator mentions the tamales served at the baptism party for her little cousin. A tamale is a Mexican dish that is highly seasoned. Chopped meat and peppers are first rolled in corn meal dough, then in corn husks, and steamed. If you consult a dictionary, you will find that the origin of the word can be traced to a word in Nahuatl, a language of Indian peoples in central Mexico.

Making Connections: Activities

1. Take a tour of a local supermarket or grocery store and make a list of all the foods of Hispanic origin that are on display. Which of these foods are new to you? Bring your list to class and compare it with the lists of others to see how many different foods have been identified.

2. In a college or an unabridged dictionary, find the definition and origin of each of the following words. Check with a Spanish-speaking authority (either a student or a teacher) for the correct pronunciation of each word. Then choose the most interesting word history for the class bulletin board.

burrito	frijol	salsa
enchilada	nacho	tortilla

FOCUS ON DESCRIPTIVE WRITING
You might want to furnish students with some old greeting cards for this activity. Or students can bring their own cards from home. Students might enjoy sharing their revised greetings in small groups.

CONNECTING CULTURES
Foods of Hispanic Origin
You might plan a food-fair day during which students can bring samples of foods from Hispanic cultures. Students might also look for recipes for Hispanic foods to share with the class or to use to create a recipe book.

Making Connections: Activities
After students have researched foods of Hispanic origin, they might create collages or posters about the foods and their origins.

The overall aim is for students to distinguish between **denotation** and **connotation** and to explore the connotations of selected words.

To introduce this section, you might write the word *thirteenth* on the chalkboard and engage students in a discussion of the literal, or **denotative**, meaning of the word versus its **connotative** meanings. Then you may want to read

Durrell's description aloud while students follow in the textbook. Students can answer the questions that follow and share their responses orally.

FOCUS ON Reading and Critical Thinking

EXPLORING CONNOTATIONS

A word's **denotations** are its literal, dictionary definitions. Its **connotations** are the emotions and associations that it arouses. In descriptive writing, the connotations of words and phrases can be powerful tools.

The following humorous description tells about the first time that Gerald Durrell, a world-famous naturalist, saw an aye-aye. Aye-ayes are small, badly endangered primates that live in only a few areas of the island of Madagascar. Read the passage that follows, paying special attention to the underlined words. Then use a separate sheet of paper to answer the questions that follow.

In the gloom it came along the branches towards me, its round hypnotic eyes blazing, its spoon-like ears turning to and fro independently like radar dishes, its white whiskers twitching and moving like sensors; its black hands, with their thin, attenuated fingers, the third seeming prodigiously elongated, tapping delicately on the branches as it moved along, like those of a pianist playing a complicated piece by Chopin. It looked like a Walt Disney witch's black cat with a touch of E.T. thrown in for good measure. If ever a flying saucer came from Mars, you felt that this is what would emerge from it. It was Lewis Carroll's Jabberwocky come to life. . . .

It lowered itself on to my shoulder, gazed into my face with its huge hypnotic eyes and ran slender fingers through my beard and hair as gently as any barber. In its under-slung jaw, I could see giant chisel-like teeth, teeth which grow constantly, and I sat quite still. . . .

Then, to my alarm, it discovered my ear. "Here," it seemed to say to itself, "must lurk a beetle larva of royal proportions and of the utmost succulence." It fondled my ear as a gourmet fondles a menu and then, with great care, it inserted its thin finger. I resigned myself to deafness—move over, Beethoven, I said to myself, here I come. To my astonishment, I could hardly feel the finger as it searched my ear like a radar probe for hidden delicacies. Finding my ear bereft of tasty and fragrant grubs, it uttered another faint "humph" of annoyance and climbed into the branches again.

—Gerald Durrell,
The Aye-Aye and I

Exploring Connotations

1. What associations do you have with the word *blazing?*

2. What kinds of creatures or things would have *sensors?*

3. How does the phrase *a touch of E.T.* make you feel about the aye-aye?

4. How does Durrell create a conflict by using the word *gently* in the same paragraph as the phrase *chisel-like?*

5. What does the word *delicacies* suggest to you?

OBJECTIVES
The overall aim is for students to write a description on a topic of their choice.

PRESENTATION
To begin this section, you may want to have students review the selections in this unit to find descriptive passages they especially enjoyed to share with the class. Have students discuss what elements make these descriptions so effective.

You might want to conduct class brainstorming sessions to help students in recalling and imagining details during the prewriting of their descriptions. As students proceed with their drafts, establish conferencing time so that you can assess their understanding of the writing process

FOCUS ON *Writing*

WRITING A DESCRIPTION

*I*n **description** you use words to paint a picture in the minds of your readers. Description is common in poetry. As you have seen from this unit, however, descriptive writing also appears in short stories and non-fiction. You can use description in letters, news stories, and advertisements. Now that you have explored some of the elements of a description, you will have a chance to write one on a topic of your choice.

Prewriting

1. Your first job is to find a subject and a focus. You will find these hints helpful:

- Think of a familiar person, place, or thing.
- Choose a subject that you can observe directly.
- Find a focus by limiting your subject to one that you can cover in a few paragraphs.

[See **Focus** assignment on page 20.]

2. Decide on your **purpose.** Is your primary goal to be creative or to inform? The chart shown above right lists some of the features of **subjective** and **objective description.**

Also think about your **audience.** How much do they already know about your subject? Do you need to give them any background? [See **Focus** assignment on page 29.]

	Subjective	Objective
Purpose	creative	informative
Point of View	first-person: uses *I*	third-person
Tone	informal, personal	formal, businesslike
Type of Writing	letters, poems, stories, essays, journals	reports, articles, speeches
Details	factual and sensory; writer's thoughts and feelings; figures of speech	factual and sensory

3. Use these techniques to gather **factual** and **sensory details** for your description:

- observing
- recalling
- researching
- imagining

Factual details can be measured or checked. Sensory details appeal to one of the five senses: sight, sound, taste, touch, and smell. List your details on a chart like this one.

Subject of Description: _____

Factual Details	Sensory Details
_____	_____
_____	_____
_____	_____
_____	_____

[See **Focus** assignments on pages 39 and 45.]

HOLT WRITER'S WORKSHOP

This computer program provides help for all types of writing through guided instruction for each step of the writing process. (Program available separately.)

See *Elements of Writing, Second Course,* Chapter 5, for more instruction on descriptive writing.

WRITING A DESCRIPTION
In addition to creating clear pictures in the minds of readers, good descriptive writing can create **mood** and **atmosphere** and evoke emotions and associations. To accomplish this, students will need to breathe life into their descriptions by using fresh images and precise, vivid language.

Prewriting
After students have chosen their subjects and gathered details, suggest that they experiment with their details to make them as specific and concrete as possible. Point out that there are degrees of specificity and concreteness. For example, *vegetable* is general; *potato* is more specific; but "mashed potatoes drowning in cream gravy" is even more concrete and specific.

and of descriptive writing in particular. Peer groups may be useful during the evaluating, revising, and proofreading stages. Ideas for publishing essays may be discussed early in the process to provide students with motivation and focus.

Writing

Because writing done in one sitting often has better continuity and more life, suggest that once students have started writing they continue until they have completed first drafts. Remind students that they will be evaluating and revising later and should not be concerned with grammar, usage, or mechanics at this stage.

Evaluating And Revising

During this stage, students should rework their descriptions until they are satisfied that the content, organization, and style represent the best they can do with the topic they have chosen. Encourage students to try to look at their writing from the perspective of a critical reader, and to read their essays aloud once or twice, listening for rough transitions and dull or inappropriate words. As a final step, students might work in small groups using the **Checklist for Evaluation and Revision.**

4. Organize the details for your description so that your essay is easy to follow. Choose one of these three organizational methods:

- **Spatial Order:** Arrange details in the order you see them.
- **Order of Importance:** Put the most important details either first or last.
- **Chronological Order:** Arrange details in the order that you notice them.

[See **Focus** assignment on page 67.]

Writing

1. Use **precise words**—nouns, verbs, adjectives, and adverbs—to create a sharp, clear image of your subject. Avoid general, fuzzy words like *go, walk, thing, interesting, really,* and *nice.* [See **Focus** assignment on page 71.]

2. You may occasionally want to use a **figure of speech** for a special effect in your description. Figures of speech are imaginative comparisons that are not meant to be taken literally.

- A **simile** compares two basically unlike things, using the words *like* or *as:* "The desert wind was like a blast furnace."
- A **metaphor** makes a direct comparison without using *like* or *as:* "The desert wind was a blast furnace."
- **Personification** gives human characteristics to nonhuman things. "The desert wind stalked us during our whole journey."

3. Be sure that all the details you include in your description contribute to a main feeling or impression. Cut any details that do not fit the focus and overall mood of your essay.

4. Use **transitional words and phrases** to show the connections between things and ideas in your essay. Below is a list of useful transitions:

above	first	most important
across	here	over
around	inside	then
before	into	there
behind	last	under
down	mainly	up

Evaluating and Revising

1. Put your first draft aside for a while. Then evaluate it as objectively as you can. Pay special attention to your choice of words and details. Are all your words as precise as you can make them? Do all the details in your description contribute to a main impression?

2. Use the following checklist to evaluate and revise your writing.

Checklist for Evaluation and Revision

✓ Do I clearly identify my subject at the beginning of the essay?

✓ Do I use sensory and factual details to create a clear picture of my subject?

✓ Do I use precise words and fresh, imaginative figures of speech?

✓ Have I included my own thoughts and feelings in a subjective description?

✓ Do all my details contribute to a single, main impression?

✓ Have I organized the details in a way that makes sense?

TRANSPARENCY 5

Writing Process
Writing a Description – helps students to plan and write an effective description.

Here is an example of how one writer revised the opening paragraph for a descriptive essay.

Writer's Model

The rays of a first-quarter moon ~~shone~~ *pale shimmered* on the bay's inky ripples as we edged away from the dock. ~~The~~ *Although* water was calm for my first fishing trip. ~~My~~ stomach felt ~~bad~~ *antsy*. Three other boats ~~were~~ *glided* beside us ~~.~~ *like thirty-foot-long ghosts* I glanced over at Dave, ~~and he~~ *who* was whistling cheerfully as he sliced up ~~fish~~ *sardine-sized silvery whiting* into chunks for bait. The fresh, clean smell of the bay ~~early in the morning~~ *just before dawn* mingled with the ~~smells~~ *stale aromas* of scraps from yesterday's catch.

Proofreading and Publishing

1. Proofread your essay to correct errors in grammar, usage, capitalization, and punctuation. (You may find it helpful to refer to the **Handbook for Revision** on pages 712–755.) Then prepare a final version of your essay by making a clean copy.

2. Consider some of the following ways of publishing and sharing your essay:

- illustrate your essay with a photo, cartoon, or drawing, and then join with other students to create a class anthology
- send your essay to the school newspaper or magazine
- deliver your essay orally in class

Portfolio If your teacher approves, you may wish to keep a copy of your work in your writing folder or portfolio.

Proofreading and Publishing
You may want to provide a proofreading focus by having students look for specific kinds of errors that may appear in descriptive writing, such as ungrammatical usage of adjectives and adverbs. Have students exchange papers with at least one other student for proofreading purposes.

GENERATIONS

OVERVIEW OF THE UNIT

Learning to understand and accept other points of view is a big part of growing up. The six selections in this unit seek to build such understanding and acceptance by illustrating different perspectives on matters of importance to young people.

This unit opens with "A Cap for Steve," a serious story in which the reader sees a conflict through the eyes of a father. In "The Apprentice," Dorothy Canfield tells the story of a girl's painful lesson in responsibility. Next comes the poem "old age sticks" in which E. E. Cummings juxtaposes views of different generations. In "Gentleman of Río en Medio," Juan A. A. Sedillo portrays the dignity of old age. The excerpt from *My Family and Other Animals* tells of a famous naturalist's early fascination with scorpions—a fascination not shared by his startled family. The unit closes with "My Friend Flicka," the touching story of a boy and his horse.

OBJECTIVES OF THE UNIT

The aims of the unit are for the student:

- To demonstrate recognition of differing points of view on selected topics and to identify characters' points of view concerning themes and conflicts presented in the short stories in this unit
- To analyze the elements of characterization, tone, plot, setting, conflict, and theme in individual selections in this unit
- To identify cause-and-effect relationships, point of view, sequence of events, and main idea within the stories in this unit
- To determine the meanings of selected words and phrases by using a dictionary and context clues
- To write a personal narrative

CONCEPTS AND SKILLS

The following concepts and skills are treated in this unit:

LANGUAGE AND VOCABULARY SKILLS

Recognizing Multiple Meanings of Words 86
Recognizing Words That Create Tone 103
Using Context Clues 121

OPPORTUNITIES FOR WRITING

Writing About Literature
Comparing Values 103

Focus on Personal Narrative
Choosing a Topic 87
Gathering Details 97
Using Vivid Verbs and Dialogue 107
Reflecting on Meanings 121

FOCUS ON READING AND CRITICAL THINKING

Recognizing the Causes of a Character's Actions 86
Understanding the Poet's Technique 99

Understanding the Title of a Story 96
Making Generalizations About Theme 122

FOCUS ON WRITING

Writing a Personal Narrative 123

TRANSPARENCIES

The following unit support materials with specific correlations to literature selections are available in the **Fine Art and Instructional Transparencies with Teacher's Notes and Blackline Masters** section of your *Audiovisual Resource Binder*.

FINE ART TRANSPARENCIES

Theme: It's My Time
6 *Cumpleaños de Lala y Tudie,* Carmen Lomas Garza
7 *The Reading*, Sharon Wilson

READER RESPONSE

8 High Five

LITERARY ELEMENTS

9 Plot

WRITING PROCESS

10 Writing a Personal Narrative

INTRODUCING THE UNIT

LEARNING OPTIONS

A day or two before the unit is to begin, ask each student to bring a story from a newspaper or magazine. (Stipulate that the story must involve more than one person.) In class, ask students to rewrite the stories from two points of view—a robbery could be described, for example, from the viewpoint of the bank teller and then of the robber; a rescue from the viewpoint of the firefighter and then of the person being rescued. Advanced students might even write their stories a third time from the viewpoint of an outside observer who presents a subjective account. For example, the rescue might be presented from the viewpoint of someone who dislikes the firefighter involved.

PORTFOLIO ASSESSMENT

Suggestions for use of portfolios as support for this unit are described in the **Portfolio Assessment and Professional Support Materials** booklet accompanying this program. Specific suggestions are provided for a variety of student projects that may be suitable for inclusion in a portfolio. In addition, copying masters are provided for guides that may be used for evaluation and assessment of student projects.

PLANNING GUIDE

For Unit Planning

- Transparencies 6–10: *Audiovisual Resources Binder*
- *Portfolio Assessment: Professional Support Materials*
- Test Generator
- Mastery Tests: Teaching Resources B, pp. 72, 74
- Analogy Test: Teaching Resources B, p. 78
- Composition Test: Teaching Resources B, p. 79

| SELECTION (Pupil's Page) | TEACHING RESOURCES B (page numbers shown below) | | | | | | | AV BINDER |
	Teacher's Notes	Reading Check	Study Guide	Language Skills	Building Vocabulary	Selection Vocab. Test	Selection Test	Audio-cassette
GENERATIONS *Introduction* (p. 77)	1							
Morley Callaghan *A Cap for Steve* (p. 78)	2	5	6		9	11	12	
Dorothy Canfield *The Apprentice* (p. 88)	14	16	17	20	23	24	25	
E. E. Cummings *old age sticks* (p. 98)	26		33		27		41	
Juan A. A. Sedillo *Gentleman of Río en Medio* (p. 100)	29	32	33	35	39		41	
Gerald Durrell from *My Family and Other Animals* (p. 104)	43	46	41		49	51	52	
Mary O' Hara *My Friend Flicka* (p. 108)	54	57	59	62	66		68	

Student Learning Options

GENERATIONS

1. Understanding Point of View

Mount pictures of people on poster board. Allow students to examine the pictures and then label two columns on a sheet of paper **first-person** and **third-person**. Ask students to pick a character and write on this sheet a short paragraph telling what is happening from first-person point of view, then write another paragraph from third-person point of view. Students can use these paragraphs to begin a short story.

2. Creating a Foreshadowing Poster

As students proceed with this unit, they will find that foreshadowing is often used to interest the reader of a story. Ask students to label a poster board *FORESHADOWING*. For each example of foreshadowing that they find, students should include the name of the story, the page on which they found the example, and a simple illustration associated with the foreshadowing event. Students can add a short essay to the back of their poster explaining how foreshadowing made the plot suspenseful. Students can present posters and essays to the class.

3. Presenting Irony

To help students distinguish the difference among the three types of irony, ask them to make a three-column chart with each type of irony written above a column. Help students think of several types of irony that they might have encountered, and then allow them to think of additional examples of irony on their own. After students have finished, they can read the ironic situation to a partner and allow the partner to guess what type of irony is being used.

TRANSPARENCIES 6 & 7

Fine Art

Theme: *It's My Time* – invites students to explore artwork portraying relationships among people of different generations.

VISUAL CONNECTIONS

About the Artist

Eastman Johnson, born in Maine to well-to-do parents, showed his artistic skill early in life in portraits done in crayon. He later worked in the same Boston lithography studio where Winslow Homer (1836–1910) served his apprenticeship. Interestingly, only Homer is considered Johnson's equal or superior as a genre painter in capturing without sentimentality the commonplace American life. In 1849, Johnson traveled to Europe and remained for six years, frequenting museums and studying oil painting in Holland and in Germany. Upon his return to the United States, he traveled in the South, studying the lives of blacks; several of his most famous works were inspired by his experiences there. His paintings of slave life may have stuck some abolitionists as too idyllic, but he was one of the few artists of the period willing to deal with social issues at all. Johnson is also known for his portraits of famous persons, including Daniel Webster, Henry Wadsworth Longfellow, Ralph Waldo Emerson, and Presidents Arthur, Cleveland, and Harrison.

Exploring the Subject

Some critics consider this painting a valuable historical document because it captures the nature of affluent New York family life in the mid-to-late nineteenth century. Ask students to consider how the family depicted in this portrait is similar to and different from a late twentieth-century family. Students might consider the presence of several generations and the great number of children.

GENERATIONS

How many generations of the Hatch family can you identify in this painting? What is each person doing? What inferences can you draw from the objects in the room, from the style of dress, from facial expressions? Is there a drama unfolding?

Choose one of the characters in the painting and write a brief monologue, or speech, revealing that person's thoughts. If you wish, put yourself in the painting and imagine that you are one of the family. Share your ideas with classmates.

The Hatch Family (1871) by Eastman Johnson (1824–1906). Oil on canvas (26.97).
The Metropoliton Museum of Art, gift of Frederic H. Hatch, 1926

GENERATIONS

The short stories and the poem in this unit seek to build understanding and acceptance of other points of view. Each selection presents a **conflict** of opinions that often arises because of generational differences—the unique perspective of one's age and experience.

Throughout the unit, students answer questions related to a character's viewpoint and motivation. The **Literary Elements** features maintain this focus by helping students to understand motivation and **point of view.** In addition, these exercises focus on understanding how a story's title may be a clue to its main idea and on understanding ways poetic technique may be used to reinforce meaning. The **Language and Vocabulary** features offer practice in using context clues to understand word meaning and in recognizing words that create **tone.** The unit writing activities focus on prewriting techniques that can be used to help students prepare for writing personal narratives.

OBJECTIVES

The overall aim is for students to analyze main characters, their attitudes, and their actions. For a complete list of objectives, see the **Teacher's Notes**.

VOCABULARY

The underlined words are in the Glossary. The **Language and Vocabulary** exercise on p. 86 gives students practice in determining the meanings of words from context.

FOCUS / MOTIVATION

Ask students if they have ever owned a seemingly insignificant possession that they would not sell for any price. Introduce "A Cap for Steve" as a story about such a possession.

PREREADING FOCUS

The headnote suggests that Callaghan's story concerns a father and son who will be divided and then united because of an incident involving a baseball cap. Ask students if they have ever argued with a relative or friend over something trivial. Also, ask if they have owned or wanted to own something very important to them even though others thought it trivial.

A Cap for Steve

1

Symbolism. "Diamond" represents both precious gem and baseball infield.

2 Drawing Conclusions
What does this suggest about mother? She serves as mediator.

3

Characterization. Both father and son feel guilty for not talking.

4

Condon, a stranger, is first to call Steve "son."

A Cap for Steve

MORLEY CALLAGHAN

How can something as trivial as a baseball cap divide and then unite a father and son?

1 Dave Diamond, a poor man, a carpenter's assistant, was a small, wiry, quick-tempered individual who had learned how to make every dollar count in his home. His wife, Anna, had been sick a lot, and his twelve-year-old son, Steve, had to be kept in school. Steve, a big-eyed, shy kid, ought to have known the value of money as well as Dave did. It had been ground into him.

But the boy was crazy about baseball, and after school, when he could have been working as a delivery boy or selling papers, he played ball with the kids. His failure to appreciate that the family needed a few extra dollars disgusted Dave. Around the house he wouldn't let Steve talk about baseball, and he scowled when he saw him hurrying off with his glove after dinner.

When the Phillies came to town to play an exhibition game with the home team and Steve pleaded to be taken to the ballpark, Dave, of course, was outraged. Steve knew they couldn't **2** afford it. But he had got his mother on his side. Finally Dave made a bargain with them. He said that if Steve came home after school and worked hard helping to make some kitchen shelves, he would take him that night to the ballpark.

Steve worked hard, but Dave was still resentful. They had to coax him to put on his good suit. When they started out, Steve held aloof, **3** feeling guilty, and they walked down the street like strangers; then Dave glanced at Steve's face and, half ashamed, took his arm more cheerfully.

As the game went on, Dave had to listen to Steve's recitation of the batting average of every Philly that stepped up to the plate; the time the boy must have wasted learning these averages began to appall him. He showed it so plainly that Steve felt guilty again and was silent.

After the game Dave let Steve drag him onto the field to keep him company while he tried to get some autographs from the Philly players, who were being hemmed in by gangs of kids blocking the way to the clubhouse. But Steve, who was shy, let the other kids block him off from the players. Steve would push his way in, get blocked out, and come back to stand mournfully beside Dave. And Dave grew impatient. He was wasting valuable time. He wanted to get home; Steve knew it and was worried.

Then the big, blond Philly outfielder, Eddie Condon, who had been held up by a gang of kids tugging at his arm and thrusting their score cards at him, broke loose and made a run for the clubhouse. He was jostled, and his blue cap with the red peak, tilted far back on his head, fell off. It fell at Steve's feet, and Steve **4** stooped quickly and grabbed it. "Okay, son,"

MOTIVATIONAL SUMMARY
The Diamonds are a working-class family. Their son, Steve, does not seem to understand their financial problems and spends his time playing baseball. Steve's father, Dave, resents Steve's interest in the sport, but Steve wishes his father would take more of an interest in the game. Their **conflict** intensifies when Steve is offered twenty dollars for a cap he received at a Phillies game. It is his most prized possession, but the money is difficult for Dave to resist.

PRESENTATION
The first selection in this unit introduces the **theme** of **conflict** between generations. In the story "A Cap for Steve," the conflict centers on the relationship between a father and his twelve-year-old son. Students may initially identify with

VISUAL CONNECTIONS
Exploring the Subject
Baseball, sometimes called America's national pastime, may not have originated in the United States. Although some researchers maintain that the game was invented by Abner Doubleday in 1839 in Cooperstown, New York, others, probably in the majority, believe the game is derived from an English game called "rounders." The British began to play rounders—a sport in which players used a bat to slug a ball and went around bases—in the seventeenth century. The game crossed the Atlantic with the colonists.

People in different settlements played the game and called it by different names, one of which was "baseball." Wherever the game originated, it is a matter of record that the first club for baseball playing was started in New York City in 1845. When Alexander Cartwright organized the club, he also wrote rules for the game.

Ideas for Writing
Have students write an "internal monologue," either humorous or serious, describing one fan's thoughts and feelings about the two teams in competition, the food and drink, and the level of interest he or she feels toward the game.

the outfielder called, turning back. But Steve, holding the hat in both hands, only stared at him.

5   "Give him his cap, Steve," Dave said, smiling apologetically at the big outfielder, who towered over them. But Steve drew the hat closer to his chest. In an awed trance he looked up at big Eddie Condon. It was an embarrassing moment. All the other kids were watching. Some shouted, "Give him his cap."

"My cap, son," Eddie Condon said, his hand out.

"Hey, Steve," Dave said, and he gave him a shake. But he had to jerk the cap out of Steve's hands.

"Here you are," he said.

5

Foreshadowing. Apologetic manner suggests awkwardness Dave will feel when he meets Mr. Hudson.

and defend the position of the son. Through a careful study of the story, many will realize that the major problem the characters have is a lack of communication, which is a shared responsibility.

MEETING INDIVIDUAL NEEDS
Visual Learners • To assist students in exploring the central conflict in "A Cap for Steve," you might show how a name may be seen as a symbol for characters' opposing values in the story. Write the name *Diamond* on the chalkboard and draw two large diamond shapes beneath it. Ask students what is most important to each of the two Diamonds, Steve and Dave, at the beginning of the story. As they reply, sketch in the two shapes to represent a baseball diamond and a gem in a setting. Lead students in a

The outfielder, noticing Steve's white, worshiping face and pleading eyes, grinned and then shrugged. "Aw, let him keep it," he said.

"No, Mister Condon, you don't need to do that," Steve protested.

"It's happened before. Forget it," Eddie Condon said, and he trotted away to the clubhouse.

Dave handed the cap to Steve; envious kids circled around them and Steve said, "He said I could keep it, Dad. You heard him, didn't you?"

"Yeah, I heard him," Dave admitted. The wonder in Steve's face made him smile. He took the boy by the arm and they hurried off the field.

6 On the way home Dave couldn't get him to talk about the game; he couldn't get him to take his eyes off the cap. Steve could hardly believe in his own happiness. "See," he said suddenly, and he showed Dave that Eddie Condon's name was printed on the sweatband. Then he went on dreaming. Finally he put the cap on his head and turned to Dave with a slow, proud smile. The cap was away too big for him; it fell down over his ears. "Never mind," Dave said. "You can get your mother to take a tuck in the back."

When they got home, Dave was tired and his wife didn't understand the cap's importance, and they couldn't get Steve to go to bed. He swaggered around wearing the cap and looking in the mirror every ten minutes. He took the cap to bed with him.

Dave and his wife had a cup of coffee in the kitchen, and Dave told her again how they had **7** got the cap. They agreed that their boy must have an attractive quality that showed in his face, and that Eddie Condon must have been drawn to him—why else would he have singled Steve out from all the kids?

But Dave got tired of the fuss Steve made over that cap and of the way he wore it from the time he got up in the morning until the **12**

time he went to bed. Some kid was always coming in, wanting to try on the cap. **8** It was childish, Dave said, for Steve to go around assuming that the cap made him important in the neighborhood, and to keep telling them how he had become a leader in the park a few blocks away where he played ball in the evenings. And Dave wouldn't stand for Steve's keeping the cap on while he was eating. He was always scolding his wife for accepting Steve's explanation that he'd forgotten he had it on. Just the same, it was remarkable what a little thing like a ball **9** cap could do for a kid, Dave admitted to his wife as he smiled to himself.

One night Steve was late coming home from the park. Dave didn't realize how late it was until he put down his newspaper and watched his wife at the window. Her restlessness got on **10** his nerves. "See what comes from encouraging the boy to hang around with those park loafers," he said. "I don't encourage him," she protested. "You do," he insisted irritably, for he was really worried now. A gang hung around the park until midnight. It was a bad park. It was true that on one side there was a good district with fine, expensive apartment houses, but the kids from that neighborhood left the park to the kids from the poorer homes. When his wife went out and walked down to the corner, it was his turn to wait and worry and watch **11** at the open window. Each waiting moment tortured him. At last he heard his wife's voice and Steve's voice, and he relaxed and sighed; then he remembered his duty and rushed angrily to meet them.

"I'll fix you, Steve, once and for all," he said. "I'll show you you can't start coming into the house at midnight."

"Hold your horses, Dave," his wife said. "Can't you see the state he's in?" Steve looked utterly exhausted and beaten.

"What's the matter?" Dave asked quickly.

"I lost my cap," Steve whispered; he walked

6
Again, father and son have difficulty communicating.

7
Characterization. Indicative of parents' pride in Steve.

8
Irony. Steve is only twelve years old—he should behave like a child.

9
One moment Dave criticizes his son's obsession with the cap, and the next moment, he remarks favorably on cap's effect.

10
Dave blames his wife for child's behavior.

11
Dave's intense worry indicates his love for Steve.

12 Making Inferences
What does "whispered" suggest about Steve's feelings at this moment? Responses will vary. He is heartbroken about loss and perhaps fearful of father's reaction.

COOPERATIVE LEARNING
Many families experience conflict over money and how it should be spent. To acquaint students with the universality of disagreements about money, you might divide the class into three or four groups. Have the groups talk about things that cost money—clothing, tapes and CDs, movies, extracurricular school activities, school fees, eating out, and others—that are important to them. Then have the groups survey other members of their families to determine what their spending priorities are.

past his father and threw himself on the couch in the living room and lay with his face hidden.

"Now, don't scold him, Dave," his wife said.

13 "Scold him. Who's scolding him?" Dave asked, indignantly. "It's his cap, not mine. If it's not worth his while to hang on to it, why should I scold him?" But he was implying resentfully that he alone recognized the cap's value.

"So you are scolding him," his wife said. "It's his cap. Not yours. What happened, Steve?"

Steve told them he had been playing ball and he found that when he ran the bases the cap fell off; it was still too big despite the tuck his mother had taken in the band. So the next time he came to bat he tucked the cap in his hip pocket. Someone had lifted it, he was sure.

"And he didn't even know whether it was still in his pocket," Dave said sarcastically.

"I wasn't careless, Dad," Steve said. For the last three hours he had been wandering around to the homes of the kids who had been in the park at the time; he wanted to go on, but he was too tired. Dave knew the boy was apolo-

14 gizing to him, but he didn't know why it made him angry.

"If he didn't hang on to it, it's not worth worrying about now," he said, and he sounded offended.

After that night they knew that Steve didn't go to the park to play ball; he went to look for the cap. It irritated Dave to see him sit around listlessly, or walk in circles, trying to force his memory to find a particular incident which would suddenly recall to him the moment when the cap had been taken. It was no attitude for a growing, healthy boy to take, Dave

15 complained. He told Steve firmly once and for all that he didn't want to hear any more about the cap.

One night, two weeks later, Dave was walking home with Steve from the shoemaker's. It

16 was a hot night. When they passed an ice-

17 cream parlor, Steve slowed down. "I guess I

couldn't have a soda, could I?" Steve said. "Nothing doing," Dave said firmly. "Come on now," he added as Steve hung back, looking in the window.

"Dad, look!" Steve cried suddenly, pointing at the window. "My cap! There's my cap! He's coming out!"

18 A well-dressed boy was leaving the ice-cream parlor; he had on a blue ball cap with a red peak, just like Steve's cap. "Hey, you!" Steve cried, and he rushed at the boy, his small face fierce and his eyes wild. Before the boy could

VISUAL CONNECTIONS
Exploring the Subject
"Batter up!" The catcher and outfielders in position, the pitcher throws his best pitch. This is a familiar scene in vacant lots and school and community baseball fields throughout the country. Baseball began as an amateur sport played with unofficial rules, oftentimes in any available place. Now, however, the game is mostly played in a 90-foot-square field, or "diamond," like the one pictured here.

13
Refers to son in third person; Dave's not speaking directly to Steve indicates separation.

14 Expressing an Opinion
Why is Dave so angry with his son? Responses will vary. Perhaps Dave believes Steve should be more concerned with pressing "adult" matters (like finances) rather than placing such great importance on cap.

15
Lack of communication widens gap between father and son.

16
Hot night mirrors emotional level.

17
Steve does not comprehend family's financial problems; Dave cannot relate to needs of a twelve-year-old.

18
Inference. "Well-dressed" indicates boy comes from a well-to-do family.

After groups gather their information, ask each group to select two recorders to list the various uses for money on the chalkboard. Students might find it interesting to list the priorities of parents in a separate column and then compare and contrast their responses to those of the students. Ask students to analyze the different uses for money and to suggest why different priorities exist.

19

Characterization. Steve's willingness to fight illustrates how important cap is to him.

20

Irony. First time Dave uses word "son," it is addressed to unknown boy.

21

Other boy uses his father for help.

22   Analyzing

Why does the boy point out that his father is a lawyer? Stresses wealth and legal knowledge in attempt to intimidate Dave.

23

Dave's removal of his hat suggests he is intimidated by wealth surrounding him.

24

Dave's use of "us" suggests difficult situation brings him and his son closer together.

25

Smoking jacket is sign of wealth and emphasizes class differences.

26

Irony. Dave has never understood bond to cap.

back away, Steve had snatched the cap from his head. "That's my cap!" he shouted.

"What's this?" the bigger boy said. "Hey, give me my cap or I'll give you a poke on the nose."

19   Dave was surprised that his own shy boy did not back away. He watched him clutch the cap in his left hand, half crying with excitement as he put his head down and drew back his right fist: he was willing to fight. And Dave was proud of him.

20   "Wait, now," Dave said. "Take it easy, son," he said to the other boy, who refused to back away.

"My boy says it's his cap," Dave said.

"Well, he's crazy. It's my cap."

"I was with him when he got this cap. When the Phillies played here. It's a Philly cap."

"Eddie Condon gave it to me," Steve said. "And you stole it from me, you jerk."

"Don't call me a jerk, you little squirt. I never saw you before in my life."

"Look," Steve said, pointing to the printing on the cap's sweatband. "It's Eddie Condon's cap. See? See, Dad?"

"Yeah. You're right, Son. Ever see this boy before, Steve?"

"No," Steve said reluctantly.

The other boy realized he might lose the cap. "I bought it from a guy," he said. "I paid him. My father knows I paid him." He said he got the cap at the ballpark. He groped for some magically impressive words and suddenly

21   found them. "You'll have to speak to my father," he said.

"Sure, I'll speak to your father," Dave said. "What's your name? Where do you live?"

"My name's Hudson. I live about ten minutes away on the other side of the park." The boy appraised Dave, who wasn't much bigger than he was and who wore a faded blue windbreaker and no tie. "My father is a lawyer," he

22   said boldly. "He wouldn't let me keep the cap if he didn't think I should."

"Is that a fact?" Dave asked belligerently.

"Well, we'll see. Come on. Let's go." And he got between the two boys and they walked along the street. They didn't talk to each other. Dave knew the Hudson boy was waiting to get to the protection of his home, and Steve knew it, too, and he looked up apprehensively at Dave. And Dave, reaching for his hand, squeezed it encouragingly and strode along, cocky and belligerent, knowing that Steve relied on him.

The Hudson boy lived in that row of fine apartment houses on the other side of the park. At the entrance to one of these houses, Dave tried not to hang back and show he was impressed, because he could feel Steve hanging back. When they got into the small elevator,

23   Dave didn't know why he took off his hat. In the carpeted hall on the fourth floor, the Hudson boy said, "Just a minute," and entered his own apartment. Dave and Steve were left alone in the corridor, knowing that the other boy was preparing his father for the encounter. Steve looked anxiously at his father, and Dave said, "Don't worry, Son," and he added resolutely,

24   "No one's putting anything over on us."

25   A tall, balding man in a brown velvet smoking jacket suddenly opened the door. Dave had never seen a man wearing one of those jackets, although he had seen them in department store windows. "Good evening," he said, making a deprecatory[1] gesture at the cap Steve clutched tightly in his hand. "My boy didn't get your name. My name is Hudson."

"Mine's Diamond."

"Come on in," Mr. Hudson said, putting out his hand and laughing good-naturedly. He led Dave and Steve into his living room. "What's

26   this about that cap?" he asked. "The way kids can get excited about a cap. Well, it's understandable, isn't it?"

"So it is," Dave said, moving closer to Steve, who was awed by the broadloom rug and the

---

1. **deprecatory** (dĕp′rə-kə-tôr′ē): apologetic.

MATHEMATICS LINK
Students may have a difficult time comprehending the relative value of money in this story because prices are low in comparison to those of today. You might ask them to speculate on what a professional ball player's cap might be worth today. What might a ball signed by players on a favorite team be worth? In discussing sports paraphernalia, you could include a discussion of sports cards collections. You might also take this opportunity to talk about inflation and how the value of money changes over time.

fine furniture. He wanted to show Steve he was at ease himself, and he wished Mr. Hudson wouldn't be so polite. That meant Dave had to be polite and affable, too, and it was hard to manage when he was standing in the middle of **27** the floor in his old windbreaker.

"Sit down, Mr. Diamond," Mr. Hudson said.

28 Dave took Steve's arm and sat him down beside him on the chesterfield.[2] The Hudson boy watched his father. And Dave looked at Steve and saw that he wouldn't face Mr. Hudson or the other boy; he kept looking up at Dave, putting all his faith in him.

"Well, Mr. Diamond, from what I gathered from my boy, you're able to prove this cap belonged to your boy."

"That's a fact," Dave said.

"Mr. Diamond, you'll have to believe my boy bought that cap from some kid in good faith."

"I don't doubt it," Dave said. "But no kid can sell something that doesn't belong to him. You know that's a fact, Mr. Hudson."

"Yes, that's a fact," Mr. Hudson agreed. "But that cap means a lot to my boy, Mr. Diamond."

"It means a lot to my boy, too, Mr. Hudson."

29 "Sure it does. But supposing we called in a policeman. You know what he'd say? He'd ask you if you were willing to pay my boy what he paid for the cap. That's usually the way it works **30** out," Mr. Hudson said, friendly and smiling, as he eyed Dave shrewdly.

"But that's not right. It's not justice," Dave protested. "Not when it's my boy's cap."

31 "I know it isn't right. But that's what they do."

"All right. What did you say your boy paid for the cap?" Dave said reluctantly.

"Two dollars."

"Two dollars!" Dave repeated. Mr. Hudson's smile was still kindly, but his eyes were shrewd, and Dave knew the lawyer was counting on his not having the two dollars; Mr. Hudson

thought he had Dave sized up; he had looked at him and decided he was broke. Dave's pride was hurt, and he turned to Steve. What he saw in Steve's face was more powerful than the hurt to his pride: it was the memory of how difficult it had been to get an extra nickel, the talk he heard about the cost of food, the worry in his mother's face as she tried to make ends meet, and the bewildered embarrassment that he was here in a rich man's home, forcing his father to confess that he couldn't afford to **32** spend two dollars. Then Dave grew angry and reckless. "I'll give you the two dollars," he said.

Steve looked at the Hudson boy and grinned brightly. The Hudson boy watched his father.

"I suppose that's fair enough," Mr. Hudson said. "A cap like this can be worth a lot to a kid. You know how it is. Your boy might want to sell—I mean be satisfied. Would he take five dollars for it?"

"Five dollars?" Dave repeated. "Is it worth five dollars, Steve?" he asked uncertainly.

Steve shook his head and looked frightened.

"No, thanks, Mr. Hudson," Dave said firmly. "I'll tell you what I'll do," Mr. Hudson said. "I'll **33** give you ten dollars. The cap has a sentimental value for my boy, a Philly cap, a big-leaguer's cap. It's only worth about a buck and a half really," he added. But Dave shook his head **34** again. Mr. Hudson frowned. He looked at his own boy with indulgent concern, but now he was embarrassed. "I'll tell you what I'll do," he said. "This cap—well, it's worth as much as a day at the circus to my boy. Your boy should be recompensed.[3] I want to be fair. Here's twenty dollars," and he held out two ten-dollar bills to Dave.

That much money for a cap, Dave thought, and his eyes brightened. But he knew what the cap had meant to Steve; to deprive him of it now that it was within his reach would be

---

2. **chesterfield** (chĕs′tər-fēld): a kind of sofa.

3. **recompensed** (rĕk′əm-pĕnst′): paid.

27
Clothes of the two men, like their occupations, show status differences.

28
Dave tries to reassure his son by taking him by the arm.

29
Hudson's mentioning policeman is subtle threat.

30
Characterization. Hudson's outward friendliness masks his shrewdness.

31 Analyzing
To whom does "they" refer? Probably not just hypothetical policemen, but a general absent authority.

32
Dave becomes emotional.

33
Irony. Hudson mentions "sentimental value." Steve has stronger emotional attachment to cap.

34
For first time, Hudson shows doubt and concern about his ability to obtain cap.

35

35

Conflict. Dave struggles with difficult decision. He suspects that he should not sell cap, but he rationalizes decision for sake of money.

36

Hudson is quite pleased with his victory.

37

Characterization. "Whispering" suggests Dave's fear. First time father has called son "Stevie."

38

Both characters are afraid to talk about situation.

39

Dave again uses "us" to suggest unity between father and son, but the word now sounds false.

40

Steve's words hurt his father deeply.

41 Analyzing

Why does Dave want to hit his son? Responses will vary. Dave is not necessarily angry with Steve. Perhaps he feels guilty about his decision to sell cap or frustrated by his inability to communicate with his son or angry at injustice of being poor.

---

35 unbearable. All the things he needed in his life gathered around him; his wife was there, saying he couldn't afford to reject the offer, he had no right to do it; and he turned to Steve to see if Steve thought it wonderful that the cap could bring them twenty dollars.

"I don't know," Steve said. He was in a trance. When Dave smiled, Steve smiled too, and Dave believed that Steve was as impressed as he was, only more bewildered, and maybe even more aware that they could not possibly turn away that much money for a ball cap.

"Well, here you are," Mr. Hudson said, and he put the two bills in Steve's hand. "It's a lot of money. But I guess you had a right to expect as much."

With a dazed, fixed smile Steve handed the money slowly to his father, and his face was white.

36 Laughing jovially, Mr. Hudson led them to the door. His own boy followed a few paces behind.

In the elevator Dave took the bills out of his **37** pocket. "See, Stevie," he whispered eagerly. "That windbreaker you wanted! And ten dollars for your bank! Won't Mother be surprised?"

"Yeah," Steve whispered, the little smile still on his face. But Dave had to turn away quickly so their eyes wouldn't meet, for he saw that it was a scared smile.

Outside, Dave said, "Here, you carry the money home, Steve. You show it to your mother."

"No, you keep it," Steve said, and then there **38** was nothing to say. They walked in silence.

"It's a lot of money," Dave said finally. When Steve didn't answer him, he added angrily, "I turned to you, Steve. I asked you, didn't I?"

"That man knew how much his boy wanted that cap," Steve said.

39 "Sure. But he recognized how much it was worth to us."

"No, you let him take it away from us," Steve blurted.

"That's unfair," Dave said. "Don't dare say that to me."

40 "I don't want to be like you," Steve muttered, and he darted across the road and walked along on the other side of the street.

"It's unfair," Dave said angrily, only now he didn't mean that Steve was unfair. He meant that what had happened in the prosperous Hudson home was unfair, and he didn't know quite why. He had been trapped, not just by Mr. Hudson, but by his own life.

Across the road Steve was hurrying along with his head down, wanting to be alone. They walked most of the way home on opposite sides of the street, until Dave could stand it no longer. "Steve," he called, crossing the street. "It was very unfair. I mean, for you to say . . ." but Steve started to run. Dave walked as fast as he could and Steve was getting beyond him, and he felt enraged and suddenly he yelled, "Steve!" and he started to chase his son. He **41** wanted to get hold of Steve and pound him, and he didn't know why. He gained on him, he gasped for breath and he almost got him by the shoulder. Turning, Steve saw his father's face in the streetlight and was terrified; he circled away, got to the house, and rushed in, yelling, "Mother!"

"Son, Son!" she cried, rushing from the kitchen. As soon as she threw her arms around Steve, shielding him, Dave's anger left him and he felt stupid. He walked past them into the kitchen.

"What happened?" she asked anxiously. "Have you both gone crazy? What did you do, Steve?"

"Nothing," he said sullenly.

"What did your father do?"

"We found the boy with my ball cap, and he let the boy's father take it from us."

"No, no," Dave protested. "Nobody pushed

TRANSPARENCY 8
Reader Response
High Five – compares and contrasts the distinguishing traits of two characters from a selection in the unit.

TRANSPARENCY 9
Literary Elements
Plot – invites students to identify and analyze the sequence of events in a selection.

us around. The man didn't put anything over on us." He felt tired and his face was burning. He told what had happened; then he slowly took the two ten-dollar bills out of his wallet **42** and tossed them on the table and looked up guiltily at his wife.

It hurt him that she didn't pick up the money and that she didn't rebuke him. "It is a lot of money, Son," she said slowly. "Your father was only trying to do what he knew was right, and it'll work out, and you'll understand." She was soothing Steve, but Dave knew she felt that she needed to be gentle with him, too, and he was ashamed.

When she went with Steve to his bedroom, Dave sat by himself. His son, for the first time, had seen how easy it was for another man to handle him, and he had judged him and had wanted to walk alone on the other side of the street. He looked at the money and he hated the sight of it.

43 His wife returned to the kitchen, made a cup of tea, talked soothingly, and said it was incredible that he had forced the Hudson man to pay him twenty dollars for the cap, but all Dave could think of was Steve was scared of me.

Finally, he got up and went into Steve's room. **44** The room was in darkness, but he could see the outline of Steve's body on the bed, and he sat down beside him and whispered, "Look, Son, it was a mistake. I know why. People like us—in circumstances where money can scare us. No, no," he said, feeling ashamed and shaking his head apologetically; he was taking the wrong way of showing the boy they were together; he was covering up his own failure. The failure **45** had been his, and it had come out of being so separated from his son that he had been blind to what was beyond the price in a boy's life. He longed now to show Steve he could be with him

from day to day. His hand went out hesitantly to Steve's shoulder. "Steve, look," he said eagerly. "The trouble was I didn't realize how much I enjoyed it that night at the ballpark. If I had watched you playing for your own team—the kids around here say you could be a great pitcher. We could take that money and **46** buy a new pitcher's glove for you, and a catcher's mitt. Steve, Steve, are you listening? I could catch for you, work with you in the lane. Maybe I could be your coach . . . watch you become a great pitcher." In the half-darkness he could see the boy's pale face turn to him.

Steve, who had never heard his father talk like this, was shy and wondering. All he knew was that his father, for the first time, wanted to be with him in his hopes and adventures. He said, "I guess you do know how important that **47** cap was." His hand went out to his father's arm. "With that man the cap was—well, it was just something he could buy, eh, Dad?" Dave gripped his son's hand hard. The wonderful generosity of childhood—the price a boy was willing to pay to be able to count on his father's admiration and approval—made him feel humble, then strangely exalted.

Reading Check

1. What does Steve do after school instead of working?
2. What does Dave promise to do if Steve helps make kitchen shelves?
3. Why doesn't Steve get autographs after the game?
4. What does the outfielder give Steve?
5. How much does Mr. Hudson pay Steve for the cap?

42 Analyzing
What does "tossed" suggest?
Suggests Dave now feels contempt for the money.

43
Irony. Dave did not force Hudson to pay twenty dollars; Hudson forced Dave to sell cap.

44
Symbol. Darkness represents emotions of father and son.

45
Dave fully realizes distance between him and his son.

46
Dave is finally saying right things to his son, and, just as importantly, Steve is finally listening—they are communicating.

47
First time Steve makes effort to touch his father.

READING CHECK
1. Plays baseball (p. 78).
2. Take him to Phillies game (p. 78).
3. Other boys surround players, keeping Steve away from them (p. 78).
4. His cap (p. 80).
5. Twenty dollars (p. 84).

Letter writing provides an opportunity for the writer to express his or her feelings in a manner that he or she might not use in oral communication. Students may want to write letters to Steve in which they relate experiences similar to those Steve goes through with his father. Letters could describe students' feelings before, during, and after the experiences. Some students may want to write their letters on stationery they created for that purpose. Revised letters could be added to student portfolios. Consult with students individually to agree on whether and on how their letters will be assessed. (See *Portfolio Assessment and Professional Support Materials* for additional information on student portfolios.)

FOR STUDY AND DISCUSSION

1a. Dave has had to worry about money and must make careful spending decisions. **1b.** Dave feels Steve should be more concerned about family's financial difficulties.

2a. Responses will vary. Steve may believe Condon possesses heroic qualities that Dave lacks.

2b. Dave feels son is childish for believing cap makes him important.

3a. He does not understand how important cap is to Steve. **3b.** Refused money and taken cap back.

4. Love and respect of his son.

5. Apologizes for not understanding. Also shows interest in helping Steve become a better baseball player.

6. Responses will vary. Dave and Steve seem to solve their communication problem at story's end.

FOCUS ON READING

1. Dave thinks of the family needs that the money could alleviate.

2. Steve wants his father's admiration and approval.

LANGUAGE AND VOCABULARY

1. Know meaning of "loafers" from its context.

2. *Ground:* instructed repeatedly.
Drawn: attracted.
Sized: inspected, appraised.
Broke: without money.
Pitcher: one who throws baseballs to batters.

3. Responses will vary. Students can probably come up with many meanings for *ground* (grind), *drawn,* and *broke* (break). *Sized* and *pitcher* also have several meanings.

For Study and Discussion

Analyzing and Interpreting the Story

1. In this story, Dave Diamond and his son, Steve, are divided and then brought closer together because of a conflict over money. **a.** What does the first paragraph tell about the father's attitude toward money? **b.** According to the second paragraph, how has money caused hard feelings between father and son?

2. The baseball cap has a meaning for Steve that his father does not understand. **a.** Why does the cap mean so much to Steve? **b.** What does Dave think of Steve's attachment to the cap at first?

3. The bargaining for the cap that takes place at the Hudson apartment becomes a kind of test for the two fathers. Mr. Hudson "passes" the test because he has enough money to pay any price for the cap. **a.** Why does Dave "fail" the test? **b.** What should Dave have done in order to "pass" the test in his son's eyes?

4. Later, Dave looks at the money he has accepted for the cap and hates the sight of it. What has Dave realized is more important than money?

5. What does Dave finally say to make Steve see that he does know what is "beyond the price" in his son's life?

6. This story begins with a conflict. Do you think it ends with peace? Explain your answer.

Focus on Reading

Recognizing the Causes of a Character's Actions

An important moment in this story occurs when the two fathers bargain for the baseball cap. At first, Dave offers to pay two dollars for the cap. But by the end of the scene, he has decided to give up the cap entirely.

1 What causes Dave to change his mind and take the money instead of the cap? The answer is in this paragraph.

That much money for a cap, Dave thought, and his eyes brightened. But he knew what the cap had meant to Steve; to deprive him of it now that it was within his reach would be unbearable. All the things he needed in his life gathered around him; his wife was there, saying he couldn't afford to reject the offer, he had no right to do it; and he turned to Steve to see if Steve thought it wonderful that the cap could bring them twenty dollars.

The turning point of the story occurs when Dave goes into Steve's bedroom and tries to explain why he gave up the cap. Steve is angry with his father. He has already said, "I don't **2** want to be like you." According to the last paragraph of the story, what causes Steve to forgive his father and to forget about the cap?

Language and Vocabulary

Recognizing Multiple Meanings of Words

The meaning of a word is usually clear from its **context**—that is, from the other words in the sentence or paragraph. On page 80, Dave says, "See what comes from encouraging the boy to **1** hang around with those park *loafers.*" Clearly, *loafers* doesn't mean a pair of shoes; it means a group of lazy people. How do you know?

2 What does each italicized word or phrase mean in the following quotations from the story? Write a sentence using each word or phrase in another context, to indicate a **3** different meaning. Do some words have more than two meanings? Your dictionary will help.

Steve . . . ought to have known the value of money as well as Dave did. It had been *ground* into him.

. . . Eddie Condon must have been *drawn* to him . . .

. . . Mr. Hudson thought he had Dave *sized* up; he had looked at him and decided he was *broke.*

". . . the kids around here say you could be a great *pitcher.*"

CLOSURE
Ask students to identify and analyze passages that show how the **conflict** between Steve and Dave begins, intensifies, and then is resolved. Have students identify the motives behind the characters' attitudes and actions.

EXTENSION AND ENRICHMENT
Students may wish to write an account, from the mother's point of view, of the scene in which Dave and Steve return from the Hudsons'. What are her feelings about the cap and the twenty dollars?

Students who enjoy ''A Cap for Steve'' might enjoy reading two collections of Callaghan's short stories, *A Native Argosy* and *Close to the Sun Again*.

Focus on Personal Narrative

Choosing a Topic

Imagine how Steve might have recalled the incident of the cap a few years later. Do you think it would still have been so important to him? How do you think he might have written about it from his own point of view?

A **personal narrative** tells about an experience that happened to you and shows the meaning of the experience. In a personal narrative, you usually tell events according to the order in which they happened. You also include specific details about events, people, places, and thoughts and feelings.

When you select a topic for a personal narrative, use these guidelines:

1. Choose an experience that was important to you.
2. Choose an experience that you remember clearly and vividly.
3. Choose an experience that you are willing to share with others.

Explore some topics for a personal narrative by listing ideas and memories on a chart like the one below. Feel free to change one or more of the column heads. Save your notes.

Holidays	Meetings	Arguments	Challenges
————	————	————	————
————	————	————	————
————	————	————	————
————	————	————	————

About the Author

Morley Callaghan (1903–1990)

Morley Callaghan was born in Toronto and lived there for most of his life. Although he received a law degree, he never practiced. After publishing his first book, *Strange Fugitive* (1928), he briefly joined the "lost generation"—a group of expatriate writers and artists who went to Paris in search of new ways to express their ideas. In a famous boxing match in Paris, he beat his mentor Ernest Hemingway when F. Scott Fitzgerald, the timekeeper, mistakenly let a round go on too long. Callaghan once lamented that he was better known for this boxing match than for his writing.

Following his return to Canada, Callaghan wrote his most successful novels: *Such Is My Beloved* (1934), *They Shall Inherit the Earth* (1935), and *More Joy in Heaven* (1937). Much of Callaghan's work explores the human condition and conscience. Like Ernest Hemingway, the writer he admired the most, Callaghan wrote in a simple and direct style. In *That Summer in Paris,* he explained that a good writer was one who could "tell the truth cleanly."

FOCUS ON PERSONAL NARRATIVE
Students might enjoy collecting ideas for personal narratives through a brainstorming activity. Using the headings from the text in additon to headings that students suggest, do the following procedure with the whole class: Call out one heading and ask students to list all the experiences that come to mind. Give students about a minute to write. Then have each student choose one of the experiences and brainstorm for another minute everything he or she can remember about the experience. Continue this process for as long as necessary in order for students to collect possible topics.

ABOUT THE AUTHOR
Morley Callaghan worked with Ernest Hemingway as a reporter for the *Toronto Star;* more than this, however, the relationship between the two writers is evident in their fiction and especially in the dialogue of their fiction. Callaghan is best known for his short stories although he has written ten novels.

OBJECTIVES

The overall aim is for students to identify the changes that take place within the main character. For a complete list of objectives, see the **Teacher's Notes.**

VOCABULARY

The underlined words are in the Glossary. You probably will want to make sure that all students understand the definition of "apprentice" before reading this selection.

FOCUS / MOTIVATION

In almost everyone's life, there comes a time for a crucial **internal conflict** when responsibility and maturity are tested. Have students give examples of such situations from characters in books or movies.

TEACHING RESOURCES B

Teacher's Notes, p. 14
Reading Check, p. 16
Study Guide, p. 17
Language Skills, p. 20
Building Vocabulary, p. 23
Selection Vocabulary Test, p. 24
Selection Test, p. 25

PREREADING FOCUS

The headnote refers to an apprentice as a "learner or beginner." Ask students to write a brief paragraph about a lesson they learned that will be valuable to them for a long time. Perhaps they learned on their own or perhaps a friend or adult served as teacher. The experience may have been happy or sad. It may have involved acquiring a skill, gaining an insight into life, or learning about relationships among people. Volunteers may read paragraphs if they wish.

VISUAL CONNECTIONS

Exploring the Subject

Dogs are noted for their devotion to their human owners, and this photograph illustrates the close ties that may develop between them. The first animals to be domesticated, dogs make excellent pets because they are social pack animals. If they are exposed to human care and handling during the crucial socialization phase of their development (which occurs between three and twelve weeks), they come to see their human owner as their "pack leader."

Relating Expression Skills

Lead a discussion about the scene in the photograph. Ask students to make guesses about the relationship between the girl and her dog. Do you think the dog is the girl's pet or just a family dog? Examine the girl's expression. Would you describe it as a look of contentment, joy, or great relief? Why might she be so happy to see the dog?

The Apprentice

DOROTHY CANFIELD

As you read this story, think of an apprentice as a learner or beginner. What do you think this apprentice learns by the end of the story?

MOTIVATIONAL SUMMARY

Peg is thirteen years old and resentful of what she sees as unfair restrictions her parents place on her. Having been chastised for being irresponsible, she seeks comfort from her dog, Rollie, a half-grown collie. When she cannot find him, she remembers with horror the neighbors' collie that had to be shot because he was killing sheep. Peg's parents had warned her that Rollie must be taught or might also be killed. While searching for Rollie, Peg learns a lesson about responsibility.

PRESENTATION

Dorothy Canfield's "The Apprentice" is a "coming of age" story. The thirteen-year-old protagonist, Peg, comes to the realization that many of the attitudes and characteristics she once associated with her parents have been unwittingly

The day had been one of those unbearable ones, when every sound had set her teeth on **1** edge like chalk creaking on a blackboard, when every word her father or mother said to her or did not say to her seemed an intentional injustice. And of course it would happen, as the end to such a day, that just as the sun went down back of the mountain and the long twilight began, she noticed that Rollie was not around.

Tense with exasperation—she would simply explode if Mother got going—she began to call him in a carefully casual tone: "Here, Rollie! He-ere, boy! Want to go for a walk, Rollie?" Whistling to him cheerfully, her heart full of wrath at the way the world treated her, she made the rounds of his haunts; the corner of the woodshed, where he liked to curl up on the wool of Father's discarded old windbreaker; the hay barn, the cow barn, the sunny spot on the side porch—no Rollie.

Perhaps he had sneaked upstairs to lie on her bed where he was not supposed to go—not that *she* would have minded! That rule was a part of Mother's fussiness, part too of Mother's bossiness. It was *her* bed, wasn't it? But was she allowed the say-so about it? Not on your life. They told her she could have things the way she wanted in her own room, now she was in her teens, but—her heart raged against unfairness as she took the stairs stormily, two steps at a time, her pigtails flopping up and down on her back. If Rollie was on her bed, she was just going to let him stay right there, and Mother could shake her head and frown all she wanted to.

But he was not there. The bedspread and pillow were crumpled, but not from his weight. She had flung herself down to cry there that afternoon. And then she couldn't. Every nerve **2** in her had been twanging, but she couldn't cry. She could only lie there, her hands doubled up hard, furious that she had nothing to cry about. Not really. She was too big to cry just over Father's having said to her, severely, "I told you if I let you take the chess set you were to put it away when you got through with it. One of the pawns was on the floor of our bedroom this morning. I stepped on it. If I'd had my shoes on, I'd have broken it."

Well, he *had* told her to be sure to put them away. And although she had forgotten and left them, he hadn't forbidden her ever to take the **3** set again. No, the instant she thought about that, she knew she couldn't cry about it. She could be, and she was, in a rage about the way Father kept on talking, long after she'd got his point, "It's not that I care so much about the chess set," he said, just leaning with all his **4** weight on being right, "it's because if you don't learn how to take care of things, you yourself will suffer for it, later. You'll forget or neglect something that will be really important, for **5** *you*. We *have* to try to teach you to be responsible for what you've said you'll take care of. If we . . ." on and on, preaching and preaching.

She heard her mother coming down the hall, and hastily shut her door. She had a right to **6** shut the door to her own room, hadn't she? She had *some* rights, she supposed, even if she was only thirteen and the youngest child. If her mother opened it to ask, smiling, "What are you doing in here that you don't want me to see?" she'd say—she'd just say—

She stood there, dry-eyed, by the bed that Rollie had not crumpled, and thought, "I hope Mother sees the spread and says something about Rollie—I just hope she does."

But her mother did not open the door. Her feet went steadily on along the hall, and then, carefully, slowly, down the stairs. She probably **7** had an armful of winter things she was bringing down from the attic. She was probably thinking that a tall, thirteen-year-old daughter was big enough to help with a chore like that.

The Apprentice

1
Simile. Comparison to irritating noise heightens tension.

2
"Twanging" indicates discord and irritability.

3 Summarizing
Why can't Peg cry about the incident with the chessboard? Peg acknowledges father's fairness.

4
Use to answer **study question 1**, p. 96.

5
Father indicates that responsibility is learned behavior.

6
Conflict. Peg has entered adolescence; however, as youngest, she is still "baby of family." She feels so moody she would almost welcome trouble.

7
Symbol. Winter, end of seasonal cycle, comes before new growth of spring. Symbolic of the physical and emotional changes Peg is experiencing.

The Apprentice **89**

adopted by her, primarily their concept of responsibility. The author skillfully reveals to the reader the universal conflicts between parent/child and experience/naiveté. Also, an element of **suspense** is provided, making this a very readable and rewarding story.

CREATIVE WRITING LINK

Ask students who has the easiest tasks to do in their families—the youngest child, an older brother or sister, a grandparent, or someone else. Who does the most work to make the household run smoothly? Tell students to pretend they could trade responsibilities with anyone in their home for a day. Ask each to write a paragraph about trading places that addresses questions such as these: Who would students trade with? What would they do all day? What would they not have to do?

8

Characterization. Peg does not want to be treated like a child, yet she stamps her foot childishly. Indicates she is experiencing changes she does not comprehend.

9

Symbol. Giving up dolls represents Peg's leaving childhood.

10 Expressing an Opinion
Analyzing
Do you think Peg is being realistic and honest in her statement? Why? Responses will vary. Although Peg's parents love her, there are times when she truly feels as if Rollie is her only friend. She does not yet realize that parents scold her out of love.

11

Peg is annoyed by parents' instructions simply because they were given by parents. Indicates breakdown in communication between generations.

12

Reemphasizes concept of responsibility. Foreshadows potential crisis.

13

Indicates seriousness of possible consequences.

But she wouldn't *say* anything. She would just get out that insulting look of a grown-up silently putting up with a crazy, unreasonable kid. She had worn that expression all day; it was too much to be endured.

Up in her bedroom behind her closed door **8** the thirteen-year-old stamped her foot in a rage, none the less savage and heart-shaking because it was mysterious to her.

But she had not located Rollie. Before she would let her father and mother know she had lost sight of him, forgotten about him, she would be cut into little pieces. They would not scold her, she knew. They would do worse. They would look at her. And in their silence she would hear droning on reproachfully what they had repeated and repeated when the sweet, woolly collie puppy had first been in her arms and she had been begging to keep him for her own.

How warm he had felt! Astonishing how warm and alive a puppy was compared to a **9** doll! She had never liked her dolls much, after she had held Rollie, feeling him warm against her breast, warm and wriggling, bursting with life, reaching up to lick her face—he had loved her from that first instant. As he felt her arms around him, his beautiful eyes had melted in trusting sweetness. And they did now, when **10** ever he looked at her. "My dog is the only one in the whole world who *really* loves me," she thought passionately.

Even then, at the very minute when as a darling baby dog he was beginning to love her, her father and mother were saying, so cold, so rea **11** sonable—gosh! how she *hated* reasonable **12** ness!—"Now, Peg, remember that, living where we do, with sheep on the farms around us, it is a serious responsibility to have a collie dog. If you keep him, you've got to be the one to take care of him. You'll have to be the one to train **13** him to stay at home. We're too busy with you

children to start bringing up a puppy too." Rollie, nestling in her arms, let one hind leg drop awkwardly. It must be uncomfortable. She looked down at him tenderly, tucked his dangling leg up under him and gave him a hug. He laughed up in her face—he really did laugh, his mouth stretched wide in a cheerful grin.

All the time her parents kept hammering away: "If you want him, you can have him. But you must be responsible for him. If he gets to running sheep, he'll just have to be shot, you know that."

COOPERATIVE LEARNING

Students might relate to Peg's growing pains by comparing her conflicts with her parents to their own family relationships. First, ask students to scan the story to locate Peg's complaints about her parents. As they find these complaints, have volunteers write summarized versions on the chalkboard.

Then, divide the class into small groups. Invite each group to talk about conversations with parents that are repeated over and over again. Have each group make a list titled, "What I wish my parents would stop saying." Then have each group prepare a sheet to survey parents about their exasperations, "What I wish my teenager would do without being told."

Ask the groups to collate responses and to create a bulletin board to display them.

They had not said, aloud, "Like the Wilsons' collie." They never mentioned that awfulness—her racing unsuspectingly down across the fields just at the horrible moment when Mr. Wilson shot his collie caught in the very act of killing sheep. They probably thought that if they never spoke about it, she would forget it—

14 *forget* the crack of that rifle, and the collapse of the great beautiful dog! Forget the red, red blood spurting from the hole in his head. She hadn't forgotten. She never would. She knew as well as they did how important it was to train a

15 collie puppy about sheep. They didn't need to rub it in like that. They always rubbed everything in. She had told them, fervently, indignantly, that of *course* she would take care of him, be responsible for him, teach him to stay at home. Of course, of course. *She* understood!

16 And now, this afternoon, when he was six months old, tall, rangy,[1] powerful, standing up far above her knee, nearly to her waist, she didn't know where he was. But of course he must be somewhere around. He always was. She composed her face to look natural and went downstairs to search the house. He was probably asleep somewhere. She looked every room over carefully. Her mother was nowhere visible. It was safe to call him again, to give the special piercing whistle which always brought him racing to her, the white-feathered plume of his tail waving in elation that she wanted him.

But he did not answer. She stood still on the front porch to think.

Could he have gone up to their special place in the edge of the field where the three young pines, their branches growing close to the ground, made a triangular, walled-in space, completely hidden from the world? Sometimes he went up there with her. When she lay down on the dried grass to dream, he too lay down

quietly, his head on his paws, his beautiful eyes fixed adoringly on her. He entered into her every mood. If she wanted to be quiet, all right, he did too.

It didn't seem as though he would have gone

17 alone there. Still——She loped up the steep slope of the field rather fast, beginning to be anxious.

No, he was not there. She stood, irresolutely,[2] in the roofless, green-walled triangular hideout, wondering what to do next.

Then, before she knew what thought had come into her mind, its emotional impact knocked her down. At least her knees crumpled under her. Last Wednesday the Wilsons had brought their sheep down to the home farm from the upper pasture! She herself had

18 seen them on the way to school, and like an idiot had not thought of Rollie. She had seen them grazing on the river meadow.

She was off like a racer at the crack of the

19 starting pistol, her long, strong legs stretched in great leaps, her pigtails flying. She took the shortcut down to the upper edge of the meadow, regardless of the brambles. Their thorn-spiked, wiry stems tore at her flesh, but she did not care. She welcomed the pain. It was something she was doing for Rollie, for her Rollie.

20 She was tearing through the pine woods now, rushing down the steep, stony path, tripping over roots, half falling, catching herself just in time, not slackening her speed. She burst out on the open knoll above the river meadow, calling wildly, "Rollie, here, Rollie, here, boy! here! here!" She tried to whistle, but she was crying too hard to pucker her lips. She had not, till then, known she was crying.

There was nobody to see or hear her. Twilight was falling over the bare knoll. The sunless evening wind slid down the mountain like an

---

1. **rangy** (răn´jē): thin and long-limbed.

2. **irresolutely** (ĭ-rĕz´ə-lōōt´lē): in an undecided way.

14
Violent image creates tension, prepares reader for worst.

15 Summarizing
What is Peg's reaction to her parents' attempts to teach her the importance of responsibility? She is childishly resentful.

16
Rollie, also an adolescent, is in that sense similar to Peg.

17
Suspense. Peg's anxiety increases tension.

18
Characterization. Peg is self-critical for first time. She realizes her grave error.

19
Again, physical comparison between Peg and Rollie. Though "starting pistol" is harmless, mention of gun may be subtle reminder of the collie shot with a rifle.

20
"Tearing," "rushing," "tripping," "falling," and "catching," heighten tension and excitement.

SPORTS LINK
You may have students in your classroom who ride horses recreationally or who work around, live near, or own horses. Encourage those students who are familiar with horses to share information with the class.

You might want to suggest topics they could discuss, such as the role of horses in human history, names for and characteristics of various breeds, equipment for different kinds of riding, care and grooming of horses, horse racing, uses for horses on a farm or ranch, or other subjects

appropriate to your community.

21

Characterization. Peg assumes responsibility of caretaker for Rollie. Emphasizes closeness between two and, of course, also suggests relationship between Peg and her own mother.

22

Peg is imagining this scene. Experiences anxiety about not teaching Rollie difference between right and wrong.

23

Simile. Her wildness mirrors Rollie's nature.

24

Peg finally assumes full responsibility for earlier carelessness. Shows increased maturity.

25

Use to answer **study question 2a,** p. 96.

VISUAL CONNECTIONS
Exploring the Subject
This picture suggests the scene in which Peg reflects on her responsibilities toward her collie, realizes that she has been negligent, and takes an important step in understanding the nature of adulthood. In most stories that involve character development, such a moment of reflection and realization occurs. Ask students to decide if such moments occur in stories they have read so far. (In "Raymond's Run," for example, Squeaky's moment of reflection and growth occurs during the race when she sees Raymond running with her and realizes she could help him succeed as a runner.)

invisible river, engulfing her in cold. Her teeth began to chatter. "Here, Rollie, here, boy, here!" She strained her eyes to look down into the meadow to see if the sheep were there. She could not be sure. She stopped calling him as if he were a dog, and called out his name despair-
21 ingly, as if he were her child, "Rollie! oh, *Rollie,* where are you!"

The tears ran down her cheeks in streams. She sobbed loudly, terribly. Since there was no one to hear, she did not try to control herself.

"Hou! hou! hou!" she sobbed, her face contorted grotesquely. "Oh, Rollie! Rollie! Rollie!" She had wanted something to cry about. Oh, how terribly now she had something to cry about.

22 She saw him as clearly as if he were there beside her, his muzzle and gaping mouth all smeared with the betraying blood (like the Wilsons' collie). "But he didn't *know* it was
23 wrong!" she screamed like a wild creature. "Nobody *told* him it was wrong. It was my fault. I
24 should have taken better care of him. I will now. I will!"

But no matter how she screamed, she could not make herself heard. In the cold gathering darkness, she saw him stand, poor, guiltless victim of his ignorance, who should have been protected from his own nature, his soft eyes looking at her with love, his splendid plumed tail waving gently. "It was my fault. I promised I would bring him up. I should have *made* him stay at home. I was responsible for him. It was my fault."

But she could not make his executioners hear her. The shot rang out, Rollie sank down, his beautiful liquid eyes glazed, the blood spurting from the hole in his head—like the Wilsons' collie. She gave a wild shriek, long,
25 soul-satisfying, frantic. It was the scream at sudden, unendurable tragedy of a mature, full-blooded woman. It drained dry the girl of thirteen. She came to herself. She was standing on the knoll, trembling and quaking with cold, the darkness closing in on her.

Her breath had given out. For once in her life she had wept all the tears there were in her body. Her hands were so stiff with cold she could scarcely close them. How her nose was running! Simply streaming down her upper lip. And she had no handkerchief. She lifted her skirt, fumbled for her slip, stooped, blew her nose on it, wiped her eyes, drew a long quavering breath—and heard something! Far off in the distance, a faint sound, like a dog's muffled bark.

She whirled on her heels and bent her head to listen. The sound did not come from the meadow below the knoll. It came from back of her higher up, from the Wilsons' maple grove. She held her breath. Yes, it came from there.

26 She began to run again, but now she was not sobbing. She was silent, absorbed in her effort to cover ground. If she could only live to get there, to see if it really were Rollie. She ran steadily till she came to the fence and went over this in a great plunge. Her skirt caught on a nail. She impatiently pulled at it, not hearing or not heeding the long sibilant[3] tear as it came **27** loose. She was in the dusky maple woods, stumbling over the rocks as she ran. As she tore on up the slope, she heard the bark again, and knew it was Rollie's.

She stopped short and leaned weakly against a tree. She was sick with the breathlessness of her straining lungs, sick in the reaction of **28** relief, sick with anger at Rollie, who had been here having a wonderful time while she had been dying, just dying in terror about him.

For she could now not only hear that it was Rollie's bark. She could hear, in the dog language she knew as well as he, what he was saying in those excited yips—that he had run a woodchuck into a hole in the tumbled stone wall, that he had almost had him, that the intoxicating wild-animal smell was as close to him—almost—as if he had his jaws on his **29** quarry. Yip! Woof! Yip! Yip!

The wildly joyful quality of the dog-talk enraged the girl. She had been trembling in exhaustion. Now it was indignation. So that was where he had been—when *she* was *killing* herself trying to take care of him. Plenty near enough if he had paid attention to hear her calling and whistling to him. Just so set on hav-

3. **sibilant** (sĭb′ə-lənt): making a hissing sound.

ing his foolish good time, he never thought to listen for her call.

She stooped to pick up a stout stick. She **30** would teach him. She was hot with anger. It was time he had something to make him remember to listen. She started forward on a run.

31 But after a few steps she stopped, stood thinking. One of the things to remember about collies, everybody knew that, was that a collie who had been beaten was never "right"

Exploring the Subject
Collies, like the one pictured here, are excellent sheepherders and watchdogs, as well as good pets. Originally, dogs used for herding were selected for their size and ferocity since they were expected to protect their charges from predatory attacks. In modern times, however, the most desirable trait of a collie is its ability to learn complicated commands.

26
Peg no longer cries like a child.

27
Peg disregards physical comfort.

28
Characterization. Peg's reactions are similar to those that parents might experience after finding lost child.

29
Rollie's voice is in process of changing, like that of adolescent—"yip" of puppy mixed with "woof" of adult dog.

30 Expressing an Opinion
Is Peg's anger at Rollie totally justified? Responses will vary. Rollie did not know to behave differently because Peg had not taught him to stay home.

31
Characterization. Peg, who earlier complained about "reasonable" parents, now begins to reason with greater maturity.

32

Peg is having similar thoughts about Rollie that her parents have about her.

33

Characterization. Peg comprehends meaning of change she has experienced—a sign of maturity in itself.

34 Comparing/Contrasting

To what can Peg's grave voice and severe speech be compared? Her father's earlier use of "severe" voice in dealing with her about chess set.

35

Nearly exact words her father had spoken to her earlier, further indicating change of role.

36

Earlier, Peg's emotions were "mysterious" to her, like Rollie's at this point.

37

Imagery. "Wriggled," "lick," "warm," and "pulsing" appeal to sense of touch—connote warm and loving emotions.

again. His spirit was broken. "Anything but a broken-spirited collie"—she had often heard a farmer say that. They were no good after that.

She threw down her stick. Anyhow, she thought, he was really too young to know that he had done wrong. He was still only a puppy. Like all puppies, he got perfectly crazy over wild-animal smells. Probably he truly hadn't heard her calling and whistling.

All the same, all the same—she stood stock-still, staring intently into the twilight—you **32** couldn't let a puppy grow up just as he wanted to. It wouldn't be safe—for *him.* Somehow she would have to make him understand that he mustn't go off this way, by himself. He must be trained to know how to do what a good dog does—not because *she* wanted it, but for his own sake.

She walked on now, steady, purposeful, gath- **33** ering her inner strength together, Olympian[4] in her understanding of the full meaning of the event.

When he heard his own special young god approaching, he turned delightedly and ran to meet her, panting, his tongue hanging out. His eyes shone. He jumped up on her in an ecstasy of welcome and licked her face.

34 She pushed him away. Her face and voice were grave. "No, Rollie, *no!*" she said severely. "You're *bad.* You know you're not to go off in the woods without me! You are—a—*bad—dog.*"

He was horrified. Stricken into misery. He stood facing her, frozen. The gladness went out of his eyes, the waving plume of his tail slowly lowered to slinking, guilty dejection.

"I know you were all wrapped up in that woodchuck. But that's no excuse. You *could* have heard me, calling you, whistling for you,

4. **Olympian** (ō-lĭm′pē-ən): godlike. The ancient Greek gods were believed to live on Mount Olympus in northeastern Greece.

35 if you'd paid attention," she went on. "You've got to learn, and I've got to teach you."

With a shudder of misery he lay down, his tail stretched out limp on the ground, his head flat on his paws, his ears drooping—ears ringing with the doomsday awfulness of the voice he loved and revered. To have it speak so to him, he must have been utterly wicked. He trembled, he turned his head away from her august[5] look of blame, he groveled in remorse **36** for whatever mysterious sin he had committed.

As miserable as he, she sat down by him. "I don't *want* to scold you. But I have to! I have to bring you up right or you'll get shot, Rollie. You mustn't go away from the house without me, do you hear, *never.*"

His sharp ears, yearning for her approval, caught a faint overtone of relenting affection in her voice. He lifted his eyes to her, humbly, soft in imploring fondness.

"Oh, Rollie!" she said, stooping low over him, "I *do* love you. I do. But I *have* to bring you up. I'm responsible for you, don't you see."

He did not see. Hearing sternness, or something else he did not recognize, in the beloved voice, he shut his eyes tight in sorrow, and made a little whimpering lament in his throat.

She had never heard him cry before. It was too much. She sat down by him and drew his head to her, rocking him in her arms, soothing him with inarticulate small murmurs.

37 He leaped into her arms and wriggled happily as he had when he was a baby; he reached up to lick her face as he had then. But he was no baby now. He was half as big as she, a great, warm, pulsing, living armful of love. She clasped him closely. Her heart was brimming full, but calmed, quiet. The blood flowed strongly, steadily, all through her body. She was deliciously warm. Her nose was still running, a little. She sniffed and wiped it on her sleeve.

5. **august** (ô-gŭst′): dignified; inspiring respect.

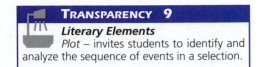

TRANSPARENCIES 6 & 7
Fine Art
Theme: *It's My Time* – invites students to explore artwork portraying relationships among people of different generations.

TRANSPARENCY 9
Literary Elements
Plot – invites students to identify and analyze the sequence of events in a selection.

38 It was almost dark now. "We'll be late to supper, Rollie," she said, responsibly. Pushing him gently off she stood up. "Home, Rollie, home."

Here was a command he could understand. At once he trotted along the path towards home. His tail, held high, waved plumelike. His short dog-memory had forgotten the suffering just back of him.

39 Her human memory was longer. His prancing gait was as carefree as a young child's. She plodded behind him like a serious adult. Her very shoulders seemed bowed by what she had **40** lived through. She felt, she thought, like an old woman of thirty. But it was all right now, she knew she had made an impression on him.

When they came out into the open pasture, Rollie ran back to get her to play with him. He leaped around her in circles, barking in cheerful yawps, jumping up on her, inviting her to run a race with him, to throw him a stick, to come alive.

41 His high spirits were ridiculous. But infectious. She gave one little leap to match his. Rollie took this as a threat, a pretend play-threat. He planted his forepaws low and barked loudly at her, laughing between yips. He was so funny, she thought, when he grinned that way. She laughed back, and gave another mock-threatening leap at him. Radiant that his sky was once more clear, he sprang high on his steel-spring muscles in an explosion of happiness, and bounded in circles around her.

Following him, not noting in the dusk where she was going, she felt the grassy slope drop steeply. Oh, yes, she knew where she was. They had come to the rolling-down hill just back of the house. All the kids rolled down there, even the littles ones, because it was soft grass without a stone. She had rolled down that slope a **42** million times—years and years before, when she was a kid herself, six or seven years ago. It was fun. She remembered well the whirling dizziness of the descent, all the world turning crazily over and over. And the delicious giddy staggering when you first stood up, the earth still spinning under your feet.

43 "All right, Rollie, let's go," she cried, and flung herself down in the rolling position, her arms straight up over her head.

Rollie had never seen this skylarking before. It threw him into almost hysterical amusement. He capered around the rapidly rolling figure, half scared, mystified, enchanted.

His wild frolicsome barking might have come from her own throat, so accurately did it sound the way she felt—crazy, foolish—like a

VISUAL CONNECTIONS
Ideas for Writing
Children and young people often have close relationships with pets. Students might write about why they value their pets. What makes their pets so special to them? Students who do not have pets might write about imagined pets. What kind of pets would they choose and why?

38
Symbol. Near darkness represents Peg's near abandonment of childhood.

39
Use to answer **study question 4a,** p. 96.

40
Although Peg is growing up, she still considers thirty old.

41
She cannot stay angry at her "child."

42 Analyzing
What is ironic about "years and years before"? Peg views her childhood as if it had taken place in distant past.

43
Characterization. Peg reverts to youthful behavior; she realizes joys of childhood.

44
Peg's attitude toward her mother has matured.

45
Last sentence indicates Peg's transition from childhood to adolescence is complete.

READING CHECK
1. In her room (p. 89).
2. She left out chess set (p. 89).
3. Recalls Rollie as pup and parents' warning to teach him (p. 90).
4. In Wilsons' maple grove (p. 93).
5. Remembers that beating collie breaks its spirit (p. 94).

FOR STUDY AND DISCUSSION
1. Begins "if you don't learn . . ." and ends with "that will be really important, for *you*."
2a. It was "scream at sudden, unendurable tragedy of a mature, full-blooded woman." 2b. Peg is reaching adulthood; has faced tragedy.
3a. She scolds him for his own sake. 3b. He is hurt when Peg scolds him, as Peg was hurt. Rollie and Peg both want to play later, having forgotten scolding.
4a. Rollie prances while Peg plods behind him. 4b. Responses will vary. Seems to have newfound respect.
5. Responses will vary. After experience with responsibility, happy still to be adolescent.

FOCUS ON READING
1. Because she is learning responsible adulthood from older, experienced persons. She learns this "craft" by watching the way her parents behave toward her, just as an apprentice carpenter learns to prepare wood by observing techniques used by a master carpenter.
2. Her parents.

little kid, no more than five years old, the age she had been when she had last rolled down that hill.

At the bottom she sprang up, on muscles as steel-strong as Rollie's. She staggered a little, and laughed aloud.

The living-room windows were just before them. How yellow the lighted windows looked when you were in the darkness going home. How nice and yellow. Maybe Mother had **44** waffles for supper. She was a swell cook, Mother was, and she certainly gave her family all the breaks, when it came to meals.

"Home, Rollie, home!" She burst open the door to the living room. "Hi, Mom, what'you got for supper?"

From the kitchen her mother announced coolly, "I hate to break the news to you, but it's waffles."

"Oh, *Mom!*" she shouted in ecstasy.

Her mother could not see her. She did not need to. "For goodness' sakes, go and wash," she called.

In the long mirror across the room she saw herself, her hair hanging wild, her long bare legs scratched, her broadly smiling face dirt-streaked, her torn skirt dangling, her dog **45** laughing up at her. Gosh, was it a relief to feel your own age, just exactly thirteen years old!

Reading Check

1. At the opening of the story, where does Peg expect to find her dog?
2. Why has her father been severe with her?
3. What makes Peg think of the Wilsons' collie?
4. Where does she find Rollie?
5. Why does Peg decide not to beat her dog for running off?

For Study and Discussion

Analyzing and Interpreting the Story

1. At the beginning of the story, Peg is angry with her parents because they have been trying to teach her to take care of the things entrusted to her. What words spoken by her father on page 89 predict what actually does happen to Peg later that day?

2a. How does the author describe Peg's scream on page 92? **b.** What does this statement tell about the change that has taken place in Peg?

3. Peg is enraged at Rollie when she finds him. **a.** In what ways do Peg's actions become just like those she had resented in her parents? **b.** How is Rollie like Peg herself?

4. Look back at the passage describing Peg and Rollie's return home. **a.** What details indicate that Peg feels she is a different person? **b.** Do you think Peg has changed her attitude toward her mother? Why?

5. By the end of the story, why do you think Peg is relieved to feel thirteen again?

Focus on Reading

Understanding the Title of a Story

One clue to the main idea of a story may be in its title. This story, for example, is called "The Apprentice." Yet no one in the story is an apprentice in the strict sense of the word. No one is really bound to some experienced person for a period of time in order to learn a trade or business.

But if we think of an apprentice as a learner, or beginner, we can understand why the story **1** was given this title. Why can Peg be called an **2** "apprentice"? Who are her teachers?

Often a story expresses some truth about life or people. Think about how the apprentice in

CLOSURE
Have students trace Peg's search for Rollie. They should list the different places she searched, as well as her thoughts along the way. Ask them to identify and analyze changes in Peg's character.

EXTENSION AND ENRICHMENT
Small groups might improvise the scene they think will most likely occur when Peg comes down to dinner at the end of the story. The class can then decide which version is most consistent with the story.

Students who enjoyed ''The Apprentice'' might like to read other works by Canfield, particularly *Gunhild* and *The Deepening Stream*.

3 this story learns her lesson. What idea do you think the story expresses about the way young people learn to be adults?

Focus on Personal Narrative

Gathering Details

Details are the small, specific parts of an experience. **Factual details** provide objective information, such as the fact that Peg is thirteen in Canfield's story. **Sensory details** appeal to one or more of the five senses: sight, hearing, touch, taste, and smell. Canfield uses sensory details in the paragraph beginning "How warm he had felt!" to describe the first time Peg held Rollie in her arms (page 90).

To collect details for a personal narrative, use one or more of these techniques:

Fill in a chart like the one below to gather as many factual and sensory details as you can for a personal narrative. Save your notes.

Topic of Narrative: _____

	Events	Details	Thoughts/ Feelings
Background			
Beginning			
Middle			
End			

About the Author

Dorothy Canfield (1879–1958)

At the age of eighteen, Dorothy Canfield, also known as Dorothy Canfield Fisher, wrote, "I've lived long enough to know that life is a thing that can be saved or spent, but that it has value only as it's spent!" She spent her life in activity, and wrote constantly. She was born in Kansas, the daughter of an educator and an artist. She attended Ohio State University and in 1904 received a doctoral degree in philology (historical linguistics) from Columbia University. She married and began to raise a family in the country in Vermont. During World War I, she and her children joined her husband in France. She spent three years doing war work there. After the war she returned with her family to Vermont.

Whatever happened in her life, Canfield found time to write. She wrote many books for children. For adults she wrote novels, short stories, poems, and nonfiction on such topics as education and Vermont. She received many honors and awards for her writings. "The Apprentice" is one of her most famous stories, along with "The Heyday of the Blood" and "The Old Soldier." Canfield once said that no piece of fiction is "worth the reading unless it grapples with some problem of living."

3. Students will have different opinions on the **theme** of the story. Allowing for variations, you might say that the story points out how young people learn to be responsible adults—not in isolation, but through the example of others.

FOCUS ON PERSONAL NARRATIVE
If students completed the **Focus on Personal Narrative** activity on p. 87, suggest that they choose a topic from their notes to use for this activity. Encourage them to use each of the techniques suggested in the text to help them thoroughly explore their topics for details. Before filling out their charts, students might want to develop time lines based on their experiences. You may want to assign a minimum number of details as a goal. Also, to help students write down their feelings about events, give them an example. You might point out that in the paragraph referred to on p. 90, Peg describes feeling warm and loved. Check students' charts to make sure they understand the process of collecting details for personal narratives.

ABOUT THE AUTHOR
In her long career, Canfield wrote numerous novels including *Gunhild* (1907), set in Norway, *The Bent Twig* (1915), about a Midwestern professor, and *The Deepening Stream* (1930), tracing a woman's life from her youth in the U.S. to adulthood in France. Collections of short stories include *Hillsboro People* (1915) and *The Real Motive* (1916). Canfield served on the editorial board of The Book-of-the-Month Club from its founding in 1926 until her death. In 1959, the Club established annual awards in her name to public libraries in small cities across the United States. Vermont organizations also established an award in her name to be given annually to distinguished children's books.

TEACHING RESOURCES B

Teacher's Notes, p. 26
Study Guide, p. 33
Building Vocabulary, p. 27
Selection Test, p. 41

PREREADING FOCUS

The headnote may be used to introduce a discussion of the unusual way Cummings divides and combines words, phrases, and sentences to communicate his ideas about **conflict** between generations.

old age sticks

1
Connotation. "Sticks" is used as verb but could refer to walking canes or old age as something that "sticks" to a person.

2 Analyzing
What do "Keep Off" signs symbolize? Authority and law, control and limitations.

3
Youth often rebels against tradition (old ways) and authority.

4
"Tres" and "pas" are French for "very" and "not" or "step"; also first two syllables of word *trespassing,* completed in l. 11 with "sing."

5
Theme. Youth, so different at one time, ultimately becomes old, exactly like elders that youth had rebelled against.

6
Division of word suggests long process of aging and that youth "owes" age.

old age sticks

E. E. CUMMINGS

Many of E. E. Cummings' poems look like puzzles. Often he does not begin his sentences with capital letters or end them with periods. Sometimes he stretches words out across a line, or squeezes them together, or divides them up in unusual ways.

This poem is made up of three sentences, each beginning with the words old age. *The first part of each sentence, in parentheses, tells what old age does to youth. The second part, the part not in parentheses, tells how youth responds.*

1 old age sticks
  up Keep
  Off
2 signs)&

3 youth yanks them   5
  down(old
  age
  cries No

4 Tres)&(pas)
  youth laughs   10
  (sing
  old age

  scolds Forbid
  den Stop
  Must   15
  n't Don't

5 &)youth goes
  right on
6 gr
  owing old   20

PRESENTATION

Cummings' poem is obviously a statement about the universal **conflict** that separates the young and the old; it ends, however, with the poignant message that youth will gradually acquire the rigid rules and conservatism of the older genera-tion they now ridicule. The poem points out the cyclical nature of the ''generation gap.'' Like the seasons and tides, youth ages as new youth emerges.

CLOSURE

Have students analyze the contrasts between age and youth presented in the poem, and explain how Cummings depicts these differences through his unusual **diction** and violation of the rules of standard English usage.

For Study and Discussion

Analyzing and Interpreting the Poem

1. In this poem about the differences between generations, old age sticks up "Keep Off" signs. How does youth respond?

2. "No Trespassing" and "Keep Off" signs warn outsiders to keep off private property. However, in this poem, "No Trespassing" prob-ably means more than this kind of warn-ing. **a.** What else do you think old age is warning youth not to interfere with? **b.** How does youth respond to this cry of "No Trespass-ing"?

3a. Which lines in the poem suggest that the difference between generations will go on and on forever? **b.** Why will this happen?

Focus on Reading

Understanding the Poet's Technique

Notice how Cummings divides the word *grow-ing* in lines 19–20. By stretching out the word in such a way, he suggests that growing old is a long, slow process. How would you read these lines aloud?

The words *No Trespassing* are spread out over lines 8, 9, and 11. They are interrupted by *&* and *youth laughs.* Shifting back and forth from *No Trespassing* to *& youth laughs* creates the same effect as that of a motion-picture camera focusing first on one character and then on another. We see what both characters are doing at the same time. How would you read these lines aloud?

About the Author

E. E. Cummings (1894–1962)

The Granger Collection, New York

By nature E. E. Cum-mings, whose full name was Edward Estlin Cummings, was shy and sensitive. A painter as well as a poet, he created many new ways of present-ing a poem on a page. Some of his poems looked so unusual that they baffled typesetters and threw some readers into confusion.

Before the United States entered World War I, Cummings went to France as an ambulance driver. Because of a censor's error, he was placed in a French prison camp. There he gathered material for his book *The Enormous Room*, which has been called one of the best direct-observation books to come out of that war.

Cummings, however, is best known for his lyric poems, which are witty, emotional, and filled with striking images. He can make us look at the tiniest words and symbols in new ways. One of his books of poetry is called *&* [and].

FOR STUDY AND DISCUSSION

1. Youth yanks them down.
2a. Responses will vary. Old age could be saying ''Don't bother me with your modern attitudes, new ways.'' **2b.** Youth laughs.
3a. Last four lines. **3b.** As ''youth'' becomes ''old,'' set in its ways and jealous of its privileges, new group of young people will clamor to take over.

FOCUS ON READING

1. Responses will vary. One way to approach this exercise is to write the poem in more conven-tional form.
2. Responses will vary.

ABOUT THE AUTHOR

Cummings was born and raised in Cambridge, Massachusetts. His father was a Harvard professor who later became a Unitarian minister in Boston. Cummings graduated from Harvard in 1915, lived in Paris, France, for a period after World War I, and even-tually settled in New York's Greenwich Village. He was a pro-lific writer, producing many col-lections of poems as well as a travel book expressing his out-rage at the suppression of individ-ual freedoms in the Soviet Union.

At first glance, the unusual ar-rangement of Cummings' poems on the page may suggest that they are difficult and abstract. The reader soon discovers, how-ever, that his poems are often about uncomplicated feelings and warm human relationships.

OBJECTIVES

The overall aim is for students to analyze Don Anselmo's character and contrasting viewpoints concerning property. For a complete list of objectives, see the **Teacher's Notes.**

VOCABULARY

The underlined words are in the Glossary. The **Language and Vocabulary** exercise on p. 103 gives students an opportunity to analyze the effectiveness of formal speech.

FOCUS / MOTIVATION

Before reading, pass around pictures of the town of Santa Fe, the Sangre de Cristo (Blood of Christ) Range, and adobe houses. Perhaps students can bring such pictures, or you can borrow them from your library or media center.

TEACHING RESOURCES B

Teacher's Notes, p. 29
Reading Check, p. 32
Study Guide, p. 33
Language Skills, p. 35
Building Vocabulary, p. 39
Selection Test, p. 41

PREREADING FOCUS

The headnote might be used to get students to think about how they view property. List on the chalkboard their answers to the question.

Gentleman of Río en Medio

1

Río en Medio: River in the middle.

2

Setting. Located in mountains outside New Mexico's capital, Santa Fe. Many villages still observe traditions.

3

Don Anselmo's house described with contrasting adjectives. Reinforces **theme** of differing points of view, especially about old and new.

4

Again, adjectives describing orchard are in opposition.

5

"Green" carries a **connotation** of life and living things; yet, like man's life, coat's color is fading.

6

Old man removes gloves in dignified manner, but young lawyer finds actions dated and somewhat comical.

7

Ironic that lawyer refers to buyers as "Americans" when old man's people have lived in area for hundreds of years.

Gentleman of Río en Medio

JUAN A. A. SEDILLO

Why would a man sell his land but not the trees on it?

It took months of negotiation to come to an understanding with the old man. He was in no hurry. What he had the most of was time. He lived up in Río en Medio, where his people had been for hundreds of years. He tilled the same land they had tilled. His house was small and wretched, but quaint. The little creek ran through his land. His orchard was gnarled and beautiful.

The day of the sale he came into the office. His coat was old, green and faded. I thought of Senator Catron,[1] who had been such a power with these people up there in the mountains. Perhaps it was one of his old Prince Alberts.[2] He also wore gloves. They were old and torn and his fingertips showed through them. He carried a cane, but it was only the skeleton of a worn-out umbrella. Behind him walked one of his innumerable kin—a dark young man with eyes like a gazelle.

The old man bowed to all of us in the room. Then he removed his hat and gloves, slowly and carefully. Chaplin[3] once did that in a picture, in a bank—he was the janitor. Then he handed his things to the boy, who stood obediently behind the old man's chair.

There was a great deal of conversation about rain and about his family. He was very proud of his large family. Finally we got down to business. Yes, he would sell, as he had agreed, for twelve hundred dollars, in cash. We would buy, and the money was ready. "Don[4] Anselmo," I said to him in Spanish, "we have made a discovery. You remember that we sent that surveyor, that engineer, up there to survey your land so as to make the deed. Well, he finds that you own more than eight acres. He tells us that your land extends across the river and that you own almost twice as much as you thought." He didn't know that. "And now, Don Anselmo," I added, "these Americans are *buena gente,* they are good people, and they are willing to pay you for the additional land as well, at the same rate per acre, so that instead of twelve hundred dollars you will get almost twice as much, and the money is here for you."

The old man hung his head for a moment in thought. Then he stood up and stared at me.

1. **Senator Catron:** Thomas Benton Catron, a Senator from New Mexico (1912–1917).
2. **Prince Alberts:** long, double-breasted coats named after Prince Albert, who later became King Edward VII of Great Britain.
3. **Chaplin:** Charlie Chaplin, a comic star of silent movies.

4. **Don:** a title of respect in Spanish, like *Sir* in English.

New Mexico Landscape (1929) by John Marin (1870–1953). Watercolor on paper.

100

MOTIVATIONAL SUMMARY

Don Anselmo has agreed to sell his house and property to non-Hispanic buyers. After the buyers move onto the property, they are bothered by the village children who come on the land everyday to play under the trees. Anselmo explains that when he sold the land, he did not sell the trees because they were not his to sell. He had planted one tree for each child born in the village. The trees belong to the children. It is up to the "Americans" to understand and settle the issue of each tree.

PRESENTATION

By reading "Gentleman of Río en Medio," students may gain a better understanding of the contrasting ideas different cultures and generations can have about money and property. You may want to begin by pointing out the contrasts

Courtesy of Kennedy Galleries, Inc., New York

VISUAL CONNECTIONS
About the Artist

American artist John Marin (1870–1953) first studied architecture. However, from the age of twenty-eight, when he entered the Pennsylvania Academy to work under artists such as William Merritt Chase, he devoted himself to drawing and painting. From 1905 to 1911, Marin lived in Europe and made his reputation sketching monuments such as the cathedral at Rouen, France. He also studied exhibitions of water colors by both Cézanne and Picasso, and began to experiment with abstract expressionism.

After 1911, Marin returned to New York, painting newly completed landmarks such as the Manhattan Bridge and the Woolworth Building, huge structures that Marin felt represented the energy and power of America. Later, however, he turned to more lyrical work, painting elemental forms—land, sea, sky—especially along the coast of Maine.

Between 1928 and 1930, he spent much of his time in New Mexico, the setting of this painting, and tried to capture the state's vast landscapes.

in the opening paragraphs—first describing the house and orchard and then describing the old man (faded coat and worn gloves contrasted with formal language and gentlemanly manners). Point out the old man's unwillingness to accept more money for his property after hav-

ing given his word and also his feeling that he cannot sell the trees planted at the birth of each new child in the village. You may want students to discuss positive and negative results of the old man's sense of community. Also, have students discuss whether or not the "Americans" match

the old man's integrity with their willingness to buy each tree individually.

8
Characterization. Emphasizes Don Anselmo's integrity and honesty. He values honor and commitment.

9
Use to answer **study question 1**, p. 103.

10
Youth follows old man out as he followed him in. Stresses importance of respect of young for the old and wise.

11 Making Inferences
Why do you think Don Anselmo plants a tree for each of his descendants? Responses will vary. Most will agree that Don Anselmo loves his relatives and wants them to share his feelings for the land.

12
Use to answer **study question 2**, p. 103.

13
That which is legal and supposedly "rational" contrasts with that which is moral, right, and good.

14 Expressing an Opinion
Why do the owners buy the trees from each descendant rather than taking what is legally theirs? Responses will vary. Perhaps Americans feel obligated because Don Anselmo refused to accept all the money he deserved, or they may admire his commitment to his relatives.

"Friend," he said, "I do not like to have you speak to me in that manner." I kept still and let him have his say. "I know these Americans are good people, and that is why I have agreed to **8** sell to them. But I do not care to be insulted. I have agreed to sell my house and land for **9** twelve hundred dollars and that is the price."

I argued with him but it was useless. Finally he signed the deed and took the money but refused to take more than the amount agreed upon. Then he shook hands all around, put on his ragged gloves, took his stick and walked **10** out with the boy behind him.

A month later my friends had moved into Río en Medio. They had replastered the old adobe house, pruned the trees, patched the fence, and moved in for the summer. One day they came back to the office to complain. The children of the village were overrunning their property. They came every day and played under the trees, built little play fences around them, and took blossoms. When they were spoken to, they only laughed and talked back good-naturedly in Spanish.

I sent a messenger up to the mountains for Don Anselmo. It took a week to arrange another meeting. When he arrived he **11** repeated his previous preliminary perform- **12** ance. He wore the same faded cutaway,[5] carried the same stick and was accompanied by the boy again. He shook hands all around, sat down with the boy behind his chair, and talked about the weather. Finally I broached the subject. "Don Anselmo, about the ranch you sold **13** to these people. They are good people and want to be your friends and neighbors always. When you sold to them you signed a document, a deed, and in that deed you agreed to **14** several things. One thing was that they were to have the complete possession of the property.

Now, Don Anselmo, it seems that every day the children of the village overrun the orchard and spend most of their time there. We would like to know if you, as the most respected man in the village, could not stop them from doing so in order that these people may enjoy their new home more in peace."

Don Anselmo stood up. "We have all learned to love these Americans," he said, "because they are good people and good neighbors. I sold them my property because I knew they were good people, but I did not sell them the trees in the orchard."

This was bad. "Don Anselmo," I pleaded, "when one signs a deed and sells real property one sells also everything that grows on the land, and those trees, every one of them, are on the land and inside the boundaries of what you sold."

"Yes, I admit that," he said. "You know," he added, "I am the oldest man in the village. Almost everyone there is my relative and all the children of Río en Medio are my *sobrinos* and *nietos*,[6] my descendants. Every time a child has been born in Río en Medio since I took possession of that house from my mother I have planted a tree for that child. The trees in that orchard are not mine, *señor*, they belong to the children of the village. Every person in Río en Medio born since the railroad came to Santa Fe owns a tree in that orchard. I did not sell the trees because I could not. They are not mine."

There was nothing we could do. Legally we owned the trees but the old man had been so generous, refusing what amounted to a fortune for him. It took most of the following winter to buy the trees, individually, from the descendants of Don Anselmo in the valley of Río en Medio.

---

5. **cutaway:** a long coat with part of the lower front cut away, used for formal occasions.

6. *sobrinos* (sō-brē′nōs) **and** *nietos* (nyĕ′tōs): Spanish for "nephews and nieces" and "grandchildren."

🖥 **TRANSPARENCIES 6 & 7**
Fine Art
Theme: *It's My Time* – invites students to explore artwork portraying relationships among people of different generations.

🖥 **TRANSPARENCY 8**
Reader Response
High Five – compares and contrasts the distinguishing traits of two characters from a selection in the unit.

Reading Check

1. For how much money does Don Anselmo agree to sell his land?
2. Why do the Americans return to the lawyer's office and complain?
3. What reason does Don Anselmo give the lawyer for not being able to sell the trees?
4. How do the Americans finally come to own the trees?

For Study and Discussion

Analyzing and Interpreting the Story

1. Don Anselmo and the Americans have dif-ferent views about money and property. What surprising reply does Don Anselmo make when he is offered more money for his prop-erty?

2. The Americans believe they have a legal right to the entire property, but Don Anselmo has another surprise for them. Why does Don Anselmo feel he has no right to sell the trees?

3. Because of the unexpected turn of events, Don Anselmo's descendants receive some money at the end of this story. Do you think this solution is fair to everyone? Why or why not?

4. Don Anselmo is dressed in faded and tat-tered clothing. **a.** What details reveal that he wears these clothes like a dignified gentle-man? **b.** In what other ways does Don Anselmo show that he is a true gentleman?

Language and Vocabulary

Recognizing Words That Create Tone

Formal speech is language that has a dignified tone. It is the language you use to write a seri-

▶ Before students begin this writing assignment, you may want to refer them to the **Writing About Literature** section on p. 672.

ous paper or make an important speech. To use formal speech or writing, you must follow the rules of grammar, sentence construction, and spelling for standard English.

In "Gentleman of Río en Medio," the author uses language that reflects the dignity of his main character, Don Anselmo. The words of Don Anselmo are simple and direct, yet they command respect from those around him. His language clearly characterizes him as a gentleman.

Included in the dialogue are words and phrases from the Spanish language which con-tribute to the story's overall dignified tone. The social formalities which are observed by Don Anselmo also add to the feeling of formal-ity. Find two examples of dialogue which show **1** the author's use of formal tone. Tell why you think the overall tone of formality expressed in Don Anselmo's language makes the outcome of the story believable.

Writing About Literature

▶ **Comparing Values**

In a brief essay compare Don Anselmo's ideas about money and property with those of the lawyer and his clients.

About the Author

Juan A. A. Sedillo   (1902–1982)

Juan A. A. Sedillo was born in New Mexico and was a descendant of early Spanish colonists. He was a lawyer and judge, and he held several public offices. For a number of years he wrote a weekly article on Mexico for New Mexico newspapers. The story "Gentle-man of Río en Medio" is based on an incident that took place in his law office.

READING CHECK
1. $1,200 (p. 100).
2. Complain about children play-ing under trees (p. 102).
3. Trees belong to children, not to him (p. 102).
4. Americans buy trees individu-ally from children (p. 102).

FOR STUDY AND DISCUSSION
1. "I do not care to be insulted." Insists agreed price stands.
2. Says trees belong to children of village since he planted one for each of them.
3. Responses will vary. Most will probably think solution is fair. Buyers can spend the money they saved from old man's generosity to buy the trees from the chil-dren.
4a. He bows to everyone in office and removes hat and gloves; he shakes hands all around before leaving; walks out with young relative behind him.
4b. He is never in a hurry, speaks courteously about Americans, lets others have their say, keeps his word, and is generous.

LANGUAGE AND VOCABULARY
1. Formality of language under-scores dignity of Don Anselmo's character. He commands respect, and people go out of their way to respect his wishes. This serves to make the outcome of the story believable.

WRITING ABOUT LITERATURE
This assignment can be used with students in pairs or in small groups. To do this, ask one part-ner (or half the group), using examples from the story for sup-port, to express Don Anselmo's ideas about money and property. The other partner (or half of the group) does the same for the law-yer and his clients. Partners (or group members) then compare the information they have gath-ered and produce a collaborative essay.

FROM
My Family and Other Animals

GERALD DURRELL

Durrell, who became a famous naturalist, was ten when this adventure took place. Even at that age, he was fascinated by all forms of life—including a community of scorpions he found one day in a plaster wall.

I grew very fond of these scorpions. I found them to be pleasant, unassuming creatures with, on the whole, the most charming habits. Provided you did nothing silly or clumsy (like putting your hand on one) the scorpions treated you with respect, their one desire being to get away and hide as quickly as possible. They must have found me rather a trial, for I was always ripping sections of the plaster away so that I could watch them, or capturing them and making them walk about in jam jars so that I could see the way their feet moved. By means of my sudden and unexpected assaults on the wall I discovered quite a bit about scorpions. I found that they would eat bluebottles[1] (though how they caught them was a mystery I never solved), grasshoppers, moths, and lacewing flies. Several times I found one of them eating another, a habit I found most distressing in a creature otherwise so impeccable.[2]

By crouching under the wall at night with a torch,[3] I managed to catch some brief glimpses of the scorpions' wonderful courtship dances. I saw them standing, claws clasped, their bodies raised to the skies, their tails lovingly entwined; I saw them waltzing slowly in circles among the moss cushions, claw in claw. But my view of these performances was all too short, for almost as soon as I switched on the torch the partners would stop, pause for a moment, and then, seeing that I was not going to extinguish the light, would turn round and walk firmly away, claw in claw, side by side. They were definitely beasts that believed in keeping themselves *to* themselves. If I could have kept a colony in captivity I would probably have been able to see the whole of the courtship, but the family had forbidden scorpions in the house, despite my arguments in favor of them.

Then one day I found a fat female scorpion in the wall, wearing what at first glance appeared to be a pale fawn fur coat. Closer inspection proved that this strange garment was made up of a mass of tiny babies clinging to the mother's back. I was enraptured by this family, and I made up my mind to smuggle them into the house and up to my bedroom so that I might keep them and watch them grow up. With infinite care I maneuvered the mother and family into a matchbox, and then

1. **bluebottles:** bluish flies.
2. **impeccable** (ĭm-pĕk′ə-bəl): faultless; perfect.
3. **torch:** here, a flashlight.

PRESENTATION

You may want to point out to students that although the essay is told from the viewpoint of a ten-year-old boy, the language is that of an accomplished adult writer. Also point out that much of the essay's humor relies on this adult

hurried to the villa. It was rather unfortunate that just as I entered the door lunch should be served; however, I placed the matchbox care-
5 fully on the mantelpiece in the drawing room, so that the scorpions should get plenty of air, and made my way to the dining room and joined the family for the meal. Dawdling over my food, feeding Roger[4] surreptitiously under the table, and listening to the family arguing, I
6 completely forgot about my exciting new captures. At last, Larry,[5] having finished, fetched the cigarettes from the drawing room, and lying back in his chair he put one in his mouth and picked up the matchbox he had brought. Oblivious of my impending doom I watched him interestedly as, still talking glibly, he opened the matchbox.

Now I maintain to this day that the female scorpion meant no harm. She was agitated and a trifle annoyed at being shut up in a matchbox for so long, and so she seized the first opportunity to escape. She hoisted herself out of the box with great rapidity, her babies clinging on desperately, and scuttled onto the back of Larry's hand. There, not quite certain what to do next, she paused, her sting curved up at the ready. Larry, feeling the movement of her claws, glanced down to see what it was, and from that moment things got increasingly confused.

7 He uttered a roar of fright that made Lugaretzia[6] drop a plate and brought Roger out from beneath the table, barking wildly. With a flick of his hand he sent the unfortunate scorpion flying down the table, and she landed midway between Margo and Leslie,[7]

---

4. **Roger:** the narrator's big, black, woolly dog.
5. **Larry:** the narrator's twenty-three-year-old brother, who tends to be very dramatic.
6. **Lugaretzia** (lōō′gə-rĕt′sē-ə): the family's Greek maid, who is always worried about her health.
7. **Margo and Leslie:** Margo is the eighteen-year-old sister, and Leslie the nineteen-year-old brother.

8 scattering babies like confetti as she thumped onto the cloth. Thoroughly enraged at this treatment, the creature sped towards Leslie,
9 her sting quivering with emotion. Leslie leaped to his feet, overturning his chair, and flicked out desperately with his napkin, sending the scorpion rolling across the cloth towards Margo, who promptly let out a scream that any railway engine would have been proud to produce. Mother, completely bewildered by this sudden and rapid change from peace to chaos, put on her glasses and peered down the table to see what was causing the pandemonium, and at that moment Margo, in a vain attempt to stop the scorpion's advance, hurled a glass of water at it. The shower missed the animal completely, but successfully drenched Mother, who, not being able to stand cold water, promptly lost her breath and sat gasping at the end of the table, unable even to protest. The scorpion had now gone to ground under Leslie's plate, while her babies swarmed wildly all over the table. Roger, mystified by the panic, but determined to do his share, ran round and round the room, barking hysterically.

10 "It's that bloody boy again . . ." bellowed Larry.

"Look out! Look out! They're coming!" screamed Margo.

"All we need is a book," roared Leslie; "don't panic, hit 'em with a book."

"What on earth's the *matter* with you all?" Mother kept imploring, mopping her glasses.

"It's that bloody boy . . . he'll kill the lot of us.
11 . . . Look at the table . . . knee-deep in scorpions. . . ."

"Quick . . . quick . . . do something. . . . Look out, look out!"

"Stop screeching and get a book. . . . You're worse than the dog. . . . Shut *up*, Roger. . . ."

"By the grace of God I wasn't bitten. . . ."

"Look out . . . there's another one. . . . Quick . . . quick . . ."

language: Durrell's calling scorpions "impeccable" is funny partly because we do not expect a young boy to use such a difficult word.

Discuss details about the character that make his bringing scorpions into the house believable. Also analyze the table scene to show how Durrell uses **description, dialogue,** and vivid verbs to create comic chaos.

This brief story is too much fun not to be shared. Have the class read it aloud, perhaps assigning different readers to the lines spoken by Larry, Margo, Leslie, and Mother. (You will need to sort out in advance the designated speakers on p. 105.)

VISUAL CONNECTIONS
Exploring the Subject
This photograph shows Durrell in a natural setting befitting his reputation as a naturalist and zoologist. Zoology is a branch of biology concerned with animal life. Although zoologists often work in laboratories, they are also interested in studying animals in the wild and preserving natural habitats.

12
Eventually dialogue becomes confused. No one knows who is saying what to whom; adds to feeling of pandemonium and to humor.

13
Use to answer **study question 3b,** p. 107.

14
Letting family calm down is good idea. Protagonist knows human animal's behavior, also.

15
Use to answer **study question 4,** p. 107.

READING CHECK
1. In a plaster wall (p. 104).
2. In a matchbox (p. 104).
3. Threw glass of water at scorpion (p. 105).
4. He bit maid on ankle (p. 106).
5. He took scorpions outside and freed them (p. 106).

"Oh, shut up and get me a book or something. . . ."

"But *how* did the scorpions get on the table, dear?"

"That bloody boy. . . . Every matchbox in the house is a deathtrap. . . ."

12 "Look out, it's coming towards me. . . . Quick, quick, do something. . . ."

"Hit it with your knife . . . *your knife*. . . . Go on, hit it. . . ."

Since no one had bothered to explain things to him, Roger was under the mistaken impression that the family were being attacked, and that it was his duty to defend them. As **13** Lugaretzia was the only stranger in the room, he came to the logical conclusion that she must be the responsible party, so he bit her in the ankle. This did not help matters very much.

By the time a certain amount of order had been restored, all the baby scorpions had hidden themselves under various plates and bits of cutlery.[8] Eventually, after impassioned pleas on my part, backed up by Mother, Leslie's suggestion that the whole lot be slaughtered was quashed. While the family, still simmering with rage and fright, retired to the drawing room, I spent half an hour rounding up the babies, picking them up in a teaspoon, and returning them to their mother's back. Then I carried them outside on a saucer and, with the utmost reluctance, released them on the garden wall. Roger and I went and spent the afternoon on the hillside, for I felt it would be **14** prudent to allow the family to have a siesta before seeing them again.

The results of this incident were numerous. Larry developed a phobia about matchboxes and opened them with the utmost caution, a handkerchief wrapped round his hand. Lugaretzia limped around the house, her ankle enveloped in yards of bandage, for

8. **cutlery:** knives, forks, and spoons.

©Quentin Bloxam, Jersey Wildlife Preservation Trust

Gerald Durrell shown with an aye-aye, an endangered primate.

weeks after the bite had healed, and came round every morning, with the tea, to show us how the scabs were getting on. But, from my point of view, the worst repercussion of the whole affair was that Mother decided I was **15** running wild again, and that it was high time I received a little more education.

Reading Check

1. Where did Gerald find the scorpion colony?
2. Where did he put the mother scorpion and her babies?
3. What did Margo do in an attempt to stop the mother scorpion?
4. What did Roger do to the maid?
5. What did Gerald finally do with the scorpions?

CLOSURE
Have students describe in their own words the comic events that follow the scorpions' release from the matchbox. Ask them to point out details that show Durrell's inquiring and affectionate attitude toward animals.

EXTENSION AND ENRICHMENT
Students might narrate the events of the story from the point of view of one of the victims: Larry, perhaps, or Mother or even Roger the dog. A clever student might find the mother scorpion's point of view interesting. In addition, students might like to write **parodies** in which a household riot is caused by another animal. These parodies might begin, ''I grew very fond of these. . . .''

For Study and Discussion

Analyzing and Interpreting the Selection

1. Living with the Durrells was like being in a comic movie. This part of the comedy began when Gerald found the scorpions.   **a.** How did Gerald feel about scorpions?   **b.** Why were his feelings rather unusual?

2. The rest of the family didn't share Gerald's fascination with the scorpions. In a comic sequence, we are told about their reactions. The first one to react was Larry. What did he do?

3a. What did each of the other family members do?   **b.** How did Lugaretzia get bitten in the ankle?

4. From the family's point of view, the scorpion invasion was bad enough. But from Gerald's point of view, what was the worst result of the whole affair?

5. What did Mother fail to realize about the kind of education Gerald was getting on his own?

Focus on Personal Narrative

Using Vivid Verbs and Dialogue

To bring his personal narrative to life, Gerald Durrell uses two techniques that you can apply in your own writing.

First, notice the lively, **vivid verbs** Durrell uses to describe events. Look at the paragraph on page 105, beginning "He uttered a roar of fright...." Here are some of the verbs that make us see this scene full of frenzy: *barking, flying, scattering, thumped, sped, quivering, leaped, overturning, flicked, rolling, peered, hurled, drenched, gasping, swarmed, ran.*

Second, Durrell gives his characters passages of **dialogue,** or direct speech, to make the scene vivid and dramatic. Here are some guidelines to follow when you create dialogue for your own characters in a narrative:

> Use informal language.
> Use "dialogue tags" that show *how* a character speaks: for example, "he complained" or "she murmured."

Write a paragraph in which you narrate a series of related events that you remember from your own experience. Use verbs that will help your reader see lively movement. Use dialogue to show the thoughts and feelings of the characters, including your own. Save your writing.

About the Author

Gerald Durrell   (1925–   )

Gerald Durrell is an internationally respected zoologist and naturalist. He was born in India. His lifelong interest in animals began on the Greek island of Corfu, where he lived with his parents for five years before World War II. His books *My Family and Other Animals* (1956), *Birds, Beasts, and Relatives* (1969), and *Fauna and Family* (1978) are about those years.

In 1958 Durrell and his wife founded a zoo on the isle of Jersey in the English Channel, which they devote to the conservation of endangered species. He has led zoological expeditions to places all over the world, including Cameroon, Sierra Leone, Nigeria, Argentina, Paraguay, Mexico, New Zealand, and India. At the end of his novel *The Mockery Bird* (1981), Durrell expresses his purpose as a naturalist: "We are pleading on behalf of these plants and creatures because they cannot plead for themselves, and it is, after all, your world which we are asking you to preserve." His other works include *The Overloaded Ark* (1958), *A Zoo in My Luggage* (1960), *A Bevy of Beasts* (1973), *Ark on the Move* (1983), and *The Aye-Aye and I* (1992).

FOR STUDY AND DISCUSSION
1a. Gerald was very fond of scorpions and interested in their behavior. **1b.** Most people find scorpions frightening.
2. He roared with fright and shook scorpion and her babies off his hand.
3a. Leslie jumped up, overturned his chair, and flicked napkin at scorpions. Margo screamed and hurled glass of water at them, drenching her mother instead. Mother lost breath and sat gasping. **3b.** Dog bit her, thinking she was a stranger attacking family.
4. His mother decided that it was ''high time'' he received ''a little more education.''
5. He was learning much about zoology and forming excellent habits of study, including the skill of careful observation.

FOCUS ON PERSONAL NARRATIVE
To help students with their narrative passages, ask the class to suggest all the vivid verbs, in addition to the ones in the text, that can be used in place of *go.* Write their suggestions on the chalkboard. Then do the same for *say.* You might have students create on butcher paper a master list of vivid verbs for each overused verb and post these in the classroom. Encourage students to use these verbs in their paragraphs.

ABOUT THE AUTHOR
Durrell's first zoological trip, in 1947–48, was to the rain forests of the British Cameroons where he collected over one hundred crates of mammals, reptiles, and birds for English zoos. *The Overloaded Ark* is an account of this trip. He began writing to finance his expeditions.

The overall aim is for students to analyze the main characters' **conflicts** and the development of these characters throughout the story. For a complete list of objectives, see the **Teacher's Notes**.

The underlined words are in the Glossary. The **Language and Vocabulary** exercise on p. 121 gives students practice in using context clues to define words.

Ask students to recall "The Apprentice." How did Peg's collie teach her a lesson on responsibility? Encourage students to share similar experiences they have had with pets.

TEACHING RESOURCES B

Teacher's Notes, p. 54
Reading Check, p. 57
Study Guide, p. 59
Language Skills, p. 62
Building Vocabulary, p. 66
Selection Test, p. 68

PREREADING FOCUS

The headnote focuses on Kennie's dilemma, his desires, and his hopes. It also foreshadows the resolution of the story. Ask volunteers to share their own or others' experiences with failure and disappointment and how they overcame that failure.

My Friend Flicka

1

Characterization. Kennie's father is a no-nonsense sort. His comment is sarcastic.

2 Analyzing
Making Inferences
What does the author mean by this statement about Kennie? What might be inferred about Kennie from this line? Kennie is not only upset by this episode but also he apparently has a history of taking unpleasant situations to heart. Responses will vary to the second question. Kennie is a sensitive boy, a fact that will be important later in story.

3

Imagery. Author uses poetic language to describe the colors, details, and **atmosphere** of the **setting**.

4

"Disgusted" is a particularly strong indication of **conflict** between father and son.

My Friend Flicka

MARY O'HARA

Kennie never seemed to do anything right. "If I could have a colt all for my own," he said, "I might do better."

Report cards for the second semester were sent out soon after school closed in mid-June.

Kennie's was a shock to the whole family.

"If I could have a colt all for my own," said Kennie, "I might do better."

1 Rob McLaughlin glared at his son. "Just as a matter of curiosity," he said, "how do you go about it to get a *zero* in an examination? Forty in arithmetic; seventeen in history! But a *zero*? Just as one man to another, what goes on in your head?"

"Yes, tell us how you do it, Ken," chirped Howard.

"Eat your breakfast, Howard," snapped his mother.

Kennie's blond head bent over his plate until his face was almost hidden. His cheeks burned.

McLaughlin finished his coffee and pushed his chair back. "You'll do an hour a day on your lessons all through the summer."

Nell McLaughlin saw Kennie wince as if something had actually hurt him.

Lessons and study in the summertime, when the long winter was just over and there weren't hours enough in the day for all the things he wanted to do!

2 Kennie took things hard. His eyes turned to the wide-open window with a look almost of despair.

The hill opposite the house, covered with arrow-straight jack pines, was sharply etched in the thin air of the eight-thousand-foot alti-
3 tude. Where it fell away, vivid green grass ran up to meet it; and over range and upland poured the strong Wyoming sunlight that stung everything into burning color. A big jack rabbit sat under one of the pines, waving his long ears back and forth.

Ken had to look at his plate and blink back tears before he could turn to his father and say carelessly, "Can I help you in the corral with the horses this morning, Dad?"

"You'll do your study every morning before you do anything else." And McLaughlin's scarred boots and heavy spurs clattered across
4 the kitchen floor. "I'm disgusted with you. Come, Howard."

Howard strode after his father, nobly refraining from looking at Kennie.

"Help me with the dishes, Kennie," said Nell McLaughlin as she rose, tied on a big apron, and began to clear the table.

Kennie looked at her in despair. She poured steaming water into the dishpan and sent him for the soap powder.

"If I could have a colt," he muttered again.

"Now get busy with that dish towel, Ken. It's eight o'clock. You can study till nine and then go up to the corral. They'll still be there."

At supper that night, Kennie said, "But Dad, Howard had a colt all of his own when he was only eight. And he trained it and schooled it all

MOTIVATIONAL SUMMARY

Kennie McLaughlin wants a colt that is all his own. His father thinks Kennie is too irresponsible, but he finally gives in. Kennie chooses a feisty yearling—no horse of the colt's line has ever been successfully broken.

PRESENTATION

O'Hara's story is delightful reading for your students. Like the other selections in this unit, there is an underlying **theme** in "My Friend Flicka." Even when old and young (father and son) are so much alike, conflicts can arise. O'Hara's major emphasis, however, is placed on the maturation of the **protagonist,** Kennie, and on his filly, Flicka. Through the repeated use of comparisons, O'Hara shows how the blossoming relationship between Kennie and Flicka changes both of them.

himself; and now he's eleven and Highboy is three, and he's riding him. I'm nine now, and even if you did give me a colt now, I couldn't catch up to Howard because I couldn't ride it till it was a three-year-old and then I'd be twelve."

5 Nell laughed, "Nothing wrong with that arithmetic."

But Rob said, "Howard never gets less than seventy-five average at school, and hasn't disgraced himself and his family by getting more **6** demerits than any other boy in his class."

Kennie didn't answer. He couldn't figure it out. He tried hard; he spent hours poring over his books. That was supposed to get you good **7** marks, but it never did. Everyone said he was bright; why was it that when he studied he didn't learn? He had a vague feeling that perhaps he looked out the window too much, or looked through the walls to see clouds and sky and hills and wonder what was happening out there. Sometimes it wasn't even a wonder but just a pleasant drifting feeling of nothing at all, as if nothing mattered, as if there was always plenty of time, as if the lessons would get done of themselves. And then the bell would ring and study period was over.

If he had a colt . . .

When the boys had gone to bed that night, Nell McLaughlin sat down with her overflowing mending basket and glanced at her husband.

He was at his desk as usual, working on account books and inventories.

8 Nell threaded a darning needle and thought, "It's either that whacking big bill from the vet for the mare that died or the last half of the tax bill."

It didn't seem just the auspicious moment to plead Kennie's cause. But then, these days, **9** there was always a line between Rob's eyes and a harsh note in his voice.

"Rob," she began.

He flung down his pencil and turned around.

"That law!" he exclaimed.

"What law?"

"The state law that puts high taxes on pedigreed stock. I'll have to do as the rest of 'em do—drop the papers."

"Drop the papers! But you'll never get decent prices if you don't have registered horses."

"I don't get decent prices now."

"But you will someday, if you don't drop the papers."

10 "Maybe." He bent again over the desk.

Rob, thought Nell, was a lot like Kennie himself. He set his heart. Oh, how stubbornly he set his heart on just some one thing he wanted above everything else. He had set his heart on horses and ranching way back when he had been a crack rider at West Point; and he had resigned and thrown away his army career just for the horses. Well, he'd got what he wanted.

She drew a deep breath, snipped her thread, laid down the sock, and again looked across at her husband as she unrolled another length of darning cotton.

To get what you want is one thing, she was thinking. The three-thousand-acre ranch and the hundred head of horses. But to make it pay—for a dozen or more years they had been trying to make it pay. People said ranching hadn't paid since the beef barons ran their herds on public land; people said the only prosperous ranchers in Wyoming were the **11** dude ranchers; people said . . .

But suddenly she gave her head a little rebel-**12** lious, gallant shake. Rob would always be fighting and struggling against something, like Kennie, perhaps like herself too. Even those first years when there was no water piped into the house, when every day brought a new difficulty or danger, how she had loved it! How she still loved it!

5
Characterization. Mother's sense of humor during potentially tense situation indicative of her optimistic character. She is voice of compassion and compromise.

6
"Demerits" are assigned as punishment for inappropriate behavior.

7
Conflict. Kennie experiences internal conflict between his desire for freedom and constraints of school and expectations.

8
Darning: method of mending socks by weaving over the hole with thread.

9
Father preoccupied and beleaguered with business of ranching.

10
Father's hope for better future suggests parallel between him and Kennie. Father also frustrated by **conflict** between his desires and constraints of outside world.

11
"Dude ranchers" enhance their profits by lodging guests, giving riding lessons, and renting horses for pleasure riding.

12
Another indication that Kennie and his father are similar to each other.

MEETING INDIVIDUAL NEEDS
Visual, Auditory, and Kinesthetic Learners •
To help students unravel the conflicts in the story, you might use an approach that appeals to students with various learning styles. Ask students to make tagboard name cards for the characters in the story—Kennie; Rob McLaughlin, his father; Howard, his brother; Flicka; Nell McLaughlin, his mother—and one labeled "Other Problems."

Have kinesthetic learners select two cards, display them for the class, and pantomime the conflict that exists. Auditory learners might make suggestions as to why each conflict exists. (For example, Kennie versus his brother could be a conflict related to sibling rivalry, a difference in personalities, or an age difference.) Visual learners will benefit from watching the pantomime

13
Author draws parallel between Kennie and colt. Kennie is in fact "colt" of sorts who needs to be trained and to mature.

14
Foreshadowing. Mother's theory is prophetic. Ownership and responsibility for horse will indeed "make a big difference in him."

15 Summarizing
Comparing/Contrasting
What is Rob's attitude toward Kennie? How does his attitude contrast with the mother's?
Rob has no confidence in Kennie; he seems rather harsh. Mother is more compassionate and much less willing to give up on Kennie.

16
Irony. Rob previously spoke highly of Howard's ability to take responsibility. In his disciplining of Howard, he seems to reverse himself. Ironic that the son Rob deems most capable and responsible shows irresponsibility.

17
Merely planning to get horse causes change in Kennie. Suddenly he is center of attention on ranch, a position he never experienced before.

She ran the darning ball into the toe of a sock, Kennie's sock. The length of it gave her a shock. Yes, the boys were growing up fast, and now Kennie—Kennie and the colt . . . **13**

After a while she said, "Give Kennie a colt, Rob."

"He doesn't deserve it." The answer was short. Rob pushed away his papers and took out his pipe.

"Howard's too far ahead of him; older and bigger and quicker and his wits about him, and . . ."

"Ken doesn't half try, doesn't stick at anything."

She put down her sewing. "He's crazy for a colt of his own. He hasn't had another idea in his head since you gave Highboy to Howard."

"I don't believe in bribing children to do their duty."

"Not a bribe." She hesitated.

"No? What would you call it?"

She tried to think it out. "I just have a feeling Ken isn't going to pull anything off, and"—her eyes sought Rob's—"it's time he did. It isn't the school marks alone, but I just don't want things to go on any longer with Ken never coming out at the right end of anything."

"I'm beginning to think he's just dumb."

"He's not dumb. Maybe a little thing like this—if he had a colt of his own, trained him, rode him . . ." **17**

Rob interrupted. "But it isn't a little thing, nor an easy thing, to break and school a colt the way Howard has schooled Highboy. I'm not going to have a good horse spoiled by Ken's careless ways. He goes woolgathering. He never knows what he's doing."

14 "But he'd *love* a colt of his own, Rob. If he could do it, it might make a big difference in him."

15 "*If* he could do it! But that's a big if."

At breakfast next morning, Kennie's father said to him, "When you've done your study, come out to the barn. I'm going in the car up to section twenty-one this morning to look over the brood mares.[1] You can go with me."

"Can I go too, Dad?" cried Howard.

16 McLaughlin frowned at Howard. "You turned Highboy out last evening with dirty legs."

Howard wriggled. "I groomed him. . . ."

"Yes, down to his knees."

"He kicks."

"And whose fault is that? You don't get on his back again until I see his legs clean."

The two boys eyed each other, Kennie secretly triumphant and Howard chagrined.[2] McLaughlin turned at the door, "And, Ken, a week from today I'll give you a colt. Between now and then you can decide what one you want."

Kennie shot out of his chair and stared at his father. "A—a—spring colt, Dad, or a yearling?"

McLaughlin was somewhat taken aback, but his wife concealed a smile. If Kennie got a yearling colt, he would be even up with Howard.

"A yearling colt, your father means, Ken," she said smoothly. "Now hurry with your lessons. Howard will wipe."

Kennie found himself the most important personage on the ranch. Prestige lifted his head, gave him an inch more of height and a bold stare, and made him feel different all the way through. Even Gus and Tim Murphy, the ranch hands, were more interested in Kennie's choice of a colt than anything else.

Howard was fidgety with suspense. "Who'll you pick, Ken? Say—pick Doughboy, why don't you? Then when he grows up, he'll be sort of twins with mine, in his name anyway. Doughboy, Highboy, see?"

---

1. **brood mares:** female horses kept for breeding.
2. **chagrined** (shə-grĭnd′): embarrassed.

110

MEETING INDIVIDUAL NEEDS

ESL/LEP • To facilitate comprehension, have students target vocabulary that refers to horses. Which words pertain to the age of the horse? Which are specific to gender? Which word describes the coloring of the horse? Write these terms on the chalkboard and, if necessary, provide definitions. Students' vocabulary "maps" should include the following words: *colt, spring (colt), mare, stallion, filly, sorrel,* and *pony*.

Scenes on pages 111, 113, 115, and 118 from the film *My Friend Flicka*.

The boys were sitting on the worn wooden step of the door which led from the tack room into the corral, busy with rags and polish, shining their bridles.

Ken looked at his brother with scorn. Doughboy would never have half of Highboy's speed.

"Lassie, then," suggested Howard. "She's black as ink, like mine. And she'll be fast. . . ."

18 "Dad says Lassie'll never go over fifteen hands."[3]

Nell McLaughlin saw the change in Kennie and her hopes rose. He went to his books in the morning with determination and really studied. A new alertness took the place of the day-**19** dreaming. Examples in arithmetic were neatly written out, and, as she passed his door before breakfast, she often heard the monotonous drone of his voice as he read his American history aloud.

20 Each night, when he kissed her, he flung his arms around her and held her fiercely for a moment, then, with a winsome and blissful smile into her eyes, turned away to bed.

21 He spent days inspecting the different bands of horses and colts. He sat for hours on the corral fence, very important, chewing straws. He rode off on one of the ponies for half the day, wandering through the mile-square pastures that ran down toward the Colorado border.

And when the week was up, he announced his decision. "I'll take that yearling filly of Rocket's. The sorrel[4] with the cream tail and mane.

His father looked at him in surprise. "The one that got tangled in the barbed wire?— that's never been named?"

22 In a second all Kennie's new pride was gone. He hung his head defensively. "Yes."

"You've made a bad choice, Son. You couldn't have picked a worse."

"She's fast, Dad. And Rocket's fast. . . ."

23 "It's the worst line of horses I've got. There's never one among them with real sense. The mares are hellions[5] and the stallions outlaws; they're untamable."

"I'll tame her."

Rob guffawed. "Not I, nor anyone, has ever really been able to tame any one of them."

Kennie's chest heaved.

"Better change your mind, Ken. You want a horse that'll be a real friend to you, don't you?"

"Yes"—Kennie's voice was unsteady.

---

3. **fifteen hands:** 60 inches (about 150 centimeters) in height.

4. **sorrel:** a horse of reddish-brown color.
5. **hellions:** troublemakers.

VISUAL CONNECTIONS
Exploring the Subject
Ask students how the boy in the photograph compares to the mental pictures of Kennie they have formed.

18 Expressing an Opinion
Why does Kennie disregard his brother's suggestions? Responses will vary. While brother encourages Kennie to choose horse most like his own, Kennie resists because he longs to differentiate himself from his brother.

19
Apparently mother's theory was correct: New responsibility of choosing horse and satisfaction of having wish fulfilled have caused Kennie to change for the better.

20 Analyzing
Why does Kennie act so lovingly? Responses will vary. Perhaps he is aware of mother's role in his receiving horse and is showing gratitude for her confidence.

21
Characterization. Indicative of Kennie's new attitude about himself—his self-esteem is increasing.

22
Pride disappears because father's line of questioning causes Kennie to anticipate father's characteristic disapproval.

23
Conflict. Father's comments mirror his attitude toward Kennie, thereby strengthening parallel between Kennie and colt.

MEETING INDIVIDUAL NEEDS
ESL/LEP • Encourage students to pay special attention to Gus's speech. The author has used phonetic spelling to approximate the way Gus's Swedish accent sounds when he talks. Challenge students to identify the phonetically
spelled words and give their standard spellings. You might want to frame this activity as a game or a scavenger hunt. Afterwards, write the variations with corresponding standard forms on the chalkboard.

24

Theme. Passage highlights one theme of story that love, understanding, and loyalty inspire great change. Love, as exemplified by mother's love for Ken and Ken's love for colt, makes a "difference."

25

Subtle parallel between colt and Ken, who are both wavering.

26

Dialect. Author creates Swedish accent to add dimension to **characterization** of Gus.

Making Generalizations
27 Making Inferences

What is the tone of Ken's announcement? What might be inferred about Ken from his manner here? He is confident and assertive. Responses to the second question will vary. It might be inferred that Kennie is changing from wavering, unconfident little boy into more self-assured young man.

28

Imagery. Lyrical **description** of Flicka in wild, natural **setting** makes her seem magical and sends Ken into his dream world. Image sets up contrast between free Flicka and corralled Flicka.

29

Kennie reverts to daydreaming. Detail emphasizes reality that changes in attitudes, personality, and behavior are not automatic and sudden. On path to maturity, Kennie backslides.

"Well, you'll never make a friend of that filly. **27** She's all cut and scarred up already with tearing through barbed wire after that no-good mother of hers. No fence'll hold 'em. . . ."

"I know," said Kennie, still more faintly.

"Change your mind?" asked Howard briskly. "No."

Rob was grim and put out. He couldn't go back on his word. The boy had to have a reasonable amount of help in breaking and taming the filly, and he could envision precious hours, whole days, wasted in the struggle.

Nell McLaughlin despaired. Once again Ken seemed to have taken the wrong turn and **28** was back where he had begun, stoical, silent, defensive.

24 But there was a difference that only Ken could know. The way he felt about his colt. The way his heart sang. The pride and joy that filled him so full that sometimes he hung his **29** head so they wouldn't see it shining out of his eyes.

He had known from the very first that he would choose that particular yearling because he was in love with her.

The year before, he had been out working with Gus, the big Swedish ranch hand, on the irrigation ditch, when they had noticed Rocket standing in a gully on the hillside, quiet for once and eyeing them cautiously.

"Ay bet she got a colt," said Gus, and they walked carefully up the draw.[6] Rocket gave a wild snort, thrust her feet out, shook her head wickedly, then fled away. And as they reached **25** the spot, they saw standing there the wavering, pinkish colt, barely able to keep its feet. It gave a little squeak and started after its mother on crooked, wobbling legs.

26 "Yee whiz! Luk at de little *flicka!*" said Gus.

"What does *flicka* mean, Gus?"

"Swedish for 'little gurl,' Ken. . . ."

6. **draw:** gully.

Ken announced at supper, "You said she'd never been named. I've named her. Her name is Flicka."

The first thing to do was to get her in. She was running with a band of yearlings on the saddleback,[7] cut with ravines and gullies, on section twenty.

They all went out after her, Ken, as owner, on old Rob Roy, the wisest horse on the ranch.

Ken was entranced to watch Flicka when the wild band of youngsters discovered that they were being pursued and took off across the mountain. Footing made no difference to her. **28** She floated across the ravines, always two lengths ahead of the others. Her pink mane and tail whipped in the wind. Her long, delicate legs had only to aim, it seemed, at a particular spot for her to reach it and sail on. She seemed to Ken a fairy horse.

He sat motionless, just watching and holding Rob Roy in, when his father thundered past on Sultan and shouted, "Well, what's the matter? Why didn't you turn 'em?"

Kennie woke up and galloped after.

Rob Roy brought in the whole band. The corral gates were closed, and an hour was spent shunting the ponies in and out through the chutes, until Flicka was left alone in the small round corral in which the baby colts were branded. Gus drove the others away, out of the gate, and up the saddleback.

But Flicka did not intend to be left. She hurled herself against the poles which walled the corral. She tried to jump them. They were seven feet high. She caught her front feet over the top rung, clung, scrambled, while Kennie held his breath for fear the slender legs would be caught between the bars and snapped. Her hold broke; she fell over backward, rolled, screamed, tore around the corral. Kennie had

7. **saddleback:** a hill or ridge with a depression at the top, like the back of a horse that has worn a saddle too long.

This scene is one of great **conflict**—Flicka fights for her freedom, and Kennie struggles to prove to his father that the horse is not worthless. During this tense episode, reader should be able to guess, based on their previous behavior, what is going through Kennie's mind and what the father is thinking. Have students write a paragraph from either Kennie's or his father's viewpoint in which they capture the sights, sounds, and smells of the scene as well as the character's inner thoughts during the episode.

a sick feeling in the pit of his stomach, and his father looked disgusted.

30 One of the bars broke. She hurled herself again. Another went. She saw the opening and, as neatly as a dog crawls through a fence, inserted her head and forefeet, scrambled through, and fled away, bleeding in a dozen places.

As Gus was coming back, just about to close the gate to the upper range, the sorrel whipped through it, sailed across the road and ditch with her inimitable floating leap, and **31** went up the side of the saddleback like a jack rabbit.

From way up the mountain, Gus heard **32** excited whinnies, as she joined the band he had just driven up, and the last he saw of them they were strung out along the crest running like deer.

"Yee whiz!" said Gus, and stood motionless and staring until the ponies had disappeared over the ridge. Then he closed the gate, remounted Rob Roy, and rode back to the corral.

Rob McLaughlin gave Kennie one more chance to change his mind. "Last chance, Son. Better pick a horse that you have some hope of riding one day. I'd have got rid of this whole line of stock if they weren't so fast that I've had the fool idea that some day there might turn out one gentle one in the lot—and I'd have a racehorse. But there's never been one so far, and it's not going to be Flicka."

"It's not going to be Flicka," chanted Howard.

"Perhaps she *might* be gentled," said Kennie; and Nell, watching, saw that although his lips quivered, there was fanatical determination in his eye.

"Ken," said Rob, "it's up to you. If you say you want her, we'll get her. But she wouldn't be

30

Style. Language used to mimic action of Flicka's escape. First three short, choppy sentences indicate separate actions. Last long, flowing sentence creates effect of continuous, frenzied action.

31

Simile. Flicka's running style and swiftness compared to that of jack rabbit, suggesting Flicka is wild animal. Reminiscent of mention of jack rabbit as part of rustic **setting** described earlier in story (p. 108).

32

Kennie's statement about Flicka reminiscent of his earlier statement about himself, "I might do better" (p. 108). **Repetition** of phrase strengthens connection between Kennie and Flicka.

My Friend Flicka **113**

READING SKILLS PRACTICE
The underlined passage can be used to give students practice in the reading skill of determining the sequence of events. Ask students to read the passage, paying attention to the events that occur. Then ask students to identify the event which occurs immediately before Flicka shoots into the air. **A.** She turned when she reached the south pasture boundary. (Incorrect. This is the first event in the passage.) **B.** She raced south toward the range. (Correct.) **C.** She narrowly missed the barn. (Irrelevant. This contradicts details in the passage.) **D.** She investigated all possibilities. (Incorrect. This does not occur immediately before the event.)

33 Analyzing

What does Rob mean? Responses will vary. He is giving Kennie last chance to change his mind and telling him that there will be no more chances or choices. Trying to break Flicka may cost her life.

34
Suspense. Just as readers believe Flicka is captured for good, this detail leads them to believe she has escaped again.

35
Foreshadowing. These three statements together hint at what will happen next. All three statements are correct: She is like her mother and will go through the wire; she will try to jump the wire; and she will not be able to do so.

36
Use to answer **study question 4b,** p. 121.

37
Imagery. Description of Flicka's motions and appearance suggestive of wild animal snared in hunter's trap.

---

the first of that line to die rather than give in. They're beautiful and they're fast, but let me tell you this, young man, they're *loco!*"[8]

Kennie flinched under his father's direct glance.

33 "If I go after her again, I'll not give up whatever comes, understand what I mean by that?"

"Yes."

"What do you say?"

"I want her."

They brought her in again. They had better luck this time. She jumped over the Dutch half door of the stable and crashed inside. The men slammed the upper half of the door shut and she was caught.

The rest of the band were driven away, and Kennie stood outside the stable, listening to the wild hoofs beating, the screams, the crashes. His Flicka inside there! He was drenched with perspiration.

"We'll leave her to think it over," said Rob when dinnertime came. "Afterward, we'll go up and feed and water her."

34 But when they went up afterward there was no Flicka in the barn. One of the windows, higher than the mangers, was broken.

The window opened into a pasture an eighth of a mile square, fenced in barbed wire six feet high. Near the stable stood a wagonload of hay. When they went around the back of the stable to see where Flicka had hidden herself, they found her between the stable and the hay wagon, eating.

At their approach she leaped away, then headed east across the pasture.

35 "If she's like her mother," said Rob, "she'll go right through the wire."

"Ay bet she'll go over," said Gus. "She yumps like a deer."

"No horse can jump that," said McLaughlin.

Kennie said nothing because he could not

8. *loco:* the Spanish word for "crazy."

speak. It was, perhaps, the most terrible moment of his life. He watched Flicka racing toward the eastern wire.

A few yards from it, she swerved, turned, and raced diagonally south.

"It turned her! It turned her!" cried Kennie, almost sobbing. It was the first sign of hope for Flicka. "Oh, Dad! She has got sense. She has! She has!"

▶Flicka turned again as she met the southern boundary of the pasture; again at the northern; she avoided the barn. Without abating anything of her whirlwind speed, following a precise, accurate calculation and turning each time on a dime, she investigated every possibility. Then, seeing that there was no hope, she raced south toward the range where she had spent her life, gathered herself, and shot into the air. ◀

Each of the three men watching had the impulse to cover his eyes, and Kennie gave a sort of howl of despair.

36 Twenty yards of fence came down with her as she hurled herself through. Caught on the upper strands, she turned a complete somersault, landing on her back, her four legs dragging the wire down on top of her, and tangling herself in them beyond hope of escape.

"Blasted wire!" said McLaughlin. "If I could afford decent fences . . ."

Kennie followed the men miserably as they walked to the filly. **37** They stood in a circle, watching while she kicked and fought and thrashed until the wire was tightly wound and knotted about her, cutting, piercing, and tearing great three-cornered pieces of flesh and hide. At last she was unconscious, streams of blood running on her golden coat, and pools of crimson widening and spreading on the grass beneath her.

With the wire cutter which Gus always carried in the hip pocket of his overalls, he cut all the wire away, and they drew her into the pasture, repaired the fence, placed hay, a box of oats, and a tub of water near her, and called it a day.

38 "I don't think she'll pull out of it," said McLaughlin.

Next morning Kennie was up at five, doing his lessons. At six he went out to Flicka.

She had not moved. Food and water were untouched. She was no longer bleeding, but **39** the wounds were swollen and caked over.

Kennie got a bucket of fresh water and poured it over her mouth. Then he leaped away, for Flicka came to life, scrambled up, got her balance, and stood swaying.

Kennie went a few feet away and sat down to watch her. When he went into breakfast, she **40** had drunk deeply of the water and was mouthing the oats.

There began, then, a sort of recovery. She ate, drank, limped about the pasture; stood for hours with hanging head and weakly splayed-out[9] legs, under the clump of cottonwood trees.

9. **splayed-out:** spread outward.

The swollen wounds scabbed and began to heal.

Kennie lived in the pasture, too. He followed her around; he talked to her. He too lay snoozing or sat under the cottonwoods; and often, coaxing her with hand outstretched, he walked very quietly toward her. But she would not let him come near her.

Often she stood with her head at the south fence, looking off to the mountain. It made the tears come to Kennie's eyes to see the way she longed to get away.

Still Rob said she wouldn't pull out of it. There was no use putting a halter on her. She had no strength.

One morning, as Ken came out of the house, Gus met him and said, "De filly's down."

Kennie ran to the pasture, Howard close behind him. The right hind leg, which had been badly swollen at the knee joint, had opened in a festering wound, and Flicka lay flat and motionless, with staring eyes.

"Don't you wish now you'd chosen Dough-boy?" asked Howard.

tle. She stood with her head hanging, but when he stroked it and talked to her, she pressed her face into his chest and was content. He could feel the burning heat of her body. It didn't seem possible that anything so thin could be alive.

Presently Kennie saw Gus come into the pasture, carrying the Marlin. When he saw Ken, he changed his direction and sauntered along as if he were out to shoot some cottontails.

Ken ran to him. "When are you going to do it, Gus?"

"Ay was goin' down soon now, before it got dark. . . ."

51 "Gus, don't do it tonight. Wait till morning. Just one more night, Gus."

"Vell, in de morning, den, but it got to be done, Ken. Yer fader gives de order."

"I know. I won't say anything more."

An hour after the family had gone to bed, Ken got up and put on his clothes. It was a warm moonlit night. He ran down to the brook, calling softly, "Flicka! Flicka!"

But Flicka did not answer with a little nicker, and she was not in the nursery nor hopping about the pasture. Ken hunted for an hour.

At last he found her down the creek, lying in the water. Her head had been on the bank, but as she lay there, the current of the stream had sucked and pulled at her, and she had had no strength to resist; and little by little her head had slipped down until when Ken got there only the muzzle was resting on the bank, and the body and legs were swinging in the stream.

Kennie slid into the water, sitting on the bank, and he hauled at her head. But she was heavy, and the current dragged like a weight; 52 and he began to sob because he had no strength to draw her out.

Then he found a leverage for his heels against some rocks in the bed of the stream, and he braced himself against these and 54 pulled with all his might; and her head came

53 up onto his knees, and he held it cradled in his arms.

He was glad that she had died of her own accord, in the cool water, under the moon, instead of being shot by Gus. Then, putting his face close to hers and looking searchingly into her eyes, he saw that she was alive and looking back at him.

And then he burst out crying and hugged her and said, "Oh, my little Flicka, my little Flicka."

The long night passed.

The moon slid slowly across the heavens.

The water rippled over Kennie's legs and

need for a father figure's approval. Have groups present their quotations and discuss the ideas they represent.

over Flicka's body. And gradually the heat and fever went out of her. And the cool running water washed and washed her wounds.

When Gus went down in the morning with the rifle, they hadn't moved. There they were, Kennie sitting in water over his thighs and hips, with Flicka's head in his arms.

Gus seized Flicka by the head and hauled her out on the grassy bank, and then, seeing that Kennie couldn't move, cold and stiff and half paralyzed as he was, lifted him in his arms and carried him to the house.

"Gus," said Ken through chattering teeth, "don't shoot her, Gus."

"It ain't fur me to say, Ken. You know dat."

"But the fever's left her, Gus."

"Ay wait a little, Ken. . . ."

Rob McLaughlin drove to Laramie to get the **55** doctor, for Ken was in violent chills that would not stop. His mother had him in bed, wrapped in hot blankets, when they got back.

He looked at his father imploringly as the doctor shook down the thermometer.

"She might get well now, Dad. The fever's left her. It went out of her when the moon went down."

"All right, Son. Don't worry. Gus'll feed her, morning and night, as long as she's . . ."

56 "As long as I can't do it," finished Ken happily.

The doctor put the thermometer in his mouth and told him to keep it shut.

All day Gus went about his work, thinking of Flicka. He had not been back to look at her. He had been given no more orders. If she was alive, the order to shoot her was still in effect. But Kennie was ill; McLaughlin, making his second trip to town, taking the doctor home, would not be back till long after dark.

After their supper in the bunkhouse, Gus and Tim walked down to the brook. They did not speak as they approached the filly, lying

stretched out flat on the grassy bank, but their eyes were straining at her to see if she was dead or alive.

She raised her head as they reached her.

"By the powers!" exclaimed Tim; "there she is!"

She dropped her head, raised it again, and moved her legs and became tense as if struggling to rise. But to do so she must use her right hind leg to brace herself against the earth. That was the damaged leg, and at the first bit of pressure with it, she gave up and fell back.

"We'll swing her onto the other side," said Tim. "Then she can help herself."

"Ja. . . ."

Standing behind her, they leaned over, grabbed hold of her left legs, front and back, **57** and gently hauled her over. Flicka was as lax and willing as a puppy. But the moment she found herself lying on her right side, she began to scramble, braced herself with her good left leg, and tried to rise.

"Yee whiz!" said Gus. "She got plenty strength yet."

"Hi!" cheered Tim. "She's up!"

58 But Flicka wavered, slid down again, and lay flat. This time she gave notice that she would not try again by heaving a deep sigh and closing her eyes.

Gus took his pipe out of his mouth and **59** thought it over. Orders or no orders, he would try to save the filly. Ken had gone too far to be let down.

"Ay'm goin' to rig a blanket sling fur her, Tim, and get her on her feet and keep her up."

There was bright moonlight to work by. They brought down the posthole digger and set two aspen poles deep into the ground on either side of the filly, then, with ropes attached to the blanket, hoisted her by a pulley.

Not at all disconcerted, she rested comfortably in the blanket under her belly, touched

55
Kennie has sacrificed own health to save his beloved horse.

56 Analyzing
Drawing Conclusions
What does Kennie mean by this statement? What does this show about him? Responses will vary. Tone of Kennie's response indicates he fully expects Flicka to be alive when he recovers from his own illness, at which time he can care for her again. Indicates his heroic optimism.

57
Simile. Flicka is once again compared to another animal, this time a puppy. Comparison suggests her total helplessness and innocence.

58
Conflict. Flicka is totally exhausted and has given up.

59
Characterization. Gus is understanding, compassionate character, as evidenced by his willingness to disobey orders to aid horse and Kennie.

My Friend Flicka   **119**

Interested students may want to participate in a panel discussion about "the generation gap." Suggest that students present specific examples from the selections in this unit and from their own experiences. Panel discussions may be videotaped or audiotaped. Afterward, have students write paragraphs describing their contributions and self-assessing their participation in the discussion. These can be included in their writing portfolios. (See *Portfolio Assessment and Professional Support Materials,* especially the section entitled **Suggestions for Portfolio Projects.**)

60
Theme. Power of nature and unwavering love and faith combine to heal horse's injuries, Kennie's self-esteem, and rift between father and son.

61
Ken's life has turned around. His dreams have come true.

62 Making Inferences
What might be inferred from this description of Rob? "Strange expression" might be subtle smile, and his eyes might reflect pride he seldom felt or showed before. Father is also changed due to experience with Flicka.

63
Simile. Final comparison of Flicka to another animal, this time a kitten, a very gentle and domestic pet, suggests that Flicka has changed significantly.

READING CHECK
1. Having colt of his own (p. 108).
2. Kennie's mother (p. 110).
3. He has loved her ever since seeing her as a newborn foal (p. 112).
4. By trying to escape through barbed wire fence (p. 114).
5. With poultice his mother prepares (p. 116).

FOR STUDY AND DISCUSSION
1. Kennie gets low grades, always daydreams, and does not stick to anything. Flicka is from worst line of horses and has been cut by barbed wire.

---

her feet on the ground, and reached for the bucket of water Gus held for her.

Kennie was sick a long time. He nearly died. But Flicka picked up. Every day Gus passed the word to Nell, who carried it to Ken. "She's cleaning up her oats.... She's out of the sling. ... She bears a little weight on the bad leg."

Tim declared it was a real miracle. They argued about it, eating their supper.

60 "Na," said Gus. "It was de cold water, washin' de fever outa her. And more dan dot—it was Ken—you tink it don't count? All night dot boy sits dere and says, 'Hold on, Flicka, Ay'm here wid you. Ay'm standin' by, two of us togedder.'...."

Tim stared at Gus without answering, while he thought it over. In the silence, a coyote yapped far off on the plains, and the wind made a rushing sound high up in the jack pines on the hill.

Gus filled his pipe.

"Sure," said Tim finally. "Sure, that's it."

Then came the day when Rob McLaughlin stood smiling at the foot of Kennie's bed and said, "Listen! Hear your friend?"

Ken listened and heard Flicka's high, eager whinny.

"She don't spend much time by the brook any more. She's up at the gate of the corral half the time, nickering for you."

"For me!"

Rob wrapped a blanket around the boy and carried him out to the corral gate.

Kennie gazed at Flicka. There was a look of marveling in his eyes. He felt as if he had been living in a world where everything was dreadful and hurting but awfully real; and *this* couldn't be real; this was all soft and happy, nothing to struggle over or worry about or **61** fight for any more. Even his father was proud of him! He could feel it in the way Rob's big arms held him. It was all like a dream and far away.

He couldn't, yet, get close to anything.

But Flicka—Flicka—alive, well, pressing up to him, recognizing him, nickering...

Kennie put out a hand—weak and white— and laid it on her face. His thin little fingers straightened her forelock the way he used to do, while Rob looked at the two with a strange **62** expression about his mouth and a glow in his eyes that was not often there.

"She's still poor, Dad, but she's on four legs now."

"She's picking up."

Ken turned his face up, suddenly remembering. "Dad! She did get gentled, didn't she?"

63 "Gentle—as—a kitten...."

They put a cot down by the brook for Ken, and boy and filly got well together.

Reading Check

1. What does Kennie believe will help him do better in school?
2. Who persuades Kennie's father to give him a colt?
3. Why does Kennie pick Rocket's yearling filly?
4. How does Flicka injure herself?
5. How does Kennie treat Flicka's infection?

For Study and Discussion

Analyzing and Interpreting the Story

1. In this story, both Kennie and Flicka have to go through long and painful ordeals before they prove themselves to the people around them. Give examples to show how both the boy and filly are considered "misfits" or "losers" when we first meet them.

CLOSURE
Have students identify and analyze details that show the gradual character development of Kennie and his father as well as the change in Flicka. Also, ask them to identify the main conflicts in the story.

EXTENSION AND ENRICHMENT
Students might write before-and-after character sketches of Kennie to show how he changes during the story. Be sure they explain reasons for the changes.
Students interested in reading other stories that feature animals as their subject might enjoy *The Yearling* by Marjorie Kinnan Rawlings, *The Bat-Poet* by Randall Jarrell, and *The Jungle Books* by Rudyard Kipling.

2. Kennie's father tries to get his son to change his mind about Flicka. Why does Kennie insist on his choice?

3. In what ways is Kennie like his father?

4a. What was perhaps "the most terrible moment" in Kennie's life (page 114)? **b.** What happens to Flicka in her leap for freedom?

5. On page 116 you are told: "This was the happiest month of Kennie's life." What makes this time so special for Kennie?

6a. What does Kennie do on the night before the filly is to be shot that proves his love for his "friend" Flicka? **b.** According to Gus, what saved Flicka?

7a. How do we know by the end of the story that Rob McLaughlin has changed his mind about Kennie and Flicka? **b.** How have Kennie and Flicka changed by the end of the story?

Language and Vocabulary

Using Context Clues

1 What context clues in the following sentences help you define the italicized words? Check your answers in a dictionary.

a Nell McLaughlin saw Kennie *wince* as if something had actually hurt him.

b "I'm not going to have a good horse spoiled by Ken's careless ways. He goes *woolgathering*. He never knows what he's doing."

c ...she often heard the monotonous *drone* of his voice as he read his American history aloud.

Focus on Personal Narrative

Reflecting on Meanings

What do you think was the meaning for Ken of his experience with Flicka? What did he learn from the experience, and how did it change him?

When you write a personal narrative, you want to be sure that your audience understands the meaning that the experience you describe has for you. When you **reflect on the meaning** of your experience, you can ask yourself questions like these:

1. What was I like before the experience?
2. How did I change?
3. What did I learn from the experience about myself and others?
4. How did I feel after the experience?

Explore the meaning of a personal experience by filling out a chart like the one below.

Experience: _____		
	Before	**After**
Thoughts:	_____	_____
	_____	_____
Feelings:	_____	_____
	_____	_____
Views of Self and Others:	_____	_____
	_____	_____

About the Author

Mary O'Hara (1885-1980)

Mary O'Hara is a name special to readers of all ages who love horses. She created a classic story of a boy and his horse, *My Friend Flicka,* in 1941. The story grew out of her experiences and impressions while living in Wyoming. A critic wrote that the story "makes you smell the grass and feel the coolness of the wind." She followed its success with two more novels about the Wyoming range country, *Thunderhead, Son of Flicka* and *The Green Grass of Wyoming*, and a diary, *Wyoming Summer*. The three novels were made into successful motion pictures, and *My Friend Flicka* also became a television series. O'Hara was a native of New Jersey. She worked for a time as a screenwriter in California and also composed piano music.

2. Kennie had seen Flicka as foal and fallen in love with her.
3. Both are stubborn in setting their hearts on one thing they want above everything else.
4a. When Kennie watched Flicka race for barbed wire. **4b.** She cuts her flesh terribly as she jumps into barbed wire.
5. He feels that Flicka has become his friend.
6a. He sits in creek all night holding Flicka's head out of water.
6b. Cool running water and Ken's love and loyalty.
7a. Father smiles at Kennie and takes him out to see Flicka in corral. **7b.** Both have proved themselves: Kennie by his steadfastness to a task; Flicka by becoming gentle.

LANGUAGE AND VOCABULARY
1a. *Wince:* to shrink back or grimace as if in pain. Clue is word "hurt."
1b. *Woolgathering:* absent-mindedness or daydreaming. Clue is word "careless."
1c. *Drone:* continuous and monotonous humming sound. Clue is word "monotonous."

FOCUS ON PERSONAL NARRATIVE
Remind students that a personal narrative does not have to be about an earthshaking experience. The narrative can deal with a time when the writer merely came to some simple understanding about life or about himself or herself. Help students by filling out an example chart on the chalkboard. Explore a personal experience they will relate to or an anecdote from one of the stories they have read. If students have difficulty distinguishing between thoughts and feelings, you could lead them in brainstorming a list of words that describe feelings, such as *joyous, envious, lonely, bored, terrified, giddy, content,* and *nervous*.

OBJECTIVES
The overall aim is for students to determine the **theme** of a story.

PRESENTATION
After students have read the introductory material, you might want to use the questions in the text to determine, with students' help, the theme of a popular movie. Students then might find it beneficial to work in small groups and

discuss answers to the questions for each story before they begin work individually. Have students share and explain their theme statements.

MAKING GENERALIZATIONS ABOUT THEME

MAKING GENERALIZATIONS ABOUT THEME
Students are on their way to determining the **theme** of a literary work when they ask the question, "What is it about?" Determining a work's subject is the first step toward being able to state the work's main idea about life or human nature.

Answers
Answers will vary. Possible statements of theme for "The Apprentice": Being mature means realizing that actions have consequences; sometimes it takes personal experience, rather than other people's advice, to teach lessons about the world. Possible statement of theme for "Gentleman of Río en Medio": To be good neighbors, people must maintain their integrity and uphold what is moral, right, and good.

*T*he **theme** of a story is its main idea about life or human nature. Usually, an author does not state the theme of a work directly. Readers must infer or make a reasonable guess about the theme from evidence in the story. When you make a **generalization** about theme, you use a broad statement to sum up a story's significance. Making valid generalizations can help you analyze and appreciate literature better. It can also help you reflect on the meaning of an experience you write about in a personal narrative.

To make valid generalizations, you need to use sufficient, reliable evidence and sound reasoning. To find the theme of a story, first determine the story's central purpose or what the writer is trying to show about human nature. Ask yourself questions such as the following:

- *How have the characters changed through the story?* For example, does an irresponsible character become responsible? Does a coward save someone's life?

- *What major conflicts occur during the story?* Do the conflicts end with characters understanding more about themselves or with your understanding the characters better?
- *Does the title give a clue to the theme?*

After you determine the theme, state it in a complete sentence as a *generalization* about life. This means that the statement will apply to many people, not just to those in the story. For example, the theme of Morley Callaghan's story "A Cap for Steve" (page 78) might be stated as the following generalization: *Winning and keeping the love and respect of a son can prove to be more important to a parent than having money.*

Using the questions on this page as guidelines, state, as a generalization, the theme of either Dorothy Canfield's "The Apprentice" (page 88) or Juan A. A. Sedillo's "Gentleman of Río en Medio" (page 100).

OBJECTIVES
The overall aim is for students to write a narrative about a personal experience that shows the event's meaning to them.

PRESENTATION
Students can find ideas for their personal narratives in the notes they have taken during their study of this unit. You might want to have students work in small groups throughout the stages of the writing process. However, be sensitive to the wishes of students who might feel uncomfortable sharing their personal narratives with peers. As closure, have students identify the steps in the writing process, listing elements especially important to consider when writing personal narratives.

FOCUS ON Writing

WRITING A PERSONAL NARRATIVE

Writing about a personal experience is one of the best ways to find out more about yourself. In a **personal narrative** you tell about an experience that happened to you and show the event's meaning for you.

Prewriting

1. As a subject for your personal narrative, choose an experience

- that was important to you
- that you remember clearly
- that you want to share with others

You may want to use a chart such as the one below to identify possible topics. What associations do the words prompt in your mind? Feel free to use different memory prompts if you wish.

Family _____

Birthday _____

Party _____

School _____

Friend _____

[See **Focus** assignment on page 87.]

2. After you have identified an experience to tell about in your narrative, think about your purpose and audience. Your **purpose** in this kind of writing is to express yourself. Therefore, when you plan your narrative, remember to make notes about your own thoughts and feelings as you experienced events. Your **audience** may be your classmates, your friends, or a group of adults. Think about the background information your audience will need.

3. Start to recall **factual** and **sensory details** for your narrative. You can use techniques like freewriting, clustering, brainstorming, and visualizing. As you jog your memory, make notes on a chart like the one below.

Details Chart	
Events _____	Places _____
_____	_____
_____	_____
People _____	Thoughts/ _____
_____	Feelings _____
	_____

[See **Focus** assignment on page 97.]

4. Arrange your details in **chronological** or **time order.** Plan to use **transitional words and phrases** in your personal narrative. Some useful words include the following: *first, second, then, next, at last,* and *finally.*

5. Reflect on the **overall meaning** that the experience had for you. Ask yourself questions such as the following, and make notes on your answers:

HOLT WRITER'S WORKSHOP

This computer program provides help for all types of writing through guided instruction for each step of the writing process. (Program available separately.)

See *Elements of Writing, Second Course,* Chapter 4, for more instruction on expressive writing.

WRITING A PERSONAL NARRATIVE
Students can avoid many problems with personal narratives by limiting themselves to a single incident. Otherwise, their narratives may only summarize events, and not reflect on them as well.

Prewriting
To help students make sure that they have not left out any important details, you might suggest that they look over their various charts and notes and then use the **5W-How questions** to analyze all the parts of their narratives. Remind students that the stages of the writing process are fluid and that they may need to return to the prewriting stage later.

TRANSPARENCY 10

Writing Process
Writing a Personal Narrative – helps students plan and write an effective personal narrative.

- What was I like before the experience?
- What did I learn from the experience about myself and others?
- How did I feel after the experience?

[See **Focus** assignment on page 121.]

Writing

1. Follow an outline like the one below to write your narrative.

 I. Introduction
  A. Grab reader's attention
  B. Give any necessary background information
 II. Body
  A. Event 1: Give details about event, people, places; describe your thoughts and feelings
  B. Event 2: Give details about event, people, places; describe your thoughts and feelings
  C. Event 3: Give details about event, people, places; describe your thoughts and feelings
  D. Possibly more events
 III. Conclusion: Tell meaning of experience

2. Use **vivid verbs** and **dialogue** to make your narrative more graphic and lifelike. Lively verbs help readers to *see* the action. Dialogue can help you to *show* events and characters, rather than merely *tell* about them. Here are some guidelines to use when you create dialogue:

- Be sure that your dialogue sounds natural—the way people talk in real life.
- Use "dialogue tags" to show *how* a character speaks.

Evaluating and Revising

1. After putting your narrative aside for a while, reread it as objectively as you can. You may want to trade papers with a classmate and then exchange suggestions about each other's writing. Check to see that your narrative reads smoothly. Have you arranged the events in chronological order? Also reread your conclusion. Have you clearly shown the meaning that the personal experience has for you?

2. You may find the following checklist helpful as you revise your narrative.

Checklist for Evaluation and Revision

✓ Do I grab the reader's attention in the introduction?
✓ Do I supply any necessary background?
✓ Are the events arranged in chronological order?
✓ Does the narrative include vivid details that bring the people, places, and events to life?
✓ Do I include details about my own thoughts and feelings?
✓ Do I include comments about the meaning of the experience?

Here is how one writer revised the opening paragraph of a personal narrative.

Writer's Model

It was late Friday afternoon. When

Mom casually referred to my little sis-

ter Gretchen's ~~party~~ *birthday* the following day,

I gulped. *and* ~~The~~ holiday rush in the

stores *turned* ~~made~~ them *into* ~~like~~ sardine cans.

My sister was going to be seven years

old in less than eight hours. *and* I had for-

gotten to buy her a present. I *dashed* ~~went~~

out the door. ¶ "Never put off till tomor-

row what you can do today." One day

last winter, I found out how true that

saying is.

Proofreading and Publishing

1. Proofread your personal narrative and correct any errors you find in grammar, usage, and mechanics. (Here you may find it helpful to refer to the **Handbook for Revision** on pages 712–755.) Then prepare a final version of your narrative by making a clean copy.

2. Consider some of the following publication methods for your narrative:

- share a copy with a trusted friend or relative
- deliver your narrative orally in a story theater for younger students
- send your narrative to the school magazine or newspaper

Portfolio If your teacher approves, you may wish to keep a copy of your work in your writing folder or portfolio.

Evaluating and Revising
Encourage students to read their narratives aloud several times. They might record their stories on an audiocassette and use the **Checklist for Evaluation and Revision** for self-assessment. You might want to use a class period to help students work specifically on **vivid verbs**.

Proofreading and Publishing
Students will probably need to focus on punctuation, capitalization, and paragraphing of dialogue when proofreading this assignment. Students might enjoy creating a class anthology of their narratives to display in the room or share with other classes.

AMERICAN HERITAGE

OVERVIEW OF THE UNIT

This unit invites young readers to step back and view their own country as it is reflected in literature. That reflection goes beyond the dusty images of times gone by to capture the country that has learned to celebrate the diversity of its people. The unit begins with Joseph Bruchac's "Ellis Island"; it ends with the still timely challenge made by Martin Luther King, Jr., in "I Have a Dream." Between lie the perennial favorites: Longfellow's "Paul Revere's Ride," Hale's "The Man Without a Country," Lincoln's Gettysburg Address, Whitman's "O Captain! My Captain!," Johnson's "Too Soon a Woman," and Ferber's "The Oklahoma Land Run." Also featured are familiar folk tales about Paul Bunyan and John Henry as well as Mexican American and American Indian folk tales. Other glimpses of American life outside the cultural mainstream include Ernesto Galarza's *Barrio Boy* and Dwight Okita's "In Response to Executive Order 9066." The total impression is that of a young nation that encompasses a variety of people and experiences.

Questions and activities throughout the unit challenge students to respond more fully to each selection and to practice skills important to close reading and critical thinking—including such higher-level skills as responding to poetic language, drawing inferences and determining purpose, noting details used for authenticity, interpreting an extended metaphor, and sensing the mood and tone created by choice of details and vocabulary.

Each selection can function as a springboard for classroom discussion and writing. Discussions offer students opportunities to sharpen their critical thinking and speaking skills. By enabling students to exchange ideas, discussions can also be one of the best ways to improve students' attitudes toward literature. Sometimes, you may wish to structure discussions around an important aspect of a particular work. At other times, you might allow discussions to develop from questions that arise as students read. Spontaneous discussions are often the most stimulating and enlightening ones for your students.

Formal discussions, such as panel discussions and symposiums, also make excellent class and small-group projects. In a panel discussion, group members discuss an issue or problem in a literary work, such as the theme of patriotism in Edward Everett Hale's "The Man Without a Country." A symposium is similar to a panel discussion except that group members, often presenting opposing viewpoints, give formal presentations on different aspects of a literary work. Either form provides an opportunity for students to think, write, and talk about literature.

Writing activities in the unit focus on persuasive writing but also challenge students to relate fiction to history and to write a tall tale and a ballad. **Focus on Reading and Critical Thinking** provides practice in distinguishing fact from opinion. **Focus on Writing** guides students through the process of writing a persuasive essay.

OBJECTIVES OF THE UNIT

The aims of the unit are for the student:

◆ To demonstrate recognition of themes important to American literature and to identify authors' purposes for writing
◆ To interpret the meanings of poems, addresses, speeches, short stories, and folk tales and to relate these meanings to the overall theme of this unit
◆ To analyze theme, setting, and elements of plot and characterization, in individual selections in this unit
◆ To evaluate a selected author's use of sensory details, historical facts, comparisons, word choices, dialogue, exaggeration, and imagery
◆ To demonstrate recognition of rhythm, onomatopoeia, and figurative language in poems and stories
◆ To make an oral presentation of a well-known American poem
◆ To write a persuasive essay
◆ To write original folk songs and folk tales

CONCEPTS AND SKILLS

The following concepts and skills are treated in this unit:

LITERARY ELEMENTS/TERMS AND TECHNIQUES

Responding to a Narrative Poem   140
Recognizing Figures of Speech   178

OPPORTUNITIES FOR WRITING

Writing About Literature
Relating Fiction to History   166

Creative Writing
Writing a Tall Tale   178
Writing a Ballad   185

Focus on Persuasive Writing
Choosing a Topic   157
Writing an Opinion Statement   172
Thinking About Your Audience   174
Using Logical Appeals   180
Using Emotional Appeals   195

CONNECTIONS

Literature and History   135, 141
Connecting Cultures   185

FOR ORAL READING

Preparing a Presentation   141

FOCUS ON READING AND CRITICAL THINKING

Noting Details that Suggest Authenticity   157
Distinguishing Fact From Opinion   196

PLANNING GUIDE

FOR UNIT PLANNING

- Transparencies 11–17: *Audiovisual Resources Binder*
- *Portfolio Assessment: Professional Support Materials*
- Test Generator
- Mastery Tests: Teaching Resources B, pp. 198, 200
- Analogy Test: Teaching Resources B, p. 205
- Composition Test: Teaching Resources B. p. 206

SELECTION (Pupil's Page)	TEACHING RESOURCES B (page numbers shown below)							AV BINDER
	Teacher's Notes	Reading Check	Study Guide	Language Skills	Building Vocabulary	Selection Vocab. Test	Selection Test	Audio-cassette
AMERICAN HERITAGE *Introduction* (p. 127)	81							
Joseph Bruchac *Ellis Island* (p. 134)	82		83				86	
Henry Wadsworth Longfellow *Paul Revere's Ride* (p. 136)	87		89		91		93	
Edward Everett Hale *The Man Without a Country* (p. 142)	95	98	99, 101	106	106		108	
Abraham Lincoln *The Gettysburg Address* (p. 158)	110		112		120		114	
Walt Whitman *O Captain! My Captain!* (p. 160)	116		118		120			
Dorothy M. Johnson *Too Soon a Woman* (p. 162)	122	124	125	127			130	
Edna Ferber *The Oklahoma Land Run* (p. 167)	131	133	134	137	141	193	143	
Dwight Okita *In Response to Executive Order 9066* (p. 173)	145		146				149	
retold by Maurice Dolbier *Paul Bunyan's Been There* (p.175)	150	152	154		156		158	
retold by Rudolfo A. Anaya *The Deer Thief* (p.179)	160		162	165			167	
retold by Barry Lopez *Coyote Shows How He Can Lie* (p. 181)	160		162	165			167	
Anonymous *John Henry* (p. 183)	168		169				171	
Ernesto Galarza *Barrio Boy* (p. 186)	173	175	176	178	182	193	184	
Martin Luther King, Jr. *I Have a Dream* (p. 192)	189		188		191	193	194	

CONCEPTS AND SKILLS (continued)

FOCUS ON WRITING

Writing a Persuasive Essay   197

TRANSPARENCIES

The following unit support materials with specific correlations to literature selections are available in the **Fine Art and Instructional Transparencies with Teacher's Notes and Blackline Masters** section of your *Audiovisual Resources Binder.*

FINE ART TRANSPARENCIES

Theme: An Emerging Nation and an Evolving People

11 *Life on the Prairie/The Trapper's Defense, "Fire Fight Fire,"* after Arthur F. Tait

12 *Foreigners Sightseeing at Famous Spots in Edo: American Couple at Ryogokee Bridge,* Sadahide

READER RESPONSE

13 Just Wanted to Tell You
14 Put up a Statue
15 What Do You Know?

LITERARY ELEMENTS

16 Imagery

WRITING PROCESS

17 Writing a Persuasive Essay

INTRODUCING THE UNIT

To generate interest in the unit, you may wish to begin with one of these activities:

Ask each student to choose a figure from early American history—such as Abigail Adams, George Washington, Betsy Ross, or John Smith—and to write that person a "letter" reporting the highlights of what has happened in America since colonial times.

Alternatively, you might have each student imagine that he or she has been asked to participate in a space probe by writing an open letter to the unknown inhabitants of a distant galaxy. (Pretend that language is no problem since the unknown recipient will live in civilization that is advanced enough to decipher any language.) The purpose of the letter is to tell how the United States is unique.

In either case, limit letters to two pages and let students form small groups to share what they have written. Each group may then share highlights with the class. Relate these highlights to the introductory comments on p. 127 and suggest that students look for "echoes" of their own images of America as they read the selections in the unit.

Direct students' attention to the photographic essay on pp. 128–133. Discuss with them what "image" of America is suggested by each of these pictures. How do they suggest the country's diversity? You might ask students to add to this photographic essay by bringing additional pictures from magazines. Students might be able to think of an appropriate title for the essay. As a beginning, you may wish to suggest "As American as . . ."

After noting the comments on p. 127, involve the class in describing their images of America. You might display a large map of the United States and let students mark with small personalized flags any cities and towns in which they have lived. Then ask each student to make a poster or collage of pictures that represent life in the hometown he or she knows best. Display and discuss these visual images, noting the similarities and the differences in life in various regions. Keep these posters and collages for reference during the course of the unit.

Observe that the old "melting pot" philosophy has yielded to the idea of preserving ethnic and cultural identity. In what ways is American life enriched by the cultural diversity of American people? In reading throughout the unit, ask students to consider this question and to note examples of such diversity.

You might request that students think of ethnic images as presented in the media, for example, in television programs, current movies, and music. To increase student awareness of cultural diversity, suggest that they collect newspaper articles on various American minority groups and discuss these in class.

Since students' appreciation of these selections is often enhanced by background information that illuminates the text, you may want to incorporate student research into introductory activities for each selection.

Before beginning Longfellow's "Paul Revere's Ride," you may wish to assign several students to present brief reports about the events that led to the ride or about the following encounters with the British at Concord and Lexington.

Before beginning Edward Everett Hale's "The Man Without a Country," you may wish to assign an individual or small-group research project concerning Aaron Burr. Be sure that the oral presentation includes the story of Burr's planned invasion of Mexico that caused Burr to be accused of treason.

Abraham Lincoln's Gettysburg Address might be introduced with student reports on the battle itself and an explanation of why it was so significant to the outcome of the Civil War.

You may wish to introduce Walt Whitman's "O Captain! My Captain!" by explaining that Lincoln was the first American president to be assassinated. The event was devastating to a nation still suffering from a bitter and bloody war. Even Southerners, many of whom had had no great love for Lincoln, were saddened because Lincoln had promised fair treatment to the South. Remind students that the murder of a national leader is always a cause for mourning; it calls for expressions of grief that are both public and personal. In this selection, Whitman gives voice to the nation's pain as well as his own.

You might combine introductory activities for Dorothy M. Johnson's "Too Soon a Woman" and Edna Ferber's "The Oklahoma Land Run." Many students find frontier life fascinating, and they would probably enjoy hearing excerpts from diaries or letters written by pioneers in their own area of the country. Many university presses publish collections of diaries and letters by the area's first European settlers, and your librarian should be able to help you find an appropriate collection. One example is *Covered Wagon Women: Diaries and Letters from the Western Trails, 1840–1849,* Kenneth L. Holmes, ed. (A H Clark, 1983).

To introduce the section on folk tales, you might have students report on folk tales that pertain to their region and then discuss what these tales might reveal about the history of the area.

Before beginning the excerpt from Ernesto Galarza's *Barrio Boy*, students might conduct interviews with family members or other people in the community who immigrated to this country. Students should enjoy learning about immigrant perspectives on American life.

To introduce Martin Luther King, Jr.'s "I Have a Dream," have students present reports on the 1963 March on Washington. They might research newspaper articles that appeared at the time or interview parents or others who remember the event in order to learn about contemporary reactions to the speech and to the rally.

Student Learning Options

AMERICAN HERITAGE

1. Dramatizing an Inspection

Between 1880 and 1920, more than twenty million immigrants arrived in the United States, mainly from European countries. After they arrived, they had to endure the inspections at Ellis Island. Students could reenact the inspection process. For example, three official "inspectors" can mark "immigrants" with chalk to identify sickness, and they can form lines of those who are educated, uneducated, without proper documentation, or without good vision. After inspectors have finished grouping immigrants into categories, discuss as a class why these inspections might have been necessary.

2. Making an American Dream Collage

In his speech "I Have a Dream," Martin Luther King, Jr., refers to "the American Dream" and describes his dream for this country to free itself of segregation and discrimination. Ask students to think about their own version of the American dream and to create collages using articles or pictures cut from magazines and newspapers. Students' collages might focus on their own personal dreams for the future or on their dreams for the nation, such as a home for every family. After students have finished, ask each student to explain his or her American dream collage to a partner. Then ask partners to write a comparison/contrast journal entry on the two collages.

3. Learning About an Artist

A small group of students can look in an encyclopedia or art book located in their school library to find the art of George Catlin. Catlin, who traveled through Native American areas between 1830 and 1836, produced more than five hundred paintings. Have the students bring examples of Catlin's art to class. All students can then write descriptive paragraphs, commenting on what they see in the pictures.

4. Presenting History as Drama

Numerous events led to the American Revolution and the subsequent Second Continental Congress and signing of the Declaration of Independence. Students can bring these events to life by working in small groups to create and act out short skits of the following scenarios:

- Thomas Jefferson telling his wife, Martha, he is a delegate to attend the Second Continental Congress in Philadelphia
- The first meeting between John Adams and Thomas Jefferson at the Colonial State House, later known as Independence Hall
- Benjamin Franklin's arrival in Philadelphia in 1775 and a conversation between him and a local shopkeeper who is preparing for war
- John Hancock discussing the signing of the Declaration of Independence with his secretary, Charles Thomson, on July 4, 1776

5. Exploring Medicine of the Civil War

To help students understand the suffering of the soldiers at Gettysburg, ask students to work in small groups to find out what medical procedures and tools were available to treat injuries during the Civil War. For example, amputations were performed with saws, and cuts might have been stitched with any available threadlike material, such as a horse hair. Ask students to present their findings to the class. Some students might want to draw medical instruments and describe their possible uses.

6. Imagining Relocation

Challenge students to imagine that all Americans of their ethnic background are about to be relocated to an internment camp. Have students decide what possessions they would most want to take with them. Ask each student to bring to class the one possession he or she would most want to take and to explain to the class why that possession is so important.

7. Comparing Lifestyles

To help students understand the difficulties and harsh lives of pioneer families, ask them to list all the conveniences of modern-day life they use regularly. Next to these, students should list methods pioneers might have used to achieve the same goals. For example, instead of a washing machine, a pioneer might have used a washboard or some rocks in a stream to do laundry.

8. Creating and Illustrating an Original Folk Tale

Ask students to create their own larger-than-life characters and stories that describe how the characters helped create local land formations. Students should illustrate their stories and use irony and exaggeration to add humor to their tales. Students can share their stories with one another or with an elementary school class.

9. Creating an Agricultural Chart

The Homestead Act of 1862 granted 160 acres of land to any settler who would spend five years on the land. The resulting movement of settlers to the Middle West created an increase in agricultural production. Each student could gather information on this increase in production and create a chart of successful agricultural products and their possible uses. Students could then write short paragraphs explaining the effects of successful agricultural production in this area on the nation as a whole.

Exploring the Subject

An oxbow is a bend in a river that is rounded like the collar an ox wears to support the yoke. Land within such a curve in a river is also called an oxbow, and lakes that are formed when a river changes course are known as oxbow lakes.

About the Artwork

The painting contrasts the ordered rural landscape of the valley, sunny and tranquil, with the turbulent landscape of the highlands, upon which a storm is raging.

About the Artist

Thomas Cole was born in England and came to America when he was nineteen (1820). He was the founder of a group of landscape painters known as the Hudson River school, which lasted from 1825 to 1875. These painters were particularly attracted to the beauty of the rivers and mountains of the New England area.

Cole's paintings, though representative of real landscapes, were often composites of various sketches of the most striking mountains, storms, or trees he could find. He saw the vast grandeur of America as a revelation of God, and it was this mystical vision of nature that he tried to convey in his work.

AMERICAN HERITAGE

The literature in this unit reveals something about how Americans—past and present—have seen themselves and their society. Here are images of heroic people, of national ordeals, of the frontier, and of our institutions. Certain beliefs expressed in these selections have been part of America's heritage for centuries. These are beliefs in independence, tolerance, and personal freedom.

Each of the images on pages 126–133 says something about America's heritage. Try writing a poem or a brief story that connects these different illustrations.

The Oxbow (The Connecticut River near Northampton) (1836) by Thomas Cole (1801–1848). Oil on canvas (08.288).
The Metropolitan Museum of Art, gift of Mrs. Russell Sage, 1908

AMERICAN HERITAGE

Along with nineteenth-century classics that celebrate the nation's beginnings, the unit includes **folk tales, ballads,** and stories of and about ordinary people who worked to settle and develop the country. Twentieth-century selections reveal increasing awareness of and appreciation for the nation's racial and ethnic diversity. Students will find poetry written in response to historical events, stories with distinctive American characters and settings, American folk tales, a ballad, and two speeches that made a difference in American thought. These selections and the picture essay at the beginning of the unit present an overview of the American experience from the nation's founding to the present.

Explain to students that a nation's literary heritage is not static, and that this unit will present an expansive view of what constitutes America's heritage. Invite students to look at the paintings and photographs on pp. 126–133 and to relate them to what they know and believe about America. Give students the opportunity to discuss their responses to these images. Students might also like to respond by writing a poem or story, by drawing their own illustrations, or by compiling a tape recording of musical pieces to express the nation's heritage. Create a class anthology of their finished pieces for display.

Questions and activities throughout the unit challenge students to respond more fully to each selection and to practice important skills of close reading—especially such higher-level skills as responding to poetic language, drawing inferences and determining purpose, noting details used for authenticity, interpreting an extended **metaphor,** and sensing the **mood** and **tone** that choices of details and vocabulary create. The **Focus on Writing** features teach the elements of persuasive writing.

The photo essay on these pages shows important aspects of U.S. heritage. Students may want to compose photo essays showing their family's heritage. Students could use family photos or magazine pictures to create their es-says. Suggest that students include a caption for each image. Photo essays may be displayed in the classroom and then included in student scrapbooks or portfolios. Consult with students in the planning stages to agree on how their essays will be assessed. The photo essay is one of many projects students might complete as part of a contract. (See *Portfolio Assessment and Professional Support Materials* for additional information on student portfolios.)

VISUAL CONNECTIONS

About the Artwork

In *Mission San Carlos de Rio Carmelo,* showing a mission at what is now Carmel, California, wagons are piled high with supplies as two priests and two officers lead a party on an expedition. Missions played an important role in colonizing the New World. This mission was founded in 1770 by Spanish Franciscan missionary Junípero Serra.

The Old House of Representatives shows a semicircular chamber inspired by the shape of classical Roman theaters. The classical influence is also displayed in the columns with their ornate capitals (uppermost portion of the columns). In the center of the chamber, a chandelier, lowered from the ceiling, is being lighted.

About the Artist

Samuel Finley Breese Morse wanted to be known as a painter; however, he is best known for his invention of the telegraph. Born in Massachusetts, he studied in England with well-known artist Benjamin West and today his paintings are to be found in both Europe and the United States. In *The Old House of Representatives,* Morse shows the legislators at candle-lighting time when the evening session begins. The eighty-six figures in the painting represent the actual legislators, all but one of whom were willing to sit for a likeness.

Relating Expression Skills

You might have students sketch other Spanish missions or any buildings they have visited that were important to or representative of periods in American history.

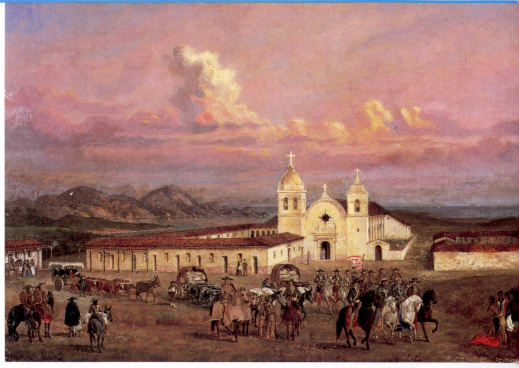

Mission San Carlos de Rio Carmelo by Oriana Day.
Oil on canvas.
By Permission of The Fine Arts Museums of San Francisco, gift of Mrs. Eleanor Martin

The Old House of Representatives (1822)
by Samuel Finley Breese Morse (1791–1872).
Oil on canvas.
The Corcoran Gallery of Art, Museum purchase, Gallery Fund, 1911

During your study of this unit, you might ask students to interpret American experience themselves. To get them started, have them look through the artwork in this introduction to see how American heritage has been represented. Then ask students to plan a related project.

Visual learners could browse through magazines and other picture sources for photographs or illustrations to use in a collage. You might suggest that students use a copier for artwork they cannot cut out or remove. Auditory learners might select recordings that they think represent America's heritage. Kinesthetic learners might enjoy expressing their experience through dance or possibly a dramatic reading.

The Jolly Flatboatmen (1846) by George Caleb Bingham (1811–1879). Oil on canvas.
Private Collection, on loan to the National Gallery of Art, Washington

The County Election (1851–1852) by George Caleb Bingham (1811–1879). Oil on canvas.
The Saint Louis Art Museum, Museum purchase

The Clipper Ship "Flying Cloud" by Frank Vining Smith (1879–1967). Oil on canvas on masonite.
Courtesy of the Seamen's Bank for Savings, FSB

VISUAL CONNECTIONS

About the Artist

George Caleb Bingham was born near the Blue Ridge Mountains in Virginia and, as a child, moved to an area just west of St. Louis, Missouri. After trying numerous trades, Bingham turned to painting as a result of meeting Chester Harding (1792-1866), a frontiersman artist who was in Missouri to do a portrait of Daniel Boone. Bingham, too, began to paint scenes of rugged life on the frontier. As a man who would eventually hold several political offices, Bingham was particularly interested in public elections and painted several pictures capturing the rustic and rowdy activities of election day.

Relating Expression Skills

Flatboats like the the one in *The Jolly Flatboatmen* are flatbottomed boats used to transport goods on inland waterways. You might have students prepare reports for the class about the lives and work of flatboatmen in the 1800s.

Some of the activities depicted in *The County Election* are now prohibited by law at or near polling places (such as drinking, campaigning, loitering). You might have students discuss what they know about present-day elections and how they differ from the election in Bingham's painting.

Life on clipper ships was often harsh and cruel. The view in *The Clipper Ship "Flying Cloud,"* however, is romanticized. You could ask students what elements of the painting contribute to this feeling (for instance, clear sky, soft colors, sails billowing, birds flying).

TRANSPARENCIES 11 & 12

Fine Art

Theme: *An Emerging Nation and an Evolving People* – explores artwork reflecting America's early growth as a nation.

VISUAL CONNECTIONS

About the Artwork

In *Indian Council,* four decorated tepees form an impressive background to the events in the foreground. Feathers played an important role in Indian decoration and ceremonies.

About the Artist

George Catlin, born in Pennsylvania, studied law but decided to become a painter. He spent eight years traveling among Indian tribes in North and South America, sketching and painting them and portraying their ways of life. His determination to record in art these people and their customs made an invaluable contribution to American history.

Relating Expression Skills

You might ask students how *Westward Ho* makes them feel. Does the painting depict moving west as adventurous and romantic? Responses will vary, but the muted colors, the worn look of the men and animals, the scrubby land, and the hazy sky suggest an unromantic life.

Sioux War Council by George Catlin (1796–1872). Oil on canvas.
John F. Eulich Collection, Dallas, Texas

Westward Ho (1867–1868) by Otto Sommer. Oil on canvas.
Private Collection

Cincinnati, Queen of the West in 1876 (1972) by John Stobart (1929–   ).
Oil on canvas.
Private Collection

The Bowery at Night (c. 1895) by W. Louis Sonntag, Jr. (1822–1900).
Watercolor.
The Museum of the City of New York

Exploring the Subject

Cincinnati, on the Ohio River, is an industrial city and also the commercial and cultural center of western Ohio. Its history can be traced back to 1802 when it began as a village in what shortly before had been wilderness. Stobart's *Cincinnati, Queen of the West in 1876* celebrates the astonishing progress made by Americans in the nineteenth century in creating a thriving commercial civilization out of virgin territory. Rivers were the highways of civilization, with the ubiquitous paddle boat providing a relatively rapid form of transportation. As the century progressed, railroads took over this function. They traveled across the rivers on bridges built by ingenious Victorian engineers. The bridge that dominates this picture is a splendid example of their work.

"Bowery" is the Dutch word for estate or farm. The Bowery in New York City was originally the road to Peter Stuyvesant's farm in lower Manhattan. The street and area are still known by the name, and even in 1895, the Bowery was a densely populated, busy area of the city. The painting *The Bowery at Night* dates from the period just before the introduction of the automobile. Transportation was provided by horse-drawn carriages, streetcars, and in larger cities, elevated railroads with steam locomotives. Today in America, most surviving steam locomotives are preserved as tourist attractions and retain a romance about them that diesel locomotives have never been able to capture.

Exploring the Subject

Although no country has laid claim to the moon, the American astronauts who visited the moon in the late sixties and seventies followed the ancient custom of planting the flag. When much of the world was unexplored, this action symbolized the claiming of new territory. American missions to the moon reflected a continuation of the pioneering spirit that was so important in the development of America in the nineteenth century.

Ideas for Writing

You could ask students to imagine what it would be like to walk on the moon as Mitchell does in the photograph. They might then write short essays describing how they think they would feel upon their return to Earth.

Students who have played baseball in both places might enjoy writing essays describing the differences between playing with friends on an empty lot, as in Fasanella's *Sandlot Game,* and playing an organized game on a real baseball field. Is the sense of competition as strong in a sandlot game? Which is more fun? Why?

American Astronaut Edgar D. Mitchell standing on the moon's surface in the hilly upland region north of the Fra Mauro crater (February 5, 1971).

Sandlot Game (1954) by Ralph Fasanella (1914–   ). Oil on canvas.
Collection of Mr. and Mrs. John DePolo

Centennial of Statue of Liberty
(July 4, 1986).

Reverend Martin Luther King, Jr., in
Jackson, Mississippi, 1966. Reverend
King was awarded
a Nobel Peace Prize
in 1964.

Independence Hall, Philadelphia
(September 18, 1987). Bicentennial
celebration of signing of the United
States Constitution.

VISUAL CONNECTIONS
Exploring the Subject
The centennial of the Statue of Liberty was televised extensively. You might ask students who saw parts of it to discuss what they remember about the ceremonies, the tall ships, the fireworks, etc. Students might report on the origins of the Statue. Finally, ask students what the Statue of Liberty represents for them.

Dr. King advocated nonviolent means for changing the racial situation in the United States. He was influenced by the writings of Mohandas K. Gandhi, who had encountered racial prejudice in South Africa and in his native India. Both men had dreams of achieving acceptance for all races.

Philadelphia was founded in 1682 by English Quaker William Penn. The city soon became the financial and political center of the American colonies, and by 1770, it was the third most prosperous city in the British Empire—after London and Liverpool. Independence Hall (originally called the provincial state house) has been the site of some of the most important events in American history. The Declaration of Independence was signed there on July 4, 1776, and, four days later, the Liberty Bell rang in celebration from the steeple of Independence Hall. The U.S. Congress met in Independence Hall during much of the American Revolution. In the summer of 1787, the Constitutional Convention, under the leadership of George Washington, met there and drafted the U.S. Constitution. Philadelphia served as the American capital from 1790 to 1800.

133

OBJECTIVES

The overall aim is for students to analyze the poem's figurative language in relationship to the meaning of the poem. For a complete list of objectives, see the **Teacher's Notes**.

FOCUS / MOTIVATION

Ask students what the Statue of Liberty means to them. Then, have students think of immigrants seeing the Statue of Liberty for the first time. Lead a discussion of any differences between the two sets of responses.

PRESENTATION

A good way to present this poem is to read it aloud while students follow along in their texts. You could use the **For Study and Discussion** questions as points of departure for discussing Bruchac's use of imagery and figurative lan-

TEACHING RESOURCES B
Teacher's Notes, p. 82
Study Guide, p. 83
Selection Test, p. 86

AV RESOURCES BINDER
Audiocassette 1, Side B

PREREADING FOCUS
The headnote stresses the multiethnic heritage of the poet. You might ask students to speculate on how their own heritage affects their conceptions of the American Dream.

Ellis Island

1
Slovaks come from present-day Slovakia, which was part of Czechoslovakia until the early 1990s.

2
Metaphor. Compares old country to sickness. Also plays on word "quarantine," which is isolation for a prescribed period of time to prevent spread of disease.

3
The island is Liberty Island in New York harbor, where the Statue of Liberty is located.

4
Symbolism. The color green is often used to symbolize innocence, youth, and inexperience. May be used here to suggest innocence of both newly arrived immigrants and their dreams. The Statue of Liberty is green from oxidation.

5
People in Slovakia worked hard under a feudal system for generations and were not able to buy land of their own.

6 Drawing Conclusions
What does speaker imply about these people? That they were in touch with cycles of nature.

Ellis Island

JOSEPH BRUCHAC

From 1892 to 1954, Ellis Island was the port of entry for European immigrants seeking the American Dream. In this poem, Joseph Bruchac (broō′shăk) considers the quest for this dream from the viewpoint of someone whose heritage is both European and Native American.

Beyond the red brick of Ellis Island
1 where the two Slovak children
who became my grandparents
waited the long days of quarantine,°
2 after leaving the sickness,   5
the old Empires of Europe,
a Circle Line ship° slips easily
3 on its way to the island
4 of the tall woman,° green
as dreams of forests and meadows   10
5 waiting for those who'd worked
a thousand years
yet never owned their own.

Like millions of others,
I too come to this island,   15
nine decades the answerer
of dreams.

Yet only one part of my blood loves that memory.
Another voice speaks
of native lands   20
within this nation.
Lands invaded
when the earth became owned.
Lands of those who followed
the changing Moon,   25
6 knowledge of the season
in their veins.

4. **quarantine** (kwôr′ən-tēn′): a period of isolation to prevent contagious diseases from spreading.

7. **Circle Line ship:** a sightseeing ferry to the Statue of Liberty.

9. **tall woman:** the Statue of Liberty, which overlooks the New York port of entry.

CLOSURE

Ask students to suggest reasons that the poet may have visited Ellis Island.

EXTENSION AND ENRICHMENT

Students might conduct a "literature hunt" for other poems, stories, or essays written about the Statue of Liberty or Ellis Island; have them share their findings with the class.

For Study and Discussion

Analyzing and Interpreting the Poem

1. What do you think the word *sickness* in line 5 refers to? Consider whether the speaker is referring to a literal or a figurative illness.

2. Why did those who worked "a thousand years" never own anything?

3. How does the mood of the poem shift after line 18?

4a. What does the speaker mean by the "Lands invaded" in line 22? **b.** What historical events might he be thinking of?

About the Author

Joseph Bruchac   (1942–   )

Joseph Bruchac was born in Saratoga Springs, New York. He holds degrees from Cornell and Syracuse universities and Union Graduate School. During his school years he worked as a laborer, surveyor, and tree surgeon. Bruchac also taught secondary-school English and literature in Ghana, West Africa, and creative writing and African literature in the United States. Bruchac has said that being part Abenaki has profoundly influenced his writing. Nature inspires him as well. He once said, "I like to work outside, in the earthmother's soil, with my hands…but maintain my life as an academic…to write…and share my insights into the beautiful and all too fragile world of men and living things we have been granted." Among his well-known poetry collections are *Indian Mountain* (1971) and *Remembering the Dawn* (1983). He has also published a novel, *Dawn Land* (1993), and retellings of Native American folklore, such as *Iroquois Stories* (1985) and *The First Strawberries* (1993), a Cherokee story.

Literature and History

Ports of Entry

Ellis Island was an immigration station for sixty years. In 1965 it became part of the Statue of Liberty National Monument. It was not the only port of entry for immigrants. Angel Island, an immigration station in San Francisco Bay, processed immigrants from Asia for many years.

Making Connections: Activities

1. The words inscribed on the Statue of Liberty are from "The New Colossus," a poem by Emma Lazarus. Write a biographical sketch of the poet and include the full text of her sonnet.

2. Read some firsthand accounts by immigrants to the United States and compare their experiences. Some titles to consider are *The Promised Land* (1912) by Mary Antin; *Songs of Gold Mountain* (1987), translated by Marlon K. Hom; and "Steerage" from *The Uprooted* (1951) by Oscar Handlin. *American Mosaic* (1980) is a collection of interviews with recent immigrants to the United States.

FOR STUDY AND DISCUSSION

1. Answers may vary. Speaker is probably making a figurative reference to crumbling societies or areas torn apart by unemployment, food shortages, and threats of war.
2. Answers may vary. Most of Europe operated under a feudal system of land ownership for centuries, in which the majority of the population was unable to buy land. When that system began to dissolve in the sixteenth century, most people still could not acquire enough money to buy expensive land.
3. The mood shifts from hopefulness to a darker point of view as speaker considers the fate of Native Americans.
4a. He is probably referring to the early colonizers who eventually pushed Native Americans onto reservations and settled on their lands. **4b.** He might be thinking of the nineteenth-century Indian wars.

LITERATURE AND HISTORY

As an optional activity students might work in small groups to research current immigration into the United States. Some aspects they might explore are laws, current ports of entry, the process for attaining citizenship, and problems with immigration policy. You might want to offer groups several options for presenting their findings.

The overall aim is for students to explain Paul Revere's "message" and to analyze the function of **rhythm** and sensory details in the poem. For a complete list of objectives, see the **Teacher's Notes**.

The underlined words are in the Glossary. Students should pay particular attention to the use of words connoting action and movement to create a **rhythm** that captures the cadence of hoof beats.

You could ask a volunteer to present a biographical report on Paul Revere, stressing his importance as a silversmith. Discuss whether his ride would have been considered as extraordinary if he had been a military man.

TEACHING RESOURCES B

Teacher's Notes, p. 87
Study Guide, p. 89
Building Vocabulary, p. 91
Selection Test, p. 93

PREREADING FOCUS

The headnote stresses the historical significance of the incident described in the poem. Students might be asked to name other historical incidents that would be suitable subjects for poems.

Paul Revere's Ride

1 Analyzing
What does the use of "children" indicate? Implies speaker has firsthand knowledge of these events and wishes to ensure that story (poem) will be told to present and future generations as part of their heritage.

2
Setting. North Church is in Boston. General Thomas Gage, commander of British forces there, knew colonists were collecting and storing guns in Concord. He decided to march there secretly to destroy war materials and to arrest Samuel Adams and John Hancock. Fortunately, colonists learned of plan.

3
Narrative poetry. Use of adverbs, such as "then" and "meanwhile" in next stanza, provides transitional devices throughout poem.

4
Simile. Image of "prison bar" suggests intent of British forces to deny freedom to colonies.

Paul Revere's Ride

HENRY WADSWORTH LONGFELLOW

Some say "the United States" began on the night of April 18, 1775. On that night, British soldiers went to raid the Massachusetts towns of Lexington and Concord. But the colonists had been warned that the soldiers were coming. Fully armed, they met the British in battle the next morning. About eighty years after this first battle of the American Revolution, Longfellow wrote the following poem.

1 Listen, my children, and you shall hear
  Of the midnight ride of Paul Revere,
  On the eighteenth of April, in Seventy-five;
  Hardly a man is now alive
  Who remembers that famous day and year.   5

  He said to his friend, "If the British march
  By land or sea from the town tonight,
  Hang a lantern aloft in the belfry arch
2 Of the North Church tower as a signal light—
  One, if by land, and two, if by sea;   10
  And I on the opposite shore will be,
  Ready to ride and spread the alarm
  Through every Middlesex° village and farm,
  For the country folk to be up and to arm."

13. **Middlesex:** a county in Massachusetts.

3 Then he said "Good night!" and with muffled oar   15
  Silently rowed to the Charlestown° shore,
  Just as the moon rose over the bay,
  Where swinging wide at her moorings lay
  The *Somerset,* British man-of-war;
4 A phantom ship, with each mast and spar   20
  Across the moon, like a prison bar,
  And a huge black hulk, that was magnified
  By its own reflection in the tide.

16. **Charlestown:** a former city on Boston Harbor, now a part of Boston.

[handwritten annotations: "a place where a boat is docked"; "poles used to support a ship's rigging"; "Pole used to support the sails of a ship"]

  Meanwhile, his friend, through alley and street,
  Wanders and watches with eager ears,
  Till in the silence around him he hears   25

MOTIVATIONAL SUMMARY

British troops march through the dark night to-ward Concord. As Paul Revere waits impatiently beside his horse, one light appears and then another in the tower of the North Church. Revere springs into the saddle and begins to ride.

PRESENTATION

The reading of Longfellow's narrative poem is generally enjoyed by students because of its ability to capture their imaginations. You could play a recording of the poem, read the poem aloud as students follow in their books, or assign good oral readers from the class to present the poem. Point out how the **rhythm** suggests the hoof beats of Revere's horse. The poem provides an opportunity to comment on how history and art may complement each other and how the author selects and incorporates historical facts and

The muster of men at the barrack door,
The sound of arms, and the tramp of feet,
And the measured tread of the grenadiers
Marching down to their boats on the shore.   30

5 Then he climbed the tower of the Old North Church,
   By the wooden stairs, with stealthy tread,
   To the belfry chamber overhead,
   And startled the pigeons from their perch
   On the somber rafters, that round him made   35
6 Masses and moving shapes of shade—
   By the trembling ladder, steep and tall,
   To the highest window in the wall,
   Where he paused to listen and look down
   A moment on the roofs of the town,   40
   And the moonlight flowing over all.

7 Beneath, in the churchyard, lay the dead,
   In their night encampment on the hill,
   Wrapped in silence so deep and still
8 That he could hear, like a sentinel's tread,   45
9 The watchful night wind, as it went
   Creeping along from tent to tent,
   And seeming to whisper, "All is well!"
   A moment only he feels the spell
   Of the place and the hour, and the secret dread 50
   Of the lonely belfry and the dead;
   For suddenly all his thoughts are bent
   On a shadowy something far away,
   Where the river widens to meet the bay—
   A line of black that bends and floats   55
   On the rising tide, like a bridge of boats.

10 Meanwhile, impatient to mount and ride,
   Booted and spurred, with a heavy stride
   On the opposite shore walked Paul Revere.
   Now he patted his horse's side.   60
   Now gazed at the landscape far and near,
   Then, impetuous, stamped the earth,
   And turned and tightened his saddle girth;
   But mostly he watched with eager search
   The belfry tower of the Old North Church,   65
   As it rose above the graves on the hill,

[handwritten note:] a soldier in a special regiment; originally a soldier trained to use grenades

[handwritten note:] a tower in which a bell is hung

[handwritten note:] eager to act, impatient

5
Suspense. Visual description of slow ascent heightens tension.

6
Alliteration. Repetition of *m* and *sh* sounds draws attention to words that connote darkness and mystery.

7
Figurative language. Describing dead "in their night encampment" suggests even they would be willing to join forces against enemy.

8
Sentinel: guard.

9 Drawing Conclusions
On whose side is the wind? Wind is given human characteristics; like the dead, wind supports colonists.

10
Even though reader is not sure British ships have been sighted, narrator switches scene to Revere anxiously waiting for signal. Increases **suspense.**

details which lend themselves to his or her work. You could also discuss the **setting** and historical background of this famous event.

HISTORY LINK

Students might be more interested in reading "Paul Revere's Ride" if they can see the places mentioned in the poem (Middlesex County, Old North Church, Medford, and Lexington) on a map. You might obtain a copy of a road map of

the greater Boston area and have students use it to create their own map showing the route of Paul Revere's ride.

If you have time before your study of this unit, you might obtain copies of other maps of the area. The National Park Service, which oper-

— ghost like

Lonely and spectral and somber and still.
And lo! as he looks, on the belfry's height
A glimmer, and then a gleam of light!
He springs to the saddle, the bridle he turns,   70
But lingers and gazes, till full on his sight
A second lamp in the belfry burns!

11
Rhythm. Words connoting action and movement are stressed, building readers' excitement. Rhythm suggests beating of horse's hoofs. The "fate of a nation" refers to fact that upcoming skirmish is first battle in American Revolution. "Spark" turning into "flame" mirrors colonists' passions after this night.

11 A hurry of hoofs in a village street,
A shape in the moonlight, a bulk in the dark,
And beneath, from the pebbles, in passing, a spark   75
Struck out by a steed flying fearless and fleet:
That was all! And yet, through the gloom and the light,
The fate of a nation was riding that night;
And the spark struck out by that steed, in his flight,
Kindled the land into flame with its heat.   80

He has left the village and mounted the steep,
12
Setting. Mystic River flows into Atlantic near Boston.

12 And beneath him, tranquil and broad and deep,
Is the Mystic, meeting the ocean tides;
13 And under the alders that skirt its edge,
Now soft on the sand, now loud on the ledge,   85
Is heard the tramp of his steed as he rides.

13
Alders are deciduous shrubs or trees.

14 It was twelve by the village clock,
When he crossed the bridge into Medford town.
He heard the crowing of the cock,
And the barking of the farmer's dog,   90
And felt the damp of the river fog,
That rises after the sun goes down.

14
Narrative poetry. Clock indicates passing of time; adds to narrative technique. Repeated report of time increases tension.

It was one by the village clock,
When he galloped into Lexington.
15 He saw the gilded weathercock   95
Swim in the moonlight as he passed,
And the meetinghouse windows, blank and bare,
Gaze at him with a spectral glare,
As if they already stood aghast
At the bloody work they would look upon.   100

15
Finding Details
Analyzing
What sort of characteristics are given to the weathercock and the windows? What idea of Longfellow's does this enhance? They are given human qualities. Enhances idea that entire world is observing events of that night.

16
Concord is twenty miles northwest of Boston; setting for "shot heard round the world."

It was two by the village clock,
16 When he came to the bridge in Concord town.
He heard the bleating of the flock,
And the twitter of birds among the trees,

138

ates the Boston National Historical Park and the Minute Man National Historical Park (between Lexington and Concord) publishes brochures for visitors that include historical maps and information about Paul Revere's ride.

VISUAL CONNECTIONS
About the Artwork
Longfellow's poem is addressed to children, and in his *Midnight Ride of Paul Revere*, Grant Wood offers a childlike vision of what the ride was like. Revere gallops through a freshly painted, toyland landscape. As he passes, people emerge from the snug security of their homes, wondering what is happening to disturb the tranquility of a moonlit night. The tidy village, dominated by a church steeple, reflects the values of a society that is devout and industrious.

About the Artist
Iowan Grant Wood studied art in Europe where he was influenced by early Flemish painting. After returning to Iowa, he developed his own realistic American style and painted many works depicting historical events. He is noted for fine detail and wry humor in paintings such as *American Gothic* and *Parson Weem's Fable*.

And felt the breath of the morning breeze 105
17 Blowing over the meadows brown.
And one was safe and asleep in his bed
Who at the bridge would be first to fall,
Who that day would be lying dead,
Pierced by a British musket ball. 110

18 You know the rest. In the books you have read
How the British Regulars fired and fled—
How the farmers gave them ball for ball,
From behind each fence and farmyard wall,
Chasing the redcoats down the lane, 115
Then crossing the fields to emerge again
Under the trees at the turn of the road,
And only pausing to fire and load.

Midnight Ride of Paul Revere
(1931) by Grant Wood
(1892–1942).
Oil on masonite, 50.117.
The Metropolitan Museum of Art,
Arthur Hoppock Hearn Fund, 1950

17
Inversion. "Brown" following instead of preceding "meadows" fits with poem's flowing **rhythm.**

18
Narrative poetry. Stanza summarizes battle. The "ride" remains the dominant event in the poem.

TRANSPARENCIES 11 & 12
Fine Art
Theme: *An Emerging Nation and an Evolving People* – explores artwork reflecting America's early growth as a nation.

TRANSPARENCY 16
Literary Elements
Imagery – examines the use of imagery that appeals to the reader's senses.

So through the night rode Paul Revere;
And so through the night went his cry of alarm   120
To every Middlesex village and farm—
A cry of defiance and not of fear,
A voice in the darkness, a knock at the door,
And a word that shall echo forevermore!
For, borne on the night wind of the Past,   125
19 Through all our history, to the last,
In the hour of darkness and peril and need,
The people will waken and listen to hear
The hurrying hoofbeats of that steed,
And the midnight message of Paul Revere.   130

19
Suggests reason for speaker's opening statement. He wants story to be told to future generations because it will serve as an inspiration in perilous times.

FOR STUDY AND DISCUSSION
1a. It was turning point for colonists, leading to first battle in American Revolution and birth of nation. **1b.** United States of America never would have been reality; suggests British would have overpowered colonists.
2a. American Revolution. **2b.** Inflamed feelings of colonists had effect of fire, which begins as a spark and spreads into a devouring blaze.
3. Responses will vary. Could be spirit of defiance and love of freedom; words of warning, cautioning us to be vigilant in guarding freedoms.

LITERARY ELEMENTS
1. Possible answers: "in the silence around him," "sound of arms," "tramp of feet," "startles" pigeons, "masses and moving shapes of shade," "moonlight flowing over all," "a shadowy something," "a line of black that bends and floats"; many others.
2. Cock crowing, dog barking, sheep bleating, birds twittering.
3. Yes. Cadence of hoof-beats maintains reader interest.

For Study and Discussion

Analyzing and Interpreting the Poem

1. The poet says in line 78: "The fate of a nation was riding that night." **a.** What do you think this line means? **b.** What does it suggest *might* have happened if Paul Revere had not been successful?

2. In lines 79–80, the poet says that "the spark struck out" by Paul Revere's horse "kindled the land into flame with its heat." You know that the horse's iron horseshoes did not actually set the land on fire. **a.** What event in American history is the poet comparing to a fire? **b.** How is this a good comparison?

3. In the last six lines of the poem, the poet says that Paul Revere's message will be heard by people throughout our history. What do you think this "message" is? Try to express it in your own words.

Literary Elements

Responding to a Narrative Poem

A **narrative poem** is a poem that tells a story. Like all good storytellers, Longfellow wants to hold your attention and keep you in suspense. In fact, the first word of his poem is a direction: "Listen."

Beginning with line 15, the poet gives details that help you experience the tension felt by Revere and his friend as they wait for the British to reveal their plans. **1** Which details in lines 24–56 help you see and hear what Revere's friend sees and hears as he walks the streets, climbs the tower, and waits?

Once the British plans are known, the **2** famous ride begins. Which details in lines 87–110 help you hear the country sounds that Revere hears as he gallops through the sleeping villages?

This poem has a strong, galloping rhythm. **3** Does the rhythm help hold your attention? Why or why not?

CLOSURE
Ask students to explain the historical and symbolic importance of Paul Revere's "message" and to identify various poetic techniques used by Longfellow to dramatize the event.

EXTENSION AND ENRICHMENT
Some students might want to read other long historical poems by Longfellow and report on their readings to the class. Individuals or small groups might like to choose another famous event in American history and use it as the basis for an original narrative poem. The **rhythm** of the students' poems could imitate the rhythm of Longfellow's, and they could imitate his opening line.

For Oral Reading

Preparing a Presentation

Plan an oral reading of "Paul Revere's Ride" that will convey the changes in mood. What tone of voice will you use for the opening stanza? How will you shift that tone in line 6? How will you convey the sense of mystery and danger as Paul Revere and his friend wait for the British to reveal their plans? How will you signal the change in line 57 as the scene switches? How will you show the rider's impatience and the excitement of the ride?

If you like, practice reading with a partner or with a group of students who will join in a choral reading of the poem.

About the Author

Henry Wadsworth Longfellow (1807–1882)

Henry Wadsworth Longfellow was the most popular poet America has ever had. During his lifetime, people eagerly awaited each new poem, and his works were translated into twenty-four languages. In addition to writing, Longfellow taught at Harvard University for eighteen years. He then retired to lead a quiet life, devoting himself fully to writing poetry for his admiring public. But a catastrophe almost destroyed his desire to create. His wife died as a result of a fire in their home, and the poet needed great courage and patience to overcome his grief and begin writing again.

Longfellow was inspired by the American past. His long poems, *The Courtship of Miles Standish, Evangeline,* and *The Song of Hiawatha,* show Longfellow's talent for using history as a background for poems of action and romance.

Literature and History

Facts or Fiction

Paul Revere was a well-known patriot, but if Longfellow had not written this poem, Revere's ride might be only a footnote in history books. In fact, his companions that night are little known because Longfellow decided not to name them.

Making Connections: Activities

1. In a history book or an encyclopedia, look up the historical facts about all the riders who warned the farmers to arm and meet the British. In a paragraph tell how the details in the poem differ from the details in history. What were the names of the other riders? Did Paul Revere ever reach Concord? Why do you think people have remembered the poem long after they have forgotten the historical facts?

2. Read Stephen Vincent Benét's short story "A Tooth for Paul Revere." Check the different references in the story to events leading up to the American Revolution. How does Benét combine facts with fiction?

FOR ORAL READING
Inexperienced oral interpreters commonly believe that they are introducing far more vocal variety into a reading than is the case. You can help students overcome this problem by suggesting that they attempt to exaggerate changes in rate, pitch, and volume. Explain to them that while they may feel that they are exaggerating, this will not be apparent to listeners.

ABOUT THE AUTHOR
Longfellow based "Paul Revere's Ride" on stories his grandfather, Revolutionary War General Wadsworth, told about the war and his friendship with Paul Revere.

Longfellow studied languages in Europe and taught Spanish, French, Italian, and German at Harvard. He also translated many works of literature.

Longfellow's poems presented American history in memorable form to the world. He was considered America's foremost poet when he died at the age of seventy-five. There is a monument to Longfellow in Poet's Corner in Westminster Abbey, London.

LITERATURE AND HISTORY
Allow students to choose one of the activities to work on independently. To evaluate students' paragraphs, you might develop an analytical scoring guide that emphasizes the paragraphs' content, organization, and use of concrete details to support ideas. You might ask students to look for similarities as well as differences between the poem and historical facts.

The Man Without a Country

EDWARD EVERETT HALE

"Prisoner, hear the sentence of the court! The court decides, subject to the approval of the President, that you never hear the name of the United States again."

I suppose that very few readers of the New York Herald of August 13, 1863, observed in an obscure corner, among the "Deaths," the announcement:

1 NOLAN. Died on board the U.S. Corvette *Levant*, Lat. 2° 11′ S., Long. 131° W., on May *2* 11, PHILIP NOLAN.

Hundreds of readers would have paused at that announcement, if it had read thus: "DIED, MAY 11, THE MAN WITHOUT A COUNTRY." For it was as "The Man Without a Country" that poor Philip Nolan had generally been known by the officers who had him in charge during some fifty years, as, indeed, by all the men who sailed under them.

There can now be no possible harm in *3* telling this poor creature's story. Reason enough there has been till now for very strict secrecy, the secrecy of honor itself, among the gentlemen of the navy who have had Nolan in charge. And certainly it speaks well for the profession and the personal honor of its members that to the press this man's story has been *4* wholly unknown—and, I think, to the country at large also. This I do know, that no naval officer has mentioned Nolan in his report of a cruise.

But there is no need for secrecy any longer. Now the poor creature is dead, it seems to me *5* worthwhile to tell a little of his story, by way of showing young Americans of today what it is to be "A Man Without a Country."

Nolan's Fatal Wish

Philip Nolan was as fine a young officer as there was in the "Legion of the West," as the Western division of our army was then called. When Aaron Burr[1] made his first dashing expedition down to New Orleans in 1805, he met this gay, bright, young fellow. Burr marked[2] him, talked to him, walked with him, took him a day or two's voyage in his flatboat, and, in short, fascinated him. For the next year, barrack life was very tame to poor Nolan. He occasionally availed himself of the permission the great man had given him to write to

1. **Aaron Burr:** a controversial American political figure (1756–1836). Burr was Vice-President of the United States from 1801 to 1805. He killed Alexander Hamilton in a duel in 1804. At one time he was suspected of plotting to set up an empire in the Southwest.
2. **marked:** here, noticed.

PRESENTATION

After reading aloud enough of the story to excite curiosity, you might ask students to finish reading the story by themselves. Since the story is fairly long and divided into topical episodes, the reading may be assigned in two installments, perhaps breaking between "The Ball" and "The Battle."

Before discussing the **For Study and Discussion** questions, encourage students to comment spontaneously on the story and to ask questions about any details they find puzzling. If the story

Seascape (1906) by Thomas Moran (1837–1926). Oil on canvas.
The Brooklyn Museum, gift of the Executors, Estate of Michael Friedsam

VISUAL CONNECTIONS
About the Artist
Moran was born in Lancashire, England. While he was still young, his parents moved to America and settled in Philadelphia. Moran worked as an apprentice to an engraver and studied art before venturing out on his own as an artist. In 1860, while on a long trek through the Great Lake region, Moran discovered that his greatest talent lay in depicting the American wilderness. He immediately began a series of sketches and paintings that captured the area around Lake Superior, and later he became well known for his dramatic portraits of the Far West. Moran's most famous accomplishment was a grandiose painting of the Grand Canyon, completed in 1871. The painting measured more that seven feet by nine feet and was one of the largest American pictures painted to that time. The painting *The Grand Canyon of Yellowstone* so impressed the U.S. Congress that they bought it for 10,000 dollars and, in 1872, made Yellowstone a national park. As a further honor, a peak in the Teton Range was named after Moran.

him. Long, stilted letters the poor boy wrote and rewrote and copied. But never a line did he have in reply. The other boys in the garrison sneered at him, because he lost the fun which they found in shooting or rowing while he was
6 working away on these grand letters to his grand friend. But before long, the young fellow had his revenge. For this time His Excellency, Honorable Aaron Burr, appeared again under a very different aspect. There were rumors that he had an army behind him and

an empire before him. At that time the youngsters all envied him. Burr had not been talking twenty minutes with the commander before he asked him to send for Lieutenant Nolan. Then, after a little talk, he asked Nolan if he could
7 show him something of the great river and the plans for the new post. He asked Nolan to take him out in his skiff to show him a canebrake[3] or a cottonwood tree, as he said—really to win

3. **canebrake:** a dense growth of cane plant.

6
Connotation. Use of "grand" twice seems sarcastic, suggests "not so grand."

7
"Great river" is Mississippi River.

is read in the two installments suggested above, you may wish to deal with **study questions 1–3** at the end of the first installment and **study questions 4–7** at the end of the second.

Students would benefit from background information on Aaron Burr and the scheme that caused Burr to be accused of treason. Be sure students realize Nolan's is a fictitious story about a young man who admires Burr greatly and wishes to participate in his grand adventures.

The story gives you an opportunity to emphasize the use of verisimilitude (appearance of authenticity in fiction). You could begin discussion by considering the **Literary Elements** feature on p. 157 on noting details that suggest authenticity.

VISUAL CONNECTIONS
About the Artist
Everett Shinn was a newspaper artist-reporter in the 1890s before the days of reproducing photographs quickly and cheaply. He covered accidents, fires, and other news events, sketching in detail, essentially working as a human camera. Illustrations for ''The Man Without a Country,'' although done much later in his career, show Shinn's skill as an artist-reporter.

8 Analyzing
Why is Nolan's total commitment to Burr significant? Nolan totally supports Burr yet becomes responsible for his own actions.

9
Richmond is the capital of Virginia. Fort Adams is located at southwestern corner of Mississippi.

10
Connotation. Use of ''little'' indicates Nolan was not a major figure in conspiracy.

11
Plot. Irrational statement becomes Nolan's downfall.

12
Use to answer **study question 2,** p. 156.

Illustrations on pages 144–145, 148 149, 150, 152, and 154 by Everett Shinn (1876–1953) from *The Man Without a Country* (1940).

him over; and by the time the sail was over, **8** Nolan was enlisted body and soul. From that time, though he did not yet know it, he lived as a man without a country.

What Burr meant to do I know no more than you. It is none of our business just now. Only, when the grand catastrophe came, Burr's **9** treason trial at Richmond, Fort Adams[4] got up a string of courts-martial on the officers there. One and another of the colonels and majors **10** were tried, and, to fill out the list, little Nolan, against whom there was evidence enough that he was sick of the service, had been willing to be false to it, and would have obeyed any order to march anywhere had the order been signed, "By command of his Exc. A. Burr." The courts dragged on. The big flies[5] escaped—rightly for all I know. Nolan was proved guilty enough, yet you and I would never have heard of him but that, when the president of the court asked him at the close whether he wished to say anything to show that he had always been faithful **11** to the United States, he cried out in a fit of frenzy: "Damn the United States! I wish I may never hear of the United States again!"

Nolan's Punishment
I suppose he did not know how the words shocked old Colonel Morgan, who was holding the court. Half the officers who sat in it had served through the Revolution, and their lives had been risked for the very idea which he **12** cursed in his madness. He, on his part, had grown up in the West of those days. He had

been educated on a plantation where the finest company was a Spanish officer or a French merchant from Orleans. His education had been perfected in commercial expeditions to Veracruz,[6] and I think he told me his father once hired an Englishman to be a private tutor for a winter on the plantation. He had spent half his youth with an older brother, hunting horses in Texas; and to him *United States* was

4. **Fort Adams:** the fort where Nolan was stationed.
5. **the big flies:** Burr and the other important men who may have plotted with him.

6. **Veracruz** (věr′ə-krōōz′): a seaport in Mexico.

George," Morgan would not have felt worse. He called the court into his private room and returned in fifteen minutes, with a face like a sheet, to say: "Prisoner, hear the sentence of the court! The court decides, subject to the approval of the President, that you never hear the name of the United States again."

Nolan laughed. But nobody else laughed. Old Morgan was too solemn, and the whole room was hushed dead as night for a minute. Even Nolan lost his swagger in a moment. Then Morgan added: "Mr. Marshal, take the prisoner to Orleans, in an armed boat, and deliver him to the naval commander there."

The marshal gave his orders and the prisoner was taken out of court.

"Mr. Marshal," continued old Morgan," see that no one mentions the United States to the prisoner. Mr. Marshal, make my respects to Lieutenant Mitchell at Orleans, and request him to order that no one shall mention the United States to the prisoner while he is on board ship. You will receive your written orders from the officer on duty here this evening. The court is adjourned."

Before the *Nautilus*[7] got round from New Orleans to the northern Atlantic coast with the prisoner on board, the sentence had been approved by the President, and he was a man without a country.

The plan then adopted was substantially the same which was necessarily followed ever after. The Secretary of the Navy was requested to put Nolan on board a government vessel bound on a long cruise, and to direct that he should be only so far confined there as to make it certain that he never saw or heard of the country. We had few long cruises then, and I do not know certainly what his first cruise was. But the commander to whom he was entrusted regulated the etiquette and the precautions of

scarcely a reality. I do not excuse Nolan; I only explain to the reader why he damned his country and wished he might never hear her name again.

From that moment, September 23, 1807, till the day he died, May 11, 1863, he never heard her name again. For that half-century and more, he was a man without a country.

Old Morgan, as I said, was terribly shocked. If Nolan had compared George Washington to Benedict Arnold, or had cried, "God save King

7. *Nautilus:* the naval ship to which Nolan was delivered.

13 Synthesizing
How might Nolan's behavior be explained? He had an unusual upbringing, growing up in the West and having more contact with foreigners than with Americans.

14
Use to answer **study question 3a,** p. 156.

15
Characterization. Nolan laughs because sentence seems so mild or perhaps as act of defiance.

16
Symbol. Nautilus is derived from Greek word *nautilo,* meaning sailor. Symbolic of life Nolan will spend at sea.

17
Theme. Repetition of "man without a country" reinforces idea that Nolan's situation is a horrible state of affairs.

18
Narrator's ignorance of all the facts gives story additional authenticity.

The Man Without a Country   **145**

19
Use to answer **study question 1,** p. 156.

20
Letters or official documents are a method of establishing authenticity. The fact that narrator has not copied document and must paraphrase it offers further evidence of authenticity.

21
Officers were expected to conduct themselves as gentlemen, and in the nineteenth century, this meant following code of unfailing courtesy towards others. Nolan was to be treated as a gentleman.

22
Exposition. Paragraph describes method and difficulty of carrying out the sentence.

23
Indicates how much of usual conversation contains talk of home and country.

24
Characterization. Nolan grows shy because he is aware of difficulty in carrying on conversation with shipmates.

25 Finding Details
Why were sailors allowed to socialize with Nolan? It was believed Nolan's punishment would be example to persuade sailors to avoid misconduct and to remain patriotic.

the affair, and according to his scheme they were carried out till Nolan died.

19 When I was second officer of the *Intrepid,* some thirty years after, I saw the original **20** paper of instructions. I have been sorry ever since that I did not copy the whole of it. It ran, however, much in this way:

> Washington [with a date, which must have been late in 1807]

Sir:

You will receive from Lieutenant Neale the person of Philip Nolan, late a lieutenant in the United States Army.

This person on trial by court-martial expressed, with an oath, the wish that he might "never hear of the United States again."

The court sentenced him to have his wish fulfilled.

For the present, the execution of the order is entrusted by the President to this department.

You will take the prisoner on board your ship, and keep him there with such precautions as shall prevent his escape.

21 You will provide him with such quarters, rations, and clothing as would be proper for an officer of his late rank, if he were a passenger on your vessel on the business of his government.

The gentlemen on board will make any arrangements agreeable to themselves regarding his society. He is to be exposed to no indignity of any kind, nor is he ever unnecessarily to be reminded that he is a prisoner.

But under no circumstances is he ever to hear of his country or to see any information regarding it; and you will especially caution all the officers under your command to take care that this rule, in which his punishment is involved, shall not be broken.

It is the intention of the government that he shall never again see the country which he has disowned. Before the end of your cruise, you will receive orders which will give effect to this intention.

> Respectfully yours,
> W. Southard,
> for the Secretary of the Navy

The rule adopted on board the ships on which I have met "The Man Without a Country" was, I think, transmitted from the begin-**22** ning. No mess[8] liked to have him permanently, because his presence cut off all talk of home or of the prospect of return, of politics or letters, **23** of peace or of war—cut off more than half the talk men liked to have at sea. But it was always thought too hard that he should never meet the rest of us, except to touch hats, and we finally sank into one system. He was not permitted to talk with the men unless an officer was by. With officers he had unrestrained inter-**24** course, as far as they and he chose. But he grew shy, though he had favorites: I was one. Then the captain always asked him to dinner on Monday. Every mess in succession took up the invitation in its turn. According to the size of the ship, you had him at your mess more or less often at dinner. His breakfast he ate in his own stateroom. Whatever else he ate or drank, he ate or drank alone. Sometimes, when the marines or sailors had any special jollification,[9] they were permitted to invite Plain Buttons, as they called him. Then Nolan was sent with some officer, and the men were forbidden to speak of home while he was there. I believe the **25** theory was that the sight of his punishment did them good. They called him Plain Buttons, because, while he always chose to wear a regulation army uniform, he was not permitted to wear the army button, for the reason that it bore either the initials or the insignia of the country he had disowned.

8. **mess:** a group of people who eat meals together.
9. **jollification:** merrymaking.

The Reading

I remember, soon after I joined the navy, I was on shore with some of the older officers from our ship, and some of the gentlemen fell to talking about Nolan, and someone told the system which was adopted from the first about his books and other reading. As he was almost never permitted to go on shore, even though the vessel lay in port for months, his time at the best hung heavy. Everybody was permitted to lend him books, if they were not published in America and made no allusion to it. These were common enough in the old days. He had almost all the foreign papers that came into the ship, sooner or later; only somebody must go over them first, and cut out any advertisement or stray paragraph that referred to America. This was a little cruel sometimes, when the back of what was cut out might be **26** innocent. Right in the midst of one of Napoleon's battles poor Nolan would find a great hole, because on the back of the page of that paper there had been an advertisement of a packet[10] for New York, or a scrap from the President's message. This was the first time I ever heard of this plan. I remember it, because poor Phillips, who was of the party, told a story of something which happened at the Cape of **30** Good Hope[11] on Nolan's first voyage. They had touched at the Cape, paid their respects to the English admiral and the fleet, and then Phillips had borrowed a lot of English books **27** from an officer. Among them was *The Lay of the Last Minstrel*,[12] which they had all of them heard of, but which most of them had never seen. I think it could not have been published long. Well, nobody thought there could be any **31** risk of anything national in that. So Nolan was

10. **packet:** a boat that travels a regular route, carrying passengers, freight, and mail.
11. **Cape of Good Hope:** a projection of land on the southwestern coast of Africa.
12. *The Lay of the Last Minstrel:* a long narrative poem by Sir Walter Scott (1771–1832).

permitted to join the circle one afternoon when a lot of them sat on deck smoking and reading aloud. In his turn, Nolan took the book and read to the others; and he read very well, as I know. Nobody in the circle knew a line of the poem, only it was all magic and chivalry, and was ten thousand years ago. Poor Nolan read steadily through the fifth canto,[13] stopped a minute and drank something, and **28** then began, without a thought of what was coming:

> Breathes there the man with soul so dead,
> Who never to himself hath said . . .

It seems impossible to us that anybody ever heard this for the first time; but all these fellows did then, and poor Nolan himself went on, still unconsciously or mechanically:

> This is my own, my native land!

Then they all saw that something was to pay; but he expected to get through, I suppose, turned a little pale, but plunged on:

> Whose heart hath ne'er within him burned,
> As home his footsteps he hath turned
> From wandering on a foreign strand!
> If such there breathe, go, mark him well . . .

By this time, the men were all beside themselves, wishing there was any way to make him turn over two pages; but he had not quite presence of mind for that; he gagged a little, colored crimson, and staggered on:

> For him no minstrel raptures swell;
> High though his titles, proud his name,
> Boundless his wealth as wish can claim;
> Despite these titles, power, and pelf.[14]
> The wretch, concentered all in self . . .

13. **canto:** a main division of certain long poems.
14. **pelf:** wealth.

26
Irony. Napoleon, like Nolan, was exiled from his country.

27
Setting. Romantic era. One trait of Romanticism is nationalism with much of reading material of the time containing this element.

28
That Nolan has no warning of the poem's content and is enjoying a brief moment of camaraderie with the other men adds to the poignancy of the scene.

29
In this poem, Scott states that feelings of love of country, growing out of one's natural attachment to home and culture, are universal.

30
Strand: land bordering a body of water. Scott states that we are most likely to feel love of country when we are away from home.

31
Nolan sees himself described in poem, which states that one who is more concerned with himself than with his country is an essentially miserable person.

148

32 Making Inferences
Why would Nolan read aloud only the Bible, Shakespeare, or something he knew well? Responses will vary. Probably these works remind him least of the United States, and he knows them so well that he will not be overwhelmed by emotion or surprised by the content.

33
Characterization. Nolan's spirit is broken. Furthermore, Nolan is discovering he does love his country intensely, and these feelings will make his punishment more severe.

34
"Boys" refers to sailors.

35
Symbol. Joseph Warren was a prominent leader of the American Revolution and the one who sent Paul Revere on his famous ride. Warren died in the Battle of Bunker Hill. Name of ship is symbolic of patriotic stirrings Nolan is beginning to feel.

36
"Signs of the sky" refers to constellations, and Nolan can roughly judge latitude by positions of constellations in sky. For example, if Little Dipper and polestar were not visible, Nolan would know ship was in Southern Hemisphere.

37 Analyzing
What does "even to a prison" suggest? Prison in own country would be pleasure for him.

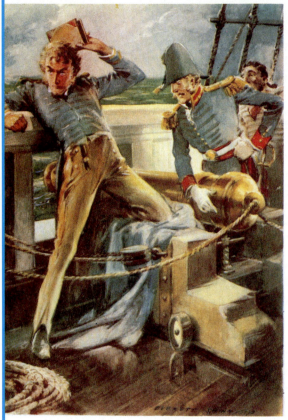

Here the poor fellow choked, could not go on, but started up, swung the book into the sea, vanished into his stateroom, "And by Jove," said Phillips, "we did not see him for two months again. And I had to make up some story to that English surgeon why I did not return his Walter Scott to him."

That story shows about the time when Nolan's braggadocio[15] must have broken down. At first, they said, he took a very high tone, considered his imprisonment a mere <u>farce</u>, <u>affected</u> to enjoy the voyage, and all that; but Phillips said that after he came out of his state-

15. **braggadocio** (brăg′ə-dō′shē-ō): pretended courage; in this case, Nolan's pretense that he does not mind his punishment.

room he never was the same man again. He **32** never read aloud again, unless it was the Bible or Shakespeare, or something else he was sure **33** of. But it was not that merely. He never entered in with the other young men exactly as a companion again. He was always shy afterward, when I knew him—very seldom spoke unless he was spoken to, except to a very few friends. He lighted up occasionally, but generally he had the nervous, tired look of a heart-wounded man.

The Ball

When Captain Shaw was coming home, rather to the surprise of everybody they made one of the Windward Islands,[16] and lay off and on for **34** nearly a week. The boys said the officers were sick of salt junk,[17] and meant to have turtle soup before they came home. But after several **35** days, the *Warren* came to the same <u>rendezvous</u>; they exchanged signals; she told them she was outward bound, perhaps to the Mediterranean, and took poor Nolan and his traps[18] on the boat to try his second cruise. He looked very blank when he was told to get ready to **36** join her. He had known enough of the signs of the sky to know that till that moment he was going "home." But this was a distinct evidence of something he had not thought of, perhaps— **37** that there was no going home for him, even to a prison. And this was the first of some twenty such transfers, which brought him sooner or later into half our best vessels, but which kept him all his life at least some hundred miles from the country he had hoped he might never hear of again.

It may have been on that second cruise—it was once when he was up the Mediterranean —that Mrs. Graff, the celebrated Southern

16. **Windward Islands:** a group of islands in the West Indies.
17. **salt junk:** dried beef salted for preservation.
18. **traps:** here, luggage.

beauty of those days, danced with him. The ship had been lying a long time in the Bay of Naples, and the officers were very intimate in the English fleet, and there had been great festivities, and our men thought they must give a great ball on board the ship. They wanted to use Nolan's stateroom for something, and they hated to do it without asking him to the ball; so the captain said they might ask him, if they would be responsible that he did not talk with the wrong people, "who would give him intelligence."[19] So the dance went on. For ladies they had the family of the American consul, one or two travelers who had adventured so far, and a nice bevy of English girls and matrons.

Well, different officers relieved each other in standing and talking with Nolan in a friendly way, so as to be sure that nobody else spoke to him. The dancing went on with spirit, and after a while even the fellows who took this honorary guard of Nolan ceased to fear any trouble.

As the dancing went on, Nolan and our fellows all got at ease, as I said—so much that it seemed quite natural for him to bow to that splendid Mrs. Graff, and say, "I hope you have not forgotten me, Miss Rutledge. Shall I have the honor of dancing?"

He did it so quickly that Fellows, who was with him, could not hinder him. She laughed and said, "I am not Miss Rutledge any longer, Mr. Nolan; but I will dance all the same." She nodded to Fellows, as if to say he must leave Mr. Nolan to her, and led Nolan off to the place where the dance was forming.

38 Nolan thought he had got his chance. He had known her at Philadelphia. He said bold-
39 ly—a little pale, she said, as she told me the story years after— "And what do you hear from home, Mrs. Graff?"

And that splendid creature looked *through*

40 him. Jove! How she *must* have looked through him!

"Home! Mr. Nolan! I thought you were the man who never wanted to hear of home
41 again!"—and she walked directly up the deck
42 to her husband and left poor Nolan alone. He did not dance again.

The Battle

A happier story than either of these I have told is of the war.[20] That came along soon after. I have heard this affair told in three or four ways—and, indeed, it may have happened

---

19. **intelligence:** here, information about his country.

20. **the war:** the War of 1812, between the United States and Great Britain.

VISUAL CONNECTIONS
Exploring the Subject
The officers depicted in this illustration are wearing full military dress for the grand ball. At other times, during battle or while running the ship, they wore more casual uniforms. Students might research the changing uniforms that the American military has worn from the time of the American Revolution to the present.

38
Irony. Graff is first person Nolan meets whom he knew previously. Ironic that he had known her in Philadelphia, the first capital of the United States.

39 Drawing Conclusions
Why is Nolan a little pale? He is nervous, hoping Mrs. Graff does not know of his punishment.

40
"Jove," shortened form of "by Jove," mild oath of surprise (Jove another Roman name for god Jupiter).

41
Significant that Southern woman is supporting United States' position against Nolan, considering Hale wrote story during Civil War when South no longer recognized United States. Hale is implying that Southerners can be as patriotic as anyone else.

42
Inference. Last sentence is understatement. Nolan was most likely crushed by Mrs. Graff's actions. Also, implies that Nolan never again surreptitiously attempted to gain information about United States.

43

Although there had been some fighting at sea in the American Revolution, unofficial navy was discarded until creation of United States Navy in 1797. Narrator's use of "baptized" stresses that this is first war United States Navy had seen.

44

Characterization. Nolan acts with courage and authority. He remains cheerful in adversity, maintaining good morale among other sailors. By making important contributions toward defeating enemy, Nolan confirms his patriotism.

45

Raw hands: new recruits.

46 Analyzing

What does the commodore mean by saying Nolan is "one of us today"? Refers to Nolan being an American, but commodore does not mention the country by name.

VISUAL CONNECTIONS
Exploring the Subject

The frigate was developed in the late 1700s as an escort for merchant ships. It was designed to patrol and protect coastlines and shipping lanes although some frigates carried as many as sixty guns and were more than a match for the largest warships of the time. In 1794, six frigates became the first naval ships commissioned by the U.S. Congress. They were used to fight pirates off the coast of North Africa.

more than once. In one of the great frigate[21] duels with the English, in which the navy was **43** really baptized, it happened that a round shot[22] from the enemy entered one of our ports[23] square, and took right down the officer of the gun himself and almost every man of the gun's crew. Now you may say what you choose about courage, but that is not a nice thing to see. But, as the men who were not killed picked themselves up, and as they and the surgeon's people **44** were carrying off the bodies, there appeared Nolan, in his shirtsleeves, with the rammer in

21. **frigate** (frĭg'ĭt): a sailing ship equipped with war guns.
22. **round shot:** a cannonball.
23. **ports:** here, portholes for cannons.

his hand, and, just as if he had been the officer, told them off with authority—who should go to the cockpit with the wounded men, who should stay with him—perfectly cheery, and with that way which makes men feel sure all is right and is going to be right. And he finished loading the gun with his own hands, aimed it, and bade the men fire. And there he stayed, captain of that gun, keeping those fellows in spirits, till the enemy struck[24]—sitting on the carriage while the gun was cooling, though he was exposed all the time, showing them easier ways **45** to handle heavy shot, making the raw hands laugh at their own blunders, and when the gun cooled again, getting it loaded and fired twice as often as any other gun on the ship. The captain walked forward by way of encouraging the men, and Nolan touched his hat and said, "I am showing them how we do this in the artillery, sir."

And this is the part of the story where all the legends agree; the commodore said, "I see you are, and I thank you, sir; and I shall never forget this day, sir, and you never shall, sir."

After the whole thing was over, and the commodore had the Englishman's sword,[25] in the midst of the state and ceremony of the quarterdeck, he said, "Where is Mr. Nolan? Ask Mr. Nolan to come here."

And when Nolan came, he said, "Mr. Nolan, we are all very grateful to you today; you **46** are one of us today; you will be named in the dispatches."

And then the old man took off his own sword of ceremony, gave it to Nolan, and made him put it on. The man who told me this saw it. Nolan cried like a baby, and well he might. He had not worn a sword since that infernal day at Fort Adams. But always afterward on occasions

24. **struck:** struck their colors, or lowered their flag to admit defeat.
25. **the Englishman's sword:** A defeated commander used to give up his sword to the victor.

47 of ceremony he wore that quaint old sword of the commodore.

The captain did mention him in the dis-
48 patches. It was always said he asked that Nolan might be pardoned. He wrote a special letter to the Secretary of War, but nothing ever came of it.

All that was nearly fifty years ago. If Nolan was thirty then, he must have been near eighty when he died. He looked sixty when he was forty. But he never seemed to me to change a hair afterward. As I imagine his life, from what I have seen and heard of it, he must have been in every sea, and yet almost never on land. Till
49 he grew very old, he went aloft a great deal. He always kept up his exercise, and I never heard
50 that he was ill. If any other man was ill, he was the kindest nurse in the world; and he knew more than half the surgeons do. Then if any-body was sick or died, or if the captain wanted him to, or on any other occasion, he was always ready to read prayers. I have said that he read beautifully.

The Slaves

My own acquaintance with Philip Nolan began six or eight years after the English war, on my first voyage after I was appointed a midship-man. From the time I joined, I believe I thought Nolan was a sort of lay chaplain—a chaplain with a blue coat. I never asked about him. Everything in the ship was strange to me. I
51 knew it was green to ask questions, and I sup-pose I thought there was a Plain Buttons on every ship. We had him to dine in our mess once a week, and the caution was given that on that day nothing was to be said about home. But if they had told us not to say anything about the planet Mars or the Book of Deuteronomy,[26] I should not have asked why;

52 there were a great many things which seemed to me to have as little reason. I first came to understand anything about "The Man Without a Country" one day when we overhauled a dirty little schooner which had slaves[27] on board. An officer named Vaughan was sent to take charge of her, and, after a few minutes, he sent back his boat to ask that someone might be sent who could speak Portuguese. None of the officers did; and just as the captain was sending forward to ask if any of the people could, Nolan stepped out and said he should be glad to interpret, if the captain wished, as he understood the language. The captain thanked him, fitted out another boat with him, and in this boat it was my luck to go.

When we got there, it was such a scene as you seldom see—and never want to. Nastiness beyond account, and chaos ran loose in the midst of the nastiness. There were not a great many of the Negroes. By way of making what
53 there were understand that they were free, Vaughan had had their handcuffs and ankle-cuffs knocked off. The Negroes were, most of them, out of the hold and swarming all around the dirty deck, with a central throng surround-ing Vaughan and addressing him in every dialect.

As we came on deck, Vaughan looked down from a hogshead,[28] which he had mounted in desperation, and said, "Is there anybody who can make these wretches understand some-thing?"

Nolan said he could speak Portuguese, and one or two fine-looking Krumen[29] who had worked for the Portuguese on the coast were dragged out.

---

26. **Book of Deuteronomy** (do͞o′tə-rŏn′ə-mē): the fifth book of the Bible.

27. **slaves:** In 1808 the United States made it illegal to bring slaves into the country. In 1842 America and Great Britain agreed to patrol the African coast with ships to prevent any more people from being shipped off as slaves.
28. **hogshead** (hôgz′hĕd′): a large cask.
29. **Krumen** (kro͞o′mĕn): members of a tribe in northern Africa.

47
Symbol. Sword symbolic of No-lan's desire to belong, if only in spirit.

48
Narrator is not only one who pit-ies Nolan. Indicates Nolan has vindicated himself, at least to his peers.

49
"Went aloft" refers to climbing rigging and masts of ship; per-haps hoping for glimpse of land, particularly American shore.

50
Characterization. Despite own circumstances, Nolan tends to crew's physical and spiritual needs.

51
"Green" here means untrained and inexperienced.

52
Although **narrator** loves country, he does not seem to possess great affection for military regu-lations.

53
Again, reminder that Hale wrote story during Civil War.

VISUAL CONNECTIONS
Exploring the Subject
Sailing ships originated in the Mediterranean around 2000 B.C. and reached their greatest development by the late Middle Ages. In the story, Nolan, on his deathbed, is told of Robert Fulton, the inventor of the steam engine. The first steam-powered warship in the U.S. Navy was the U.S.S. Fulton, built for the War of 1812. It inaugurated a new age of ships, and within decades, the wooden sailing ship had all but vanished from naval and commercial fleets.

54
Irony. Nolan last touched United States (home) in New Orleans.

55 Analyzing
What is ironic about Nolan's position? Perpetually separated from his native country, he is put in position of helping others to regain their home.

56
"Gray" suggests not only pallor but also age. Experiences such as these age Nolan.

57
Figurative language. Nolan consumed with emotion. Even the elements, supposedly the basic building materials of the universe, "melt" from the heat of passion.

58
Vaughan's fervent desire to return slaves to their homeland is actually a vicarious fulfillment of Nolan's dream. Captain, overwhelmed by Nolan's agony, quickly agrees.

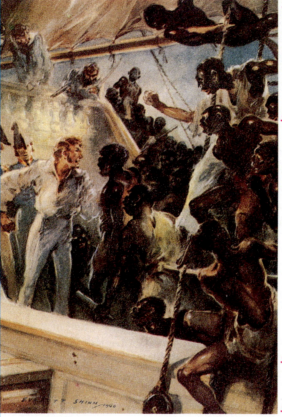

"Tell them they are free," said Vaughan.

Nolan explained it in such Portuguese as the Krumen could understand, and they in turn to such of the Negroes as could understand them. Then there was a yell of delight, clenching of **58** fists, leaping and dancing, and kissing of Nolan's feet by way of spontaneous celebration of the occasion.

"Tell them," said Vaughan, well pleased, "that I will take them all to Cape Palmas."[30]

This did not answer so well. Cape Palmas was practically as far from the homes of most

54 of them as New Orleans or Rio de Janeiro was; that is, they would be eternally separated from home there. And their interpreters, as we could understand, instantly said, "*Ah, non Palmas*" and began to protest loudly. Vaughan was rather disappointed at this result of his liberality, and he asked Nolan eagerly what they said.

55 The drops stood on poor Nolan's white forehead, as he hushed the men down, and said, "He says, 'Not Palmas.' He says, 'Take us home; take us to our own country; take us to our own house; take us to our own children and our own women.' He says he has an old father and mother who will die if they do not see him. And this one says that he left his people all sick, and paddled down to Fernando to beg the white doctor to come and help them, and that these devils caught him in the bay just in sight of home, and that he has never seen anybody from home since then. And this one says," choked out Nolan, "that he has not heard a word from his home in six months."

56 Vaughan always said Nolan grew gray himself while he struggled through this interpretation. I, who did not understand anything of the passion involved in it, **57** saw that the very elements were melting with fervent heat and that something was to pay somewhere. Even the Negroes themselves stopped howling as they saw Nolan's agony and Vaughan's almost equal agony of sympathy. As quick as he could get words, Vaughan said, "Tell them yes, yes, yes; tell them they shall go to the Mountains of the Moon,[31] if they will. If I sail the schooner through the Great White Desert,[32] they shall go home!"

And after some fashion, Nolan said so. And then they all fell to kissing him again and wanted to rub his nose with theirs.

30. **Cape Palmas** (päl′məs): a point on the southern border of Liberia, on the western coast of Africa—about 2,000 miles (about 3,200 kilometers) from the home of these Africans.

31. **Mountains of the Moon:** a mountain range in East Central Africa.
32. **Great White Desert:** probably the Great Salt Desert in Iran.

But he could not stand it long; and getting Vaughan to say he might go back, he beckoned me down into our boat. As we started back he **59** said to me: "Youngster, let that show you what it is to be without a family, without a home, and without a country. If you are ever tempted to say a word or to do a thing that shall put a bar between you and your family, your home, and your country, pray God in His mercy to take you that instant home to His own heaven. Think of your home, boy; write and send and talk about it. Let it be nearer and nearer to your thought the farther you have to travel from it, and rush back to it when you are free, as that poor slave is doing now. And for your country, boy," and the words rattled in his throat, "and for that flag," and he pointed to the ship, "never dream a dream but of serving her as she bids you, though the service carry you through a thousand hells. No matter what happens to you, no matter who flatters you or who abuses you, never look at another flag, never let a night pass but you pray God to bless **60** the flag. Remember, boy, that behind all these men you have to do with, behind officers, and government, and people even, there is the Country herself, your Country, and that you belong to her as you belong to your own mother. Stand by her, boy, as you would stand by your mother!"

I was frightened to death by his calm, hard passion; but I blundered out that I would, by all that was holy, and that I had never thought of doing anything else. He hardly seemed to hear me; but he did, almost in a whisper, say, "Oh, if anybody had said so to me when I was of your age!"

I think it was this half-confidence of his, which I never abused, that afterward made us great friends. He was very kind to me. Often he sat up, or even got up, at night, to walk the deck with me when it was my watch. He explained to me a great deal of my mathemat-

ics, and I owe him my taste for mathematics. He lent me books and helped me about my reading. He never referred so directly to his story again; but from one and another officer, I **61** have learned, in thirty years, what I am telling.

Nolan's Repentance

After that cruise I never saw Nolan again. The other men tell me that in those fifteen years he aged very fast, but he was still the same gentle, uncomplaining, silent sufferer that he ever was, bearing as best he could his self-appointed punishment. And now it seems that the dear old fellow is dead. He has found a home at last, and a country.

Since writing this, and while considering **62** whether or not I would print it, as a warning to the young Nolans of today of what it is to throw away a country, I have received from Danforth, who is on board the *Levant*, a letter which gives an account of Nolan's last hours. It removes all my doubts about telling this story.

Here is the letter:

Dear Fred,

I try to find heart and life to tell you that it is **63** all over with dear old Nolan. I have been with him on this voyage more that I ever was, and I can understand wholly now the way in which you used to speak of the dear old fellow. I could see that he was not strong, but I had no idea the end was so near. The doctor has been watching him very carefully, and yesterday morning he came to me and told me that Nolan was not so well and had not left his state-room—a thing I never remember before. He had let the doctor come and see him as he lay there—the first time the doctor had been in the stateroom—and he said he should like to see me. Do you remember the mysteries we boys used to invent about his room in the old *Intrepid* days? Well, I went in, and there, to be

59
Characterization. Nolan does not mention "home" or "country" by name; perhaps he now believes he does not have the right.

60
Nolan's advice based on involvement with Burr; also it is Hale's own statement against divisions caused by the Civil War.

61   Drawing Conclusions
Why does the narrator make frequent references to how he came to learn the story? To reinforce idea that story is true.

62
In 1863, the year this story was written, United States was in the midst of Civil War, outcome of which was by no means certain. While not specifically mentioning the war, Hale is clearly comparing "young Nolans" to Confederates.

63
Inference. Nolan, now dead, is referred to as "dear" rather than "poor." Implies change from feeling of pity to one of respect.

The Man Without a Country   **153**

VISUAL CONNECTIONS
Ideas for Writing
Readers may be surprised at the end of the story to learn that Nolan has, for fifty-five years, said a prayer twice daily for the United States. Students might write a short paper from Nolan's point of view, explaining the reasons why he might secretly love his country and yet not apologize publicly and hope to return home. Is Nolan justified in his reasoning or not?

64
Symbol. Nolan's cabin is coffin-like, reflecting his living death while in exile.

65
Characterization. First time Nolan uses "America" in story. Illustrates transformation he has undergone, from condemning United States to praising it.

66
Story's first readers would have been vividly aware that this was no longer true. In 1860 and 1861, eleven states had seceded from Union, signaling beginning of Civil War.

67 Summarizing
Expressing an Opinion
What is the captain doing that is forbidden? Do you think the captain is doing the right thing? Captain is answering questions about America. Seems appropriate humanitarian deed; Nolan certainly seems to have suffered enough and learned from his punishment.

sure, the poor fellow lay in his berth, smiling pleasantly as he gave me his hand but looking very frail. I could not help a glance round, **64** which showed me what a little shrine he had made of the box he was lying in. The Stars and Stripes were draped up above and around a picture of Washington, and he had painted a majestic eagle, with lightnings blazing from his beak and his foot just clasping the whole globe, which his wings overshadowed. The dear old boy saw my glance, and said, with a sad smile, "Here, you see, I have a country!" Then he pointed to the foot of his bed, where I had not seen before a great map of the United States, as he had drawn it from memory, and which he had there to look upon as he lay. Quaint, queer old names were on it, in large letters: "Indiana Territory," "Mississippi Territory," and "Louisiana Territory," as I suppose our fathers learned such things: but the old fellow had patched in Texas, too; he had carried his western boundary all the way to the Pacific, but on that shore he had defined nothing.

"O Captain," he said, "I know I am dying. I cannot get home. Surely you will tell me something now? . . . Stop! Stop! . . . Do not speak till I say what I am sure you know, that there is not **65** in this ship, that there is not in America—God bless her!—a more loyal man than I. There cannot be a man who loves the old flag as I do, **67** or prays for it as I do, or hopes for it as I do. There are thirty-four stars in it now, Danforth. I thank God for that, though I do not know what their names are. There has never been **66** one taken away; I thank God for that. I know by that that there has never been any successful Burr. O Danforth, Danforth," he sighed out, "how like a wretched night's dream a boy's idea of personal fame or of separate sovereignty seems, when one looks back on it after such a life as mine! But tell me—tell me something—tell me everything, Danforth, before I die!"

I swear to you that I felt like a monster because I had not told him everything before. "Mr. Nolan," said I, "I will tell you everything you ask about. Only, where shall I begin?"

Oh, the blessed smile that crept over his white face! He pressed my hand and said, "God bless you! Tell me their names," and he pointed to the stars on the flag. "The last I know is Ohio. My father lived in Kentucky. But I have guessed Michigan, and Indiana, and Mississippi—that is where Fort Adams was—they make twenty. But where are your other fourteen? You have not cut up any of the old ones, I hope?"

Well, that was not a bad text, and I told him the names in as good order as I could, and he

154

TRANSPARENCY 15

Reader Response

What Do You Know? – asks students to identify specific information they have learned about a character from a selection.

68 bade me take down his beautiful map and draw them in as I best could with my pencil. He was wild with delight about Texas, told me how his cousin died there; he had marked a gold cross near where he supposed his grave was; and he had guessed at Texas. Then he was delighted as he saw California and Oregon—that, he said, he had suspected partly, because he had never been permitted to land on that shore, though the ships were there so much. Then he asked about the old war—told me the story of his serving the gun the day we took the *Java*. Then he settled down more quietly, and very happily, to hear me tell in an hour the history of fifty years.

69 How I wish it had been somebody who knew something! But I did as well as I could. I told him of the English war. I told him of Fulton[33] and the steamboat beginning. I told him about old Scott,[34] and Jackson,[35] told him all I could think of about the Mississippi, and New Orleans, and Texas, and his own old Kentucky.

I tell you, it was a hard thing to condense the history of half a century into that talk with a sick man. And I do not now know what I told him—of emigration and the means of it—of steamboats, and railroads, and telegraphs—of inventions and books, and literature—of the colleges, and West Point, and the Naval School, but with the queerest interruptions that ever

70 you heard. You see it was Robinson Crusoe asking all the accumulated questions of fifty-six years!

I remember he asked, all of a sudden, who was President now; and when I told him, he asked if Old Abe was General Benjamin Lincoln's son. He said he met old General

33. **Fulton:** Robert Fulton (1765–1815), the inventor of the steamboat.
34. **Scott:** General Winfield Scott (1786–1866), a commander in the War of 1812 and in the Mexican War.
35. **Jackson:** Andrew Jackson (1767–1845), a general in the War of 1812 and the seventh President of the United States (1829–1837).

Lincoln, when he was quite a boy himself, at **71** some Indian treaty. I said no, that Old Abe was a Kentuckian like himself, but I could not tell him of what family; he had worked up from the ranks. "Good for him!" cried Nolan; "I am glad of that." Then I got talking about my visit to Washington. I told him everything I could think of that would show the grandeur of his country and its prosperity.

And he drank it in and enjoyed it as I cannot tell you. He grew more and more silent, yet I never thought he was tired or faint. I gave him a glass of water, but he just wet his lips, and told me not to go away. Then he asked me to bring the Presbyterian Book of Public Prayer which lay there, and said, with a smile, that it would open at the right place—and so it did. There was his double red mark down the page; and I knelt down and read, and he repeated with me:

For ourselves and our country, O gracious God, we thank Thee, that, notwithstanding our manifold transgressions of Thy Holy laws, Thou hast continued to us Thy marvelous kindness . . .

72 and so to the end of that thanksgiving. Then he turned to the end of the same book, and I read the words more familiar to me:

Most heartily we beseech Thee with Thy favor to behold and bless Thy servant, the President of the United States, and all others in authority.

"Danforth," said he, "I have repeated those **73** prayers night and morning—it is now fifty-five years." And then he said he would go to sleep. He bent me down over him and kissed me; and he said, "Look in my Bible, Captain, when I am gone." And I went away.

But I had no thought it was the end. I

68 Analyzing
Why does Danforth refer to the dated map as "beautiful"?
He has great respect for Nolan's passionate view of America.

69
Danforth has taken the history of his country for granted, whereas even the most obvious pieces of news about America are treasured by Nolan.

70
Allusion. *Robinson Crusoe*, an enormously popular novel by Daniel Defoe (1660–1731), tells the story of a man shipwrecked on an uninhabited island. After twenty-four years, he is able to return to his native England.

71
Irony. Nolan had once had opportunities to work up from ranks.

72
Thanksgiving not only refers to the prayer but alludes to the American holiday commemorating the Pilgrims' first feast.

73
Nolan's punishment has lasted fifty-five years.

Have students use the first-person point of view to write about people who have been banished from their countries. Students who are interested in science fiction might enjoy writing stories in which the narrators have been banished from this planet, or even from the solar system.

Ask students to analyze the changes in the main character during the time spent at sea and to select lines from the poem "The Lay of the Last Minstrel" that express the main idea of "The Man Without a Country."

---

74 Analyzing
What is meant by Nolan's epitaph? Responses will vary. Nolan loved his country and accepted his punishment as being fair.

READING CHECK
1. Philip Nolan (p. 142).
2. Plantation in West (p. 144).
3. Plain Buttons (p. 146).
4. His sword (p. 150).
5. To hear all that had happened in the United States since his exile (p. 154).

FOR STUDY AND DISCUSSION
1. Sailor in United States Navy. Wants young Americans to know what it is to be man without a country.
2. Early company was primarily with foreigners; spent time in Veracruz and Texas; may have had English tutor.
3a. Exiled to sea, never to hear name of United States again.
3b. Lived fifty-five years on ships, never coming near United States; reading material censored; no one permitted to speak to him of homeland.
4. From considering imprisonment as farce and pretending to enjoy journey, to shy, nervous-looking man who was gentle, selfless, uncomplaining, silent sufferer.

thought he was tired and would sleep. I knew he was happy, and I wanted him to be alone.

But in an hour, when the doctor went in gently, he found Nolan had breathed his life away with a smile.

We looked in his Bible, and there was a slip of paper at the place where he had marked the text:

They desire a country, even a heavenly: where God is not ashamed to be called their God: for he hath prepared for them a city.[36]

On this slip of paper he had written this:

Bury me in the sea; it has been my home, and I love it. But will not someone set up a stone for my memory, that my disgrace may not be more than I ought to bear? Say on it:

In Memory of
PHILIP NOLAN
Lieutenant in the Army
of the United States

74

HE LOVED HIS COUNTRY
AS NO OTHER MAN HAS LOVED HER;
BUT NO MAN DESERVED LESS
AT HER HANDS.

36. **They desire . . . a city:** The passage is from Hebrews 11:16.

The Star Spangled Banner published by Currier and Ives. Colored lithograph.

Print Collection, Miriam and Ira D. Wallach Division, Division of Art, Prints and Photographs, The New York Public Library, Astor, Lenox and Tilden Foundations

For Study and Discussion

Analyzing and Interpreting the Story

1. Who is telling this story? Why does he believe the story of Philip Nolan should be told?

2. What facts does the narrator give about Nolan's early life that might explain why he joined Aaron Burr and why he later renounced the United States?

3a. What was Nolan's punishment? **b.** How was the punishment carried out?

4. How did Nolan change during his years at sea?

5. After Nolan dies, the narrator tells you on page 153: "He has found a home at last, and a

---

Reading Check

1. What was the name of the man without a country?
2. Where was he educated?
3. What did the men on the ships call him?
4. What did he receive from the commodore after the battle with the English?
5. What was his last request?

Panel discussions could be held on such questions as these: (A) If Philip Nolan had uttered the same disrespectful oath in a United States courtroom sometime during the last three years, would his punishment have been as severe? (B) Would modern audiences find themselves moved to greater patriotism on reading this story? (C) Were the naval men who helped carry out the sentence of silence for more than fifty years correct in their actions?

Students particularly interested in music might like to investigate the opera Arthur Guiterman and Walter Damrosch based on this story.

---

country." What do you think the narrator means by "home" and "country" here?

6. This story was written in 1863, when the United States was in danger of being destroyed by the Civil War. Which passages in the story show that the author wants to impress upon the reader the importance of national unity?

7. Look back at the passage from *The Lay of the Last Minstrel* on page 147. Which lines from this poem could be used to express the main idea of this story?

Focus on Reading

Noting Details That Suggest Authenticity

"The Man Without a Country" is not a true story. However, the author uses certain techniques to make the reader think it is true, or to give it the appearance of *authenticity*. For example, the story opens with a quotation from the "Deaths" column of a real newspaper, a source most people trust. The author cites the date of the newspaper and even the name and the exact position of the ship. What real people and historical events does the author use to suggest authenticity?

Focus on Persuasive Writing

Choosing a Topic

One of Edward Everett Hale's goals in writing his story was persuasive: he wanted to encourage patriotism during the Civil War. In **persuasive writing** you state a clear opinion on a topic and then support your opinion with reasons and with appeals to the emotions of your audience. Your purpose is to persuade the audience to agree with you. Sometimes your purpose is also to get your audience to take action.

To find a topic for persuasive writing, follow these two steps:

1. Be sure that the issue you choose is a matter of opinion, rather than a matter of fact. An *opinion* is a belief or an attitude; a *fact* can be checked for truth. Choose an issue about which people can or do disagree.

2. Be sure the topic is an issue that matters, both to you and to your audience. Don't choose an issue that isn't worth arguing about!

Explore topics for persuasion by listening to radio, watching television, looking through some recent issues of magazines, or brainstorming with a small group of classmates. Make some notes on two or three topics that interest you. Save your writing.

About the Author

Edward Everett Hale   (1822–1909)

Edward Everett Hale, a grandnephew of the famous Nathan Hale of the American Revolution, was a highly respected clergyman, journalist, and teacher. Hale worked for many social reforms in his lifetime, including education, housing, and world peace. In 1863 he published "The Man Without a Country" to try to inspire greater patriotism during the Civil War. The story became very popular as a blend of fiction and history. In 1903 Hale was named chaplain of the United States Senate.

---

5. Perhaps heaven.
6. Nolan's speech about love of country (p. 153); comments on his life (p. 154).
7. Responses will vary; first three lines good possibility.

FOCUS ON READING
1. Real details include: Aaron Burr and his failed conspiracy; *The Lay of the Last Minstrel;* slave incident based on actual law; Danforth uses real names, places, events when telling Nolan what happened during years of his exile.

FOCUS ON PERSUASIVE WRITING
You might want to provide students with a supply of current magazines and newspapers to skim for possible topics for a persuasive essay. Also, since effective persuasion deals with topics about which the writer cares, you might want to have students brainstorm a list of issues of special concern to them.

ABOUT THE AUTHOR
Edward Everett Hale was born in Boston and began his prolific writing career at an early age by publishing stories and even his own newspaper. He graduated from Harvard in 1839 and worked as a teacher, minister, and writer. His literary output included a wide range of novels, stories, and essays. "The Man Without a Country" first appeared in the December 1863 issue of the *Atlantic Monthly.* The story caused a stir at the time because many readers believed it was true and were outraged.

OBJECTIVES

The overall aim is for students to explain the nation's purpose as set forth in the Gettysburg Address. For a complete list of objectives, see the **Teacher's Notes**.

FOCUS / MOTIVATION

The Gettysburg Address is perhaps the single most famous speech given by an American. Much of the speech's impact comes from its beauty.

PRESENTATION

You might begin by reminding students that Gettysburg was an especially important battle in the Civil War. After the Confederate troops lost there, the South had no real hope of winning the war. More than 55,000 men were killed,

TEACHING RESOURCES B

Teacher's Notes, p. 110
Study Guide, p. 112
Building Vocabulary, p. 120
Selection Test, p. 114

AV RESOURCES BINDER

Audiocassette 1, Side B

PREREADING FOCUS

The Gettysburg Address was in response to the terrible loss of life at Gettysburg. Ask students to be alert to Lincoln's references to the sacrifices of those who died.

The annotations will help you analyze the speech from a modern perspective.

The Gettysburg Address

1

A "score" is twenty.

2

Birth of nation compared to birth of baby.

3

Repetition of "we cannot" adds cumulative force to idea that those who dedicate are unable to bestow honors befitting those who fought.

4

Readers view this statement ironically today because of speech's enduring popularity.

5

Metaphor. Birth is metaphorically used to describe cause of freedom to which survivors must rededicate themselves.

6

Lincoln stresses that democracy, like a living thing, may perish. It must be protected and defended.

The Gettysburg Address

ABRAHAM LINCOLN

On November 19, 1863, President Abraham Lincoln delivered this speech at a ceremony to dedicate the Soldiers' National Cemetery at Gettysburg, Pennsylvania. Gettysburg had been the scene of one of the most terrible battles of the Civil War. Edward Everett, who spoke before Lincoln, said that the President came closer to expressing the importance of the occasion in two minutes than Everett himself had done in two hours.

1 Four score and seven years ago our fathers brought forth on this continent a new nation, **2** conceived in liberty, and dedicated to the proposition that all men are created equal.

Now we are engaged in a great civil war, testing whether that nation, or any nation so conceived and dedicated, can long endure. We are met on a great battlefield of that war. We have come to dedicate a portion of that field as a final resting place for those who here gave their lives that that nation might live. It is altogether fitting and proper that we should do this. **3** But, in a larger sense, we cannot dedicate — we cannot consecrate — we cannot hallow — this ground. The brave men, living and dead, who struggled here, have consecrated it far above our poor power to add or detract. The world **4** will little note nor long remember what we say here, but it can never forget what they did here. It is for us, the living, rather, to be dedicated here to the unfinished work which they who fought here have thus far so nobly advanced. It is rather for us to be here dedicated to the great task remaining before us — that from these honored dead we take increased devotion to that cause for which they gave the last full measure of devotion — that we here highly resolve that these dead shall not have died in vain — that this **5** nation, under God, shall have a new birth of freedom — and that government of the people, **6** by the people, for the people, shall not perish from the earth.

wounded, or missing at Gettysburg. You could explain that "four score and seven" means eighty-seven and that Lincoln refers to the American Revolution in the first sentence. You may want to read the address aloud while students follow in their textbooks.

Abraham Lincoln, November 15, 1863. This photograph was taken by Alexander Gardner (1821–1882) four days before the Gettysburg Address was delivered.

For Study and Discussion

Analyzing and Interpreting the Speech

1. In the Gettysburg Address, Abraham Lincoln presents three images of America— one from the past, one of the present, one for the future. In the first paragraph how does he describe the nation that was created "four score and seven years ago"?

2. In the second and third paragraphs, Lincoln speaks of the present time. Why can't the people at the ceremony make the battleground any more sacred than it already is?

3. The last part of the third paragraph focuses on the future. What national purpose does the President set for the people?

4. Where does President Lincoln present an image of the nation as something alive?

OBJECTIVES
The overall aim is for students to make comparisons between the President and a ship's captain and the nation and a ship. For a complete list of objectives, see the **Teacher's Notes.**

FOCUS / MOTIVATION
Ask students how they felt on hearing of the death of someone they liked and respected. Alternatively, ask them if they can think of instances where happiness has changed abruptly into sadness.

PRESENTATION
You could read the poem aloud as students follow in their books. Begin discussion by having students comment upon the obvious **extended metaphor** (the President as a ship's captain and the nation as a ship). You may want to have stu-

TEACHING RESOURCES B

Teacher's Notes, p. 116
Study Guide, p. 118
Building Vocabulary, p. 120

AV RESOURCES BINDER

Audiocassette 1, Side B

PREREADING FOCUS
The headnote stresses that the poem was prompted by the assassination of Lincoln. Alert students to the fact that Lincoln's name is never mentioned even though the poem is about him.

O Captain! My Captain!

1
Metaphor. Trip is metaphor for Civil War. Lincoln has served as "Captain" or leader. Nation, like ship, has weathered storm.

2
Repetition of "heart" reinforces poet's feelings of remorse.

3
Prizes for successfully navigating through war are of no use to dead; paradox—a time of joy and of mourning.

4
Use to answer **study question 1c,** p. 161.

5 Making Inferences
Why does Whitman refer to Lincoln's death as a dream?
Responses will vary. Poet has difficulty accepting reality of tragedy.

O Captain! My Captain!

WALT WHITMAN

Walt Whitman wrote this poem during a tragic time in America's history. In 1865 the American people were relieved that the Civil War was ending. But the relief turned to sadness again when the news came that President Abraham Lincoln had been assassinated.

1 O Captain! my Captain! our fearful trip is done,
The ship has weathered every rack,° the prize we sought is won,
The port is near, the bells I hear, the people all exulting,
While follow eyes the steady keel, the vessel grim and daring;
2   But O heart! heart! heart!   5
      O the bleeding drops of red,
         Where on the deck my Captain lies,
           Fallen cold and dead.

O Captain! my Captain! rise up and hear the bells;
Rise up— for you the flag is flung— for you the bugle trills,   10
3 For you bouquets and ribboned wreaths— for you the shores
    a-crowding,
For you they call, the swaying mass, their eager faces turning;
4   Here Captain! dear father!
      This arm beneath your head!
5   It is some dream that on the deck   15
          You've fallen cold and dead.

My Captain does not answer, his lips are pale and still,
My father does not feel my arm, he has no pulse nor will,
The ship is anchored safe and sound, its voyage closed and done,
From fearful trip the victor ship comes in with object won;   20
    Exult O shores! and ring O bells!
      But I with mournful tread
        Walk the deck my Captain lies,
          Fallen cold and dead.

2. **rack:** here an upheaval caused by a storm.

160

dents give oral answers to the **For Study and Discussion** exercise on this page. You could tell students that Whitman's poem reflects personal and public grief over Lincoln's death.

CLOSURE

Ask students to point out ways in which the poem expresses the grief and shock the nation felt after Lincoln's assassination. Have them discuss the poem's use of **metaphor**, especially **extended metaphor.**

EXTENSION AND ENRICHMENT

If resources are available, students could research the responses of various political leaders and newspaper editors to Lincoln's assassination. Students might word their own tributes to leaders they admire.

For Study and Discussion

Analyzing and Interpreting the Poem

1. Whitman does not tell you directly who the "Captain" is. However, the readers of his day knew that the "Captain" was President Lincoln, and that the "ship" was the country. **a.** In what ways are a President and a ship's captain alike? **b.** In what ways is a nation like a ship? **c.** What else does Whitman call Lincoln?

2. This ship has been through a "fearful trip." What does this "fearful trip" stand for?

3. The ship is coming into "port." The "port" is the peace that the country has finally found. Is "port" a good way to describe peace? Why or why not?

Photograph of Lincoln's funeral showing the catafalque passing through the streets of Springfield, Illinois.

About the Author

Walt Whitman   (1819–1892)

Walt Whitman was born on Long Island, New York. For several years he worked as a journalist, but he was fired from his job for his strong antislavery views. Trips to Chicago and New Orleans intensified his appreciation of his country, and he soon began to write poetry. In 1855 Whitman published a collection of his own poems called *Leaves of Grass*. It was an extraordinary work, unlike any poetry that had appeared before. The public was astonished by the driving rhythms, the enthusiastic statements, and the frank language. Throughout his life Whitman continued to revise and add poems to *Leaves of Grass*. The book has had a tremendous influence on later poets.

During the Civil War, Whitman served as a volunteer nurse, caring for the wounded who filled the military hospitals. A great lover of America, Whitman was deeply affected by the assassination of Abraham Lincoln. His greatest poem about Lincoln's death is "When Lilacs Last in the Dooryard Bloomed."

O Captain! My Captain! **161**

Too Soon a Woman

DOROTHY M. JOHNSON

We left the home place behind, mile by slow mile, heading for mountains, across the prairie where the wind blew forever.

At first there were four of us with the one-horse wagon and its skimpy load. *1* Pa and I walked, because I was a big boy of eleven. My two little sisters romped and trotted until they got tired and had to be boosted up into the wagon bed.

That was no covered Conestoga,[1] like Pa's folks came West in, but just an old farm wagon, drawn by one weary horse, creaking and rumbling westward to the mountains, toward the little woods town where Pa thought he had an old uncle who owned a little two-bit sawmill.

2 Two weeks we had been moving when we picked up Mary, who had run away from somewhere that she wouldn't tell. Pa didn't want her along, but she stood up to him with no fear in her voice.

3 "I'd rather go with a family and look after kids," she said, "but I ain't going back. If you won't take me, I'll travel with any wagon that will."

Pa scowled at her, and her wide blue eyes stared back.

"How old are you?" he demanded.

"Eighteen," she said. "There's teamsters come this way sometimes. I'd rather go with you folks. But I won't go back."

4 "We're prid'near out of grub," my father told her. "We're clean out of money. I got all I can handle without taking anybody else." He turned away as if he hated the sight of her. "You'll have to walk," he said.

So she went along with us and looked after the little girls, but Pa wouldn't talk to her.

On the prairie, the wind blew. But in the mountains, there was rain. When we stopped at little timber claims along the way, the home-*5* steaders said it had rained all summer. Crops among the blackened stumps were rotted and spoiled. There was no cheer anywhere, and little hospitality. The people we talked to were past worrying. They were scared and desperate.

So was Pa. He traveled twice as far each day as the wagon, ranging through the woods with his rifle, but he never saw game. He had been depending on venison,[2] but we never got any except as a grudging gift from the homesteaders.

He brought in a porcupine once, and that was fat meat and good. Mary roasted it in chunks over the fire, half crying with the smoke. Pa and I rigged up the tarp sheet for a shelter to keep the rain from putting the fire clean out.

The porcupine was long gone, except for some of the tried-out fat[3] that Mary had saved, when we came to an old, empty cabin. Pa said

---

1. **Conestoga** (kŏn'ĭs-tō'gə): a covered wagon with broad wheels, used by American pioneers in crossing the prairies.

2. **venison** (vĕn'ə-sən, -zən): deer meat.
3. **tried-out fat:** fat that is rendered, or melted down.

MOTIVATIONAL SUMMARY

A pioneer family, consisting of a poor but resourceful man and his three children, travel west, first across arid prairie and then through mountains. They are joined by Mary, an eighteen-year-old runaway. They cannot find game, and they run out of food. Desperate, the father goes in search of food, leaving the children with Mary.

PRESENTATION

You could assign this story for reading out of class. Tell students to be alert as they read to facts that contribute to the **setting** of the story, including the narrator's **dialect**. After the class has read the story, you could give some historical

we'd have to stop. The horse was wore out, couldn't pull anymore up those grades on the deep-rutted roads in the mountains.

At the cabin, at least there was shelter. We had a few potatoes left and some corn meal. There was a creek that probably had fish in it, if a person could catch them. Pa tried it for half a day before he gave up. To this day I don't care for fishing. I remember my father's
6 sunken eyes in his gaunt, grim face.

He took Mary and me outside the cabin to talk. Rain dripped on us from branches overhead.

"I think I know where we are," he said. "I calculate to get to old John's and back in about four days. There'll be grub in the town, and they'll let me have some whether old John's still there or not."

7 He looked at me. "You do like she tells you," he warned. It was the first time he had admitted Mary was on earth since we picked her up two weeks before.

"You're my pardner," he said to me, "but it might be she's got more brains. You mind what she says."

He burst out with bitterness. "There ain't anything good left in the world, or people to care if you live or die. But I'll get grub in the town and come back with it."

He took a deep breath and added, "If you
8 get too all-fired hungry, butcher the horse. It'll be better than starvin'."

He kissed the little girls goodbye and plodded off through the woods with one blanket and the rifle.

The cabin was moldy and had no floor. We kept a fire going under a hole in the roof, so it was full of blinding smoke, but we had to keep the fire so as to dry out the wood.

9 The third night we lost the horse. A bear scared him. We heard the racket, and Mary and I ran out, but we couldn't see anything in the pitch-dark.

In gray daylight I went looking for him, and I must have walked fifteen miles. It seemed like I had to have that horse at the cabin when Pa came or he'd whip me. I got plumb lost two or three times and thought maybe I was going to die there alone and nobody would ever know it, but I found the way back to the clearing.

That was the fourth day, and Pa didn't come. That was the day we ate up the last of the grub.

The fifth day, Mary went looking for the horse. My sisters whimpered, huddled in a quilt by the fire, because they were scared and hungry.

I never did get dried out, always having to bring in more damp wood, and going out to yell to see if Mary would hear me and not get
10 lost. But I couldn't cry like the little girls did, because I was a big boy, eleven years old.

It was near dark when there was an answer to my yelling, and Mary came into the clearing.

Mary didn't have the horse—we never saw hide nor hair of that old horse again—but she was carrying something big and white that looked like a pumpkin with no color to it.

She didn't say anything, just looked around and saw Pa wasn't there yet, at the end of the fifth day.

"What's that thing?" my sister Elizabeth demanded.

"Mushroom," Mary answered. "I bet it hefts[4] ten pounds."

"What are you going to do with it now?" I
11 sneered. "Play football here?"

"Eat it—maybe," she said, putting it in a corner. Her wet hair hung over her shoulders. She huddled by the fire.

My sister Sarah began to whimper again. "I'm hungry!" she kept saying.

"Mushrooms ain't good eating," I said. "They can kill you."

4. **hefts:** weighs.

6
Alliteration. Repetition of *g* sound in one-syllable words creates stark, harsh sound to mirror **description** of father's fatigue and despair.

7
Father refuses to address Mary by name, but he knows her to be strong person.

8 Finding Cause and Effect
What would be the consequences of killing the horse?
Responses will vary. May include thoughts of family's being stranded, perhaps resulting in eventual death.

9
Conflict. People-versus-nature conflict, seen earlier in references to wind and rain, continues with bear.

10
Characterization. Second time narrator mentions himself as a big boy of eleven, indicating his attempts to be grown up and the pressure inherent in his situation to grow up quickly.

11
Narrator's sneering is sarcastic. Ill humor no doubt is result of hunger.

TRANSPARENCY 14
Reader Response
Put up a Statue – invites students to plan a commemorative statue of a character from the unit.

TRANSPARENCY 16
Literary Elements
Imagery – examines the use of imagery that appeals to the reader's senses.

18
Nature's hostilities subside.

19
Symbol. Sun suggests life, hope.

20 Expressing an Opinion
Could this story be titled "Too Soon a Man," indicating narrator's coming of age? Responses will vary. Narrator learns from experiences.

READING CHECK
1. Eleven (p. 162).
2. West to mountains, to town where father's uncle may live (p. 162).
3. Bear frightens horse away (p. 163).
4. Six (p. 163).
5. Food (p. 166).

FOR STUDY AND DISCUSSION
1. Pa angry at Mary; may feel she has taken advantage of him; family's provisions low, but he feels he cannot in good conscience leave her behind.
2. Rained so much crops have spoiled; no game available.
3. Must get food or family will starve; knows children probably would not survive walk to town.
4. Must terrify them so they will not eat mushroom until she determines if it is poisonous.
5. She has no money but has run away from abusers; does not back down when asking Pa to let her travel with family; endures hardship without complaint; cares for girls, cooks even though Pa ignores her; shows no self-pity.
6. Responses may vary.

ABOUT THE AUTHOR
Dorothy Johnson was as well-known for her children's books as for her westerns. Her books have been translated into over a dozen languages.

Mary ruled, "That'll hold you," and would not cook any more. She didn't touch any of the mushroom herself.

That was a strange day in the moldy cabin. Mary laughed and was gay; she told stories, and we played "Who's Got the Thimble?" with a pine cone.

In the afternoon we heard a shout, and my sisters screamed and I ran ahead of them across the clearing.

18 The rain had stopped. My father came plunging out of the woods leading a pack horse—and well I remember the treasures of food in that pack.

He glanced at us anxiously as he tore at the ropes that bound the pack.

"Where's the other one?" he demanded.

Mary came out of the cabin then, walking *19* sedately. As she came toward us, the sun began to shine.

20 My stepmother was a wonderful woman.

Reading Check

1. How old is the boy in the story?
2. What is the family's destination?
3. What happens to the horse?
4. How many days do the children and Mary spend in the cabin?
5. What does the father bring on the pack horse?

For Study and Discussion

Analyzing and Interpreting the Story

1. Pa allows Mary to travel with his wagon. Why, then, won't he speak to her?
2. Why is it difficult for the family to find food?
3. Why is the father forced to leave his family in Mary's care?

4. Consider Mary's behavior after she finds the mushroom. Why is her harsh treatment of the children necessary?
5. How are you prepared early in the story for the strength in Mary's character?
6. Were you surprised by the conclusion of the story? Tell why or why not.

Writing About Literature

▶ **Relating Fiction to History**

In a short essay, show how this story reveals the hardships faced by many early settlers in moving west across the prairie.

About the Author

Dorothy Johnson   (1905–1984)

Dorothy Johnson was born in McGregor, Iowa. After graduating from the University of Montana in 1928, she worked as a magazine editor in New York City for many years. She then moved back to Montana, where she worked as a news editor, professor of journalism, and secretary-manager for the Montana State Press Association. Johnson also became an honorary member of the Blackfeet tribe of Montana. Her stories are famous for their realistic and respectful portrayal of Native Americans and the American West. Several of her novels were made into films, such as *The Man Who Shot Liberty Valence* (1953), *The Hanging Tree* (1957), and *A Man Called Horse* (1968). Her other well-known works include *Warrior for a Lost Nation* (1969), a biography of the Sioux chief Sitting Bull, and the novels *Buffalo Woman* (1977) and *All the Buffalo Returning* (1977).

▶Before students begin this writing assignment, you may want to refer them to the **Writing About Literature** section on p. 672.

The Oklahoma Land Run

EDNA FERBER

Exactly at noon on April 22, 1889, two million acres of Oklahoma territory were opened for settlement. On the border, some 50,000 land-seekers massed for the biggest stampede in the history of the West. This was the Oklahoma Land Run, a historical event that Edna Ferber used in her famous novel Cimarron.

The following selection is a scene from that novel. The Venables, a wealthy Kansas family, are listening to Yancey Cravat, a son-in-law, as he relates his adventures in the Land Run.

"I had planned to try and get a place on the Santa Fe train that was standing, steam up, ready to run into the Nation.[1] But you couldn't get on. There wasn't room for a flea. They were hanging on the cowcatcher[2] and swarming all over the engine, and sitting on top of the cars. It was keyed down to make no more speed than a horse. It turned out they didn't even do that. They went twenty miles in ninety minutes. I decided I'd use my Indian pony. I knew I'd get endurance, anyway, if not speed. And that's what counted in the end.

"There we stood, by the thousands, all night. Morning, and we began to line up at the Border, as near as they'd let us go. Militia all along to keep us back. They had burned the prairie ahead for miles into the Nation, so as to keep the grass down and make the way clearer. To smoke out the Sooners,[3] too, who had sneaked in and were hiding in the scrub oaks, in the draws,[4] wherever they could. Most of the killing was due to them. They had crawled in and staked the land and stood ready to shoot those of us who came in, fair and square, in the Run. I knew the piece I wanted. An old freighters' trail, out of use, but still marked with deep ruts, led almost straight to it, once you found the trail, all overgrown as it was. A little creek ran through the land, and the prairie rolled a little there, too. Nothing but blackjacks[5] for miles around it, but on that section, because of the water, I suppose, there were elms and persimmons and cottonwoods and even a grove of pecans. I had noticed it many a time, riding the range. . . .

"Ten o'clock, and the crowd was nervous and restless. Hundreds of us had been followers of Payne and had gone as Boomers[6] in the old Payne colonies, and had been driven out, and had come back again. Thousands from all parts of the country had waited ten years for

1. **the Nation:** the territory formerly occupied by five American Indian nations—the Cherokees, Creeks, Choctaws, Chickasaws, and Seminoles.
2. **cowcatcher:** a metal frame set on the front of a locomotive to remove obstructions, such as cows, from the tracks.
3. **Sooners:** people who occupied homestead land "sooner" than the authorized time for doing so.
From *Cimarron* by Edna Ferber. Copyright © 1930 by Edna Ferber; copyright © renewed 1957 by Edna Ferber. Reprinted by permission of Harriet F. Pilpel, as trustee and attorney for the Ferber Proprietors.

4. **draws:** gullies or ravines.
5. **blackjacks:** short oaks with black bark.
6. **Payne . . . Boomers:** David L. Payne was one of the leaders of the Boomers, people who settled illegally on the Unassigned Lands of central Oklahoma, but who were evicted by United States soldiers.

MOTIVATIONAL SUMMARY
It is April 22, 1889. The Oklahoma border is now open for settlement. Though the land is free, the stakes are high; selecting a good piece of land as opposed to a bad one can mean the difference between success and failure. A young man named Yancey Cravat and a young woman race toward the same piece of land. She is determined to get the property.

PRESENTATION
To establish the conversational tone of this extended monologue, to ease students past a few unfamiliar vocabulary words, and to build suspense, you may want to read aloud to the point at which the starting gun is fired to begin the

VISUAL CONNECTIONS
About the Artist
John Steuart Curry, of Kansas City, was an American Scene realist painter like Grant Wood. Reacting to abstract modernism, the American Scene painters of the 1920s and 1930s created a school of art that consciously set out to celebrate the old-fashioned virtues of city and small town life. After the Great Depression began in 1929, the painters of this school became increasingly socially conscious. The Federal Government's WPA (Works Progress Administration) was created to ease unemployment through instituting public works projects. The WPA hired many of these painters and encouraged the use of this style. Curry specialized in large, sweeping murals romanticizing American life, primarily western migration. Many of his murals are in government buildings in Washington, D. C.

National Gallery of Art

5

Simile. Numerous similes are found in this story.

6

Use to answer **study question 2a**, p. 172.

this day when the land-hungry would be fed. 5 They were like people starving. I've seen the same look exactly on the faces of men who were <u>ravenous</u> for food.

"Well, eleven o'clock, and they were crowding and cursing and fighting for places near the Line. They shouted and sang and yelled and argued, and the sound they made wasn't human at all, but like thousands of wild animals penned up. The sun blazed down. It was cruel. The dust hung over everything in a thick cloud, blinding you and choking you. The black dust of the burned prairie was over

6 everything. We were like a <u>horde</u> of fiends with our red eyes and our cracked lips and our blackened faces. Eleven thirty. It was a picture straight out of hell. The roar grew louder. People fought for an inch of gain on the Border. Just next to me was a girl who looked about eighteen—she turned out to be twenty-five—and a beauty she was, too—on a coal-black thoroughbred. . . .

"On the other side was an old fellow with a long gray beard—a plainsman, he was—a six-shooter in his belt, one wooden leg, and a flask of whiskey. He took a pull out of that every

The Oklahoma Land Rush (1938). Sketch for mural for Department of Interior Building, Washington, D.C., by John Steuart Curry (1847–1946). Oil on canvas.

of anyone that saw her, even in that crazy mob. The better to cut the wind, she had shortened sail and wore a short skirt, black tights, and a skullcap. . . .

9 "It turned out that the three of us, there in the front line, were headed down the old freighters' trail toward the creek land. I said, 'I'll be the first in the Run to reach Little Bear.' That was the name of the creek on the section. The girl pulled her cap down tight over her ears. 'Follow me,' she laughed. 'I'll show you the way.' Then the old fellow with the wooden leg and the whiskers yelled out, 'Whoop-ee! I'll tell 'em along the Little Bear you're both a-comin'."

"There we were, the girl on my left, the old plainsman on my right. Eleven forty-five. Along the Border were the soldiers, their guns in one hand, their watches in the other. Those last five minutes seemed years long; and funny, they'd quieted till there wasn't a sound. Listening. The last minute was an eternity. Twelve o'clock. There went up a roar that drowned the crack of the soldiers' musketry as they fired in the air as the signal of noon and the start of the Run. You could see the puffs of smoke from their guns, but you couldn't hear a sound. The thousands surged over the Line. It was like water going over a broken dam. The rush had started, and it was devil take the hindmost. We swept across the prairie in a cloud of black and red dust that covered our faces and hands **10** in a minute, so that we looked like black demons from hell. Off we went, down the old freight trail that was two wheel ruts, a foot wide each, worn into the prairie soil. The old man on his pony kept in one rut, the girl on her thoroughbred in the other, and I on my White-

minute or two. He was mounted on an Indian **7** pony like mine. Every now and then he'd throw back his head and let out a yell that would curdle your blood, even in that chorus of fiends. As we waited we fell to talking, the three of us, though you couldn't hear much in that uproar. The girl said she had trained her thoroughbred for the race. He was from Kentucky, and **10** **8** so was she. She was bound to get her hundred and sixty acres, she said. She had to have it. She didn't say why, and I didn't ask her. We were all too keyed up, anyway, to make sense. Oh, I forgot. She had on a get-up that took the attention

7
Foreshadowing. Foreshadows old man's violent death.

8
Characterization. Urgency of young woman's attitude toward land is important to ending of story. Sense of mystery adds touch of realism to story; so many people wanting land for various unknown reasons.

9
Conflict. All three vying for land in same area. Good-natured kidding belies danger, seriousness of their pursuit.

10
"Black demons from hell" describes mass intensity of land-seekers. Tremendous danger of falling and being trampled by horde of people, horses, wagons.

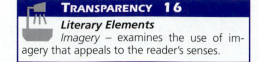

foot on the raised place in the middle. That first half mile was almost a neck-and-neck race. The old fellow was yelling and waving one arm and hanging on somehow. He was beating his pony with the flask on his flanks. Then he began to drop behind. Next thing I heard a terrible scream and a great shouting behind me. I threw a quick glance over my shoulder. The old plainsman's pony had stumbled and fallen. His bottle smashed into bits, his six-shooter flew in another direction, and he lay sprawling full length in the rut of the trail. The next instant he was hidden in a welter[7] of pounding hoofs and flying dirt and cinders and wagon wheels."

A dramatic pause. . . . The faces around the table were balloons pulled by a single string. They swung this way and that with Yancey Cravat's pace as he strode the room, his Prince Albert[8] coattails billowing. This way—the faces turned toward the sideboard. That way—they turned toward the windows. Yancey held the little moment of silence like a jewel in the circlet of faces. Sabra Cravat's voice, high and sharp with suspense, cut the stillness.

"What happened? What happened to the old man?"

Yancey's pliant hands flew up in a gesture of inevitability. "Oh, he was trampled to death in the mad mob that charged over him. Crazy. They couldn't stop for a one-legged old whiskers with a quart flask. . . .

"The girl and I—funny, I never did learn her name—were in the lead because we had stuck to the old trail, rutted though it was, rather than strike out across the prairie that by this time was beyond the burned area and was covered with a heavy growth of blue stem grass almost six feet high in places. A horse could only be forced through that at a slow pace.

That jungle of grass kept many a racer from winning his section that day.

"The girl followed close behind me. That thoroughbred she rode was built for speed, not distance. A racehorse, blooded. I could hear him blowing. He was trained to short bursts. My Indian pony was just getting his second wind as her horse slackened into a trot. We had come nearly sixteen miles. I was well in the lead by that time, with the girl following. She was crouched low over his neck, like a jockey, and I could hear her talking to him, low and sweet and eager, as if he were a human being. We were far in the lead now. We had left the others behind, hundreds going this way, hundreds that, scattering for miles over the prairie. Then I saw that the prairie ahead was afire. The tall grass was blazing. Only the narrow trail down which we were galloping was open. On either side of it was a wall of flame. Some skunk of a Sooner, sneaking in ahead of the Run, had set the blaze to keep the Boomers off, saving the land for himself. The dry grass burned like oiled paper. I turned around. The girl was there, her racer stumbling, breaking and going on, his head lolling now. I saw her motion with her hand. She was coming. I whipped off my hat and clapped it over White-foot's eyes, gave him the spurs, crouched down low and tight, shut my own eyes, and down the trail we went into the furnace. Hot! It was hell! The crackling and snapping on either side was like a fusillade.[9] I could smell the singed hair on the flanks of the mustang. My own hair was singeing. I could feel the flames licking my legs and back. Another hundred yards and neither the horse nor I could have come through it. But we broke out into the open choking and blinded and half suffocated. I looked down the lane of flame. The girl hung on her horse's neck. Her skullcap was pulled down over her

---

7. **welter:** great confusion or turmoil.
8. **Prince Albert:** a long, double-breasted coat.

9. **fusillade** (fyōō´sə-lād´): a burst of firearms.

11
Metaphor. Faces-as-balloons metaphor cleverly sustained throughout paragraph. Metaphors and **similes** become more literary and fresh when no longer from Yancey's "voice."

12
Narrator purposely breaks off story about old man so listeners anxiously left wondering about his fate.

13
Presents old man's death in matter-of-fact manner. One man's death meaningless to "mad mob."

14
Foreshadowing. Hint that thoroughbred will not make it to end of race.

15 Drawing Conclusions
What is the significance of the horse's head lolling? "Lolling" refers to hanging or drooping of head, clear indication horse is exhausted.

16
Metaphor. "Furnace" and "It was hell" used to emphasize tremendous heat of lane of fire.

eyes. She was coming through, game. I knew that my land—the piece that I had come through hell for—was not more than a mile ahead. I knew that hanging around here would probably get me a shot through the head, for the Sooner that started that fire must be lurking somewhere in the high grass ready to kill anybody that tried to lay claim to his **17** land. I began to wonder, too, if that girl wasn't headed for the same section that I was bound for. I made up my mind that, woman or no woman, this was a race, and devil take the hindmost. My poor little pony was coughing and sneezing and trembling. Her racer must have been ready to drop. I wheeled and went on. I kept thinking how, when I came to Little Bear Creek, I'd bathe my little mustang's nose and face and his poor heaving flanks, and how I mustn't let him drink too much, once he got his muzzle in the water.

"Just before I reached the land I was riding for I had to leave the trail and cut across the **19** prairie. I could see a clump of elms ahead. I knew the creek was nearby. But just before I got to it I came to one of those deep gullies you **20** find in the plains country. Drought does it—a crack in the dry earth to begin with, widening with every rain until it becomes a small canyon. Almost ten feet across this one was, and deep. No way around it that I could see, and no time to look for one. I put Whitefoot to the leap and . . . he took it, landing on the other side with hardly an inch to spare. I heard a wild scream **21** behind me. I turned. The girl on her spent racer had tried to make the gulch. He had actually taken it—a thoroughbred and a gentleman, that animal—but he came down on his knees just on the farther edge, rolled, and slid down the gully side into the ditch. The girl had flung herself free. My claim was fifty yards away. So was the girl, with her dying horse. She **18** lay there on the prairie. As I raced toward her—my own poor little mount was nearly

gone by this time—she scrambled to her knees. I can see her face now, black with cinders and soot and dirt, her hair all over her shoulders, her cheek bleeding where she had struck a stone in her fall, her black tights torn, her little short skirt sagging. She sort of sat up and looked around her, and stood there swaying, and pushing her hair out of her eyes like someone who'd been asleep. She pointed down the gully. The black of her face was streaked with tears.

"'Shoot him!' she said, 'I can't. His two forelegs are broken. I heard them crack. Shoot him!' . . .

"So I off my horse and down to the gully's edge. There the animal lay, his eyes all whites, his poor legs doubled under him, his flanks black and sticky with sweat and dirt. He was done for, all right. I took out my six-shooter and aimed right between his eyes. He kicked once, sort of leaped—or tried to, and then lay still. I stood there a minute, to see if he had to have another. He was so game that, some way, I didn't want to give him more than he needed.

"Then something made me turn around. The girl had mounted my mustang. She was off toward the creek section. Before I had moved ten paces she had reached the very piece I had marked in my mind for my own. She leaped from the horse, ripped off her skirt, tied it to her riding whip that she still held tight in her hand, dug the whip butt into the soul of the prairie—planted her flag—and the land was hers by right of claim."

Reading Check

1. Why had the prairie been burned?
2. What dangers did the Sooners represent?
3. What was the signal to begin the Run?
4. What happened to the plainsman?
5. Which piece of land did the girl get?

17
Suspense. Listeners (readers) strongly suspect woman and Yancey are in close competition.

18 Summarizing
Analyzing
What choice does Yancey make? What can be inferred of his character by this choice? He stops to help woman and dying horse. Responses will vary to second question. His choice is an unselfish one.

19
Conflict. Yancey admired and respected horse for its exceptional performance even though it belongs to his rival.

20 Analyzing
What does the woman's choice say about her character? Responses will vary. She looked after herself.

21
Clearly, right does not always win; he has underestimated her determination.

READING CHECK
1. Keep grass down to make way clearer (p. 167).
2. They were prepared to shoot those who came in Land Run (p. 167).
3. Soldiers fired shots (p. 169).
4. Trampled to death (p. 170).
5. Land that Yancey wanted (p. 171).

For Study and Discussion

Analyzing and Interpreting the Selection

1. This realistic description of the Oklahoma Land Run shows how desperate people were for new, free land. What does Yancey say the land-hungry people were like, in the third and fourth paragraphs?

2a. Which details in the fourth paragraph make you picture the scene as something from hell? **b.** How do you think the author wants you to feel about the Land Run?

3. The girl next to Yancey turns out to be his chief competitor in the race. What does Yancey tell you about the girl?

4a. How does the girl manage to stake her claim ahead of Yancey? **b.** What personal qualities cause Yancey's failure? **c.** What qualities make the girl the winner?

5. What do you think of the girl's actions?

Focus on Persuasive Writing

Writing an Opinion Statement

An **opinion statement** is a one-sentence sum-mary of how you feel or what you think about a topic. Writers often use the word *should* in an opinion statement. Here are some examples:

> An introduction to computers should be a required course for eighth-graders.
> Video games should be rated for their violence content.
> There should be a term limitation for all members of Congress.

Choose one of the topics for the assignment on page 157, or select a new topic. Write a one-sentence opinion statement that sums up your position. Save your notes.

About the Author

Edna Ferber (1885–1968)

Edna Ferber, one of the most popular nov-elists in America, at first wanted to be an actress. She aban-doned this ambition after her father became blind and she had to take a job as a newspaper reporter for three dollars a week. She threw her first novel away, but her mother rescued the manuscript and sent it to a pub-lisher. Edna Ferber later admitted that she had never written a book she was fully satisfied with. Her first best seller, *Show Boat*, was made into a stage musical and three movies. She won the Pulitzer Prize for *So Big*, a novel about a woman whose rugged individualism helps her triumph over disaster. *Cimarron* was a big hit as a movie, as was *Giant*, a novel about modern life in Texas. Though she had never intended to be a writer, Edna Ferber loved her profession. She once remarked that "life can't ever defeat a writer who is in love with writing."

OBJECTIVES
The overall aim is for students to show an understanding of the feelings of the speaker in the poem and to analyze how the poet uses **symbol** and **tone** to express those feelings. For a complete list of objectives, see the **Teacher's Notes.**

FOCUS / MOTIVATION
Ask students to imagine how they might feel if they were suddenly seen as "the enemy" by their classmates and even close friends. How would they react?

PRESENTATION
After students have shared their thoughts about being seen as "the enemy," read the poem aloud as students follow in their textbooks. Before you read, alert students to the fact that the poem is written in the form of a letter. You

In Response to Executive Order 9066:
ALL AMERICANS OF JAPANESE DESCENT MUST REPORT TO RELOCATION CENTERS

DWIGHT OKITA°

The title and subtitle of this poem refer to an order that was issued during World War II. More than 100,000 people on the West Coast were evacuated from their homes and relocated in internment camps. What insight does this poem give you into the feelings of young people whose lives were disrupted by this order?

Dear Sirs:
1 Of course I'll come. I've packed my galoshes
and three packets of tomato seeds. Janet calls them
"love apples." My father says where we're going
they won't grow.   5

I am a fourteen-year-old girl with bad spelling
and a messy room. If it helps any, I will tell you
I have always felt funny using chopsticks
and my favorite food is pizza.
My best friend is a white girl named Denise—   10
2 we look at boys together. She sat in front of me
all through grade school because of our names:
O'Connor, Ozawa. I know the back of Denise's head very well.
I tell her she's going bald. She tells me I copy on tests.
We are best friends.   15

I saw Denise today in Geography class.
3 She was sitting on the other side of the room.
"You're trying to start a war," she said, "giving secrets away
to the Enemy, Why can't you keep your big mouth shut?"
I didn't know what to say.   20
4 I gave her a packet of tomato seeds
and asked her to plant them for me, told her
when the first tomato ripens
to miss me.

°**Dwight Okita** (dwīt ō′kē-tä).

TEACHING RESOURCES B
Teacher's Notes, p. 145
Study Guide, p. 146
Selection Test, p. 149

AV RESOURCES BINDER
Audiocassette 1, Side B

PREREADING FOCUS
Point out that the word *executive* in the title refers to the executive branch of government, the presidency. President Franklin Roosevelt approved this order in 1942, after the bombing of Pearl Harbor. Then discuss with students why the President might have signed such an order.

In Response to Executive Order 9066

1
Irony. Name "love apples" is ironic considering situation. Father's statement that they will not grow at internment camps is ominous and emphasizes this irony.

2
Irony. Denise's Irish last name and speaker's Japanese last name are next to one another in alphabetical order, and names' pronunciations are similar. Implication is that only a few letters arranged in different order separate the two girls.

3 Drawing Conclusions
Why is it significant that Denise sits on other side of room? Emphasizes that Denise wants to distance herself from speaker, whom she now considers an enemy.

4
Symbol. Tomato, or "love apples," seeds symbolize friendship that speaker hopes she and Denise can somehow maintain.

could use the discussion questions to focus class discussion.

CLOSURE
Ask students to discuss the effectiveness of the central symbol of the poem—the tomato seeds. Or, have them suggest reasons that the poet might have chosen to use a fourteen-year-old girl as the speaker of this poem.

EXTENSION AND ENRICHMENT
Students might enjoy looking for other poems, stories, and artwork related to the relocation of Japanese Americans during World War II.

FOR STUDY AND DISCUSSION
1. Answers may vary. They symbolize the relationships that she hopes she can maintain even through distance and prejudice.
2. To emphasize that she is not an enemy agent plotting against the United States.
3. Answers may vary. Students might point out that the speaker and Denise have known each other a long time and are best friends.
4. Answers will vary. Students might say the speaker seems more confused than anything else. She does not understand how she can feel so American and yet be so ostracized.

FOCUS ON PERSUASIVE WRITING
You may want to suggest that students work in small groups to fill out their audience charts. Students can discuss with their group members possible topics and potential audiences for those topics. You might want to model the procedure before students work on their individual charts.

For Study and Discussion

Analyzing and Interpreting the Poem

1. The tomato seeds are mentioned in the first stanza and again at the end of the poem. What importance do they have for the speaker?

2. The speaker claims that she behaves just like any other girl her age. Why does she think that this information may help (line 7)?

3. Although Denise accuses her of aiding "the Enemy," the speaker wants to remain friends. Why?

4. How would you describe the speaker's tone in the poem? Is she angry? confused? hurt? Explain.

Focus on Persuasive Writing

Thinking About Your Audience

The **audience** for the "response" in Dwight Okita's poem was the United States government, which ordered Japanese Americans to be relocated in World War II.

When you plan a persuasive essay, consider your audience. How much do they already know about your topic? What are their interests and concerns? What person or group in the audience might disagree with your opinion, and why?

Choose one of the topics you have explored for earlier assignments in this unit. Fill out an audience chart like the one that follows. Save your notes.

Audience Chart

Topic: _____

Position/Opinion: _____
_____

Audience: _____

Prior Knowledge About Topic: _____
_____

Interests and Concerns: _____
_____

Possible Opposing Opinions: _____
_____

Likely Reasons for Opposition: _____
_____
_____

About the Author

Dwight Okita (1958–   )

Dwight Okita is a third-generation Japanese American who grew up in Chicago. In 1988 he received an Illinois Arts Fellowship in poetry. Besides poems he has written four stage plays. In 1992 Okita's collection of poetry *Crossing with the Light* was published. He has also collaborated on a video by the same title. He has said of his poetry: "I write the kind of poems that I like to read: visual and approachable. The sort of thing that might be fun finding in an old whiskey bottle along the shore, if you were stranded on an island."

American Folk Tales

Paul Bunyan's Been There

Retold by
MAURICE DOLBIER

Tales about Paul Bunyan, the giant logger, were first told in the northern lumber camps. Paul became popular with the general public when a logging company began using the stories in advertising brochures, to attract new workers. Since then, generations of storytellers have helped old Paul's tales grow taller and taller.

1 Wherever you go in this big country, you're likely to find somebody who'll tell you that Paul Bunyan's been there. Been there and 2 done things. Like digging the Great Lakes so that Babe would have watering troughs that wouldn't run dry, or digging a canal that turned out to be the Mississippi River.

You'll hear that the dirt he threw off to the right became the Rocky Mountains, and the dirt he threw off to the left became the Appalachians.

You'll hear that Kansas used to be full of mountains before Paul Bunyan came. He turned it upside-down. Now it's flat as a pancake because all its mountain peaks are inside the ground, pointing to the center of the earth.

3 You'll hear that Paul got so sad at what he saw going on in New York City that he fell to crying, and his tears started the Hudson River.

Western deserts or Southern swamps, Eastern shores or Northern forests, Paul is said to have been there and done things. And if by chance you can't find any stories about his hav- 4 ing been in your neck of the woods, fix some up. Everybody else has.

Right now, let's stick to the Northern forests, because we know for sure that Paul was there. 5 Paul and his men and the Blue Ox. They logged all through Michigan and Minnesota and the Dakotas, North and South, and they were always pushing westward to where the redwoods waited.

6 Maybe you'd like to know what life was like in those lumber camps of Paul Bunyan?

Well, the day started when the owls in the woods thought it was still night. The Little Chore Boy would blow his horn, and the men would tumble out of their bunks for chow.

There were always flapjacks for breakfast.

The legendary giant logger Paul Bunyan created the Great Lakes, the Mississippi River, the Appalachians, the Rocky Mountains, and flattened Kansas. There was not a job too big nor a problem too difficult for Paul Bunyan to handle. That

Students can read this story on their own, but you may want to read it aloud to add to the fun and to capture the zest of the colloquial style. You could let students discuss their favorite exaggerations in the story as well as any other tall

---

7
Intentional, obvious exaggeration is called **hyperbole**, characteristic of tall tales.

8
Sourdough bread common on frontier because yeast was rarely available.

9
Irony. Reader already is reading yarn "so whopping" it is unbelievable; adds to humor.

10
More exaggeration of weather, common subject of "whoppers."

11
Description. Frozen flames typical of creative details found in **tall tales.**

12 Analyzing
What is the effect of all this exaggeration? Adds to tale's humor as details become more and more outlandish.

---

7 These were made on a big round griddle about two city blocks wide. Before the batter was poured on, five men used to skate up and down and around on it with slabs of bacon tied on their feet. It'd take an ordinary man a week to eat one of the flapjacks that came off that griddle. Paul used to eat five or six every morning.

After breakfast came the work. The loggers tramped off to the woods. One crowd cleared the paths, another cut down the trees, another cut them up into logs, another piled them on carts or sledges. Then Babe the Blue Ox hauled the carts down to the water.

Soon after sunset, the men would all be back at the camp for supper. That was either baked beans or pea soup. Sometimes the cooks would surprise them, and serve pea soup or baked beans.

Sourdough Sam never liked to work very hard. One time he just dumped some split peas in the lake and then boiled the lake water and served it.

8 Matter of fact, Sam didn't stay with Paul Bunyan long. The men didn't mind that he was lazy, but they got almighty tired of sourdough. That's a kind of fermented dough that rises like yeast, and Sam used it in all his recipes. He put it in the coffee one morning. The Little Chore Boy drank a cup, and then started to rise into the air and float across the lake. They had to lasso him and pull him down.

9 After supper, they'd sit around and talk and sing and tell yarns so whopping that you'd never believe them.

Then, about nine o'clock, they turned in.

Of course, it wasn't all work at Paul's camp. The men would hunt and fish, and sometimes they'd have logrolling contests. That's when you **12** stand on a log in the middle of the water and start the log rolling under you, trying to keep your balance as long as you can. Joe Murfraw used to win, mostly. Paul Bunyan himself never took part, except to demonstrate, because

nobody could beat him anyway. He used to get the logs rolling so fast under foot that they set up a foam solid enough for him to walk to the shore on.

These are the things that went on fairly regularly, but I couldn't tell you what a typical day at Paul's camp was like. No day was typical. They were all special, and so was the weather.

10 There were fogs so thick that you could cut houses out of them, the way they do with snow and ice in the far north.

There were winds that blew up and down and in every direction at once.

There were thaws so quick that when the snow melted it just stayed there in big drifts of water for a week.

There was one time when all four seasons hit at once, and the whole camp came down with frostbite, sunstroke and spring fever.

There was another time when the rain didn't come from the skies at all. It came up from China, away underneath the world. Up from the ground it came, first in a drizzle and then in a pour, and it went straight up into the air. It got the sky so wet that the clouds were slipping and slopping around in the mud for a month.

But most of the stories you hear are about the winters that Paul Bunyan's loggers had to put up with. No one ever had winters like them before or since.

The cold was mighty intense. It went down to 70 degrees below zero, and each degree was 16 **11** inches long. The men couldn't blow out the candles at night, because the flames were frozen, so they had to crack the flames off and toss them outdoors. (When the warm weather came, the flames melted and started quite a forest fire.)

It was so cold that the words froze in mid-air right after they'd come out of people's mouths, and all the next summer nobody had to talk. They had a winter's supply of conversation on hand.

The cold wasn't the only thing that was pecul-

tales that come to mind. Emphasize that the story evolved from life in a lumber camp before the days of power saws, trucks, and even railroads. Ask students to think about what kind of person a logger had to be and have them comment on how these very traits are magnified to

create this larger-than-life logger. You may wish to point out that the North American tradition of exaggerating natural formations, weather, and encounters with inhabitants dates to early writings, such as those by Virginia colonist Captain John Smith.

MEETING INDIVIDUAL NEEDS
ESL/LEP • The story contains several colloquial words and expressions that may require explanation. These include *neck of the woods* (region or locality), *chow* (food), *almighty* (extremely), and *hotfoot* (to move in a hurry).

iar. Sometimes the snow was too. One winter it came down in big blue flakes, and Johnny Inkslinger used the icicles to write down the figures in his books. That's how he got the idea for inventing fountain pens. And the men used to have snowball fights until they were blue in the face.

Yes, the weather did all it could to upset Paul Bunyan's operations. And when the weather gave up, the mosquitoes tried.

One spring day, the men were working in a swamp, near a lake in northern Michigan, when **13** they heard a droning noise. They looked up to see the whole stretch of western horizon black with flying creatures heading right toward them. The men didn't stop to inquire. They dropped their tools and went hotfoot back to the camp and locked themselves up in the bunkhouse.

Pretty soon they heard a terrible racket over- **14** head, and then long things like sword blades began piercing through the tin roof. Paul Bunyan grabbed a sledgehammer and began pounding those stingers flat, so the mosquitoes couldn't get out. The rest of the mosquito army saw that it was no use and flew away.

Paul figured they'd be back with some new ideas, and he'd better have a new idea, too, just in case. So he sent Swede Charlie on a trip

down into Indiana. He'd heard they had a special kind of monster bumblebee there. Charlie brought some of these back, and Paul trained them to fly in a protective circle around the camp. He thought that the next time the mosquitoes came they'd have a surprise. They **15** did, and he did too. The bumblebees and the mosquitoes liked each other so much that they married and had children, and the children grew up with stingers in back and in front.

You won't hear anyone say that Paul Bunyan was ever stumped by any problem that came up. I won't say, either. But that section of timberland up in Michigan was the only place that Bunyan's men moved away from while there were still trees to be cut. I suppose they got a better offer.

Reading Check

1. According to this tale, how did Paul Bunyan create the Rocky Mountains?
2. What was the name of Bunyan's ox?
3. Identify Sourdough Sam.
4. What happened when Bunyan brought in monster bumblebees?

13
In fact, many settlers did experience insects in such hordes that they darkened sky; an example of realistic details that serve as basis for fanciful exaggeration.

14 Finding Details
What simile is used to describe the mosquitoes' stingers? Stingers are "long things like sword blades."

15
Personification. Mosquitoes and bumblebees given human characteristics, which adds to exaggeration and humor.

READING CHECK
1. As he dug canal that became Mississippi River, dirt thrown off to right became Rocky Mountains (p. 175).
2. Babe the Blue Ox (p. 175).
3. Lazy cook who used sourdough in all his recipes (p. 176).
4. Bees and mosquitoes fell in love and married (p. 177).

CLOSURE
Ask students to cite specific details that serve to characterize Paul Bunyan and tell how he is typical of a **tall tale** hero.

EXTENSION AND ENRICHMENT
Students might write a sequel to "Paul Bunyan's Been There" in which Paul and company return to defeat the mosquito-bees.

After reviewing the outlandish claims made for northern winters, some students might de-scribe an extreme tropical summer. Have them exaggerate the ways in which the heat affects people and the environment. Students who read other Bunyan stories from the suggested collections might tell their favorite to the class.

FOR STUDY AND DISCUSSION
1. Very tall, big, strong; tears formed Hudson River; every day ate five or six times as many flapjacks as ordinary man could eat in week; logrolled so fast, he set up foam solid enough to walk on.
2. Pounds stingers flat so they cannot get them out of tin roof; has monster bumblebees fly in protective circle around camp.
3. Dug Great Lakes as watering troughs for Babe; made Mississippi River when digging a canal: dirt thrown became Rocky Mountains and Appalachians; tears made Hudson River; flattened out Kansas by turning it upside down.
4. Became sad and cried over what he saw in New York City.

LITERARY ELEMENTS
1a. *Your neck of the woods:* your neighborhood or locality.
1b. *Blue in the face:* literally refers to one having no breath; figuratively means "exhausted or speechless."
1c. *Went hotfoot:* raced, rushed (as if fire burning one's feet).

CREATIVE WRITING
A relief map of your state might help generate ideas for this activity. So might a short brainstorming session about problems in your area. After this warm-up, students should work independently on their tall tales. Be sure to allow time for sharing completed stories.

178

For Study and Discussion

Analyzing and Interpreting the Selection

1. A **tall tale** is an exaggerated humorous story. Like the heroes of myths and legends, tall-tale figures often have superhuman characteristics. What exaggerated characteristics does the super-logger Paul Bunyan have?

2. Americans have become known as a people who are good problem-solvers. It isn't surprising that Paul Bunyan also has a reputation for being skilled at solving problems. How does he solve the mosquito problem?

3. Some tall-tale figures are so gigantic and powerful that their casual movements form lakes, rivers, deserts, and mountains. According to this tale, how did Paul Bunyan affect the geography of North America?

4. Tall-tale heroes of the frontier always live in the wilderness. Many of their stories show a distrust of city life and of the "city slicker." What passage in this story reveals that Paul dislikes city life?

Literary Elements

Recognizing Figures of Speech

Every language has expressions called **figures of speech.** Figures of speech are not literally, or factually, true. For example, the expression *on hand* in this sentence is used as a figure of speech:

> They had a winter's supply of conversation *on hand.*

The supply of conversation is not literally on top of anybody's hand. *On hand* here means "available; ready for use."

This story is told in a relaxed, informal style, the way that a storyteller might tell it aloud. It uses several figures of speech that are common **1** in informal American usage. Explain the

meaning of each of the italicized figures of speech in the following sentences from the story. Use your imagination to explain how each one might have originated.

a And if by chance you can't find any stories about his having been in *your neck of the woods,* fix some up.

b And the men used to have snowball fights until they were *blue in the face.*

c They dropped their tools and *went hotfoot* back to the camp and locked themselves up in the bunkhouse.

Creative Writing

Writing a Tall Tale

The teller of these tall tales about Paul Bunyan says: "And if by chance you can't find any stories about his having been in your neck of the woods, fix some up. Everybody else has."

Make up a brief story about Paul Bunyan that is set in your state or community. What natural features (mountain, river, cave, lake, swamp, cliff) can you explain with a tall tale about Paul Bunyan? What problems are perplexing people in your area? What does ol' Paul do to solve them?

You might want to read more about Paul Bunyan. Two good collections are *Ol' Paul* by Glen Rounds and *Paul Bunyan* by Esther Shephard.

The Deer Thief

Retold by
RUDOLFO A. ANAYA

As you read this Mexican American folk tale, notice how the hunter keeps his wits about him and, by using logic, recovers his losses.

1 A hunter was out hunting one day and killed a deer. Since it was very late in the day, he couldn't take the deer home, so he skinned it 2 and hung it as high as he could from the branch of a tall pine tree. The following day he returned for his deer, but the deer was gone. He searched the area for tracks. He inspected everything very carefully, and then he went to 3 the Justice of the Peace to seek redress.

The Justice of the Peace asked him if he had any idea who stole the deer. The hunter replied that he had not seen the thief and he didn't know who it was, but he could give an accurate description of the man who stole the deer.

"If you know something, tell me what kind of man he is," the Justice of the Peace said.

4 "Well, he is shorter than I. He is older, and he had a yellow bulldog with him."

"But how do you know all that?"

"I know he is shorter than I because he had to put some logs beneath the tree to reach the deer," replied the hunter.

"And how do you know he is old?"

5 "Because he took short steps, like an old man."

"And how do you know he had a yellow dog?"

"I followed his tracks and I found yellow hair where the dog passed beneath low branches."

"But how do you know it was a bulldog?" the exasperated judge asked.

6 "Because when the old man was lowering the deer, the dog sat nearby and the way the stub of his tail dug into the ground told me it was a bulldog."

The judge was convinced and granted permission to look for a man fitting that description. After searching for some time the hunter and the Justice of the Peace arrived at a house where they saw a yellow bulldog. They knocked on the door and a small, old man appeared. Then they searched his barn and found the stolen deer. So the hunter, by using his wits, had tracked down the thief who had stolen his deer.

Man with Deer. Painted clay figurine, Carajá, Brazil.

Courtesy National Museum of the American Indian, Smithsonian Institution #3189

179

to formulate his description of the thief. He examines specific evidence and then comes to a more general conclusion. Ask students to think of instances when they have used this process. Are there any occupations that require this type of logical reasoning? (scientists, researchers)

CLOSURE
Have students identify the motives behind each character's actions.

EXTENSION AND ENRICHMENT
Students might find newspaper and magazine articles that relate how investigators used evidence to solve a criminal case. Other students might enjoy creating cartoons based on this tale.

FOR STUDY AND DISCUSSION

1. He inspects the surroundings very carefully.
2. The hunter notices the stack of logs under the tree, indicating thief's height; the short distance between footprints, showing thief's possible age; and the yellow hair and indention of the dog's tail, indicating color and type of dog.
3. With logical evidence, he convinces Justice of the Peace to look for a man who fits his detailed description.
4. Answers will vary. Students might mention Pecos Bill, Paul Bunyan, Davy Crockett, Robin Hood, and Bruh Rabbit.

FOCUS ON PERSUASIVE WRITING

Ask students to choose a topic from their earlier notes. Or you might brainstorm with students a list of other controversial issues. Help students to make sure they are identifying real issues and not just personal preferences. Then students can write their opinion statements and list their reasons. Before they start, provide examples of each type of logical appeal. You may want to provide students time outside class to consult sources for their reasons.

For Study and Discussion

Analyzing and Interpreting the Selection

1. When the hunter found that someone had stolen his deer, what was the first thing he did?

2. The hunter noted that the thief was shorter and older than himself. He also knew that the thief had a yellow bulldog with him. How did he determine these things?

3. How did the hunter succeed in recovering his stolen property?

4. The central character in a folk tale is often someone who uses his or her wits to outsmart or outmaneuver someone else. Think of some other folk tales in which the main character outwits others.

Focus on Persuasive Writing

Using Logical Appeals

The hunter in "The Deer Thief" uses a number of reasons to convince the Justice of the Peace that he knows what the thief looks like. In the same way, when you try to persuade an audience to adopt your opinion about an issue, your argument will carry more weight if you use **logical appeals** to support it.

The diagram below shows three useful types of logical appeal:

Logical Appeals →
- Reasons (telling why)
- Facts (information that can be checked)
- Expert Opinions (statements by authorities on a subject)

Choose a position you would like to support in a persuasive speech to a group in your neighborhood or at your school. Write a one-sentence statement of opinion. Then list as many reasons, facts, and expert opinions as you can to support your view logically. Save your notes.

About the Author

Rudolfo A. Anaya (1937–)

As a writer, Anaya has been greatly influenced by his New Mexican heritage. The mystical qualities of Spanish folk tales have especially inspired his novels. Anaya's highly praised first work, *Bless Me, Ultima* (1972), describes a struggle between good and evil and portrays characters typical of Spanish legends, like the healer Ultima. Although Anaya's work is based on folklore, it also deals with the problems of a young Mexican American boy growing up in a small New Mexican village during World War II. *Bless Me, Ultima, Heart of Aztlán* (1976), and *Tortuga* (1979) form a loosely connected trilogy about the Hispanic experience in America over several decades. Critics have praised Anaya for skillfully using the extraordinary elements of myth to tell a tale of realistic human experience. "The Deer Thief" uses a similar approach: The hunter applies his superior powers of observation and reasoning to solve a common problem, the disappearance of a stolen item.

Anaya holds a bachelor's and master's degree from the University of New Mexico, where he teaches creative writing. He has received a number of awards and fellowships, including the Before Columbus American Book Award and a National Endowment for the Arts Fellowship.

OBJECTIVES
The overall aim is for students to identify details that characterize Coyote and to analyze the irony of the end of the tale. For a complete list of objectives, see the **Teacher's Notes.**

FOCUS / MOTIVATION
Ask students to think of movies or television shows they have seen in which animals seem to be smarter than humans. List some of their responses on the chalkboard and discuss why these animal tales may have been so popular over the years.

PRESENTATION
This tale could be assigned as independent reading, either in class or at home, or could be quickly read aloud. Tell students that this folk tale is also a fable and that fables often have animal characters and are designed to teach people

Coyote Shows How He Can Lie

Retold by
BARRY LOPEZ

In the folk tales of many cultures, the fox, coyote, owl, jackal, and other animals are characterized as shrewd and mischievous. As you read this Native American tale, pay particular attention to the cunning ways of Coyote and think about other folk tales in which animals appear wiser than people.

1 Coyote came into a group of camps. The men were all sitting around. They knew Coyote was always telling lies.

The men called Coyote over. "Coyote," they said, "you are the biggest liar we've ever known."

"How do you know I lie?"

"Oh, you always make trouble and then you lie. You get away with things like that. You are very good at it. Why don't you teach us how to lie so we can lie successfully too?"

"Well," said Coyote, "I had to pay a big price for that power. I learned it from my enemy."

"What did you pay?"

"One horse. But it was my best buffalo horse, with a fine bridle."

"Is that all?"

"Yes."

2 They did not think that was much, for in those days there were plenty of horses. One man brought out a fine white buffalo horse, his best.

"Yes," said Coyote. "This is a good-looking horse. This is the kind I mean. It was with a horse like this that I paid for my power."

3 Then Coyote said, "Let me try the horse. If he doesn't buck, I'll explain my power."

They agreed and Coyote got up on the horse. Coyote had never been on a horse before and **4** he dug in with his claws to hold on. The horse began to buck.

"Oh! This horse needs a blanket, that is the trouble," said Coyote.

They put a blanket on the horse.

But Coyote's claws were sharp and they went through the blanket and the horse jumped again.

"Oh! He wants something more over his back. He wants a good saddle on."

So they got a good saddle and helped Coyote put it on the horse. Coyote got on again and then turned his head as though he were listening for something.

"That is my power speaking," he said. "That voice tells me he wants a whip too."

They gave him one.

He said, "I'm going around now and try this horse to see if he still bucks. I'll come right back and tell you about it."

5 He rode off a little way and then turned around and shouted back, "This is the way I lie. I get people to give me horses and blankets and saddles and other fine things." Then he rode away.

Coyote Shows How He Can Lie **181**

TEACHING RESOURCES B
Teacher's Notes, p. 160
Study Guide, p. 162
Language Skills, p. 165
Selection Test, p. 167

AV RESOURCES BINDER
Audiocassette 1, Side B

PREREADING FOCUS
The headnote says that the fox, coyote, owl, and jackal are characterized as shrewd and mischievous in many cultures. Ask students to consider what traits these animals possess that may have led to their being characterized in this way.

Coyote Shows How He Can Lie

1
Personification. Coyote is given human characteristics, including ability to talk.

2
Phrase "in those days" implies that events of story happened long ago, and that there are not plenty of horses anymore.

3
Coyote places a condition on his agreement to explain his power.

4 Making Inferences
Does Coyote dig in his claws on purpose to make the horse buck, thereby releasing himself from the agreement? Answers will vary. Have students explain their opinions.

5 Finding Main Ideas
Does Coyote fulfill his part of bargain? Answers will vary. Students might point out that Coyote says he will tell men how he lies if the horse does not buck and that since the horse stops bucking, Coyote does not renege on his promises.

lessons about how to behave. After students have read the tale, ask what lessons it teaches. Use the **For Study and Discussion** questions to help students to analyze the tale.

CLOSURE

Have students compare how the coyote uses his wits to how the hunter uses his in "The Deer Thief."

EXTENSION AND ENRICHMENT

Students might look for other folk tales or fables to present orally or as short plays to the class. Other students can research the contributions of folklore to music, art, drama, film, and other literature.

6

Irony. Coyote's lies do not pay off in the long run because the horse runs away. Use to answer **study question 4**, p. 182.

FOR STUDY AND DISCUSSION

1. He always makes trouble and then lies and gets away with it.
2. He tells lies.
3a. The power of lying successfully. **3b.** Answers will vary; perhaps he is referring to another animal or even man, who is the coyote's predator.
4. The horse runs away and returns to its owner.

CREATIVE WRITING

Students might work in pairs for this activity. Encourage students to do some improvisational role-playing to get ideas for their writing. Allow time for students to share or act out their dialogues.

The people couldn't do anything about it. Coyote went home and showed his wife what he had.

"Look at this fine horse," he said. "I took it away from an enemy out on the plains. It was some fight."

6 But Coyote did not know how to take care of the horse. When he got off, the horse walked away, back to its owner.

For Study and Discussion

Analyzing and Interpreting the Selection

1. Why is Coyote admired by the men at the camps?

2. What are the tricks Coyote uses to cheat the people of their possessions?

3. In the beginning of the tale, Coyote says, "I had to pay a big price for that power. I learned it from my enemy." **a.** What "power" is he referring to? **b.** Who do you think is the "enemy"?

4. In some stories about Coyote, he is punished for his mischief. What is ironic about the end of this folk tale?

Creative Writing

Writing a Dialogue

Fables and folk tales often have animal characters with the ability to speak. Below are several animal pairs. Pick a pair and write a dialogue between the two characters, in which one is trying to persuade the other to do something. Remember to use quotation marks to enclose each speaker's words.

> coyote and jackal
> hedgehog and fox
> bear and squirrel
> dolphin and shark
> butterfly and horse

About the Author

Barry Lopez (1945–   )

When Barry Holstun Lopez moved from New York to southern California as a child, he discovered images that greatly moved him—wild animals, the Mojave Desert, and the San Bernardino Mountains. He eventually left California, but when he returned years later, he felt "exhilarated, brought back to life, by the landscapes of the West." As a full-time writer and freelance photographer, he has devoted his career to observing and portraying the behavior of wild animals. His popular book *Of Wolves and Men* (1978) is both a scientific study of wolves and a history of their role in mythology, folklore, and fairy tales. In 1986 his book *Arctic Dreams,* inspired by trips to Alaska to study wildlife, won the American Book Award. In his acceptance speech Lopez said, "Even though I appear to write largely about other landscapes and animals, what is in my gut as a writer is a concern with the fate of the country I live in and the dignity and morality of the people I live with."

Lopez has traveled to northern Hokkaido in Japan, the Galápagos Islands, Africa, Antarctica, and China. He says that these journeys will be the subject of future works.

OBJECTIVES
The overall aim is for students to identify details that make "John Henry" a famous **folk tale**. For a complete list of objectives, see the **Teacher's Notes**.

VOCABULARY
All words in this **ballad** should be well within the independent reading range of most eighth graders. You may wish to discuss how the ballad's rich mountain **dialect** adds to the color and melody.

FOCUS / MOTIVATION
Have one student prepare a short oral report about a steel driver's work before mechanized railroad construction. Another might tell about automatic drills' capabilities. Then present John Henry as another legend drawn from life.

John Henry

John Henry was a real person, a steel driver, who is remembered for what he did and how he died. In 1870 John Henry raced an automatic steam drill in the Big Bend Tunnel of the Chesapeake and Ohio Railroad in the West Virginia mountains. What happened? The story is immortalized in this famous folk ballad.

John Henry was a little baby boy,
You could hold him in the palm of your hand,
He gave a long and lonesome cry,
"Gonna be a steel-drivin' man, Lawd, Lawd,
Gonna be a steel-drivin' man."   5

They took John Henry to the tunnel,
Put him in the lead to drive,
The rock was so tall, John Henry so small,
That he lied down his hammer and he cried, Lawd, Lawd,
Lied down his hammer and he cried.   10

John Henry started on the right hand,
The steam drill started on the left,
"Fo' I'd let that steam drill beat me down,
I'd hammer my fool self to death, Lawd, Lawd,
I'd hammer my fool self to death."   15

John Henry told his Captain,
"A man ain't nothin' but a man,
Fo' I let your steam drill beat me down
I'll die with this hammer in my hand, Lawd, Lawd,
I'll die with this hammer in my hand."   20

John Henry had a little woman
Her name were Polly Anne,
John Henry took sick and he had to go to bed,
Polly Anne drove steel like a man, Lawd, Lawd,
Polly Anne drove steel like a man.   25

TEACHING RESOURCES B
Teacher's Notes, p. 168
Study Guide, p. 169
Selection Test, p. 171

AV RESOURCES BINDER
Audiocassette 1, Side B

PREREADING FOCUS
The headnote emphasizes that John Henry was a real person. Suggest to students that they notice, as they read, elements in the **ballad** that exaggerate real life.

John Henry

1
"Lonesome cry" indicates job will be very hard.

2
Use to answer **study question 1,** p. 185.

3   Making Generalizations
What do you expect the conflict of the ballad to be? People versus machine.

4
Foreshadowing. John Henry eventually works himself to death.

5
Irony. The image conveyed by "little woman," a slang term for wife that suggests a small, delicate person, contrasts with her ability to drive steel like a man.

6
Use to answer **study question 4a,** p. 185.

A skillful dramatic reading or singing is a must for this **ballad,** which has a moderate blues tempo. The ballad originally was not written down, and there are many variations to the lyrics. Students should realize that although many of the events in the ballad are factual, exaggeration has affected the interpretation of those events. Follow the **For Study and Discussion** questions on p. 185 to clarify any hazy points without weighing the ballad down with too much analysis.

Now the Captain told John Henry,
"I b'lieve my tunnel's sinkin' in."
"Stand back, Captain, and doncha be afraid,
That's nothin' but my hammer catchin' wind, Lawd, Lawd,
That's nothin' but my hammer catchin' wind."   30

John Henry he told his shaker,°
"Now shaker, why don't you sing?
I'm throwin' nine pounds from my hips on down,
Just listen to the cold steel ring, Lawd, Lawd,
Just listen to the cold steel ring."   35

John Henry he told his shaker,
"Now shaker, why don't you pray?
For if I miss this six-foot steel
Tomorrow'll be your buryin' day, Lawd, Lawd,
Tomorrow'll be your buryin' day."   40

7 John Henry he told his Captain,
"Looky yonder, boy, what do I see?
Your drill's done broke and your hole's done choke,
And you can't drive steel like me, Lawd, Lawd,
8 And you can't drive steel like me."   45

John Henry hammerin' in the mountain
Till the handle of his hammer caught on fire,
He drove so hard till he broke his poor heart,
Then he lied down his hammer and he died, Lawd, Lawd,
Then he lied down his hammer and he died.   50

Women in the West heard of John Henry's death
They couldn't hardly stay in bed,
9 Stood in the rain, flagged that eastbound train
"Goin' where that man fell dead, Lawd, Lawd,
Goin' where that man fell dead."   55

10 They took John Henry to the tunnel,
And they buried him in the sand,
An' every locomotive come rollin' by
Say, "There lays a steel-drivin' man, Lawd, Lawd,
There lays a steel-drivin' man."   60

31. **shaker:** steel driver's assistant.

7

Conflict. John Henry has defeated drilling machine.

8 Analyzing Synthesizing
Why is the Captain using a steam drill? What social conflict does the ballad reflect? Captain thinks he can replace men with more efficient machines. **Ballad** evolved during Industrial Revolution when many industrialists replaced workers with machines, changing the nature of work and leading to social upheaval and eventually to some labor reform.

9
Use to answer **study question 4b,** p. 185.

10
Use to answer **study question 3,** p. 185.

CLOSURE
Ask students to identify the ambitions of John Henry and to cite the lines in the song that tell how his legendary reputation is kept alive.

EXTENSION AND ENRICHMENT
Some students may enjoy creating a modern version of John Henry in which the hero confronts another speedy machine—the computer. Ambitious students might like to conduct research concerning the **folk tales** of other lands.

Each interested student might select the tales of a different culture. Folk tales from Africa, Scandinavian countries, Greece, Germany, and Japan should prove of interest.

Now some say he come from England,
And some say he come from Spain,
11 But I say he's nothin' but a Lou'siana man,
Leader of a steel-drivin' gang, Lawd, Lawd,
Leader of a steel-drivin' gang.

65

For Study and Discussion

Analyzing and Interpreting the Song

1. Many folk heroes show unusual talents or promise when they are only babies. What ambition did John Henry reveal when he was so little he could be held in the palm of a hand?

2. The famous contest with the machine starts in the third stanza. How was John Henry both a winner and a loser in that battle?

3. According to the next-to-last stanza, how is John Henry's memory kept alive?

4a. How is Polly Anne also a heroic figure?
b. How did the actions of other women show how people felt about John Henry's tragic death?

Creative Writing

Writing a Ballad

Make up a brief song that tells a story about a colorful hero or heroine, real or imaginary. The words to many ballads are composed to old melodies. Here are three good ones:

"On Top of Old Smoky"
"My Darling Clementine"
"Sweet Betsy from Pike"

Connecting Cultures

Tall Tales

Improbable and exaggerated tales have existed since earliest times. Tall stories can be found in works more than two thousand years old as well as in recent writing. A long-winded tale with an absurd ending is called a *shaggy dog story*. A long, improbable story is sometimes called a *yarn*.

Making Connections: Activities

1. Consult a book on American folklore or an encyclopedia for information on one of these tall-tale figures:

Mike Fink
Casey Jones
Joe Margarac
Stormalong
Davy Crockett
Pecos Bill
Slue-Foot Sue

One source for stories is *Yankee Doodle's Cousins* by Anne Malcolmson. Another source is *Homespun: Tales from America's Favorite Storytellers*, edited by Jimmy Neil Smith.

2. Investigate tall-tale figures in different cultures and see what characteristics they share.

11
Emphasis placed on John Henry's being an American.

FOR STUDY AND DISCUSSION
1. He wanted to be a steel driver, even then.
2. He beat drill but lost his life.
3. He is buried where locomotives pass, and every one that passes says "there lays a steel-drivin' man."
4a. When John Henry became ill, she took over and drove steel like a man. **4b.** When women in West heard of his death, they stood in rain, flagged eastbound train, and went to "where that man fell dead."

CONNECTING CULTURES
As with previous research activities, you may want to work with your school's librarian in preparing for this project. Plan some tall-tales days on which students can share the stories they find and make comparisons among tall tales.

OBJECTIVES

The overall aim is for students to analyze the "lesson" taught by the teachers and to describe reactions by other characters. For a complete list of objectives, see the **Teacher's Notes.**

VOCABULARY

The underlined words are in the Glossary. The **Language and Vocabulary** exercise on p. 191 gives students practice in comparing words that imitate sounds.

FOCUS / MOTIVATION

Ask volunteers to share reminiscences of entering a school for the first time. What memories or apprehensions remain most vivid? Why would these apprehensions be even stronger if the new school were in a foreign country?

PREREADING FOCUS

The headnote emphasizes that this selection deals with the process of becoming an American. Students might discuss the ways public schools contribute to the Americanization process.

Barrio Boy

1

Being in an unfamiliar environment, narrator is focusing on what is different.

2

Galarza's close attention to details reflects first-grader's keen curiosity.

3

In Mexico, a *director* is almost always a man.

4

Portraits of Washington and Lincoln, presidents identified with strong American ideals. School named for Lincoln.

186

Barrio Boy

ERNESTO GALARZA

"The melting pot" is an expression often used to describe the United States. In "the melting pot," all nationalities are mixed together, so that they assimilate, or absorb, one another's ways. Ernesto Galarza says that his public school was not a melting pot. He thinks of it as a griddle, where knowledge was warmed into students and racial hatreds roasted out of them.

In this excerpt from Barrio° Boy, *his autobiography, Ernesto and his mother have just arrived in Sacramento, California, from their native Mexico. They are on their way to enroll Ernesto in public school.*

The two of us walked south on Fifth Street one morning to the corner of Q Street and turned right. Half of the block was occupied by the Lincoln School. It was a three-story wooden building, with two wings that gave it the shape of a double-T connected by a central hall. It was a *1* new building, painted yellow, with a shingled roof that was not like the red tile of the school in Mazatlán.[1] I noticed other differences, none of them very reassuring.

We walked up the wide staircase hand in hand and through the door, which closed by *2* itself. A mechanical contraption screwed to the top shut it behind us quietly.

Up to this point the adventure of enrolling me in the school had been carefully rehearsed. Mrs. Dodson[2] had told us how to find it and we had circled it several times on our walks. *3* Friends in the barrio explained that the *director*

°**Barrio:** the neighborhood or district of a city where Spanish-speaking people live.
1. **Mazatlán** (mä′sät-län′): a city in Mexico, where Ernesto lived before coming to the United States.
2. **Mrs. Dodson:** the landlady of the boardinghouse in which the Galarzas lived.

was called a principal, and that it was a lady and not a man. They assured us that there was always a person at the school who could speak Spanish.

Exactly as we had been told, there was a sign on the door in both Spanish and English: "Principal." We crossed the hall and entered the office of Miss Nettie Hopley.

Miss Hopley was at a roll-top desk to one side, sitting in a swivel chair that moved on wheels. There was a sofa against the opposite wall, flanked by two windows and a door that opened on a small balcony. Chairs were set *4* around a table and framed pictures hung on the walls of a man with long white hair and another with a sad face and a black beard.

The principal half turned in the swivel chair to look at us over the pinch glasses crossed on the ridge of her nose. To do this she had to duck her head slightly as if she were about to step through a low doorway.

What Miss Hopley said to us we did not know but we saw in her eyes a warm welcome and when she took off her glasses and straightened up she smiled wholeheartedly, like Mrs. Dod-

MOTIVATIONAL SUMMARY
Ernesto, who has recently arrived from Mexico and speaks no English, is enrolled at Lincoln School. He struggles to learn English from loving, though demanding, teachers. But Ernesto and the other immigrant children at his school

must learn something more than English from their teachers.

PRESENTATION
You could let students read this story independently, either in class or as homework. Allow time for students to comment spontaneously on parts of the story they liked best and to recount personal experiences similar to those recalled by

son. We were, of course, saying nothing, only catching the friendliness of her voice and the sparkle in her eyes while she said words we did not understand. She signaled us to the table. Almost tiptoeing across the office, I maneuvered myself to keep my mother between me and the gringo[3] lady. In a matter of seconds I had to decide whether she was a possible friend or a menace. We sat down.

Then Miss Hopley did a <u>formidable</u> thing. She stood up. Had she been standing when we entered she would have seemed tall. But rising from her chair she soared. And what she carried up and up with her were firm shoulders, a straight sharp nose, full cheeks slightly molded by a curved line along the nostrils, thin lips that moved like steel springs, and a high forehead topped by hair gathered in a bun. Miss Hopley was not a giant in body but when she <u>mobilized</u> it to a standing position she seemed a match for giants. I decided I liked her.

She strode to a door in the far corner of the office, opened it and called a name. A boy of about ten years appeared in the doorway. He sat down at one end of the table. He was brown like us, a plump kid with shiny black hair combed straight back, neat, cool, and faintly <u>obnoxious</u>.

Miss Hopley joined us with a large book and some papers in her hand. She, too, sat down and the questions and answers began by way of our interpreter. My name was Ernesto. My mother's name was Henriqueta. My birth certificate was in San Blas. Here was my last report card from the Escuela Municipal Número 3 para Varones of Mazatlán, and so forth. Miss Hopley put things down in the book and my mother signed a card.

As long as the questions continued, Doña Henriqueta could stay and I was secure. Now

3. **gringo:** a Spanish-American term for a foreigner.

that they were over, Miss Hopley saw her to the door, dismissed our interpreter and without further ado took me by the hand and strode down the hall to Miss Ryan's first grade.

Miss Ryan took me to a seat at the front of the room, into which I shrank—the better to survey her. She was, to skinny, somewhat runty me, of a withering height when she patrolled the class. And when I least expected it, there she was, crouching by my desk, her blond, radiant face level with mine, her voice patiently maneuvering me over the awful idiocies of the English language.

During the next few weeks Miss Ryan overcame my fears of tall, energetic teachers as she bent over my desk to help me with a word in the preprimer. Step by step, she loosened me and my classmates from the safe anchorage of the desks for recitations at the blackboard and consultations at her desk. Frequently she burst into happy announcements to the whole class. "Ito can read a sentence," and small Japanese Ito slowly read aloud while the class listened in wonder: "Come, Skipper, come. Come and run." The Korean, Portuguese, Italian, and Polish first-graders had similar moments of glory, no less shining than mine the day I conquered *butterfly*, which I had been persistently pronouncing in standard Spanish as "boo-ter-flee." "Children," Miss Ryan called for attention. "Ernesto has learned how to pronounce *butterfly!*" And I proved it with a perfect imitation of Miss Ryan. From that celebrated success, I was soon able to match Ito's progress as a sentence reader with "Come, butterfly, come fly with me."

Like Ito and several first-graders who did not know English, I received private lessons from Miss Ryan in the closet, a narrow hall off the classroom with a door at each end. Next to one of these doors Miss Ryan placed a large chair for herself and a small one for me. Keeping an eye on the class through the open door

5
Imagery. Details of Miss Hopley's appearance recall a soaring bird; as she stands, she seems to become larger than life.

6 Analyzing
What might this boy's demeanor convey to Galarza? That a Hispanic child can become comfortable at the school.

7
Doña: Title of respect used before a woman's given name.

8
Theme. Provides evidence to support his idea that children of different nationalities at the school were engaged in a common enterprise.

9
Symbol. Butterfly is result of a transformation (metamorphosis); Ernesto is also undergoing transformation.

the author—particularly their first impressions of a school principal or a first-grade teacher.

Galarza's "melting pot" **theme** reinforces the idea that it has taken all types of people from all walks of life to make America what it is today. Galarza's story also illustrates how a person can overcome obstacles (in his case, language and social barriers).

GEOGRAPHY LINK

Lincoln School hosted students from all over the world. Students might enjoy looking at a world map and identifying all the countries mentioned in the story. These include Japan, China, Italy, Mexico, Portugal, Poland, Yugoslavia, and Ireland.

VISUAL CONNECTIONS

Exploring the Subject

Before the advent of photography, only the wealthy could afford portraits. With the widespread use of photography in the nineteenth century, most people could afford to have a likeness of themselves made. Soon, even schools were able to afford to have photographers come to take class pictures.

Relating Expression Skills

You could suggest that interested students bring photographs of their parents' or grandparents' early group school pictures to share with the class. What similarities and differences do students see in these photographs compared to their own class pictures?

10 Summarizing

What quality does Miss Ryan have that is important to Galarza? He senses that her sympathies are with her students and that she cares about them.

11

"Lower part of town" indicates poor section.

12

Use to answer **study question 3a,** p. 191.

13

Use to answer **study question 4,** p. 191.

EACH PUPIL REPRESENTS A DIFFERENT RACE—21 DIFFERENT NATIONALITIES

Photographs of the Lincoln School on pages 190 and 191 from the Sacramento City School District's Superintendent's Annual Reports for 1913–14 and 1917–18.

she read with me about sheep in the meadow and a frightened chicken going to see the king, coaching me out of my phonetic ruts in words like *pasture, bow-wow-wow, hay* and *pretty,* which to my Mexican ear and eye had so many unnecessary sounds and letters. She made me watch her lips and then close my eyes as she repeated words I found hard to read. When we came to know each other better, I tried interrupting to tell Miss Ryan how we said it in Spanish. It didn't work. She only said "oh" and went on with *pasture, bow-wow-wow,* and *pretty.* It was as if in that closet we were both discovering together the secrets of the English language and grieving together over the tragedies of Bo-Peep. The main reason I was graduated with honors from the first grade was that I had fallen in love with Miss Ryan. **10** Her radiant, no-nonsense character made us either afraid not to love her or love her so we would not be afraid, I am not sure which. It was not only that we sensed she was with it, but also that she was with us.

Like the first grade, the rest of the Lincoln **11** School was a sampling of the lower part of town where many races made their home. My pals in the second grade were Kazushi, whose parents spoke only Japanese; Matti, a skinny Italian boy; and Manuel, a fat Portuguese who would never get into a fight but wrestled you to the ground and just sat on you. Our assortment of nationalities included Koreans, Yugoslavs, Poles, Irish, and home-grown Americans.

Miss Hopley and her teachers never let us forget why we were at Lincoln: for those who **12** were alien, to become good Americans; for those who were so born, to accept the rest of us. Off the school grounds we traded the same insults we heard from our elders. On the playground we were sure to be marched up to the principal's office for calling someone an insulting name. The school was not so much a melting pot as a griddle where Miss Hopley and her helpers warmed knowledge into us and roasted racial hatreds out of us.

At Lincoln, making us into Americans did not mean scrubbing away what made us originally **13** foreign. The teachers called us as our parents did, or as close as they could pronounce our names in Spanish or Japanese. No one was ever scolded or punished for speaking in his native tongue on the playground. Matti told the class about his mother's down quilt, which she had made in Italy with the fine feathers of a thousand geese. Encarnación acted out how boys learned to fish in the Philippines. I astounded the third grade with the story of my travels on a stagecoach, which nobody else in the class had seen except in the museum at Sutter's Fort. After a visit to the Crocker Art Gallery and its collection of heroic paintings of the golden age of California, someone showed a silk scroll with a Chinese painting. Miss Hopley herself had a way of expressing wonder over these matters before a class, her eyes wide open until they popped slightly. It was easy for me to feel that becoming a proud American, as she said we should, did not mean feeling ashamed of being a Mexican.

14

15 The Americanization of Mexican me was no smooth matter. I had to fight one lout[4] who made fun of my travels on the *diligencia*,[5] and my barbaric translation of the word into "diligence." He doubled up with laughter over the word until I straightened him out with a kick. In class I made points explaining that in Mexico roosters said *"qui-qui-ri-qui"* and not "cock-a-doodle-doo," but after school I had to put up with the taunts of a big Yugoslav who said Mexican roosters were crazy.

4. **lout:** a clumsy, stupid person.
5. *diligencia* (dē′lē-hĕn′syä): a Spanish word meaning "a fast coach." At one time, the English word *diligence* meant "speed" or "haste." Now *diligence* means "careful effort" or "hard work."

14 Finding Main Ideas
Why is it important that Ernesto not be ashamed of his Mexican heritage? Because it is a part of him; rejecting his past would mean rejecting a part of himself.

15
Conflict. He meets taunts from fellow students head-on.

VISUAL CONNECTIONS
Exploring the Subject
A pleasingly proportioned building, Lincoln Primary School was designed by an architect inspired by the graceful lines of classical and Renaissance architecture. This style reflects a belief in traditional values and implies that the community values education.

LINCOLN PRIMARY.

graphs describing the event and telling what, if anything, it taught them.

16
Characterization. Description of Homer's dress and hair style effectively characterize him.

17
Tune of "America" ("My Country 'Tis of Thee") borrowed from English "God Save the King (Queen)."

18
Miss Hopley effectively gives the children another lesson in what it means to be an American: Rules are to be obeyed by all regardless of social class or position.

19 Expressing an Opinion
Do you think Miss Hopley was reprimanded for her actions?
Responses will vary. Probably not since her actions seem in keeping with the school's purpose.

READING CHECK
1. Miss Nettie Hopley (p. 186).
2. Through interpreter (p. 187).
3. "Butterfly" (p. 187).
4. In the closet, a narrow hall off classroom (p. 187).
5. To become good Americans (p. 188).

But it was Homer who gave the most lasting lesson for a future American.

16 Homer was a chunky Irishman who dressed as if every day was Sunday. He slicked his hair between a crew cut and a pompadour.[6] And **17** Homer was smart, as he clearly showed when he and I ran for president of the third grade.

Everyone understood that this was to be a demonstration of how the American people vote for president. In an election, the teacher explained, the candidates could be generous and vote for each other. We cast our ballots in a shoebox and Homer won by two votes. I polled my supporters and came to the conclusion that I had voted for Homer and so had he. After class he didn't deny it, reminding me of what the teacher had said—we could vote for each **18** other but didn't have to.

The lower part of town was a collage[7] of nationalities in the middle of which Miss Nettie Hopley kept school with discipline and compassion. She called assemblies in the upper hall to introduce celebrities like the police sergeant or the fire chief, to lay down the law of the school, to present awards to our athletic champions, and to make important announcements. **19** One of these was that I had been proposed by my school and accepted as a member of the newly formed Sacramento Boys Band. "Now, isn't that a wonderful thing?" Miss Hopley asked the assembled school, all eyes on me. And everyone answered in a chorus, including myself, "Yes, Miss Hopley."

It was not only the parents who were summoned to her office and boys and girls who served sentences there who knew that Nettie Hopley meant business. The entire school witnessed her sizzling Americanism in its awful majesty one morning at flag salute.

All the grades, as usual, were lined up in the courtyard between the wings of the building, ready to march to class after the opening bell. Miss Shand was on the balcony of the second floor off Miss Hopley's office, conducting us in our lusty singing of "My Country tiz-a-thee." Our principal, as always, stood there like us, joining in the song.

Halfway through the second stanza she stepped forward, held up her arm in a sign of command, and called loud and clear: "Stop the singing." Miss Shand looked flabbergasted. We were frozen with shock.

Miss Hopley was now standing at the rail of the balcony, her eyes sparking, her voice low and resonant, the words coming down to us distinctly and loaded with indignation.

"There are two gentlemen walking on the school grounds with their hats on while we are singing," she said, sweeping our ranks with her eyes. "We will remain silent until the gentlemen come to attention and remove their hats." A minute of awful silence ended when Miss Hopley, her gaze fixed on something behind us, signaled Miss Shand and we began once more the familiar hymn. That afternoon, when school was out, the word spread. The two gentlemen were the Superintendent of Schools and an important guest on an inspection.

6. **pompadour:** a hair style in which the hair is combed or brushed up high away from the forehead.
7. **collage** (kō-läzh′): a collection of bits and pieces.

Reading Check
1. Who was the principal at Lincoln School?
2. How did the principal communicate with Ernesto?
3. What word did Ernesto struggle to pronounce correctly?
4. Where did Ernesto receive private tutoring from his teacher?
5. What was the goal set for the students at Lincoln?

This selection provides a fine opportunity for students of different ethnic and cultural backgrounds to share their heritage. Schedule a modified show-and-tell in which students display examples of arts or crafts, tell about special holidays or heroes, describe typical foods (perhaps sharing samples), model ceremonial clothing, or teach the class certain words in the language of their cultures.

Many students might like to write their own reminiscences of early school experiences, especially experiences that seem, in retrospect, humorous. Suggest that they pay particular attention to the specific details they want to share with the reader. Notice, for example, the way Galarza helps us see Miss Hopley's office on p. 186.

For Study and Discussion

Analyzing and Interpreting the Selection

1. When Ernesto came to school in the United States, he did not understand English. How did Miss Hopley, the principal, make him feel at ease?

2. Miss Ryan was a patient and encouraging teacher with a "blond, radiant face." What did she do to make Ernesto and the other first-graders enjoy learning English?

3. The teachers at the Lincoln School never let the students forget why they were there. **a.** According to the teachers, what was the purpose of school? **b.** In your own words, explain what you think the teachers meant by "good Americans" (page 190).

4. Ernesto and his classmates also kept their pride in their own backgrounds. How did the teachers encourage the students to remember their own cultures?

5a. What lesson in "sizzling Americanism" did Miss Hopley give to the Superintendent of Schools and his important guest? **b.** How would you describe what Ernesto and his classmates learned from this "lesson"?

Language and Vocabulary

Comparing Words That Imitate Sounds

Ernesto discovered something about language when he realized that a Mexican rooster and an American rooster make different sounds. An American rooster is supposed to say "cock-a-doodle-doo." What does a Mexican rooster say? If there were Norwegians in Ernesto's class, they could have told him that Norwegian roosters go *"kykkeliky."*

Here are some other words that are supposed to echo natural sounds. Notice that people in different lands seem to "hear" the sounds in different ways.

bow-wow: *oua-oua* (French); *wan-wan* (Japanese); *bu-bu* (Italian)
bang: *pum* (Spanish)
knock-knock: *pom-pom* (French)
purr: *ron-ron* (French); *schnurr* (German)

The English words *hiss, rustle,* and *tap* are supposed to echo or imitate natural sounds. Do any of your classmates know the words for these sounds in another language?

About the Author

Ernesto Galarza   (1905–1984)

Ernesto Galarza's popular autobiography *Barrio Boy* began as stories he told his own children about Jalcocotán, the remote mountain village in Mexico where he was born. The Galarza family suffered great hardship during the Mexican revolution, and some of them finally made their way to Sacramento, California. There young Ernesto had his first experience with American education. Galarza went on to receive a Ph.D. from Columbia University and become a teacher and writer. His other books include several textbooks on the Mexican American heritage.

FOR STUDY AND DISCUSSION
1. She welcomed him warmly and smiled at him; had friendly voice, sparkle in her eyes.
2. Sometimes crouched by their desks to help; praised them for their successes; gave private lessons.
3a. Purpose was "for those who were alien, to become good Americans; for those who were so born, to accept the rest of us."
3b. Responses will vary. Details suggest good American accepts people of every country and does not harbor racial hatreds.
4. Children called by names families had given them; no one ever scolded for speaking in native language on playground; students encouraged to tell stories in class about their families and ways they lived.
5a. Stopped singing of "My Country, 'Tis of Thee" until two officials had removed their hats and come to attention. 5b. Responses will vary. Probably learned that no one should be above the rules; they should apply equally to all at all times.

LANGUAGE AND VOCABULARY
1. "Qui-qui-ri qui" (p. 189).

ABOUT THE AUTHOR
In addition to being a writer and teacher, Galarza had a notable career as a labor leader. His experiences as a youthful farm worker, a cannery worker, and a packing shed laborer made him deeply concerned with the plight of poor Mexican field hands. In 1950, he led a strike of San Joaquin tomato pickers and, in 1951, of Imperial Valley cantaloupe pickers. Among his many books is *Strangers in Our Field* (1955).

192

I Have a Dream

MARTIN LUTHER KING, JR.

On August 28, 1963, a quarter of a million Americans marched peacefully to Washington, D.C., to urge Congress to pass civil rights legislation. This is the speech delivered by Dr. King on that summer day.

Martin Luther King, Jr., speaking to crowd at Freedom Rally, 1963.

I am happy to join with you today in what will go down in history as the greatest demonstration for freedom in the history of our nation.

1 Five score years ago, a great American, in whose symbolic shadow we stand, signed the Emancipation Proclamation. This momentous decree came as a great beacon light of hope to millions of Negro slaves who had been seared in the flames of withering injustice. It came as a joyous daybreak to end the long night of captivity.

2 But one hundred years later, we must face the tragic fact that the Negro is still not free. One hundred years later, the life of the Negro is still sadly crippled by the manacles of segregation and the chains of discrimination. One hundred years later, the Negro lives on a lonely island of poverty in the midst of a vast ocean of

PRESENTATION
The full power of "I Have a Dream" can only be understood through hearing it. If possible, use a recording of the speech. You might want to concentrate discussion on two points: how King's dream was rooted in the larger American dream and how King used **allusions** in the speech to heighten emotional responses of his listeners. The **For Study and Discussion** questions on p. 195 lend themselves to either class or small-group discussions.

material prosperity. One hundred years later, the Negro is still languishing in the corners of American society and finds himself an exile in his own land. So we have come here today to dramatize an appalling condition.

3   In a sense we have come to our nation's Capital to cash a check. When the architects of our republic wrote the magnificent words of the Constitution and the Declaration of Independence, they were signing a promissory note[1] to which every American was to fall heir. This note was a promise that all men would be guaranteed the unalienable[2] rights of life, liberty, and the pursuit of happiness.

It is obvious today that America has defaulted on this promissory note insofar as her citizens of color are concerned. Instead of honoring this sacred obligation, America has given the Negro people a bad check; a check which has come back marked "insufficient funds." But we refuse to believe that the bank of justice is bankrupt. We refuse to believe that there are insufficient funds in the great vaults of opportunity of this nation. So we have come to cash this check—a check that will give us upon demand the riches of freedom and the security of justice. We have also come to this hallowed spot to remind America of the fierce

4 urgency of *now*. This is no time to engage in the luxury of cooling off or to take the tranquilizing drug of gradualism. *Now* is the time to make real the promises of Democracy. *Now* is the time to rise from the dark and desolate valley of segregation to the sunlit path of racial justice. *Now* is the time to open the doors of opportunity to all of God's children. *Now* is the time to lift our nation from the quicksands of racial injustice to the solid rock of brotherhood.

It would be fatal for the nation to overlook the urgency of the moment and to underesti-

5 mate the determination of the Negro. This sweltering summer of the Negro's legitimate discontent will not pass until there is an invigorating autumn of freedom and equality. 1963 is not an end, but a beginning. Those who hope that the Negro needed to blow off steam and will now be content will have a rude awakening if the Nation returns to business as usual. There will be neither rest nor tranquility in America until the Negro is granted his citizenship rights. The whirlwinds of revolt will continue to shake the foundations of our Nation until the bright day of justice emerges.

But there is something that I must say to my people who stand on the warm threshold which leads into the palace of justice. In the process of gaining our rightful place we must not be guilty

6 of wrongful deeds. Let us not seek to satisfy our thirst for freedom by drinking from the cup of bitterness and hatred. We must forever conduct our struggle on the high plane of dignity and

7 discipline. We must not allow our creative protest to degenerate into physical violence. Again and again we must rise to the majestic heights of meeting physical force with soul force. The marvelous new militancy which has engulfed the Negro community must not lead us to a distrust of all white people, for many of our white brothers, as evidenced by their presence here today, have come to realize that their destiny is tied up with our destiny and their freedom is inextricably[3] bound to our freedom. We cannot walk alone.

And as we walk, we must make the pledge that we shall march ahead. We cannot turn back. There are those who are asking the devotees of civil rights, "When will you be satisfied?" We can never be satisfied as long as the Negro is the victim of the unspeakable horrors of

3
Extended Metaphor. King compares the demand for equality to the act of collecting on a payment owed by the government.

4
Repetition. Repetition of *now* emphasizes urgency of the situation.

5
Allusion to "Now is the winter of our discontent. . . ." from Shakespeare's *Richard III*.

6
Metaphor. Compares desire for freedom to physical sensation of thirst.

7
King echoes Gandhi, whose teachings about nonviolent civil disobedience rooted in love rather than hatred were a major influence.

---

1. **promissory note:** a written promise to pay a sum of money at a specified time.
2. **unalienable** (ŭn-āl′yən-ə-bəl): that cannot be taken away.

3. **inextricably** (ĭn′ĕx-strĭ′kə-blē): in a manner that cannot be untied.

police brutality. We can never be satisfied as long as our bodies, heavy with the fatigue of travel, cannot gain lodging in the motels of the highways and the hotels of the cities. We cannot be satisfied as long as the Negro's basic mobility is from a smaller ghetto to a larger one. We can never be satisfied as long as a Negro in Mississippi cannot vote and a Negro in New York believes he has nothing for which to vote. No, no, we are not satisfied, and we will not be satisfied until justice rolls down like waters and righteousness like a mighty stream.

I am not unmindful that some of you have come here out of great trials and tribulations. Some of you have come fresh from narrow jail cells. Some of you have come from areas where your quest for freedom left you battered by the storms of persecution and staggered by the winds of police brutality. You have been the veterans of creative suffering. Continue to work with the faith that unearned suffering is redemptive.

Go back to Mississippi, go back to Alabama, go back to South Carolina, go back to Georgia, go back to Louisiana, go back to the slums and ghettos of our modern cities, knowing that somehow this situation can and will be **8** changed. Let us not wallow in the valley of despair.

I say to you today, my friends, that in spite of the difficulties and frustrations of the moment I **9** still have a dream. It is a dream deeply rooted **10** in the American dream.

I have a dream that one day this nation will rise up and live out the true meaning of its **11** creed: "We hold these truths to be self-evident; that all men are created equal."

12 I have a dream that one day on the red hills of Georgia the sons of former slaves and the sons of former slaveowners will be able to sit down together at the table of brotherhood.

I have a dream that one day even the state of Mississippi, a desert state sweltering with the heat of injustice and oppression, will be transformed into an oasis of freedom and justice.

I have a dream that my four little children will one day live in a nation where they will not be judged by the color of their skin but by the content of their character.

I have a dream today.

I have a dream that one day the state of Alabama, whose governor's[4] lips are presently dripping with the words of interposition and nullification[5] will be transformed into a situation where little black boys and black girls will be able to join hands with little white boys and white girls and walk together as sisters and brothers.

I have a dream today.

13 I have a dream that one day every valley shall be exalted, every hill and mountain shall be made low, the rough places will be made plains, and the crooked places will be made straight, and the glory of the Lord shall be revealed, and all flesh shall see it together.

This is our hope. This is the faith with which I return to the South. With this faith we will be able to hew out of the mountain of despair a **14** stone of hope. With this faith we will be able to transform the jangling discords of our nation into a beautiful symphony of brotherhood. With this faith we will be able to work together, to pray together, to struggle together, to go to jail together, to stand up for freedom together, knowing that we will be free one day.

This will be the day when all of God's children will be able to sing with new meaning "My country 'tis of thee, sweet land of liberty, of thee I sing. Land where my fathers died, land

4. **Alabama . . . governor:** George Wallace, who was a segregationist. In 1963, he stood in the doorway of the University of Alabama to prevent the enrollment of black students.
5. **interposition** (ĭn′tər-pə-zĭsh′ən): the doctrine that a state may reject a federal order that it considers to be invading its rights; **nullification** (nŭl′ə-fĭ-kā′shən): the refusal of a state to recognize or enforce a federal law that it considers a violation of its authority.

PORTFOLIO ASSESSMENT
Time to reflect about what has been accomplished is an important part of learning. Suggest that students take time to review and assess the selections they have chosen to include in their portfolios for Part One. Encourage them to ask themselves if their collections (1) include the best of the works from which they have to choose, (2) are decorated appropriately, and (3) meet the assessment requirements they may have agreed to.

CLOSURE
Ask students to describe the America of King's dream, citing specific examples from the speech of what King felt was necessary for America to become "a great nation."

of the pilgrim's pride, from every mountain-side, let freedom ring."

And if America is to be a great nation this
15 must become true. So let freedom ring from the prodigious hilltops of New Hampshire. Let freedom ring from the mighty mountains of New York. Let freedom ring from the heightening Alleghenies of Pennsylvania!

Let freedom ring from the snowcapped Rockies of Colorado!

Let freedom ring from the curvaceous peaks of California!

But not only that; let freedom ring from Stone Mountain of Georgia!

Let freedom ring from Lookout Mountain of Tennessee!

Let freedom ring from every hill and mole hill of Mississippi. From every mountainside, let freedom ring.

When we let freedom ring, when we let it ring from every village and every hamlet, from every state and every city, we will be able to speed up that day when all of God's children, black men and white men, Jews and Gentiles, Protestants and Catholics, will be able to join hands and sing in the words of the old Negro spiritual, "Free at last! free at last! thank God almighty, we are free at last!"[6]

6. **"Free at last!":** Dr. King is recalling the words of a famous spiritual.

For Study and Discussion

Analyzing and Interpreting the Selection

1. Martin Luther King, Jr., uses several images, or pictures, to express his dream. What are some of the pictures that he sees when he dreams of the perfect America?
2. King repeats "Let freedom ring!" **a.** What song is this line from? **b.** How do you think King's use of this line would affect an audience?

Focus on Persuasive Writing

Using Emotional Appeals

When Dr. King described his dream of racial equality as "deeply rooted in the American dream" (page 194), he appealed powerfully to the emotions of his audience.

In a persuasive essay or speech, you can support your argument further by using **emotional appeals** that stir the feelings of readers or listeners. Some of the most effective emotional appeals are specific examples or personal experiences with which an audience can identify.

Write a one-sentence opinion statement on an issue you care deeply about. Jot down notes for two emotional appeals you could make in a speech or essay to support your opinion. When you have finished, get together with a partner and discuss each other's ideas. Save your notes.

About the Author

Martin Luther King, Jr. (1929–1968)

Martin Luther King, Jr., was a Baptist minister with a doctorate in theology from Boston University. During his graduate studies, he read from the works of the American writer Henry David Thoreau and the Indian leader Mahatma Gandhi. Both of these men advocated using nonviolent resistance to bring about social and political change. Their writings convinced King that these principles could be used to win civil rights for black people in America. Dr. King worked tirelessly for his goals. In 1957 alone, he traveled 700,000 miles and delivered 200 speeches. He spent time in jail. He preached, he marched, he wrote. In 1964 Dr. King was awarded the Nobel Prize for Peace. In 1968 he was killed by an assassin's bullet.

15
Repetition of "let freedom ring" from song "My Country, 'Tis of Thee" designed to evoke strong emotional response, love of freedom and of nation.

FOR STUDY AND DISCUSSION
1. People sitting down together at table of brotherhood; landscape of America; people working, praying, struggling, going to jail (for civil rights), standing up for freedom together; "all of God's children" joining hands, singing.
2a. "My Country, 'Tis of Thee."
2b. Using line out of context may jolt audience into thinking about what line really means.

FOCUS ON PERSUASIVE WRITING
Explain to students that emotional appeals are enhanced by careful use of specific words and details. Suggest that students review their notes for topics for which they can provide specific examples or personal experiences that might appeal to an audience. Then, encourage students to draw on their descriptive and narrative skills to create imagery that paints vivid pictures and to use language that evokes emotion.

ABOUT THE AUTHOR
King's crusade for civil rights began in December of 1955 in Montgomery, Alabama. Rosa Parks, a black woman, had refused to give up her bus seat to a white and was arrested for violating a segregation law. Under King's leadership, blacks organized to boycott the transit system. King's house was dynamited, his family threatened, but a little more than a year later the city of Montgomery desegregated its buses.

OBJECTIVES
The overall aim is for students to demonstrate the ability to distinguish between fact and opinion.

PRESENTATION
You might wish to read the passage aloud as students follow along in their textbooks. After students have had time to respond individually to the questions, discuss their responses. To close, ask students to consider and discuss why writers often mix facts and opinions. What type of writing would include only facts?

DISTINGUISHING FACT FROM OPINION
The ratio of facts to opinions in a piece of writing often depends on its author's purpose. Writing that is primarily informative usually contains many facts, while persuasive and expressive writing may contain more opinions.

Answers
Answers may vary.
1. Students might list any of the details that Whitman observed firsthand.
2. The latter part of the passage includes numerous opinions about Lincoln's demeanor.
3. "Mr. Lincoln on the saddle generally rides a good-sized, easy-going gray horse, is dressed in plain black, somewhat rusty and dusty, wears a black stiff hat, and looks about as ordinary in attire as the commonest man. . . ." Here Whitman includes several facts based on what he has seen, but adds his own interpretation of them.

FOCUS ON
Reading and Critical Thinking

DISTINGUISHING FACT FROM OPINION

As a reader and as a listener, you need to know whether you are being presented with facts or opinions. A **fact** is something that has happened or is true. An **opinion** is a statement that represents a belief or judgment that cannot be proved. There is nothing wrong with opinions so long as they are not presented or mistaken for facts.

The following excerpt about Abraham Lincoln is from a journal by Walt Whitman. Read the journal entry and then use a separate sheet of paper for the activity below.

August 12th.—I see the President almost every day, as I happen to live where he passes to or from his lodgings out of town. He never sleeps at the White House during the hot season, but has quarters at a healthy location some three miles north of the city, the Soldiers' home, a United States military establishment. I saw him this morning about 8½ coming in to business, riding on Vermont Avenue, near L Street. He always has a company of twenty-five or thirty cavalry, with sabers drawn and held upright over their shoulders. They say this guard was against his personal wish, but he let his counselors have their way. The party makes no great show in uniform or horses. Mr. Lincoln on the saddle generally rides a good-sized, easy-going gray horse, is dressed in plain black, somewhat rusty and dusty, wears a black stiff hat, and looks about as ordinary in attire as the commonest man. . . . I see very plainly Abraham Lincoln's dark brown face, with the deep-cut lines, the eyes, always to me with a deep latent sadness in the expression. We have got so that we exchange bows, and very cordial ones. . . . Earlier in the summer I occasionally saw the President and his wife, toward the latter part of the afternoon, out in a barouche,[1] on a pleasure ride through the city. . . . They passed me once very close, and I saw the President in the face fully, as they were moving slowly, and his look, though abstracted, happened to be directed steadily in my eye. He bowed and smiled, but far beneath his smile I noticed well the expression I have alluded to. None of the artists or pictures has caught the deep, though subtle and indirect expression of this man's face. There is something else there. One of the great portrait painters of two or three centuries ago is needed.

1. **barouche** (bə-rōōsh'): a four-wheeled carriage with two double seats and a folding top.

Distinguishing Fact from Opinion

1. List three or more facts in the passage.
2. List three or more opinions.
3. List one or more statements that combine fact with opinion.

OBJECTIVES
The overall aim is for students to write a persuasive essay.

PRESENTATION
To motivate students for this writing activity, you might bring to class samples of the types of persuasion listed in the opening paragraph, then analyze and evaluate the kinds of support used. You may want to schedule library time for stu-dents as they work on their essays. You may also want to allow time for conferencing with stu-dents as needed throughout the writing pro-cess. In closing, ask students what tips they would give to another student trying to write a persuasive essay.

FOCUS ON *Writing*

WRITING A PERSUASIVE ESSAY

*W*hat do a television commercial, a cam-paign speech, a newspaper ad, and an edito-rial have in common? They are all examples of persuasion. In **persuasive writing,** you state a clear opinion on a topic and try to get your readers or listeners to agree with you. This unit has presented some of the key ele-ments of persuasion. Now you will have a chance to write a persuasive essay of your own.

Prewriting

1. What are the issues you care about? Explore possible topics for your essay by list-ing some topics about which you have an opinion. Make sure that these subjects really *are* matters of opinion, rather than cut-and-dried matters of fact. Remember how to dis-tinguish fact from opinion.

- A **fact** is something that has happened or is true.
- An **opinion** is a statement of belief or judgment.

Choose an issue that matters, both to you and to your audience. [See **Focus** assignment on page 157.]

2. Write a one-sentence statement of your opinion on the issue. This statement will serve as the **main idea** for your essay. [See **Focus** assignment on page 172.]

3. Analyze your **audience** by making a chart like the following one.

Audience Chart

Topic: _____

Position/Opinion: _____

Audience: _____

Audience's Knowledge About Topic: _____
_____

Audience's Interests and Concerns: _____
_____

Possible Opposing Opinions: _____
_____

Reasons for Opposition: _____
_____

[See **Focus** assignment on page 174.]

4. Gather support for your opinion. Here are some kinds of support you can use in a persuasive essay or speech:

■ logical appeals	■ emotional appeals
reasons	examples
facts	personal experiences
expert opinions	

[See **Focus** assignments on pages 180 and 195.]

5. Evaluate your support. Pay particular attention to emotional appeals that may backfire. Here are three specific examples:

- **Bandwagon:** urging people to think or do something because "everybody" believes or does it. Example: "Don't be the only kid on your block not to own a Vivid Video!"

HOLT WRITER'S WORKSHOP

This computer program provides help for all types of writing through guided instruction for each step of the writing process. (Program available separately.)

See *Elements of Writing, Sec-ond Course,* Chapter 8, for more instruction on persuasive writing.

WRITING A PERSUASIVE ESSAY
In writing their persuasive essays, students should become more aware of how important it is for writers to consider their audi-ence. Writers whose aim is to persuade will vary types of sup-port, method of organization, level of usage, diction, and style depending upon their intended audience.

Prewriting
Students can use their notes from the **Focus on Persuasive Writing** features in the unit to find topics for their essays. Give students plenty of time to gather support. They may benefit from working in small groups to help one another with evaluating their support.

TRANSPARENCY 17

Writing Process
Writing a Persuasive Essay – helps students plan and write an effective persuasive essay.

Writing

You may want to suggest that students start with their body paragraphs. Encourage students to fully develop each reason with evidence and appeals. Students can then decide on the order of the paragraphs and can experiment with the appropriate transitions. Stress that the outline given is meant to be suggestive only, and that they may want to order reasons from least to most important. Once students have drafted the bodies of their essays, they can write their introductions and conclusions.

Evaluating and Revising

Students may want to focus their self-evaluations on their sentences. Students can evaluate each sentence to decide if it furthers their main idea, and if it logically follows from the previous sentence. If the function of a sentence is not clear to students, they can ask themselves whether to omit it, move it, or revise. Then students might work with partners to use the **Checklist for Evaluation and Revision** and for additional suggestions to improve their essays. Encourage students to read their essays aloud several times during the revision process.

- **Flattery:** appealing to people's desire to think highly of themselves. "Vivid Videos are for special kids, like you."
- **Testimonial:** using the endorsement of a celebrity or another person who doesn't know very much about the topic. "Baseball Coach Dave Allen says that Vivid Videos are tops for kids."

Writing

1. Follow an **outline** like the one below as you write your first draft.

I. Introduction
   A. Attention-grabber
   B. Background (if needed)
   C. Statement of opinion
II. Body
   A. Most important reason, with evidence + emotional appeal (if appropriate)
   B. Next reason, with evidence + emotional appeal (if appropriate)
   C. Additional reasons, with evidence + emotional appeals (if appropriate)
III. Conclusion
   A. Restatement of opinion
   B. Call for action (if appropriate)

2. Remember to use **transitional words and phrases** in your essay to make the relationship of ideas clear. Some helpful transitions include the following:

also	first	most important
another	however	then
because	last	therefore
but	likewise	to begin with
finally	moreover	

Evaluating and Revising

1. When you revise your essay, pay special attention to your **credibility,** or your believability in the eyes of your audience. Make sure you have presented a balanced mix of logical and emotional appeals. See if you can recognize and respond to some of your audience's reasons for holding a different opinion on the issue.

This is how one writer revised a persuasive paragraph to combine a logical appeal with an emotional appeal.

Writer's Model

The most important reason for increasing the school library budget is that many books need to be replaced. *In a random sample of fifty titles in the catalog, five volumes were* ~~Many books are~~ missing *seven had torn or* ~~or torn. Some~~ *missing pages, and three lacked* ~~books lack~~ covers. In interviews conducted with ten students, four reported that they could not find the materials they needed for their assign- *"I wanted to write my report on the Human* ments. ~~One student complained in an~~ *Genome Project," declared Randy Pilsic,* *"but the best references were either* ~~interview that the best materials for~~ *missing or hadn't even been ordered yet* *by the library."* ~~his project weren't there.~~

2. You may find the following checklist helpful as you revise your essay.

Checklist for Evaluation and Revision

✓ Do I grab the audience's attention in the introduction?

✓ Do I state my opinion clearly?

✓ Do I use both logical and emotional appeals to support my opinion?

✓ Is my reasoning sound?

✓ Have I organized my support in a way that makes sense?

✓ Do I end with a strong conclusion?

Proofreading and Publishing

1. Proofread your persuasive essay and correct any errors you find in grammar, usage, and mechanics. (Here you may find it helpful to refer to the **Handbook for Revision** on pages 712–755.) Then prepare a final version of your essay by making a clean copy.

2. Consider some of the following ways to publish and share your essay:

■ send your essay to a newspaper as a letter to the editor

■ get together with a group of classmates and use your essays as the basis for an opinion forum or a debate

■ deliver your essay as a speech in class

Portfolio If your teacher approves, you may wish to keep a copy of your work in your writing folder or portfolio.

Proofreading and Publishing

You might engage students in a whole-class proofreading procedure in which each student is responsible for checking for a specific type of error, such as comma usage, pronoun agreement, and spelling. Students can then form a kind of proofreading assembly line in which each essay is read by each student in the class.

SHORT STORIES

OVERVIEW OF THE UNIT

Because short stories are so compact, immediate, and accessible, they make an ideal starting point for a study of literary forms. Study of form in the short story, however, should not preempt the content of the stories themselves. Together, the stories in the unit invite readers to explore fantasy, horror, the nature of reality, and human values.

The unit concludes with **Focus on Reading and Critical Thinking** and **Focus on Writing.** The first activity provides students with a set of questions to consider when evaluating any short story. The second activity offers students the opportunity to write their own stories.

OBJECTIVES OF THE UNIT

The aims of the unit are for the student:
- To develop the ability to identify and analyze literary elements such as characterization, plot, setting, and theme in shorter works of fiction
- To analyze an author's use of irony, foreshadowing, and figurative language in selected short stories
- To solve word problems using synonyms and antonyms and to identify the etymology, denotation, and connotation of selected words in the unit
- To distinguish between standard and nonstandard English
- To identify the Latin and Greek roots of selected words
- To write an original story and a letter

CONCEPTS AND SKILLS

The following concepts and skills are treated in this unit:

CLOSE READING OF A SHORT STORY

LITERARY ELEMENTS/TERMS AND TECHNIQUES

LANGUAGE AND VOCABULARY SKILLS

OPPORTUNITIES FOR WRITING

Creative Writing

Focus on Writing a Short Story

FOR ORAL READING

FOCUS ON READING AND CRITICAL THINKING

FOCUS ON WRITING

TRANSPARENCIES

The following unit support materials with specific correlations to literature selections are available in the **Fine Art and Instructional Transparencies with Teacher's Notes and Blackline Masters** section of your *Audiovisual Resources Binder.*

FINE ART TRANSPARENCIES

Theme: Slice of Life
18 *Folding Laundry,* Terry Furchgott
19 *Tar Beach 2,* Faith Ringgold

READER RESPONSE

20 Charting a Response

LITERARY ELEMENTS

21 Story Map

WRITING PROCESS

22 Writing a Short Story

INTRODUCING THE UNIT

Provide recent newspapers and let each student clip a front-page story of interest and then underline the first sentence, which usually tells *what, who, where, when,* and perhaps *why* or *how.* Ask students to look at the opening of one of the short stories in the anthology. Do writers of fiction usually provide as much information as reporters do in their first sentences? Why not? Ask each student to write the first paragraph of a short story that could be based on events in the news story they have chosen. Post clippings and story openers in pairs on the bulletin board. Have students finish their stories using the techniques gleaned from the unit.

PLANNING GUIDE

FOR UNIT PLANNING
- Transparencies 18–22: *Audiovisual Resources Binder*
- *Portfolio Assessment: Professional Support Materials*
- Test Generator

- Mastery Tests: *Teaching Resources C,* pp. 139, 141, 144
- Analogy Tests: *Teaching Resources C,* pp. 146, 147
- Composition Test: *Teaching Resources C,* p. 148

SELECTION (Pupil's Page)	TEACHING RESOURCES C (page numbers shown below)							AV BINDER
	Teacher's Notes	Reading Check	Study Guide	Language Skills	Building Vocabulary	Selection Vocab. Test	Selection Test	Audio-cassette
SHORT STORIES *Introduction* (p. 203)	1							
Ray Bradbury *The Gift* (p. 204)	3						4	
O. Henry *A Retrieved Reformation* (p. 210)	6	9	10	15, 17	21	23	24	
Ursula K. Le Guin *The Rule of Names* (p. 220)	26	29	30	34, 37	40	41	42	
Langston Hughes *Thank You, M'am* (p. 230)	44	46	47	50	53		55	
D'Arcy Niland *The Parachutist* (p. 235)	57	60	61	65	68, 70	73, 75, 77	78	
Daniel Keyes *Flowers for Algernon* (p. 240)	80	85	86, 90, 94		98	100, 101	102	
Shirley Ann Grau *The Land and the Water* (p. 265)	104	107	109		112		114	
Edgar Allan Poe *The Tell-Tale Heart* (p. 273)	116	119	120	123, 127	131	133	135	

Student Learning Options

SHORT STORIES

1. Creating a Plot Chart
Students could create plot charts for a favorite short story. Students' charts could include brief explanations and illustrations of each story's primary conflict, its climax, and its resolutions. Students could then present their plot charts to the class, thereby giving other students the opportunity to note other stories they might enjoy.

2. Experimenting with New Settings
Ask students to divide a sheet of paper into two columns and label one column **setting** and the other **alternate setting.** Have students write down elements of a story's setting in the first column and then write the corresponding elements of an alternate setting in the other column. Students might then write paragraphs about how the story's plot would change or how the resolution might differ if the new setting were used.

3. Presenting Objects to Represent Characters
Students could bring to class objects that represent a character from a short story. The objects could be things the character used in the story or that the character might have in his or her possession. Or, an object might simply express an aspect of the character's personality. In short presentations to the class, students should be able to explain why each object could belong to or represent a particular character.

VISUAL CONNECTIONS

About the Artwork
The artist's early work, of which this painting is an example, is characterized by the use of colored contours (tan hill and foreground) that enclose areas of strong color (pool and figure). He also uses distortion (elongation of figure) for emphasis and decorative effect.

About the Artist
Augustus Edwin John was born in Wales and studied art in London as a teen-ager. He became one of the leaders of the modern art movement in England, developing an original style that featured brilliant color and a free, sketchy technique. John painted portraits of famous people, drew cartoons, and created murals. His paintings and etchings of scenes of gypsy life, based on his own nomadic experiences on the moors of Essex, England, are among his most popular works.

Ideas for Writing
This unit includes tales of horror, **suspense,** fantasy, realism, nature, and human interest. You might have students study "The Blue Pool" and then write their own short stories based on the painting.

202

SHORT STORIES

Think about what is happening in this painting. Who is the figure in the foreground? Describe what she is wearing. Imagine what she is thinking as she looks toward the blue pool. What is her mood? Does she come to this place often? Is she waiting for someone?

Judging from details in the painting, where do you think the pool is located? What memories are associated with the blue pool?

Write the first paragraph of a story in which you describe the scene in the painting. Then give your readers hints about what is going to happen next. Share your opening paragraph with other students and invite ideas for developing your story.

The Blue Pool (1911) by Augustus John (1878–1961). Oil on panel.
Aberdeen Art Gallery and Museums

SHORT STORIES
Focus students on the short-story genre by asking them to list characteristics of the short story while you write them on the chalkboard. What is their previous experience with reading short stories? Are they looking forward to studying this unit? Preview the material by telling them that the seven stories in this unit provide readers with varied glimpses of life and deal with both realistic and fanciful characters and events.

In fact, the stories in this unit are ideal representatives of the short-story genre, demonstrating both creativity of form and variety of subject matter. Some stories in the unit—O. Henry's "A Retrieved Reformation"; Hughes's "Thank You, M'am"; Keyes's "Flowers for Algernon"; and Grau's "The Land and the Water"—make strong statements about human values and life. Niland's "The Parachutist" takes a look at animal nature. Le Guin's "The Rule of Names" is a fantastic tale of wizards and dragons, and Poe's "The Tell-Tale Heart" is a classic psychological horror story.

Questions at the end of each selection encourage students to make personal connections with characters and their conflicts. Vocabulary exercises focus on **denotation** and **connotation**, word histories, identifying levels of usage, and recognizing analogies. Exercises on literary elements discuss **plot, suspense, characterization, theme,** and **atmosphere.** Exercises for improving oral and written expression include writing to an imaginary character, analyzing **foreshadowing**, using realistic details for **characterization**, creating descriptive details for **setting,** writing from a different **point of view,** exploring a **theme,** reading a story aloud to try to portray the narrator's emotions, and writing a short story.

203

FOCUS / MOTIVATION

Ask students to recall their favorite short stories and to tell what aspects of the stories appealed to them. Then invite students to match their own impressions with those of another reader as they read "The Gift."

PRESENTATION

This section focuses on developing the skills needed in understanding a short story. You may wish to have students read "The Gift" silently in class after you have discussed the **Guidelines for Close Reading.** Alternatively, you may pre-fer to read the story aloud, stopping to ask questions that will help students to identify and analyze the elements of the story. In any case, encourage students to make their own notes to compare with the **One Reader's Response** notes. As students compare their impressions

TEACHING RESOURCES C

Teacher's Notes, p. 3
Selection Test, p. 4

CLOSE READING OF A SHORT STORY

1
Good writers create stories that convey ideas about life. Their content reflects something of value or importance about human experience.

2
Le Guin's story is a fantasy and is told for entertainment. There are, however, substantive obser-vations about life and human ex-perience to be gleaned from a close reading.

3
For example, even a clock can be a character in a story if it is given human qualities—a "face," the ability to think and feel, perhaps some ability to move.

4
These are the basic tools of the writer, the primary "elements" of his or her **fiction.** Fictional prose is created through careful and creative blending of these ele-ments.

Close Reading OF A SHORT STORY

1 *A short story is like a little piece of life. A short-story writer creates characters and places them in a situation. In a good story you keep on reading because you are eager to find out what happens to the characters. You have become interested in them as if they were living people.*

2 *Some stories are told purely for fun. "The Rule of Names" in this unit is an example of a story that is told just to entertain you. Most stories, however, also have something serious to say about life and people.*

A short story is made up of certain basic elements: plot *(the sequence*
3 *of related events);* characters *(persons, animals, or things presented as persons);* point of view *(the standpoint from which the writer tells the*
4 *story);* setting *(the time and place of the action); and* theme *(the under-lying idea about human life). The better you, the individual reader, understand how these elements work together, the better you will understand and appreciate the author's intent and meaning.*

In order to enter imaginatively into a short story, you need to read actively, asking questions as you read and noting your own reactions to characters and events. The following guidelines can help you develop skill as a reader.

with the printed comments that appear alongside the story, remind them that this examination represents only one reader's interpretation. After students have had an opportunity to discuss their ideas in small groups, encourage students to share their own conclusions with the class and to support their assertions with evidence from the story.

Guidelines for Close Reading

1. Read actively, questioning the author's purpose and method. Ask yourself what significance there might be to details that the author gives you.

2. Ask questions about unfamiliar words and references. If you feel uncertain about the meaning of a word and cannot get the meaning from context clues, be sure to check in a standard dictionary or other reference work.

3. Draw inferences as you read. Authors often do not tell us things directly but allow us to draw our own conclusions from evidence in their stories.

4. Make predictions as you read. Ask yourself, "What will happen next?" Be aware of your own response to characters and actions.

5. Relate what you are reading to your own life and experiences. Put together your responses to determine the central idea or underlying meaning of the story. The theme of a story is seldom stated directly. Generally, it must be inferred from the characters and their actions. Try to state the central idea of the story in your own words.

Here is a brief story that has been read carefully by one reader. The comments in the margin show how this reader has responded to the story. If you like, cover up the printed notes as you read and make notes of your own on a separate sheet of paper. You may wish to compare your responses with the printed comments at a later point.

5
Details may serve to **fore-shadow,** to develop **character,** to establish **setting,** to describe vivid **images,** and to create **suspense.**

6
Students should consider the type of story they are reading and think about not only **denotation** of words but also **connotation.**

7
For example, readers must draw **inferences** from characters' actions and **dialogue** in Langston Hughes's "Thank You, M'am" because author offers little direct **characterization.**

8
To predict outcomes, good readers consider clues provided by details of **character, plot, setting,** and details that may **fore-shadow** events. Good readers also use their personal knowledge and experience, and they look for **cause-and-effect** relationships.

9
Theme, the central idea of a story, is often an important message about life and human nature. The **Literary Elements** section, p. 271, explores differences between **theme** and **plot.**

To help students begin the unit with a good understanding of the short story form, you might try the following activity. Divide the class into several small groups. Read aloud or write on the chalkboard the intriguing opening lines of a short story such as O. Henry's "The Gift of the Magi," which opens, "One dollar and eighty-seven cents. That was all." Have students work together in their groups to develop stories suggested by the opening lines and then encourage each group to share its version with the class. Discuss the group stories in terms of the basic elements of the short story discussed on p. 204. Finally, read the original story aloud.

Close Reading
OF A SHORT STORY

ONE READER'S RESPONSE

10
First sentence establishes **setting**, suggests central **characters**, and foreshadows **conflict**.

11
Point of view. Bradbury uses an **omniscient third-person point of view** to tell his story. As a result, reader knows more about what each member of family is thinking than if the story had been told from one family member's point of view.

12
Plot. Leaving behind boy's gift and Christmas tree introduces conflict.

13
Symbol. Tree may represent Earth and life there that family is leaving behind.

14
Family's fear and helplessness is emphasized by details such as the "great howl" of the siren, the press of people, the description of son as "small" and "pale," their being "flung headlong into dark space."

15
Suggestion that time holds no meaning in outer space further threatens significance of a specific time of celebration.

16
Foreshadowing. That father delays boy's desire to look out porthole and has "reason" for doing so suggests father has thought of a possible solution to problem.

A rocket port? Is this a science-fiction story?

They have to leave behind his Christmas present. Where are they going?

Don't they need spacesuits to go to Mars?

This is great. Space travelers don't have to worry about weightlessness. They can move around normally.

The Gift
RAY BRADBURY

10 Tomorrow would be Christmas, and even while the three of **11** them rode to the rocket port the mother and father were worried. It was the boy's first flight into space, his very first time in **12** a rocket, and they wanted everything to be perfect. So when, at the customs table,[1] they were forced to leave behind his gift, which exceeded the weight limit by no more than a few ounces, and the little tree with the lovely white candles, they felt themselves deprived of the season and their love.

The boy was waiting for them in the Terminal room. Walking toward him, after their unsuccessful clash with the Interplanetary officials, the mother and father whispered to each other.

"What shall we do?"

"Nothing, nothing, What *can* we do?"

"Silly rules!"

13 "And he so wanted the tree!"

14 The siren gave a great howl and people pressed forward into the Mars Rocket. The mother and father walked at the very last, their small pale son between them, silent.

"I'll think of something," said the father.

"What...?" asked the boy.

And the rocket took off and they were flung headlong into dark space.

15 The rocket moved and left fire behind and left Earth behind on which the date was December 24, 2052, heading out into a place where there was no time at all, no month, no year, no hour. They slept away the rest of the first "day." Near midnight, by their Earthtime New York watches, the boy awoke and said, "I want to go look out the porthole."

There was only one port, a "window" of immensely thick glass of some size, up on the next deck.

"Not quite yet," said the father. "I'll take you up later."

"I want to see where we are and where we're going."

16 "I want you to wait for a reason," said the father.

1. **customs table:** an area in an airport or pier where goods and baggage coming into or leaving a country are inspected and duties are paid.

He had been lying awake, turning this way and that, thinking of the abandoned gift, the problem of the season, the lost tree and the white candles. And at last, sitting up, no more than five minutes ago, he believed he had found a plan. He need only carry it out and this journey would be fine and joyous indeed.

"Son," he said, "in exactly one half hour it will be Christmas."

"Oh," said the mother, dismayed that he had mentioned it. Somehow she had rather hoped that the boy would forget.

The boy's face grew feverish and his lips trembled. "I know, I know. Will I get a present, will I? Will I have a tree? Will I have a tree? You promised—"

"Yes, yes, all that, and more," said the father.

The mother started. "But—"

"I mean it," said the father. "I really mean it. All and more, much more. Excuse me, now. I'll be back."

He left them for about twenty minutes. When he came back, he was smiling. "Almost time."

What is the father's plan? How will he replace the boy's present and the Christmas tree?

I wonder how the father will keep his promise.

17
Plot. Revealing that father has developed a plan moves the plot forward. Failure to reveal specifics of plan creates suspense.

18
Suspense. Mother's and boy's anxious tones add to suspense.

19
Father is certain awesome sight of stars will create a powerful impression and evoke beauty and meaning of Christmas.

20
Father's attention to time stands in contrast to earlier statement about meaninglessness of time in space. Emphasizes his determination to bring comforting elements of life on earth with them into space.

A view of our own galaxy as seen from a distant planet. Interstellar dust causes the patchy appearance of the Milky Way.

Chris Butler, Science Photo Library/ Science Source/Photo Researchers, Inc.

207

21
Symbol. Watch may be seen as symbolizing family's efforts to retain celebration of specific time in void of space.

22
Suspense. Darkness and whispering create air of mystery, intensifying suspense.

Close Reading
OF A SHORT STORY

How can they celebrate Christmas in deep space?

Whispering. What kind of surprise is coming?

"Can I hold your watch?" asked the boy, and the watch was handed over and he held it ticking in his fingers as the rest of
21 the hour drifted by in fire and silence and unfelt motion.

"It's Christmas *now!* Christmas! Where's my present?"

"Here we go," said the father and took his boy by the shoulder and led him from the room, down the hall, up a rampway, his wife following.

"I don't understand," she kept saying.

"You will. Here we are," said the father.

They had stopped at the closed door of a large cabin. The father tapped three times and then twice in a code. The door
22 opened and the light in the cabin went out and there was a whisper of voices.

"Go on in, son," said the father.

"It's dark."

The Milky Way seen edge-on.   David A. Hardy, Science Photo Library/Science Source/Photo Researchers, Inc.

208

CLOSURE

Ask students to point out major literary elements in "The Gift" and to identify several passages where **inferences** may be drawn. Ask students to state the **theme** to be inferred from the actions and **dialogue** of the characters.

"I'll hold your hand. Come on, Mama."

23   They stepped into the room and the door shut, and the room was very dark indeed. And before them loomed a great glass eye, the porthole, a window four feet high and six feet wide, from which they could look out into space.

The boy gasped.

Behind him, the father and the mother gasped with him, and then in the dark room some people began to sing.

24   "Merry Christmas, son," said the father.

And the voices in the room sang the old, the familiar carols, and the boy moved slowly until his face was pressed against the
25   cool glass of the port. And he stood there for a long, long time, just looking and looking out into space and the deep night at the burning and the burning of ten billion billion white and lovely candles....

This is like one of the scenes on TV space shows, where the crew look out a giant porthole into space.

*They're singing Christmas carols. I guess they want to hold on to their heritage.
The boy's Christmas gift must be the beauty of the stars. I like that.*

23
Atmosphere. Description of room and porthole creates excited, suspenseful mood.

24
Climax. Conflict introduced at beginning of story is resolved.

25
Repetition. Bradbury uses repetition of words to suggest viewers' sense of wonder and awe.

Looking at Yourself as a Reader

If you have made your own notes on Bradbury's story, compare them with the printed comments that appear alongside the story. Are the two sets of responses similar in any way? Are there important differences in these responses?

Meet with several of your classmates and compare responses. What did you think of the author's idea for the story? Did the story make you think about gift-giving in a new way? Would this story make a good episode for a TV program?

Looking at Yourself as a Reader

Responses to story and to questions should provide the framework for diverse small- and large-group discussions. Encourage students to be open to each others' interpretations. Students might also think of other stories related to gift giving and compare them with "The Gift."

OBJECTIVES
The overall aim is for students to analyze the protagonist's actions, attitudes, and changes in character throughout "A Retrieved Reformation." For a complete list of objectives, see the **Teacher's Notes.**

VOCABULARY
The underlined words are in the Glossary. The **Language and Vocabulary** exercise on p. 219 gives students practice in understanding **denotations** and **connotations** of words.

FOCUS / MOTIVATION
Observe that one stock character in **fiction** and in movies is the tough guy "with a heart of gold." Ask students to recall and describe some lovable bad guys; then present Jimmy Valentine as such a character.

TEACHING RESOURCES C
Teacher's Notes, p. 6
Reading Check, p. 9
Study Guide, p. 10
Language Skills, pp. 15, 17
Building Vocabulary, p. 21
Selection Vocabulary Test, p. 23
Selection Test, p. 24

AV RESOURCES BINDER
Audiocassette 2, Side A

PREREADING FOCUS
The headnote emphasizes that people often act in surprising ways. Ask students to recall times when people they know behaved in an unexpected manner and whether students later understood the reasons for the behavior.

A Retrieved Reformation

1
O. Henry served three years in prison for embezzlement. Many of his stories were inspired by tales told by prison inmates.

2 Summarizing
What is meant by "it is hardly worthwhile to cut his hair"? Jimmy's friends will get him out of prison very quickly.

3 Analyzing
How does the warden, who understands Jimmy and his ways, make his point? He uses sarcasm.

4
Characterization. Jimmy's response helps indirectly characterize him as sly but affable.

5
Connotation. The word *villainously* here means "badly or obnoxiously," but it connotes "criminally," appropriate for Jimmy's character.

A Retrieved Reformation

O. HENRY

People don't always behave in predictable ways—in fact, they often do things that can't be easily explained. In this story, a sequence of events leads more than one character to a change of heart.

1 A guard came to the prison shoeshop, where Jimmy Valentine was assiduously[1] stitching uppers, and escorted him to the front office. There the warden handed Jimmy his pardon, which had been signed that morning by the Governor. Jimmy took it in a tired kind of way. He had served nearly ten months of a four-year sentence. He had expected to stay only about three months, at the longest. When a man with as many friends on the outside as **2** Jimmy Valentine had is received in the "stir," it is hardly worthwhile to cut his hair.

"Now, Valentine," said the warden, "you'll go out in the morning. Brace up, and make a man of yourself. You're not a bad fellow at heart. Stop cracking safes, and live straight."

"Me?" said Jimmy, in surprise. "Why, I never cracked a safe in my life."

3 "Oh, no," laughed the warden. "Of course not. Let's see, now. How was it you happened to get sent up on that Springfield job? Was it because you wouldn't prove an alibi for fear of compromising somebody in extremely high-toned society? Or was it simply a case of a mean old jury that had it in for you? It's always one or the other with you innocent victims."

4 "Me?" said Jimmy, still blankly virtuous. "Why, Warden, I never was in Springfield in my life!"

"Take him back, Cronin," smiled the warden, "and fix him with outgoing clothes. Unlock him at seven in the morning, and let him come to the bullpen.[2] Better think over my advice, Valentine."

At a quarter past seven on the next morning **5** Jimmy stood in the warden's outer office. He had on a suit of the villainously fitting, ready-made clothes and a pair of the stiff, squeaky shoes that the state furnishes to its discharged compulsory guests.

The clerk handed him a railroad ticket and the five-dollar bill with which the law expected him to rehabilitate himself into good citizenship and prosperity. The warden gave him a cigar, and shook hands. Valentine, 9762, was chronicled on the books "Pardoned by Governor," and Mr. James Valentine walked out into the sunshine.

Disregarding the song of the birds, the waving green trees, and the smell of the flowers, Jimmy headed straight for a restaurant. There

---

1. **assiduously** (ə-sĭj′ōō-əs-lē): steadily and busily.

2. **bullpen:** a barred room where prisoners are held temporarily.

6 he tasted the first sweet joys of liberty in the shape of a broiled chicken and a bottle of white wine—followed by a cigar a grade better than the one the warden had given him. From there he proceeded leisurely to the depot. He tossed a quarter into the hat of a blind man sitting by the door and boarded his train. Three hours set him down in a little town near the state line. He went to the café of one Mike Dolan and shook hands with Mike, who was alone behind the bar.

7 "Sorry we couldn't make it sooner, Jimmy, me boy," said Mike. "But we had that protest from Springfield to buck against, and the Governor nearly balked. Feeling all right?"

"Fine," said Jimmy. "Got my key?"

He got his key and went upstairs, unlocking the door of a room at the rear. Everything was just as he had left it. There on the floor was still Ben Price's collar button that had been torn from that eminent detective's shirt band when they had overpowered Jimmy to arrest him.

Pulling out from a wall a folding bed, Jimmy slid back a panel in the wall and dragged out a

8 dust-covered suitcase. He opened this and gazed fondly at the finest set of burglar's tools in the East. It was a complete set, made of specially tempered steel, the latest designs in drills, punches, braces and bits, jimmies, clamps, and augers,[3] with two or three novelties invented by Jimmy himself, in which he took pride. Over nine hundred dollars they had cost him to have made at——, a place where they make such things for the profession.

In half an hour Jimmy went downstairs and through the café. He was now dressed in tasteful and well-fitting clothes and carried his dusted and cleaned suitcase in his hand.

"Got anything on?" asked Mike Dolan genially.

___
3. **drills . . . augers** (ô′gərz): tools for working with metal.

9 "Me?" said Jimmy, in a puzzled tone. "I don't understand. I'm representing the New York Amalgamated Short Snap Biscuit Cracker and Frazzled Wheat Company."

This statement delighted Mike to such an extent that Jimmy had to take a seltzer and milk on the spot. He never touched "hard" drinks.

10 A week after the release of Valentine, 9762, there was a neat job of safe burglary done in Richmond, Indiana, with no clue to the author. A scant eight hundred dollars was all that was secured. Two weeks after that a patented, improved, burglarproof safe in Logansport was opened like a cheese to the tune of fifteen hundred dollars, currency; securities and silver untouched. That began to interest the rogue-catchers.[4] Then an old-fashioned bank safe in Jefferson City became active and threw out of its crater an eruption of bank notes amounting to five thousand dollars. The losses were now high enough to bring the matter up into Ben Price's class of work. By comparing notes, a remarkable similarity in the methods of the burglaries was noticed. Ben Price investigated the scenes of the robberies and was heard to remark:

"That's Dandy Jim Valentine's autograph. He's resumed business. Look at that combination knob—jerked out as easy as pulling up a radish in wet weather. He's got the only clamps that can do it. And look how clean those tumblers were punched out! Jimmy never has to drill but one hole. Yes, I guess I want Mr. Valentine. He'll do his bit next time without any short-time or clemency foolishness."

Ben Price knew Jimmy's habits. He had learned them while working up the Springfield case. Long jumps, quick getaways, no confederates,[5] and a taste for good society—these ways

___
4. **rogue-catchers:** an elaborate way of describing the police.
5. **confederates:** accomplices.

Encourage students to find out about careers in the banking industry. Students could consult school librarians and counselors for information about positions available in banking such as teller, data entry clerk, bookkeeper, accountant, loan officer, and other bank jobs. Encourage students to record the information they learn in their journals or learning logs.

VISUAL CONNECTIONS
Exploring the Subject
You might ask students if they have ever seen the inside of a real safe or a bank vault. Did the vault look like the one in this painting?

Many of the bills shown are silver certificates: paper money in exchange for which the bearer could demand silver. Silver certificates were taken out of circulation in the United States in the 1960s.

You might also ask students if they have foreign currencies or old United States currency that they could bring to show in class. Currency in the U.S. never depicts anyone still living, but foreign currency often does: Queen Elizabeth's likeness appears on British coins and paper money. If old U.S. currency is available, the class could compare it with today's.

Ideas for Writing
You might have students write essays about what the class would do with this safe full of money. There are many possibilities, such as dividing the money among class members, buying things for the school or city, helping people in need, investing in stocks, or putting the money into savings.

READING SKILLS PRACTICE
The passage underscored in the page below can be used to give students practice in the reading skill of identifying an accurate generalization. Before students try to answer the following question, ask them to read the passage very carefully. Which of the following statements is supported by the information given in this passage? **A.** Jimmy Valentine is ignored by the young lady. (Contradicted.) **B.** Jimmy Valentine has fallen in love with the young lady and wants to know as much as possible about her. (Correct.) **C.** When Jimmy Valentine asks the boy questions, he is trying to get information that will enable him to rob the bank. (Unsupported.) **D.** Jimmy Valentine's college football sweater makes him very attractive to the young lady. (Irrelevant.)

had helped Mr. Valentine to become noted as a successful dodger of retribution.[6] It was given out that Ben Price had taken up the trail of the elusive cracksman, and other people with burglarproof safes felt more at ease.

▶ One afternoon Jimmy Valentine and his suitcase climbed out of the mail hack[7] in Elmore, a little town five miles off the railroad down in **11** the blackjack country of Arkansas. Jimmy, looking like an athletic young senior just home from college, went down the board sidewalk toward the hotel.

A young lady crossed the street, passed him at the corner, and entered a door over which **12** was the sign "The Elmore Bank." Jimmy Valentine looked into her eyes, forgot what he was, and became another man. She lowered her eyes and colored slightly. Young men of Jimmy's style and looks were scarce in Elmore.

Jimmy collared a boy that was loafing on the steps of the bank as if he were one of the stockholders, and began to ask him questions about the town, feeding him dimes at intervals. By and by the young lady came out, looking royally unconscious of the young man with the suitcase, and went her way.

"Isn't that young lady Miss Polly Simpson?" asked Jimmy with specious guile.[8] ◀

"Naw," said the boy. "She's Annabel Adams. **13** Her pa owns this bank. What'd you come to Elmore for? Is that a gold watch chain? I'm going to get a bulldog. Got any more dimes?"

Jimmy went to Planters' Hotel, registered as Ralph D. Spencer, and engaged a room. He leaned on the desk and declared his platform[9] to the clerk. He said he had come to Elmore to look for a location to go into business. How was the shoe business, now, in the town? He had thought of the shoe business. Was there an opening?

14 The clerk was impressed by the clothes and manner of Jimmy. He, himself, was something of a pattern of fashion to the thinly gilded[10] youth of Elmore, but now he perceived his shortcomings. While trying to figure out Jimmy's manner of tying his four-in-hand,[11] he cordially gave information.

Yes, there ought to be a good opening in the shoe line. There wasn't an exclusive shoe store in the place. The dry goods and general stores handled them. Business in all lines was fairly good. Hoped Mr. Spencer would decide to locate in Elmore. He would find it a pleasant town to live in, and the people very sociable.

Mr. Spencer thought he would stop over in the town a few days and look over the situation. No, the clerk needn't call the boy. He would carry up his suitcase, himself; it was rather heavy.

15 Mr. Ralph Spencer, the phoenix[12] that arose from Jimmy Valentine's ashes—ashes left by the flame of a sudden and alterative[13] attack of love—remained in Elmore and prospered. He opened a shoe store and secured a good run of trade.

Socially he was also a success and made many friends. And he accomplished the wish of his heart. He met Miss Annabel Adams and

6. **retribution:** (rĕt′rə-byōō′shən): punishment.
7. **mail hack:** a horse-drawn carriage used to carry mail from one town to another.
8. **with specious** (spē′shəs) **guile** (gīl): in a tricky way that appears to be innocent.

9. **platform:** here, intentions; plans.
10. **thinly gilded:** only seeming to be well-dressed. To be *gilded* is to be covered with a layer of gold.
11. **four-in-hand:** a necktie.
12. **phoenix:** (fē′nĭks): a bird in ancient Egyptian mythology. It was believed that the phoenix burned itself up and that from its ashes a new bird arose.
13. **alterative** (ôl′tə-rā′tĭv): causing an alteration, or change. Jimmy's love changed him.

Safe Money (c. 1889) by Victor Dubreuil.
Oil on canvas.
Collection of The Corcoran Gallery of Art, Museum Purchase through a gift from the heirs of George E. Lemon

11 American South is recurring setting for O. Henry's short stories.

12 Jimmy's falling in love provides motivation for Jimmy's actions throughout remainder of story.

13 Irony. That Jimmy, a safecracker, should fall in love with a banker's daughter is ironic.

14 Expressing an Opinion
Is Jimmy's interest in operating a shoe business surprising? Responses will vary. Having fallen in love with Annabel, Jimmy may want work that is less exciting and dangerous than cracking safes. His clothes suggest he knows and appreciates fashion.

15 Allusion. Jimmy, like phoenix, is reborn. Reader can infer source of funds to open store.

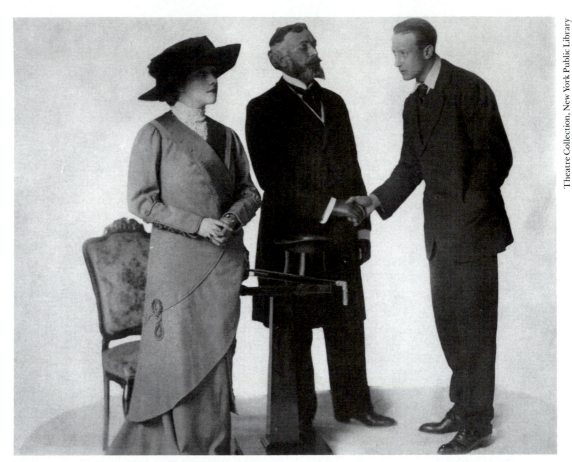

Theatre Collection, New York Public Library

Scenes on pages 214 and 217 are from the Broadway theater production of *Alias Jimmy Valentine* (1910).

became more and more captivated by her charms.

At the end of a year the situation of Mr. Ralph Spencer was this: he had won the respect of the community, his shoe store was flourishing, and he and Annabel were **16** engaged to be married in two weeks. Mr. Adams, the typical, plodding country banker, approved of Spencer. Annabel's pride in him **17** almost equaled her affection. He was as much **18** at home in the family of Mr. Adams and that of Annabel's married sister as if he were already a member.

One day Jimmy sat down in his room and wrote this letter, which he mailed to the safe address of one of his old friends in St. Louis:

Dear Old Pal:

I want you to be at Sullivan's place in Little Rock, next Wednesday night, at nine o'clock. I want you to wind up some little matters for me. And, also, I want to make you a present of my little kit of tools. I know you'll be glad to get them—you couldn't duplicate the lot for a thousand dollars. Say, Billy, I've quit the old business—a year ago. I've got a nice store. I'm making an honest living, and I'm going to marry the finest girl on earth two weeks from now. It's the only life, Billy—the straight one. I wouldn't touch a dollar of another man's money now for a million. **19** After I get married I'm going to sell out and go West, where there won't be so much danger of having old scores brought up against me. I tell you, Billy, she's an angel. She believes in me; and I wouldn't do another crooked thing for the whole world. Be sure to be at Sully's, for I must see you. I'll bring along the tools with me.

> Your old friend,
> Jimmy

On the Monday night after Jimmy wrote this **20** letter, Ben Price jogged unobtrusively[14] into Elmore in a livery buggy.[15] He lounged about town in his quiet way until he found out what he wanted to know. From the drugstore across the street from Spencer's shoe store, he got a good look at Ralph D. Spencer.

"Going to marry the banker's daughter, are you, Jimmy?" said Ben to himself softly. "Well, I don't know!"

The next morning Jimmy took breakfast at the Adamses'. He was going to Little Rock that **23** day to order his wedding suit and buy something nice for Annabel. That would be the first time he had left town since he came to Elmore. It had been more than a year now since those last professional "jobs," and he thought he **24** could safely venture out.

After breakfast quite a family party went downtown together—Mr. Adams, Annabel, Jimmy, and Annabel's married sister with her two little girls, aged five and nine. They came

by the hotel where Jimmy still boarded, and he ran up to his room and brought along his suitcase. Then they went on to the bank. There stood Jimmy's horse and buggy and Dolph Gibson, who was going to drive him over to the railroad station.

21 All went inside the high, carved oak railings into the banking room—Jimmy included, for Mr. Adams' future son-in-law was welcome anywhere. The clerks were pleased to be greeted by the good-looking, agreeable young man who was going to marry Miss Annabel. Jimmy set his suitcase down. Annabel, whose heart was bubbling with happiness and lively youth, put on Jimmy's hat and picked up the suitcase. "Wouldn't I make a nice drummer?"[16] asked Annabel. "My! Ralph, how heavy it is! **22** Feels like it was full of gold bricks."

"Lot of nickel-plated shoehorns in there," said Jimmy coolly, "that I'm going to return. Thought I'd save express charges by taking them up. I'm getting awfully economical."

The Elmore Bank had just put in a new safe and vault. Mr. Adams was very proud of it and insisted on an inspection by everyone. The vault was a small one, but it had a new patented door. It fastened with three solid steel bolts thrown simultaneously with a single handle, and had a time lock. Mr. Adams beamingly **23** explained its workings to Mr. Spencer, who showed a courteous but not too intelligent interest. The two children, May and Agatha, were delighted by the shining metal and funny clock and knobs.

24 While they were thus engaged, Ben Price sauntered in and leaned on his elbow, looking casually inside between the railings. He told the teller that he didn't want anything; he was just waiting for a man he knew.

Suddenly there was a scream or two from the women and a commotion. Unperceived by

---

14. **unobtrusively** (ŭn′əb-trōō′sĭv-lē): without attracting attention.

15. **livery buggy:** a hired horse and carriage.

16. **drummer:** here, a traveling salesman.

the elders, May, the nine-year-old girl, in a spirit of play had shut Agatha in the vault. She had then shot the bolts and turned the knob of the combination as she had seen Mr. Adams do.

The old banker sprang to the handle and tugged at it for a moment. "The door can't be opened," he groaned. "The clock hasn't been wound nor the combination set."

Agatha's mother screamed again, hysterically.

"Hush!" said Mr. Adams, raising his trembling hand. "All be quiet for a moment. Agatha!" he called as loudly as he could. "Listen to me." During the following silence they could just hear the faint sound of the child wildly shrieking in the dark vault in a panic of terror.

"My precious darling!" wailed the mother. "She will die of fright! Open the door! Oh, break it open! Can't you men do something?"

25 "There isn't a man nearer than Little Rock who can open that door," said Mr. Adams, in a shaky voice. "Spencer, what shall we do? That child—she can't stand it long in there. There isn't enough air, and, besides, she'll go into convulsions from fright."

Agatha's mother, frantic now, beat the door of the vault with her hands. Somebody wildly **28** suggested dynamite. Annabel turned to Jimmy, her large eyes full of anguish, but not yet despairing. To a woman nothing seems quite impossible to the powers of the man she worships.

"Can't you do something, Ralph—*try*, won't you?"

He looked at her with a queer, soft smile on his lips and in his keen eyes.

26 "Annabel," he said, "give me that rose you are wearing, will you?"

Hardly believing that she heard him aright, she unpinned the bud from the bosom of her dress, and placed it in his hand. Jimmy stuffed it into his vest pocket, threw off his coat, and **27** pulled up his shirt sleeves. With that act Ralph D. Spencer passed away, and Jimmy Valentine took his place.

"Get away from the door, all of you," he commanded, shortly.

He set his suitcase on the table, and opened it out flat. From that time on he seemed to be unconscious of the presence of anyone else. He laid out the shining, queer implements swiftly and orderly, whistling softly to himself as he always did when at work. In a deep silence and immovable, the others watched him as if under a spell.

In a minute Jimmy's pet drill was biting smoothly into the steel door. In ten minutes—breaking his own burglarious record—he threw back the bolts and opened the door.

Agatha, almost collapsed, but safe, was gathered into her mother's arms.

Jimmy Valentine put on his coat, and walked outside the railings toward the front door. As he went he thought he heard a faraway voice that he once knew call "Ralph!" But he never hesitated.

At the door a big man stood somewhat in his way.

"Hello, Ben!" said Jimmy, still with his strange smile. "Got around at last, have you? Well, let's go. I don't know that it makes much difference, now."

And then Ben Price acted rather strangely.

29 "Guess you're mistaken, Mr. Spencer," he said. "Don't believe I recognize you. Your buggy's waiting for you, ain't it?"

And Ben Price turned and strolled down the street.

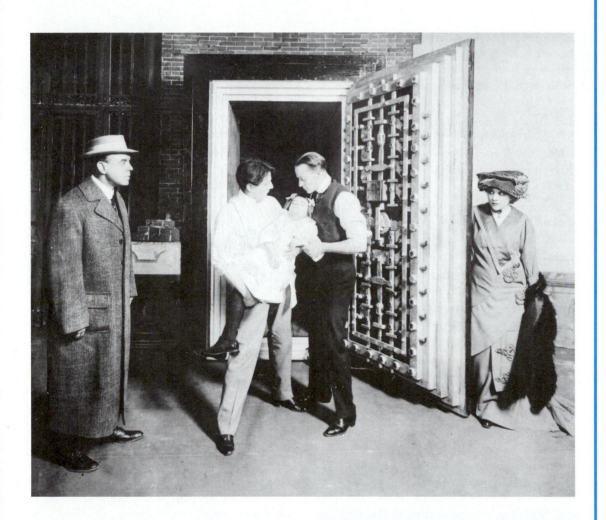

Reading Check

1. Why had Jimmy Valentine been in prison?
2. What is unusual about the contents of Jimmy's suitcase?
3. Identify Ben Price.
4. What business does Jimmy go into in Elmore?
5. How does Agatha get locked in the vault?

For Study and Discussion

Analyzing and Interpreting the Story

1. At the beginning of the story, the prison warden tells Jimmy Valentine to stop cracking safes and reform. What does Jimmy do after his release that shows he plans to ignore the warden's advice?

2a. How does the power of love make Jimmy decide to "go straight"? **b.** Describe the new life that Jimmy has created for himself at the end of a year in Elmore.

A Retrieved Reformation **217**

TRANSPARENCIES 18 & 19
Fine Art
Theme: *Slice of Life* – highlights art-work depicting a situation that captures a meaningful scene from life, as a short story does.

TRANSPARENCY 20
Reader Response
Charting A Response – invites students to examine a selection from several different perspectives.

3. Through letter Jimmy wrote to pal. Intercepts letter or pal tells. Letter's postmark would reveal address.

4. Jimmy's actions prove to Price that he has reformed.

5a. When he got out tools to open safe, he risked discovery and imprisonment. 5b. Ironically, by the same act, opening the safe. He convinces Price of his reformation, and Price refuses to recognize him as Jimmy.

6. Responses will vary.

LITERARY ELEMENTS
Following the Plot

1. With society's laws and detective Price.

2. He must decide whether to reveal his identity and lose Annabel or to save Agatha.

3. When Jimmy sees Price in doorway. Students most likely feared that Jimmy would be arrested.

4. Responses will vary. Some may like happy ending in which good deed and true reformation of character are rewarded; others may not like fact Jimmy will not be punished for crimes.

Recognizing Irony

1. Prisoners are opposite of guests: uninvited, not there of own free will or to be entertained.

2. If Annabel had known Jimmy's true identity, she would not have chosen to marry him, someone who normally would be one of her father's greatest enemies.

3. If Jimmy had not opened safe, Price would have arrested him.

---

3. The reader knows that Ben Price, the great detective, is on Jimmy's trail. But Jimmy himself is unaware of this danger. How do you think Ben Price finds out that Jimmy is in Elmore?

4. When he opens the safe to free Agatha, Jimmy believes he is destroying his chances for a new life. However, opening the safe actually *saves* Jimmy's happiness. Why doesn't Ben Price arrest Jimmy?

5. *Retrieved* means "brought back" or "recaptured." A *reformation* is a "change" or "improvement." **a.** How was Jimmy's reformation endangered? **b.** How was it "retrieved"?

6. What other stories, films, or television shows do you know that feature a good-hearted detective like Ben Price, or a tough character like Jimmy Valentine transformed by the power of love?

Literary Elements

Following the Plot

At the beginning of this story, you meet Jimmy Valentine in jail, where he has already spent ten months for breaking the law. At the end of the story, Jimmy is a reformed character. The series of events in the story, or the **plot,** tells you how this change occurs in the hero. In other words, plot is "what happens" in a story.

At the heart of every plot there is a **conflict,** or struggle. Often the character wants something that pits him or her in a struggle against someone or something else.

Conflicts with another person, an animal, or a force of nature, such as a hurricane, are **1** called **external conflicts.** What is Jimmy's external conflict? Many stories also include **internal conflicts.** These are struggles that take place within a character's mind or feel-

---

ings. Internal conflicts often involve decisions.
2 How does Agatha's imprisonment in the vault force Jimmy into a difficult internal conflict?

In most stories there is a **climax,** or turning point. At this point you know whether the story will end happily or unhappily. The climax is a time of great suspense or emotion. It is usually the most exciting and tense part of the **3** story. Which scene in this story would you say is the climax? What were your feelings at that point?

One of Jimmy's conflicts is finally resolved when he meets Ben Price after the safecrack-**4** ing scene. Were you surprised at Ben's actions at the end of the story? Did this ending satisfy you? Why or why not?

Recognizing Irony

If you were to say "That's just great!" when you really mean that something is terrible, you would be using **irony.** When people speak ironically, they are saying just the opposite of what **1** they mean, or the opposite of what is true. Can you explain the irony in O. Henry's description of prisoners as "compulsory guests"?

Often an entire situation is ironic. In other words, it turns out to be exactly the opposite of what should happen, or the opposite of what we would expect to happen. O. Henry is famous for the humorously ironic situations in his stories.

2 Why is it ironic that Jimmy Valentine, the notorious safecracker, should win the hand of the banker's daughter, with the banker's approval?

3 Why is it ironic that Jimmy thought that opening the safe to free Agatha would ruin his chances for happiness? (Would Ben Price have let Jimmy go if he hadn't observed what Jimmy did to save Agatha?)

CLOSURE
Ask students to identify and analyze passages that suggest Jimmy's initial character and then analyze passages of action and **dialogue** by which they can infer that character change is taking place.

EXTENSION AND ENRICHMENT
Students might like to write stories with surprise endings, original stories about ironic situations, or essays in which they give their opinions about Ben Price's decision to let Jimmy go free.
   Students who enjoyed this story may want to read other favorites by O. Henry, such as "The Cop and the Anthem" and "The Last Leaf."

Language and Vocabulary

Understanding Denotation and Connotation

In addition to their dictionary meanings, or **denotations,** words have suggested meanings, or **connotations.** We are told that when Jimmy leaves the prison, he is wearing *ready-made* clothes. The literal meaning, or denotation, of *ready-made* is "ready for use" or "not made for any particular customer." The suggested meaning, or connotation, of *ready-made* is "ordinary" or "commonplace." We can infer from context that Jimmy has been accustomed to having his clothes made to order.

1 In these sentences from the story, what do the italicized words denote, and what additional feelings and qualities do they connote?

a A guard came to the prison shoeshop, where Jimmy Valentine was assiduously stitching uppers, and *escorted* him to the front office.

b Then an old-fashioned bank safe in Jefferson City became active and threw out of its crater an *eruption* of bank notes amounting to five thousand dollars.

c There wasn't an *exclusive* shoe store in the place.

Creative Writing

Writing a Letter to an Imaginary Character

"A Retrieved Reformation" ends with the idea that Jimmy has truly reformed and will not go back to jail. Imagine that Jimmy and Annabel marry and have children and that Jimmy decides to explain his former life and his change of heart to their children. Assume that you are Jimmy. Write a letter to your children in which you explain your life of crime and why you decided to "go straight." You might enjoy reading your letter to a small group of your classmates.

About the Author

O. Henry (1862–1910)

The Granger Collection, New York

O. Henry wrote "A Retrieved Reformation" while he was a prisoner in the Ohio federal penitentiary, serving time for embezzling funds from a Texas bank. The character of Jimmy Valentine—the criminal with a heart—was based on a safecracker that O. Henry knew in prison. As *Alias Jimmy Valentine*, O. Henry's story became a successful Broadway play.

   O. Henry was the pen name of William Sydney Porter, who grew up in Greensboro, North Carolina, and became an apprentice to a pharmacist. He moved to Texas to work on an uncle's ranch. Later he was a bookkeeper, a bank teller, a newspaper writer, and owner of a weekly newspaper called *The Rolling Stone*. When he was summoned for trial on the embezzlement charge, he jumped bail and fled to Honduras. A year and a half later, when he returned to Texas to visit his dying wife, he was arrested and spent the next three years in jail. By 1903 he was in New York City, where he roamed the parks, streets, and restaurants, talking to people and collecting story material. His stories—more than two hundred fifty in all—became immensely popular.

   You can almost count on an O. Henry story to have a surprise ending. Two of his other stories that you might enjoy are "The Gift of the Magi" and "The Ransom of Red Chief."

LANGUAGE AND VOCABULARY
1a. *Escorted:* accompanied by a person or protective guard. It connotes situation in which person is accompanied by another out of respect; ironic because Jimmy has "a taste for good society," but his escort here is not of a social nature.
1b. *Eruption:* the act, process, or instance of erupting or exploding. Humorously continuing to ignore Jimmy's association with these burglaries, O. Henry uses word *eruption* and analogy of volcano to suggest that money suddenly came out of safe as if result of natural causes. *Eruption* also connotes large quantity of whatever is erupted.
1c. *Exclusive:* single or independent. Basic idea is that there was not a store specializing in shoes; suggests high quality, refinement, and respectability.

CREATIVE WRITING
Most students should have little difficulty with this assignment. You might suggest they "get into character" and imagine the number and ages of the children to whom they are writing. Ask students what they think Jimmy's biggest fear might be in revealing his past to his children.

ABOUT THE AUTHOR
The now-famous embezzlement charge was filed against O. Henry in 1896, two years after he ceased working in an Austin bank. (He served as a teller from 1891 to 1894.) An otherwise unexplained shortage in funds was blamed on O. Henry. While serving his prison sentence for this charge, O. Henry wrote his first short story.

OBJECTIVES
The overall aim is for students to analyze specific details concerning characters, their identities and actions, and important events in "The Rule of Names." For a complete list of objectives, see the **Teacher's Notes.**

VOCABULARY
The underlined words are in the Glossary. The **Language and Vocabulary** exercise on p. 229 gives students practice in looking up word histories.

FOCUS / MOTIVATION
Ask students what they know of the origins of surnames. Discuss the origins of common surnames such as *Miller* (profession) and *Hill* (geography). Tell students to notice how people in this story got their names.

TEACHING RESOURCES C
Teacher's Notes, p. 26
Reading Check, p. 29
Study Guide, p. 30
Language Skills, pp. 34, 37
Building Vocabulary, p. 40
Selection Vocabulary Test, p. 41
Selection Test, p. 42

PREREADING FOCUS
The headnote prepares students for the central character of the story—a dragon in disguise. Encourage students to evaluate the author's use of clues about the disguise and to decide whether the clues are too subtle or not subtle enough.

The Rule of Names

1
Symbol. Name *Underhill* suggests hidden place.

2
Foreshadowing. Steam from his nostrils is clue to Mr. Underhill's true identity.

3
Atmosphere. Vivid **description** of **setting**, a mixture of realism and fantasy, sets stage for story.

4
Evidently, the spoken word is very powerful on this island.

5 Making Generalizations
What can you tell about the inhabitants of Sattins Island? They appear to be superstitious (although their beliefs may be well-founded).

6
Foreshadowing. Underhill's dislike of being visited in his "cave" is another hint at his true identity.

The Rule of Names

URSULA K. LE GUIN

In this story of magic and mystery, one of the characters is a mighty dragon in disguise. As you read the story, pay attention to the author's clever clues about the dragon's disguise.

1 Mr. Underhill came out from under his hill, **2** smiling and breathing hard. Each breath shot out of his nostrils as a double puff of steam, snow-white in the morning sunshine. Mr. Underhill looked up at the bright December sky and smiled wider than ever, showing snow-white teeth. Then he went down to the village.

3 "Morning, Mr. Underhill," said the villagers as he passed them in the narrow street between houses with conical, overhanging roofs like the fat red caps of toadstools. "Morning, **4** morning!" he replied to each. (It was of course bad luck to wish anyone a *good* morning; a simple statement of the time of day was quite enough, in a place so permeated with Influences as Sattins Island, where a careless adjective might change the weather for a week.) All of them spoke to him, some with affection, some with affectionate disdain. He was all the little island had in the way of a wizard, and so deserved respect—but how could you respect a little fat man of fifty who waddled along with his toes turned in, breathing steam and smiling? He was no great shakes as a workman either. His fireworks were fairly elaborate but his elixirs[1] were weak. Warts he charmed off frequently reappeared after three days; tomatoes he enchanted grew no bigger

than cantaloupes; and those rare times when a strange ship stopped at Sattins Harbor, Mr. Underhill always stayed under his hill—for **5** fear, he explained, of the evil eye. He was, in other words, a wizard the way walleyed[2] Gan was a carpenter: by default. The villagers made do with badly-hung doors and inefficient spells, for this generation, and relieved their annoyance by treating Mr. Underhill quite familiarly, as a mere fellow villager. They even asked him to dinner. Once he asked some of them to dinner, and served a splendid repast, with silver, crystal, damask,[3] roast goose, sparkling Andrades '639,[4] and plum pudding with hard sauce; but he was so nervous all through the meal that it took the joy out of it, and besides, everybody was hungry again half **6** an hour afterward. He did not like anyone to visit his cave, not even the anteroom, beyond which in fact nobody had ever got. When he saw people approaching the hill he always came trotting out to meet them. "Let's sit out here under the pine trees!" he would say, smiling and waving towards the fir grove, or if it was raining, "Let's go have a drink at the inn,

1. **elixirs** (ĭ-lĭk′sərz): magic remedies.

2. **walleyed** (wôl′īd′): having eyes that turn outward.
3. **damask** (dăm′əsk): a fine fabric, which has a design woven into it. Here, the word refers to a tablecloth and napkins made from this fabric.
4. **Andrades '639:** a vintage of wine. The number '639 indicates the year.

MOTIVATIONAL SUMMARY

Blackbeard, who calls himself a wizard and sea-lord, arrives on Sattins Island in search of stolen treasures. He suspects that the island's wizard, Mr. Underhill, is the thief. Mr. Underhill, however, may be more than he seems.

PRESENTATION

Although students may enjoy sharing at least part of this whimsical story through a spirited oral reading, "The Rule of Names" is easy enough to be assigned as independent reading either in class or at home. You may wish to divide the class into six small groups and assign each group the task of answering one of the first six **For Study and Discussion** questions. Have each group report its consensus to the rest of the class and compare the responses. Accept any answer that is consistent with details in the story, and

Illustration by Wayne Anderson for *The Flight of Dragons* by Peter Dickinson (1979).

7
Le Guin blends normal activities of curious young boys with magical events—"roar of wrath" and "purple steam."

8
Alliteration. Repetition of *h* sound suggests sound of Mr. Underhill's steaming bellow.

9 Analyzing
How does Mr. Underhill's grocery list foreshadow the revelation that he is a dragon? Grocery list—three dozen eggs and a pound of liver—is more fitting for a dragon than for a man.

eh?" though everybody knew he drank nothing stronger than well-water.

Some of the village children, teased by that locked cave, poked and pried and made raids while Mr. Underhill was away; but the small door that led into the inner chamber was spell-shut, and it seemed for once to be an effective **7** spell. Once a couple of boys, thinking the wizard was over on the West Shore curing Mrs. Ruuna's sick donkey, brought a crowbar and a hatchet up there, but at the first whack of the hatchet on the door there came a roar of wrath from inside, and a cloud of purple steam. Mr. Underhill had got home early. The boys fled. He did not come out, and the boys came to no harm, though they said you couldn't believe **8** what a huge hooting howling hissing horrible bellow that little fat man could make unless you'd heard it.

9 His business in town this day was three dozen fresh eggs and a pound of liver; also a stop at Seacaptain Fogeno's cottage to renew the seeing-charm on the old man's eyes (quite useless when applied to a case of detached

guide students to see the richness of interpretation that a good writer makes possible. Finally, you might ask each student to write an individual response to the seventh question.

Have one or more small groups of students work together to adapt the story for television by writing a scenario upon which a script might be based. Suggest that students cast well-known actors and actresses in the key roles. En-

courage students who are interested in writing a complete script to do so and, if they are particularly ambitious, to attempt a video production with student actors.

---

10 Summarizing Analyzing
How do girls act around Mr. Underhill? Why? They are nervous around Mr. Underhill. Perhaps they instinctively realize that he is a threat. Le Guin slowly reveals Mr. Underhill's nature through reactions of others.

11
Le Guin broadly characterizes all the island's inhabitants as illiterates. Informal school routine and roving teacher seem indicative of islanders' relaxed life style.

12
Mr. Underhill is captivated by Palani. The hungry dragon in him thinks she looks "plump, pretty."

13
Suspense. Mr. Underhill's arrival is shrouded in mystery, creating suspense.

14 Finding Main Ideas
Why is the "truename" so important? Knowing a person's or thing's real name or truename gives one power and control over it.

---

retina,[5] but Mr. Underhill kept trying), and finally a chat with old Goody[6] Guld, the concertina[7]-maker's widow. Mr. Underhill's friends were mostly old people. He was timid with the **10** strong young men of the village, and the girls were shy of him. "He makes me nervous he smiles so much" they all said, pouting, twisting silky ringlets round a finger. *Nervous* was a newfangled word, and their mothers all replied grimly, "Nervous my foot, *silliness* is the word for it. Mr. Underhill is a very respectable wizard!"

After leaving Goody Guld, Mr. Underhill passed by the school, which was being held this **11** day out on the common. Since no one on Sattins Island was literate, there were no books to learn to read from and no desks to carve initials on and no blackboards to erase, and in fact no schoolhouse. On rainy days the children met in the loft of the Communal Barn, and got hay in their pants; on sunny days the schoolteacher, Palani, took them anywhere she felt like. Today, surrounded by thirty interested children under twelve and forty uninterested sheep under five, she was teaching an important item on the curriculum: the Rules of Names. Mr. Underhill, smiling shyly, paused **12** to listen and watch. Palani, a plump, pretty girl of twenty, made a charming picture there in the wintry sunlight, sheep and children around her, a leafless oak above her, and **14** behind her the dunes and sea and clear, pale sky. She spoke earnestly, her face flushed pink by wind and words. "Now you know the Rules of Names already, children. There are two, and they're the same on every island in the world. What's one of them?"

---

5. **detached retina** (rĕt′n-ə): a serious visual disorder caused by damaged nerve tissue at the back of the eyeball.
6. **Goody:** a shortened form of *goodwife,* a title once used for married women of low social status.
7. **concertina:** a musical instrument similar to a small accordion.

"It ain't polite to ask anybody what his name is," shouted a fat, quick boy, interrupted by a little girl shrieking, "You can't never tell your own name to nobody, my ma says!"

"Yes, Suba. Yes, Popi dear, don't screech. That's right. You never ask anybody his name. You never tell your own. Now think about that a minute and then tell me why we call our wizard Mr. Underhill." She smiled across the curly heads and the woolly backs at Mr. Underhill, who beamed, and nervously clutched his sack of eggs.

" 'Cause he lives under a hill!" said half the children.

"But is it his truename?"

"No!" said the fat boy, echoed by little Popi shrieking, "No!"

"How do you know it's not?"

13 " 'Cause he came here all alone and so there wasn't anybody knew his truename so they couldn't tell, and *he* couldn't—"

"Very good, Suba. Popi, don't shout. That's right. Even a wizard can't tell his truename. When you children are through school and go through the Passage, you'll leave your childnames behind and keep only your truenames, which you must never ask for and never give away. Why is that the rule?"

The children were silent. The sheep bleated gently. Mr. Underhill answered the question: "Because the name is the thing," he said in his shy, soft, husky voice, "and the truename is the true thing. To speak the name is to control the thing. Am I right, Schoolmistress?"

She smiled and curtsied, evidently a little embarrassed by his participation. And he trotted off towards his hill, clutching his eggs to his bosom. Somehow the minute spent watching Palani and the children had made him very hungry. He locked his inner door behind him with a hasty incantation,[8] but there must

---

8. **incantation:** a series of magic words used to cast a spell.

---

have been a leak or two in the spell, for soon the bare anteroom of the cave was rich with the smell of frying eggs and sizzling liver.

The wind that day was light and fresh out of the west, and on it at noon a little boat came skimming the bright waves into Sattins Harbor. Even as it rounded the point a sharp-eyed boy spotted it, and knowing, like every child on the island, every sail and spar of the forty boats of the fishing fleet, he ran down the street calling out, "A foreign boat, a foreign boat!" Very seldom was the lonely isle visited by a boat from some equally lonely isle of the East Reach, or an adventurous trader from the Archipelago.[9] By the time the boat was at the pier half the village was there to greet it, and fishermen were following it homewards, and cowherds and clam-diggers and herb-hunters were puffing up and down all the rocky hills, heading towards the harbor.

But Mr. Underhill's door stayed shut.

There was only one man aboard the boat. Old Seacaptain Fogeno, when they told him that, drew down a bristle of white brows over his unseeing eyes. "There's only one kind of man," he said, "that sails the Out Reach alone. A wizard, or a warlock, or a Mage. . . ."

So the villagers were breathless hoping to see for once in their lives a Mage, one of the mighty White Magicians of the rich, towered, crowded inner islands of the Archipelago. They were disappointed, for the voyager was quite young, a handsome black-bearded fellow who hailed them cheerfully from his boat, and leaped ashore like any sailor glad to have made port. He introduced himself at once as a sea-peddler. But when they told Seacaptain Fogeno that he carried an oaken walking-stick around with him, the old man nodded. "Two wizards in one town," he said. "Bad!" And his mouth snapped shut like an old carp's.

9. **Archipelago** (är′kə-pĕl′ə-gō′): a large group of islands.

As the stranger could not give them his name, they gave him one right away: Blackbeard. And they gave him plenty of attention. He had a small mixed cargo of cloth and sandals and piswi feathers for trimming cloaks and cheap incense and levity stones and fine herbs and great glass beads from Venway—the usual peddler's lot. Everyone on Sattins Island came to look, to chat with the voyager, and perhaps to buy something—"Just to remember him by!" cackled Goody Guld, who like all the women and girls of the village was smitten with Blackbeard's bold good looks. All the boys hung round him too, to hear him tell of his voyages to far, strange islands of the Reach or describe the great rich islands of the Archipelago, the Inner Lanes, the roadsteads white with ships, and the golden roofs of Havnor. The men willingly listened to his tales; but some of them wondered why a trader should sail alone, and kept their eyes thoughtfully upon his oaken staff.

But all this time Mr. Underhill stayed under his hill.

"This is the first island I've ever seen that had no wizard," said Blackbeard one evening to Goody Guld, who had invited him and her nephew and Palani in for a cup of rushwash tea. "What do you do when you get a toothache, or the cow goes dry?"

"Why, we've got Mr. Underhill!" said the old woman.

"For what that's worth," muttered her nephew Birt, and then blushed purple and spilled his tea. Birt was a fisherman, a large, brave, wordless young man. He loved the schoolmistress, but the nearest he had come to telling her of his love was to give baskets of fresh mackerel to her father's cook.

"Oh, you do have a wizard?" Blackbeard asked. "Is he invisible?"

"No, he's just very shy," said Palani. "You've only been here a week, you know, and we see so

15
Setting. Island is small and lonely—so small that children are familiar with all the fishing boats, and half the townspeople can gather together at one place.

16 Making Inferences
      Drawing Conclusions
Why is Mr. Underhill's door shut? Why does the author state this fact in a separate paragraph? Perhaps Mr. Underhill's door is shut because he has something to hide; perhaps he is afraid of something. That the fact is revealed in a one-sentence paragraph indicates its significance.

17
All masters and makers of magic.

18
Symbol. Oaken walking stick is associated with magic. Since ancient times, the oak has been considered a sacred tree with magical properties.

19
Characterization. Blackbeard's impressive physical appearance and aura of mystery captivate islanders.

20
Blackbeard is beginning to obtain information he needs to complete his quest. Although he seems to be asking innocent questions, he has a serious purpose.

few strangers here. . . ." She also blushed a little, but did not spill her tea.

Blackbeard smiled at her. "He's a good Sattinsman, then, eh?"

21 "No," said Goody Guld, "no more than you are. Another cup, nevvy?[10]— keep it in the cup this time. No, my dear, he came in a little bit of a boat, four years ago was it?— just a day after the end of the shad-run, I recall, for they was taking up the nets over in East Creek, and Pondi Cowherd broke his leg that very morning—five years ago it must be. No, four. No, five it is, 'twas the year the garlic didn't sprout. So he sails in on a bit of a sloop loaded full up with great chests and boxes and says to Seacaptain Fogeno, who wasn't blind then, though old enough goodness knows to be blind twice over, 'I hear tell,' he says, 'you've got no wizard nor warlock at all, might you be wanting one?' 'Indeed, if the magic's white!' says the Captain, and before you could say 'cuttlefish' Mr. Underhill had settled down in the cave under the hill and was charming the mange off Goody Beltow's cat. Though the fur grew in gray, and 'twas an orange cat. Queer-looking thing it was after that. It died last winter in the cold spell. Goody Beltow took on so at the cat's death, poor thing, worse than when her man was drowned on the Long Banks, the year of the long herring-runs, when nevvy Birt here was but a babe in petticoats." Here Birt spilled his tea again, and Blackbeard grinned, but Goody Guld proceeded undismayed, and talked on till nightfall.

22 Next day Blackbeard was down at the pier, seeing after the sprung board in his boat which he seemed to take a long time fixing, and as usual drawing the taciturn[11] Sattinsmen into talk. "Now which of these is your wizard's craft?" he asked. "Or has he got one of those

10. **nevvy:** a dialectal form of *nephew.*
11. **taciturn** (tăs'ə-tərn): quiet; having little to say.

the Mages fold up into a walnut shell when they're not using it?"

"Nay," said a stolid fisherman. "She's oop in his cave, under hill."

"He carried the boat he came in up to his cave?"

"Aye. Clear opp. I helped. Heavier as lead she was. Full oop with great boxes, and they full oop with books o' spells, he says. Heavier as lead she was." And the stolid fisherman turned his back, sighing stolidly. Goody Guld's nephew, mending a net nearby, looked up from his work and asked with equal stolidity, "Would ye like to meet Mr. Underhill, maybe?"

23 Blackbeard returned Birt's look. Clever black eyes met candid blue ones for a long moment; then Blackbeard smiled and said, "Yes. Will you take me up to the hill, Birt?"

"Aye, when I'm done with this," said the fisherman. And when the net was mended, he and the Archipelagan set off up the village street towards the high green hill above it. But as they crossed the common Blackbeard said, **24** "Hold on awhile, friend Birt, I have a tale to tell you, before we meet your wizard."

"Tell away," says Birt, sitting down in the shade of a live oak.

"It's the story that started a hundred years ago, and isn't finished yet—though it soon will be, very soon. . . . In the very heart of the Archipelago, where the islands crowd thick as flies on honey, there's a little isle called Pendor. The sealords of Pendor were mighty men, in **25** the old days of war before the League. Loot and ransom and tribute came pouring into Pendor, and they gathered a great treasure there, long ago. Then from somewhere away out in the West Reach, where dragons breed on the lava isles, came one day a very mighty **26** dragon. Not one of those overgrown lizards most of you Outer Reach folk call dragons, but a big, black, winged, wise, cunning monster, full of strength and subtlety, and like all dragons loving gold and precious stones above all things. He killed the Sealord and his soldiers, and the people of Pendor fled in their ships by night. They all fled away and left the dragon coiled up in Pendor Towers. And there he stayed for a hundred years, dragging his scaly belly over the emeralds and sapphires and coins of gold, coming forth only once in a year or two when he must eat. He'd raid nearby islands for his food. You know what dragons eat?"

Birt nodded and said in a whisper, "Maidens."

"Right," said Blackbeard. "Well, that couldn't be endured forever, nor the thought of his sitting on all that treasure. So after the League grew strong, and the Archipelago wasn't so busy with wars and piracy, it was decided to attack Pendor, drive out the dragon, and get the gold and jewels for the treasury of the League. They're forever wanting money, the League is. So a huge fleet gathered from fifty islands, and seven Mages stood in the **27** prows of the seven strongest ships, and they sailed towards Pendor. . . . They got there. They landed. Nothing stirred. The houses all stood empty, the dishes on the tables full of a hundred years' dust. The bones of the old Sealord and his men lay about in the castle courts and on the stairs. And the Tower rooms reeked of dragon. But there was no dragon. And no treasure, not a diamond the size of a poppyseed, not a single silver bead. . . . Knowing that he couldn't stand up to seven Mages, **28** the dragon had skipped out. They tracked him, and found he'd flown to a deserted island up north called Udrath; they followed his trail there, and what did they find? Bones again. **29** His bones—the dragon's. But no treasure. A wizard, some unknown wizard from somewhere, must have met him singlehanded, and defeated him—and then made off with the treasure, right under the League's nose!"

The fisherman listened, attentive and expressionless.

"Now that must have been a powerful wizard and a clever one, first to kill a dragon, and second to get off without leaving a trace. The lords and Mages of the Archipelago couldn't track him at all, neither where he'd come from nor where he'd made off to. They were about to give up. That was last spring; I'd been off on a three-year voyage up in the North Reach, and got back about that time. And they asked me to help them find the unknown wizard. That was clever of them. Because I'm not only a wizard myself, as I think some of the oafs here have guessed, but I am also a descendant of the Lords of Pendor. That treasure is mine. It's mine, and knows that it's mine. Those fools of the League couldn't find it, because it's not theirs. It belongs to the House of Pendor, and the great emerald, the star of the hoard, Inalkil the Greenstone, knows its master. Behold!" Blackbeard raised his oaken staff and cried aloud, "Inalkil!" The tip of the staff began to glow green, a fiery green radiance, a dazzling haze the color of April grass, and at the same moment the staff tipped in the wizard's hand, leaning, slanting till it pointed straight at the side of the hill above them.

"It wasn't so bright a glow, far away in Havnor," Blackbeard murmured, "but the staff pointed true. Inalkil answered when I called. **30** The jewel knows its master. And I know the thief, and I shall conquer him. He's a mighty wizard, who could overcome a dragon. But I am mightier. Do you want to know why, oaf? Because I know his name!"

As Blackbeard's tone got more arrogant, Birt had looked duller and duller, blanker and blanker, but at this he gave a twitch, shut his **31** mouth, and stared at the Archipelagan. "How did you . . . learn it?" he asked very slowly.

Blackbeard grinned, and did not answer.

"Black magic?"

The Rule of Names **225**

27
Since ancient times, *seven* has been considered a sacred, mystical number by some. Its use here suggests fleet is magical, special.

28
Le Guin's use of lighthearted phrase "skipped out" to describe dragon's exit creates humorous image.

29 Drawing Conclusions
What is Blackbeard leading up to? He believes Mr. Underhill is the wizard for whom he is searching.

30
Characterization. Blackbeard is rash to boast of victory prematurely.

31 Drawing Conclusions
Why does Birt suddenly become concerned about Blackbeard's story? Birt begins to fear that Blackbeard's motives are dishonorable.

"How else?"

Birt looked pale, and said nothing.

"I am the Sealord of Pendor, oaf, and I will have the gold my fathers won, and the jewels my mothers wore, and the Greenstone! For they are mine. Now, you can tell your village boobies the whole story after I have defeated this wizard and gone. Wait here. Or you can come and watch, if you're not afraid. You'll never get the chance again to see a great wizard in all his power." Blackbeard turned, and without a backward glance strode off up the hill towards the entrance to the cave.

Very slowly, Birt followed. A good distance from the cave he stopped, sat down under a hawthorn tree, and watched. The Archipelagan had stopped; a stiff, dark figure alone on the green swell of the hill before the gaping cave-mouth, he stood perfectly still. All at once he swung his staff up over his head, and the emerald radiance shone about him as he shouted, "Thief, thief of the Hoard of Pendor, **35** come forth!"

There was a crash, as of dropped crockery, from inside the cave, and a lot of dust came spewing out. Scared, Birt ducked. When he looked again he saw Blackbeard still standing **32** motionless, and at the mouth of the cave, dusty and disheveled, stood Mr. Underhill. He looked small and pitiful, with his toes turned in as usual, and his little bowlegs in black **33** tights, and no staff—he never had had one, Birt suddenly thought. Mr. Underhill spoke. "Who are you?" he said in his husky little voice.

"I am the Sealord of Pendor, thief, come to claim my treasure!"

At that, Mr. Underhill slowly turned pink, as he always did when people were rude to him. **34** But he then turned something else. He turned yellow. His hair bristled out, he gave a coughing roar—and was a yellow lion leaping down the hill at Blackbeard, white fangs gleaming.

But Blackbeard no longer stood there. A

gigantic tiger, color of night and lightning, bounded to meet the lion. . . .

The lion was gone. Below the cave all of a sudden stood a high grove of trees, black in the winter sunshine. The tiger, checking himself in mid-leap just before he entered the shadow of the trees, caught fire in the air, became a tongue of flame lashing out at the dry black branches. . . .

But where the trees had stood a sudden cataract[12] leaped from the hillside, an arch of silvery crashing water, thundering down upon the fire. But the fire was gone. . . .

For just a moment before the fisherman's staring eyes two hills rose—the green one he knew, and a new one, a bare, brown hillock ready to drink up the rushing waterfall. That passed so quickly it made Birt blink, and after blinking he blinked again, and moaned, for what he saw now was a great deal worse. Where the cataract had been there hovered a dragon. Black wings darkened all the hill, steel claws reached groping, and from the dark, scaly, gaping lips fire and steam shot out.

Beneath the monstrous creature stood Blackbeard, laughing.

"Take any shape you please, little Mr. Underhill!" he taunted. "I can match you. But the game grows tiresome. I want to look upon my treasure, upon Inalkil. Now, big dragon, little wizard, take your true shape. I command you **36** by the power of your truename—Yevaud!"

Birt could not move at all, not even to blink. He cowered, staring whether he would or not. He saw the black dragon hang there in the air above Blackbeard. He saw the fire lick like many tongues from the scaly mouth, the steam jet from the red nostrils. He saw Blackbeard's face grow white, white as chalk, and **37** the beard-fringed lips trembling.

"Your name is Yevaud!"

---

12. **cataract** (kăt′ə-răkt′): a waterfall.

TRANSPARENCY 21

Literary Elements
Elements of the Short Story – invites students to examine some of the basic elements of fiction.

"Yes," said a great, husky, hissing voice. "My truename is Yevaud, and my true shape is this shape."

"But the dragon was killed—they found dragon bones on Udrath Island—"

"That was another dragon," said the dragon, and then stooped like a hawk, <u>talons</u> outstretched. And Birt shut his eyes.

38 When he opened them the sky was clear, the hillside empty, except for a reddish-blackish trampled spot, and a few talon-marks in the grass.

Birt the fisherman got to his feet and ran.

He ran across the common, scattering sheep to right and left, and straight down to the village street to Palani's father's house. Palani was out in the garden weeding the nasturtiums. "Come **39** with me!" Birt gasped. She stared. He grabbed her wrist and dragged her with him. She screeched a little, but did not resist. He ran with her straight to the pier, pushed her into his fishing sloop the *Queenie,* untied the **40** painter,[13] took up the oars and set off rowing like a demon. The last that Sattins Island saw

13. **painter:** here, a rope attached to a boat.

Lacquer chest with incised design (Cheng Te Reign 1306–1321).

Private Collection

38
Use to answer **study question 4,** p. 228.

39
Birt realizes that the maiden Palani would be in danger from the dragon.

40
Simile. Birt's rowing "like a demon" suggests furious, frenzied activity. Use of "demon" adds touch of humor in story of wizards and dragons.

VISUAL CONNECTIONS
Exploring the Subject
Dragons are mythical beasts, found, since ancient times, in the lore of almost all cultures. Some cultures regard these creatures as evil and some as good. Dragons originated as monster sea serpents in the folklore of the Sumerians, and many dragons are associated with water. Some dragons are credited with guarding sacred places. In China and Japan, dragons are usually benevolent and are wingless although they are regarded as powers of the air. The dragon was the badge of the imperial family in China.

41

Irony. Villagers quickly have occasion to stop talking about it. Disappearance of Birt and Palani not associated with danger until Mr. Underhill reappears.

42 Drawing Conclusions
What does the dragon intend as his "real meal"? Maiden from village.

READING CHECK
1. Wizardry (p. 220).
2. No one is literate (p. 222).
3. After they go through the Passage (p. 222).
4. To defeat wizard and recover his family's treasure (p. 225).
5. Yevaud, dragon (p. 227).

FOR STUDY AND DISCUSSION
1a. Gold and precious stones from Pendor, including Inalkil the Greenstone. 1b. To recover his treasure; his staff points toward Inalkil.
2. Mr. Underhill is little, fat, fifty years old. He waddles; his toes turn in. Blackbeard is young, handsome, black-bearded.
3a. Call him by his truename. 3b. He does not realize Yevaud is a dragon.
4. Le Guin tells that "the sky was clear, the hillside empty, except for a reddish-blackish trampled spot, and a few talon-marks in the grass" (p. 227).
5a. Maidens. 5b. He realizes Palani, a maiden whom he loves, is in danger.
6a. Does not need a disguise as his truename is no longer secret; walking is harder than flying; he wants a good meal. 6b. Maidens, at least, will be in danger.
7. Rule of names did not work for Blackbeard.

---

of him and Palani was the *Queenie*'s sail vanishing in the direction of the nearest island westward.

41   The villagers thought they would never stop talking about it, how Goody Guld's nephew Birt had lost his mind and sailed off with the schoolmistress on the very same day that the peddler Blackbeard disappeared without a trace, leaving all his feathers and beads behind. But they did stop talking about it, three days later. They had other things to talk about, when Mr. Underhill finally came out of his cave.

Mr. Underhill had decided that since his truename was no longer a secret, he might as well drop his disguise. Walking was a lot harder than flying, and besides, it was a long, *42* long time since he had had a real meal.

Reading Check

1. What kind of work does Mr. Underhill do on Sattins Island?
2. Why are there no books on Sattins Island?
3. When are the children allowed to keep their truenames?
4. Why has the Sealord of Pendor come to Sattins Island?
5. What is Mr. Underhill's true identity?

For Study and Discussion

Analyzing and Interpreting the Story

1. By the end of this story we know that Yevaud, the powerful dragon, came to Sattins Island disguised as Mr. Underhill. **a.** What does Mr. Underhill keep hidden in his cave? **b.** Why does Blackbeard, the Sealord of Pendor, come to Sattins Island?

2. Mr. Underhill does not seem to be much of an opponent for Blackbeard. How do they differ in appearance?

3. According to the magical Rule of Names, if you say someone's "truename," you can gain control over that person. **a.** How does Blackbeard plan to conquer Mr. Underhill? **b.** Why doesn't his plan work?

4. The author doesn't tell you directly what happened to Blackbeard. Find the passage toward the end of the story that reveals what became of the handsome stranger.

5a. According to Blackbeard, what do dragons eat? **b.** At the end of the story, Birt runs away with Palani, the schoolteacher. Why do you think he does this?

6a. After destroying Blackbeard, why does Mr. Underhill decide to drop his disguise? **b.** What do you think this decision will mean for the people living on Sattins Island?

7. Perhaps you've heard the saying: "There's an exception to every rule." How does this saying apply to the story?

Literary Elements

Noting Techniques That Create Suspense

Ursula Le Guin gains interest and creates suspense by dropping clues about what is going to happen. This technique is called **foreshadowing**.

For example, the opening paragraph of this story describes Mr. Underhill breathing a "double puff of steam" and showing "snow-white teeth." These clues hint that he is a dragon. You get another hint of his true nature when you are told that "the minute spent watching Palani and the children had made him very hungry." Later you learn that a dragon eats maidens. **1** Can you find other clues that foreshadow Mr. Underhill's identity?

CLOSURE
Ask students to evaluate the actions, motives, and plans of Mr. Underhill and Blackbeard and to describe what happens to the characters at the end of the story.

EXTENSION AND ENRICHMENT
Students might research the origins of their own names or investigate customs related to giving names in another culture. Students might also be asked to narrate the story Birt and Palani had to tell when they arrived at one of the westward islands. Some students might like to describe the scene that is left to the reader's imagination when Birt's eyes are shut.

Sometimes this author drops false clues to put you off balance and to keep you in suspense. For example, from Blackbeard's story, you are led to think that a great wizard killed the dragon, stole its treasure, and fled to Sattins

2 Island. What actually happened?

Language and Vocabulary

Looking Up Word Histories

In this story of fantasy, Seacaptain Fogeno knows that the mysterious Blackbeard is a wizard when he hears that the stranger carries an "*oaken* walking stick." Thousands of years ago in Europe, many people considered the oak to be a sacred tree with magical properties. In ancient Greece, the oak was the special tree of Zeus, the chief god.

1 Using a dictionary or an encyclopedia, find the meaning and history of these words:

dragon	mage	warlock
incantation	magic	wizard

Focus on Writing a Short Story

Building a Story Plot

Good stories always involve a **conflict** or struggle. In "The Rule of Names" the main conflict is between two characters, Yevaud and Blackbeard. In the plot of a short story, the conflict leads to a **climax** or **high point.** This is the most exciting, tense part of the story. The climax settles the main conflict in a story, one way or the other. In "The Rule of Names" the climax occurs when Yevaud destroys Blackbeard. Below is a plot diagram for a short story:

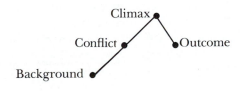

Choose an event that could be the climax of a story plot: for example, the winning shot in a close game or the discovery of a lost pet. Try building a plot around this event by filling out a chart like the one below. Save your notes.

About the Author

Ursula K. Le Guin (1929–   )

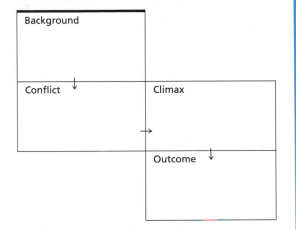

Ursula K. Le Guin is considered one of today's most important writers of science fiction and fantasy. Some of her best-known stories deal with events on the planet Hain and on the dream landscape of Earthsea. "The Rule of Names" is from her short-story collection *The Wind's Twelve Quarters* (1975) and is, Le Guin says, one of her first "explorations" of Earthsea. She is the author of such award-winning novels as *The Left Hand of Darkness* (1969) and *The Dispossessed* (1974). Her most recently published books include *Always Coming Home* (1985), *Tehanu: The Last Book of Earthsea* (1990), and *Dancing at the Edge of the World* (1992), a collection of essays.

LITERARY ELEMENTS
1. Some other clues: puffs of steam come from his nostrils (p. 220); cloud of purple steam, hissing, bellowing sound from his cave (p. 221); he gets hungry watching Palani, children (p. 222); he arrived in village with chests, boxes (p. 224); he never had a staff (p. 226). His failures as wizard suggest he is not what he seems to be.
2. Yevaud, the dragon, defeated the wizard and kept treasure hidden on Sattins Island.

LANGUAGE AND VOCABULARY
1. *Dragon:* from Greek word *drakōn,* "dragon or serpent," literally "the seeing one," from verb *derkesthai,* "to see." Winged creature in mythical stories, often a reptile with wings and claws, exhaling fire and smoke.
Incantation: from Latin verb *incantare,* "to enchant or bewitch." Usually a chant of magical words or formulas to cast spells.
Mage: from Old Persian word *magus* or *magu,* "a member of a priestly caste, one of the Magi." Today means "a magician or wizard" in different sense.
Magic: same root as *mage.* Magic, strictly speaking, is use of charms, spells, and rituals to control events. Now any mysterious or extraordinary power or influence.
Warlock: from Old English word *waerloga,* "traitor or liar." Today person practicing black magic; male equivalent of witch.
Wizard: from Middle English word *wisard,* "sage." Now refers to magician or sorcerer but also to gifted, clever person. In England, means "excellent."

Thank You, M'am

LANGSTON HUGHES

Sometimes characters do not act as you might expect they would. As you read this story, notice how the characters gradually reveal themselves through what they do, say, and think.

She was a large woman with a large purse that had everything in it but hammer and nails. It had a long strap and she carried it slung across her shoulder. It was about eleven o'clock at night, and she was walking alone, when a boy ran up behind her and tried to snatch her purse. The strap broke with the single tug the boy gave it from behind. But the boy's weight, and the weight of the purse combined, caused him to lose his balance so, instead of taking off full blast as he had hoped, the boy fell on his back on the sidewalk, and his legs flew up. The large woman simply turned around and kicked him right square in his blue-jeaned sitter. Then she reached down, picked the boy up by his shirt front, and shook him until his teeth rattled.

After that the woman said, "Pick up my pocketbook, boy, and give it here."

She still held him. But she bent down enough to permit him to stoop and pick up her purse. Then she said, "Now ain't you ashamed of yourself?"

Firmly gripped by his shirt front, the boy said, "Yes'm."

The woman said, "What did you want to do it for?"

The boy said, "I didn't aim to."

She said, "You a lie!"

By that time two or three people passed, stopped, turned to look, and some stood watching.

"If I turn you loose, will you run?" asked the woman.

"Yes'm," said the boy.

"Then I won't turn you loose," said the woman. She did not release him.

"I'm very sorry, lady, I'm sorry," whispered the boy.

"Um-hum! And your face is dirty. I got a great mind to wash your face for you. Ain't you got nobody home to tell you to wash your face?"

"No'm," said the boy.

"Then it will get washed this evening," said the large woman starting up the street, dragging the frightened boy behind her.

He looked as if he were fourteen or fifteen, frail and willow-wild, in tennis shoes and blue jeans.

The woman said, "You ought to be my son. I

Mother Courage II (1974) by Charles White (1918–1979). Oil on canvas.
The National Academy of Design, New York
Courtesy Heritage Gallery, Los Angeles

MOTIVATIONAL SUMMARY

Roger, a teen-aged boy, tries to steal the purse of a woman who is walking home alone late one night. The woman, Mrs. Luella Bates Washington Jones, kicks him, picks him up, and takes him home with her. What now?

PRESENTATION

To ensure maximum impact, you should be certain that students have no interruptions or distractions as they read the story silently in class, immediately after it has been introduced. Begin class discussion by asking students what significance they attach to the title of the story. Ask them if they think this story could be a "thank you" to people like Mrs. Luella Bates Washington Jones. This is a good story with which to review indirect **characterization**. You may want to use the **Literary Elements** and **Focus on**

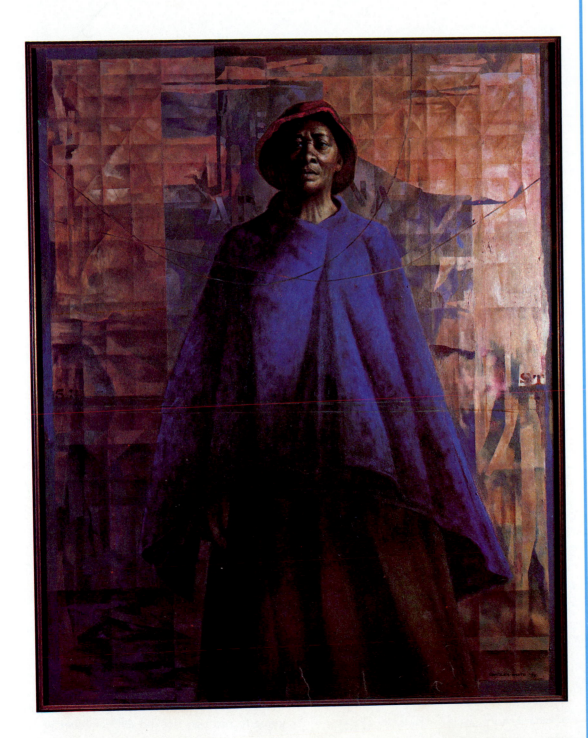

VISUAL CONNECTIONS

About the Artwork

Although this painting is not based on the woman in the story, you could ask students if they think Mrs. Luella Bates Washington Jones looks like this. The perspective of the painting makes the woman appear larger, as she would to someone shorter or to someone like Roger who had fallen backwards.

Relating Expression Skills

The background of this painting is primarily geometric shapes. You might ask students what other backgrounds could have been used and have them design alternatives with pencil, paint, collage, etc. Figures similar to this woman could be traced or drawn, colored, and then laid on the backgrounds. Ask students how different backgrounds change the mood of the pictures. Does the background make any difference in accepting the woman in the textbook figure as the sort of person Mrs. Luella Bates Washington Jones was? The color blue often represents loyalty and sincerity. Ask students if they think a different color cloak would change the mood of the painting.

Ideas for Writing

Students might write a character sketch in which they imagine, based on the woman's expression, clothes, and the way she carries herself, what sort of person she is. What does she care about, what would she fight for, what does she value, and what does she dislike?

Writing a Short Story sections on p. 234 in presenting the topic.

MEETING INDIVIDUAL NEEDS
ESL/LEP • Students learning English may find Hughes's use of dialect confusing. You might want to call students' attention to examples of dialect and provide clarification if necessary.

CREATIVE WRITING LINK
Encourage students to write a diary or journal entry that Mrs. Jones might have made on the day the story takes place. You could use the following questions to help students get started. What does she think about Roger when he tries

6 Analyzing
What is the woman's motive for stressing that he initiated their relationship? She puts responsibility for boy's predicament squarely on him.

7
Setting. Description of Mrs. Jones's home indicates she lives in a city and probably has modest income. She lives in a rear room of a large house.

8
Dialect. Natural patterns of speech, informal words used in conversation help reveal the two characters here and throughout story.

9 Making Inferences
Expressing an Opinion
What tone do you think the boy used to say this? Is he being honest? Responses will vary. Perhaps tone is defensive, angry, sullen. Probably telling truth as he did earlier when admitting he would run.

10
Mrs. Jones's comment presents completely unthought-of possibility for boy; he reacts in question and confusion. She wants to show him an alternative behavior.

11
Characterization. Mrs. Jones has enough strength and confidence to reveal her own frailties.

would teach you right from wrong. Least I can do right now is to wash your face. Are you hungry?"

"No'm," said the being-dragged boy. "I just **9** want you to turn me loose."

"Was I bothering *you* when I turned that corner?" asked the woman.

"No'm."

"But you put yourself in contact with *me*," **6** said the woman. "If you think that that contact is not going to last awhile, you got another thought coming. When I get through with you, sir, you are going to remember Mrs. Luella Bates Washington Jones."

Sweat popped out on the boy's face and he **10** began to struggle. Mrs. Jones stopped, jerked him around in front of her, put a half nelson[1] about his neck, and continued to drag him up **7** the street. When she got to her door, she dragged the boy inside, down a hall, and into a large kitchenette-furnished room at the rear of the house. She switched on the light and left the door open. The boy could hear other roomers laughing and talking in the large house. Some of their doors were opened, too, so he knew he and the woman were not alone. The woman still had him by the neck in the middle of her room.

She said, "What is your name?"

"Roger," answered the boy.

"Then, Roger, you go to that sink and wash your face," said the woman, whereupon she turned him loose—at last. Roger looked at the door—looked at the woman—looked at the **11** door—*and went to the sink.*

"Let the water run until it gets warm," she said. "Here's a clean towel."

"You gonna take me to jail?" asked the boy, **8** bending over the sink.

"Not with that face, I would not take you nowhere," said the woman. "Here I am trying

1. **half nelson:** a wrestling hold made with one arm.

to get home to cook me a bite to eat and you snatch my pocketbook! Maybe you ain't been to your supper either, late as it be. Have you?"

"There's nobody home at my house," said the boy.

"Then we'll eat," said the woman. "I believe you're hungry—or been hungry—to try to snatch my pocketbook."

"I wanted a pair of blue suede shoes," said the boy.

"Well, you didn't have to snatch *my* pocketbook to get some suede shoes," said Mrs. Luella Bates Washington Jones. "You could of asked me."

"M'am?"

The water dripping from his face, the boy looked at her. There was a long pause. A very long pause. After he had dried his face and not knowing what else to do dried it again, the boy turned around, wondering what next. The door was open. He could make a dash for it down the hall. He could run, run, run, run, *run!*

The woman was sitting on the daybed. After a while she said, "I were young once and I wanted things I could not get."

There was another long pause. The boy's mouth opened. Then he frowned, but not knowing he frowned.

The woman said, "Um-hum! You thought I was going to say *but*, didn't you? You thought I was going to say, *but I didn't snatch people's pocketbooks.* Well, I wasn't going to say that." Pause. Silence. "I have done things, too, which I would not tell you, son—neither tell God, if he didn't already know. So you set down while I fix us something to eat. You might run that comb through your hair so you will look presentable."

In another corner of the room behind a screen was a gas plate and an icebox. Mrs. Jones got up and went behind the screen. The woman did not watch the boy to see if he was going to run now, nor did she watch her purse

PORTFOLIO ASSESSMENT
Have students pretend that they are Roger and write letters to Mrs. Jones from his point of view. Letters might reveal Roger's feelings about how he was treated by Mrs. Jones, tell what he did or will do with the ten dollars she gave him, or describe how the experience has made a difference in his life. Consult with students to agree on how their letters will be assessed. (For more information on student portfolios see *Portfolio Assessment and Professional Support Materials.*)

which she left behind her on the daybed. But the boy took care to sit on the far side of the room where he thought she could easily see him out of the corner of her eye, if she wanted **12** to. He did not trust the woman *not* to trust him. And he did not want to be mistrusted now.

"Do you need somebody to go to the store," asked the boy, "maybe to get some milk or something?"

"Don't believe I do," said the woman, "unless you just want sweet milk yourself. I was going to make cocoa out of this canned milk I got here."

"That will be fine," said the boy.

She heated some lima beans and ham she had in the icebox, made the cocoa, and set the table. The woman did not ask the boy anything about where he lived, or his folks, or anything else that would embarrass him. Instead, as they ate, she told him about her job in a hotel beauty shop that stayed open late, what the work was like, and how all kinds of women came in and out, blondes, redheads, and Spanish. Then she cut him a half of her ten-cent cake.

"Eat some more, son," she said.

When they were finished eating she got up **13** and said, "Now, here, take this ten dollars and buy yourself some blue suede shoes. And next time do not make the mistake of latching on to *my* pocketbook *nor nobody else's*—because shoes come by devilish like that will burn your feet. I got to get my rest now. But I wish you would behave yourself, son, from here on in."

She led him down the hall to the front door and opened it. "Good night! Behave yourself, boy!" she said, looking out into the street.

The boy wanted to say something else other than, "Thank you, m'am," to Mrs. Luella Bates Washington Jones, but he couldn't do so as he turned at the barren stoop and looked back at the large woman in the door. He barely managed to say, "Thank you," before she shut the door. And he never saw her again.

Reading Check

1. What does Roger try to do to Mrs. Jones?
2. How old is Roger?
3. Why does Mrs. Jones take Roger home?
4. What does Roger want to buy?
5. What does Mrs. Jones give to Roger?

For Study and Discussion

Analyzing and Interpreting the Story

1. Many people who are robbed would call for help or call the police. What does Mrs. Jones do instead?

2. Most people in Roger's situation would run when they had a chance. Why do you think Roger decides not to run away when he can?

3a. What does Mrs. Jones reveal about her past when she and Roger are in her home? **b.** How do you think this information makes Roger feel?

4a. During the time that Roger is in her apartment, how does Mrs. Jones show that she does not want to embarrass him or hurt his feelings? **b.** What does this concern reveal about her character?

5. What do Mrs. Jones's home and the meal she serves reveal about her own financial situation?

6a. In your opinion, why does Mrs. Jones give Roger the ten dollars? **b.** What do you think he learns from her warmth and generosity?

7. Why do you suppose Roger cannot say more than "Thank you, m'am"?

12
Conflict. Roger apparently has resolved his inner conflict and does not try to run away. He responds to Mrs. Jones' apparent sincerity in offering to help him.

13   Synthesizing
Why does Mrs. Jones give him ten dollars to buy shoes? Responses will vary. She sees his need and believes he is basically a good boy; perhaps someone was kind to her during a troubled time in her life. She wants to show him someone cares.

READING CHECK
1. Snatch her purse (p. 230).
2. Fourteen or fifteen (p. 230).
3. To wash his face (p. 230).
4. Blue suede shoes (p. 232).
5. Ten dollars, advice (p. 233).

FOR STUDY AND DISCUSSION
1. Kicks him, picks him up, shakes him, drags him home.
2. Responses will vary. Mrs. Jones is tough but fair; she pays attention and talks to him. He probably wants to show her that trust in him is justified.
3a. Also young once, she wanted things she could not get and did things for which she is ashamed. 3b. Probably feels she understands him because she has had similar temptations; also feels he has chance to change.
4a. She does not ask about his family or himself. 4b. She is sensitive, generous, understands what Roger needs.
5. She does not have much money.
6a. Perhaps to show him that money is not as important as compassion. 6b. Perhaps closer to becoming compassionate person.
7. Probably wants to say more but cannot express feelings.

LITERARY ELEMENTS
1. Opening incident when she kicks Roger, picks him up, shakes him, and drags him home with her.

FOCUS ON WRITING A SHORT STORY
Encourage students to use vivid language and cite specific details in creating their **character.** Because concrete examples can help stimulate ideas, you might provide pictures of interesting-looking people and tape recordings of people with diverse ways of speaking. You might also have students develop pairs of characters with opposite qualities.

ABOUT THE AUTHOR
James Langston Hughes was born in Joplin, Missouri, but grew up in Lawrence, Kansas, and Cleveland, Ohio. He was elected class poet in grammar school and wrote poems for his high-school magazine. He was an avid reader. He traveled widely in Africa and Europe and lived for a while in France and Italy. In later years, he traveled in the Soviet Union, Japan, China, and Spain. Continuing to write poems, novels, short stories, and humorous sketches throughout his life, he had a strong influence on the development of black literature in America. His books of poetry include *The Weary Blues* (1926), *The Dream Keeper* (1932), *Shakespeare in Harlem* (1942), *One Way Ticket* (1949), *Ask Your Mama* (1961), and *The Panther and the Lash* (1967). *The Ways of White Folks* (1934), *Laughing to Keep from Crying* (1952), and *Something in Common* (1963) are collections of Hughes's short stories.

Literary Elements

Recognizing Techniques of Characterization

Characterization is the means an author uses to reveal the characters in a story. When writers *tell* what characters are like through description, they are using **direct characterization.** For example, in the first sentence of this story, Langston Hughes describes Mrs. Jones as "a large woman with a large purse that had everything in it but hammer and nails." Later he also describes Roger, saying, "He looked as if he were fourteen or fifteen, frail and willow-wild, in tennis shoes and blue jeans." These are examples of direct characterization. They are the only direct statements made about the two characters in the story.

Yet you know much more about these two characters because you have watched their actions and listened to their conversations and thoughts. When writers let you know characters in this way—they are using **indirect characterization.** What incident in the story lets you know, for example, that Mrs. Jones is physically strong?

Focus on Writing a Short Story

Creating Characters

In "Thank You, M'am," Langston Hughes uses **realistic details** to help you "see" Mrs. Jones and Roger. When you create characters for a short story of your own, fill out a chart like this one for each character.

Character Chart

Name: _____ Age: _____

Appearance: _____

Movements: _____

Way of Speaking: _____

Personality Traits: _____

Habits: _____

Review the notes for the assignment on page 229 or choose another story idea. Create at least two characters for your story by filling out a character chart for each one. Save your notes.

About the Author

Langston Hughes   (1902-1967)

"Mightily did he use the street," poet Gwendolyn Brooks has written about her friend Langston Hughes. During his long and diverse career, Hughes wrote poems, short stories, novels, plays, songs, and essays. He attended Columbia University in New York City for a year, but left to write and travel. He worked as a seaman on transatlantic ships and as a cook in Paris. In 1925 he took a job as a busboy in a Washington, D.C., hotel where the poet Vachel Lindsay was staying. Hughes left three of his poems next to Lindsay's plate one day. Lindsay, recognizing their merit, read them to his audience that night and introduced a new young poet to the world of literature. One critic has said that Hughes has written "some of the saddest, most humorous, and beautiful insights ever given into the heart of a race." One of his famous poems is "Mother to Son."

OBJECTIVES

The overall aim is for students to identify and analyze the **setting, conflicts,** and actions of the characters in "The Parachutist." For a complete list of objectives, see the **Teacher's Notes.**

VOCABULARY

The underlined words are in the Glossary. Students may have difficulty with Niland's use of specific words to describe **setting** and animals. Point out the value of these specific words in creating vivid images.

FOCUS / MOTIVATION

You might invite students to tell about their own observations of animals hunting for food and have them describe predators' methods. The story describes the natural order of things in the animal kingdom.

TEACHING RESOURCES C

Teacher's Notes, p. 57
Reading Check, p. 60
Study Guide, p. 61
Language Skills, p. 65
Building Vocabulary, pp. 68, 70
Selection Vocabulary Test, pp. 73, 75, 77
Selection Test, p. 78

VISUAL CONNECTIONS
About the Artwork
A photograph of an object that is moving may be taken by "panning," that is, moving the camera at the same speed as the object. This blurs or streaks the background, giving an effect of motion. Another effect is achieved by holding the camera still and using a slower shutter speed. The background, if it is not moving, will appear sharp, and the moving object will be blurred.

PREREADING FOCUS
The headnote may be used to alert students to the **conflict** of "The Parachutist." As they read, have students look for details which show what the two creatures want.

The Parachutist

1
Imagery. Niland uses strong sensory images to establish **setting.** The images appeal to the senses of sight, touch, and hearing.

2 Summarizing
How does Niland characterize the hawk? Hawk is characterized by hatred and sets out like a warrior to claim his stake, yet the hawk also is viewed as a pathetic creature, miserable because it cannot find its customary food.

3
Simile. The swollen body of the bull killed in the storm is compared to a wet, inflated bladder.

The Parachutist

D'ARCY NILAND

In this story, the fierce conflict between a hawk and a kitten reflects the fierceness of the setting—a land ravaged by a hurricane. As you read, notice how the natural environment brings out each animal's instinct for survival.

The hurricane came down from Capricorn,[1] and for two days and a night it rained.

1 In the darkness of the second night, softening away to dawn, there was silence. There was only the gurgle and drip of the wet world, and the creatures that lived on the earth began to appear, freed from the tyranny of the elements.

1. **Capricorn:** the Tropic of Capricorn. The story is set in the Southern Hemisphere.

2 The hawk, ruffled in misery, brooding in ferocity, came forth in hunger and hate. It struck off into the abyss of space, scouring the earth for some booty of the storm—the sheep lying like a heap of wet kapok[2] in the sodden *3* paddocks,[3] the bullock like a dark bladder carried down on the swollen stream and washing

2. **kapok** (kā'pŏk'): silky fiber from the seeds of a tropical tree, used for padding in pillows and mattresses.
3. **paddocks** (păd'əks): fenced-in land.

MOTIVATIONAL SUMMARY

A hungry hawk, scouring a hurricane-ravaged land for food, spots a kitten playing in a field. The hawk swoops down and carries the kitten off. The two desperate animals engage in a spectacular aerial battle.

PRESENTATION

To be sure that students understand the **setting** and the hawk's extreme hunger, you might read the story aloud up to the point where the hawk comes down to carry off the kitten. Stop as you think necessary to clarify what is happening. You may want to let students read the rest of the story silently in class and then allow time for discussion.

VISUAL CONNECTIONS

Exploring the Subject

Hawks are of the same family as eagles but are smaller birds, ranging in length from twelve to twenty-four inches. They have strong, curved beaks, long legs with powerful claws, and long tails. They primarily eat poultry, rodents, reptiles, and insects. They build loosely constructed nests of bark and twigs in the tops of trees or on high, rocky ledges.

4

Rooster found temporary refuge on piece of floating debris. Evidently, few animals are out due to storm. Hawk is in **conflict** with environment.

5 Finding Details

How does Niland emphasize the fierce bird's tension and misery? With descriptions of hunger and lice.

6

Imagery. Vivid visual **description** of hawk's surroundings. Niland uses simile "like a battlefield of bones" to describe effects of storm. Storm has made food scarce.

7 Expressing an Opinion

Is it possible for a hawk to "hate" anything? Answers may vary. Most students will probably agree hawk cannot hate something as a human might. The hawk, after all, is merely hungry. Point out to students that hatred is a particularly human emotion.

8

Description. Savage hunger of hawk described through vivid accounts of past meals. That rabbit's eyes are put out will add tension and **suspense** to later struggle with kitten.

---

against a tree on the river flats, the rabbit, driven from its flooded warren[4] and squeezed dead against a log.

With practiced eye it scrutinized the floating islands of rubble and the wracks[5] of twigs lying askew on the banks for sign of lizard or snake, dead or alive. But there was nothing. Once, in **4** the time before, there had been a rooster, daggled,[6] forlorn derelict riding a raft of flotsam: too weak to fight and too sick to care about dying or the way it died.

5 The hawk rested on a crag of the gorge and conned the terrain with a fierce and frowning eye. The lice worried its body with the sting of nettles. Savagely it plucked with its beak under the fold of its wings, first on one side, then on the other. It rasped its bill on the jagged stone, and dropped over the lip. It climbed in a gliding circle, widening its field of vision.

The earth was yellow and green. On the flats were chains of lagoons as if the sky had broken and fallen in sheets of blue glass. The sun was hot and the air heavy and humid.

6 Swinging south, the hawk dropped over a vast graveyard of dead timber. The hurricane had ravaged the gaunt trees, splitting them, felling them, tearing off their naked arms and strewing the ground with pieces, like a battlefield of bones, gray with exposure and decay.

A rabbit sprang twenty yards like a bobbing wheel, and the sight drew the hawk like a plummet, but the rabbit vanished in a hollow log, and stayed there, and there was no other life.

Desperate, weak, the hawk alighted on a **7** bleak limb and glared in hate. The sun was a fire on its famished body. Logs smoked with steam and the brightness of water on the earth reflected like mirrors. The telescopic eye

---

4. **warren** (wôr′ən, wŏr′-): a place where rabbits live in their burrows.
5. **wracks** (răks): fragments.
6. **daggled** (dă′gəld): wet and dirty.

inched over the ground—crawled infallibly over the ground, and stopped. And then suddenly the hawk swooped to the ground and tore at the body of a dead field mouse—its belly bloated and a thin vapor drifting from the gray, plastered pelt.

8 The hawk did not sup as it supped on the hot running blood of the rabbit in the trap—squealing in eyeless terror; it did not feast in stealthy leisure as it did on the sheep paralyzed in the drought, tearing out bit by bit its steaming entrails. Voraciously it ripped at the mouse, swallowing fast and finishing the meal in a few seconds.

But the food was only a tantalization, serving to make the hawk's appetite more fierce, more lusty. It flew into a tree, rapaciously scanning the countryside. It swerved into space and climbed higher and higher in a vigilant circle, searching the vast expanse below, even to its uttermost limits.

9 Hard to the west something moved on the earth, a speck: and the hawk watched it: and the speck came up to a walnut, and up to a plum, and up to a ball striped with white and gray.

The hawk did not strike at once. Obedient to instinct, it continued to circle, peering down at the farmhouse and outbuildings, suspicious; seeing the draft horses in the yard and the fowls in the hen coop, the pigs in the sty, and the windmill twirling, and watching for human life in their precincts.

10 Away from them all, a hundred yards or more, down on the margin of the fallowed[7] field, the kitten played, leaping and running and tumbling, pawing at a feather and rolling on its back biting at the feather between its forepaws.

Frenzied with hunger, yet ever cautious, the hawk came down in a spiral, set itself, and **11** swooped. The kitten propped[8] and froze with its head cocked on one side, unaware of danger but startled by this new and untried sport. It was no more than if a piece of paper had blown past it in a giant brustle[9] of sound. But in the next moment the hawk fastened its talons in the fur and the fat belly of the kitten, and the kitten spat and twisted, struggling against the power that was lifting it.

Its great wings beating, paddling with the rhythm of oars, the hawk went up a slope of space with its cargo, and the kitten, airborne **14** for the first time in its life, the earth running under it in a blur, wailed in shrill terror. It squirmed frantically as the world fell away in

12 the distance, but the hawk's talons were like the grabs of an iceman.

The air poured like water into the kitten's eyes and broke against its triangular face, streaming back against its rippling furry sides. It howled in infinite fear, and gave a sudden desperate twist, so that the hawk was jolted in its course and dropped to another level, a few feet below the first.

13 Riding higher and higher on the wind, the hawk went west by the dam like a button of silver far below. The kitten cried now with a new note. Its stomach was wambling.[10] The air gushing into its mouth and nostrils set up a humming in its ears and an aching dizziness in its head. As the hawk turned on its soundless orbit, the sun blazed like flame in the kitten's eyes, leaving its sight to emerge from a blinding grayness.

The kitten knew that it had no place here in the heart of space, and its terrified instincts told it that its only contact with solidity and safety was the thing that held it.

Then the hawk was ready to drop its prey. It was well practiced. Down had gone the rabbit, a whistle in space, to crash in a quiver of death on the ruthless earth. And the hawk had followed to its gluttonous repast.

Now there at two thousand feet the bird hovered. The kitten was alarmingly aware of the change, blinking at the pulsations of beaten air as the wings flapped, hearing only that sound. Unexpectedly, it stopped, and the wings were still—outstretched, but rigid, tilting slightly with the poised body, only the fanned tail lifting and lowering with the flow of the currents.

14 The kitten felt the talons relax slightly, and that was its warning. The talons opened, but in the first flashing shock of the movement the kitten completed its twist and slashed at the hawk's legs and buried its claws in the flesh like

---

7. **fallowed** (făl′ōd): plowed.
8. **propped** (prŏpt): stopped suddenly.
9. **brustle:** a dialect variation of *bristle*.

10. **wambling** (wŏm′blĭng, wăm′-): turning.

9
Niland creates dramatic effect by using hawk's perspective in flight. Comparison of object hawk sees to foods suggests hawk's hunger.

10 Comparing/Contrasting
How does the description of the kitten contrast ironically with the later life-and-death struggle with the feathered hawk? Depiction of kitten playing with soft feather emphasizes animal's fragility and softness.

11
Kitten, an innocent, playful creature, displays no sense of danger. Its captor is mistaken for a playmate.

12
Simile. Effective comparison to describe hawk's sharp claws. A *grab* is a mechanical device for gripping an object such as an iceman would use for gripping a large block of ice.

13
Description. Passage conveys hawk's sense of soaring victory and kitten's sense of puzzlement and fright.

14
Conflict. Feeling that it is about to be dropped, kitten instinctively holds on and fights for its own survival.

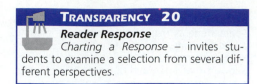

15

Imagery. Brutal aspect of nature dramatically illustrated by Niland's graphic picture of kitten's condition.

16   Drawing Conclusions
Why does the hawk want to dislodge the kitten? It knows fall will kill its prey.

17

Irony. Kitten originally had thought hawk was an "untried sport" and now finds itself an unwilling participant in sport of parachuting.

18

Suspense. Author creates tension near end of story as kitten loses grip and legs dangle in space.

19   Analyzing
What is ironic about this situation? One would expect hawk to be in control in air, but kitten is pilot and parachutist. Kitten uses hawk, which had carried it off to kill it, to return safely to earth. Emphasizes surprises that nature may hold.

20

Innocent, childlike kitten cries at recognition of home territory, as if calling its child owner for help.

READING CHECK
1. Southern hemisphere, probably Australia (p. 235).
2. Food (p. 235).
3. It has rained for two days and a night, few animals have come out, and hawk cannot find any dead animals caught in debris of storm (pp. 235–236).
4. Buries its claws in hawk's flesh and keeps them there (pp. 237–238).

238

---

fishhooks. In the next fraction of a second the kitten had consolidated its position, securing its hold, jabbing in every claw except those on one foot which thrust out in space, pushing against insupportable air. And then the claws on this foot were dug in the breast of the hawk.

With a cry of pain and alarm the bird swooped crazily, losing a hundred feet like a dropping stone. And then it righted itself, flying in a drunken sway that diminished as it circled.

15   Blood from its breast beaded and trickled down the paw of the kitten and spilled into one eye. The kitten blinked, but the blood came and congealed, warm and sticky. The kitten could not turn its head. It was frightened to risk a change of position. The blood slowly built over its eye a blinding pellicle.[11]

The hawk felt a spasm of weakness, and out of it came an accentuation of its hunger and a lust to kill at all costs the victim it had claimed and carried to this place of execution. Lent an access of power by its ferocity, it started to

16 climb again, desperately trying to dislodge the kitten. But the weight was too much and it could not ascend. A great tiredness came in its dragging body; an ache all along the frames of its wings. The kitten clung tenaciously, staring down at the winding earth and mewling in terror.

For ten minutes the hawk gyrated on a level, defeated and bewildered. All it wanted to do now was to get rid of the burden fastened to its legs and body. It craved respite, a spell on the tallest trees, but it only flew high over these trees, knowing it was unable to perch. Its beak gaped under the harsh ruptures of its breath.

17 It descended three hundred feet. The kitten, with the wisdom of instinct, never altered its position, but rode down like some fantastic parachutist.

11. **pellicle** (pĕl′ ĭ-kəl): a thin film.

In one mighty burst the hawk with striking beak and a terrible flapping of its wings tried finally to cast off its passenger—and nearly succeeded. The kitten miauled[12] in a frenzy of fear at the violence of the sound and the agita-

18 tion. Its back legs dangled in space, treading air, and like that it went around on the curves of the flight for two minutes. Then it secured a foothold again, even firmer than the first.

In a hysterical rage, the hawk tried once more to lift itself, and almost instantly began to sweep down in great, slow, gliding eddies that became narrower and narrower.

19 The kitten was the pilot now and the hawk no longer the assassin of the void, the lord of the sky and the master of the wind. The ache coiled and throbbed in its breast. It fought against the erratic disposition of its wings and the terror of its waning strength. Its heart bursting with the strain, its eyes dilated wild and yellow, it came down until the earth

20 skimmed under it; and the kitten cried at the silver glare of the roofs not far off, and the expanding earth, and the brush of the grass.

The hawk lobbed and flung over, and the kitten rolled with it. And the hawk lay spraddled in exhaustion, its eyes fiercely, cravenly aware of the danger of its forced and alien position. The kitten staggered giddily, unhurt, towards the silver roofs, wailing loudly as if in answer to the voice of a child.

12. **miauled** (mē-ôld′): meowed.

Reading Check

1. Where does the story take place?
2. What is the hawk searching for?
3. Why is the hawk's search so difficult?
4. What does the kitten do to save itself?

CLOSURE
Ask students to analyze the effect of the **setting** on the **plot** and to identify the **conflicts** in Niland's story.

EXTENSION AND ENRICHMENT
Students might create their own stories about events in "The Parachutist" from the viewpoint of either the hawk or the kitten. Students also could write stories that tell what happens next to the hawk or to the kitten. Some students might

select books from the library about hawks and read more about their habits in the wild. Others might produce a series of sketches to illustrate the story as if for a magazine or picture book.

For Study and Discussion

Analyzing and Interpreting the Story

1. Sometimes a writer suggests certain details of setting in a story.   **a.** At what time of day does this story occur?   **b.** How do you know?

2. Every story centers on **conflict,** the struggle between two opposing forces.   **a.** What is the conflict in this story?   **b.** Is there more than one conflict?

3. Although the hawk is lord of the sky at the beginning of the story, its rule is challenged by the end of the story. How does the situation of control change?

4. Why do you think the author ends the story with the kitten crying as if in answer to a child's voice?

5. The characters an author chooses convey a certain message to the reader.   **a.** Why do you think the author chose a hawk and a kitten as the characters in this story?   **b.** How would you feel about the story if the author had used a bobcat instead of a kitten?

6. A reader learns a great deal about characters through the words the author uses to describe them. **a.** Considering how Niland describes the hawk, how would you characterize it?   **b.** What kind of character is the kitten?

7. Why do you think the author titled this story "The Parachutist"?

Literary Elements

Recognizing the Importance of Setting

Setting is the time and place in which a story occurs. The setting also includes background information that relates to the action of a story. In "The Parachutist," the general setting is the countryside, but, as the hawk travels, the specifics of the setting change.

1 How many different settings are actually described in the story? What are the conditions 2 of the hawk's environment before it comes 3 across the kitten? How is the environment different after the hawk spots the kitten? How do 4 you think the story would change if the setting were in the city and the kitten were a household animal instead of a farm animal?

Focus on Writing a Short Story

Listing Details of Setting

Create a **setting** for a short story of your own. List as many descriptive details as you can: for example, time of day, weather, and sensory details such as sights, smells, and sounds. Your setting could be realistic: for example, an urban street corner or a country meadow at twilight. The setting could be entirely imaginary or fantastic: for example, the inside of a mainframe computer. Save your notes.

About the Author

D'Arcy Niland   (1920–1967)

D'Arcy Niland's birthplace of Glen Innes, New South Wales, Australia, serves as a backdrop for many of his works. It has been said that his writing presents an authentic picture of life in the Australian outback—vigorous and harsh, lonely, and sometimes heartbreaking. Throughout his career as a writer and journalist, Niland wrote for radio and television. He contributed many of his short stories to anthologies and periodicals while writing articles for newspapers and magazines. His other works include *The Shiralee* (1955) and his autobiography, *The Drums Go Bang* (1956).

OBJECTIVES

The overall aim is for students to identify specific events, characters' actions, and details important to the main idea of "Flowers for Algernon." For a complete list of objectives, see the **Teacher's Notes.**

VOCABULARY

The underlined words are in the Glossary. The **Language and Vocabulary** exercise on p. 262 gives students practice in identifying levels of usage (nonstandard English and standard English).

FOCUS / MOTIVATION

You could plunge directly into this appealing story by having students read the first diary entry. Then stop reading and compare impressions of Charlie Gordon. How have only ten lines conveyed so much information?

TEACHING RESOURCES C

Teacher's Notes, p. 80
Reading Check, p. 85
Study Guide, pp. 86, 90, 94
Building Vocabulary, p. 98
Selection Vocabulary Test, pp. 100, 101
Selection Test, p. 102

PREREADING FOCUS

The headnote points out that "Flowers for Algernon" is written from **first-person point of view.** As students read, have them consider how effective the story would be if it were related by an **omniscient** narrator.

Flowers for Algernon
Part One
Progress Reports
March 5–April 20, 1965

1

Point of view. Science fiction story told from **first-person point of view.** Charlie keeps account of events and responses in journal. Reader learns about characters and events in story only through what Charlie reports.

2
Analyzing
Drawing Conclusions
What does the first entry reveal about Charlie's character? Why does he reveal his name and birthdate? Charlie is a sincere person with one wish: to be smart. He reveals his name and his birthdate because he believes they establish his character; his thought processes are not well developed.

3
Rorschach tests given to determine emotional characteristics, personality traits, and impulses.

4
Characterization. Even at this stage of his intellect, Charlie shows concern for others and a sensitive nature.

Flowers for Algernon

DANIEL KEYES

The doctors told Charlie that if he volunteered for this experiment he might "get smart." If the operation worked, Charlie would be the first of a new breed of intellectual supermen. As you read, notice how the first-person point of view helps us to understand the remarkable but tragic changes that Charlie undergoes.

progris riport—martch 5 1965

1 Dr. Strauss says I shud rite down what I think and evrey thing that happins to me from now on. I dont know why but he says its importint so they will see if they will use me. I hope they use me. Miss Kinnian says maybe they can **2** make me smart. I want to be smart. My name is Charlie Gordon. I am 37 years old and 2 weeks ago was my brithday. I have nuthing more to rite now so I will close for today.

progris riport 2—martch 6

3 I had a test today. I think I faled it. and I think that maybe now they wont use me. What happind is a nice young man was in the room and he had some white cards with ink spillled all over them. He sed Charlie what do you see on this card. I was very skared even tho I had my rabits foot in my pockit because when I was a kid I always faled tests in school and I spilled ink to.

I told him I saw an inkblot. He said yes and it made me feel good. I thot that was all but when I got up to go he stopped me. He said now sit down Charlie we are not thru yet. Then I dont remember so good but he wantid me to say what was in the ink. I dint see nuthing in the ink but he said there was picturs there other pepul saw some picturs. I coudnt see any picturs. I reely tried to see. I held the card close up and then far away. Then I said if I had my glases I coud see better I usally only ware my glases in the movies or TV but I said they are in the closit in the hall. I got them. Then I said let me see that card agen I bet Ill find it now.

I tryed hard but I still coudnt find the picturs I only saw the ink. I told him maybe I need new glases. He rote somthing down on a paper and I got skared of faling the test. I told him it was a very nice inkblot with littel points **4** all around the eges. He looked very sad so that wasnt it. I said please let me try agen. Ill get it in a few minits becaus Im not so fast somtimes. Im a slow reeder too in Miss Kinnians class for slow adults but I'm trying very hard.

MOTIVATIONAL SUMMARY
Charlie is mentally handicapped but eager to learn. His enthusiasm is one reason he is selected for experimental surgery that may raise his intelligence. Only a mouse has had this operation, and there are unanswered questions.

PRESENTATION
Since this story is long, you probably should break it into three installments—the first up to Progress Report 10 on p. 248, the second up to Progress Report 12 on p. 255, and the third to the end of the story. Since misspellings make the

early sections a bit difficult, you may want to schedule class time for silent reading so that you can circulate through the class, offering help as needed. If reading is assigned in installments, you might discuss **For Study and Discussion** questions 1 and 2 after the first installment,

He gave me a chance with another card that had 2 kinds of ink spilled on it red and blue.

He was very nice and talked slow like Miss Kinnian does and he explained to me that it was a *raw shok*.[1] He said pepul see things in the ink. I said show me where. He said think. I told him I think a inkblot but that wasnt rite eather. He said what does it remind you—pretend

5 something. I closd my eyes for a long time to pretend. I told him I pretned a fowntan pen with ink leeking all over a table cloth. Then he got up and went out.

I dont think I passd the *raw shok* test.

progris report 3—martch 7

Dr Strauss and Dr Nemur say it dont matter about the inkblots. I told them I dint spill the ink on the cards and I coudnt see anything in the ink. They said that maybe they will still use me. I said Miss Kinnian never gave me tests

6 like that one only spelling and reading. They said Miss Kinnian told that I was her bestist pupil in the adult nite scool becaus I tryed the hardist and I reely wantid to lern. They said how come you went to the adult nite scool all by yourself Charlie. Ilow did you find it. I said I askd pepul and sumbody told me where I shud go to lern to read and spell good. They said why did you want to. I told them becaus all my life I wantid to be smart and not dumb. But its very hard to be smart. They said you know it will probly be tempirery. I said yes. Miss Kin-

7 nian told me. I dont care if it herts.

Later I had more crazy tests today. The nice lady who gave it me told me the name and I asked her how do you spellit so I can rite it in

8 my progris riport. THEMATIC APPERCEPTION TEST. I dont know the frist 2 words but I know

what *test* means. You got to pass it or you get bad marks. This test lookd easy becaus I coud see the picturs. Only this time she dint want me to tell her the picturs. That mixd me up. I said the man yesterday said I shoud tell him what I saw in the ink she said that dont make no difrence. She said make up storys about the pepul in the picturs.

9 I told her how can you tell storys about pepul you never met. I said why shud I make up lies. I never tell lies any more becaus I always get caut.

She told me this test and the other one the raw-shok was for getting personalty. I laffed so hard. I said how can you get that thing from inkblots and fotos. She got sore and put her picturs away. I dont care. It was sily. I gess I faled that test too.

Later some men in white coats took me to a difernt part of the hospitil and gave me a game to play. It was like a race with a white mouse.

10 They called the mouse Algernon. Algernon was in a box with a lot of twists and turns like all kinds of walls and they gave me a pencil and a paper with lines and lots of boxes. On one side it said START and on the other end it said FINISH. They said it was *amazed*[2] and that Algernon and me had the same *amazed* to do. I dint see how we could have the same *amazed* if Algernon had a box and I had a paper but I dint say nothing. Anyway there wasnt time because the race started.

One of the men had a watch he was trying to hide so I wouldnt see it so I tryed not to look and that made me nervus.

Anyway that test made me feel worser than all the others because they did it over 10 times with difernt *amazeds* and Algernon won every time. I dint know that mice were so smart.

---

1. **raw shok:** Charlie means the *Rorschach* (rôr′shäk) test, a personality test in which people tell what is suggested to them by a series of inkblot designs.

2. *amazed:* Charlie means *a maze*, a series of winding paths with one exit and many dead ends. The intelligence of laboratory animals is measured by the amount of time it takes them to find the exit.

5
Characterization. Charlie's imagination is severely limited. He can relate only to physical existence of the blots.

6
Characterization. Charlie's reputation reveals his concern with bettering himself through education.

7 Analyzing
To what does "herts" refer?
Refers to pain of experiment—surgical technique to increase intelligence. Willingness to withstand pain shows his strong desire to learn.

8
Test consists of thirty picture cards of people engaged in various activities. Person being tested reveals elements of personality by responses.

9 Analyzing
What does Charlie's response reveal about his moral standards? Moral code is uncomplicated. Test conflicts with what he has been taught about lying.

10
Algernon is Charlie's counterpart in story; his fate is Charlie's fate. Name is Old French, meaning "with whiskers."

MEETING INDIVIDUAL NEEDS

ESL/LEP • Charlie's "progress reports" (1–9) may be especially difficult for those students working to acquire English. Create small study groups, pairing ESL students and native English speakers. Ask each group to rewrite one of the progress reports according to standard usage. Then, as a whole-class activity, review one of the revisions, inviting discussion and writing standard forms on the chalkboard.

11

White mice are standard laboratory animals for medical research.

12

I.Q., intelligence quotient, arrived at by multiplying tested mental age by 100 and dividing result by chronological age.

13 Analyzing

What motivates Charlie? Desire to be intelligent.

14

Characterization. As Dr. Strauss points out, Charlie is not hostile, uncooperative, or apathetic; he is unusually motivated. Charlie is able to write part of difficult words but not all.

15

Use to answer **study question 1,** p. 261.

16

Conflict. Antagonism between Dr. Nemur and Dr. Strauss becomes clear during course of story.

11 Maybe thats because Algernon is a white mouse. Maybe white mice are smarter then other mice.

progris riport 4 — Mar 8

Their going to use me! Im so exited I can hardly write. Dr Nemur and Dr Strauss had a argament about it first. Dr Nemur was in the office when Dr Strauss brot me in. Dr Nemur was worryed about using me but Dr Strauss told him Miss Kinnian rekemmended me the best from all the people who she was teaching. I like Miss Kinnian becaus shes a very smart teacher. And she said Charlie your going to have a second chance. If you volenteer for this experament you mite get smart. They dont know if it will be perminint but theirs a chance. Thats why I said ok even when I was scared because she said it was an operashun. She said dont be scared Charlie you done so much with so little I think you deserv it most of all.

So I got scaird when Dr Nemur and Dr Strauss argud about it. Dr Strauss said I had something what was very good. He said I had a good *motor-vation.*[3] I never even knew I had that. I felt proud when he said that not every body with an eye-q of 68 had that thing. I dont know what it is or where I got it but he said Algernon had it too. Algernons *motor-vation* is the cheese they put in his box. But it cant be that because I didnt eat any cheese this week.

Then he told Dr Nemur something I dint understand so while they were talking I wrote down some of the words.

He said Dr Nemur I know Charlie is not what you had in mind as the first of your new brede of intelek** (couldnt get the word)

14 superman. But most people of his low ment** are host** and uncoop** they are usualy dull apath** and hard to reach. He has a good natcher hes intristed and eager to please.

15 Dr Nemur said remember he will be the first human beeng ever to have his inteljence trippled by surgicle meens.

Dr Strauss said exakly. Look at how well hes lerned to read and write for his low mentel age its as grate an acheve** as you and I lerning einstines therey of **vity without help. That shows the intenss motor-vation. Its comparat** a tremen** achev** I say we use Charlie.

16 I dint get all the words and they were talking to fast but it sounded like Dr Strauss was on my side and like the other one wasnt.

Then Dr Nemur nodded he said all right maybe your right. We will use Charlie. When he said that I got so exited I jumped up and shook his hand for being so good to me. I told him thank you doc you wont be sorry for giving me a second chance. And I mean it like I told him. After the operashun Im gonna try to be smart. Im gonna try awful hard.

progris ript 5 — Mar 10

Im skared. Lots of people who work here and the nurses and the people who gave me the tests came to bring me candy and wish me luck. I hope I have luck. I got my rabits foot and my lucky penny and my horse shoe. Only a black cat crossed me when I was comming to the hospitil. Dr Strauss says dont be supersitis Charlie this is sience. Anyway Im keeping my rabits foot with me.

I asked Dr Strauss if Ill beat Algernon in the race after the operashun and he said maybe. If the operashun works Ill show that mouse I can be as smart as he is. Maybe smarter. Then Ill be abel to read better and spell the words good and know lots of things and be like other peo-

---

3. ***motor-vation:*** Charlie means *motivation* (mō′tə-vā′shən), the inner drive to work hard at something.

PORTFOLIO ASSESSMENT
Reader's journals can contain plot summaries, questions that arise while reading, interesting or new words and phrases, and personal comments. Because of the length of "Flowers for Algernon," you may want to have students keep a reader's journal to help them keep track of what happens in the story and how the dynamic characters change. Students could keep written or taped journals. Since the story itself is told within the framework of a journal or diary, students may want to maintain divisions similar to those in the story. Consult with students individually to agree on how their reader's journals will be assessed. (See *Portfolio Assessment and Professional Support Materials*, especially the section entitled **Suggestions for Portfolio Projects**.)

ple. I want to be smart like other people. If it works perminint they will make everybody smart all over the wurld.

They dint give me anything to eat this morning. I dont know what that eating has to do with getting smart. Im very hungry and Dr Nemur took away my box of candy. That Dr Nemur is a grouch. Dr Strauss says I can have it back after the operashun. You cant eat befor a operashun . . .

Progress Report 6 — Mar 15

The operashun dint hurt. He did it while I was sleeping. They took off the bandijis from my eyes and my head today so I can make a PRO- **17** GRESS REPORT. Dr Nemur who looked at some of my other ones says I spell PROGRESS wrong and he told me how to spell it and REPORT too. I got to try and remember that.

I have a very bad memary for spelling. Dr Strauss says its ok to tell about all the things that happin to me but he says I shoud tell more about what I feel and what I think. When I told **18** him I dont know how to think he said try. All the time when the bandijis were on my eyes I tryed to think. Nothing happened. I dont know what to think about. Maybe if I ask him he will tell me how I can think now that Im suppose to get smart. What do smart people think about. Fancy things I suppose. I wish I knew some fancy things alredy.

Progress Report 7 — mar 19

Nothing is happining. I had lots of tests and **19** different kinds of races with Algernon. I hate that mouse. He always beats me. Dr Strauss said I got to play those games. And he said some time I got to take those tests over again. Those inkblots are stupid. And those pictures **20** are stupid too. I like to draw a picture of a man and a woman but I wont make up lies about people.

Scenes on pages 243, 246, 250, 253 and 260 are from the film *Charly*.

17 Analyzing
How is Charlie already demonstrating his ability to learn? His spelling is improving. Keyes uses spelling, vocabulary level, and sentence complexity to show changes in Charlie's intelligence.

18
Charlie thinks about thinking, a new realm for him.

19
Charlie's sense of competition is another result of his operation.

20
Characterization. Charlie's desire to create a drawing demonstrates his new desire to express ideas, but he says he still will not make up lies. No matter what happens to him, Charlie maintains certain values and strengths.

VISUAL CONNECTIONS
Relating Expression Skills
You might have students draw mazes after discussing how mazes are made difficult by the addition of many false paths leading to dead ends. The start and finish points should be labeled. Students then could exchange mazes and find solutions as Charlie did. Graph paper could be helpful, but you might explain that mazes can be any shape, including round.

COOPERATIVE LEARNING

"Flowers for Algernon" is written from the first-person **point of view**. To help students understand point of view, have them work in small groups to rewrite a portion of the story from third-person point of view. Each group could choose a journal entry from the story to rewrite, or you could assign entries. Ask a member of each group to read that group's rewrite to the class.

SOCIAL STUDIES LINK

Have interested students do research on the IQ (intelligence quotient) test developed by Alfred Binet in 1905. Encourage them to explore how the test purports to measure intelligence as well as to learn about the debate surrounding its

21
Characterization. Charlie begins to make judgments about people and about what he is told to do; his responses are becoming more complex.

22 Drawing Conclusions
What unpleasant situation awaits Charlie when he returns to work? He does not realize that his responses to friends and job will change because of increased intelligence.

23
As long as Algernon demonstrates intelligence, Charlie can believe operation is successful.

24 Drawing Conclusions
What does this passage reveal about Charlie's "friends" at work? Although Charlie thinks they are being nice, they are actually ridiculing him.

21   I got a headache from trying to think so much. I thot Dr Strauss was my frend but he dont help me. He dont tell me what to think or when Ill get smart. Miss Kinnian dint come to see me. I think writing these progress reports are stupid too.

Progress Report 8—Mar 23

Im going back to work at the factery. They said it was better I shud go back to work but I cant tell anyone what the operashun was for and I have come to the hospitil for an hour evry night after work. They are gonna pay me mony every month for lerning to be smart.

22   Im glad Im going back to work because I miss my job and all my frends and all the fun we have there.

Dr Strauss says I shud keep writing things down but I dont have to do it every day just when I think of something or something speshul happins. He says dont get discoridged because it takes time and it happins slow. He says it took a long time with Algernon before he got 3 times smarter than he was before. Thats why Algernon beats me all the time because he had that operashun too. That makes me feel better. I coud probly do that *amazed* faster than a reglar mouse. Maybe some day Ill beat Algernon. Boy that would be some-

23 thing. So far Algernon looks like he mite be smart perminent.

Mar 25   (I dont have to write PROGRESS REPORT on top any more just when I hand it in once a week for Dr Nemur to read. I just have to put the date on. That saves time)

24   We had a lot of fun at the factery today. Joe Carp said hey look where Charlie had his operashun what did they do Charlie put some brains in. I was going to tell him but I remembered Dr Strauss said no. Then Frank Reilly said what did you do Charlie forget your key and open your door the hard way. That made me laff. Their really my friends and they like me.

Sometimes somebody will say hey look at Joe or Frank or George he really pulled a Charlie Gordon. I dont know why they say that but they always laff. This morning Amos Borg who is the 4 man at Donnegans used my name when he shouted at Ernie the office boy. Ernie lost a packige. He said Ernie what are you trying to be a Charlie Gordon. I dont understand why he said that. I never lost any packiges.

Mar 28   Dr Strauss came to my room tonight to see why I dint come in like I was suppose to. I told him I dont like to race with Algernon any more. He said I dont have to for a while but I shud come in. He had a present for me only it wasnt a present but just for lend. I thot it was a little television but it wasnt. He said I got to turn it on when I go to sleep. I said your kidding why shud I turn it on when Im going to sleep. Who ever herd of a thing like that. But he said if I want to get smart I got to do what he says. I told him I dint think I was going to get smart and he put his hand on my sholder and said Charlie you dont know it yet but your getting smarter all the time. You wont notice for a while. I think he was just being nice to make me feel good because I dont look any smarter.

Oh yes I almost forgot. I asked him when I can go back to the class at Miss Kinnians school. He said I wont go their. He said that soon Miss Kinnian will come to the hospitil to start and teach me speshul. I was mad at her for not comming to see me when I got the operashun but I like her so maybe we will be frends again.

Mar 29   That crazy TV kept me up all night. How can I sleep with something yelling crazy

things all night in my ears. And the nutty pictures. Wow. I dont know what it says when Im up so how am I going to know when Im sleeping.

Dr Strauss says its ok. He says my brains are lerning when I sleep and that will help me when Miss Kinnian starts my lessons in the hospitl (only I found out it isnt a hospitil its a labatory). I think its all crazy. If you can get smart when your sleeping why do people go to school. That thing I dont think will work. I use to watch the late show and the late late show on TV all the time and it never made me smart. Maybe you have to sleep while you watch it.

PROGRESS REPORT 9—April 3

Dr Strauss showed me how to keep the TV turned low so now I can sleep. I dont hear a thing. And I still dont understand what it says. A few times I play it over in the morning to find out what I lerned when I was sleeping and I dont think so. Miss Kinnian says Maybe its another langwidge or something. But most times it sounds american. It talks so fast faster than even Miss Gold who was my teacher in 6 grade and I remember she talked so fast I couldnt understand her.

I told Dr Strauss what good is it to get smart in my sleep. I want to be smart when Im awake. He says its the same thing and I have two minds. Theres the *subconscious* and the *conscious* (thats how you spell it). And one dont tell the other one what its doing. They dont even talk to each other. Thats why I dream. And boy have I been having crazy dreams. Wow. Ever since that night TV. The late late late late late show.

I forgot to ask him if it was only me or if everybody had those two minds.

(I just looked up the word in the dictionary Dr Strauss gave me. The word is *subconscious.*

adj. Of the nature of mental operations yet not present in consciousness; as, subconscious conflict of desires.) Theres more but I still don't know what it means. This isnt a very good dictionary for dumb people like me.

Anyway the headache is from the party. My frends from the factery Joe Carp and Frank Reilly invited me to go with them to Muggsys Saloon for some drinks. I dont like to drink but they said we will have lots of fun. I had a good time.

Joe Carp said I shoud show the girls how I mop out the toilet in the factory and he got me a mop. I showed them and everyone laffed when I told that Mr Donnegan said I was the best janiter he ever had because I like my job and do it good and never come late or miss a day except for my operashun.

I said Miss Kinnian always said Charlie be proud of your job because you do it good.

Everybody laffed and we had a good time and they gave me lots of drinks and Joe said Charlie is a card. I dont know what that means but everybody likes me and we have fun. I cant wait to be smart like my best friends Joe Carp and Frank Reilly.

I dont remember how the party was over but I think I went out to buy a newspaper and coffe for Joe and Frank and when I came back there was no one their. I looked for them all over till late. Then I dont remember so good but I think I got sleepy or sick. A nice cop brot me back home. Thats what my landlady Mrs Flynn says.

But I got a headache and a big lump on my head and black and blue all over. I think maybe I fell. Anyway I got a bad headache and Im sick and hurt all over. I dont think Ill drink anymore.

April 6 I beat Algernon! I dint even know I beat him until Burt the tester told me. Then the second time I lost because I got so exited I fell off the chair before I finished. But after that I beat him 8 more times. I must be getting smart to beat a smart mouse like Algernon. But I dont *feel* smarter.

I wanted to race Algernon some more but Burt said thats enough for one day. They let me hold him for a minit. Hes not so bad. Hes soft like a ball of cotton. He blinks and when he opens his eyes their black and pink on the eges.

I said can I feed him because I felt bad to beat him and I wanted to be nice and make frends. Burt said no Algernon is a very specshul mouse with an operashun like mine, and he was the first of all the animals to stay smart so long. He told me Algernon is so smart that **31** every day he has to solve a test to get his food. Its a thing like a lock on a door that changes every time Algernon goes in to eat so he has to **29** lern something new to get his food. That made me sad because if he couldnt lern he woud be hungry.

30 I dont think its right to make you pass a test to eat. How woud Dr Nemur like it to have to pass a test every time he wants to eat. I think Ill be frends with Algernon.

April 9 Tonight after work Miss Kinnian was at the laboratory. She looked like she was glad to see me but scared. I told her dont worry Miss Kinnian Im not smart yet and she laffed. She said I have confidence in you Charlie the way you struggled so hard to read and right better than all the others. At werst you will have it for a little wile and your doing somthing for sience.

We are reading a very hard book. I never **31** read such a hard book before. Its called *Robinson Crusoe* about a man who gets merooned on a dessert Iland. Hes smart and figers out all kinds of things so he can have a house and food and hes a good swimmer. Only I feel sorry because hes all alone and has no frends. But I think their must be somebody else on the iland because theres a picture with

32 his funny umbrella looking at footprints. I hope he gets a frend and not be lonly.

April 10   Miss Kinnian teaches me to spell better. She says look at a word and close your eyes and say it over and over until you remember. I have lots of truble with *through* that you say *threw* and *enough* and *tough* that you dont say *enew* and *tew*. You got to say *enuff* and *tuff*. Thats how I use to write it before I started to get smart. Im confused but Miss Kinnian says theres no reason in spelling.

Apr 14   Finished *Robinson Crusoe*. I want to find out more about what happens to him but Miss **33** Kinnian says thats all there is. *Why*

Apr 15   Miss Kinnian says Im lerning fast. She read some of the Progress Reports and she looked at me kind of funny. She says Im a fine person and Ill show them all. I asked her why. **34** She said never mind but I shouldnt feel bad if I find out that everybody isnt nice like I think. She said for a person who god gave so little to you done more then a lot of people with brains they never even used. I said all my frends are smart people but there good. They like me and they never did anything that wasnt nice. Then she got something in her eye and she had to run out to the ladys room.

Apr 16   Today, I lerned, the *comma*, this is a comma (,) a period, with a tail, Miss Kinnian, says its important, because it makes writing, better, she said, somebody, coud lose, a lot of money, if a comma, isnt, in the, right place, I dont have, any money, and I dont see, how a comma, keeps you, from losing it,

But she says, everybody, uses commas, so Ill use, them too,

Apr 17   I used the comma wrong. Its punctuation. Miss Kinnian told me to look up long

words in the dictionary to lern to spell them. I said whats the difference if you can read it anyway. She said its part of your education so now on Ill look up all the words Im not sure how to spell. It takes a long time to write that way but I think Im remembering. I only have to look up once and after that I get it right. Anyway thats how come I got the word *punctuation* right. (Its that way in the dictionary). Miss Kinnian says a period is punctuation too, and there are lots of other marks to lern. I told her I thot all the periods had to have tails but she said no.

35   You got to mix them up, she showed? me" how. to mix! them(up,. and now; I can! mix up all kinds" of punctuation, in! my writing? There, are lots! of rules? to lern; but Im gettin'g them in my head.

One thing I? like about, Dear Miss Kinnian: (thats the way it goes in a business letter if I ever go into business) is she, always gives me' a reason" when—I ask. She's a gen'ius! I wish! I cou'd be smart" like, her;

(Punctuation, is ; fun!)

Apr 18   What a dope I am! I didn't even **36** understand what she was talking about. I read the grammar book last night and it explanes the whole thing. Then I saw it was the same way as Miss Kinnian was trying to tell me, but I didn't get it. I got up in the middle of the night, and the whole thing straightened out in my mind.

Miss Kinnian said that the TV working in my sleep helped out. She said I reached a plateau. Thats like the flat top of a hill.

After I figgered out how punctuation worked, I read over all my old Progress Reports from the beginning. Boy, did I have crazy spelling and punctuation! I told Miss Kinnian I ought to go over the pages and fix all the mistakes but she said, "No, Charlie, Dr. Nemur wants them just as they are. That's why he let you keep them after they were photo-

32
Crusoe's situation parallels Charlie's—they are both alone in a strange and new environment. Notice, too, Charlie's compassion for another's situation.

33
Charlie's question "Why?" seems very poignant here. At this point, Charlie apparently has trouble understanding difference between fiction and reality. However, the question shows Charlie's new intelligence and interest in increasingly complex questions.

34
Miss Kinnian tries to prepare Charlie for future discoveries about people. She knows Charlie will be hurt by people as his perceptions and intelligence increase. His unjaded response touches her.

35   Making Inferences
Is Charlie, as he is writing, aware of how humorous his punctuation is? Charlie probably believes he is using punctuation correctly.

36
Inference. Charlie reads an entire book in one night; suggests his intelligence is growing at a very rapid rate.

37 Finding Cause and Effect
Why does Charlie feel sick?
Feels effects of realization that his
co-workers are cruel.

38 Making Inferences
*Why did Charlie's soft drink
taste funny?* Joe tampered with
Charlie's drink.

39
Use to answer **study question 3,**
p. 261.

**Part Two
Progress Reports
April 21–May 18**

1
Foreshadowing. Mrs. Flynn's
fear suggests that others will respond in same way to Charlie's
change.

2
Theme. A dramatic comment on
social values. Charlie realizes how
he has been treated and why.

3
Charlie is developing a photographic memory.

stated, to see your own progress. You're coming along fast, Charlie."

That made me feel good. After the lesson I
went down and played with Algernon. We don't
race any more.

37 *April 20* I feel sick inside. Not sick like for a
doctor, but inside my chest it feels empty like
getting punched and a heartburn at the same
time.

I wasn't going to write about it, but I guess I
got to, because it's important, Today was the
first time I ever stayed home from work.

Last night Joe Carp and Frank Reilly invited
me to a party. There were lots of girls and
some men from the factory. I remembered how
sick I got last time I drank too much, so I told
Joe I didn't want anything to drink. He gave
38 me a plain Coke instead. It tasted funny, but I
thought it was just a bad taste in my mouth.

We had a lot of fun for a while. Joe said I
should dance with Ellen and she would teach
me the steps. I fell a few times and I couldn't
understand why because no one else was dancing besides Ellen and me. And all the time I
was tripping because somebody's foot was
always sticking out.

Then when I got up I saw the look on Joe's
face and it gave me a funny feeling in my stom-
ack. "He's a scream," one of the girls said.
Everybody was laughing.

Frank said, "I ain't laughed so much since
we sent him off for the newspaper that night at
Muggsy's and ditched him."

"Look at him. His face is red."

"He's blushing. Charlie is blushing."

"Hey, Ellen, what'd you do to Charlie? I
never saw him act like that before."

39 I didn't know what to do or where to turn.
Everyone was looking at me and laughing and
I felt naked. I wanted to hide myself. I ran out
into the street and I threw up. Then I walked
home. It's a funny thing I never knew that Joe

and Frank and the others liked to have me
around all the time to make fun of me.

Now I know what it means when they say "to
pull a Charlie Gordon."

I'm ashamed.

PROGRESS REPORT 10

April 21 Still didn't go into the factory. I told
Mrs. Flynn my landlady to call and tell Mr.
1 Donnegan I was sick. Mrs. Flynn looks at me
very funny lately like she's scared of me.

I think it's a good thing about finding out
how everybody laughs at me. I thought about it
a lot. It's because I'm so dumb and I don't even
2 know when I'm doing something dumb. People
think it's funny when a dumb person can't do
things the same way they can.

Anyway, now I know I'm getting smarter
every day. I know punctuation and I can spell
good. I like to look up all the hard words in the
dictionary and I remember them. I'm reading
a lot now, and Miss Kinnian says I read very
fast. Sometimes I even understand what I'm
reading about, and it stays in my mind. There
are times when I can close my eyes and think
3 of a page and it all comes back like a picture.

Besides history, geography, and arithmetic,
Miss Kinnian said I should start to learn a few
foreign languages. Dr. Strauss gave me some
more tapes to play while I sleep. I still don't
understand how that conscious and unconscious mind works, but Dr. Strauss says not to
worry yet. He asked me to promise that when I
start learning college subjects next week I
wouldn't read any books on psychology—that
is, until he gives me permission.

I feel a lot better today, but I guess I'm still a
little angry that all the time people were laughing and making fun of me because I wasn't so
smart. When I become intelligent like Dr.
Strauss says, with three times my I.Q. of 68,

then maybe I'll be like everyone else and people will like me and be friendly.

I'm not sure what an I.Q. is. Dr. Nemur said it was something that measured how intelligent you were—like a scale in the drugstore weighs pounds. But Dr. Strauss had a big argument with him and said an I.Q. didn't weigh intelligence at all. He said an I.Q. showed how much intelligence you could get, like the numbers on the outside of a measuring cup. You still had to fill the cup up with stuff.

Then when I asked Burt, who gives me my intelligence tests and works with Algernon, he said that both of them were wrong (only I had to promise not to tell them he said so). Burt says that the I.Q. measures a lot of different things including some of the things you learned already, and it really isn't any good at all.

4 So I still don't know what I.Q. is except that mine is going to be over 200 soon. I didn't want to say anything, but I don't see how if they don't know *what* it is, or *where* it is—I don't see how they know *how much* of it you've got.

Dr. Nemur says I have to take a *Rorschach Test* tomorrow. I wonder what *that* is.

April 22 I found out what a *Rorschach* is. It's the test I took before the operation—the one with the inkblots on the pieces of cardboard. The man who gave me the test was the same one.

5 I was scared to death of those inkblots. I knew he was going to ask me to find the pictures and I knew I wouldn't be able to. I was thinking to myself, if only there was some way of knowing what kind of pictures were hidden there. Maybe there weren't any pictures at all. Maybe it was just a trick to see if I was dumb enough to look for something that wasn't there. Just thinking about that made me sore at him.

"All right, Charlie," he said, "you've seen these cards before, remember?"

6 "Of course I remember."

The way I said it, he knew I was angry, and he looked surprised. "Yes, of course. Now I want you to look at this one. What might this be? What do you see on this card? People see all sorts of things in these inkblots. Tell me what it might be for you—what it makes you think of."

I was shocked. That wasn't what I had expected him to say at all. "You mean there are no pictures hidden in those inkblots?"

He frowned and took off his glasses. "What?"

"Pictures. Hidden in the inkblots. Last time you told me that everyone could see them and you wanted me to find them too."

He explained to me that the last time he had used almost the exact same words he was using now. I didn't believe it, and I still have the suspicion that he misled me at the time just for the fun of it. Unless—I don't know any more—could I have been *that* feeble-minded?

7 We went through the cards slowly. One of them looked like a pair of bats tugging at something. Another one looked like two men fencing with swords. I imagined all sorts of things. I guess I got carried away. But I didn't trust him any more, and I kept turning them around and even looking on the back to see if there was anything there I was supposed to catch. While he was making his notes, I peeked out of the corner of my eye to read it. But it was all in code that looked like this:

8 WF + A   DdF − Ad orig.   WF − A   SF + obj

The test still doesn't make sense to me. It seems to me that anyone could make up lies about things that they didn't really see. How could he know I wasn't making a fool of him by mentioning things that I didn't really imagine? Maybe I'll understand it when Dr. Strauss lets me read up on psychology.

4
Such intelligence, at the top range of human potential, would be difficult to test.

5
Characterization. Charlie is now able to ponder nature and purpose of test.

6 Finding Cause and Effect
Why is Charlie angry? He remembers his reaction the first time he took test and is afraid that he is being made fun of in much the same way his "friends" made fun of him.

7
Symbol. Charlie's responses show the unrest created within his own mind by his new feelings and capabilities.

8
The tester uses codes to record Charlie's responses. Score will be compared to established norms and used to identify Charlie's new personality traits.

9
Charlie begins to solve problems creatively. Ironic contrast between Donnegan's savings and Charlie's bonus.

10 Analyzing
Drawing Conclusions
Do Joe Carp and Frank Reilly actually have other plans? Why would they invent excuses? They have no plans. They are now uneasy around Charlie and want to avoid having lunch with him.

11
Charlie is becoming more confident as his intelligence increases.

12
Conflict. Argument between Dr. Nemur and Dr. Strauss shows the personal interests of the doctors in Charlie's case. Both appear selfish and unconcerned about Charlie as a person.

9 *April 25*   I figured out a new way to line up the machines in the factory, and Mr. Donnegan says it will save him ten thousand dollars a year in labor and increased production. He gave me a twenty-five-dollar bonus.

I wanted to take Joe Carp and Frank Reilly out to lunch to celebrate, but Joe said he had to **12** buy some things for his wife, and Frank said he **10** was meeting his cousin for lunch. I guess it'll take a little time for them to get used to the changes in me. Everybody seems to be frightened of me. When I went over to Amos Borg and tapped him on the shoulder, he jumped up in the air.

People don't talk to me much any more or kid around the way they used to. It makes the job kind of lonely.

11 *April 27*   I got up the nerve today to ask Miss Kinnian to have dinner with me tomorrow night to celebrate my bonus.

At first she wasn't sure it was right, but I asked Dr. Strauss and he said it was okay. Dr. Strauss and Dr. Nemur don't seem to be getting along so well. They're arguing all the time. This evening when I came in to ask Dr. Strauss about having dinner with Miss Kinnian, I heard them shouting. Dr. Nemur was saying that it was *his* experiment and *his* research, and Dr. Strauss was shouting back that he contributed just as much, because he found me through Miss Kinnian and he performed the operation. Dr. Strauss said that someday thousands of neurosurgeons might be using his technique all over the world.

Dr. Nemur wanted to publish the results of the experiment at the end of this month. Dr. Strauss wanted to wait a while longer to be sure. Dr. Strauss said that Dr. Nemur was more interested in the Chair[4] of Psychology at

4. **Chair:** here, a professorship.

Princeton than he was in the experiment. Dr. Nemur said that Dr. Strauss was nothing but an opportunist who was trying to ride to glory on *his* coattails.

When I left afterwards, I found myself trembling. I don't know why for sure, but it was as if I'd seen both men clearly for the first time. I remember hearing Burt say that Dr. Nemur had a shrew of a wife who was pushing him all the time to get things published so that he could become famous. Burt said that the dream of her life was to have a big-shot husband.

Was Dr. Strauss really trying to ride on his coattails?

13 *April 28* I don't understand why I never noticed how beautiful Miss Kinnian really is. She has brown eyes and feathery brown hair that comes to the top of her neck. She's only thirty-four! I think from the beginning I had the feeling that she was an unreachable genius—and very, very old. Now, every time I see her she grows younger and more lovely.

We had dinner and a long talk. When she said that I was coming along so fast that soon I'd be leaving her behind, I laughed.

"It's true, Charlie. You're already a better reader than I am. You can read a whole page at a glance while I can take in only a few lines at a time. And you remember every single thing you read. I'm lucky if I can recall the main thoughts and the general meaning."

"I don't feel intelligent. There are so many things I don't understand."

She took out a cigarette and I lit it for her. "You've got to be a *little* patient. You're accomplishing in days and weeks what it takes normal people to do in half a lifetime. That's what makes it so amazing. You're like a giant sponge now, soaking things in. Facts, figures, general knowledge. And soon you'll begin to connect them, too. You'll see how the different branches

14

of learning are related. There are many levels, Charlie, like steps on a giant ladder that take you up higher and higher to see more and more of the world around you.

"I can see only a little bit of that, Charlie, and I won't go much higher than I am now, but you'll keep climbing up and up, and see more and more, and each step will open new worlds that you never even knew existed." She frowned. "I hope . . . I just hope to God—"

"What?"

"Never mind, Charles. I just hope I wasn't wrong to advise you to go into this in the first place."

16 I laughed. "How could that be? It worked, didn't it? Even Algernon is still smart."

We sat there silently for a while and I knew what she was thinking about as she watched me toying with the chain of my rabbit's foot and my keys. I didn't want to think of that possibility any more than elderly people want to think of death. I *knew* that this was only the beginning. I knew what she meant about levels because I'd seen some of them already. The thought of leaving her behind made me sad.

I'm in love with Miss Kinnian.

15

PROGRESS REPORT 11

April 30 I've quit my job with Donnegan's Plastic Box Company. Mr. Donnegan insisted that it would be better for all concerned if I left. What did I do to make them hate me so?

The first I knew of it was when Mr. Donnegan showed me the petition. Eight hundred and forty names, everyone connected with the factory, except Fanny Girden. Scanning the list quickly, I saw at once that hers was the only missing name. All the rest demanded that I be fired.

Joe Carp and Frank Reilly wouldn't talk to me about it. No one else would either, except

17

13 Analyzing
Why is Miss Kinnian now described as a person, not as a professional? Charlie's feelings now focus on her personal qualities as he and Miss Kinnian become more intellectually equal.

14
Important characteristic of genius—ability to relate one thing to another and to perceive new relationships.

15
Foreshadowing. That Charlie could regress is a continuing threat. Such fears suggest likelihood that Charlie will regress.

16
Charlie dismisses idea that his intellect might decline; he clings to security that Algernon has maintained high intelligence.

17
Irony. Although Charlie does not know why he is a threat, he quickly locates one missing name on list of 840 names.

Keyes makes point that it is rare to find people who have enough courage to stand up for their beliefs.

19
Dialogue. Fanny's nonstandard English contrasts with Charlie's perfect syntax.

20
Allusion. In referring to story of Adam and Eve, Fanny is saying she believes that original sin is connected with desire for knowledge and is root of evil.

21 Analyzing
Why is Charlie "more alone than ever before"? Responses will vary. He finds loneliness on both ends of intelligence spectrum. He doesn't fit in with uneducated people at the factory or with educated acquaintances such as Drs. Strauss and Nemur.

22
Names of organizations lend credibility to events of story and make story seem real.

23 Comparing/Contrasting
In what way have the situations of Charlie and the doctors been reversed? Charlie now has ability to assess personality traits of men who had been assessing him.

18 Fanny. She was one of the few people I'd known who set her mind to something and believed it no matter what the rest of the world proved, said, or did—and Fanny did not believe that I should have been fired. She had been against the petition on principle and despite the pressure and threats she'd held out.

19 "Which don't mean to say," she remarked, "that I don't think there's something mighty strange about you, Charlie. Them changes. I don't know. You used to be a good, dependable, ordinary man—not too bright maybe, but honest. Who knows what you done to yourself to get so smart all of a sudden. Like everybody around here's been saying, Charlie, it's not right."

"But how can you say that, Fanny? What's wrong with a man becoming intelligent and wanting to acquire knowledge and understanding of the world around him?"

She stared down at her work and I turned to **20** leave. Without looking at me, she said: "It was evil when Eve[5] listened to the snake and ate from the tree of knowledge. It was evil when she saw that she was naked. If not for that none of us would ever have to grow old and sick, and die."

Once again now I have the feeling of shame burning inside me. This intelligence has driven a wedge between me and all the people I once knew and loved. Before, they laughed at me and despised me for my ignorance and dullness; now, they hate me for my knowledge and understanding. What do they want of me?

They've driven me out of the factory. Now **21** I'm more alone than ever before. . . .

May 15 Dr. Strauss is very angry at me for not having written any progress reports in two weeks. He's justified because the lab is now pay-

ing me a regular salary. I told him I was too busy thinking and reading. When I pointed out that writing was such a slow process that it made me impatient with my poor handwriting, he suggested that I learn to type. It's much easier to write now because I can type nearly seventy-five words a minute. Dr. Strauss continually reminds me of the need to speak and write simply so that people will be able to understand me.

I'll try to review all the things that happened to me during the last two weeks. Algernon and **22** I were presented to the American Psychological Association sitting in convention with the World Psychological Association last Tuesday. We created quite a sensation. Dr. Nemur and Dr. Strauss were proud of us.

I suspect that Dr. Nemur, who is sixty—ten **23** years older than Dr. Strauss—finds it necessary to see tangible results of his work. Undoubtedly the result of pressure by Mrs. Nemur.

Contrary to my earlier impressions of him, I realize that Dr. Nemur is not at all a genius. He has a very good mind, but it struggles under the specter of self-doubt. He wants people to take him for a genius. Therefore, it is important for him to feel that his work is accepted by the world. I believe that Dr. Nemur was afraid of further delay because he worried that someone else might make a discovery along these lines and take the credit from him.

Dr. Strauss on the other hand might be called a genius, although I feel that his areas of knowledge are too limited. He was educated in the tradition of narrow specialization; the broader aspects of background were neglected far more than necessary—even for a neurosurgeon.

I was shocked to learn that the only ancient languages he could read were Latin, Greek, and Hebrew, and that he knows almost nothing of mathematics beyond the elementary levels of the calculus of variations. When he admit-

5. **Eve:** The story of Adam and Eve is told in Genesis 2–3.

TRANSPARENCIES 18 & 19

Fine Art
Theme: *Slice of Life* – highlights artwork depicting a situation that captures a meaningful scene from life, as a short story does.

VISUAL CONNECTIONS

Exploring the Subject

This photograph shows actor Cliff Robertson as Charles Gordon in the 1968 film *Charly*, directed by Ralph Nelson. Robertson's performance earned him an Academy Award as best actor. Robertson also portrayed John F. Kennedy in the famous 1963 film *PT 109*. *Charly* is available on videotape, and you could show it to the class or suggest that students view it, if possible, after reading the story.

Ideas for Writing

You might have students write short essays in which they contrast and compare the appearance of the character Charlie (actor Cliff Robertson) in this picture and in the picture on p. 246. This photograph shows Charlie after his intelligence level has improved dramatically. Students should notice the neatly cut hair, professional-looking clothing, and serious, intent look. The scene on p. 246 shows Charlie shortly after the operation, and he still has informal clothes, an unkempt appearance, and an unworried expression.

24

Characterization. Charlie has very quickly gone from a simple, innocent person to a jaded, analytical one. His ability to assess character has become almost frightening.

25

Charlie has struck upon an unsettling truth. Even Strauss has become uncomfortable with his insights.

26 Comparing/Contrasting
How is Miss Kinnian's reaction different from that of the two doctors? Her laughter no doubt directed more at herself than at Charlie; she does not seem defensive about his superior intelligence.

27

Metamorphosis. Charlie's transformation from mentally handicapped man to mental giant has been so successful that he can no longer communicate with people and is becoming alienated. His intelligence level is above that of his former teacher and his doctors, so he now spends time alone absorbing information.

28

Charlie sees his own past recreated. Boy is mocked by owner and customers. Author develops **theme** of discrimination and cruelty.

---

ted this to me, I found myself almost annoyed. It was as if he'd hidden this part of himself in order to deceive me, pretending—as do many people I've discovered—to be what he is not. **24** No one I've ever known is what he appears to be on the surface.

Dr. Nemur appears to be uncomfortable around me. Sometimes when I try to talk to him, he just looks at me strangely and turns away. I was angry at first when Dr. Strauss told me I was giving Dr. Nemur an inferiority complex. I thought he was mocking me and I'm oversensitive at being made fun of.

How was I to know that a highly respected psychoexperimentalist like Nemur was unacquainted with Hindustani and Chinese? It's absurd when you consider the work that is being done in India and China today in the very field of his study.

I asked Dr. Strauss how Nemur could refute Rahajamati's attack on his method and results if Nemur couldn't even read it in the first place. **25** The strange look on Dr. Strauss's face can only mean one of two things. Either he doesn't want to tell Nemur what they're saying in India, or else—and this worries me—Dr. Strauss doesn't **28** know either. I must be careful to speak and write clearly and simply so that people won't laugh.

May 18 I am very disturbed. I saw Miss Kinnian last night for the first time in over a week. I tried to avoid all discussions of intellectual concepts and to keep the conversation on a simple, everyday level, but she just stared at me blankly and asked me what I meant about the mathematical variance equivalent in Dobermann's Fifth Concerto.

26 When I tried to explain she stopped me and laughed. I guess I got angry, but I suspect I'm approaching her on the wrong level. No matter what I try to discuss with her, I am unable to communicate. I must review Vrostadt's equa- **27** tions on *Levels of Semantic Progression*. I find that I don't communicate with people much any more. Thank God for books and music and things I can think about. I am alone in my apartment at Mrs. Flynn's boardinghouse most of the time and seldom speak to anyone.

May 20 I would not have noticed the new dishwasher, a boy of about sixteen, at the corner diner where I take my evening meals if not for the incident of the broken dishes.

They crashed to the floor, shattering and sending bits of white china under the tables. The boy stood there, dazed and frightened, holding the empty tray in his hand. The whistles and catcalls from the customers (the cries of "Hey, there go the profits!" . . . *"Mazel tov!"*[6] . . . and "Well, *he* didn't work here very long. . . ." which invariably seem to follow the breaking of glass or dishware in a public restaurant) all seemed to confuse him.

When the owner came to see what the excitement was about, the boy cowered as if he expected to be struck and threw up his arms as if to ward off the blow.

"All right! All right, you dope," shouted the owner, "don't just stand there! Get the broom and sweep that mess up. A broom . . . a broom, you idiot! It's in the kitchen. Sweep up all the pieces."

The boy saw that he was not going to be punished. His frightened expression disappeared and he smiled and hummed as he came back with the broom to sweep the floor. A few of the rowdier customers kept up the remarks, amusing themselves at his expense.

"Here, sonny, over here there's a nice piece behind you. . . ."

"C'mon, do it again. . . ."

"He's not so dumb. It's easier to break 'em than to wash 'em. . . ."

6. *Mazel tov!* (mä′zəl tôf): Hebrew for "Congratulations!"

As his vacant eyes moved across the crowd of amused onlookers, he slowly mirrored their smiles and finally broke into an uncertain grin at the joke which he obviously did not understand.

I felt sick inside as I looked at his dull, vacuous smile, the wide, bright eyes of a child, uncertain but eager to please. They were laughing at him because he was mentally retarded.

And I had been laughing at him too.

29 Suddenly, I was furious at myself and all those who were smirking at him. I jumped up and shouted, "Shut up! Leave him alone! It's not his fault he can't understand! He can't help what he is! But . . . he's still a human being!"

The room grew silent. I cursed myself for losing control and creating a scene. I tried not to look at the boy as I paid my check and walked out without touching my food. I felt ashamed for both of us.

30 How strange it is that people of honest feelings and sensibility, who would not take advantage of a man born without arms or legs or eyes—how such people think nothing of abusing a man born with low intelligence. It infuriated me to think that not long ago, I, like this boy, had foolishly played the clown.

And I had almost forgotten.

I'd hidden the picture of the old Charlie Gordon from myself because now that I was intelligent it was something that had to be pushed out of my mind. But today in looking at that boy, for the first time I saw what I had been. *I was just like him!*

Only a short time ago, I learned that people laughed at me. Now I can see that unknowingly I had joined with them in laughing at myself. That hurts most of all.

I have often reread my progress reports and seen the illiteracy, the childish naiveté, the **31** mind of low intelligence peering from a dark room, through the keyhole, at the dazzling light outside. I see that even in my dullness I knew that I was inferior, and that other people had something that I lacked—something denied me. In my mental blindness, I thought that it was somehow connected with the ability to read and write, and I was sure that if I could get those skills I would automatically have intelligence too.

32 Even a feebleminded man wants to be like other men.

A child may not know how to feed itself, or what to eat, yet it knows of hunger.

This then is what I was like; I never knew. Even with my gift of intellectual awareness, I never really knew.

This day was good for me. Seeing the past **33** more clearly, I have decided to use my knowledge and skills to work in the field of increasing human intelligence levels. Who is better equipped for this work? Who else has lived in both worlds? These are my people. Let me use my gift to do something for them.

Tomorrow, I will discuss with Dr. Strauss the manner in which I can work in this area. I may be able to help him work out the problems of widespread use of the technique which was used on me. I have several good ideas of my own.

There is so much that might be done with this technique. If I could be made into a genius, what about thousands of others like myself? What fantastic levels might be achieved by using this technique on normal people? On *geniuses?*

34 There are so many doors to open. I am impatient to begin.

PROGRESS REPORT 12

1 *May 23* It happened today. Algernon bit me. I visited the lab to see him as I do occasionally,

READING SKILLS PRACTICE
The underlined passage can be used to give students practice in drawing logical conclusions. Ask students to read over the selection carefully before trying to answer the question: Which of the following can be concluded from this passage? **A.** Dr. Strauss and Dr. Nemur are becoming unable to continue their research, and Charlie wants to help them. (Unsupported.) **B.** Charlie senses that he will soon suffer from the same problems Algernon has and wants to find whether surgically increased intelligence can last. (Correct.) **C.** Charlie wants to finish his research before he is locked out of the laboratory. (Irrelevant.) **D.** Charlie is very excited because of the improvement in Algernon's behavior. (Contradicted.)

and when I took him out of his cage, he snapped at my hand. I put him back and watched him for a while. He was unusually disturbed and vicious.

▶ *May 24*   Burt, who is in charge of the experimental animals, tells me that Algernon is changing. He is less cooperative; he refuses to run the maze any more; general motivation has decreased. And he hasn't been eating. Everyone is upset about what this may mean.

May 25   They've been feeding Algernon, who now refuses to work the shifting-lock problem. Everyone identifies me with Algernon. In a way we're both the first of our kind. They're all pretending that Algernon's behavior is not necessarily significant for me. But it's hard to hide the fact that some of the other animals who were used in the experiment are showing strange behavior.

Dr. Strauss and Dr. Nemur have asked me not to come to the lab any more. I know what they're thinking but I can't accept it. I am going ahead with my plans to carry their research forward. With all due respect to both of these fine scientists, I am well aware of their limitations. If there is an answer, I'll have to find it out for myself. Suddenly, time has become very important to me. ◀

May 29   I have been given a lab of my own and permission to go ahead with the research. I'm on to something. Working day and night. I've had a cot moved into the lab. Most of my writing time is spent on the notes which I keep in a separate folder, but from time to time I feel it necessary to put down my moods and my thoughts out of sheer habit.

I find the *calculus of intelligence* to be a fascinating study. Here is the place for the application of all the knowledge I have acquired. In a

sense it's the problem I've been concerned with all my life.

May 31   Dr. Strauss thinks I'm working too hard. Dr. Nemur says I'm trying to cram a lifetime of research and thought into a few weeks. I know I should rest, but I'm driven on by something inside that won't let me stop. I've got to find the reason for the sharp regression in Algernon. I've got to know *if* and *when* it will happen to me.

June 4
LETTER TO DR. STRAUSS (*copy*)

Dear Dr. Strauss

Under separate cover I am sending you a copy of my report entitled "The Algernon-Gordon Effect: A Study of Structure and Function of Increased Intelligence," which I would like to have you read and have published.

As you can see, my experiments are completed. I have included in my report all of my formulae, as well as mathematical analysis in the appendix. Of course, these should be verified.

Because of its importance to both you and Dr. Nemur (and need I say to myself, too?) I have checked and rechecked my results a dozen times in the hope of finding an error.

I am sorry to say the results must stand. Yet for the sake of science, I am grateful for the little bit that I here add to the knowledge of the function of the human mind and of the laws governing the artificial increase of human intelligence.

I recall your saying to me once that an experimental *failure* or the *disproving* of a theory was as important to the advancement of learning as a success would be. I know now that this is true. I am sorry, however,

---

2
Conflict. Charlie is in a race against time, realizing he may lose his intelligence before he can accomplish his goals.

3
Connotation. "Calculus of intelligence" possibly means a method of analyzing how intelligence is acquired; at any rate, it *sounds* impressive.

4
As a person directly affected and as a member of a scientific team, Charlie wants to discover causes and predictability of regression.

5   Summarizing
Analyzing
What is the major conclusion Charlie has reached? Why does he not feel emotionally devastated? Main conclusion is that regression is inevitable and—for him—imminent. Responses to second question will vary. Surely he feels personal fear and grief, yet is gratified to know that he has contributed to scientific and medical progress.

TRANSPARENCY **20**

Reader Response
Charting a Response – invites students to examine a selection from several different perspectives.

that my own contribution to the field must rest upon the ashes of the work of two men I regard so highly.

Yours truly,
Charles Gordon

6 *June 5* I must not become emotional. The facts and the results of my experiments are clear, and the more sensational aspects of my own rapid climb cannot obscure the fact that the tripling of intelligence by the surgical technique developed by Drs. Strauss and Nemur must be viewed as having little or no practical applicability (at the present time) to the increase of human intelligence.

As I review the records and data on Algernon, I see that although he is still in his physical infancy, he has regressed mentally. Motor activity[7] is impaired; there is a general reduction of glandular activity; there is an accelerated loss of coordination.

There are also strong indications of progressive amnesia.

7 As will be seen by my report, these and other physical and mental deterioration syndromes can be predicted with statistically significant results by the application of my formula.

The surgical stimulus to which we were both subjected has resulted in an intensification and acceleration of all mental processes. The unforeseen development, which I have taken the liberty of calling the "Algernon-Gordon Effect," is the logical extension of the entire intelligence speedup. The hypothesis here proven may be described simply in the following terms: Artificially increased intelligence deteriorates at a rate of time directly proportional to the quantity of the increase.

8 I feel that this, in itself, is an important discovery.

7. **Motor activity:** movement.

As long as I am able to write, I will continue to record my thoughts in these progress reports. It is one of my few pleasures. However, by all indications, my own mental deterioration will be very rapid.

I have already begun to notice signs of emotional instability and forgetfulness, the first symptoms of the burnout.

June 10 Deterioration progressing. I have **9** become absent-minded. Algernon died two days ago. Dissection shows my predictions were right. His brain had decreased in weight and there was a general smoothing out of cerebral **10** convolutions[8] as well as a deepening and broadening of brain fissures.[9]

I guess the same thing is or soon will be happening to me. Now that's it's definite, I don't want it to happen.

I put Algernon's body in a cheese box and buried him in the backyard. I cried.

June 15 Dr. Strauss came to see me again. I wouldn't open the door and told him to go away. I want to be left to myself. I have become touchy and irritable. I feel the darkness closing in. It's hard to throw off thoughts of suicide. I keep telling myself how important this introspective journal will be.

It's a strange sensation to pick up a book that you've read and enjoyed just a few months ago and discover that you don't remember it. I remembered how great I thought John Milton **11** was, but when I picked up *Paradise Lost* I couldn't understand it at all. I got so angry I threw the book across the room.

I've got to try to hold on to some of it. Some of the things I've learned. Oh, God, please don't take it all away.

8. **cerebral** (sə-rē′brəl) **convolutions** (kŏn′və-loo′shənz): irregular folds in the cerebrum, the part of the brain where thinking takes place.
9. **fissures** (fĭsh′ərz): deep cracks or grooves.

6
Irony. That Charlie says he must not become emotional indicates he already has become emotional.

7
Charlie realizes course his deterioration will take. He strives to maintain a scientific, detached view of his future. Presentation of story in diary form lets reader feel close to Charlie's suffering.

8
Recognition of the significance of his findings gives Charlie a sense of contribution and accomplishment.

9 Drawing Conclusions
What does Algernon's death portend? Algernon has been linked with Charlie throughout experiment; Algernon's death suggests experiment on Charlie may end in his death, too.

10
These details are the physical evidence of decreased brain function.

11
Symbol. Title of book suggests the loss of the "paradise" his increased intelligence represents. As Charlie's intelligence decreases, he loses scientific objectivity and feels full trauma of loss.

12
Charlie is torn between past and present as he gradually regresses to the person he was.

12
Charlie is torn between past and present as he gradually regresses to the person he was.

13
Humiliation of becoming helpless again is horrifying to Charlie. Boy represents old Charlie Gordon—and a rapidly approaching new one. Ironic that his determination to fight loss is symptom of regression; in his genius state Charlie would know struggle is useless.

14
Simile. Description of his intelligence as slipping "like sand" through his fingers suggests rapid, irretrievable loss. Ability to create figure of speech sign of intelligence remaining.

15
Charlie now feels helpless, disoriented. Spelling errors, such as omitting apostrophe and reversing *a* and *u* in *because* are also signs of deterioration.

16 Analyzing
What do Charlie's thoughts of his early years signify? Responses will vary. May indicate his rapid mental regression from thinking of scientific experiments to remembering childhood; may also signify a longing for the better life that might have been his if his father had kept promises.

June 19 Sometimes, at night, I go out for a **12** walk. Last night I couldn't remember where I lived. A policeman took me home. I have the strange feeling that this has all happened to me before—a long time ago. I keep telling myself I'm the only person in the world who can describe what's happening to me.

June 21 Why can't I remember? I've got to fight. I lie in bed for days and I don't know who or where I am. Then it all comes back to me in a flash. Fugues of amnesia.[10] Symptoms of senility—second childhood. I can watch them coming on. It's so cruelly logical. I learned so **13** much and so fast. Now my mind is deteriorating rapidly. I won't let it happen. I'll fight it. I can't help thinking of the boy in the restaurant, the blank expression, the silly smile, the people laughing at him. No—please—not that again . . .

June 22 I'm forgetting things that I learned recently. It seems to be following the classic pattern—the last things learned are the first things forgotten. Or is that the pattern? I'd better look it up again. . . .

I reread my paper on the "Algernon-Gordon Effect" and I get the strange feeling that it was written by someone else. There are parts I don't even understand.

Motor activity impaired. I keep tripping over things, and it becomes increasingly difficult to type.

June 23 I've given up using the typewriter completely. My coordination is bad. I feel that I'm moving slower and slower. Had a terrible shock today. I picked up a copy of an article I used in my research, Krueger's "Über psychi-

10. **Fugues** (fyōōgz) **of amnesia** (ăm-nē'zhə): periods of time in which a person behaves normally but later has no memory of what has happened.

sche Ganzheit," to see if it would help me understand what I had done. First I thought there was something wrong with my eyes. Then I realized I could no longer read German. I tested myself in other languages. All gone.

June 30 A week since I dared to write again. **14** It's slipping away like sand through my fingers. Most of the books I have are too hard for me now. I get angry with them because I know that I read and understood them just a few weeks ago.

I keep telling myself I must keep writing these reports so that somebody will know what is happening to me. But it gets harder to form the words and remember spellings. I have to look up even simple words in the dictionary now and it makes me impatient with myself.

Dr. Strauss comes around almost every day, but I told him I wouldn't see or speak to anybody. He feels guilty. They all do. But I don't blame anyone. I knew what might happen. But how it hurts.

15 *July 7* I don't know where the week went. Todays Sunday I know becuase I can see through my window people going to church. I think I stayed in bed all week but I remember Mrs. Flynn bringing food to me a few times. I keep saying over and over I've got to do something but then I forget or maybe its just easier not to do what I say Im going to do.

16 I think of my mother and father a lot these days. I found a picture of them with me taken at a beach. My father has a big ball under his arm and my mother is holding me by the hand. I dont remember them the way they are in the picture. All I remember is my father arguing with mom about money. He never shaved much and he used to scratch my face when he hugged me. He said he was going to take me to see cows on a farm once but he never did. He never kept his promises . . .

July 10   My landlady Mrs Flynn is very worried about me. She said she doesnt like loafers. If Im sick its one thing, but if Im a loafer thats another thing and she wont have it. I told her I think Im sick.

17   I try to read a little bit every day, mostly stories, but sometimes I have to read the same thing over and over again because I dont know what it means. And its hard to write. I know I should look up all the words in the dictionary but its so hard and Im so tired all the time.

Then I got the idea that I would only use the easy words instead of the long hard ones. That **18** saves time. I put flowers on Algernons grave about once a week. Mrs Flynn thinks Im crazy to put flowers on a mouses grave but I told her that Algernon was special.

July 14   Its sunday again. I dont have anything to do to keep me busy now because my television set is broke and I dont have any money to get it fixed. (I think I lost this months check from the lab. I don't remember)

I get awful headaches and asperin doesnt help me much. Mrs Flynn knows Im really sick and she feels sorry for me. Shes a wonderful woman whenever someone is sick.

July 22   Mrs Flynn called a strange doctor to see me. She was afraid I was going to die. I told the doctor I wasnt too sick and that I only forget sometimes. He asked me did I have any friends or relatives and I said no I dont have **19** any. I told him I had a friend called Algernon once but he was a mouse and we used to run races together. He looked at me kind of funny like he thought I was crazy.

He smiled when I told him I used to be a genius. He talked to me like I was a baby and he winked at Mrs Flynn. I got mad and chased him out because he was making fun of me the way they all used to.

July 24   I have no money and Mrs Flynn says I got to go to work somewhere and pay the rent because I havent paid for over two months. I dont know any work but the job I used to have at Donnegans Plastic Box Company. I dont want to go back there because they all knew me when I was smart and maybe theyll laugh at me. But I dont know what else to do to get money.

July 25   I was looking at some of my old progress reports and its very funny but I cant read what I wrote. I can make out some of the words but they don't make sense.

20   Miss Kinnian came to the door but I said go away I dont want to see you. She cried and I cried too but I wouldnt let her in because I didnt want her to laugh at me. I told her I didn't like her any more. I told her I didnt want to be smart any more. Thats not true. I still love her and I still want to be smart but I had to say that so shed go away. She gave Mrs Flynn money to pay the rent. I dont want that. I got to get a job.

Please . . . please let me not forget how to read and write . . .

July 27   Mr Donnegan was very nice when I came back and asked him for my old job of janitor. First he was very suspicious but I told him **21** what happened to me and then he looked very sad and put his hand on my shoulder and said Charlie Gordon you got guts.

Everybody looked at me when I came downstairs and started working in the toilet sweep- **22** ing it out like I used to. I told myself Charlie if they make fun of you dont get sore because you remember their not so smart as you once thot they were. And besides they were once your friends and if they laughed at you that doesn't mean anything because they liked you too.

One of the new men who came to work there

17
Loss of intellectual powers is accompanied by loss of physical strength. Reminder that Algernon eventually died.

18
Symbol. Flowers on grave commemorate Algernon's death and Charlie's own loss.

19
Charlie still identifies with Algernon because Algernon was only other living thing that shared his experience. He remembers enough to know he is being made fun of, and it is worse now because he knows he once was intelligent.

20   Analyzing
Why does Charlie tell Miss Kinnian to go away? To allow Miss Kinnian to see him would be humiliating. He remembers glimpses of his former self.

21
Donnegan recognizes Charlie's great personal courage and treats him with sympathy and understanding.

22   Summarizing
What gives Charlie the strength to return to work? Knowledge that his co-workers' insensitivities arose from ignorance.

TRANSPARENCY 21

Literary Elements
Elements of the Short Story – invites students to examine some of the basic elements of fiction.

23
Characterization. Joe represents change in attitude of Charlie's old co-workers. They have learned compassion through knowing Charlie.

24
Loyalty of his friends touches Charlie deeply. His intellectual degeneration has not affected his ability to feel emotions.

25 Making Generalizations
What does Charlie's return to class demonstrate? He has lost touch with his previous experiences. He has picked up where he left off before surgery.

26 Drawing Conclusions
Analyzing
Why does Charlie use the expression, "I reely pulled a Charlie Gordon"? What effect does this phrase have? He perceives his actions as dumb and makes fun of himself. Used here, the expression is particularly poignant; Charlie has obviously retained some of the self-awareness of his intelligent phase, yet he can only helplessly observe his own behavior.

VISUAL CONNECTIONS
Ideas for Writing
Charlie enters Miss Kinnian's class when he is no longer a student there. You might have students write about how they would react to finding themselves in a class in which they did not belong. Students who change schools must deal with similar feelings during their first few days among strangers. Some students might write about a time they did something embarrassing. How did their friends react?

---

after I went away made a nasty crack he said hey Charlie I hear your a very smart fella a real quiz kid. Say something intelligent. I felt bad **23** but Joe Carp came over and grabbed him by the shirt and said leave him alone or Ill break your neck. I didnt expect Joe to take my part so I guess hes really my friend.

Later Frank Reilly came over and said Charlie if anybody bothers you or trys to take advantage you call me or Joe and we will set em **24** straight. I said thanks Frank and I got choked up so I had to go into the supply room so he wouldn't see me cry. Its good to have friends.

July 28 I did a dumb thing today I forgot I wasnt in Miss Kinnians class at the adult center any more like I use to be. I went in and sat down in my old seat in the back of the room and she looked at me funny and she said **25** Charles. I dint remember she ever called me that before only Charlie so I said hello Miss Kinnian Im redy for my lesin today only I lost my reader that we was using. She startid to cry and run out of the room and everybody looked at me and I saw they wasnt the same pepul who used to be in my class.

Then all of a suddin I rememberd some things about the operashun and me getting **26** smart and I said holy smoke I reely pulled a Charlie Gordon that time. I went away before she came back to the room.

Thats why Im going away from New York for

Encourage students to ask their school librarians and guidance counselors for help in exploring the careers of some of the characters in the story, specifically in the fields of psychology, medicine (especially psychiatry and neuro-

surgery), and special education. Have students share what they learn in brief, oral reports to the class or record it in their journals or learning logs.

---

good. I dont want to do nothing like that agen. I dont want Miss Kinnian to feel sorry for me. Evry body feels sorry at the factery and I dont want that eather so Im going someplace where nobody knows that Charlie Gordon was once a genus and now he cant even reed a book or rite good.

Im taking a cuple of books along and even if I cant reed them Ill practise hard and maybe I wont forget every thing I lerned. If I try reel hard maybe Ill be a littel bit smarter then I was before the operashun. I got my rabits foot and my luky penny and maybe they will help me.

If you ever reed this Miss Kinnian dont be sorry for me Im glad I got a second chanse to be smart becaus I lerned a lot of things that I never even new were in this world and Im **27** grateful that I saw it all for a littel bit. I dont know why Im dumb agen or what I did wrong maybe its becaus I dint try hard enuff. But if I try and practis very hard maybe Ill get a littl smarter and know what all the words are. I remember a littel bit how nice I had a feeling with the blue book that has the torn cover when I red it. Thats why Im gonna keep trying to get smart so I can have that feeling agen. Its a good feeling to know things and be smart. I wish I had it rite now if I did I would sit down **28** and reed all the time. Anyway I bet Im the first dumb person in the world who ever found out something importent for sience. I remember I did somthing but I dont remember what. So I guess its like I did it for all the dumb pepul like me.

Good-by Miss Kinnian and Dr Strauss and evreybody. And P.S. please tell Dr Nemur not to be such a grouch when pepul laff at him and he woud have more frends. Its easy to make frends if you let pepul laff at you. Im going to have lots of frends where I go. P.P.S. Please if you get a chanse put some flowrs on Algernons grave in the bak yard . . .

Reading Check

1. Who suggests that Charlie volunteer for the experiment?
2. What is Charlie's job at the factory?
3. How does Charlie learn while he is asleep?
4. What is the first sign of change in Algernon?
5. What are the first symptoms of the deterioration of Charlie's intelligence?

For Study and Discussion

Analyzing and Interpreting the Story

1. "Flowers for Algernon" is a story about a young man who undergoes a remarkable transformation, or change, through surgery. According to the Progress Report dated March 8, what are the doctors planning to do with their daring techniques?

2. What evidence in the entries of March 10 through April 18 shows Charlie's increase in intelligence?

3. In the entry of April 20, Charlie's feelings change. What happens to make him feel ashamed?

4a. As Charlie becomes *more* intelligent, how do his relations with other people change? b. How do the doctors, Miss Kinnian, and the people at the factory treat him when he *loses* his intelligence?

5. Charlie feels shame again in the entry of May 20. a. What does Charlie learn about himself in the scene with the dishwasher? b. What resolution does he make at the end of this entry?

6. The entry of May 23 opens with the dramatic words: "It happened today." What hap-

27
Characterization. Charlie still believes trying hard will get him ahead. His blaming himself needlessly makes his situation all the more poignant.

28 Finding Main Ideas
What thought comforts Charlie? Knowledge that his pain served greater purpose of helping others like him.

READING CHECK
1. Miss Kinnian (p. 242).
2. Janitor (p. 245).
3. Machine feeds information to his subconscious mind (pp. 244–245).
4. He bites Charlie (p. 255).
5. Emotional instability and absent-mindedness (p. 257).

FOR STUDY AND DISCUSSION
1. Triple Charlie's intelligence by surgical means.
2. On March 29, distinguishes between hospital and laboratory. Syntax, usage improved by April 3. Learns difference between conscious and subconscious on April 3. By April 6, has beaten Algernon. Becomes involved with story of Robinson Crusoe on April 9. Asks question *why* on April 14. Corrects himself, learns from trial and error on April 17.
3. Realizes friends like to have him around so they can laugh at him; learns what it means "to pull a Charlie Gordon."
4a. He becomes lonelier, more aware of his isolation. 4b. Dr. Strauss feels guilty; Miss Kinnian cries; factory people support him.
5a. Realizes he once was willing to be humiliated for acceptance. 5b. To use his knowledge to help increase human intelligence levels.
6. Algernon bit him; regression, change in behavior probably will occur in Charlie.

Students who are interested in film might want to watch the movie *Charly* and compare it to the short story. Suggest that students compare only one aspect of the two versions, such as the characterization of Charlie or the plot.

Require evaluations that tell which version the students liked better and why. Comparisons may be presented as speeches that can be videotaped or audiotaped for inclusion in student portfolios. Consult with students to agree on how their comparisons will be assessed. (See

Portfolio Assessment and Professional Support Materials for additional information on student portfolios.)

---

7. He has regressed completely to former state, being the fool to win what he mistakenly believes is friendship.

8a. Perhaps warning Charlie that desire for knowledge may cost him happiness of innocent state, that humans should not try to assume powers of gods. **8b.** His new intelligence isolates him from other people; he is lonely, angry.

9a. Will lose new intelligence; may die prematurely. **9b.** When Algernon bites Charlie, failure of experiment seems clear; June 10 entry says, "I guess the same thing is or will soon be happening to me."

10. Algernon has had same operation, and his future is Charlie's future; Charlie sympathizes, identifies with Algernon.

11a. Responses will vary. Probably, given his strong motivation to learn, he would have done it under any circumstances. **11b.** On March 7, told it might be temporary, says he knows, but "I don't care if it herts." In last entry, he says he learned about things he had never known existed and is "grateful that I saw it all for a littel bit."

LITERARY ELEMENTS
1. She is crying.
2. Focuses sympathy more on Charlie.
3. Increases immediacy, personal feeling of story.

LANGUAGE AND VOCABULARY
1. Spelling, punctuation, word usage.
2. His intelligence is increasing.
3. Can discuss own case, describe details.

---

pened, and why does Charlie see such significance in it?

7. In his P.S., Charlie says, "Its easy to make frends if you let pepul laff at you. Im going to have lots of frends where I go." Why is this statement sad?

8. In the entry of April 30, one of Charlie's co-workers, Fanny, says that it was evil when Eve listened to the snake and ate from the tree of knowledge. **a.** Why do you think she reminds Charlie of the temptation of Adam and Eve? **b.** How does Charlie, like Adam and Eve, have to pay a terrible price for his decision?

9a. What is going to happen to Charlie? **b.** How do you know?

10. Why is Algernon so important to Charlie?

11a. If Charlie had understood what would happen to him, do you think he would still have chosen to be intelligent, or to be limited mentally, as he is in the beginning and the end of this story? **b.** What evidence from his own reports can you find to support your answer?

Literary Elements

Understanding Point of View

"Flowers for Algernon" is written from the point of view of Charlie Gordon, the narrator. You learn about the characters and events in the story only through what Charlie writes in his reports. A story told by one of its characters is written in the **first-person point of view.** (The first-person pronoun is *I*, and it is an *I* who tells the story.)

The first-person point of view enables you to learn the narrator's thoughts and feelings, but it limits your understanding of other characters. First-person narrators can report only conversations and events they are aware of. Charlie's limited understanding of the people

around him is clear at the beginning of his story. For example, what is really happening to Miss Kinnian in this entry of April 15?

> I said all my frends are smart people but there good. They like me and they never did anything that wasnt nice. Then she got something in her eye and she had to run out to the ladys room.

A writer may choose any of the characters in the story to be the narrator. Why do you think Daniel Keyes made Charlie Gordon the narrator, instead of Miss Kinnian or one of the doctors? Why do you think he chose to write the story in the form of personal reports, which are like diary entries?

Language and Vocabulary

Identifying Levels of Usage

As Charlie Gordon's intelligence changes, his use of language also changes. Notice the dramatic contrast in the following sentences.

> I dint see nuthing in the ink but he said there was picturs there other pepul saw some picturs.

> I am sorry, however, that my own contribution to the field must rest upon the ashes of the work of two men I regard so highly.

What mistakes can you find in the first sentence? This type of language, or level of usage, is called **nonstandard English** because it does not follow the generally accepted rules of English usage and English spelling.

The second sentence is an example of **standard English,** the level of usage most widely accepted by English-speaking people. When Charlie Gordon begins to write in standard English, what do you realize is happening to him mentally?

Charlie's command of vocabulary also changes in this story. His intelligence is probably at its peak on June 4 and 5. How do the reports written on these two days show that he has acquired an extensive scientific vocabu-

4 lary? Contrast these reports with the one written on March 8.

Despite the different levels of usage in his Progress Reports, Charlie Gordon retains the **5** same human feelings. Did your own feelings for Charlie change after his writing improved? Why or why not?

Focus on Writing a Short Story

Experimenting with Point of View

The **point of view** of a story is the vantage point from which readers see the events and characters. When you write a story, you can choose between these points of view.

First-person point of view: The narrator is a character in the story and tells it in his or her own words. This point of view uses the first-person pronouns *I, me, my, we, our,* and so on. (Example: "Flowers for Algernon")

Third-person point of view: The narrator is outside the story. Characters are referred to with third-person pronouns, such as *he, she,* and *they.* (Example: "The Parachutist")

Experiment with **point of view** by writing the first paragraph for the same story in two different ways. For example, you might want to retell the story of a movie or television show that you saw recently. In your first version, use first-person point of view. In your second version, use third-person point of view. When you have finished writing, exchange papers with a classmate and offer each other suggestions. Save your notes.

About the Author

Daniel Keyes   (1927–   )

Daniel Keyes says he is "fascinated by the complexities of the human mind," as "Flowers for Algernon" shows. The story won the Hugo Award given by the Science Fiction Writers of America in 1959, and it has been translated into many languages. Keyes expanded the story into a novel, which won the Nebula Award for science fiction in 1966. The story was also successful as a television play called *The Two Worlds of Charlie Gordon* and as a movie called *Charly.* The novel was adapted into a stage musical in 1980. Keyes won a special award from the Mystery Writers of America for *The Minds of Billy Milligan* (1981), which continues his interest in psychological themes.

Keyes was born in New York City and graduated from Brooklyn College. He has worked as a merchant seaman, a fiction editor, and a photographer. He has taught English at Ohio University in Athens, Ohio, since 1962, and is director of the university's creative writing center.

About the Artwork

Photographing fog is not difficult, but it is important to have the camera no colder than the outside air. If the lens is colder, fog will condense on it, blurring the view and not giving a true picture of the scene. It is best to photograph with natural light, as flash will bounce back, diminishing any depth in the picture.

Ideas for Writing

Fog blurs images and muffles sound. You might have students write about an experience they have had with fog or make up a story based on how the photograph makes them feel.

Relating Expression Skills

You may wish to lead a discussion relating the mood of this photograph to music. Ask students what music makes them feel the way the photograph does. Perhaps some students could bring records or tapes to class and discuss the relationship between the music and the photograph.

The Land and The Water

SHIRLEY ANN GRAU

At some point in our lives, we all realize that death can touch us at any time. Read the story to see how the author explores this theme.

1 From the open Atlantic beyond Timbalier Head[1] a few scattered foghorns grunted, muffled and faint. That bank[2] had been hanging offshore for days. We'd been watching the big draggers[3] chug up to it, get dimmer and dimmer, and finally disappear in its grayness, leaving only the stifled sounds of their horns behind. It had been there so long we got used to it, and came to think of it as always being there, like another piece of land, maybe.

2 The particular day I'm thinking about started out clear and hot with a tiny breeze—a perfect day for a snipe or a sailfish.[4] There were a few of them moving on the big bay, not many. And they stayed close to shore, for the

3 barometer was drifting slowly down in its tube and the wind was shifting slowly backward around the compass.[5]

Larger sailboats never came into the bay—it was too shallow for them—and these small ones, motorless, moving with the smallest stir of air, could sail for home, if the fog came in, by following the shore—or if there was really no wind at all, they could be paddled in and beached. Then their crews could walk to the nearest phone and call to be picked up. You had to do it that way, because the fog always came in so quick. As it did that morning.

My sister and I were working by our dock, scraping and painting the little dinghy.[6]

4 Because the spring tides washed over this stretch, there were no trees, no bushes even, just snail grass and beach lettuce and pink flowering sea lavender, things that liked salt. All morning it had been bright and blue and shining. Then all at once it turned gray and wet, like an unfalling rain, moveless and still. We went right on sanding and from being sweaty hot we turned sweaty cold, the fog chilling and dripping off our faces.

5 "It isn't worth the money," my sister said. She is ten and that is her favorite sentence. This time it wasn't even true. She was the one who'd talked my father into giving us the job.

I wouldn't give her the satisfaction of an answer, though I didn't like the wet any more

---

1. **Timbalier** (tăm′bəl-yā′) **Head:** the part of Louisiana that juts into Tambalier Bay.
2. **bank:** a mass of fog.
3. **draggers:** trawlers, or fishing boats that use huge nets to catch fish.
4. **snipe . . . sailfish:** sailboats.
5. **the barometer . . . compass:** A drop in atmospheric pressure and a change in wind direction are signs that a storm is approaching.
6. **dinghy** (dĭng′ē): a small rowboat.

PREREADING FOCUS

The headnote emphasizes that this author is writing about a topic that can be particularly difficult. Ask students to discuss the problems inherent in writing about a difficult subject.

The Land and the Water

1
Title of story originally was "The Reach of Fog."

2
Narration. Story told from **first-person point of view.** Reader knows incidents in the story have made lasting impression on narrator since she is still thinking about them some time after the events.

3 Summarizing
Why are the boats staying close to shore? There are signs of an approaching storm, and boaters do not want to be too far from shore when storm comes.

4
Vegetation is determined by tidal amplitude. Only salt-tolerant plants survive even occasional inundation by tides.

5
Narrator's sister is apparently younger than narrator.

With a storm approaching, the narrator's father and brother help search for three young neighbors who have not returned from sailing. Hours later, the men return exhausted but without finding the boat or the neighbors.

You might allow uninterrupted class time for silent reading of this moving, sensitive story. Exploring the **For Study and Discussion** questions on p. 271 in class will allow careful handling of sensitive issues that may surface. You may wish to use the **Literary Elements** section on p. 271 in considering the **theme** of the story.

6
Setting. Descriptive details that include cultural artifacts ("hard metal curlers") give a concrete sense of when (1950s–1960s) and where the story occurs.

7 Drawing Conclusions
What does the detail "summer house" in the description reveal? Family evidently is able to spend summers on the coast; this is not their year-round home.

8
Oilskin: waterproof cloth, typically worn by sailors and fishers.

9
In this paragraph, author presents pleasing picture of leisurely afternoon with such images as "minnow-flecked water," "tumbled heap of rocks," swooping sea gull, and shells skipped along water.

10 Making Generalizations
What does Robert's reply suggest about his character? He is sarcastic; does not volunteer much information.

than she did. It was sure to make my hair roll up
6 in tight little curls all over my head and I would have to wash it again and sleep on the hard metal curlers to get it back in shape.

Finally my sister said, "Let's go get a Coke."

When we turned around to go back up to the house, we found that it had disappeared. It was only a couple of hundred yards away, right behind us and up a little grade, a long slope of beach plum and poison ivy, saltburned and scrubby. You couldn't see a thing now, except gray. The land and the water all looked the same; the fog was that thick.

There weren't any Cokes. Just some bottles of Dr. Pepper and a lot of empties waiting in cases on the back porch. "Well," my sister said, "let's go tell her."

She meant my mother, of course, and we didn't have to look for her very hard. The house wasn't
7 big, and being a summer house, it had very thin walls: we could hear her playing cards with my father in the living room.

They were sitting by the front window. On a clear day there was really something to see out there: the sweep of the bay and the pattern of the inlets and, beyond it all, the dark blue of the Atlantic. Today there was nothing, not even a bird, if you didn't count the occasional yelp of a sea gull off high overhead somewhere.

"There's no Cokes," my sister said. "Not a single one."

"Tomorrow's grocery day," my mother said. "Go make a lemonade."

"Look," my father said, "why not go back to work on the dinghy? You'll get your money faster."

8 So we went, only stopping first to get our oilskin hats. And pretty soon, fog was dripping from the brims like a kind of gentle rain.

But we didn't go back to work on the dinghy.
9 For a while we sat on the edge of the dock and looked at the minnow-flecked water, and then we got out the crab nets and went over to the tumbled heap of rocks to see if we could catch anything. We spent a couple of hours out there, skinning our knees against the rough barnacled[7] surfaces. Once a sea gull swooped down so low he practically touched the tops of our hats. Almost but not quite. I don't think we even saw a crab, though we dragged our nets around in the water just for the fun of it. Finally we dug a dozen or so clams, ate them, and tried to skip the shells along the water. That was how the afternoon passed, with one thing or the other, and us not hurrying, not having anything we'd rather be doing.

We didn't have a watch with us, but it must have been late afternoon when they all came down from the house. We heard them before we saw them, heard the brush of their feet on the grass path.

It was my mother and my father and Robert, my biggest brother, the one who is eighteen. My father had the round black compass and a coil of new line. Robert had a couple of gas lanterns and a big battery one. My mother had the life jackets and a little wicker basket and a thermos bottle. They all went out along the narrow rickety dock and began to load the gear into my father's *Sea Skiff.* It wasn't a big boat and my father had to take a couple of minutes to pack it, stowing the basket way up forward under the cowling[8] and wedging the thermos bottle on top of that. Robert, who'd left his lanterns on the ground to help him, came back to fetch them.

"I thought you were at the McKays," I said. "How'd you get over here?"

"Dad called me." He lifted one eyebrow.
10 "Remember about something called the telephone?" And he picked up his gear and walked away.

"Well," my sister said.

They cast off; the big outboard sputtered gen-

---
7. **barnacled** (bär′nə-kəld): covered with barnacles, tiny shellfish that cling to rocks and wood.
8. **cowling:** a metal lid that covers an engine.

MEETING INDIVIDUAL NEEDS
ESL/LEP • Several references are made in the story to types of boats. Ask students how many they can find mentioned in the text (sailboat, dinghy, skiff, launch). Invite students to use a dictionary to find the meaning of each. What distinguishes the different types of boats? Challenge students to name five more specific types of boat. (Responses could include barge, catamaran, battleship, galleon, rowboat, yacht, clipper, sloop, trawler, and canoe.)

VISUAL CONNECTIONS
Exploring the Subject
Fog is no more than ground-level clouds—tiny water droplets suspended in the air. There are two main types of fog, advection and radiation. Advection fog forms when the sea and land are different temperatures or when currents, such as the warm Gulf Stream and cold Labrador Current, cause moisture-laden air to condense as it moves from warm to cold. Radiation fog is formed as moisture evaporated from lakes and streams cools and condenses after sunset. The fog in this story would be advection fog.

11
Foreshadowing. Fog's effect on visibility of boaters suggests trouble.

12 Drawing Conclusions
What is suggested by the fact that the father and Robert leave in the fog and by the sound of other boats out in the fog? Since boats come in when it is foggy, something unusual is happening.

13
Foreshadowing. Narrator's mother behaves unexpectedly, which also suggests something significant is happening.

14
Girls are curious but maintain show of outward disinterest.

11 tly, throttled way down. They would have to move very slowly in the fog. As they swung away, Robert at the tiller, we saw my father set out his compass and take a bearing off it.

My mother watched them out of sight, which didn't take more than a half-minute. Then she stood watching the fog for a while and, I guess, following the sound of the steady put-put. It seemed to me, listening to it move off and blend with the sounds of the bay—the sounds of a lot of water, of tiny waves and fish feeding—that I **12** could pick out two or three other motors.

Finally my mother got tired of standing on the end of the dock and she turned around and **13** walked up to us. I expected her to pass right by and go on up to the house. But she didn't. We could hear her stop and stand looking at us. My sister and I just scraped a little harder, pretending we hadn't noticed.

"I guess you're wondering what that was all about?" she said finally.

"I don't care," my sister said. She was lying. She was just as curious as I was.

My mother didn't seem to have heard her. "It's Linda Holloway and Stan Mitchell and Butch Rodgers."

We knew them. They were sailing people, a little older than I. A little younger than my brother Robert. They lived in three houses lined up one by the other on the north shore of Marshall's Inlet. They were all-right kids, nothing special either way, sort of a gang, living as close

Have students do research on storms, including hurricanes, that occur in coastal regions of the United States. You could have students work in groups. One group might find out about barometric pressure—what it is, how it is measured, and how it relates to storms. Another group might research wind, rain, and ocean conditions during storms. Encourage groups to come up with their own storm-related topics to research and then have them make short presentations to the class.

GEOGRAPHY LINK

Have students locate Louisiana, Timbalier Bay, the Gulf of Mexico, and the Atlantic Ocean on a map of the United States. Interested students might also use encyclopedias and other references to find information about the terrain,

15 Drawing Conclusions
What do sister's comments indicate? She does not appreciate the possible consequences of the situation.

16 Analyzing
What does the mother mean? Responses will vary. Mother refers to barometer's steady drop in pressure; dangerous storm is probable. Young girl seems oblivious to children's peril and the anxiety their parents must be experiencing.

17
Onomatopoeia. "Grumble" suggests sound of thunder.

18
Sister shows concern for first time.

19
Atmosphere. Descriptions of rain, thunder, and fog create gloomy, unsettling mood.

20
Narrator's father wearily explains why their search has ended.

as they did. This year they had turned up with a new sailboat, a twelve-foot fiberglass job that somebody had designed and built for Stan Mitchell as a birthday present.

"What about them?" my sister asked, forgetting that she wasn't interested.

"They haven't come home."

"Oh," I said.

"They were sailing," my mother said. "The Brewers think they saw them off their place just before the fog. They were sort of far out."

"You mean Dad's gone to look for them?"

She nodded.

15 "Is that all?" my sister said. "Just somebody going to have to sit in their boat and wait until the fog lifts."

My mother looked at us. Her curly red hair was dripping with the damp of the fog and her **16** face was smeared with dust. "The Lord save me from children," she said quietly. "The glass is twenty-nine eighty and it's still going down fast."

We went back up to the house with her, to help fix supper—a quiet nervous kind of supper. The thick luminous fish-colored fog turned into deep solid night fog. Just after supper, while we were drying the dishes, the wind sprang up. It shook the whole line of windows in the kitchen and knocked over every single pot of geraniums on the back porch.

"Well," my mother said, "it's square into the east now."

A low barometer and a wind that had gone backwards into the east—there wasn't one of us didn't know what that meant. And it wasn't more **17** than half an hour before there was a grumble of approaching thunder and the fog began to swirl around the windows, streaming like torn cotton as the wind increased.

18 "Dad'll come back now, huh?" my sister asked.

"Yes," my mother said. "All the boats'll have to come back now."

We settled down to television, half watching it and half listening to the storm outside. In a little while, an hour or so, my mother said, "Turn off that thing."

"What?"

"Turn if off, quick." She hurried on the porch, saying over her shoulder: "I hear something."

19 The boards of the wide platform were wet and slippery under our feet, and the eaves of the house poured water in steady small streams that the wind grabbed and tore away. Between the crashes of thunder, we heard it too. There was a boat coming into our cove. By the sound of it, it would be my father and Robert.

"Is that the motor?" my mother asked.

"Sure," I said. It had a little tick and it was higher pitched than any of the others. You couldn't miss it.

Without another word to us she went scuttling across the porch and down the stairs toward the cove. We followed and stood close by, off the path and a little to one side. It was tide marsh there, and salt mud oozed over the tops of our sneakers. The cove itself was sheltered—it was in the lee[9] of Cedar Tree Neck—but even so it was pretty choppy. Whitecaps were beginning to run high and broken, wind against tide, and the spume from them stung as it hit your face and your eyes. You could hear the real stuff blowing overhead, with the peculiar sound wind has when it gets past half a gale.

My father's boat was sidling up to the dock now, pitching and rolling in the broken water. Its motor sputtered into reverse and then the hull rubbed gently against the pilings. They had had a bad time. In the quick lightning flashes you could see every scupper[10] pouring water. You could see the slow weary way they made the lines fast.

20 "There wasn't anything else to do," my father was saying as they came up the path, beating their arms for warmth; "with it blowing straight

---

9. **lee:** the side away from the wind; the protected side.
10. **scupper:** an opening in a ship's side at deck level that allows water to run off the deck.

climate, and wildlife of coastal Louisiana. Suggest that students record the information they learn in their journals or learning logs.

MEETING INDIVIDUAL NEEDS
Auditory Learners • Have students find sound effect recordings of fog horns, howling winds, loud thunder, and crashing waves. Listening to such sounds might help students better understand the setting of this story. Students might also enjoy using these sound effects to enhance an oral reading of the entire story or the portion of the story about the storm (p. 268).

out of the east, we had to come in."

Robert stopped a moment to pull off his oilskins. Under them his shirt was as drenched as if he hadn't had any protection at all.

21 "We came the long way around," my father said, "hugging the lee as much as we could."

"We almost swamped," Robert said.

Then we were at the house and they went off to dry their clothes, and that was that. They told us later that everybody had come in, except only for the big Coast Guard launch. And with only one boat it was no wonder they didn't find them.

22 The next morning was bright and clear and a lot cooler. The big stretch of bay was still shaken and tousled-looking, spotted with whitecaps. Soon as it was light, my father went to the front porch and looked and looked with his glasses. He checked the anemometer[11] dial and shook his head. "It's still too rough for us." In a bit the coast Guard boats—two of them—appeared, and a helicopter began its chopping noisy circling.

It was marketing day too, so my mother, my sister, and I went off, as we always did. We stopped at the laundromat and the hardware, and then my mother had to get some pine trees for the slope behind the house. It was maybe four o'clock before we got home.

The wind had dropped; the bay was almost quiet again. Robert and my father were gone, and so was the boat. "I thought they'd go out again," my mother said. She got a cup of coffee and the three of us sat watching the fleet of boats work their way back and forth across the bay, **26** searching.

23 Just before dark—just when the sky was beginning to take its twilight color—my father **24** and Robert appeared. They were burned lobster-red with great white circles around their eyes where their glasses had been.

11. **anemometer** (ăn′ə-mŏm′ə-tər): an instrument that measures wind speed.

"Did you find anything?" my sister asked.

My father looked at my mother, who was opening a can of beer for him.

"You might as well tell them," she said. "They'll know anyway."

"Well," my father said, "they found the boat."

"That's what they were expecting to find, wasn't it?" my mother asked quietly.

He nodded. "It's kind of hard to say what happened. But it looks like they got blown on East Shoal with the tide going down and the chop tearing the keel out."[12]

"Oh," my mother said.

"Oh," my sister said.

"They found the boat around noon."

My mother said: "Have they found them?"

"Not that I heard."

25 "You think," my mother said, "they could have got to shore way out on Gull Point or some place like that?"

"No place is more than a four-hour walk," my father said. "They'd have turned up by now."

And it was later still, after dark, ten o'clock or so, that Mr. Robinson, who lived next door, stopped on the porch on his way home. "Found one," he said wearily. "The Mitchell boy."

"Oh," my mother said, "oh, oh."

"Where?" my father asked.

"Just off the shoal, they said, curled up in the eelgrass."

"My God," my mother said softly.

Mr. Robinson moved off without so much as a goodbye. And after a while my sister and I went to bed.

But not to sleep. We played cards for an hour or so, until we couldn't stand that any more. Then we did a couple of crossword puzzles **27** together. Finally we just sat in our beds, in the chilly night, and listened. There were the usual sounds from outside the open windows, sounds of the land and the water. Deer moving about in

12. **the chop tearing the keel out:** the choppy waves tearing out the keel, or supporting beam at the bottom of the boat.

21
Severity of storm is indicated again by course men were forced to travel home.

Drawing Conclusions
22 Analyzing
What does this description indicate? How does this description affect the story's mood? It is still windy but the storm is over. Mood seems more hopeful with clear morning.

23
Darkness symbolizes death; foreshadows fate of the missing teenagers.

24
Imagery. Description of sunburned father and brother creates vivid image.

25
Inference. Because they should have been found or should have been able to get home by this time, all three of the missing are presumed dead.

26
Sisters play cards and do crossword puzzles to take their minds off tragedy.

27
Girls' vague yet intense fear heightens their sense of uncertainty.

Encourage interested students to find out about the U.S. Coast Guard and its functions in peacetime and in war. Students might also be interested in learning about the typical day of a U.S. Coast Guard officer. Students may find such information in encyclopedias and in books about the Coast Guard as well as by requesting information directly from the nearest U.S. Coast Guard installation. If possible, invite a Coast Guard officer to speak to your class.

28 Drawing Conclusions
What does girls' awareness of surrounding sounds indicate? They are feeling vulnerable.

29
Characterization. Narrator is sensitive; her thoughts and emotions trigger physical responses.

30
Symbol. Dawn symbolizes awakening; in this case, symbolizes girl's early awakening to concept of death.

31
Theme. Narrator has come to realize that death can come unexpectedly and even when one is young; now, because of her new awareness, the sea, which had been an enjoyable place to spend an afternoon, seems dangerous.

32
Girl is running from her understanding of death's inevitability.

33 Drawing Conclusions
What does the mother's reaction indicate? She apparently understands what has affected her daughter.

---

the brush on their way to eat the wild watercress and wild lettuce that grew around the spring. The deep pumping sounds of an owl's wings in the air. Little splashes from the bay—the fishes and the muskrats and the otters.

28 "I didn't know there'd be so many things moving at night," my sister said.

"You just weren't ever awake."

"What do you reckon it's like," she said, "being on the bottom in the eelgrass?"

"Shut up," I told her.

"Well," she said, "I just asked. Because I was wondering."

"Don't."

29 Her talking had started a funny shaking quivering feeling from my navel right straight back to my backbone. The tips of my fingers hurt too, the way they always did.

"I thought the dogs would howl," she said.

"They can't smell anything from the water," I told her. "Now quit."

She fell asleep then and maybe I did too,
30 because the night seemed awful short. Or maybe the summer dawns really come that quick. Not dawn, no. The quiet deep dark that means dawn is just about to come. The birds started whistling and the gulls started shrieking. I got up and looked out at the dripping beach plum bushes
32 and the twisted, salt-burned jack pines, then I slipped out the window. I'd done it before. You lifted the screen and lowered yourself down. It wasn't anything of a drop—all you had to watch was the patch of poison ivy. I circled around the house and took the old deer trail down to the bay. It was chilly, and I began to wish I had brought
33 my robe or a coat. With just cotton pajamas my teeth would begin chattering very soon.

I don't know what I expected to see. And I didn't see anything at all. Just some morning fog in the hollows and around the spring. And the dock, with my father's boat bobbing in the run of the tide.

The day was getting close now. The sky over-

head turned a sort of luminous dark blue. As it did, the water darkened to a lead-colored gray. It looked heavy and oily and impenetrable.[13] I tried to imagine what would be under it. I always thought I knew. There would be horseshoe crabs and hermit crabs and blue crabs, and scallops squirting their way along, and there'd be all the different kinds of fish, and the eels. I kept telling myself that that was all.

But this time I couldn't seem to keep my thoughts straight. I kept wondering what it must be like to be dead and cold and down in the sand and mud with the eelgrass brushing you and the crabs bumping you and the fish—I had felt their little sucking mouths sometimes when I swam.

The water was thick and heavy and the color of a mirror in a dark room. Minnows broke the surface right under the wharf. I jumped. I couldn't help it.

31 And I got to thinking that something might come out of the water. It didn't have a name or a shape. But it was there.

I stood where I was for a while, trying to fight down the idea. When I found I couldn't do that, I decided to walk slowly back to the house. At least I thought I was going to walk, but the way the boards of the wharf shook under my feet I know that I must have been running. On the path up to the house my bare feet hit some of the sharp cut-off stubs of the rosa rugosa bushes, but I didn't stop. I went crashing into the kitchen because that was the closest door.

The room was thick with the odor of frying bacon, the softness of steam: my mother had gotten up early. She turned around when I came in, not seeming surprised—as if it was the most usual thing in the world for me to be wandering around before daylight in my pajamas.

"Go take those things off, honey," she said. "You're drenched."

13. **impenetrable** (ĭm-pĕn′ə-trə-bəl): Unable to be penetrated or pierced; also, unable to be understood.

CLOSURE

Ask students to identify the effect of the teen-agers' drownings on the main characters' atti-tudes and actions. Have them identify the **theme** of "The Land and the Water."

EXTENSION AND ENRICHMENT

Students who feel comfortable doing so might recount in writing the first close encounter of a young person (themselves or someone else) with the reality of someone's death. Students might also enjoy reading Grau's novels. *The Hard Blue*

Sky (1958) tells of life in an isolated Louisiana island community. *The House on Coliseum Street* (1961), set in New Orleans, tells of an unloved girl's sad experiences. Short story collections are *The Black Prince* (1955) and *The Wind Shifting West* (1973).

"Yes ma'am," I told her.

I stripped off the clothes and saw that they really were soaking. I knew it was just the dew 34 and the fog. But I couldn't help thinking it was something else. Something that had reached for me, and missed. Something that was wet, that had come from the water, something that had splashed me as it went past.

Reading Check

1. Which ocean serves as the setting in the story?

2. What are the narrator and her sister doing at the beginning of the story?

3. Why do the narrator's father and brother go out in the boat?

4. What news does Mr. Robinson bring?

For Study and Discussion

Analyzing and Interpreting the Story

1. At the beginning of this story, a girl and her sister are peacefully scraping their dinghy near a dock on a bright, sunny day. At the end of the story, the girl runs in terror from the same dock in the darkness just before dawn. **a.** What tragedy has occurred to bring about this change in her feelings? **b.** What details show that she now views the water as a fright-ening place, a place where death lives?

2. The land and the water produce very dif-ferent feelings in this story. Find passages in the story that suggest that the land is a safe and com-fortable place.

3. Why do you suppose the girl goes down to the dock in the darkness before dawn?

4. A young person's first reaction to death is a common subject in stories. Do you think the

girl's reactions in this story are believable? Why or why not?

5. Why do you think the author titled the story "The Land and the Water"?

Literary Elements

Stating the Theme

Many stories are written purely for entertain-ment. Detective stories, Westerns, love stories—many of these are written just to be enjoyed. But many stories are also written to illustrate some central idea or truth about human life or experi-ence. This central idea is called the **theme** of the story. Writers do not generally state the theme in their stories. They expect the reader to derive the theme from all the events that take place in the story.

The theme of a story is different from the **plot**, which is the sequence of events that occur in the story. Plot is what happens in the story. Theme is what the story means.

Here are two statements about this story. One is a statement of the plot. The other is a state-ment about the theme. **Which one states the theme?**

1. The narrator hears that three of her young neighbors are missing on a sailboat. The fog is coming in, and a storm is expected. She waits while her father and older brother aid in the search. Late the next day she hears that the three young people have been lost. One of them is found dead in the eelgrass. Shortly before dawn the next day, she goes to the dock. There she feels some terror in the water and rushes home.

2. A girl learns for the first time that death can touch young people like her. She discovers how fragile and vulnerable human life is. Though nature can seem mild and pleasant, beneath its sur-face are destructive forces which can destroy with-out warning and without reason. She has escaped death this time, but she realizes that it can reach out for her just as it has reached out and caught her young neighbors.

34

Theme. She feels same wetness that touched sea's victims; real-izes her own mortality.

READING CHECK
1. Atlantic, specifically Gulf of Mexico (p. 265).
2. Scraping, painting dinghy (p. 265).
3. To look for three young neigh-bors missing on sailboat (pp. 267–268).
4. Mitchell boy's body found (p. 269).

FOR STUDY AND DISCUSSION
1a. Drowning of Mitchell boy.
1b. Descriptions of water; her feeling that something in water "had reached for me, and missed" (pp. 270–271).
2. Living room is a comforting, secure sight (p. 266); in house drying dishes as wind picks up outside (p. 268); kitchen is haven (p. 270).
3. Responses will vary. Perhaps she thought she would find some explanation for the deaths or that she might be able to *know* what it was like to be "dead and cold and down in the sand and mud."
4. Responses will vary. Person's first real encounter with death of-ten a combination of horror, puz-zlement, and curiosity. People commonly associate events with places or things; image of boy curled up in eelgrass has changed narrator's feelings about the wa-ter.
5. Responses will vary. Title em-phasizes that land and water are separate entities, perhaps repre-senting life and death; serves to illustrate narrator's new aware-ness of fragile barrier between life and death, the land and the water.

LITERARY ELEMENTS
1. Second statement.

2. Perhaps because water is formless, boundless, takes any shape; humans need water to live, but water can cause death. Thus, water can seem mysterious and unknowable, like death.

3. Responses will vary. May include *Moby-Dick*, movie *Jaws*, Loch Ness Monster, sea-dragons slain by Beowulf, monsters Scylla and Charybdis from the *Odyssey*.

LANGUAGE AND VOCABULARY

1. *Anemone:* from Greek word *anemone*, meaning "altered," after *anemos*, "wind."
Barometer: from Greek words *baros*, meaning "weight," and *metron*, meaning "a measure."
Meter: from *metron.*
Pedometer: from Latin words *pedis*, meaning "foot," and *metron.*
Thermometer: from Greek words *therme*, meaning "heat, warmth," and *metron.*
Thermos: from *therme.*

FOCUS ON WRITING A SHORT STORY

Students might create story wheels around their **themes**. Have students draw large circles and write their theme statements in the center. Then have them divide their circles into three pie-shaped parts labeled **characters**, **setting**, and **plot**. Students can complete their wheels by listing their notes in the appropriate areas. This activity will illustrate how the characters, setting, and plot of a story must revolve around its center—the theme.

ABOUT THE AUTHOR

Shirley Grau's first collection of short stories, *The Black Prince and Other Stories,* was considered one of the most important American fiction works of 1955. Her work is characterized by careful craftsmanship.

This story might have suggested other meanings to you. **2** Why do you think the author associates death with *water*? **3** Do you know of any other stories where something evil and fearful is associated with the sea?

Language and Vocabulary

Analyzing Words with Greek and Latin Roots

At one point in this story, the father checks the *anemometer* dial. As the footnote on page 269 indicates, an *anemometer* is a device for measuring the speed of wind. It comes from *anemos*, a Greek root word meaning "wind," and *metron*, a Greek word meaning "a measure."

1 What Latin and Greek roots are used to form these words? A dictionary will help.

anemone	meter	thermometer
barometer	pedometer	thermos

Focus on Writing a Short Story

Exploring a Theme

The **theme** of a story is its central idea about life or human experience. Some writers have a theme in mind before they begin to write a story. For other writers, the theme of a story may emerge during the writing process. Some stories are written purely for entertainment and do not have a serious theme.

Choose a theme for a short story of your own. You may use one of the following suggestions, or you may choose another theme.

1. A true friend brings out the best in you.
2. Nature can be destructive.
3. Happiness comes from giving more than from receiving.
4. It takes courage to admit one's mistakes.

When you have chosen a theme, make some notes about a plot, a setting, and some characters that you might use to develop the theme into a story. Save your notes.

About the Author

Shirley Ann Grau   (1929–   )

Shirley Ann Grau was born in New Orleans, Louisiana, and graduated from Tulane University. Grau has said that she gets many ideas for her novels and short stories from reading newspapers: "It's the quickest, easiest way to store up characters in your head. I read the back pages and the obituaries....I'm convinced that writers are rather inefficient computers. You store bits of characters away and then wait. Eventually your little computer clicks and multiple pieces fit together."

Grau won the Pulitzer Prize for fiction in 1965 for her third novel, *The Keepers of the House.* The story is set in a small Alabama town and revolves around three generations of a family. She said the book considers "the whole human plight of how do you cope with evil." Her novels and short-story collections have established Grau as an important Southern writer. She says that the goal of all her fiction is to make the muddle of human life more understandable, more bearable. Grau's novels include *The Condor Passes* (1971) and *Evidence of Love* (1977).

The Tell-Tale Heart

EDGAR ALLAN POE

Edgar Allan Poe's stories linger in our memories. As you read, try to figure out how Poe creates an unforgettable atmosphere for a chilling tale.

1 True!—nervous—very, very dreadfully nervous I had been and am; but why *will* you say that I am mad? The disease had sharpened my senses—not destroyed—not dulled them. Above all was the sense of hearing acute. I heard all things in the heaven and in the earth. I heard many things in hell. How, then, am I mad? Hearken! and observe how healthily—how calmly I can tell you the whole story.

It is impossible to say how first the idea entered my brain; but once conceived, it haunted me day and night. Object there was

2 none. Passion there was none. I loved the old man. He had never wronged me. He had never given me insult. For his gold I had no desire. I think it was his eye! yes, it was this! He had the eye of a vulture—a pale blue eye, with a film over it. Whenever it fell upon me, my blood ran cold; and so by degrees—very gradually—I made up my mind to take the life of the old

3 man, and thus rid myself of the eye forever.

4 Now this is the point. You fancy[1] me mad. Madmen know nothing. But you should have seen *me.* You should have seen how wisely I proceeded—with what caution—with what foresight—with what dissimulation[2] I went to work! I was never kinder to the old man than during the whole week before I killed him. And every

night, about midnight, I turned the latch of his door and opened it—oh, so gently! And then, when I had made an opening sufficient for my head, I put in a dark lantern,[3] all closed, closed, so that no light shone out, and then I thrust in my head. Oh, you would have laughed to see how cunningly I thrust it in! I moved it slowly—very, very slowly, so that I might not disturb the old man's sleep. It took me an hour to place my whole head within the opening so far that I could see him as he lay upon his bed. Ha!—would a madman have been so wise as this? And then, when my head was well in the room, I undid the lantern cautiously—oh, so cautiously—cautiously (for the hinges creaked)—I undid it just so much that a single thin ray fell upon the vulture eye. And

5 this I did for seven long nights—every night just at midnight—but I found the eye always closed; and so it was impossible to do the work; for it was not the old man who vexed me, but

6 his Evil Eye. And every morning, when the day broke, I went boldly into the chamber, and spoke courageously to him, calling him by name in a hearty tone, and inquiring how he had passed the night. So you see he would have been a very profound old man, indeed, to suspect that every night, just at twelve, I looked in upon him while he slept.

---

1. **fancy:** imagine.
2. **dissimulation** (dĭ-sĭm′yə-lā′shən): concealment of plans or intentions.

3. **dark lantern:** a lantern with a shutter that can conceal its light.

MOTIVATIONAL SUMMARY
The narrator, declaring that he is not mad, tells how and why he skillfully murdered an old man to get rid of his cold, blue eye. Policemen visiting with him at first suspect nothing, but the narrator begins to hear a strange sound.

PRESENTATION
This story is a dramatic monologue with great auditory impact. Horror—like humor—is more intense and satisfying when shared. You may want to read the story aloud or have another skilled reader do it. An oral presentation will be helpful for students because the vocabulary and sentence structure will challenge eighth graders. After reading the story, allow time for spontaneous questions and comments, possibly introducing the **For Study and Discussion** questions on p. 277 for class discussion. The class should enjoy

7
Characterization. "Fairly chuckled," in this situation, suggests madness. Narrator perceives himself outwitting not the man, but the dark power manifested in the eye.

8 Summarizing
What happens that is different when the narrator enters the room this time? He makes a noise and the man calls out. Since he "chuckled" before, the narrator may have secretly intended to wake the old man this time.

9
Motivation. Narrator, like old man, is afraid of death—no doubt in part a cause of his insanity and motive for crime.

10
Imagery. "Mournful influence of the unperceived shadow"—meaning Death—creates a menacing, frightening image.

11
Simile. Poe's comparison of beam of light to a spider's thread increases the horror of scene.

12 Analyzing
Does the narrator really hear the old man's heartbeat? Responses will vary. The narrator is insane; he may be hearing or feeling his own heartbeat.

Upon the eighth night I was more than usually cautious in opening the door. A watch's minute hand moves more quickly than did mine. Never before that night had I *felt* the extent of my own powers—of my sagacity.[4] I could scarcely contain my feelings of triumph. To think that there I was, opening the door, little by little, and he not even to dream of my **7** secret deeds or thoughts. I fairly chuckled at the idea; and perhaps he heard me; for he moved on the bed suddenly, as if startled. Now you may think that I drew back—but no. His room was black as pitch with the thick darkness (for the shutters were close fastened, through fear of robbers), and so I knew that he could not see the opening of the door, and I kept pushing it on steadily, steadily.

I had my head in, and was about to open the **8** lantern, when my thumb slipped upon the tin fastening, and the old man sprang up in bed, crying out—"Who's there?"

I kept quite still and said nothing. For a whole hour I did not move a muscle, and in the meantime I did not hear him lie down. He was still sitting up in the bed listening—just as I have done, night after night, hearkening to the deathwatches[5] in the wall.

Presently I heard a slight groan, and I knew it was the groan of mortal terror. It was not a groan of pain or of grief—oh, no!—it was the low stifled sound that arises from the bottom **9** of the soul when overcharged with awe. I knew the sound well. Many a night, just at midnight, when all the world slept, it has welled up from my own bosom, deepening, with its dreadful echo, the terrors that distracted me. I say I knew it well. I knew what the old man felt, and pitied him, although I chuckled at heart. I

knew that he had been lying awake ever since the first slight noise, when he had turned in the bed. His fears had been ever since growing upon him. He had been trying to fancy them causeless, but could not. He had been saying to himself, "It is nothing but the wind in the chimney—it is only a mouse crossing the floor," or "It is merely a cricket which has made a single chirp." Yes, he had been trying to comfort himself with these suppositions: but he had **10** found all in vain. *All in vain;* because Death, in approaching him, had stalked with his black shadow before him, and enveloped the victim. And it was the mournful influence of the unperceived shadow that caused him to feel—although he neither saw nor heard—to *feel* the presence of my head within the room.

When I had waited a long time, very patiently, without hearing him lie down, I resolved to open a little—a very, very little crevice[6] in the lantern. So I opened it—you cannot imagine how stealthily, stealthily— **11** until, at length, a simple dim ray, like the thread of the spider, shot from out the crevice and fell full upon the vulture eye.

It was open—wide, wide open—and I grew furious as I gazed upon it. I saw it with perfect distinctness—all a dull blue, with a hideous veil over it that chilled the very marrow in my bones; but I could see nothing else of the old man's face or person: for I had directed the ray as if by instinct, precisely upon the damned spot.

And have I not told you that what you mistake for madness is but overacuteness of the senses?—now, I say, there came to my ears a low, dull, quick sound, such as a watch makes when enveloped in cotton. I knew *that* sound well, too. It was the beating of the old man's heart. It increased my fury, as the beating of a drum stimulates the soldier into courage.

---

4. **sagacity** (sə-găs′ə-tē): keen intelligence and good judgment.
5. **deathwatches:** small insects which make a ticking sound, believed by superstitious people to be a forewarning of death.

6. **crevice:** an opening. The shutter opens to let the light shine out.

finding instances where Poe creates a "single overwhelming impression" as described in the **Literary Elements** section on p. 278.

MEETING INDIVIDUAL NEEDS

ESL/LEP • Poe makes liberal use of adverbs. Remind students that many adverbs can be identified by their *–ly* endings. Invite students to find as many adverbs in the story as they can. Then call on individual students to use these adverbs in original sentences.

13 But even yet I refrained and kept still. I scarcely breathed. I held the lantern motionless. I tried how steadily I could maintain the ray upon the eye. Meantime the hellish tattoo[7] of the heart increased. It grew quicker and quicker, and louder and louder every instant. The old man's terror *must* have been extreme! It grew louder, I say, louder every moment!—do you mark[8] me well? I have told you that I am nervous: so I am. And now at the dead hour of the night, amid the dreadful silence of that old house, so strange a noise as this excited me to uncontrollable terror. Yet, for some minutes longer I refrained and stood still. But the beating grew louder, louder! I thought the heart **14** must burst. And now a new anxiety seized me—the sound would be heard by a neighbor! The old man's hour had come! With a loud yell, I threw open the lantern and leaped into the room. He shrieked once—once only. In an instant I dragged him to the floor, and pulled the heavy bed over him. I then smiled gaily, to find the deed so far done. But, for many minutes, the heart beat on with a muffled sound. This, however, did not vex me; it would not be heard through the wall. At length it ceased. The old man was dead. I removed the bed and examined the corpse. Yes, he was stone, stone dead. I placed my hand upon the heart and held it there many minutes. There was no pulsation. He was stone dead. His eye would trouble me no more.

15 If still you think me mad, you will think so no longer when I describe the wise precautions I took for the concealment of the body. The night waned,[9] and I worked hastily, but in silence. First of all I dismembered the corpse. I cut off the head and the arms and the legs.

I then took up three planks from the flooring of the chamber, and deposited all between the scantlings.[10] I then replaced the boards so cleverly, so cunningly, that no human **16** eye—not even *his*—could have detected anything wrong. There was nothing to wash out—no stain of any kind—no blood spot whatever. I had been too wary for that. A tub had caught all—ha! ha!

When I had made an end of these labors, it was four o'clock—still dark as midnight. As the bell sounded the hour, there came a knocking **17** at the street door. I went down to open it with a light heart, for what had I *now* to fear? There entered three men, who introduced themselves, with perfect suavity,[11] as officers of the police. A shriek had been heard by a neighbor during the night; suspicion of foul play had been aroused; information had been lodged at the police office, and they (the officers) had been deputed to search the premises.

I smiled, for *what* had I to fear? I bade the gentlemen welcome. The shriek, I said, was my own in a dream. The old man, I mentioned, **18** was absent in the country. I took my visitors all over the house. I bade them search—search *well*. I led them, at length, to *his* chamber. I showed them his treasures, secure, undisturbed. In the enthusiasm of my confidence, I brought chairs into the room, and desired them *here* to rest from their fatigues, while **19** I myself, in the wild audacity[12] of my perfect triumph, placed my own seat upon the very spot beneath which reposed the corpse of the victim.

The officers were satisfied. My *manner* had convinced them. I was singularly at ease. They sat, and while I answered cheerily, they chatted of familiar things. But, ere long, I felt myself getting pale and wished them gone. My head ached, and I fancied a ringing in my ears; but still they sat and still they chatted. The

---

7. **tattoo:** here, a rhythmic beating.
8. **mark:** here, pay attention to.
9. **waned** (wānd): drew to a close.

10. **scantlings:** crosspieces of wood.
11. **suavity** (swäv′ə-tē): politeness.
12. **audacity** (ô-dăs′ə-tē): daring.

13
Symbol. Sound of the heart represents fear, perhaps guilt, and drives narrator into "uncontrollable terror."

14
Foreshadowing. The narrator's morbid fear that the old man's heartbeat will be heard by others will be his undoing.

15
Irony. Narrator's actions merely convince reader of his insanity.

16 Analyzing
Why does the narrator emphasize the word "his"? He imagines that old man's eye has extraordinary powers.

17
Irony. Narrator has "light heart," believing his worries are over now that he has rid himself of the old man's "evil eye."

18
Characterization. Overconfident, narrator imagines himself in total control of situation.

19
Narrator sets stage for exposure of crime.

Have students write the events of the story in the form of an official police report that might have been made by one of the officers who came to search the house. Ask students to consider how and why the police officer's version of the story might differ from the narrator's.

VISUAL CONNECTIONS

About the Artist

Arthur Rackham, English illustrator and watercolorist, was born in London. He studied art formally for a short time but was mainly self-taught. He was well known as an illustrator of the fantastic. In addition to Poe's work, he illustrated *Grimm's Fairy Tales, Aesop's Fables, Rip Van Winkle, Peter Pan, Andersen's Fairy Tales,* and many other literary works. He won gold medals for his work in Milan (1906), Barcelona (1911), and Paris (1912).

About the Artwork

The coloring, perspective, and expressions of characters in this painting contribute to its dark mood. Rackham's use of muted color and dramatic, dark shading produces a terrifying somber effect. The painting's perspective is unusual; it not only shows, center stage, the narrator's attempts to conceal the evidence of his crime, it also reveals the evidence he has hidden beneath the floor boards. The expressions of the three policemen let the viewer know they are not fooled, and the narrator's expression clearly shows his insanity.

ringing became more distinct—it continued and became more distinct; I talked more freely to get rid of the feeling; but it continued and gained definiteness—until, at length, I found that the noise was *not* within my ears.

No doubt, I now grew *very* pale—but I talked more fluently, and with a heightened voice. Yet the sound increased—and what could I do? It **20** was *a low, dull, quick sound—much such a sound as a watch makes when enveloped in cotton.* I gasped for breath—and yet the officers heard it not. I talked more quickly—more vehemently; but the noise steadily increased. I arose and argued about trifles, in a high key and with violent gesticulations;[13] but the noise steadily increased. Why *would* they not be gone? I paced the floor to and fro with heavy strides, as if excited to fury by the observations of the men—but the noise steadily increased. Oh **21** what *could* I do? I foamed—I raved—I swore! I swung the chair upon which I had been sitting, and grated it upon the boards, but the noise arose over all and continually increased. It grew louder—louder—*louder!* And still the men chatted pleasantly, and smiled. Was it possible they heard not? No, no! They heard!—they suspected—they *knew!*—they were making a *mockery* of my horror—this I thought, and this I think. But anything was better than this agony! Anything was more tolerable than this derision![14] I could bear those hypocritical smiles no longer! I felt that I must scream or die!—and now—again!—hark! louder! louder! louder! *louder!*—

13. **gesticulations** (jĕ-stĭk'yə-lā'shənz): gestures; movements of the arms and legs.
14. **derision** (dĭ-rĭzh'ən): mockery.

Frontispiece by Arthur Rackham (1867–1939) from *Tales of Mystery and Imagination* (1935) by Edgar Allan Poe.
Print Collection, Miriam and Ira D. Wallach Division, Division of Art, Prints and Photographs, The New York Public Library, Astor, Lenox and Tilden Foundations

22 "Villains!" I shrieked, "dissemble[15] no more! I admit the deed!—tear up the planks!—here, here!—it is the beating of his hideous heart!"

15. **dissemble** (dĭ-sĕm'bəl): pretend.

Reading Check

1. What is the narrator's sharpest sense?
2. What is it about the old man that disturbs the narrator?
3. How does the narrator treat the old man during the week before he kills him?
4. How does the narrator try to hide his crime?
5. What causes the narrator to admit his crime?

For Study and Discussion

Analyzing and Interpreting the Story

1. In the first sentence of this horror story, the narrator asks a question: ". . . but why *will* you say that I am mad?" How does the narrator try to convince you that he is sane?

2. What does the narrator claim is his motive for killing the old man?

3. The narrator tells how he opens the old man's door every night for seven nights. Why doesn't he kill the man until the eighth night?

4. Find the passage in which the narrator first describes hearing the sound of the old man's heart (page 274). How does this sound affect him?

5. At first, the narrator is able to convince the three police officers that nothing is wrong. What do you think makes him reveal where the old man's body is hidden?

20 Finding Details
When has the narrator previously described this sound? He described the old man's heart as beating with a sound like this and said that this noise drove him into a fury.

21
Increased use of italics, exclamation marks, dashes, and shorter and shorter phrases mirrors tension and chaos of madman's thoughts.

22
Irony. Narrator earlier claims old man's loud heartbeat propelled him into committing murder; here, it forces him to confess the crime.

READING CHECK
1. Hearing (p. 273).
2. His "vulture" eye (p. 273).
3. Kinder than ever (p. 273).
4. Dismembers corpse, hides it under floor planks, uses tub to catch blood (p. 275).
5. Imagines he hears old man's heart beating and loses control (p. 277).

FOR STUDY AND DISCUSSION
1. Explains how disease has sharpened his senses, noting how "healthily—how calmly" he tells story; tells how wisely, cautiously he planned murder.
2. To rid himself forever of the "vulture" eye that made his blood run cold.
3. Could kill old man only if "vulture" eye was open.
4. It increases the narrator's "fury."
5. Responses will vary. He thinks they hear sound but pretend not to in order to torture him until he cannot stand it. Some students may suggest that his conscience makes him imagine heartbeat.

Visual Learners • As an extension of the Literary Elements section below, ask students to interpret the atmosphere of the story visually, either in a collage or in an original painting or poster. What colors best express the emotional effect of the story? What images?

1. Repetition of words *very* and *nervous;* dashes; emphasis on word *will.*
2. Dashes, exclamation points, stressed words; repetition of words *increased* and *louder;* repeated anxious questions, use of specific words to describe his actions: "heightened voice," "gasped for breath," "talked more quickly—more vehemently," "in a high key," argued with "violent gesticulations," "paced," "heavy strides," "foamed," "raved," "swore," "grated it [chair] over floor," "agony," "scream," "shrieked."
3. It feeds on dead, rotting animals; connotes death.
4. Effect would be of innocence, harmlessness, not of menace.
5. Responses will vary. Most students will be horrified by story.

LANGUAGE AND VOCABULARY

Synonyms
1. a—annoy
2. d—clever
3. d—smother

Antonyms
4. b—shallow
5. c—unemotional
6. d—honest

Literary Elements

Responding to Atmosphere

Poe once said that he wanted to give the readers of his stories a "single overwhelming impression." In other words, he wanted to create a certain **atmosphere**, or emotional effect. Poe uses several techniques to create the atmosphere in this unusual story.

1 The very first word of the first sentence is set off with an exclamation point: "True!" In what other ways does the first sentence emphasize the narrator's nervousness?

Sometimes Poe uses short, jerky sentences and dashes to create an effect of nervousness and tension. Look back at the passage on page 277 beginning "No doubt, I now grew *very* pale. . . ." 2 Which details in this passage make you feel the narrator's excitement and increasing nervousness?

A single word can help create atmosphere. For example, Poe compares the old man's eye 3 to the eye of a *vulture*. What kind of bird is a vulture? Suppose Poe had compared the eye to the eye of a robin, or the eye of a kitten. 4 How would the effect be different?

5 If you had to identify the "single overwhelming impression" that this story created for you, what would you say it was: horror, pity, sadness, fear, or something entirely different?

Language and Vocabulary

Recognizing Analogies

Vocabulary questions that ask you to identify synonyms or antonyms usually involve a pair of words. Some other vocabulary questions, called **analogies**, involve two pairs of words. You must first decide what relationship exists between the words in the first pair. The same relationship applies to the second pair.

An analogy question has a special format and uses special symbols. This is one type of analogy question:

bright : cheerful :: fierce : _____

a. happy **b.** gentle **c.** savage **d.** fearful

The two dots (:) stand for "is to"; the four dots (::) stand for "as." The example, therefore, reads "Bright *is to* cheerful *as* fierce *is to* _____ ." Since the first two words, *bright* and *cheerful*, are synonyms, the correct answer is **c.** The word *savage* means the same thing as *fierce*.

Complete the following analogies:

Synonyms

1. coax : persuade :: vex : _____
   a. annoy **c.** walk
   b. rave **d.** dare
2. alien : foreign :: cunning : _____
   a. soothing **c.** sad
   b. alarming **d.** clever
3. savor : enjoy :: stifle : _____
   a. squirm **c.** confess
   b. move **d.** smother

Antonyms

4. courageous : cowardly :: profound : _____
   a. deep **c.** simply
   b. shallow **d.** brave
5. good : evil :: vehement : _____
   a. reckless **c.** unemotional
   b. tricky **d.** angry
6. brief : lengthy :: hypocritical : _____
   a. unusual **c.** envious
   b. friendly **d.** honest

For Oral Reading

Reading a Story Aloud

Read "The Tell-Tale Heart" aloud. Make your voice sound the way you imagine the narrator would sound. At different points in the story, he sounds nervous, calm, excited, frightened, pleased with himself, or almost hysterical.

CLOSURE
Ask students to identify and analyze the narrator's motives and the thoughts and actions that reveal his growing madness and that create **atmosphere.**

EXTENSION AND ENRICHMENT
Some students could tape-record "The Tell-Tale Heart," using appropriate background music and sound effects. Students may want to read other horror stories by Poe. "The Fall of the House of Usher," "The Pit and the Pendulum,"

"The Cask of Amontillado" and "The Masque of the Red Death" are recommended. You might suggest that they make posters featuring key images from these stories.

Be sure to notice the punctuation marks as you read. The dashes signal places where the narrator interrupts his thoughts, and the exclamation marks signal strong feeling or excitement. Notice especially the last paragraphs of the story. How would you read these sentences to suggest the narrator's panic?

Focus on Writing a Short Story

Making a Story Map

A **story map** is an outline that shows all the key elements of a short story. Here is a sample story map:

Story Map

Title: _____
Point of View: _____
Setting
   Time: _____
   Place: _____
Characters
   1: _____
   2: _____
   3: _____
Plot
   Background: _____
   Conflict: _____
      Event 1: _____
      Event 2: _____
      Event 3: _____
   Climax: _____
   Outcome: _____

Create a story map for your own short story. You may either develop one of the story ideas you have explored in this unit, or you may choose a new idea. When you have finished your story map, share your work with a small group of classmates. Offer each other comments on your ideas for stories. Save your notes.

About the Author

Edgar Allan Poe (1809–1849)

The Granger Collection, New York

Edgar Allan Poe—poet, short-story writer, and literary critic—is one of the most important American writers of the nineteenth century. He is called "the father of the American short story" and "the inventor of the detective story."

Poe was the son of professional actors. He was orphaned by the age of three and was raised and educated by a wealthy couple in Richmond, Virginia, named Allan. As Poe grew older, he came into conflict with his foster father, who disapproved of his literary ambitions. Poe attended the University of Virginia briefly and then enlisted in the army. Hoping to win back the favor of his foster father, he served for a short time as a West Point cadet. But he purposely got himself dismissed when he realized that reconciliation with the Allan family was impossible.

Marriage to his young cousin Virginia Clemm provided Poe with some affection and family life. He eked out a meager living by writing for newspapers and literary magazines. Though he was a good editor, Poe was unable to hold a job for long. His temper was erratic, and he always seemed to be exhausted and underfed. In 1847 his young wife died of tuberculosis. Poe, grief-stricken and ill, survived her by only two years.

One of Poe's most famous poems is "The Raven." Some of Poe's other famous horror stories are "The Fall of the House of Usher," "The Pit and the Pendulum," "The Cask of Amontillado," and "The Masque of the Red Death."

FOCUS ON WRITING A SHORT STORY
Remind students that they do not necessarily have to start with a title to fill out their story maps. Suggest that they start with whatever element they feel is their strongest idea and work up and down their maps from there. For example, a student might start with a character, then go to conflict, then to setting, back to character, and so forth. A title will probably be one of the last elements to consider.

ABOUT THE AUTHOR
Poe wrote more than sixty short stories, nearly fifty poems, plus books of literary criticism. He felt he was primarily a poet; he believed that poetry should not arouse passions or offer moral guidance but instead be the "rhythmical creation of beauty." His poems are noted for their sound and rhythm and are therefore best read aloud. In addition to "The Raven," his most popular poems are "Annabel Lee" and "The Bells."

Of Poe's short stories, the horror stories remain the best-known. His original detective stories such as "The Gold Bug" and "The Murders in the Rue Morgue," feature clever detectives who, through the use of deductive reasoning, unravel mysteries. In his short stories, Poe liked to create intellectual excitement, something he deliberately avoided in his poetry.

The overall aim is for students to demonstrate an understanding of criteria that can be used to evaluate short stories.

You may want to begin by listing and discussing the basic elements of the short story: **plot, character, setting, point of view,** and **theme.** You might also refer students to **Close Reading of a Short Story** at the beginning of this unit.

Then students might work in small groups to answer the questions for each story. Have a member of each group share the group's response.

FOCUS ON *Reading and Critical Thinking*

EVALUATING SHORT STORIES

EVALUATING SHORT STORIES

This section offers students the opportunity to become more conscious of the basic elements of the short story. It is important to note that in most stories, one or more of these elements may be developed more fully than the others. For example, a story might be primarily character-driven, with plot being of much less importance.

Answers

Answers will vary. Have students support their conclusions with evidence from the stories.
1. Students will probably find the conflict in O. Henry's story well-developed and believable.
2. Le Guin's descriptions of Mr. Underhill provide hints that he is a dragon and create interest and suspense.
3. Charlie's character is revealed through his words and actions and is clearly distinct from the characters of Miss Kinnian and Dr. Strauss, which are not fully developed.
4. The coastal setting is crucial in developing the conflict through which the narrator learns that the sea can be deadly. The heavy fog, dark skies, and other aspects of setting create a somber atmosphere and ominous mood.
5. Have students explain how the first-person point of view brings the reader closer to the terrible events in "The Tell-Tale Heart."
6. The survival instinct is powerful, causing the land and its creatures to struggle for life against all odds.

*I*n this unit you have studied the elements that make up short stories. Below are some standards you can use to *evaluate,* or judge, the quality of any short story you read. Use a separate sheet of paper to answer the questions marked with this symbol ■.

Plot

1. *Is the conflict in the story clear, well-developed, and believable?* Even stories with surprise endings, such as O. Henry's "A Retrieved Reformation," should end with a believable solution to the conflict.

2. *Is foreshadowing used to create interest and suspense?*

■ How does Ursula K. Le Guin hint in the first paragraph of "The Rule of Names" that Mr. Underhill is actually a dragon (page 220)?

Characters

3. *Do the characters' actions match their words and thoughts and the author's descriptions of them? Are their actions clearly motivated by events in the story? Are the characters clearly individuals, or are they merely predictable and shallow?*

■ Think about Charlie Gordon in "Flowers for Algernon" (page 240). How is Charlie revealed as a unique character, different from Miss Kinnian or Dr. Strauss?

Setting

4. *What role does the setting play? Does it have an important connection to the plot, or could the story have been set in any time and place?*

■ In "The Land and the Water" (page 265), how is the setting related to the lesson the narrator learns? How does the setting create atmosphere or mood in this story?

Point of View

5. *How does the point of view contribute to the story?* For example, Edgar Allan Poe uses the first-person point of view to bring the reader closer to the terrible events in "The Tell-Tale Heart" (page 273).

Theme

6. *Does the story offer some insight into human experience?* Some stories merely tell about an exciting episode. In others, the main character learns a valuable lesson. More often than not, the reader draws a conclusion about the theme from what happens in the story.

■ How would you state the message or theme of "The Parachutist" (page 235)? Test your statement by seeing if it includes all the important aspects of the story.

OBJECTIVES
The overall aim is for students to use key literary elements to write an original short story.

PRESENTATION
You may want to begin by leading a class discussion on **conflict.** Ask students to identify some of the conflicts they have encountered in their lives and write their responses on the chalkboard. Emphasize that these conflicts can

be the seeds for good stories. Encourage students to use situations, events, and **characters** from their own lives or the lives of people they know and to develop or rewrite conflicts with which they are already familiar. Students can use the prewriting questions and charts to gather

FOCUS ON Writing

WRITING A SHORT STORY

A good **short story** entertains the reader, develops a conflict or problem, and holds the reader's interest through well-developed characters, setting, and plot. In this unit you have studied some of the key elements of short stories. Now you will have the chance to write a short story of your own.

Prewriting

1. One strategy to find a story idea is to think about the people, places, and events that are most familiar to you. Another technique is to ask yourself some "What if?" questions like the following:

You can also explore story ideas by brainstorming with a small group of classmates, looking in family albums, and reviewing the notes you have made for writing assignments in this unit.

2. When you have identified a promising idea, explore the **plot** of your story in more detail by making some notes on these key elements:

- background
- conflict
- climax
- outcome

Focus especially on the main **conflict** of your story, and plan to introduce it early in order to hook the reader's interest. You can choose from these kinds of conflicts:

- a person versus another person (external conflict)
- a person versus a force of nature (external conflict)
- struggles within a character's mind or feelings (internal conflict)

Also decide in advance what the **climax** or **high point** of your story will be—the point where the conflict is settled one way or the other. This is usually the point of greatest suspense or emotion. [See **Focus** assignment on page 229.]

3. Make some notes about the **characters** in your story. A short story usually has at least two characters. Fill out a character chart like the one below for each character you plan to include:

Name: _____ Age: _____
Appearance: _____
Way of Moving and Speaking: _____
Personality Traits: _____
Likes and Dislikes: _____
Habits: _____

[See **Focus** assignment on page 234.]

HOLT WRITER'S WORKSHOP

This computer program provides help for all types of writing through guided instruction for each step of the writing process. (Program available separately.)

See *Elements of Writing, Second Course,* Chapter 6, for more instruction on creative writing.

WRITING A SHORT STORY
Nowhere is the writing process more circular and fluid than in creative writing. New ideas about plot, character, setting, point of view, and theme will surface even as students proofread. In this type of writing, structure can be helpful but should not be allowed to become rigid.

Prewriting
Have students consult the notes they kept from the **Focus on Writing** activities in this unit. If they do not find ideas for stories in their notes, have them use the techniques mentioned here. Students may benefit by summarizing the conflicts in their stories in single sentences. You may want to have students write theme statements on their story maps. Assess students' maps before they begin the writing stage.

details and ideas for their stories. The story map will be a useful aid for students when they are ready to write. Give students time to write several drafts and to experiment with **point of view** and **dialogue**. Peer groups can evaluate, suggest revisions, and proofread. To close this lesson, ask students to list the key elements of the short story and to identify which elements are strongest in their stories.

Writing

Remind students that they need to capture their readers' interest at the beginning of their stories. You might suggest that they experiment with strategies to "hook" their readers, such as vivid descriptions of setting to establish mood, dialogue that foreshadows conflict, or exciting action relevant to conflict.

Evaluating and Revising

You might set up peer-evaluation sessions and have students use the **Checklist for Evaluation and Revision**. Suggest that students incorporate as much direct dialogue as possible and read it aloud to determine whether it sounds natural. Encourage students to add, revise, and delete whole blocks of text, not just a few words or sentences here and there.

4. Sketch notes for the **setting** of your story—the time and place of the events. Make a list of descriptive details. Focus especially on **sensory details** that appeal to sight, hearing, taste, smell, and touch. [See **Focus** assignment on page 239.]

5. Decide on the **point of view,** or vantage point, from which you will tell the story. In **first-person point of view,** your narrator will be a character in the story who uses first-person pronouns, such as *I, me, my, we, our,* and so on. In **third-person point of view,** the narrator will be outside the story, and characters will be referred to with third-person pronouns, such as *he, she,* and *they.*

Each point of view has certain advantages as well as drawbacks. For example, first-person point of view brings your readers close to one character, the storyteller. On the other hand, a first-person narrator is limited to telling only about the events that he or she witnesses. [See **Focus** assignment on page 263.]

6. Using all your notes so far, make a **story map,** a plan that outlines all the main elements of your story. [See the **Focus** assignment on page 279.]

Writing

1. Use **chronological** or **time order** to tell the events of your story in the order they happened. Remember that **transitional words and phrases** can help the audience understand relationships of events and ideas. Here are some useful transitional expressions for time order:

after	finally	suddenly
at once	first	then
before	meanwhile	when
eventually	next	

2. Make your story as vivid and lifelike as you can by showing characters in action, not just telling about them. For example, you can use **dialogue** to show what your characters say and what other people say about them. Use **dialogue tags**—phrases like "he yelled" or "she laughed"—to show *how* a character speaks. Also remember to use **vivid verbs** and **sensory details** in your writing.

Evaluating and Revising

1. When you have finished your first draft, put it aside for a while. Then evaluate it with a critical eye. Pay special attention to showing events vividly and specifically.

2. You may find the following checklist helpful as you revise your short story.

Checklist for Evaluation and Revision

✓ Do I present a strong conflict for the main character at the beginning?
✓ Do I tell the story from a consistent point of view?
✓ Are the characters lifelike and believable? Is the setting clear and vivid?
✓ Does the plot have a clear high point and a satisfying outcome?

Here is how one writer revised a passage from a short story.

Writer's Model

Ramona had been avoiding Toni all
day. ~~but~~ *literally collided* They ~~ran into each other~~ *on the* outside
frozen steps of
the neighborhood library.

"You knew how much I wanted to go
blurted out angrily
on the ski trip!" Toni ~~said.~~ "Why did

you tell Mom that you thought I

should stay home instead to take care

of Paul?"

a burning in her cheeks
Ramona felt ~~very embarrassed.~~ She
took a deep breath and
~~paused for a minute. She~~ then faced

her younger sister. "I'm sorry, Toni. I

was just being selfish, I guess."

Proofreading and Publishing
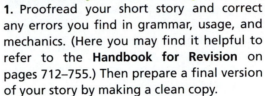

1. Proofread your short story and correct any errors you find in grammar, usage, and mechanics. (Here you may find it helpful to refer to the **Handbook for Revision** on pages 712–755.) Then prepare a final version of your story by making a clean copy.

2. Consider some of the following publication methods for your story:

- illustrate your story and post it on the class bulletin board
- read your story aloud to a class of younger students
- volunteer to read your story to someone who is visually impaired

Portfolio If your teacher approves, you may wish to keep a copy of your work in your writing folder or portfolio.

Proofreading and Publishing
You might have the class develop a proofreading checklist that focuses on errors common in narrative writing, such as inconsistent point of view and verb tense, and incorrect punctuation and capitalization in dialogue. Students can use the checklist to proofread each other's stories.

DRAMA

OVERVIEW OF THE UNIT

Plays are comfortably familiar to a generation brought up on television. Watching television, however, requires less imagination than reading and breathing life into a script. The plays in this unit challenge students to read creatively, as a reader of drama must. The first selection of the unit is A. A. Milne's zany comedy *The Ugly Duckling*. This enjoyable spoof is followed by *Pyramus and Thisby*, an excerpt from Shakespeare's comedy *A Midsummer Night's Dream*. The unit closes with the two-act drama *The Diary of Anne Frank*, an adaptation of a tragic first-person account of the Holocaust. Questions and exercises following each play focus on skills of reading dramatic literature. Special activities deal with recognizing the elements of comedy and tragedy, understanding stage terms and dramatic terms, and recreating a scene from a play. The drama unit closes with an opportunity to write an informative essay.

OBJECTIVES OF THE UNIT

The aims of the unit are for the student:

- To identify the elements of comedy and tragedy and to analyze comic and tragic themes
- To identify theatrical conventions such as stage directions and sound effects and to apply these conventions to selected plays
- To evaluate a play using an accepted method of analysis
- To identify and analyze the elements of plot, subplot, characterization, and setting in selected plays
- To determine the effects of the playwright's use of dialogue, monologue, disguise, suspense, and flashbacks in a selected play
- To identify the use of alliteration, rhyme, and parody in selected plays
- To write an informative essay
- To present a dramatic scene

CONCEPTS AND SKILLS

The following concepts and skills are treated in this unit:

CLOSE READING OF A PLAY

Guidelines for Close Reading   286
One Reader's Response   287
Looking at Yourself as a Reader   299

LITERARY ELEMENTS/TERMS AND TECHNIQUES

Recognizing the Elements of a Comedy   317
Understanding Stage Terms   317
Recognizing the Elements of a Tragedy   393
Understanding Dramatic Terms   394

LANGUAGE AND VOCABULARY SKILLS

Understanding Meanings of Words   332
Recognizing Exact Meanings   370

OPPORTUNITIES FOR WRITING

Writing About Literature
Discussing Aspects of the Play   333
Writing a Review of a Play   394

Focus on Informative Writing
Explaining a Process   318, 333
Exploring Cause and Effect   370

FOR DRAMATIZATION

Presenting a Scene   318

FOCUS ON READING AND CRITICAL THINKING

Understanding Cause and Effect   396

FOCUS ON WRITING

Writing an Informative Essay   397

TRANSPARENCIES

The following unit support materials with specific correlations to literature selections are available in the **Fine Art and Instructional Transparencies with Teacher's Notes and Blackline Masters** section of your *Audiovisual Resources Binder*.

FINE ART TRANSPARENCIES

Theme: "As If" Real Life
23 *Aria After the Ballet,* Edgar Degas
24 *The Riverbed at Shijō,* Anonymous

READER RESPONSE

25 Silent Movie Storyboard

LITERARY ELEMENTS

26 Evaluating a Play

WRITING PROCESS

27 Writing an Informative Essay

INTRODUCING THE UNIT

If possible, plan a field trip to a local theater and arrange to have the manager, director, or an actor conduct a tour. If this is not possible, invite someone from a professional theater or a drama instructor from a local high school or college as a guest speaker to preview forthcoming productions and to tell the class how a director or an actor approaches a script.

If these options are unavailable, you might work with a student committee to arrange in advance a display of theatrical posters, playbills, and reviews clipped from newspapers and magazines. Ask volunteers to tell the class about stage plays they have seen. If any students have performed in plays, ask them to share their

FOR UNIT PLANNING

◆ Transparencies 23–27: *Audiovisual Resources Binder*
◆ *Portfolio Assessment: Professional Support Materials*
◆ Test Generator

◆ Mastery Tests: Teaching Resources C, pp. 225, 227, 230
◆ Analogy Test: Teaching Resources C, p. 233
◆ Composition Test: Teaching Resources C, p. 234

SELECTION (Pupil's Page)	TEACHING RESOURCES A (page numbers shown below)							AV BINDER
	Teacher's Notes	Reading Check	Study Guide	Language Skills	Building Vocabulary	Selection Vocab. Test	Selection Test	Audio-cassette
DRAMA *Introduction* (p. 285)	150							
Van Dusen Rickert, Jr. *The Bishop's Candlesticks* (p. 287)	151				152		153	
A. A. Milne *The Ugly Duckling* (p. 300)	155	158	159	161	164	166	167	
William Shakespeare *Pyramus and Thisby* (p. 319)	169	172	174, 176, 178	180	183		185	
Frances Goodrich and Albert Hackett *The Diary of Anne Frank* (p. 334)	187	193	195, 197, 200, 202	204, 208	212, 214	216	217, 219, 221	

experiences. Discuss the differences between watching television, seeing a movie, attending a play, and reading a script.

PORTFOLIO ASSESSMENT

Suggestions for use of portfolios as support for this unit are described in the *Portfolio Assessment and Professional*

Support Materials booklet accompanying this program. Specific suggestions are provided for a variety of student projects that may be suitable for inclusion in a portfolio. In addition, copying masters are provided for guides that may be used for evaluation and assessment of student projects.

Student Learning Options

DRAMA

1. Building a Hiding Place Replica

Students might enjoy building models of the hidden rooms in which Anne Frank lived. Students could use cardboard and other materials and should base their models on Anne's description and on the stage descriptions.

2. Performing a Play

You might want to involve your students in producing a play. Some students can perform in the play while others act as directors, costume designers, stage designers, and technicians. Draw names from a box or assign responsibilities for the play. Students could present the play live to other classes or videotape it.

3. Choosing Possessions

The day before they are to read *The Diary of Anne Frank,* ask students to come to school with possessions they feel they would want with them to live happily for two years in a small place. Tell students they can bring no more than what they can physically carry in their everyday book bag. Ask students to discuss their choice of items and what they wish they could have brought but could not carry with them.

4. Experiencing a Wartime Shortage

Divide the class and give one half three pencils each and one half three ration coupons for milk. Then give every student three cards labeled with everyday objects, such as a radio, flour, or trousers that will represent illegal-market items. Explain to students that they can trade coupons, pencils, or cards representing objects for one week, trying to collect as many goods as possible. Students should not discuss their trades, so no student knows what the others are collecting, and should have a minimum of three trades. At the end of one week, students will display what they have accumulated and have a better understanding of illegal trading created by wartime shortages. Then ask students to recollect what they have heard recently in the news to determine what modern-day country might have an illegal market and what the desired illegal items might be.

VISUAL CONNECTIONS
Exploring the Subject
This eclectic production of *Two Gentlemen of Verona* combines eighteenth-century costuming with modern lighting and staging. Some of the costumes, such as those of the actors on the stairway, show the influence of the *commedia dell'arte,* an Italian dramatic form of the sixteenth century.

This Shakespearean comedy makes use of disguises and mistaken identities. The two "gentlemen," Valentine and Proteus, love Silvia, the Duke's daughter. Proteus forces Valentine into banishment, but Valentine returns in time to rescue Silvia from Proteus' assault. The Duke, impressed by Valentine's valor, bestows Silvia on him.

In order to convey the universal themes and difficult language of Shakespeare's plays to modern audiences, stage directors often present their productions with more contemporary settings. For example, *Macbeth* actually deals with medieval Scottish monarchy, but modern productions of the play have set the action among more recognizable characters, such as 1930s Chicago gangsters, Japanese feudal lords, and modern American motorcycle gangs.

284

DRAMA

The curtain has opened and the audience sees a striking *tableau vivant* (tă-blō′vē-väɴ′), a group in costume, posing silently as if in a picture.

Look at the different groups of actors and actresses. What do you think these characters will do when the play begins?

Choose one group of figures and give the characters names. Judging from their costumes, when and where do you think they live? Write the dialogue for a brief dramatic scene.

Join with other members of the class and combine ideas. See if you can come up with an idea for a play that will include all the characters onstage.

Scene from a modern production of Shakespeare's *Two Gentlemen of Verona* at the Oregon Shakespeare Festival in Ashland.

TEACHING RESOURCES C
Teacher's Notes, p. 150

DRAMA

The focus of this unit is on the analysis, interpretation, and appreciation of **drama** as literature. The activities suggested in **Introducing the Unit** will give students the opportunity to be engaged actively in the internal workings of a drama and will prepare them for the challenges of this unit, which include reading creatively and imagining plays as if they were being presented on stage. The plays encompass a wide variety of settings, styles, and genres. A. A. Milne's one-act comedy, *The Ugly Duckling,* offers a delightful **parody** of the fairy-tale genre. *Pyramus and Thisby,* from Shakespeare's *A Midsummer Night's Dream,* presents a hilariously inept performance of a tragic love story. Finally, *The Diary of Anne Frank* offers a first-person account of one family's harrowing efforts to escape the Holocaust.

Following each play, questions and activities will help students recognize and analyze elements of drama such as **flashback** and **dialogue,** and understand stage terms such as **stage directions** and **monologue.** Writing assignments allow students to focus on informative writing, to analyze aspects of a play, and to review a play. Language and vocabulary exercises give students practice in understanding the precise meanings of words. Students will also be given the opportunity to perform a scene from *The Ugly Duckling.*

The drama unit closes with **Focus on Reading and Critical Thinking** and **Focus on Writing.** The first activity helps students to examine cause-and-effect relationships, while the writing activity takes students through the process of writing an informative essay.

Ask students to consider how a director turns the playwright's script into a finished production. Tell them they are going to learn how to analyze and visualize the following play as if they were directors.

In this section, students will develop close reading skills as they read the play *The Bishop's Candlesticks*. After you have discussed the **Guidelines for Close Reading**, you might guide students through the first part of the play by reading it aloud and pausing to ask questions that will help students identify and analyze the elements of the play. Encourage students to visualize the **setting** and ask what may be learned from it. Be sure they know that the action takes place in the nineteenth century and

---

TEACHING RESOURCES C

Teacher's Notes, p. 151
Building Vocabulary, p. 152
Selection Test, p. 153

CLOSE READING OF A PLAY

1
Stage directions can also establish tone, as in *The Ugly Duckling* and *The Diary of Anne Frank*.

2
Generally, stage directions give only very general information about characters, such as that given in the stage directions for *The Bishop's Candlesticks*.

3
In addition to explicit stage directions, plays often contain implicit stage directions in **dialogue** to show actors how to play their parts. Mme. Magloire's line ". . . Let me stir up that fire a little. Such a cold night!" tells the reader that Mme. Magloire is stirring up the fire.

4
In *The Ugly Duckling* the contrast between the confident princess and her worried parents lets the audience anticipate that she will solve her own problems. Anne Frank's monologues foreshadow events; her predictions that her family will be found creates continuous **suspense**.

5
Shakespeare punctuated even his tragedies with comic scenes. *Pyramus and Thisby* is a comic scene, from the play *A Midsummer Night's Dream*.

6
The **theme** of a play must be inferred from dialogue and actions of characters.

7
Playgoers are not given this background information immediately. The playwright reveals information to the audience a little at a time.

286

Close Reading OF A PLAY

While many of the elements studied in connection with short stories are relevant to the study of drama, there are several additional elements that need to be taken into account. Dramatists fre-**1**quently make use of stage directions to create setting and to give players instructions for acting. Sound effects are often important in creating setting and mood. Sometimes a dramatist may use a narrator to comment on the action. Generally, however, dialogue is the dramatist's most important device for presenting character and for moving the action along.

Guidelines for Close Reading

2 **1.** Note any information that tells you about the setting and the characters' backgrounds. This information may be given by the playwright in stage directions, or it may be revealed during the opening scenes of the play.

3 **2.** Note clues that tell you what the players are doing or how the lines are spoken. This information is often revealed in stage directions. Sometimes you will need to infer actions, gestures, and tone from the dialogue.

4 **3.** Try to predict the action that will develop out of each scene.

5 **4.** Be alert to the mood of the play and shifts in tone. A comedy may have serious scenes, and a serious play may have scenes that are humorous. Ask yourself how these shifts in tone and mood affect your response.

6 **5.** Using your responses to the characters and events, write a statement of the theme or the underlying idea of the play.

The following play, *The Bishop's Candlesticks* by Van Dusen Rickert, Jr., is based on a famous episode in a nineteenth-century French novel, *Les Misérables (The Unfortunate Ones)*, by Victor Hugo. The central figure in **7** this story is a man named Jean Valjean, who is sentenced to prison for stealing food. During this time, ex-convicts were required to carry yellow passports, which made it difficult for them to find shelter or to earn a living.

that the candlesticks are not merely decoration: there is no electricity. Using the **One Reader's Response** notes, ask students why they think this reader focused on these details and whether or not they agree with the conclusions drawn. Ask what they would add or change, and why. Conclude the analysis of the play with a discussion of the questions asked in **Looking at Yourself as a Reader.**

The comments in the margins alongside the play represent one reader's responses. If you wish, cover up these notes and take notes of your own on a separate sheet of paper. You may wish to compare both sets of responses at a later point.

The Bishop's Candlesticks

VAN DUSEN RICKERT, JR.

CHARACTERS

1 Monseigneur   Bienvenu   (môn-sĕ-nyœr′ byȧɴ′və-nü), Bishop of Digne (dēn′yə)[1]

Mademoiselle   Baptistine   (mȧd′mwȧ-zĕl′ bȧp′tē-stēn′), his sister

Madame Magloire (mȧ-dȧm′ mȧ-glwȧr′), their servant

Jean Valjean (zhȧɴ vȧl-zhȧɴ′), an ex-convict

A Sergeant and Two Police Officers

SCENE 1

2 *The living room of the Bishop of Digne, a large oblong room plainly furnished, scrupulously[2] neat. The walls are whitewashed. There is no carpet. A fire burns in the fireplace down right; an alcove, closed by portières,[3] occupies the upstage center. A door leading outdoors is in the wall left of the alcove. Against the wall up left stands a sturdy dresser. Down left a door leads to a passage.*

The Bishop *and his* Sister *are finishing their supper. It is late evening of a winter day. The room is lighted by firelight and two can-*
3 *dles which stand on the table in* handsome silver candlesticks.

---

1. **Digne:** in southeast France, northeast of Marseilles.
2. **scrupulously** (skroo′pyə-ləs-lē): with utmost care.
3. **portières** (pôr-tyȧrz′): heavy curtains.

The Bishop's Candlesticks

1
Pronunciation of the characters' names is given so that actors will pronounce them correctly.

ONE READER'S RESPONSE

The Bishop's house is very plain except for the silver candlesticks. I wonder if all bishops in France lived this way during the nineteenth century.

2
Mood. The scene described here establishes a tranquil mood.

3
Symbol. The silver candlesticks, the only valuable items in view, represent wealth.

4 Summarizing
What do we learn about Mme. Magloire through this dialogue? She has worked for the Bishop and his sister for a long time. She knows them well, and they treat her with respect.

5
Conflict. The Bishop and his sister regard the poor differently.

6
Foreshadowing. The mention of another person suggests that he might soon appear. Audience's attention is directed toward candlesticks.

7
Characterization. The Bishop believes people may be victims of ill fortune but are not "brutes."

The servant takes very good care of the Bishop and his sister. She seems to admire the Bishop.

They had homeless people then too.

There are some people who feel this way today about homeless people.

It sounds like there's only one hotel. Where will he go?

The Bishop is kinder than the women.

Mlle.[4] **Baptistine.** Will you have coffee, brother?
The Bishop. If you please.
Mlle. Baptistine. I'll ring for Madame Magloire....

[Mme.[5] Magloire *enters from the passage.*]

The Bishop. But here she is—and bringing our coffee. Madame Magloire, you are wonderful; you read our minds.
Mme. Magloire. I should be able to, after all these years.
The Bishop. Of faithful service—and mind reading.
Mme. Magloire. Thank you, my lord.
Mlle. Baptistine. We'll drink our coffee in front of the fire, Madame Magloire.
Mme. Magloire. Yes, mademoiselle. Let me stir up that fire a little. Such a cold night!
Mlle. Baptistine. I'm glad all our poor have fuel and food. (*Sits at fireplace and pours coffee*)
The Bishop. Not all, I'm afraid.
Mlle. Baptistine. I meant all in the parish.
The Bishop. If we could only help them all! My heart aches on a night like this to think of poor homeless wanderers, lonely, hungry—
Mlle. Baptistine. Not all of them deserve help, I'm afraid. Some of them are good-for-nothing, ungrateful vagabonds.
Mme. Magloire. They say there's a tough-looking fellow in town now. He came along the boulevard and tried to get in to spend the night at the hotel. Of course they threw him out. A tramp with a sack over his shoulder and a terrible face. An ugly brute! (*She brings the candlesticks from the table and sets them on the mantelpiece above the fireplace.*)
The Bishop. There are no human brutes; there are only miserable men who have been unfortunate.
Mme. Magloire (*she is clearing the table*). You are as kindhearted as the good Lord himself, Bishop; but when there are fellows like that around, we say—mademoiselle and I...
Mlle. Baptistine. I have said nothing.
Mme. Magloire. Well...we say that this house isn't safe. If you don't mind, I'm going to send for the locksmith to put bolts on

4. **Mlle.:** an abbreviation for mademoiselle.
5. **Mme.:** an abbreviation for madame.

A scene from a 1935 film version of *Les Misérables*.

Photofest

Characterization. The Bishop's willingness to open his door to everyone is a sign of generous nature.

9

Man fits description given by Mme. Magloire. Audience has been prepared for his entrance. Character reactions—gasps, suppressed cries, silence—accent the effect of Valjean's rough appearance and lead the audience to react similarly.

10   Summarizing
What is the significance of the yellow passport? It is a warning that the bearer is a convict. Valjean refers to it a second time as if the Bishop has not understood its significance.

11

Irony. Convict is going out of his way to be honest with the Bishop. Not what we would expect from thief. Valjean is almost belligerent; obviously expects to be refused.

12   Expressing an Opinion
The stage directions do not reveal Mlle. Baptistine's reactions. If you were playing her part, how might you choose to act as Valjean begins to eat? Students might interpret Mlle. Baptistine's part in various ways. They might predict she would recoil in disgust, stare at Valjean, or begin to pray silently.

13

Characterization. The Bishop calls himself a priest, rather than a bishop. The playwright is reinforcing Bishop's humility. Also Bishop may have instinctively known Valjean would feel more comfortable with a priest than with a bishop.

Close Reading OF A PLAY

The Bishop doesn't seem worried about his safety or his possessions.

This must be the "ugly brute" the servant was talking about.

The Bishop actually offers him food.

The man doesn't believe that anyone would let him stay. I can imagine the expressions on the women's faces.

Valjean isn't used to being treated with respect.

these doors. It's terrible to leave these doors unfastened, so that **8** anybody can walk in. And the Bishop always calls "Come in!" the minute anyone knocks.

[*There is a loud knock.*]

The Bishop. Come in.

9 [Jean Valjean *appears in the doorway.* Mlle. Baptistine *gasps;* Mme. Magloire *suppresses a cry. There is a silence.*]

Valjean. My name's Jean Valjean. I'm a convict. I've been nineteen years in prison at hard labor. I got out four days ago, and I'm on my way to Pontarlier.[6] I've come twenty-five miles on foot today, and I'm tired and hungry. Nobody'll take me in, because I've got a convict's passport—yellow. See! They've kicked me out like a dog everywhere I stopped. I even went to the jail and asked for lodging, but the turnkey said. "Get yourself arrested, if you want to spend the night here." Then a good woman pointed out your door to me and said, "Knock there." So I did. I'm tired. Can I stay?
The Bishop. Madame Magloire, will you set another place and bring some food?
10 Valjean. Wait a minute. Did you understand? I'm a convict.
11 There's my yellow passport. Take a look at it. It says nineteen years in prison—five years for burglary and fourteen for attempted escape. It says, "This man is dangerous." Dangerous! Well, are you going to take me in?
The Bishop. Won't you sit down, monsieur?[7] Madame Magloire, you may make up the bed in the alcove.
Valjean (*lowers his sack to the floor*). "Monsieur!" You call me "monsieur!" And you're not going to put me out! (Mme. Magloire *places food on the table.*) That looks good. (*He sits.*) I've **12** been starving for four days. (*He begins to eat avidly.*) I'll pay you for this. I've got some money to pay you with.…You're an innkeeper, aren't you?
13 The Bishop. I'm a priest.
Valjean. Oh, a priest…a good priest.…That's a good one! Then you don't want me to pay—

6. **Pontarlier** (pôn′tär-lyā′): in eastern France, near the Swiss border.
7. **monsieur** (mə-syœ′): a title like "Mister" or "Sir" in English.

The Bishop. No, no. Keep your money. How much have you?

Valjean. One hundred and nine francs.

The Bishop. And how long did it take you to earn that?

Valjean. Nineteen years.

14 The Bishop. (*sighing*) Nineteen years.

Valjean. Yes, they pay us something for the work we do in prison. Not much, of course; but we get a little out of it. I really earned one hundred and seventy-one francs, but they didn't give me that much. I've still got all they paid me.

15 The Bishop. Madame Magloire, will you bring the candles to the table? It is a little dark over here.

16 Mlle. Baptistine (*timidly*). Did you . . . could you ever go to Mass while you were—in there?

Valjean. Yes, ma'am. They said Mass at an altar in the middle of the courtyard. You'll be interested in this, monsieur, since you're a priest. Once we had a bishop come to say Mass—"my lord," they called him. He's a priest who's over a lot of other

17 priests. He said Mass and wore a pointed gold thing on his head. He wasn't close to us. We were drawn up in lines on three sides of the courtyard. We couldn't understand what he said. That was the only time we ever saw a bishop.

18 The Bishop. That's very interesting.

Mlle. Baptistine. How happy your family will be to see you again after so many years.

19 Valjean. I haven't got any family.

Mlle. Baptistine. Haven't you any relatives at all? Is there no one waiting for you?

Valjean. No, nobody. I had a sister. I used to live with her and her children, but I don't know what's become of her. She may have gone to Paris.

Mlle. Baptistine. Didn't she write to you sometimes?

Valjean. I haven't heard from her in twelve years. I'll never bother her again.

The Bishop. And you're going to Pontarlier. Do you know anyone there?

Valjean. No, I don't. It's not my part of the country; but I visited there once when I was young, and I liked it—high mountains, good air, and not too many people. I thought about it often in prison and made up my mind to go there if ever—if I ever was free.

That doesn't sound like much money for nineteen years of work.

He thinks he was cheated.

He still doesn't know he's talking to a bishop.

The ex-convict wants to start a new life.

---

14 Making Inferences
Why does Bishop sigh here? Students might say Bishop sighs out of empathy with Valjean.

15
Audience's attention is drawn toward candlesticks, this time through **dialogue**. Also, act of bringing light to table as Valjean speaks about prison foreshadows Bishop's later actions that bring hope and goodness into Valjean's life.

16
Mlle. Baptistine probably hoping, though doubting, that Valjean has some religious impulses.

17
Miter: tall, decorated cap with peaks in front and back worn by high church officials as a badge of office.

18
Irony. Actor's tone of voice important here; reveals to audience how the Bishop feels about the priest whose visit to prison seems to have been done out of duty, not out of concern for prisoners.

19
Characterization. Valjean is completely alone in the world.

A scene from the Broadway production of *Les Misérables*.

Joan Marcus

The Bishop. You're going to a fine country, and there is plenty of work there: paper mills, tanneries, copper and iron foundries; and there are dairy farms all through the region. You'll have to find work, of course. What do you want to do?

Valjean. It doesn't matter. I can do any kind of work. I'm as

20 tough as steel. But, with a yellow passport, I don't know whether I can get a job.

The Bishop (*writing*). Here, take this card. If you will give it to

21 Monsieur Doumic from me…he has a tannery at Pontarlier and, what is more important, he has a heart. He will not ask you too many questions.

22 **Valjean.** Thank you, monsieur. You've been so kind, giving me this good dinner and taking me in—and all….I ought to tell you my name.

The Bishop. You have a name I know without your telling me.

Valjean. Is that right? You already knew my name?

23 **The Bishop.** Yes. Your name is…my brother. You need not tell me who you are. Those who come to this door are not asked "What is your name?" but "What is your need…or sorrow?"

Valjean. I've seen plenty of that. There's nothing else in prison. If you complain—solitary confinement. Double chains, just for nothing at all. A dog is better off than a convict! I had nineteen

24 years of it—because I stole some food. And now I'm forty-six, and I have a yellow passport.

The Bishop. You have left behind you a sad and terrible place. If you have come from it with a little kindness or peace in your heart, then you are better than any one of us.

Mme. Magloire. The bed is made now.

The Bishop. Thank you, Madame Magloire. You may clear the

25 table. And, monsieur, we know you are very tired. My sister and I will leave you to your rest. Do you need anything else?

Valjean. No…thanks.

The Bishop. Then good night, monsieur.

Mlle. Baptistine. Good night, monsieur.

[*Exit left, followed by the* Bishop. Jean Valjean *carries his sack to the bed.* Mme. Magloire *comes from the kitchen carrying silver, which she*

26 *puts away in the dresser.* Jean Valjean *watches her. When she leaves the room, he goes to the table and takes up one of the candlesticks. He looks toward the dresser. The* Bishop *enters.*]

The Bishop is going to help him get a job.

Nineteen years for stealing food. What a harsh sentence.

This is suspenseful. Is he going to steal the silver?

20
This is the third time yellow passport has been mentioned. Playwright wants to emphasize that criminal record is very difficult to overcome.

21 Summarizing Comparing/Contrasting
How does the Bishop show faith in Valjean and humanity in general? How is Monsieur Doumic like the Bishop? Bishop gives recommendation to exconvict he has just met. Like the Bishop, Doumic will not prejudge person and will be generous enough to employ ex-convict.

22
Characterization. Valjean expresses his gratitude. Reinforces the Bishop's earlier statement that people are not "brutes" but are victims of misfortune.

23
The Bishop asserts Christian ideal that people should regard one another as brothers and sisters.

24 Drawing Conclusions
What does Valjean's admission that his imprisonment was for stealing food suggest about the circumstances of his crime? Suggests that he stole out of necessity, not out of greed.

25
Characterization. The Bishop displays trust by leaving Valjean alone with silver that could be easily stolen.

26
Suspense. Since audience knows Valjean is a thief, his actions suggest that he is thinking of stealing the silver and the candlesticks.

The Bishop. I've brought you an extra cover, monsieur. It is a doeskin I bought in Germany, in the Black Forest. This is better than a blanket for warmth.

[Jean Valjean *puts down the candlestick as the* Bishop *speaks*.]

27 **Valjean** (*harshly*). Are you going to let me sleep in your house like this? You'd better think it over. I'm a thief, you know. How do you know I'm not a murderer?
The Bishop. That is as God wills it, brother.

[*He blesses* Jean Valjean *and goes slowly out of the room.* Jean Valjean *looks after the* Bishop, *motionless and unyielding. Then he blows out the candles and goes to the alcove, where he lies down on the bed without undressing.*]

[*Curtain.*]

Scene 2

28 *The room is dark.* Jean Valjean *sits on the bed. After a moment he rises and takes up his pack and tiptoes toward the door. He hesitates, looking at the dresser; then he goes to it, opens it, and takes out silver; he crouches beside his pack, putting the silver into it. There is a sound as he thrusts the silver into the pack. Alarmed, he starts up, leaving the silver basket on the floor, catches up the pack, and goes hastily out of the door.*

[*Curtain.*]

29 **Scene 3**

30 *It is morning.* Mme. Magloire *enters with dishes. Going directly to the table, she notices that the bed is unoccupied. Without seeing the basket, she runs to the dresser and finds that the silver is gone.*

Mme. Magloire. Good heavens! Oh, good heavens! Made-
31 moiselle! Monseigneur! What will the Bishop say! Oh, Mademoiselle!

27
Conflict. Valjean's words and tone (harshly) suggest **internal conflict**.

28
Suspense. Play has no **dialogue** to help create suspense here; it comes as a result of situation, actor's movements, and audience's imagination. The dark stage lighting that the stage directions specify will help.

29
The stage direction "curtain" before and after Scene 2 may not indicate the actual closing of the stage curtain. Instead, directors may merely dim and then brighten the lights. Such light changes may last only a few seconds.

30
Mme. Magloire's actions emphasize her uneasiness about Valjean's visit. Her worst suspicions are confirmed.

31
Mme. Magloire has been characterized as being able to read the Bishop's mind. Her speech helps create **suspense**. When she is unsure of what the Bishop will say, the audience is also apprehensive.

Valjean seems to be warning the Bishop, but the Bishop's strength is in his faith.

I knew he would steal the silver.

A scene from a television production of *Les Misérables* (1978).

Photofest

32 Analyzing
What is ironic about the Bishop's answer? It is literal; he has seen the basket on the floor and seems unconcerned that it is empty and out of place.

33 Drawing Conclusions
Did the Bishop really fail to understand that she was concerned about the silver? Responses will vary. Some students will say that he did, because he himself is so unconcerned. Others might say that he is trying to calm Mme. Magloire.

34
Characterization. The Bishop's reasoned response suggests that he expected the theft and that he is not merely naive.

35
For the Bishop, ownership seems to be a temporary state. Objects of value should be shared with others.

36 Analyzing
What does the Bishop's reaction to the theft show about him? He has a humane concern for others.

37
Characterization. The Bishop's humility contrasts with Mme. Magloire's disdain.

The Bishop doesn't care about the silver.

The Bishop comes to the ex-convict's defense. Since Valjean is one of the poor, the silver belongs to him.

Does this mean that the Bishop thinks it's all right for the poor to take what they need?

[Mlle. Baptistine *enters.*]

Mlle. Baptistine. Good morning, Madame Magloire. What's the matter?

Mme. Magloire. Mademoiselle! The dresser is open—and that man is gone! The silver—all our knives and forks! Where are they?

Mlle. Baptistine. You put them away there last night?

Mme. Magloire. Yes, yes, just as I always do. And now there's nothing here! Oh, my lord.

[*The* Bishop *enters. He sees the silver basket and the empty alcove.*]

The Bishop. What is it, Madame Magloire?

Mme. Magloire. The silver! Does your lordship know where the silver basket is?

32 The Bishop. Yes.

Mme. Magloire. Oh, thank heaven! I didn't know what had become of it.

The Bishop (*picking up the empty basket and handing it to her*).
33 Here it is.

Mme. Magloire. Well, but—there's nothing in it. Where's the silver?

The Bishop. Oh, then it's the silver you're worried about. I don't know where it is.

Mme. Magloire. Then it's stolen! Knives, forks, spoons—all gone. That vagabond stole them. He's gone, you see—cleared out before any of us were awake. The scoundrel!

34 The Bishop. Well, let's consider. In the first place, was the silver ours?

Mme. Magloire. Ours? And why not?

35 The Bishop. Madame Magloire, I had no right to keep that silver so long. It belonged to the poor. And this man was one of
36 the poor, wasn't he?

Mme. Magloire. Oh, it isn't that I mind for myself or mademoiselle. But, my lord, what will you eat with?

37 The Bishop. There are tin spoons.

Mme. Magloire (*with great disgust*). Tin smells.

The Bishop. And there are iron spoons.

Mme. Magloire. Iron tastes!

296

The Bishop (*chuckling*). Well, well—then there are wooden spoons. Tell me, sister, do you regret having given that poor fellow food and shelter?

38 **Mme. Magloire.** Not at all. I shall pray for him. Somehow I have a feeling that we may hear more from him.

[*They sit at the table.*]

Mme. Magloire. When I think of that cutthroat spending the night here! Suppose he had taken it into his head to kill us instead of stealing from us.

Mlle. Baptistine. He'll probably make haste to get as far away as he can. He wouldn't try to sell the silver in this neighborhood.

Mme. Magloire. I hope he'll take good care never to come this way again.

[*There is a knock at the door.* Mme. Magloire *and* Mlle. Baptistine *are startled.*]

The Bishop. Come in.

[*A Sergeant* and two Policemen, *guarding* Jean Valjean, *appear at the door.*]

Sergeant. Your excellency—
The Bishop. Come in, officer.

39 **Valjean** (*he looks up, surprised*). Excellency? Then he isn't a priest?

Policeman. Be quiet you. This is the Bishop.

40 **The Bishop.** Oh, it's you. I'm glad to see you. Why did you go off so early and without the candlesticks? They're solid silver and I gave them to you, as well as the other pieces. You can easily get two hundred francs for the pair.

Sergeant. Your excellency, we wanted to know if this fellow was telling the truth. We stopped him on suspicion and found that he had a yellow passport and this silver.

41 **The Bishop.** And he told you the silver was given him by a good old priest at whose house he spent last night.

Sergeant. He did, your excellency.

Valjean now finds out that the priest is really a bishop.

38
Mme. Magloire's response is no doubt sarcastic. Hearing more from him probably refers to belief that he will steal again. She probably is praying that he will not take more from them.

39
The term *Excellency* is used to address bishops, ambassadors, and other important officials.

40
Plot. The Bishop, to Valjean's surprise, offers him the candlesticks in addition to the stolen silver. By freely giving these items to Valjean, the Bishop exonerates him from theft.

41
The Bishop has guessed correctly that when Valjean was caught, he lied and said that the silver was given to him.

Close Reading of a Play   **297**

297

Close Reading
OF A PLAY

42
The word "misunderstanding" is ironic. The Bishop understands the situation perfectly.

The Bishop claims it was a misunderstanding. I wonder if the police suspect that he's protecting their prisoner.

43 Drawing Conclusions
Why does Valjean stammer? Having experienced years of excessive punishment for a minor crime, he is tongue-tied and confused by the Bishop's generosity.

The Bishop must feel that this man has already suffered enough. He's trying to change him into an honest man.

I think Valjean is going to change.

44
Conflict. Struggle between good and evil in Valjean is resolved. His quiet tone of voice and his gesture of kneeling suggest that the Bishop's faith in him is not misplaced. **Theme** of play is that kindness toward others can reawaken their essential goodness.

This author believed that kindness and understanding could change a hardened criminal into an honest person.

The Bishop. I see it all. Then you brought him back here. Well,
42 it's just a misunderstanding.
Sergeant. Then we can let him go?
The Bishop. Of course, let him go.

[*The* Sergeant *hands the silver to* Valjean.]

Valjean. You mean I'm free?
Policeman. Yes, it's all right. You're free.
The Bishop. But, before you go, here are your candlesticks. Take them with you.
43 **Valjean.** Monsieur…monseigneur…I…(*he stands silent, with bowed head.*)
The Bishop. Ah—good morning, officer. You and your men were quite right in doing your duty. Good morning.
Sergeant. Good day, your excellency.

[*The* Sergeant *and* Policemen *close the door and leave.*]

Mlle. Baptistine (*very softly*). Come in Madame Magloire.

[*They slip discreetly out the door down left.*]

The Bishop. Now, Jean Valjean, you may go in peace. But never forget that you have promised to use that silver to make yourself an honest man.
Valjean (*slowly*). I didn't promise.…But I…
The Bishop. Jean Valjean, my brother, you no longer belong to evil, but to good. It is your soul that I am buying for you. It belongs to God. Will you give it to Him?
44 **Valjean** (*almost inaudibly*). Yes, Father. (*He kneels.*)

[*Curtain.*]

TRANSPARENCIES 23 & 24

Fine Art

Theme: *"As If" Real Life* – explores artworks showing a public performance or one that conveys meaningful messages.

CLOSURE

Ask students to identify **dialogue** and actions that characterize the Bishop, Valjean, and Mme. Magloire. Also, have students identify the **theme** of the play.

Woodcut of Jean Valjean by Onorio Ruofolo.
The Bettmann Archive

Looking at Yourself as a Reader

As you came to the end of the play, were all your questions answered, or did you have some new questions about the characters? What do you think will happen to Jean Valjean after he leaves the Bishop's house?

If you took notes of your own as you were reading, compare your notes with those alongside the selection. Are the two sets of responses similar in some respects? Are they different in others?

Review your responses carefully. Did you find your opinions of the characters changing as the action developed? Did you find the characters believable? Meet with several classmates in a group and compare reactions. Do you find that any of your impressions are changed by listening to others' responses?

Looking at Yourself as a Reader

Students might form small groups to share their responses to the play and to compare them with the **One Reader's Response** notes. You might assign each group one of the questions in the text to discuss. Then have a representative from each group share with the class the group's consensus.

300

The Ugly Duckling

A. A. MILNE

Nothing in this comical fairy-tale kingdom is quite the way we expect it to be. The King is not very kingly. The Queen is very bossy. The Princess is not beautiful, and the Prince can't swim. As you read, think about the details Milne has used to create a story that is not at all like the usual fairy tale. Can you predict what will happen after the play ends?

Characters

The King
The Queen
The Princess Camilla
The Chancellor
Dulcibella
Prince Simon
Carlo
A Voice

Scene: *The Throne Room of the palace, a room of many doors, or, if preferred, curtain openings, simply furnished with three thrones for Their Majesties and Her Royal Highness the* Princess Camilla—*in other words, with three handsome chairs. At each side is a long seat, reserved, as it might be, for His Majesty's Council (if any), but useful, as today, for other purposes.*

The King *is asleep on his throne, with a handkerchief over his face. He is a king of any country from any storybook, in whatever costume you please. But he should be wearing his crown.*

A Voice (*announcing*). His Excellency, the Chancellor!

[*The* Chancellor, *an elderly man in horn-rimmed spectacles, enters bowing. The* King *wakes up with a start and removes the handkerchief from his face.*]

King (*with simple dignity*). I was thinking.
Chancellor (*bowing*). Never, Your Majesty, was greater need for thought than now.
King. That's what I was thinking. (*He struggles into a more dignified position.*) Well, what is it? More trouble?
Chancellor. What we might call the old trouble, Your Majesty.
King. It's what I was saying last night to the Queen. "Uneasy lies the head that wears a crown,"[1] was how I put it.
Chancellor. A profound and original thought, which may well go down to posterity.
King. You mean it may go down well with posterity. I hope so. Remind me to tell you some time of another little thing I said to Her Majesty: something about a fierce light beating

---

1. **"Uneasy . . . crown":** This line is a quotation from *Henry IV, Part II* by William Shakespeare. Throughout the play, the King quotes from famous poets and claims to have made up the lines himself. He probably really thinks he has.

The King and Queen have had no luck in finding someone to marry their plain daughter Princess Camilla until now. Not only do they have a likely candidate, Prince Simon, but they have also devised a plot to trick him into a royal wedding.

Prince Simon, however, has his own plan for the wedding day. The only person who does not seem worried about the nuptials is the Princess, who knows something special about magic spells and beauty.

To be enjoyed fully, this farce probably should be read aloud or performed. You might hold tryouts and assign parts in advance. In addition, you might appoint a "costume" committee to make something for each character to wear—perhaps

Scenes on pages 301, 304, 307, 311, 314–315 are from *The Ugly Duckling* performed by Music Mosaics, Canmore, Alberta, Canada. Puppets designed by Felix Mirbt. The King and the Chancellor are shown above.

VISUAL CONNECTIONS
Exploring the Subject

Portraying the King as an owl makes the opening scene of this production especially funny. Not only does audience catch him sleeping in the daytime, as owls do, but finds him in nightshirt and slippers. Point out to students that the puppeteer has given the King human legs, suggesting that he is more sympathetic than the Chancellor, who looks like a bird of prey. It is easy to imagine the Chancellor's fussing over the details of running the Kingdom, begrudging the small amount of money needed to oil the drawbridge. His elegant, rather formal costume gives a clue about his character; he looks as if he believes that appearance is important. His costume makes the King in his nightshirt and crown look ridiculous and out of place.

on a throne.[2] Posterity would like that, too. Well, what is it?

Chancellor. It is in the matter of Her Royal Highness' wedding.

2. **a fierce . . . throne:** These words are an approximate quotation from *Idylls of the King* by Alfred, Lord Tennyson.

King. Oh . . . yes.

Chancellor. As Your Majesty is aware, the young Prince Simon arrives today to seek Her Royal Highness' hand in marriage. He has been **6** traveling in distant lands and, as I understand, has not—er—has not——

King. You mean he hasn't heard anything.

6 Drawing Conclusions
Why does the Chancellor hesitate to speak directly? He is careful not to anger the King by referring to ugliness of the Princess.

an oversized paper-bag crown for the King and huge pipe-cleaner glasses for the Chancellor. Instead of reading stage directions aloud, have actors follow the directions as they read.

COOPERATIVE LEARNING
Have students refer to the definition of *parody* in the **Literary Terms and Techniques** at the back of their textbooks, and lead a brief discussion of what the term means. Tell students that this play is a parody of the traditional "hap-

pily-ever-after" fairy tale. Then divide the class into smaller groups and have students look back at the play to find instances of parody. (For example, Camilla's plainness parodies the fact that all fairy tale princesses are beautiful.)

Extend this activity by having students note

7
Characterization. Chancellor's halting speech reveals that he fears offending King.

8 Analyzing
What does the Chancellor mean by "elusive" beauty? Diplomatic way of saying she is ugly.

9
Inference. Although it is not stated directly, audience may infer that Court Painter was executed for failing to capture Princess' elusive beauty. His replacement avoids painting Princess for health reasons.

10 Making Inferences
What probably happened to the Chancellor's predecessor? When he mentioned resemblance of King and ugly Princess, he was removed from office and probably executed. Witty **dialogue** and comic **tone** make such talk of violence humorous instead of horrifying.

11 Summarizing
How does the King think people choose marriage partners? On basis of looks, not character.

12
Comparison of hidden character and hidden beauty is funny since beautiful face would have to be surface feature.

13
Even King notices Chancellor's fawning attitude.

14 Analyzing
Does the King mean the same thing when he repeats "ill-chosen"? He expects a grander adjective for himself but apparently thinks "nice" accurately describes Queen.

Chancellor. It is a little difficult to put this tactfully, Your Majesty.

King. Do your best, and I will tell you afterwards how you got on.

7 Chancellor. Let me put it this way. The Prince Simon will naturally assume that Her Royal Highness has the customary—so customary as to be, in my own poor opinion, slightly monotonous—has what one might call the inevitable—so inevitable as to be, in my opinion again, almost mechanical—will assume, that she has the, as *I* think of it, faultily faultless, icily regular, splendidly—

King. What you are trying to say in the fewest words possible is that my daughter is not beautiful.

8 Chancellor. Her beauty is certainly elusive, Your Majesty.

King. It is. It has eluded you, it has eluded me, it has eluded everybody who has seen her. It **9** even eluded the Court Painter. His last words were, "Well, I did my best." His successor is now painting the view across the water meadows from the West Turret. He says that his doctor has advised him to keep to landscape.

Chancellor. It is unfortunate, Your Majesty, but there it is. One just cannot understand how it could have occurred.

King. You don't think she takes after *me*, at all? You don't detect a likeness?

Chancellor. Most certainly not, Your Majesty.

King. Good. . . . Your predecessor did.

10 Chancellor. I have often wondered what happened to my predecessor.

King. Well, now you know.

[*There is a short silence.*]

Chancellor. Looking at the bright side, although Her Royal Highness is not, strictly speaking, beautiful——

King. Not, truthfully speaking, beautiful——
Chancellor. Yet she has great beauty of character.

11 King. My dear Chancellor, we are not considering her Royal Highness' character, but her chances of getting married. You observe that there is a distinction.

Chancellor. Yes, Your Majesty.

12 King. Look at it from the suitor's point of view. If a girl is beautiful, it is easy to assume that she has, tucked away inside her, an equally beautiful character. But it is impossible to assume that an unattractive girl, however elevated in character, has, tucked away inside her, an equally beautiful face. That is, so to speak, not where you want it—tucked away.

Chancellor. Quite so, Your Majesty.

King. This doesn't, of course, alter the fact that the Princess Camilla is quite the nicest person in the kingdom.

Chancellor (*enthusiastically*). She is indeed, Your Majesty. (*Hurriedly*) With the exception, I need hardly say, of Your Majesty—and Her Majesty.

13 King. Your exceptions are tolerated for their loyalty and condemned for their extreme fatuity.[3]

Chancellor. Thank you, Your Majesty.

King. As an adjective for your King, the word **14** *nice* is ill-chosen. As an adjective for Her Majesty, it is—ill-chosen.

[*At which moment the* Queen *comes in. The* King *rises. The* Chancellor *puts himself at right angles.*]

Queen (*briskly*). Ah. Talking about Camilla? (*She sits down.*)

King (*returning to his throne*). As always, my dear, you are right.

Queen (*to the* Chancellor). This fellow, Simon—what's he like?

Chancellor. Nobody has seen him, Your Majesty.

Queen. How old is he?

3. **fatuity** (fə-tōo′ə-tē): stupidity.

examples of parody they find in advertisements, television shows, and movies.

Both of these activities will help prepare students to understand the parody in the next play, *Pyramus and Thisby,* which is more difficult.

MEETING INDIVIDUAL NEEDS
Visual and Kinesthetic Learners • Have students study the pictures of the puppet production of *The Ugly Duckling* on pp. 301, 304, 307, 311, and 314–315. Have them note the details of dress and the imaginative treatment of physi-

cal characteristics that convey the personalities of the characters in the play. Encourage students to create, without imitating those pictured, one or more of their own puppet characters for the play.

Chancellor. Five-and-twenty, I understand.

Queen. In twenty-five years he must have been seen by somebody.

King (*to the* Chancellor). Just a fleeting glimpse?

Chancellor. I meant, Your Majesty, that no detailed report of him has reached this country, save that he has the usual personal advantages and qualities expected of a prince and has been traveling in distant and dangerous lands.

15 **Queen.** Ah! Nothing gone wrong with his eyes? Sunstroke or anything?

Chancellor. Not that I am aware of, Your Majesty. At the same time, as I was venturing to say to His Majesty, Her Royal Highness' character and disposition are so outstandingly——

Queen. Stuff and nonsense. You remember what happened when we had the Tournament of Love last year.

Chancellor. I was not myself present, Your Majesty. I had not then the honor of—I was abroad, and never heard the full story.

Queen. No, it was the other fool. They all rode up to Camilla to pay their homage—it was the first time they had seen her. The heralds blew their trumpets and announced that she would marry whichever prince was left master of the field when all but one had been unhorsed. The trumpets were blown again, they charged enthusiastically into the fight, and——(*The* King *looks nonchalantly at the ceiling and whistles a few bars.*) Don't do that.

King. I'm sorry, my dear.

Queen (*to the* Chancellor). And what happened?

16 They all simultaneously fell off their horses and assumed the posture of defeat.

King. One of them was not quite so quick as the others. I was very quick. I proclaimed him the victor.

Queen. At the Feast of Betrothal held that night——

King. We were all very quick.

Queen. ——the Chancellor announced that by the laws of the country the successful suitor had

17 to pass a further test. He had to give the correct answer to a riddle.

Chancellor. Such undoubtedly is the fact, Your Majesty.

18 **King.** There are times for announcing facts, and times for looking at things in a broad-minded way. Please remember that, Chancellor.

Chancellor. Yes, Your Majesty.

Queen. I invented the riddle myself. Quite an easy one. What is it that has four legs and barks like a dog? The answer is, "A dog."

King (*to the* Chancellor). You see that?

Chancellor. Yes, Your Majesty.

King. It isn't difficult.

Queen. He, however, seemed to find it so. He

19 said an eagle. Then he said a serpent; a very high mountain with slippery sides; two peacocks; a moonlight night; the day after tomorrow——

King. Nobody could accuse him of not trying.

Queen. *I* did.

King. I *should* have said that nobody could fail to recognize in his attitude an appearance of doggedness.

Queen. Finally he said death. I nudged the King——

20 **King.** Accepting the word *nudge* for the moment, I rubbed my ankle with one hand, clapped him on the shoulder with the other, and congratulated him on the correct answer. He disappeared under the table, and, personally, I never saw him again.

Queen. His body was found in the moat next morning.

Chancellor. But what was he doing in the moat, Your Majesty?

21 **King.** Bobbing about. Try not to ask needless questions.

Chancellor. It all seems so strange.

Queen. What does?

15 Drawing Conclusions
Analyzing
Why would the Queen want to know if there were anything wrong with the Prince's eyes? What is ironic about her hopes? She is hoping Prince will be unable to see Princess' face. Ironic that she would hope future son-in-law has physical problems.

16
Tone. Tone is comic. Princess is so ugly that all potential suitors wanted to lose tournament by being unseated. Snappy dialogue between characters should be read at brisk pace.

17
Solution of complex riddle as means of coming to power is feature of both serious (*Oedipus*) and fairy-tale ("Rumpelstiltskin") literature. Queen's riddle is, however, intentionally easy.

18
Chancellor is stickler for detail. King prefers to ignore facts if ignoring them helps Camilla get married.

19
Suitor, trying to avoid marriage, intentionally gave wrong answers.

20
Queen apparently kicked King quite sharply. King was willing to accept wrong answer, law or no law.

21
King avoids question. Though he "personally" never saw suitor again, King may have had him killed for trying to avoid marriage, or perhaps suitor drowned himself.

Milne's reference to *christening* may require clarification for students from religious or cultural backgrounds that do not practice Christianity. Explain that a *christening* is a ceremony in which an infant is received into the Christian church and is given a name.

VISUAL CONNECTIONS

Exploring the Subject
As soon as audience sees the Queen, they know that the King is henpecked. The puppeteers have utilized many stereotypes in choosing the birds for this production. The Queen is a matronly hen whose size dwarfs the wise owl, her husband.

Relating Expression Skills
Students might like to draw pictures of human faces to match the King, Queen, Princess Camilla, and other main characters. As an alternative activity, they might choose photographs of actors and actresses from newspapers or movie magazines that would fit the parts. Have students explain their choices.

22
Chancellor tactfully points out that all fairy-tale princesses except Camilla are beautiful.

23
Characterization. King depends on Chancellor to compute even a simple mathematical problem.

24
The promise is humorous because King will have happiness his wife deserves. King probably believes promise has come true, that he has little happiness because his wife deserves little happiness.

22 Chancellor. That Her Royal Highness, alone of all the princesses one has ever heard of, should lack that <u>invariable</u> attribute of royalty, **23** supreme beauty.
Queen. (*to the* King). That was your Great-Aunt Malkin. She came to the christening. You know what she said.
King. It was cryptic.[4] Great-Aunt Malkin's

4. **cryptic** (krĭp'tĭk): puzzling.

besetting weakness. She came to *my* christening—she was one hundred and one then, and that was fifty-one years ago. (*To the* Chancellor) How old would that make her?
Chancellor. One hundred and fifty-two, your Majesty.
24 King (*after thought*). About that, yes. She promised me that when I grew up I should have all the happiness which my wife deserved. It struck me at the time—well, when I say "at

the time," I was only a week old—but it did strike me as soon as anything could strike me—I mean of that nature—well, work it out for yourself, Chancellor. It opens up a most interesting field of speculation. Though naturally I have not liked to go into it at all deeply with Her Majesty.

25 **Queen.** I never heard anything less cryptic. She was wishing you extreme happiness.

King. I don't think she was *wishing* me anything. However.

Chancellor. (*to the* Queen). But what, Your Majesty, did she wish Her Royal Highness?

Queen. Her other godmother—on my side—had promised her the dazzling beauty for which all the women in my family are famous.

26 [*She pauses, and the* King *snaps his fingers surreptitiously[5] in the direction of the* Chancellor.]

Chancellor (*hurriedly*). Indeed, yes, Your Majesty.

[*The* King *relaxes.*]

Queen. And Great-Aunt Malkin said——(*To the* King) What were the words?

King. I give you with this kiss
A wedding-day surprise.
27 Where ignorance is bliss
'Tis folly to be wise.[6]

I thought the last two lines rather neat. But what it *meant*——

Queen. We can all see what it meant. She was given beauty—and where is it? Great-Aunt **28** Malkin took it away from her. The wedding-day surprise is that there will never be a wedding day.

King. Young men being what they are, my dear, it would be much more surprising if there *were* a wedding day. So how——

5. **surreptitiously** (sûr′əp-tĭsh′əs-lē): secretly.
6. **Where . . . wise:** These lines come from a poem called "A Distant Prospect of Eton College" by Thomas Gray.

[*The* Princess *comes in. She is young, happy, healthy, but not beautiful. Or let us say that by some trick of makeup or arrangement of hair she seems plain to us, unlike the princesses of the storybooks.*]

Princess (*to the* King). Hallo, darling! (*Seeing the others*) Oh, I say! Affairs of state? Sorry.
King (*holding out his hand*). Don't go, Camilla.

[*She takes his hand.*]

Chancellor. Shall I withdraw, Your Majesty?
Queen. You are aware, Camilla, that Prince Simon arrives today?
Princess. He has arrived. They're just letting down the drawbridge.
King (*jumping up*). Arrived! I must——
29 **Princess.** Darling, you know what the drawbridge is like. It takes at *least* half an hour to let it down.
King (*sitting down*). It wants oil. (*To the* Chancellor) Have *you* been grudging it oil?
Princess. It wants a new drawbridge, darling.
Chancellor. Have I Your Majesty's permission——
King. Yes, yes.

[*The* Chancellor *bows and goes out.*]

Queen. You've told him, of course? It's the only chance.
King. Er—no. I was just going to, when——
Queen. Then I'd better. (*She goes to the door.*) You can explain to the girl; I'll have her sent to you. You've told Camilla?
King. Er—no. I was just going to, when——
Queen. Then you'd better tell her now.
King. My dear, are you sure——
30 **Queen.** It's the only chance left. (*Dramatically to heaven*) My daughter! (*She goes out. There is a little silence when she is gone.*)
King. Camilla, I want to talk seriously to you about marriage.

Princess. Yes, Father.
King. It is time that you learned some of the facts of life.
Princess. Yes, Father.
31 King. Now the great fact about marriage is that once you're married you live happy ever after. All our history books affirm this.
Princess. And your own experience too, darling.
32 King (*with dignity*). Let us confine ourselves to history for the moment.
Princess. Yes, Father.
King. Of course, there *may* be an exception here and there, which, as it were, proves the rule; just as—oh, well, never mind.
Princess (*smiling*). Go on, darling. You were going to say that an exception here and there proves the rule that all princesses are beautiful.
King. Well—leave that for the moment. The point is that it doesn't matter *how* you marry, or *who* you marry, as long as you *get* married. Because you'll be happy ever after in any case. Do you follow me so far?
Princess. Yes, Father.
King. Well, your mother and I have a little plan——
Princess. Was that it, going out of the door just now?
King. Er—yes. It concerns your waiting-maid.
Princess. Darling, I have several.
33 King. Only one that leaps to the eye, so to speak. The one with the—well, with everything.
Princess. Dulcibella?
King. That's the one. It is our little plan that at the first meeting she should pass herself off as
34 the Princess—a harmless ruse,[7] of which you will find frequent record in the history books—and allure Prince Simon to his—that is to say, bring him up to the—— In other words,

7. **ruse** (rōōz): trick.

the wedding will take place immediately afterwards, and as quietly as possible—well, naturally in view of the fact that your Aunt Malkin is one hundred and fifty-two; and since you
35 will be wearing the family bridal veil—which is no doubt how the custom arose—the surprise after the ceremony will be his. Are you following me at all? Your attention seems to be wandering.
Princess. I was wondering why you needed to tell me.
King. Just a precautionary measure, in case you happened to meet the Prince or his attendant before the ceremony; in which case, of course, you would pass yourself off as the maid——
36 Princess. A harmless ruse, of which, also, you will find frequent record in the history books.
King. Exactly. But the occasion need not arise.
A Voice (*announcing*). The woman Dulcibella!
King. Ah! (*To the* Princess) Now, Camilla, if you will just retire to your own apartments, I will come to you there when we are ready for the actual ceremony. (*He leads her out as he is talking, and as he returns calls out.*) Come in, my dear! (Dulcibella *comes in. She is beautiful, but dumb.*) Now don't be frightened, there is nothing to be frightened about. Has Her Majesty told you what you have to do?
Dulcibella. Y-yes, Your Majesty.
King. Well now, let's see how well you can do it. You are sitting here, we will say. (*He leads her to a seat.*) Now imagine that I am Prince Simon.
37 (*He curls his mustache and puts his stomach in. She giggles.*) You are the beautiful Princess Camilla whom he has never seen. (*She giggles again.*) This is a serious moment in your life, and you will find that a giggle will not be helpful. (*He goes to the door.*) I am announced: "His Royal Highness Prince Simon!" That's me being announced. Remember what I said about giggling. You should have a faraway look upon the face. (*She does her best.*) Farther away than that.

The King giving lessons to Dulcibella.

38 (*She tries again.*) No, that's too far. You are sit-ting there, thinking beautiful thoughts—in maiden meditation, fancy-free,[8] as I remember saying to Her Majesty once—speaking of somebody else—fancy-free, but with the

8. **in . . . fancy-free:** The King is quoting from Shakespeare again—this time from *A Midsummer Night's Dream.*

39 mouth definitely shut—that's better. I advance and fall upon one knee. (*He does so.*) You extend your hand graciously—*graciously*; you're not trying to push him in the face—that's better, and I raise it to my lips—so—and I kiss it (*He kisses it warmly*)—no, perhaps not so ardently as

40 that, more like this (*He kisses it again*), and I say,

VISUAL CONNECTIONS
Exploring the Subject
Dulcibella is both a "silly goose" and a "dumb blonde," two stereotypes that playwrights often exploit. Her waist is made of rods that allow her to "waft," and the fringe on the hem of her costume helps create an illusion of silliness and purposeless movement.

38
Dulcibella cannot convey "distant" look believably.

39
When a character's speech reveals how another character is to act on stage, speech is known as internal stage direction. Dulcibella's mouth hanging open suggests her stupidity; King has her shut it.

40
King still enjoys playing role of suitor. Finds excuse to kiss Dulcibella's hand again.

41
King seems unable to say anything truly romantic.

42
Dialect. After King's long, tedious explanation of proper behavior, "coo" should get a big laugh. This British working-class expression is not expected from a princess.

43
King mistakes Dulcibella's explanation for another reply which she might give Prince Simon.

44
Doves are normally associated with love, but Dulcibella's loud voice and unrefined manners remind the King of stampeding elephants.

45
Dulcibella's limited mental capacity continues as basis of humor.

46
Characterization. Dulcibella's speech is long and garbled, showing her to be emotional but dumb.

47 Finding Main Ideas
Why is Camilla now strangely beautiful? Prophecy that only Princess understands comes true. On wedding day her beauty is revealed, first to Prince who loves her.

41 "Your Royal Highness this is the most—er—Your Royal Highness, I shall ever be—no—Your Royal Highness, it is the proudest—" Well, the point is that *he* will say it, and it will be something complimentary, and then he will take your hand in both of his and press it to his heart. (*He does so.*) And then—what do *you* say?
42 Dulcibella. Coo!
King. No, *not* "Coo."
Dulcibella. Never had anyone do *that* to me before.
43 King. That also strikes the wrong note. What you want to say is, "Oh, Prince Simon!" . . . Say it.
Dulcibella (*loudly*). Oh, Prince Simon!
King. No, no. You don't need to shout until he has said "What?" two or three times. Always consider the possibility that he *isn't* deaf. Softly, and giving the words a dying fall, letting them play around his head like a flight of doves.
Dulcibella (*still a little overloud*). O-o-o-o-h, Prinsimon!
44 King. Keep the idea in your mind of a flight of *doves* rather than a flight of panic-stricken elephants, and you will be all right. Now I'm going to get up, and you must, as it were, *waft*[9] me into a seat by your side. (*She starts wafting.*) *Not* rescuing a drowning man, that's another idea altogether, useful at times, but at the moment inappropriate. Wafting. Prince Simon will put the necessary muscles into play—all you require to do is indicate by a gracious movement of the hand the seat you require him to take. Now! (*He gets up, a little stiffly, and sits next to her.*) That was better. Well, here we are. Now, I think you give me a look: something, let us say, halfway between breathless adoration and regal dignity, touched, as it were, with good comradeship. Now try that.
45 (*She gives him a vacant look of bewilderment.*) Frankly, that didn't quite get it. There was just a little something missing. An absence, as it were, of all the qualities I asked for, and in their place an odd resemblance to an unsatisfied fish. Let us try to get at it another way. Dulcibella, have you a young man of your own?
46 Dulcibella (*eagerly, seizing his hand*). Oo, yes, he's ever so smart, he's an archer, well, not as you might say a real archer, he works in the armory, but old Bottlenose, *you* know who I mean, the Captain of the Guard, says the very next man they ever has to shoot, my Eg shall take his place, knowing Father and how it is with Eg and me, and me being maid to Her Royal Highness and can't marry me till he's a real soldier, but ever so loving, and funny like, the things he says, I said to him once, "Eg," I said—
King (*getting up*). I rather fancy, Dulcibella, that if you think of Eg all the time, *say* as little as possible, and, when thinking of Eg, see that the mouth is not more than partially open, you will do very well. I will show you where you are to sit and wait for His Royal Highness. (*He leads her out. On the way he is saying*) Now remember—waft—waft—not *hoick*.[10]

[*Prince Simon wanders in from the back unannounced. He is a very ordinary-looking young man in rather dusty clothes. He gives a deep sigh of relief as he sinks into the throne of the King. . . . Camilla,* **47** *a new and strangely beautiful Camilla, comes in.*]

Princess (*surprised*). Well!
Prince. Oh, hallo!
Princess. Ought you?
Prince (*getting up*). Do sit down, won't you?
Princess. Who are you, and how did you get here?
Prince. Well, that's rather a long story. Couldn't

---

9. **waft** (wäft): carry gently, as if through the air.

10. **hoick:** yank or pull abruptly.

we sit down? You could sit here if you liked, but it isn't very comfortable.

Princess. That is the King's Throne.

48 Prince. Oh, is that what it is?

Princess. Thrones are not meant to be comfortable.

Prince. Well, I don't know if they're meant to be, but they certainly aren't.

Princess. Why were you sitting on the King's Throne, and who are you?

49 Prince. My name is Carlo.

Princess. Mine is Dulcibella.

Prince. Good. And now couldn't we sit down?

Princess (*sitting down on the long seat to the left of the throne, and, as it were, wafting him to a place next to her*). You may sit here, if you like. Why are you so tired?

[*He sits down.*]

Prince. I've been taking very strenuous exercise.

Princess. Is that part of the long story?

Prince. It is.

Princess (*settling herself*). I love stories.

Prince. This isn't a story really. You see, I'm attendant on Prince Simon, who is visiting here.

Princess. Oh? I'm attendant on Her Royal Highness.

Prince. Then you know what he's here for.

Princess. Yes.

Prince. She's very beautiful, I hear.

50 Princess. Did you hear that? Where have you been lately?

Prince. Traveling in distant lands—with Prince Simon.

Princess. Ah! All the same, I don't understand. Is Prince Simon in the palace now? The drawbridge *can't* be down yet!

Prince. I don't suppose it is. *And* what a noise it makes coming down!

Princess. Isn't it terrible?

Prince. I couldn't stand it any more. I just had to get away. That's why I'm here.

Princess. But how?

Prince. Well, there's only one way, isn't there? That beech tree, and then a swing and a grab for the battlements, and don't ask me to remember it all—— (*He shudders.*)

Princess. You mean you came across the moat by that beech tree?

Prince. Yes. I got so tired of hanging about.

Princess. But it's terribly dangerous!

51 Prince. That's why I'm so exhausted. Nervous shock. (*He lies back and breathes loudly.*)

52 Princess. Of course, it's different for *me*.

Prince (*sitting up*). Say that again. I must have got it wrong.

Princess. It's different for me, because I'm used to it. Besides, I'm so much lighter.

Prince. You don't mean that you——

Princess. Oh yes, often.

Prince. And I thought I was a brave man! At least, I didn't until five minutes ago, and now I don't again.

Princess. Oh, but you are! And I think it's wonderful to do it straight off the first time.

Prince. Well, *you* did.

Princess. Oh no, not the first time. When I was a child.

Prince. You mean that you crashed?

Princess. Well, you only fall into the moat.

Prince. Only! Can you *swim*?

Princess. Of course.

Prince. So you swam to the castle walls, and yelled for help and they fished you out and walloped you. And next day you tried again. Well, if *that* isn't pluck——

Princess. Of course I didn't. I swam back, and did it at once; I mean I tried again at once. It wasn't until the third time that I actually did it. You see, I was afraid I might lose my nerve.

Prince. Afraid she might lose her nerve!

Princess. There's a way of getting over from this side, too; a tree grows out from the wall and you jump into another tree—I don't think it's quite so easy.

48
Either Prince is ignorant of rules of etiquette or he is doing good job acting part of Carlo.

49
Plot. Story depends upon disguise and mistaken identity. Prince and Princess, however, fall in love with each other despite deception.

50
Princess is surprised; wants to know where he heard she is beautiful.

51
Prince admits he is tired, scared, not the usual behavior of fairy-tale Prince.

52
Irony. Normally in fairy tales, Prince attempts daring deeds that leave Princess in "nervous shock."

53 Analyzing
What does the Prince mean by saying he thought he was a brave man for five minutes?
He thought he had done something dangerous until Princess told him that she often crosses the moat in similar way.

Prince. Not quite so easy. Good. You must show me.

Princess. Oh, I will.

Prince. Perhaps it might be as well if you taught me how to swim first. I've often heard about swimming, but never——

Princess. You can't swim?

54 Prince. No. Don't look so surprised. There are a lot of other things that I can't do. I'll tell you about them as soon as you have a couple of years to spare.

Princess. You can't swim and yet you crossed by the beech tree! And you're *ever* so much heavier than I am! Now who's brave?

Prince (*getting up*). You keep talking about how light you are. I must see if there's anything in it. Stand up! (*She stands obediently and he picks her up.*) You're right, Dulcibella. I could hold you here forever. (*Looking at her*) You're very lovely. Do you know how lovely you are?

55 Princess. Yes. (*She laughs suddenly and happily.*)

Prince. Why do you laugh?

Princess. Aren't you tired of holding me?

56 Prince. Frankly, yes. I exaggerated when I said I could hold you forever. When you've been hanging by the arms for ten minutes over a very deep moat, wondering if it's too late to learn how to swim—— (*He puts her down.*) What I meant was that I should *like* to hold you forever. Why did you laugh?

Princess. Oh, well, it was a little private joke of mine.

Prince. If it comes to that, I've got a private joke too. Let's exchange them.

Princess. Mine's very private. One other woman in the whole world knows, and that's all.

Prince. Mine's just as private. One other man knows, and that's all.

60 Princess. What fun. I love secrets. . . . Well, here's mine. When I was born, one of my godmothers promised that I should be very beautiful.

Prince. How right she was.

Princess. But the other one said this:

> I give you with this kiss
> A wedding-day surprise.
> Where ignorance is bliss
> 'Tis folly to be wise.

And nobody knew what it meant. And I grew up very plain. And then, when I was about ten, I met my godmother in the forest one day. It was my tenth birthday. Nobody knows this—except you.

Prince. Except us.

Princess. Except us. And she told me what her gift meant. It meant that I *was* beautiful—but everybody else was to go on being ignorant and thinking me plain, until my wedding day. Because, she said, she didn't want me to grow up spoiled and willful and vain, as I should have done if everybody had always been saying

57 how beautiful I was; and the best thing in the world, she said, was to be quite sure of yourself, but not to expect admiration from other people. So ever since then my mirror has told

58 me I'm beautiful, and everybody else thinks

59 me ugly, and I get a lot of fun out of it.

Prince. Well, seeing that Dulcibella is the result, I can only say that your godmother was very, very wise.

Princess. And now tell me *your* secret.

Prince. It isn't such a pretty one. You see, Prince Simon was going to woo Princess Camilla, and he'd heard that she was beautiful and haughty and imperious—all *you* would have been if your godmother hadn't been so wise. And being a very ordinary-looking fellow himself, he was afraid she wouldn't think much of him, so he suggested to one of his attendants, a man called Carlo, of extremely attractive appearance, that *he* should pretend to be the Prince and win the Princess' hand; and then at the last moment they would change places——

VISUAL CONNECTIONS
Exploring the Subject
The Prince and the Princess in this photograph are more conventionally human; they are the "real people" in the play. The puppets' eyebrows and noses, however, give even these two characters appearances much like birds. Perhaps the puppeteers are suggesting that the Prince and the Princess, too, are capable of some of the "bird-brain" behavior of the others. The similarity of their costumes carries out the idea, suggested in the play that they are very much alike.

Princess. How would they do that?
Prince. The Prince was going to have been married in full armor—with his visor down.
61 Princess (*laughing happily*). Oh, what fun!
Prince. Neat, isn't it?
Princess (*laughing*). Oh, very . . . very . . . very.
Prince. Neat, but not so terribly *funny*. Why do you keep laughing?

Princess. Well, that's another secret.
Prince. If it comes to that, *I've* got another one up my sleeve. Shall we exchange again?
Princess. All right. You go first this time.
62 Prince. Very well....I am not Carlo. (*Standing up and speaking dramatically*) I am Simon!—*ow!* (*He sits down and rubs his leg violently.*)
Princess (*alarmed*). What is it?

61 Finding Cause and Effect
Why is the Princess delighted with the Prince's plan? It is almost identical to her father's plan.

62
Irony. In trying to make a gallant, dramatic announcement, the Prince is pained by a cramp in his leg.

The Ugly Duckling **311**

312

63
Repetition of announcement suggests that Prince expects Dulcibella to be surprised.

64
We have heard this statement before from Princess' father. The echo is humorous.

65
Plot. By suggesting that Dulcibella is her maid, Camilla implies that she is Princess; Prince is not surprised.

66
Prince humorously reverses earlier claim that he has never read history. Camilla appreciates his humor.

67
Plot. This part of secret is new; means that as soon as Prince told Camilla she was lovely, she knew his identity.

68
For Prince, it was also "love at first sight," without knowing Princess' identity.

69
Dulcibella is not as quick as Carlo; has to be prompted.

Prince. Cramp. (*In a mild voice, still rubbing*) I was saying that I was Prince Simon.

Princess. Shall I rub it for you? (*She rubs.*)

Prince (*still hopefully*). I am Simon.

Princess. Is that better?

63 **Prince** (*despairingly*). I am Simon.

Princess. I know.

Prince. How did you know?

Princess. Well, you told me.

Prince. But oughtn't you to swoon or something?

64 **Princess.** Why? History records many similar ruses.

Prince (*amazed*). Is that so? I've never read history. I thought I was being profoundly original.

Princess. Oh, no! Now I'll tell you *my* secret. For reasons very much like your own, the Princess Camilla, who is held to be extremely plain, feared to meet Prince Simon. Is the drawbridge down yet?

Prince. Do your people give a faint, surprised cheer every time it gets down?

Princess. Naturally.

Prince. Then it came down about three minutes ago.

65 **Princess.** Ah! Then at this very moment your man Carlo is declaring his passionate love for my maid, Dulcibella. That, I think, is funny. (*So does the* Prince. *He laughs heartily.*) Dulcibella, by the way, is in love with a man she calls Eg, so I hope Carlo isn't getting carried away.

Prince. Carlo is married to a girl he calls "the little woman," so Eg has nothing to fear.

Princess. By the way, I don't know if you heard, but I said, or as good as said, that I am the Princess Camilla.

66 **Prince.** I wasn't surprised. History, of which I read a great deal, records many similar ruses.

Princess (*laughing*). Simon!

Prince (*laughing*). Camilla! (*He stands up.*) May I try holding you again? (*She nods. He takes her in his arms and kisses her.*) Sweetheart!

67 **Princess.** You see, when you lifted me up before, you said, "You're very lovely," and my godmother said that the first person to whom I would seem lovely was the man I should marry; so I knew then that you were Simon and I should marry you.

68 **Prince.** I knew directly[11] I saw you that I should marry you, even if you were Dulcibella. By the way, which of you *am* I marrying?

Princess. When she lifts her veil, it will be Camilla. (*Voices are heard outside.*) Until then it will be Dulcibella.

Prince (*in a whisper*). Then goodbye, Camilla, until you lift your veil.

Princess. Goodbye, Simon, until you raise your visor.

[*The* King *and* Queen *come in arm-in-arm, followed by* Carlo *and* Dulcibella *also arm-in-arm. The* Chancellor *precedes them, walking backwards, at a loyal angle.*]

Prince (*supporting the* Chancellor *as an accident seems inevitable*). Careful!

[*The* Chancellor *turns indignantly round.*]

King. Who and what is this? More accurately who and what are all these?

Carlo. My attendant, Carlo, Your Majesty. He will, with Your Majesty's permission, prepare me for the ceremony.

[*The* Prince *bows.*]

King. Of course, of course!

Queen (*to* Dulcibella). Your maid, Dulcibella, is **69** it not, my love? (Dulcibella *nods violently.*) I thought so. (*To* Carlo) *She* will prepare Her Royal Highness.

[*The* Princess *curtsies.*]

11. **directly:** here, as soon as.

King. Ah, yes. Yes. *Most* important.

Princess (*curtsying*). I beg your pardon, Your Majesty, if I've done wrong, but I found the gentleman wandering——

King (*crossing to her*). Quite right, my dear, quite right. (*He pinches her cheek and takes advantage of this kingly gesture to speak in a loud whisper.*) We've pulled it off!

[*They sit down:* the King *and* Queen *on their thrones,* Dulcibella *on the* Princess' *throne.* Carlo *stands behind* Dulcibella, *the* Chancellor *on the right of the* Queen, *and the* Prince *and* Princess *behind the long seat on the left.*]

Chancellor (*consulting documents*). H'r'm! Have I Your Majesty's authority to put the final test to His Royal Highness?

Queen (*whispering to the* King). Is this safe?

King (*whispering*). Perfectly, my dear. I told him the answer a minute ago. (*Over his shoulder, to* Carlo) Don't forget. "Dog." (*Aloud*) Proceed, Your Excellency. It is my desire that the affairs of my country should ever be conducted in a strictly constitutional manner.

Chancellor (*oratorically*). By the constitution of the country, a suitor to Her Royal Highness' hand cannot be deemed successful until he has given the correct answer to a riddle. (*Conversationally*) The last suitor answered incorrectly, and thus failed to win his bride.

King. By a coincidence he fell into the moat.

Chancellor (*to* Carlo). I have now to ask Your Royal Highness if you are prepared for the ordeal?

Carlo (*cheerfully*). Absolutely.

Chancellor. I may mention, as a matter possibly of some slight historical interest to our visitor, that by the constitution of the country, the same riddle is not allowed to be asked on two successive occasions.

King (*startled*). What's that?

Chancellor. This one, it is interesting to recall, was propounded exactly a century ago, and we must take it as a fortunate omen that it was well and truly solved.

King (*to the* Queen). I may want my sword directly.

Chancellor. The riddle is this: What is it that has four legs and mews like a cat?

Carlo (*promptly*). A dog.

King (*still more promptly*). Bravo, bravo! (*He claps loudly and nudges the* Queen, *who claps too.*)

Chancellor (*peering at his documents*). According to the records of the occasion to which I referred, the correct answer would seem to be——

Princess (*to the* Prince). Say something, quick!

Chancellor.——not "dog," but——

Prince. Your Majesty, have I permission to speak? Naturally His Royal Highness could not think of justifying himself on such an occasion, but I think that with Your Majesty's gracious permission, I could——

King. Certainly, certainly.

Prince. In our country, we have an animal to which we have given the name "dog," or, in the local dialect of the more mountainous districts, "doggie." It sits by the fireside and purrs.

Carlo. That's right. It purrs like anything.

Prince. When it needs milk, which is its staple food, it mews.

Carlo (*enthusiastically*). Mews like nobody's business.

Prince. It also has four legs.

Carlo. One at each corner.

Prince. In some countries, I understand, this animal is called a "cat." In one distant country to which His Royal Highness and I penetrated, it was called by the very curious name of "hippopotamus."

Carlo. That's right. (*To the* Prince) Do you remember that ginger-colored hippopotamus which used to climb onto my shoulder and lick my ear?

70
Everyone is playing along with plan. King has no idea real Prince and Princess have met.

71
King is taking no chances; unashamedly tells Carlo the answer to riddle again.

72 Analyzing Making Inferences
Why does the King mention that the last suitor fell into the moat? Was this a coincidence? It is a threat of what will happen if Prince backs out. Not coincidental at all.

73
Chancellor unwisely changes riddle. As usual, he adheres to law.

74 Drawing Conclusions
Why does the King want his sword? He is thinking of using it on Chancellor. The reader may now know what happened to Chancellor's predecessor.

75
Scene is comic. Carlo blurts out prearranged answer, and King immediately applauds it even though it is ludicrous and wrong.

76
The comic coverup is allowed so that everyone can agree on marriage. Prince shows quick thinking. Drawing out tale provides humor.

Exploring the Subject

This is probably curtain call that the entire cast takes at end of the play. The Prince and the Princess are now wearing their crowns, so we know they are married. Secret of Prince Simon's deception is revealed. It seems natural that Carlo is a rooster, one of the handsomest of birds, but feather-duster tail makes him farcical. These puppets parody cast of characters just as the play parodies the fairy tale.

Ideas for Writing

Students might like to write their own parodies of their favorite television programs or movies. Possibilities include game shows, westerns, crime dramas, karate movies, and other popular genres.

The entire cast: (*left*) the Prince and the Princess; (*center*) the Chancellor, the King, and the Queen; (*right*) Dulcibella and Carlo.

COOPERATIVE LEARNING
Have students work in groups to create extra editions of a royal newspaper filled with stories of Camilla and Simon's wedding; human interest stories about other characters, such as Dulcibella; and editorials on such subjects as love or beauty.

Prince. I shall never forget it, sir. (*To the* King) So you see, Your Majesty——

King. Thank you. I think that makes it perfectly clear. (*Firmly, to the* Chancellor) You are about to agree?

77 Chancellor. Undoubtedly, Your Majesty. May I be the first to congratulate His Royal Highness on solving the riddle so accurately?

King. You may be the first to see that all is in order for an immediate wedding.

Chancellor. Thank you, Your Majesty.

[*He bows and withdraws. The* King *rises, as do the* Queen *and* Dulcibella.]

King (*to* Carlo). Doubtless, Prince Simon, you will wish to retire and prepare yourself for the ceremony.

Carlo. Thank you, sir.

Prince. Have I Your Majesty's permission to attend His Royal Highness? It is the custom of his country for princes of the royal blood to be married in full armor, a matter which requires a certain adjustment——

King. Of course, of course. (Carlo *bows to the* King *and* Queen *and goes out. As the* Prince *is* **78** *about to follow, the* King *stops him.*) Young man, you have a quality of quickness which I admire. It is my pleasure to reward it in any way which commends itself to you.

Prince. Your Majesty is ever gracious. May I ask for my reward *after* the ceremony?

[*The* Prince *catches the eye of the* Princess, *and they give each other a secret smile.*]

King. Certainly. (*The* Prince *bows and goes out.* **79** *To* Dulcibella) Now, young woman, make yourself scarce. You have done your work excel- **80** lently, and we will see that you and your——What was his name?

Dulcibella. Eg, Your Majesty.

King.——that you and your Eg are not forgotten.

77
Chancellor, who perhaps remembers fate of predecessor, declares answer correct.

78
Irony. King believes he is indebted to a servant who has helped him. Dramatic irony occurs because the reader realizes King is addressing Prince, who explained problem of wrong answer to riddle so that he could marry Princess.

79
The reader would expect King to grant someone permission to withdraw, not tell her to make herself "scarce." King's manner of speaking parodies that of usual fairy-tale ruler.

80 Summarizing
What will happen now if all goes according to the plan?
Princess, wearing her veil, will be married to Prince, whose face will be hidden by armor.

TRANSPARENCY 26

Literary Elements
Evaluating a Play – examines the various elements of fiction that contribute to the reader's experience of a play.

CLOSURE
Ask students to identify and explain characteristics of traditional fairy tales that Milne parodies in *The Ugly Duckling*. Also, have students state the **theme** of the play.

EXTENSION AND ENRICHMENT
Students might create comic-book versions of *The Ugly Duckling* or create playbills for a performance complete with a cast of well-known actors and actresses.

81
King once again takes credit for origin of an old saying.

82
Irony. Queen is correct, but she is talking of Carlo.

83
The King almost recognizes that looks may not be "the important thing."

84
Ironically, Milne ends parody of fairy tale with fairy-tale ending.

READING CHECK
1. They fear he will reject their ugly daughter (p. 303).
2. Have Dulcibella pretend to be Camilla; veil Camilla at wedding (p. 306).
3. Has handsome servant pose for him; will marry in armor (pp. 310–311).
4. Accidentally, while waiting for imposters to meet (p. 308).
5. What has four legs, mews like cat (p. 313).

FOR STUDY AND DISCUSSION
1. Everyone will see her as beautiful.
2a. He sleeps on throne, is henpecked, whistles, needs help with simple arithmetic. 2b. She interrupts, acts as if she knows everything, corrects King. 2c. He is exhausted, frightened, cannot swim, admits other faults.
3. Suitors fell off horses, tried to lose. Slowest was declared winner; he guessed the riddle wrong, ended up in moat.

Dulcibella. Coo! (*She curtsies and goes out.*)
Princess (*calling*). Wait for me, Dulcibella!
King (*to the* Queen). Well, my dear, we may con-
81 gratulate ourselves. As I remember saying to somebody once, "You have not lost a daughter, you have gained a son." How does he strike you?
82 **Queen.** Stupid.
King. They made a very handsome pair, I thought, he and Dulcibella.
Queen. Both stupid.
King. I said nothing about stupidity. What I *said* was that they were both extremely handsome. That is the important thing. (*Struck by a*
83 *sudden idea*) Or isn't it?
Queen. What do *you* think of Prince Simon, Camilla?
84 **Princess.** I adore him. We shall be so happy together.
King. Well, of course you will. I told you so. Happy ever after.
Queen. Run along now and get ready.
Princess. Yes, Mother. (*She throws a kiss to them and goes out.*)
King (*anxiously*). My dear, have we been wrong about Camilla all this time? It seemed to me that she wasn't looking *quite* so plain as usual just now. Did *you* notice anything?
Queen (*carelessly*). Just the excitement of the marriage.
King (*relieved*). Ah, yes, that would account for it.

[*Curtain.*]

Reading Check

1. Why are the King and the Queen worried about Prince Simon's arrival?
2. How do the King and Queen plan to trick Prince Simon?
3. How does Prince Simon plan to trick the Princess?
4. How do Prince Simon and Princess Camilla meet each other?
5. What riddle must the Prince solve in order to win the hand of Princess Camilla?

For Study and Discussion

Analyzing and Interpreting the Play

1. In the fairy tale "The Ugly Duckling" by Hans Christian Andersen, a young bird believes he is ugly until he grows into a beautiful swan. In this play, a young woman is believed to be very plain until love reveals her beauty. In the scene on page 310, what does the Princess say will happen on her wedding day?

2. Fairy tales are filled with characters such as a dignified king, a serene and ladylike queen, a beautiful princess, and a fearless and strong prince. But the characters in this humorous play are not at all what they would be in the usual fairy tale. **a.** What actions of the King show that he is undignified and a bit foolish? **b.** How does the Queen show she is bossy and quick-tempered? **c.** How do you learn that the Prince is not fearless and strong?

3. Fairy tales are also filled with trials and tests such as tournaments and riddles. But this comedy is filled with surprising twists. What humorous unexpected events occurred in the Tournament of Love that the King and Queen gave for Camilla?

316

You could expand on **Understanding Stage Terms** below by having students work in small groups to make Director's Notebooks for *The Ugly Duckling*. The notebooks might be organized according to the four topics given in this section and should contain set diagrams, sketches showing character placement in each scene, lists of props, plans for lighting, and drawings of costumes. Have groups compare completed notebooks and discuss the various choices each group made. This approach will help students recognize the importance of the director in interpreting a script.

---

4. The most important part of this story will take place after the play ends. **a.** What will happen then? **b.** What surprising discoveries will be made when all the disguises are removed?

5. Most comedies end with all problems solved and everyone living "happily ever after." **a.** Do you believe that Simon and Camilla will live "happily ever after"? **b.** What will happen to Dulcibella to help her and Eg live "happily ever after"?

Literary Elements

Recognizing the Elements of a Comedy

The Ugly Duckling is a **comedy**. In a comedy the characters often include some young lovers, the plot ends happily, and the theme often has something to do with love.

Comic Characters. One of the basic elements of humor is the unexpected. Characters like a king who is nagged by his queen and a prince who is timid are funny because they are different from what you expect them to be. **1** Why is Dulcibella's attempt to act like a **2** princess so funny? Why is it humorous to see a fairy-tale chancellor in horn-rimmed glasses?

Comic Plot. In every play, the characters face some struggle or conflict. The plot tells what they do to solve their problem. In a comedy, the characters solve the problem happily. In every play there is also a **climax**, or turning point, when we know whether the play will end happily or unhappily. The climax in this play comes when the Chancellor tests the fake **3** "Prince" with the riddle (page 313). How does the real Prince win his bride and make the play end happily?

Comic Theme. Most comedies are about love **4** or happiness. What does *The Ugly Duckling* say about the power of love? Look at the Princess' speech on page 310, in which she reveals her

5 secret to the Prince. Which line sums up what this play says about happiness?

Understanding Stage Terms

The theater has its own technical terminology, just as baseball, medicine, and electronics do. If you ever stage a play, you'll have to know the vocabulary of the stage.

Almost every production of a play has people in charge of *sets, props, lighting,* and *costumes*. The *director* of the play supervises all aspects of the play's production.

Set: all the scenery and furniture used on the stage. Some plays use more than one set. Each time a play is produced, it usually has a different set. Describe (or draw) the set you **1** would design for *The Ugly Duckling*. Would it be a reversal of what the audience expects a castle to be like, or would it be a typical fairy-tale castle?

Props: the properties, or objects that the characters need to use as they act out the play. Props may include a handkerchief, a glass of **2** water, a sword, or a paper bag. Make a list of the props needed for this play. Start with the handkerchief.

Lighting: all the lights that are focused on the stage, including footlights and spotlights. Lighting must be planned to create the right **3** mood for the play. What kind of lighting would you use for *The Ugly Duckling*?

Costumes: the clothes the characters wear. Each time a play is produced, the costumes may differ. If you were the costume designer for a production of *The Ugly Duckling*, you would need to tell exactly what each character would wear. Using words or drawings (or both), describe the costumes you would design for the **4** characters in *The Ugly Duckling*. Would you have the King wear a business suit, a typical fairy-tale costume, or a humorous combination of both? (Notice that the stage direction at the opening

---

4a. The wedding. **4b.** That Princess and Prince have met, are in love, and have deceived everyone.
5a. Yes, since this is fairy tale.
5b. Dulcibella will be rewarded.

LITERARY ELEMENTS
Recognizing the Elements of a Comedy
1. She is dumb, silly; incongruous in role of fairy-tale princess.
2. They are modern inventions, out of place.
3. Prince makes up story that cats are called dogs in his country.
4. Love can transform people; transforms Camilla into beautiful woman.
5. That "the best thing in the world . . . was to be quite sure of yourself, but not to expect admiration from other people."

Understanding Stage Terms
1. Milne gives hint (p. 300) that "curtain openings" could serve as doors. Because this is a parody, elaborate set is not needed.
2. Handkerchief, horn-rimmed spectacles, crowns, "thrones," and documents for the Chancellor.
3. Responses will vary. Lighting might soften during Prince and Princess' romantic scene.
4. Responses will vary. Because play is a parody, King should look slightly ridiculous.

draft, and revise their posters on drawing paper before doing final drafts on larger poster board. Each poster should include the name of the play, time and place of its presentation, and names of the leading actors. Consult with students in the planning stages to agree on how their posters

will be assessed. Students could include photos of their posters in their portfolios. (For more information on student portfolios see the *Portfolio Assessment and Professional Support Materials* booklet in your teaching resources.)

---

5. Responses will vary. Dulcibella must be dressed as maid, but her costume should accentuate her physical beauty. Camilla's should be plain, but dignified.

FOR DRAMATIZATION
1. She giggles.
2. Staring off into space, her mouth hanging open.

FOCUS ON INFORMATIVE WRITING
To emphasize the importance of audience in informative writing, you might want to suggest that students brainstorm first for audiences they might address, such as their classmates, students in a local elementary school, and their parents. Then have students list suitable topics for those audiences. Alternatively, you might do this activity on the chalkboard as a whole-class activity. Encourage students to be thorough and specific in listing their steps.

ABOUT THE AUTHOR
Students may be familiar with Milne's work, which includes *Winnie-the-Pooh, The House at Pooh Corner,* and two books of children's poems, *When We Were Very Young* and *Now We Are Six.* Milne's poems are often included in literature textbooks; animated movies have been made of his stories of Pooh.

---

of the play says, *"But he should be wearing his crown."*) **5** How would you make Dulcibella's costume differ from Camilla's?

For Dramatization

Presenting a Scene

Perhaps the funniest scene in this play is the one in which the King tries to teach the giggling Dulcibella to act like a princess (page 306). Dulcibella tries hard—too hard—but she is a hilarious flop as a princess. You might try presenting this scene in class.

Read the scene carefully to find out what props you will need.

Pay close attention to the stage directions in parentheses. One stage direction to the King reads:

(He curls his mustache and puts his stomach in.)

1 What does Dulcibella do in response to this action?

You will also get clues to actions from the speeches of the characters. For example, the King tells Dulcibella to be "thinking beautiful thoughts." Then he adds, "but with the mouth **2** definitely shut." What is Dulcibella doing to look as if she is having beautiful thoughts?

Focus on Informative Writing

Explaining a Process

In informative or expository writing, you often explain a **process:** how to do something or how something works. A director's process of preparing to present a dramatic scene, for example, might be outlined this way:

Cast parts →
Identify and prepare props →
Prepare costumes and lighting →
Rehearse actors' lines and movements

When you choose a topic for a process explanation, use the following guidelines:

1. Choose a suitable topic for your audience—something that will have interest and value for them.
2. Choose a topic with which you are familiar—something you know how to do well.

Brainstorm with a small group of classmates to choose *two* topics for informative essays. One topic should be on how to do something, while the other should be on how something works. For each topic, make a chart like the one below. List each step or stage of the process in the correct order. Save your notes.

| Topic: _____ |
| Audience: _____ |
| Steps/Stages |
| 1: _____ |
| 2: _____ |
| 3: _____ |
| 4: _____ |

About the Author

A. A. Milne   (1882–1956)

The Granger Collection, New York

A. A. Milne was a British novelist and playwright whose stories of Winnie-the-Pooh and Christopher Robin (a character based on his own son) have overshadowed everything else he wrote. Milne worked for the British humor magazine *Punch.* He wrote his first play at the front lines during World War I. His plays were huge successes. Among them are *Mr. Pim Passes By* and a mystery called *The Perfect Alibi.*

OBJECTIVES

The overall aim is for students to analyze character, to examine types and use of language, and to identify the use of **parody** in *Pyramus and Thisby.* For a complete list of objectives, see the **Teacher's Notes.**

VOCABULARY

The **Language and Vocabulary** exercise on p. 332 provides students with practice in using the dictionary to find meanings of archaic words.

FOCUS / MOTIVATION

Ask students to speculate on the skills needed to produce, direct, and act in a play. Ask what kind of production they would expect from actors without experience. Tell them the play they will now read is about such a production.

Pyramus and Thisby

WILLIAM SHAKESPEARE

In Shakespeare's comedy A Midsummer Night's Dream, *a group of workingmen plan a play as entertainment for the wedding of their ruler, the Duke of Athens. The men can hardly read or write. They have difficulty figuring out the meaning of their lines and memorizing them. They decide to dramatize a tragic story that was well known in Shakespeare's day—a tale of two young lovers named Pyramus and Thisby. As you read, notice how seriously these actors take themselves and how the audience responds to their play.*

Characters

Peter Quince, a carpenter, the director of the play, who also delivers
   the Prologue
Nick Bottom, a weaver, who takes the part of the lover Pyramus
Francis Flute, a bellows-mender, who takes the part of Thisby
Robin Starveling, a tailor, who presents Moonshine
Tom Snout, a tinker, who plays the Wall
Snug, a joiner, or cabinetmaker, who plays the Lion
Theseus (thē′sē-əs, -syoōs′), Duke of Athens
Hippolyta (hǐ-pŏl′ə-tə), queen of the Amazons and bride of Theseus
Philostrate (fǐ′lŏs-strä′tē), master of the revels
Courtiers, Ladies, and Attendants

Scene 1

[*Quince's house. Enter* Quince, Snug, Bottom, Flute, Snout, *and* Starveling.]

Quince. Is all our company here?
Bottom. You were best to call them generally,° man by man, according to the scrip.°
Quince. Here is the scroll of every man's name which is thought fit, through all Athens, to play in our interlude° before the Duke and the Duchess on his wedding day at night.
Bottom. First, good Peter Quince, say what the play treats on. Then read the names of the actors, and so grow to a point.°   5

2. **generally:** Bottom means "severally" or "separately."   **scrip:** list.   4. **interlude:** play.   6. **grow to a point:** conclude.

TEACHING RESOURCES C
Teacher's Notes, p. 169
Reading Check, p. 172
Study Guide, pp. 174, 176, 178
Language Skills, p. 180
Building Vocabulary, p. 183
Selection Test, p. 185

AV RESOURCES BINDER
Audiocassette 2, Side B

PREREADING FOCUS
The headnote focuses on the characters' misunderstanding of the play they stage. Shakespeare parodies the characters, whose good intentions are overshadowed by their ineptness.

Pyramus and Thisby

1
Bellows: tool used to pump air to keep fire going and increase temperature.

2
A *tinker* is one who works with metals; repairs household utensils.

3
Philostrate decides that entertainment will be presented at ceremonies.

4
Pyramus and Thisby is a play within a play. Scene 1 is actually Act One, Scene 2 of *A Midsummer Night's Dream.*

5
Characterization. Bottom is loud, egocentric character who often upstages Quince, the director.

MOTIVATIONAL SUMMARY

The Duke of Athens has taken a wife. A group of humble, nearly illiterate workmen decide to honor the occasion with a play, *Pyramus and Thisby,* a classic tragedy of lost love. Quince, the director, has his hands full: None of his actors have ever been on stage. However, one actor, Bottom, is convinced that he can play any part. The result would certainly have surprised the ancient Greek playwrights.

PRESENTATION

Discuss the **plot** of *A Midsummer Night's Dream* and the legendary story of *Pyramus and Thisby.* (The *Teacher's Manual* gives a summary and suggestions for further reading.) Then you may want to discuss the cast of characters on p. 319

6
Verbal irony. Quince has called the play a *"lamentable comedy."* It is, in fact, a **tragedy** made comic by the ineptness of the players.

7 Analyzing
What does Bottom mean when he says the play is a "merry"? The play is entertaining.

8
The legend of Pyramus and his lover would have been familiar to Shakespeare's audience. Bottom reveals his ignorance by asking "What is Pyramus?"

9
Parody. Bottom is attempting to demonstrate his ability to act a tyrant's part. In stately poetry, however, rhymes do not follow each other so rapidly. Bottom mispronounces "Phoebus," and his "poem" ends nonsensically. Nevertheless, he immediately declares his own performance to be first rate: "This was lofty."

10
Characterization. Flute would obviously like to play the role of a heroic "wandering knight." He is given a female part instead.

11
Characterization. Bottom wants to play Flute's part also. He strives persistently to be the center of attention. He is the stereotypical "ham," an incompetent actor who overacts.

12
"A play fitted" means the cast is complete.

---

6 **Quince.** Marry,° our play is *The most lamentable comedy* and most cruel death of Pyramus and Thisby.

7 **Bottom.** A very good piece of work, I assure you, and a merry. Now, good Peter Quince, call forth your actors by the scroll. Masters, spread yourselves. 10

Quince. Answer as I call you. Nick Bottom, the weaver.

Bottom. Ready. Name what part I am for, and proceed.

Quince. You, Nick Bottom, are set down for Pyramus.

8 **Bottom.** What is Pyramus? A lover, or a tyrant?

Quince. A lover, that kills himself most gallant for love. 15

Bottom. That will ask some tears in the true performing of it. If I do it, let the audience look to their eyes, I will move storms, I will condole° in some measure. To the rest. Yet my chief humor° is for a tyrant. I could play Ercles° rarely, or a part to tear a cat in,° to make all split.

9
"The raging rocks 20
And shivering shocks
Shall break the locks
   Of prison gates.
And Phibbus' car°
Shall shine from far, 25
And make and mar
   The foolish Fates."

This was lofty! Now name the rest of the players. This is Ercles' vein, a tyrant's vein.° A lover is more condoling.

Quince. Francis Flute, the bellows-mender. 30

Flute. Here, Peter Quince.

Quince. Flute, you must take Thisby on you.

10 **Flute.** What is Thisby? A wandering knight?

Quince. It is the lady that Pyramus must love.

Flute. Nay, faith, let not me play a woman. I have a beard coming. 35

Quince. That's all one. You shall play it in a mask, and you may speak as small° as you will.

11 **Bottom.** An° I may hide my face, let me play Thisby too. I'll speak in a monstrous little voice, "Thisne, Thisne." "Ah Pyramus, my lover dear! Thy Thisby dear, and lady dear!"

Quince. No, no. You must play Pyramus, and Flute, you Thisby.

Bottom. Well, proceed.

Quince. Robin Starveling, the tailor. 40

Starveling. Here, Peter Quince.

Quince. Robin Starveling, you must play Thisby's mother. Tom Snout, the tinker.

Snout. Here, Peter Quince.

Quince. You, Pyramus' father. Myself, Thisby's father. Snug, the joiner, you, the lion's part. 45

12 And, I hope, here is a play fitted.

---

7. **Marry:** an exclamation.   17. **condole:** Bottom means "lament."   18. **humor:** whim.   **Ercles:** Hercules.   **tear a cat in:** to overact.   24. **Phibbus' car:** the chariot of Phoebus, the sun god.   28. **tyrant's vein:** In the old drama, Hercules was portrayed as a ranting character.   36. **small:** shrilly.   37. **An:** if.

13 Snug. Have you the lion's part written? Pray you, if it be, give it me, for I am slow of study.

Quince. You may do it extempore, for it is nothing but roaring.

14 Bottom. Let me play the lion too. I will roar that I will do any man's heart good to hear me; I will roar that I will make the Duke say, "Let him roar again, let him roar again." 50

Quince. An you should do it too terribly, you would fright the Duchess and the ladies, that they would shriek; and that were enough to hang us all.

All. That would hang us, every mother's son.

Bottom. I grant you, friends, if you should fright the ladies out of their wits, they would have

15 no more discretion but to hang us. But I will aggravate° my voice so that I will roar you 55 as gently as any sucking dove, I will roar you an 'twere any nightingale.

16 Quince. You can play no part but Pyramus; for Pyramus is a sweet-faced man, a proper° man as one shall see in a summer's day, a most lovely, gentlemanlike man. Therefore you must needs play Pyramus.

Bottom. Well, I will undertake it. What beard were I best to play it in? 60

Quince. Why, what you will.

17 Bottom. I will discharge it in either your straw-color beard, your orange-tawny beard, your purple-in-grain° beard, or your French-crown-color beard, your perfect yellow.

Quince. Masters, here are your parts. And I am to entreat you, request you, and desire you, to con° them by tomorrow night; and meet me in the palace wood, a mile without the 65 town, by moonlight. There will we rehearse, for if we meet in the city, we shall be dogged with company, and our devices known. In the meantime I will draw a bill of properties such as our play wants. I pray you, fail me not.

18 Bottom. We will meet, and there we may rehearse most obscenely° and courageously. Take pains, be perfect. Adieu. 70

Quince. At the Duke's Oak we meet.

Scene 2

[*A wood near Athens. Enter* Quince, Snug, Bottom, Flute, Snout, *and* Starveling.]

Bottom. Are we all met?

Quince. Pat,° pat, and here's a marvelous convenient place for our rehearsal. This green plot shall be our stage, this hawthorn brake° our tiring-house;° and we will do it in action as we will do it before the Duke.

Bottom. Peter Quince —— 5

19 Quince. What sayest thou, bully Bottom?

Bottom. There are things in this comedy of Pyramus and Thisby that will never please. First, Pyramus must draw a sword to kill himself, which the ladies cannot abide. How answer you that?

---

55. **aggravate:** Bottom means "restrain." 57. **proper:** handsome. 63. **purple-in-grain:** dyed purple. 65. **con;** learn. 69. **obscenely:** Bottom means "obscurely" or "off the scene."
2. **Pat:** right on time. 3. **hawthorn brake:** thicket of hawthorn bushes. **tiring-house:** dressing room.

Pyramus and Thisby **321**

13
Characterization. The actors are all simpletons. Snug, admitting he is "slow of study," asks for the script so that he can have time to learn the lion's part. All he will have to do is roar.

14
Bottom also wishes to play the lion's part. The other actors fear that his roaring would frighten the ladies and cause the whole cast to be executed.

15
Characterization. Bottom often misuses words. Here he uses "aggravate" and "roar" in senses opposite to their meanings. His intent is revealed in the **similes** ("as gently as any sucking dove," "an 'twere any nightingale").

16
Quince flatters Bottom, perhaps to assure him that he is perfect for the role of Pyramus.

17 Making Generalizations
What is humorous about Bottom's comments? An actor's performance does not depend upon the type of beard he wears.

18
Another example of Bottom's misuse of words.

19
In Shakespeare's day, the word *bully* meant roughly "good friend."

MEETING INDIVIDUAL NEEDS

ESL/LEP • Several archaic words and phrases may require explanation. These include "You . . . are *set down for*" (assigned), "That will *ask* some tears . . ." (require), "Flute, you must *take Thisby on you.*" (play the role of Thisby), "*Pray you*" (I ask/beg of you), "I will *undertake* it." (do) and "a mile *without the* town" (outside of).

You should also familiarize students with two archaic verb forms. First, call their attention to the *–st* ending in the second-person singular present tense, as in "What *sayest* thou . . .?"

Then point out Shakespeare's use of the third-person singular present tense *–eth/–th* ending, as in "This man . . . *presenteth* Moonshine" and "*Doth* the moon shine that night . . .?" Make sure students know that these forms are no longer used today.

20
Good theater creates the illusion of real life. Bottom, however, fears that the audience would be disturbed to see suicides acted out on stage, so he recommends that members of the troupe emphasize that they are only "playing."

21
"I fear it" means "I think so" or "I'm afraid so." May also mean Starveling fears the roaring.

22 Summarizing
How will the lion avoid scaring the ladies? The lion will explain to the audience that he does not want to scare anyone and will give his name to prove that he is only a harmless actor.

23
Quince, Snout, and Bottom talk about technical problems: How does one represent moonlight and a wall? Shakespeare is mocking the literalism of actors' solutions.

24
Bottom is consistently confused by words that sound similar. He uses "odious" (repugnant) for "odors." The lines humorously refer to Thisby's breath.

Snout. By'r lakin, a parlous° fear! 10

Starveling. I believe we must leave the killing out, when all is done.

20 Bottom. Not a whit. I have a device to make all well. Write me a prologue, and let the prologue seem to say we will do no harm with our swords, and that Pyramus is not killed indeed. And, for the more better assurance, tell them that I Pyramus am not Pyramus, but Bottom, the weaver. This will put them out of fear. 15

Quince. Well, we will have such a prologue, and it shall be written in eight and six.°

Bottom. No, make it two more. Let it be written in eight and eight.

Snout. Will not the ladies be afeard of the lion?

21 Starveling. I fear it, I promise you.

Bottom. Masters, you ought to consider with yourselves. To bring in—God shield us—a lion 20 among ladies is a most dreadful thing; for there is not a more fearful wildfowl than your lion living, and we ought to look to 't.

Snout. Therefore another prologue must tell he is not a lion.

22 Bottom. Nay, you must name his name, and half his face must be seen through the lion's neck. And he himself must speak through, saying thus, or to the same defect°—"Ladies"—or 25 "Fair ladies—I would wish you"—or "I would request you"—or "I would entreat you—not to fear, not to tremble. My life for yours. If you think I come hither as a lion, it were pity of my life. No, I am no such thing. I am a man as other men are." And there indeed let him name his name, and tell them plainly he is Snug the joiner.

23 Quince. Well, it shall be so. But there is two hard things: that is, to bring the moonlight into a 30 chamber, for you know, Pyramus and Thisby meet by moonlight.

Snout. Doth the moon shine that night we play our play?

Bottom. A calendar, a calendar! Look in the almanac, find out moonshine, find out moonshine!

Quince. Yes, it doth shine that night. 35

Bottom. Why, then may you leave a casement of the great-chamber° window, where we play, open, and then the moon may shine in at the casement.

Quince. Aye, or else one must come in with a bush of thorns and a lantern,° and say he comes to disfigure,° or to present, the person of moonshine. Then, there is another thing. We must have a wall in the great chamber, for Pyramus and Thisby, says the story, did talk 40 through the chink of a wall.

Snout. You can never bring in a wall. What say you, Bottom?

Bottom. Some man or other must present wall. And let him have some plaster, or some loam, or some roughcast° about him, to signify wall. And let him hold his fingers thus, and through that cranny shall Pyramus and Thisby whisper. 45

Quince. If that may be, then all is well. Come, sit down, every mother's son, and rehearse your parts. Pyramus, you begin. When you have spoken your speech, enter into that brake. And so everyone according to his cue. Speak, Pyramus, Thisby, stand forth.

24 Bottom (*as* **Pyramus**). "Thisby, the flowers of odious savors sweet —— "

---

10. **parlous:** perilous.   16. **eight and six:** Ballads were written in alternate lines of eight and six syllables.   25. **defect:** Bottom means "effect."   36. **great-chamber:** hall of a great house.   38. **bush . . . lantern:** supposedly carried by the man in the moon.   39. **disfigure:** Quince means "figure" or "portray."   44. **roughcast:** rough plaster.

Shakespeare wrote his plays in the vernacular—in other words, in the English that was commonly spoken at that time. However, because English has changed over the years, students often find his language stilted and difficult to understand. Have students paraphrase scenes from *Pyramus and Thisby* using modern English or even slang. Suggest that students ask peers to evaluate their completed paraphrases based on how well they convey the original meaning. Some students may want to present to the class dramatic readings of their paraphrases.

Scene from *A Midsummer Night's Dream* performed at the Stratford Shakespeare Festival, Stratford, Ontario, Canada.

Quince. Odors, odors.   50

Bottom (*as* **Pyramus**). " ⎯ odors savors sweet.
    So hath thy breath, my dearest Thisby dear.
    But hark, a voice! Stay thou but here awhile,
    And by and by I will to thee appear."   [*Exit.*]

25 **Flute.** Must I speak now?   55

Quince. Aye, marry must you, for you must understand he goes but to see a noise that he
    heard, and is to come again.

26 **Flute** (*as* **Thisby**). "Most radiant Pyramus, most lily-white of hue,
    Of color like the red rose on triumphant brier,
    Most briskly juvenal,° and eke° most lovely too,   60

60. **juvenal:** youthful.   **eke:** also.

VISUAL CONNECTIONS
Exploring the Subject
Theater can be simple or complex. In its simplest form, theater needs only an actor, a story, and an audience. In its most sophisticated form, every element of theater—setting, lighting, costuming, makeup, and so on—is carefully controlled as in this production of *A Midsummer Night's Dream.* Notice especially that the floor is not bare boards but is carefully contoured to create an unusually harmonious impression.

25
Humor. Flute does not know what a cue is and must ask if he should speak his lines.

26
Parody. Thisby describes Pyramus in words normally reserved for praising women. Notice the absurd mixture of colors to describe Pyramus' complexion.

27   As true as truest horse, that yet would never tire,
         I'll meet thee, Pyramus, at Ninny's tomb."
28 **Quince.** "Ninus' tomb," man. Why, you must not speak that yet. That you answer to Pyramus.
         You speak all your part at once, cues and all. Pyramus enter. Your cue is past. It is "never
         tire."   65
Flute (*as* **Thisby**). Oh—
         "As true as truest horse, that yet would never tire."

                                [*Reenter* Bottom.]

Bottom (*as* **Pyramus**). "If I were fair, Thisby, I were only thine."

29 [*At this point the rehearsal is broken up and the players scatter. They next meet to perform their play before the Duke and his court.*]

Scene 3

[*Athens. The palace of* Theseus. *Enter* Theseus, Hippolyta, Philostrate, Lords, *and* Attendants.]

Theseus. Where is our usual manager of mirth?
         What revels are in hand? Is there no play?
         Call Philostrate.
Philostrate.   Here, mighty Theseus.
Theseus. Say, what abridgement° have you for this evening?
30   What masque?° What music? How shall we beguile   5
         The lazy time, if not with some delight?
31 **Philostrate.** A play there is, my lord, some ten words long,
         Which is as brief as I have known a play.
         But by ten words, my lord, it is too long,
         Which makes it tedious; for in all the play   10
         There is not one word apt, one player fitted.
         And tragical, my noble lord, it is,
         For Pyramus therein doth kill himself.
         Which, when I saw rehearsed, I must confess,
         Made mine eyes water, but more merry tears   15
         The passion of loud laughter never shed.
Theseus. What are they that do play it?
32 **Philostrate.** Hardhanded men that work in Athens here,
         Which never labored in their minds till now,

---

4. **abridgement:** entertainment (to abridge, or shorten, the evening.)   5. **masque:** court entertainment.

And now have toiled their unbreathed° memories 20
With this same play, against° your nuptial.
33 Theseus. I will hear that play,
For never anything can be amiss,
When simpleness and duty tender it.
Go, bring them in, and take your places, ladies. 25

[*As* Philostrate *leaves to get the players,* Theseus *and the others arrange themselves on the side of the stage as an audience.* Philostrate *reenters.*]

Philostrate. So please your Grace, the Prologue is addressed.°

[*Flourish of trumpets. Enter* Quince *for the* Prologue.]

Quince (*as* **Prologue**). If° we offend, it is with our good will.
34   That you should think, we come not to offend,
But with good will. To show our simple skill,
That is the true beginning of our end.
Consider, then, we come but in despite.° 30
We do not come, as minding to content you,
Our true intent is. All for your delight,
We are not here. That you should here repent you,
The actors are at hand, and, by their show, 35
You shall know all, that you are like to know.
35 Theseus. This fellow does not stand upon points.°
First Courtier. He hath rid° his prologue like a rough colt, he knows not the stop. A good
moral, my lord. It is not enough to speak, but to speak true.
36 Hippolyta. Indeed he hath played on his prologue like a child on a recorder—a sound, but 40
not in government.°
Theseus. His speech was like a tangled chain—nothing impaired, but all disordered. Who is
next?

[*Enter* Pyramus *and* Thisby, Wall, Moonshine, *and* Lion.]

37 Quince (*as* **Prologue**). Gentles, perchance you wonder at this show,
But wonder on, till truth makes all things plain. 45
This man is Pyramus, if you would know.
This beauteous lady, Thisby is certáin.
This man, with lime and roughcast, doth present
Wall, that vile Wall which did these lovers sunder,°

20. **unbreathed:** unpracticed, inexperienced.   21. **against:** in anticipation of.   26. **addressed:** ready.   27. **If . . .:** Because the prologue is mispunctuated, the meaning of Quince's speech is comically distorted.   31. **despite:** ill will.   37. **stand upon points:** pay attention to punctuation marks.   38. **rid:** ridden.   41. **not in government:** undisciplined.   49. **sunder:** separate.

33
Theseus respects his subjects' loyalty.

34
The punctuation in the text represents the way Quince speaks the words. He pauses in all the wrong places, so the speech says the opposite of what it is meant to say. For example, the two phrases in the third line should not be separated by a period. He means "We come not to offend but with good will to show our simple skill." Altering punctuation radically alters meaning.

35
Theseus realizes that Quince's meaning is lost in misreading punctuation.

36
Simile. Quince's performing the Prologue is compared to a child's making noises on a recorder (a wind instrument): The resulting discordant sound shows his lack of training and experience.

37
Though Prologues were used in plays in Shakespeare's day, none so obviously had to introduce the main characters or explain that one character would be playing a wall. Prologues usually conveyed thematic issues.

38
Although characters look ridiculous in their costumes, this is most serious part of play. Quince gives an excellent summary of legend.

Scene from *A Midsummer Night's Dream* performed at the New York Shakespeare Festival, New York City.

38

And through Wall's chink, poor souls, they are content   50
To whisper. At the which let no man wonder.
This man, with lantern, dog, and bush of thorn,
Presenteth Moonshine; for, if you will know,
By moonshine did these lovers think no scorn
To meet at Ninus' tomb, there, there to woo.   55
This grisly beast, which Lion hight° by name,
The trusty Thisby, coming first by night,
Did scare away, or rather did affright.
And, as she fled, her mantle she did fall,
Which Lion vile with bloody mouth did stain.   60

56. **hight:** is called.

Anon comes Pyramus, sweet youth and tall,
And finds his trusty Thisby's mantle slain.

39 Whereat, with blade, with bloody blameful blade,

40 He bravely broached° his boiling bloody breast.
And Thisby, tarrying in mulberry shade,   65
His dagger drew, and died. For all the rest,
Let Lion, Moonshine, Wall, and lovers twain
At large° discourse, while here they do remain.

[*Exeunt* Prologue, Pyramus, Thisby, Lion *and* Moonshine.]

Theseus. I wonder if the lion be to speak.

41 Second Courtier. No wonder, my Lord. One lion may when many asses do.   70

Snout (*as* **Wall**). In this same interlude it doth befall
That I, one Snout by name, present a wall,
And such a wall, as I would have you think,
That had in it a crannied hole or chink,
Through which the lovers, Pyramus and Thisby,   75
Did whisper often very secretly.
This loam, this roughcast, and this stone doth show
That I am that same wall. The truth is so.

42 And this the cranny is, right and siníster,°
Through which the fearful lovers are to whisper.   80

43 Theseus. Would you desire lime and hair to speak better?

Second Courtier. It is the wittiest partition that I have ever heard discourse, my lord.

Theseus. Pyramus draws near the wall! Silence!

[*Reenter* Pyramus.]

44 Bottom (*as* **Pyramus**). O grim-looked night! O night with hue so black!
O night, which ever art when day is not!   85
O night, O night! alack, alack, alack,
I fear my Thisby's promise is forgot!
And thou, O wall, O sweet, O lovely wall,
That stand'st between her father's ground and mine!
Thou wall, O wall, O sweet and lovely wall,   90
Show me thy chink, to blink through with mine eyne!

[*Wall holds up his fingers.*]

Thanks, courteous wall. Jove shield thee well for this!

64. **broached:** stabbed. 68. **at large:** in full. 79. **siníster:** left.

39
Pyramus jumps to wrong conclusion; kills himself as Romeo does in Shakespeare's tragedy *Romeo and Juliet*.

40
Alliteration. Shakespeare is poking fun at overuse of this poetic device. Properly used, repetition of sound complements meaning without drawing undue attention to itself.

41
Pun. Since all the actors are "asses" that speak their lines, it would be no surprise to hear a lion speak.

42
Snout signifies hole in wall by holding apart two fingers of his hand.

43
Irony. Theseus and the Courtier praise the wall, not Snout, for its wit and acting ability.

44
Repetition of "O" and "alack" shows that Bottom is "hamming it up" for audience.

45

Irony. No sooner does Pyramus finish praising the wall than he curses it.

46

Theseus facetiously says that the wall should curse back.

47

Bottom does something an actor should never do; he comes out of character and responds directly to the audience. Such conduct destroys the illusion that action in the play is real.

48

Bottom confuses references to hearing and seeing; he obviously does not listen to what he says.

49

The company humorously solves the problem of making a quick change of **setting**.

50 Finding Main Ideas

What does Theseus mean in l. 120? Responses will vary. His point is that if the audience uses its imagination, a bad play, such as the one he is watching, might seem as good as any.

But what see I? No Thisby do I see.
45 O wicked wall, through whom I see no bliss!
Cursed be thy stones for thus deceiving me! 95
46 Theseus. The wall, methinks, being sensible,° should curse again.
47 Bottom. No, in truth, sir, he should not. "Deceiving me" is Thisby's cue. She is to enter now, and I am to spy her through the wall. You should see it will fall pat as I told you. Yonder she comes.

[*Reenter* Thisby.]

Flute (*as* **Thisby**). O wall, full often has thou heard my moans, 100
For parting my fair Pyramus and me!
My cherry lips have often kissed thy stones,
Thy stones with lime and hair knit up in thee.
48 Bottom (*as* **Pyramus**). I see a voice. Now will I to the chink,
To spy an I can hear my Thisby's face. 105
Thisby!
Flute (*as* **Thisby**). My love thou art, my love I think.
Bottom (*as* **Pyramus**). Think what thou wilt, I am thy lover's grace;
And like Limander,° am I trusty still.
Flute (*as* **Thisby**). And I, like Helen,° till the Fates° me kill. 110
Bottom (*as* **Pyramus**). Oh, kiss me through the hole of this vile wall!
Flute (*as* **Thisby**). I kiss the wall's hole, not your lips at all.
Bottom (*as* **Pyramus**). Wilt thou at Ninny's tomb meet me straightway?
Flute (*as* **Thisby**). 'Tide° life, 'tide death, I come without delay.

[*Exeunt* Pyramus *and* Thisby.]

49 Snout (*as* **Wall**). Thus have I, Wall my part dischargèd so; 115
And, being done, thus Wall away doth go. [*Exit* Wall.]
Theseus. Now is the mural° down between the two neighbors.
Second Courtier. No remedy, my lord, when walls are so willful to hear without warning.
Hippolyta. This is the silliest stuff that I ever heard.
50 Theseus. The best in this kind are but shadows, and the worst are no worse if imagination 120
amend them.
Hippolyta. It must be your imagination then, and not theirs.
Theseus. If we imagine no worse of them than they of themselves, they may pass for excellent men. Here come two noble beasts in, a man and a lion.

[*Reenter* Lion *and* Moonshine.]

---

96. **being sensible:** having feeling.   109. **Limander:** instead of *Leander*, a legendary Greek lover.   110. **Helen:** instead of *Hero*, Leander's love. Helen was in another legend.   **Fates:** in Greek mythology, the three goddesses who controlled the future.   114. **'Tide:** betide; happen.   117. **mural:** wall.

51 Snug (*as* **Lion**). You, ladies, you, whose gentle hearts do fear 125
  The smallest monstrous mouse that creeps on floor,
  May now perchance° both quake and tremble here,
  When lion rough in wildest rage doth roar.
  Then know that I, one Snug, the joiner, am
  A lion fell,° nor else no lion's dam; 130
  For, if I should as lion come in strife
  Into this place, 'twere pity on my life.°

Theseus. A very gentle beast, and of a good conscience.

Second Courtier. The very best at a beast, my lord, that e'er I saw.

First Courtier. This lion is a very fox for his valor. 135

Starveling (*as* **Moonshine**). This lantern doth the hornèd moon present,
  Myself the man i' the moon do seem to be.

52 Theseus. This is the greatest error of all the rest. The man should be put into the lantern.
  How is it else the man i' the moon?

First Courtier. Proceed, Moon. 140

53 Starveling. All that I have to say is, to tell you that the lantern is the moon; I, the man i' the
  moon; this thornbush, my thornbush; and this dog, my dog.

Second Courtier. Why, all these should be in the lantern, for all these are in the moon. But
  silence! Here comes Thisby.

[*Reenter* Thisby.]

54 Flute (*as* **Thisby**). This is old Ninny's tomb. Where is my love? 145

Snug (*as* **Lion**, *roaring*). Oh—— [Thisby *runs off.*]

55 Second Courtier. Well roared, Lion.

Theseus. Well run, Thisby.

Hippolyta. Well shone, Moon. Truly, the moon shines with a good grace.

[*Lion shakes* Thisby's *mantle and exits.*]

56 Theseus. Well moused, Lion. 150

First Courtier. And so the lion vanished.

Second Courtier. And then came Pyramus.

[*Reenter* Pyramus.]

57 Bottom (*as* **Pyramus**). Sweet Moon, I thank thee for thy sunny beams,
  I thank thee, Moon, for shining now so bright.
  For by thy gracious, golden, glittering gleams, 155
  I trust to take of truest Thisby sight.
    But stay, oh spite!

---

127. **perchance:** perhaps.   130. **fell:** fierce. *Fell* also refers to an animal's hide or skin.   132. **'twere . . . life:** I should be
hanged for it.

Summarizing
Drawing Conclusions
51 *How does Snug play the role of the Lion? Why does he play it so unusually?* Plays role cautiously. Does not want to give offense or scare audience.

52 Theseus, mocking the actors' literalism, suggests that Starveling should be inside the lantern if he is to represent man in the moon.

53 Starveling is confused by the criticism and responds in literal fashion by pointing out that his thornbush and his dog play themselves.

54 As in the rehearsal, Flute blunders by referring to Ninus as "Ninny."

55 Dramatic irony. Audience knows that the compliments from Theseus and wedding party are made in jest, but the players do not know they are being mocked.

56 Theseus refers to the way Lion shakes Thisby's mantle as the way a cat would shake a mouse.

57 Verbal irony. Bottom refers to the moon's beams as "sunny."

58

Parody. Intentionally bad verse filled with frivolous **rhymes** and **alliterations,** and made laughable by its blend of incongruous language levels (lofty, poetic language: "poor king," "dreadful dole," "furies fell"; common language: "dainty duck," "mantle good," "cut thread").

59

Bottom "hams up" the dying scene, even though he speaks absurd lines such as "Where heart doth hop" and "Tongue, lose thy light."

60

The moon does not rise or set upon human command, but Moonshine exits on Bottom's command.

61

Theseus' statement would be reminder of what happened during the rehearsal, when Puck put an ass's head on Bottom.

58

> But mark, poor knight,
> What dreadful dole° is here!
> Eyes, do you see?   160
> How can it be?
> Oh dainty duck! Oh dear!
> Thy mantle good,
> What, stained with blood!
> Approach, ye Furies fell!°   165
> O Fates, come, come,
> Cut thread and thrum°
> Quail, crush, conclude, and quell!°

Theseus. This passion,° and the death of a dear friend, would go near to make a man look
    sad.   170

Hippolyta. Beshrew my heart, but I pity the man.

Bottom (*as* **Pyramus**). O wherefore, Nature, didst thou lions frame?
> Since lion vile hath here deflowered my dear,
> Which is—no, no—which was the fairest dame
> That lived, that loved, that liked, that looked with cheer.   175
>> Come, tears, confound.°
>> Out, sword, and wound
>> The pap° of Pyramus.
>> Aye, that left pap,

59
>> Where heart doth hop. [*Stabs himself.*]   180
>> Thus die I, thus, thus, thus.
>> Now am I dead,
>> Now am I fled,
>> My soul is in the sky.
>> Tongue, lose thy light,   185

60
>> Moon, take thy flight, [*Exit* Moonshine.]
>> Now die, die, die, die, die. [*Dies.*]

61 **Theseus.** With the help of a surgeon he might yet recover, and prove an ass.

Hippolyta. How chance Moonshine is gone before Thisby comes back and finds her lover?

Theseus. She will find him by starlight. Here she comes, and her passion ends the play.   190

[*Reenter* Thisby.]

Flute (*as* **Thisby**). Asleep, my love?
> What, dead, my dove?
> O Pyramus, arise!

---

159. **dole:** sorrow.   165. **Furies fell:** In Greek mythology, the Furies avenged unpunished crimes.   167. **thrum:** the very end of the thread. One of the goddesses spun the thread of life, a second goddess determined its length, and a third cut it.   168. **quell:** slay.   169. **passion:** display of sorrow.   176. **confound:** destroy.   178. **pap:** breast.

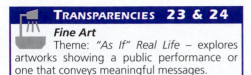

TRANSPARENCIES 23 & 24
Fine Art
Theme: "As If" Real Life – explores artworks showing a public performance or one that conveys meaningful messages.

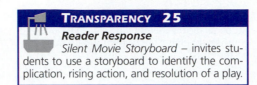

TRANSPARENCY 25
Reader Response
Silent Movie Storyboard – invites students to use a storyboard to identify the complication, rising action, and resolution of a play.

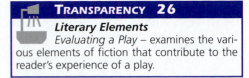

TRANSPARENCY 26
Literary Elements
Evaluating a Play – examines the various elements of fiction that contribute to the reader's experience of a play.

62 Speak, speak. Quite dumb?
Dead, dead? A tomb   195
Must cover thy sweet eyes.
These lily lips,
This cherry nose,
These yellow cowslip cheeks,
Are gone, are gone.   200
Lovers, make moan.
His eyes were as green as leeks.
O Sisters Three,°
Come, come to me,
With hands as pale as milk,   205
Lay them in gore,
Since you have shore°
With shears his thread of silk.
Tongue, not a word.
Come trusty sword,   210
Come, blade, my breast imbrue.° [*Stabs herself.*]
And, farewell, friends.
Thus Thisby ends.
Adieu, adieu, adieu! [*Dies.*]

63 Theseus. Moonshine and Lion are left to bury the dead.   215
Second Courtier. Aye, and Wall too.

64 Bottom (*starting up*). No, I assure you; the wall is down that parted their fathers. Will it please you to see the epilogue?

65 Theseus. No epilogue, I pray you, for your play needs no excuse. Never excuse, for when the players are all dead, there need none to be blamed. Marry, if he that writ it had played   220
Pyramus and hanged himself in Thisby's garter, it would have been a fine tragedy. And so it is, truly, and very notably discharged.

203. **Sisters Three:** the Fates.   207. **shore:** cut.   211. **imbrue:** drench with blood.

62

Parody. Thisby's farewell speech is like a lighthearted nursery rhyme rather than the words of someone who will soon commit suicide. Her description of the dead Pyramus makes him sound like a clown or a court jester.

63

In the final scenes of most Renaissance tragedies, major characters, who serve as stabilizing forces, typically come on stage to bury the slain tragic figures. In this play, no human characters remain to bury the dead or reestablish order. Only Moonshine, Lion, and Wall are alive.

64

Bottom cannot resist a last chance to address the audience, but the Duke has had enough.

65

Duke says the author should have played Pyramus and hanged himself. The performance has been a "lamentable comedy" as Quince indicated (Scene 1, l. 7).

READING CHECK

1. The Duke's wedding (p. 319).
2. To avoid scaring ladies (pp. 321–322).
3. Actors: one with plaster for wall, one with lantern for moon (p. 322).
4. Laugh, joke (pp. 325–331).
5. They stab themselves (pp. 330–331).

FOR STUDY AND DISCUSSION

Scene 1

1. Misuse language; mix legends; fail to see contradictions in their thoughts.
2. Description of cruel deaths as "lamentable comedy" is contradiction.
3. Line 2: "generally" for "separately"; l. 37: "monstrous little voice," a contradiction; l. 69: "obscenely" for "off the scene."
4. Eager to do each part; overacts.
5. It is senseless.

Scene 2

1a. That ladies will fear suicide, lion. 1b. A prologue to explain action; Snug's face must show.
2. Actors will represent moonlight and wall.
3. Bottom and Flute misread parts and cues.

Scene 3

1a. Says play is tedious, ridiculous. 1b. Respects subjects' loyalty. 1c. He is wise, benevolent.
2. For summary, see p. 160 in *Teacher's Manual*.
3. He parodies alliteration, ll. 63–64, 158–169; invocations, ll. 84–91; allusions, ll. 109–110. For poetry that puts meter, rhyme before sense, see ll. 57–58, 79–80, 100–104, 129–130, 194–214.
4. See ll. 155, 162 for use of alliteration and words that rhyme without making sense.
5a. Bottom in ll. 97–99, 217. Starveling in ll. 141–142. 5b. The actors do not see how silly the play is.

Reading Check

1. What is the occasion for the interlude the workingmen present?
2. Why does Bottom ask for a prologue to the play?
3. What do the players use to represent the wall and the moon?
4. How do Theseus and the other members of the audience react to the play?
5. In the play, how do Pyramus and Thisby die?

For Study and Discussion

Analyzing and Interpreting the Play

Scene 1

1. How can you tell that these workingmen are simple and uneducated?

2. How does the title of the interlude contribute to the humor of this scene?

3. Bottom often uses words without understanding what they mean. For example, in line 55 he says he will *aggravate* his voice when he means he will *restrain* it. Find several comic examples of his misuse of language.

4. How does Bottom show he is a "ham," a performer who tends to exaggerate his roles?

5. In lines 20–27, Bottom treats us to poetry in the "lofty" vein. Why is this speech so comical?

Scene 2

1a. What fears does Bottom express about the audience's reaction to certain parts of the play? **b.** What solution does he offer to these problems?

2. Quince says in line 30 that there are "two hard things" to present in the interlude. How do the actors decide to handle these difficulties?

Scene 3

1a. Why does Philostrate try to dissuade Theseus from having the play performed? **b.** Why does Theseus decide, nevertheless, to hear it? **c.** What does his decision reveal about him as a ruler?

2. Retell the story of Pyramus and Thisby in your own words. Be sure to include the roles played by the wall and by the lion.

3. **Parody** is a humorous imitation of a serious work or style of writing for the purpose of amusement. In this play Shakespeare parodies certain techniques of his contemporaries. Find instances where he pokes fun at flowery language and ridiculous comparisons.

4. Read aloud Bottom's speech, lines 153–168. How does Bottom overuse such poetic devices as alliteration and rhyme?

5a. Find instances where the actors drop out of character to address members of the audience. **b.** Why do these interruptions add to the comedy?

Language and Vocabulary

Understanding Meanings of Words

Notice that many words in *Pyramus and Thisby* are glossed at the bottom of the page. Some of the words are explained as comic misuse of language by one of the characters. Others are defined because their meanings in the play are either out of use (**archaic**) or not commonly used. Shakespeare wrote *Pyramus and Thisby* about four hundred years ago, and a number of the words he used have changed in meaning over the centuries.

1 Use an unabridged dictionary to answer the following questions about words used in *Pyramus and Thisby:*

a Does your dictionary list the same definition for the word *proper* as is listed on page 321? Is the definition marked *archaic?*

CLOSURE

Ask students to explain how Shakespeare parodies bad writing, acting, and directing. Also, ask them to cite humorous examples of the characters' misuse of language.

EXTENSION AND ENRICHMENT

Ask students to pick the scene they think is funniest and share their insights into humor with a group. Ask each group to determine what makes a scene funny and then explain these ideas to the class.

Some students might want to illustrate scenes from the play. See the *Teacher's Manual* for suggested scenes. Advanced students might enjoy comparing the **plot** with the original legend from Ovid's *Metamorphoses* and reporting on the differences to the class.

b The meaning of *con* given on page 321 is "to learn." This meaning is not commonly used today. Explain the relationship between this meaning and the French word *conduire,* meaning "to guide."

c On page 325, the definition provided for *against* is "in anticipation of." Is that meaning archaic or is it just infrequently used?

d The meaning given for *sinister* (page 327) is "left." That meaning for *sinister,* though rare today, is derived from the Latin word *sinister,* meaning "left." Can you think of any connection between the meaning of *left* and the meaning of *evil,* the common definition of *sinister* today?

Writing About Literature

▶ **Discussing Aspects of the Play**

1. Shakespeare was an actor as well as a playwright. What aspects of his profession might he be poking fun at in this "interlude"? In your discussion refer to specific speeches.

2. Bottom is one of Shakespeare's great comic characters. Write an analysis of Bottom's character. Be sure to include his treatment of language.

3. All the workingmen are simple and uneducated. However, they are presented as individuals with distinguishing characteristics. Explain the differences you note in this group.

Focus on Informative Writing

Explaining a Process

When you write an informative paper, it is important to evaluate and organize the details you include. Ask yourself these questions to **evaluate** the information you gather:

1. Is this detail something that my audience already knows?
2. Without this detail, would readers make a mistake or become confused?

You should also **organize** information clearly so that readers can follow your explanation. When you explain a process, use **chronological** or **time order.** Explain the steps or stages in exact order. Use **transitional words and phrases** like these:

after	finally	meanwhile	then
before	first	next	when

Choose one of the topics below, or select a "how-to" topic of your own. Write a paragraph of directions. Evaluate and organize your details carefully. Save your writing.

> how to start work on a jigsaw puzzle
> how to go grocery shopping
> how to plant a small flower garden
> how to make your favorite sandwich

About the Author

William Shakespeare   (1564–1616)

William Shakespeare is generally regarded as the greatest English writer and the world's greatest dramatist. He was the son of a prominent merchant in the town of Stratford-on-Avon in England. When he was in his twenties, he went to London to seek his fortune. There he joined a famous acting company. For this company, he wrote thirty-seven brilliant plays, including tragedies, comedies, and history plays. Plays such as *Hamlet* and *Romeo and Juliet,* which were great successes in their own day, still are being read and performed all over the world. Shakespeare also wrote two narrative poems and many sonnets. Most of Shakespeare's plays were not published during his lifetime.

LANGUAGE AND VOCABULARY

1a. *Proper* as used in play means "handsome." In most modern dictionaries, this usage is marked archaic or dialectal.

1b. *Con* as used in the play means "learn." Students will find that this meaning does not relate directly to the French word *conduire.* Students will discover, however, that **con** in another sense, "to direct the steering of," does relate directly to *conduire.* Because this exercise requires in-depth investigation of word histories, it might best be completed only by advanced students.

1c. *Against* as used in the play means "in anticipation of." This definition is listed in the dictionary, so it is probably infrequently used rather than archaic.

1d. *Sinister* as used in the play means "left," the opposite of "right." The Romans considered thunder on the left an omen of evil. Thus, the word *sinister* gained a connotation which over the centuries has become a denotation.

WRITING ABOUT LITERATURE

1. Shakespeare pokes fun at unimaginative use of properties, excessive and undisciplined use of rhetorical devices (**alliteration, rhyme, metaphor, allusion,** and other figures of speech), failure to preserve decorum (careless misuse of language), and inept delivery of lines.

2. Students might consider Quince's discussion with Bottom (pp. 321–322), each character's delivery of his speeches, and audience's reactions (pp. 328–331).

3. A good way to begin is to examine each character's reaction when Quince assigns roles.

▶ Before students begin this writing assignment, you may want to refer them to the **Writing About Literature** section on page 672.

Page 334: Anne Frank (May 1939).
Page 335: The building where the Franks, the Van Daans, and Mr. Dussel were hidden.

The Diary of Anne Frank

FRANCES GOODRICH
AND
ALBERT HACKETT

The Diary of Anne Frank *is a play based upon a diary found at the end of World War II in a pile of rubbish in an old warehouse in Amsterdam. A young Jewish girl named Anne Frank had kept this diary for twenty-five months. In it, she had recorded the small details of domestic life and her own thoughts during the last years of one of the most terrible wars in history.*

For two years, Otto Frank hid from the Nazis with seven others, seeing the same faces each day, sharing food and fears, keeping frustrations under control as well as he could. Now the war is over, and Otto Frank is the only member of the group who survives. He has come to take a last look at the apartment that was both their shelter and prison and finds there a diary his young daughter had kept. What was it like for a thirteen-year-old to live under such conditions?

PRESENTATION

It is extremely important to lay a good foundation for this drama. You might wish to invite a guest speaker on the Holocaust or assign some research to the class. Be sure students understand that, during World War II, Holland was

To escape the Nazis, Anne Frank's family had moved from Germany to the Netherlands. But when the Nazis took over the Netherlands in 1940, they immediately began persecuting the Jews there.

In July 1942 Anne's family went into hiding in a secret apartment. Their hiding place was on the top floors of a building that Otto Frank, Anne's father, had used as his warehouse and business office. It was in these hidden rooms that Anne kept the diary that has since been translated into many languages. It was here that, in the midst of fear and suffering, she could write: "In spite of everything, I still believe that people are really good at heart."

As you read this play, consider how the characters deal with the terrible forces that are seeking to destroy them.

Characters

Mr. Frank	Mrs. Frank
Miep (mēp)	Margot Frank
Mrs. Van Daan	Anne Frank
Mr. Van Daan	Mr. Kraler
Peter Van Daan	Dussel

The Time: During the years of World War II and immediately thereafter.
The Place: Amsterdam.
There are two acts.

Act One

Scene 1

1 *The scene remains the same throughout the play. It is the top floor of a warehouse and office building in Amsterdam, Holland. The sharply peaked roof of the building is outlined against a sea of other rooftops, stretching away into the distance. Nearby is the* belfry *of a church tower, the* Westertoren, *whose* carillon *rings out the hours. Occasionally faint sounds float up from below: the voices of children playing in the street, the tramp of marching feet, a boat whistle from the canal.*

VISUAL CONNECTIONS
Exploring the Subject
This building, once a commercial property and the last home of the Frank family, is now a museum. Although the original furniture has been removed, models of the secret rooms are displayed in glass cases. The ground floor now houses an organization that monitors anti-Semitic incidents. Farther down the street is a small statue of Anne Frank.

The Diary of Anne Frank

**Act One
Scene One**

1
Setting. In many plays, the setting will change from scene to scene. In this drama, the single setting and the inability of the actors to escape it will contribute to the **atmosphere** of repression.

occupied by the Nazis and that there was an active resistance, that families like the Franks could not have survived as long as they did without the help of the Dutch. Explain that people in the play are waiting for the Allies to invade Europe, bring down Hitler, and end the occupation. Point out that the play's **suspense** depends in part on the reader's awareness that in 1944 the Allies were very close to liberating Holland. The Green Police found this particular hiding place only months before the occupants would have been freed. Although we know that Anne Frank did not survive the persecution, the diary format of the play allows the reader to share her deeply personal reaction to the ordeal. Suggest to students that they try to put themselves in Anne's place as they read.

VISUAL CONNECTIONS
Exploring the Subject
This is a traditional box set, open to full view of audience. It is unrealistic only in that we can see its surroundings and through its "fourth wall." Aronson received good reviews for his design, and reviewers credited the director, Garson Kanin, for making full use of it.

2
Atmosphere. The sparse furnishings and the coverings on the windows create a somber mood. The characters are hemmed in; they have few personal comforts.

3 Making Inferences
What do these clues suggest to the audience? Some time has passed since people have been here; people left in a hurry, or violent action occurred here.

4
Those who know background of play will remember that Otto Frank was wealthy German who fled from Nazi persecution to Holland in 1933, that he would be coming from Auschwitz where he was imprisoned during the war.

The stage set for the original production of *The Diary of Anne Frank* (1955). Designed by Boris Aronson.

The three rooms of the top floor and a small attic space above are exposed to our view. The largest of the rooms is in the center, with two small rooms, slightly raised, on either side. On the right is a bathroom, out of sight. A narrow, steep flight of stairs at **2** *the back leads up to the attic. The rooms are sparsely furnished with a few chairs, cots, a table or two. The windows are painted over, or covered with makeshift blackout curtains. In the main room there is a sink, a gas ring for cooking, and a wood-burning stove for warmth.*

The room on the left is hardly more than a closet. There is a skylight in the sloping ceiling. Directly under this room is a small steep stairwell, with steps leading down to a door. This is the only entrance from the building below. When the door is opened we see that it has been concealed on the outer side by a bookcase attached to it.

The curtain rises on an empty stage. It is late afternoon, November, 1945.

3 *The rooms are dusty, the curtains in rags. Chairs and tables are overturned.*

The door at the foot of the small stairwell swings **4** *open.* Mr. Frank *comes up the steps into view. He is a gentle, cultured European in his middle years. There is still a trace of a German accent in his speech.*

He stands looking slowly around, making a supreme effort at self-control. He is weak, ill. His clothes are threadbare.

Divide the class into small groups to research Holland before, during, and after World War II. Ask each group to select a topic of interest, such as culture, industry, geography, or politics. Have students report orally on their topics, either dividing the presentation among all members of the group or selecting one or two members to present for the group. Encourage students to prepare and use at least one visual aid, such as a picture, drawing, or model to illustrate the information they present.

After a second he drops his <u>rucksack</u> *on the couch and moves slowly about. He opens the door to one of the smaller rooms and then abruptly closes it again, turning away. He goes to the window at the back, looking off at the Westertoren as its carillon strikes the hour of six; then he moves restlessly on.*

5 *From the street below we hear the sound of a barrel organ and children's voices at play. There is a many-colored scarf hanging from a nail. Mr. Frank takes it, putting it around his neck. As he starts back for his rucksack, his eye is caught by something lying on the floor. It is a woman's white glove. He holds it in his hand and suddenly all of his self-control is gone.*

6 *He breaks down, crying.*

We hear footsteps on the stairs. Miep Gies comes up, looking for Mr. Frank. Miep *is a Dutch girl of about twenty-two. She wears a coat and hat, ready to go home. She is pregnant. Her attitude toward* Mr. Frank *is protective, compassionate.*

Miep. Are you all right, Mr. Frank?

Mr. Frank (*quickly controlling himself*). Yes, Miep, yes.

Miep. Everyone in the office has gone home. . . . It's after six. (*Then pleading*) Don't stay up here, Mr. Frank. What's the use of torturing yourself like this?

Mr. Frank. I've come to say goodbye. . . . I'm leaving here, Miep.

Miep. What do you mean? Where are you going? Where?

Mr. Frank. I don't know yet, I haven't decided.

Miep. Mr. Frank, you can't leave here! This is your home! Amsterdam is your home. Your business is here, waiting for you. . . . You're needed here. . . . Now that the war is over, there are things that . . .

Mr. Frank. I can't stay in Amsterdam, Miep. It has too many memories for me. Everywhere there's something . . . the house we lived in . . . the school . . . that street organ playing out

there . . . I'm not the person you used to know,

7 Miep. I'm a bitter old man. (*Breaking off*) Forgive me. I shouldn't speak to you like this . . .

8 after all that you did for us . . . the suffering . . .

9 **Miep.** No. No. It wasn't suffering. You can't say we suffered. (*As she speaks, she straightens a chair which is overturned.*)

Mr. Frank. I know what you went through, you and Mr. Kraler. I'll remember it as long as I live. (*He gives one last look around.*) Come, Miep. (*He starts for the steps, then remembers his rucksack, going back to get it.*)

Miep (*hurrying up to a cupboard*). Mr. Frank, did you see? There are some of your papers here. (*She brings a bundle of papers to him.*) We found them in a heap of rubbish on the floor after . . . after you left.

Mr. Frank. Burn them. (*He opens his rucksack to put the glove in it.*)

Miep. But, Mr. Frank, there are letters, notes . . .

10 **Mr. Frank.** Burn them. All of them.

Miep. Burn *this*? (*She hands him a paperbound notebook.*)

Mr. Frank (*quietly*). Anne's diary. (*He opens the diary and begins to read.*) "Monday, the sixth of

11 July, nineteen forty-two." (*To* Miep) Nineteen forty-two. Is it possible, Miep? . . . Only three years ago. (*As he continues his reading, he sits down on the couch.*) "Dear Diary, since you and I are going to be great friends, I will start by telling you about myself. My name is Anne Frank. I am thirteen years old. I was born in Germany the twelfth of June, nineteen twenty-nine. As my family is Jewish, we emigrated to Holland when Hitler came to power."

[*As* Mr. Frank *reads on, another voice joins his, as if coming from the air. It is* Anne's *voice.*]

Mr. Frank and **Anne.** "My father started a business, importing spice and herbs. Things went well for us until nineteen forty. Then the

5 As the play begins, these every-day sounds have no special meaning. Later, to the trapped family, they will become tantalizing sounds of freedom.

6 These rooms seem to hold painful memories; it seems that the glove reminds Mr. Frank of an overwhelming grief.

7 **Characterization.** Mr. Frank characterizes himself as a "bitter old man"; he has lost his family to Nazi injustices.

8 Miep was part of Dutch Resistance that gave help to Jews.

9 Analyzing
Why does Miep deny having suffered? Miep was not Jewish and did not experience the deprivation of living in cramped quarters directly. By helping Jews, however, she lived in constant fear of discovery.

10 Finding Cause and Effect
Why does Mr. Frank want all the papers burned? His memories are so painful and bitter that he does not want to be reminded of the past.

11 **Flashback.** Almost the entire play is a flashback. Mr. Frank has come to the warehouse in 1945. The action will return to 1942 and move forward until the last scene returns to 1945. The diary serves as the means for reliving the past.

Hate crimes, crimes whose victims are chosen because they belong to a particular racial or ethnic group, still happen throughout the world today. Ask students to collect and bring to class newspaper or magazine articles about such crimes. Engage students in a discussion on why people commit hate crimes and on some possible solutions. Solutions might include ways to encourage acceptance of people's differences, ways to build self-esteem, and ways to get beyond stereotypes. Extend this activity by asking students to identify examples of racism and stereotyping in books, films, television, and advertising. You might wish to show the video documentary "A Class Divided," a 1970 case

---

12 Making Generalizations

What impressions of Anne do the first passages give? Responses will vary. She seems intelligent, aware. She writes well. She is likely to tell story honestly.

13

The audience is unable to see anything on the stage; it hears only Anne's voice. The technique serves to disorient viewers enough to make the transition back in time seem natural.

14

Atmosphere. Anne's lines, telling of the denial of basic freedoms, are spoken in total darkness to create a sense of ominous isolation.

Scene Two

1

Although a play program usually tells audience the time frame of a play's action, audience should be alert to changes in **setting** and appearance of characters.

2 Analyzing Drawing Conclusions

What do the Van Daans' clothes and actions reveal about them? Will the Van Daans be easy to get along with? They are well-to-do, fashionable. Mrs. Van Daan seems more excitable than her husband, but both are high-strung. Their temperaments and apparent concern with themselves may make them difficult to live with.

3

Suspense. Throughout the play, characters live in fear. The first spoken lines of the **flashback** establish this sense of foreboding.

---

12 war came, and the Dutch capitulation,[1] followed by the arrival of the Germans. Then things got very bad for the Jews."

13 [Mr. Frank's *voice dies out. Anne's voice continues alone. The lights dim slowly to darkness. The curtain falls on the scene.*]

14 **Anne's Voice.** You could not do this and you could not do that. They forced Father out of his business. We had to wear yellow stars. I had to turn in my bike. I couldn't go to the movies, or ride in an automobile, or even on a streetcar, and a million other things. But somehow we children still managed to have fun. Yesterday Father told me we were going into hiding. Where, he wouldn't say. At five o'clock this morning Mother woke me and told me to hurry and get dressed. I was to put on as many clothes as I could. It would look too suspicious if we walked along carrying suitcases. It wasn't until we were on our way that I learned where we were going. Our hiding place was to be upstairs in the building where Father used to have his business. Three other people were coming in with us . . . the Van Daans and their son Peter. . . . Father knew the Van Daans but we had never met them. . . .

[*During the last lines the curtain rises on the scene. The lights dim on. Anne's voice fades out.*]

Scene 2

1 *It is early morning, July, 1942. The rooms are bare, as before, but they are now clean and orderly.*

Mr. Van Daan, a tall, portly man in his late forties, is in the main room, pacing up and down, ner-

---

1. **capitulation** (kə-pĭ′chŏŏ-lā′shən): surrender. The Netherlands was taken over by the Nazis in May 1940. The Dutch underground, however, was active in helping escaped Allied prisoners and Jewish refugees.

---

2 *vously smoking a cigarette. His clothes and overcoat are expensive and well cut.*

Mrs. Van Daan sits on the couch, clutching her possessions—a hatbox, bags, etc. She is a pretty woman in her early forties. She wears a fur coat over her other clothes.

Peter Van Daan is standing at the window of the room on the right, looking down at the street below. He is a shy, awkward boy of sixteen. He wears a cap, a raincoat, and long Dutch trousers, like "plus fours."[2] At his feet is a black case, a carrier for his cat.

The yellow Star of David[3] is conspicuous on all of their clothes.

3 **Mrs. Van Daan** (*rising, nervous, excited*). Something's happened to them! I know it!

Mr. Van Daan. Now, Kerli!

Mrs. Van Daan. Mr. Frank said they'd be here at seven o'clock. He said . . .

Mr. Van Daan. They have two miles to walk. You can't expect . . .

Mrs. Van Daan. They've been picked up. That's what's happened. They've been taken. . . .

[Mr. Van Daan *indicates that he hears someone coming.*]

Mr. Van Daan. You see?

[Peter *takes up his carrier and his schoolbag, etc., and goes into the main room as* Mr. Frank *comes up the stairwell from below.* Mr. Frank *looks much younger now. His movements are brisk, his manner confident. He wears an overcoat and carries his hat and a small cardboard box. He crosses to the* Van Daans, *shaking hands with each of them.*]

Mr. Frank. Mrs. Van Daan, Mr. Van Daan,

---

2. **"plus fours":** baggy trousers that are gathered in under the knee; also called *knickers*.
3. **Star of David:** a six-pointed star, an ancient symbol of Judaism. The Nazis required Jews to sew the Star of David onto all their clothing so that they would be immediately identifiable as Jews.

study of a third grade teacher who tried to help her students understand discrimination through an innovative class experiment.

PORTFOLIO ASSESSMENT
Students may want to keep readers' journals as they read *The Diary of Anne Frank*. Recording their responses as they read will help students gain a deeper understanding of the play and of themselves. Suggest that students include relevant drawings, photographs, and collages in their journals. Some students might benefit from recording their journals on audiotape rather than in writing. Consult with students individually to agree on how their journals will be assessed.

Peter. (*Then, in explanation of their lateness*) There were too many of the Green Police[4] on the streets. . . . We had to take the long way around.

4 [*Up the steps come* Margot Frank, Mrs. Frank, Miep (*not pregnant now*), *and* Mr. Kraler. *All of them carry bags, packages, and so forth. The Star of David is conspicuous on all of the* Franks' *clothing.* Margot *is eighteen, beautiful, quiet, shy.* Mrs. Frank *is a young mother, gently bred, reserved. She, like* Mr. Frank, *has a slight German accent.* Mr. Kraler *is a Dutchman, dependable, kindly.*

As Mr. Kraler *and* Miep *go upstage to put down their parcels,* Mrs. Frank *turns back to call* Anne.]

Mrs. Frank. Anne?

5 [Anne *comes running up the stairs. She is thirteen, quick in her movements, interested in everything, mercurial[5] in her emotions. She wears a cape, long wool socks, and carries a schoolbag.*]

Mr. Frank (*introducing them*). My wife, Edith. Mr. and Mrs. Van Daan

[Mrs. Frank *hurries over, shaking hands with them.*]

. . . their son, Peter . . . my daughters, Margot and Anne.

6 [Anne *gives a polite little curtsy as she shakes* Mr. Van Daan's *hand. Then she immediately starts off on a tour of investigation of her new home, going upstairs to the attic room.*

Miep *and* Mr. Kraler *are putting the various things they have brought on the shelves.*]

Mr. Kraler. I'm sorry there is still so much confusion.

Mr. Frank. Please. Don't think of it. After all, **7** we'll have plenty of leisure to arrange everything ourselves.

Miep (*to* Mrs. Frank). We put the stores of food you sent in here. Your drugs are here . . . soap, linen here.

Mrs. Frank. Thank you, Miep.

Miep. I made up the beds . . . the way Mr. Frank and Mr. Kraler said. (*She starts out.*) Forgive me. I have to hurry. I've got to go to the **8** other side of town to get some ration books[6] for you.

Mrs. Van Daan. Ration books? If they see our names on ration books, they'll know we're here.

Mr. Kraler. There isn't anything . . .   ⎫

Miep. Don't worry. Your names won't be on them. (*As she hurries out*) I'll be up later.   ⎬ (*Together*)

Mr. Frank. Thank you, Miep.

9 **Mrs. Frank** (*to* Mr. Kraler). It's illegal, then, the ration books? We've never done anything illegal.

Mr. Frank. We won't be living here exactly according to regulations.

[*As* Mr. Kraler *reassures* Mrs. Frank, *he takes various small things, such as matches, soap, etc., from his pockets, handing them to her.*]

10 **Mr. Kraler.** This isn't the black market,[7] Mrs. Frank. This is what we call the white market . . . helping all of the hundreds and hundreds who are hiding out in Amsterdam.

[*The carillon is heard playing the quarter-hour before eight.* Mr. Kraler *looks at his watch.* Anne *stops at the window as she comes down the stairs.*]

6. **ration books:** books given to each citizen during wartime, containing a certain number of stamps for various items such as food, clothing, and gasoline. These items could not be purchased without the stamps. Ration books were used to make sure that scarce items would be rationed, or evenly distributed.

7. **black market:** an illegal system for buying and selling goods without ration stamps.

4. **Green Police:** the Nazi police, who wore green uniforms.

5. **mercurial** (mər-kyoŏr′ē-əl): quickly changeable.

4
The audience can assume everyone is nervous, not just at thought of going into hiding, but at thought of spending time with people they hardly know.

5
Characterization. Anne is a healthy, inquisitive young teenager.

6
Use to answer **study question 3b**, p. 369.

7 Drawing Conclusions
To what leisure is Mr. Frank referring? The families are in hiding and will have little to occupy their time.

8
Many Dutch citizens took risks and made great sacrifices to save the lives of the Jews among them. Sharing rations was only one of the sacrifices.

9 Analyzing
Why does it seem strange that Mrs. Frank worries about doing something illegal? They are fighting for their lives, so this infraction seems trivial. Mrs. Frank has always been law-abiding; she does not fully realize the situation yet.

10
Black markets thrive because of shortages, especially during war. Mr. Kraler alludes to the help given to persecuted Jews as a "white market," which contrasts with the illegal "black market."

11
Symbol. The carillon, which rings periodically, is a symbol of the freedom which has been denied these families.

12
The discussion of details makes clear the kind of imprisonment to which these Jewish families are committing themselves.

13   Analyzing
What does Mr. Kraler mean by his comment about Mr. Frank?
He sees Mr. Frank as respectable citizen.

14
Characterization. Mrs. Frank clearly does not comprehend the situation as well as her husband does. She is unaware of the need to avoid making the slightest of noises which might disclose their location.

15
It seems that material possessions do not mean as much to Mr. and Mrs. Frank as they do to the Van Daans.

16
Suspense. Mr. Frank's explanation of the dangers helps the audience understand just how cautious the families have to be.

17
Irony. For Mrs. Frank, the ordeal will end in imprisonment and, ultimately, death.

11 **Anne.** It's the Westertoren!

Mr. Kraler. I must go. I must be out of here and downstairs in the office before the workmen get here. (*He starts for the stairs leading out.*) Miep or I, or both of us, will be up each day to bring you food and news and find out what your needs are. Tomorrow I'll get you a better **12** bolt for the door at the foot of the stairs. It needs a bolt that you can throw yourself and open only at our signal. (*To* Mr. Frank) Oh . . . You'll tell them about the noise?

Mr. Frank. I'll tell them.

Mr. Kraler. Goodbye then for the moment. I'll come up again, after the workmen leave.

Mr. Frank. Goodbye, Mr. Kraler.

Mrs. Frank (*shaking his hand*). How can we thank you?

[*The others murmur their goodbyes.*]

Mr. Kraler. I never thought I'd live to see the **13** day when a man like Mr. Frank would have to go into hiding. When you think——

[*He breaks off, going out,* Mr. Frank *follows him down the steps, bolting the door after him. In the interval before he returns,* Peter *goes over to* Margot, *shaking hands with her. As* Mr. Frank *comes back up the steps,* Mrs. Frank *questions him anxiously.*]

14 **Mrs. Frank.** What did he mean, about the noise?

Mr. Frank. First let us take off some of these clothes.

[*They all start to take off garment after garment. On each of their coats, sweaters, blouses, suits, dresses, is another yellow Star of David.* Mr. *and* Mrs. Frank **15** *are underdressed quite simply. The others wear several things—sweaters, extra dresses, bathrobes, aprons, nightgowns, etc.*]

Mr. Van Daan. It's a wonder we weren't arrested, walking along the streets . . . Petronella with a fur coat in July . . .

and that cat of Peter's crying all the way.

Anne. (*as she is removing a pair of panties*). A cat?

Mrs. Frank (*shocked*). Anne, please!

Anne. It's all right. I've got on three more.

[*She pulls off two more. Finally, as they have all removed their surplus clothes, they look to* Mr. Frank, *waiting for him to speak.*]

16 **Mr. Frank.** Now. About the noise. While the men are in the building below, we must have complete quiet. Every sound can be heard down there, not only in the workrooms, but in the offices too. The men come at about eight thirty, and leave at about five thirty. So, to be perfectly safe, from eight in the morning until six in the evening we must move only when it is necessary, and then in stockinged feet. We must not speak above a whisper. We must not run any water. We cannot use the sink, or even, forgive me, the w.c.[8] The pipes go down through the workrooms. It would be heard. No trash . . . (Mr. Frank *stops abruptly as he hears the sound of marching feet from the street below. Everyone is motionless, paralyzed with fear.* Mr. Frank *goes quietly into the room on the right to look down out of the window.* Anne *runs after him, peering out with him. The tramping feet pass without stopping. The tension is relieved.* Mr. Frank, *followed by* Anne, *returns to the main room and resumes his instructions to the group.*) . . . No trash must ever be thrown out which might reveal that someone is living up here . . . not even a potato paring. We must burn everything in the stove at night. This is the way we must live until it is over, if we are to survive.

[*There is silence for a second.*]

17 **Mrs. Frank.** Until it is over.

---

8. **w.c.:** water closet, or toilet.

Mr. Frank (*reassuringly*). After six we can move
about . . . we can talk and laugh and have our
supper and read and play games . . . just as we
would at home. (*He looks at his watch.*) And now
I think it would be wise if we all went to our
rooms, and were settled before eight o'clock.
Mrs. Van Daan, you and your husband will be
upstairs. I regret that there's no place up there
for Peter. But he will be here, near us. This will
be our common room, where we'll meet to talk
and eat and read, like one family.

Mr. Van Daan. And where do you and Mrs.
Frank sleep?

Mr. Frank. This room is also our bedroom.

Mrs. Van Daan. That isn't right.
We'll sleep here and you take the } (*Together*)
room upstairs.

Mr. Van Daan. It's your place.

Mr. Frank. Please. I've thought this out for
weeks. It's the best arrangement. The only
arrangement.

Mrs. Van Daan (*to Mr. Frank*). Never, never can
we thank you. (*Then, to* Mrs. Frank) I don't
know what would have happened to us, if it
hadn't been for Mr. Frank.

Mr. Frank. You don't know how your husband
helped me when I came to this country . . .
knowing no one . . . not able to speak the language. I can never repay him for that. (*Going to*
Mr. Van Daan) May I help you with your
things?

Mr. Van Daan. No. No. (*To* Mrs. Van Daan)
Come along, *liefje*.[9]

Mrs. Van Daan. You'll be all right, Peter?
You're not afraid?

Peter (*embarrassed*). Please, Mother.

[*They start up the stairs to the attic room above.* Mr.
Frank *turns to* Mrs. Frank.]

Mr. Frank. You too must have some rest, Edith.

---

9. *liefje* (lēf'hyə): Dutch for "little loved one."

You didn't close your eyes last night. Nor you,
Margot.

Anne. I slept, Father. Wasn't that funny? I
knew it was the last night in my own bed, and
yet I slept soundly.

Mr. Frank. I'm glad, Anne. Now you'll be able
to help me straighten things in here. (*To* Mrs.
Frank *and* Margot) Come with me. . . . You and
Margot rest in this room for the time being.
(*He picks up their clothes, starting for the room on
the right.*)

Mrs. Frank. You're sure . . . ? I could help . . .
And Anne hasn't had her milk . . .

Mr. Frank. I'll give it to her. (*To* Anne *and*
Peter) Anne, Peter . . . it's best that you take off
your shoes now, before you forget. (*He leads the
way to the room, followed by* Margot.)

Mrs. Frank. You're sure you're not tired,
Anne?

Anne. I feel fine. I'm going to help Father.

Mrs. Frank. Peter, I'm glad you are to be with
us.

Peter. Yes, Mrs. Frank.

[Mrs. Frank *goes to join* Mr. Frank *and* Margot.

During the following scene Mr. Frank *helps* Margot *and* Mrs. Frank *to hang up their clothes. Then
he persuades them both to lie down and rest. The* Van
Daans *in their room above settle themselves. In the
main room* Anne *and* Peter *remove their shoes.*
Peter *takes his cat out of the carrier.*]

Anne. What's your cat's name?

Peter. Mouschi.

Anne. Mouschi! Mouschi! Mouschi! (*She picks
up the cat, walking away with it. To* Peter) I love
cats. I have one . . . a darling little cat. But they
made me leave her behind. I left some food
and a note for the neighbors to take care of
her. . . . I'm going to miss her terribly. What is
yours? A him or a her?

18
Characterization. Mr. Frank
tries to be as positive as possible
about the situation.

19 Drawing Conclusions
*Why does Mr. Frank want cen-
ter room as his bedroom?* The
arrangement will give him quick
access to door, allow him to mon-
itor noises, comings and goings.
The Franks have kept the least
private room for themselves.

20
Apparently, Mr. Frank is repaying
a favor. Mr. Van Daan had helped
him when he first came to Holland.

21
At the outset of the imprisonment, everyone is extremely gracious and helpful. As the close
quarters become confining and
fear produces tension, **conflict**
will develop.

22 Finding Cause and Effect
Why is Peter embarrassed? He
is sixteen years old, wants to be
considered a man.

23
Everyone will have to establish
new habits. Audience can assume that such a routine will be
hard on young people.

24
Jewish children were segregated into Jewish schools in 1940.

25
Irony. None of them can go out. Anne still has not grasped the meaning of being in hiding; it is still adventure for her.

26 Making Inferences
What are their friends apt to think? That they either have escaped or have been arrested.

27
Symbol. Star reminds audience that problems of the families cannot be solved easily.

28 Summarizing
Why is Anne unable to throw the star away? Although it has been used to oppress her, it is a powerful **symbol** of her religion, which is important part of her identity.

Photographs (pages 342, 344, 347, 351, 353, 360, 364, 371, 379, 381, 387, 388, 391, and 392) of the original stage production of *The Diary of Anne Frank,* which opened on Broadway on October 5, 1955.

Peter. He's a tom. He doesn't like strangers. (*He takes the cat from her, putting it back in its carrier.*) **27**
Anne (*unabashed*). Then I'll have to stop being a stranger, won't I? Is he fixed?
Peter (*startled*). Huh?
Anne. Did you have him fixed?
Peter. No.
Anne. Oh, you ought to have him fixed—to keep him from—you know, fighting. Where did you go to school?
24 Peter. Jewish Secondary.
Anne. But that's where Margot and I go! I never saw you around.
Peter. I used to see you . . . sometimes . . .

Anne. You did?
Peter. . . . in the schoolyard. You were always in the middle of a bunch of kids. (*He takes a penknife from his pocket.*)
Anne. Why didn't you ever come over?
Peter. I'm sort of a lone wolf. (*He starts to rip off his Star of David.*)
Anne. What are you doing?
Peter. Taking it off.
25 Anne. But you can't do that. They'll arrest you if you go out without your Star. (*He tosses his knife on the table.*)
Peter. Who's going out?
Anne. Why, of course! You're right! Of course we don't need them any more. (*She picks up his knife and starts to take her Star off.*) I wonder **26** what our friends will think when we don't show up today?
Peter. I didn't have any dates with anyone.
Anne. Oh, I did. I had a date with Jopie to go and play ping-pong at her house. Do you know Jopie de Wall?
Peter. No.
Anne. Jopie's my best friend. I wonder what she'll think when she telephones and there's no answer? . . . Probably she'll go over to the house. . . . I wonder what she'll think . . . we left everything as if we'd suddenly been called away . . . breakfast dishes in the sink . . . beds not made. . . . (*As she pulls off her Star the cloth underneath shows clearly the color and form of the Star.*) Look! It's still there! (*Peter goes over to the stove with his Star.*) What're you going to do with yours?
Peter. Burn it.
Anne. (*She starts to throw hers in, and cannot.*) It's funny, I can't throw mine away. I don't know why.
Peter. You can't throw . . . ? Something they branded you with . . . ? That they made you wear so they could spit on you?
28 Anne. I know. I know. But after all, it *is* the Star of David, isn't it?

[*In the bedroom, right,* Margot *and* Mrs. Frank *are lying down.* Mr. Frank *starts quietly out.*]

Peter. Maybe it's different for a girl.

[Mr. Frank *comes into the main room.*]

29 **Mr. Frank.** Forgive me, Peter. Now let me see. We must find a bed for your cat. (*He goes to a cupboard.*) I'm glad you brought your cat. Anne was feeling so badly about hers. (*Getting a used small washtub*) Here we are. Will it be comfortable in that?

Peter (*gathering up his things*). Thanks.

Mr. Frank (*opening the door of the room on the left*). And here is your room. But I warn you, Peter, you can't grow any more. Not an inch, or you'll have to sleep with your feet out of the skylight. Are you hungry?

Peter. No.

Mr. Frank. We have some bread and butter.

Peter. No, thank you.

Mr. Frank. You can have it for luncheon then. And tonight we will have a real supper . . . our first supper together.

Peter. Thanks. Thanks. (*He goes into his room. During the following scene he arranges his possessions in his new room.*)

Mr. Frank. That's a nice boy, Peter.

Anne. He's awfully shy, isn't he?

Mr. Frank. You'll like him, I know.

30 **Anne.** I certainly hope so, since he's the only boy I'm likely to see for months and months.

[Mr. Frank *sits down, taking off his shoes.*]

Mr. Frank. Annele,[10] there's a box there. Will you open it?

[*He indicates a carton on the couch.* Anne *brings it to the center table. In the street below there is the sound of children playing*].

10. **Annele** (än′ə-lə): an affectionate form of the name Anne in Yiddish.

Anne (*as she opens the carton*). You know the way I'm going to think of it here? I'm going to think of it as a boardinghouse. A very peculiar summer boardinghouse, like the one that we ——(*She breaks off as she pulls out some photo-* **31** *graphs.*) Father! My movie stars! I was wondering where they were! I was looking for them this morning . . . and Queen Wilhelmina![11] How wonderful!

Mr. Frank. There's something more. Go on. Look further. (*He goes over to the sink, pouring a glass of milk from a thermos bottle.*)

Anne (*pulling out a pasteboard-bound book*). A diary! (*She throws her arms around her father.*) I've **32** never had a diary. And I've always longed for one. (*She looks around the room.*) Pencil, pencil, pencil, pencil. (*She starts down the stairs.*) I'm going down to the office to get a pencil.

Mr. Frank. Anne! No! (*He goes after her, catching her by the arm and pulling her back.*)

Anne (*startled*). But there's no one in the building now.

Mr. Frank. It doesn't matter. I don't want you ever to go beyond that door.

Anne (*sobered*). Never . . . ? Not even at night-time, when everyone is gone? Or on Sundays? Can't I go down to listen to the radio?

Mr. Frank. Never, I am sorry, Anneke.[12] It isn't safe. No, you must never go beyond that door.

33 [*For the first time* Anne *realizes what "going into hiding" means.*]

Anne. I see.

Mr. Frank. It'll be hard, I know. But always **34** remember this, Anneke. There are no walls, there are no bolts, no locks that anyone can put on your mind. Miep will bring us books. We will read history, poetry, mythology. (*He gives*

11. **Queen Wilhelmina:** queen of the Netherlands from 1890 to 1948. She died in 1962.
12. **Anneke** (än′ə-kə): an affectionate form of the name Anne.

29
Characterization. Mr. Frank is kind and considerate. Tries to make Peter comfortable by showing consideration for his cat.

30
Anne begins to see the reality of her future.

31
These pictures of favorite movie stars will help distract Anne from the harsh reality of her condition.

32   Analyzing
Anne actually started her diary before she went into hiding. Why would the playwrights alter this fact? It makes a more dramatic beginning and end to the story.

33
Actor's timing is important here. Audience needs moment to consider what hiding will mean.

34
Use to answer study questions 6a and 6b, p. 369.

The underlined passage may be used to give students practice in the reading skill of identifying the main idea. Ask students to read the passage carefully and choose the answer that best states the main idea of the passage: **A.** Mr. Frank chastises Anne for battling with her mother. (Irrelevant. Introduces information not in passage.) **B.** Mr. Frank tells Anne she does not have to practice the piano. (Inappropriate in scope. Does not encompass all information in passage.) **C.** Mr. Frank tells Anne that her life in hiding will be one of endless misery. (Contradicted. Contradicts information in passage.) **D.** Mr. Frank explains the advantages of living in hiding to Anne. (Correct.)

35 Finding Details

What does Mr. Frank point out as advantages for Anne as he tries to lighten the harshness of their situation? She will not have to wear overshoes, or coat, or practice on piano.

36

Carillon warns the occupants to be silent: Workers will soon arrive below.

37

Characterization. Through such small acts, audience sees friendly, generous side of Anne.

VISUAL CONNECTIONS
Exploring the Subject
In this photograph, Otto Frank, played by Joseph Schildkraut, gives Anne his pen. Anne's pen was actually sent to her by her grandmother. By having Mr. Frank give it to her, the playwrights are able to demonstrate his loving, kindly nature.

Ideas for Writing
You might ask students to speculate on Mr. Frank's reasons for giving Anne a diary. Have students consider his statement "There are no walls, there are no bolts, no locks that anyone can put on your mind" and write a short essay on the part writing plays in this freedom.

her the glass of milk.). Here's your milk. (*With his arm about her, they go over to the couch, sitting down side by side.*) ▶As a matter of fact, between us, Anne, being here has certain advantages for you. For instance, you remember the battle you had with your mother the other day on the subject of overshoes? You said you'd rather die than wear overshoes? But in the end you had to wear them? Well now, you see, for as long as we are here you will never have to wear overshoes! Isn't that good? And the coat that you inherited from Margot, you won't have to wear that any more. And the piano! You won't have to practice on the piano. I tell you, this is going to be a fine life for you! ◀

[*Anne's panic is gone.* Peter *appears in the doorway of his room, with a saucer in his hand. He is carrying his cat.*]

Peter. I . . . I . . . I thought I'd better get some water for Mouschi before . . .
Mr. Frank. Of course.

[*As he starts toward the sink the carillon begins to chime the hour of eight. He tiptoes to the window at the back and looks down at the street below. He turns to* Peter, *indicating in pantomime that it is too late.* Peter *starts back for his room. He steps on a creaking board. The three of them are frozen for a minute in fear. As* Peter *starts away again,* Anne *tiptoes over to him and pours some of the milk from her glass into the saucer for the cat.* Peter *squats on the floor, putting the milk before the cat.* Mr. Frank *gives* Anne *his fountain pen and then goes into the room at the right. For a second* Anne *watches the cat; then she goes over to the center table and opens her diary.*

In the room at the right, Mrs. Frank *has sat up*

▶Reading Skills Objective: Identifying the Main Idea

quickly at the sound of the carillon. Mr. Frank comes in and sits down beside her on the settee, his arm comfortingly around her.

Upstairs, in the attic room, Mr. and Mrs. Van Daan have hung their clothes in the closet and are now seated on the iron bed. Mrs. Van Daan leans back exhausted. Mr. Van Daan fans her with a newspaper.

38 *Anne starts to write in her diary. The lights dim out; the curtain falls.*

In the darkness Anne's voice comes to us again, faintly at first, and then with growing strength.]

Anne's Voice. I expect I should be describing what it feels like to go into hiding. But I really don't know yet myself. I only know it's funny never to be able to go outdoors . . . never to breathe fresh air . . . never to run and shout and jump. It's the silence in the nights that frightens me most. Every time I hear a creak in the house, or a step on the street outside, I'm sure they're coming for us. The days aren't so **39** bad. At least we know that Miep and Mr. Kraler are down there below us in the office. Our protectors, we call them. I asked Father what would happen to them if the Nazis found **40** out they were hiding us. Pim said that they would suffer the same fate that we would. . . . Imagine! They know this, and yet when they come up here, they're always cheerful and gay as if there were nothing in the world to bother them. . . . Friday, the twenty-first of August, nineteen forty-two. Today I'm going to tell you **41** our general news. Mother is unbearable. She insists on treating me like a baby, which I loathe. Otherwise things are going better. The weather is . . .

[*As Anne's voice is fading out, the curtain rises on the scene.*]

Scene 3

It is a little after six o'clock in the evening, two months later.

Margot is in the bedroom at the right, studying. Mr. Van Daan is lying down in the attic room above.

The rest of the "family" is in the main room. Anne and Peter sit opposite each other at the center table, where they have been doing their lessons. Mrs. Frank is on the couch. Mrs. Van Daan is seated with her fur coat, on which she has been sewing, in **1** *her lap. None of them are wearing their shoes.*

Their eyes are on Mr. Frank, waiting for him to give them the signal which will release them from their day-long quiet. Mr. Frank, his shoes in his hand, stands looking down out of the window at the back, watching to be sure that all of the workmen have left the building below.

After a few seconds of motionless silence, Mr. Frank turns from the window.

Mr. Frank (*quietly, to the group*). It's safe now. The last workman has left.

[*There is an immediate stir of relief.*]

2 Anne (*Her pent-up energy explodes*). WHEE!
Mrs. Frank (*startled, amused*). Anne!
Mrs. Van Daan. I'm first for the w.c.

[*She hurries off to the bathroom. Mrs. Frank puts on her shoes and starts up to the sink to prepare sup-* **3** *per. Anne sneaks Peter's shoes from under the table and hides them behind her back. Mr. Frank goes into Margot's room.*]

Mr. Frank (*to Margot*). Six o'clock. School's over.

[*Margot gets up, stretching. Mr. Frank sits down to put on his shoes. In the main room Peter tries to find his.*]

38
The passage of time is indicated by the dimming of lights and falling of curtain, conventional transitional devices. Anne's writing in the diary and speaking what she writes are devices more particular to this play.

39 Summarizing
What would happen to Miep and Mr. Kraler if they were discovered helping the fugitives? They would be jailed or killed.

40 Drawing Conclusions
What does the use of a nickname for her father suggest? That she may be closer to her father than to her mother or sister. She does not call them by nicknames.

41
Conflict. Anne's statement is the first indication of conflicts that will build among the characters in hiding.

Scene Three

1
Their going barefooted reminds audience of the necessity for silence.

2
Anne's outburst shows that she is still young and finds it hard to control her emotions.

3
Plot. Anne's teasing Peter begins the **subplot** of the play. At first they seem to dislike each other, but each will gradually show affection for the other.

4 Finding Cause and Effect
Why is Peter embarrassed? He is sixteen years old, young enough to enjoy a game, but old enough to feel foolish for responding.

5 Making Generalizations
Comparing/Contrasting
Why does Peter resist Anne's overtures? How is Anne different from him? Responses will vary. He is shy, insecure, and unaccustomed to female companions. She is aggressive and slightly childish. As yet, they have little in common.

6
Characterization. Anne points out they need to keep up with more than lessons; they must remember how to have fun.

7
Margot never says anything to upset people. The contrast makes Anne seem even more unruly.

8
The close relationship between Anne and her father becomes even more apparent.

9 Summarizing
Why is Mr. Van Daan so strict about Peter's lessons? He hopes they will be free soon. Peter will need to have kept up with his classmates.

10
Symbol. Mrs. Van Daan often works on her fur coat. It is obviously extremely important to her—a connection with her past life.

Peter (*to* Anne). Have you seen my shoes?
Anne (*innocently*). Your shoes?
Peter. You've taken them, haven't you?
Anne. I don't know what you're talking about.
Peter. You're going to be sorry!
Anne. Am I?

[Peter *goes after her.* Anne, *with his shoes in her hand, runs from him, dodging behind her mother.*]

Mrs. Frank (*protesting*). Anne, dear!
Peter. Wait till I get you!
Anne. I'm waiting! (Peter *makes a lunge for her. They both fall to the floor.* Peter *pins her down, wrestling with her to get the shoes.*) Don't! Don't! Peter, stop it. Ouch!
Mrs. Frank. Anne! . . . Peter!

4 [*Suddenly* Peter *becomes self-conscious. He grabs his shoes roughly and starts for his room.*]

Anne (*following him*). Peter, where are you going? Come dance with me.
5 **Peter.** I tell you I don't know how.
Anne. I'll teach you.
Peter. I'm going to give Mouschi his dinner.
Anne. Can I watch?
Peter. He doesn't like people around while he eats.
Anne. Peter, please.
Peter. No!

[*He goes into his room.* Anne *slams his door after him.*]

Mrs. Frank. Anne, dear, I think you shouldn't play like that with Peter. It's not dignified.
Anne. Who cares if it's dignified? I don't want to be dignified.

[Mr. Frank *and* Margot *come from the room on the right.* Margot *goes to help her mother.* Mr. Frank *starts for the center table to correct* Margot's *school papers.*]

Mrs. Frank (*to* Anne). You complain that I don't treat you like a grown-up. But when I do, you resent it.
6 **Anne.** I only want some fun . . . someone to laugh and clown with. . . . After you've sat still all day and hardly moved, you've got to have some fun. I don't know what's the matter with that boy.
Mr. Frank. He isn't used to girls. Give him a little time.
Anne. Time? Isn't two months time? I could cry. (*Catching hold of* Margot) Come on, Margot . . . dance with me. Come on, please.
7 **Margot.** I have to help with supper.
Anne. You know we're going to forget how to dance. . . . When we get out we won't remember a thing.

8 [*She starts to sing and dance by herself.* Mr. Frank *takes her in his arms, waltzing with her.* Mrs. Van Daan *comes in from the bathroom.*]

Mrs. Van Daan. Next? (*She looks around as she starts putting on her shoes.*) Where's Peter?
Anne (*as they are dancing*). Where would he be!
Mrs. Van Daan. He hasn't finished his lessons,
9 has he? His father'll kill him if he catches him in there with that cat and his work not done. (Mr. Frank *and* Anne *finish their dance. They bow to each other with extravagant formality.*) Anne, get him out of there, will you?
Anne (*at* Peter's *door*). Peter? Peter?
Peter (*opening the door a crack*). What is it?
Anne. Your mother says to come out.
Peter. I'm giving Mouschi his dinner.
Mrs. Van Daan. You know what your father
10 says. (*She sits on the couch, sewing on the lining of her fur coat.*)
Peter. For heaven's sake, I haven't even looked at him since lunch.

Mrs. Van Daan. I'm just telling you, that's all.
Anne. I'll feed him.
Peter. I don't want you in there.
Mrs. Van Daan. Peter!
Peter (*to* Anne). Then give him his dinner and come right out, you hear?

[*He comes back to the table. Anne shuts the door of Peter's room after her and disappears behind the curtain covering his closet.*]

11 **Mrs. Van Daan** (*to* Peter). Now is that any way to talk to your little girlfriend?
Peter. Mother . . . for heaven's sake . . . will you please stop saying that?

Mrs. Van Daan. Look at him blush! Look at him!
Peter. Please! I'm not . . . anyway . . . let me alone, will you?
Mrs. Van Daan. He acts like it was something to be ashamed of. It's nothing to be ashamed of, to have a little girlfriend.
Peter. You're crazy. She's only thirteen.
Mrs. Van Daan. So what? And you're sixteen. Just perfect. Your father's ten years older than I am. (*To* Mr. Frank) I warn you, Mr. Frank, if
12 this war lasts much longer, we're going to be related and then . . .
Mr. Frank. *Mazel tov!*[13]
Mrs. Frank (*deliberately changing the conversa-*
13 *tion*). I wonder where Miep is. She's usually so prompt.

[*Suddenly everything else is forgotten as they hear the sound of an automobile coming to a screeching stop in the street below. They are tense, motionless in their terror. The car starts away. A wave of relief sweeps over them. They pick up their occupations*
14 *again.* Anne *flings open the door of* Peter's *room, making a dramatic entrance. She is dressed in* Peter's *clothes.* Peter *looks at her in fury. The others are amused.*]

Anne. Good evening, everyone. Forgive me if I don't stay. (*She jumps up on a chair.*) I have a friend waiting for me in there. My friend Tom. Tom Cat. Some people say that we look alike. But Tom has the most beautiful whiskers, and
15 I have only a little fuzz. I am hoping . . . in time . . .
Peter. All right, Mrs. Quack Quack!
Anne (*outraged—jumping down*). Peter!
Peter. I heard about you. . . . How you talked so much in class they called you Mrs. Quack
16 Quack. How Mr. Smitter made you write a composition . . . " 'Quack, quack,' said Mrs. Quack Quack."

13. *Mazel tov!* (mä′zəl tôf′): Hebrew for "Congratulations!"

17 Anne. Well, go on. Tell them the rest. How it was so good that he read it out loud to the class and then read it to all his other classes!
Peter. Quack! Quack! Quack . . . Quack . . . Quack . . .

[Anne *pulls off the coat and trousers.*]

18 Anne. You are the most intolerable, insufferable boy I've ever met!

[*She throws the clothes down the stairwell. Peter goes down after them.*]

Peter. Quack, quack, quack!
Mrs. Van Daan (*to* Anne). That's right, Anneke! Give it to him!
Anne. With all the boys in the world . . . Why I had to get locked up with one like you! . . .
Peter. Quack, quack, quack, and from now on stay out of my room!

[*As* Peter *passes her,* Anne *puts out her foot, tripping him. He picks himself up and goes on into his room.*]

Mrs. Frank (*quietly*). Anne, dear . . . your hair. (*She feels* Anne's *forehead.*) You're warm. Are you feeling all right?
Anne. Please, Mother. (*She goes over to the center table, slipping into her shoes.*)
Mrs. Frank (*following her*). You haven't a fever, have you?
Anne (*pulling away*). No. No.
Mrs. Frank. You know we can't call a doctor here, ever. There's only one thing to do . . . watch carefully. Prevent an illness before it comes. Let me see your tongue.
19 Anne. Mother, this is perfectly absurd.
Mrs. Frank. Anne, dear, don't be such a baby. Let me see your tongue. (*As* Anne *refuses,* Mrs. Frank *appeals to* Mr. Frank.) Otto . . . ?
Mr. Frank. You hear your mother, Anne.

[Anne *flicks out her tongue for a second, then turns away.*]

Mrs. Frank. Come on—open up! (*As* Anne *opens her mouth very wide*) You seem all right . . . but perhaps an aspirin . . .
Mrs. Van Daan. For heaven's sake, don't give
20 that child any pills. I waited for fifteen minutes this morning for her to come out of the w.c.
Anne. I was washing my hair!
Mrs. Frank. I think there's nothing the matter with our Anne that a ride on her bike or a visit with her friend Jopie deWaal wouldn't cure. Isn't that so, Anne?

[Mr. Van Daan *comes down into the room. From outside we hear faint sounds of bombers going over and a burst of ack-ack.*[14]]

Mr. Van Daan. Miep not come yet?
Mrs. Van Daan. The workmen just left, a little while ago.
Mr. Van Daan. What's for dinner tonight?
Mrs. Van Daan. Beans.
21 Mr. Van Daan. Not again!
Mrs. Van Daan. Poor Putti! I know. But what can we do? That's all that Miep brought us.

[Mr. Van Daan *starts to pace, his hands behind his*
22 *back.* Anne *follows behind him, imitating him.*]

Anne. We are now in what is known as the "bean cycle." Beans boiled, beans en casserole, beans with strings, beans without strings . . .

[Peter *has come out of his room. He slides into his place at the table, becoming immediately absorbed in his studies.*]

Mr. Van Daan (*to* Peter). I saw you . . . in there, playing with your cat.

14. **ack-ack:** antiaircraft fire.

Mrs. Van Daan. He just went in for a second, putting his coat away. He's been out here all the time, doing his lessons.

Mr. Frank (*looking up from the paper*). Anne, you got an excellent in your history paper today . . . and very good in Latin.

Anne (*sitting beside him*). How about algebra?

Mr. Frank. I'll have to make a confession. Up until now I've managed to stay ahead of you in algebra. Today you caught up with me. We'll leave it to Margot to correct.

Anne. Isn't algebra *vile*, Pim!

Mr. Frank. Vile!

Margot (*to Mr. Frank*). How did I do?

23 Anne (*getting up*). Excellent, excellent, excellent, excellent!

Mr. Frank (*to Margot*). You should have used the subjunctive here. . . .

Margot. Should I? . . . I thought . . . look here . . . I didn't use it here. . . .

[*The two become absorbed in the papers.*]

Anne. Mrs. Van Daan, may I try on your coat?

Mrs. Frank. No, Anne.

Mrs. Van Daan (*giving it to* Anne). It's all right . . . but careful with it. (Anne *puts it on and struts* **24** *with it.*) My father gave me that the year before he died. He always bought the best that money could buy.

Anne. Mrs. Van Daan, did you have a lot of boyfriends before you were married?

Mrs. Frank. Anne, that's a personal question. It's not courteous to ask personal questions.

25 Mrs. Van Daan. Oh, I don't mind. (*To* Anne) Our house was always swarming with boys. When I was a girl we had . . .

26 Mr. Van Daan. Oh, God. Not again!

Mrs. Van Daan (*good-humored*). Shut up! (*Without a pause, to* Anne. Mr. Van Daan *mimics Mrs. Van Daan, speaking the first few words in unison with her.*) One summer we had a big house in Hilversum. The boys came buzzing round like

bees around a jam pot. And when I was sixteen! . . . We were wearing our skirts very short those days and I had good-looking legs. (*She pulls up her skirt, going to* Mr. Frank) I still have 'em. I may not be as pretty as I used to be, but I **27** still have my legs. How about it, Mr. Frank?

Mr. Van Daan. All right. All right. We see them.

Mrs. Van Daan. I'm not asking you. I'm asking Mr. Frank.

Peter. Mother, for heaven's sake.

Mrs. Van Daan. Oh, I embarrass you, do I? Well, I just hope the girl you marry has as good. (*Then, to* Anne) My father used to worry about me, with so many boys hanging round. He told me, if any of them gets fresh, you say to him . . . "Remember, Mr. So-and-So, remember I'm a lady."

Anne. "Remember, Mr. So-and-So, remember I'm a lady." (*She gives* Mrs. Van Daan *her coat.*)

Mr. Van Daan. Look at you, talking that way in **28** front of her! Don't you know she puts it all down in that diary?

Mrs. Van Daan. So, if she does? I'm only telling the truth!

[Anne *stretches out, putting her ear to the floor, listening to what is going on below. The sound of the bombers fades away.*]

Mrs. Frank (*setting the table.*) Would you mind, Peter, if I moved you over to the couch?

Anne (*listening*). Miep must have the radio on.

[Peter *picks up his papers, going over to the couch beside* Mrs. Van Daan.]

Mr. Van Daan (*accusingly, to* Peter). Haven't you finished yet?

Peter. No.

Mr. Van Daan. You ought to be ashamed of yourself.

23
Irony. Anne would speak this line mockingly. She is jealous of Margot's grades and the praise she gets.

24
Audience sees the importance of Mrs. Van Daan's fur coat. She has a strong interest in material things, is proud it is best coat money can buy. The coat also has sentimental value as gift from father.

25 Analyzing
Why is Mrs. Van Daan so patient with Anne's personal questions? Mrs. Van Daan is vain, still wants to be considered beautiful, feels she has had little opportunity to talk about herself.

26
Mr. Van Daan is irritated by his wife's vanity. Evidently has heard this story often.

27
Mrs. Van Daan knows that she still has pretty legs; she takes this opportunity to flirt with Mr. Frank, perhaps to "get back" at her husband for mocking her.

28
Conflict. For Mr. Van Daan, Anne's presence is a disturbing one. Her personal questions have led to the present trouble, and her diary becomes a source of friction.

29

The Van Daans are demanding parents. Peter feels that he cannot please them regardless of how hard he tries.

30

Conflict. Mrs. Van Daan continues to flirt with Mr. Frank and to praise him as a way of criticizing Mr. Van Daan, a selfish tactic that increases tensions unnecessarily.

31

Peter is glad to get away from his father and mother and the uncomfortable scene.

32

Mrs. Frank may be jealous, but it would be out of character for her to say anything.

33

Considering the limited availability of food and goods, especially luxury items such as chocolate and cigarettes, Mr. Van Daan's complaint ("only" one package) seems unwarranted.

34 Summarizing
Drawing Conclusions

Why is Anne so interested in the Van Daans' argument? What might the audience assume about Anne's parents by her interest in the quarrel? She is not used to hearing adults quarrel. Audience can assume her parents do not quarrel.

35

Whenever she can, Mrs. Frank tries to avoid confrontation.

36

Characterization. Anne is sensitive to problems their hiding is causing for others. Miep is a person to her, not just a convenience.

29 Peter. All right. I'm a dunce. I'm a hopeless case. Why do I go on?

Mrs. Van Daan. You're not hopeless. Don't talk that way. It's just that you haven't anyone to help you, like the girls have. (*To* Mr. Frank) Maybe you could help him, Mr. Frank?

Mr. Frank. I'm sure that his father . . . ?

Mr. Van Daan. Not me. I can't do anything with him. He won't listen to me. You go ahead . . . if you want.

Mr. Frank (*going to* Peter). What about it, Peter? Shall we make our school coeducational?

30 Mrs. Van Daan (*kissing* Mr. Frank). You're an angel, Mr. Frank. An angel. I don't know why I didn't meet you before I met that one there. Here, sit down, Mr. Frank. . . . (*She forces him down on the couch beside* Peter.) Now, Peter, you listen to Mr. Frank.

Mr. Frank. It might be better for us to go into Peter's room.

31 [Peter *jumps up eagerly, leading the way.*]

Mrs. Van Daan. That's right. You go in there, Peter. You listen to Mr. Frank. Mr. Frank is a highly educated man.

[As Mr. Frank *is about to follow* Peter *into his* **32** *room,* Mrs. Frank *stops him and wipes the lipstick from his lips. Then she closes the door after them.*]

Anne (*on the floor, listening*). Shh! I can hear a man's voice talking.

Mr. Van Daan. (*to* Anne). Isn't it bad enough here without your sprawling all over the place?

[Anne *sits up.*]

Mrs. Van Daan (*to* Mr. Van Daan). If you didn't smoke so much, you wouldn't be so bad-tempered.

Mr. Van Daan. Am I smoking? Do you see me smoking?

Mrs. Van Daan. Don't tell me you've used up all those cigarettes.

33 Mr. Van Daan. One package. Miep only brought me one package.

Mrs. Van Daan. It's a filthy habit anyway. It's a good time to break yourself.

Mr. Van Daan. Oh, stop it, please.

Mrs. Van Daan. You're smoking up all our money. You know that, don't you?

Mr. Van Daan. Will you shut up? (*During this,* Mrs. Frank *and* Margot *have studiously kept their* **34** *eyes down. But* Anne, *seated on the floor, has been following the discussion interestedly.* Mr. Van Daan *turns to see her staring up at him.*) And what are you staring at?

Anne. I never heard grown-ups quarrel before. I thought only children quarreled.

Mr. Van Daan. This isn't a quarrel! It's a discussion. And I never heard children so rude before.

Anne. (*rising* indignantly). I, rude!

Mr. Van Daan. Yes!

35 Mrs. Frank (*quickly*). Anne, will you get me my knitting? (Anne *goes to get it.*) I must remember, when Miep comes, to ask her to bring me some more wool.

Margot (*going into her room*). I need some hairpins and some soap. I made a list. (*She goes into her bedroom to get the list.*)

Mrs. Frank (*to* Anne). Have you some library books for Miep when she comes?

36 Anne. It's a wonder that Miep has a life of her own, the way we make her run errands for us. Please, Miep, get me some starch. Please take my hair out and get it cut. Tell me all the latest news, Miep. (*She goes over, kneeling on the couch beside* Mrs. Van Daan.) Did you know she was engaged? His name is Dirk, and Miep's afraid the Nazis will ship him off to Germany to work in one of their war plants. That's what they're doing with some of the young Dutchmen . . . they pick them up off the streets ——

Mr. Van Daan. (*interrupting*). Don't you ever get tired of talking? Suppose you try keeping still for five minutes. Just five minutes.

37 [*He starts to pace again. Again* Anne *follows him, mimicking him.* Mrs. Frank *jumps up and takes her by the arm up to the sink, and gives her a glass of milk.*]

Mrs. Frank. Come here, Anne. It's time for your glass of milk.

Mr. Van Daan. Talk, talk, talk. I never heard such a child. Where is my . . . ? Every evening it's the same, talk, talk, talk. (*He looks around.*) Where is my . . . ?

Mrs. Van Daan. What're you looking for?

Mr. Van Daan. My pipe. Have you seen my pipe?

Mrs. Van Daan. What good's a pipe? You haven't got any tobacco.

Mr. Van Daan. At least I'll have something to hold in my mouth! (*Opening* Margot's *bedroom door*) Margot, have you seen my pipe?

Margot. It was on the table last night.

38 [Anne *puts her glass of milk on the table and picks up his pipe, hiding it behind her back.*]

Mr. Van Daan. I know. I know. Anne, did you see my pipe? . . . Anne!

Mrs. Frank. Anne, Mr. Van Daan is speaking to you.

Anne. Am I allowed to talk now?

Mr. Van Daan. You're the most aggravating . . . The trouble with you is, you've been spoiled. What you need is a good old-fashioned spanking.

39 **Anne** (*mimicking* Mrs. Van Daan). "Remember, Mr. So-and-So, remember I'm a lady." (*She thrusts the pipe into his mouth, then picks up her glass of milk.*)

Mr. Van Daan. (*restraining himself with difficulty*). Why aren't you nice and quiet like your sister Margot? Why do you have to show off all the time? Let me give you a little advice, young lady. Men don't like that kind of thing in a girl. You know that? A man likes a girl who'll listen to him once in a while . . . a domestic girl, who'll keep her house shining for her husband . . . who loves to cook and sew and . . .

40 Anne. I'd cut my throat first! I'd open my veins! I'm going to be remarkable! I'm going to Paris . . .

Mr. Van Daan (*scoffingly*). Paris!

Anne. . . . to study music and art.

Mr. Van Daan. Yeah! Yeah!

41 Anne. I'm going to be a famous dancer or singer . . . or something wonderful.

[*She makes a wide gesture, spilling the glass of milk on the fur coat in* Mrs. Van Daan's *lap.* Margot *rushes quickly over with a towel.* Anne *tries to brush the milk off with her skirt.*]

37
Stress is affecting everyone. Anne is unable to control her playful nature, does not know when to stop.

38
In this scene, Anne is sassy, immature, and intentionally rebellious. She will outgrow this childishness later in the play.

39
Anne mocks Mrs. Van Daan by repeating the lady's words in an altered context.

40 Finding Cause and Effect
Why does Mr. Van Daan's advice make Anne angry? In part, she dislikes comparison to Margot; mostly, she envisions different kind of life for herself.

41
Use to answer **study question 8a,** p. 369.

VISUAL CONNECTIONS
Exploring the Subject
This is a dramatic moment on stage. The playwrights have prepared the audience for it carefully by developing the importance of the coat to Mrs. Van Daan and by allowing Anne's actions to become more uncontrolled. The tension keeps building. The audience expects something to happen and is almost relieved when Anne spills milk on Mrs. Van Daan's fur coat.

Mrs. Van Daan. Now look what you've done . . . you clumsy little fool! My beautiful fur coat my father gave me . . .

Anne. I'm so sorry.

Mrs. Van Daan. What do you care? It isn't yours. . . . So go on, ruin it! Do you know what that coat cost? Do you? And now look at it! Look at it!

Anne. I'm very, very sorry.

Mrs. Van Daan. I could kill you for this. I could just kill you!

[Mrs. Van Daan *goes up the stairs, clutching the coat.* Mr. Van Daan *starts after her.*]

Mr. Van Daan. Petronella . . . *liefje! Liefje!* . . . Come back . . . the supper . . . come back!

Mrs. Frank. Anne, you must not behave in that way.

Anne. It was an accident. Anyone can have an accident.

Mrs. Frank. I don't mean that. I mean the answering back. You must not answer back. They are our guests. We must always show the greatest courtesy to them. We're all living under terrible tension. (*She stops as* Margot *indicates that* Mr. Van Daan *can hear. When he is gone, she continues.*) That's why we must control ourselves. . . . You don't hear Margot getting into arguments with them, do you? Watch Margot. She's always courteous with them. Never familiar. She keeps her distance. And they respect her for it. Try to be like Margot.

Anne. And have them walk all over me, the way they do her? No, thanks!

Mrs. Frank. I'm not afraid that anyone is going to walk all over you, Anne. I'm afraid for other people, that you'll walk on them. I don't know what happens to you, Anne. You are wild, self-willed. If I had ever talked to my mother as you talk to me . . .

Anne. Things have changed. People aren't like that any more. "Yes, Mother." "No, Mother."

"Anything you say, Mother." I've got to fight things out for myself! Make something of myself!

Mrs. Frank. It isn't necessary to fight to do it. Margot doesn't fight, and isn't she . . . ?

Anne (*violently, rebellious*). Margot! Margot! Margot! That's all I hear from everyone . . . how wonderful Margot is . . . "Why aren't you like Margot?"

Margot (*protesting*). Oh, come on, Anne, don't be so . . .

Anne (*paying no attention*). Everything she does is right, and everything I do is wrong! I'm the goat around here! . . . You're all against me! . . . And you worst of all!

[*She rushes off into her room and throws herself down on the settee, stifling her sobs.* Mrs. Frank *sighs and starts toward the stove.*]

Mrs. Frank (*to* Margot). Let's put the soup on the stove . . . if there's anyone who cares to eat. Margot, will you take the bread out? (Margot *gets the bread from the cupboard.*) I don't know how we can go on living this way . . . I can't say a word to Anne . . . she flies at me. . . .

Margot. You know Anne. In half an hour she'll be out here, laughing and joking.

Mrs. Frank. And . . . (She makes a motion upwards, indicating the Van Daans.) I told your father it wouldn't work . . . but no . . . no . . . he had to ask them, he said . . . he owed it to him, he said. Well, he knows now that I was right! These quarrels! . . . This bickering!

Margot (*with a warning look*). Shush. Shush.

[*The buzzer for the door sounds.* Mrs. Frank *gasps, startled.*]

Mrs. Frank. Every time I hear that sound, my heart stops!

Margot (*starting for* Peter's *door*). It's Miep. (*She knocks at the door.*) Father?

TRANSPARENCIES 23 & 24

Fine Art

Theme: *"As If" Real Life* – explores art-works showing a public performance or one that conveys meaningful messages.

[Mr. Frank *comes quickly from* Peter's room.]

Mr. Frank. Thank you, Margot. (*As he goes down the steps to open the outer door*) Has everyone his list?

Margot. I'll get my books. (*Giving her mother a list*) Here's your list. (Margot *goes into her and* Anne's *bedroom on the right.* Anne *sits up, hiding her tears, as* Margot *comes in.*) Miep's here.

49 [Margot *picks up her books and goes back.* Anne *hurries over to the mirror, smoothing her hair.*]

Mr. Van Daan (*coming down the stairs*). Is it Miep?

Margot. Yes. Father's gone down to let her in.

Mr. Van Daan. At last I'll have some cigarettes!

Mrs. Frank (*to Mr. Van Daan*). I can't tell you how unhappy I am about Mrs. Van Daan's coat. Anne should never have touched it.

50 **Mr. Van Daan.** She'll be all right.

Mrs. Frank. Is there anything I can do?

Mr. Van Daan. Don't worry.

[*He turns to meet* Miep. *But it is not* Miep *who comes up the steps. It is* Mr. Kraler, *followed by* Mr. 51 Frank. *Their faces are grave.* Anne *comes from the bedroom.* Peter *comes from his room.*]

Mrs. Frank. Mr. Kraler!

Mr. Van Daan. How are you, Mr. Kraler?

Margot. This is a surprise.

Mrs. Frank. When Mr. Kraler comes, the sun begins to shine.

Mr. Van Daan. Miep is coming?

Mr. Kraler. Not tonight. (Mr. Kraler *goes to* Margot *and* Mrs. Frank *and* Anne, *shaking hands with them.*)

Mrs. Frank. Wouldn't you like a cup of coffee? . . . Or, better still, will you have supper with us?

Mr. Frank. Mr. Kraler has something to talk

49
Anne shows her resilience. The crisis of moments ago is forgotten.

50
Characterization. Mr. Van Daan's brief reply reveals a lack of concern about his wife's dearest possession.

51
Foreshadowing. Grim expressions of characters suggest something terrible has happened.

VISUAL CONNECTIONS
Exploring the Subject
Pictured with briefcase is Victor Kraler, played by Clinton Swindberg. Kraler, Otto Frank's longtime friend and business associate, was arrested for hiding the Franks and for other work in the Dutch underground. He was sent to a Dutch concentration camp but survived his imprisonment and returned to the business after the liberation.

52
Addition of another character increases opportunity for tension.

53
Characterization. Mr. Frank blurts out answer without hesitation, despite the disadvantages of having another boarder.

54
Conflict. Hints of increased tension come almost immediately.

55 Finding Cause and Effect
Why is Peter ashamed of his father? Mr. Van Daan sounds selfish about food.

56
Characterization. Peter begins to show the same kind of generosity as Mr. Frank does. Inevitably, Peter and Anne will grow close, both having learned values from Mr. Frank.

57 Drawing Conclusions
Why must Anne share room with Dussel? Margot is too old to sleep in same room with adult man. In Mrs. Frank's eyes, Anne is still young enough; arrangement would be proper.

over with us. Something has happened, he says, which demands an immediate decision.
Mrs. Frank (*fearful*). What is it?

[Mr. Kraler *sits down on the couch. As he talks he takes bread, cabbages, milk, etc., from his briefcase, giving them to* Margot *and* Anne *to put away.*]

Mr. Kraler. Usually, when I come up here, I try **52** to bring you some bit of good news. What's the use of telling you the bad news when there's nothing that you can do about it? But today something has happened. . . . Dirk . . . Miep's Dirk, you know, came to me just now. He tells me that he has a Jewish friend living near him. A dentist. He says he's in trouble. He begged me, could I do anything for this man? Could I find him a hiding place? . . . So I've come to **52** you. . . . I know it's a terrible thing to ask of you, living as you are, but would you take him in with you?

53 Mr. Frank. Of course we will.
Mr. Kraler (*rising*). It'll be just for a night or two . . . until I find some other place. This happened so suddenly that I didn't know where to **57** turn.
Mr. Frank. Where is he?
Mr. Kraler. Downstairs in the office.
Mr. Frank. Good. Bring him up.
Mr. Kraler. His name is Dussel . . . Jan Dussel.
Mr. Frank. Dussel . . . I think I know him.
Mr. Kraler. I'll get him.

[*He goes quickly down the steps and out.* Mr. Frank *suddenly becomes conscious of the others.*]

Mr. Frank. Forgive me. I spoke without consulting you. But I knew you'd feel as I do.
Mr. Van Daan. There's no reason for you to consult anyone. This is your place. You have a **54** right to do exactly as you please. The only thing I feel . . . there's so little food as it is . . . and to take in another person . . .

55 [Peter *turns away, ashamed of his father.*]

Mr. Frank. We can stretch the food a little. It's only for a few days.
Mr. Van Daan. You want to make a bet?
Mrs. Frank. I think it's fine to have him. But, Otto, where are you going to put him? Where?
56 Peter. He can have my bed. I can sleep on the floor. I wouldn't mind.
Mr. Frank. That's good of you, Peter. But your room's too small . . . even for *you*.
Anne. I have a much better idea. I'll come in here with you and Mother, and Margot can take Peter's room, and Peter can go in our room with Mr. Dussel.
Margot. That's right. We could do that.
Mr. Frank. No, Margot. You mustn't sleep in that room . . . neither you nor Anne. Mouschi has caught some rats in there. Peter's brave. He doesn't mind.
Anne. Then how about *this?* I'll come in here with you and Mother, and Mr. Dussel can have my bed.
57 Mrs. Frank. No. No. *No!* Margot will come in here with us and he can have her bed. It's the only way. Margot, bring your things in here. Help her, Anne.

[Margot *hurries into her room to get her things.*]

Anne (*to her mother*). Why Margot? Why can't I come in here?
Mrs. Frank. Because it wouldn't be proper for Margot to sleep with a . . . Please, Anne. Don't argue. Please.

[Anne *starts slowly away.*]

Mr. Frank (*to* Anne). You don't mind sharing your room with Mr. Dussel, do you, Anne?
Anne. No. No, of course not.
Mr. Frank. Good. (Anne *goes off into her bedroom, helping* Margot. Mr. Frank *starts to search in the cupboards.*) Where's the cognac?

Mrs. Frank. It's there. But, Otto, I was saving it in case of illness.

58 Mr. Frank. I think we couldn't find a better time to use it. Peter, will you get five glasses for me?

[Peter *goes for the glasses.* Margot *comes out of her bedroom, carrying her possessions, which she hangs behind a curtain in the main room.* Mr. Frank *finds the cognac and pours it into the five glasses that* Peter *brings him.* Mr. Van Daan *stands looking on sourly.* Mrs. Van Daan *comes downstairs and looks around at all of the bustle.*]

Mrs. Van Daan. What's happening? What's going on?

Mr. Van Daan. Someone's moving in with us.

59 Mrs. Van Daan. In here? You're joking.

Margot. It's only for a night or two . . . until Mr. Kraler finds him another place.

Mr. Van Daan. Yeah! Yeah!

[Mr. Frank *hurries over as* Mr. Kraler *and* Dussel **60** *come up.* Dussel *is a man in his late fifties, meticulous, finicky . . . bewildered now. He wears a raincoat. He carries a briefcase, stuffed full, and a small medicine case.*]

Mr. Frank. Come in, Mr. Dussel.

Mr. Kraler. This is Mr. Frank.

Dussel. Mr. Otto Frank?

Mr. Frank. Yes. Let me take your things. (*He takes the hat and briefcase, but* Dussel *clings to his medicine case.*) This is my wife Edith . . . Mr. and Mrs. Van Daan . . . their son, Peter . . . and my daughters, Margot and Anne.

[Dussel *shakes hands with everyone.*]

Mr. Kraler. Thank you, Mr. Frank. Thank you all. Mr. Dussel, I leave you in good hands. Oh . . . Dirk's coat.

[Dussel *hurriedly takes off the raincoat, giving it to* Mr. Kraler. *Underneath is his white dentist's jacket, with a yellow Star of David on it.*]

Dussel (*to* Mr. Kraler). What can I say to thank you . . . ?

Mrs. Frank (*to* Dussel). Mr. Kraler and Miep . . . They're our lifeline. Without them we couldn't live.

61 Mr. Kraler. Please, please. You make us seem very heroic. It isn't that at all. We simply don't like the Nazis. (*To* Mr. Frank, *who offers him a drink*) No, thanks. (*Then going on*) We don't like their methods. We don't like . . .

Mr. Frank (*smiling*). I know. I know. "No one's going to tell us Dutchmen what to do with our damn Jews!"

Mr. Kraler (*to* Dussel). Pay no attention to Mr. Frank. I'll be up tomorrow to see that they're treating you right. (*To* Mr. Frank) Don't trouble to come down again. Peter will bolt the door after me, won't you, Peter?

Peter. Yes, sir.

Mr. Frank. Thank you, Peter. I'll do it.

Mr. Kraler. Good night, Good night.

Group. Good night, Mr. Kraler. We'll see you tomorrow, *etc. etc.*

[Mr. Kraler *goes out with* Mr. Frank. Mrs. Frank *gives each one of the "grown-ups" a glass of cognac.*]

Mrs. Frank. Please, Mr. Dussel, sit down.

[Mr. Dussel *sinks into a chair.* Mrs. Frank *gives him a glass of cognac.*]

62 Dussel. I'm dreaming. I know it. I can't believe my eyes. Mr. Otto Frank here! (*To* Mrs. Frank) You're not in Switzerland then? A woman told me . . . She said she'd gone to your house . . . the door was open, everything was in disorder, dishes in the sink. She said she found a piece of paper in the wastebasket with an address scrib-

58
Mr. Frank thinks the decision should be celebrated, expects others to share his emotions.

59
The Van Daans are clearly critical. Audience can expect trouble.

60
Characterization. Actor has complicated task. Must show Dussel's thankfulness, nervousness, and fear of rejection.

61
Irony. Mr. Kraler acts as if his primary motivation is dislike for Nazis—as if what he is doing is not heroic. Mr. Frank's comment indicates that the motivations run deeper.

62
Dussel must have mixed feelings. Although he would rather have the Franks safe, had they escaped they could not now help him.

The Diary of Anne Frank Act One, Scene 3 **355**

355

63 Finding Cause and Effect
How would this information affect the Frank family? Would be relieved that their ploy worked, lessening police suspicion.

64 Analyzing
What may Dussel's bolting his drink show? Responses will vary. He may have been under such stress that he thinks a drink will relax him.

65
Conflict. Peter is again humiliated by his father's selfishness.

66
Use to answer **study question 9**, p. 369.

67
Anne is personally touched by the tragedy when she discovers that the Nazis have taken her best friend.

68 Making Inferences
Why does Dussel have so little with him? It is likely he has just avoided capture in one of the block searches. He also may have been informed about the close quarters.

bled on it . . . an address in Zurich. She said you must have escaped to Zurich.

Anne. Father put that there purposely . . . just so people would think that very thing!

Dussel. And you've been *here* all the time?

Mrs. Frank. All the time . . . ever since July.

[Anne *speaks to her father as he comes back.*]

63 Anne. It worked, Pim . . . the address you left! Mr. Dussel says that people believe we escaped to Switzerland.

Mr. Frank. I'm glad . . . And now let's have a little drink to welcome Mr. Dussel. (*Before they can* **64** *drink,* Dussel *bolts his drink.* Mr. Frank *smiles and raises his glass.*) To Mr. Dussel. Welcome. We're very honored to have you with us.

Mrs. Frank. To Mr. Dussel, welcome.

[*The* Van Daans *murmur a welcome. The "grown-ups" drink.*]

Mrs. Van Daan. Um. That was good.

Mr. Van Daan. Did Mr. Kraler warn you that you won't get much to eat here? You can imagine . . . three ration books among the seven of us . . . and now you make eight.

65 [Peter *walks away, humiliated. Outside a street organ is heard dimly.*]

Dussel (*rising*). Mr. Van Daan, you don't realize what is happening outside that you should warn me of a thing like that. You don't realize what's going on. . . . (*As* Mr. Van Daan *starts his characteristic pacing,* Dussel *turns to speak to the* **66** *others.*) Right here in Amsterdam every day hundreds of Jews disappear. . . . They surround a block and search house by house. Children come home from school to find their parents gone. Hundreds are being deported . . . people that you and I know . . . the Hallensteins . . . the Wessels . . .

Mrs. Frank (*in tears*). Oh, no. No!

Dussel. They get their call-up notice . . . come to the Jewish theater on such and such a day and hour . . . bring only what you can carry in a rucksack. And if you refuse the call-up notice, then they come and drag you from your home and ship you off to Mauthausen. The death camp!

Mrs. Frank. We didn't know that things had got so much worse.

Dussel. Forgive me for speaking so.

Anne (*coming to* Dussel). Do you know the deWaals? . . . What's become of them? Their daughter Jopie and I are in the same class. Jopie's my best friend.

Dussel. They are gone.

Anne. Gone?

Dussel. With all the others.

67 Anne. Oh, no. Not Jopie!

[*She turns away, in tears.* Mrs. Frank *motions to* Margot *to comfort her.* Margot *goes to* Anne, *putting her arms comfortingly around her.*]

Mrs. Van Daan. There were some people called Wagner. They lived near us . . . ?

Mr. Frank (*interrupting with a glance at* Anne). I think we should put this off until later. We all have many questions we want to ask. . . . But I'm sure that Mr. Dussel would like to get settled before supper.

68 Dussel. Thank you. I would. I brought very little with me.

Mr. Frank (*giving him his hat and briefcase*). I'm sorry we can't give you a room alone. But I hope you won't be too uncomfortable. We've had to make strict rules here . . . a schedule of hours. . . . We'll tell you after supper. Anne, would you like to take Mr. Dussel to his room?

Anne (*controlling her tears*). If you'll come with me, Mr. Dussel? (*She starts for her room.*)

Dussel (*shaking hands with each in turn*). Forgive me if I haven't really expressed my gratitude to all of you. This has been such a shock to me. I'd always thought of myself as Dutch. I was **69** born in Holland. My father was born in Holland, and my grandfather. And now . . . after all these years . . . (*He breaks off.*) If you'll excuse me.

[Dussel *gives a little bow and hurries off after* Anne. Mr. Frank *and the others are subdued.*]

Anne (*turning on the light*). Well, here we are.

[Dussel *looks around the room. In the main room* Margot *speaks to her mother.*]

Margot. The news sounds pretty bad, doesn't it? It's so different from what Mr. Kraler tells us. Mr. Kraler says things are improving.

70 Mr. Van Daan. I like it better the way Kraler tells it.

[*They resume their occupations, quietly.* Peter *goes off into his room. In* Anne's *room,* Anne *turns to* Dussel.]

Anne. You're going to share the room with me. **74**

Dussel. I'm a man who's always lived alone. I haven't had to adjust myself to others. I hope you'll bear with me until I learn.

Anne. Let me help you. (*She takes his briefcase.*) Do you always live all alone? Have you no family at all?

71 Dussel. No one. (*He opens his medicine case and* **75** *spreads his bottles on the dressing table.*)

72 Anne. How dreadful. You must be terribly **76** lonely.

Dussel. I'm used to it.

Anne. I don't think I could ever get used to it. Didn't you even have a pet? A cat, or a dog?

Dussel. I have an allergy for fur-bearing animals. They give me asthma.

Anne. Oh, dear. Peter has a cat.

Dussel. Here? He has it here?

Anne. Yes. But we hardly ever see it. He keeps it in his room all the time. I'm sure it will be all right.

Dussel. Let us hope so. (*He takes some pills to fortify himself.*)

Anne. That's Margot's bed, where you're going to sleep. I sleep on the sofa there. (*Indicating the clothes hooks on the wall*) We cleared these off for your things. (*She goes over to the window.*) The best part about this room. . . you can look down and see a bit of the street and the canal. **73** There's a houseboat . . . you can see the end of it . . . a bargeman lives there with his family. . . . They have a baby and he's just beginning to walk and I'm so afraid he's going to fall into the canal some day. I watch him. . . .

Dussel (*interrupting*). Your father spoke of a schedule.

Anne (*coming away from the window*). Oh, yes. It's mostly about the times we have to be quiet. And times for the w.c. You can use it now if you like.

Dussel (*stiffly*). No, thank you.

Anne. I suppose you think it's awful, my talking about a thing like that. But you don't know how important it can get to be, especially when you're frightened. . . . About this room, the way Margot and I did . . . she had it to herself in the afternoons for studying, reading . . . lessons, you know . . . and I took the mornings. Would that be all right with you?

Dussel. I'm not at my best in the morning.

Anne. You stay in here in the mornings then. I'll take the room in the afternoons.

Dussel. Tell me, when you're in here, what happens to me? Where am I spending my time? In there, with all the people?

Anne. Yes.

Dussel. I see. I see.

Anne. We have supper at half past six.

Dussel (*going over to the sofa*). Then, if you don't mind . . . I like to lie down quietly for ten minutes before eating. I find it helps the digestion.

69
Not all Jews in Holland were refugees; in 1940, over 100,000 were native-born citizens. Dussel seems to feel more Dutch than Jewish.

70
Like most people, Mr. Van Daan would like to see a more optimistic picture, even if it is untrue.

71 Drawing Conclusions
What do these props tell audience about Dussel? Responses will vary. He may be a hypochondriac.

72
Dussel lives alone, does not like living with people.

73
Symbol. The family on the houseboat is a symbol of freedom. Anne's fears for the baby show her concern for the welfare of others.

74
Anne tries to befriend Dussel.

75
Anne is being unusually cooperative, gives Dussel his choice of time.

76
Characterization. Dussel is not flexible. Prospect of being with others does not appeal to him. He seems more concerned about his own convenience than others' needs. He may not yet realize how restricted their lives are.

Anne. Of course. I hope I'm not going to be too much of a bother to you. I seem to be able to get everyone's back up.

[Dussel *lies down on the sofa, curled up, his back to her.*]

77 **Dussel.** I always get along very well with children. My patients all bring their children to me, because they know I get on well with them. So don't you worry about that.

[Anne *leans over him, taking his hand and shaking it gratefully.*]

Anne. Thank you. Thank you, Mr. Dussel.

[*The lights dim to darkness. The curtain falls on the scene. Anne's voice comes to us faintly at first, and then with increasing power.*]

Anne's Voice. . . . And yesterday I finished Cissy Van Marxvelt's latest book. I think she is a first-class writer. I shall definitely let my children read her. Monday, the twenty-first of Sep-
78 tember, nineteen forty-two. Mr. Dussel and I had another battle yesterday. Yes, Mr. Dussel! According to him, nothing, I repeat . . . nothing, is right about me . . . my appearance, my character, my manners. While he was going on at me I thought . . . sometime I'll give you such a smack that you'll fly right up to the ceiling! Why is it that every grown-up thinks he knows the way to bring up children? Particularly the grown-ups that never had any. I keep wishing that Peter was a girl instead of a boy. Then I would have someone to talk to. Margot's a darling, but she takes everything too seriously. To pause for a moment on the subject of Mrs. Van Daan. I must tell you that her attempts to flirt
79 with Father are getting her nowhere. Pim, thank goodness, won't play.

[*As she is saying the last lines, the curtain rises on the darkened scene. Anne's voice fades out.*]

Scene 4

It is the middle of the night, several months later. The stage is dark except for a little light which comes through the skylight in Peter's *room.*

Everyone is in bed. Mr. *and* Mrs. Frank *lie on the couch in the main room, which has been pulled out to serve as a makeshift double bed.*

Margot *is sleeping on a mattress on the floor in the main room, behind a curtain stretched across for privacy. The others are all in their accustomed rooms.*

From outside we hear two drunken soldiers singing "Lili Marlene." A girl's high giggle is heard. The sound of running feet is heard coming closer and then fading in the distance. Throughout the scene there is the distant sound of airplanes passing overhead.

A match suddenly flares up in the attic. We dimly
1 *see* Mr. Van Daan. *He is getting his bearings. He comes quickly down the stairs and goes to the cupboard where the food is stored. Again the match flares up, and is as quickly blown out. The dim figure is seen to steal back up the stairs.*

There is quiet for a second or two, broken only by the sound of airplanes, and running feet on the street below.

Suddenly, out of the silence and the dark, we hear Anne *scream.*

2 **Anne** (*screaming*). No! No! Don't . . . don't take me!

[*She moans, tossing and crying in her sleep. The other people wake, terrified.* Dussel *sits up in bed, furious.*]

3 **Dussel.** Shush! Anne! Anne, for God's sake, shush!

Anne (*still in her nightmare*). Save me! Save me!

77
Irony. Dussel prides himself on getting along with children, but he will be a source of friction.

78
Narration. During the blackout, Anne's narration reveals that friction has developed with Dussel.

79
Anne's father remains a force of stability. Friction would become unbearable if he responded to Mrs. Van Daan's flirtations.

Scene Four

1 Making Inferences
What is Mr. Van Daan doing at the food cupboard in the middle of the night? He might be just checking, since he worries about food so much, but because he is so selfish, audience might guess he is stealing.

2
Foreshadowing. Anne's nightmare foreshadows the arrest by Nazis.

3
Dussel does not show Anne any compassion.

358

358 DRAMA

[*She screams and screams.* Dussel *gets out of bed, going over to her, trying to wake her.*]

Dussel. For God's sake! Quiet! Quiet! You want someone to hear?

[*In the main room* Mrs. Frank *grabs a shawl and pulls it around her. She rushes in to* Anne, *taking her in her arms.* Mr. Frank *hurriedly gets up, putting on his overcoat.* Margot *sits up, terrified.* Peter'*s light goes on in his room.*]

4 **Mrs. Frank** (*to* Anne, *in her room*). Hush, darling, hush. It's all right. It's all right. (*Over her shoulder, to* Dussel) Will you be kind enough to turn on the light, Mr. Dussel? (*Back to* Anne) It's nothing, my darling. It was just a dream.

[Dussel *turns on the light in the bedroom.* Mrs. Frank *holds* Anne *in her arms. Gradually* Anne *comes out of her nightmare, still trembling with hor-*
5 *ror.* Mr. Frank *comes into the room and goes quickly to the window, looking out to be sure that no one outside has heard* Anne'*s screams.* Mrs. Frank *holds* Anne, *talking softly to her. In the main room* Mar-got *stands on a chair, turning on the center hanging*
6 *lamp. A light goes on in the* Van Daans' *room overhead.* Peter *puts his robe on, coming out of his room.*]

Dussel (*to* Mrs. Frank, *blowing his nose*). Something must be done about that child, Mrs. Frank. Yelling like that! Who knows but there's somebody on the streets? She's endangering all our lives.
Mrs. Frank. Anne, darling.
7 **Dussel.** Every night she twists and turns. I don't sleep. I spend half my night shushing her. And now it's nightmares!

[Margot *comes to the door of* Anne'*s room, followed by* Peter. Mr. Frank *goes to them, indicating that everything is all right.* Peter *takes* Margot *back.*]

Mrs. Frank (*to* Anne). You're here, safe, you see? Nothing has happened. (*To* Dussel) Please, Mr. Dussel, go back to bed. She'll be herself in a minute or two. Won't you, Anne?
Dussel (*picking up a book and a pillow*). Thank you, but I'm going to the w.c. The one place where there's peace!

[*He stalks out.* Mr. Van Daan, *in underwear and trousers, comes down the stairs.*]

Mr. Van Daan (*to* Dussel). What is it? What happened?
Dussel. A nightmare. She was having a nightmare!
Mr. Van Daan. I thought someone was murdering her.
8 **Dussel.** Unfortunately, no.

[*He goes into the bathroom.* Mr. Van Daan *goes back up the stairs.* Mr. Frank, *in the main room, sends* Peter *back to his own bedroom.*]

Mr. Frank. Thank you, Peter. Go back to bed.

[Peter *goes back to his room.* Mr. Frank *follows him, turning out the light and looking out the window. Then he goes back to the main room and gets up on a chair, turning out the center hanging lamp.*]

Mrs. Frank (*to* Anne). Would you like some water? (Anne *shakes her head.*) Was it a very bad dream? Perhaps if you told me . . . ?
9 **Anne.** I'd rather not talk about it.
Mrs. Frank. Poor darling. Try to sleep then. I'll sit right here beside you until you fall asleep. (*She brings a stool over, sitting there.*)
Anne. You don't have to.
Mrs. Frank. But I'd like to stay with you . . . very much. Really.
Anne. I'd rather you didn't.
Mrs. Frank. Good night, then. (*She leans down to kiss* Anne. Anne *throws her arm up over her face,*

4

Characterization. Although Anne does not get along well with her mother, audience sees Mrs. Frank's deep concern for Anne's well-being.

5

Suspense. Even though Mr. Frank does not speak, his actions keep up the fear and suspense which pervade the play.

6

Reaching for the lamp will be important later.

7 Comparing/Contrasting
How has Dussel changed since the audience first saw him? He was grateful, humble; now he complains about sharing room with Anne.

8

Irony. Dussel's comment is painfully ironic; murdering Jews is a Nazi goal.

9 Summarizing
How does Anne react to her mother? She rejects her attempts to provide comfort. Anne does not feel close to her mother because of mother's criticism.

Scene Five

1

Hanukkah prayer celebrates victory over oppression. Audience is reminded that faith has brought Jewish people through many trials. Hanukkah is a **symbol** of hope for the Franks, the Van Daans, and Dussel in that they might also eventually win liberty from oppressors.

2 Drawing Conclusions

What does Dussel's action tell the audience? Dussel is unaccustomed to this ritual. His ancestry is Jewish, but he does not practice Judaism.

3

Dussel has been raised as a Christian. The Nazis, however, hunt anyone with Jewish ancestors.

---

the scene. The lights dim on as Anne's *voice fades away.*]

Scene 5

It is the first night of the Hanukkah[19] celebration. Mr. Frank *is standing at the head of the table, on which is the menorah.[20] He lights the shamas,[21] or servant candle, and holds it as he says the blessing. Seated listening is all of the "family," dressed in their best. The men wear hats;* Peter *wears his cap.*

1 Mr. Frank (*reading from a prayer book*). "Praised be Thou, O Lord our God, Ruler of the universe, who hast sanctified us with Thy commandments and bidden us kindle the Hanukkah lights. Praised be Thou, O Lord our God, Ruler of the universe, who hast wrought wondrous deliverances for our fathers in days of old. Praised be Thou, O Lord our God, Ruler of the universe, that Thou hast given us life and sustenance and brought us to this happy season." (Mr. Frank *lights the one candle of the menorah as he continues.*) "We kindle this Hanukkah light to celebrate the great and wonderful deeds wrought through the zeal with which God filled the hearts of the heroic Maccabees, two thousand years ago. They fought against indifference, against <u>tyranny</u> and <u>oppression</u>, and they restored our Temple to us. May these lights remind us that we should ever look to God, whence cometh our help." Amen. (*Pronounced "O-mayn"*)

---

19. **Hanukkah** (ᴋʜä′noŏ-kə): a joyful holiday lasting eight days, usually in December, which celebrates a victorious fight for religious liberty in 165 B.C. At that time, a Greek king of Syria who ruled the Jews had been forcing them to worship Greek gods. Led by a family known as the Maccabees, the Jews won their independence from Syria and restored their holy Temple, which the Syrians had used to make offerings to Zeus.
20. **menorah** (mə-nôr′ə): a ritual candleholder. The Hanukkah menorah holds nine candles.
21. **shamas** (shä′məs): the central candle in the menorah, which is used to light the others.

All. Amen.

[Mr. Frank *hands* Mrs. Frank *the prayer book.*]

Mrs. Frank (*reading*). "I lift up mine eyes unto the mountains, from whence cometh my help. My help cometh from the Lord who made heaven and earth. He will not suffer thy foot to be moved. He that keepeth thee will not slumber. He that keepeth Israel doth neither slumber nor sleep. The Lord is thy keeper. The Lord is thy shade upon thy right hand. The sun shall not smite thee by day, nor the moon by night. The Lord shall keep thee from all evil. He shall keep thy soul. The Lord shall guard thy going out and thy coming in, from this time forth and forevermore." Amen.
All. Amen.

[Mrs. Frank *puts down the prayer book and goes to get the food and wine.* Margot *helps her.* Mr. Frank *takes the men's hats and puts them aside.*]

2 Dussel (*rising*). That was very moving.
Anne (*pulling him back*). It isn't over yet!
Mrs. Van Daan. Sit down! Sit down!
Anne. There's a lot more, songs and presents.
Dussel. Presents?
Mrs. Frank. Not this year, unfortunately.
Mrs. Van Daan. But always on Hanukkah everyone gives presents . . . everyone!
3 Dussel. Like our St. Nicholas' Day.[22]

[*There is a chorus of* no's *from the group.*]

Mrs. Van Daan. No! Not like St. Nicholas! What kind of a Jew are you that you don't know Hanukkah?
Mrs. Frank (*as she brings the food*). I remember

---

22. **our St. Nicholas' Day:** Christian children in the Netherlands receive gifts on St. Nicholas' Day, December 6. Mr. Dussel considers himself a Christian. However, he is one of the many people who were hunted by the Nazis because they had Jewish ancestry.

particularly the candles. . . . First one, as we have tonight. Then the second night you light two candles, the next night three . . . and so on until you have eight candles burning. When there are eight candles it is truly beautiful.

Mrs. Van Daan. And the potato pancakes.

4 Mr. Van Daan. Don't talk about them!

Mrs. Van Daan. I make the best *latkes* you ever tasted!

5 Mrs. Frank. Invite us all next year . . . in your own home.

Mr. Frank. God willing.

Mrs. Van Daan. God willing.

Margot. What I remember best is the presents we used to get when we were little . . . eight days of presents . . . and each day they got better and better.

Mrs. Frank. (*sitting down*). We are all here, alive. That is present enough.

6 Anne. No, it isn't. I've got something. . . . (*She rushes into her room, hurriedly puts on a little hat improvised from the lampshade, grabs a satchel bulging with parcels and comes running back.*)

Mrs. Frank. What is it?

Anne. Presents!

Mrs. Van Daan. Presents!

Dussel. Look!

Mr. Van Daan. What's she got on her head?

Peter. A lampshade!

Anne. (*She picks out one at random*). This is for Margot. (*She hands it to* Margot, *pulling her to her feet.*) Read it out loud.

Margot (*reading*).
"You have never lost your temper.
You never will, I fear,
You are so good.
But if you should,
Put all your cross words here."
(*She tears open the package.*) A new crossword puzzle book! Where did you get it?

7 Anne. It isn't new. It's one that you've done. But I rubbed it all out, and if you wait a little and forget, you can do it all over again.

Margot (*sitting*). It's wonderful, Anne. Thank you. You'd never know it wasn't new.

[*From outside we hear the sound of a streetcar passing.*]

Anne (*with another gift*). Mrs. Van Daan.

Mrs. Van Daan (*taking it*). This is awful. . . . I haven't anything for anyone. . . . I never thought . . .

Mr. Frank. This is all Anne's idea.

Mrs. Van Daan (*holding up a bottle*). What is it?

Anne. It's hair shampoo. I took all the odds and ends of soap and mixed them with the last of my toilet water.

8 Mrs. Van Daan. Oh, Anneke!

Anne. I wanted to write a poem for all of them, but I didn't have time. (*Offering a large box to* Mr. Van Daan) Yours, Mr. Van Daan, is *really* something . . . something you want more than anything. (*As she waits for him to open it*) Look! Cigarettes!

Mr. Van Daan. Cigarettes!

Anne. Two of them! Pim found some old pipe tobacco in the pocket lining of his coat . . . and we made them . . . or rather, Pim did.

Mrs. Van Daan. Let me see . . . Well, look at that! Light it, Putti! Light it.

[Mr. Van Daan *hesitates.*]

Anne. It's tobacco, really it is! There's a little fluff in it, but not much.

[*Everyone watches as* Mr. Van Daan *cautiously lights it. The cigarette flares up. Everyone laughs.*]

Peter. It works!

Mrs. Van Daan. Look at him.

9 Mr. Van Daan (*spluttering*). Thank you, Anne. Thank you.

[Anne *rushes back to her satchel for another present.*]

---

4 Analyzing
Why does Mr. Van Daan not want his wife to talk about potato pancakes? They obviously will not have them this year, and he does not want to be reminded of the deprivation.

5
Eternal optimism essential to survival.

6
Anne has devised a way to give presents.

7
Characterization. Anne's actions demonstrate not only generosity but also ingenuity and a willingness to forgive. Anne recycles old materials to create a spirit of giving. She does not withhold gifts from anyone, even those with whom she has quarreled.

8
Mrs. Van Daan's use of endearing nickname for Anne shows that she is deeply moved by the gift.

9
Tone. There is absolutely no hint of **irony** in any of the expressions of gratitude made to Anne. Tension, which has been building steadily under the pressure of the close quarters, is relieved by Anne's generous spirit.

Anne (*handing her mother a piece of paper.*) For Mother, Hanukkah greeting. (*She pulls her mother to her feet.*)

Mrs. Frank. (*She reads*).

10 "Here's an IOU that I promise to pay.
Ten hours of doing whatever you say.
Signed Anne Frank." (*Mrs. Frank, touched, takes Anne in her arms, holding her close.*)

Dussel. (*to* Anne). Ten hours of doing what you're told? *Anything* you're told?

Anne. That's right.

Dussel. You wouldn't want to sell that, Mrs. Frank?

Mrs. Frank. Never! This is the most precious gift I've ever had.

[*She sits, showing her present to the others. Anne hurries back to the satchel and pulls out a scarf, the scarf that* Mr. Frank *found in the first scene.*]

Anne (*offering it to her father*). For Pim.

Mr. Frank. Anneke . . . I wasn't supposed to have a present! (*He takes it, unfolding it and showing it to the others.*)

11 Anne. It's a muffler . . . to put round your neck . . . like an ascot, you know. I made it myself out of odds and ends. . . . I knitted it in the dark each night, after I'd gone to bed. I'm afraid it looks better in the dark!

12 Mr. Frank (*putting it on*). It's fine. It fits me perfectly. Thank you, Annele.

[Anne *hands* Peter *a ball of paper, with a string attached to it.*]

Anne. That's for Mouschi.

Peter (*rising to bow*). On behalf of Mouschi, I thank you.

Anne (*hesitant, handing him a gift*). And . . . this **13** is yours . . . from Mrs. Quack Quack. (*As he holds it gingerly in his hands*) Well . . . open it. . . . Aren't you going to open it?

Peter. I'm scared to. I know something's going to jump out and hit me.

Anne. No. It's nothing like that, really.

Mrs. Van Daan (*as he is opening it*). What is it, Peter? Go on. Show it.

Anne (*excitedly*). It's a safety razor!

Dussel. A what?

Anne. A razor!

Mrs. Van Daan (*looking at it*). You didn't make that out of odds and ends.

Anne (*to Peter*). Miep got it for me. It's not new. It's secondhand. But you really do need a razor now.

Dussel. For what?

Anne. Look on his upper lip . . . you can see the beginning of a mustache.

Dussel. He wants to get rid of that? Put a little milk on it and let the cat lick it off.

Peter (*starting for his room*). Think you're funny, don't you.

Dussel. Look! He can't wait! He's going to try it!

Peter. I'm going to give Mouschi his present! (*He goes into his room, slamming the door behind him.*)

Mr. Van Daan (*disgustedly*). Mouschi, Mouschi, Mouschi.

15 [*In the distance we hear a dog persistently barking. Anne brings a gift to Dussel.*]

Anne. And last but never least, my roommate, Mr. Dussel.

Dussel. For me? You have something for me? (*He opens the small box she gives him.*)

Anne. I made them myself.

Dussel. (*puzzled*). Capsules! Two capsules!

Anne. They're earplugs!

Dussel. Earplugs?

16 **Anne.** To put in your ears so you won't hear me when I thrash around at night. I saw them advertised in a magazine. They're not real ones. . . . I made them out of cotton and candle wax. Try them. . . . See if they don't work . . . see if you can hear me talk. . . .

Dussel (*putting them in his ears*). Wait now until I get them in . . . so.

Anne. Are you ready?

Dussel. Huh?

Anne. Are you ready?

Dussel. Good God! They've gone inside! I can't get them out! (*They laugh as Dussel jumps about, trying to shake the plugs out of his ears. Finally he gets them out. Putting them away*)

17 Thank you, Anne! Thank you!

Mr. Van Daan. A real Hanukkah!

Mrs Van Daan. Wasn't it cute of her?

Mrs. Frank. I don't know when she did it.

Margot. I love my present.

(*Together*)

Anne (*sitting at the table*). And now let's have the song, Father . . . please. . . . (*To Dussel*) Have you heard the Hanukkah song, Mr. Dussel? The song is the whole thing! (*She sings.*) "Oh, Hanukkah! Oh, Hanukkah! The sweet celebration. . . ."

Mr. Frank (*quieting her*). I'm afraid, Anne, we shouldn't sing that song tonight. (*To Dussel*) It's a song of jubilation, of rejoicing. One is apt to become too enthusiastic.

Anne. Oh, please, please. Let's sing the song. I promise not to shout!

Mr. Frank. Very well. But quietly now . . . I'll keep an eye on you and when . . .

13 Analyzing
Why does Anne remind Peter he once called her "Mrs. Quack Quack"? She is saying she likes Peter even though he made fun of her, that she is no longer angry.

14
Conflict. Dussel's sarcastic humor has sounded the only discordant note in this Hanukkah celebration. Yet, tensions are only suppressed. Now Peter is angry at Dussel.

15
Background noises are important throughout the play. Dog's barking reminds characters and audience of outside world, and it warns of danger.

16
Anne's gifts have all promoted reconciliation. Although she cannot stop her nightmares, she wishes not to disturb Dussel's sleep.

17
Although the earplugs will not be useful, even Dussel recognizes that Anne's intent is good. His enthusiastic thank you, however, no doubt partly includes emotion of relief that plugs came out.

[*As Anne starts to sing, she is interrupted by Dussel, who is snorting and wheezing.*]

Dussel (*pointing to* Peter). You . . . you! (Peter *is coming from his bedroom,* ostentatiously *holding a bulge in his coat as if he were holding his cat, and dangling* Anne's *present before it.*) How many times . . . I told you . . . Out! Out!

Mr. Van Daan (*going to* Peter). What's the matter with you? Haven't you any sense? Get that cat out of here.

Peter (*innocently*). Cat?

Mr. Van Daan. You heard me. Get it out of here!

18 **Peter.** I have no cat.

[*Delighted with his joke, he opens his coat and pulls*
19 *out a bath towel. The group at the table laugh, enjoying the joke.*]

Dussel (*still wheezing*). It doesn't need to be the cat . . . his clothes are enough . . . when he comes out of that room. . . .

Mr. Van Daan. Don't worry. You won't be bothered any more. We're getting rid of it.

Dussel. At last you listen to me. (*He goes off into his bedroom.*)

Mr. Van Daan (*calling after him*). I'm not doing it for you. That's all in your mind . . . all of it! (*He starts back to his place at the table.*) I'm doing it because I'm sick of seeing that cat eat all our food.

Peter. That's not true! I only give him bones . . . scraps . . .

Mr. Van Daan. Don't tell me! He gets fatter every day! Damn cat looks better than any of us. Out he goes tonight!

Peter. No! No!

20 **Anne.** Mr. Van Daan, you can't do that! That's Peter's cat. Peter loves that cat.

Mrs. Frank (*quietly*). Anne.

Peter (*to* Mr. Van Daan). If he goes, I go.

21 **Mr. Van Daan.** Go! Go!

Mrs. Van Daan. You're not going and the cat's not going! Now please . . . this is Hanukkah . . . Hanukkah . . . this is the time to celebrate. . . . What's the matter with all of you? Come on, Anne. Let's have the song.

Anne (*singing*).
"Oh, Hanukkah! Oh, Hanukkah!
The sweet celebration."

Mr. Frank (*rising*). I think we should first blow out the candle . . . then we'll have something for tomorrow night.

Margot. But, Father, you're supposed to let it burn itself out.

22 **Mr. Frank.** I'm sure that God understands shortages. (*Before blowing it out*) "Praised be Thou, O Lord our God, who hast sustained us and permitted us to celebrate this joyous festival."

[*He is about to blow out the candle when suddenly there is a crash of something falling below. They all freeze in horror, motionless. For a few seconds there is complete silence. Mr. Frank slips off his shoes. The others noiselessly follow his example. Mr. Frank turns out a light near him. He motions to* Peter *to turn off the center lamp.* Peter *tries to reach it, real-*
23 *izes he cannot and gets up on a chair. Just as he is touching the lamp he loses his balance. The chair goes out from under him. He falls. The iron lampshade crashes to the floor. There is a sound of feet below, running down the stairs.*]

Mr. Van Daan (*under his breath*). God almighty! (*The only light left comes from the Hanukkah candle.* Dussel *comes from his room.* Mr. Frank *creeps over to the stairwell and stands listening. The dog is heard barking excitedly.*) Do you hear anything?

Mr. Frank (*in a whisper*). No. I think they've gone.

24 **Mrs. Van Daan.** It's the Green Police. They've found us.

Mr. Frank. If they had, they wouldn't have left. They'd be up here by now.

Mrs. Van Daan. I know it's the Green Police. They've gone to get help. That's all, they'll be back.

Mr. Van Daan. Or it may have been the Gestapo,[23] looking for papers. . . .

Mr. Frank (*interrupting*). Or a thief, looking for money.

Mrs. Van Daan. We've got to do something. . . . Quick! Quick! Before they come back.

Mr. Van Daan. There isn't anything to do. Just wait.

[Mr. Frank *holds up his hand for them to be quiet.* **25** *He is listening intently. There is complete silence as they all strain to hear any sound from below. Suddenly* Anne *begins to sway. With a low cry she falls to the floor in a faint.* Mrs. Frank *goes to her quickly, sitting beside her on the floor and taking her in her arms.*]

Mrs. Frank. Get some water, please! Get some water!

[Margot *starts for the sink.*]

Mr. Van Daan (*grabbing* Margot). No! No! No one's going to run water!

Mr. Frank. If they've found us, they've found us. Get the water. (Margot *starts again for the sink.* Mr. Frank, *getting a flashlight*) I'm going down.

[Margot *rushes to him, clinging to him.* Anne *struggles to consciousness.*]

Margot. No, Father, no! There may be someone there, waiting. . . . It may be a trap!

26 Mr. Frank. This is Saturday. There is no way for us to know what has happened until Miep or Mr. Kraler comes on Monday morning. We cannot live with this uncertainty.

Margot. Don't go, Father!

23. **Gestapo** (gə-stä′pō): the Nazi secret police.

Mrs. Frank. Hush, darling, hush. (Mr. Frank *slips quietly out, down the steps and out through the door below.*) Margot! Stay close to me.

[Margot *goes to her mother.*]

Mr. Van Daan. Shush! Shush!

[Mrs. Frank *whispers to* Margot *to get the water.* Margot *goes for it.*]

27 Mrs. Van Daan. Putti, where's our money? Get our money. I hear you can buy the Green Police off, so much a head. Go upstairs quick! Get the money!

Mr. Van Daan. Keep still!

Mrs. Van Daan (*kneeling before him, pleading*). Do you want to be dragged off to a concentration camp? Are you going to stand there and wait for them to come up and get you? Do something, I tell you!

Mr. Van Daan (*pushing her aside*). Will you keep still!

[He *goes over to the stairwell to listen.* Peter *goes to his mother, helping her up onto the sofa. There is a second of silence. Then* Anne *can stand it no longer.*]

Anne. Someone go after Father! Make Father come back!

Peter (*starting for the door*). I'll go.

28 Mr. Van Daan. Haven't you done enough?

[He *pushes* Peter *roughly away. In his anger against his father* Peter *grabs a chair as if to hit him with it, then puts it down, burying his face in his hands.* Mrs. Frank *begins to pray softly.*]

Anne. Please, please, Mr. Van Daan. Get Father.

Mr. Van Daan. Quiet! Quiet!

25

Suspense. Dramatic pause heightens suspense as all listen in fear. Next sound could be Green Police crashing through door.

26

Characterization. Mr. Frank is still in charge. He is courageous, practical, and insightful. He recognizes that going for two days without knowing whether they are discovered would cause too much stress.

27 Analyzing
Expressing an Opinion

Why is it in character for Mrs. Van Daan to think of money as solution? Is it a logical solution? Seems in character since she is vain, values material possessions. Responses to second question will vary. Probably not a solution. Police could take money, arrest them anyway. Shows her fear and desperation.

28

Conflict. Tension and fear have turned members of the Van Daan family against one another. Mr. Van Daan blames Peter for falling from chair and pulling down lampshade.

29

Mrs. Frank's prayer is repetition from memory of words she had read in Hanukkah service.

30

It is unusual to hear Mr. Frank speak sharply.

31

In his fear, Dussel must find a scapegoat.

32

Foreshadowing. Although Mrs. Van Daan's argument seems more plausible, Dussel's fears turn out to be well-founded. Ironic that with all their precautions, uncontrollable event (burglary) will lead to their discovery.

33

Characterization. Mr. Frank's clear thinking and strong faith prevent panic.

34

Atmosphere. Mood has changed greatly from just a few minutes earlier when Anne began to sing. Audience realizes how fragile families' safety is, wonders how much longer they can escape detection.

[Anne *is shocked into silence.* Mrs. Frank *pulls her closer, holding her protectively in her arms.*]

29 **Mrs. Frank** (*softly, praying*). "I lift up mine eyes unto the mountains, from whence cometh my help. My help cometh from the Lord who made heaven and earth. He will not suffer thy foot to be moved. . . . He that keepeth thee will not slumber. . . .

[*She stops as she hears someone coming. They all watch the door tensely.* Mr. Frank *comes quietly in.* Anne *rushes to him, holding him tight.*]

Mr. Frank. It was a thief. That noise must have scared him away.

Mrs. Van Daan. Thank God.

Mr. Frank. He took the cashbox. And the radio. He ran away in such a hurry that he didn't stop to shut the street door. It was swinging wide open. (*A breath of relief sweeps over them.*) I think it would be good to have some light.

Margot. Are you sure it's all right?

Mr. Frank. The danger has passed. (Margot *goes to light the small lamp.*) Don't be so terrified, Anne. We're safe.

Dussel. Who says the danger has passed? Don't you realize we are in greater danger than ever?

30 **Mr. Frank.** Mr. Dussel, will you be still! (Mr. Frank *takes* Anne *back to the table, making her sit down with him, trying to calm her.*)

31 **Dussel** (*pointing to* Peter). Thanks to this clumsy fool, there's someone now who knows we're up here! Someone now knows we're up here, hiding!

Mrs. Van Daan (*going to* Dussel). Someone knows we're here, yes. But who is the someone? A thief! A thief! You think a thief is going to go to the Green Police and say . . . I was robbing a place the other night and I heard a noise up over my head? You think a thief is going to do that?

Dussel. Yes. I think he will.

Mrs. Van Daan (*hysterically*). You're crazy!

[*She stumbles back to her seat at the table.* Peter *follows protectively, pushing* Dussel *aside.*]

32 **Dussel.** I think someday he'll be caught and then he'll make a bargain with the Green Police . . . if they'll let him off, he'll tell them where some Jews are hiding!

[*He goes off into the bedroom. There is a second of appalled silence.*]

Mr. Van Daan. He's right.

Anne. Father, let's get out of here! We can't stay here now . . . Let's go. . . .

Mr. Van Daan. Go! Where?

Mrs. Frank (*sinking into her chair at the table*). Yes. Where?

33 **Mr. Frank** (*rising, to them all*). Have we lost all faith? All courage? A moment ago we thought that they'd come for us. We were sure it was the end. But it wasn't the end. We're alive, safe. (Mr. Frank *prays.*) "We thank Thee, O Lord our God, that in Thy infinite mercy Thou hast again seen fit to spare us." (*He blows out the candle, then turns to* Anne.) Come on, Anne. The song! Let's have the song!

[*He starts to sing.* Anne *finally starts faltering to sing as* Mr. Frank *urges her on. Her voice is hardly audible at first.*]

Anne (*singing*).
"Oh, Hanukkah! Oh, Hanukkah!
The sweet . . . celebration. . . ."

34 [*As she goes on singing, the others gradually join in, their voices still shaking with fear.* Mrs. Van Daan *sobs as she sings.*]

Group.
"Around the feast . . . we . . . gather

In complete . . . jubilation. . . .
Happiest of sea . . . sons
Now is here.
Many are the reasons for good cheer.
(Dussel *comes from the bedroom. He comes over to the table, standing beside* Margot, *listening to them as they sing.*)
"Together
We'll weather
Whatever tomorrow may bring.
(*As they sing on with growing courage, the lights start to dim.*)
"So hear us rejoicing
And merrily voicing
The Hanukkah song that we sing.
Hoy!
(*The lights are out. The curtain starts slowly to fall.*)
35 "Hear us rejoicing
And merrily voicing
The Hanukkah song that we sing."

[*They are still singing as the curtain falls.*]

Reading Check

1. Why were Anne and her family forced into hiding?
2. Where did the Frank family hide?
3. Who else was forced into hiding with the Franks?
4. Who helped the Franks and the others to survive?
5. How old was Anne when she started her diary?

Analyzing and Interpreting the Play

ACT ONE

Scene 1

1. *The Diary of Anne Frank* is about a group of people who are forced to leave the outside world and to retreat into a small, secret hiding place. What details of the set indicate that this will be a realistic, or lifelike, story?

2a. The play opens in November 1945. But in what year does most of this act take place? **b.** What prompts Mr. Frank's thoughts to flash back in time?

Scene 2

3. Anne's entrance is an important moment in the play. **a.** How does the stage direction on page 339, before her entrance, describe her personality? **b.** What does Anne do as soon as she comes onstage?

4. Why do you think Anne cannot destroy the Star of David, as Peter does?

5. When does Anne first realize what "going into hiding" means?

6a. What does Mr. Frank say cannot be locked up? **b.** What does he suggest he and Anne can do to hold on to one kind of freedom?

Scene 3

7. After several months together in their enclosed world, the "family" members find their tempers growing shorter. **a.** What do Anne and Peter argue about in this scene? **b.** What do the Van Daans quarrel about?

8. Anne has grown lonely and frustrated in the last several months. **a.** What are Anne's dreams for her future? **b.** What does she accuse her family of feeling about her?

9. Mr. Dussel brings the group the harsh news which they have been ignorant of. What

---

35
Irony. Closing this scene of near-discovery with a song of joy should make audience acutely aware of difference between what these people deserve and what is sure to happen to them.

READING CHECK
1. To escape Nazi persecution (p. 335).
2. Secret apartment in Otto Frank's warehouse (p. 335).
3. Mr. and Mrs. Van Daan, son Peter, and Mr. Dussel (pp. 338, 354).
4. Mr. Kraler, Miep (p. 337).
5. Thirteen (p. 337).

FOR STUDY AND DISCUSSION
Scene 1
1. Furnishings, props suggest real life.
2a. In 1942. 2b. Anne's diary.

Scene 2
3a. Quick, interested, mercurial.
3b. Meets Mr. Van Daan, investigates new home.
4. Sees it as symbol of her heritage.
5. When father tells her she can never go through door.
6a. The mind. 6b. Read books.

Scene 3
7a. She teases him about cat, wears his clothes; he calls her Mrs. Quack Quack. She wants playmate; he wants privacy.
7b. Mrs. Van Daan's vanity, Mr. Van Daan's smoking.
8a. To study music, art; become dancer, singer. 8b. They are against her. She is always wrong, and Margot is always right.

Ask students to describe briefly the **setting** and the incidents that illustrate how each character is affected by the confinement.

EXTENSION AND ENRICHMENT

Some students might design posters that capture the play's **mood** and **theme**. Others might design stage sets of the attic room or make and display scale models of it.

Small groups might like to perform selected scenes of the play. Have students pay careful attention to the **stage directions** as they interpret the lines.

Students may want to write and present reports on the Nazi atrocities against the Jews during World War II.

9. Hundreds of Jews are disappearing, being deported, being sent to death camps. He names friends, including Anne's friend Jopie.

Scene 4
10a. Green Police drag her away as they did Jopie. **10b.** Others are in control, not she. Fear instead of joy.
11a. Sweeter, nicer "good Anne." **11b.** Fears being ridiculed.

Scene 5
12a. Crossword book, razor, homemade shampoo, cigarettes, IOU, cat toy, earplugs. **12b.** Anne shows love, generosity; reminds them of possibilities.
13a. Little food. Few reasons for cheer. They sing with fear. **13b.** Responses will vary. Perhaps sad; perhaps optimistic.
14. Green Police, Gestapo, or thief.

LANGUAGE AND VOCABULARY
1. *Tyranny:* cruel, unjust use of power.
Oppression: being burdened or kept down by unjust use of force or authority.
2. Sentences will vary.

FOCUS ON INFORMATIVE WRITING
You might help students brainstorm cause-and-effect topics that affect them directly in their school, community, and families. List students' responses on the chalkboard and then work with students to select the best topic for a cause-and-effect essay. Model the process of making preliminary notes for the selected topic, engaging students' help as much as possible. Then encourage students to choose topics of their own that they have some firsthand knowledge or experience of.

does he tell them has been happening in the outside world?

Scene 4
10a. What is Anne's nightmare? **b.** How is it completely different from the dreams of her future that she expressed in Scene 3?

11. Anne says that there is a person inside her that is different from the one that people see. **a.** What kind of person remains hidden inside her? **b.** Why doesn't Anne allow this side of her nature to show?

Scene 5
12a. What gifts has Anne managed to gather together for the members of her "family"? **b.** How does the celebration help unite them in the midst of their suffering?

13. The Hanukkah song gives the characters hope and courage. Yet the words of the song do not at all describe their true situation. **a.** Tell how each of the following lines from the song differs from the real conditions of the singers:

Around the feast . . . we . . . gather
Many are the reasons for good cheer.
So hear us rejoicing

b. Knowing what you do of the actual circumstances of the characters, tell how their singing of the Hanukkah song makes you feel.

14. Act One ends with the characters (and the audience) in a state of worry and suspense. What do the characters fear caused the noise downstairs?

Language and Vocabulary

Recognizing Exact Meanings

During the Hanukkah celebration in Scene 5, Mr. Frank tells about the Maccabees, who fought against "tyranny and oppression." The words *tyranny* and *oppression* are close in meaning but they are not synonyms. <u>What is the exact meaning of each word?</u> Check your

1

answers in a dictionary. <u>Show that you understand the precise meaning of each word by using it in a sentence.</u>

2

Focus on Informative Writing

Exploring Cause and Effect

A **cause-and-effect** explanation is another type of informative writing. This kind of essay focuses on an event or situation and answers one or both of these questions:

Why does that happen? (cause)
What is the result? (effect)

When you explore cause and effect, you will often find that a single event can have more than one cause. Likewise, a single event can lead to more than one effect.

For example, what are the causes for the growing tension among the characters in Act One of *The Diary of Anne Frank*? You might show the causes in a chart like the one below:

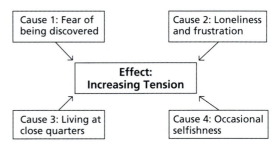

Make notes for a cause-and-effect essay on a topic that interests you. To get started, ask yourself questions like the following. Save your notes.

I wonder why . . .
What would happen if . . . ?

OBJECTIVES
The overall aim is for students to analyze the development of Anne's character and to identify the **theme** of the play. For a complete list of objectives, see the **Teacher's Notes**.

VOCABULARY
The underlined words are in the Glossary. Encourage students to notice the use of German and Hebrew words and references to political events of the time that give the play a greater sense of realism.

FOCUS / MOTIVATION
Ask students whether they have ever been nervous about a future event (perhaps a test or performance) and then suddenly realized something that gave them complete confidence in the future. Anne Frank has such a realization.

Act Two

Scene 1

In the darkness we hear Anne's *voice, again reading from the diary.*

1 **Anne's Voice.** Saturday, the first of January, nineteen forty-four. Another new year has begun and we find ourselves still in our hiding place. We have been here now for one year, five months and twenty-five days. It seems that our life is at a standstill.

2 [*The curtain rises on the scene. It is late afternoon. Everyone is bundled up against the cold. In the main room* Mrs. Frank *is taking down the laundry, which is hung across the back.* Mr. Frank *sits in the chair down left, reading.* Margot *is lying on the couch with a blanket over her and the many-colored knitted scarf around her throat.* Anne *is seated at the center table, writing in her diary.* Peter, Mr. *and* Mrs. Van Daan, *and* Dussel *are all in their own rooms, reading or lying down.*]

As the lights dim on, Anne's voice continues, without a break.]

Anne's Voice. We are all a little thinner. The Van Daans' "discussions" are as violent as ever. Mother still does not understand me. But then I don't understand her either. There is one great change, however. A change in myself. I read somewhere that girls of my age don't feel quite certain of themselves. That they become quiet within and begin to think of the miracle that is taking place in their bodies. I think that what is happening to me is so wonderful . . . not only what can be seen, but what is taking place inside. Each time it has happened I have a feeling that I have a sweet secret. (*We hear the chimes and then a hymn being played on the carillon outside.*) And in spite of any pain, I long for the time when I shall feel that secret within me again.

3 [*The buzzer of the door below suddenly sounds.*

Everyone is startled; Mr. Frank *tiptoes cautiously to the top of the steps and listens. Again the buzzer* **4** *sounds, in* Miep's *V-for-Victory signal.*[1]]

Mr. Frank. It's Miep!

[*He goes quickly down the steps to unbolt the door.* Mrs. Frank *calls upstairs to the* Van Daans *and then to* Peter.]

Mrs. Frank. Wake up, everyone! Miep is here! (Anne *quickly puts her diary away.* Margot *sits up, pulling the blanket around her shoulders.* Dussel *sits on the edge of his bed, listening, disgruntled.* Miep *comes up the steps, followed by* Mr. Kraler. *They bring flowers, books, newspapers, etc.* Anne *rushes to* Miep, *throwing her arms affectionately around her.*) Miep . . . *and* Mr. Kraler . . . What a delightful surprise!

1. **V-for-Victory signal:** three short rings and one long ring, the Morse code for V, used as the Allied symbol for victory.

VISUAL CONNECTIONS
Ideas for Writing
Each scene of the play is based on Anne's diary descriptions of life in hiding. You may ask students to write a diary entry that expresses Anne's feelings about one of the scenes in this act, perhaps Peter's loss of Mouschi, Mr. Van Daan's sale of his wife's coat, or the news of a possible blackmailer.

**Act Two
Scene One**

1
A year and a half has passed since first entry in Anne's diary in July, 1942.

2
Atmosphere. Stage direction suggests that everyone is suffering from boredom.

3
Sounds at door immediately create tension and fear. Capture and death are constant possibilities.

4
Miep has chosen a positive, hopeful signal. All are hoping for liberation by the Allied forces.

MOTIVATIONAL SUMMARY

The Franks and their friends have spent nearly a year and a half in hiding but now are threatened by a serious and unsolvable problem: Someone knows that there are people on the top floor of the warehouse.

PRESENTATION

In Act One, the audience learns about the people and the **setting**. Each has become a part of the life of every other in this tiny community, just as each of them becomes a part of every reader and viewer of this play.

Act Two focuses on the physical, emotional, and intellectual growth of Anne and Peter and on the sudden capture of the whole group by police.

In this act, Anne resolves the **conflict** between "good" Anne and "bad" Anne. Physically, she

---

5
Symbol. Anne yearns for freedom of outdoors, symbolized by smell of wind and cold on Miep's clothes.

6 Drawing Conclusions
Has the cat run away, or is Mr. Van Daan responsible for its disappearance? Audience never knows for sure, but Mr. Van Daan's increasing belligerence and his remarks about the cat suggest that he is responsible.

7
Only food lures Dussel into company of others.

8
Irony. Cake, meant to lift spirits and celebrate New Year, reminds them how long they have been in hiding.

9
Mr. Van Daan becomes more difficult as time passes. His selfishness, especially about food, contrasts sharply with Miep's generosity.

10
Conflict. Apparently the Van Daans have not been sharing all things fairly.

Mr. Kraler. We came to bring you New Year's greetings.

Mrs. Frank. You shouldn't . . . you should have at least one day to yourselves. (*She goes quickly to the stove and brings down teacups and tea for all of them.*)

Anne. Don't say that, it's so wonderful to see
5 them! (*Sniffing at* Miep's *coat*) I can smell the wind and the cold on your clothes.

Miep (*giving her the flowers*). There you are. (*Then, to* Margot, *feeling her forehead*) How are you, Margot? . . . Feeling any better?

Margot. I'm all right.

Anne. We filled her full of every kind of pill so she won't cough and make a noise.

[*She runs into her room to put the flowers in water. Mr. and Mrs. Van Daan come from upstairs. Outside there is the sound of a band playing.*]

Mrs. Van Daan. Well, hello, Miep. Mr. Kraler.

Mr. Kraler (*giving a bouquet of flowers to* Mrs. Van Daan). With my hope for peace in the New Year.

6 **Peter** (*anxiously*). Miep, have you seen Mouschi? Have you seen him anywhere around?

Miep. I'm sorry, Peter. I asked everyone in the neighborhood had they seen a gray cat. But they said no.

[Mrs. Frank *gives* Miep *a cup of tea.* Mr. Frank *comes up the steps, carrying a small cake on a plate.*]

Mr. Frank. Look what Miep's brought for us!

Mrs. Frank (*taking it*). A cake!

Mr. Van Daan. A cake! (*He pinches* Miep's *cheeks gaily and hurries up to the cupboard.*) I'll get some
plates.

7 [Dussel, *in his room, hastily puts a coat on and starts out to join the others.*]

Mrs. Frank. Thank you, Miepia. You shouldn't

---

have done it. You must have used all of your sugar ration for weeks. (*Giving it to* Mrs. Van Daan) It's beautiful, isn't it?

8 **Mrs. Van Daan.** It's been ages since I even saw a cake. Not since you brought us one last year. (*Without looking at the cake, to* Miep) Remember? Don't you remember, you gave us one on New Year's Day? Just this time last year? I'll never forget it because you had "Peace in nineteen forty-three" on it. (*She looks at the cake and reads.*) "Peace in nineteen forty-four!"

Miep. Well, it has to come sometime, you know. (*As* Dussel *comes from his room*) Hello, Mr. Dussel.

Mr. Kraler. How are you?

Mr. Van Daan (*bringing plates and a knife*). Here's the knife, *liefje.* Now, how many of us are there?

Miep. None for me, thank you.

Mr. Frank. Oh, please. You must.

Miep. I couldn't.

9 **Mr. Van Daan.** Good! That leaves one . . . two . . . three . . . seven of us.

Dussel. Eight! Eight! It's the same number as it always is!

Mr. Van Daan. I left Margot out. I take it for granted Margot wouldn't eat any.

Anne. Why wouldn't she?

Mrs. Frank. I think it won't harm her.

Mr. Van Daan. All right! All right! I just didn't want her to start coughing again, that's all.

Dussel. And please, Mrs. Frank should cut the cake.

Mr. Van Daan. What's the difference?
Mrs. Van Daan. It's not Mrs. Frank's cake, is it, Miep? It's for all of us. ⎫ (*Together*)

10 **Dussel.** Mrs. Frank divides things better.

Mrs. Van Daan (*going to* Dussel). What are you trying to say?
Mr. Van Daan. Oh, come on! Stop wasting time! ⎫ (*Together*)

Mrs. Van Daan (*to* Dussel). Don't I always give everybody exactly the same? Don't I?

---

enters adulthood. Its arrival coincides with her emotional, spiritual, and intellectual maturation. Her ambitions are less self-centered. No longer does she want just to be famous, a dancer or something "wonderful." Her new outlook is more intellectual and socially responsible—to be a writer or journalist. She outgrows her fear of being ridiculed for being too serious and learns to give love as she has received love. Although she is under constant threat of capture and death, she chooses to believe that people are basically good.

Peter, also a dynamic character, grows not as quickly or as much as Anne, but his presence helps to stimulate Anne's emotional development. Anne's sympathetic understanding and romantic feelings for him help Peter learn to have a friend. Both young people mature under

---

Mr. Van Daan. Forget it, Kerli.

Mrs. Van Daan. No. I want an answer! Don't I?

Dussel. Yes. Yes. Everybody gets exactly the
11 same . . . except Mr. Van Daan always gets a little bit more.

[Mr. Van Daan *advances on* Dussel, *the knife still in his hand.*]

Mr. Van Daan. That's a lie!

[Dussel *retreats before the* onslaught *of the* Van Daans.]

12 **Mr. Frank.** Please, please! (*Then, to* Miep) You see what a little sugar cake does to us? It goes right to our heads!

Mr. Van Daan (*handing* Mrs. Frank *the knife*). Here you are, Mrs. Frank.

Mrs. Frank. Thank you. (*Then, to* Miep *as she goes to the table to cut the cake*) Are you sure you won't have some?

Miep (*drinking her tea*). No, really, I have to go in a minute.

[*The sound of the band fades out in the distance.*]

Peter (*to* Miep). Maybe Mouschi went back to our house . . . they say that cats . . . Do you ever get over there . . . ? I mean . . . do you suppose you could . . . ?

Miep. I'll try, Peter. The first minute I get I'll try. But I'm afraid, with him gone a week . . .

13 **Dussel.** Make up your mind, already someone has had a nice big dinner from that cat!

[Peter *is furious,* inarticulate. *He starts toward* Dussel *as if to hit him.* Mr. Frank *stops him.* Mrs. Frank *speaks quickly to ease the situation.*]

Mrs. Frank (*to* Miep). This is delicious, Miep!

Mrs. Van Daan (*eating hers*). Delicious!

14 **Mr. Van Daan** (*finishing it in one gulp*). Dirk's in luck to get a girl who can bake like this!

Miep (*putting down her empty teacup*). I have to run. Dirk's taking me to a party tonight.

Anne. How heavenly! Remember now what everyone is wearing, and what you have to eat and everything, so you can tell us tomorrow.

Miep. I'll give you a full report! Goodbye, everyone!

Mr. Van Daan (*to* Miep). Just a minute. There's something I'd like you to do for me. (*He hurries off up the stairs to his room.*)

Mrs. Van Daan (*sharply*). Putti, where are you going? (*She rushes up the stairs after him, calling hysterically.*) What do you want? Putti, what are you going to do?

Miep (*to* Peter). What's wrong?

15 **Peter** (*His sympathy is with his mother*). Father says he's going to sell her fur coat. She's crazy about that old fur coat.

Dussel. Is it possible? Is is possible that anyone is so silly as to worry about a fur coat in times like this?

16 **Peter.** It's none of your darn business . . . and if you say one more thing . . . I'll, I'll take you and I'll . . . I mean it . . . I'll . . .

[*There is a piercing scream from* Mrs. Van Daan *above. She grabs at the fur coat as* Mr. Van Daan *is starting downstairs with it.*]

Mrs. Van Daan. No! No! No! Don't you dare take that! You hear? It's mine! (*Downstairs* Peter *turns away, embarrassed, miserable.*) My father gave me that! You didn't give it to me. You have no right. Let go of it . . . you hear?

[Mr. Van Daan *pulls the coat from her hands and hurries downstairs.* Mrs. Van Daan *sinks to the floor*
17 *sobbing. As* Mr. Van Daan *comes into the main room the others look away, embarrassed for him.*]

Mr. Van Daan (*to* Mr. Kraler). Just a little—discussion over the advisability of selling this coat. As I have often reminded Mrs. Van Daan, it's

---

11
This comment reveals Dussel's previously unexpressed resentment. When there is so little enjoyment in life, size of a slice of cake becomes important.

12
Mr. Frank, ever the peacemaker, diplomatically intervenes. He is embarrassed by childish squabble over Miep's gift.

13
Because of wartime shortages, pets were sometimes eaten. Dussel's comment is quite insensitive.

14
Characterization. Mr. Van Daan's gulping of cake shows his greed. His craving for food goes beyond his body's hunger.

15   Making Inferences
Why is Mr. Van Daan selling his wife's coat? At this point, audience does not know. Audience might assume Mr. Van Daan's reasons are selfish.

16
Conflict. Tension is increasing. This is third threat of violence within minutes. The speech is interrupted by a scream.

17
The others are embarrassed because Mr. Van Daan is so insensitive to his wife's feelings.

the kindly guidance of Mr. Frank.

The growth of Anne and Peter takes place against the backdrop of the daily events of their confined world. From these events, the audience learns, as do Anne and Peter, about people and life, about human conduct and values.

The other characters are largely static. They serve as foils to one another and to the young people. The Van Daans are both preoccupied with selfish interests—he with food and cigarettes, she with money and her fading beauty. Mr. Dussel sees mostly the negative in life. He

keeps a whole arsenal of pills to ward off imagined diseases. Mr. and Mrs. Frank and Margot are generous, helpful, considerate; they provide the moral and social standards by which others are judged. At the end of the play, Mr. Frank returns to the locale of the play's action to re-

---

18

Characterization. Although Mr. Van Daan pretends to be selling coat because of others' needs, he is interested in only two things: money it will bring and cigarettes that money will buy. His action shows he is both selfish and cruel.

19 Synthesizing

Why is it hard to see a doctor at this time? Most are serving in army.

20

It seems unlikely that Mr. Kraler would need Mr. Frank's help with contracts. Margot sees through thin excuse to get Mr. Frank alone.

21

Irony. Mr. Frank is correct—the imagination can intensify fear. The horrible irony of this play is that the reality of Nazi atrocities staggers human imagination.

22

New threat to safety comes at a bad time; tension is already causing problems.

23

Mr. Frank refuses to jump to conclusions. This is small sum, perhaps only a request for raise.

---

very selfish of her to keep it when people outside are in such desperate need of clothing. . . .

18 (*He gives the coat to* Miep.) So if you will please to sell it for us? It should fetch a good price. And by the way, will you get me cigarettes. I don't care what kind they are . . . get all you can.

Miep. It's terribly difficult to get them, Mr. Van Daan. But I'll try. Goodbye.

[*She goes.* Mr. Frank *follows her down the steps to bolt the door after her.* Mrs. Frank *gives* Mr. Kraler *a cup of tea.*]

Mrs. Frank. Are you sure you won't have some cake, Mr. Kraler?

Mr. Kraler. I'd better not.

Mr. Van Daan. You're still feeling badly? What does your doctor say?

Mr. Kraler. I haven't been to him.

Mrs. Frank. Now Mr. Kraler! . . .

19 **Mr. Kraler** (*sitting at the table*). Oh, I tried. But you can't get near a doctor these days . . . they're so busy. After weeks I finally managed to get one on the telephone. I told him I'd like an appointment . . . I wasn't feeling very well. You know what he answers . . . over the telephone . . . Stick out your tongue! (*They laugh. He turns to* Mr. Frank *as* Mr. Frank *comes back.*) I have some contracts here. . . . I wonder if you'd look over them with me. . . .

Mr. Frank (*putting out his hand*). Of course.

Mr. Kraler (*He rises*). If we could go downstairs . . . (Mr. Frank *starts ahead;* Mr. Kraler *speaks to the others.*) Will you forgive us? I won't keep him but a minute. (*He starts to follow* Mr. Frank *down the steps.*)

20 **Margot** (*with sudden foreboding*). What's happened? Something's happened! Hasn't it, Mr. Kraler?

[Mr. Kraler *stops and comes back, trying to reassure* Margot *with a pretense of casualness.*]

Mr. Kraler. No, really. I want your father's advice. . . .

Margot. Something's gone wrong! I know it!

Mr. Frank (*coming back, to* Mr. Kraler). If it's something that concerns us here, it's better that we all hear it.

Mr. Kraler (*turning to him, quietly*). But . . . the children . . . ?

21 **Mr. Frank.** What they'd imagine would be worse than any reality.

[*As* Mr. Kraler *speaks, they all listen with intense apprehension.* Mrs. Van Daan *comes down the stairs and sits on the bottom step.*]

Mr. Kraler. It's a man in the storeroom. . . . I don't know whether or not you remember him . . . Carl, about fifty, heavyset, near-sighted . . . He came with us just before you left.

Mr. Frank. He was from Utrecht?

22 **Mr. Kraler.** That's the man. A couple of weeks ago, when I was in the storeroom, he closed the door and asked me . . . how's Mr. Frank? What do you hear from Mr. Frank? I told him I only knew there was a rumor that you were in Switzerland. He said he'd heard that rumor too, but he thought I might know something more. I didn't pay any attention to it . . . but then a thing happened yesterday. . . . He'd brought some invoices to the office for me to sign. As I was going through them, I looked up. He was standing staring at the bookcase . . . your bookcase. He said he thought he remembered a door there. . . . Wasn't there a door there that used to go up to the loft? Then he told me he wanted more money. Twenty guilders² more a week.

Mr. Van Daan. Blackmail!

23 **Mr. Frank.** Twenty guilders? Very modest blackmail.

Mr. Van Daan. That's just the beginning.

2. **Twenty guilders:** about five dollars at the time.

HISTORY LINK
Encourage students to read related books. You could suggest the following first-hand accounts: *Night* by Elie Wiesel, the memoirs of a survivor of two concentration camps, and *Anne Frank Remembered: The Story of the Woman Who* *Helped to Hide the Frank Family* by Miep Gies and Alison Leslie Gold.

Dussel (*coming to* Mr. Frank). You know what I think? He was the thief who was down there that night. That's how he knows we're here.

Mr. Frank (*to* Mr. Kraler). How was it left? What did you tell him?

Mr. Kraler. I said I had to think about it. What shall I do? Pay him the money? . . . Take a chance on firing him . . . or what? I don't know.

Dussel (*frantic*). For God's sake don't fire him! Pay him what he asks . . . keep him here where you can have your eye on him.

24 Mr. Frank. Is it so much that he's asking? What are they paying nowadays?

Mr. Kraler. He could get it in a war plant. But this isn't a war plant. Mind you, I don't know if he really knows . . . or if he doesn't know.

25 Mr. Frank. Offer him half. Then we'll soon find out if it's blackmail or not.

Dussel. And if it is? We've got to pay it, haven't we? Anything he asks we've got to pay!

Mr. Frank. Let's decide that when the time comes.

26 Mr. Kraler. This may be all imagination. You get to a point, these days, where you suspect everyone and everything. Again and again . . . on some simple look or word, I've found myself . . .

[*The telephone rings in the office below.*]

Mrs. Van Daan (*hurrying to* Mr. Kraler). There's the telephone! What does that mean, the telephone ringing on a holiday?

Mr. Kraler. That's my wife. I told her I had to go over some papers in my office . . . to call me there when she got out of church. (*He starts out.*) I'll offer him half then. Goodbye . . . we'll hope for the best!

[*The group call their goodbyes halfheartedly. Mr. Frank follows Mr. Kraler, to bolt the door below. During the following scene, Mr. Frank comes back up and stands listening, disturbed.*]

27 Dussel (*to* Mr. Van Daan). You can thank your son for this . . . smashing the light! I tell you, it's just a question of time now. (*He goes to the window at the back and stands looking out.*)

28 Margot. Sometimes I wish the end would come . . . whatever it is.

Mrs. Frank (*shocked*). Margot!

[*Anne goes to Margot, sitting beside her on the couch with her arms around her.*]

Margot. Then at least we'd know where we were.

Mrs. Frank. You should be ashamed of yourself! Talking that way! Think how lucky we are! Think of the thousands dying in the war, every day. Think of the people in concentration camps.

Anne (*interrupting*). What's the good of that? What's the good of thinking of misery when you're already miserable? That's stupid!

Mrs. Frank. Anne!

[*As Anne goes on raging at her mother, Mrs. Frank tries to break in, in an effort to quiet her.*]

29 Anne. We're young. Margot and Peter and I! You grown-ups have had your chance! But look at us. . . . If we begin thinking of all the horror in the world, we're lost! We're trying to hold on to some kind of ideals . . . when everything . . . ideals, hopes . . . everything, are being destroyed! It isn't our fault that the world is in such a mess! We weren't around when all this started! So don't try to take it out on us! (*She rushes off to her room, slamming the door after her. She picks up a brush from the chest and hurls it to the floor. Then she sits on the settee, trying to control her anger.*)

Mr. Van Daan. She talks as if we started the war! Did we start the war?

30 [*He spots Anne's cake. As he starts to take it, Peter anticipates him.*]

24 Mr. Frank remains calm and rational.

25 Summarizing
How will Mr. Frank's recommendation work? If Carl is blackmailer, he will use what he knows to force issue, get his full demand. Mr. Frank's logic settles situation for now.

26 Atmosphere. Under tyranny, fear is a way of life. Everything is interpreted as a threat. The point is proved immediately by Mrs. Van Daan's panicky response to the ringing telephone.

27 Dussel continues to be unlikable character, devoid of all social grace and compassion.

28 The anxiety is almost more than Margot can endure. She admits her fear, desire for any kind of end to their plight. She has apparently kept her feelings from her mother.

29 Conflict. Anne loses her temper, but this is not the type of childish outburst she was given to earlier. She is struggling with play's central issue—how to maintain ideals and dignity in a corrupt world.

30 Mr. Van Daan intends to eat Anne's cake. Peter, perhaps motivated by his feelings for Anne, shows courage in dealing with his father.

31 Comparing/Contrasting
Making Generalizations
How have Peter's feelings changed toward Anne? What is it about Anne that appeals to Peter? He respects her, has grown to care about her. She bravely speaks her mind, something Peter cannot do before adults.

32
Anne sees herself as the child that first went into hiding. She does not see how she has matured. Anne has poor image of herself, has not learned to trust her instincts.

33
Peter aggressively backs Dussel out of the room. Peter is still resorting to physical threat. He will mature as he discusses life with Anne.

34
Conflict. Peter explains why he keeps to himself so much. His parents' arguments upset him.

35
Characterization. Anne is more mature than most fourteen-year-olds. She has been forced to grow up quickly, but she also recognizes that she does not have the answers to their problems.

36
Anne cannot see that Mr. Frank loves, protects his wife. He cannot take sides.

Peter. She left her cake. (*He starts for Anne's room with the cake. There is silence in the main room. Mrs. Van Daan goes up to her room, followed by Mr. Van Daan. Dussel stays looking out the window. Mr. Frank brings Mrs. Frank her cake. She eats it slowly, without relish. Mr. Frank takes his cake to Margot and sits quietly on the sofa beside her. Peter stands in the doorway of Anne's darkened room, looking at her, then makes a little movement to let her know he is there. Anne sits up, quickly, trying to hide the signs of her tears. Peter holds out the cake to her.*) You left this.

Anne (*dully*). Thanks.

[Peter *starts to go out, then comes back.*]

31 Peter. I thought you were fine just now. You know just how to talk to them. You know just how to say it. I'm no good . . . I never can think . . . especially when I'm mad. . . . That Dussel . . . when he said that about Mouschi . . . someone eating him . . . all I could think is . . . I wanted to hit him. I wanted to give him such a . . . a . . . that he'd . . . That's what I used to do when there was an argument at school. . . . That's the way I . . . but here . . . And an old man like that . . . it wouldn't be so good.

32 Anne. You're making a big mistake about me. I do it all wrong. I say too much. I go too far. I hurt people's feelings. . . .

[Dussel *leaves the window, going to his room.*]

Peter. I think you're just fine. . . . What I want to say . . . if it wasn't for you around here, I don't know. What I mean . . .

[Peter *is interrupted by* Dussel's *turning on the light. Dussel stands in the doorway, startled to see Peter. Peter advances toward him forbiddingly.*
33 Dussel *backs out of the room. Peter closes the door on him.*]

Anne. Do you mean it, Peter? Do you really mean it?

Peter. I said it, didn't I?

Anne. Thank you, Peter!

[*In the main room* Mr. *and* Mrs. Frank *collect the dishes and take them to the sink, washing them. Margot lies down again on the couch. Dussel, lost, wanders into* Peter's *room and takes up a book, starting to read.*]

Peter (*looking at the photographs on the wall*). You've got quite a collection.

Anne. Wouldn't you like some in your room? I could give you some. Heaven knows you spend enough time in there . . . doing heaven knows what. . . .

34 Peter. It's easier. A fight starts, or an argument . . . I duck in there.

Anne. You're lucky, having a room to go to. His Lordship is always here. . . . I hardly ever get a minute alone. When they start in on me, I can't duck away. I have to stand there and take it.

Peter. You gave some of it back just now.

Anne. I get so mad. They've formed their **35** opinions . . . about everything . . . but we . . . we're still trying to find out. . . . We have problems here that no other people our age have ever had. And just as you think you've solved them, something comes along and bang! You have to start all over again.

Peter. At least you've got someone you can talk to.

Anne. Not really. Mother . . . I never discuss anything serious with her. She doesn't understand. Father's all right. We can talk about everything . . . everything but one thing.
36 Mother. He simply won't talk about her. I don't think you can be really intimate with anyone if he holds something back, do you?

Peter. I think your father's fine.

Anne. Oh, he is, Peter! He is! He's the only one

376

who's ever given me the feeling that I have any sense. But anyway, nothing can take the place of school and play and friends of your own age . . . or near your age . . . can it?

Peter. I suppose you miss your friends and all.

Anne. It isn't just . . . (*She breaks off, staring up at him for a second.*) Isn't it funny, you and I? Here we've been seeing each other every minute for almost a year and a half, and this is the first time we've ever really talked. It helps a lot to have someone to talk to, don't you think? It helps you to let off steam.

37 Peter (*going to the door*). Well, any time you want to let off steam, you can come into my room.

Anne (*following him*). I can get up an awful lot of steam. You'll have to be careful how you say that.

Peter. It's all right with me.

38 Anne. Do you really mean it?

Peter. I said it, didn't I?

39 [*He goes out.* Anne *stands in her doorway looking after him. As* Peter *gets to his door, he stands for a minute looking back at her. Then he goes into his room.* Dussel *rises as he comes in, and quickly passes him, going out. He starts across for his room.* Anne *sees him coming and pulls her door shut.* Dussel *turns back toward* Peter's *room.* Peter *pulls his door shut.* Dussel *stands there, bewildered, forlorn.*

The scene slowly dims out. The curtain falls on the scene. Anne's *voice comes over in the darkness . . . faintly at first, and then with growing strength.*]

Anne's Voice. We've had bad news. The people from whom Miep got our ration books have been arrested. So we have had to cut down on **40** our food. Our stomachs are so empty that they rumble and make strange noises, all in different keys. Mr. Van Daan's is deep and low, like a bass fiddle. Mine is high, whistling like a flute. As we all sit around waiting for supper, it's like an orchestra tuning up. It only needs

Toscanini[3] to raise his baton and we'd be off in the "Ride of the Valkyries."[4] Monday, the sixth of March, nineteen forty-four. Mr. Kraler is in the hospital. It seems he has ulcers. Pim says **41** we are his ulcers. Miep has to run the business and us too. The Americans have landed on the southern tip of Italy. Father looks for a quick finish to the war. Mr. Dussel is waiting every day for the warehouseman to demand more money. Have I been skipping too much from one subject to another? I can't help it. I feel **42** that spring is coming. I feel it in my whole body and soul. I feel utterly confused. I am longing . . . so longing . . . for everything . . . for friends . . . for someone to talk to . . . someone who understands . . . someone young, who feels as I do. . . .

[*As these last lines are being said, the curtain rises on the scene. The lights dim on.* Anne's *voice fades out.*]

Scene 2

It is evening, after supper. From the outside we hear **1** *the sound of children playing. The "grown-ups," with the exception of* Mr. Van Daan, *are all in the main room.* Mrs. Frank *is doing some mending.* Mrs. Van Daan *is reading a fashion magazine.* Mr. Frank *is going over business accounts.* Dussel, *in his dentist's jacket, is pacing up and down, impatient to get into his bedroom.* Mr. Van Daan *is upstairs working on a piece of embroidery in an embroidery frame.*

In his room Peter *is sitting before the mirror, smoothing his hair. As the scene goes on, he puts on his tie, brushes his coat and puts it on, preparing himself meticulously for a visit from* Anne. *On his*

3. **Toscanini** (tŏs′kə-nē′nē): Arturo Toscanini, a famous conductor.
4. **"Ride of the Valkyries"** (văl-kîr′ēz): a rousing piece of music from an opera by the German composer Richard Wagner.

37
Peter's invitation indicates he likes her very much; he may have a "crush" on her.

38
Anne is pleased, surprised; she wants to be sure Peter means what he says.

39 Analyzing
What does this scene show the audience about Anne and Peter? They can draw on each other for support, courage.

40
Characterization. One of Anne's most important traits is her ability to make the best of a bad situation. While starvation is no laughing matter, her ironic and humorous treatment of it is a method of coping.

41 Drawing Conclusions
What does Pim (Mr. Frank) mean by "we are his ulcers"? Ulcers are often result of worry; Mr. Kraler has lived in constant fear for harboring the Franks.

42
Plot. Anne is an adolescent now; she yearns for romance.

Scene Two

1 Comparing/Contrasting
How does what the audience sees here differ from the beginning of Scene One? Everyone seems to have more direction; boredom, tensions are under control.

378

What is Anne doing? What is unusual about this date? Anne is getting ready for date with Peter. Unusual because she lives with him every day.

3

Inference. Margot assumes that Anne is "fishing" for a compliment. Anne seems to be self-conscious, unsure of her attractiveness.

4 Analyzing
    Drawing Conclusions
Why does Anne comment on the vagueness of Margot's response? What is Anne implying to her sister? Anne quickly notices what is *not* said. She is implying that Margot is being diplomatic, not totally honest. Nice eyes and animation do not add up to physical beauty.

5

Mrs. Frank is trying to be subtle, will not say what she really means.

6 Expressing an Opinion
Does Mrs. Frank trust Anne? Responses will vary. Mrs. Frank probably trusts Anne, but she is concerned about what others will think. She knows Mrs. Van Daan can twist situation against Anne.

7

Characterization. Mrs. Frank would rather avoid confrontation than oppose Mrs. Van Daan. She lets Mrs. Van Daan intimidate her.

8

Margot understands her mother's nature; seems to admire Anne's fighting spirit but dislikes her judgment of mother.

---

wall are now hung some of Anne's *motion-picture stars.*

2 *In her room* Anne *too is getting dressed. She stands before the mirror in her slip, trying various ways of dressing her hair.* Margot *is seated on the sofa, hemming a skirt for* Anne *to wear.*

In the main room Dussel *can stand it no longer. He comes over, rapping sharply on the door of his and* Anne's *bedroom.*

Anne (*calling to him*). No, no, Mr. Dussel! I am not dressed yet. (Dussel *walks away, furious, sitting down and burying his head in his hands.* Anne
3 *turn to* Margot.) How is that? How does that look?
Margot (*glancing at her briefly*). Fine.
Anne. You didn't even look.
Margot. Of course I did. It's fine.
Anne. Margot, tell me, am I terribly ugly?
Margot. Oh, stop fishing.
Anne. No. No. Tell me.
Margot. Of course you're not. You've got nice eyes . . . and a lot of animation, and . . .
4 **Anne.** A little vague, aren't you?

[*She reaches over and takes a brassière out of* Margot's *sewing basket. She holds it up to herself, studying the effect in the mirror. Outside,* Mrs. Frank, *feeling sorry for* Dussel, *comes over, knocking at the girls' door.*]

Mrs. Frank (*outside*). May I come in?
Margot. Come in, Mother.
Mrs. Frank (*shutting the door behind her*). Mr. Dussel's impatient to get in here.
Anne (*still with the brassière*). Heavens, he takes the room for himself the entire day.
Mrs. Frank (*gently*). Anne, dear, you're not going in again tonight to see Peter?
Anne (*dignified*). That is my intention.
Mrs. Frank. But you've already spent a great deal of time in there today.
Anne. I was in there exactly twice. Once to get

---

the dictionary, and then three quarters of an hour before supper.
5 **Mrs. Frank.** Aren't you afraid you're disturbing him?
Anne. Mother, I have some intuition.
Mrs. Frank. Then may I ask you this much, Anne. Please don't shut the door when you go in.
Anne. You sound like Mrs. Van Daan!

[*She throws the brassière back in* Margot's *sewing basket and picks up her blouse, putting it on.*]

6 **Mrs. Frank.** No. No. I don't mean to suggest anything wrong. I only wish that you wouldn't expose yourself to criticism . . . that you wouldn't give Mrs. Van Daan the opportunity to be unpleasant!
Anne. Mrs. Van Daan doesn't need an opportunity to be unpleasant!
Mrs. Frank. Everyone's on edge, worried about Mr. Kraler. This is one more thing. . . .
Anne. I'm sorry, Mother. I'm going to Peter's room. I'm not going to let Petronella Van Daan spoil our friendship.

[Mrs. Frank *hesitates for a second, then goes out, closing the door after her. She gets a pack of playing cards and sits at the center table, playing solitaire. In* Anne's *room* Margot *hands the finished skirt to* Anne. *As* Anne *is putting it on,* Margot *takes off her high-heeled shoes and stuffs paper in the toes so that* Anne *can wear them.*]

Margot (*to* Anne). Why don't you two talk in
7 the main room? It'd save a lot of trouble. It's hard on Mother, having to listen to those remarks from Mrs. Van Daan and not say a word.
Anne. Why doesn't she say a word? I think it's ridiculous to take it and take it.
Margot. You don't understand Mother at all, do you? She can't talk back. She's not like you. It's just not in her nature to fight back.
Anne. Anyway . . . the only one I worry about is

you. I feel awfully guilty about you. (*She sits on the stool near* Margot, *putting on* Margot's *high-heeled shoes.*)

Margot. What about?

9 **Anne.** I mean, every time I go into Peter's room, I have a feeling I may be hurting you. (Margot *shakes her head.*) I know if it were me, I'd be wild. I'd be desperately jealous, if it were me.

Margot. Well, I'm not.

Anne. You don't feel badly? Really? Truly? You're not jealous?

10 **Margot.** Of course I'm jealous . . . jealous that you've got something to get up in the morning for . . . But jealous of you and Peter? No.

[Anne *goes back to the mirror.*]

Anne. Maybe there's nothing to be jealous of. Maybe he doesn't really like me. Maybe I'm just taking the place of his cat. . . . (*She picks up a pair of short, white gloves, putting them on.*)

11 Wouldn't you like to come in with us?

Margot. I have a book.

[*The sound of the children playing outside fades out. In the main room* Dussel *can stand it no longer. He jumps up, going to the bedroom door and knocking sharply.*]

Dussel. Will you please let me in my room!

Anne. Just a minute, dear, dear Mr. Dussel. (*She picks up her mother's pink stole and adjusts it elegantly over her shoulders, then gives a last look in*

12 *the mirror.*) Well, here I go . . . to run the gantlet.[5] (*She starts out, followed by* Margot.)

Dussel (*as she appears—sarcastic*). Thank you so much.

[Dussel *goes into his room.* Anne *goes toward* Peter's *room, passing* Mrs. Van Daan *and her parents at the center table.*]

Mrs. Van Daan. My God, look at her! (Anne *pays no attention. She knocks at* Peter's *door.*) I don't know what good it is to have a son. I

5. **run the gantlet** (gônt'lĭt): go forward under attack from both sides.

13 never see him. He wouldn't care if I killed myself. (Peter *opens the door and stands aside for* Anne *to come in.*) Just a minute, Anne. (*She goes to them at the door.*) I'd like to say a few words to my son. Do you mind? (Peter *and* Anne *stand waiting.*) Peter, I don't want you staying up till all hours tonight. You've got to have your sleep. You're a growing boy. You hear?

Mrs. Frank. Anne won't stay late. She's going to bed promptly at nine. Aren't you, Anne?

Anne. Yes, Mother . . . (*to* Mrs. Van Daan) May we go now?

VISUAL CONNECTIONS
Exploring the Subject
In earlier scenes, Anne's hair has been combed like a schoolgirl's, and Anne has worn loose, childish clothing. Here, she wears her hair in a more sophisticated style, and her clothing is attractive. These minor changes suggest to audience that Anne has grown up.

9
Characterization. Anne, who assumes that Margot may have feelings for Peter, wants to treat others as she would want to be treated.

10 Analyzing
What does Margot mean when she says "you've got something to get up in the morning for"? Anne's new friendship has given meaning to her life, something Margot's life lacks.

11
Anne's offer is generous. She has developed strong feelings for Peter but is willing to risk sharing him with her sister.

12
Symbol. By walking past the adults dressed in a stole, Anne is declaring that she has become a woman. Anne is particularly likable in this scene because she takes an emotional risk in visually declaring her romantic interests.

13
Mrs. Van Daan, who earlier tried to flirt with Mr. Frank, is now jealous of attention Peter pays to Anne.

25
Anne is hinting to Peter that she is ready to be kissed.

26 Analyzing
Anne is very honest with Peter about how she used to feel about him.

27
Plot. Kiss is handled suddenly and awkwardly, but it shows that Peter has romantic feelings for Anne.

28
Symbol. Act of kissing Mrs. Van Daan, with whom Anne has not gotten along, is a symbolic expression of acceptance of her as the mother of her boyfriend.

29
Anne denies being in love and then describes classical symptoms of the condition.

30
Showing changes in age is always difficult. This passage allows playwrights to show that time has passed and that Anne has grown.

---

engaged to them. And I'm sure too that Mother never touched a man before Pim. But I don't know . . . things are so different now. . . . **25** What do you think? Do you think a girl shouldn't kiss anyone except if she's engaged or something? It's so hard to try to think what to do, when here we are with the whole world falling around our ears and you think . . . well . . . you don't know what's going to happen tomorrow and . . . What do you think?

Peter. I suppose it'd depend on the girl. Some girls, anything they do's wrong. But others . . . well . . . it wouldn't necessarily be wrong with them. (*The carillon starts to strike nine o'clock.*) I've always thought that when two people . . .

Anne. Nine o'clock. I have to go.

Peter. That's right.

Anne (*without moving*). Good night.

[*There is a second's pause; then* Peter *gets up and moves toward the door.*]

Peter. You won't let them stop you coming?

Anne. No. (*She rises and starts for the door.*) Sometime I might bring my diary. There are so many things in it that I want to talk over with **29** you. There's a lot about you.

Peter. What kind of thing?

26 Anne. I wouldn't want you to see some of it. I thought you were a nothing, just the way you thought about me.

Peter. Did you change your mind, the way I changed my mind about you?

Anne. Well . . . You'll see. . . .

[*For a second* Anne *stands looking up at* Peter, *longing for him to kiss her. As he makes no move she* **30** **27** *turns away. Then suddenly* Peter *grabs her awkwardly in his arms, kissing her on the cheek.* Anne *walks out dazed. She stands for a minute, her back to the people in the main room. As she regains her poise she goes to her mother and father and* Margot, *silently kissing them. They murmur their good-nights*

28 *to her. As she is about to open her bedroom door, she catches sight of* Mrs. Van Daan. *She goes quickly to her, taking her face in her hands and kissing her first on one cheek and then on the other. Then she hurries off into her room.* Mrs. Van Daan *looks after her and then looks over at* Peter's *room. Her suspicions are confirmed.*]

Mrs. Van Daan (*She knows*). Ah hah!

[*The lights dim out. The curtain falls on the scene. In the darkness* Anne's *voice comes faintly at first, and then with growing strength.*]

Anne's Voice. By this time we all know each other so well that if anyone starts to tell a story, the rest can finish it for him. We're having to cut down still further on our meals. What makes it worse, the rats have been at work again. They've carried off some of our precious food. Even Mr. Dussel wishes now that Mouschi was here. Thursday, the twentieth of April, nineteen forty-four. Invasion fever is mounting every day. Miep tells us that people outside talk of nothing else. For myself, life has become much more pleasant. I often go to Peter's room after supper. Oh, don't think I'm in love, because I'm not. But it does make life more bearable to have someone with whom you can exchange views. No more tonight. P.S. . . . I must be honest. I must confess that I actually live for the next meeting. Is there anything lovelier than to sit under the skylight and feel the sun on your cheeks and have a darling boy in your arms? I admit now that I'm glad the Van Daans had a son and not a daughter. I've outgrown another dress. That's the third. I'm having to wear Margot's clothes after all. I'm working hard on my French and am now reading *La Belle Nivernaise*.[6]

6. *La Belle Nivernaise:* a novel by the French writer Alphonse Daudet.

[*As she is saying the last lines, the curtain rises on the scene. The lights dim on as Anne's voice fades out.*]

Scene 3

It is night, a few weeks later. Everyone is in bed. There is complete quiet. In the Van Daans' room a match flares up for a moment and then is quickly put out. Mr. Van Daan, in bare feet, dressed in underwear and trousers, is dimly seen coming stealthily down the stairs and into the main room, where Mr. and Mrs. Frank and Margot are sleeping. He goes to the food safe and again lights a match. Then he cautiously opens the safe, taking out a half-loaf of bread. As he closes the safe, it creaks. He stands rigid. Mrs. Frank sits up in bed. She sees him.

Mrs. Frank (*screaming*). Otto! Otto! Komme schnell!*[7]

[*The rest of the people wake, hurriedly getting up.*]

Mr. Frank. Was ist los? Was ist passiert?*[8]

[*Dussel, followed by Anne, comes from his room.*]

Mrs. Frank (*as she rushes over to Mr. Van Daan*). Er stiehlt das Essen!*[9]
Dussel (*grabbing Mr. Van Daan*). You! You! Give me that.
Mrs. Van Daan (*coming down the stairs*). Putti . . . Putti . . . what is it?
Dussel (*his hands on Van Daan's neck*). You dirty thief . . . stealing food . . . you good-for-nothing . . .
Mr. Frank. Mr. Dussel! For God's sake! Help me, Peter!

---

7. **Komme schnell!:** Come quickly.
8. **Was ist los? Was ist passiert?:** What's wrong? What happened?
9. **Er stiehlt das Essen!:** He's stealing the food!

[*Peter comes over, trying, with Mr. Frank, to separate the two struggling men.*]

Peter. Let him go! Let go!

[*Dussel drops Mr. Van Daan, pushing him away. He shows them the end of a loaf of bread that he has taken from Mr. Van Daan.*]

Dussel. You greedy, selfish . . .

[*Margot turns on the lights.*]

Mrs. Van Daan. Putti . . . what is it?

[*All of Mrs. Frank's gentleness, her self-control, is gone. She is outraged, in a frenzy of indignation.*]

Mrs. Frank. The bread! He was stealing the bread!
Dussel. It was you, and all the time we thought it was the rats!
Mr. Frank. Mr. Van Daan, how could you!
Mr. Van Daan. I'm hungry.
Mrs. Frank. We're all of us hungry! I see the children getting thinner and thinner. Your own son Peter . . . I've heard him moan in his sleep, he's so hungry. And you come in the night and steal food that should go to them . . . to the children!
Mrs. Van Daan (*going to Mr. Van Daan protectively*). He needs more food than the rest of us. He's used to more. He's a big man.

[*Mr. Van Daan breaks away, going over and sitting on the couch.*]

Mrs. Frank (*turning on Mrs. Van Daan*). And you . . . you're worse than he is! You're a mother, and yet you sacrifice your child to this man . . . this . . . this . . .
Mr. Frank. Edith! Edith!

The Diary of Anne Frank Act Two, Scene 3 **383**

Scene Three

1
Anne's diary does not indicate that this bread-stealing incident actually happened.

2
Atmosphere. Part of this scene is played in almost total darkness, adding to the sense of secrecy and tension.

3
The Franks speak in German when emotional.

4
Conflict. Incident, along with pent-up emotions of two years, sparks violent reaction from Dussel. Although physical violence has often been threatened, this is first occurrence.

5
Mrs. Frank uncharacteristically rages at Mr. Van Daan. Mr. Van Daan's selfishness and lack of concern for his own son reveal not only the shallowness of his character but also the desperation to which deprivation has driven him.

6
Despite Mr. Van Daan's poor treatment of her, Mrs. Van Daan defends her husband.

7 **Finding Cause and Effect**
Why is Mrs. Frank so angry over a piece of bread? Mrs. Frank knows that part of a parent's role is to sacrifice for one's children, not to steal from them.

[Margot *picks up the pink woolen stole, putting it over her mother's shoulders.*]

Mrs. Frank (*paying no attention, going on to* Mrs. Van Daan). Don't think I haven't seen you! Always saving the choicest bits for him! I've watched you day after day and I've held my tongue. But not any longer! Not after this! Now I want him to go! I want him to get out of here!
Mr. Frank. Edith!
Mr. Van Daan. Get out } (*Together*)
of here?
Mrs. Van Daan. What do you mean?
Mrs. Frank. Just that! Take your things and get out!
Mr. Frank (*to* Mrs. Frank). You're speaking in anger. You cannot mean what you are saying.
8 Mrs. Frank. I mean exactly that!

[Mrs. Van Daan *takes a cover from the* Franks' *bed, pulling it about her.*]

9 Mr. Frank. For two long years we have lived here, side by side. We have respected each other's rights . . . we have managed to live in peace. Are we now going to throw it all away? I know this will never happen again, will it, Mr. Van Daan?
Mr. Van Daan. No. No.
Mrs. Frank. He steals once! He'll steal again!

[Mr. Van Daan, *holding his stomach, starts for the* **10** *bathroom.* Anne *puts her arms around him, helping him up the step.*]

11 Mr. Frank. Edith, please. Let us be calm. We'll all go to our rooms . . . and afterwards we'll sit down quietly and talk this out . . . we'll find some way . . .
Mrs. Frank. No! No! No more talk! I want them to leave!
Mrs. Van Daan. You'd put us out, on the streets?

Mrs. Frank. There are other hiding places.
Mrs. Van Daan. A cellar . . . a closet. I know. And we have no money left even to pay for that.
Mrs. Frank. I'll give you money. Out of my own pocket I'll give it gladly. (*She gets her purse from a shelf and comes back with it.*)
Mrs. Van Daan. Mr. Frank, you told Putti you'd never forget what he'd done for you when you came to Amsterdam. You said you could never repay him, that you . . .
Mrs. Frank (*counting out money*). If my husband had any obligation to you, he's paid it, over and over.
12 Mr. Frank. Edith, I've never seen you like this before. I don't know you.
Mrs. Frank. I should have spoken out long ago.
Dussel. You can't be nice to some people.
Mrs. Van Daan (*turning on* Dussel). There would have been plenty for all of us, if *you* hadn't come in here!
13 Mr. Frank. We don't need the Nazis to destroy us. We're destroying ourselves.

[*He sits down, with his head in his hands.* Mrs. Frank *goes to* Mrs. Van Daan.]

Mrs. Frank (*giving* Mrs. Van Daan *some money*). Give this to Miep. She'll find you a place.
Anne. Mother, you're not putting *Peter* out. Peter hasn't done anything.
14 Mrs. Frank. He'll stay, of course. When I say I must protect the children, I mean Peter too.

[Peter *rises from the steps where he has been sitting.*]

Peter. I'd have to go if Father goes.

[Mr. Van Daan *comes from the bathroom.* Mrs. Van Daan *hurries to him and takes him to the couch. Then she gets water from the sink to bathe his face.*]

Mrs. Frank (*while this is going on*). He's no

father to you . . . that man! He doesn't know what it is to be a father!

15 **Peter** (*starting for his room*). I wouldn't feel right. I couldn't stay.

Mrs. Frank. Very well, then. I'm sorry.

Anne (*rushing over to* Peter). No, Peter! No! (Peter *goes into his room, closing the door after him.* Anne *turns back to her mother, crying.*) I don't care about the food. They can have mine! I don't want it! Only don't send them away. It'll be daylight soon. They'll be caught. . . .

Margot (*putting her arms comfortingly around* Anne). Please, Mother!

16 **Mrs. Frank.** They're not going now. They'll stay here until Miep finds them a place. (*To* Mrs. Van Daan) But one thing I insist on! He must never come down here again! He must never come to this room where the food is stored! We'll divide what we have . . . an equal share for each! (Dussel *hurries over to get a sack of potatoes from the food safe.* Mrs. Frank *goes on, to* Mrs. Van Daan.) You can cook it here and take it up to him.

[Dussel *brings the sack of potatoes back to the center table.*]

Margot. Oh, no. No. We haven't sunk so far that we're going to fight over a handful of rotten potatoes.

17 **Dussel** (*dividing the potatoes into piles*). Mrs. Frank, Mr. Frank, Margot, Anne, Peter, Mrs. Van Daan, Mr. Van Daan, myself . . . Mrs. Frank . . .

[*The buzzer sounds in* Miep's *signal.*]

Mr. Frank. It's Miep! (*He hurries over, getting his overcoat and putting it on.*)

Margot. At this hour?

Mrs. Frank. It is trouble.

18 **Mr. Frank** (*as he starts down to unbolt the door*). I beg you, don't let her see a thing like this!

Mr. Dussel (*counting without stopping*). . . . Anne, Peter, Mrs. Van Daan, Mr. Van Daan, myself . . .

Margot (*to* Dussel). Stop it! Stop it!

Dussel. . . . Mr. Frank, Margot, Anne, Peter, Mrs. Van Daan, Mr. Van Daan, myself, Mrs. Frank . . .

Mrs. Van Daan. You're keeping the big ones for yourself! All the big ones . . . Look at the size of that! . . . And that! . . .

[Dussel *continues on with his dividing.* Peter, *with his shirt and trousers on, comes from his room.*]

Margot. Stop it! Stop it!

[*We hear* Miep's *excited voice speaking to* Mr. Frank *below.*]

19 **Miep.** Mr. Frank . . . the most wonderful news! . . . The invasion has begun!

Mr. Frank. Go on, tell them! Tell them!

[Miep *comes running up the steps, ahead of* Mr. Frank. *She has a man's raincoat on over her night-clothes and a bunch of orange-colored flowers in her hand.*]

Miep. Did you hear that, everybody? Did you hear what I said? The invasion has begun! The invasion!

[*They all stare at* Miep, *unable to grasp what she is telling them.* Peter *is the first to recover his wits.*]

Peter. Where?

Mrs. Van Daan. When? When, Miep?

Miep. It began early this morning. . . .

[*As she talks on, the realization of what she has said*
20 *begins to dawn on them. Everyone goes crazy. A wild demonstration takes place.* Mrs. Frank *hugs* Mr. Van Daan.]

15
Though humiliated several times by his father's actions, Peter feels he must remain loyal to his family. Anne's one happiness may be taken away from her. Peter has become more important than food to her.

16
Mrs. Frank relents somewhat but still bans Mr. Van Daan from common room.

17
Symbol. Dussel is not helping matters. His dividing of potatoes symbolizes their distrust of one another.

18
Mr. Frank does not want Miep to see the fighting and Dussel's pettiness.

19
Use to answer **study question 7a,** p. 393.

20
Irony. Squabbling bitterly only moments before, Mrs. Frank and Mr. Van Daan hug each other in celebration of the news.

Mrs. Frank. Oh, Mr. Van Daan, did you hear that?

[Dussel *embraces* Mrs. Van Daan. Peter *grabs a frying pan and parades around the room, beating on it, singing the Dutch national anthem.* Anne *and* Margot *follow him, singing, weaving in and out among the excited grown-ups.* Margot *breaks away to take the flowers from* Miep *and distribute them to everyone. While this pandemonium is going on* Mrs. Frank *tries to make herself heard above the excitement.*]

Mrs. Frank (*to* Miep). How do you know?
21 Miep. The radio . . . The B.B.C.![10] They said they landed on the coast of Normandy!
Peter. The British?
Miep. British, Americans, French, Dutch, Poles, Norwegians . . . all of them! More than **24** four thousand ships! Churchill[11] spoke, and **22** General Eisenhower![12] D-Day they call it!
Mr. Frank. Thank God, it's come!
Mrs. Van Daan. At last!
Miep (*starting out*). I'm going to tell Mr. Kraler. This'll be better than any blood transfusion.
Mr. Frank (*stopping her*). What part of Normandy did they land, did they say?
Miep. Normandy . . . that's all I know now. . . . I'll be up the minute I hear some more! (*She goes hurriedly out.*)
Mr. Frank (*to* Mrs. Frank). What did I tell you? What did I tell you?

[Mrs. Frank *indicates that he has forgotten to bolt the door after* Miep. *He hurries down the steps.* Mr. Van Daan, *sitting on the couch, suddenly*

---

10. **B.B.C.:** British Broadcasting Corporation, a British radio network.
11. **Churchill:** Sir Winston Churchill (1874–1965), a British prime minister (1940–1945; 1951–1955).
12. **General Eisenhower:** Dwight D. Eisenhower (1890–1969), the commander of the Allied forces in Europe during World War II, and later the thirty-fourth President of the United States (1953–1961).

---

breaks into a convulsive sob. Everybody looks at him, bewildered.]

Mrs. Van Daan (*hurrying to him*). Putti! Putti! What is it? What happened?
23 Mr. Van Daan. Please. I'm so ashamed.

[Mr. Frank *comes back up the steps.*]

Dussel. Oh, for God's sake!
Mrs. Van Daan. Don't, Putti.
Margot. It doesn't matter now!
Mr. Frank (*going to* Mr. Van Daan). Didn't you hear what Miep said? The invasion has come! We're going to be liberated! This is a time to celebrate. (*He embraces* Mrs. Frank *and then hurries to the cupboard and gets the cognac and a glass.*)
Mr. Van Daan. To steal bread from children!
24 Mrs. Frank. We've all done things that we're ashamed of.
25 Anne. Look at me, the way I've treated Mother . . . so mean and horrid to her.
26 Mrs. Frank. No, Anneke, no.

[Anne *runs to her mother, putting her arms around her.*]

Anne. Oh, Mother, I was. I was awful.
Mr. Van Daan. Not like me. No one is as bad as me!
Dussel (*to* Mr. Van Daan). Stop it now! Let's be happy!
Mr. Frank (*giving* Mr. Van Daan *a glass of cognac*). Here! Here! *Schnapps! L'chaim![13]*

[Mr. Van Daan *takes the cognac. They all watch him. He gives them a feeble smile.* Anne *puts up her fingers in a V-for-Victory sign. As* Mr. Van Daan *gives an answering* V-*sign, they are startled to hear a loud sob from behind them. It is* Mrs. Frank,

---

13. *Schnapps!* (shnäps) *L'chaim!* (lə-KHä′yĭm): *Schnapps* means "a drink" in German. *L'chaim* is a toast in Hebrew, meaning "To life!"

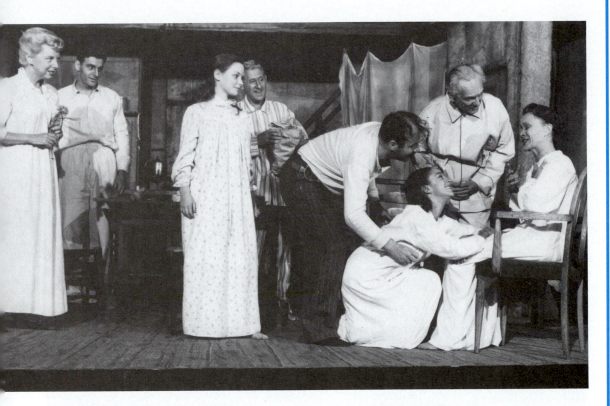

VISUAL CONNECTIONS
Exploring the Subject
Staging such a scene is more complicated than it looks. One of the first things a director does is "block" the play; that is, each character's movement is worked out for every scene, insuring that actors will be in the right place at the right time and that the scene will present a pleasing composition to the audience. The director must be familiar with the "sight lines" of the theater to make sure that the important action of each scene can be viewed from all parts of the theater.

stricken with remorse. She is sitting on the other side of the room.]

Mrs. Frank (*through her sobs*). When I think of the terrible things I said . . .

[Mr. Frank, Anne *and* Margot *hurry to her, trying*
27 *to comfort her.* Mr. Van Daan *brings her his glass of cognac.*]

28 Mr. Van Daan. No! No! You were right!
Mrs. Frank. That I should speak that way to **29** you! . . . Our friends! . . . Our guests! (*She starts to cry again.*)
Dussel. Stop it, you're spoiling the whole invasion!

[*As they are comforting her, the lights dim out. The curtain falls.*]

Anne's Voice (*faintly at first, and then with growing strength*). We're all in much better spirits these days. There's still excellent news of the invasion. The best part about it is that I have a feeling that friends are coming. Who knows? Maybe I'll be back in school by fall. Ha, ha! The joke is on us! The warehouseman doesn't know a thing and we are paying him all that money! . . . Wednesday, the second of July, nineteen forty-four. The invasion seems temporarily to be bogged down. Mr. Kraler has to have an operation, which looks bad. The Gestapo have found the radio that was stolen. Mr. Dussel says they'll trace it back and back to the thief, and then, it's just a matter of time till they get to us. Everyone is low. Even poor Pim can't raise their spirits. I have often been downcast myself . . . but never in despair. I can shake off everything if I write. But . . . and that

27
Mr. Van Daan comforts Mrs. Frank by offering his share of the drink.

28
The shameful behavior of families obviously was motivated by fear, tension. Real feelings are resurfacing; both Mrs. Frank and Mr. Van Daan regret their actions.

29
In the same diary entry, Anne says they are in better spirits; later she notes everyone is feeling low because invasion is slow. Circumstances take the families on an emotional roller coaster. Anne feels that with discovery of radio their capture is likely.

30 is the great question . . . will I ever be able to write well? I want to so much. I want to go on living even after my death. Another birthday has gone by, so now I am fifteen. Already I know what I want. I have a goal, an opinion.

[*As this is being said, the curtain rises on the scene, the lights dim on, and Anne's voice fades out.*]

Scene 4

It is an afternoon a few weeks later. . . . Everyone but Margot is in the main room. There is a sense of great tension.

1 *Both* Mrs. Frank *and* Mr. Van Daan *are nervously pacing back and forth;* Dussel *is standing at the window, looking down fixedly at the street below.* Peter *is at the center table, trying to do his lessons.* Anne *sits opposite him, writing in her diary.* Mrs. Van Daan *is seated on the couch, her eyes on* Mr. Frank *as he sits reading.*

The sound of a telephone ringing comes from the office below. They all are rigid, listening tensely. Dussel *rushes down to* Mr. Frank.

Dussel. There it goes again, the telephone! Mr. Frank, do you hear?
Mr. Frank (*quietly*). Yes. I hear.
2 Dussel (*pleading, insistent*). But this is the third time, Mr. Frank! The third time in quick succession! It's a signal! I tell you it's Miep, trying to get us! For some reason she can't come to us and she's trying to warn us of something!

Mr. Frank. Please. Please.

Mr. Van Daan (*to* Dussel). You're wasting your breath.

3 **Dussel.** Something has happened, Mr. Frank. For three days now Miep hasn't been to see us! And today not a man has come to work. There hasn't been a sound in the building!

Mrs. Frank. Perhaps it's Sunday. We may have lost track of the days.

Mr. Van Daan (*to* Anne). You with the diary there. What day is it?

Dussel (*going to* Mrs. Frank). I don't lose track of the days! I know exactly what day it is! It's Friday, the fourth of August. Friday, and not a man at work. (*He rushes back to* Mr. Frank, *pleading with him, almost in tears.*) I tell you Mr. Kraler's dead. That's the only explanation. He's dead and they've closed down the building, and Miep's trying to tell us!

4 **Mr. Frank.** She'd never telephone us.

Dussel (*frantic*). Mr. Frank, answer that! I beg you, answer it!

Mr. Frank. No.

Mr. Van Daan. Just pick it up and listen. You don't have to speak. Just listen and see if it's Miep.

Dussel (*speaking at the same time*). For God's sake . . . I ask you.

Mr. Frank. No. I've told you, no. I'll do nothing that might let anyone know we're in the building.

5 **Peter.** Mr. Frank's right.

Mr. Van Daan. There's no need to tell us what side you're on.

Mr. Frank. If we wait patiently, quietly, I believe that help will come.

6 [*There is silence for a minute as they all listen to the telephone ringing.*]

Dussel. I'm going down. (*He rushes down the steps.* Mr. Frank *tries ineffectually to hold him.* Dussel *runs to the lower door, unbolting it. The telephone*

stops ringing. Dussel *bolts the door and comes slowly back up the steps.*) Too late.

[Mr. Frank *goes to* Margot *in* Anne's *bedroom.*]

Mr. Van Daan. So we just wait here until we die.

7 **Mrs. Van Daan** (*hysterically*). I can't stand it. I'll kill myself! I'll kill myself!

Mr. Van Daan. For God's sake, stop it!

8 [*In the distance, a German military band is heard playing a Viennese waltz.*]

Mrs. Van Daan. I think you'd be glad if I did! I think you want me to die!

Mr. Van Daan. Whose fault is it we're here? (Mrs. Van Daan *starts for her room. He follows, talking at her.*) We could've been safe somewhere . . . in America or Switzerland. But no! No! You wouldn't leave when I wanted to. You couldn't leave your things. You couldn't leave your precious furniture.

Mrs. Van Daan. Don't touch me!

[*She hurries up the stairs, followed by* Mr. Van Daan. Peter, *unable to bear it, goes to his room.* Anne *looks after him, deeply concerned.* Dussel *returns to his post at the window.* Mr. Frank *comes back into the main room and takes a book, trying to read.* Mrs. Frank *sits near the sink, starting to peel some potatoes.* Anne *quietly goes to* Peter's *room, closing the door after her.* Peter *is lying face down on*
9 *the cot.* Anne *leans over him, holding him in her arms, trying to bring him out of his despair.*]

10 **Anne.** Look, Peter, the sky. (*She looks up through the skylight.*) What a lovely, lovely day! Aren't the clouds beautiful? You know what I do when it seems as if I couldn't stand being cooped up for one more minute? I *think* myself out. I think myself on a walk in the park where I used to go with Pim. Where the jonquils and

---

11 Analyzing
What does Anne mean by "You can have roses and violets and chrysanthemums all blooming at the same time"? The three flowers bloom in different seasons. In one's imagination, such limitations can be ignored.

12
Peter reduces Anne's philosophical comment to a practical one—feels he is about to lose his mind.

13
Theme. Anne's statement encompasses the theme of the play. One must have faith, and the basis of faith is the goodness of people and the beauty of nature.

14
Peter is bitter, frustrated over losing two important years of his life. He is not yet consoled by Anne's words.

15
Use to answer **study questions 9a and 9b,** p. 393.

16
Allusion. Hitler predicted that the Third Reich would last for a thousand years.

17
Anne believes this horror only fragment of pattern, that world is changing for better. Perhaps not in her lifetime, but eventually, good will triumph.

the crocuses and violets grow down the slopes. You know the most wonderful part about *thinking* yourself out? You can have it any way you **11** like. You can have roses and violets and chrysanthemums all blooming at the same time. . . . It's funny . . . I used to take it all for granted . . . and now I've gone crazy about everything to do with nature. Haven't you?

12 **Peter.** I've just gone crazy. I think if something doesn't happen soon . . . if we don't get out of here . . . I can't stand much more of it!

Anne (*softly*). I wish you had a religion, Peter.

Peter. No, thanks! Not me!

Anne. Oh, I don't mean you have to be Orthodox[14]. . . or believe in heaven or hell and purgatory and things . . . I just mean some religion . . . **13** it doesn't matter what. Just to believe in something! When I think of all that's out there . . . the trees . . . the flowers . . . and sea gulls . . . when I think of the dearness of you, Peter . . . and the goodness of the people we know . . . Mr. Kraler, Miep, Dirk, the vegetable man, all risking their lives for us every day . . . When I think of these good things, I'm not afraid any more . . . I find myself, and God, and I . . .

[Peter *interrupts, getting up and walking away.*]

14 **Peter.** That's fine! But when I begin to think, I get mad! Look at us, hiding out for two years. Not able to move! Caught here like . . . waiting for them to come and get us . . . and all for what?

Anne. We're not the only people that've had to suffer. There've always been people that've had to . . . sometimes one race . . . sometimes another . . . and yet . . .

Peter. That doesn't make me feel any better!

Anne (*going to him*). I know it's terrible, trying to have any faith . . . when people are doing such horrible . . . But you know what I some-

14. **be Orthodox:** follow the most strictly traditional branch of Judaism.

15 times think? I think the world may be going through a phase, the way I was with Mother. It'll pass, maybe not for hundreds of years, but someday . . . I still believe, in spite of everything, that people are really good at heart.

16 **Peter.** I want to see something now. . . . Not a thousand years from now!

[*He goes over, sitting down again on the cot.*]

17 **Anne.** But, Peter, if you'd only look at it as part of a great pattern . . . that we're just a little minute in the life . . . (*She breaks off.*) Listen to us, going at each other like a couple of stupid grown-ups! Look at the sky now. Isn't it lovely? (*She holds out her hand to him.* Peter *takes it and rises, standing with her at the window looking out, his arms around her.*) Someday, when we're outside again, I'm going to . . .

[*She breaks off as she hears the sound of a car, its brakes squealing as it comes to a sudden stop. The people in the other rooms also become aware of the sound. They listen tensely. Another car roars up to a screeching stop.* Anne *and* Peter *come from* Peter's *room.* Mr. *and* Mrs. Van Daan *creep down the stairs.* Dussel *comes out from his room. Everyone is listening, hardly breathing. A doorbell clangs again and again in the building below.* Mr. Frank *starts quietly down the steps to the door.* Dussel *and* Peter *follow him. The others stand rigid, waiting, terrified.*

In a few seconds, Dussel *comes stumbling back up the steps. He shakes off* Peter's *help and goes to his room.* Mr. Frank *bolts the door below and comes slowly back up the steps. Their eyes are all on him as he stands there for a minute. They realize what they feared has happened.* Mrs. Van Daan *starts to whimper.* Mr. Van Daan *puts her gently in a chair, and then hurries off up the stairs to their room to collect their things.* Peter *goes to comfort his mother. There is a sound of violent pounding on a door below.*]

18 Mr. Frank (*quietly*). For the past two years we have lived in fear. Now we can live in hope.

[*The pounding below becomes more insistent. There are muffled sounds of voices, shouting commands.*]

Men's Voices. *Aufmachen! Da drinnen! Aufmachen! Schnell! Schnell! Schnell!*[15] *etc., etc.*

[*The street door below is forced open. We hear the*
19 *heavy tread of footsteps coming up.* Mr. Frank *gets two schoolbags from the shelves and gives one to* Anne *and the other to* Margot. *He goes to get a bag for* Mrs. Frank. *The sound of feet coming up grows louder.* Peter *comes to* Anne, *kissing her goodbye; then he goes to his room to collect his things. The buzzer of their door starts to ring.* Mr. Frank *brings* Mrs. Frank *a bag. They stand together, waiting. We hear the thud of gun butts on the door, trying to break it down.*

20   Anne *stands, holding her school satchel, looking over at her father and mother with a soft, reassuring smile. She is no longer a child, but a woman with courage to meet whatever lies ahead.*

     The lights dim out. The curtain falls on the scene. We hear a mighty crash as the door is shattered. After a second Anne's *voice is heard.*]

Anne's Voice. And so it seems our stay is over. They are waiting for us now. They've allowed us five minutes to get our things. We can each take a bag and whatever it will hold of clothing.
21 Nothing else. So, dear Diary, that means I must leave you behind. Goodbye for a while. P.S. Please, please, Miep, or Mr. Kraler, or anyone else. If you should find this diary, will you please keep it safe for me, because someday I hope . . .

[*Her voice stops abruptly. There is silence. After a second the curtain rises.*]

15. *Aufmachen! . . . Schnell!:* Open up! You in there! Open up! Quick! Quick! Quick!

Scene 5

It is again the afternoon in November 1945. The rooms are as we saw them in the first scene. Mr. Kraler *has joined* Miep *and* Mr. Frank. *There are coffee cups on the table. We see a great change in* Mr. Frank. *He is calm now. His bitterness is gone. He slowly turns a few pages of the diary. They are blank.*

Mr. Frank. No more. (*He closes the diary and puts it down on the couch beside him.*)
Miep. I'd gone to the country to find food.

VISUAL CONNECTIONS
Exploring the Subject
Anne appears ready to face whatever is coming. Although she is dressed in schoolgirl clothes and carries a book bag, she looks unmistakably mature. This portrayal of a little girl growing into a woman should touch the hearts of the members of the audience as they see the character for the last time and think beyond the play to Anne's fate.

18 Finding Main Ideas
What does Mr. Frank mean?
Now that they have been discovered they must not live in fear but in hope that someday they will be free.

19
Atmosphere. Everyone behaves calmly. Now that worst has happened they are more in control than they have been in two years.

20
Characterization. In stage direction, the authors explicitly explain what they have dramatically shown: Anne has grown into a courageous woman, resigned to accept whatever is in store for her on the strength of her dignity and faith.

Summarizing
21 Drawing Conclusions
Why does Anne not take her diary with her? What hope does she have for herself? She is not permitted to take diary with her. She hopes to return for it someday.

Have interested students select a scene from the play and rewrite it as a diary entry that one of the minor characters—such as Peter, Mr. Dussel, or Mr. or Mrs. Van Daan—might have made. Remind students to maintain the personality and point of view of the character they select and to include the specific details of the scene they choose.

VISUAL CONNECTIONS

Exploring the Subject

There are strong religious overtones in this last scene. The diary looks much like a prayer book, and the scarf which Anne had knitted gives the impression of a prayer shawl. The director has found a way to make this a visually uplifting end for the play.

Scene Five

1
Dussel was right the night he said the thief would get caught and tell the police.

2
Theme. Her father's statement confirms that Anne lived with courage and optimism.

3
Allusion. Auschwitz and Bergen-Belsen were concentration camps in which large numbers of people died from execution and disease. It is miraculous that Mr. Frank survived.

4
Since the Nazis commonly separated family members, survivors of the camps had to try to learn of relatives' whereabouts by word-of-mouth.

5
Repetition of Anne's words to Peter.

6
Irony. In spite of this assertion of his inferiority to Anne, Mr. Frank has been a model of virtue throughout the play. Anne, in fact, learned to be a generous and loving person from her father. Her death, therefore, ironically spares her from the pain, grief, and desolation that he must feel. Having lost Anne, he finds it difficult to share her optimism.

When I got back the block was surrounded by police. . . .

Mr. Kraler. We made it our business to learn **1** how they knew. It was the thief . . . the thief who told them.

[Miep *goes up to the gas burner, bringing back a pot of coffee.*]

2 **Mr. Frank** (*after a pause*). It seems strange to say this, that anyone could be happy in a concentration camp. But Anne was happy in the camp in Holland where they first took us. After two years of being shut up in these rooms, she could be out . . . out in the sunshine and the fresh air that she loved.

Miep (*offering the coffee to* Mr. Frank). A little more?

Mr. Frank (*holding out his cup to her*). The news of the war was good. The British and Americans were sweeping through France. We felt sure that they would get to us in time. In September we were told that we were to be shipped to Poland. . . . The men to one camp. **3** The women to another. I was sent to Auschwitz. They went to Belsen. In January we were freed, the few of us who were left. The war wasn't yet over, so it took us a long time to get home. We'd be sent here and there behind the lines where we'd be safe. Each time our train **4** would stop . . . at a siding, or a crossing . . . we'd all get out and go from group to group. . . . Where were you? Were you at Belsen? At Buchenwald? At Mauthausen? Is it possible that you knew my wife? Did you ever see my husband? My son? My daughter? That's how I found out about my wife's death . . . of Margot, the Van Daans . . . Dussel. But Anne . . . I still hoped . . . Yesterday I went to Rotterdam. I'd heard of a woman there . . . She'd been in Belsen with Anne. . . . I know now.

[*He picks up the diary again and turns the pages back to find a certain passage. As he finds it we hear Anne's voice.*]

5 **Anne's Voice.** In spite of everything, I still believe that people are really good at heart.

[Mr. Frank *slowly closes the diary.*]

6 **Mr. Frank.** She puts me to shame.

[*They are silent. The curtain falls.*]

Anne's actual diary ends on August 1, 1944. On August 4 the Nazis broke into the warehouse and sent all occupants to concentration camps. Anne's father was the only one to survive. Anne died of typhus fever at Bergen-Belsen in March 1945, two months before the liberation of the Netherlands.

The tragedy of Anne Frank's story is about intolerance toward those who are "different." The Nazis put to death millions of people whose cultural and/or religious backgrounds differed from their own, including Jews, Catholics, Gypsies, and homosexuals. Invite the class to discuss the following questions: What causes a person to be afraid of or angry with someone who is, in some way, *different* (that is, who speaks a different language, observes different religious customs, eats different foods, and so on)? Have *you* ever felt afraid of or angry with someone who was very different from yourself? What happened? Have you ever been treated badly because *you* were in some way different? How did this feel? How can each of us prevent Anne Frank's experience from ever happening again?

Reading Check

1. What does Miep bring on New Year's Day, 1944?
2. What does Mr. Van Daan want to do with his wife's fur coat?
3. What does Anne offer to give Peter for his room?
4. What good news does Miep bring as the families are arguing?
5. Why does Mr. Frank refuse to answer the telephone?

For Study and Discussion

Analyzing and Interpreting the Play

ACT TWO

Scene 1

1. Anne's voice reading from her diary provides basic information about the story. What facts does the diary relate at the opening of Act Two?

2. Most of the characters own a few small possessions that are very precious to them. **a.** What do you think Peter's cat means to him? **b.** Why is Mrs. Van Daan's coat so important to her?

3. The suspense in the play is increased by a new worry. What fear does Mr. Kraler's news bring?

Scene 2

4. Love, which unites some of the characters, also divides them. How would you describe Mrs. Van Daan's reaction to the interest that Anne and Peter show in each other?

5. Peter says that Anne has changed from the kind of girl she was when they first met. **a.** How has Anne changed? **b.** How does she explain her new relationship with Peter in her diary?

Scene 3

6. Mr. Frank says, "We don't need the Nazis to destroy us. We're destroying ourselves." The constant threat of the Nazis on the outside terrifies the characters. What human fears and weaknesses attack them from the inside?

7. In one moment the "family" realizes that their quarrels are unimportant compared to the greater evil in the outside world. **a.** What event changes their fear to hope, and their hatred to forgiveness? **b.** What is the first reaction of Mrs. Frank and Mr. Van Daan?

Scene 4

8. In spite of the great tension around her, Anne still has a way to escape to a happy and beautiful world. **a.** What does she do? **b.** Where does she go?

9a. How does Anne explain the war and the world's madness? **b.** What belief, in spite of everything, gives her hope?

10. At the opening of the play, Anne is a girl just beginning to understand the world around her. How has she changed by the end of the play?

Scene 5

11. This scene returns to the first scene of the play. Mr. Frank tells Miep about the concentration camps. What does he say happened to all the other members of the "family"?

12. Mr. Frank feels ashamed because he cannot share Anne's belief in the goodness of people. Do you think any events in the play support Anne's belief?

Literary Elements

Recognizing the Elements of a Tragedy

The Diary of Anne Frank is a **tragedy.** Most tragedies end with the hero or heroine suffering death or defeat.

READING CHECK
1. Flowers, books, newspapers, a cake (pp. 371–372).
2. Sell it (p. 373).
3. Photographs from magazines (p. 376).
4. That invasion has begun (p. 385).
5. Does not want to alert outsiders they are in building (p. 389).

FOR STUDY AND DISCUSSION
Scene 1
1. They've been hiding one year, five months, twenty-five days; they are thinner. The Van Daans still fight; Anne and mother disagree.
2a. Responses will vary. Cat was Peter's friend. **2b.** Symbolizes comfortable lifestyle before going into hiding.
3. Man in storeroom may be blackmailer; could turn them in.

Scene 2
4. Annoyed, suspicious, jealous.
5a. Has grown up, thinks more seriously about life, future; wants to be writer. **5b.** Says she is not in love but lives for their next meeting.

Scene 3
6. Fear of hunger, death, discovery; selfishness, anger, jealousy.
7a. News of D-Day. **7b.** They hug.

Scene 4
8a. "Thinks" herself outside, using her imagination. **8b.** To park.
9a. As part of pattern, a phase. **9b.** "People are really good at heart."
10. Has philosophy of life, can reassure others, has grown up.

Scene 5
11. All are dead.
12. Responses will vary. Miep's, Kraler's many risks; Anne's support of Peter; Mr. Frank's constant selflessness.

Anne Frank's diary was found in Amsterdam after the war and published in its original form in 1947. Students may be interested in reading it for the purpose of comparing it to the play. Suggest that students look for at least three differences and three similarities between the two, and have them cite examples from each of the works to support their assertions. You may also want to encourage students to consider the reasons for any differences. Were the two pieces written with the same purpose?

Ask students to include in their comparisons which form of the story they preferred and why. Consult with students to agree on what form their comparisons will take and how they will be assessed.

LITERARY ELEMENTS

Recognizing the Elements of a Tragedy

1. Responses will vary.

2. Responses will vary. Students might mention Anne's innocence and exuberance or Mr. Frank's generosity and strength of character.

3. The Nazi police are looking for all Jews in hiding.

4. Answers will vary. Even though audiences know how the play will end, they still can be interested in how characters will cope with situation and what this may reveal about life and human nature.

5. Answers will vary. One possible theme is that a person can find faith and a reason for living in even the most dire circumstances.

6. She keeps her mind free, develops philosophy that sustains her. Her diary makes it possible for part of herself to endure.

Understanding Dramatic Terms

1. Shows love can persist in spite of deprivation, misery, tension.

2. Anne's father as he reads the diary.

3. "I want to so much [write well]. I want to go on living even after my death."

Tragic Characters. In tragedies, attention is focused on one or two outstanding characters. These are people whose courage, dignity, or other heroic qualities strongly distinguish them from the rest of the people in the play. **1 Which characters in this play are you most 2 interested in? What makes you admire them?**

Tragic Plot. In tragedies, the characters face some powerful force that finally overcomes **3** them. **What terrible outside forces are seeking to destroy the characters in this play?** You knew from the beginning of the play that **4** Anne would not survive. **Did you want to read on, even though you knew that the story would end sadly for her?**

Tragic Theme. Tragedies need not be depressing, even though they show people facing overwhelming odds and often death. In fact, many tragedies lift up our spirits. They make us see nobility and courage and dignity in people, despite the terrible things that hap- **5** pened to them. **What would you say is the theme, or main idea about life, that this play expresses?**

6 In what ways is Anne victorious, despite her tragedy?

Understanding Dramatic Terms

Here are some terms that are useful in understanding *The Diary of Anne Frank* and other plays.

Subplot: a second plot or "story" within the larger main plot. In *The Diary of Anne Frank,* the main plot tells what happens as the "family" hides from the Nazis. The subplot tells what happens between Anne and Peter. Plot and subplot are often related. Anne and Peter, for instance, must hide their world of love from the grown-ups, just as the whole "family" must **1** hide from the hostile outside world. **How does this subplot involving Anne and Peter add a hopeful mood to the play?**

Flashback: a way of taking the audience back in time, in order to recall events already past. Almost all of *The Diary of Anne Frank* is a **2** flashback. **Who is remembering these events?**

Monologue: a long speech delivered by one character. In English, the suffix *-logue* means "words." *Monologue* means "words spoken by one person." *Dialogue* means "conversation, or words exchanged between characters." Monologues often contain ideas that are important in the play. In this play, Anne delivers several **3** monologues. **Which sentence in Anne's monologue in Act Two, Scene 3, expresses an important wish?**

Writing About Literature

▶ Writing a Review of a Play

The review of *The Diary of Anne Frank* reproduced on page 395 was written by Walter F. Kerr for the *New York Herald Tribune.* Kerr begins his review with an evaluation of the play itself. He then describes what he thinks is the most touching scene in the play. Write your own review of the play. Include your personal reactions to the play and a description of the scene you think is the most touching. End your review with a comment about the appropriateness of the play for a teenage audience.

▶Before students begin this writing assignment, you may want to refer them to the **Writing About Literature** section on p. 672.

CLOSURE
Ask students to explain briefly the major changes in Anne and to tell how these changes are related to the **theme** of the play.

EXTENSION AND ENRICHMENT
Students might enjoy reading *Anne Frank: The Diary of a Young Girl*, the book on which the play is based. Several students might work together on a small research project, reporting on how the playwright adapted the diary into dramatic form.

As an exercise in **point of view**, students might rewrite a scene of the play as the diary entry of one of the minor characters—perhaps Peter, Mr. or Mrs. Van Daan, or Mr. Dussel.

New York Herald Tribune
October 6, 1955

THEATER

'The Diary of Anne Frank'
By WALTER F. KERR

NEARLY all of the characters in "The Diary of Anne Frank"—they are Dutch Jews hiding out from Hitler in a dingy and overcrowded garret—are doomed to death. Yet the precise quality of the new play at the Cort is the quality of glowing, ineradicable life—life in its warmth, its wonder, its spasms of anguish, and its wild and flaring humor.

Perhaps no scene in the play is more touching than that in which a fifteen-year-old girl and a nineteen-year-old boy enter into the formalities of courtship. They have, with their families, been cooped up on the top floor of an Amsterdam office building for nearly two years. They have seen each other morning, noon and night during all this time, eaten together, squabbled together, been terrified together, simply grown up together.

When the time comes, though, for each to seek the other out in a shy, faltering, heartbreak-ing romance, they at once begin to behave like lovers who have just been introduced. In her own little corner of the densely populated living quarters, the girl piles her hair on top of her head and hopefully drapes a scarf about her shoulders; in his cubbyhole the boy puts on a jacket, straightens his tie, and trembles in expectation. The girl 'goes out' for the evening to see him—just across the room, past her chess-playing parents, past the boy's greedy father and frivolous mother—to a door that opens gently not more than twenty feet away.

• • •

The circumstances around her are the circumstances of despair and decay. In the midst of this, a fresh and shining dignity, a springtime innocence and an instinctive honor rise to fill the shabby room. Since you know that Anne Frank's life is to end in the horrors of Belsen, the play cannot help but break your heart. But along the way it takes great care to let you know that the moments of living—short as they were—were all moments of growth and discovery and very great joy.

Frances Goodrich and Albert Hackett have fashioned a wonderfully sensitive and theatrically craftsmanlike narrative out of the real-life legacy left us by a spirited and straight-forward Jewish girl. Garson Kanin has not so much staged it as orchestrated it—from the simple and homely rhythms of a silent couple doing the dinner dishes to the sudden, catlike tensions of an alarmed household listening in panic to a telephone bell that may be a warning.

Authors and director together have given us a series of vivid, utterly lifelike yet colorfully dramatic pictures: the happy new refugees stripping off layer after layer of concealed clothing, the night-time stir that responds to an adolescent's scream, the religious ritual by candlelight that turns into an antic round of gift-giving.

• • •

And Mr. Kanin has found a superb company for the purpose. A few seasons ago young Susan Strasberg suggested, in an off-Broadway performance, that she had the magic of which stars are made. That star is beginning to shine now—not with absolute authority, perhaps, but with a puppyish efferve-scence that is like a promise of the world on a platter.

If Miss Strasberg has a little difficulty still with the reflective passages that come with the girl's new maturity, she has nothing but enchantment to bring the earlier scenes of tom-boy fire and prankish ebullience. Clambering over the furniture, pounding her hands against her head excitedly, dancing demure-ly with her father, or donning oversize trousers for a flash of mimic impudence, she is breath-taking.

• • •

Joseph Schildkraut's controlled and confident father is a tower of strength to the family—and to the play—he must hold to-gether. David Levin's boy-next-door is quietly moving, Jack Gilford's fussy dentist, Lou Jacobi's eternally hungry busi-ness man, Dennie Moore's vain and pathetic wife, and Clinton Sundberg's restrained friend of the oppressed are all crystal-clear portraits. And you aren't likely to forget Gusti Huber's drawn face across a festive table as she realizes with absolute cer-tainty that they are all bound to be discovered.

Boris Aronson's gabled setting, from which the homeless look out on a thousand homes, is bril-liantly drawn, a stunning back-ground for a play that is—for all its pathos—as bright and shin-ing as a banner.

About the Authors

Frances Goodrich (1891–1984)
Albert Hackett (1900–)

Frances Goodrich and Albert Hackett, a hus-band-and-wife team, made an abrupt change in their careers with the writing of the play *The Diary of Anne Frank*. They had been writing scripts for light comedy movies since 1933. They began *The Thin Man* series in 1934. They also wrote the script for the popular movie musical *Seven Brides for Seven Brothers*. Writing Anne Frank's story took the couple two years. The script went through eight rewrites. The play won the Pulitzer Prize for drama in 1956.

WRITING ABOUT LITERATURE
Walter Kerr was a well-respected drama critic. His review was one that the playwrights would have stayed up to read on the morning after opening night. It could make or break a play at the box office.

Remind students that they should include not only their reactions to the play but also references to specific scenes or lines that sup-port their reactions.

ABOUT THE AUTHORS
Goodrich and Hackett began col-laborating in 1927 before they were married. They were em-ployed by movie studios, wrote scripts from 1933–1952. Their procedure was that each would write a scene and then show it to the other. They would discuss and evaluate and then choose the best parts. They claimed that they could not identify their individual writing in the final draft. To-gether they earned the New York Drama Critics Award and a Tony Award. *The Diary of Anne Frank* was one of their last efforts. They are credited with having re-searched carefully, writing a script that was faithful to the spirit of Anne's writing.

OBJECTIVES

The overall aim is for students to demonstrate an ability to determine causes and effects.

PRESENTATION

You might introduce this section by asking students to recall some of the cause-effect relationships in the plays they have just read. Then have students read the passage silently and respond to the questions that follow. Students might share their answers in small groups before you initiate a class discussion of cause and effect in the selection.

UNDERSTANDING CAUSE AND EFFECT

To show a cause and effect relationship, a writer must supply concrete, relevant details organized in a logical manner that connects **cause** to **effect** in the mind of the reader.

Answers

1. Dutch Christians show their support of Jews by wearing yellow stars and flowers. Signs appear in shops asking Christians to show respect for Jews by lifting their hats in cheerful greeting.
2. Their solidarity angers the Germans who retaliate with brutality, arrests, and threats.

FOCUS ON Reading and Critical Thinking

UNDERSTANDING CAUSE AND EFFECT

*W*riters often develop ideas by explaining causes and effects. In her autobiography, *Anne Frank Remembered,* Miep Gies, the woman who helped hide the Frank family, describes life under the Nazi occupation of Holland. In the following passage she tells about the Nazi edict ordering Jews to sew a yellow Magen David (Star of David) on their clothing and how this order affected the Dutch people.

In the spring of 1942 came yet another edict. This one was printed in the Dutch newspaper, not just in the *Jewish Weekly.* From one week hence, all Jews were ordered to sew a yellow six-pointed star the size of an adult's palm onto their clothing above the heart. This meant *all* Jewish men, women, and children. Each star cost a clothing coupon from the ration book and 4 cents. On the yellow star was printed JOOD—"Jew."

On the day that this order was to begin, many Dutch Christians, deeply rankled by this humiliation of our Jews, also wore yellow stars on their coats. Many wore yellow flowers, as emblems of solidarity, in their lapels or in their hair. Signs appeared in some shops asking Christians to show special respect for our Jewish neighbors, suggesting,

for instance, that we lift our hats to them in a cheerful greeting—anything to show them that they were not alone.

Many Dutch did what they could to show their solidarity. This edict, somehow so much more enraging than all the others, was bringing our fierce Dutch anger to a boil. The yellow stars and yellow flowers those first few days were so common that our River Quarter was known as the Milky Way. The Jewish Quarter was laughingly called Hollywood. A surge of pride and solidarity swelled briefly until the Germans started cracking heads and making arrests. A threat was delivered to the population at large: anyone assisting Jews in any way would be sent to prison and possibly executed.

—Miep Gies,
Anne Frank Remembered

Understanding Cause and Effect

1. What were the effects of the Nazi edict ordering Jews to identify themselves by wearing a six-pointed star on their clothing?

2. How did the Dutch people's reactions to this edict become the cause of still other effects?

OBJECTIVES
The overall aim is for students to write an informative essay in the form of a process paper or cause-and-effect explanation.

PRESENTATION
Write the headings "process" and "cause-and-effect" on the chalkboard and list an example of a possible topic for each type of expository writing. Ask students to brainstorm more topics and list those under the appropriate heading. Students might choose topics from this list or from notes they have already taken, or they can think of new topics. You may want to stress the importance of the prewriting step, perhaps approving students' topics to be sure they are suitable. During the writing and revising stages,

FOCUS ON *Writing*

WRITING AN INFORMATIVE ESSAY

*I*n **informative** or **expository writing,** your purpose is to share information. One important type of informative writing is the **process paper.** In this kind of paper, you explain how to do something or how something works. Another kind of informative essay is the **cause-and-effect explanation.** In this type of essay, you explore the causes and/or the effects of an event, a situation, or a trend. This unit has presented some of the important elements of informative writing. You will now have the chance to write on a topic of your own choice.

Prewriting

1. Here is a strategy to find a good topic for a "how-to" essay:

- make a list of your interests →
- pick something you do well →
- make sure the topic fits the audience

To explore topics for a cause-and-effect essay, ask yourself questions like these:

- What interesting events or trends have I heard or read about?
- What natural processes am I curious about?
- What would happen if . . . ?

2. After you've made some notes about possible topics, think about your **audience.** What information can you offer them? Why is your topic either interesting or valuable for readers? Also, be sure that your topic is suitable for the length of your essay. Reject topics that are either too broad ("how farmers grow food," "what causes wars") or too narrow ("how to address an envelope").

3. If you have chosen a "how-to" topic, list the steps or stages in the process carefully. Remember to arrange them in exact order. Make a chart like the one below.

Topic: _____
Audience: _____
Steps/Stages of Process
1. _____   3. _____
2. _____   4. _____

For a cause-and-effect essay, you may wish to make a cluster diagram to explore all the major causes or effects of a single event or situation. The sample diagram below lists causes.

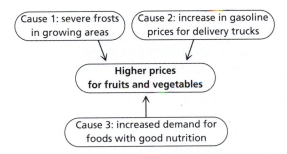

Cause 1: severe frosts in growing areas

Cause 2: increase in gasoline prices for delivery trucks

Higher prices for fruits and vegetables

Cause 3: increased demand for foods with good nutrition

[See **Focus** assignments on pages 318 and 370.]

HOLT WRITER'S WORKSHOP

This computer program provides help for all types of writing through guided instruction for each step of the writing process. (Program available separately.)

See *Elements of Writing, Second Course,* Chapter 7, for more instruction on informative writing.

WRITING AN INFORMATIVE ESSAY

Students are exposed to informative or expository writing often—in textbooks, newspapers, and magazines. Students may think that this kind of writing must be serious and dull. But good exposition often is entertaining and lively as well as informative. Students should be aware that they can use vivid descriptions and lively verbs to enhance their essays.

Prewriting

Encourage students to be thorough in their prewriting, listing as many details for the process and as many causes and effects as they can think of. You might want to have students work in small groups to help each other collect ideas. Remind students that even though these two papers may differ in many ways, both require that students include all necessary details so that the process or relationship they are describing can be understood.

TRANSPARENCY 27

Writing Process
Writing an Informative Essay – helps students plan and write an effective informative essay.

students might benefit from examining some models of expository writing that are developed through process or cause-and-effect. In closing, ask students to compare and contrast the elements of the process essay and the cause-and-effect essay.

Writing

Before students write their first drafts, you might suggest that they write their main idea statements on the top lines of their first pages. Keeping their main ideas in mind will help students to focus their essays. For example, a writer whose main idea is "There are three important causes for the recent price hikes for fruit and vegetables" should focus only on those three causes, rather than digressing to any other causes or effects.

Evaluating and Revising

You might divide the class into groups of six and have the groups use the **Checklist for Evaluation and Revision** in the following manner: As students evaluate each other's papers, each student should be responsible for only one question from the checklist. Students could alternate the questions they address each time the members exchange papers. Rather than simply answering "yes" or "no" to the questions, have students give one another constructive suggestions. After this procedure, students should spend time revising, based on their peers' suggestions.

---

4. Your next task is to **evaluate** or judge your information. For a process paper, ask yourself these questions to evaluate details:

- Is this detail something that my audience already knows? (If the answer is "yes," omit the detail.)

- Without this detail, would readers make a mistake or be confused? (If the answer is "yes," include the detail.)

[See **Focus** assignment on page 333.]

For a cause-and-effect paper, make sure you do not fall into the error of **false cause and effect,** or assuming that one event caused another just because the first happened before the second in time.

5. You will focus your details and ideas better if you identify a **main idea** for your essay and state it in one or two sentences. For example, you might state the main idea of a process essay this way: "Grocery shopping can be simple and fun if you follow these five hints." The following sentence states the main idea for a cause-and-effect essay: "There are three important causes for the recent price hikes for fruit and vegetables."

Writing

1. Follow an **outline** when you write your first draft. Below are two sample outlines that you will find helpful.

Process Paper
  I. Introduction
    A. Grab reader's attention
    B. State main idea
  II. Body
    A. List necessary materials
    B. Explain each step in order
  III. Conclusion
    Summarize value of process

Cause-and-Effect Explanation
  I. Introduction
    A. Grab reader's attention
    B. State main idea
  II. Body
    Discuss causes/effects in a logical order
  III. Conclusion
    Sum up main points and add comment

2. Help your readers understand the connections of ideas in your writing by using **transitional words and phrases.**

Process Paper

after	next	third
at first	second	when
before	then	

Cause-and-Effect Explanation

as a result	for	so that
because	since	therefore
consequently	so	

Evaluating and Revising

1. When you have finished the first draft of your essay, look it over as critically as you can. Be sure that you have presented the steps of a process or the causes or effects of an event in a logical order.

2. You may find the following checklist helpful as you revise your essay.

Checklist for Evaluation and Revision

✓ Does the introduction catch the reader's interest?

✓ Do I give readers information they may need?

✓ Do I clearly state the main idea of my essay?

✓ Do I discuss the stages in a process or the causes and effects of an event logically?

✓ Do I end with a strong conclusion?

Here is an example of how one writer revised the opening paragraph of an informative essay.

Writer's Model

Most of the world's ^30,000 species of fish are cold-blooded. ~~The way they live their lives~~ ^Life is less work for them that way. ~~They~~ ^because lose body heat to the cold ocean water when they take in oxygen. How can ^then we explain that a small number of fish, including the ~~tuna,~~ ^bluefin tuna, the butterfly mackerel, and the swordfish are warm-blooded like mammals? Scientists think they now know the cause for ~~this.~~ ^puzzling phenomenon

Proofreading and Publishing

1. Proofread your essay and correct any errors you find in grammar, usage, and mechanics. (Here you may find it helpful to refer to the **Handbook for Revision** on pages 712–755.) Then prepare a final version of your essay by making a clean copy.

2. Consider some of the following publication methods for your essay:

- send your essay to a hobby magazine
- illustrate your essay with drawings, diagrams, or other suitable graphics, and then post it on the class bulletin board
- enter your essay in a writing contest

Portfolio If your teacher approves, you may wish to keep a copy of your work in your writing folder or portfolio.

NONFICTION

OVERVIEW OF THE UNIT

The unit opens with Gerald Carson's story about Old Abe, a patriotic eagle mascot of the Civil War period. Next comes "The Dog That Bit People," James Thurber's remembrances of an unforgettable canine. Ann Petry's "They Called Her Moses" follows, providing a vivid look at the heroic Harriet Tubman. The rest of the unit includes Kim Yong Ik's "A Book-Writing Venture" as well as autobiographical material from Mark Twain's *Life on the Mississippi* and Maya Angelou's *I Know Why the Caged Bird Sings.* Each selection offers the opportunity to focus on key reading skills, such as drawing inferences and recognizing main ideas.

As they work to become better readers of nonfiction, students are also challenged to become better writers by practicing techniques used in the selections. Students are then challenged to integrate and apply the skills they have practiced as the unit concludes with **Focus on Writing,** in which students are asked to write a biographical report.

OBJECTIVES OF THE UNIT

The aims of the unit are for the student:
◆ To identify the types of informal and formal nonfiction and to interpret the writer's purpose within an essay
◆ To apply an accepted method of analysis to determine the purpose, tone, style, and main idea of an essay
◆ To identify and analyze elements of characterization and setting in the essays
◆ To recognize jargon within a selection
◆ To write a biographical report
◆ To make connections between literature and history

CONCEPTS AND SKILLS

The following concepts and skills are treated in this unit:

CLOSE READING OF AN ESSAY

LITERARY ELEMENTS/TERMS AND TECHNIQUES

LANGUAGE AND VOCABULARY SKILLS

OPPORTUNITIES FOR WRITING
Focus on Biographical Report

CONNECTIONS

FOCUS ON READING AND CRITICAL THINKING

FOCUS ON WRITING

TRANSPARENCIES

The following unit support materials with specific correlations to literature selections are available in the **Fine Art and Instructional Transparencies with Teacher's Notes and Blackline Masters** section of your *Audiovisual Resources Binder.*

FINE ART TRANSPARENCIES
Theme: Ideas and People
28 *Paul Revere,* John Singleton Copley
29 *Harriet Tubman Series No. 21,* Jacob Lawrence

READER RESPONSE
30 Tell Me 1—2—3

LITERARY ELEMENTS
31 Distinguishing Between Facts and Opinion

WRITING PROCESS
32 Writing a Biographical Report

INTRODUCING THE UNIT

To spark interest in the many forms of nonfiction, you might engage students in one of the following activities:

Several days before the unit is to be introduced, ask students to list everything they have read for at least three days. Stress the importance of logging every item, from textbooks and paperbacks to newspapers and television program guides. On the day the unit is to be introduced, divide students into small groups to make composite lists, and mark items that may be categorized as nonfiction. As the class reconvenes and compares composite logs, list the different kinds of nonfiction represented and ask students to estimate the proportion of total reading time occupied by each category. Why is nonfiction such an important part of daily life? After briefly discussing the utility and lifelong importance of nonfiction, call attention to the comments on p. 402.

Another approach is to enlist the help of students and colleagues in collecting a stack of newspapers and popular magazines for the classroom. Have students browse through a newspaper and at least one magazine. Ask each student to find and list as many different kinds of nonfiction as possible—for example, news articles,

FOR UNIT PLANNING

- Transparencies 28–32: *Audiovisual Resources Binder*
- *Portfolio Assessment: Professional Support Materials*
- Test Generator

- Mastery Tests: Teaching Resources D, pp. 99, 102, 105
- Analogy Test: Teaching Resources D, p. 108
- Composition Test: Teaching Resources D, p. 109

SELECTION (Pupil's Page)	TEACHING RESOURCES D (page numbers shown below)							AV BINDER
	Teacher's Notes	Reading Check	Study Guide	Language Skills	Building Vocabulary	Selection Vocab. Test	Selection Test	Audio-cassette
NONFICTION *Introduction* (p. 402)	1							
Fabiola Cabeza de Baca *Pioneer Women* (p. 403)	2				3	5	6	
Gerlald Carson *The Glorious Bird* (p. 407)	8	11	12	16	19	20	22	
James Thurber *The Dog That Bit People* (p. 413)	25	27	28	31	35	53	37	
Ann Petry *They Called Her Moses* (p. 419)	39	41	42	48	51	53	54	
Mark Twain *Cub Pilot on the Mississippi* (p. 428)	56	59	60	64	67	69	70	
Maya Angelou *I Know Why The Caged Bird Sings* (p. 437)	72	75	76	81	83	84	85	
Kim Yong Ik *A Book-Writing Venture* (p. 443)	87	89	91		94		96	

interviews, editorials, book and movie reviews, letters, speeches, biographical articles, personal essays, and even advertisements. If time permits, each student may select a favorite example to share briefly with the class as types are listed on the board. The class may also discuss examples of nonfiction on radio and television. Relate this activity to the introductory comments on p. 402.

PORTFOLIO ASSESSMENT

Suggestions for use of portfolios as support for this unit are described in the *Portfolio Assessment and Professional Support Materials* booklet accompanying this program. Specific suggestions are provided for a variety of student projects that may be suitable for inclusion in a portfolio. In addition, copying masters are provided for guides that may be used for evaluation and assessment of student projects.

Student Learning Options

NONFICTION

1. Writing About Art

Find a picture of a painting by Thomas Hart Benton to share with the class. Explain to students that Benton painted realistic scenes portraying everyday life, such as paintings of miners and sharecroppers. Ask students to write short journal entries explaining why Benton's art might be compared to the non-fiction pieces in this unit. Do these paintings help the viewer to understand everyday life for twentieth-century Americans?

2. Writing to Harriet Tubman

Ask students to write letters to Harriet Tubman. Students could express their feelings about her courageous acts, inform her of the struggles for freedom of some modern-day people in various countries, or relate their own personal struggles for freedom.

3. Creating a Word Search

Students could create word search puzzles of terminology or new vocabulary from this unit. Each puzzle should have a theme. For example, a puzzle might have the theme "Steamboats" and include only words related to that theme. Ask students to include at least fifteen words in their word searches and to list the words below their puzzles.

About the Artwork

This photograph by Cartier-Bresson is much like a painting. It does not attempt to record a specific place or to give a portrait of the little girl; it concentrates on patterns. The pattern of the door is repeated in the square shapes of the buildings, in the rectangular steps and shadows, and in the square of sky at the very top of the picture. The viewer's eyes are led up the narrow channel of the stairway to the running figure that seems about to escape from the photograph. You may ask the class for reasons this particular scene may have appealed to the photographer. What mood does the picture convey? What does the presence of so many doors suggest to the imagination? In what ways does this picture resemble a piece of nonfiction?

About the Artist

Cartier-Bresson is a well-known French photojournalist and fine-art photographer. In World War II, he worked with the French Resistance as an underground photographer. He has photographed many important political and social events and has published book-length photographic essays on Russia and China.

Ideas for Writing

This photograph represents a nonfiction scene—the girl and place are real although the setting and the character are not identified. You might ask students to write in nonfiction style an account of the event captured in the photograph. Students could consider who the girl is, where she is going, and why she is going there.

NONFICTION

Imagine yourself a traveler to the scene shown in this photograph. If you were keeping a record of your journey or writing a postcard to someone at home, how would you describe the scene in this photograph? What words could you use to describe the steps in the foreground? How would you describe the areas of light and shadow? What impression would you want to give of the buildings?

Write a journal entry, a postcard, or an informal letter in which you note what you see in this picture. Then compare your responses with those of other students. Did you miss any details? Did you find yourself looking at the photograph more carefully after listening to others' responses?

Little Greek Girl Mounting a Staircase (c. 1963)
by Henri Cartier-Bresson (1908–   ). Photograph.

NONFICTION
Invite students to examine the photograph and to note their impressions. Encourage them to note not only what they see but also the thoughts and feelings that the scene evokes. Then have students write brief journal entries, postcards, or informal letters based on their notes. After students have shared their writing, explain that the writers represented in this unit probably followed a process similar to the one students used: they began with information (often gathered from a variety of sources), noted their responses to the information, and combined the information with these responses to create works of nonfiction. Students might want to skim through the unit to preview the selections. They include two essays about animals (Gerald Carson's "affectionate legend" of a patriotic eagle and James Thurber's humorous sketch "The Dog That Bit People"), a biographical essay on a historical figure (an excerpt from Ann Petry's biography *Harriet Tubman: Conductor on the Underground Railroad*), and three autobiographical essays whose authors share difficulties they faced as young people (excerpts from Mark Twain's *Life on the Mississippi*, Maya Angelou's *I Know Why the Caged Bird Sings*, and Kim Yong Ik's "A Book-Writing Venture"). Suggested activities give students practice in drawing **inferences** and recognizing main ideas and purpose. Students are also encouraged to identify and analyze literary elements such as **style** and **tone**. **Language and Vocabulary** exercises focus on recognizing the use of jargon and tracing etymologies, and a special feature helps students make connections between literature and history. Finally, **Focus on Writing** (Writing a Biographical Report) leads students through the process of exploring subjects, gathering details, developing a main idea, and creating an outline for a biographical report.

401

The writings in this unit are *nonfiction*—that is, they are about actual people and actual events. Nonfiction can be about almost anything—sports, wars, inventions, adventures, disasters, people's lives. It can take the form of diaries, letters, biographies, magazine articles, speeches, or interviews.

Like all literature, nonfiction helps you share experiences. This unit includes an article about an eagle that became the mascot for a Wisconsin infantry company during the Civil War; a humorous essay about living with a bad-tempered dog; an excerpt from a biography of Harriet Tubman, a conductor on the Underground Railroad; a true narrative about a fight on a Mississippi steamboat; an autobiographical recollection of growing up in the South; and a true story of a young writer's efforts to be published.

You will be reading nonfiction all of your life. It is a form of writing that can give you information about the world and personal pleasure as well.

Santa Fe (1925) by Edward Hopper (1882-1967). Watercolor.   The Phillips Collection, Washington, D.C.

FOCUS / MOTIVATION

Ask students to discuss what they know about the lives of frontier women from family stories, reading, or television and movies. Tell them to be alert to new information as they read the **Close Reading** selection.

PRESENTATION

You might find it effective to read the essay aloud, stopping to ask questions that will help students identify and analyze elements of the selection. After the reading, lead students in a discussion of **One Reader's Response** and the

questions that follow the essay. Remind students that the sidenotes represent only one reader's interpretation. Encourage students to offer their own conclusions and to support their ideas with evidence from the essay.

Close Reading OF AN ESSAY

1 *The essay is a type of nonfiction that can be adapted to several purposes. An essay can be informative or instructive; it can be entertaining; it can be persua-*2*sive. Essays may be* formal or informal. The formal essay is serious and impersonal. The informal essay is light, personal, and often humorous.*

Guidelines for Close Reading

3 **1.** Ask yourself what the purpose of the essay is. The purpose may be to inform, to explain, to entertain, to persuade, or some combination of these objectives.

4 **2.** Determine the tone of the essay. A formal essay is serious in tone and is generally objective. An informal essay is told from a personal point of view and may be humorous.

5 **3.** Pay close attention to style. Writers make use of different kinds of writing in order to give pictures and communicate sensory impressions, to relate a series of events, to present information, and to influence the reader's ideas.

6 **4.** Clarify your own responses as you read. What is your impression of the writer? Do you find yourself agreeing or disagreeing with the writer's ideas?

7 **5.** Look for the single idea that gives focus to the essay. This idea may be stated directly or it may be implied. Try to state this idea in a sentence or two.

Read the following essay carefully. The notes alongside the essay represent one reader's responses. If you like, cover these notes and write your own comments on a separate sheet of paper as you read. At a later point you may wish to compare your responses with the printed comments.

CLOSE READING OF AN ESSAY

1
Essays can also be primarily expressive or creative.

2
The French philosopher Michel Eyquem de Montaigne (1533–1592), is credited with inventing the **essay**. People of his day often gathered thematic collections of proverbs, sayings, and adages. Montaigne, adding personal reflection and self-analysis, became first essayist.

3
Purpose is writer's reason for writing. Answers question: Why did writer write this?

4
Tone of an essay is often reflected in writer's **style**, which includes word choice and arrangement, sentence length, **imagery, figurative language,** and **rhythm.**

5
Writers often combine writing strategies—**description** (to communicate sensory impressions), **narration** (to relate a series of events), **classification** (to organize information) and **evaluation**—to develop style.

6
Cabeza de Baca's essay is informative; however, it is also designed to persuade reader that pioneer women were important.

7
The main idea is often stated at the beginning of an **essay** and paraphrased at the end. However, if idea is implied, reader must infer from writer's **tone, style,** and content. The main idea of "The Pioneer Women" is stated explicitly in the first sentence of the essay.

The Pioneer Women

1
Setting. Opening sentence establishes location, which strongly influences women's choices and roles.

2
Women often traveled long distances from their homes to the frontier to accompany or join their husbands.

3
Women around the world have acted as midwives for one another for millenia.

4
Interest in plant medicine dates back more than eight thousand years to time of Assyrians, ancient Egyptians, and pre-Inca Peruvians.

5
First Spanish colonizers came to New Mexico in 1500s; first Spanish colony was established in 1598.

6
Most of these women were probably Roman Catholic.

7
Cabeza de Baca was born in 1898 in La Liendre, New Mexico. She weaves story of grandmother with general information about pioneer women of the area, thus establishing her authority on this subject.

8
Many common herbs are thought to have healing properties. These include thyme, garlic, ginger, and mint.

Close Reading
OF AN ESSAY

ONE READER'S RESPONSE

According to the footnotes, the author is talking about the Southwest. These Spanish words are new to me.

I think the subject of the essay will be the contributions of pioneer women.

Women really had to be self-sufficient and courageous.

I didn't know this.

Lots of people today use home remedies.

These women were substitutes for doctors.

The wives of ranchers had responsibility for the welfare of the workers and their families.

The Pioneer Women

FABIOLA CABEZA DE BACA

1 The women on the *Llano*[1] and *Ceja*[2] played a great part in the history of the land. It was a difficult life for a woman, but she had made her choice when in the marriage ceremony she had promised to obey and follow her husband. It may not have been her choice, since parents may have decided for her. It was the Spanish custom to make matches for the children. Whether **2** through choice or tradition, the women had to be a hardy lot in order to survive the long trips by wagon or carriage and the separation from their families, if their families were not among those who were settling on the Llano.

3 The women had to be versed in the curative powers of plants and in midwifery, for there were no doctors for two hundred miles or more.

4 The knowledge of plant medicine is an inheritance from the **5** Moors[3] and brought to New Mexico by the first Spanish colonizers. From childhood, we are taught the names of herbs, weeds and plants that have curative potency; even today when we have doctors at immediate call, we still have great faith in plant medicine. Certainly this knowledge of home remedies was a source of comfort to the women who went out to the *Llano*, yet **6** their faith in God helped more than anything in the survival.

Every village had its *curandera* or *medica*[4] and the ranchers rode many miles to bring the medicine woman or midwife from a distant village or neighboring ranch.

Quite often, the wife of the *patron*[5] was well versed in plant **7** medicine. I know that my grandmother, Dona Estefana Delgado de Baca, although not given the name of *medica*, because it was not considered proper in her social class, was called every day by some family in the village, or by their *empleados* (servants, or *hacienda* workers), to treat a child or some other person in the family. In the fall of the year, she went out to the hills **8** and valleys to gather her supply of healing herbs. When she

1. *Llano* (lyä'nō): a large grassy plain in southwestern United States.
2. *Ceja* (sā'hä): top of a mesa.
3. **Moors** (mŏŏrz): a Muslim people who invaded Spain in the eighth century.
4. *curandera* or *medica:* medicine woman, or doctor.
5. *patron* (pä-trōn'): the owner of a large ranch.

went to live in La Liendre, there were terrible outbreaks of smallpox, and she had difficulty convincing the villagers that **9** vaccination was the solution. Not until she had a godchild in every family was she able to control the dreaded disease. In Spanish tradition, a godmother takes the responsibility of a real mother, and in that way grandmother conquered many superstitions which the people had. At least she had the power to decide what should be done for her godchildren.

10   From El Paso, Texas, she secured vaccines from her cousin, Doctor Samaniego. She vaccinated her children, grandchildren and godchildren against the disease. She vaccinated me when I was three years old and the vaccination has passed any doctor's inspections.

As did my grandmother, so all the wives of the *patrones* held a very important place in the villages and ranches on the *Llano.* **11** The *patron* ruled the *rancho,* but his wife looked after the spiri-

I didn't realize that Spanish godmothers had that kind of influence.

Women were responsible for bringing progress to settlements in the Southwest.

The author is speaking from personal experience.

9
Godmothers traditionally vow, during the baptism ceremony, to look after their godchildren's spiritual development, although the role differs from culture to culture.

10
Although El Paso lies near the border between Texas and New Mexico, the vaccines would have had to be transported quite a distance.

11
Connotation. The verb *ruled* carries a very different connotation from that of the verb phrase *looked after,* suggesting the difference between these two roles.

Red and Yellow Cliffs—Ghost Ranch (1940) by Georgia O'Keeffe (1887–1986). Oil on canvas.

Close Reading
OF AN ESSAY

This is history we don't usually find in our textbooks.

This was true of most pioneer communities. In lots of places there were no public schools, and mothers had to teach their own children to read.

I think I know the purpose of this essay. It's to make the reader appreciate the contributions of pioneer women to the colonizing of the Southwest.

This was an interesting essay. I learned a lot from it.

tual and physical welfare of the *empleados* and their families. She was the first one called when there was death, illness, misfortune or good tidings in a family. She was a great social force in the community—more so than her husband. She held the purse strings, and thus she was able to do as she pleased in her charitable enterprises and help those who might seek her assistance. . . .

The women in these isolated areas had to be resourceful in every way. They were their own doctors, dressmakers, tailors and advisers.

12   The settlements were far apart and New Mexico was a poor territory trying to adapt itself to a new rule. The *Llano* people **13** had no opportunity for public schools, before statehood, but there were men and women who held classes for the children of the *patrones* in private homes. They taught reading in Spanish and sometimes in English. Those who had means sent their children to school in Las Vegas, Santa Fe, or Eastern states. If no teachers were available, the mothers taught their own children to read and many of the wealthy ranchers had private teachers for their children until they were old enough to go away to boarding schools. . . .

14   Without the guidance and comfort of the wives and mothers, life on the *Llano* would have been unbearable, and a great debt is owed to the brave pioneer women who ventured into the cruel life of the plains, far from contact with the outside world. Most of them have gone to their eternal rest, and God must have saved a very special place for them to recompense them for their contribution to colonization and religion in an almost **15** savage country.

12
New Mexico became a United States territory in 1850; current boundaries set in 1863.

13
Children educated at home either by mothers or by other members of the community. Wealthy families hired tutors and sent children to boarding school.

14
Theme. Author concludes we are indebted to pioneer women; her purpose has been to explain that debt.

15
Diction. Author's use of word *savage*, rather than *uncivilized*, emphasizes hardships endured by pioneer women and debt owed by their descendants.

Looking at Yourself as a Reader
The questions given here could provide stimulus for small-group or class discussions. Students could also use them to write paragraphs in which they state and explain their opinions about the essay.

Looking at Yourself as a Reader
Did you find the essay informative? entertaining? persuasive? Did you enjoy reading it? Would you want to read more essays of this kind?

Did the essay arouse your interest in learning more about the role of pioneer women in the Southwest? What sources would you consult to get more information?

If you wrote your own responses while you were reading the essay, compare your notes with the printed notes. Did you arrive at the same conclusions or did you have differences of opinion? Did the printed responses clarify any of your own reactions to the essay?

OBJECTIVES
The overall aim is for students to interpret reactions of characters to "Old Abe" and to differentiate between fact and **legend**. For a complete list of objectives, see the **Teacher's Notes**.

VOCABULARY
The underlined words are in the Glossary. Students may need help with the pronunciation of *Flambeau* (flam'bō) and *Eau Claire* (ō kler').

FOCUS / MOTIVATION
Ask students why schools and teams have mascots. If your school has a mascot, discuss its symbolic meaning; point out that it generates school spirit much as Old Abe inspires patriotism in "The Glorious Bird."

The Glorious Bird

GERALD CARSON

Although some of the stories about Old Abe may have been exaggerated, no one questions the fact that he performed his patriotic duties well. As you read this essay, note how Gerald Carson interweaves historical information with legend.

1 From time immemorial, birds have been held in particular esteem as omens and as totems, especially the eagle, whose soaring flights were interpreted in Homer's *Odyssey*[1] as signs of events yet to come in human affairs. And the eagle has been the symbol of Saint John the Evangelist, of imperial Rome, and of other proud empires that have since risen and passed away.

2 In our own American annals, no individual member of the zoological world can rival Old Abe, the Wisconsin Civil War eagle, in the nation's affections, although one might get an argument in favor of Jumbo, P. T. Barnum's[2] celebrated elephant, or of a magnificent,

3 shaggy, American bull bison whose name may or may not have been Black Diamond and whose home was probably, but not certainly, New York's Central Park Zoo. The bison was real, all right, but the high regard in which he was held was due in part to an unfair advantage: he represented money since his profile appeared on the reverse of the "buffalo" nickel.

But on to our eagle, who was, after all, designated our national bird in 1782. Early in 1861,

4 at sugar-making time, a Chippewa Indian called Chief Sky captured a young bald eagle at the headwaters of the Flambeau River near the line between Wisconsin's Ashland and Pierce counties. Finding a large, tublike nest of mud and sticks in a tall pine, the Indian felled the tree amid the screams and menaces of the parent birds. A few weeks later, when the Flambeau band moved south to dispose of baskets, furs, and moccasins, Chief Sky carried the young bird to Eagle Point. There a farmer named Dan McCann acquired the bird, now nearly grown and handsome, for a bushel of corn. McCann, in turn, took the eagle to Eau Claire, where members of the Eau Claire Badgers, later Company C of the Eighth Wisconsin Volunteer Infantry, chipped in to buy the appealing raptor for $5.00, although a

5 variant account says the price was $2.50. The captain of the company gave the bird the felicitous name Old Abe in compliment to President Abraham Lincoln.

Old Abe was formally sworn into the service of the United States in a ceremony that included placing red, white, and blue ribbons around his graceful neck and a rosette of the same colors on his breast. A new rank, eagle

---

1. ***Odyssey*** (ŏd'ə-sē): a Greek epic poem about the wanderings of Odysseus. See the introduction to the epic on page 624.
2. **P. T. Barnum:** Phineas Taylor Barnum (1810–1891), a circus producer and showman.

TEACHING RESOURCES D
Teacher's Notes, p. 8
Reading Check, p. 11
Study Guide, p. 12
Language Skills, p. 16
Building Vocabulary, p. 19
Selection Vocabulary Test, p. 20
Selection Test, p. 22

PREREADING FOCUS
The headnote mentions that Carson combines historical information and **legend** in "The Glorious Bird." Encourage students to be on the lookout for information in the essay that is probably legend.

The Glorious Bird

1
Tone. Lofty sound of "time immemorial," intriguing mention of "omens" and "totems," **epic** and historical **allusions** in first paragraph establish immediate feeling that while Carson takes his subject seriously, he recognizes the humorous aspects of the **legend**.

2 Summarizing
What are "our own American annals"? Recorded history of our country.

3
This story is not well documented and may not be true. Author's comment about "high regard" because bison associated with money is a tongue-in-cheek comment.

4
"Sugar-making time" is spring.

5
Discrepancies between reported facts surface right from start of Old Abe's army career.

Old Abe and Color Guard of the Eighth Wisconsin Volunteer Infantry, Vicksburg, Mississippi (July 1863).
State Historical Society of Wisconsin

6 bearer, was created, and a soldier was detailed to carry the eagle beside the regimental colors on a special perch. Little flags made by two patriotic ladies were placed on each side when the regiment was on the march. The bearer wore a belt with a socket to receive the butt end of the staff. The pole was about five feet long, which made it possible to carry the eagle three feet above the heads of the men. This, a member of Company C recalled, "made him quite conspicuous."

Early in September 1861, the Eau Claire Eagles (formerly Badgers) boarded the steamer *Stella Whipple* with banners flying. People shouted and wept, as they paid farewell to the young recruits departing for the war. The little steamer carried the soldiers downriver to **7** the Mississippi where it was made fast to the levee at La Crosse. There the First Wisconsin Battery[3] boomed a salute. As the spectators **8** shouted greetings, the war eagle was carried proudly above the line of march, the color bearer and the eagle bearer heading the column—the colors on the right, eagle on the left. At this time an offer for Old Abe, the first of many, was made and refused. The bird could not be bought, even for $200 on the barrelhead.[4]

The company traveled by rail from La Crosse to Madison, to join the regiment forming at Camp Randall, moving briskly at the quickstep past the capitol building to the gates of the camp. At that moment Old Abe became **10** a celebrity. As the men of the Seventh Wisconsin lined up on each side of the entrance to

greet the new men of the Eighth, and the band played "Yankee Doodle," the majestic bird cast an eye on the American flag floating above him, seized its starry folds in his beak, and spread his wings to their full extent—six and a half feet. It was an irresistible *tableau vivant.*[5] The crowds went wild when they grasped the symbolism—our national bird, the bird of free- **9** dom, aligning the natural world with the **10** Union cause. Omen indeed!

At the time, Old Abe weighed about ten and a half pounds. His breast was broad and heavy;

3. **Battery:** heavy artillery.
4. **on the barrelhead:** in cash only.

5. *tableau vivant* (tă-blō′ vē-vän′): French for "a living picture," a scene in which figures pose without moving or making a sound.

ways in which the author anthropomorphizes the bird, making him seem like another patriotic soldier.

MEETING INDIVIDUAL NEEDS
ESL/LEP • You may want to review several idiomatic expressions. These include *to chip in* (to share in giving money, to contribute), *to make fast* (to secure, tie up, or fasten), *quickstep* (a marching step in quick time), *to go wild* (to be very enthusiastic).

ECOLOGY LINK
Invite students to research and report on the problems eagles have encountered, especially after World War II, because of the use of DDT and other changes to the environment.

his body <u>symmetrical</u> with a white tail, well rounded. He had a large, well-developed head, **11** bright yellow legs, and talons sharp as grappling irons. The <u>plumage</u> was brown with hints of gold, the greater part of the neck a snowy white, the iris of the eyes a brilliant straw color, the pupils a piercing black. For this splendid creature a new, more elaborate, round wooden perch was designed. At each end were clusters of golden arrows, and underneath the crossbar, a shield with painted stars and stripes was attached. Below, there appeared the <u>legend</u>, "8th Reg. W.V." A leather ring was attached to one of the eagle's legs, with a stout cord about **12** twenty feet long. On a march or during a bat-tle, the eagle bearer took in the <u>slack</u>, giving the bird a free play of about three feet. . . .

13 The Eighth Wisconsin was assigned to the western theater of war, where it did railroad guard duty, manned rifle pits, and engaged in a number of skirmishes. On various occasions it took heavy <u>casualties</u>, being under heavy fire at the battles of Farmington and Corinth; the capture of Island No. 10; the assault on Jackson, Mississippi; the siege of Vicksburg. It took part in the Red River expedition, and later, toward the end of its period of enlistment, in **14** the two-day battle at Nashville in 1864. The eagle was in the thick of it all, carried high on all marches, present at every battle in which the Eighth was engaged, spreading his wings when he heard the bugle calls, and screaming through the smoke and roar of battle. At Corinth, according to one version of the story, Old Abe's cord was cut by a bullet and the war eagle soared high above the battle, even drop- **15** ping rocks upon the rebel forces. This may be carrying anthropomorphism[6] pretty far, but it is a fact that the phenomena[7] of war—the drums and rattle of musketry and the roar of cannon—did excite the bird, and the rest is, well, a matter of the will to believe. At any rate, the eagle undoubtedly lifted up the spirits of a **16** whole regiment. And he survived. Once he <u>wavered</u> in the sky, but a <u>solicitous</u> examination showed that only a few tail feathers had been shot away.

Like all soldiers, Old Abe found that in war there is more waiting than fighting. When in quarters, Abe was allowed a good deal of free- **17** dom. He amused himself catching bugs, fishing in a creek, tipping over water pails, stealing baseballs, sneaking into the sutler's[8] tent for dainties. Old Abe never forgot a

6. **anthropomorphism** (ăn′thrə-pō-môr′fĭz′əm): assigning human behavior and characteristics to objects or animals.
7. **phenomena** (fĭ-nŏm′ə-nə): events.
8. **sutler** (sŭt′lər): camp cook.

11
Simile. Comparison gives reader good idea of strength and sharpness of Old Abe's talons. Grappling irons, sharp, hooked, and much like anchors in appearance, were used to raise sunken ships.

12   Summarizing
Why were two cords of different length used to tie Old Abe? Twenty-foot cord kept eagle from escaping but gave him room to spread wings; shorter rein needed during battle.

13
Theater: area of military operations.

14
Imagery. Sights and sounds of eagle during battle effectively conveyed in one sentence.

15
Use to answer **study question 2,** p. 412.

16
As **symbol,** eagle's survival helped men retain will to survive.

17
Like most soldiers, Abe kept himself entertained when not in battle.

grudge and punished any soldier foolish

18 enough to "get fresh" with him. In general he was as independent as a hog on ice. Abe disliked dogs, except for Frank, the regimental dog, who brought in rabbits, squirrels, rats,

19 and mice; as a gourmet, however, his preference was for Confederate chicken, which seemed to agree with his constitution remarkably well. Once Abe discovered a cup of peach brandy and swallowed it, thus rounding out his military experience by finding out what it was like to be drunk. . . .

20 A furlough home enabled the war eagle to celebrate the Fourth of July, 1864, in Chippewa Falls, and the *Wisconsin State Journal* noticed that he had put on weight and "acquired dignity and ease of bearing . . . the impersonation of haughty defiance." The eagle participated in his final battle at Hurricane Creek, Mississippi, in the late summer of 1864. At the time he was mustered out of service, P. T. Barnum, the great showman of the age, made an unsuccess-

21 ful bid of $20,000 for the sacred bird. Governor Lewis received the bald eagle as an honored charge of the state. A large, airy cage in a special room was prepared for Old Abe in the capitol building, and he was given life tenancy in his quarters and the right to draw rations in perpetuity. On nice summer days, Abe, with his attendant, enjoyed the freedom of the capitol grounds under the shade of venerable oak trees.

▶But Old Abe's career was not over; he still had public duties to perform as a civilian. He

22 was in demand as a star feature of sanitary fairs (to raise money for medical care for soldiers) and encampments of the Grand Army of the Republic, where the boys cheered,

23 marched, ate hardtack and sowbelly, sang Civil War marching songs, and cheered for Old Abe—while he cheered back, after his fashion. On these occasions, devoted to nostalgia and charity, Abe lent a photograph or a tail feather

Old Abe, the Live Wisconsin War Eagle, Taking a Sun Bath (1879). Stereograph.
State Historical Society of Wisconsin

(worth $10) to raise funds for sick and wounded veterans. At a great fair in Chicago, for example, in 1865, the eagle raised about $16,000. In fact, in a souvenir book written about Old Abe, the author explained in a note that the volume was "prepared to furnish a means whereby a few veterans, maimed in the service of their country, might turn an honest penny." . . .◀

Eighteen-hundred and seventy-six—the centennial of American independence. It goes without saying that Old Abe attended the great

Centennial Exhibition in Philadelphia, the first of our great World's Fairs, in the United States. Abe was one of the chief attractions during that centennial summer, feted especially on Wisconsin Day. Standing on the national escutcheon,[9] supported on a lofty pole, he **24** behaved with the dignity of a hero of some forty-two battles and skirmishes. Crowds were always at hand, and the bird surveyed the animated scene around him, a historian of the exposition wrote, "with an air of royal majesty."

25 Old Abe's death and apotheosis[10] were spectacular, not to say, Wagnerian,[11] and fully consistent with his extraordinary life. He didn't peg out until March 1881, when a paint-and-oil smudge fire in the capitol basement created a suffocating volume of oily smoke. The eagle was rescued but never recovered from smoke inhalation, refused all food, and died on March 26 in the arms of his keeper. A gracefully posed image of the bird was preserved by the art of taxidermy and displayed in the Capitol War Museum until February 1904. Then another fire swept through much of the museum, this time destroying all that remained of **26** Old Abe. "The vision ends," wrote an amateur poet, "and we will leave him there,/And trust

9. **escutcheon** (ĕ-skŭch′ən, ĭ-): shield or emblem.
10. **apotheosis** (ə-pŏth′ē-ō′sĭs, ăp′ə-thē′ə-sĭs):glorification.
11. **Wagnerian** (väg-nîr′ē-ən): referring to Richard Wagner (1813–1883), a German composer whose operas are known for their grand and often theatrical climaxes.

in God with faith and earnest prayer/That Victory's dream be fully realized,/And all the world be nobly eagleized!"

Old Abe's memory endures. Today on state highway 178, approximately eight miles northeast of Chippewa Falls and the Chippewa River, a historical marker commemorates the **27** "glorious bird" at a wayside that is part of the old McCann farm, and an oil portrait by an unknown artist hangs in the state capitol in **28** Madison, Wisconsin. It perpetuates a legend, yes, not of the Paul Bunyan[12] school of unnatural natural history, such as the Black Hodag,[13] *Bovinis spiritualis*, subject of many tall tales, but an affectionate legend, mostly true, based upon verifiable fact.

12. **Paul Bunyan:** in American folk tales, a giant logger. See page 173.
13. **Black Hodag** (hō′dăg): a mythical creature with horns and a hooked tail, known for its ugliness and ferocity.

Reading Check

1. How was the young eagle captured?
2. What group purchased the eagle?
3. How was Old Abe displayed in parades?
4. What did Old Abe do when he heard bugle calls?
5. What happened to Old Abe after he left military service?

---

24 Finding Details
What characteristics made the eagle look heroic on these occasions? He was high up; stood with dignity, looked majestic.

25
Allusion. Comparison to Wagner's works is in keeping with enthusiastic yet tongue-in-cheek opening **tone** of **essay**.

26
Uneven **rhythm** and awkward **end rhyme** make this poem sound like work of amateur.

27
Historical marker is source of title, calling Abe a "glorious bird."

28
Legend. Most legends seem to have some basis, however slight, in history and fact. Author reminds reader in closing that aspects of Old Abe's life are well documented.

READING CHECK
1. Chippewa Indian cut down tree that held nest (p. 407).
2. Eau Claire Badgers, Company C of 8th Wisconsin Volunteer Infantry (p. 407).
3. On a perch carried above soldiers' heads (p. 408).
4. Spread his wings (p. 409).
5. Appeared at fairs and encampments to raise money for medical assistance for soldiers (p. 410).

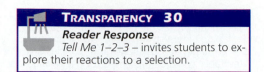

TRANSPARENCY 30
Reader Response
Tell Me 1–2–3 – invites students to explore their reactions to a selection.

TRANSPARENCY 31
Literary Elements
Distinguishing Between Facts and Opinion – asks students to differentiate between facts and opinions in nonfiction.

FOR STUDY AND DISCUSSION

1. An omen indicating that "natural world" agreed with Union cause.
2. Says this "may be carrying anthropomorphism pretty far," that it is "a matter of the will to believe."
3. Appeared at events raising money for soldiers needing medical care.
4. Responses will vary. Old Abe was a spirited patriot, represented courage, loyalty, pride.
5a. Answers will vary. Old Abe's reported actions at Camp Randall, at Corinth, and in camp awaiting battle are examples of bird's legendary exploits. 5b. Responses will vary. Actions are exaggerated, given human attributes.

FOCUS ON BIOGRAPHICAL REPORT

You may want to help students choose subjects for biographical reports by modeling the process described here. Write on the chalkboard the name of a possible subject with whom students might be familiar. Then enlist students' help to answer the suggested questions for that person. You may want to lead students through this process more than once.

For Study and Discussion

Analyzing and Interpreting the Essay

1. When the company moved to Camp Randall, Old Abe put on quite a show for the crowd. What were Old Abe's actions interpreted to mean?

2. During the battle at Corinth, Old Abe was rumored to have bombed the rebel forces with rocks. How does the author indicate that this story may not actually be true?

3. What public duties did Old Abe perform as a "civilian"?

4. What do you think made Old Abe so appealing and memorable to people?

5. At the close of the essay, Gerald Carson says that the story of Old Abe is an "affectionate legend, mostly true, based upon verifiable fact." **a.** In your view, what in the essay is more legend than fact? **b.** Why do you think so?

Focus on Biographical Report

Choosing a Subject

Although Old Abe was a nonhuman mascot rather than a person, Gerald Carson uses many of the techniques of biography in "The Glorious Bird." A biography is the life story of a person written by someone else. A shorter form of biography is the biographical report. In a **biographical report,** you present information about a real person's life, personality, and achievements.

When you choose a subject for this kind of informative writing, ask yourself questions like these:

1. What is interesting and special about the person? Why would other people be interested in her or him?
2. What are the person's achievements?
3. What kinds of sources are available about the person? Can you get the information you need?

Make a list of three possible subjects for a biographical report of your own. You can choose famous people from history, living celebrities, or people in your own family. Jot down some notes explaining why you think that readers would be interested in learning more about each person. Save your notes.

About the Author

Gerald Carson (1899–1989)

Gerald Carson was born in Carrollton, Illinois. After graduating from the University of Illinois, he worked as a reporter, an editor, and an advertising copywriter. After 1951 he devoted himself to writing full time. He said he left advertising because it had become too surreal. An avid reader, Carson was especially interested in American folkways, culture, and history. Among the many subjects of his books are the treatment of animals, American manners, income tax, and breakfast cereals. His most popular books are *The Old Country Store* (1954) and *The Dentist and the Empress: The Adventures of Dr. Tom Evans in Gas-Lit Paris* (1983).

OBJECTIVES

The overall aim is for students to analyze the use of **anecdotes** in "The Dog That Bit People" and to discuss the personalities of the main characters. For a complete list of objectives, see the **Teacher's Notes.**

VOCABULARY

The underlined words are in the Glossary. You may want students to check the variant pronunciations of *Greenwich.*

FOCUS / MOTIVATION

You might display a few of Thurber's dog cartoons or present a sampling from *Thurber's Dogs* (Simon and Schuster). Explain that Thurber found dogs so fascinating that he made his cartoons of them his hallmark.

The Dog That Bit People

JAMES THURBER

An informal essay often reveals as much about the personality of the author as it does about its subject. What impression do you form of Thurber from this informal essay?

1 Probably no one man should have as many dogs in his life as I have had, but there was more pleasure than distress in them for me except in the case of an Airedale named Muggs. He gave me more trouble than all the other fifty-four or -five put together, although *2* my moment of keenest embarrassment was the time a Scotch terrier named Jeannie, who had just had four puppies in the shoe closet of a fourth-floor apartment in New York, had the fifth and last at the corner of—but we shall get around to that later on. Then, too, there was the prizewinning French poodle, a great big black poodle—none of your little, untrouble- *3* some white miniatures—who got sick riding in the rumble seat[1] of a car with me on her way to the Greenwich Dog Show. She had a red rubber bib tucked around her throat and, since a rainstorm came up when we were halfway through the Bronx, I had to hold over her a small green umbrella, really more of a parasol.

The rain beat down fearfully, and suddenly the driver of the car drove into a big garage filled with mechanics. It happened so quickly that I forgot to put the umbrella down, and I shall always remember the look of incredulity[2] that came over the face of the garageman who came over to see what we wanted. "Get a load of this, Mac," he called to someone behind him.

4 But the Airedale, as I have said, was the worst of all my dogs. He really wasn't my dog, as a matter of fact; I came home from a vacation one summer to find that my brother Robert had brought him while I was away. A big, burly, choleric[3] dog, he always acted as if he thought I *5* wasn't one of the family. There was a slight advantage in being one of the family, for he didn't bite the family as often as he bit strangers. Still, in the years that we had him he bit everybody but Mother, and he made a pass at her once but missed. That was during the

---

1. **rumble seat:** an open seat in the back of some early automobiles. It could be folded shut when not in use.

2. **incredulity** (ĭn′krə-dōō′lə-tē): disbelief.
3. **choleric** (kŏl′ər-ĭk): bad-tempered.

TEACHING RESOURCES D

Teacher's Notes, p. 25
Reading Check, p. 27
Study Guide, p. 28
Language Skills, p. 31
Building Vocabulary, p. 35
Selection Vocabulary Test, p. 53
Selection Test, p. 37

PREREADING FOCUS

The headnote directs students' attention to the personality of Thurber himself as revealed in this **essay** about a dog. Encourage students to "sit back" and enjoy Thurber's humor as they read the essay and also to think about the personalities of the author, his mother, and Muggs.

The Dog That Bit People

1
Thurber did own a number of dogs during his life. "Fifty-four or -five" is, of course, comic exaggeration.

2
Humor. Part of Thurber's humorous style is his digression to related but not actually pertinent details.

3 Analyzing
What does this anecdote reveal about Thurber's character? Shows comical extent to which he will go for his pets.

4
An Airedale is a large black and tan terrier developed in England. It is about 22 inches high, 35–45 pounds, with hard, wiry coat.

5
Tone. Author's calm acceptance of Muggs's biting habits puts this irritating behavior in humorous light. Advantage of being family member only "slight."

In this humorous **essay**, Thurber focuses on Muggs, a memorable family dog that was preoccupied with biting. Only Thurber's mother was safe from the canine's wrath, and she adored the dog, making excuses for his inexcusable behavior. How do you live with a dog that bites neighbors, congressmen, and lieutenant governors, and who has the garbage man, the laundry man, and the ice man too terrified to approach the house? The Thurber family shows to what extremes animal lovers will go.

PRESENTATION

While students should have no trouble reading this on their own, it is funny enough to share with the whole class. The class will want to discuss their own "horror" stories of the inconveniences pets can impose on a family. You may

6 Expressing an Opinion
Do you think the mice and Muggs really acted in the manner Thurber describes? Responses will vary. Hard to tell how far the author's exaggeration for comic effect extends.

7
Characterization. Mother is a major comic figure of this **essay.** Her explanations of dog's behavior contribute to humor.

8 Analyzing
Why is this odd Christmas list funny? Responses will vary. Most people would rather forget an unpleasant circumstance like the dog's having bitten a guest in the home, rather than commemorating it in this way.

9
Even as old, crippled dog, Muggs rallies his energies. Mother again has good excuse for Muggs's behavior.

10
Anecdote. Thurber's narration gives reader a graphic picture of Robert's actions and Muggs's technique.

11
Another example of Mother's unusual nature.

month when we suddenly had mice, and Muggs refused to do anything about them. Nobody ever had mice exactly like the mice we had that **6** month. They acted like pet mice, almost like mice somebody had trained. They were so friendly that one night when Mother entertained at dinner the Friraliras, a club she and my father had belonged to for twenty years, she put down a lot of little dishes with food in them on the pantry floor so that the mice would be satisfied with that and wouldn't come into the dining room. Muggs stayed out in the pantry with the mice, lying on the floor, growling to himself—not at the mice, but about all the people in the next room that he would have liked to get at. Mother slipped out into the pantry once to see how everything was going. Everything was going fine. It made her so mad to see Muggs lying there, oblivious of[4] the mice—they came running up to her—that she slapped him **7** and he slashed at her, but didn't make it. He was sorry immediately, Mother said. He was always sorry, she said, after he bit someone, but we could not understand how she figured this out. He didn't act sorry.

8 Mother used to send a box of candy every Christmas to the people the Airedale bit. The list finally contained forty or more names. Nobody could understand why we didn't get rid of the dog. I didn't understand it very well myself, but we didn't get rid of him. I think that one or two people tried to poison Muggs—he acted poisoned once in a while—and old Major Moberly fired at him once with his service revolver near the Seneca Hotel on East Broad Street—but Muggs lived to be almost eleven **9** years old, and even when he could hardly get around, he bit a congressman who had called to **11** see my father on business. My mother had never liked the congressman—she said the signs of his horoscope showed he couldn't be

trusted (he was Saturn with the moon in Virgo)—but she sent him a box of candy that Christmas. He sent it right back, probably because he suspected it was trick candy. Mother persuaded herself it was all for the best that the dog had bitten him, even though Father lost an important business association because of it. "I wouldn't be associated with such a man," Mother said. "Muggs could read him like a book."

We used to take turns feeding Muggs to be on his good side, but that didn't always work. He was never in a very good humor, even after a meal. Nobody knew exactly what was the matter with him, but whatever it was it made him **10** irascible,[5] especially in the mornings. Robert never felt very well in the morning either, especially before breakfast, and once when he came downstairs and found that Muggs had moodily chewed up the morning paper, he hit him in the face with a grapefruit and then jumped up on the dining-room table, scattering dishes and silverware and spilling the coffee. Muggs's first free leap carried him all the way across the table and into a brass fire screen in front of the gas grate, but he was back on his feet in a moment, and in the end he got Robert and gave him a pretty vicious bite in the leg. Then he was all over it; he never bit anyone more than once at a time. Mother always mentioned that as an argument in his favor; she said he had a quick temper but that he didn't hold a grudge. She was forever defending him. I think she liked him because he wasn't well. "He's not strong," she would say, pityingly, but that was inaccurate; he may not have been well, but he was terribly strong.

11 One time my mother went to the Chittenden Hotel to call on a woman mental healer who was lecturing in Columbus on the subject of "Harmonious Vibrations." She wanted to find out if it

4. **oblivious of:** forgetful of; not mindful of.

5. **irascible** (ĭ-răs′ə-bəl): irritable.

was possible to get harmonious vibrations into a dog. "He's a large, tan-colored Airedale," Mother explained. The woman said she had **12** never treated a dog, but she advised my mother to hold the thought that he did not bite and would not bite. Mother was holding the thought the very next morning when Muggs got the iceman, but she blamed that slip-up on the iceman. "If you didn't think he would bite you, he wouldn't," Mother told him. He stomped out of the house in a terrible jangle of vibrations.

One morning when Muggs bit me slightly, more or less in passing, I reached down and grabbed his short stumpy tail and hoisted him into the air. It was a foolhardy thing to do, and the last time I saw my mother, about six months ago, she said she didn't know what possessed me. I don't know either, except that I was pretty mad. As long as I held the dog off the floor by his tail he couldn't get at me, but he twisted and jerked so, snarling all the time, that I realized I couldn't hold him that way very long. I carried him to the kitchen and flung him onto the floor and shut the door on him just as he crashed **13** against it. But I forgot about the back stairs. Muggs went up the back stairs and down the front stairs and had me cornered in the living room. I managed to get up onto the mantelpiece above the fireplace, but it gave way and came down with a tremendous crash, throwing a large marble clock, several vases, and myself heavily to the floor. Muggs was so alarmed by the racket that when I picked myself up he had disappeared. We couldn't find him anywhere, although we whistled and shouted, until old Mrs. Detweiler called after dinner that night. Muggs had bitten her once, in the leg, and she came into the living room only after we assured her that Muggs had run away. She had just seated herself when, with a great growling and scratching of claws, Muggs emerged from under a davenport where he had been quietly hiding all the time and bit her again. Mother

examined the bite and put arnica[6] on it and told Mrs. Detweiler that it was only a bruise. "He just bumped you," she said. But Mrs. Detweiler left the house in a nasty state of mind.

Lots of people reported our Airedale to the police, but my father held a municipal office at the time and was on friendly terms with the police. Even so, the cops had been out a couple of times—once when Muggs bit Mrs. Rufus Sturtevant and again when he bit Lieutenant **14** Governor Malloy—but Mother told them that it hadn't been Muggs's fault but the fault of the people who were bitten. "When he starts for them, they scream," she explained, "and that excites him." The cops suggested that it might be a good idea to tie the dog up, but Mother **15** said that it mortified him to be tied up and he wouldn't eat when he was tied up.

Muggs at his meals was an unusual sight. Because of the fact that if you reached toward the floor he would bite you, we usually put his **16** food plate on top of an old kitchen table with a bench alongside the table. Muggs would stand **17** on the bench and eat. I remember that my mother's Uncle Horatio, who boasted that he was the third man up Missionary Ridge,[7] was splutteringly indignant when he found out that we fed the dog on a table because we were afraid to put his plate on the floor. He said he wasn't afraid of any dog that ever lived and that he would put the dog's plate on the floor if we would give it to him. Robert said that if Uncle Horatio had fed Muggs on the ground just before the battle, he would have been the first man up Missionary Ridge. Uncle Horatio was furious. "Bring him in! Bring him in now!" he shouted. "I'll feed the——on the floor!" Robert was all for giving him a chance, but my father wouldn't hear of it. He said that Muggs had

6. **arnica:** a preparation for sprains and bruises made from the arnica plant.
7. **Missionary Ridge:** a ridge in Tennessee and Georgia, the site of an important Civil War battle.

12
Conflict. Muggs bites iceman, and Mother blames iceman for not using positive thinking. Punch line is iceman leaving in "terrible jangle of vibrations."

13
Characterization. Muggs shows determination and resourcefulness by finding alternative route.

Summarizing
14 Analyzing
Why, according to Mother, are people to blame for being bitten by Muggs? Is Mother serious? People excite Muggs by screaming when he starts for them (a perfectly logical reaction). Mother is apparently blind to all Muggs's faults.

15
Mortified: humiliated.

16
Example of ridiculous allowances family makes for dog. Muggs has own dining table.

17
Anecdote. This story of Uncle Horatio demonstrates that the humans in Thurber's family are just as eccentric as the pets. His military pride is stung by the idea that the family is afraid of a dog.

MEETING INDIVIDUAL NEEDS
Visual and Auditory Learners • Thurber emphasizes the human characteristics of his dog Muggs. To help students to relate personally to the story, you might ask auditory learners to collect anecdotes from their classmates about their pets, especially those that illustrate human characteristics the pets have. Students could tape the stories their classmates tell them or organize and plan presentations for the class.

Visual learners might enjoy collecting humorous drawings or cartoons of dogs or other pets.

Students could then create a bulletin board on which to post their favorite animal cartoons.

VISUAL CONNECTIONS
Relating Expression Skills
Thurber's line drawing is rough and simple but captures a great deal of personality and action. You might have students who enjoy Thurber's line drawing try their own skills in depicting a scene from the essay using their own simple line drawings. Students also may enjoy captioning this drawing or adding a "conversational balloon" to it.

Copr. © 1933, 1961 James Thurber.
From *My Life and Hard Times*, published by Harper & Row.

18 Analyzing
Why are the family's extraordinary efforts unusual? Most people would not be willing to rearrange their lives to suit their pets.

19
Use to answer **study question 2b**, p. 417.

20
Explanation of elaborate scheme to trick Muggs into coming into house illustrates again how far family is willing to go for its pet.

21
Connotation. Use of *stalk* is humorous because it suggests an image of Muggs sneaking up carefully on someone who is not there.

already been fed. "I'll feed him again!" bawled Uncle Horatio. We had quite a time quieting him.

In his last year Muggs used to spend practically all of his time outdoors. He didn't like to stay in the house for some reason or other—perhaps it held too many unpleasant memories for him. Anyway, it was hard to get him to come in, and as a result, the garbage man, the iceman, and the laundryman wouldn't come near **18** the house. We had to haul the garbage down to the corner, take the laundry out and bring it back, and meet the iceman a block from home. After this had gone on for some time, we hit on an ingenious arrangement for getting the dog **19** in the house so that we could lock him up while the gas meter was read, and so on. Muggs was afraid of only one thing, an electrical storm.

Thunder and lightning frightened him out of his senses (I think he thought a storm had broken the day the mantelpiece fell). He would rush into the house and hide under a bed or in **20** a clothes closet. So we fixed up a thunder machine out of a long narrow piece of sheet iron with a wooden handle on one end. Mother would shake this vigorously when she wanted to get Muggs into the house. It made an excellent imitation of thunder, but I suppose it was the most roundabout system for running a household that was ever devised. It took a lot out of Mother.

A few months before Muggs died, he got to **21** "seeing things." He would rise slowly from the floor, growling low, and stalk stiff-legged and menacing toward nothing at all. Sometimes the Thing would be just a little to the right or left of

TRANSPARENCY 30

Reader Response
Tell Me 1–2–3 – invites students to explore their reactions to a selection.

a visitor. Once a Fuller brush salesman got hysterics. Muggs came wandering into the room like Hamlet following his father's ghost. His eyes were fixed on a spot just to the left of the Fuller brush man, who stood it until Muggs was about three slow, creeping paces from him. Then he shouted. Muggs wavered on past him into the hallway, grumbling to himself, but the Fuller brush man went on shouting. I think Mother had to throw a pan of cold water on him before he stopped. That was the way she used to stop us boys when we got into fights.

Muggs died quite suddenly one night. Mother wanted to bury him in the family plot under a marble stone with some such inscription as "Flights of angels sing thee to thy rest,"[8] but we persuaded her it was against the law. In the end we just put up a smooth board above his grave along a lonely road. On the board I wrote with an indelible pencil *"Cave Canem."*[9] Mother was quite pleased with the simple, classic dignity of the old Latin epitaph.

8. **"Flights . . . rest":** words spoken to the dead Hamlet in Shakespeare's play.
9. *Cave Canem* (kä′vā kän′ĕm): Latin for "Beware of the dog." In ancient Rome, this warning was often put on the doorways of homes.

Reading Check

1. What family member was never bitten by the Airedale?
2. What did Thurber's mother do at Christmastime for the people that the Airedale had bitten?
3. Why did she refuse to keep the dog tied up?
4. Why was Muggs fed on a table?
5. What was the only thing that the Airedale feared?

For Study and Discussion

Analyzing and Interpreting the Essay

1. This essay is made up of a series of **anecdotes,** or amusing stories, about a particular subject—here, a dog. Thurber pokes fun at himself and his family as he tells how they tried to keep Muggs in a good mood. How does the opening incident with the prize poodle prepare you for a story about people who would do anything for their pets?

2. Part of the fun of this story lies in the ridiculous lengths a whole family went to, in order to stay on the good side of their dog. **a.** What did the family do about Muggs's food, and about their garbage, their laundry, and the iceman? **b.** Why did they rig up the thunder machine?

3. Thurber's mother saw Muggs as having human characteristics. **a.** What were some of the excuses she made for his behavior? **b.** Do you think many people see their pets in the same way that Mother saw Muggs? Explain your answer.

4a. What does Thurber reveal about himself in this essay? **b.** Would you say that he likes or dislikes dogs? **c.** Does he seem tolerant of people's (and dogs') quirks?

Ask students to analyze the **anecdotes** that characterize Muggs and that show the accomodations made for the dog by the Thurber household. Also, ask students to explain Thurber's use of Mother's "excuses" to create humor.

EXTENSION AND ENRICHMENT
As an experiment in viewpoint, students might rewrite one of the incidents as it would be told by one of Muggs's victims.

Students might collect examples of comic-strip animals such as Snoopy, Marmaduke, Garfield, Heathcliff, and Fred Basset. Students could discuss these animals' personality differences and their relationships with their owners.

ABOUT THE AUTHOR
Thurber was born in Columbus, Ohio. He started his career as a journalist and in 1927 began his lifelong association with *The New Yorker*. Most of his work was printed first in this magazine. Thurber's book *The Years with Ross* (1959) is a memoir about the relationship between Thurber and long-time *New Yorker* editor Harold Ross. Other Thurber books, whose titles reflect his distinct brand of humor, include *The Owl in the Attic and Other Perplexities* (1931), *The Seal in the Bedroom & Other Predicaments* (1932), *My Life and Hard Times* (1933), *The Middle-Aged Man on the Flying Trapeze* (1935), *My World—and Welcome to It* (1942), *The Beast in Me and Other Animals* (1948), and *Lanterns and Lances* (1961). He also wrote several children's books, including *Many Moons* (1943) and *The 13 Clocks* (1950). Thurber illustrated many of his essays and stories with his own line drawings.

Focus on Biographical Report

Gathering Details

The details about Muggs in "The Dog That Bit People" come from the narrator's own memories. When you gather details for a biographical report, however, you will usually need to consult **sources** about your subject.

If your subject is a famous person, past or present, you will often be able to consult books and magazine articles about the person. Keep a list of your sources as you take notes. If you are writing about a family member, interview the person, as well as other people who know him or her. Try to use a minimum of three sources for a biographical report.

Choose one of the subjects identified for a report in the assignment on page 412, or select a new subject. As you gather details about your subject, fill out a chart like the one below. Save your notes.

Details Chart

Date and Place of Birth: _____

Education: _____

Job/Profession: _____
_____

Achievements/Special Awards: _____
_____

Family: _____
_____

Opinions/Outlook on Life: _____
_____

Statements/Quotations: _____
_____

About the Author

James Thurber   (1894–1961)

James Thurber wrote about all kinds of animals—seals, dolphins, unicorns, polar bears, fiddler crabs, wombats, woggle-bugs, bowerbirds, bandicoots, and bristle worms. But he wrote enough dog stories to collect them into an entire book, called *Thurber's Dogs*. Thurber also wrote stories about the kind of person who is victimized by life and its problems. He gave this character a shape and a name in one of his most famous humorous stories, "The Secret Life of Walter Mitty."

Thurber was blinded in one eye in a childhood accident, and he became completely blind during the last years of his life. Nevertheless, he continued to write and he even appeared nightly as himself in *A Thurber Carnival*, a Broadway show based on his work. Thurber once said that humor was a serious thing, one of our greatest national resources, which must be preserved at all cost. One of his humorous twists on a familiar fairy-tale plot is called "The Princess and the Tin Box."

They Called Her Moses

ANN PETRY

This selection is from a biography called Harriet Tubman: Conductor on the Underground Railroad. *After Harriet Tubman made the perilous journey out of slavery herself, she returned to conduct others along the Underground Railroad to freedom. As you read, find out how she came to be called Moses.*

1 Along the Eastern Shore of Maryland, in Dorchester County, in Caroline County, the **2** masters kept hearing whispers about the man named Moses, who was running off slaves. At first they did not believe in his existence. The stories about him were fantastic, unbelievable. Yet they watched for him. They offered rewards for his capture.

3 They never saw him. Now and then they heard whispered rumors to the effect that he was in the neighborhood. The woods were searched. The roads were watched. There was never anything to indicate his whereabouts. But a few days afterward, a goodly number of slaves would be gone from the plantation. Neither the master nor the overseer had heard or seen anything unusual in the quarter. Sometimes one or the other would vaguely remember having heard a whippoorwill call somewhere in the woods, close by, late at night. Though it was the wrong season for whippoorwills.

Sometimes the masters thought they had heard the cry of a hoot owl, repeated, and would remember having thought that the intervals between the low moaning cry were wrong, that it had been repeated four times in

succession instead of three. There was never anything more than that to suggest that all was not well in the quarter. Yet when morning came, they invariably discovered that a group of the finest slaves had taken to their heels.

4 Unfortunately, the discovery was almost always made on a Sunday. Thus a whole day was lost before the machinery of pursuit could be set in motion. The posters offering rewards for the fugitives could not be printed until Monday. The men who made a living hunting for runaway slaves were out of reach, off in the woods with their dogs and their guns, in pursuit of four-footed game, or they were in camp meetings saying their prayers with their wives and families beside them.

Harriet Tubman could have told them that there was far more involved in this matter of running off slaves than signaling the would-be **5** runaways by imitating the call of a whippoorwill, or a hoot owl, far more involved than a matter of waiting for a clear night when the North Star was visible.

In December, 1851, when she started out with the band of fugitives that she planned to take to Canada, she had been in the vicinity of the plantation for days, planning the trip, care-

Harriet Tubman, an ex-slave who led small groups of slaves on foot to Canada, began one such journey in December 1851, after quietly singing the forbidden "Go Down, Moses" to reveal her presence. She gathered eleven willing slaves for the long trek toward freedom. It would be a perilous journey, one in which she would have to draw her gun on one of her party and threaten, "Go with us, or die."

PRESENTATION

Introduce "They Called Her Moses" as the true story of a courageous black woman who risked her life to lead others to freedom in the years before the Civil War. A dramatic introduction to this story would be to play a recording of "Go

VISUAL CONNECTIONS

Exploring the Subject

Harriet Tubman (1820–1913), who was born in Bucktown, Maryland, escaped from slavery in 1849 and subsequently led more than 300 slaves into freedom. She made nineteen trips to Maryland to take runaways along the Underground Railroad. At one time, there was up to $40,000 in rewards on her head. She led her parents to freedom in 1857. She later worked as a scout, nurse, and spy for the Union army. After the war, she was active in Auburn, New York, where she raised money for schools and helped create a home for elderly and needy blacks.

Relating Expression Skills

One of the ways that slaves resisted their oppressors and expressed their feelings was through singing spirituals. (Petry notes that some spirituals were forbidden by slaveholders.) Find a recording of black spirituals and play it for your class after giving them a copy of the lyrics. Point out the songs' potent emotions and the metaphorical allusions to the slaves' anguish and hopes.

TRANSPARENCIES 28 & 29

Fine Art
Theme: *Ideas and People* – features artworks that show real people, emphasizing their unique characteristics and personalities.

Down, Moses.'' Before discussing the study questions, you might want students to trace on a map Tubman's journey from the Eastern Shore of Maryland to St. Catherines, Ontario, clarifying details and reinforcing the sequence of events. If you want students to read this selection silently, provide class time so that you can circulate and offer help as needed.

6 fully selecting the slaves that she would take with her.

She had announced her arrival in the quarter by singing the forbidden spiritual[1]—"Go down, Moses, way down to Egypt Land"— singing it softly outside the door of a slave **7** cabin, late at night. The husky voice was beautiful even when it was barely more than a murmur borne on the wind.

Once she had made her presence known, word of her coming spread from cabin to cabin. The slaves whispered to each other, ear to mouth, mouth to ear, "Moses is here." "Moses has come." "Get ready. Moses is back again." The ones who had agreed to go North **8** with her put ashcake and salt herring in an old bandanna, hastily tied it into a bundle, and then waited patiently for the signal that meant it was time to start.

There were eleven in this party, including one of her brothers and his wife. It was the **9** largest group that she had ever conducted, but **10** she was determined that more and more slaves should know what freedom was like.

She had to take them all the way to Canada. The Fugitive Slave Law[2] was no longer a great many incomprehensible words written down

---

1. **forbidden spiritual:** In 1831, a slave named Nat Turner led an unsuccessful uprising in Virginia. Turner used the Biblical account of the Israelites' escape from Egypt to encourage the rebellion. After this, slaves were forbidden to sing certain spirituals. It was feared that the songs about the Israelites' march to freedom would encourage more uprisings.
2. **Fugitive Slave Law:** part of the Compromise of 1850. According to this law, escaped slaves, even if found in free states, could be forced to return to their masters. Thus, the fugitives were not really safe until they reached Canada. Anyone caught aiding a fugitive slave could be punished with six months in prison and a thousand-dollar fine.

Harriet Tubman by H. B. Lindsley.
Photograph.
Library of Congress

on the country's lawbooks. The new law had become a reality. It was Thomas Sims, a boy, picked up on the streets of Boston at night and shipped back to Georgia. It was Jerry and Shadrach, arrested and jailed with no warning.

11 She had never been in Canada. The route beyond Philadelphia was strange to her. But she could not let the runaways who accompanied her know this. As they walked along she told them stories of her own first flight, she kept painting vivid word pictures of what it would be like to be free.

But there were so many of them this time. She knew moments of doubt when she was half afraid, and kept looking back over her shoulder, imagining that she heard the sound of pursuit. They would certainly be pursued. Eleven of them. Eleven thousand dollars' worth of flesh and bone and muscle that belonged to Maryland planters. If they were caught, the eleven runaways would be whipped and sold South, but she—she would probably be hanged.

They tried to sleep during the day but they never could wholly relax into sleep. She could tell by the positions they assumed, by their restless movements. And they walked at night. Their progress was slow. It took them three nights of walking to reach the first stop. She had told them about the place where they would stay, promising warmth and good food, holding these things out to them as an incentive to keep going.

When she knocked on the door of a farmhouse, a place where she and her parties of runaways had always been welcome, always been given shelter and plenty to eat, there was no answer. She knocked again, softly. A voice from within said, "Who is it?" There was fear in the voice.

She knew instantly from the sound of the voice that there was something wrong. She

---

Drawing Conclusions
6 **Making Inferences**
Why has Tubman been in the vicinity of the plantation for days? Why was this necessary?
She is selecting slaves to take with her. Considering dangers, Tubman probably looks for people with courage, strength, will to be free, and special skills.

7
Author's effective description of Tubman's soft, husky voice as a ''murmur borne on the wind'' allows reader to imagine its quality.

8
''Ashcake and salt herring'' are corn bread (made in an open fire; thus the ash) and fish (preserved with salt) that the fugitives take along for food.

9
Word *conducted* is used because Harriet Tubman is ''conducting'' (leading her ''passengers'') from stop to stop on Underground Railroad.

10
Theme. Tubman's motive is to help slaves know freedom. Most of her charges have been slaves all their lives.

11
Characterization. Tubman, committed to helping her people know freedom, hides her own doubts and remains outwardly strong for others. Reader begins to see her strength.

They Called Her Moses **421**

In discussing the Underground Railroad with students, you might want to explain the origins of the term. The metaphor was first used in print in the early 1840s. After the term Underground Railroad was used, other railroad comparisons were made. The escaping slaves were called passengers; the homes that sheltered them were called stations; those who guided them were called conductors. Ask students if they can think of other railroad terms that could be used metaphorically in connection with the runaway slaves. For example, what might *tickets, berths, caboose, sleeper car,* or *reservations* refer to?

12

Figurative language. Tubman hopes nourishment for their souls will take place of physical nourishment for a while.

13   Summarizing
What is contradictory about Tubman's actions? She must calm her runaways so they can function but instill fear to motivate them to keep going.

14

Quaker: member of the Christian Society of Friends, founded in England about 1650.

15

Tubman tries to convince runaways they will reach freedom; knows strong faith required to continue despite fatigue, hunger, doubt, fear.

16

Inference. Reader can imagine fugitives' depressed and skeptical attitude since they were turned away at last stop.

17   Finding Cause and Effect
Why do the fugitives hide? For safety and to cushion impact of seeing eleven desperate faces when door opens.

18

Suspense. Tubman can never be sure door of next rest stop will be open to her group. Break in sentence adds to feeling of uncertainty about reception.

---

said, "A friend with friends," the password on the Underground Railroad.

The door opened, slowly. The man who stood in the doorway looked at her coldly, looked with unconcealed astonishment and fear at the eleven disheveled runaways who were standing near her. Then he shouted, "Too many, too many. It's not safe. My place was searched last week. It's not safe!" and slammed the door in her face.

She turned away from the house, frowning. She had promised her passengers food and rest and warmth, and instead of that there would be hunger and cold and more walking over the frozen ground. Somehow she would have to instill courage into these eleven people, most of them strangers, would have to feed them on hope and bright dreams of freedom instead of the fried pork and corn bread and milk she had promised them.

They stumbled along behind her, half dead for sleep, and she urged them on, though she was as tired and as discouraged as they were. She had never been in Canada, but she kept painting wondrous word pictures of what it would be like. She managed to dispel their fear of pursuit, so that they would not become hysterical, panic-stricken. Then she had to bring some of the fear back, so that they would stay awake and keep walking though they drooped with sleep.

Yet during the day, when they lay down deep in a thicket, they never really slept, because if a twig snapped or the wind sighed in the branches of a pine tree, they jumped to their feet, afraid of their own shadows, shivering and shaking. It was very cold, but they dared not make fires because someone would see the smoke and wonder about it.

She kept thinking, eleven of them. Eleven thousand dollars' worth of slaves. And she had to take them all the way to Canada. Sometimes she told them about Thomas Garrett, in Wilmington. She said he was their friend even though he did not know them. He was the friend of all fugitives. He called them God's poor. He was a Quaker and his speech was a little different from that of other people. His clothing was different, too. He wore the wide-brimmed hat that the Quakers wear.

She said that he had thick white hair, soft, almost like a baby's, and the kindest eyes she had ever seen. He was a big man and strong, but he had never used his strength to harm anyone, always to help people. He would give all of them a new pair of shoes. Everybody. He always did. Once they reached his house in Wilmington, they would be safe. He would see to it that they were.

She described the house where he lived, told them about the store where he sold shoes. She said he kept a pail of milk and a loaf of bread in the drawer of his desk so that he would have food ready at hand for any of God's poor who should suddenly appear before him, fainting with hunger. There was a hidden room in the store. A whole wall swung open, and behind it was a room where he could hide fugitives. On the wall there were shelves filled with small boxes—boxes of shoes—so that you would never guess that the wall actually opened.

While she talked, she kept watching them. They did not believe her. She could tell by their expressions. They were thinking, New shoes, Thomas Garrett, Quaker, Wilmington—what foolishness was this? Who knew if she told the truth? Where was she taking them anyway?

That night they reached the next stop—a farm that belonged to a German. She made the runaways take shelter behind trees at the edge of the fields before she knocked at the door. She hesitated before she approached the door, thinking, suppose that he, too, should refuse shelter, suppose— Then she thought, Lord, I'm going to hold steady on to You and You've got to see me through—and knocked softly.

▶ She heard the familiar guttural[3] voice say, "Who's there?"

She answered quickly, "A friend with friends."

He opened the door and greeted her warmly. "How many this time?" he asked.

"Eleven," she said and waited, doubting, wondering.

He said, "Good. Bring them in."

He and his wife fed them in the lamplit kitchen, their faces glowing, as they offered food and more food, urging them to eat, saying there was plenty for everybody, have more milk, have more bread, have more meat.

They spent the night in the warm kitchen. They really slept, all that night and until dusk the next day. When they left, it was with reluctance. They had all been warm and safe and well-fed. It was hard to exchange the security offered by that clean, warm kitchen for the darkness and the cold of a December night. ◀

Harriet had found it hard to leave the warmth and friendliness, too. But she urged them on. For a while, as they walked, they seemed to carry in them a measure of contentment; some of the serenity and the cleanliness of that big, warm kitchen lingered on inside them. But as they walked farther and farther away from the warmth and light, the cold and the darkness entered into them. They fell silent, sullen, suspicious. She waited for the moment when someone of them would turn mutinous. It did not happen that night.

Two nights later she was aware that the feet behind her were moving slower and slower. She heard the irritability in their voices, knew that soon someone would refuse to go on.

She started talking about William Still and the Philadelphia Vigilance Committee.[4] No one commented. No one asked any questions. She told them the story of William and Ellen Craft and how they escaped from Georgia. Ellen was so fair that she looked as though she were white, and so she dressed up in a man's clothing and she looked like a wealthy young planter. Her husband, William, who was dark, played the role of her slave. Thus they traveled from Macon, Georgia, to Philadelphia, riding on the trains, staying at the finest hotels. Ellen pretended to be very ill—her right arm was in a sling, and her right hand was bandaged, because she was supposed to have rheumatism. Thus she avoided having to sign the register at the hotels, for she could not read or write. They finally arrived safely in Philadelphia, and then went on to Boston.

No one said anything. Not one of them seemed to have heard her.

She told them about Frederick Douglass, the most famous of the escaped slaves, of his eloquence, of his magnificent appearance. Then she told them of her own first vain effort at running away, evoking the memory of that miserable life she had led as a child, reliving it for a moment in the telling.

But they had been tired too long, hungry too long, afraid too long, footsore too long. One of them suddenly cried out in despair, "Let me go back. It is better to be a slave than to suffer like this in order to be free."

She carried a gun with her on these trips. She had never used it—except as a threat. Now as she aimed it, she experienced a feeling of guilt, remembering that time, years ago, when she had prayed for the death of Edward Brodas, the Master, and then not too long afterward had heard that great wailing cry that

---

3. **guttural** (gŭt′ər-əl): a reference to the man's German language, which uses many guttural sounds—that is, sounds produced in the back of the throat.

4. **Philadelphia Vigilance Committee:** a committee of citizens who offered assistance to slaves who had escaped. William Still, a free black man, was secretary of the Committee.

19 Analyzing
Why does Petry repeat "have more"? To stress generosity of German couple.

20
Imagery. Petry uses contrasting images to depict group starting out in high spirits and then faltering as they go farther from German couple's house.

21 Drawing Conclusions
Why do you think Tubman tells them this story? To motivate group, to encourage them with information that other slaves have overcome obstacles and succeeded.

22
Douglass (1817–1895) was born a slave in Maryland and escaped from slavery to the North in 1838. Three years later he began attracting attention as lecturer for the abolitionist cause.

23
Inference. Although she does not say so directly, Tubman's story implies that the group's current sufferings are worthwhile in order to escape slavery. Tubman shares her personal story to encourage group.

24
Repetition of "too long" emphasizes discomfort and danger runaways endured.

Harriet Tubman refers to Thomas Garrett as a Quaker. You might want to explain to students that the Quakers (also known as The Society of Friends) are a Christian religious group that began in the 1600s in England. In the 1750s, Quakers denounced slavery in the United States and, thereafter, played important roles in the abolition movement. According to the Quakers, each "friend" or believer holds the light of God within and has no need for priests or clergy, not even in ceremonies and rituals.

25 Expressing an Opinion
Are you surprised when Tubman threatens one of the fugitives with gun? Responses will vary. Some may think action goes against her concern for human dignity, freedom; others may view it as logical extension of her commitment to succeed. Petry gives explanation in next paragraph.

26
Use to answer **study question 3b,** p. 427.

27
Theme. Tubman's belief in importance of freedom to individuals and her knowledge that freedom is not easily won are evident in this statement.

28
Tubman takes an almost parental role, encouraging them and enforcing discipline.

29
That the group waits for her to continue shows they know she has their best interests at heart.

30
In Underground Railroad terminology, fugitives were called "freight."

came from the throats of the field hands, and knew from the sound that the Master was dead.

One of the runaways said, again, "Let me go back. Let me go back," and stood still, and then turned around and said, over his shoulder, "I am going back."

25 She lifted the gun, aimed it at the despairing slave. She said, "Go on with us or die." The husky low-pitched voice was grim.

He hesitated for a moment and then he joined the others. They started walking again.

26 She tried to explain to them why none of them could go back to the plantation. If a runaway returned, he would turn traitor, the master and the overseer would force him to turn traitor. The returned slave would disclose the stopping places, the hiding places, the cornstacks they had used with the full knowledge of the owner of the farm, the name of the German farmer who had fed them and sheltered them. These people who had risked their own security to help runaways would be ruined, fined, imprisoned.

27 She said, "We got to go free or die. And freedom's not bought with dust."

This time she told them about the long agony of the Middle Passage on the old slave ships, about the black horror of the holds, about the chains and the whips. They too knew these stories. But she wanted to remind them of the long, hard way they had come, about the long hard way they had yet to go. She told them about Thomas Sims, the boy picked up on the streets of Boston and sent back to Georgia. She said when they got him back to Savannah, got him in prison there, they whipped him until a doctor who was standing by watching said, "You will kill him if you strike him again!" His master said, "Let him die!"

28 Thus she forced them to go on. Sometimes she thought she had become nothing but a voice speaking in the darkness, cajoling, urging, threatening. Sometimes she told them things to make them laugh, sometime she sang to them, and heard the eleven voices behind her blending softly with hers, and then she knew that for the moment all was well with them.

She gave the impression of being a short, muscular, indomitable woman who could never be defeated. Yet at any moment she was liable to be seized by one of those curious fits of sleep, which might last for a few minutes or for hours.[5]

29 Even on this trip, she suddenly fell asleep in the woods. The runaways, ragged, dirty, hungry, cold, did not steal the gun, as they might have, and set off by themselves, or turn back. They sat on the ground near her and waited patiently until she awakened. They had come to trust her implicitly, totally. They, too, had come to believe her repeated statement, "We got to go free or die." She was leading them into freedom, and so they waited until she was ready to go on.

Finally, they reached Thomas Garrett's house in Wilmington, Delaware. Just as Harriet had promised, Garrett gave them all new shoes, and provided carriages to take them on to the next stop.

By slow stages they reached Philadelphia, **30** where William Still hastily recorded their names, and the plantations whence they had come, and something of the life they had led in slavery. Then he carefully hid what he had written, for fear it might be discovered. In 1872 he published this record in book form and called it *The Underground Railroad.* In the foreword to his book he said: "While I knew the danger of keeping strict records, and while

5. **sleep . . . hours:** When Harriet was about thirteen, she accidentally received a severe blow on the head from a two-pound weight that an overseer was hurling at a man trying to escape. After the accident, Harriet frequently lost consciousness. When this happened, she could not be roused until the episode passed of its own accord.

Twenty-Eight Fugitives Escaping from the Eastern Shore of Maryland.
Illustration from *Underground Railroad* by William Still (1872).

Picture Collection, The Branch Libraries, The New York Public Library

I did not then dream that in my day slavery would be blotted out, or that the time would come when I could publish these records, it **31** used to afford me great satisfaction to take them down, fresh from the lips of fugitives on the way to freedom, and to preserve them as they had given them."

William Still, who was familiar with all the **32** station stops on the Underground Railroad, supplied Harriet with money and sent her and her eleven fugitives on to Burlington, New Jersey.

Harriet felt safer now, though there were danger spots ahead. But the biggest part of her **33** job was over. As they went farther and farther north, it grew colder; she was aware of the wind on the Jersey ferry and aware of the cold damp in New York. From New York they went on to Syracuse, where the temperature was even lower.

In Syracuse she met the Reverend J. W. Loguen, known as "Jarm" Loguen. This was the beginning of a lifelong friendship. Both Harriet and Jarm Loguen were to become friends and supporters of Old John Brown.[6]

From Syracuse they went north again, into a colder, snowier city—Rochester. Here they almost certainly stayed with Frederick Douglass, for he wrote in his autobiography: "On one occasion I had eleven fugitives at the same time under my roof, and it was necessary for them to remain with me until I could collect sufficient money to get them to Canada. It was the largest number I ever had at any one time, and I had some difficulty in providing so many with food and shelter, but, as may well be imag-

6. **John Brown:** a famous white abolitionist (1800–1859). He was hanged for leading an attack on the federal arsenal at Harper's Ferry, Virginia, in order to get arms to start a slave uprising.

VISUAL CONNECTIONS
About the Artwork
We do not know if the engraver was actively involved with the Underground Railroad, and heard firsthand accounts, or if he worked from Still's notes. Still does not identify the artist in his book. You may ask students to examine the engraving carefully and decide if the artist captured the details and mood of an escape like the one Petry describes.

31
While interviewing one escapee, Still discovered the brother he had not seen since childhood.

32
Stations: hidden rest and help stops along route of Underground Railroad.

33
Conflict. The fugitives, although making good progress, must now face bitter Northeast winter.

They Called Her Moses **425**

TRANSPARENCY 31

Literary Elements
Distinguishing Between Facts and Opinion – asks students to differentiate between facts and opinions in nonfiction.

34
Fugitives become pioneers by carving out a place to live in Canada.

35 Finding Details
In what ways does Tubman continue to be a leader once the group reaches its destination? Tubman does not merely deliver fugitives to Canada. With great dedication, she teaches them and helps them build new lives.

36 Finding Details
What features of their new home do the fugitives dislike? The climate is harsh and cold; land is bleak and barren.

37 Finding Details
What rights does Tubman enjoy in Canada? She can work for pay, run for office, get an education, own a home, choose where to live.

38
Characterization. That she made journey twice a year for six years is reason we read her story today. Tubman's life was dedicated to the ideal of freedom.

READING CHECK
1. Sunday (p. 419).
2. Almost a month (p. 426).
3. Two trips a year (p. 426).
4. Returned slave would be forced to reveal the escape route (p. 424).
5. *The Underground Railroad* (p. 424).

ined, they were not very fastidious in either direction, and were well content with very plain food, and a strip of carpet on the floor for a bed, or a place on the straw in the barnloft."

Late in December, 1851, Harriet arrived in St. Catharines, Canada West (now Ontario), with the eleven fugitives. It had taken almost a month to complete this journey; most of the time had been spent getting out of Maryland.

That first winter in St. Catharines was a terrible one. Canada was a strange, frozen land, snow everywhere, ice everywhere, and a bone-biting cold the like of which none of them had ever experienced before. Harriet rented a small frame house in the town and set to work to make a home. The fugitives boarded with her. They worked in the forests, felling trees, and so did she. Sometimes she took other jobs, cooking or cleaning house for people in the town. She cheered on these newly arrived fugitives, working herself, finding work for them, finding food for them, praying for them, sometimes begging for them.

Often she found herself thinking of the beauty of Maryland, the mellowness of the soil, the richness of the plant life there. The climate itself made for an ease of living that could never be duplicated in this bleak, barren countryside.

In spite of the severe cold, the hard work, she came to love St. Catharines, and the other towns and cities in Canada where black men lived. She discovered that freedom meant more than the right to change jobs at will, more than the right to keep the money that one earned. It was the right to be elected to office. In Canada there were black men who were country officials and members of school boards. St. Catharines had a large colony of ex-slaves, and they owned their own homes. They lived in whatever part of town they chose and sent their children to the schools.

When spring came she decided that she would make this small Canadian city her home—as much as any place could be said to be home to a woman who traveled from Canada to the Eastern Shore of Maryland as often as she did.

In the spring of 1852, she went back to Cape May, New Jersey. She spent the summer there, cooking in a hotel. That fall she returned, as usual, to Dorchester County, and brought out nine more slaves, conducting them all the way to St. Catharines, in Canada West, to the bone-biting cold, the snow-covered forests—and freedom.

She continued to live in this fashion, spending the winter in Canada, and the spring and summer working in Cape May, New Jersey, or in Philadelphia. She made two trips a year into slave territory, one in the fall and another in the spring. She now had a definite crystallized purpose, and in carrying it out, her life fell into a pattern which remained unchanged for the next six years.

Reading Check

1. On what day of the week did the slave owners usually discover that slaves were missing?
2. How long did it take the slaves to make the trip from Maryland to Canada?
3. How many trips between Maryland and Canada did Harriet Tubman make each year?
4. Why wouldn't she allow a slave to go back after starting the trip?
5. What was the name of the book in which the stories of the escaping slaves were recorded?

CLOSURE
Ask students to explain why Harriet Tubman is compared to Moses and to discuss Tubman's reasons for being involved in the Underground Railroad. Have them also identify the hardships involved in her work.

EXTENSION AND ENRICHMENT
Students of all abilities should be able to read Petry's book *Harriet Tubman, Conductor on the Underground Railroad* and report on highlights of the **biography.**

Some students might like to write poems about the heroic deeds of Harriet Tubman as described in "They Called Her Moses."

After recalling the stories of heroism Tubman told to restore morale, the class might like to compile its own scrapbook or tape recording of inspirational tales.

For Study and Discussion

Analyzing and Interpreting the Selection

1. Moses was the great Biblical hero who led the Israelites out of slavery in Egypt. Moses took his people on a long, perilous journey and brought them to the "Promised Land." How was Harriet Tubman another Moses?

2. The forbidden spiritual "Go Down, Moses" was a code song used by Harriet to announce her presence. What other signals did Harriet use to announce that she had returned?

3a. In what ways did Harriet keep hope alive in her group and instill courage in them? **b.** Why did she have to tell them, "Go on with us or die?"

4. The Underground Railroad, of course, was really not a railroad at all, and it was not literally "underground." Railroad terminology was part of the code. **a.** From what you've read here, tell what a "station" on the railroad was. **b.** In what sense was Harriet a "conductor" on the railroad?

5. "Freedom's not bought with dust," Harriet told her band of fugitives. What price did all these people, including Harriet, pay in order to purchase freedom?

Focus on Biographical Report

Identifying a Main Idea

People's lives consist of thousands of details and events. In order to focus your biographical report, you need to develop a **main idea.** The main idea in "They Called Her Moses," for example, is that Harriet Tubman needed courage and determination to lead her bands of fugitive slaves to freedom.

Reread the notes for the writing assignments on pages 412 and 418, or make notes on a new subject for a biographical report. Use your notes to develop a specific main idea. Then state this idea as clearly as you can in one or two sentences. Save your writing.

About the Author

Ann Petry (1911–   )

Ann Petry was born in Connecticut. She attended the University of Connecticut and Columbia University. Petry has been a pharmacist, a reporter, an advertising salesperson, and an editor. *The Street* (1946) was the first novel by an African American woman to address the experiences of African American women in urban areas. One critic described Petry's writing in this way: "Her novels protest against the entire society which would contrive to make any individual less than human, or even less than he can be." In addition to novels, Petry has written biographies, short stories, and poems. Her works include *Legends of the Saints* (1970) and *Miss Muriel and Other Stories* (1971).

Cub Pilot on the Mississippi

MARK TWAIN

A hundred years ago many boys living along the Mississippi dreamed of becoming steamboat pilots. One of them was the famous American writer, Mark Twain, who realized his ambition. In this excerpt from Life on the Mississippi, *Twain recalls events from his days as an apprentice to a riverboat pilot. What impression do you get of Twain from his attitude toward these events?*

1 When I was a boy, there was but one permanent ambition among my comrades in our village on the west bank of the Mississippi River. That was to be a steamboatman. We had transient[1] ambitions of other sorts, but they were **2** only transient. When a circus came and went, it left us all burning to become clowns; the first minstrel show that ever came to our section left us all suffering to try that kind of life; now and then we had a hope that, if we lived and were **3** good, God would permit us to be pirates. These ambitions faded out, each in its turn; but the ambition to be a steamboatman always remained.

4 I first wanted to be a cabin boy, so that I could come out with a white apron on and shake a tablecloth over the side, where all my old comrades could see me; later I thought I would rather be the deckhand who stood on the end of the stage plank with the coil of rope in his hand, because he was particularly conspicuous.

Boy after boy managed to get on the river. The minister's son became an engineer. The

1. **transient** (trăn'shənt): temporary; passing.

MOTIVATIONAL SUMMARY

When Mark Twain was young, he served as an apprentice to many pilots on the Mississippi River, but none was as mean and malicious as Brown. Twain refrained from hitting Brown only because he believed it to be a Federal offense for a cub to strike or threaten a pilot on duty, but when Brown threatened his brother, Twain could no longer control his temper.

PRESENTATION

Because of Twain's rich vocabulary and his occasionally complex sentence structure, eighth-grade students probably will benefit from a spirited oral reading of this selection. You might want to preface the reading by a discussion of

doctor's and the postmaster's sons became
5 "mud clerks";[2] the wholesale liquor dealer's son became a barkeeper on a boat; four sons of the chief merchant, and two sons of the county judge, became pilots. Pilot was the grandest position of all. The pilot, even in those days of trivial wages, had a princely salary—from a hundred and fifty to two hundred and fifty
6 dollars a month, and no board to pay. Two

2. **mud clerks:** the lowest of several clerks who assisted the purser, the officer in charge of financial accounts. A mud clerk was paid very little.

Rounding a Bend on the Mississippi,
The Parting Salute (1866) by
Currier and Ives. Lithograph.

months of his wages would pay a preacher's salary for a year. Now some of us were left disconsolate. We could not get on the river—at least our parents would not let us.

So, by and by, I ran away. I said I would never come home again until I was a pilot and could come in glory.

During the two or two and a half years of my
7 apprenticeship I served under many pilots, and had experience of many kinds of steamboatmen and many varieties of steamboats. I am to this day profiting somewhat by that experience; for in that brief, sharp schooling, I got personally and familiarly acquainted with about all the different types of human nature

5
Twain uses jargon here and throughout narrative to convey **atmosphere** of the river and riverboat life.

6
No board to pay: room and meals provided as part of job.

7   Summarizing
What is an apprenticeship?
Study of a particular skill or trade; on-the-job training.

VISUAL CONNECTIONS
About the Artists
American lithographers Nathaniel Currier (1813–1888) and James Merritt Ives (1824–1895) produced inexpensive lithographs which showed many scenes that interested the American public. Their printed images dealt with the popular culture of the day and were very affordable. They hung in modest as well as affluent homes and sold for five to twenty-five cents.

About the Artwork
At the beginning of the nineteenth century, the Mississippi Valley was considered the frontier. Pictures of the river and of steamboats were very popular. The pictures were often stock pictures, portraying encounters that did not actually happen. This shows the steamers *Queen of the West, Morning Star,* and an unidentified third ship. The advent of photography diminished the public's interest in lithographs, but today some Currier and Ives prints bring thousands of dollars from collectors.

the attraction of being a riverboat pilot and compare it to the attraction of a modern profession like space exploration. Point out that Twain found that even the most exciting ambition is based on hard work and, frequently, unpleasant experiences. Ask students to consider whether or not the hardships of a glamorous profession are offset by the rewards.

The **For Study and Discussion** questions on p. 435 will be helpful in presenting the basic **conflict** in the story. Use the **Literary Elements** feature in considering the **tone** of the selection and the **Language and Vocabulary** feature in pointing out how Twain uses language to create a strong impression of the **atmosphere** of the river.

8
Characterization. Long string of adjectives tells much about Brown's appearance and personality. Also reveals Twain's attitude toward him.

9
Metaphor. Comparison of soul to lead conveys Twain's heavy sense of dread.

10
Riverboat jargon tells reader that boat had backed out and was now turning to head downriver.

11
Suspense. Twain exaggerates to emphasize tension as Brown looks him over.

12
Cub: an apprentice.

13
Twain's use of jargon again serves to convey sense of **setting** and suggests importance of pilot's position at wheel.

14 Summarizing
Why does Brown resent the cub pilot? He seems to feel Twain is a snobbish and pampered, upper-class boy. Brown may be showing his insecurity.

---

that are to be found in fiction, biography, or history.

The figure that comes before me oftenest, out of the shadows of that vanished time, is
8 that of Brown, of the steamer *Pennsylvania*. He was a middle-aged, long, slim, bony, smooth-shaven, horsefaced, ignorant, stingy, malicious, snarling, fault-hunting, mote³-magnifying tyrant. I early got the habit of coming on watch with dread at my heart. No matter how good a time I might have been having with the off-watch below, and no matter how high my spir-
9 its might be when I started aloft, my soul became lead in my body the moment I approached the pilothouse.

I still remember the first time I ever entered
10 the presence of that man. The boat had backed out from St. Louis and was "straightening **13** down." I ascended to the pilothouse in high feather, and very proud to be semiofficially a member of the executive family of so fast and famous a boat. Brown was at the wheel. I paused in the middle of the room, all fixed to make my bow, but Brown did not look around. I thought he took a furtive glance at me out of the corner of his eye, but as not even this notice was repeated, I judged I had been mistaken. By this time he was picking his way among some dangerous "breaks" abreast the woodyards; therefore it would not be proper to interrupt him; so I stepped softly to the high **14** bench and took a seat.

11 There was silence for ten minutes; then my new boss turned and inspected me deliberately and painstakingly from head to heel for about—as it seemed to me—a quarter of an hour. After which he removed his countenance, and I saw it no more for some seconds; then it came around once more, and this question greeted me: "Are you Horace Bixby's
12 cub?"

3. **mote:** a small particle, such as a speck of dust.

"Yes, sir."

After this time there was a pause and another inspection. Then: "What's your name?"

I told him. He repeated it after me. It was probably the only thing he ever forgot; for although I was with him many months he never addressed himself to me in any other way than "Here!" and then his command followed.

"Where was you born?"

"In Florida, Missouri."

A pause. Then: "Dern sight better stayed there!"

By means of a dozen or so of pretty direct questions, he pumped my family history out of me.

The leads⁴ were going now in the first crossing. This interrupted the inquest.

It must have been all of fifteen minutes—fifteen minutes of dull, homesick silence—before that long horseface swung round upon me again—and then what a change! It was as red as fire, and every muscle in it was working. Now came this shriek: "Here! You going to set there all day?"

I lit in the middle of the floor, shot there by the electric suddenness of the surprise. As soon as I could get my voice I said apologetically: "I have had no orders, sir."

"You've had no *orders!* My, what a fine bird we are! We must have *orders!* Our father was a *gentleman*—and *we've* been to *school.* Yes, *we* are a gentleman, *too,* and got to have *orders!* ORDERS, is it? ORDERS is what you want! Dod dern my skin, *I'll* learn you to swell yourself up and blow around *here* about your dod-derned *orders!* G'way from the wheel!" (I had approached it without knowing it.)

I moved back a step or two and stood as in a

4. **leads** (lĕdz): weights lowered to test the depth of the river.

The Pilothouse of a Mississippi Steamboat (1875). Illustration by Edward W. King.

dream, all my senses stupefied by this frantic assault.

15 "What you standing there for? Take that ice pitcher down to the texas tender![5] Come, move along, and don't you be all day about it!"

The moment I got back to the pilothouse Brown said:

"Here! What was you doing down there all this time?"

"I couldn't find the texas tender; I had to go all the way to the pantry."

"Derned likely story! Fill up the stove."

5. **texas tender:** the waiter in the officers' quarters. The rooms on Mississippi steamboats were named after the states. Since the officers' area was the largest, and since Texas was the largest state at this time, it was called the *texas.*

I proceeded to do so. He watched me like a cat. Presently he shouted: "Put down that shovel! Derndest numskull I ever saw—ain't even got sense enough to load up a stove."

All through the watch this sort of thing went on. Yes, and the subsequent watches were much like it during a stretch of months. As I have said, I soon got the habit of coming on duty **16** with dread. The moment I was in the presence, even in the darkest night, I could feel those yellow eyes upon me and knew their owner was watching for a pretext to spit out some venom on me. Preliminarily he would say: "Here! Take the wheel."

17 Two minutes later: "*Where* in the nation you going to? Pull her down! Pull her down!"

MEETING INDIVIDUAL NEEDS

ESL/LEP • Twain points out the "advantages of pure English grammar" over Brown's dialect. Discuss the following nonstandard patterns and invite students to suggest corresponding standard forms:

1. Substitution of singular for plural verb forms

   "Where *was* you born?" (p. 430)
   "ORDERS *is* what you want!" (p. 430)

2. Substitution of "Dern sight better" for "You should have"

"*Dern sight better* stayed there." (p. 430)

3. Substitution of "set" for "sit"

   "You going to *set* there all day?" (p. 430)

4. Substitution of "ain't" for "don't" / "got" for "have"

   "— *ain't* even *got* enough sense..." (p.

After another moment: "Say! You going to hold her all day? Let her go—meet her! Meet her!"

Then he would jump from the bench, snatch the wheel from me, and meet her himself, pouring out wrath upon me all the time.

George Ritchie was the other pilot's cub. He was having good times now, for his boss, George Ealer, was as kindhearted as Brown wasn't. Ritchie had steered for Brown the season before; consequently, he knew exactly how to entertain himself and plague me, all by the **18** one operation. Whenever I took the wheel for a moment on Ealer's watch, Ritchie would sit back on the bench and play Brown, with continual ejaculations of "Snatch her! Snatch her! Derndest mudcat I ever saw!" "Here! Where are you going *now*? Going to run over that snag?" "Pull her *down!* Don't you hear me? Pull her *down!*" "There she goes! *Just* as I expected! I told you not to cramp that reef. G'way from the wheel!"

So I always had a rough time of it, no matter **22** whose watch it was; and sometimes it seemed to me that Ritchie's good-natured badgering was pretty nearly as aggravating as Brown's **23** dead-earnest nagging.

I often wanted to kill Brown, but this would not answer. A cub had to take everything his boss gave, in the way of vigorous comment and criticism; and we all believed that there was a United States law making it a penitentiary offense to strike or threaten a pilot who was on duty.

Two trips later, I got into serious trouble. Brown was steering; I was "pulling down." My younger brother [Henry] appeared on the hurricane deck, and shouted to Brown to stop at some landing or other, a mile or so below. Brown gave no intimation that he had heard anything. But that was his way: he never condescended to take notice of an underclerk. The wind was blowing; Brown was deaf (although he always pretended he wasn't), and I very much doubted if he had heard the order. If I **19** had had two heads, I would have spoken; but as I had only one, it seemed judicious to take care of it; so I kept still.

Presently, sure enough, we went sailing by that plantation. Captain Klinefelter appeared on the deck, and said: "Let her come around, sir, let her come around. Didn't Henry tell you to land here?"

20 "*No,* sir!"

"I sent him up to do it."

"He *did* come up; and that's all the good it done, the dod-derned fool. He never said anything."

"Didn't *you* hear him?" asked the captain of me.

21 Of course I didn't want to be mixed up in this business, but there was no way to avoid it; so I said: "Yes, sir."

I knew what Brown's next remark would be, before he uttered it. It was: "Shut your mouth! You never heard anything of the kind."

I closed my mouth, according to instruc- **23** tions. An hour later Henry entered the pilothouse, unaware of what had been going on. He was a thoroughly inoffensive boy, and I was sorry to see him come for I knew Brown would have no pity on him. Brown began, straightway. "Here! Why didn't you tell me we'd got to land at that plantation?"

"I did tell you, Mr. Brown."

"It's a lie!"

I said: "You lie, yourself. He did tell you."

Brown glared at me in unaffected surprise; and for as much as a moment he was entirely speechless; then he shouted to me: "I'll attend to your case in a half a minute!"; then to Henry, "And you leave the pilothouse; out with you!"

It was pilot law, and must be obeyed. The boy started out, and even had his foot on the

---

18 Summarizing Analyzing

What does it mean that Ritchie would "play Brown"? What effect does this have on Twain's characterization of Brown? Ritchie impersonates Brown. Twain characterizes him as tyrant but comic; impersonation adds to humorous picture of Brown.

19

Humor. Twain says in roundabout, humorous way that he did not want to get his head knocked off.

20

Hard of hearing, Brown evidently missed Henry's telling him to stop at landing.

21

Characterization. Narrator tells truth even though he knows it will get him in trouble.

22 Analyzing

Why does Brown order the boy to keep quiet? Responses will vary. Brown may think boy is just humiliating him, or may want boy to cover up for him.

23

Suspense. Reader wonders how unaware, "thoroughly inoffensive" Henry will cope with explosive situation he is entering.

431)
5. Substitution of "what for" for "why" and deletion of "are" in present progressive "*What* you standing there *for*?" (p. 431)

The Mississippi River supplied Twain with ample material for his delightful stories. Students may be interested to know that the name *Mississippi* was originally a Native American word; specifically, it is Algonquian for "big river." Encourage students to research the origins of other place names mentioned in the story, such as *Missouri*, *Florida*, and *Pennsylvania*.

Mark Twain's steamboat pilot certificate (1859).
The Mariners Museum

24 upper step outside the door, when Brown, with a sudden <u>access</u> of fury, picked up a ten-pound lump of coal and sprang after him; but I was between, with a heavy stool, and I hit Brown a good honest blow which stretched him out.

I had committed the crime of crimes—I had lifted my hand against a pilot on duty! I supposed I was booked for the penitentiary sure, and couldn't be booked any surer if I went on and squared my long account with this person while I had the chance; consequently I stuck to him and pounded him with my fists a consider-

25 able time. I do not know how long; the pleasure of it probably made it seem longer than it really was; but in the end he struggled free and jumped up and sprang to the wheel: a very natural <u>solicitude</u>, for, all this time, here was this steamboat tearing down the river at the rate of fifteen miles an hour and nobody at the helm! However, Eagle Bend was two miles wide at this bank-full stage, and correspondingly long and deep; and the boat was steering herself straight down the middle and taking no chances. Still, that was only luck—a body *might* have found her charging into the woods.

Perceiving at a glance that the *Pennsylvania* was in no danger, Brown gathered up the big spyglass, war-club fashion, and ordered me out

26 of the pilothouse with more than <u>bluster</u>. But I was not afraid of him now; so, instead of going, I <u>tarried</u> and criticized his grammar. I reformed his ferocious speeches for him and put them into good English, calling his attention to the advantages of pure English over the dialect of the Pennsylvania collieries[6] whence he was <u>extracted</u>. He could have done his part to admiration in a crossfire of mere vituperation,[7] of course; but he was not equipped for this species of controversy; so he presently laid aside his glass and took the wheel, muttering and shaking his head; and I retired to the bench. The racket had brought everybody to

27 the hurricane deck, and I trembled when I saw the old captain looking up from amid the crowd. I said to myself, "Now I *am* done for!" for although, as a rule, he was so fatherly and <u>indulgent</u> toward the boat's family, and so patient of minor shortcomings, he could be stern enough when the fault was worth it.

I tried to imagine what he *would* do to a cub pilot who had been guilty of such a crime as mine, committed on a boat that was guard-

---

6. **collieries** (kŏl′yǝr-ēz): coal mines.
7. **vituperation** (vī-tōō′pǝ-rā′shǝn): abusive language.

VISUAL CONNECTIONS
Exploring the Subject
According to Twain, getting a pilot's license was not difficult. When a cub could get two pilots to approve his performance and sign an application to that effect, he sent it to the United States Inspector. The license was usually granted with no questions asked.

24
Use to answer **study question 3,** p. 435.

25
Tone. The physical **conflict** is serious, but Twain's attitude is not. He humorously relates his feeling of pleasure and describes steamboat "tearing down the river" on its own.

26
Conflict. Now Twain fights *his* way, throwing grammatical punches at Brown instead of physical ones. The pilot is helpless in fighting against the boy's better command of the language. "Retired to the bench" recalls a prizefighter resting between rounds.

27
Hurricane deck: upper deck of the steamboat.

TRANSPARENCY 31

Literary Elements
Distinguishing Between Facts and Opinions – asks students to differentiate between facts and opinions in nonfiction.

28 Summarizing
Analyzing

What does the narrator plan to do? Does his plan seem surprising? Intends to run away. Narrator has been shown to be honest and upright, but he believes—with some justification—he has committed a severe crime.

29

Suspense. Reader, like narrator, is anxious, suspects worst. "Impressively" implies captain spoke authoritatively.

30

Twain uses words a boy might use—"pounded him."

31

Irony. The captain says one thing, probably so others will hear and believe Twain has been severely reprimanded, but means another. He is glad of boy's "great crime."

32

Metaphor. Boy feels like emancipated slave because Brown seemed like slave master.

---

deep[8] with costly freight and alive with passen-
28 gers. Our watch was nearly ended. I thought I
would go and hide somewhere till I got a
29 chance to slide ashore. So I slipped out of the
pilothouse, and down the steps, and around to
the texas door, and I was in the act of gliding
within, when the captain confronted me! I
dropped my head, and he stood over me in
silence a moment or two, then said impressively: "Follow me."

I dropped into his wake; he led the way to
his parlor in the forward end of the texas. We
were alone now. He closed the afterdoor, then
moved slowly to the forward one and closed
that. He sat down; I stood before him. He
looked at me some little time, then said: "So
you have been fighting Mr. Brown?"

I answered meekly: "Yes, sir."

"Do you know that that is a very serious
matter?"

"Yes, sir."

"Are you aware that this boat was plowing
down the river fully five minutes with no one at
the wheel?"

"Yes, sir."

"Did you strike him first?"

"Yes, sir."

"What with?"

"A stool, sir."

"Hard?"

"Middling, sir."

"Did it knock him down?"

"He—he fell, sir."

"Did you follow it up? Did you do anything
32 further?"

"Yes, sir."

---

8. **guard-deep:** The *guard* of a ship is an extension of the deck. In this case, it refers to a wooden frame protecting the paddle wheel.

"What did you do?"

"Pounded him, sir."
30
"Pounded him?"

"Yes, sir."

"Did you pound him much? That is,
severely?"

"One might call it that, sir, maybe."
31
"I'm deuced glad of it! Hark ye, never mention that I said that. You have been guilty of a
great crime; and don't you ever be guilty of it
again, on this boat. *But*—lay for him ashore!
Give him a good sound thrashing, do you
hear? I'll pay the expenses. Now go—and mind
you, not a word of this to anybody. Clear out
with you! You've been guilty of a great crime,
you whelp!"[9]

I slid out, happy with the sense of a close
shave and a mighty deliverance, and I heard
him laughing to himself and slapping his fat
thighs after I had closed his door.

When Brown came off watch he went
straight to the captain, who was talking with
some passengers on the boiler deck, and
demanded that I be put ashore in New
Orleans—and added: "I'll never turn a wheel
on this boat again while that cub stays."

The captain said: "But he needn't come
round when you are on watch, Mr. Brown."

"I won't even stay on the same boat with him.
One of us has got to go ashore."

"Very well," said the captain, "let it be
yourself," and resumed his talk with the
passengers.

32 During the brief remainder of the trip I
knew how an emancipated slave feels, for I was
an emancipated slave myself.

---

9. **whelp:** a puppy or cub; here, a disrespectful young
man.

PORTFOLIO ASSESSMENT
Life on the Mississippi is an autobiographical reminiscence that Twain wrote over a period of several years. Interested students may want to read and respond to the book in a manner of their choosing. Suggest options such as artwork, speeches, reflective or informative essays, and dramatizations. After they have completed their reading, discuss with students the form their responses will take and how they will be assessed. (See *Portfolio Assessment and Professional Support Materials* for additional information on student portfolios.)

Reading Check

1. Why did Twain want to be the cabin boy or the deckhand on a steamboat?
2. Which position on a steamboat was considered to be the grandest of all?
3. Why was it essential for Twain to obey Brown's orders?
4. What was considered the most serious crime on a steamboat?
5. What advice did the captain give Twain?

For Study and Discussion

Analyzing and Interpreting the Selection

1. Twain tells a story in this part of his recollections. At the heart of the story is a conflict between two very different people. **a.** What was the conflict? **b.** How did the captain settle it?

2. Brown seemed to be furious at Twain the first time they met. Why do you think the old pilot disliked the young cub so much?

3. Why did Twain finally attack Brown?

4. People seem to enjoy reading about a conflict between an underdog and a bully–when the underdog wins. **a.** Were your sympathies with the cub or with Brown? **b.** With whom did the captain sympathize?

Literary Elements

Recognizing the Writer's Tone

Tone is the attitude a writer takes toward a subject. Tone can be serious, humorous, sarcastic, affectionate, and so on.

The events that Twain narrates here are certainly unpleasant. Yet the overall effect is not heavy and tragic because of the tone of the writing—the attitude that Twain takes toward these events.

Twain begins by itemizing the ambitions of
1 his childhood comrades on page 428. What details here would make a reader smile?

Brown is clearly a bully and a villain. Yet a reader has to smile at his conflict with the cub. Look again at the first description of Brown on page 430. The sentence has twelve adjectives and one noun describing Brown. The first few adjectives seem unbiased; *middle-aged, long, slim, smooth-shaven.* Even *bony* and *horsefaced* might be considered neutral. But then the list builds to a comic crescendo: *ignorant, stingy, malicious, snarling, fault-hunting, mote-magnifying.* The final noun, *tyrant,* finishes the list off perfectly. Part of the fun is the exaggeration.
2 We are used to the term *fault-finding.* How does *fault-hunting* differ from that?

3 A *mote* is a tiny speck, a bit of dust. What would a *mote-magnifying* person be like?

4 What is unusual about the way in which the cub humiliates the bully after attacking him? (Have you ever heard of a person using grammar to win a battle?)

5 How would you describe this story's tone?

Language and Vocabulary

Recognizing Jargon

Throughout this selection, Mark Twain uses words drawn from his experiences on a Mississippi steamboat. He refers to mud clerks, pilots, and texas tenders, and to "straightening down" and "pulling down." These words and phrases are examples of *jargon,* the specialized vocabulary of an occupation or field of knowl-
1 edge. What other examples of jargon can you
2 find in the selection? How do they contribute to the feeling Twain creates about his experiences as a cub pilot?

READING CHECK
1. To gain public attention (p. 428).
2. Pilot (p. 429).
3. Pilot was in position of authority (p. 432).
4. To attack a pilot on duty (p. 432).
5. To fight Brown on shore (p. 434).

FOR STUDY AND DISCUSSION
1a. Between bully and underdog, middle age and youth, boss and "slave." **1b.** Sided with Twain.
2. Probably felt threatened by any cub.
3. Brown sprang after Twain's brother.
4a. Probably with cub. **4b.** With cub.

LITERARY ELEMENTS
1. Boys' ambitions romantic; "burned" to join circus; "suffered" for try at minstrels, hoped "God would permit" them to be pirates.
2. "Fault-hunting" is looking for faults, not just noticing them.
3. "Mote-magnifying" person exaggerates small problems.
4. Unusual to find knowledge of grammar helping one win fight.
5. Students may describe tone of story as humorous, nostalgic, or something similar.

LANGUAGE AND VOCABULARY
1. Jargon: *stage plank, below, aloft, off-watch, breaks, abreast the woodyards, pilothouse, watch, hold her, meet her, pilot's cub, mudcat, snag, cramp the reef, hurricane deck, bank-full stage, spyglass, guard-deep, boiler deck.*
2. Creates atmosphere of Mississippi River steamboating; shows Twain's knowledge, enthusiasm for vocation of steamboat pilot.

CLOSURE

Ask students to analyze how Twain establishes humorous **tone** and **atmosphere** through his use of language. Have them discuss the characters' attitudes toward each other.

EXTENSION AND ENRICHMENT

Pairs of students might act out the scene between the boy and captain, concentrating on capturing the boy's nervousness and the captain's repressed glee.

Students may wish to read *The Adventures of* *Tom Sawyer.* Advanced readers may be ready for *Roughing It, A Connecticut Yankee in King Arthur's Court,* or *The Adventures of Huckleberry Finn.* All of these are available in paperback editions.

FOCUS ON BIOGRAPHICAL REPORT

You may want to provide copies of newspapers and magazines in which students can find anecdotes to evaluate, or students might want to focus on anecdotes about people they have researched. Model the process by leading students in an analysis of the anecdote in "Cub Pilot on the Mississippi" in which Twain describes his first meeting with Brown. What does the anecdote reveal about each character?

ABOUT THE AUTHOR

Twain grew up near the Mississippi River and was strongly influenced by it. As a pilot from 1857–1861, Twain kept extensive notebooks about the river; he wrote a series of articles about his experiences for the *Atlantic Monthly* in 1874.

The river is an important motif in *Huckleberry Finn,* considered Twain's best work. Twain started *Huckleberry Finn* in 1876, wrote the first sixteen chapters, and laid the work aside. In 1882, Twain returned to the Mississippi River to write a travel book, *Life on the Mississippi.* Twain then returned to, and finished, the story of young Huckleberry Finn.

LITERATURE AND HISTORY

Making Connections: Activities
You might extend these activities by having students create visual presentations that can then be displayed in the classroom. For **Activity 1,** students could create posters or collages of the water vehicles of the nineteenth century. For **Activity 2,** students could provide illustrations of the passages they select.

Focus on Biographical Report

Using Anecdotes

An **anecdote** is a brief story about a single incident. Your purpose in an anecdote can be to entertain your audience, or you can tell an anecdote to make a serious point. You can find examples of both kinds of anecdotes in Mark Twain's "Cub Pilot on the Mississippi," as well as in James Thurber's "The Dog That Bit People" (page 413). You may find anecdotes useful in a biographical report, especially if they reveal important personality traits of your subject.

Look through recent issues of newspapers and magazines to find two or three brief stories about a celebrity who interests you. Then make notes to evaluate these stories as anecdotes. Do they reveal significant character features? How could you use them in a biographical report about the subject? Save your notes.

About the Author

Mark Twain (1835–1910)

Mark Twain is the pen name of Samuel Langhorne Clemens. The name came from the steamboatmen's cry: "By the mark, twain!" This cry meant that by their *mark* (measure), the river was *twain* (two) fathoms deep, which was a safe depth.

Twain was born in Missouri and lived an adventuresome boyhood, which he later made use of in his novels *The Adventures of Tom Sawyer* and *Adventures of Huckleberry Finn.* For a while, he worked for a newspaper, but he gave up this occupation to apprentice himself to a steamboat pilot on the Mississippi. He stayed on the river until the Civil War brought the steamboats nearly to a standstill. After the war, Twain started his career as a traveler and journalistic humorist in the frontier style. He was soon one of the most popular writers and lecturers in America, perhaps because he showed typical American irreverence for stuffiness and tradition.

Financial difficulties and the deaths of his wife and two daughters caused Twain great unhappiness. This is reflected in the bitter tone of some of his later writings. But he is remembered chiefly for his earlier, comic writings—his Western tales and his two great novels of American boyhood.

Literature and History

The Mississippi River

The Mississippi River has played an important role in American history. The Spanish explorer Hernan de Soto was the first European to travel on the Mississippi in the sixteenth century. The French later claimed the entire Mississippi Valley. The Mississippi became an important transportation and trade route. After 1815, when the steamship *Enterprise* made a trip upstream from New Orleans to Pittsburgh, travel by steamboat became a rapid and efficient means of transportation.

Making Connections: Activities

1. During the nineteenth century, people traveled the Mississippi River on flatboats, keelboats, rafts, and steamboats. Try to find illustrations of these different forms of transportation and explain how they were used.

2. Mark Twain has left a record of his experience as a cub pilot in *Life on the Mississippi.* You might enjoy reading about Mr. Bixby, "a lightning pilot," in Chapter 2. Select passages to read aloud to a group or to the class as a whole.

OBJECTIVES

The overall aim is for students to draw **infer-ences** about the influence Mrs. Flowers has on the young Maya Angelou. For a complete list of objectives, see the **Teacher's Notes**.

VOCABULARY

The underlined words are in the Glossary. Students should be encouraged to listen for the rhythm of Southern speech in the selection.

TEACHING RESOURCES D

Teacher's Notes, p. 72
Reading Check, p. 75
Study Guide, p. 76
Language Skills, p. 81
Building Vocabulary, p. 83
Selection Vocabulary Test, p. 84
Selection Test, p. 85

AV RESOURCES BINDER

Audiocassette 2, Side B

PREREADING FOCUS

The headnote mentions a "life-line" thrown to young Angelou. Tell students to consider as they read the story why the adult Angelou feels she needed a "life-line" and needed to be "uncaged" as a child.

VISUAL CONNECTIONS

Ideas for Writing

In this photograph, a young person holds a small bird, often a symbol of freedom. However, this bird is a canary, a species that is bred in captivity and usually lives without ever tasting freedom. Ask students to write a short essay in which they explore one of the ways that people are kept from being completely free. Suggest that they consider such things as shyness, traditions, political situations, and economics.

I Know Why the Caged Bird Sings

MAYA ANGELOU

1 In this part of her true story, Maya Angelou and her older brother, Bailey, lived
2 with their grandmother in the small rural town of Stamps, Arkansas. As you
read the selection, note how Maya as a young girl felt lonely and unloved until
she met an unusual woman who threw her a "lifeline."

I Know Why The Caged Bird Sings

1
The title, an **allusion** to Paul Laurence Dunbar's poem "Sympathy," catches attention because it intimates an answer to an intriguing question.

2
Stamps is in southwestern Arkansas, east of Texarkana.

17
Mrs. Flowers' words are sophisticated, philosophical.

18
Through speech, meaning of words is created, interpreted, and infused with emotion.

19 Analyzing
Why does Mrs. Flowers ask her to read aloud? Probably to increase her self-confidence and enrich her understanding of literature. Maya's potential is "caged" and must be set free.

20
Figurative language. Exaggeration emphasizes her earnest determination never to abuse Mrs. Flowers' trust.

21
Setting. Mrs. Flowers' home seems to be as much an expression of her character as are her clothes and manner.

22
Use to answer **study question 2,** p. 442.

23
Sometimes these are called proverbs, maxims, or adages.

17 sibly no one can. But bear in mind, language is man's way of communicating with his fellow-man and it is language alone which separates him from the lower animals." That was a totally new idea to me, and I would need time to think about it.

▶ "Your grandmother says you read a lot. Every chance you get. That's good, but not good enough. Words mean more than what is **18** set down on paper. It takes the human voice to infuse them with the shades of deeper meaning."

I memorized the part about the human voice infusing words. It seemed so valid and poetic. ◀

She said she was going to give me some **19** books and that I not only must read them, I must read them aloud. She suggested that I try to make a sentence sound in as many different ways as possible.

"I'll accept no excuse if you return a book to **20** me that has been badly handled." My imagination boggled at the punishment I would deserve if in fact I did abuse a book of Mrs. Flowers'. Death would be too kind and brief.

The odors in the house surprised me. Somehow I had never connected Mrs. Flowers with food or eating or any other common experience of common people. There must have been an outhouse, too, but my mind never recorded it.

The sweet scent of vanilla had met us as she opened the door.

"I made tea cookies this morning. You see, I had planned to invite you for cookies and **23** lemonade so we could have this little chat. The lemonade is in the icebox."

It followed that Mrs. Flowers would have ice on an ordinary day, when most families in our town bought ice late on Saturdays only a few times during the summer to be used in the wooden ice cream freezers.

She took the bags from me and disappeared through the kitchen door. I looked around the room that I had never in my wildest fantasies **21** imagined I would see. Browned photographs leered or threatened from the walls and the white, freshly done curtains pushed against themselves and against the wind. I wanted to gobble up the room entire and take it to Bailey, who would help me analyze and enjoy it.

"Have a seat, Marguerite. Over there by the table." She carried a platter covered with a tea towel. Although she warned that she hadn't tried her hand at baking sweets for some time, I was certain that like everything else about her the cookies would be perfect.

They were flat round wafers, slightly browned on the edges and butter-yellow in the center. With the cold lemonade they were sufficient for childhood's lifelong diet. Remembering my manners, I took nice little ladylike bites off the edges. She said she had made them expressly for me and that she had a few in the kitchen that I could take home to my brother. So I jammed one whole cake in my mouth and the rough crumbs scratched the insides of my jaws, and if I hadn't had to swallow, it would have been a dream come true.

As I ate she began the first of what we later **22** called "my lessons in living." She said that I must always be intolerant of ignorance but understanding of illiteracy. That some people, unable to go to school, were more educated and even more intelligent than college professors. She encouraged me to listen carefully to what country people called mother wit. That in **23** those homely[6] sayings was couched the collective wisdom of generations.

When I finished the cookies she brushed off the table and brought a thick, small book from the bookcase. I had read *A Tale of Two Cities* and found it up to my standards as a romantic novel. She opened the first page and I heard poetry for the first time in my life.

6. **homely:** ordinary; everyday.

TRANSPARENCIES 28 & 29

Fine Art
Theme: *Ideas and People* – features artworks that show real people, emphasizing their unique characteristics and personalities.

24 "It was the best of times, it was the worst of times . . . ." Her voice slid in and curved down through and over the words. She was nearly singing. I wanted to look at the pages. Were they the same that I had read? Or were there notes, music, lined on the pages, as in a hymnbook? Her sounds began cascading gently. I knew from listening to a thousand preachers that she was nearing the end of her reading, and I hadn't really heard, heard to understand, a single word.

"How do you like that?"

It occurred to me that she expected a response. The sweet vanilla flavor was still on my tongue and her reading was a wonder in my ears. I had to speak.

I said, "Yes, ma'am." It was the least I could do, but it was the most also.

"There's one more thing. Take this book of poems and memorize one for me. Next time you pay me a visit, I want you to recite."

25 I have tried often to search behind the sophistication of years for the enchantment I so easily found in those gifts. The essence escapes but its aura[7] remains. To be allowed, no, invited, into the private lives of strangers, and to share their joys and fears, was a chance **26** to exchange bitter wormwood[8] for a cup of mead with Beowulf[9] or a hot cup of tea and milk with Oliver Twist. When I said aloud, "It is a far, far better thing that I do, than I have ever done . . . "[10] tears of love filled my eyes at **27** my selflessness.

On that first day, I ran down the hill and into the road (few cars ever came along it) and had

the good sense to stop running before I reached the Store.

27 I was liked, and what a difference it made. I was respected not as Mrs. Henderson's grandchild or Bailey's sister but for just being Marguerite Johnson.

28 Childhood's logic never asks to be proved (all conclusions are absolute). I didn't question why Mrs. Flowers had singled me out for attention, nor did it occur to me that Momma might have asked her to give me a little talking to. All I cared about was that she had made tea cookies for *me* and read to *me* from her favorite book. It was enough to prove that she liked me.

---

7. **aura** (ôr′ə): an atmosphere; a general feeling or quality.
8. **wormwood:** a bitter-tasting plant.
9. **Beowulf:** the hero of an old Anglo-Saxon epic. In this epic, people drink mead, a sweet drink made with honey.
10. **"It is . . . than I have ever done":** The speech is from *A Tale of Two Cities* by Charles Dickens. The narrator of this novel imagines that the hero says these words as he heroically goes to die on the guillotine so that another man can live.

VISUAL CONNECTIONS
Exploring the Subject
The outside world has ceased to exist for this child absorbed in a book. The photographer has caught the mood of quiet concentration with which the author may have taken "a hot cup of tea and milk with Oliver Twist."

24
Tone. Angelou's poetic **descriptions** and excited questions convey wonder she feels because of Mrs. Flowers' readings.

25
The author's love for literature, expressed in her own writing, shows that early influence was beneficial and lasting.

26
Allusion. References to Beowulf and Oliver Twist indicate she has become acquainted with many literary works since lessons with Mrs. Flowers.

Finding Details
27 Analyzing
What identity does Mrs. Flowers like for her? Why is this important to her? Being herself. Gives her feeling of self-worth. After Mrs. Flowers shares food, her time, her ideas as a friend, the author feels valued as a person with individual worth.

28
Theme. The reason for Mrs. Flowers' taking an interest in her is not really important, but it does matter that this encounter gave the author a sense of self-worth.

Reading Check

1. What work did the narrator do in her grandmother's store?
2. How did she punish herself for errors in judgment?
3. What food did the family have only at Christmas?
4. What complaint did teachers have about the narrator's schoolwork?
5. What "assignment" did Mrs. Flowers give her before she left?

For Study and Discussion

Analyzing and Interpreting the Selection

1. In this part of her autobiography, Maya Angelou tells about a place and a person that were important in her childhood. The place was the Store. She compares the Store to a "Fun House of Things." **a.** What does she say the Store looked like in the morning? **b.** What do these descriptions tell you about her feelings for the Store?

2. The important person in Maya's childhood was Mrs. Flowers. How did Mrs. Flowers teach her to have compassion for other people in her first "lesson in living"?

3. How did Mrs. Flowers show that she "liked" and "respected" Maya?

4. Maya eventually grew up to become a well-known writer. What details in this story show that Mrs. Flowers probably awakened her love of language?

5. Maya compares herself to an old biscuit. **a.** What beautiful fruit does she compare Mrs. Flowers' skin to? **b.** What do these two comparisons tell you of Maya's feelings about herself and Mrs. Flowers?

About the Author

Maya Angelou (1928–   )

Maya Angelou was born in St. Louis, Missouri, and grew up in Stamps, Arkansas. She lived in San Francisco for a while and studied to become a professional dancer and an actress. She toured Europe and Africa in a production of *Porgy and Bess* for the State Department. She also worked in the civil-rights movement for Dr. Martin Luther King, Jr., and wrote for newspapers in Egypt and Ghana.

Angelou has written about her own life and feelings as an African American woman in the twentieth century in four autobiographical books, beginning with *I Know Why the Caged Bird Sings* (1970), which was nominated for a National Book Award. She took the title of the work from a poem called "Sympathy" by the African American poet Paul Laurence Dunbar. Like Dunbar, Angelou identified with the songbird that sings because it wants to be free. In 1972 her book of poems *Just Give Me a Cool Drink of Water 'fore I Diiie* was nominated for a Pulitzer Prize. She has also written a number of plays, screenplays, television productions, and magazine articles and made several recordings, including *The Poetry of Maya Angelou*. A recent book is *Wouldn't Take Nothing for My Travels* (1993). In 1993 she recited her poem "On the Pulse of Morning" at President Clinton's inauguration.

A Book-Writing Venture

KIM YONG IK

In this autobiographical essay, Kim Yong Ik tells us that English was his third language—he had begun studying it while he was in high school in Korea. He was determined to master English and have his writing published. As you read this true narrative, put yourself in Kim Yong Ik's place. Would you be able to show so much persistence and determination, or would you give up?

In 1948 when I started to write a novel apart from my regular school work at Florida Southern College, Lakeland, Florida, my roommate in the dormitory told me, "If I were you, I wouldn't waste time in this country. I'll give you five hundred dollars if you publish one book in America. Breaking into that racket is nearly impossible even for an American writer who has mastered his own language." I was far from a master of English, but I didn't listen to him inside. I had studied English literature during the Second World War when it was a most unpopular subject to take up in the Orient, but I wanted to study it. Once in America, I wanted to write so much that I refused to accept the fact that my English was far from being adequate to write a novel. I put in three hours early every morning writing a book.

1 The language problem that I was attacking loomed larger and larger as I began to learn more. When I would describe in English certain concepts and objects enmeshed in Korean emotion and imagination, I became slowly **2** aware of nuances,[1] of differences between two languages even in simple expression. The remark "Kim entered the house" seems to be simple enough, yet, unless a reader has a clear visual image of a Korean house, his under-

standing of the sentence is not complete. When a Korean says he is "in the house," he may be in his courtyard, or on his porch, or in his small room! If I wanted to give a specific picture of entering the house in the Western sense, I had to say "room" instead of house—sometimes. I say "sometimes" because many Koreans entertain their guests on their porches and still are considered to be hospitable, and in the Korean sense, going into the "room" may be a more intimate act than it would be in the English sense. Such problems! That is merely an example. My Florida friends tried to help.

After three years in Florida, I moved to the University of Kentucky to continue my book-writing venture. During a holiday season when I was hired by the library to wax some leather-bound books, for fifty cents an hour, **3** I often daydreamed that some day I would have my book published and bound in that shining, aro-**4** matic leather. I was all by myself in the Precious Books section upstairs. While working with the bindings with my hands full of grease and wax, I would read aloud from a book of poetry open before me. Reading poetry did not require me **5** to turn pages often. I also loved the rhythmical voice in it. Each time my reading was interrupted because with dirty hands I could not turn the page immediately, I was frustrated, as though a phonograph record got stuck in a

---

1. **nuances** (nōō-äns′əs): slight variations.

Kim Yong Ik, born in Korea, attended college in the United States. His greatest dream was to write a novel in English and have it published, despite the fact that English was his third language. For more than six years he developed his skills by writing daily and reading extensively.

The product of those six years was a novel that he sent to many publishers, only to have it rejected again and again. Then one day as he sat dejectedly listening to music and watching the falling snow, he had a "strange fantasy" from which came a story. The first of his many publications was born.

6

Allusion. Quotation is last line of Robert Frost's "The Road Not Taken." In the poem, the line suggests that the speaker's decision to follow the lesser traveled of two roads has made a significant difference in his life.

7

It is not unusual for a book to be rejected many times before a publisher agrees to publish it.

8 Drawing Conclusions

Why was author embarrassed? Express agent knew that author had not yet had his book accepted by a publisher. Author may have imagined that agent thought less of him because his book was not published yet.

9

Japan occupied Korea from 1904 to 1945, when Korea became an independent country.

10

Suspense. The agent's words build suspense by suggesting that the author, too, may die before achieving his goal.

11

Diction. Author's use of the word *ritual* suggests that he was as faithful to his routine as some people are to religious observance.

12

Becoming fluent in a language requires knowledge of how that language is spoken as well as how it is written. Spoken language is often less formal, including more idioms and slang, and is more fluid than written language.

13 Making Inferences

Why was author fired? Trying to memorize poems as he worked made author less efficient doing his job.

scratch on a recording of my favorite song. As I was reading Robert Frost's "The Road Not Taken,"[2] I saw the librarian in charge of the section standing right behind me. I knew that she would chide me or even dismiss me, for the library was strict about student workers reading during their work hours. I couldn't look up at her to say hello. I saw her dry hand reach for the book, as though she would take it away; instead, her fingers turned the page for me to go on, and she left the room without saying a word! I was deeply moved as I finished the **6** poem—"And that has made all the difference."

I did go on to finish writing my book. In 1953 when I enrolled in the Writers Workshop of the University of Iowa, I had been writing fiction for six years and had completed one novel. I started to send it to various publishers in New York.

I had to send it by railway express and had to pay return postage. This amounted to nearly five dollars for each mailing. Since it took about **7** a month for the rejected manuscript to reach me, this turned out to be a regular monthly expense. I would walk to the outskirts of Iowa City to the railroad station to save the bus fare that would help pay for mailing the manuscript. The railway express man was quite curious about the mysterious package that kept reappearing, and finally he asked me what was in it.

I explained to him, and he told me there was an old man in Iowa City who kept on mailing his manuscript about every month, just as I did.

Still I appeared so often that finally I was **8** embarrassed whenever I met the express agent. We got to know each other rather well. By this time, he knew that Korean was my mother **9** tongue; Japanese my second (I had learned this under the Japanese occupation); and English my third (I started to learn English during my

2. **"The Road Not Taken":** a famous poem about making choices. See page 471.

high school days in Korea). One day I asked him what had become of the old man and his **10** manuscript, and he said "That fellow's manuscript always came back but he is now dead."

I kept up the game of mailing and receiving my novel manuscript, as well as several short stories. I felt I was making some progress in mastering the English language even if my collection of rejection slips seemed to shout otherwise. As days and seasons passed, I became more desperate. I read and wrote harder than before. Even on the train on the way to Maine **11** to work for a family for the summer, I kept up my morning ritual of three hours of writing. By day, I read stories for their children, enjoying the rhythm of the English language. At night, I stayed up late writing. Word got around that the Korean "liked to sleep with his light on."

I returned to school that fall only to write. My landlady in Iowa City would complain that I did not leave the room on the weekend so she could properly clean my room, and further remarked that she wouldn't like her boy to go abroad just to stay in a room always. I listened **12** to her advice only to learn living language.

I would walk around with a night watchman or with janitors on night duty, and from them I would have free lessons of English—by listening. When I went to work at the University Hospital cafeteria across the Iowa River, I used to copy a poem or two on a slip of paper to read on the way. In the cafeteria I kept the slip of paper hidden under the counter and tried to memorize it while serving food. Of course, I **13** was fired after two weeks.

I actually cared very little about a degree, so there was very small satisfaction in academic success. I wanted to have one story accepted. I was beginning to feel that perhaps this would never happen. I had only my many rejection slips to contemplate—after so many years of labor.

One Saturday it was snowing really hard outside. I was filled with self-doubt and wondered how in the world I had acquired the fantastic idea that I could write the drama of human emotion in fiction in a second language—no, in my third. I was feeling so dejected that I went out and spent nearly all my money on a record player. At least I could have music. Then I borrowed a record of Anthony Vivaldi's[3] *Four Seasons* from the library and played it over and over that day, not even stopping to eat.

14 As I sat listening and watching the falling snow, I had a strange fantasy. I imagined that I saw a pair of Korean wedding shoes walking away from me in the snow. I followed the shoes in my mind, but I was always behind the figure who wore them, watching the back of the silk brocade shoes and the white muslin socks. The **15** silken wedding shoes walked on and on toward the distant hills. I wanted to discover the person who wore the shoes, but she and her shoes wouldn't turn so I could see her. I heard my heart beat as I ran after the footmarks not to lose sight of the beautiful shoes, fearing that the snow might be wetting the finest silk.

I thought that if only I could see the elusive owner of these shoes, then I could write a real story! I came out of my reverie and got up determined to do just that. I went out.

By then I had begun to feel the effects of my day's fast, so my first stop was the corner grocery store. I went to the back to see the butcher who greeted me with a cheering "Merry Christmas" and a few words of encouragement.

I asked for a few slices of sandwich meat. (After my extravagances with my manuscripts and the impulsive purchase of the record player, there wasn't much left for food.)

I was surprised when the butcher took out a huge hunk of meat, and I reminded him "only

3. **Vivaldi:** Antonio Vivaldi (c. 1675–1743), a Venetian composer known chiefly for his concertos.

a few slices, please." But he quickly wrapped it up and marked it twenty cents. I was sure that this was really about two dollars' worth of meat and I asked, "Is this really only twenty cents?"

He answered, "Yes, sir."

When I went to pay the cashier, she looked closely at the package and then at me, but she accepted the twenty cents without comment.

After that, whenever I returned to the butcher, the package of meat seemed to grow even larger but the price was still twenty cents. Because of this kindness of the butcher, I had a high protein diet for the month and a half when I was writing my story of "The Wedding Shoes."

In my story, the butcher in a Korean valley is a very kind man who would give a very generous amount whenever a poor shoemaker's daughter came in with too little money. I wrote the story as if seen through the eyes of the butcher's son. While chasing the coveted shoes **16** in my mind, I tried to capture the rhythm of my own language in English writing and tried not to take a chance of any misunderstanding by putting everything in concrete terms. Whenever I found it difficult to describe a certain scene, I had my usual temptation to delete it. But by this time I knew better than "to glide over" any scene or word that belonged in my **17** work; more often than not, the thorny word or passage that does pose a language problem is the one that breathes pulsing life into the story.

When I completed "The Wedding Shoes," I gave it to Paul Eagle, the director of the Writers Workshop, but he was busy at the time and gave it to Margarette Young, author of *The Angel of the Forest*. She called me up and said with great enthusiasm, "This is wonderful. You must send this story to *Harper's Bazaar* right away." I did.

A few weeks later I found a letter in my mail box instead of the familiar ugly yellowed package. Alice Morris, the literary editor of *Harper's Bazaar*, wrote me that she wanted to print my

14
Imagery. The concrete images in this passage—wedding shoes, snow, silk brocade, white muslin socks—work together to create a beautiful dreamlike picture.

15
Symbol. Shoes and woman symbolize story author has been trying to write but that continues to elude him.

16
Author uses his knowledge of another language to his advantage in writing this story.

17
Metaphor. Compares difficult writing task to thorns that are hard to handle.

story and would pay me $250. It was a time of great joy, but I had no one to share it with.

Soon after my story appeared, *London Bazaar* cabled me: "Offer twenty-five guineas[4] for 'The Wedding Shoes.'" About the same time, an amateur ballet group in Iowa City planned a ballet based on my story—so, on an electric light pole in front of the grocery store was posted an advertising poster: "A Ballet: The Silken Brocade Shoes."

After my stories had been accepted by *Mademoiselle, Botteghe Oscure,*[5] and *The New Yorker,* I returned to my homeland after spending ten years in America. Besides my teaching at a university, I continued to write in English as well as in my native tongue. In 1960 I revisited the United States to see my old friends. I was happy to find the librarian at the Precious Books section when I dropped in at the University of Kentucky. She remembered my reading poetry during my work hours and even the incident of turning the page for me. She asked me what I had been doing. When I mentioned what I had written for magazines, that I'd had juvenile books published by Little, Brown, and that an adult novel of mine was to be published by Alfred A. Knopf, she did not believe me until she looked them up in the publication index of the library. Then she was so happy for me that she invited me for dinner in a Chinese restaurant, and later we drove around in that bluegrass country.

18 That winter, I received a Christmas gift from Little, Brown—a copy of my first juvenile fiction book, written in Florida and Kentucky—*The Happy Days,* bound in beautiful leather.

---

4. **guineas** (gĭn'ēz): a former coin of Great Britain, worth one pound and one shilling, at that time a considerable sum.
5. ***Botteghe Oscure*** (bŏ-tā'gā ŏs-kōō'rā): a magazine published in Rome from 1949 to 1960, which featured articles on commerce as well as contemporary literature.

dents who speak two or more languages fluently to discuss their experiences in switching from one language to another. What kinds of problems do they deal with? What do they like best about speaking more than one language?

Ask students to list the obstacles Kim Yong Ik had to overcome and the specific ways that the people around him helped. Also, ask students to speculate on why he achieved his dream.

Students might like to find and read other works by Kim Yong Ik or other nonfiction works that deal with the struggles of immigrants to this country. Other students might enjoy an oral reading of Frost's poem "The Road Not Taken."

Focus on Reading

Understanding the Role of Anecdotes

An **anecdote** is a brief story about a single incident that is told to make a point. Most anecdotes are drawn from personal experience. Anecdotes appear in different kinds of writing. Often they are humorous.

In "A Book-Writing Venture" Kim Yong Ik tells several anecdotes, each of which makes a point that you the reader are expected to grasp. What, for example, is the point of the anecdote about reading Frost's poem aloud in the library? Locate another anecdote in the essay and explain what you think is the point of the anecdote.

Focus on Biographical Report

Organizing a Biographical Report

Chronological order is usually a good way to organize your material in a biographical report. When you use this method, you present events as they happened. You can also help your reader to understand the connections of events and ideas in your report by using **transitional words and phrases.** Notice, for example, how Kim Yong Ik uses these transitions in the third paragraph of "A Book-Writing Venture": *after, during, when, often, while, each time,* and *as* (see page 443).

Write an outline like the one shown on this page for a biographical report of three or four paragraphs. You might get some ideas for the subject and details of your report by skimming recent issues of newspapers and magazines or by looking at a family album. Save your notes.

I. Introduction
   A. Attention grabber: _____
   B. Statement of main idea: _____
II. Body
   Facts/Anecdotes: _____
   _____
   _____
   _____
   _____
III. Conclusion
   A. Restatement of main idea: _____
   B. Summary of person's importance:
   _____

About the Author

Kim Yong Ik (1920–   )

Kim Yong Ik was born in South Korea. He attended college in Japan, where he studied English. At twenty-eight, he came to the United States to study English literature at Florida Southern College. He also attended the University of Kentucky and participated in a creative writing program at Iowa Writers' Workshop. His short stories have been published in *Harper's Bazaar, The New Yorker,* and *The Atlantic.* He has won a number of awards, and many of his works have been translated into several languages. Some of his best-known books are *Love in Winter* (1962), *Blue in the Seed* (1964), and *The Shoes from Wing San Valley* (1970). A Book-Writing Venture" concerns the writing of "Wedding Shoes," the story that first convinced him of his potential as a writer. Kim Yong Ik is now an English teacher at the University of Korea.

Students might look for their favorite anecdotes from the selection. Encourage students to support their ideas with details from the story. For example, students might say that the point of the anecdote about reading Frost's poem aloud is that a single kind gesture can make a significant difference in another person's life.

You may want to use this activity to review different kinds of outlines with your students. They can practice topic and sentence outlines or formal and informal outlines. Remind students that the facts and anecdotes they include in their outlines should directly support their main ideas. Students might want to organize their facts and anecdotes in chronological order.

OBJECTIVES
The overall aim is for students to analyze details in a biographical selection.

PRESENTATION
You might read the passage from *I Know Why the Caged Bird Sings* aloud while students listen with their textbooks closed. As they listen, students should make mental note of details they hear. Then students can open their books, read the selection silently, and answer the questions that follow. Engage students in a discussion of the effectiveness of Maya Angelou's details in this excerpt.

FOCUS ON Reading and Critical Thinking

USING DETAILS IN BIOGRAPHY

*D*etails are the flesh and blood of biography. It is through vivid, specific details that we come to "see" another person. Read (or reread) the following passage carefully, and then answer the questions that follow. In this passage from *I Know Why the Caged Bird Sings* (page 439), Maya Angelou uses vivid details to re-create an important person in her childhood.

Mrs. Bertha Flowers was the aristocrat of Black Stamps. She had the grace of control to appear warm in the coldest weather, and on the Arkansas summer days it seemed she had a private breeze which swirled around, cooling her. She was thin without the taut look of wiry people, and her printed voile dresses and flowered hats were as right for her as denim overalls for a farmer.

Her skin was a rich black that would have peeled like a plum if it snagged, but then no one would have thought of getting close enough to Mrs. Flowers to ruffle her dress, let alone snag her skin. She didn't encourage familiarity. She wore gloves too.

I don't think I ever saw Mrs. Flowers laugh, but she smiled often. A slow widening of her thin black lips to show even, small white teeth, then the slow effortless closing.

When she chose to smile on me, I always wanted to thank her. The action was so graceful and inclusively benign.

She was one of the few gentlewomen I have ever known, and has remained throughout my life the measure of what a human being can be.

Using Details in Biography

1 ■ List three details about Mrs. Flowers' physical appearance.
   1. _____
   2. _____
   3. _____

2 ■ List three details about Mrs. Flowers' clothing.
   1. _____
   2. _____
   3. _____

3 ■ What details in the second paragraph show you that Mrs. Flowers was a formal person? _____

4 ■ What detail in the third paragraph helps to make the author's feelings about Mrs. Flowers vivid and concrete?
   _____
   _____

OBJECTIVES
The overall aim is for students to write a biographical report that presents information about a person's life, character traits, and achievements.

PRESENTATION
To introduce writing based on research, you might initiate a class discussion on specific occasions when students do research (to find out about family history, to explore career options, to plan an itinerary for a vacation). Tell students

that the aim of a research report is to inform. When they are doing the research, they are informing themselves and learning more about their subjects. When they write and publish their reports, they will be communicating what they have learned to others. You may want to work

FOCUS ON *Writing*

HOLT WRITER'S WORKSHOP

This computer program provides help for all types of writing through guided instruction for each step of the writing process. (Program available separately.)

See *Elements of Writing, Second Course,* Chapter 6, for more instruction on report writing.

WRITING A BIOGRAPHICAL REPORT

A **biographical report** is an informative paper that presents information about a person's life, character traits, and achievements. Now that you have studied some of the elements of this kind of paper, you will have the chance to write a biographical report on a subject of your choice.

Prewriting

1. Brainstorm for subjects for your report by skimming recent issues of magazines, looking at family albums, and talking about celebrities with a small group of classmates. Ask yourself these questions about possible subjects for your report:

- What is interesting or special about this person?
- What has the person achieved or accomplished?
- Can I get the information I need about this person?

[See **Focus** assignment on page 412.]

2. After you have identified a subject, start to gather details. Your **sources** of information can include some or all of the following:

- books
- interviews
- letters
- encyclopedias
- newspaper articles
- photograph albums
- magazine articles
- photo essays

Try to consult at least three different sources about your subject. While you gather

details, fill out a chart like the one shown here.

Details Chart for a Biographical Report
Date and Place of Birth: _____
Education: _____
Job/Profession: _____
Achievements/Special Awards: _____
Family: _____
Opinions/Outlook on Life: _____
Statements/Quotations: _____   _____

As you consult your sources, remember to keep an accurate record showing where you found each piece of information about your subject. For each note you take, list the title of the source, the author, the date and place of publication, and the page number where you found the item. If your teacher requires you to create a "Works Cited" list for a biographical report, you will need all this information later. [See **Focus** assignment on page 417.]

3. Identify a **main idea** for your report, and state this idea as clearly as you can in one or two sentences. Stating a main idea will help you to evaluate and organize your details. For example, here is the way you might state the main idea for a report on poet Gwendolyn Brooks: "Throughout her career, Gwendolyn Brooks has used her life experience as an African American to suggest new angles of vision for the readers of her

WRITING A BIOGRAPHICAL REPORT
Students should consider their audiences as they plan their biographical reports. Remind students that people who read research reports usually want to come away from the report with a better understanding of the topic. As students explore their subject and write their report, they should consider their readers' interest in and previous knowledge of their subject. Students might experiment with fresh, unusual approaches to their subject to try to take their readers beyond what they may already know.

Prewriting
You may want to ensure that students have access to the format for a "Works Cited" page before they begin consulting their sources. Also, students might benefit from a lesson on taking notes—summarizing, paraphrasing, and quoting directly.

with your school librarian to arrange an orientation to the school library. You might also plan to teach a library skills unit in conjunction with this writing project. Also, give students time outside of class to engage in other kinds of research such as interviewing, watching videotapes, and consulting family members.

Writing
Point out to students that they will probably discover they are unable to include in their reports everything that they learned about their subject. However, if students are unsure about the relevance of some details, they should include them in their early drafts. During the revising stage, students can delete or change details that do not contribute to the main idea of their essay. Also, remind students that a good title often provides an effective attention-getter. Encourage students to experiment with titles that entice the reader and relate to the main ideas, or angles, of their report.

Evaluating And Revising
Remind students that informative writing should be objective. Encourage students to analyze their word choices for loaded words and words with misleading connotations. Also remind students not to present misleading portraits by including only facts and anecdotes that create a one-sided impression. Students can work in small groups using the Checklist for Evaluation and Revision.

poems." [See **Focus** assignment on page 427.]

4. Think about how you might use **anecdotes,** or brief stories about a single incident, in your report. The best anecdotes are both entertaining and revealing, in that they show important personality traits about your subject.

Writing

1. You will normally find that **chronological** or **time order** is the most convenient way to organize your material in a biographical report. Be sure to use **transitional words and phrases** to clarify the relationships of events and ideas.

   I. Introduction
      A. Attention grabber
      B. Statement of main idea
  II. Body: Facts/Anecdotes in chronological order
 III. Conclusion
      A. Restatement of main idea
      B. Summary of person's importance

2. You may wish to follow an **outline** such as the one below as you write your first draft: [See **Focus** assignment on p. 447.]

Evaluating and Revising

1. When you have finished the first draft of your report, trade papers with a classmate and ask your partner to give you suggestions about your work. As you exchange comments, take notes about revisions to make your report clearer, more specific, and more interesting.

   Here is an example of how a writer revised a paragraph in a biographical report about Gwendolyn Brooks.

Writer's Model

When
^ Gwendolyn Brooks won the Pulitzer
in 1950
Prize for her book Annie Allen. She
^   ,
became the first black writer to

receive one of America's most famous
                  Three
awards. Several years after this mile-
       ^
                her novel Maud Martha
stone, she published a novel, which
                  ,
Brooks's native city of
was set in Chicago. Both of these
                ^   of

works revealed Brooks's keen insight
                    coming of age for
into the experience of ^ African
                              ^
American women.

2. You may find the following checklist helpful as you revise your report.

Checklist for Evaluation and Revision
✓ Do I capture the reader introduction?
✓ Do I clearly identify the subject of my report and state my main idea?
✓ Have I researched my subject adequately in a number of different sources?
✓ Do I present my information clearly?
✓ Have I checked my facts for accuracy? Have I recorded all my sources?
✓ Do I end with a strong conclusion?

Proofreading and Publishing ᵔᵔ

1. Proofread your report and correct any errors you find in grammar, usage, and mechanics. (Here you may find it helpful to refer to the **Handbook for Revision** on pages 712–755.) Then prepare a final version of your report by making a clean copy.

2. Consider some of the following publication methods for your report:

- submit your report to the school newspaper or magazine
- join with other students to make a portfolio of biographies
- assemble slides, photographs, and other visual aids, and present your report to the class as an illustrated lecture

Portfolio If your teacher approves, you may wish to keep a copy of your work in your writing folder or portfolio.

POETRY

OVERVIEW OF THE UNIT

Poetry is written in a highly metaphorical and evocative language. The purpose of this unit is to help young readers experience the full power of such language. To do so, they must encounter poems that spark a response.

The poems in this unit, all chosen to appeal to young readers, have been grouped into three subsections: **Language and Meaning, Sound and Meaning,** and **Types of Poetry.** The first section opens with May Swenson's "Southbound on the Freeway," a poem about modern freeways and cars as seen by a visitor from outer space. Discussion questions and other activities focus on the use of imagery and point of view. Langston Hughes's "Mother to Son" concerns poverty and the transcendent courage a parent strives to transmit to her child. Exercises focus on the use of diction. "Sugar Poem" by Aurora Levins Morales is about poetry—the process of writing it and its role in the world. After Cathy Song's "Easter: Wahiawa, 1959," which concerns family relationships, comes Emily Dickinson's "I Like to See It Lap the Miles," rich in both imagery and figurative language. Exercises for these poems focus on imagery, metaphor, and simile. The study of figurative language continues with the analysis of "Food" by Victor M. Valle. The section ends with Robert Frost's "The Road Not Taken," which is followed by a **Literary Elements** exercise that explores the use of poetic symbols.

The second section, **Sound and Meaning,** features two dramatic poems, Edgar Allan Poe's "The Raven" and Sir Walter Scott's "Lochinvar." Activities for these poems help students become attuned to the musical effects of rhyme, alliteration, and rhythm.

The final section focuses on **Types of Poetry** and begins with a narrative poem, Robert Service's "The Cremation of Sam McGee." Lyric poetry is studied using William Shakespeare's "When Icicles Hang by the Wall," Elizabeth Coatsworth's "Calling in the Cat," and Simon J. Ortiz's "Speaking." The example of dramatic poetry in this section is "Incident of the French Camp" by Robert Browning. Study questions concern relationships between narrative and dramatic poetry. The section on comic verse includes anonymous limericks, Ogden Nash's light verse, Arthur Guiterman's "On the Vanity of Earthly Greatness," the ever-popular "Casey at the Bat" by Ernest Lawrence Thayer, and Lewis Carroll's "Jabberwocky." Questions and activities for these poems explore the ways poets use language to create humor.

Throughout the unit, activities challenge students to try some of the techniques illustrated in various poems. Writing activities focus on writing a poem.

The unit concludes with **Focus on Reading and Critical Thinking** and **Focus on Writing.** The critical thinking exercise gives students practice at relating sound to meaning in a poem. The writing section guides students through the process of writing a poem—prewriting, writing, evaluating and revising, and proofreading.

OBJECTIVES OF THE UNIT

The aims of the unit are for the student:

◆ To demonstrate a recognition of sound devices, rhythm, and rhyme within selected poems in this unit

◆ To demonstrate understanding of the poet's use of metaphor, simile, figurative language, symbolism, allusion, and sensory details in individual poems in this unit

◆ To identify the mood, setting, and point of view of specific poems in this unit

◆ To prepare an oral reading of a poem

◆ To analyze the poet's choice and ordering of words and phrases within a poem

◆ To paraphrase a stanza of a poem

◆ To write original poetry

CONCEPTS AND SKILLS

The following concepts and skills are treated in this unit:

FOR UNIT PLANNING
- Transparencies 33–37: *Audiovisual Resources Binder*
- *Portfolio Assessment: Professional Support Materials*
- Test Generator
- Mastery Tests: Teaching Resources E, pp. 124, 127, 130
- Analogy Test: Teaching Resources E, p. 132
- Composition Test: Teaching Resources E, p. 133

SELECTION (Pupil's Page)	TEACHING RESOURCES E (page numbers shown below)							AV BINDER
	Teacher's Notes	Reading Check	Study Guide	Language Skills	Building Vocabulary	Selection Vocab. Test	Selection Test	Audio-cassette
POETRY *Introduction* (p. 453)	1							
E.A. Robinson *The Dark Hills* (p. 455)	2							
May Swenson *Southbound on the Freeway* (p. 457)	3		5		7		25	TAPE 3 SIDE A
Langston Hughes *Mother to Son* (p. 461)	9		21	11	13		25	TAPE 3 SIDE A
Aurora Levins Morales *Sugar Poem* (p. 463)	15		16				25	TAPE 3 SIDE A
Cathy Song *Easter: Wahiawa, 1959* (p. 465)	20		21				25	
Emily Dickinson *I Like to See It Lap the Miles* (p. 468)	27		32		29		42	TAPE 3 SIDE A
Victor M. Valle *Food* (p. 470)	31		32		35		42	
Robert Frost *The Road Not Taken* (p. 471)	36		38		40		42	TAPE 3 SIDE A
Edgar Allan Poe *The Raven* (p. 474)	44		47		51	64	66	TAPE 3 SIDE A
Sir Walter Scott *Lochinvar* (p. 482)	53		56	60	63	64	66	TAPE 3 SIDE B
Robert Service *The Cremation of Sam McGee* (p. 486)	68		69				72	
William Shakespeare *When Icicles Hang by the Wall* (p. 492)	73		76		74			
Elizabeth Coatsworth *Calling in the Cat* (p. 494)	75		76		78			
Simon J. Ortiz *Speaking* (p. 495)	80		81				84, 86	TAPE 3 SIDE B
Robert Browning *Incident of the French Camp* (p. 497)	87		89		91		93	
Anonymous *Limericks* (p. 500)	95		98		96		120	

| SELECTION (Pupil's Page) | TEACHING RESOURCES E (page numbers shown below) | | | | | | | AV BINDER |
	Teacher's Notes	Reading Check	Study Guide	Language Skills	Building Vocabulary	Selection Vocab. Test	Selection Test	Audio-cassette
Ogden Nash *The Octopus* (p. 501)	97		98				120	
Ogden Nash *The Panther* (p. 501)	97		98				120	
Ogden Nash *The Rhinoceros* (p. 501)	97		98				120	
Arthur Guiterman *On the Vanity of Earthly Greatness* (p. 502)	101		104				120	
Ernest Lawrence Thayer *Casey at the Bat* (p. 503)	102		104	108	110		120	TAPE 3 SIDE B
Lewis Carroll *Jabberwocky* (p. 506)	112		114	116	118		120	TAPE 3 SIDE B

Experimenting with Sound Effects 481
Controlling Rhythm for Effect 499
Organizing Details 505
Coining Words and Phrases 507

ORAL READING

Using Clues to Interpretation 462
Avoiding Singsong 481
Preparing a Reading of the Poem 491

FOCUS ON READING AND CRITICAL THINKING

Relating Sound to Meaning 509

FOCUS ON WRITING

Writing a Poem 510

TRANSPARENCIES

The following unit support materials with specific correlations to literature selections are available in the **Fine Art and Instructional Transparencies with Teacher's Notes and Blackline Masters** section of your *Audiovisual Resources Binder.*

FINE ART TRANSPARENCIES

Theme: Packing Good Things into Small Packages

33 *Apart From the Crowd,* Mary Close
34 *Tied Ties,* Wayne Thiebaud

READER RESPONSE

35 Consult Your Mood Ring

LITERARY ELEMENTS

36 Sound Effects in Poetry

WRITING PROCESS

37 Writing a Poem

INTRODUCING THE UNIT

Since some young people are wary of poetry, you may want to begin with a high-interest activity inviting personal response and avoiding technical analysis.

For example, you might read aloud "The Cow" by John Ciardi in *Some Haystacks Don't Even Have Any Needles,* Dunning, Lueders, and Smith, eds. (Lothrop, Lee and Shepard). Ask students to contrast this poet's-eye view of a cow with the first paragraph of an encyclopedia entry for "cow." Which description brings the reader closer to the subject? How does the poem provide an experience, rather than a collection of facts? After noting that poems may be about commonplace subjects, ask what makes "The Cow" a poem.

Another introductory activity is to present and discuss two or three poems in which poets express their feelings about what poetry is and how it works. Possibilities include "Poem: A Reminder" by Robert Graves and "The Secret" by Denise Levertov, both in *Zero Makes Me Hungry,* Lueders and St. John, eds. (Scott, Foresman); "Your Poem, Man" by Edward Lueders in *Some Haystacks Don't Even Have Any Needles* (Lothrop, Lee and Shepard); "Ars Poetica" by Archibald MacLeish in *Collected Poems* (Houghton Mifflin) and "Poetry" by Marianne Moore in *Collected Poems* (Macmillan); MacLeish's and Moore's poems are also available in *Major American Poetry,* Louis Untermeyer, ed. (Harcourt Brace Jovanovich). "On Poetry" from Emily Dickinson's 1870 letter to Colonel T. W. Higginson in *The Life and Letters of Emily Dickinson* (Houghton Mifflin) would also provide an interesting point of view. Students might even write their own poetic definitions of poetry.

A final possibility that is especially popular with young people is to bring to class a recording of a favorite popular song that has been selected by the class. Write the lyrics on the board. After listening to the record, students may share their reasons for liking the song enough to enjoy hearing it over and over. Ask students to consider the lyrics apart from the music. Can these lyrics by considered a poem? Can they stand alone without the music? Do they have musical qualities of their own? Use this discussion to lead into the introductory comments on p. 454.

Materials booklet accompanying this program. Specific suggestions are provided for a variety of student projects that may be suitable for inclusion in a portfolio. In addition, copying masters are provided for guides that may be used for evaluation and assessment of student projects.

PORTFOLIO ASSESSMENT

Suggestions for use of portfolios as support for this unit are described in the *Portfolio Assessment and Professional Support*

Student Learning Options

POETRY

1. Changing Diction
After discussing the differences between formal and informal language, ask students to write poems using informal language. Then have students rewrite their poems using formal diction. Divide the class into small groups and ask students to read their poems to their groups and discuss how the changes in diction change the meanings of the poems.

2. Using Different Modes of Expression
Ask students to imagine a creature. Students could then both write a poem and draw a picture of the creature. Collect both, display the pictures, and hand out the poems randomly. Students can then try to match the poems they receive with the corresponding drawings. Afterward, encourage students to discuss which mode of expression was easier for them. Some students will probably find writing easier, while others can draw more easily.

3. Exploring Figurative Language
Students can write riddles using similes and metaphors. For example, a riddle whose solution is "a tomato" could consist of a metaphor—"this red-skinned sac of sun"—and a simile—"is like a vegetable but nevertheless a fruit." Students might enjoy compiling a booklet of such riddles.

4. Explicating Poetry of Frost
Ask students to find and read other nature poems by Robert Frost, such as "Birches." Students could cut pictures from magazines to make collages that reflect the images found in Frost's poems. Students should base their collages on a minimum of five poems.

6. Alphabetizing Alliteration
To help students understand alliteration, ask them to write all the letters of the alphabet vertically on a sheet of paper. Then ask students to write a sentence next to each letter, such as "Brown baby bunnies bounce buoyantly," in which as many words as possible begin with that letter.

7. Using Onomatopoeia to Describe an Experience
Have students think of an experience they have had in which sound played an important role. Students can describe their experiences in a poem using onomatopoeia. Students might begin by listing sounds associated with their experiences and then trying to think of words that reflect the sounds. Have students read their poems aloud and let the class guess what experiences are being described.

8. Hunting Rhymes
Rhyme is an important element of poetry, but it is also found in advertising, popular songs, cheers, and sayings. Have students keep a rhyme journal over the course of a week. In their journals, students should note every example of rhyme that they encounter in their daily lives.

While they are studying this unit, students may be interested in writing their own poems. Students could write poems that imitate the styles of poems in the unit or that illustrate the aspects of poetry emphasized in subsections of the unit, such as **speaker, diction, imagery, figurative language, repetition and rhyme, rhythm,** and the various types of poetry. Suggest that students illustrate their collections, place them in booklet form, and add them to their portfolios. (For more information on student portfolios see the *Portfolio Assessment and Professional Support Materials* booklet in your teaching resources.)

VISUAL CONNECTIONS

About the Artist

The French impressionist painter Claude-Oscar Monet specialized in the seascapes and landscapes that he had grown to love as a youth in Le Havre, France. In the 1870s, along with Renoir, he developed the painterly style of *impressionism*. As illustrated here in Monet's *A Field of Poppies*, impressionism seeks to capture the artist's visual experience rather than photographic detail and accuracy. Reflecting the dominant romantic mood of the age, Monet's paintings are filled with patches of color and shimmering light.

Relating Expression Skills

Discuss how Monet's painting re-creates an impression, or visual image, not realistically but as Monet subjectively perceived it. Begin a class ''impressionistic mural'' in which students re-create on a long strip of butcher block paper visual images from various poems that they read throughout this unit. Good poems for impressionistic illustration include ''The Dark Hills,'' ''The First Spring Day,'' and ''The Road Not Taken.''

Students might write poems of their own describing a portion of the world from a different point of view—that of a small animal (such as a dog, cat, or bird) or something mechanical (such as a toaster, vacuum cleaner, or airplane) that seems to have a life of its own.

TRANSPARENCY 35
Reader Response
Consult Your Mood Ring – invites students to identify and analyze significant words or phrases from a poem.

Creative Writing

Using an Unusual Point of View

In Swenson's poem a speaker looks down at cars on the freeway and describes them as if they were living creatures. Imagine that you are a visitor from outer space. How would you describe the mechanical things you see around you? A radio might be a small, rigid creature that talks and sings in different voices. A subway might be a serpent that screams. A bicycle and its rider might be a creature that moves on two round feet.

Choose an ordinary object or device. Try to think of something that moves or makes noise. In two or three sentences, describe it as though you were a tourist from another planet.

About the Author

May Swenson   (1919–1989)

May Swenson was born in Logan, Utah, but spent most of her life in New York City. She is known for her playful use of language, humor, and careful observation of nature. The poet Howard Moss once said that Swenson "speaks for animals and birds, for astronauts and trees, for statues and cities...." Swenson often played with the shape of poems, arranging lines to suit a poem's subject. She also enjoyed creating poetic riddles to challenge her readers. During her writing career Swenson received many of the country's most important literary honors and awards. Her last book of poetry, *The Love Poems of May Swenson,* was published posthumously in 1991.

Literary Elements

Identifying the Speaker

Identifying the speaker is an important step in understanding a poem's meaning. For example, May Swenson's poem would be difficult to understand if you didn't know that the
1 "tourist" is a visitor from outer space. Who is the speaker in "Paul Revere's Ride" (page 136)?
2 What characteristics has Longfellow given his speaker?

LITERARY ELEMENTS
1. Speaker in "Paul Revere's Ride" is a storyteller, one of the few men still alive who remembers that famous day and year.
2. He knows the smallest details of the day's events from an American's point of view, but of all the men, he names only Paul Revere.

CREATIVE WRITING
As an introduction to this writing exercise, students might enjoy a role-playing activity. With a partner, students can take turns playing the confused space visitor and a helpful earthling who explains the use of different mechanical devices. Having an opportunity to discuss this exercise with a partner should help students generate details and encourage originality.

ABOUT THE AUTHOR
Writing for young and old alike, Swenson specialized in visual detail; many of her poems, however, such as "Southbound on the Freeway," also include serious themes. Her poetry frequently employs wit and sound imagery. Two of her books for young readers are *Poems to Solve* (1966) and *More Poems to Solve* (1971).

The overall aim is for students to analyze the use of diction in Hughes's "Mother to Son" and in Morales' "Sugar Poem." For a complete list of objectives, see the **Teacher's Notes.**

The vocabulary exercise in the **Teacher's Notes** gives students practice in distinguishing between the **denotative** and **connotative** meanings of words.

Tell students that poets sometimes create "word pictures." Focus on images of a stairway and of a springtime scene. Have students speculate about how poets might create "word pictures" of such scenes.

VISUAL CONNECTIONS

Ideas for Writing

Both before and after reading Hughes's poem, ask students to observe closely the stairway pictured in this photograph. Then have them discuss the characteristics of an old wooden stairway such as this one and the "crystal" stairway referred to in the poem, listing characteristics of each on sheets of paper. Perhaps some students will point out that this stairway, although old and surrounded by cracked plaster and peeling paint, has a beauty and character of its own. Other students might point out the warmth, beauty, and individuality of wood (no two pieces of wood have the same grain) as contrasted to the coldness and hardness of crystal. After students have freely shared their ideas about both kinds of stairways, have them write a paper in which they compare and contrast the two stairways and the two different kinds of people they might represent.

Direct students' attention to the photograph on p. 460. Ask students how they feel when they look at this staircase. What makes this hallway look old and run-down? What is the effect of the shadows? Hughes's poem compares life to

such a stairway.

Use the **For Oral Reading** section on p. 462 to help you arrange for an oral presentation of this poem by one or more of your students. Encourage the students to emphasize the language and character of the speaker. Continue

with the study questions and other supplemental activities on p. 462. To check fundamental interpretive skills, you may wish to have each student write responses to the questions.

TEACHING RESOURCES E

Teacher's Notes, p. 9
Study Guide, p. 21
Language Skills, p. 11
Building Vocabulary, p. 13
Selection Test, p. 25

AV RESOURCES BINDER

Audiocassette 3, Side A

PREREADING FOCUS

The introduction points out the importance of diction to poetry. Tell students to notice how the diction of the following two poems evokes specific, concrete images, and ask them to think about how these poetic sentiments might be expressed in prose.

Mother to Son

1
Metaphor. Speaker, a mother talking to her son, compares life to a flight of stairs.

2
Speaker extends **metaphor,** pointing out that the steps she has had to climb have been rough, beset with "tacks," or problems, rather than smooth like "crystal"; **connotations** of *crystal* contrast with connotations of other words.

3 Drawing Conclusions
Why did Hughes place "bare" on a line by itself? Isolating word visually reinforces its meaning, emphasizing the bareness of the speaker's life.

4 Drawing Conclusions
Why does the mother say "don't you turn back"? Because she does not want her son to give up.

5
Characterization. Diction in ll. 15–19 reflects warmth, strength, determination as well as dialectal speech.

6
Repetition of central **metaphor** "frames" poem.

DICTION

Diction refers to a writer's choice of words. Poets choose words for precise effects. They depend on the associations, or *connotations,* of words as well as on their literal meanings, or *denotations.* Consider the phrases "three little pigs" and "three diminutive mammals with long, broad snouts." What is your reaction to the diction in each phrase?

The diction of a poem may be formal or informal. In "Southbound on the Freeway," the speaker refers to "their guts" in line 6. More formal usage would be *entrails.*

Poets may make up words, use unusual word order, or run words together. In "old age sticks" (page 98), E. E. Cummings achieves interesting effects by stretching out words. This freedom with language is called *poetic license.*

Mother to Son

LANGSTON HUGHES

Well, son, I'll tell you:
1 Life for me ain't been no crystal stair.
2 It's had tacks in it,
  And splinters,
  And boards torn up,
  And places with no carpet on the floor— 5
3 Bare.
  But all the time
  I'se been a-climbin' on,
  And reachin' landin's
  And turnin' corners, 10
  And sometimes goin' in the dark
  Where there ain't been no light.
4 So boy, don't you turn back.
5 Don't set you down on the steps
  'Cause you finds it's kinder hard. 15
  Don't you fall now—
  For I'se still goin', honey,
  I'se still climbin',
6 And life for me ain't been no crystal stair. 20

Auditory Learners • The diction in "Mother to Son" is noticeably dissimilar from that in "Sugar Poem." Auditory learners might notice the differences more easily if they hear the poems read aloud, one following the other. You might want to point out word choices in both poems and discuss the differences between the two. Invite each student to find two poems with contrasting styles in diction and to prepare a reading of both for the class.

FOR STUDY AND DISCUSSION

1. To a difficult, shabby, and often dark staircase that she has been steadily climbing.

2. Some parts of staircase have tacks and splinters and torn-up boards (her life's dangers and pains). Some places are bare (perhaps she's been poor), and sometimes the light is out on the stair (she cannot see where she is going or has lost faith or hope). She has reached landings (good times, easier times) and turned corners (unforeseen changes when future was unknown and perhaps frightening).

3. To not give up, to keep moving up through life no matter what obstacles block his way. He must not fall, because it is better to keep going, as she does.

LITERARY ELEMENTS

1. Repetition of word *and* suggests long climb up staircase because it is as if each *and* is a step.

2. By putting "bare" on its own line, speaker emphasizes unadorned, worn-out quality of floor.

3. Spoken, this word would come after pause indicated by the dash after *floor*. It would be noticeably dramatic and emphatic.

4. Lines spoken softly and tenderly include 1, 14, and 18.

FOR ORAL READING

Second pause would receive greater emphasis. Throughout the poem, stress words that describe staircase and any direct advice that the mother gives her son. In an oral presentation, students should lower their voices to reflect sadness or tenderness in ll. 1, 12, 14, 18, and 20. (Interpretations may vary. Encourage students to explain how individual performances reflect each reader's personal understanding of the poem.)

For Study and Discussion

Analyzing and Interpreting the Poem

1. In this poem, a mother talks to her son about her life. What does she compare her life to?

2. What images does the mother use to describe the difficulties she has faced?

3. Although the mother has often been "Where there ain't been no light" (line 13), she is "still climbin' " (line 19). What advice does she give her son?

Literary Elements

Understanding Diction

The language that we use in conversation has a rhythm and a music of its own. "Mother to Son" is an example of how plain speech can be made into poetry.

Langston Hughes uses the natural rhythms of everyday speech to create a poetic effect:

It's had tacks in it,
And splinters,
And boards torn up,
And places with no carpet on the floor—
Bare.

The poet uses these ordinary speech patterns in a careful, deliberate way. How does the repetition of *and* suggest the climb up a long, winding staircase?

The poet puts the word *bare* on a line by itself. What does he want to emphasize? How would you say this line aloud?

Plain speech can be used to suggest strong emotions. Which lines of this poem do you think should be spoken softly and tenderly?

Focus on Writing a Poem

Choosing a Subject

The speaker in Langston Hughes's poem talks to her son about a subject that she knows very well: her own life. When you choose a subject for your own poem, start by thinking about familiar people, objects, events, and experiences. Here are some examples of subjects you might consider:

a favorite relative	an apple
riding your bike	lemonade
a tree in springtime	a pet

Remember that practically anything can be a subject for a poem. It is often easier to write something new and fresh about an unexpected subject (an onion, for example) than about a typically "poetic" topic (such as a sunset).

Make a list of four possible subjects for a poem of your own. Then trade lists with a partner and exchange comments on each other's subjects. Save your notes.

For Oral Reading

Using Clues to Interpretation

Present an oral reading of "Mother to Son," using a conversational tone. Before reading aloud, look carefully at the clues for phrasing within the poem. In the first line, for example, the two commas and the colon indicate pauses. Which of these pauses would you give greater emphasis? Which words in the poem do you think should be stressed? Where would you lower your voice to reflect the speaker's sadness or tenderness?

PRESENTATION
You may want to begin by having students read the footnotes so that they will not be confused when they encounter these Spanish words. In addition to the definitions, students should pay close attention to the pronunciations.

If possible, ask a student who speaks Spanish to model correct pronunciation. Read this poem aloud as students follow in their textbooks. Discuss with students the effect of the Spanish words and their relationship to the subject matter and emotion of the poem.

TEACHING RESOURCES E
Teacher's Notes, p. 15
Study Guide, p. 16
Selection Test, p. 25

AV RESOURCES BINDER
Audiocassette 3, Side A

Sugar Poem

AURORA LEVINS MORALES

As you read this poem, think about how the physical labor of harvesting sugar cane is like the mental exercise of writing poetry. How does the poet see the success of her labors? To what does she compare her final product?

Poetry
is something refined
in your vocabulary,
taking its place at the table
in a silver bowl: essence   5
of culture.

I come from the earth
where the cane was grown.
I know
the knobbed rooting,   10
green spears, heights of
caña°
against the sky,
purple plumed.
I know the backache   15
of the machetero,°
the arc of steel
cutting, cutting,
the rhythm of harvest
leaving acres of sharp spikes   20
that wound the feet—
and the sweet smoke
of the llamarada:°
rings of red fire burning
dark sugar into the wind.   25

My poems grow from the ground.
I know what they are made of:
heavy, raw and green.

Sugar,
you say, is sweet.   30
One teaspoon in a cup of coffee . . .
life's not so bad.

12. **caña** (kä'nyä): Spanish for "cane."   16. **machetero** (mä-chĕ-tä'rō): one who uses a machete, a large heavy knife for cutting vegetation.   23. **llamarada** (yä-mä-rä'thä): blaze of fire.

© Eddie Adams/The Stock Market

Sugar Poem

1
Table sugar is produced from sugar cane through a process known as "refining." Thus, poet compares refined (that is, polished) language to refined sugar.

2 Drawing Conclusions
Who is speaker addressing? Speaker is addressing mainstream culture.

3
Diction. Speaker uses "earth," instead of "place" or "land," to suggest she grows from her home like sugar cane grows from earth.

4 Analyzing
Why does poet repeat word "cutting"? To imitate **rhythm** and sound of sugar cane being cut.

5
Sugar cane fields are set on fire after harvest to burn away remaining stubble.

6
Metaphor. Speaker compares her poems to raw sugar cane.

463

CLOSURE

Ask students to provide brief definitions of diction, **denotation,** and **connotation**—perhaps supporting their definitions with previously discussed examples from Hughes's and Morales' poems.

EXTENSION AND ENRICHMENT

After reading Langston Hughes's poem, students might choose to assume the role of the son and write a letter to the mother explaining how her advice has helped him.

TRANSPARENCIES 33 & 34

Fine Art
Theme: *Packing Good Things into Small Packages* – highlights artworks that are compact expressions of an idea, like a poem.

7

Speaker lists products other than refined sugar that are made from sugar cane.

8 Drawing Conclusions
What does speaker mean in these lines? Poems are not meant to be "sweet."

9

Metaphor. Speaker compares poems to torches, flame throwers, and spears to suggest their power to build, destroy, and change.

Caña, I reply,
7 yields many things:
molasses   35
for the horses,
rum for the tiredness
of the machetero,
industrial
alcohol to cleanse,   40
distil, to burn
as fuel.

8 I don't write my poems
for anybody's sweet tooth.

9 My poems are acetylene° torches   45
welding steel.
My poems are flamethrowers
cutting paths through the world.
My poems are bamboo spears
opening the air.   50
They come from the earth,
common and brown.

45. **acetylene** (ə-sĕt′l-ēn′): highly flammable gas.

For Study and Discussion

Analyzing and Interpreting the Poem

1. Can you think of a poem that the speaker might classify as "refined," like the sugar found in silver bowls?

2. In what ways are the speaker's poems different from the poems written for someone's "sweet tooth"?

3a. To what different things does the speaker compare her poems? **b.** What do all these comparisons suggest?

4. The poet uses several Spanish words in the poem. Try substituting the word *cane* for *caña* in lines 12 and 33. What is lost?

About the Author

Aurora Levins Morales (1954–   )

Aurora Levins Morales was born in Puerto Rico. Her mother taught her to read when she was five years old. She has been writing poetry since she was seven. When she was thirteen, she began keeping a journal and filled four books a year.

In 1976 Levins Morales began publishing both poetry and nonfiction. Her work appears in *Cuentos: Stories by Latinas* (1983), *The Courage to Heal* (1989), and *Reconstructed American Literature* (1990). She has also co-authored with her mother, Rosario Morales, a collection of poetry and prose called *Getting Home Alive* (1986). The book explores the lives of two Puerto Rican women with different backgrounds. Levins Morales now lives in Oakland, California.

The Author Comments on Her Poem

I wrote "Sugar Poem" many years ago in a writing workshop in response to a very complicated assignment that had nothing to do with my life. I like to write about real events and people whose lives move me, and I want my poems to be of use to other people—not just as a decoration, but to make them see things in a new way. Some people think poems have to be hard to understand in order to be good. I think a good poem is one that lets us see the world differently. I grew up loving poetry, but I was fourteen before I saw a poem that was about people like my friends and family. So one way I like to open people's eyes is by putting those people in my poems and using ordinary language. This poem uses images from my childhood in Puerto Rico to express this attitude about poetry.

FOR STUDY AND DISCUSSION

1. Answers will vary. Students might mention poems that include sophisticated or formal **diction.**
2. Answers may vary. Students might point out that the poems are described as being powerful rather than sweet or entertaining.
3a. Raw sugar cane, torches, flame-throwers, and bamboo spears. **3b.** Comparisons suggest that poems are elemental and powerful.
4. Answers will vary. Students might suggest that the substitution affects the **rhythm** and weakens the **theme.**

IMAGERY

We learn about the world through our senses—sight, touch, smell, taste, and hearing. *Imagery* is language that appeals to the senses. Poets use imagery to involve the reader and to convey meaning.

Although imagery can appeal to any of the five senses, it is most often visual. Swenson (page 457) uses visual imagery when she describes the police car as "a five-eyed / one, with a red eye turning / on the top of his head." In a later line she uses the imagery of sound: "They all hiss as they glide." As you read the following poem by Cathy Song, note how she uses imagery to appeal to your senses.

1 Easter: Wahiawa, 1959

CATHY SONG

1

The rain stopped for one afternoon.
Father brought out
his movie camera and for a few hours
we were all together
under a thin film   5
that separated the rain showers
from that part of the earth
like a hammock
held loosely by clothespins.

Grandmother took the opportunity   10
to hang the laundry
and Mother and my aunts
filed out of the house
2 in pedal pushers and poodle cuts,
carrying the blue washed eggs.   15

3 Grandfather kept the children
penned in on the porch,
clucking at us in his broken English

whenever we tried to peek
4 around him. There were bread crumbs   20
stuck to his blue gray whiskers.

I looked from him to the sky,
a membrane of egg whites
straining under the weight
of the storm that threatened   25
to break.

We burst loose from Grandfather
when the mothers returned
from planting the eggs
around the soggy yard.   30
5 He followed us,
walking with stiff but sturdy legs.
We dashed and disappeared
into bushes,
searching for the treasures;   35
the hard-boiled eggs
which Grandmother had been simmering
in vinegar and blue color all morning.

TRANSPARENCY 35

Reader Response
Consult Your Mood Ring – invites students to identify and analyze significant words or phrases from a poem.

PRESENTATION
Explain to students that this poem is divided into two sections. The first section relates a family Easter gathering in which the children hunt for colored eggs. The second section gives background information about Grandfather and remarks on the poet's special feelings for him.

You may want to read aloud the first section of the poem, stopping to point out the poet's use of imagery. Use the study questions, margin annotations, and **Literary Elements** exercise to focus your discussion of the poem.

6
Simile. Compares quail eggs to gigantic pearls.

7 Drawing Conclusions
Why does poet relate parts of Grandfather's past? She respects how hard he has worked through the years.

8
That she and her grandfather skip supper together shows the closeness of their relationship.

FOR STUDY AND DISCUSSION
1. Rain showers, laundry hanging out, threatening storm, soggy yard, sugar cane fields, gardenia hedge, sitting on the porch.
2. Planting gives an impression of nurturing, a gesture of love.
3. Grandmother hanging out laundry, women filing out of house carrying eggs, Grandfather clucking at anxious, peeking children, children dashing around searching for eggs.
4. A feeling of freshness and serenity.
5a. She sees him as a protector and a friend. Respects his hardworking past and wants him to reap rewards of a loving family.
5b. In first section, he detains children while eggs are being hidden and follows them in their search. In second section, poet reveals his past and present lives.

2

When Grandfather was a young boy
in Korea,   40
it was a long walk
to the riverbank,
where, if he were lucky,
6 a quail egg or two
would gleam from the mud   45
like gigantic pearls.
He could never eat enough
of them.

7 It was another long walk
through the sugarcane fields   50
of Hawaii,
where he worked for eighteen years,
cutting the sweet stalks
with a machete. His right arm
grew disproportionately large   55
to the rest of his body.
He could hold three
grandchildren in that arm.

I want to think
that each stalk that fell   60
brought him closer
to a clearing,
to that palpable field
where from the porch
to the gardenia hedge   65
that day he was enclosed
by his grandchildren,
scrambling around him,
for whom he could at last buy
cratefuls of oranges,   70
basketfuls of sky blue eggs.

I found three that afternoon.
By evening, it was raining hard.
8 Grandfather and I skipped supper.
Instead, we sat on the porch   75
and I ate what he peeled
and cleaned for me.
The scattering of the delicate
marine-colored shells across his lap
was something like what the ocean gives   80
the beach after a rain.

For Study and Discussion

Analyzing and Interpreting the Poem

1. Wahiawa is located on the island of Oahu. Which details in the poem give you a vivid picture of the setting?

2. In line 29 why are the mothers said to be "planting the eggs" rather than hiding them?

3. The speaker mentions a home movie camera. What images does she use that suggest movement, as in a movie, rather than a static scene, as in a photograph?

4. In the final lines of the poem, the speaker says that the scattering of shells on grandfather's lap "was something like what the ocean gives / the beach after a rain." What picture does this comparison put in your mind?

5. The speaker never states directly how she feels about her grandfather. **a.** How would you describe her feelings for him? **b.** What parts does the grandfather play in the first and second sections of the poem?

CLOSURE
Ask students to recall their favorite image from Song's poem and to explain why they like it.

EXTENSION AND ENRICHMENT
Students might list memorable things that a grandparent or older relative has done for them. This list may then be used as the basis for an original poem written in the style of "Easter: Wahiawa, 1959."

Literary Elements

Responding to Imagery

Cathy Song uses imagery that appeals to different senses. One of her most vivid images occurs in lines 44–46, when she describes the

1 discovery of the quail eggs. How does she use both color and shape to help you imagine what

2 her grandfather saw? Find another vivid visual image in the poem.

3 Where does the poet appeal to your sense of smell? hearing? Are there any images that appeal to your sense of touch?

4 What do all the images associated with the grandfather suggest about him as a person?

5 How do the images help reveal the importance of the grandfather to his granddaughter?

Focus on Writing a Poem

Exploring Imagery

Imagery is language that appeals to the five senses: sight, sound, smell, taste, and touch. Images are an important tool for a poet in communicating meaning.

Choose *two* of the subjects for a poem identified for the assignment on page 462, or select a different pair of subjects. For each subject make an image chart like the one below. Try to fill in a specific image for each sense. Save your notes.

Subject	Sense	Image
_____	sight	_____
	sound	_____
	smell	_____
	taste	_____
	touch	_____

About the Author

Cathy Song (1955–   )

Cathy Song was born and raised in Honolulu, Hawaii, the daughter of a Chinese mother and a Korean father. She earned her B.A. from Wellesley College in 1981 and her M.A. from Boston University in 1988. Her first book of poetry was *Picture Bride*, from which "Easter: Wahiawa, 1959" is taken. The volume earned Song the prestigious Yale Series of Younger Poets Award in 1982 and was nominated for the National Book Critics Circle Award. The title refers to the practice of mail-ordering brides through photographs; Song's Korean grandmother was one of those who came to America as a mail-order bride. *Frameless Windows, Squares of Light*, her second book of poetry, appeared in 1988. She presently lives and teaches in Honolulu.

LITERARY ELEMENTS
1. Uses contrasting images of gigantic pearls lying in mud.
2. Some other visual images occur in ll. 20–21, 23–25, 54–56, and 78–81.
3. Lines 37–38 appeal to sense of smell, l. 18 appeals to sense of hearing, and ll. 57–58 appeal to sense of touch.
4. He is a good, caring man who loves his family and has worked hard to provide for them.
5. Since speaker presents positive image, reader knows that she adores her grandfather.

FOCUS ON WRITING A POEM
After students have filled in their image charts, you might suggest they ask the following questions about each image: Is it concrete? Is it precise? Is there another image that better expresses this subject? Can I think of a more original image? After students have evaluated their images, encourage them to revise as necessary.

The overall aim is for students to explain how **figurative language** contributes to the effectiveness of selected poems by Dickinson, Valle, and Frost. For a complete list of objectives, see the **Teacher's Notes.**

Write on the chalkboard clichés such as "as loud as thunder" or "as cold as ice." Ask students to think of more original ways to express these ideas. Tell them that good poetry uses original figures of speech to describe experiences.

Ask students whether any of them have ever watched a train's progress through the countryside or ridden on a train. What did the train look like? How did it sound? Tell the class that in her poem Dickinson looks at trains in an unexpected

TEACHING RESOURCES E

Teacher's Notes, p. 27
Study Guide, p. 32
Building Vocabulary, p. 29
Selection Test, p. 42

AV RESOURCES BINDER

Audiocassette 3, Side A

PREREADING FOCUS

The introduction explains that **figurative language** is not factual and points out that two common figures of speech are **similes** and **metaphors.** Tell students to look for two meanings as they read the poems in this section: the literal and the figurative.

I Like to See It Lap the Miles

1

Metaphor. The central metaphor is established by having the train, like a horse, "lap the miles" and "lick the valleys up" as it speeds through them. Note **alliteration** of *l*'s in these two lines.

2 Synthesizing
Keeping in mind that this poem was written in the mid-nineteenth century, why must "animal" stop at tanks to feed? Steam-driven engines of the day had to stop to take on more water.

3

Train has one bright headlight that "peers" at "shanties" (crude shacks) by tracks.

4

"Quarry" has steep sides, which train appears to "pare," or cut, and "crawl between."

FIGURATIVE LANGUAGE

Figurative language is language that is not intended to be understood as factually or literally true. When we say, "March came in like a lion and went out like a lamb," we are speaking figuratively. What we are referring to is a change in weather. Many expressions in everyday language are figurative.

The term *figure of speech* refers to a particular kind of figurative language. Two figures of speech commonly used in poetry are *simile* and *metaphor.* Each figure expresses a likeness between two different things. However, a simile uses a word such as *like* or *as* to express the comparison. In "The Dark Hills" (page 455), Robinson says that "sunset hovers like a sound / Of golden horns." A metaphor identifies two things. Robinson uses a metaphor when he refers to the rays of the sun as *legions*, soldiers marching to battle.

As you read the following poems, look for the figures of speech. Think about how they appeal to your imagination and how they add to your understanding of the poems.

I Like to See
It Lap the Miles

EMILY DICKINSON

This poem describes a train. Yet the speaker never mentions the word train, *and, in fact, seems to be describing an animal. She appears to be looking at this great noisy train from above, watching it as it goes through the New England mountains.*

1 I like to see it lap the miles,
And lick the valleys up,
2 And stop to feed itself at tanks;
And then, prodigious,° step

Around a pile of mountains   5
3 And, supercilious,° peer
In shanties by the sides of roads;
4 And then a quarry pare°

4. **prodigious** (prə-dĭj'əs): huge.

6. **supercilious** (sŌŌ'pər-sĭl'ē-əs): proud and scornful.

8. **pare**: trim or peel away.

You might try reading this poem aloud. Phrase carefully to show units of thought, observing the punctuation and run-on lines to maintain the intended rhythm. Use the study questions and **Literary Elements** exercise to help students see how Dickinson uses **diction, imagery,** and **figurative language** to compare a train to a horse. Point out that Dickinson never mentions the word *train;* the reader must infer her subject.

TRANSPARENCIES 33 & 34

Theme: *Packing Good Things into Small Packages* – highlights artworks that are compact expressions of an idea, like a poem.

To fit its sides, and crawl between,
Complaining all the while   10
5 In horrid, hooting stanza;
Then chase itself down hill

6 And neigh like Boanerges;°
Then, punctual as a star,
Stop—docile and omnipotent°—   15
7 At its own stable door.

13. **Boanerges** (bō'ə-nûr'jēz): any loud, thunderous public speaker.

15. **omnipotent** (ŏm-nĭp'ə-tənt): all-powerful.

For Study and Discussion

Analyzing and Interpreting the Poem

1. The speaker in this poem uses images that seem to describe an animal. What words and phrases help you picture this animal's activities as it moves along?

2. What words and phrases help you picture the animal as something huge and powerful?

3a. What words in the last stanza identify the animal with a horse? **b.** Could it be a horse in the other stanzas? Why or why not?

4. The poet never names what she is describing. What reveals that her subject is a train?

5. This train is both "docile" (manageable) and "omnipotent" (all-powerful) at the same time. What other things can be both docile and omnipotent at the same time?

6. How does the speaker feel about this train?

Literary Elements

Recognizing Metaphors

When you compare two different things by using a word such as *like* or *as,* you are using a **simile:** "Russell is like a lamb"; "Her eyes are like stars"; "The dog is like a devil." When you identify two different things, without using a word such as *like* or *as,* you are using a **metaphor:** "Russell is a lamb"; "Her eyes are stars"; "The dog is a devil."

Metaphors, of course, are not literally, or factually, true. Russell is not really a lamb; her eyes are not really stars; the dog is not really a devil. However, metaphors are very powerful. Like similes, they help us use our imagination to see surprising likenesses between things that are basically different.

In its simplest form, a metaphor says directly that one thing *is* another, different thing. In "Mother to Son" (page 461), the speaker says, "Life for me ain't been no crystal stair." This is a metaphor, even though it is expressed nega-
1 tively. What kind of stairway would you say the
2 mother's life has been? In what ways are life
3 and a stairway alike? What do you think the
mother means when she says her stairway has
4 had "bare" spots in it? What is "the dark"?
Emily Dickinson's poem is built around a
5 metaphor. How would you state the metaphor
in her poem?

5
Onomatopoeia. Phrase "horrid, hooting" imitates the sounds of a train.

6
Simile. Sound of train is compared to that of "Boanerges," an **allusion** to thunderous speakers in New Testament. Train's punctuality is compared to that of stars, the clocks of ancient times.

7 Finding Details

What clues in this stanza make clear the comparison between a horse and a train? "Creature" neighs and has a stable.

FOR STUDY AND DISCUSSION
1. It laps, licks, feeds itself, steps around mountains, peers, crawls, complains, chases itself.
2. It is prodigious, omnipotent, supercilious, loud; it eats up miles and valleys, steps over mountains, cuts quarries.
3a. It neighs and stops at stable door. 3b. Horses do stop and feed and step around obstacles but do not lick or lap food like cats or crawl like snakes.
4. Hooting is a train sound; train cars follow one another downhill like segmented animal.
5. Cars, steam engines, fire, water.
6. Looks with admiration, wonder, humor.

LITERARY ELEMENTS
1. Perhaps a rickety wooden stair, not very pretty.
2. Both are a progression of steps, have a beginning and an end, and are "traveled."
3. Times of deprivation.
4. Times that seemed hopeless; when she could not see ahead.
5. Train is powerful, noisy creature.

Ask students if they have eaten Mexican food. If they have, tell them that according to Victor Valle, they have eaten the earth, moon, and sun. Invite students to think of ways in which some Mexican foods might resemble the earth, moon, or sun. Suggest that as students read this poem, they compare their responses to the poet's.

Many students will be familiar with the Mexican words in this poem, but to ensure comprehension, review the meaning of *tortilla* (a pancakelike bread), *frijoles* (beans), and *chile* (hot pepper). Tell students to imagine the sight, taste, and feel of these foods as they read Valle's poem silently. Then discuss the study questions in small groups.

VISUAL CONNECTIONS
About the Artist
A leading Mexican artist, Diego Rivera was influenced by Cézanne, Rousseau, and Gauguin. He is well known for his large murals in public buildings in Mexico City and in the United States. His style makes use of bold, clearly delineated shapes and flat textures.

TEACHING RESOURCES E
Teacher's Notes, p. 31
Study Guide, p. 32
Building Vocabulary, p. 35
Selection Test, p. 42

Food

1
Metaphor. The moon is compared to a tortilla because both are round and whitish-yellow.

2
Imagery of sight and touch is strong in comparison of beans and earth.

3 Analyzing
To what senses does the image of the chile appeal? Those of taste and touch.

Finding Details
4 Analyzing
To what is water compared? What is the effect of this final comparison? Water is compared to the sky. It has a cooling and refreshing effect after the image of fiery food.

FOR STUDY AND DISCUSSION
1a. Both are round and flat.
1b. The color of both is off-white or yellow.
2. Both are a reddish-brown.
3. All are red, hot, fiery.
4. Both sky and water are blue; sky is source of rainwater.

The Grinder (1924) by Diego M. Rivera (1886–1957) Encaustic on canvas.

Courtesy Museo de Arte Moderno (INBA), Mexico City. © Dirk Bakker, Photographer.

Food

VICTOR M. VALLE

1 One eats
the moon in a tortilla
2 Eat frijoles°
and you eat the earth
3 Eat chile
and you eat the sun and fire
4 Drink water
and you drink sky

3. **frijoles** (frē-hōl′ĕs): beans.

For Study and Discussion

Analyzing and Interpreting the Poem

1. The poet makes a comparison between things that one eats or drinks and elements of nature. **a.** What is the similarity in shape between the moon and a tortilla? **b.** What is the similarity in color?

2. What is the similarity in the color of beans and of the earth?

3. Chile is compared to both the sun and fire. What similarities are there?

4. In what way is water like the sky?

The Road Not Taken

ROBERT FROST

Many readers feel that the roads in this poem have a significance that applies to life. What meaning do you see in them?

Two roads diverged° in a yellow wood,
And sorry I could not travel both
And be one traveler, long I stood
And looked down one as far as I could
To where it bent in the undergrowth;   5

Then took the other, as just as fair,
And having perhaps the better claim,
Because it was grassy and wanted wear;
Though as for that the passing there
Had worn them really about the same,   10

And both that morning equally lay
In leaves no step had trodden black.
Oh, I kept the first for another day!
Yet knowing how way leads on to way,
I doubted if I should ever come back.   15

I shall be telling this with a sigh
Somewhere ages and ages hence:
Two roads diverged in a wood, and I—
I took the one less traveled by,
And that has made all the difference.   20

1. **diverged** (dĭ-vûrjd′): branched off.

Visual Learners • Students might like to visually represent in artwork the metaphor of a road not taken. Suggest that their pieces show decisions that they have made in their own lives. You could ask students the following questions to help them get started: Did the decision mark a major turning point? Did you know what the outcome of the decision might be, or was it hidden from view? Ask for volunteers to explain their pictures to the class.

CLOSURE

Write on the chalkboard the terms **simile** and **metaphor**. Ask students to define and give an example of each. You might continue this exercise by writing **symbol** and asking for examples of this term as well.

FOR STUDY AND DISCUSSION

1. Sorry that cannot travel both.

2. Second road is less traveled.

3. One choice will lead to another, and each choice will take him farther from the point of divergence.

4a. Since this is a poem, we might think that speaker could be talking about choosing between a life in the arts and a business or professional career. **4b.** Choosing to be poet rather than doctor or farmer or teacher, for example, would make great difference in a person's life. Almost any choice might be named.

5. Reflective, thoughtful, a bit regretful. Note the use of word *sigh* in l. 16.

LITERARY ELEMENTS

1. Phrase might mean person has come to end of some venture (probably unsuccessful) or is going to die.

2. Choices in life, like roads, lead in different directions, and we rarely "go back."

3. "Way leads on to way" suggests that some turns in the road will fade in memory and retracing old routes will become impossible.

4. Less common way of life.

5. Seems to feel regret at not trying other roads ("sigh"). Perhaps will always wonder where others would have led.

FOCUS ON WRITING A POEM

If **figurative language** does not come easily to students, get them started by modeling this activity for several different subjects. You might enlist students' help and write responses on the chalkboard in chart form. If further help is needed, you might add structure by suggesting subjects to practice with, such as rain, fireworks, and homework.

For Study and Discussion

Analyzing and Interpreting the Poem

1. How does this speaker feel when he has to choose one road instead of the other?

2. Why does the second road seem to be a better choice?

3. The speaker hopes to take the first road on "another day." Yet why does he doubt that he will ever be able to do this?

4a. What larger choices in life do you think the poet could be talking about here? **b.** Name some choices that could "make all the difference" in a person's life.

5. How would you describe the mood, or feeling, of this poem?

Literary Elements

Recognizing Symbols

When you see the colors red, white, and blue together, you probably think of the United States. These colors stand for the United States, just as a dove stands for peace and a red rose stands for love or beauty. These are examples of **symbols.** A **symbol** is anything that represents, or stands for, something else.

1   A road is a common symbol for life. What would we mean, for example, if we said "It's the end of the road for him"? The forked road in this poem is a symbol for a choice that the

2 speaker has to make. Why is a forked road a good symbol for choices in life?

The speaker says that "way leads on to way."

3 How does this suggest that life is a maze of roads that cannot be retraveled?

4   If a road is symbol for life, what kind of life does the speaker choose when he takes a road "less traveled by"?

The title of the poem is "The Road *Not*

5 Taken." How do you think the speaker feels about the road he did *not* take and can never find again? Does he have any regrets?

Focus on Writing a Poem

Using Figurative Language

Figurative language is language that is not meant to be taken literally. Poets use figures of speech to describe subjects or to express ideas in a fresh, memorable way.

The chart below shows four of the most common figures of speech. You may want to use one or more of these in poems that you write.

Figures of Speech	
Simile: uses *like* or *as* to compare two different things	The snow was like a pale, fluffy blanket.
Metaphor: compares two different things directly	The snow was a pale, fluffy blanket.
Personification: gives human qualities to something nonhuman	The snow gently lulled the dark earth to sleep.
Symbol: something that stands for something else beyond itself	For the children, snow meant paradise: sledding, snowball fights, and no school.

Choose a familiar subject: for example, a potato chip, a tree, or a nighttime street. Create a chart like the one above by making up four figures of speech to describe your subject. Save your notes.

About the Authors

Emily Dickinson (1830–1886)

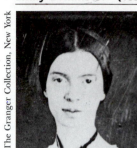

The Granger Collection, New York

A seventh-generation New Englander, Emily Dickinson lived and died in the house in which she was born, in Amherst, Massachusetts. For most of her adult life, she traveled no farther than her own garden. She wrote her poems in the rhythms she found in her Bible and hymnbook. A few friends knew that she had written some poems, but after her death, even her sister was amazed to discover almost eighteen hundred poems tied in bundles in her bedroom. Emily Dickinson might have lacked worldly experience, but she lived an intense inner life. In her imagination, the smallest, most ordinary object or scene could be a sign of something deep and mysterious.

Víctor M. Valle (1950–)

Víctor Manuel Valle, a native of California, is a poet, translator, and journalist. His family originally were dairy workers, followers of Pancho Villa and other political exiles. Born a third-generation Mexican American, he has said that the oral tradition of his grandparents and aunts gave him insight into Mexican history.

After studying anthropology at California State University, Valle received a master's degree in comparative literature. His thesis, a translation of the short stories of Peruvian writer José María Arguedas, received an award from the Translation Center of Columbia University. But Valle was already known as a poet for his book *Illegal* (1977), which won the Third Irvine Chicano Prize for poetry. In 1979 he received the *Caracol* Poetry Prize. In the poem "To the Students of Hollenbeck Junior High" (1979), Valle explains his view of poetry:

Poetry is a tool
because it helps you take things apart;
loosen people up.
But it's also a telephone for sending secrets,
or a radio blaring loud
making everyone listen.

Robert Frost (1874–1963)

After working as a country schoolteacher, a newspaper editor, and a cobbler, Robert Frost tended a small chicken farm in New Hampshire. In 1912, having had little success as a farmer, he sold the farm and moved to England with his family. There he devoted all his time to writing. He soon published his first two volumes of poems. These books were so highly praised that when Frost returned to America in 1915, he was recognized as a major poet. The rest of his long and productive life was spent living quietly on a small farm in Vermont, writing poetry and occasionally lecturing and teaching. Though Robert Frost's poems reflect the quiet dignity and simplicity of the countryside, they often give us a glimpse into the tragic and puzzling sides of life.

OBJECTIVES
The overall aim is for students to identify and analyze the effect of **rhyme, repetition,** and other sound devices. For a complete list of objectives, see the **Teacher's Notes.**

VOCABULARY
The underlined words are in the Glossary. The **Vocabulary Activity** in the **Teacher's Notes** provides practice in determining the **denotations** and **connotations** of words.

FOCUS / MOTIVATION
Ask students to jot down words they associate with these birds: robin, lark, dove, eagle, vulture, raven. Then discuss what might be expected in a poem called "The Raven" as opposed to a poem called "The Lark."

TEACHING RESOURCES E

Teacher's Notes, p. 44
Study Guide, p. 47
Building Vocabulary, p. 51
Selection Vocabulary Test, p. 64
Selection Test, p. 66

AV RESOURCES BINDER

Audiocassette 3, Side A

PREREADING FOCUS
Like music, poetry employs both repetition and variation. The introduction emphasizes that sound contributes to meaning and briefly explains various types of repetition such as **rhyme** and **alliteration.** Encourage students to look for both as they read "The Raven."

The Raven

1

Setting. The fairy tale opening "Once upon a" prepares for fantasy; "midnight" is also the time most commonly associated with mysterious or supernatural occurrences. Midnight also has **connotations** associated with death, dread, and gloom that help create poem's **atmosphere** of foreboding.

2

The speaker, who "pondered" over unusual and strange books, seems to be an intelligent but saddened ("weak and weary") man.

3 Summarizing
Drawing Conclusions
What has the speaker been doing before the tapping? What does this suggest about the events in the poem? He has been nodding, "nearly napping." He may have dreamed all that follows.

474

Sound and Meaning

REPETITION AND RHYME

In addition to such elements as diction, imagery, and figurative language, poets use devices of sound to convey meaning. One important sound device is *repetition*. Repetition may occur in different forms. It may occur in the form of *rhyme*, in which similar sounds are repeated within or at the end of lines. Repetition may also occur with a single letter or group of letters, as in these lines from Emily Dickinson's poem (page 468): "I *l*ike to see it *l*ap the miles, / And *l*ick the valleys up." This kind of repetition is known as *alliteration* (ə-lĭt′ə-rā′shən). Poets may also choose to repeat a single word, a phrase, or an entire line. In the short poem "Food" (page 470), Victor Valle repeats the word *eat* five times. Repetition is a way of emphasizing and communicating meaning as well as giving pleasure.

The Raven

EDGAR ALLAN POE

This poem is famous for its mood and for its dazzling musical effects. How does Poe use sound to create a mood of mystery?

1 Once upon a midnight dreary, while I pondered, weak and weary,
2 Over many a quaint and curious volume of forgotten lore°—
3 While I nodded, nearly napping, suddenly there came a tapping,
    As of someone gently rapping, rapping at my chamber door.
    " 'Tis some visitor," I muttered, "tapping at my chamber door—   5
               Only this and nothing more."

2. **lore:** knowledge.

PRESENTATION
This challenging poem will require more than one reading. First, you might ask students to follow along in their textbooks as you read the poem in sections—perhaps **stanzas** 1, 2, 3–6, 7, 8, 9–12, 13–16, and 17–18. After each section, ask brief questions to be sure that students have followed the poem to that point. After the first two stanzas, for example, you might ask where and when the action took place, what the speaker was doing, and why. When this preliminary reading has been completed, ask students to close their books and listen closely as you play a recording of the poem or as you read it yourself.

4 Ah, distinctly I remember it was in the bleak December;
   And each separate dying ember wrought its ghost upon the floor.
   Eagerly I wished the morrow—vainly I had sought to borrow
5 From my books surcease° of sorrow—sorrow for the lost Lenore—   10
   For the rare and radiant maiden whom the angels name Lenore—
                              Nameless *here* forevermore.

6 And the silken, sad, uncertain rustling of each purple curtain
7 Thrilled me—filled me with fantastic terrors never felt before;
   So that now, to still the beating of my heart, I stood repeating,   15
   " 'Tis some visitor entreating entrance at my chamber door—
   Some late visitor entreating entrance at my chamber door—
                              That it is and nothing more."

8 Presently my soul grew stronger; hesitating then no longer,
   "Sir," said I, "or Madam, truly your forgiveness I implore;   20
   But the fact is I was napping, and so gently you came rapping,
   And so faintly you came tapping, tapping at my chamber door,
   That I scarce was sure I heard you"—here I opened wide the door—
9   Darkness there and nothing more.

10. **surcease:** an end.

Illustrations on pages 475, 476, 477, and 479 by W.L. Taylor for an 1883 edition of *The Raven*.
General Research Division, The New York Public Library, Astor, Lenox and Tilden Foundations

4
Atmosphere. "The bleak December" and the flickering, ghostly shadows from the dying fire create an eerie mood.

5 Summarizing
What "sorrow" is the speaker hoping to escape? Responses will vary, but he is mourning the loss, or death, of Lenore, a woman he loved.

6
Alliteration. The repetition of *s* in this line suggests the sound of the rustling curtain.

7
"Fantastic" refers to the strange or weird as well as the imaginary and exaggerated.

8
Rhyme. Internal rhyme occurs in the first and third lines of each **stanza.** "Stronger" rhymes with "longer," and "napping" rhymes with "rapping."

9 Summarizing
     Drawing Conclusions
What does the speaker see as he opens the door? What is suggested by what he sees? He sees nothing, only darkness. Perhaps something strange is happening, or perhaps speaker imagined "rapping" and is losing sanity.

VISUAL CONNECTIONS
About the Artist
For more than forty years—from the 1880s through the 1920s—W. L. Taylor was a popular and respected illustrator for *The Ladies Home Journal*.

The Raven **475**

475

10 Drawing Conclusions
Expressing an Opinion
What does "dreams" suggest about the speaker? What kind of dreams has "no mortal ever dared to dream before"? Suggests that speaker is hopeful, at least momentarily. Responses to second question will vary; one possibility is that his lost love has returned to him.

11
Rhyme. After speaker whispers Lenore's name, the echo repeats it; the rhyme pattern is uniquely suited to allow "echoes" of this type.

12
Soul is "burning" because speaker hears the name "Lenore" when he never expected to hear the name again (see l. 12).

13 Finding Details
What evidence is there that the speaker is attempting to be rational? He tells his heart to "be still" and tries to believe that the "mystery" is just the wind.

VISUAL CONNECTIONS
About the Artist
W. L. Taylor's work for *The Ladies Home Journal* included illustrations for old songs, passages from Shakespeare, and familiar poems. Strongly influenced by the Bible, his "sweet" style came to be identified with the journal. Subscribers frequently ordered copies of his prints and illustrations.

Deep into that darkness peering, long I stood there wondering, fearing,   25
10 Doubting, dreaming dreams no mortal ever dared to dream before;
But the silence was unbroken, and the stillness gave no token,
11 And the only word there spoken was the whispered word, "Lenore?"
This I whispered, and an echo murmured back the word "Lenore!"—
                        Merely this and nothing more.   30

12 Back into the chamber turning, all my soul within me burning,
Soon again I heard a tapping somewhat louder than before.
"Surely," said I, "surely that is something at my window lattice;
13 Let me see, then, what thereat is, and this mystery explore—
Let my heart be still a moment and this mystery explore—   35
                        'Tis the wind and nothing more!"

Open here I flung the shutter, when, with many a flirt and flutter,

14 In there stepped a stately Raven of the saintly days of yore;

Not the least obeisance° made he; not a minute stopped or stayed he;

But, with mien° of lord or lady, perched above my chamber door— 40

15 Perched upon a bust of Pallas° just above my chamber door—

Perched, and sat, and nothing more.

16 Then this ebony bird beguiling my sad fancy into smiling,

By the grave and stern decorum of the countenance it wore,

"Though thy crest be shorn and shaven, thou," I said, "art sure no craven,° 45

17 Ghastly, grim, and ancient Raven wandering from the Nightly shore—

Tell me what thy lordly name is on the Night's Plutonian shore!"°

18 Quoth the Raven, "Nevermore."

Much I marveled this ungainly fowl to hear discourse so plainly,

Though its answer little meaning—little relevancy bore; 50

For we cannot help agreeing that no living human being

Ever yet was blessed with seeing bird above his chamber door—

Bird or beast upon the sculptured bust above his chamber door,

With such name as "Nevermore."

But the Raven, sitting lonely on the placid bust, spoke only 55

19 That one word, as if his soul in that one word he did outpour.

20 Nothing further then he uttered, not a feather then he fluttered—

21 Till I scarcely more than muttered, "Other friends have flown before—

On the morrow *he* will leave me, as my Hopes have flown before."

Then the bird said, "Nevermore." 60

Startled at the stillness broken by reply so aptly spoken,

"Doubtless," said I, "what it utters is its only stock and store

22 Caught from some unhappy master whom unmerciful Disaster

Followed fast and followed faster till his songs one burden° bore—

Till the dirges of his Hope that melancholy burden bore 65

Of 'Never—nevermore.'"

39. **obeisance** (ō-bā′səns): a gesture of respect; a bow. 40. **mien** (mēn): man- ner. 41. **bust of Pallas:** a statue of the head of Pallas Athena, the Greek goddess of wisdom. 45. **craven:** coward. 47. **Plutonian shore:** the shore of the river leading to the underworld, ruled by Pluto. 64. **burden:** here, a repeated word or phrase in a song.

14

Ancient legends of knights tell of messenger ravens; "saintly" may refer to Crusades.

15

Symbol. Bust of Pallas Athena, Greek goddess of wisdom, sym- bolizes reason and intelligence.

Summarizing
16 Making Inferences
What does the speaker do when he sees the Raven's "grave and stern" appear- ance? Why does the Raven's appearance make him smile? The speaker smiles upon seeing the Raven. Speaker may be re- lieved to see source of sounds if he suspects he is losing sanity.

17

Use to answer **study question 3,** p. 480.

18

Refrain. This sentence is refrain in poem that helps build up mood of despair. Also, reminds reader of sound of Lenore's name.

19

Inversion. Poe probably reversed normal word order of "as if he did outpour his soul in that one word" to fit the **rhyme** scheme.

20

Example of **alliteration** in repeti- tions of *f, th,* and *t* sounds.

21

Speaker believes bird, perhaps messenger from Lenore, will leave as Lenore, his friends, and his hopes have.

22

Speaker decides that some "un- happy master" taught bird its phrase; if speaker is dreaming, he could be tormenting himself with memories of Lenore.

Visual, Auditory, and Kinesthetic Learners •
You might involve students in interpreting "The Raven" by asking them to plan a multimedia presentation that emphasizes movement, sound, and sight. They might plan slides or graphics, develop sound effects, and choreograph movement for a dramatic reading of the poem. Presentations may be audiotaped or videotaped for inclusion in portfolios. You may also want to have students include in their portfolios paragraphs that describe their experience of this activity. (For more information on student portfolios, see the *Portfolio Assessment and Professional Support Materials* booklet in your teaching resources.)

23

In ll. 69–72, speaker tries to use reason to explain bird's message.

24

Alliteration. Repetition of *g* sounds serves to emphasize speaker's **description** of Raven.

25

"Bosom's core" suggests speaker's heart or soul; bird's eyes see into speaker's inner self.

26

In this stanza, speaker's imagination and obsession with Lenore cause him to lose control.

27

Speaker calls himself (not bird) a "wretch" (miserable person).

28 Analyzing

What does the Raven's answer mean? Speaker will never be able to forget Lenore.

29 Finding Main Ideas

Why is the speaker's home a "Horror haunted" "desert land"? It is barren without Lenore, haunted with memories.

30

Calling on Heaven and God indicates speaker's intense feelings.

31

Speaker wants to know whether his soul will join Lenore's in the afterlife.

But the Raven still beguiling all my fancy° into smiling,
Straight I wheeled a cushioned seat in front of bird and bust and
    door;
23 Then, upon the velvet sinking, I betook myself to linking
Fancy unto fancy, thinking what this ominous° bird of yore—   70
24 What this grim, ungainly, ghastly, gaunt, and ominous bird of yore
                  Meant in croaking, "Nevermore."

This I sat engaged in guessing, but no syllable expressing
25 To the fowl, whose fiery eyes now burned into my bosom's core;
This and more I sat divining, with my head at ease reclining   75
On the cushion's velvet lining that the lamplight gloated o'er,
But whose velvet violet lining with the lamplight gloating o'er,
                  She shall press, ah, nevermore!

26 Then, methought, the air grew denser, perfumed from an unseen
    censer°
Swung by seraphim° whose footfalls tinkled on the tufted floor.   80
27 "Wretch," I cried, "thy God hath lent thee—by these angels he hath
    sent thee
Respite°—respite and nepenthe° from thy memories of Lenore!
Quaff,° oh, quaff this kind nepenthe and forget this lost Lenore!"
28   Quoth the Raven, "Nevermore."

"Prophet!" said I, "thing of evil—prophet still, if bird or devil!—   85
Whether Tempter° sent, or whether tempest tossed thee here ashore,
29 Desolate yet all undaunted, on this desert land enchanted—
On this home by Horror haunted—tell me truly, I implore—
Is there—*is* there balm in Gilead?°—tell me—tell me, I implore!"
                 Quoth the Raven, "Nevermore."   90

"Prophet!" said I, "thing of evil!—prophet still, if bird or devil!
30 By that Heaven that bends above us—by that God we both adore—
31 Tell this soul with sorrow laden if, within the distant Aidenn,°
It shall clasp a sainted maiden whom the angels name Lenore—
Clasp a rare and radiant maiden whom the angels name Lenore."   95
                 Quoth the Raven, "Nevermore."

---

67. **fancy:** imagination.   70. **ominous** (ŏm'ə-nəs): threatening.   79. **censer:** a container for incense.   80. **seraphim** (sĕr'ə-fĭm): angels.   82. **Respite** (rĕs'pĭt): relief or rest.   **nepenthe** (nĭ-pĕn'thē): a drug thought to banish sorrow.   83. **Quaff** (kwŏf): drink.   86. **Tempter:** Satan.   89. **Is there...Gilead** (gĭl'ē-əd): This line is from the Bible, where it means "Is there any relief from pain?"   93. **Aidenn** (ā'dən): Paradise.

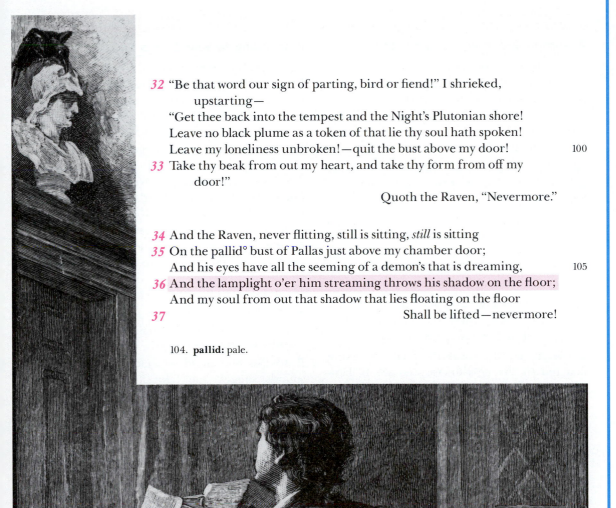

TRANSPARENCY 36

Literary Elements
Sound Effects in Poetry – invites students to explore poetic sound effects, such as rhyme, rhythm, repetition, alliteration, and onomatopoeia.

32 "Be that word our sign of parting, bird or fiend!" I shrieked, upstarting—

"Get thee back into the tempest and the Night's Plutonian shore!
Leave no black plume as a token of that lie thy soul hath spoken!
Leave my loneliness unbroken!—quit the bust above my door!   100
33 Take thy beak from out my heart, and take thy form from off my door!"

                            Quoth the Raven, "Nevermore."

34 And the Raven, never flitting, still is sitting, *still* is sitting
35 On the pallid° bust of Pallas just above my chamber door;

And his eyes have all the seeming of a demon's that is dreaming,   105
36 And the lamplight o'er him streaming throws his shadow on the floor;

And my soul from out that shadow that lies floating on the floor
37   Shall be lifted—nevermore!

104. **pallid:** pale.

32 Comparing/Contrasting
How has the speaker's mood changed? Earlier the speaker was amused by bird, trying to explain its presence reasonably; now he screams uncontrollably for the Raven to leave.

33
The Raven's "beak" in speaker's heart represents the knowledge that he will never be united with his lost, beloved Lenore.

34 Analyzing
What two meanings does "still" have here? Bird sits without moving and has never left.

35
The bust of Pallas is now pale beneath the ominous Raven; the speaker's reason and wisdom are overwhelmed by the irrational.

36
Symbol. The Raven and its dark shadow symbolize harsh reality, death, evil.

37
Speaker is condemned to eternal sorrow and grief.

VISUAL CONNECTIONS
About the Artwork
You might ask students to consider the composition of this drawing. Students might discuss why the artist positioned the speaker in the foreground with the speaker's back toward the viewer. Some students may suggest that the composition gives the viewer a perspective similar to the one the speaker has, thus bringing the viewer closer to the speaker's point of reference.

479

CLOSURE
Ask students to identify words that express the mood of Poe's poem and to tell which sound devices contribute most to the poem's overall effect.

EXTENSION AND ENRICHMENT
Writing assignments that may be based on "The Raven" include the following: a translation of the poem into a television scenario with notes about casting and costumes as well as set and camera angles; a narrative telling how the young

FOR STUDY AND DISCUSSION
1a. A December midnight in narrator's purple-curtained chamber. **1b.** Rustling of curtain terrifies narrator; dying fire casts shadows; there is a tapping at the door, but no one is there. Midnight suggests mystery, dread.

2a. He has lost his beloved Lenore. **2b.** Speaker is sorrowful and sits alone reading, trying to forget his pain and loss.

3. He asks what the Raven is named on "Night's Plutonian shore" (l. 47) and tells him to return (l. 98). He thinks Satan may have sent Raven (l. 86).

4a. Asks the Raven's name, if there is relief from pain, and if he will see Lenore in Paradise.

4b. Answers "Nevermore" to each question. (Speaker's reaction moves from a humorous comment on first answer to despair at the last one.)

5a. Demands that the Raven leave his chamber and return to the underworld. Finally, he tells Raven to "take thy beak from out my heart." **5b.** Raven says "Nevermore" and in last stanza is still sitting above chamber door. Speaker says that his soul shall "nevermore" be free of the Raven's shadow.

6. Responses will vary.

LITERARY ELEMENTS
Responding to Sounds in a Poem

1. Suggests that her name also echoes over and over again in the speaker's mind.

2. Internal rhyme in l. 3 is found with the words *napping/tapping.* First and third lines of each stanza contain internal rhymes.

3. Examples of onomatopoeia: *rustling, beating, whispered, murmured, flutter, croaking, tinkled, flitting.*

For Study and Discussion

Analyzing and Interpreting the Poem

1. In this mysterious poem, a man is driven to hysteria by a Raven that enters his room and refuses to leave. **a.** What is the poem's setting, or the time and place of the action? **b.** How does the setting create a mood of mystery?

2a. What tragic loss has the speaker suffered? **b.** How does this create a mood of loneliness?

3. The mystery increases when the Raven enters the room (line 38). Ravens are often associated with death and evil. What evidence in the poem tells you that the speaker thinks this bird is a visitor from the land of the dead?

4a. What three questions does the speaker ask the Raven (see lines 47, 89, and 93–95)? **b.** How does the Raven answer?

5a. What is the speaker's final, shrieking demand in the next-to-last stanza? **b.** How do you know that the Raven will never leave the speaker's chamber?

6. Some people say that this poem describes a nightmare. Others say it tells of a man going insane. What do you think?

Literary Elements

Responding to Sounds in a Poem

The speaker talks about a woman named Lenore. The name *Lenore* is repeated throughout the poem. Each stanza also has words that rhyme with *Lenore.* Identify these rhyming **1** words in each stanza. How does the echoing of the dead woman's name suggest what is going on in the speaker's mind?

Rhymes are heard in every line of this poem. Poe even rhymes words within the same line. In the first line, the word *weary* rhymes **2** with *dreary.* Find another example of this **internal rhyme** in line 3. Read aloud the first and third lines of every stanza to hear the internal rhymes.

Poe creates other musical effects by using alliteration:

> And the silken, sad, uncertain rustling of each purple curtain

Read this line aloud so that the repeated **s** sounds suggest the faint "rustling" of the curtains. If you look closely at each stanza of this poem, you will find other lines that use alliteration. Read some of these lines aloud.

In addition to alliteration and rhyme, Poe uses words that suggest or echo mysterious and frightening sounds. Here are some from the first stanza alone:

> tapping   rapping   muttered

Add words from other stanzas to this list.

In the first stanza of "The Raven," Poe describes the sounds of *rapping* and *tapping* at the speaker's chamber door. These words to some degree imitate the actual sounds made. Poe is making use of **onomatopoeia** **3** (ŏn′ə-mătə-pēə). Find other examples of this technique in "The Raven."

man lost his beloved Lenore; a monologue in which the man, years later, recalls his encounter with the Raven and tells what happened afterwards.

Ensembles might present choral readings of "The Raven," each introduced by an original prologue to set the mood and perhaps to tell something about the author.

Several students might present readings of other Poe favorites such as "Annabel Lee," "The Bells," and "Eldorado."

A number of students might like to illustrate a manuscript of "The Raven," either a favorite **stanza** or the whole poem. Another possibility for an art activity is the creation of a shoebox diorama of the narrator's gloomy study.

Understanding Allusions

In Greek and Roman mythology, the underworld—the land of the dead—was ruled by a god known as Pluto. It was believed that the spirits of the dead reached the underworld by being ferried across the River Styx. When Poe refers to "Night's Plutonian shore" (line 47), he has in mind the shore of the river leading to the underworld. Such a reference to a place, a character, or an event is called an **allusion**.

In line 89 the speaker cries out, "Is there—*is* there balm in Gilead?" This line is an allusion to the Bible, in which the prophet Jeremiah, in his sorrow, asks the same question. Gilead was a region of ancient Palestine where balm, a soothing ointment, was made. You will find the source of this allusion in Jeremiah 8:22.

In Dickinson's poem "I Like to See It Lap the Miles" (page 468) there is another allusion **1** to the Bible. Look in Mark 3:17. How does this Biblical passage explain the allusion in line 13?

Focus on Writing a Poem

Experimenting with Sound Effects

Reading "The Raven" aloud will show you how important **sound effects** can be in a poem. Sound effects that you can use in your own poem include the following:

repetition	rhyme
alliteration	onomatopoeia

Experiment with sound effects by choosing *two* of the four devices listed above. Using each device, write a few lines of prose or verse. For example, you might create a few sentences with alliteration like the following: "Silently Sam shifted the sensors so that Stan shouldn't notice the switch." Save your writing.

For Oral Reading

Avoiding Singsong

In order to stress the rhyme of a poem, people sometimes read in a monotonous pattern called *singsong*. One way to avoid singsong is to read a poem in a natural voice. Do not stress rhyme words by pausing mechanically at the end of each line. Follow the punctuation and phrasing of the poem.

Plan to read "The Raven" aloud, either as a solo performance or in an ensemble. Practice reading the poem aloud, paying attention to meaning as well as to sound.

About the Authors

Edgar Allan Poe   (1809–1849)

For a biography of Poe, see page 279.

482

RHYTHM

Rhythm is the pattern of stressed and unstressed sounds in a line of poetry. Rhythm not only contributes to the musical quality of a poem, but also gives emphasis to important words and ideas. Sometimes the rhythm of a poem actually suggests its subject matter. This is the case with the poem you are about to read.

Lochinvar

SIR WALTER SCOTT

This story takes place in the fifteenth century, when "Border" wars raged between England and Scotland. Lochinvar had gone off to battle. But shocking news brings him home . . .

Oh, young Lochinvar is come out of the west,
Through all the wide Border his steed was the best;
And, save his good broadsword, he weapons had none,
He rode all unarmed, and he rode all alone.
So faithful in love, and so dauntless in war,   5
There never was knight like the young Lochinvar.

He stayed not for brake,° and he stopped not for stone,
He swam the Eske River where ford there was none;
But ere he alighted at Netherby gate,
The bride had consented, the gallant came late: 10
For a laggard° in love, and a dastard° in war,
Was to wed the fair Ellen of brave Lochinvar.

So boldly he entered the Netherby Hall,
Among bridesmen, and kinsmen, and brothers, and all.
Then spoke the bride's father, his hand on his sword   15
(For the poor craven° bridegroom said never a word),
"Oh, come ye in peace here, or come ye in war,
Or to dance at our bridal, young Lord Lochinvar?"

7. **brake:** a clump of bushes or trees.

11. **laggard:** a slow person.
dastard: a sneak.

16. **craven:** cowardly.

After you explain the poem's basic **setting** and **plot** and give students an opportunity to predict what will happen in the poem, tell them to check their predictions as the poem is read to them. You may want to underscore the dramatic quality of the poem by having different students take the roles of the father, Lochinvar, and the bridesmaids as you read the narrative parts of the poem aloud.

Return to the conjectures offered before the reading. Did anyone predict what the young knight would do to win his bride? Before you consider the study questions, you may want to ask students to write in their journals a paraphrase of the first **stanza (Writing About Literature)** or perhaps of the complete poem. Then discuss student paraphrases, the study

VISUAL CONNECTIONS
Exploring the Subject
Sir Walter Scott loved Scotland's romantically beautiful lakes, rivers, and castles. In 1811 he bought Abbotsford, a rambling mansion overlooking the Tweed River in Roxburghshire, Scotland, thirty-five miles southeast of Edinburgh. He enlarged the original building, duplicating parts of various Scottish castles and mansions that appealed to him. Scott went bankrupt in 1828, but a gentleman to the last, he wrote furiously to pay his debts and still keep his dream mansion for his children.

6
Conflict. Lochinvar's "suit" (request to marry Ellen, the maiden he loves) has been denied. By poem's end, Lochinvar has resolved that conflict.

7 Making Inferences
Why might Lochinvar show indifference to Ellen? To put her family off guard and to prepare for their escape.

8
Use to answer **study question 3a,** p. 484.

9
Rhythm. The "measure" of dancing and galloping is suggested by Scott's strong, active rhythm.

6 "I long wooed your daughter, my suit you denied—
7 Love swells like the Solway,° but ebbs like its tide—
And now I am come, with this lost love of mine,
To lead but one measure,° drink one cup of wine.
There are maidens in Scotland more lovely by far,
That would gladly be bride to the young Lochinvar."

The bride kissed the goblet; the knight took it up;
He quaffed off° the wine, and he threw down the cup.
8 She looked down to blush, and she looked up to sigh,
With a smile on her lips, and a tear in her eye.
He took her soft hand, ere her mother could bar—
9 "Now tread we a measure!" said young Lochinvar.

20

25

30

20. Solway: an inlet between England and Scotland.

22. measure: a movement of the dance.

26. quaffed (kwŏft) **off:** drank deeply.

TRANSPARENCY 36

Literary Elements
Sound Effects in Poetry – invites students to explore poetic sound effects, such as rhyme, rhythm, repetition, alliteration, and onomatopoeia.

10
Bonnet: flat, brimless cap worn by men in Scotland.

11 Summarizing
What are Ellen's feelings toward Lochinvar? She is eager to leave with him; a "touch" and a "word" confirm her feelings.

12
Rhythm. Short line and **inversion** here suggest Lochinvar's speed and deliberateness; rhythm in the last **stanza** suggests galloping horses in the chase.

13 Summarizing
What is the fate of Lochinvar and Ellen? They escape and are never seen again.

So stately his form, and so lovely her face,
That never a hall such a galliard° did grace;
While her mother did fret, and her father did fume,
10 And the bridegroom stood dangling his bonnet and plume,
And the bridesmaidens whispered, "Twere better by far,   35
To have matched our fair cousin with young Lochinvar."

11 One touch to her hand, and one word to her ear,
When they reached the hall door, and the charger° stood near,
12 So light to the croup° the fair lady he swung.
So light to the saddle before her he sprung!   40
"She is won! we are gone, over bank, brush, and scaur;°
They'll have fleet steeds that follow," quoth young Lochinvar.

There was mounting 'mong Graemes of the Netherby clan;
Forsters, Fenwicks, and Musgraves, they rode and they ran.
There was racing and chasing on Cannobie Lee,°   45
13 But the lost bride of Netherby ne'er did they see.
So daring in love, and so dauntless in war,
Have ye e'er heard of gallant like young Lochinvar?

32. **galliard** (găl'yərd): a lively dance.

38. **charger:** a horse.
39. **croup** (krōōp): the horse's back, behind the saddle area.
41. **scaur** (skär): a rocky hillside.

45. **Cannobie Lee:** a meadow.

FOR STUDY AND DISCUSSION
1. Bridegroom is a cowardly sneak and slow in love (l. 11). Lochinvar is a brave, dauntless, passionate knight.
2a. Fears that Lochinvar will fight (l. 15). **2b.** Lochinvar says that love ebbs like the tide and that there are lovelier maidens in Scotland. He now wants only to dance one measure and drink one cup of wine. (See ll. 19–24.)
3a. Ellen blushes and sighs; she smiles with tears in her eyes (ll. 27–28). **3b.** She loves him.
4. They dance over to hall door; outside, horse is ready; they leap on it and gallop away (ll. 37–40).

For Study and Discussion

Analyzing and Interpreting the Poem

1. When Lochinvar arrives at Netherby Hall, Ellen is about to marry another man. How does the bridegroom contrast with Lochinvar?

2a. What does Ellen's father fear when Lochinvar arrives? **b.** What answer does Lochinvar give to reassure him?

3a. What are Ellen's reactions when Lochinvar drinks the goblet of wine? **b.** What do her reactions tell about her feelings for Lochinvar?

4. How do Lochinvar and Ellen trick everyone?

Literary Elements

Responding to Rhythm

All spoken language has rhythm. When you speak, your voice rises and falls naturally in ways that help communicate meaning. In a poem, rhythm often follows a pattern. Read the following lines from "Lochinvar" aloud, and listen to the rhythm. The symbol (') indi-

Each student might write a letter that Ellen sends back to her family, explaining her motives and telling her family what has happened to her since she left.

The class might prepare a taped choral reading of "Lochinvar" for exchange with another class.

Students might enjoy seeing how James Thurber has illustrated and gently mocked this poem in *Fables for Our Times* (Harper).

Since the characters in the poem border on stereotypes, students might like to draw cartoon-style figures of Lochinvar, Ellen, the parents, the bridegroom, and the bridesmaids. They might also create a comic-strip version of the narrative.

---

cates a stressed syllable. The symbol (˘) indicates an unstressed syllable.

> Hĕ stayĕd nŏt fŏr bráke, ănd hĕ stóppĕd nŏt
>   fŏr stóne,
> Hĕ swám thĕ Éskĕ Rívĕr whĕre fórd thĕre
>   wăs nóne;
> Bŭt ĕre hĕ ălíghtĕd ăt Néthĕrby gáte,
> Thĕ bride hăd cŏnséntĕd, thĕ gállănt cáme
>   láte:

Sometimes the rhythm of a poem suggests what the poem is about. "Lochinvar" is about a knight who gallops over the countryside. Reread the lines above and tap out the rhythm gently on your desk. **1** Does the rhythm sound like the galloping of a horse?

Recognizing Inverted Word Order

Poets, like other writers, sometimes reverse the usual order of words in their sentences. When they do, they are using **inverted word order.** For example, in line 3 Scott says, ". . . he weapons had none." A standard English sentence would use subject-verb-object order: "he had no weapons." **1** But what happens to Scott's swinging, regular rhythm when "he had no weapons" is substituted for "he weapons had none"?

2 Rewrite the following inverted lines from the poem so that they reflect standard English word order:

a . . . where ford there was none;   (line 8)
b Now tread we a measure!   (line 30)
c That never a hall such a galliard did grace;
          (line 32)
d So light to the croup the fair lady he swung.
          (line 39)
e But the lost bride of Netherby ne'er did they see.
          (line 46)

Writing About Literature

▶ Paraphrasing a Stanza

To **paraphrase** a line or passage of poetry is to restate its ideas in your own words. A paraphrase puts inverted constructions into normal order. It also restates images and figures of speech in plain language.

Paraphrase the first stanza of "Lochinvar." Then check your paraphrase to see if you have included all of Scott's details.

About the Author

Sir Walter Scott   (1771–1832)

As a boy, Sir Walter Scott was fascinated by the tales of Scotland's past that his mother and grandfather told him. When he grew older, he traveled throughout the countryside on ballad "raids," writing down the songs he heard. At the age of thirty-one, he published a collection of these old Scottish folk ballads. He then wrote three long narrative poems, of which *The Lady of the Lake* is the most famous. Scott was the best-loved poet in England when he began publishing a series of historical novels, which were filled with adventure and romance. *Ivanhoe* is one of the most famous of these novels.

▶ Before students begin this writing assignment, you may want to refer them to the **Writing About Literature** section on p. 672.

LITERARY ELEMENTS
Responding to Rhythm
1. Most students will agree that the rhythm sounds like galloping.

Recognizing Inverted Word Order
1. The rhythm is interrupted.
2a. . . . where there was no ford.
2b. Now we tread a measure!
2c. That such a galliard never did grace a hall.
2d. So light to the croup he swung the fair lady.
2e. But they never did see the lost bride of Netherby.

WRITING ABOUT LITERATURE
Student paraphrases will vary but should resemble the following sample: Young Lochinvar came from out of the west. Throughout all the Border country, his horse was the best. His only weapon was a good sword, and he rode alone. There never was a knight as faithful in love and as brave in war as young Lochinvar.

ABOUT THE AUTHOR
Although Scott was born in the city of Edinburgh, he spent much of his youth on his grandfather's farm in the Tweed River valley near the border between Scotland and England, an area rich in the history and legends of the Border raiders. He later established his home at Abbotsford there. Scott's antiquarian and Gothic interests are revealed in his novels and poetry; in both genres, his most important skill is superb storytelling.

OBJECTIVES

The overall aim is for students to analyze the poem as a "tall tale." For a complete list of objectives, see the **Teacher's Notes**.

VOCABULARY

The underlined words are in the Glossary. Some unfamiliar words are defined in the footnotes. If students encounter unfamiliar words as they read, ask them to look up the words in a dictionary and to jot down the words and their definitions.

FOCUS / MOTIVATION

Ask students to describe what it feels like to be extremely cold and to tell what they would be willing to do to get warm. Students who have never experienced extreme cold can describe what it feels like to hold an ice cube.

TEACHING RESOURCES E

Teacher's Notes, p. 68
Study Guide, p. 69
Selection Test, p. 72

PREREADING FOCUS

The introduction defines and provides examples of **narrative poetry** and points out that **ballads** and **epics** are specific kinds of narrative poetry. Folk ballads are passed orally from generation to generation; literary ballads are written by individual poets but have qualities of the oral ballad. Epics, which record the historical and mythic legends of a people, may also be passed down orally from generation to generation. Narrative poetry often includes a strong dramatic element. Tell students to look for this dramatic element as they read Service's poem.

The Cremation of Sam McGee

1

Klondike Gold Rush occurred when gold was discovered on Bonanza Creek in Klondike region of Yukon Territory, Canada. About 30,000 people took part in gold rush.

2

In Arctic region, sun is above horizon at midnight in summer.

3

Personification. Northern Lights have human ability to see.

Types of Poetry

NARRATIVE POETRY

Like a short story, a *narrative* poem tells a story. A narrative poem has characters, a setting, and action. "Paul Revere's Ride" (page 136), "The Raven" (page 474), and "Lochinvar" (page 482) are well-known narrative poems.

A special kind of narrative poem is the *ballad*. Folk ballads were not written down, but were transmitted over the centuries by word of mouth. "John Henry" (page 185) is an example of a folk ballad.

Another kind of narrative poem is the *epic*, a long poem about heroic figures and events. You will learn more about the epic in the unit that begins on page 609 of this textbook.

The Cremation of Sam McGee

ROBERT SERVICE

1 *During the Klondike Gold Rush, which started in 1896, Dawson became the center of the Klondike mining region. The temperature at Dawson is frequently 40 degrees below zero. This narrative poem tells about a man who left his home*
2 *in the South to seek his fortune in the land of the midnight sun.*

> There are strange things done in the midnight sun
>   By the men who moil° for gold;
> The Arctic trails have their secret tales
>   That would make your blood run cold;
> The Northern Lights° have seen queer sights,   5
>   But the queerest they ever did see
> Was that night on the marge° of Lake Lebarge
>   I cremated Sam McGee.

2. *moil:* work very hard.   5. *Northern Lights:* bands of light that can be seen in the night skies; also called the aurora borealis.   7. *marge:* the edge of the lake.

486

MOTIVATIONAL SUMMARY
Right before he dies, Sam McGee, who had come from Tennessee to the Arctic to look for gold, asks his partner to cremate his corpse instead of burying it. The partner agrees, but he must haul the corpse a long distance to find fuel to conduct the cremation. He finally finds a boat frozen in place on a lake, and he uses the boat's boiler to cremate Sam McGee.

PRESENTATION
Part of the fun of this poem comes from the elaborate **rhythm** and **rhyme** schemes the poet builds into it. To introduce your students to this aspect of the poem, you might read the first eight lines aloud. Point out the internal rhyme and the end

Now Sam McGee was from Tennessee, where the cotton blooms and blows.

4 Why he left his home in the South to roam 'round the Pole, God only knows.   10

5 He was always cold, but the land of gold seemed to hold him like a spell;

6 Though he'd often say in his homely way that "he'd sooner live in hell."

On a Christmas Day we were mushing° our way over the Dawson trail.

7 Talk of your cold! through the parka's fold it stabbed like a driven nail.

If our eyes we'd close, then the lashes froze till sometimes we couldn't see;   15

8 It wasn't much fun, but the only one to whimper was Sam McGee.

13. **mushing:** traveling by sled. *Mush* is a command to a dog team to move forward.

4 Analyzing
What does narrator mean by "Pole"? North Pole, or Arctic region.

5
Simile. Compares allure of gold in Yukon to a spell that controls Sam McGee.

6
Irony. Hell is believed by some people to be extremely hot. Sam McGee prefers intense heat to cold.

7
Simile. Compares cold wind to sharp nail, emphasizing wind's piercing quality.

8
Narrator understates conditions by saying "It wasn't much fun." Miners are probably miserable.

William Bacon III/Photo Researchers, Inc.

rhyme, and also point out that each line has its own distinctive rhythm. You might want to encourage students to notice the rhyme and rhythm but not to exaggerate them as they read.

After reading the first eight lines, ask students to speculate about what sight the Northern Lights saw. You should be careful not to give away the conclusion, since much of the effect of the poem depends on the surprise ending. Simply letting students guess what might happen without commenting will help increase their interest in the poem and their comprehension of it.

After students have read the poem, the items in the **For Study and Discussion** exercise will help sharpen their response to the poem. The activity in the **For Oral Reading** exercise will lead them to reread the poem several times with an eye toward interpretation.

And that very night, as we lay packed tight in our robes beneath
    the snow,
9 And the dogs were fed, and the stars o'erhead were dancing heel and
    toe,
10 He turned to me, and "Cap," says he, "I'll cash in this trip, I guess;
    And if I do, I'm asking that you won't refuse my last request."   20

11 Well, he seemed so low that I couldn't say no; then he says with a sort of
    moan:
12 "It's the cursèd cold, and it's got right hold till I'm chilled clean
    through to the bone.
13 Yet 'tain't being dead—it's my awful dread of the icy grave that pains;
14 So I want you to swear that, foul or fair, you'll cremate my last
    remains."

Aurora borealis, also called the northern lights.

Pekka Parviainen/Science Photo Library/
Science Source/Photo Researchers, Inc.

9

Personification. Stars have human ability to dance, which describes their appearance of twinkling.

10 Analyzing
What does Sam mean by "cash in this trip"? He will die. He compares dying to a gambler cashing in chips for money at end of game.

11
Some people believe they have solemn duty to honor dying person's last request.

12
Poet uses accent mark on "cursed" to make word two syllables to fit rhythm of line.

13 Making Inferences
Why does Sam fear icy grave? Answers will vary. He may feel so cold now he fears he will somehow feel cold after he is dead.

14 Analyzing
What does Sam mean by "foul or fair"? Regardless of whether it's easy or difficult to accomplish.

TRANSPARENCY 36

Literary Elements
Sound Effects in Poetry – invites students to explore poetic sound effects, such as rhyme, rhythm, repetition, alliteration, and onomatopoeia.

A pal's last need is a thing to heed, so I swore I would not fail;   25

15 And we started on at the streak of dawn; but God! he looked ghastly
        pale.

16 He crouched on the sleigh, and he raved all day of his home in
        Tennessee;
     And before nightfall a corpse was all that was left of Sam McGee.

17 There wasn't a breath in that land of death, and I hurried, horror-
        driven,
     With a corpse half hid that I couldn't get rid, because of a promise
        given;   30
     It was lashed to the sleigh, and it seemed to say: "You may tax your
        brawn and brains,

18 But you promised true, and it's up to you to cremate those last
        remains."

19 Now a promise made is a debt unpaid, and the trail has its own stern
        code.

20 In the days to come, though my lips were dumb, in my heart how I
        cursed that load.
     In the long, long night, by the lone firelight, while the huskies,° round in
        a ring,   35
     Howled out their woes to the homeless snows—O God! how I loathed
        the thing.

21 And every day that quiet clay seemed to heavy and heavier grow;
     And on I went, though the dogs were spent and the grub was getting low;
     The trail was bad, and I felt half mad, but I swore I would not give in;
     And I'd often sing to the hateful thing, and it hearkened with a grin.   40

22 Till I came to the marge of Lake Lebarge, and a derelict there lay;
     It was jammed in the ice, but I saw in a trice° it was called the "Alice
        May."
     And I looked at it, and I thought a bit, and I looked at my frozen chum;

23 Then "Here," said I, with a sudden cry, "is my cre-ma-tor-eum."

35. **huskies:** dogs used in the arctic to pull sleds.   42. **trice:** instant.

15
Figurative Language. "Streak of dawn" means first light of day.

16 Drawing Conclusions
Why does Sam rave of his home state? Answers will vary. Perhaps he misses warmth of Tennessee. Perhaps he is delirious.

17 Analyzing
What does narrator mean by "land of death"? Answers will vary. Perhaps he refers to Sam's death. Perhaps he is talking about place where snow covers everything so that it appears that nothing is alive.

18 Drawing Conclusions
What problem does narrator face in cremating corpse? Where to find fuel for fire.

19
Metaphor. Compares making a promise to assuming a debt.

20
Narrator does not express aloud how he feels.

21
Figurative Language. "Quiet clay" refers to corpse.

22
Narrator finds an abandoned boat on shore of lake.

23
Rhythm. Poet separates word into syllables to emphasize that each syllable should be pronounced individually.

possible. Suggest that in addition to performers, dramatizations will require a stage crew and, if desired, a videotaping crew. Consult with students in the planning stages to determine what roles they will play and how their participation will be assessed.

CLOSURE
Have each student write on a small slip of paper one factual question about the poem. Put all the slips into a box, draw them out one at a time, and pose them to the class. You can divide the class in half for a "fact bee" or simply

---

24 Analyzing
Why does narrator use unusual word order? To make internal rhyme scheme work.

25
"Fuel" should be pronounced as two syllables.

26
Personification. Sky has human ability to frown, meaning weather is getting bad.

27
Figurative Language. "Hot sweat" means narrator is crying.

28
Figurative Language. "Inky cloak" means smoke is black.

29
Personification. Fear has human quality of being able to wrestle, meaning narrator has to overcome fear in order to return to boat.

30
Narrator means he guesses Sam McGee's corpse is consumed by fire by now.

31
Exaggeration. Overstates distance smile can be seen to emphasize it is broad.

---

24 Some planks I tore from the cabin floor, and I lit the boiler fire;   45
25 Some coal I found that was lying around, and I heaped the fuel higher;
   The flames just soared, and the furnace roared—such a blaze you
      seldom see;
   And I burrowed a hole in the glowing coal, and I stuffed in Sam McGee.

   Then I made a hike, for I didn't like to hear him sizzle so;
26 And the heavens scowled, and the huskies howled, and the wind began
      to blow.   50
27 It was icy cold, but the hot sweat rolled down my cheeks, and I don't know
      why;
28 And the greasy smoke in an inky cloak went streaking down the sky.

29 I do not know how long in the snow I wrestled with grisly fear;
   But the stars came out and they danced about ere again I ventured near;
   I was sick with dread, but I bravely said: "I'll just take a peep inside.   55
30 I guess he's cooked, and it's time I looked"; . . . then the door I opened
      wide.

   And there sat Sam, looking cool and calm, in the heart of the furnace
      roar;
31 And he wore a smile you could see a mile, and he said: "Please close
      that door.
   It's fine in here, but I greatly fear you'll let in the cold and storm—
   Since I left Plumtree, down in Tennessee, it's the first time I've been
      warm."   60

         There are strange things done in the midnight sun
            By the men who moil for gold;
         The Arctic trails have their secret tales
            That would make your blood run cold;
         The Northern Lights have seen queer sights,   65
            But the queerest they ever did see
         Was that night on the marge of Lake Lebarge
            I cremated Sam McGee.

ask questions and have students volunteer to answer them.

For Study and Discussion

Analyzing and Interpreting the Poem

1. What did the title of the poem lead you to expect? Were you surprised by the ending of the story?

2. What images and comparisons does the narrator use to describe the arctic cold?

3. In lines 30–34 the narrator talks about the "stern code of the trail." What do you think he means?

4. Could "The Cremation of Sam McGee" be called a "tall tale"? Review the definition on page 176 before responding.

For Oral Reading

Preparing a Reading of the Poem

Imagine that you are presenting "The Cremation of Sam McGee" in a public reading. How will you prepare so that your presentation is dramatic and effective? How will you handle the voices of the two speakers? Where will you pause in reciting each stanza? Where will you raise or lower your voice?

Practice with a classmate. Use a tape recorder or cassette player to tape your reading and listen to it before you deliver your performance.

About the Author

Robert Service   (1874–1958)

Born in Lancashire, England, Robert Service is well known for his ballads of the remote Yukon territory. His ballads are characterized by regular rhythms, rhyme, and sentimentality with touches of irony. "The Cremation of Sam McGee" and "The Shooting of Dan McGrew" are two of his most popular poems. Service once claimed that his verse was not highbrow "poetry," and he even wrote a verse apologizing for any true poetry that might have crept into his work.

Service did not live quite as adventurous a life as that of his Yukon characters—he spent many years as a bank clerk, living mostly in Canada and Paris. He published a number of books over his lifetime, most of them collections of rhymes and ballads, including *Songs of a Sourdough* (1907), *Ballads of a Cheechako* (1909), and *Rhymes of a Rolling Stone* (1912). *The Trail of '98* (1910), a novel, tells a story of the Yukon gold rush and was made into a movie in 1928.

OBJECTIVES
The overall aim is for students to analyze how **imagery** and other poetic elements work together to reveal the poet's—or speaker's—mood and feelings. For a complete list of objectives, see the **Teacher's Notes.**

VOCABULARY
Call students' attention to vocabulary notes in their textbooks. In addition, the **Vocabulary Activity** in the **Teacher's Notes** gives students practice in using the dictionary.

FOCUS / MOTIVATION
Begin by writing *winter, cats,* and *nature* on the chalkboard. Ask students to freewrite about each subject. The poems in this section deal with these subjects. As they read, students could compare their responses to the poems.

TEACHING RESOURCES E
Teacher's Notes, p. 73
Study Guide, p. 76
Building Vocabulary, p. 74

PREREADING FOCUS
The introduction emphasizes that lyric poetry is personal in nature and that it is often meant to be sung. Ask students to bring to class examples of modern song lyrics. You might then read aloud several songs and discuss why they could be considered lyric poetry.

When Icicles Hang by the Wall

1 Making Generalizations
What is the setting, the time of year? It is the coldest part of winter, when "icicles hang."

2
Imagery. Cold freezes milk before it can be brought from the barn, but presence of food and logs for a fire is reassuring; both images reinforce poem's wintry **theme.**

3
Onomatopoeia. "Tu-whit,/Tu-who" suggests owl's merry song.

4
Images of fellowship contrast with cold and illness associated with winter.

5 Drawing Conclusions
Why is Marian's nose red and raw? Description suggests she has a cold.

6
Refrain. Same lines appear in both **stanzas** and suggest a cozy counterpoint to rugged weather.

492

LYRIC POETRY

Lyric poetry is generally used to express personal thoughts and feelings. In many lyrics the poet is felt to be speaking in his or her own voice. Some lyrics, like the song from Shakespeare's *Love's Labor's Lost,* were intended to be sung.

When Icicles Hang by the Wall

WILLIAM SHAKESPEARE

One of William Shakespeare's comedies, Love's Labor's Lost, *ends with two songs—the first is Spring's song and the second is Winter's. This is the song of Winter.*

1 When icicles hang by the wall,
　And Dick the shepherd blows his nail,°
2 And Tom bears logs into the hall,
　And milk comes frozen home in pail,
When blood is nipped, and ways be foul,° 5
Then nightly sings the staring owl,
3　Tu-whit,
Tu-who, a merry note,
While greasy Joan doth keel° the pot.

When all aloud the wind doth blow, 10
4　And coughing drowns the parson's saw,°
And birds sit brooding in the snow,
5　And Marian's nose looks red and raw,
When roasted crabs° hiss in the bowl,
6 Then nightly sings the staring owl, 15
　Tu-whit,
Tu-who, a merry note,
While greasy Joan doth keel the pot.

2. **blows his nail:** blows on his fingernails to warm his hands.

5. **ways be foul:** roads are muddy.

9. **keel:** cool by stirring.

11. **saw:** wise saying.

14. **crabs:** crab apples.

Ask students to imagine living four hundred years ago in a climate with severe winters. How would living conditions have differed from those in the same region today? Introduce "When Icicles Hang by the Wall" as a song that Shakespeare wrote into his play *Love's Labor's Lost* to describe such a sixteenth-century winter.

After you review with students the vocabulary in the notes, read the poem aloud. Use inflection to help students follow the long parallel sentences that compose each **stanza**. Since the study questions encourage close reading and personal responses, you may want to broaden participation and ensure an exchange of views by dividing students into small discussion groups.

VISUAL CONNECTIONS
Ideas for Writing
This photograph of ice and icicles on rocks suggests the harshness and coldness of winter. Ask students to write a paragraph describing a winter scene so that readers of the paragraph will sense the cold. Encourage students to appeal to their readers' five senses (sight, hearing, touch, taste, smell) as Shakespeare does in "When Icicles Hang by the Wall."

FOR STUDY AND DISCUSSION
1a. Icicles hang; milk is frozen; blood is nipped (chilled); roads are foul (muddy); wind blows; people cough; birds sit in snow; Marian's nose is red and raw.
1b. We hear owl singing, wind blowing, people coughing, shepherd warming hands, and roasted apples hissing.
2a. Joan is stirring something that needs cooling—perhaps a soup or stew. 2b. Roasted crab apples hissing in bowl.
3. Responses will vary. This seems a realistic but not sad picture of winter: it is cold and raw outside but warm and busy in kitchen.

For Study and Discussion

Analyzing and Interpreting the Poem

1. This poem uses images to help you imagine a cold winter scene in sixteenth-century England. For example, line 2 pictures a shepherd blowing on his fingernails to warm his hands. **a.** What other images in the poem help you picture this cold winter scene? **b.** What sounds do you hear?

2. Although the images in the poem emphasize the harshness of winter, some of them suggest warmth and comfort. Tom's logs (line 3) must be for a fire. **a.** What do you think Joan is stirring in the pot? **b.** Which image suggests that something tasty is being cooked?

3. Many poems about autumn or winter give the reader a sense of sadness or loneliness. How does this "Winter's song" affect you?

Begin a discussion of famous cats from literature and popular culture by asking students to identify their favorite celebrity cats. What qualities do these cats have? Are they independent, stealthy, lazy, tidy, or finicky? Is this "screen image" of cats an accurate one? Suggest that as students read the poem, they try to determine the personality of this particular cat.

Give an expressive first reading of the poem so that your students will sense its mysterious mood. Then use the study questions to aid discussion of this mood and to help you explore how—and why—such an everyday occurrence is made to seem serious and suspenseful. This discussion should help prepare students for the writing assignment for this poem.

Calling in the Cat

1
"Dark, a deeper dark" suggests night and mystery.

2
Imagery. Visual images of shining eyes and dew-laden hair suggest the cat's ephemeral presence.

3 Finding Details Analyzing
What both attracts and repels the cat? How do ll. 9 and 10 suggest the cat's indecision? The light from indoors (lamp, firelight) both attracts and repels cat. Lines are same, but order is reversed, indicating attraction to night *and* light.

4
Fastidiously: delicately, to a fault.

FOR STUDY AND DISCUSSION
1. Stealth (ll. 2–3), awareness (l. 3), caution (ll. 6, 7, 17), hesitancy (ll. 7, 9, 10).
2. Knows that food, comfort, warmth are inside but feels drawn to the wild.
3. "Offer up the sacrifice" (ll. 13–14), "snare" (l. 15), and "trap" (l. 18).

WRITING ABOUT LITERATURE
You might suggest that students make these headings on paper: setting, physical description, actions. Have them reread the poem and write down words, phrases, or images that fit under each category. This will provide a list of elements that show the cat as fascinating and mysterious.

Calling in the Cat

ELIZABETH COATSWORTH

1 Now from the dark, a deeper dark,
   The cat slides,
   Furtive and aware,
2 His eyes still shine with meteor spark
   The cold dew weights his hair.   5
   Suspicious,
   Hesitant, he comes
   Stepping morosely from the night,
3 Held but repelled,
   Repelled but held,   10
   By lamp and firelight.

   Now call your blandest,
   Offer up
   The sacrifice of meat,
   And snare the wandering soul with greeds,   15
   Give him to drink and eat,
4 And he shall walk fastidiously
   Into the trap of old
   On feet that still smell delicately
   Of withered ferns and mould.   20

For Study and Discussion

Analyzing and Interpreting the Poem

1. What characteristics of the cat are emphasized in this poem? Refer to specific lines in formulating your answer.

2. Why is the cat both held and repelled?

3. What words and phrases in the second stanza emphasize that the cat must be lured indoors?

Writing About Literature

▶ Discussing Elements of Mystery

From earliest times the cat has been associated with magic. One superstition, for example, claimed that witches were attended by cats that were spirits in animal form. Discuss the elements in the poem that give the cat a fascinating and mysterious character.

▶ Before students begin this writing assignment, you may want to refer them to the **Writing About Literature** section on p. 672.

PRESENTATION

Begin by asking students to recall one of their earliest childhood memories of nature. Where were they? Who were they with? How did they feel?

Have students read the poem silently, and ask a few volunteers to share their responses. Continue by discussing the study questions.

TEACHING RESOURCES E
Teacher's Notes, p. 80
Study Guide, p. 81
Selection Test, pp. 84, 86

AV RESOURCES BINDER
Audiocassette 3, Side B

PREREADING FOCUS
The introduction mentions the two relationships discussed in the poem. Ask students how they might describe their relationship with nature. Do they associate a special person with nature?

Speaking

SIMON J. ORTIZ

In this poem two relationships are discussed. One is the relationship between people and nature. The other is the relationship between a father and his son. Who or what are the different speakers in the poem?

1 I take him outside
under the trees,
have him stand on the ground.
We listen to the crickets,
2 cicadas,° million years old sound.
Ants come by us.
3 I tell them,
"This is he, my son.
This boy is looking at you.
I am speaking for him." 10

The crickets, cicadas,
4 the ants, the millions of years
are watching us,
hearing us.
5 My son murmurs infant words, 15
speaking, small laughter
bubbles from him.
Tree leaves tremble.
6 They listen to this boy
speaking for me. 20

5. **cicadas** (sĭ-kā′dəz): insects that make a high-pitched, droning sound.

Speaking

1
In first three lines, speaker sets scene for some significant event.

2 Analyzing
What does speaker mean by saying insects make "million years old sound"? Sound has not changed in a million years. Suggests link to past and to other fathers who have introduced their children to nature.

3
Personification. Speaker addresses ants as though they can comprehend. This reinforces speaker's relationship to nature.

4 Analyzing
What does speaker mean by "millions of years are watching us, hearing us"? Responses will vary. Insects represent millions of years of natural world. When insects watch and hear, all of history watches and hears through them.

5
Infant words are babblings of baby.

6
Speaker implies his infant son speaks a universal language all of nature understands.

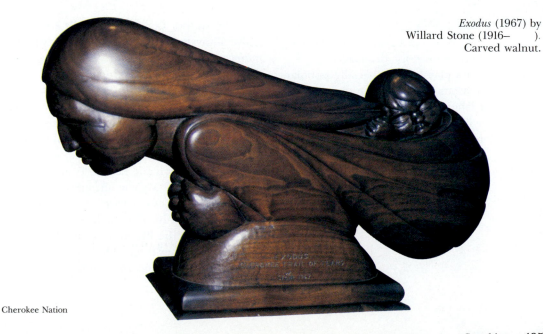

Exodus (1967) by Willard Stone (1916–   ). Carved walnut.

Cherokee Nation

Cats is a good source for poems about cats.

FOR STUDY AND DISCUSSION
Answers will vary.
1a. The father and son share a close, special bond, in which each is able to relate to nature in a way the other is not. The bond between them strengthens their bonds to nature and vice versa.
1b. The ancient bond between nature and humanity is reestablished through communication.
2. Nature "speaks" through the sounds made by the crickets, cicadas, and trees.

For Study and Discussion

Analyzing and Interpreting the Poem

1. In this poem a father is showing his infant son the beauties of nature. **a.** What kind of bond is created between the child and the father? **b.** What kind of bond is created between human beings and the natural world?

2. The father says that he speaks for his son and that his son speaks for him. In what way is nature also "speaking" in this poem?

About the Authors

William Shakespeare (1564–1616)

William Shakespeare was born in the town of Stratford-on-Avon in England. In his twenties he went to London, and after a time he joined a well-known company of actors there. For this acting company he wrote a great series of comedies, tragedies, and historic dramas.

Shakespeare's plays were especially popular for various reasons. For one thing, he wrote in magnificent language. He also had the power to create living characters of all kinds and classes. Morever, his plays have a unique kind of vitality; at each rereading they reveal new depth and meanings.

Elizabeth Coatsworth (1893–1986)

Elizabeth Coatsworth was born in Buffalo. Her work is known for blending the natural and supernatural. She first achieved recognition with *The Cat Who Went to Heaven* (1930), a story based on Japanese folklore. This book was awarded the Newbery Medal for 1931. She wrote many books for children.

Simon J. Ortiz (1941–   )

Simon J. Ortiz, of Acoma Pueblo in New Mexico, has taught at several universities, including San Diego State University, University of New Mexico, Lewis and Clark College, and Sinte Gleska College. Among his published books are *A Good Journey; Going for the Rain; Fight Back: For the Sake of the People, For the Sake of the Land; From Sand Creek* (Pushcart Prize, 1982); and *Woven Stone*.

The Author Comments on His Poem

I've always wondered about the way we communicate among ourselves....Parents teach their children, show things around them, explain experience to them, and then we, as human beings, listen as well to the world around us, the ants, crickets, trees—all life forms millions of years old. They tell us about themselves through their particular ways of living, and they watch and hear us from their own ways of existence. My son, an infant years ago when "Speaking" was written, who graduated from law school in May 1993, spoke with his childsounds to the life around us, the cicadas and trees, and they listened to him speaking for me, who was learning from him.

OBJECTIVES
The overall aim is for students to identify and analyze the dramatic elements (speaker, **setting, characterization, plot**) in Robert Browning's poem. For a complete list of objectives, see the **Teacher's Notes.**

VOCABULARY
The **Language and Vocabulary** exercise on p. 499 gives students practice in recognizing multiple meanings of words.

FOCUS / MOTIVATION
Ask students to envision an Austrian city under attack by Napoleon's troops. A French victory looks doubtful. Napoleon, watching nearby, is eager for news of battle. A boy brings that news in this dramatic poem.

TEACHING RESOURCES E
Teacher's Notes, p. 87
Study Guide, p. 89
Building Vocabulary, p. 91
Selection Test, p. 93

DRAMATIC POETRY

A *dramatic* poem resembles a play in some ways. Sometimes a dramatic poem is in the form of a dialogue between two speakers. Sometimes the speaker is addressing someone who does not respond but whose presence is understood. Narrative poems may also be dramatic, and dramatic poems may contain narrative elements.

Incident of the French Camp

ROBERT BROWNING

This poem is based upon an actual incident which occurred during Napoleon's Austrian campaign in 1809. Marshal Lannes, one of Napoleon's most trusted commanders, stormed the fortified city of Ratisbon in a battle which was crucial for the French.

1 You know, we French stormed Ratisbon.
　　A mile or so away,
On a little mound, Napoleon
　　Stood on our storming-day;
2 With neck out-thrust, you fancy how, 　　　　　　　　　　　5
　　Legs wide, arms locked behind,
As if to balance the prone brow
　　Oppressive with its mind.

Just as perhaps he mused "My plans
　　That soar, to earth may fall, 　　　　　　　　　　　　　　10
Let once my army leader Lannes
　　Waver at yonder wall"—
3 Out 'twixt the battery smokes there flew
　　A rider, bound on bound
Full galloping; nor bridle drew 　　　　　　　　　　　　　15
　　Until he reached the mound.

Incident of the French Camp

1
Frenchman who participated in battle relates poem's events; **setting** is a "mound" a mile from Austrian city of Ratisbon.

2 Drawing Conclusions
What does "oppressive" suggest about Napoleon's feelings? What does his stance suggest? He is worried about battle's outcome. He tries not to show his concern.

3
Imagery. Descriptive details suggest that horse and rider speed toward mound like flying cannonball.

You may want to focus students' attention on the events of the poem by summarizing the first few stanzas for them, but it is probably best to avoid revealing the surprise ending prematurely. After your summary, you might give a dramatic reading of the poem. Be sure that the first four stanzas are charged with the excitement of battle. Read the last stanza in such a way that students will feel its poignancy. After a little practice, good readers might perform the poem for the class.

Use the study questions to help students analyze the poem's dramatic elements. Then continue with discussion of the **Literary Elements** and **Language and Vocabulary** activities and with the **Creative Writing** assignment.

4

Use to answer **study question 4a,** p. 498.

5 Summarizing
Drawing Conclusions
Why does the boy keep his lips compressed? What does this show about his character? He keeps lips compressed to steel himself against his injury. Shows he is courageous.

6

Metaphor. Waving flag is compared to a bird flapping wings.

7

Simile. Napoleon's rising hopes compared to rekindled fire.

8

Simile. Napoleon's eyes are compared to those of a mother eagle whose young is hurt.

FOR STUDY AND DISCUSSION

1a. Frenchman who was with Napoleon. **1b.** Friends, children. **2.** Characters (Napoleon and boy); setting (battle near Ratisbon); plot (boy rides to tell Napoleon of near victory and dies). **3a.** Boy raised Napoleon's banner over city. **3b.** This courageous act would have been expected from older soldier; making hero a boy gives his deed more dramatic impact and makes his death more shocking. **4a.** Line 19. **4b.** Smoke and dust obscure identity. **4c.** Responses will vary, but most will agree that it comes at a dramatic moment, as he leaps from his horse and just before reader learns that he is injured, so that mention of injury creates sympathy. **5.** Sees concern for his cause (ll. 7–8) and for his soldiers (ll. 33–37).

Then off there flung in smiling joy,
    And held himself erect
By just his horse's mane, a boy:
    You hardly could suspect—   20
(So tight he kept his lips compressed,
    Scarce any blood came through)
You looked twice ere you saw his breast
    Was all but shot in two.

"Well," cried he, "Emperor, by God's grace   25
    We've got you Ratisbon!
The Marshal's in the market-place,
    And you'll be there anon°
To see your flag-bird flap his vans°
    Where I, to heart's desire,   30
Perched him!" The chief's eye flashed; his plans
    Soared up again like fire.

The chief's eye flashed; but presently
    Softened itself, as sheathes
A film the mother-eagle's eye   35
    When her bruised eaglet breathes;
"You're wounded!" "Nay," the soldier's pride
    Touched to the quick, he said:
"I'm killed, Sire!" And, his chief beside,
    Smiling, the boy fell dead.   40

28. **anon:** right away.

29. **vans:** wings.
The emblem on Napoleon's banner was an eagle.

For Study and Discussion

Analyzing and interpreting the Poem

1a. Who is the speaker in this poem? **b.** To whom might he be telling this incident of the French camp?

2. Many dramatic poems are also narrative poems. Show that this poem contains the three basic elements of a short story: characters, setting, and plot.

3a. According to lines 27–31, what part did the boy play in the battle? **b.** Some historians say that a man, not a boy, performed the act of bravery. Why is Browning's choice of a boy more effective in arousing the reader's sympathy?

4. Look again at the description of the boy's ride (lines 14–24). **a.** In which line do we realize that the rider is a boy? **b.** Why would an observer see him at first as simply "a rider"? **c.** Does the information that he is a boy come at the best dramatic moment?

5. What special qualities does the narrator see in Napoleon that might inspire devotion such as that of the wounded boy?

CLOSURE
Ask students to identify the speaker of the poem and to discuss the story the speaker tells in terms of the dramatic elements of **setting**, **characterization**, and **plot**.

EXTENSION AND ENRICHMENT
Some students might enjoy illustrating one or more scenes from the poem. Other students might research another famous historical event and write a story or poem from the **first-person point of view** of one of its participants. Still

others might wish to read biographical accounts of Napoleon or Robert Browning or read other poems by Browning.

Literary Elements

Understanding Simile

To describe Napoleon's reaction to the boy's injury, the poet uses a **simile** (lines 34–36). As you have seen, a simile is a figure of speech that compares one thing to another, using the word *like* or *as* to suggest the similarity the poet sees between two things. In "Incident of the French Camp," Napoleon's eye softens *as* a mother eagle's eye is sheathed by a membra-

1 nous film. What is Napoleon compared to in
2 this simile? What does this comparison suggest
3 about his reaction to the boy's wound? Can you find another effective simile in this poem?

Language and Vocabulary

Recognizing Multiple Meanings of Words

1 What is the meaning of the word *oppressive* in
2 line 8? What is another common meaning of this word? Look up the root of the word *oppress*
3 in a dictionary. What is the meaning of the
4 Latin word from which it came? Does this orig-inal meaning of the word give you a more vivid
5 sense of what it means to be oppressed? How is the oppression of a dictator, for instance,
6 different from that of Napoleon's mind? How are the two similar?

Focus on Writing a Poem

Controlling Rhythm for Effect

Rhythm is the pattern of stressed and unstressed sounds in a line of poetry or in a passage of prose. Although all language has rhythm of some sort or another, rhythm is especially important in poetry.

On a sheet of paper, copy six to ten lines from your favorite poem so far in this unit.

Then get together with a small group of class-mates. Take turns reading your favorite pas-sages aloud. Pay special attention to the rhythm of the words. Discuss with your group the different ways in which you can use the rhythm of the words to create a certain mood or to emphasize the meaning of the passage.

About the Author

Robert Browning   (1812–1889)

Robert Browning, one of England's greatest poets, is noted for the dramatic situations and vivid characters in his poems. Fasci-nated by history, he frequently drew upon the past of other coun-tries, especially Italy and France, for his sub-jects. His elopement with the English poet Elizabeth Barrett, one of the world's famous love stories, has been told by numerous biogra-phers and dramatized by Rudolf Besier in the play *The Barretts of Wimpole Street*.

LITERARY ELEMENTS
1. Compared to a mother eagle who is concerned for its bruised eaglet.
2. Suggests an instinctive con-cern for boy. He responds imme-diately upon realizing that boy is wounded.
3. Comparison of Napoleon's feelings about his plans to a soar-ing fire (ll. 31–32).

LANGUAGE AND VOCABULARY
1. *Oppressive:* weighing heavily upon.
2. Another common meaning is "tyrannical."
3. Latin derivation of *oppress* is *opprimere*, which means "to press against."
4. Original meaning makes the modern meaning more vivid.
5. Napoleon's mind is oppressed by heavy thought and worry. Dic-tator's oppression involves injus-tice—forcing people to act against their wishes.
6. One condition is mental, the other physical (involving actions), but in both, a pressure is felt or exerted.

FOCUS ON WRITING A POEM
You may want to mark on the chalkboard the stressed and un-stressed syllables in a few lines of poetry. Then students can experi-ment with marking stressed and unstressed syllables in the lines they have copied.

ABOUT THE AUTHOR
Browning's mature work was strongly influenced by three fac-tors: his experience with play-writing, the soliloquies of Shakespeare, and John Donne's poetry. His work is modern in his use of allusions to contemporary events and of the technique of beginning a dramatic narrative in the middle of the action.

COMIC VERSE

Anonymous Limericks

A limerick is a short humorous poem with a characteristic form. What is its rhythm and rhyme pattern?

There was a young man of Bengal
Who went to a fancy-dress ball.
1   He went just for fun
    Dressed up as a bun,
And a dog ate him up in the hall.

2 I sat next the Duchess at tea.
It was just as I feared it would be:
    Her rumblings abdominal
    Were simply abominable,
And everyone thought it was me.

3 There was a young fellow of Perth,
4 Who was born on the day of his birth;
    He was married, they say,
    On his wife's wedding day,
And he died when he quitted the earth.

5 A gentleman dining at Crewe
Found quite a large mouse in his stew.
    Said the waiter, "Don't shout,
    And wave it about,
Or the rest will be wanting one too!"

Creative Writing

Writing Limericks

No one knows who invented this funny five-line verse form. Some say limericks began in Limerick, Ireland, but most people there refuse to take responsibility for them. Wherever they came from, limericks seem here to stay. Some groups hold limerick contests. Great poets write limericks for fun. A former President of the United States wrote limericks.

Try writing some limericks of your own. Often limericks include the name of some town or country, or the name of a person. You could start out with a line like one of these:

There was a young lady from York
There once was a fellow named Hank

Ask each student to tell about an animal that for some reason is funny because of its name, physical characteristics, or the sounds it makes. Some examples might be the hippopotamus, the platypus, and the turkey. Tell students that the poet Ogden Nash finds humor in a variety of animals and that his poems will introduce them to a unique poetic style.

Let students read these poems silently; then call on volunteers to read them aloud. Use the margin annotations and the **Literary Elements** exercise to guide a discussion of Nash's use of humorous language in his poetry.

TEACHING RESOURCES E
Teacher's Notes, p. 97
Study Guide, p. 98
Selection Test, p. 120

Private Zoo

OGDEN NASH

The Octopus

1 Tell me, O Octopus, I begs,
Is those things arms, or is they legs?
I marvel at thee, Octopus;
2 If I were thou, I'd call me Us.

The Panther

3 The panther is like a leopard,
Except it hasn't been peppered.
Should you behold a panther crouch,
Prepare to say Ouch.
Better yet, if called by a panther,
4 Don't anther.

The Rhinoceros

The rhino is a homely beast,
For human eyes he's not a feast.
Farewell, farewell, you old rhinoceros.
5 I'll stare at something less prepocerous.

Private Zoo

1
Nash takes grammatical liberties with English language, substituting *begs* for *beg* and *is* for *are*.

2 Finding Details
Analyzing
Which pronoun does the speaker think is appropriate for the octopus? Why? The speaker thinks "us" is appropriate because the octopus has too many legs/arms for one creature.

3 Summarizing
What does Nash mean by "the panther . . . hasn't been peppered"? Panther does not have spots like leopard.

4
Rhyme. To complete rhyme with "panther" Nash invents "anther," a humorous replacement for the word *answer.*

5
Rhyme. To complete rhyme with "rhinoceros," Nash invents "prepocerous," a slurring of the word *preposterous.*

LITERARY ELEMENTS
1. A third-person singular verb (*begs*) is used with a first-person singular subject (*I*), and singular verb (*is*) is used with plural subjects (*things* and *they*).
2. "Anther" as rhyme for "panther."
3. "Prepocerous" as rhyme for "rhinoceros."
4. "Anther" sounds like *answer;* "prepocerous" sounds like *preposterous.*
5. If familiar words are used, fun and nonsense are lost.

Literary Elements

Recognizing Humorous Rhymes

Ogden Nash often creates humorous rhymes by twisting words, or by using made-up words.
1 How is the grammar in "The Octopus" misused so that the lines rhyme?
2 Which word in "The Panther" is invented to
3 fit the rhyme? Which word in "The Rhinoceros" is also original? What familiar words do
4 these two made-up words sound like? Substitute the familiar words for the made-up ones,
5 and then reread the poems. What happens to the humor?

Ask students to explain the phrase "deadpan humor." What comedians usually tell jokes without cracking a smile? Why do some jokes seem funnier when they are told with a straight face? Link the discussion to the headnote, which refers to the serious tone of Guiterman's title and its humorous nature within the context of the poem itself.

Read the poem aloud with mock eloquence until you reach the last line, which should be read with a wry informality. Be certain that students understand what Guiterman means in the title and the last line. Use the **Literary Elements** exercise to expand students' understanding of Guiterman's technique.

On the Vanity of Earthly Greatness

1
Billiards is a game similar to pool; billiard balls were once made from tusks of elephants, the descendants of mighty, now extinct, mastodons.

2
Charlemagne (Charles the Great) was King of Franks and the Holy Roman Emperor; sword turning to rust suggests that political power is fleeting and that greatness becomes trivial.

3
Rhyme. Each set of two rhyming lines in poem forms a meaningful unit.

4 Making Generalizations
What lesson does the speaker learn from the three examples in the poem? Existence of everything on earth—even great things—is temporary; therefore, his own existence must also be temporary.

LITERARY ELEMENTS
1. Charlemagne's sword, grizzly bear, and Caesar.
2. Rust, rug, and sculptured bust.
3. Realizing that he, too, will someday be "history," it is not surprising that poet feels ill.
4. After students work through this exercise, allow time for them to share lists of great and glorious things that remain only in trivial form. Students might list examples such as deadly snakes that end up as hatbands or giant ships that now rest on the ocean floor.

On the Vanity of Earthly Greatness

ARTHUR GUITERMAN

The word vanity *in this title means "uselessness." The title has a serious ring to it, but don't let it fool you.*

The tusks that clashed in mighty brawls
1 Of mastodons, are billiard balls.

2 The sword of Charlemagne the Just
Is ferric oxide, known as rust.

3 The grizzly bear whose potent hug
Was feared by all, is now a rug.

Great Caesar's bust is on the shelf,
4 And I don't feel so well myself.

Literary Elements

Recognizing the Techniques of Comic Verse

Many writers over the ages have written seriously about the passage of time and the worthlessness of earthly success. But this poem is meant to be comical. Part of its humor comes from the way in which the poet links very mighty things with very ordinary things. For example, when he thinks of the mastodon's gigantic tusks, he thinks of billiard balls, which are all that he imagines is left of them today.

1 What other mighty things from the past
2 does he think of? What does he say is left of
3 them today? Is it any wonder that the poet doesn't feel well himself?

This verse is also comical because of its strong rhymes and rhythms. Notice how the poet never skips a beat, even though he probably had to do some thinking to match up "potent hug" with "now a rug."

Perhaps you can add to the poet's comical
4 complaint. What other great and glorious things are now gone, remaining only as leather shoes, note paper, or old portraits?

MOTIVATIONAL SUMMARY

When Casey at last comes to bat for Mudville's home team, it is the final inning, and the score is 4–2, with the tying runs on second and third. A smiling and confident Casey has two strikes; now it is his last swing.

PRESENTATION

Ask what game is known as "The Great American Pastime." Then give a short, oral baseball quiz, asking for definitions of such phrases as *line drive, double play, sacrifice fly,* and so on. Introduce "Casey at the Bat" as one of the most famous poems ever written about baseball or any other game.

Preview the vocabulary and alert students to look for "high-flown language that is humorously overdone for the occasion. Be sure to provide a lively reading of this poem. A mock-serious,

Casey at the Bat

ERNEST LAWRENCE THAYER

This is one of the most famous poems ever written about baseball. When it was first recited to a group of baseball fans, the audience went wild. As you read, see if you can find reasons for the poem's enormous popularity.

1 The outlook wasn't brilliant for the Mudville nine that day;
  The score stood four to two, with but one inning more to play;
2 And so, when Cooney died at first, and Burrows did the same,
  A sickly silence fell upon the patrons of the game.

  A straggling few got up to go in deep despair. The rest   5
  Clung to the hope which springs eternal in the human breast;
3 They thought, if only Casey could but get a whack, at that,
  They'd put up even money now, with Casey at the bat.

  But Flynn preceded Casey, as did also Jimmy Blake,
4 And the former was a pudding, and the latter was a fake;   10
5 So upon that stricken multitude grim melancholy sat,
  For there seemed but little chance of Casey's getting to the bat.

  But Flynn let drive a single, to the wonderment of all,
  And Blake, the much-despised, tore the cover off the ball;
  And when the dust had lifted, and they saw what had occurred,   15
  There was Jimmy safe on second, and Flynn a-hugging third.

6 Then from the gladdened multitude went up a joyous yell;
  It bounded from the mountaintop, and rattled in the dell;
  It struck upon the hillside, and recoiled upon the flat;
  For Casey, mighty Casey, was advancing to the bat.   20

  There was ease in Casey's manner as he stepped into his place;
  There was pride in Casey's bearing, and a smile on Casey's face;
7 And when, responding to the cheers, he lightly doffed his hat,
  No stranger in the crowd could doubt 'twas Casey at the bat.

TEACHING RESOURCES E

Teacher's Notes, p. 102
Study Guide, p. 104
Language Skills, p. 108
Building Vocabulary, p. 110
Selection Test, p. 120

AV RESOURCES BINDER

Audiocassette 3, Side B

Casey at the Bat

1
Setting. Scene is set in town of "Mudville"; Mudville team has one inning left in which to score three runs it needs to win.

2 Summarizing
What is the situation with Cooney and Burrows "dead" at first? Mudville team has two outs.

3 Finding Details
What clue is there that Casey is the best player on the Mudville team? Fans would bet their money on winning if Casey were at bat.

Finding Details
4 Drawing Conclusions
What does the speaker call Flynn and Blake? What do the descriptions suggest? He calls them a "pudding" and a "fake," respectively. These descriptions suggest that they are not very good players.

5
Personification. Image of "grim melancholy" sitting on "stricken multitude" is humorous because it is more appropriate to a funeral than a baseball game.

6
Exaggerated enthusiasm of crowd as contrasted to funereal **tone** of l. 11 is humorous.

7
Casey's bearing and "doffing," or tipping, his hat suggest his pride—and set him up for a humorous fall.

almost oratorical tone is most effective.

You may want to let pairs of students or small groups work together to answer and discuss the study questions. You can provide for individual interests and abilities by dividing the class into groups, allowing some students to work on the **Creative Writing** assignment and others to prepare the pantomime suggested in the **For Dramatization** section.

8 Drawing Conclusions
What do Casey's "defiance" and "sneer" suggest? Casey is proud, arrogant.

9
Casey's informal, ungrammatical response contrasts humorously with high-flown language used to describe him. Reader can infer from his reply that he is very confident—perhaps overconfident. Casey's pride may do him in.

10
Simile. Figurative comparison of crowd's roar to beating waves is again humorous because the majesty of the image is inappropriate to reality it describes.

11 Finding Cause and Effect
What effect do phrases "Christian charity" and "Casey's visage shone" have on reader? They imply that Casey has saint-like qualities he does not have.

12
Use to answer study question 1, p. 505.

VISUAL CONNECTIONS
About the Artwork
Dorne's watercolor effectively recreates the folk, or tall tale, quality of the ballad. The exaggerated expectations of the "hero" are portrayed in his extraordinary size, in the expressions on the faces in the crowd, and in the impossible position of Casey's legs. One source of humor is the contrasting facial expressions of Casey, the catcher, and the umpire.

Ten thousand eyes were on him as he rubbed his hands with dirt; 25
Five thousand tongues applauded when he wiped them on his shirt;
Then while the writhing pitcher ground the ball into his hip,
8 Defiance gleamed in Casey's eye, a sneer curled Casey's lip.

And now the leather-covered sphere came hurtling through the air,
And Casey stood a-watching it in haughty grandeur there; 30
Close by the sturdy batsman the ball unheeded sped.
9 "That ain't my style," said Casey. "Strike one," the umpire said.

10 From the benches, black with people, there went up a muffled roar,
Like the beating of the storm waves on a stern and distant shore;
"Kill him! Kill the umpire!" shouted someone on the stand; 35
And it's likely they'd have killed him had not Casey raised his hand.

11 With a smile of Christian charity great Casey's visage shone;
He stilled the rising tumult; he bade the game go on;
12 He signaled to the pitcher, and once more the spheroid flew;
But Casey still ignored it, and the umpire said, "Strike two." 40

Mighty Casey Has Struck Out by Albert Dorne (1904–1965). Watercolor.
The National Baseball Hall of Fame and Museum, Inc.

504

"Fraud!" cried the maddened thousands, and the echo
    answered, "Fraud!"
But a scornful look from Casey, and the audience was <u>awed</u>;
They saw his face grow stern and cold, they saw his muscles strain,
13 And they knew that Casey wouldn't let that ball go by again.

14 The sneer is gone from Casey's lips, his teeth are clenched in hate,   45
He pounds with cruel violence his bat upon the plate;
And now the pitcher holds the ball, and now he lets it go,
And now the air is shattered by the force of Casey's blow.

15 Oh! somewhere in this favored land the sun is shining bright;
The band is playing somewhere, and somewhere hearts are light;   50
And somewhere men are laughing, and somewhere children shout,
16 But there is no joy in Mudville—mighty Casey has struck out!

For Study and Discussion

Analyzing and Interpreting the Poem

1. Ernest Lawrence Thayer creates a humorous effect by using high-flown, or fancy, language to describe an ordinary event—a baseball game played in a town called Mudville. For example, in line 29, the poet doesn't say "baseball"; instead, he says "leather-covered sphere." What does the poet say instead of "baseball" in line 39?

2. Casey, Mudville's hero, is also described in high-flown, heroic language. **a.** What words and phrases in lines 20–30 describe him? **b.** How does Casey's own speech in line 32 differ from the heroic language used to describe him?

3a. What image, or picture, is created in line 11? **b.** How is this image funny if you take it literally? **c.** What fancy simile is used in lines 33–34 to describe the crowd's roar?

Focus on Writing a Poem

Organizing Details

Organizing the details in a poem helps your readers to grasp your meaning better. To organize a poem effectively, you can use a number of different methods:

chronological (time) order: the order in which events happen

spatial order: the order in which things are placed

order of impression: the order in which an observer notices things

order of the senses: details of one sense, then another, and so on

Use one of the methods above to write an **outline** in note form for a short poem on a subject of your choice. When you have finished writing, exchange papers with a classmate. Offer each other comments on your outlines. Save your notes.

Jabberwocky

1 Analyzing
What atmosphere is created in the first stanza? Responses will vary. Dangerous, cheerful, mysterious, playful.

2
Foreshadowing. Advice from old man hints at future **conflict**. Conversation is between older man and boy, perhaps father and son.

3 Finding Details
Who is the "manxome foe"? The Jabberwock.

4
Onomatopoeia. "Whiffling"—blowing puffs of air—and "burbled"—made a bubbling sound—re-create their sounds; they both describe and name.

5
Galumphing, a word Carroll invented but now part of standard English vocabulary, means "marching or bounding along in a self-satisfied manner."

6
Carroll coined these words which are now considered standard English: *beamish* means "beaming, radiant, and cheerful"; *chortled* is a gleeful mixture of chuckling and snorting.

506

Jabberwocky

LEWIS CARROLL

In a book called Through the Looking Glass, *Alice steps through a mirror and into a world of reversals. She finds this poem in a "mirror-book," written backward. As you read the poem, note how the poet manages to tell a story with some very unusual words.*

1 'Twas brillig, and the slithy toves
       Did gyre and gimble in the wabe;
    All mimsy were the borogoves,
       And the mome raths outgrabe.

2 "Beware the Jabberwock, my son!   5
       The jaws that bite, the claws that catch!
    Beware the Jubjub bird, and shun
       The frumious Bandersnatch!"

    He took his vorpal sword in hand;
3   Long time the manxome foe he sought—   10
    So rested he by the Tumtum tree,
       And stood awhile in thought.

    And, as in uffish thought he stood,
       The Jabberwock, with eyes of flame,
4 Came whiffling through the tulgey wood,   15
       And burbled as it came!

    One, two! One, two! And through and through
       The vorpal blade went snicker-snack!
    He left it dead, and with its head
5   He went galumphing back.   20

    "And hast thou slain the Jabberwock?
6   Come to my arms, my beamish boy!
    O frabjous day! Callooh! Callay!"
       He chortled in his joy.

Illustration by Sir John Tenniel (1820–1914) for *Through the Looking-Glass* (1870).

'Twas brillig and the slithy toves   25
   Did gyre and gimble in the wabe;
All mimsy were the borogoves,
   And the mome raths outgrabe.

Picture Collection, The Branch Libraries, The New York Public Library

MEETING INDIVIDUAL NEEDS
ESL/LEP • Non-native speakers may find Carroll's poem especially challenging. Have students close their books while you read the poem aloud. Explain that Carroll uses standard syntax (arrangement of words in each sentence) to give the impression that the poem, despite its many made-up words, makes sense. Given contextual clues, can students guess at the action? How many characters are involved? What happens between them? Challenge students to create dictionary entries for the made-up words in the poem. The entries should include approximate definitions and parts of speech. Students might also enjoy writing original sentences that include invented words.

Language and Vocabulary

Explaining Portmanteau Words

Alice asks Humpty Dumpty to explain "Jabberwocky." Here is their conversation.

"*Brillig* means four o'clock in the afternoon—the time when you begin *broiling* things for dinner."

"That'll do very well," said Alice; "and *slithy?*"

"Well, *slithy* means 'lithe and slimy.' *Lithe* is the same as 'active.' You see it's like a portmanteau—there are two meanings packed up into one word."

"I see it now," Alice remarked thoughtfully; "and what are *toves?*"

"Well, *toves* are something like badgers—they're something like lizards—and they're something like corkscrews."

"They must be very curious-looking creatures."

"They are that," said Humpty Dumpty; "also they make their nests under sundials—also they live on cheese."

"And what's to *gyre* and to *gimble?*"

"To *gyre* is to go round and round like a gyroscope. To *gimble* is to make holes like a gimlet."

"And *the wabe* is the grass plot round a sundial, I suppose?" said Alice, surprised at her own ingenuity.

"Of course it is. It's called *wabe,* you know, because it goes a long way before it, and a long way behind it——"

"And a long way beyond it on each side," Alice added.

"Exactly so. Well then, *mimsy* is 'flimsy and miserable' (there's another portmanteau for you). And a *borogove* is a thin, shabby-looking bird with its feathers sticking out all round—something like a live mop."

"And then *mome raths?*" said Alice. "I'm afraid I'm giving you a great deal of trouble."

"Well, a *rath* is a sort of green pig; but *mome* I'm not certain about. I think it's short for 'from home'—meaning that they'd lost their way, you know."

"And what does *outgrabe* mean?"

"Well, *outgribing* is something between bellowing and whistling, with a kind of sneeze in the middle; however, you'll hear it done, maybe—down in the wood yonder—and, when you've once heard it, you'll be *quite* content. Who's been repeating all that hard stuff to you?"

"I read it in a book," said Alice.

1 A *portmanteau* is a suitcase that opens into two parts. What does Humpty Dumpty say a *portmanteau word* is?

Try to explain the two meanings "packed up into" these common portmanteau words. Check your answers in your dictionary.

2   brunch   motel   smog   transistor

Focus on Writing a Poem

Coining Words and Phrases

Have you ever made up your own words or phrases? Does your family or your group of friends use any private words, abbreviations, or colloquial expressions?

Poets not only help the rest of us to see our world more clearly. They are also usually leaders in our use of language. William Shakespeare, for example, created and used hundreds of new words.

Write a brief, humorous paragraph of prose or a few lines of verse in which you use three or four new verbs, nouns, adjectives, or adverbs. Then join with a small group of classmates and take turns reading your passages aloud. Be prepared to explain your word coinages, the way Humpty Dumpty explains "Jabberwocky" to Alice. Save your writing.

LANGUAGE AND VOCABULARY
After students have read the exercise and discussed Humpty Dumpty's explication of the poem, direct attention to the concluding exercise. Students should complete this task independently. To extend work on portmanteau words, ask your class to collect other examples or to create some. You might provide felt pens and index cards for students to use in posting their examples on the bulletin board. Periodically, allow time to discuss new additions and to use them in original sentences.

Answers
1. A word that blends two meanings.
2. *Brunch:* One meal that combines breakfast and lunch.
Motel: motor (for a car) and hotel; primarily intended for overnight lodging during automobile trips.
Smog: smoke and fog; chemical components of smoke react in presence of sunlight to form more toxic compounds.
Transistor: transfer and resistor; transfers electrical current across resistors.

FOCUS ON WRITING A POEM
Students will benefit from a whole-class brainstorming session for made-up words. As students come up with new words, they could write them on the chalkboard and identify their meanings and parts of speech. Students can then write their paragraphs individually. Afterward, students might enjoy compiling a class dictionary of made-up words.

Ask students to vote on the funniest poem in this section, providing reasons for their choices. Also have them identify the characteristics of each nominated poem.

EXTENSION AND ENRICHMENT

Students might write their own **limericks,** poems with fractured **rhymes,** or poems about confrontations with the Jubjub bird or the frumious Bandersnatch. These poems can be illustrated and used in a bulletin-board display.

ABOUT THE AUTHORS

Ogden Nash

Nash wrote light, humorous and more serious, satiric verse. Many of his poems are about animals. He used puns and uneven lines and often coined words. Among Nash's books are *Happy Days* (1933), *Many Long Years Ago* (1945), *You Can't Get There From Here* (1975), *The Christmas That Almost Wasn't* (1958), *The Old Dog Barks Backward* (1972), and *I Wouldn't Have Missed It* (1975).

Ernest Lawrence Thayer

Thayer wrote his Sunday ballads for the *San Francisco Examiner* under the pseudonym "Phin." He also wrote ballads for the New York *Journal* for a short time. Thayer later joined his father's textile firm in Worchester, Massachusetts, and ceased writing for publication.

Lewis Carroll

While Carroll is best known for his stories of Alice's adventures, he also wrote a nonsense epic poem titled *The Hunting of the Snark: An Agony in Eight Fits* (1876) and two children's novels, *Sylvie and Bruno* (1889) and *Sylvie and Bruno Concluded* (1893). He also published poetry collections, books on mathematics and logic, and puzzles and games. Carroll also was a portrait photographer and, less successfully, an illustrator.

About the Authors

Ogden Nash   (1902–1971)

Ogden Nash is America's most famous writer of comic verse. He was admired greatly during his lifetime, and his whimsical poems for adults and children still are extremely popular. Some of his lines—such as "If called by a panther, / Don't anther"—have become part of modern American folk culture. He once described himself as a "worsifier." Nash was born in Rye, New York. He worked as a teacher and a bond salesman, and then as an advertising copy writer before he could support his family with his verse. His first book of humorous verse, *Hard Lines*, was published in 1931. In addition to many books of poetry, Nash wrote three screenplays, lyrics for the successful Broadway musical *One Touch of Venus,* and lyrics for several television specials. He also made regular radio and television appearances.

Ernest Lawrence Thayer   (1863–1940)

Ernest Lawrence Thayer, a native of Lawrence, Massachusetts, was an American journalist and poet. He was a graduate of Harvard University and president of the *Harvard Lampoon* during his senior year. In 1886 he joined the staff of the *San Francisco Examiner,* where he wrote a humorous column and ballads for the Sunday editions. The newspaper printed "Casey at the Bat" in 1888. The poem became a nationwide favorite when recited all over the country by touring actor De Wolfe Hopper. Thayer devoted his later years to traveling, studying philosophy, and writing.

Lewis Carroll   (1832–1898)

The Granger Collection, New York

Lewis Carroll, whose real name was Charles Lutwidge Dodgson, was a mathematics teacher at Oxford University in England. He was friendly with a little girl named Alice Liddell, to whom he told stories. Out of this friendship came two of the most popular fantasies ever written, *Alice's Adventures in Wonderland* and *Through the Looking Glass.* Some of the other famous characters in these two books are the Mad Hatter, the March Hare, the Cheshire Cat, and Tweedledum and Tweedledee. Carroll once claimed that mathematics is the true wonderland, for "nothing is impossible" there.

OBJECTIVES

The overall aim is for students to analyze the sound devices, **theme,** and **mood** of a poem.

PRESENTATION

You might divide the class into small groups for this activity. One student should read the poem "Mount Kearsarge" aloud while other students listen and make notes based on the questions that follow. Then students can discuss the

sound patterns in the poem and agree on answers to the questions. Have a member of each group share the group's ideas with the class.

FOCUS ON *Reading and Critical Thinking*

RELATING SOUND TO MEANING

During this unit you have learned that the sounds of words in poetry can be closely related to a poem's meaning. Sound patterns include end rhyme, internal rhyme, repetition, alliteration, and onomatopoeia. Writers use sound devices in prose as well as in poetry.

Read aloud the poem below. Then join with a small group of classmates for the activity that follows.

Mount Kearsarge

Great blue mountain! Ghost.
I look at you
from the porch of the farmhouse
where I watched you all summer
as a boy. Steep sides, narrow flat
patch on top—
you are clear to me
like the memory of one day.
Blue! Blue!
The top of the mountain floats
in haze.
I will not rock on this porch
when I am old. I turn my back on you,
Kearsarge, I close
my eyes, and you rise inside me,
blue ghost.

—Donald Hall

Relating Sound to Meaning

1. Working in small groups, use a separate sheet of paper to list the sound devices that you think contribute to the vivid description in Hall's poem. List one or more specific examples from the text for each sound device.

2. Discuss with your group what you think is the theme or message of this poem. State the theme in a sentence or two.

3. How would you describe the speaker's mood in this poem? Choose an adjective from the list below that most nearly describes the mood that the poem suggests. If none of these adjectives fits, pick an adjective of your own to describe the mood.

angry	jealous	sad
dreamy	nostalgic	self-pitying
happy	regretful	

RELATING SOUND TO MEANING

Every word has both a sound and a meaning. Poets capitalize on this by choosing words whose sounds emphasize, suggest, or enhance meaning. This helps to hold the reader's attention and to strengthen the overall effect and meaning of the poem.

Answers

Answers may vary.
1. End rhyme is irregular with "Blue" in l. 9 rhyming with "you" in ll. 2 and 13. Internal rhyme appears in l. 15, "eyes" and "rise." Repetition occurs with the words "mountain," "blue," "ghost," "porch." Several lines contain alliteration— "Great. . . Ghost," and "Steep sides." Onomatopoeia does not occur.
2. Possible statement of theme: Memories of youth can haunt us forever.
3. Students might suggest the mood of the poem is dreamy, regretful, sad, or nostalgic. Encourage students to support their interpretations with evidence from the poem.

FOCUS ON *Writing*

WRITING A POEM

Poets give their readers unexpected angles of vision. We all have different ways of looking at the world. Now you will have the chance to capture an individual thought or feeling of your own by writing a short poem.

Prewriting

1. Choose a subject for your poem by brainstorming about familiar people, objects, events, and experiences. To get yourself in a creative mood, try coming up with a figure of speech to describe one of the following:

- the feeling you have when you run (or swim, or ride your bike)
- the way the earth smells after a rainfall
- what a dog sounds like when it eats
- what a dripping faucet sounds like when you are trying to sleep

Talk over possible subjects with a classmate. Remember that almost anything can be a good subject for a poem. [See **Focus** assignment on page 462.]

2. When you have found a good subject, list as many **sensory details** about it as you can. Make chart like the one below.

Sense	Image
Sight	_____
Sound	_____
Smell	_____
Taste	_____
Touch	_____

[See **Focus** assignment on page 467.]

3. Experiment with phrases that involve **figures of speech** and **sound effects**. Here are some of the devices you can use in your poem to make your language memorable:

Figures of Speech

- **simile:** uses *like* or *as* to compare two different things
- **metaphor:** compares two different things directly
- **personification:** gives human qualities to something nonhuman
- **symbol:** something that stands for something else beyond itself

Sound Effects

- **repetition**
- **rhyme**
- **alliteration:** repetition of a sound in a group of words
- **onomatopoeia:** use of a word whose sound suggests its meaning

[See **Focus** assignments on pages 472 and 481.]

4. Use one of the following methods to organize the details for your poem. If you wish, make an **outline** of your poem in note form.

- chronological order
- order of impression
- spatial order
- order of the senses

[See **Focus** assignment on page 505.]

students at the beginning of this activity how you intend to assess their poems. The class might develop a scoring guide based on the **Checklist for Evaluation and Revision.** To close, ask students to identify the poetic elements they used in their poems and to explain how they relate to the meanings of the poems.

TRANSPARENCY 37

Writing Process
Writing a Poem – helps students to generate ideas and write an imaginative poem.

Writing

As you write your poem, concentrate on using fresh, vivid phrases that will make the main impression and meaning come alive for your readers. Do not be shy about occasionally coining words and phrases in your poem. [See **Focus** assignments on pages 499 and 507.]

Evaluating and Revising

1. When you have finished your poem, put it aside for a while. Then evaluate it as objectively as you can. Add, cut, reorder, or replace words. Remember that poetry is a craft, like cabinetry or watchmaking. Polish your poem until it shines!

Here is an example of how a writer revised part of a poem.

Writer's Model

The moon ~~moves~~ *sails*

High up in the ~~sky~~ *cold, blue night*

A ~~few stars are shining~~ *shows, but fiercely*

A fox ~~hunts~~ *forages* for food, ~~scared~~ *fears* of his

own shadow.

2. You may find the following checklist helpful as you revise your poem.

Checklist for Evaluation and Revision

✓ Does the poem convey a main impression about a subject?
✓ Have I included vivid descriptions and sensory details?
✓ Do the figures of speech create fresh and lively images?
✓ Do I use sound effects that help to convey my meaning?
✓ Are all my words as precise as possible?

Proofreading and Publishing

1. Proofread your poem and correct any errors you find in grammar, usage, and mechanics. (Here you may find it helpful to refer to the **Handbook for Revision** on pages 712–755.) Then prepare a final version of your poem by making a clean copy.

2. Consider some of the following publication methods for your poem:

- illustrate your poem and post it on the class bulletin board
- submit your poem to a literary magazine
- join with classmates to create a poetry forum, and read your poems aloud

Portfolio If your teacher approves, you may wish to keep a copy of your work in your writing folder or portfolio.

Writing
For students who wish to write a rhymed poem, a rhyming dictionary will be a valuable resource. All students will find a thesaurus helpful as they look for additional words to enhance both meaning and sound. Students who feel comfortable doing so should be allowed to try freewriting their first drafts. Then, if necessary, they can experiment with various strategies for incorporating figurative language and sound devices.

Evaluating and Revising
To help students evaluate their poems, suggest that they use the **Checklist for Evaluation and Revision.** Students may also want to enlist help from individual peers. Students can revise their poems based on their own findings and their peers' responses and suggestions.

Proofreading and Publishing
Remind students that punctuation and capitalization provide the signposts for a reader's interpretation of their poems. Therefore, students want to proofread carefully for commas, end punctuation, and appropriate capitalization. Also, students should be reminded that if they stretch the rules of usage, which poets often do, it must be clear to readers that they have done so intentionally and for a specific purpose.

THE NOVEL

OVERVIEW OF THE UNIT

The coming-of-age novel is an important part of literature for young people because it touches on important aspects of growing up. In Will Hobbs' *Beardance,* students watch a Native American boy become a young man as he takes on adult responsibilities and becomes aware of his spiritual heritage as a member of the Ute people.

Published in 1993, *Beardance* is a young adult novel that deals with the relationship of human beings and nature. Hobbs thus writes in the tradition of Ralph Waldo Emerson and others who wrote on themes of philosophy and nature. *Beardance* is also a suspenseful adventure story that introduces students to problems of endangered animal species and to important aspects of a Native American culture.

The novel is divided into three parts, each of which is followed by exercises and activities that focus on close reading and on elements of the novel (including plot, character, setting, point of view, and theme). The suggested writing activities will enhance students' understanding of the novel and help them clarify their responses to it.

OBJECTIVES OF THE UNIT

The aims of the unit are for students:
◆ To identify and explain aspects of the novel related to setting, character, plot, point of view, and theme
◆ To predict probable action based on events which have already occurred
◆ To write sentences using active verbs
◆ To write essays on the development of Cloyd's character
◆ To analyze plot to determine crisis, climax, and resolution
◆ To write a letter
◆ To debate a proposition about a character's behavior
◆ To make connections between literature and culture

CONCEPTS AND SKILLS

The following concepts and skills are treated in this unit:

CLOSE READING OF A NOVEL

Guidelines for Close Reading   515

LITERARY ELEMENTS/TERMS AND TECHNIQUES

Understanding the Novel   547, 581, 610

LANGUAGE AND VOCABULARY SKILLS

Using Active Verbs   582

OPPORTUNITIES FOR WRITING

Writing About Literature
Recognizing Dynamic Characters   582

Analyzing the Quest   611

Focus on Writing a Letter
Writing a Personal Letter   548
Writing a Business Letter   611

FOR ORAL PRESENTATION

Defending a Position   611

CONNECTIONS

Connecting Cultures   549, 550
Literature and Geography   583

FOCUS ON READING AND CRITICAL THINKING

Predicting Probable Actions   547
Drawing Inferences   615

FOCUS ON WRITING

Writing a Letter   616

TRANSPARENCIES

The following unit support materials with specific correlations to literature selections are available in the **Fine Art and Instructional Transparencies with Teacher's Notes and Blackline Masters** section of your *Audiovisual Resources Binder.*

FINE ART TRANSPARENCIES

Theme: Learning to Appreciate Heritage
38 *Rain Song,* Blackbear Bosin

Theme: Facing New Challenges
39 *Spirit of the Grizzly,* Bev Doolittle

READER RESPONSE

40 Connecting to a Character
41 Dark Shadows

LITERARY ELEMENTS

42 Suspense
43 Conflict
44 Analyzing and Evaluating a Novel

WRITING PROCESS

45 Writing a Letter

INTRODUCING THE UNIT

You can introduce the unit by asking students to share with the class any experiences they may have had with bears. Most students will not have encountered bears in the wild, but some may have seen bears in other settings. Then ask students how many of them have or have had stuffed bears. Why do stuffed bears seem to

PLANNING GUIDE

FOR UNIT PLANNING

- Transparencies 38–45: *Audiovisual Resources Binder*
- *Portfolio Assessment: Professional Support Materials*
- Test Generator

- Mastery Test: Teaching Resources E, p. 50
- Analogy Test: Teaching Resources E, p. 52
- Composition Test: Teaching Resources E, p. 53

SELECTION (Pupil's Page)	TEACHING RESOURCES E (page numbers shown below)							AV BINDER
	Teacher's Notes	Reading Check	Study Guide	Language Skills	Building Vocabulary	Selection Vocab. Test	Selection Test	Audio-cassette
THE NOVEL Will Hobbs *Beardance*, Chapters 1–9 (p. 513)	1	5	7	10	13	14	16	
Beardance, Chapters 10–18 (p. 551)	18	21	23		26	27	29	
Beardance, Chapters 19–24 (p. 584)	31	35	37	40	43	44	46	

appeal to people? You can point out that people in many parts of the world have felt they have special relationships with bears and that many Native American peoples in particular have great reverence and respect for bears.

After discussing bears, ask the class if any of them have ever had to find their way to a specific destination on their own. Ask also if any students had to accomplish some important task on their own without benefit of directions or adult help. How did they feel? Were they afraid? Were they confused? Did they enjoy the adventure? Point out that *Beardance* is about a boy who has to survive on his own in the wilderness without much of the equipment we ordinarily think we need for survival. Suggest that as they

read the novel they try to imagine how Cloyd feels about the things that happen to him.

PORTFOLIO ASSESSMENT

Suggestions for use of portfolios as support for this unit are described in the *Portfolio Assessment and Professional Support Materials* booklet accompanying this program. Specific suggestions are provided for a variety of student projects that may be suitable for inclusion in a portfolio. In addition, copying masters are provided for guides that may be used for evaluation and assessment of student projects.

Student Learning Options

THE NOVEL

1. Writing a Letter to a Character
Have students write a letter that Cloyd might send to Ursa describing his experiences in the wilderness after her return to Montana. One approach is to tell of Cloyd's adventures surviving with the cubs. Another approach is to report scientific observations about the cubs' behavior that Ursa might find useful in her research. In either case students should stay close to the details in the novel.

2. Performing the Bear Dance
In several places in the novel, the narrator describes the Bear Dance in detail. Ask students to practice the Bear Dance and perform it for the class.

3. Mapping Grizzly Populations
Using a map of North America, ask students to indicate where grizzly bears can be found. Some mention of grizzly populations is made in the novel, but students may need to use library resources for an accurate census.

4. Making a Book Jacket
Have students make a book jacket for *Beardance*. The front of the jacket should include the title of the novel and an appropriate illustration or photograph. The back can feature made-up quotations from literary critics or readers praising the story, and the front and back flaps can contain a summary of the plot. You might offer a prize for the best book jacket.

5. Exploring Wildlife
Invite a representative of your state's wildlife agency, or some other knowledgeable person, to visit the class to talk about endangered animal species that live in your area. If this is not possible, have students write to the state agency that deals with endangered species for information and report their findings to the class.

6. Discovering Native American Culture
Invite Native Americans in your area to talk to students about the traditions and culture of their people. If this is not possible, ask students to research Native American peoples who do, or did, live in your locale and report to the class on their research.

THE NOVEL

This is a photograph of the Grenadier Range, part of the Rocky Mountain chain in southwestern Colorado. In the novel you are about to read, the main character journeys through a mountainous terrain close to the location shown here. There he learns to survive, adapting to the shift of seasons in a rugged landscape.

Imagine that you were placed in such a setting. What skills do you already possess that would help you overcome cold, hunger, and physical danger? Think about ways that you might get food, water, fire, and shelter. What three items would you take with you if you could? Write down your thoughts on how you might respond to your new surroundings. Then talk with your classmates about the skills that would be necessary for survival.

Stony Pass, Grenadier Range in the Weminuche Wilderness, Colorado.

© David Muench

THE NOVEL

Will Hobbs's novel *Beardance* belongs to the literary tradition of coming-of-age fiction. Because it features a main character close in age to eighth-grade students, it should appeal to students who are struggling to discover their ideals and values. The novel has the added advantage of introducing students to an aspect of Native American culture they may not otherwise be exposed to, and it offers quite a bit of information about the habits of grizzly bears. Finally, *Beardance* raises a number of important questions about wildlife preservation and endangered aspects of the natural environment.

The unit provides an opportunity for students to develop their skills in reading and responding to a long work of fiction. By encouraging students to think about aspects of **plot, setting, character, point of view, imagery,** and **theme,** the unit reinforces important literary concepts.

Several activities in the unit give students a chance to write about aspects of literature, including the author's use of imagery and the development of characters. One **Language and Vocabulary** activity focuses on the use of action verbs, and an oral language activity asks students to debate an issue. Several features provide additional information about Native American culture and the influence of the Spanish language on place names of the Southwest. The unit concludes with **Reading and Critical Thinking** activities on drawing inferences and with a **Writing** feature on writing a letter.

1

First American novel was *The Power of Sympathy,* now believed to have been written by William Hill Brown (1765–1793) of Boston. This novel is written in form of letters.

2

Novels vary greatly in length, from less than a hundred pages to more than a thousand pages. Shorter novels, sometimes called **novellas** or **novelettes,** are closer to short stories in length, but they show development of character and complexity of plot found in novels.

3

Cloyd's quest is an essential part of his growth and maturity. *Beardance* is a coming-of-age novel in which a boy becomes a young man through adventures he has in course of story.

4

Hunter claims grizzly attacked him and he killed it in self-defense. Cloyd witnessed killing and knows hunter's version of story is not true, but he does not go to authorities because it would be his word against hunter's. Cloyd feels that he betrayed grizzly, and much of what happens in *Beardance* is motivated by Cloyd's feelings of guilt.

1 The term *novel* comes from the Italian *novella,* a short realistic tale popular in medieval times. The first American novel written and published in America appeared in 1789. Since then the novel has become the most widely read form of literature in America.

2 The novel is a type of imaginative literature and shares many of the same literary elements as short stories. A novel may be defined as *a fictional narrative in prose, generally longer than a short story*. The novel allows for greater complexity of character and plot development than the short story. It can take place over a longer period of time, feature more characters, and have a wider range of settings. Since we remain with the characters for a longer stretch of time, we are able to become immersed in their world and have them enter our imagination fully.

3 In this unit you will read Will Hobbs's novel *Beardance,* which takes place in the spectacular wilderness areas around the San Juan Mountains of southwestern Colorado. You will meet Cloyd Atcitty, a fourteen-year-old Ute (yo͞ot, yo͞ot′ē), who embarks on an unusual quest. The Utes are a Native American people who live in the Southwest. During the 1800s the Utes signed several treaties with the United States government in which they were forced to give up the mountains and hunting grounds that their ancestors once roamed freely. After gold was discovered in Colorado in 1858, the Utes' land was almost completely taken over. Today many of them live on reservation lands assigned to them by the government. Cloyd is from a people called the *Weminuche* (wĕ-mĭ-no͞och′ē).

The Utes once held the grizzly bear sacred, and every spring they still celebrate a ritual called the *Bear Dance*. The dance is traditionally performed to wake the bears from their winter hibernation and prepare them for the spring hunt. The Utes have a deep relationship with animals and the natural world, and Cloyd's spiritual connection with bears and the mountains arises partly from this heritage.

It may help you in reading *Beardance* to have some background on Will Hobbs's earlier book, *Bearstone*. In *Bearstone* Cloyd is introduced to us as a boy who is angry and troubled. He has left a youth home in Durango, Colorado, to spend the summer with Walter Landis, a prospector and farmer. In an ancient burial site near Walter's farm, Cloyd discovers a turquoise stone carved in the shape of a bear. He keeps it as his personal charm and secretly calls himself Lone Bear, drawing on the power of the Ancient Ones—his ancestors—to help him overcome his difficulties. Cloyd mistakenly tells an expert hunter that he has seen a huge grizzly in the mountains—possibly the last of its kind in Colorado. When the bear is killed, Cloyd strengthens his **4** resolve to seek out any remaining grizzlies in the state. When we meet him again in *Beardance,* he is still living with Walter Landis, now his close friend. You may want to read *Bearstone* to learn more about Cloyd and Walter.

5 In *Beardance* you will learn a great deal about grizzly bears. While there once were more than 100,000 of these bears in our Western states, their numbers have been reduced drastically. A grizzly was once a hunter's greatest trophy, but since 1975 the bears have been protected under the Endangered Species Act. This act protects those species that are in danger of completely dying out. Still, whenever civilization moves in on the bear's wilderness habitat, both humans and bears can be in danger. Grizzlies have been thought to be extinct in Colorado since the 1950s, but there has been recent evidence that a small population may be living in the state. To survive and breed, these few grizzlies might need some help from humans. In *Beardance*, Will Hobbs shows us what it might be like if these Colorado grizzlies did exist.

When you read a novel, it is important to develop as complete an understanding as possible. This requires studying and reviewing what you have read. The following guidelines will help you understand the uses of literary elements found in the novel.

Guidelines for Close Reading

1. Read actively, asking questions as you read. For example, try to predict how a conflict or event will turn out. Try to determine the author's purpose for using specific events or conflicts. Be aware of your own responses to characters and actions.

2. Define all unfamiliar words. Use a dictionary to define any unfamiliar words that might cause difficulty in understanding a passage. Be sure to locate the correct definition as it applies to the word and its use in context.

3. Become aware of information that establishes the setting or background of the novel. The language of characters, for example, can help to set the time and place of the action.

4. Look for clues that reveal what the characters are like: dialogue, important actions, or descriptive details. Discover how characters develop and change as the novel progresses.

5. Determine the main action of the novel. As you read, consider how individual episodes are connected to the main plot.

6. Note the point of view of the novel. Seek to understand the author's reason for selecting a particular point of view.

7. Consider how all the elements of the novel contribute to its theme. Try to identify the various elements and how they contribute to the overall theme of the novel.

5 Grizzlies once roamed in open country from northern Alaska to central Mexico. They can grow as tall as nine feet and can weigh one thousand pounds or more. Territory of a single bear may be several hundred square miles.

GUIDELINES FOR CLOSE READING

1. You may want to encourage students to write down their questions, predictions, and responses, at least until they become familiar with this aspect of active reading. *Beardance* offers opportunities to predict events that will probably occur.

2. Many unfamiliar words are defined in footnotes or glossary of textbook. Students may find it useful to use a geographical dictionary for some of the terms in *Beardance*.

3. Some of older characters in *Beardance* use expressions that may not be familiar to students. These expressions help establish characters' ages and experiences.

4. In *Beardance*, two characters undergo major changes, and one character belies his reputation. Students should attend closely to subtle clues regarding character changes.

5. Main action in *Beardance* is a spinoff of Walter Landis' trip to mountains to look for gold.

6. Point of view of *Beardance* is mainly third-person limited as experienced by Cloyd Atcitty. At times, though, point of view shifts to omniscient third person.

7. Conflicts with nature and with other people combine with Cloyd's developing character to create **theme,** which is related to spiritual relationship between human beings and nature.

Names of Places in *Beardance*

Cañon Paso: (kän′yōn pä′sō) A rugged canyon to the west of the Pine River, south of the Rincon la Osa.

Chuska Mountains: A mountain range in the northeastern part of Arizona.

The Continental Divide: A series of mountainous ridges running from Alaska to Mexico. Water to the east of the Divide flows to the Atlantic, while water on the western side flows to the Pacific.

Durango: (do͝o-răng′gō) A city south of the Weminuche Wilderness in Colorado.

el Cerro de la Pyramide: (ĕl sâ′rō dā lä pē-rä′mē-*th*ā) "Pyramid Mountain," or the Rio Grande Pyramid, a mountain in the Continental Divide.

Ignacio: A town in southwestern Colorado, southeast of Durango.

Lake Mary Alice: A high mountain lake under the north face of Mount Oso.

Lost and Hidden Lakes: Two high mountain lakes to the west of Lake Mary Alice.

Mt. Oso: (ō′-sō) A mountain on the Pacific side and south of the Continental Divide.

Needles: A mountain range in the far southwestern corner of Colorado.

Pagosa (pə-gō′-sə) **Springs:** A town in southwestern Colorado, fifty miles east of Durango.

Piedra (pyĕ′*th*rä) **River:** The river running near Walter Landis' farm.

Pine River Trail: A trail near the Pine River, heading into the San Juan Mountains of southwestern Colorado.

Rincon la Osa: (rēn-kōn′ lä ō′sä) "Corner of the bear." A valley south of the Continental Divide.

Rincon la Vaca: (rēn-kōn′ lä bä′kä) "Corner of the cow." A valley directly south of the Continental Divide.

Rio Grande Pyramid: A mountain peak in the ridge that makes up the Continental Divide.

Rock Creek: A creek on the Pacific side of the Continental Divide, flowing into Rock Lake.

Roell Creek Basin: A high, bowl-shaped area among the mountain peaks on the Pacific side of the Continental Divide.

San Juan (sän wän′, sän hwän′) **Mountains:** A portion of the Rocky Mountains in southwestern Colorado, with the highest peak reaching 14,309 feet.

Snowslide Canyon: A canyon to the east of the Pine River and on the Pacific side of the Continental Divide.

Ute (yo͞ot, yo͞ot′ē) **Lakes Basin:** A basin between the mountain peaks where West, Middle, and Ute Creeks flow into lakes.

Vallecito (bä-yĕ-sē′-tō) **Creek:** A creek running north-south on the Pacific side of the Divide; it lies to the west of Roell Creek Basin.

Weminuche (wĕ-mĭ-no͞och′-ē) **Wilderness:** A tract of protected land in the southwestern corner of Colorado, named after the Weminuche people.

West, Middle, and East Ute Creek: Three tributaries of the Rio Grande, each flowing south into Ute Lakes Basin.

The Window: A notch in a ridge extending from the Rio Grande Pyramid, a mountain in the Continental Divide.

Wolf Creek Pass: The only road within a 200-mile area of the San Juan Mountains; near Pagosa Springs, Colorado.

The Windom and Sunlight Mountains, the Needles Range in the Weminuche Wilderness, Colorado.
©David Muench

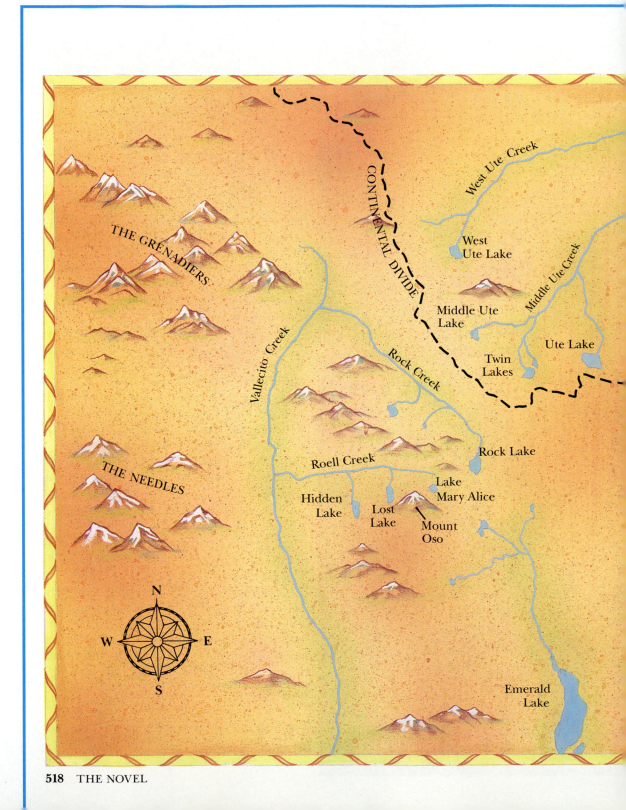

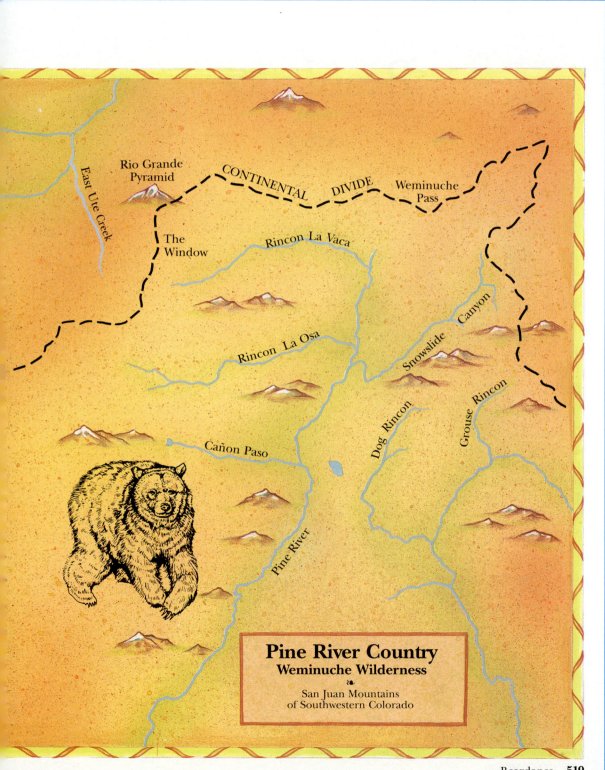

East Ute Creek

Rio Grande
Pyramid

CONTINENTAL DIVIDE

Weminuche
Pass

The
Window

Rincon La Vaca

Rincon La Osa

Snowslide Canyon

Cañon Paso

Dog Rincon

Grouse Rincon

Pine River

Pine River Country
Weminuche Wilderness

San Juan Mountains
of Southwestern Colorado

Beardance

WILL HOBBS

1

"Do you think there could still be any grizzlies in the mountains?" Cloyd asked.

Up and out of the yellow pines they rode and into the aspens, their quaky leaves shimmering with the slightest breeze. Out of the blue skies and into the clouds and the rolling thunder. Out of the heat and the stale smell of the low country and into the windblown freshness of the high.

In search of a lost Spanish gold mine.

Up ahead, the old man stroked the white bristles of his beard and rode on without answering. Cloyd knew that the old man was deep in thought. Walter wouldn't give a quick answer to his question about the grizzlies. Walter knew how important it was.

It was the middle of August, and they were following the Pine River Trail into the mountains. Walter Landis led on the sorrel mare, trailing his four packhorses. Cloyd followed on the blue roan, trailing four more.

Around a bend, the old man had reined in the mare and was waiting for him to draw up alongside.

"Dunno about your grizzlies," he said. "That one you saw Rusty kill, it really could've been the last grizzly in Colorado."

It wasn't the reply Cloyd had been hoping to hear. He'd kept his dream to himself, that there were others. There had to be. It was too hard, knowing that if he had never talked about seeing the bear, Walter's old friend would never have tracked it and killed it. It wasn't something Cloyd could get over. He had boasted to the best hunter, trapper, and tracker in the mountains that he had seen a bear, a huge brown bear.

Cloyd was surprised that Walter had mentioned Rusty's name. Maybe the old man thought enough time had gone by to blur the memory or ease the hurt. For his part, Cloyd was never going to speak the man's name. Words had power, and if he never said the outfitter's[1] name aloud, he wouldn't be giving even an ounce more power to this man who had so much and deserved so little.

The man who killed the bear.

"Of course," Walter continued, "nobody's looked under every tree for grizzes.[2] You've got to figure, there's only one road over these San Juans in a two-hundred-mile swath, and that's Wolf Creek Pass way over above Pagosa. That's a lot of wild country—big enough to have hid that bear for twenty-three years. That's how old the lab in Denver said he was, from the teeth or whatever."

Cloyd regretted that his question had led to talk of the dead bear and the man who killed the bear. He shouldn't have asked his question.

It seemed the bitter taste would never go away.

---

1. **outfitter:** someone who equips people with supplies for camping trips and expeditions.
2. **grizzes:** grizzly bears.

MOTIVATIONAL SUMMARY

Walter Landis and his young friend Cloyd Atcitty go into the mountains to look for gold, but Cloyd is more interested in locating a grizzly bear and her three cubs that he hears about. As a Native American of the Ute people, Cloyd has a special kinship with grizzlies. Hiking alone one day, Cloyd meets Ursa, a grizzly expert. She tells Cloyd and Walter stories about grizzlies, and she and Cloyd set out to look for the mother bear and her cubs. Cloyd teaches Ursa the Bear Dance that the Ute people perform every spring.

PRESENTATION

You might begin the study of the novel by asking students what the title refers to. After several students offer suggestions, you can tell them that it refers to a ritual performed every spring by the Ute people of the Southwest in

521

honor of their spiritual kinship with the grizzly bear. Then have students read the first chapter of the novel in class. When they have finished reading it, discuss the three characters who have been introduced so far. Students should understand that Walter Landis is an old man who was injured in a mine explosion the previous summer, and Cloyd Atcitty is a Native American boy of the Ute people who has been living with Walter, taking care of him as he recovers from his accident and helping him on his farm. Cloyd's mother is dead and his father is in an irreversible coma, and he came to live with Walter from a group home in Durango, Colorado.

The third character, a hunter named Rusty, killed a grizzly bear the previous summer as Cloyd watched. As a member of an endangered species, the grizzly was protected by federal law,

---

6
Red-haired man is Rusty, whose name comes from the rust color of his hair.

7 *Making Inferences*
Why might Cloyd have lived in group home? Answers will vary. Maybe he was in some kind of trouble. Maybe he does not have parents or relatives to live with.

8
Symbol. This name becomes symbolic when readers learn Cloyd does not have parents.

9
Simile. Compares size of bear to size of haystack to emphasize bear's enormous bulk.

10
Metaphor. Compares mental picture of bear to indelible mark left by fire.

11
Personification. Moment has human power to hold Cloyd.

12
Walter and Cloyd eat large number of berries quickly.

13 Summarizing
Why are Walter and Cloyd so eager to eat berries? They are a rare treat they seldom find.

14
Cloyd anticipates that clouds will make air too cool for T-shirt and that he will have to put on heavier clothes.

---

6 The red-haired man seemed to have gone away, but hating him, that had never gone away.

Rusty never came anymore to the farm on the Piedra River to check in on his old friend Walter. Cloyd understood why. It was because Cloyd was living at the farm. Cloyd was the only one who knew what really happened up there, high on the Continental Divide.

Rusty would have known that Cloyd wasn't **7** living at the Ute group home in Durango anymore, hadn't returned either to his grandmother over in Utah at White Mesa. He must have heard that Cloyd had stayed at the farm to help the old man get through the winter. But he'd never come by, not even once.

Cloyd still couldn't help feeling that the bear had showed itself to him on purpose. Because Cloyd was a Ute, because Utes and bears were kin. Because Cloyd had found a turquoise bear-stone by the burial of one of the Ancient Ones,[3] **8** and had named himself Lone Bear.

There wasn't a day that had gone by that the grizzly hadn't come to mind, almost always as Cloyd had first seen him: standing at the edge of the meadow in the Rincon La Osa with the **9** dark spruce timber behind, and big as a haystack. The bear was standing on two legs, flat on his feet the way people stand, forepaws at his sides, with those enormous claws. The brown bear was just watching him, squinting for a better look, his head swaying slightly back and forth, his forehead wide and dished out a little in the middle.

More than anything, the bear was curious. Alert and intelligent and curious. That's the way Cloyd liked to remember him.

But sometimes that other scene came to **10** mind, the one burned into his memory forever. Time and again it would return without his bidding. On one of the terraces above Ute Lake,

3. **Ancient Ones:** the ancestors of the Utes.

the bear was turning over rocks along a line of brush as the red-haired man nocked his arrow **11** and bent his bow. It was a moment that would never let go of Cloyd. He was hollering with all his might into the wind, and the wind was blowing his warning behind him, up and over the Continental Divide. The bear never heard his warning.

Up ahead, Walter was riding out of the trees, and now Cloyd also rode out into the light and the greenness of the longest meadow on the lower river. Here the Pine ran smooth over gravel beds of ground granite, and on the outside of the turns there were deep pools where the biggest cutthroat trout could be found. Cloyd paused for a moment as bits of color in the bushes lining the banks caught his eye. "Walter," he called, "hold up."

They tied their horses at the edge of the trees **12** and then they fell upon the raspberry and currant bushes like bears filling their bellies against winter. The berries were juicy and sweet. The boy and the old man were laughing at the sight of the stain all around their mouths, while their fingers kept working as fast as they could go. "Can't recall berries this prime," Walter observed when his stomach was full. "Must be all the rain."

Cloyd's fingers were still flying. He had a big- **13** ger stomach to fill, and nothing they'd brought along to eat could compare with this.

Walter's old eyes had noticed something up the valley. Cloyd looked and saw a string of horses entering the meadow. Behind, toward the peaks, the tall clouds were beginning to turn dark, and thunder was rumbling. Down on this meadow, though, the sun was still shin- **14** ing. He'd be comfortable in his T-shirt awhile.

Cloyd turned back to his berry picking as the old man kept his eyes on the trail, and when Cloyd looked again several minutes later he saw that the packstring was led by a single rider, a big man with a large face framed by a full red

but Rusty lied to the authorities and said he killed the bear in self-defense as it was attacking him. Grizzlies had been thought to be extinct in Colorado until this one appeared. Now that it is dead, though, there is not much hope any grizzlies live there. A basic **conflict** exists between Cloyd and Rusty because of what Rusty did, but Rusty tries to ease the conflict by telling Walter and Cloyd that he spotted a mother grizzly and three cubs. Cloyd receives this information as a challenge, and eventually he sets out on a quest to locate the grizzlies.

After students read Chapter 1 and discuss the characters, you might want them to read the feature **Connecting Cultures: Legends and Myths of the Bear** on pp. 549–550. This feature will give students background information on the significance of bears to Native Americans

---

beard and red hair spilling from under a dark felt Stetson.[4] A rifle was scabbarded under one leg. Cloyd's hands stopped their work, and his dark eyes locked on the face almost coming into focus down the trail.

"Could it be?" the old man wondered aloud.

Cloyd was wondering the same thing, and he was hoping the old man was mistaken. The red-haired man had never had a beard before.

The horseman rode closer and closer, close enough that recognition showed in the old man's face. Walter was smiling and shaking his head, surprised to see his old friend looking so different, pleased to be seeing him after so long even if there was reason not to be pleased.

15 "Speak of the devil," the old man said in greeting. He said it in such a way that it was friendly and it wasn't, both at the same time.

Rusty's eyes were on Cloyd, not on his old friend Walter. He nodded to Cloyd, and then he broke out in a big smile all surrounded by the deep red of his beard and mustache.

"Long time . . ." Rusty said in that unmistak-
16 able gravelly voice, as he lifted his hat and ran his hand through his wavy hair. "You're the last two people I expected to run into on this trail."

The old man played dumb. "Now why's that?"

The red-haired man's eyes ran to the picks and shovels sticking out of the gear. He was shaking his head and grinning. "Walter, don't I recall you blowing yourself up last summer? Don't tell me you're going to have another go at the Pride of the West!"[5]

"Just out for a ride," Walter replied with a
17 glint in his eye. "Never know when you might have to dig a hole in the ground."

"So what's the long gizmo[6] all wrapped in

4. **Stetson:** a hat with a wide brim and a high crown, often worn in Westerns.
5. **Pride of the West:** the name of Walter's gold mine in *Bearstone.*
6. **gizmo:** gadget.

black on top of that third horse?"

"Broom," the old man quickly replied, with his tongue in his cheek. "We keep a tidy camp."

"Got to be gold you're after," the outfitter said confidently. With another glance at Cloyd, he said, "Sorry I never came by the farm. No excuses, I guess. Glad I saw you two, though—I'm leaving for Alaska real soon."

The red-haired man tied his horses, and then he came back and sat on the edge of the stream bank with the old man. Cloyd stayed well out of the reach of Rusty's crushing handshake and kept to his berry picking. He could stay near, close enough to hear. The red-haired
18 man kept glancing his way, but he seemed to know not to try to speak to him. Walter would know why. There was something between Cloyd and Rusty, and it was because of the lie. The bear hadn't attacked the big man, as Rusty had told the game wardens and the newspapers. Rusty was the one who had surprised the bear, and he'd known it was a grizzly he was tracking.

Cloyd knew now—he'd known for a long time—that he should have told what he saw. He should have told how the bear really died. This man would have lost his outfitting license, would have had to pay a huge fine, and maybe would have even gone to jail for killing an animal that was endangered. But no one else had
19 been there. It would have been his word against Rusty's. Would they have believed him, an Indian kid from Utah who didn't have a father or a mother? Now he would never know if they would have believed him or not.

It had been a mistake to leave it up to the red-haired man to tell the truth. People knew only the lie, and people believed the worst of the bear. No one would ever know what really happened.

Rusty liked to stroke his new beard, long and shaggy like a mountain man's. Cloyd hated him for his vanity.

---

15 Finding Cause and Effect
Why is Walter's greeting friendly and not friendly at same time? It is friendly because Rusty is old friend and unfriendly because he killed bear.

16
Figurative Language. Narrator calls Rusty's voice "gravelly" because sound is rough and uneven, like gravel.

17 Drawing Conclusions
What does glint in Walter's eye suggest? That he is not telling truth.

18
Rusty keeps watching Cloyd to see his reaction to him.

19
Cloyd is aware authorities probably would not have believed him.

In a values journal, students can examine their own patterns of choosing, prizing, and acting as well as the patterns of characters in literature. Some students may want to keep a values journal while they read *Beardance* in order to clarify their values and those of the main characters. Suggest that they look for how Cloyd makes choices, what he considers important, and how he acts on what is important to him. Then they can compare those patterns in Cloyd's behavior to their own and those of the other characters. Consult with students to agree on how their journals will be assessed. Journals may be included in student portfolios. (See *Portfolio Assessment and Professional Support Materials,* especially the section entitled **Suggestions for Portfolio Projects.**)

up into the barn," the old man replied sheepishly. "Who knows, Cloyd, we might even find the Lost Mine of the Window. Now wouldn't that be something."

Then the old man confessed that he'd already sent away for "the best metal detector money can buy."

According to the story in the book, the Spanish were supposed to have left three caches of high-grade gold ore behind, two hundred and fifty years before. The old man was sure he was going to find at least one with the Cachefinder he'd seen advertised in his *Mining Gazette.* The Cachefinder was supposed to be brand-new and far better than any metal detector ever made. At least he wasn't going to try to blast open his old gold mine, Cloyd thought.

10 Cloyd rode up the Pine River Trail grinning about this old man who was always sure that tomorrow would bring greater things than today and who always dreamed his dreams on a grand scale.

11 Lightning snapped closer this time, and Cloyd snugged his red baseball cap down. Walter had found a good little bench off the side of the trail with a tight cluster of spruces that would shelter them until the storm center moved past.

"It's really steep through here," Cloyd observed as they shared a candy bar.

"Narrow too," Walter replied. "This has to be like that hill country in West Virginia where my father grew up."

"Pretty narrow back there?" Cloyd asked, because he knew the old man would expect him to ask.

The hint of a smile played on Walter's weathered features. "Never seen it myself, you understand. I was born and bred on the Pine before I made my big move to the next stream over, **12** the Piedra. According to my father, that West Virginia country was so steep, all a fellow had to do to bring in his apples was to give the trees in his backyard a shake, an' the fruit would run right down into his cellar."

"That's pretty steep," Cloyd agreed, keeping his face blank as any poker player's.

"So steep they developed a breed of cattle with legs shorter on one side for easier grazing. Even the cornfields were steep. They planted corn by firing the seed out of a gun into the opposite hillside."

Cloyd was trying as hard as he could to keep from smiling. "Did you believe him?"

13 The old man's ears were turning a little red, and the veins in his forehead and temples were standing up high. "Why, of course I believed him," Walter protested. "I asked my dad once how come his teeth were worn down so bad, like an old horse's. He explained that level ground was so scarce back where he grew up, **14** chimneys crowded the hillsides and gravel was always falling into the pot of beans set to cook in the fireplace. We think *we've* got steep and narrow in our mountains....Back there the dogs had to wag their tails up and down, and you'd have to lie down and look straight up to see the sky."

Cloyd glanced away, stifling his laughter. He wanted to make the old man laugh first. For his part, Walter was trying hard to keep a straight face. It was easy to see that the old man wasn't going to last long. "Is that true?" Cloyd insisted.

"Yes sir," Walter mused. "It was so narrow **15** back there, the moonshine had to be wheelbarrowed out every morning, and daylight wheelbarrowed in."

Now it was raining hard. The horses' rumps and the tarps over their loads were streaming wet. "Did it rain a lot?"

"Why, no," Walter said quickly. "The way I remember hearing it, that was a country so dry, if a drop of water were to hit a man, they had to throw a couple buckets of dirt on his face to bring him to...."

Cloyd couldn't help it anymore and started

---

10 Making Generalizations
What does Cloyd's grinning suggest about his character? He is more realistic than Walter, who is a dreamer.

11
Onomatopoeia. Lightning makes snapping sound when it flashes.

12
Exaggeration. Walter's father exaggerated apple-picking method to emphasize steepness of countryside in West Virginia.

13 Analyzing
What do details of Walter's appearance suggest? That he is not telling truth about believing his father's stories.

14
Walter's father's teeth were worn down from biting into gravel—or so he said.

15
Figurative Language. Moonshine is both light of moon and illegal whiskey.

laughing. Then the old man was laughing too, and his face above his thick white whiskers was all red, and his ears were turning red.

The storm passed, and the horses climbed once more. Finally Cloyd saw the first of the Pine's upper meadows, miles of meadow green and wide and long, with the spruce-covered mountainsides standing back at a distance. And there was the river, winding its way toward them in gentle oxbows.[3]

" 'He maketh me to lie down in green pastures,' "[4] the old man said <u>reverently</u>.

Cloyd said nothing, only gave Blueboy a pat on his withers and ran his eyes up the valley, up the dark slopes studded with <u>massive</u> granite outcrops. The last creek on the left, another nine or ten miles up the valley and immediately under the Pyramid—that's where Rusty had seen the grizzly and cubs, if indeed he had.

It was important to Cloyd to see those grizzlies, even if it was just as unlikely as finding Spanish treasure. He'd found everything in the school library on grizzlies. He remembered that a grizzly would cover thirty, fifty, even a hundred square miles in its territory. At least Spanish gold didn't move around every day.

Still, he might have some luck left, some bear luck. More than anything, he wanted to see those grizzlies for himself.

"Fresh fish tonight," Walter said. "Fried in cornmeal blankets. If my Ute guide can still produce, that is."

"I can produce," Cloyd assured him. "I've even got flies and lures, and I can always dig worms."

Cloyd came back into camp with six orange-jawed, orange-bellied cutthroats on his willow stringer. The old man had the old sheepherder tent set up and was limping around the fire. "Let's stay a couple of days," Walter suggested.

"It'd be a good idea for me to get used to the altitude before we go on up high."

"Gonna try out your metal detector?" Cloyd asked.

"Do you walk to school or carry your lunch?" the old man replied mysteriously. "Wouldn't think of it, Cloyd, not with hikers around. Let's keep the Cachefinder hid away in its case. There's no percentage in advertising what we're really up to. When it comes to gold, people get…peculiar."

3

The old man understood Cloyd's need to roam in search of those bears. A glimpse would satisfy him, just a glimpse to verify Rusty's words. With only his daypack on his back, Cloyd roamed away from the trail, into the deep woods, across the rockslides, up the grassy avalanche chutes,[1] and into a high basin that had no name on the map.

A little higher, Cloyd thought, and he might be able to glimpse the Rio Grande Pyramid. But he'd spent the day climbing, and now it was time to start down. Heading back for that old man always made him feel good, whether it was on the long bus ride home from school in Durango or charging down off a mountain.

The second day of Walter's rest-up on the Pine, Cloyd said good-bye and set out more deliberately. Again he would leave the trail and go places that hikers would never see, but this time he would go slowly, using his eyes and his ears and his feel for the unseen. He practiced moving like a shadow and pausing for five, ten minutes behind trees without moving at all, just watching and listening.

Cloyd even tried to <u>employ</u> his nose, though he knew that a bear's sense of smell was a hun-

---

3. **oxbows:** U-shaped bends in the river.
4. **"He maketh…pastures":** a line from Psalm 23 in the Bible.

1. **avalanche chutes:** passages or hollows on the side of a mountain where rocks, snow, or ice can fall or slide down the mountain slope.

4
Cloyd is evidently good at "moving like a shadow."

5
Personification. Hands have ability to do things on their own as though they were a whole person.

6 Analyzing
Why is Living in the Southwest Cloyd's favorite class? He is interested in his Native American ancestry and in everything about part of country he lives in.

7
Sound of sticks rubbing together believed to have magical power over bears.

8
Making Inferences
Why does Cloyd wish story were true? Answers will vary. Perhaps he would like to return to earlier time when people and nature lived in harmony.

---

dred times better than his. He watched squir-
4 rels caching seeds under the roots of the trees. He crept up so close on a marmot in a boulder field that the so-called whistle pig didn't sound its screeching alarm until Cloyd could have almost yanked the big rodent's tail.

In the afternoon he stayed in one place and watched a shallow pond in a clearing in the trees five hundred or so feet below the tree line. Someone might come to drink at this pond, he thought. Deer or elk or maybe even bears.

5 His hands found themselves whittling on a piece of spruce. He made a stick that was about a foot long, straight and smooth. It reminded him of the rubbing stick[2] the singers had used at the Bear Dance he had gone to in May at the Southern Ute Reservation[3] down in Ignacio, only thirty miles south and west of the old man's farm.

Cloyd looked around for material to make the second stick, the notched one. The singers had used axe handles, long and hard and perfect for holding deep notches.

By the pond grew a cluster of chokecherry bushes. They would be perfect, if he could find
6 a dead limb. In his favorite class at school, Living in the Southwest, Mr. Pendleton had said that the Utes used to make their bows out of juniper or especially chokecherry. No juniper grew this high, but here was chokecherry. If it would make a good bow, why not growler sticks?

Two bull elk with wide, branching antlers, all in velvet, came out of the woods and approached the pond before their eyes caught the motion he was making. Cloyd never saw them, he was so intent on his whittling. The chips were flying, and a growler stick was taking form.

2. **rubbing stick:** In the Bear Dance ceremony, two sticks are used: a smooth stick is rubbed across a notched stick called a growler to produce a grating, harsh sound.
3. **Southern Ute Reservation:** in Ignacio, Colorado; one of the three reservations of land left to the Ute Indians.

Southern Ute Bear Dance.

When Cloyd tried the smooth stick across the notched growler, he was satisfied with the sound. He wasn't worried about scaring off any bears that might be close. Maybe this rasping would attract them! It was this thunder, this scratching and growling of bears, that called to the bears in the mountains all the way from the brush corral at the Bear Dance in Ignacio. This
7 sound called them out of their big sleep with the first spring thunder into a world that was coming to life again for bears and people—kin to each other, as his grandmother often said.

In the earliest times, his grandmother had said, a person could become an animal if he wanted to and an animal could become a person. His grandmother had told him that when he was little, and it had stuck in his mind. As he grew older he realized it was only a story, even if his grandmother didn't think of it as a story.
8 But it was a story he'd always wanted to be true.

SOCIAL STUDIES LINK

Interested students might want to look up information about the Ute people to present for the class. You might suggest that students find out about the geographic area in which the Utes live, their language, the principal bands, and the

source of their current income.

TRANSPARENCY 38

Fine Art
Theme: *Learning to Appreciate Heritage* – features artwork that shows appreciation of the legacy of previous generations.

Starsmore Center for Local History, Colorado Springs Pioneers Museum

When the first people and the animals crossed back and forth, his grandmother said, it made no difference whether they started out as person or animal. Everyone spoke the same language. Back then, words were magical. A word spoken by accident could result in strange consequences. Thoughts spoken could come to life, and what people wished to happen could happen—all you had to do was say the words. Nobody could explain why this was the way it was, his grandmother said. That's the way it was in the earliest times.

9 When he was little, these stories had been just as real for him as they were for his grandmother. They were still good stories, he thought.

Cloyd kept up the rhythm, the rasping, scratching, growling rhythm of the smooth stick over the growler. It was too bad he lacked the big drum dug into the earth. Eight men rasping over that long, metal-covered drum could create a powerful thunder that ran **10** through the earth. He could remember it coming up through his feet and running through his spine.

The more Cloyd rasped, the more it took him back to May and the Bear Dance. When Walter dropped him off in Ignacio that Friday morning at the Bear Dance and he saw the brush corral, ten feet high and a hundred feet across with the one opening to the east, he realized he'd seen it before. Once, when he was little, his grandmother had taken him from White Mesa in Utah all the way to Ignacio, Colorado, for the Bear Dance. That was back when she used to **11** call him "honey paws" or "short tail." She had told him that the brush corral was round like the inside of a bear den is round.

That first day of the dance had also been the last day of school. At school, Mr. Pendleton was going to show everybody how to make fire with a bow drill.[4] Everyone had failed the day before, with their own homemade bow drills, including Cloyd. One kid had said, "Cloyd can't even do it and he's an Indian."

Cloyd had wanted to go back for the last day and learn the secret of the bow drill. But even more, he didn't want to miss any of the Bear Dance. He'd been looking forward to it all win **12** ter, for himself and for the bear who had been killed.

By the pond in the forest, high above the Pine River in the back country of the Weminuche Wilderness, Cloyd began to dance the bear dance as the clouds darkened above him and thunder began to reverberate among the peaks. Three steps forward, three steps back—like a bear dancing to a scratching-tree—as he kept up the rasping of his growler **13** sticks. His dancing took him back to that first day of the Bear Dance, and the thunder took

4. **bow drill:** a tool for making fire, using the friction of a wooden drill against another soft piece of wood.

9
Grandmother passes on traditional Ute stories to Cloyd, but he no longer believes them to be literally true.

10 Finding Cause and Effect
How can sound of drum run through Cloyd's feet and spine? Sound causes earth to vibrate, and Cloyd feels vibrations with his feet.

11
Symbol. Grandmother uses pet names that are symbolic of Cloyd's kinship with bear.

12
Cloyd sees Bear Dance as memorial to bear Rusty killed.

13
Flashback. Cloyd remembers Bear Dance months before as a way of filling in readers on what happened then.

14
Figurative Language. Narrator describes lightning as appearing in webs to suggest that bolts of lightning are interconnected, like web of a spider.

15 Making Inferences
Why do people not eat until Bear Dance is over? Answers will vary. Fasting often part of religious ritual. Perhaps people want to focus all their attention on dance.

16
Simile. Compares memory to a deep lake where events can be hidden from ordinary sight.

17
Cloyd has had mystical experience during Bear Dance.

18
Why does Cloyd realize only from above that his dance movements resemble movements of bear? His concentration is so intense he does not realize what he is doing.

19
Plot. Flashback is over, and Cloyd returns to present.

him back to the second, to the unforgettable thunder of that May night with eight men working over that long resonating drum.

He remembered that there had been a storm blowing in that last night of the Bear Dance. It was well after midnight. The storm was close, **14** with lightning displaying in wide, intricate webs and thunder rumbling. The last dance was about to begin, the endurance dance. The Cat Man[5] was advising people to have someone ready to relieve them. Cloyd didn't think he would. There was no way he was going to quit now that the Bear Dance was almost over. He had almost made it, almost danced the whole thing.

He remembered that he was so tired, he didn't feel connected to his feet anymore. He hadn't eaten anything since the dance had started Friday morning. His grandmother had told him once, that was the way they did it in **15** the old days. No eating until the feast, until the Bear Dance was all over.

Keep going, he'd told himself. Keep dancing. Three springing steps forward, three back. The singers were chanting and he felt their growler sticks reverberating up and down his spine, speaking thunder and the scratching and growling of bears. He was exhausted, utterly exhausted. Yet he kept dancing without even knowing that he was dancing.

What happened next he'd never recalled before this moment by this pond. Now that time came back so vividly, his exhaustion seemed to return full force, and he was at the Bear Dance **16** again. This memory had lain deep in his mind, as if at the bottom of a lake. *While his body was* **17** *dancing, his spirit was rising above.* That's what it was, that's what had happened.

It was an odd sensation, rising up into the air, but not unpleasant. He didn't fight it, but let his spirit drift up, up, until he was high above the

5. **Cat Man:** a figure in the Ute Bear Dance.

Bear Dance, looking down at the wide brush corral and all the dancers and the singers working their growler sticks over the long resonator. Through spirit eyes he looked down at the fire at the center of the dance, the sparks flying into the night, himself in the line of male dancers. And all around, panels of lightning were lighting up the purple clouds.

He could see one of the dancers pawing the air as he danced, just like a standing bear. He could see the woman across from that dancer, in surprise, losing the beat for a moment, and pausing before she continued.

18 That dancer so much like a bear, he realized from high above, was himself.

Suddenly he was back in his body and in the line of male dancers again. His legs kept moving despite their weariness, three steps forward, three steps back. His hands were pawing the air; he heard himself woof with a bear's voice. Still his legs had that spring in them. He'd danced so long and so hard, he'd danced himself deep into the mountains. He had the sensation that he was moving on four legs. When he looked around behind him, he noticed his tracks, and they were bear tracks!

19 Cloyd shook himself out of his dreaming and stood up. Shade was overtaking the pond, and it was time to go. It had amazed him, what he'd remembered from the Bear Dance that he had never remembered before. He knew what his grandmother would have said about what happened there. She'd always said that everyone has a "traveling soul" that could leave the body and travel in the spirit world.

He'd always thought that such things could never happen again, that they only happened a long time ago to the old Indians who were all dead now. The spirit world his grandmother had always talked about—he had never really believed in it, at least for him. Only the old people could really believe in spirit people and spirit bears who lived in a spirit world.

20 But now he knew that for a brief time, he had traveled in the spirit world. And now he wondered if the spirit world was the world of that earliest time his grandmother had talked about, when there was no difference between the people and the animals and they could **21** cross back and forth. Could it have been possible, that he'd really been in the spirit world when he'd looked over his shoulder and seen only bear tracks?

He missed the bearstone. When he'd had the turquoise grizzly in his pocket, he'd felt like one of the old Utes.

It was time to be heading back to the old man, to the camp on the Pine. The bearstone was back at the farm on Walter's nightstand. It had been a good thing to do when he'd given **22** the bearstone away to the old man. Walter got his strength back then, after the terrible accident at the mine. It was the best gift Cloyd had ever given.

"Live in a good way," his grandmother liked **23** to say. "Give something back."

4

In a few days the horses were rested, and so were the boy and the old man. They proceeded up the meadows of the Pine, separated every mile or two by hills to climb where the trees reached the river and the whitewater cascaded from one meadow down to the next.

Cloyd was in the lead when they came to the spot where Snowslide Creek flowed in from the northeast. He reined in Blueboy and asked over his shoulder, "You want to go up to the mine, just to see it?"

The old man ran his hand through the bristles of his beard. He was thinking about it one way, and then the other. "I don't think so, **1** Cloyd. The Pride of the West is a closed chapter. Point me toward *la Mina Perdida de la Ventana*. I've grown fond of the idea of just

collecting that high-grade ore that's already been brought out of the mountain."

Cloyd steered them west up the next drainage, up the steep trail that led into the Rincon La Osa.

At last they broke out into the meadow he remembered so well. They made camp, and then he led the old man to the spot along the **2** Rincon stream where he'd fished the big cutthroat out with his bare hands. All winter he'd thought about what had happened next. "This is where it happened," he told the old man. "This is where I first saw the bear. The bear was over there at the edge of the trees, standing up and sort of squinting at me."

Walter Landis took off his hat and scratched his head, and then he settled himself down on the remains of a spruce, bleached for years by the sun, that had almost been reclaimed by the meadow. "You can't unscramble eggs," the old man said softly. "There's three things that return never: the spoken word, the sped arrow, the past life."

Walter picked a shoot of grass from a clump growing out of the log and began to chew on it. **3** The words he'd spoken seemed for both of them to hang in the air and take shape and power, perhaps more than he had intended.

Return never, Cloyd thought, and he could see the arrow flying off Rusty's bow.

He hated feeling sorry for himself. It reminded him of that year in the group home in Durango when he was angry all the time, **4** when he failed all his classes on purpose, when he bullied kids out of dimes and quarters.

He used to be like that.

5 He used to be like that before he found the bearstone in the cave high above the old man's farm, before he dreamed of visiting the wilderness named after his own band of Utes. Before he'd worked for Walter, and before Walter had taken him into the mountains.

The loneliness and anger was still inside him,

20 Cloyd's experience makes him a believer in traditional Ute stories.

21 Finding Cause and Effect *What effect might Cloyd's experience have on him?* He might begin to believe all stories his grandmother told him.

22 Cloyd believes bearstone has ability to heal wounded people.

23 Summarizing *What does grandmother mean by "give something back"?* She means Cloyd should help others whenever he can.

Chapter 4

1 Metaphor. Walter compares episode with gold mine to completed chapter in story of his life.

2 Cloyd caught fish without hook or net.

3 Personification. Words are given life and power to act on their own.

4 Analyzing *Why did Cloyd purposely fail classes and bully others?* Answers will vary. Maybe he did it out of anger he could not understand. Maybe he wanted to punish someone for his being in group home but there was no one to punish but himself and other kids.

5 Finding bearstone marks beginning of change in Cloyd's life.

The San Juan National Forest, where *Beardance* takes place, is located in southwest Colorado. Interested students may want to draw a map in order to trace Cloyd and Walter's journey. Some students may want to make a relief map that shows elevations in perspective. They may have to make educated guesses about some locations, which may be too small to appear on maps. Suggest that students color their maps and mark places where important episodes occur. Some may want to illustrate the episode on the map itself. Consult with students in the planning stages to agree on how their maps will be assessed. (See *Portfolio Assessment and Professional Support Materials*, especially the section entitled **Suggestions for Portfolio Projects**.)

6 Drawing Conclusions
Why did hard work cure Cloyd's mood of self-pity? He had to concentrate on his work and not on his feelings.

7
Metaphor. Tony compares Cloyd to coyote to mean he knows how to bargain with customers.

8
Tony is evidently headed home, or at least his horse thinks he is.

9 Drawing Conclusions
Why does Walter not tell Tony real reason for trip to mountains? He does not want others to know his true purpose for fear they will try to find lost mine, too.

10
Figurative Language. Tony knows they are looking for gold but teases them by asking about goldfish.

11 Analyzing
Why does Tony use stage whisper? To pretend he is passing on secret advice.

like a poisonous desert plant waiting for a big rain. He could keep it from growing if he didn't **6** feed it. Taking care of the old man and the farm hadn't left any time for feeling sorry for himself. He'd driven the tractor in winter and summer, plowed snow and cut hay. He'd hand-shoveled the deep snow from the walks around the old farmhouse. Every day in winter, he'd taken the axe and chopped the ice to keep the hole in the pond open for Blueboy and the other horses to drink. He'd brought in the firewood all winter and irrigated the fields in the summer and done a hundred other chores. It was a good feeling, to work that hard for someone you cared about.

And here he was, back in the Rincon La Osa, the Corner of the Bear.

Blueboy had grazed close and wasn't ten feet away. The blue roan never strayed far. With his eye on Cloyd he ripped a clump of grass free, then raised his head and began to draw the long shoots across his molars, grinding noisily. The old man had chewed up his own piece of grass, just like a horse.

They heard the sound of horseshoes on stone and looked up to see a rider approaching with six pack-horses behind.

Cloyd recognized the young man who'd come twice to the farm this summer to buy hay. It was Tony Archuleta, who was always joking, **11** with the flashing smile and the thick black mustache, his hair black as Cloyd's and nearly as long. Cloyd remembered how much Tony Archuleta's eyes had approved of the hay, but Tony had never said it was good hay until he was done bargaining. Cloyd had handled all the sales of the hay; the old man had wanted him to learn. Cloyd knew he'd done well when the man had said in his English that sounded like **7** Spanish, "You're an old coyote."

Tony looked good riding down the Rincon La Osa on his buckskin horse, with his beaten felt hat and his denim jacket and the ancient leather chaps[1] on his legs. His face was dark, at least half as dark as a Ute's. "Walter Landis," the young man sang out, "and his Yuta coyote!"

Cloyd liked that, being called a Ute coyote.

8 Frustrated at being held up on the march to the barn, Tony's buckskin horse was yanking down on the reins, fighting the bit. The handsome rider's eyes went to the picks and shovels on the packhorses, and he pointed to them with his lips like an Indian. A knowing grin was spreading across his face. "Looking for treasure, eh?"

Walter Landis, who'd known this young man since he was a baby, and his parents and grandparents too on their place fifteen miles down the Piedra, replied with his best poker face, **9** "Just seein' the country, Tony, just seein' the country."

Cloyd added, "We dig a lot of worms for fishing."

10 Tony Archuleta's thick black eyebrows rose, and he said, "Goldfish, no?"

Cloyd liked this man.

"The direction you're heading, let me guess...maybe you're going to dig some worms up at *la Ventana?*"

The old man laughed through his nose, snorting like a horse.

Tony Archuleta leaned forward, cupped his lips, and spoke in a hoarse stage whisper. "You know the old Spanish sheepherders called the Window *el Portal del Diablo*—'the Devil's Gateway.' Lot of bad storms up there, lots of unusual things that have happened to people looking for that treasure. You be careful, now...."

Walter Landis winked and promised, "We'll be careful."

"You won't find Spanish treasure up there," Tony added good-naturedly. "Sixto Loco found it a long time ago, that's what I think."

1. **chaps:** leggings without a seat, worn over trousers by Western ranch hands. Also called *chaparejos*.

MEETING INDIVIDUAL NEEDS

ESL/LEP • This page contains words that are commonly used as nouns to refer to seasons. Here, however, the author uses them as verbs. Can students find them? ("... they used to winter in New Mexico and summer up in the San Juans.") Explain that in conversational English, the same idea is more frequently expressed by using the verb *spend*. For example, "They used to spend the winter in New Mexico." Ask the class if the words *autumn, fall,* and *spring* may also be used as verbs in this way. (No, only *winter* and *summer.*)

"You just resupply your uncle?" the old man asked.

"I'll be back at least two more times. Well, I gotta go—and don't let Sixto see those picks and shovels. He's crankier than ever and he's a dead shot. The old people say he knows everything that goes on in the mountains. Some still call him *la Sombra*—'the Shadow.'"

They watched Tony go. Just before he crossed the creek, he turned and called back, "Hey, Yuta coyote! I told Sixto Loco about the hay I got for him! I told him he'd probably want to eat with his sheep this winter! Too bad I robbed you on the price!"

Cloyd was grinning, and he was repeating the name, "Sixto Loco."

"I never met him," Walter said, "but I'll sure enough take Tony's warning to heart. Sixto Archuleta's reputation was made a long, long time ago. His brother disappeared in the mountains when they were both young men...some say Sixto killed his brother and buried him somewhere in the wilderness. I've heard that story too about him finding treasure—they say he killed his brother over gold."

"And he's a sheepherder?"

"Only one left in the mountains. The market's been poor for years and years, and nobody wants the life of a high-country shepherd—too lonely, too cold, too dangerous. A few of the families keep sheep on their home places, but nothing like the numbers they used to winter in New Mexico and summer up in the San Juans. Sixto's the only one left. Lives alone in the winter, with just his dogs, at his place along the San Juan River. Near the ghost town of Gato as I recollect; I've driven by it now and again. It's just a shotgun shack off the side of the old railroad bed, with pelts nailed over the cracks in the walls. Saw him once splitting wood out in his yard—there's no denying the man has a baleful look in his eye....Year after year, he takes his flock back above the timberline...that

man's been out in the wind and the cold more than any in the country, I'm sure."

"If he found the treasure, he would've built a better house."

The old man stood up to go, and limped on the leg that had been broken. "I'd agree with you, but people have an explanation for that. They say he's just too ornery to change his ways. There's a story I heard about him...every three or four years he decides to drive his old pickup into town—it's supposed to be about as old as its 1939 license plates. He'll drive into town with it, and when he gets pulled over for expired plates, he'll say, "Throw me in jail! It's nice and warm in there, and you'll have to feed me!"

5

In the night Walter had a coughing fit. He coughed so hard, he couldn't stop until he got out of his bedroll and went outside to get a drink of water. Cloyd was alarmed. Walter had to be eighty years old, and he was sick. The thin air was hard on him, and tonight they were camping at 11,600 feet, just below the tree line in the Rincon La Osa. The map showed the Window at 12,857 feet. Where the old man wanted to look for the lost mine, the storms would be fierce and the air even thinner than here. Should they be heading for "the Devil's Gateway"?

"Should've brought some water into the tent with me," Walter said when he came back inside. "I'll remember next time."

"Maybe we should turn back," Cloyd said. "Maybe it's too high up here."

"We'll rest up here another day. If I can't do it, I won't. This'll pass. I feel like a fat pony in high oats up here. You'll see."

The "fat pony" felt better in the morning, even better the next day. Early in the morning they started for the Continental Divide, and

12 Tony implies hay is of high quality, good enough for people to eat.

13 Cloyd is surprised Sixto herds sheep, especially if he has gold.

14 **Figurative Language.** A ghost town is a place where nobody lives anymore.

15 **Inference.** Cloyd draws conclusion by using logic.

16 Drawing Conclusions *What does Sixto imply by this?* Being put in jail would not really be punishment for him.

Chapter 5

1 Cloyd has doubts about wisdom of this trip for Walter.

2 **Simile.** Walter compares himself to a young, fit horse with plenty to eat to emphasize he feels good in mountains.

3

Metaphor. Narrator uses *bursting* to suggest there are so many peaks sky cannot contain them all.

4 Analyzing
What does Walter mean by "fly away like a kite"? He is light-headed, or dizzy, in thin air.

5

Metaphor. Compares large number of peaks to large number of people who take part in riot. Also, *riot* suggests lack of order, which also characterizes peaks.

6

Cloyd suspects Walter may be crying as emotional reaction to beauty of place.

7 Summarizing
Why does Walter ask Cloyd about geography of area? Cloyd has been here before and knows place.

8

Personification. Describes snow on mountain as though mountain were wearing human clothes.

9

Metaphor. Compares Walter's desire to find gold to disease that causes fever.

10 Making Generalizations
What does fact Walter and Cloyd know passage by heart suggest? They loved passage and read it many times because it describes place where Walter hopes his dreams will come true.

3 when they reached it the sky was bursting with peaks, hundreds of them. The old man said **4** he'd better sit down or he was going to fly away like a kite, and so they got off their horses. **5** Cloyd pointed out the Needles, a riot of peaks close at hand to the west, all rock and sky and straight up and down. He pointed south to the mesas of New Mexico, and southwest to the vague shapes of the Chuska Mountains of Arizona.

Then they looked east along the Divide. The **6** old man's eyes were moist. Cloyd couldn't tell if it wasn't only from the wind. Walter had his eye on a lone giant of a mountain only a few miles away. "That's got to be *el Cerro de la Piramide,* **7** as the book calls it, but where the heck is *la Ventana?*"

"In the ridge between us and the Pyramid," Cloyd said. "We can't see the Window because we're lined straight up with that ridge. But look over here."

Cloyd was looking at an immense spur off the Divide that stuck out to the north in the direc-**10** tion of the Rio Grande. He pointed it out to the old man. "From there you'd be looking straight across to the Window. Remember how it said in the book, you could see the Window from the mine?"

They made their camp a thousand feet down off the Divide on the Rio Grande side, fifteen minutes' ride below the timberline and at the head of East Ute Creek's long meadow. They pitched their sheep-herder tent at the edge of the meadow, with the forest at their back and a splendid view of the Rio Grande Pyramid towering above all the big country. "Only thing this camp's lacking is a view of the Window," the old man said. "I know it's up there somewhere."

By their campfire the old man brought out his treasure book and began to read from the chapter called *"La Mina Perdida de la Ventana."*

" 'To the Spaniards adventuring north from Santa Fe and Taos,' " the old man began, " 'the

San Juan Mountains in the Continental Divide's east-west bend must have taken on the appearance of a majestic wall spiked with hundreds of **8** towering peaks, clad in a forbidding mantle of white much of the year.' "

The old man paused for breath. His eyes were sparkling with excitement in the reflected light of the fire. Cloyd liked the way he read. He liked the way the old man's voice trembled not so much with the thin air, though that was **9** part of it, as with the effects of his gold fever, all stirred up by the closeness of the legendary mine.

" 'The Spanish of the 1700s knew from two hundred years' experience in the New World that such a range was likely to contain fabulous lodes of gold and silver. Of all the landmarks in these mountains, none rivaled the combination of one lone peak with the appearance of a pyramid, and the massive notch in the ridge to its west. The mountain they named *el Cerro de la Pyramide,* the notch *la Ventana.*' "

Cloyd knew this passage by heart, and so did the old man. But here, with the Pyramid itself looming above them, the words seemed to reverberate with power, as if it might really be true that the Spanish had toiled somewhere very close to here and left a fabulous treasure behind.

Walter handed the book over for Cloyd's turn, saying "I just wish we'd caught a glimpse of that Window even once today."

Cloyd said, "Now we're too close underneath it."

" 'The Spanish had been in nearby New Mexico since Cor-o-na-do's conquest of 1540,' "[1] Cloyd began. Once he'd caught on to reading, he could pronounce almost anything. But he had to go slow. " 'By the early 1700s they were

---

1. **Coronado's conquest of 1540:** Francisco Vásquez de Coronado (c. 1510–1554), a Spanish explorer who was the first European to explore Arizona and New Mexico.

bringing gold secretly out of southwestern Colorado's Ute frontier. The Spanish operated in secret to avoid paying "the king's fifth." ' "

Cloyd stopped reading and let his eyes show that he didn't understand the meaning.

"One-fifth of all treasure from the New World went right back to the king in Spain," Walter explained. "No wonder they were mining on the sly."

" 'They also operated in secret,' " Cloyd read, " 'because they feared the Utes.' " This part always brought a smile to his face. " 'It was known to the Utes that the Spanish made a practice of taking slaves among the Navajos and the pueblo peoples, mostly women and children to work in their households.' "

"Now you," Cloyd said, and showed the place to the old man.

"Let's remember to pay close attention," Walter said. "Listen hard for clues. It says, 'A group of six Spaniards and Frenchmen discovered a lode of high-grade gold ore in 1750 and worked their mine over the span of twenty summers. The ore was carried on mule trains toward Taos

or Santa Fe, but before it was carried out each fall it was hidden in three major caches and a number of minor caches in the district around the mine. Two of the minor caches have been found by treasure hunters, one on West Ute Creek in the summer of 1936, the other on Middle Ute Creek in 1937. The ore from both proved amazingly rich; both caches had been marked by an intricate pattern of tree blazes and rock cairns.[2] The mine itself was located west of the Window—' "

"Wait a minute," Cloyd said. "What pattern? Why doesn't it say?"

"Just doesn't," Walter said with a shrug, and threw a few more sticks onto the fire. "Maybe if the writer knew, he would've found the treasure instead of only spending years looking for it."

Cloyd's old doubts were coming back. Maybe it's just a story, he thought, but he didn't say so.

As convinced as ever, Walter continued, his

2. **cairns** (kârnz): piles of stones used as landmarks or memorials.

Ruby Lake with Weminuche Wilderness in the background.

©Tom Bean 1990/DRK Photo

voice eager with excitement: "'The mine itself was located west of the Window, which could be seen from the entrance of the mine. Over a period of twenty years the original miners made themselves rich and also made enemies of the Utes. When the Utes surprised them and the end came—'"

"It doesn't say what they did to make enemies of the Utes," Cloyd interrupted. "It should've said that."

"You're right, it should have told about that. Probably never got written down anywhere. Anyhow, we're just getting to this part here where you've been reading it so careful, your eyes almost wore the print off the page."

"Where?"

"Look, right here."

"That's just a smudge."

"Spooked me too," the old man said with a wink. "It's about Aguilar and the skeletons: 'Some of the miners died and others escaped, but none ever returned. The mine itself was never rediscovered, except perhaps by a Spanish sheepherder named Doneciano Aguilar in 1908. A teller of tales, one night he told his fellows at camp of spying two skeletons through an opening in a ledge at the foot of a cliff, in the vicinity of the Window. He said he hadn't gone in to investigate because of the darkness and his fear of *los espiritus de los antiguos*—the spirits of the ancients.' When Aguilar was laughed at, he resolved never to tell the location of the mine. Convicted of a murder the following year, he was sent to the state penitentiary in Santa Fe to serve a life sentence.'"

Walter closed the book. The fire had burned low once again. "Cloyd, do you realize," the old man said slowly, emphasizing every word, "no one has ever searched for those three major caches with a metal detector the caliber of ours."

Cloyd nodded agreeably, acknowledging the old man's faith in his secret piece of equipment.

"This Cachefinder of ours is stuffed full of microchips and all that new computer technology! Scans deeper than any metal detector ever made, anywhere in the world!"

Cloyd stretched and smiled, and shivered with the night cold. At least Walter didn't have any doubts.

6

The next morning the old man studied the lay of the mountains and pored over the maps, thinking it all out. "We know the mine should be up behind us somewhere," he said. "It should be on that slope of the ridge above us, facing the Window. We can't see the tailings[1] because they would have dropped them over a ledge, mixed them into a rockslide to disguise the location of the mine. But we're not looking for the mine so much as for the caches of high-grade ore, the ones they left behind when the survivors skedaddled[2] for Santa Fe. Now where would you look for those caches, Cloyd?"

Cloyd had been thinking about it. "If I was them, I wouldn't want to try to hide anything up on that ridge—too much rock. It would be easier to hide the ore down in the trees. The digging would be a lot easier."

"Same thing I'm thinking. Maybe you've got a nose for treasure after all."

"Besides," Cloyd added, "the book said there were markings on rocks and markings on *trees*."

"We'll keep our eyes out for those grizzlies too," Walter declared. "That mother and her three cubs."

"Brown, cocoa, and gray-black," Cloyd remembered.

"Grizzlies and gold," the old man sang,

---

1. **tailings:** waste products left after mining.
2. **skedaddled** (skə-dăd'əld): ran away in panic.

3 "that's you and me, Cloyd. Grizzlies and gold."

Cloyd was glad they weren't going to have to comb the high, steep slopes above for treasure. They couldn't camp up there. The horses had no pasture up there. Walter would never survive trying to cling to those elk trails up on the ledges.

4 Mostly, Cloyd thought, Walter needs to nurse that cough. Down in the trees we'll be protected from the weather.

Every morning Walter took off with his 5 Cachefinder, scanning the forest floor back from the meadow. For several days Cloyd went with him, and then he started to stray in search of old Spanish blazes[3] or piles of rocks that might mark one of the caches the old man was looking for. But really, he didn't believe in the gold. Even if the story was true, two hundred and more years was a long time for a tree to heal an axe wound. The marked trees might have even died and returned to the soil. Two 6 hundred years provided plenty of time for a little pile of rocks to fall down.

His eyes were searching tree bark for high claw marks that might have been left by a grizzly, and searching the ground for tracks with claws far forward of the footpad.

On an aspen, as high as his hand could reach, he found the claw marks of a bear. These marks didn't prove anything. A black bear, he knew, could reach that high or higher.

But when he found a pile of bear scat, full of seeds, bits of bone, and strands of hair, Cloyd 7 had to wonder. Could a black bear leave this big a dropping? He kept a segment in a plastic bag and brought it back to show to Walter.

"Wish I could tell you," Walter said. "I just don't know."

It began to rain every day, by two in the afternoon at the latest. Sometimes they were both back in camp, and through the fold in the door of the sheepherder tent, they would watch 8 the hail dance. Other times the weather would catch them away from camp, and they would each wait it out before returning. The temperature could drop thirty degrees in less than thirty minutes, but Cloyd was ready for it. His cold-weather clothing and his rain gear were so much better than what he'd had the year before. The old man had taken him to the Pine Needle Mountaineering store in Durango and 9 had written a big check. His red rain shell with both top and trousers wouldn't allow any moisture in, even though it would let his sweat out. His clothes were staying dry.

Later in the afternoon the sun would come back out, and they would dry their wet things on the big boulder, knee-high and flat like a table, out in the meadow halfway to the creek.

Five days had passed in their camp, and Walter had worked the trees on both sides as far as he could reach downstream. They'd dug a few holes where the old man had heard a hopeful signal, and then they filled the holes back in. "Let's move downstream a mile or so," the old man suggested. "Those caches must be just out of our reach."

Cloyd like the new camp better. It was closer to the fishing. In the late afternoons after the thunderstorms died down, he rode Blueboy a 10 few miles down the creek to the beaver ponds to find fish for dinner.

Every night it was freezing now, and the tundra grasses and flowers[4] were turning red and gold.

11 Mornings he rose early, and his breath spouted jets of vapor. It was never long before the old man hooked the Cachefinder's sending

---

3. **blazes:** trail markers, often made by cutting the bark on trees. Blazes are also used by loggers to indicate which trees are to be cut down.

4. **tundra...flowers:** vegetation that grows beyond the timberline.

---

3 Analyzing
Why does Walter refer to himself and Cloyd as "grizzlies and gold"? Those are things they are most interested in finding.

4
Once again Cloyd proves to be realistic about Walter's condition.

5
Metaphor. Compares forest to a room. Ground is floor and tops of trees form ceiling.

6 Making Inferences
What might cause rock pile to fall down? A number of things: passing animals, erosion, heavy rain, freeze.

7
Cloyd uses scientific method of close observation to track bears.

8
Personification. Hail has human ability to dance.

9 Analyzing
What's meant by Walter "had written a big check"? He paid a lot of money for Cloyd's gear, meaning he got good-quality merchandise.

10
Beaver ponds form upstream from dams beavers build as their homes.

11
Metaphor. Compares vapor made by breath to stream of gas coming out of a nozzle.

12
Metaphor. Compares Walter's hopes to a mint full of newly-made money. He has as much hope as a mint has money.

13 Drawing Conclusions
What does Walter hope to find by crevice mining? Veins of gold exposed by erosion of stream.

14 Analyzing
Would Walter really die of happiness? No. Excitement of finding treasure might cause heart attack that would kill him.

15
Fresh bear scat indicates bear was there recently and may still be in area.

16 Drawing Conclusions
Why is bear sniffing wind? It wants to detect scent of any animal in vicinity.

17
Description. Woman's appearance from sky and clouds suggests mysterious quality of goddess.

18
Cloyd is modest about his tracking skills.

and receiving unit to his belt, adjusted the headphones, and started out in search of treasure. Every day was a new adventure for the old **12** man, mint-full of promise. With Walter Landis, the harder he searched, the more the search possessed him, and the more he became convinced that the moment of discovery was imminent. From a distance, you couldn't tell that he was keeping the circular search coil slightly above the ground. It looked like he was out vacuuming the meadow or the mountainsides.

In the afternoons Walter would tire of being on his feet, and he'd pick at little cracks in the stream bottom's bedrock, cleaning all the grooves and cracks with a screwdriver bent at right angles near the tip. The old man called it **13** "crevice mining," but to Cloyd it looked like Walter was an old dentist who'd just gone crazy.

It didn't seem as crazy when the old man brought him a nugget the size of a raisin that had been caught in one of the cracks. Walter Landis was so excited, Cloyd could picture what he'd be like if he actually found a big treasure. His heart might not be able to take it. He might **14** die on the spot out of pure happiness.

▶ At the edge of a melt pond, below snowbanks that had survived the summer in the shadows, Cloyd found bear tracks in the mud. They showed five toes but lacked the grizzly's long **15** claws. Nearby, fresh bear scat. Even if it wasn't a grizzly, he wanted to track this bear.

The trail led down the mountain into the timber, where the bear had stopped to dig up a squirrel's cache and to overturn a log for the ants and grubs underneath. Cloyd tracked the bear upslope now, far from any trail, and thought he'd lost it when he emerged from the forest at the tree line. The bear wasn't above him on the open, grassy slopes as he'd hoped. But when he crouched and then crawled up to the very top of the Divide, with the wind blowing stiffly in his face, there the black bear was, not thirty feet away, sitting on its haunches and **16** sniffing the wind.

The bear couldn't see him and didn't catch his scent either, until the wind shifted a little. All it took was a look over its shoulder, and the bear exploded in flight down the mountainside. The black bear didn't stop running until it had reached the timber more than a mile below. Cloyd had read about this, how fast a bear could run, but he'd never seen it himself. ◀

As if out of the sky, a woman appeared over the grassy slope of the Divide. She was coming his way.

As the hiker approached, he could see that her eyes were shaped like his. Almond-eyed, high-cheekboned, with dark, braided hair that fell almost to her waist, she had to be Indian, though she didn't look very much like a Ute or Navajo. She was carrying a big pack, but she **17** wasn't bent under it. Her legs were sinewy and strong, and she came striding toward him across the alpine carpet of short wildflowers, out of the blue sky and billowing white clouds. From her neck hung the largest pair of binoculars he had ever seen and a camera with an extra-long lens.

"That bear was sure surprised," the woman said in greeting, with a smile at her lips. "You could've almost tapped him on the shoulder. I've been watching you. You're a good tracker." Her eyes were black, and her chin delicate like his sister's. He guessed she might be the age his mother would have been, had she lived.

"I'm just learning," he said.

She didn't offer her hand, and Cloyd was glad of that. She was curious about him, but her eyes didn't try to know him all at once. "I'm Cloyd Atcitty," he offered.

"I'm Ursa."

She took off her pack and sat quietly, and admired the view. Her eyes were on the Pyramid and the Window. Close at her throat, a small, flattened turquoise bear hung suspended from a delicate gold chain.

7

"Your necklace," Cloyd said. "It's a bear."

1 The Indian woman who'd appeared out of the sky smiled a smile that reminded him even more of his sister, who was curious and did well in school and liked to laugh. The woman touched her bear charm and said, "It's for my name, Ursa. My name means 'bear.' "

Everything about her was filling him with surprise and awe. Yet she was easy to talk to. "What are you doing up here?" he asked her. "Where did you come from?"

2 She laughed. "I was about to ask you the same question. But you asked first. This morning I came from the head of Snowslide Canyon, and I'm looking for grizzly bears in these mountains."

Ursa was watching his eyes to see his reaction. She could see how keenly he was listening.

3 Cloyd asked quickly, "Have you found any?"

The woman with the long braid shook her head. "Of course, I've only been trying for three weeks. There've been teams from the U.S. Fish and Wildlife Service looking all sum-4 mer....They've given up; they're all gone now. There's only me left, and a couple of game wardens who are somewhere west of that mountain right now."

She was pointing toward the Rio Grande Pyramid.

"Are you from around here?" Cloyd asked doubtfully.

Ursa brought out two granola bars and gave him one. "I'm a wildlife biologist—I research grizzlies. I teach at the University of Montana in Missoula. Unfortunately, I'm running out of time down here on my grizzly search—I have to be back in the classroom nine days from now."

Cloyd was wondering how much she knew.

5 Had there been more sightings? "How come everybody's looking for grizzlies?" he asked her.

Ursa paused, looking out over the moun-6 tains, nibbling at her granola bar. Cloyd had already wolfed his. He was pleased that the storm in the Needles didn't look like it was heading their way. The sun was shining on this conversation, which he didn't want to end.

"I'll go back to the beginning," Ursa said with a smile. "Last summer there was a grizzly bear killed in these mountains. It was the first grizzly confirmed in Colorado since the early 1950s. When people think of grizzlies, they think of a few places in Wyoming and Montana, but not Colorado. The story even ran in papers around the country—people were amazed. It caught people's imagination to think of grizzlies surviving in Colorado all this time."

"Grizzlies? You said *grizzlies*. There's more than that one, for sure?"

Ursa's black eyes reflected hope and doubt at the same time. "The only evidence we have so far is the word of the outfitter who killed the grizzly last summer. He claims he saw a grizzly with three cubs this May, over in that drainage there...." The grizzly woman, as Cloyd now thought of her, was pointing to the Rincon La Vaca, below the Pyramid on the Pine River side. "But I'm not sure I believe him, even if he is fully qualified to tell grizzlies apart from black 7 bears. This guy goes to Alaska to hunt grizzlies every year. He's not exactly a friend of bears."

Mention of the red-haired man was making Cloyd sick and angry. The red-haired man always seemed to be the big man in the middle of things.

8 "No one who knows bears and knows his background really believes his version of what happened last summer, when the grizzly supposedly surprised him...."

Cloyd's heart was beating fast. Not everybody had believed Rusty's story.

"There was someone who might know what really did happen," the grizzly woman said. "There was supposed to have been a boy, a Ute

Chapter 7

1
Symbol. Bear necklace is symbol of Ursa's identity.

2 Making Inferences
Why does Ursa laugh? Answers will vary. Perhaps she is amused by coincidence of wanting to ask Cloyd same question. Perhaps she is amused by Cloyd's straight-forward curiosity.

3
Cloyd hopes answer will be "yes."

4 Making Inferences
Why have people given up looking for grizzlies? Answers will vary. Maybe they have concluded there are not any. Maybe they have other duties to attend to.

5
Cloyd already knows one reason, but he is hoping someone other than Rusty has reported a sighting.

6
Metaphor. Compares Cloyd's quick, greedy eating to way wolf eats.

7
Fact that Rusty hunts grizzlies in Alaska makes Ursa suspect truth of his report of grizzly sighting.

8 Drawing Conclusions
What does this imply about behavior of grizzlies? That they do not attack people unless they are provoked.

9
Simile. Compares Cloyd's face to mask to indicate he shows no emotion.

10
Cloyd's father is in a coma.

11   Expressing an Opinion
Why does Cloyd have such warm feelings toward Ursa? Answers will vary. Perhaps her interest in grizzlies makes him realize they are much alike.

12
Metaphor. Compares sound and tone of voice to feelings speaker seems to have.

13   Drawing Conclusions
Why would existence of grizzlies encourage the possibility of breeding? Existence of bears means area is good habitat for grizzlies.

14   Analyzing
Why does Cloyd turn away when he asks Ursa to camp with them? Answers will vary. Maybe he does not want to see negative reaction on her face.

15
Cloyd's careful investigation earlier may pay off.

Chapter 8

1
Walter proves he is experienced camper and cook by making dessert on campfire.

---

boy, who was there when the bear was killed...."

9   Cloyd's face was blank, like a mask. He would let her talk.

Suddenly she stopped and looked at him. "You," she said. "You are that boy, aren't you?"

He nodded. It was time to tell her his story. She wanted to know, and he would tell her.

As he was about to begin, she said, "Start from the beginning."

Cloyd wondered where the beginning was. His mother, who died getting him born? His **10** father, in a sleep he would never waken from in the hospital in Window Rock? His grandmother, who raised him; the group home in Durango?

"I found a bearstone once," he said, pointing at the charm at her throat with a twist of his lips.

He was sparing with his words, but Cloyd told her more of himself, of his true feelings, than **11** he had ever told anyone before. He wanted to tell his story to this woman. In addition to being the grizzly woman, it felt like she was his sister, his grandmother, the mother he never knew. He told her about Walter Landis, the farm, and the gold mine, and he told her the true story of what had really happened when Rusty killed the grizzly.

"I'm not surprised," Ursa said when he was **12** done. Her voice sounded tired and sad. "It's an old story, the mountain man killing the thing he loves. Indian people have known this lesson for a long time. The People know that the hunter who only takes and gives nothing in return will one day wake up to find that all the animals have vanished. This is what comes from not recognizing that people and animals are all relatives in the spirit world."

It was strange, how closely her words echoed his grandmother's. "Do you really believe there's a spirit world?" he asked her.

Ursa's eyes shone with conviction. "Oh, yes," she said softly.

It made him feel good to hear her talk.

"Cloyd, I only hope Rusty Owens was telling the truth about the mother and cubs. Let me tell you what's at stake....If any of us can prove there are still grizzlies in Colorado, in this Weminuche Wilderness, it means they'll be given the greatest possible protection under the Endangered Species Act, and most likely more will be brought in, to insure a breeding **13** population."

At first Cloyd doubted he could have heard right. This news was almost too wonderful to believe. "That's true?" he asked her, not with a smile, but with almost desperate hope.

"True," the grizzly woman said. "Prove one, they'll bring others."

He could hardly wait to tell the old man about that. "Can you camp with us tonight?" **14** Cloyd asked her, looking away as he said it. He didn't want her to leave.

"Sounds great," she said. "And I'd love to meet your friend."

On their way down to the camp on East Ute Creek, Cloyd told her about the bear scat he'd found. Ursa was listening carefully. "I'll take **15** some hairs from it," she told him. "In the laboratory, they'll be able to tell if it's black bear or grizzly. The chromosome structures in the DNA[1] are different."

Cloyd led her down the mountainside. Behind him, he heard nothing, she walked so quietly. He could learn to go as softly. One thing she had said above all others stuck in his mind and kept repeating itself: "Prove one, they'll bring others."

8

It was a special time, this evening with the griz- **1** zly woman in camp. Walter had baked a peach

---

1. **chromosome** (krō′mə-sōm′)...**DNA:** the part of the cell that contains most of the nucleic acids that are the basis of heredity.

cobbler in the Dutch oven, and Ursa and Cloyd both ate seconds. She liked peaches and peach cobbler just as much as he did. They were finishing up their cobbler, and the old man was pouring coffee out of the old enamel pot. "Nothing like coffee out in the fresh air," Walter was saying. "Never tastes better. Warms up the old bones. Cloyd, you sure are a lucky fellow. Imagine meeting someone way back here that's as keen on bears as you are...."

The woman was eyeing both of them fondly, this unlikely combination of a Ute boy and an old white rancher. She'd been charmed by the grizzled farmer-turned-prospector and his fascination with gold, his eagerness to speak of the excitement of the search, his instinctive reluctance to tell in detail of the treasure he was after. She was sipping her coffee, and the firelight was dancing in her dark eyes.

"If I might," the old man asked the grizzly woman in a formal tone, "and I don't mean to pry...but is Ursa your entire name?"

"It is," she replied. "I gave it to myself at the time I decided to make grizzlies my life's work. The name I grew up with was Elizabeth Torsness. I grew up in southeast Alaska. My mother is Tlingit[1] and my father's people were some Tlingit and some Norwegian. His great-grandfather came from Norway during the Alaska gold rush."[2]

Alaska, Cloyd thought. The name had magic and power. Alaska was big and beautiful, he knew, but mostly what it meant to him was bears. Alaska meant huge bears.

" 'Kling-it'?" the old man repeated. "I don't believe I've heard of Kling-its." He stroked his beard with great seriousness. "Heard of Kling-ons—Cloyd and I went to one of them *Star Trek* movies."

The grizzly woman had a good laugh. "That's the way it sounds, but it has a funny spelling. Begins with a T instead of a K. We're one of the tribes that carves the totem poles. We didn't for a long time, but now we're starting to again."

Walter was shaking his head in wonder and pouring himself another cup of coffee. He held it in his hands, letting the hot cup warm them before it warmed him inside. "I always wanted to see Alaska," he said. "I guess I never will."

"Did you see bears where you grew up?" Cloyd asked her.

"Bears were our only neighbors," Ursa replied. "They were grizzly bears, though in Alaska people mostly call them brown bears or especially 'brownies.' I grew up on Admiralty Island,[3] a big island off the coast. My father was a fisherman and he built a float house about halfway between the mouths of two streams. The brownies fished too, and when the salmon were running you could see as many as twenty around the falls on one of those creeks."

"Twenty grizzlies in one place," the old man marveled. "Imagine that, Cloyd."

Cloyd was imagining, as Ursa was filling in the details. "The falls were only about six feet high," she said. "Bears would stake out their favorite fishing holes, either in the stream right below the falls or right on the edge of the falls themselves. Now and then they would have terrible fights over the best spots...but grizzlies can take as well as give horrible wounds. They have amazing powers of healing."

"And you would see them catch the fish?" Cloyd asked.

"Oh, yes. I especially liked to watch the ones standing on the lip of the falls. They'd just hang their heads out there—sometimes they'd grab one in midair. I watched them all the time.

---

1. **Tlingit**: a seafaring people who live in southeast Alaska and northern British Columbia.
2. **Alaska gold rush:** See "The Cremation of Sam McGee," page 486.

3. **Admiralty Island:** one of the chief islands in the Alexander Archipelago, off the coast of southeast Alaska.

2
Exaggeration. Coffee makes Walter feel better, but it does not really warm his bones.

3
Figurative Language. Narrator uses *eyeing* instead of *watching* or some other word to make writing more vivid.

4
Metaphor. Compares flickering of firelight to movements of dancers.

5 Analyzing
Why does the name Alaska have magic and power? Because of happy images it brings to Cloyd's mind.

6
Even though Walter is not familiar with Tlingit people, Ursa assumes he knows about their famous totem poles.

7
Metaphor. Compares migration of salmon to animal or person running.

8
Ursa probably has scientific knowledge about grizzlies' healing powers.

Cloyd's friend Ursa is a wildlife biologist who researches grizzlies at the University of Montana. Students who are interested in wildlife might want to find out more about this occupation. Suggest that students do some research in your community. If you live in an urban area, students could check with a nearby college or university to find a wildlife biologist who might be willing to talk to them about his or her career.

Students might also want to write to the National Park Service or to a national wildlife refuge. *The New York Public Library Desk Reference* has a listing of the national parks in the United States, the national wildlife refuge locations, and additional addresses which may be of benefit in their search.

Alaskan brown bear fishing.   ©Kim Heacox/DRK Photo

9   Finding Cause and Effect
What does amount of available food suggest about grizzlies' potential size? They are capable of growing very large if enough food to support large size is available.

10
Ursa states basic facts about getting along with bears.

A brownie can eat a hundred pounds of salmon in a day. There's so much food up there… **9** that's why they grow bigger than Rocky Mountain grizzlies."

Cloyd was having trouble picturing one thing. "How can you get close enough to watch them…without getting hurt?"

"Don't get me wrong," Ursa said. "Grizzlies **10** can be dangerous.…But people and bears have been sharing those salmon streams for thousands of years. It's a matter of respecting the bears' dominance, knowing how to act around them, knowing the distance that's comfortable for them."

"How close?" the old man wondered, his eyes wide.

"At the creeks, a few hundred feet. They were used to us. It was close enough—they looked enormous to me. Quite a few of them weighed upward of a thousand pounds. We'd

see them all the time on the tidal flats[4] around
our house. They'd loll around like hound
dogs."

"Holy cow!" Walter exclaimed. "I thought I
could tell a whopper,[5] Cloyd. Her actual life
story's taller'n a whopper!"

11 Ursa had a sparkle in her eye and Cloyd wondered for a moment if she was making all this
up, but he didn't think so.

"Sometimes people came to visit," she continued. "They'd want to see the bears fishing.
They were uncomfortable if my father didn't
12 carry a weapon along, so he carried a hefty stick
just to make them feel better."

"Did he ever use it?" asked Cloyd, who was
anxious to know more about how dangerous
grizzlies were.

She smiled. "If a thousand-pound bear
charged at thirty miles an hour…," the grizzly
woman calculated, "that stick wouldn't have
seemed like much of a weapon. No, he never
used it, but he did get hurt once by a bear. It
was a bear that was new to the creek. The bear
rushed him and broke his collarbone and three
ribs…."

The grizzly woman's face filled with emotion
as she paused, remembering. "It was my
mother who saved my father from a worse
mauling, or even being killed. Was that bear
ever surprised when she opened her umbrella
in his face! I'll never forget the look in that
bear's eyes and how fast it ran off."

"Well, I'll be busted to flinderjigs!" Walter
exclaimed, with a quick slap to his knee. "My,
my…And how about you, Ursa? This research
that you do among the grizzlies in Wyoming
and Montana…have you ever been hurt?"

13 Ursa gave a few raps on the log she was sitting on. "Not so far. I'm very careful not to
blunder between a mother and her cubs, but I

14 do get a lot closer than hikers who are wearing
bells, making noise, giving bears the opportunity to vanish without ever being seen. I need to
get close to make my notes and to take pictures
and movies. Grizzlies get used to me being
around, and they'll go about their business. But
I've been charged a few times over the
years…."

15 Now Cloyd's eyes were as wide as saucers.
"You were?"

"Grizzlies will bluff you into giving them the
space they feel they need. The scary part is,
their bluffs don't look like bluffs in the least. It's
the scariest thing in your life. If the bear not
only stands up, but woofs several times…if you
hear a popping sound of the jaws, and the bear
lays its ears back—look out."

"Good lord," the old man whispered
hoarsely.

Cloyd felt like he was there, and one of those
bears was charging him.

Ursa's teeth were clenched. "If you turn and
run," she said, "you'll probably get mauled. In a
short burst, they're faster than a racehorse."

"Then what do you do?" Cloyd wondered.

"You try to make yourself look as big as possible, without making any threatening gestures.
But don't look the bear in the eye. You talk
softly and apologetically. If it charges, it'll probably stop before it gets to you. Or sometimes it'll
run right past you."

The old man was pulling hard on his beard.
16 "Gives me chills just thinking about it!"

She shrugged. "I try to keep in mind that I'm
statistically much more at risk driving on the
17 highway. So, the more time I spend in grizzly
country and out of my car, the longer I'll live,
statistically speaking."

Cloyd could tell that Walter liked this woman.
Cloyd liked watching the old man's face as he
listened to her stories. Walter said with a grin,
"Must be hard to recall those statistics when a
grizzly's charging…."

---

4. **tidal flats:** muddy or marshy stretches of land.
5. **whopper:** a big lie.

11 Making Inferences
*What does sparkle in Ursa's
eye mean?* Answers will vary.
Perhaps she is exaggerating. Perhaps she is just happy to have interested audience.

12 Summarizing
*Why did people feel more
comfortable when Ursa's father carried stick?* They did not
know it was useless, and they assumed he knew what he was
doing.

13
Ursa knocks on wood of log for
good luck.

14
Exaggeration. Hikers are not literally wearing bells, but their
equipment jangles when they
walk.

15
Simile. Compares size of Cloyd's
eyes to saucers to indicate his
eyes are open very wide.

16
Exaggeration. Walter does not
literally have chills; emotional reaction makes his skin tighten,
causing goose bumps.

17
Irony. Facing a huge wild animal
is safer than driving, statistically
speaking.

18

This fact raises questions about Rusty's claim that grizzly he killed attacked him.

19 Analyzing
Why does everyone become silent? They are thinking about awesome power of grizzly bears.

20

Cloyd is obviously impressed by Ursa and her experience with grizzlies.

Chapter 9

1
Simile. Compares tree cover to blanket which covers everything.

2 Finding Main Ideas
Why does Walter urge Cloyd to go with Ursa? He knows searching with her is rare chance for Cloyd to learn about grizzlies.

3
Cloyd feels responsible for Walter's safety and well-being.

4 Analyzing
Why would believing grizzlies are half-human keep people from hunting them? Eating half-human creature would be form of cannibalism.

5 Making Inferences
Why does Ursa think that maybe she wants to know too much? Answers will vary. Maybe she thinks there should be some mystery about grizzlies that people cannot solve.

6
Plot. In story, conflict develops because girl fails to follow rules.

544

"They are simply <u>awesome</u> creatures," Ursa replied. "You never forget how powerful they are and how deadly they could be. The amaz-

18 ing thing is, ordinarily they're ferocious only when attacked. They don't take kindly to being killed, and when they are being killed, 'they're hard to put down' as the hunters in Alaska often say. They can do a lot of damage as they're dying."

19 For a while, no one spoke. Each turned within. The fire had burned low, and the chill of the late August night was reaching their bones.

20 Cloyd wondered if he could be as brave as Ursa. He wished he could see another grizzly. Even just one more, just a glimpse.

9

Cloyd stuffed as much as he could into his big daypack and he followed the grizzly woman up and out of East Ute Creek, over Gunsight Pass, and into the Ute Lakes Basin, a fifteen-mile-wide shelf in the shape of a <u>crescent</u> above the timberline.

The grizzly woman was leading him across the tundra, below the boulder fields and above

1 the swath of mountain willows that covered the entire basin like a living blanket. She would stop and scan those willows with her high-powered binoculars, and she would scan the meadows of Middle Ute Creek miles below.

2 Walter had said, "Go with her. Maybe you'll find the bears."

Cloyd was happy to be out searching with

3 Ursa, yet he'd gone with misgivings, knowing he might be away several days. When he'd left the old man alone the year before, Walter had blown himself up in his mine, even though he'd promised not to do any blasting.

They were eating from the lunch of dried fruit and nuts and cheese that Ursa had set out

on the miniature, ground-hugging wildflowers, pink and purple and white.

A marmot whistled sharply. Cloyd looked up to see a solitary bull elk grazing on the other side of the boulder field. In and out of the rocks and onto the tundra, a mother ptarmigan[1] and her half-grown young were pecking along in their mottled summer plumage.

"The Tlingit believe that grizzlies can know the future," Ursa said. "They believe that grizzlies can understand our speech and know what we are saying about them, even from great distances. Do the Utes believe this also?"

"I don't know," Cloyd said. "Maybe they did, I don't know."

"Some of the tribes would hunt grizzlies. Others wouldn't, like mine up in Alaska and many of them in your part of the country,

4 because they believed that grizzlies are half-human. The ones who hunted grizzlies did so with great respect, hoping to gain power from them. Power to be used in battle or to feed one's family was a good thing."

"You know about all the tribes?"

"I try to learn as much as I can," the grizzly woman said with a sigh. "I know very little compared to what there is to know, compared to what's been lost. When it comes to bears, I want

5 to know everything. Maybe I want to know too much. Mostly, Indian women in the past were afraid of bears, afraid that bears would come out of the woods and take them back with them to be their wives. The Tlingit tell a story about people being related to bears. It's called 'The Woman Who Married a Bear.'"

Cloyd had to think about this. He asked her, "How did it happen in the story?"

6 "A girl didn't follow the rules about the distance that people and bears should keep along

---

1. **ptarmigan:** (tär′mĭ-gən) a bird with feathered legs and feet, usually having white plumage in the winter and brown during the summer.

the salmon streams. She was picking berries and got separated from her family. A young man came along, a handsome young man, and they began talking."

"Was it…the bear?"

7 The grizzly woman nodded. "But in her eyes it was a young man. In the old times, there was magic that went back and forth between people and bears. People could look at bears and see people, and bears could look at people and see bears."

Again, the grizzly woman was echoing his grandmother's words. It was strange and wonderful to think that two tribes so far apart would tell stories so much alike.

"Her children," Cloyd wondered. "Were they bears or people?"

8 A smile played at the grizzly woman's lips. "Who knows? Maybe they were whichever was in the minds of the ones looking at them. But the story says that after her brothers came to the den and killed her husband, she returned to her people and lived with them until her brothers made fun of her for being mated to a bear. At that moment she and her children turned into bear and cubs. She killed her brothers, and all the people learned a great lesson of respect as she fled into the woods with her children."

"That's a good story," Cloyd said.

"There's wisdom in all those old stories."

"Maybe the bears around here heard you tell all this," Cloyd said with a chuckle.

9 Ursa laughed a bright, musical laugh. "That grizzly with her three cubs—maybe she'd like those old stories. She might come a little closer and give us a look."

At their camp, he wanted to ask her something. "You said Indian women were afraid of bears. How come you're different?"

"My mother wanted me to have a bear as a spirit helper. She had heard that the people

down the coast, the Kwakiutl,[2] knew how to get their daughters the power of the grizzly as food
10 gatherer. They believed that if the right forepaw of a bear is placed on the palm of the right hand of an infant girl, she will be successful in picking berries and digging clams. So my mother did this with me."

A *spirit helper,* Cloyd thought. He'd never heard this expression before. "How did they get a spirit helper, the people in the old days?"

"By dreaming," she replied. "All across the continent, people believed that when they dreamed, their souls left their bodies and trav-
11 eled about in the spirit world. In a dream you could see something that would normally be invisible. You could even visit the spirit home of the bears."

"My grandmother talked about spirit bears," he said, and then he told her what had happened at the Bear Dance, when he had lifted out of his body and up above the Bear Dance and had looked down.

She listened carefully, and when he was done, she said, "What did you learn when you were out there that you could bring back?"

He thought hard, and then he said, "I guess nothing."

"Well, at least you can dream," she said, her
12 dark eyes full of fire. "That's a great thing. On his dream journey, a hunter might learn a design for his quiver that pleased the animals, or he might meet the spirit keeper of the animal he was hunting and be shown a good place to hunt. When a dream came true, it was said that you *found* your dream."

Cloyd stretched out, with his hand behind his head, and looked at the stars. It was a lucky thing he had met this woman. These things that she knew, they were things he wanted to know.

13 "I wish I'd seen the Ute Bear Dance," Ursa

2. **Kwakiutl:** (kwä′kē-o̅o̅t′l) a North American Indian people of British Columbia.

7
Traditional story relies on magic to make its point.

8
Personification. Smile has human ability to play.

9
Metaphor. Compares Ursa's laugh to lively music.

10
Ursa's mother conducted ritual that she believed would have magical results.

11 Finding Cause and Effect
What function do dreams play in these beliefs? They provide a form of education a person cannot get any other way.

12
Figurative Language. Narrator uses *fire* to mean passion.

13
Cloyd learns from Ursa, but she learns from him, too.

TRANSPARENCY 42
Literary Elements
Suspense – invites students to explore methods of creating suspense in a novel.

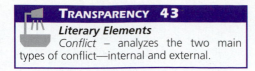

TRANSPARENCY 43
Literary Elements
Conflict – analyzes the two main types of conflict—internal and external.

14 Making Inferences
Why might Utes have stopped doing this part of dance? Maybe because all grizzlies are gone from this region.

15
Cloyd wants Ursa to experience as much of Bear Dance as possible.

16
Metaphor. Compares Ursa's smile to smile of shy girl.

17 Drawing Conclusions
Why are steps slow and small at first? Ursa is still learning dance, so they take slow and small steps until they are accustomed to dancing together.

18 Making Generalizations
What does curiosity suggest about bear's intelligence? Bear must be intelligent to want to learn as she does.

19
Bear again reveals her intelligence.

20
Irony. Readers now know that grizzly and her three cubs exist, but characters of novel do not know this. This is **dramatic irony.**

READING CHECK
1. Colorado (p. 520).
2. August (p. 520).
3. Grizzlies (p. 520).
4. Last sheepherder in mountains (p. 533).
5. Make yourself look as big as possible, avoid threatening gestures and looking in bear's eyes, speak softly and apologetically (p. 543).

said, "but I've only read about it. Do a man and a woman still appear at the end of the endurance dance, dressed in the skins of bears?"

Cloyd was shaking his head. "I don't think so. I never saw that."

14 "Maybe they don't do that part anymore. It was to show that the bears had heard the people's good wishes, that they had wakened from their hibernation and were going out into the world again. It was always held at the end of the winter, to help wake up the bears and help bring spring."

"It's late in May now," Cloyd said. "Memorial Day weekend."

"Show me how to do the bear dance," she urged.

He got to his feet, but then he hesitated. "It **15** would be better if you could hear the sounds. Let me try to make the sounds for you."

Cloyd found two sticks, and he whittled one smooth and notched the other, carefully and deliberately. The grizzly woman was done with speaking now, and watched with great interest as he whittled the sticks.

When he was ready Cloyd began to make the rasping thunder, and he was pleased that the sound coming off the sticks was much like it should be. He demonstrated the three steps forward, three steps back, and then explained, "The woman has to ask the man to dance."

She came to him, and tugged on the bottom **16** of his rain jacket, and smiled a shy, girlish smile, just like a girl of fourteen.

17 At first their steps were small and slow ones. He stepped toward her as she retreated, then she stepped toward him as he fell back.

Ursa began taking bigger steps, springing to the rhythm of his rasp. Her long braid was flying as they leaped back and forth, back and forth. After they'd danced that way awhile, he showed her his favorite form of the bear dance. Side by side, they faced in opposite directions

with his hand around her waist, her hand around his. He couldn't play the rasp, but their feet didn't need to hear the beat to keep to it. The beat seemed to be coming up out of the earth, way back out of the life of the People.

After they danced, he played the rasp for a long time, and then she played the rasp for a long time.

Miles down in the timber, in the deep spruce forest back from the long meadow down Middle **18** Ute Creek, a bear heard the unusual sound of the growler sticks. She had an innate curiosity perhaps greater than any other animal's, and she was highly curious about this sound. She had spent a good part of the afternoon on a daybed[3] she'd scratched in the earth, after feeding in the morning from the carcass of a cougar-killed deer she'd dug up from under its shallow covering of boughs and spruce needles. Following the mountain lion had paid off for **20** her and her three cubs, and when the cat had returned to feed again, it had been a simple matter to chase it off.

Curious about this unusual night sound, she led her cubs up the mountain, close enough that she could identify the forms of two human beings, both sitting cross-legged, one making the sound with two sticks. It was curious that this sound came from two human beings. She went to great lengths to avoid people, yet sometimes when she felt safe she would watch them. This sound was new and interesting, and it sounded nothing like the noises that human beings made. It sounded something like thunder, and something like bears. Her three cubs, sitting on their haunches in a straight row, listened with great interest as well. The four of them listened until the sound stopped, and then they turned silently into the night.

---

3. **daybed:** a shallow, temporary nest that bears make to rest in.

CLOSURE

Ask students to discuss which character they like best, and why. Do they feel they know one character better than others? Have they noticed any change in any of the characters since the story began?

EXTENSION AND ENRICHMENT

You might want to have students make collages of the people, places, and images of the novel. They can cut out pictures from magazines and newspapers that represent aspects of the story. You can use these to decorate the classroom.

Reading Check

1. Where does the story take place?
2. What time of year is it when the story opens?
3. What does Cloyd hope to find in the mountains?
4. Who is Sixto Loco?
5. According to Ursa, what should people do when they meet a bear in the wilderness?

For Study and Discussion

Analyzing and Interpreting the Novel

1. Before coming to work for Walter, Cloyd had lived in a group home in Durango. **a.** What was he like before he found the bearstone and dreamed of visiting the wilderness? **b.** Discuss the meaning of the simile on pages 531–532: "The loneliness and anger was still inside him, like a poisonous desert plant waiting for a big rain."

2a. In what ways is Walter like a father to Cloyd? **b.** In what ways is he also a friend?

3. How was the Bear Dance at the Ute Reservation a turning point for Cloyd?

4. Cloyd and Walter have different quests. **a.** What is the object of each one's journey into the mountains? **b.** Why are these quests important to the characters?

5. Why does Ursa, who is Tlingit, make Cloyd think about his grandmother, who is Ute?

Focus on Reading

Predicting Probable Actions

When we read, we constantly make predictions about what will happen next. A good narrative inspires us to anticipate actions. In fact, some stories leave the ending entirely to the reader's imagination.

Note these actions in the first part of *Beardance*. What do you think is going to happen?

1. Walter is searching for a lost Spanish gold mine. What are his chances of finding it? Support your answer by referring to specific details in Chapters 1–9.

2. Cloyd knows that Rusty lied about his reason for killing the grizzly. Will Cloyd tell the authorities? Judging from what you learn about Cloyd's character in the opening chapters of the book, how do you think he will act?

3. Walter is eighty years old and an accident has left him with a bad limp. Will he be able to reach the Window? Give reasons for your answer.

4. Will Ursa's news about grizzlies turn out to be true? What makes you think as you do?

Literary Elements

Understanding the Novel

Setting

1. Setting plays a significant role in this novel. Cloyd's journey into the wilderness is an attempt to heal what is troubling him. Look at the map on pages 518–519. Find the place where Walter and Cloyd are at the beginning of their trip. Then find the place where the bear and her cubs are when they hear the sound of the growler sticks.

Character

2. Novelists use the same methods of characterization as short-story writers. Some information is given directly. Most information is given indirectly. **a.** Find a descriptive statement that is an example of **direct characterization** of Cloyd. **b.** Find examples of **indirect charac-**

FOR STUDY AND DISCUSSION

1a. Cloyd was angry, bullied other kids out of money, and failed classes in school on purpose. **1b.** Cloyd has not gotten over loneliness and anger; they are just below surface and will come out if he allows them to. If they do come out, they can hurt him and others.
2a. Walter takes care of Cloyd by giving him love, food, shelter, and clothes. **2b.** He gives Cloyd advice, jokes with him, and enjoys doing recreational activities with him.
3. It made him realize his kinship with bears and helped him appreciate his Ute heritage.
4a. Walter wants to find abandoned Spanish gold mine and Cloyd wants to find grizzlies. **4b.** Finding gold has been lifelong dream of Walter, and he knows this might be his last chance. Cloyd feels guilty for betraying grizzly to Rusty last summer, and he wants to learn if any more exist in Colorado.
5. Ursa tells many of the same stories Cloyd's grandmother told, and like his grandmother, Ursa has great respect for Native American culture.

FOCUS ON READING

1. Walter's chances of finding lost mine are small. People have been looking for mine for years, and description of location in book leaves out essential details that would make finding it possible.
2. Cloyd will not tell authorities about Rusty because it would be the word of a Ute boy against the word of a white man. Cloyd will probably try to find and save grizzlies quietly in his own way.
3. Walter will probably reach Window because he is stubborn. His condition improves in mountains because he is happy there, and Cloyd helps him.
4. Story will turn out to be true. Possible reasons for thinking so include her reluctance to give up

TRANSPARENCY 40
Reader Response
Connecting to a Character – invites students to compare aspects of their own personalities to those of a literary character.

TRANSPARENCY 41
Reader Response
Dark Shadows – invites students to identify internal and external conflict experienced by a literary character.

when others have already done so and fact that mother bear and three cubs hear Ursa and Cloyd playing rasp.

LITERARY ELEMENTS

1. Walter and Cloyd begin trip at start of Pine River Trail. Bear and cubs hear growler sticks while they are in spruce forest back from long meadow down Middle Ute Creek.

2a. Possible direct statements: Rusty says of Cloyd, "Tell him he is looking lean and mean — lost his baby fat, I guess"; Ursa says to Cloyd, "You're a good tracker"; narrator says of Cloyd, "The loneliness and anger was still inside him." **2b.** Possible examples: Cloyd will not talk to Rusty; Cloyd does not believe gold stories; Cloyd teases Walter by trying not to laugh at funny stories; Cloyd searched school library for everything on grizzlies.

3. Possible classification: Round: Cloyd, Walter, Ursa; Flat: Rusty, Tony, and Sixto. Rusty and Sixto tend to be stereotypes.

4. Key plot points and cause-effect sequence they establish include the following events: Rusty tells of seeing grizzlies; Cloyd goes looking for grizzlies; Cloyd does Bear Dance; Cloyd meets Ursa and invites her back to camp; Ursa tells bear stories; Cloyd goes with Ursa to look for grizzlies.

5. First flashback comes early in Chapter 1 when Cloyd remembers day bear was killed last summer. In Chapter 2 Cloyd remembers when Walter came to him to propose trip to mountains. In Chapter 3 Cloyd remembers back to Bear Dance in previous May when his spirit had left his body.

6a. Story is about bears and relationship of human beings to nature. Cloyd is the character who is most interested in grizzlies, and he is the one obsessed with saving any that remain in Colorado. It makes sense, therefore, for the story to be told from

terization of Cloyd—actions, conversations, thoughts, or the reactions of others.

3. A **round character** is one who has a complex personality and is capable of growth and change. A round character gives the impression of having a past life outside the main action of the story. A **flat character** lacks complex emotions. A flat character usually has one dominant personality trait, such as greed or laziness. Some flat characters are **stereotypes.** Consider the characters you have met so far in the novel. How would you classify each one?

Plot

4. Plot can be defined as the series of interrelated actions within a novel. A plot is made up of scenes or episodes that form a cause-and-effect chain. One event triggers another, which then triggers another, and so on. Certain events will change the course of the action. Often an "event" that affects the plot is not dramatic. It may be simply a thought, a change of heart, or a short statement one character makes to another. Go back and list some key plot points in the first chapters of the novel. Then draw a flow chart or a story map to show how one incident has created a cause-and-effect sequence.

Flashback

5. A **flashback** is an interruption of the action in a story in order to tell about something that happened earlier. Find three instances where Hobbs uses flashback to provide us with important information and background.

Point of View

6. *Beardance* is told mainly through a point of view called **third-person limited.** The story is not told by Cloyd but by an unseen narrator who remains very close to Cloyd's thoughts and feelings. We are allowed to enter Cloyd's head, whereas we can see and hear the other characters only from the point of view of an outside

observer.   **a.** What do you think is the novelist's reason for telling the story through Cloyd's point of view?   **b.** How does the point of view change at the end of Chapter 9?   **c.** Why do you think Hobbs switches the point of view here?

Focus on Writing a Letter

Writing a Personal Letter

The purpose of a **personal letter** is usually to communicate your ideas, give an update on events in your life, or express your feelings. Personal letters may also include thank-you letters, invitations, or letters of regret. A personal letter has an informal style and tone.

The form of a personal letter is more flexible than the form of a business letter. You may find the form below convenient for a personal letter:

Your Address
Today's Date

Dear _____ ,

_____

_____

_____

_____

_____

Sincerely,

_____

Remember to keep your purpose and audience in mind as you write a personal letter.

Imagine that you are Cloyd. Write a letter that Cloyd could have sent his grandmother. In your letter use Cloyd's point of view to tell about some of the important events that have happened so far in *Beardance*. Save your writing.

Connecting Cultures

Spanish Place Names

Place names in the United States show the diversity of people who have lived in or settled in this country. There are geographical locations named by Native Americans, the French, and the Dutch, among others. Many places in the West have Spanish names. In *Beardance* there are many such place names; for example, *Rincon La Osa* (Bear's Corner) and *el Cerro de la Pyramide* (The Hill of the Pyramid).

Making Connections: Activities

1. In an atlas find a map of a southwestern state. See if you can locate Spanish place names, and make a map or a chart of the ones you find. In a Spanish-English dictionary or a history text, find out what the names mean in English.
2. Learn about the history of one of the towns on your map. Who founded it? Who named it? When was it settled? What does its name mean in English and why might have it been given that name? Prepare an illustrated report on the town you have chosen.

Legends and Myths of the Bear

Bears have long been the subject of ritual, myth, and sacred ceremony. Scientists estimate that thousands of years ago, ancestors of American Indians crossed over the Bering land bridge from Asia. They brought customs and beliefs about the bear with them. Some of their beliefs survive today among Native Americans.

Among Native American hunters, it was thought unwise to call the bear by its real name. Since hunters believed that the bear's spirit could hear them at all times, they did not want to offend it or warn it of an upcoming hunt. People might call the bear names like "Grandfather," "Honey Paws," "Black Food," or even "Takes Large Leftovers Home"! A hunter who had discovered a bear's den would have to be tricky about telling the other hunters—he might rub his back on a tree like a bear so they would get the message.

Most Native American people respected the grizzly as a wise, powerful spirit leader.

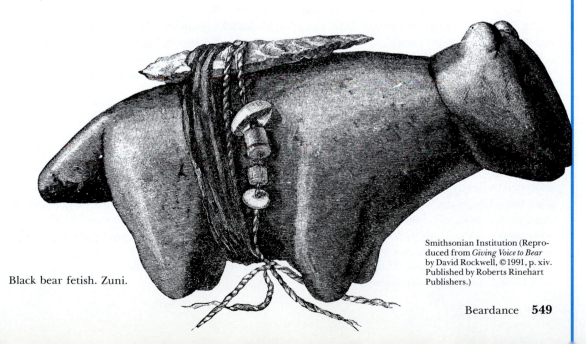

Black bear fetish. Zuni.

Smithsonian Institution (Reproduced from *Giving Voice to Bear* by David Rockwell, ©1991, p. xiv. Published by Roberts Rinehart Publishers.)

Beardance **549**

his point of view. **6b.** At the end of Chapter 9 narrator switches from Cloyd to bears. **6c.** Hobbs wants to let readers know bears really do exist, and switching point of view lets him do that efficiently.

FOCUS ON WRITING A LETTER

Before students write, you may want to have them brainstorm about the kinds of things Cloyd's grandmother might like to hear. Students' letters should follow the friendly letter form and tell important events from Cloyd's point of view.

CONNECTING CULTURES
Spanish Place Names

1. You might want to give each student or small groups of students a copy of the map. You can make a list of Spanish place names from the map and write the list on the chalkboard to help students who do not recognize Spanish words. Have students circle the place on the map.
2. If information about some towns is not available in standard library reference material, have students write to Chambers of Commerce or to schools in the area for information. Report should include basic information and pictures of area.

CONNECTING CULTURES
Legends and Myths of the Bear
You might want to clarify for students the meaning of diorama (a realistic scene with a painted background and three-dimensional figures, usually displayed in an open-faced box) and go over your specifications for the assignment (e.g., size, materials, due date, and so forth). If reference material is scarce, you might let students work in groups or use the information in the feature as the basis for their displays. Displays should depict some aspect of legend or myth about bears. In explaining their displays, students should tell which myth or legend is represented and its culture of origin.

Because the bear slept every winter, people thought it visited the spirit world during that time. The Ute bear dance is still held every spring to wake the bears from their winter sleep. Some groups, such as the Modoc, believed that humans descended from bears. Bears were a sort of cousin to humans—they walked upright, ate the same types of food, and had curious natures—so people were not supposed to kill bears or eat bear meat. Other groups did not share this taboo, and they had elaborate rituals for hunting and killing bears. A hunter hoped to dream about a bear, which was a good omen for the season's hunt. When he found the bear's den in the spring, he went to the entrance and called to it, saying something like "Grandfather, come out. I am sorry I must kill you." If the bear came out, the hunter took it as a sign that the bear was offering itself as a gift. After killing the bear, a hunter might place tobacco in its jaw as a peace offering. The bear meat was usually eaten at one huge feast—none was wasted—and the bear skull was sometimes decorated and placed in a tree or above the door to the hunter's hut.

The bear also played a part in many coming-of-age rituals. The Dakota Sioux, a plains tribe, called a young boy's initiation into manhood "making a bear." The boy would stay in a fenced-in area for several days, walking on all fours and growling like a bear. Eventually, hunters pretended to "kill" him. Women had a different relationship with bears. It was thought that a girl who strayed too close to bears or handled bearskins at the wrong time would end up marrying a bear. The story of "The woman who married the bear" is told in several versions among a large number of Native American people. Other groups thought of the bear as a healer. The Zuni and Tewa have the same words for "doctor" as for "bear." Since bears ate special herbs that aided health, the humans who watched them learned about making their own medicines.

The bear has been a powerful symbol in societies other than those of the North American Indians. In an ancient Greek myth, Callisto, whom the god Zeus loved, was changed into a bear by the jealous goddess Hera. To save her from being hunted by her own son, Zeus pulled her up into the sky and transformed her into the constellation Ursa Major. One Norwegian fairy tale, "East of the Sun and West of the Moon," tells the story of a girl who marries a man under a spell that causes him to be a bear by day and a man by night. A similar story appears in many other cultures. The oldest Finnish hero story, the *Kalevala,* tells of the mythical creation of Otso, the bear.

These different traditions, myths, and legends reveal a deep belief in nature and the world of the spirits. A bear was not just an animal—it had special spiritual powers and humanlike qualities. At the same time, it had mystery and power because it was a wild animal, and different from the human beings who named, hunted, and worshipped it.

Making Connections: Activities

Look up legends and myths about bears in a reference book such as *Giving Voice to Bear: North American Indian Myths, Rituals, and Images of the Bear* (1991) by David Rockwell or *The Sacred Paw* (1985) by Paul Shepard and Barry Sanders. Choose one ceremony or legend about the bear. Using any materials you like, illustrate the events through a diorama or model and display it in your classroom. Be prepared to explain to the class what is occurring in the scene you chose.

OBJECTIVES

The overall aim is for students to identify **static** and **dynamic characters** and to give examples of behaviors that characterize dynamic characters. For a complete list of objectives, see the **Teacher's Notes.**

VOCABULARY

The underlined words are in the Glossary. The **Language and Vocabulary** exercise on p. 582 gives students practice in using active verbs.

FOCUS / MOTIVATION

Ask students to brainstorm a list of items they would need to survive alone in the wilderness in very cold weather. When the list is complete, discuss why each item was chosen. Ask students to discuss how they might feel alone in the wild.

Grizzly sow with cubs.

©Johnny Johnson/DRK photo

TEACHING RESOURCES F

Teacher's Notes, p. 18
Reading Check, p. 21
Study Guide, p. 23
Building Vocabulary, p. 26
Selection Vocabulary Test, p. 27
Selection Test, p. 29

10

It was Cloyd who spotted them, in the morning, *1* as he glassed all he could see of the tundra fields above the chest-high willow thickets of the Ute Lakes Basin. Along the edge of a boulder field that seemed to flow like a glacier off the Continental Divide, he found them with the *2* grizzly woman's powerful binoculars. At first he thought he hadn't seen them at all, that his mind was tricking him with his greatest wish, but he blinked and held the binoculars as steadily as he could and counted the cubs that were lined up, watching their mother dig. One, two, three.

Even from this distance, over half a mile, Cloyd could catch the silver sheen on their mother's fur as she dug furiously in the tundra. He knew she was a grizzly. He could even make out the hump on her back just behind her neck. *3* There were stones flying from her claws. She seized a large stone with both forepaws and hurled it aside. Carefully, before he took *4* the field glasses from his eyes, he noted all the landmarks around the spot, the unique pattern of the Divide and the rock flow and the tundra.

"Ursa," he said as calmly as he could, and then he gave her a tug on her sleeve. He showed her where to look.

As Ursa focused the binoculars, a smile came to her lips. She looked a long time in silence. "Cloyd," she whispered, "we've brought each other luck."

Chapter 10

1
Figurative Language. Narrator uses *glassed* to mean that Cloyd looks through binoculars. This adds flavor and variety to writing.

2
Cloyd is so surprised he feels he cannot trust his eyesight.

3
Figurative Language. Narrator uses *flying* to emphasize how fast bear is digging.

4 Drawing Conclusions
Why does Cloyd note landmarks? So he can find spot again and tell Ursa where to look.

Beardance **551**

MOTIVATIONAL SUMMARY
Cloyd and Ursa spot the mother bear and her three cubs and take the photographs they need to prove grizzlies still live in Colorado. After they have done this, an ice dam breaks, with terrible consequences for the bears. After Walter and

Ursa return to their homes, Cloyd stays in the wilderness to do what he can to help the bears survive. During the time Cloyd spends alone, he learns to live as a bear lives.

PRESENTATION
You might begin the study of the second part of the novel by discussing types of **conflict** that occur in literature. Remind students that some conflicts are **internal,** that is, within a character as he or she struggles to make some kind of deci-

5
Cloyd lets Ursa take lead because she is experienced watching grizzlies and he is not.

6 Summarizing
Why are Ursa and Cloyd so careful not to make noise? Bears have keen senses, especially hearing, and humans do not want mother bear to know they are there.

7 Drawing Conclusions
How does Ursa know cubs' age and weight? She has much experience with grizzlies and can make accurate estimates.

8
Even though shutter does not make much noise, bear may have hearing keen enough to perceive it.

9 Drawing Conclusions
Why does mother grizzly toss live mice to cubs? To help them develop skill in catching live food.

10
Personification. Bear's nose has power to act on its own to test air.

5 They packed quickly, and then he followed as she used the wind and the shape of the land to find a place where they could watch without the bear catching their scent. "It's good she has three cubs," Ursa whispered. "Two's more common. Grizzlies have young only every other year at best, and cubs often die."

6 The woman made no sound as she moved toward the spot she had selected. Cloyd imitated her every move. He only hoped, when they gained the spot, that the bears would not have left.

He wasn't disappointed. Alongside the grizzly woman, he inched forward on his belly into a cluster of rocks that would shield them from view. When the moment came, he found the mother grizzly digging as vigorously as ever. She had excavated a pit five feet deep and eight to ten feet across. Now Cloyd didn't need the binoculars. He could even see the dished-out shape of her broad forehead.

The dirt was flying, and so were the stones. The bear flung a rock as big as a basketball over her shoulder.

The cubs were no longer lined up and watching. They'd fallen into a three-way boxing, wrestling, and chewing match.

Brown, cocoa, and gray-black, just as Rusty had said. Their mother would stop and look around every minute or so, constantly on the alert.

7 "The cubs look healthy," the grizzly woman whispered. "Seven months old, probably fifty pounds."

Ursa began taking pictures—two, three—very quickly. "For the proof we need, I have to risk disturbing them," she said, and indeed the mother grizzly stood up on two legs and sniffed **8** the air, looked their way. Had the bear heard the camera's shutter?

Maybe, but maybe not. After a long minute, the grizzly went back to her digging. The grizzly woman didn't take any more pictures. She

had her proof. No one could mistake the shape of the mother grizzly's head, the silver-tipped fur, the hump above her shoulders, the long claws on her front feet.

Suddenly the cubs were seizing upon small animals—three or four of them, quite alive—that their mother was throwing up and out of the pit. "Pikas,"[1] the grizzly woman said. Cloyd recognized the small rock rabbits that Walter called conies. Several minutes later their mother's mouth came up with a nest of squirming baby conies, spilling them out onto the dirt for her cubs.

The grizzly moved away from the rocks onto the open tundra and began to dig up the shallow runs that could be found in profusion everywhere on the spongy grass. Perfect little imitators, her cubs dug furiously on their own. Cloyd had seen the little meadow mice called voles scurrying above ground on occasion, but he hadn't realized how many could be found in a small area. And he never could have guessed how successfully a grizzly could dig them up. Within an hour the mother grizzly had caught **9** over thirty. Some she flicked the cubs' way for them to chase in the grass. The grizzly woman said it was the bear's hearing that told her exactly where to dig.

Even when she was catching voles, the mother grizzly kept her vigilance, standing up briefly, looking around. Her sight wasn't so good, but **10** her nose was testing the wind. The brown cub tried to nurse as she stood up, and she brushed it off as if to say, Now is not the time or the place.

After noon the bear started down toward the timber. She made a daybed just inside the trees, where she lay down, nursed her cubs, and napped.

By midafternoon the bears were on the move

1. **Pikas…conies:** A *pika* (pē′kə), also called *coney* (kō′nē) or *rock rabbit,* is a small rodent related to the rabbit.

sion. Other conflicts are **external**. These conflicts can occur between two characters or between a character and society or some force in nature. As students read these chapters, ask them to notice the kinds of conflicts that take place.

Another topic to discuss before reading is **theme**. Ask students to define **theme** (a central idea about life expressed in a work). Point out that themes are usually implied, rather than stated directly.

Because *Beardance* deals with Cloyd's coming-of-age, readers can expect to see changes occur in him as he matures and gains experience. Ask students to look for ways in which Cloyd changes in this section of the novel. They may want to make notes about the changes they notice and to use these notes later in writing about Cloyd's development.

again, and they disappeared deep into the spruce timber. Cloyd was sure he'd seen them for the last time, but the grizzly woman could detect even the faintest signs of their passage. She taught him how to tell even a grizzly's rear track apart from a black bear's. Late in the day **11** the grizzly woman was glassing a beaver pond that sat in a little bench above West Ute Creek, and she found them again.

The big grizzly was rolling and splashing in the pond with all three cubs swimming around **12** her. She began to root out pond lilies for them and for herself. Just like their mother, they held the lilies with both forepaws and crunched on the thick roots. When their mother at last began to swim across the pond, the cubs quickly followed. The brown one swam up onto her back and the cocoa clung to her tail end, while the gray-black swam along behind on its own.

Cloyd didn't know what it was, but suddenly he felt strange all over—on his arms, in his **13** spine, on the back of his neck. He began to feel **14** that he was being watched. From the corner of his eye, he tried to see if someone was watching **17** him and Ursa as they were watching the bears. For a long time he tried to look without giving himself away, but he couldn't see a thing. The strange feeling persisted. At last he spun suddenly to see if he might spy someone or something there in the forest behind him, but he saw nothing, unless it was the suggestion of a moving shadow, a shadow he glimpsed ever so briefly.

15 No, he decided. It was nothing.

The mother grizzly, in her shuffling, powerful gait, ran with her head low to the ground and disappeared with her cubs into the trees. After a while, the grizzly woman said it was **18** time to follow. At any place where bushes or boulders might have concealed the bears, Ursa angled to the side for a clear view so she wouldn't accidentally come between the grizzly and her cubs.

Cloyd and the grizzly woman were watching from the trees as the bears reappeared along the edge of the meadow of West Ute Creek. Mother and cubs were grazing on the grass and wildflowers, which surprised him. But then he remembered, from a book he'd found at school, that three-fourths of what grizzlies ate wasn't meat at all.

For a long time he watched with Ursa as the big grizzly browsed in a patch of tall cow parsnips, eating the flower tops and broad leaves and all right down to the ground. **16** Alongside her, the cubs were clasping shredded pieces of the stalks with their forepaws and eating them like celery. At last, when the shadows grew long, their mother led them into the forest on the far side of the creek, and the bears disappeared from sight.

Tomorrow, Cloyd thought, the bears might be gone for good. But that would be all right. Ursa had the pictures. Ursa had the proof of grizzlies in the San Juan Mountains.

Prove one, they'd bring others.

In their camp that night, Cloyd had the appetite of a bear. The grizzly woman was stirring the powdered cheese into a big pot of macaroni, and now she dished out two large helpings. Then she brought a small bottle of hot sauce out of her pack and sprinkled it heavily on her macaroni and cheese. Cloyd thought he'd try some too.

The spicy dish tasted good, and it warmed him up so much that he took off his jacket and even his wool cap. He was sweating, and it felt like steam was spouting out of his ears. He felt good. "How soon will they bring more grizzlies?" he asked happily.

Ursa simply shrugged.

"But they *will* bring them back here?" Cloyd asked uncertainly.

"It's a matter of time," she said. "The law is clear. The state and federal wildlife agencies will have a responsibility now to see that this

11
Personification. Pond has human ability to sit on bench. *Bench* is figurative description of part of mountain.

12
Grizzlies apparently have broad diet of meat and vegetables.

13
Suspense. Feeling of being watched creates suspense.

14
Metaphor. Compares range of vision to a room and peripheral vision to corner of room.

15
Cloyd decides not to trust his instincts.

16 Drawing Conclusions
What does cubs' behavior suggest about their experience with grazing? Even though they are young and still nursing, they have done this before.

17
Exaggeration. Compares Cloyd's appetite to bear's to make point he is very hungry.

18 Analyzing
What does "simply" imply about Ursa's attitude? She does not share Cloyd's impatience about bringing in more bears.

After students read a chapter or group of chapters, go over the basic facts of the **plot** with them to make sure they understand what has happened. The questions in **For Study and Discussion** on p. 581 will help students analyze and interpret what they have read, and the Literary Elements activities on pp. 581–582 will focus students' attention on aspects of **plot**, **characterization**, and **theme**.

19
As an experienced scientist, Ursa understands how process of wildlife preservation works.

20 Making Inferences
Why does Ursa refer to mountains as "your San Juans"? She does not live there and apparently considers herself an outsider.

21
Symbol. Ursa suggests a name that could be symbol of Cloyd's purpose in life.

22
Ursa tries to help Cloyd understand himself.

23 Making Inferences
Why does Cloyd think of Walter, his sister, and his grandmother? Answers will vary. Perhaps he misses them or is worried about them.

Chapter 11

1
Personification. In dream, bear has human ability to talk.

2
Dream bear is polite, suggesting Cloyd's special kinship with it.

3
Even though Ursa has met her goal of photographing bears, she wants to learn as much about them as she can.

4 Drawing Conclusions
Why are these bears considered rarest of North America's grizzlies? Because they live in place where no other grizzlies live.

---

19 tiny grizzly population we've discovered has a future. These four are not a breeding population. They'll die out in time. There'll be studies and hearings that could take years, but it will happen."

The grizzly woman took off her cap too, and her jacket. She sprinkled some more hot sauce onto her macaroni and cheese and broke into a smile. "I've often thought this stuff might save me from freezing to death—maybe it deserves mention in the first aid books."

"Where will they bring grizzlies from?"

20 "Probably from Yellowstone, in Wyoming. They're the closest. You know, Cloyd, your San Juans are the biggest stretch of wilderness south of Yellowstone. There's room for grizzlies here. That's why a few of them have been able to survive here for forty years after everyone thought they were gone."

When he said good night to her, she said, "I was thinking—just the same as bears are our spirit helpers, we're their spirit helpers too."

"I'm not sure I really have a spirit helper," Cloyd admitted. In his heart, he knew he didn't. Having a bearstone once wasn't the same as having a spirit helper. He hadn't done anything for bears. One had died because of his careless words.

21 "You're young," she said. "Cloyd, you could be one who fights for bears. The future looks bleak for bears, all over the world. Fights for Bears would be a good Indian name for you."

22 She read the doubt in his eyes. "You'll know when you have a spirit helper, Cloyd. You can dream, you already know that. You've traveled in the spirit world. I've never done that."

Ursa thought too much of him, Cloyd knew. He was only who he was. It was good enough to drift off to sleep knowing that there were still grizzlies in the mountains, that more would be brought, that they weren't going to die out after all.

23 He went to sleep thinking of the old man, wondering how Walter Landis was doing this night. Was he feeling well? Was his cough getting better or worse? How much was his leg hurting him? How much did it hurt to lay his body down on the ground? He thought of his sister, who was back at the boarding school in Salt Lake City, and of his grandmother. Her peaches would be ripe now on the high desert at White Mesa.

11

Cloyd woke remembering he had dreamed of bears in the night. It was a weird dream, not one he could find anything good about, not one

1 he would tell the grizzly woman about. In his dream he'd been having a conversation with a bear much like the one he'd seen the summer before. The bear in his dreams reached an enormous height and never went down on all fours. They were having a conversation about the foods they liked to eat, and the bear said that his very favorite was people. "Bears don't eat human flesh," Cloyd had said, and the

2 gigantic bear had answered, "But I do. I would like your permission to drink your blood and to eat the meat from your bones. I will leave all your bones in good condition for you to put back together."

This dream was hard to keep out of his head. He was following the grizzly woman up and out of the trees and into the brushy willows of the Ute Lakes Basin, and he kept having this crazy conversation with the dream bear over and over again. The grizzly woman was once again on the track of the mother grizzly and her three cubs. The bears were moving upslope, toward

3 the Continental Divide, and Ursa was eager to observe them as long as she could. She had only a few more days before she had to leave to travel back to Montana and begin her classes, and she wanted to spend them observing these

4 rarest of North America's grizzlies.

In the forest the grizzly woman pointed out

logs that the mother grizzly had freshly turned over. Cloyd guessed that Ursa could track bears as well as the red-haired man, or better. Ursa was pointing out bits of mushrooms left uneaten, and holes around the roots of spruce trees where the grizzly had dug up caches of nuts. Above the timberline, there were places where the bear had dug for voles and dug up bulbs and roots.

Ursa was sure the bears were moving to the southwest, in the direction of the Continental Divide. She guessed the grizzly was going to move on to another basin. "This time of year," she said as she glassed the slopes, "they have to keep on the move. They have to lay in the fat to carry them through the times when there's hardly any food around. Oh, no!" she exclaimed suddenly.

"What is it?"

The grizzly woman had her field glasses trained on the slopes above Twin Lakes, halfway around the basin between Middle Ute Lake and Ute Lake. "Sheep," she replied. "I hope our bears are steering wide of that flock. I'm sure they can smell those sheep from miles and miles away."

Cloyd could make out the motion, the moving pattern of white on the green mountainside, each individual moving in the same direction at the same speed.

"Sheepmen hate grizzlies," Ursa said. "Some kill grizzlies on sight, endangered or no."

"Sixto Loco," Cloyd said, and he told the grizzly woman about the last sheepherder in the mountains, who was a wild man and a crack shot.

"We'll just hope our bears steer well away from him. The problem is, Cloyd, the ranchers were probably grazing sheep here in the summers for a hundred years before the Weminuche was declared a wilderness area. But you tell me, who has the greater right, sheep or grizzlies?"

Cloyd had been a shepherd too. He couldn't answer without thinking about this problem. For years, he had taken his grandmother's sheep and goats across the high desert and into the fingers of the canyons. "Do grizzlies kill sheep?" he asked.

"Some do," Ursa said. "These few who've survived so long here, they must have learned to avoid sheep and man at all costs, but it didn't used to be so rare for a grizzly to become a sheep killer."

"There's lots of other places for sheep," Cloyd reasoned, "but nowhere for grizzlies. And the grizzlies were here before the sheep, no one even knows how long."

With a wink, the Tlingit woman suggested, "Why don't you walk over to that Sixto Loco's camp and tell him those things?"

Cloyd liked it when she joked with him. He had his answer ready for her. "I'm not the one named Loco."[1]

Ursa laughed and said, "We'll steer wide around him, just like we hope mother grizzly does. With a name like his, I don't imagine the man gets much company up here."

And so they followed the tracks of the grizzlies over the Continental Divide onto the Pacific side, onto the slopes that were drained by Rock Creek. At the head of the basin, the deep crater of Rock Lake sparkled in the afternoon sun at the foot of towering peaks. Rock Creek poured out of the lake, down through the trees and onto a long, boggy meadow flanked on both sides by timber and rockslides and a parade of peaks.

Cloyd and the grizzly woman sat on the short grasses of the Continental Divide, turned yellow and orange by the frosts, and admired the view. Trading the binoculars back and forth, they found the bears at last. It was the grizzly

1. **Loco:** In Spanish the word means "crazy."

5 Summarizing
When will food for bears be scarce? In winter, when snow covers everything.

6
Suspense. Ursa's reaction creates suspense.

7 Drawing Conclusions
Why do sheepmen hate grizzlies? They fear bears will kill sheep for food.

8
Conflict between bears and sheep is familiar one to Ursa.

9 Summarizing
Why does Ursa suggest this? She knows Cloyd's logic will not convince sheepmen.

10
Symbol. Cloyd realizes Loco's name is symbolic of his irrational behavior and that he will not listen to reason.

11
Metaphor. Compares line of peaks to people marching in a parade.

You might want students to keep a record of the wildlife they read about in this story. As students read, they could write in their journals the names of all the animals (or plants) they encounter.

To encourage students to learn about wildlife, you might keep a collection of field guides available in the classroom. Students could look up facts about the animals or plants and note them in their notebooks. One good resource is the Peterson Field Guide Series,

including *A Field Guide to Wildflowers of the Rocky Mountains, A Field Guide to Western Birds,* and *A Field Guide to the Mammals.*

12
Even though it is summer, there is still snow high in mountains.

13
Behavior of bear suggests ability to appreciate beauty.

14
Grizzlies apparently stay away from horses to avoid humans who ride them.

15 Finding Cause and Effect
Why is it painful for Cloyd to talk about possibility grizzly showed himself on purpose? Because it reinforces Cloyd's feelings of guilt for having told Rusty about bear.

16
Plot. Ursa introduces idea that complicates plot by giving new meaning to dead bear.

17
Plot. Ursa suggests how Cloyd can resolve complication.

18
Ability to heal sick comes from shamans' spiritual power.

19 Making Inferences
Why might students not be interested in everything Ursa has to say? Answers will vary. Perhaps students are interested only in science, not in traditional Native American beliefs.

---

12 woman who spotted them as they were sliding down a long snowbank far above the lake. Cloyd was amazed when he had his turn. He looked to Ursa for what she would say.

"I've seen them doing this lots of times in Montana and Wyoming," she said. "Some of the biologists say they do it to cool off...."

"But what do you think?"

"I don't have a very scientific explanation," she said with a laugh. "I think they slide down snowbanks just for the fun of it. I've seen them slide down the same snowbank two, three times in a row. One time in Montana, I saw a grizzly **13** sit down on his haunches and watch an especially spectacular sunset. The bear watched for twenty minutes. As soon as the sun had set, he got up and left. I remember writing in my notebook, 'Try and explain that.'"

Cloyd took his turn with the binoculars, but the bears didn't reappear. The grizzly woman thought they must be grazing or hunting marmots around the shallow meltwater lake that the map showed up there near the peaks.

Training the binoculars on the valley of Rock Creek, Cloyd discovered a white sheepherder tent in the trees below the long meadow. Ursa **18** took it to be the camp of the two game wardens who were also searching for the grizzlies Rusty had reported.

Cloyd exclaimed, "They have no idea how close the bears are!"

"They can't be very serious about their **14** search," Ursa said. "I've heard they have horses. Grizzlies can smell horses a long ways off."

"But my horse was with me last summer when I saw the grizzly...."

"I didn't realize that," Ursa said thoughtfully. Ursa seemed to be thinking hard about this. At last she said, "Maybe he showed himself to you on purpose."

Cloyd told himself, That's what I always thought. But he didn't tell this to the grizzly **15** woman. It was too painful to talk about.

"It's sometimes said that bears even know the time and place of their own death...."

Cloyd wondered if Ursa was somehow talking about the bear he had seen killed.

16 "Maybe that bear of yours," the grizzly woman said, her eyes full of conviction, "maybe that bear that is dead is your spirit bear, Cloyd, your spirit helper. Wouldn't it be true to say you haven't been the same since you met him?"

"Maybe," Cloyd said. He was remembering his dream, the one of the night before that he wasn't going to tell her. The bear in his dream wanted his blood, wanted to eat all the meat from his bones. Maybe the bear he dreamed was the same bear he had seen killed.

17 "You feel bad that he is dead, but you can turn your loss into power to do something good, like the old shamans[2] used to do."

"The medicine men?"

"The Tlingit believed that bears could change their shape to become people or other animals. Many other tribes believed this as well. Some shamans, the People said, could do the same. The shamans dreamed deeper and traveled farther than ordinary people with spirit helpers. Shamans with bears as spirit helpers healed the sick with the knowledge they brought back from the spirit world. Bears have the greatest healing powers in the animal world, and they could bestow those powers on a human being."

"I wish I knew all these things that you know," Cloyd said longingly.

19 Ursa poked him in the ribs. "I only wish my students back in Montana were half as interested as you are in everything I have to say."

"Tell me more about the shamans and the grizzlies and spirit helpers."

"Well, Tlingit shamans considered the grizzly

---

2. **shamans:** A *shaman* (shä′mən) is someone who is thought to communicate with the invisible spirit world and is believed to have powers of healing and foretelling future events.

According to the story, the old shamans believed that bears had the greatest healing powers of all the animals. Invite students to discuss beliefs, traditions, or myths from their own cultures in which certain animals represent, or symbolize, abstract properties such as healing, wisdom, freedom, peace, cleverness, mischief, and loyalty.

Blackfeet shaman. Painting by George Catlin (1796–1872).

National Museum of American Art, Washington D.C./Art Resource, NY

spirit too powerful to adopt as a spirit helper, but the shamans of some other tribes became bear-dreamers and did take grizzlies as spirit helpers. They wore the skins of grizzlies, painted themselves with bear-paw signs, and wore grizzly claws around their necks. In their medicine bundles they'd have teeth and claws…they went around the woods eating the plants that bears eat, they shuffled along like bears, they danced like bears.…"

Cloyd remembered that he'd woofed like a bear at the Bear Dance, and his fingers had felt like claws. The memory, along with her words, made the hair stand up on the back of his neck.

20 "How did a person become a shaman?" he asked hesitantly.

21 "By fasting like the bear does in its den. By enduring hardship like we can't even imagine today, cold and hunger beyond our ability to comprehend. At the extremity between life and death, the shaman met his spirit helper, and if he lived, he was changed by his ordeal and he brought back new powers with which to help the people. He, or she, could see into the spirit world for them. Sometimes women became shamans too."

Cloyd wondered if Ursa was telling him something about herself. After a long and thoughtful silence, he thought it was a question he could ask. "Are you a shaman?" he asked respectfully.

22 Ursa smiled, amused by the thought. "I withdraw from the world when I go out to study the bears, but a few weeks is about as long as I can last before I go back into town for a hot shower and restaurant food."

And then she laughed. "When they went out like that, shamans didn't come back into town every few weeks for Mexican food. To acquire power, you had to withdraw from the world like

23 a bear going into hibernation. True wisdom couldn't be found around people—shamans didn't study at the university. True wisdom could only be found in a place that was very special to the person or the tribe, far away from the village, out in the solitude. Solitude and suffering opened the pathways of knowledge that are normally closed to human beings, the pathways to the world of things that can't be seen."

"The spirit world," Cloyd said.

"I can tell you a shaman's song," she offered. "It's a grizzly bear song of the Tlingit. The shaman is singing his oneness with the bear:

"Whu! Bear!
Whu Whu!
So you say
Whu Whu Whu!

20 Expressing an Opinion
Why does Cloyd ask this question? Answers will vary. Perhaps he begins to suspect he is destined to become a shaman.

21
Symbol. In order to become a shaman, a person has to symbolically become a bear.

22
Ursa admits she enjoys comforts of modern world too much to be shaman.

23
Irony. It is ironic that true wisdom cannot be found at place of advanced learning.

lecting information about the sound elements in the story.

24
Cloyd seems to sense song is part of ritual that must be done exactly the same way each time.

25 Analyzing
Why is Cloyd willing to accept his destiny? Answers will vary. Perhaps he realizes deep spiritual nature of his calling.

26
Cloyd begins to trust his intuition about bears.

Chapter 12

1
Setting. Narrator opens new chapter with reference to morning to let reader know it is next day.

2 Drawing Conclusions
Why is trail called "manway"? Only a person on foot, not on a horse, could climb it.

3
Metaphor. Compares location of gap with respect to snowbank to position of tower with respect to ground.

4
Cloyd has to crawl on his hands and knees because of steepness of trail.

5
Metaphor. Compares lake to precious gem because of its color and shape.

6
Ursa wants Cloyd to look through binoculars to place where lake forms run-off stream, or outlet.

You come.
You're a fine young man
You grizzly bear
You crawl out of your fur.
You come
I say Whu Whu Whu!
I throw grease into the fire.
For you
Grizzly Bear
We are the same person!"

Cloyd asked her to say it two more times. He
24 learned it, every word. He didn't know why, but it was important that he have every word right. As he followed her down off the Divide toward Rock Lake, he was repeating the words to himself over and over.

He didn't know why the bears were important to him and not some other Ute kid in Ignacio or White Mesa or the group home in
25 Durango. But he would accept it, just as Ursa had accepted it. He, not someone else, had found the bearstone. He was the one that the great bear, the father of those three cubs, had shown himself to. He was the one who had spotted the mother and cubs. His grandmother would say that none of these things were acci-
26 dents. He only knew that there was something between him and those bears, something deeper than he could explain.

12

1 In the morning, the grizzly woman was going on her hunches, and she was going fast. Ursa stopped only to glass the cliffs and ledges above. "I don't see our bears on the mountainside," she told Cloyd. "They must have gone up and over. It looks like there's only a couple of routes they could have used."
2 On top of the "manway," where a foot trail wound up and through a pass considered too rough and rocky for horses, the grizzly woman

looked closely for any sign that the bears had passed this way, and found none. Ursa turned the search west, toward a small, U-shaped gap high above them between two sharp peaks. At
3 thirteen thousand feet, the gap towered above the long snowbank where the bears had been sliding.

Cloyd followed Ursa along the ledges as they worked their way through patches of tundra and across scree slides,[1] to the nameless meltwater pond high above the deep crater of Rock Lake. In the soft soil along its shore Ursa found the bear's enormous five-toed print again.

Cloyd fell to his belly and drank, then followed Ursa up the steep incline of rock and ice toward that gap in the sky. At the grizzly
4 woman's side, he inched up the final pitch on all fours. They were both going as quietly as they could. At last they bellied up to the gap and stuck their heads over.

5 At first glance Cloyd didn't see the bears. The turquoise lake far below, a rectangular jewel nearly the color of a robin's egg, captured all his attention. It was called Lake Mary Alice on the map. Its perch was so high and so forbidding, there wasn't a bit of grass around that lake, only rockflows and boulders and ice. Mary Alice lay in the shade at the foot of Mt. Oso's sheer north face, vaulting fifteen hundred feet above. An ice shelf, glowing blue, clung to the side of the lake at the bottom of the peak. It was a wild place, primitive and beautiful, unlike anything he had seen in all his days of crawling around in the canyons and the mountains.
6 "Glass the outlet," Ursa said, and handed him the big binoculars.

Cloyd found the tiny stream flowing out of the lake, and there he found his bears. Big as life through the field glasses, the mother grizzly was splashing in the tiny outlet stream. He thought she might be playing, until he saw her

---

1. **scree slides:** landslides.

pin a fish with her paw, then take it in her teeth. When she dropped it in the rocks, two of the cubs lunged for the trout at the same time, and the brown took it away from the gray-black.

7 "It's late for spawning,"[2] the grizzly woman commented, "but the ice probably hasn't been off this lake very long. In the shade of this mountain the way it sits, the surface of this lake must stay open only a few months out of the year."

Now the grizzly had caught another, and the third cub, the cocoa-colored one, claimed this fish.

The grizzly woman turned to Cloyd with a look of deep satisfaction. "The last grizzlies in 8 Colorado, making a bear living."

Ursa began to take pictures through her long telephoto lens, dozens of pictures. "We won't be able to get any closer than this," she whispered. "If we started over this edge, they'd hear us in a second. Sound would carry in this bowl like anything. But we've got plenty of proof now."

Cloyd whispered, "I don't see how we could get down."

"The map doesn't show any trails, from up 9 here or from down below. Judging by the contour lines, from down on Vallecito Creek it would be a nightmare bushwhack[3] if you tried to climb up into this Roell Creek Basin. It's a perfect refuge for bears."

The gray-black cub was chasing down a fish that was about to flip-flop its way back into the lake. Now a paw pinned the trout to the ground, and the cub took a bite out of it.

By midafternoon, the sun hadn't shone on the lake. Cloyd realized it never would again this year. The sun was too low in the sky, and the peak too high.

The cubs had long since filled their stomachs,

2. **spawning:** producing eggs or offspring; usually said of fish.
3. **bushwhack:** clearing a path through thick woods by cutting away bushes and branches.

but Cloyd could see through the binoculars that their mother was still fishing and still eating. The gray-black cub came over and attempted to nurse, but its mother with a swat sent it tumbling.

When Cloyd told the grizzly woman what he had seen, she said that besides being busy, their mother might be starting to wean them from 10 her milk. "They've come a long way since the end of January," she said. "They're so tiny when they're born—they're hardly bigger than chipmunks. The first month their mother's still snoozing, and they're nursing and growing and sleeping."

The gray-black cub was back at its mother's side, maybe hoping she would change her mind. The brown cub and the cocoa were ambling out of view, over the edge of the lake shelf.

It was an amble that saved their lives.

Cloyd didn't know what was happening, and 11 neither did Ursa. Out of the blue sky, there came a shearing, explosive crack as loud as close lightning. It sounded like trains colliding, it sounded like a mountain splitting in two. Boy and woman looked at each other in shock and in fear for their lives. "Earthquake?" Ursa muttered.

But the mountain underneath them wasn't shaking.

Motion caught Cloyd's eye, some motion high up on Mt. Oso, and he looked to see the leading edge of a titanic waterfall where no waterfall had been before. Carrying enormous blocks of ice, the waterfall was cascading down a fissure in the north face of the peak. Ice and water were tearing rock loose as it all came hurtling down; it was happening so fast that it was hard to take it all in, and it was overwhelmingly loud in this nearly closed bowl of peaks.

The mother grizzly was standing on two legs, trying to discern the source of the danger. She looked this way and that, and she couldn't tell

7 Drawing Conclusions
What does statement about spawning imply about bear's ability to catch fish? That trout are most vulnerable to bears when they are spawning.

8
Ursa means bears are able to live by their instincts and thus prosper in this territory.

9
Metaphor. Compares climb through thick brush on steep trail to terrifying nightmare.

10
Cubs were born at end of January.

11
Simile. Compares sound to loud thunder when lightning strikes near hearer.

560

---

12 which way to flee. Her death was raining down on her from above.

Helplessly, Cloyd saw it happen. In a moment the grizzly's life was snuffed out, and the life of her gray-black cub as well.

13 "Oh my God," cried the grizzly woman.

It took a minute or two for the torrent of water to become a trickle, and several more minutes for the last slides of finest rock to pour into the far side of the lake. Then it was quiet again, all quiet.

"An ice dam must have broken up," Ursa concluded. "In a crevasse[4] up near the peak."

"The cubs!" Cloyd cried. He could see the two survivors through the glasses, coming up over the edge of the lake shelf and looking around for their mother.

It wasn't long before their noses led them to their mother's scent. Through the field glasses, Cloyd could see a small dark patch among the rocks that had to be a bit of her fur showing. The gray-black cub was completely buried.

Cloyd could hear something, some new sound. The high bowl of stone around the lake
14 amplified the sound uncannily. It was the whimpering of the orphans that was coming to his ears.

Cloyd stood up and started to look for the way down. He wanted to get down there to the cubs. The bears had known a way down to the lake. Now he thought he saw it. A ledge angled down through the cliffs and onto the rockslides. "I think we can get down there," he told her, and pointed.

15 The grizzly woman was shaking her head.

13

Cloyd couldn't understand why Ursa had insisted they leave the cubs behind like they

---

1 did. He was confused, and still stunned. All he could think of was those two cubs, so alone and bewildered.

He was following Ursa back down to Rock Lake, where a sheepherder tent, tiny and white from this height, had been erected while they were on the mountain. "But can those two cubs make it on their own?" Cloyd asked doubtfully.

The grizzly woman was picking her way down from the heights in grim silence. "We just have to hope they can," she answered without taking her eyes off the ground. Ursa's voice didn't seem to have much hope at all in it. Then
2 she added, "I can't see a thing we could have done that would do them any good."

It was late in the afternoon. There would be time, during tomorrow's long walk back to East Ute Creek, to ask the grizzly woman what would happen to those cubs.

As they dropped closer to the lake, they could see two men in gray uniforms fishing down below from the grassy spot where the
3 creek ran out of the lake. "The game wardens who are looking for grizzlies," Ursa said.

"Do you think they heard the mountain cracking and the rocks falling?"

"From down there, I wouldn't think so. That mountain we were watching from is in between."

Cloyd wouldn't have spoken to the two men with starched gray shirts and brass nameplates who were fishing at the lake. He wouldn't have spoken to the gray-haired older man who stood straight as a soldier even when he was fishing. And he wouldn't have spoken to the younger one either, the one with the big smile and curly blond hair who had waved them over.
4 Cloyd had learned the hard way, the summer before, not to talk about bears that he had seen.
5 But the grizzly woman was a professor, and she was used to working with men from the fish and game departments in Wyoming and Montana, and she assumed she needed to report

---

4. **crevasse** (krĭ-văs′): a deep crack or chasm.

finding grizzlies alive in Colorado. Before Cloyd could even think to warn her, Ursa was talking to them and telling them everything.

The younger, whose nameplate said Simpson, was amazed as Ursa told them who she was, of finding the bears, of the proof in her camera. His smile was replaced by surprise and disappointment as the grizzly woman told of the death of the mother grizzly and the gray-black cub.

The older man, Haverford, showed no emotion throughout her telling. But Cloyd could see that he didn't like this Indian woman who was a professor who'd gone looking for grizzlies on her own. Haverford's bristly gray hair made him look like he'd been buzzed by a helicopter flying upside down.

"I specialized in bear biology and behavior," the younger man was saying. "Those two cubs' chances can't be good. There's starvation, predators, accidents," he explained with a glance at Haverford, "and the problem of denning.[1] Those two cubs would be denning with their mother this coming winter."

"Quote me some odds," Haverford said. It was clear who was in charge. Cloyd was afraid of this man. If only he'd been able to think more clearly. If only he had warned Ursa.

Simpson hesitated, then said, "I could be wrong, but I'd give each cub a one-in-five chance of being alive next summer. For both, if I remember my math, one-in-twenty-five."

"Slim odds," Haverford put in disapprovingly.

"What do *you* think?" Simpson asked the grizzly woman.

With a glance at Cloyd, Ursa said, "I'm afraid your odds are . . . realistic. We're going to have to go four-fifths on hope that at least one of them survives. That will keep reintroduction

alive, right? More would be brought in?"

Simpson looked at the older game warden almost apologetically and said, "That'd be the way we're all reading the Endangered Species Act, what it would mean in this case. Eventually."

Haverford, who'd said almost nothing, now said coolly and mechanically, "The Endangered Species Act requires us to protect those two cubs that survived."

Cloyd watched the confusion in the grizzly woman's face and the regret clouding the face of the younger man. "What are you getting at?" the grizzly woman asked with alarm.

"We've got to take the cubs out," Haverford stated, with no emotion at all.

Cloyd felt sick, down deep in the pit of his stomach.

"Oh, no," the grizzly woman said quickly, as she tried to catch Haverford's eyes. "If you take them out, grizzlies will be extinct in the wild in Colorado. You know how it works. The Endangered Species Act won't be applied. There has to be at least one grizzly surviving here to make a clear case for reintroduction."

"That may be the case," the man replied with an indifferent shrug, "but our job is to protect those individual grizzly cubs."

"You can't take them out," Ursa pleaded. The grizzly woman was trapped, and her eyes flashed wildly here and there as she tried to think. Cloyd could see that Ursa knew now, the younger warden knew too, that she had made a big mistake telling Haverford about the cubs. It was the same fatal mistake he had once made.

"They'll wind up in a *zoo*," she pleaded, unbelieving, angry, almost begging. "There's already plenty of grizzlies in zoos, and zoos are no place for them! These are Colorado's last grizzlies you're talking about!"

Cloyd was trying to think. "Can they be raised in a zoo and then be brought back here?"

Simpson shook his head. "No, there's no

1. **denning:** retreating to a den where animals pass the winter in hibernation.

6 Younger game warden's reaction seems mild compared to bears' tragic deaths.

7 Making Inferences
How can Cloyd tell Haverford does not like Ursa? Since he does not react, Cloyd's judgment must be based on intuition and very subtle nonverbal clues.

8 Cubs have never experienced hibernation without guidance of their mother.

9 Metaphor. Compares expression on Simpson's face with cloud blocking out sun.

10 Ursa realizes different parts of Endangered Species Act work against one another in this case.

11 Metaphor. Compares Ursa with trapped animal to suggest she and bears are victims of law.

12 Drawing Conclusions
Why is Ursa so upset at idea of cubs ending up in zoo? Zoo is not natural habitat of bears and will not allow them to follow their instincts.

Warden Haverford seems to have different ideas about upholding the Endangered Species Act from those held by Cloyd, Ursa, and Warden Simpson. Students may be interested in assuming the position of Haverford's superior in the Division of Wildlife and writing him a letter about how to handle the bear cubs in light of the Endangered Species Act. They might also evaluate Haverford's actions and reprimand or praise him. Consult with students individually to agree on how their letters will be assessed. Re- vised letters may be included in student portfolios. (See *Portfolio Assessment and Professional Support Materials,* especially the section entitled **Suggestions for Portfolio Projects.**)

---

13 Drawing Conclusions
What does Simpson mean by "problem bears"? Because they would not fear people, bears would be prone to attack hikers.

14
Wardens are trying to contact plane overhead to have pilot call Denver office for them.

15
Haverford walks away so he can concentrate on making call.

16 Analyzing
Why does Simpson not want to be quoted? What he says is implied criticism of Haverford.

17
Exaggeration. Expression "until you're blue in the face" suggests someone who has talked too much, has no more oxygen, and turns a blue color as result.

18
Irony. Trapper's job is to catch or kill animals; warden's job is to protect them from this danger.

19
Metaphor. Compares understanding spoken message to understanding written message.

20
Haverford asks for tranquilizers for cubs so they can be captured.

---

chance of that. That would never happen. They'd starve. They would've lost their fear of **13** people—they'd become problem bears. There's no chance of that happening."

"I'm going to try to call Denver," Haverford said. "They'll decide."

"The Division of Wildlife," Simpson explained.

14   The game wardens were watching the night sky for the last flight from Denver. Cloyd and the grizzly woman had set up their camp **16** nearby. Ursa was muttering to herself, and then **17** Cloyd realized she was talking to him. "Such bad luck! I'm so sorry . . . and I never for a moment considered they might have a ground-to-air radio. I should have suspected."

But Ursa hadn't given up yet. After she and Cloyd ate, she returned to the wardens' campfire.

"Been on it a number of times," Haverford was saying to the younger warden. "Half the time it flies right over Rock Lake. Gets into the Durango airport at 8:40 P.M. It should be over here fifteen minutes shy of that."

Simpson checked his watch. "That'd be ten **18** minutes from now."

Ursa was pacing in front of their fire. "Please," she pleaded. "Think about what you're doing."

15   "If you don't mind—," Haverford said. He walked a short way down the lakeshore to get away from her. The ground-to-air radio in his hand looked like a black telephone with an antenna.

"I'm sorry," the younger man said to the **19** grizzly woman.

"He doesn't understand," Ursa said. "Have him tell the Division, in all likelihood there are no other grizzlies in Colorado but those two cubs. If you take them out, there will be none left in Colorado."

Simpson rubbed his eyes wearily. "They'll **20**

know that, I assure you."

Cloyd was thinking hard. He thought it might be possible to pass close enough to the gray-haired man to grab his radio and toss it way out into the lake.

It would be a crazy thing to do. No, he couldn't do that. All he could do was hope that the plane wouldn't pass over Rock Lake tonight.

"Why doesn't he care?" Ursa was asking Simpson.

The man scratched his chin, and then he bit his lip, but finally he decided to speak. "Please don't quote me on any of this," he said. "You can talk to Tom until you're blue in the face. Before he was with the Division he worked fifteen years as a government trapper. Rifle, trap, and poison are where he's coming from. Tom's from an old Colorado ranching family, and he grew up believing there's good animals and bad animals. With the bad animals out of the way, there's more deer and elk for hunters, and no hazards for sheep and cattle on the public land. He just doesn't understand or appreciate the natural scheme of things."

The grizzly woman sat down on a rock, looking defeated. "A government trapper turned game warden." She sighed.

Now Cloyd could hear the airplane.

The older warden dashed away from the lake, into the clearing beyond the stunted spruces, and began talking into his radio. Cloyd could see the lights of the plane now as it came quickly their way.

"Emergency, emergency!" the game warden was calling "Tom Haverford, Colorado Division of Wildlife on the ground at Rock Lake. Do you read me?"

"Reading you fine," the radio crackled. "Make it quick. Be by you in a few seconds."

"Division helicopter needed at Rock Lake early tomorrow. Two grizzly bear cubs orphaned and in need of evacuation. Bring hypos with cub dosages."

WRITING LINK

In *Beardance,* Cloyd talks about things his grandmother likes to say to him. You might ask students to think of sayings they have heard from their grandparents or other older adults. Instruct students to select one or two sayings that are meaningful to them and to write about how they use these sayings as guiding principles in their lives.

"Message received," the pilot replied.

Just as the plane passed over the high peaks, Cloyd heard the word "Grizzlies!" crackling on the radio.

Ursa left the fireside and walked into the darkness. Bad luck, Cloyd thought. Such bad, bad luck.

Cloyd found her a while later up on the hillside above the lake. It was cold, and Ursa didn't have her jacket or her wool hat with her. She was crying.

21 He sat down beside her. He wasn't going to ask her not to cry. He wanted to cry too. All he could say was, "Maybe they won't be that easy to catch. Maybe there's no place to land over there."

14

1 The helicopter arrived midmorning. The pilot who climbed out wore the gray shirt and the insignia of the state wildlife department. The grizzly woman pleaded with this warden too. He had those kind of sunglasses that looked like silver mirrors, and Cloyd could see the Indian woman's round face and delicate chin in

2 those sunglasses. Ursa was shouting to be heard over the roar of the helicopter's motor and whirling blades. "There's no future for grizzlies in Colorado if you take them out!"

3 "Sorry, ma'am," he told her. "I've checked with the Division in Denver. They say we have to protect these *particular* grizzlies, not the *idea* of grizzlies. That's our responsibility."

"Name me a state," she said desperately, "name me a state where grizzlies have been brought back after the last one in the wild was gone."

4 "I'm sorry, ma'am. Some of us agree with you. I'm just following orders."

"You could kill them trying to tranquilize them! Bear cubs are tricky to sedate!"

5 The man motioned to Haverford. "I know

that," he told her. "Now if you'll excuse me...."

The new game warden knew exactly where to land in the wild basin to the west. "The northern edge of Lost Lake's the only possible place," he shouted as Haverford and Simpson started toward the helicopter. "We'll have to get to Lake Mary Alice from there on foot."

Ursa ran for her map as soon as the helicopter had taken off. She and Cloyd spread it out on the ground and studied the wild, narrow canyon of Roell Creek. The creek ran east-west, with a towering ridge high above it on the north

6 side. On the south side of the creek, three lakes were tucked in high bowls with peaks horseshoeing around them.

"Lost Lake sits in between Mary Alice and Hidden, but the peaks cut each off from the other," the grizzly woman observed. "When they land at Lost Lake, they'll have to drop down through the timber to the canyon bottom, then climb all the way up to Mary Alice. These rockslides the last half mile are awful steep. It's going to take them some time to get there. We could watch them from our spot up above."

All the way up the mountain, Cloyd kept hoping that the cubs had fled. But when he and the grizzly woman finally looked down on Lake Mary Alice, the cubs were still there by the high blue lake, still at the side of their dead mother.

"We could shout," Cloyd said. "Scare them away."

"But the only way for them to go is down. There's no cover for another mile down there. We'd only chase the cubs toward those men and save them the climb up the mountain."

The wardens didn't appear, and didn't

7 appear. Cloyd was studying the way down to the lake from this perch in the sky he shared with Ursa. Only the one ledge was difficult, and

8 it didn't look so bad, really. He wished he could go down there. If only there was something he could do.

21 Analyzing
Why does Cloyd not ask Ursa not to cry? He knows she is sad and that crying is appropriate.

Chapter 14

1
Symbol. Narrator describes man's clothes because uniform symbolizes for Ursa and Cloyd a set of attitudes they do not agree with.

2
Ursa's literal shouting to be heard over noise is comparable to her figurative shouting to be heard by wildlife officials.

3 Summarizing
Why does pilot say he checked with Division in Denver? To emphasize point he is backed up by authorities.

4
New warden appears sympathetic to Ursa's argument, but he cannot disobey orders.

5 Making Inferences
Why does warden motion to Haverford? Haverford, not new man, will shoot tranquilizer gun at cubs.

6
Metaphor. Compares mountains around lakes to horseshoe because of their shape.

7
Metaphor. By calling place where they are sitting a perch, narrator compares Ursa and Cloyd's view to view of a bird.

8 Analyzing
Why does Cloyd want to go down to where cubs are? Answers will vary. He really cannot accomplish anything, but he might feel less helpless if he were nearer cubs.

READING SKILLS PRACTICE
The underlined passage may be used to give students practice in the reading skill of identifying an accurate generalization. Before students try to answer the following question, ask them to read the passage attentively. Which of the following statements is the most reasonable generalization that can be drawn from the information given in this passage? **A.** The game wardens would stop Cloyd if they knew what he is doing. (Correct.) **B.** The cubs are asleep when Cloyd approaches them. (Contradicted.) **C.** The tent protects the wardens as they sleep. (Irrelevant.)

It was the middle of the afternoon before the three men finally appeared. They were lugging a rifle and two of those fiberglass cages people use to send their dogs on the airplanes.

The cubs scampered away onto the ice shelf, but then they edged back toward their mother. It didn't take long before Haverford's first shot rang out, and then the second. The limp forms of the cubs were loaded into the fiberglass cages, and then the men disappeared with the cubs over the rim of the high lake.

9
It wasn't a full moon. It was three-quarters of a moon, rising an hour before midnight. But it was bright enough to light Cloyd's way as he slipped out of his tent at Rock Lake. He had a lot of hard climbing to do, and he went quickly, resting only when he had to, watching his heaving breath turn to ice crystals in the freezing night air. He knew the way to the gap. He wouldn't have asked Ursa to come along; he didn't want her to get the blame.

The air was thin and burned his lungs just as badly as before. But at last he was back in the tiny gap between peaks again. Cloyd pulled his wool hat down over his ears. His hands were cold, but blowing on them helped. In the moonlight, Mary Alice shone black and silver instead of blue, and around its north side the snowbanks were shining so brightly they seemed lit **10** up with lights. He guessed it must be half an hour after midnight.

Cloyd started down, picking his way carefully down the ledge. A misstep, he knew, and he'd fall to his death. Yet the bears had come this way, and he could use all fours like a bear. He had those canyon crawling years back in Utah **11** behind him. His hands were like claws, his feet were sure. In two minutes' time the steepest, slanting part was behind him, and he was starting down, slowly picking his way down the uncertain, sliding scree.

Finally he dropped to the lakeside, at the foot of the hovering, treacherous peak of Mt. Oso, and he walked the ice-free shore on the north **12** side toward the outlet. Without pausing to locate the dead bear, he turned his back on the lake and dropped over its rim. As steep and rocky as this slope was, it wasn't nearly so difficult as above the lake. He made good time, and before long he was hastening down the very bottom of the narrow canyon.

Cloyd descended to the elevation of the first tundra and bushes and then headed through the first stunted trees at timberline, toward the shaggy shapes of the spruce forest below.

His map was in the daypack on his back, but he didn't need to pull it out. He knew that the creek coming down in waterfalls from the left, **13** in leaps through the trees, had to be flowing out of Lost Lake up where the helicopter had landed. Cloyd began to climb his way up through a maze of deadfall timber. He only hoped that the grizzly woman was right, that the game wardens would have moved slowly with those cages, returning too late to fly out. They would have had to spend the night at Lost **14** Lake. It would be too dangerous to fly out of the Roell Creek Basin in anything but good light.

▶ Carefully, carefully, he made his way out of the trees at the top of the slope and into the brushy willows. Then he saw the lake, gleaming below its horseshoe of rockflows and snowbanks and jutting peaks. Yes, there was the helicopter near the lakeside, its blades gleaming in the moonlight, in a large grassy opening among clusters of dwarf spruces. Not far away, the men's tent. And not far away from the tent, there were the two white fiberglass cages side by side.

On his elbows and knees, Cloyd crept out of his cover in the bushes. It was a good thing that the men were sleeping in a tent instead of out in the open. He crept closer, pausing to listen. One of the men was snoring. He could see the whites of the cubs' eyes as they looked his way.

9
Detail about time of moonrise lets reader know that Ursa is probably asleep and will not see Cloyd sneaking out of his tent.

10
It has taken about one and one-half hours for Cloyd to get here.

11
Simile. Compares Cloyd's hands to claws to indicate he can use them well for climbing.

12 Summarizing
Why does Cloyd not bother with dead bear? His goal is to save cubs, and he cannot waste time.

13
Personification. Compares flow of waterfall to person or animal leaping.

14 Drawing Conclusions
Why is it dangerous to fly out in poor light? Pilot would run risk of crashing into mountain in poor light.

They could see him coming, but they made no sound. ◄

Before he tried to open the cages, he studied how to do it. Just a little thumb latch beside the barred door.

15 He only hoped the cubs wouldn't make a sound. Yet, as he took a good look at them, it was apparent they weren't going to. Their eyes seemed so forlorn, so confused and so sad. The muzzles of both cubs, between their soft black noses and their eyes, were almost blond, lighter than the rest of their fur.

One, two, he let them go, and he watched them lope away, the brown and the cocoa. Before they disappeared into the woods, the
16 brown one turned and sat on its haunches a second and looked back at him. "Good luck, bear," he said under his breath. Now the brown cub vanished too, and Cloyd quickly made for the cover of the willow bushes. He had a long and hard way to go before dawn.

Even on his way back down the mountain to
17 the camp at Rock Lake it began to eat at him, what he had done. Yes, the cubs were free, but now what? Somewhere out there in the wild basin of Roell Creek, they were suddenly adrift in a frightening new world without their mother. What if, without her to lead, they were to walk right over a cliff? What if a mountain lion found them? Worse yet, what if they began to slowly, slowly starve to death?

The grizzly woman had thought that leaving **21** them to their chances was the best and only right thing to do, and he had thought so too.

But now he wasn't so sure.

Maybe the grizzly woman was wrong. Maybe he was wrong. At least the cubs would have survived if they'd been taken to a zoo.

The moon had set behind the high peaks as Cloyd was descending the last stretch of the manway down to Rock Lake. But at twelve thousand feet in the thin air, starlight alone was

sufficient to light the faint trail if he watched every single step.

18 The night lingered. The cold had even more bite as morning finally neared. At last he was off the mountain. Dawn was barely beginning to show as he slipped into his tent and collapsed in his sleeping bag.

As exhausted as he was, Cloyd couldn't sleep. Those two cubs tormented him, especially the memory of their eyes, the whites of their eyes and their forlorn faces.

19 He wouldn't tell the grizzly woman what he had done. He would wait and see what happened. It was best to be cautious now. As his grandmother always said, "If your mouth isn't open, a bee won't fly into it."

When the helicopter returned at midday with the wardens, they were baffled. Cloyd watched carefully as they told about the cages being open when they awoke, and the bears gone. They didn't suspect him or the grizzly woman.
20 It hadn't crossed their minds that one of them could have crossed the peaks in the night. They thought that the grizzly cubs had reached out through the openings in the doors and undone the latches themselves—they'd heard of raccoons doing the same kind of thing. The wardens had spent all morning looking for the bears.

The grizzly woman didn't even try to mask her feelings. "It's all for the best," she told the two men. "Now let them be."

"I won't promise that," Haverford said gruffly. "There'll have to be an official decision made about it. We still might come back and try to catch them."

Ursa turned to the younger warden. "What do you think about that?"

"Highly unlikely," he replied. "They've flown the coop now, and they're down in the trees where they'd be about impossible to catch."

The older man couldn't conceal his feelings any longer. Haverford turned on the grizzly

15
Cubs appear to understand what Cloyd is doing and want to cooperate with him.

16
Cub behaves as though it wants to thank Cloyd for freeing it.

17
Metaphor. Compares Cloyd's second thoughts to force that eats away at his confidence in his decision.

18
Metaphor. Compares discomfort of cold to painful bite.

19 Making Inferences
Why will Cloyd not tell Ursa what he is doing? Answers will vary. Maybe Cloyd is afraid she will feel need to tell warden.

20
Fact that wardens do not suspect Cloyd reinforces how difficult it was for him to do what he did.

21 Analyzing
Why does Haverford speak gruffly? He is not pleased with what has happened, and he does not agree with Ursa's statement.

You might want to find a videotape of the Ute Bear Dance or another Native American dance to show to students. Before they watch the dance, you might suggest that they try to find information about the symbolism and history of such dances.

22
Ursa calmly points out facts that dispute Haverford's concerns.

23 Analyzing
What does Ursa mean by her remarks about water and stars? Answers will vary. Perhaps she is trying to say that excitement of danger adds to experience.

Chapter 15

1
Personification. Winter has human or animal ability to bite, that is, to hurt people.

2
Fat will enable cubs to survive winter in hibernation.

3 Drawing Conclusions
What does Ursa mean by her unfinished statement? If one cub survives, other grizzlies will be brought in.

4
Cloyd has lived up to his symbolic name.

5
Metaphor. Compares expression of joy that appears on Walter's face to turning on of a light.

woman and said, "You don't care about the sheepmen, the cattlemen, and all the hikers, do you?"

Cloyd watched the Tlingit woman's face. **22** Ursa spoke calmly, with great dignity. "Ranchers can be compensated for their losses to grizzlies, and hikers wouldn't stop coming here. A quarter of a million hikers every year visit the backcountry in Yellowstone.... People who visit wilderness don't want it to be totally safe—otherwise it wouldn't be wilderness. They learn how to behave in bear country."

Haverford's jaw was set, and he wouldn't listen, but Ursa didn't seem to be talking just to him anymore. Her eyes were serene and radi- **23** ant. "In grizzly country," she explained, finding Cloyd's eyes, "the water tastes sweeter and the stars shine brighter."

Cloyd was glad he'd opened those cages.

15

Cloyd and the grizzly woman were marching back to East Ute Creek, rarely talking, walking hard, thinking about all that had happened. It was a cloudy day, but the clouds weren't the billowing thunderheads of summer. They had stopped to eat a little dried fruit and trail mix when a front[1] appeared from the southwest like an advancing wave, its clouds high and ribbed at first, but quickly following with darker, **1** thicker clouds and wind that bit like winter.

"Snow tonight?" Cloyd wondered.

"I think you're right," the grizzly woman replied. "Tomorrow's September third. But there'll be Indian summer[2] coming. It'll be a beautiful time in the mountains."

2 "Those cubs are supposed to be putting on fat now."

---

1. **front:** a term used in meteorology to describe the boundary between two air masses.
2. **Indian summer:** a period of pleasant weather after the first frost of the fall.

"If they can just get through this fall and den successfully, they'll be around for a long, long time. I only wish there was something I could do. I'll tell you one thing for sure, Cloyd. Come June, I'll be back looking for them. I'll give it **3** the entire summer. If we can find one alive..."

"I'll help you," he quickly offered. "If you want."

"I'd like that," she told him. "I'm not used to having company, but I'd like that."

She was hoisting her heavy backpack onto her knee, then her shoulders when he told her, "I let those cubs go." He hadn't known he was going to tell her, but now he had.

The grizzly woman's face reflected her astonishment, then her joy.

Cloyd told of his night crossing into the Roell **4** Creek Basin. "Fights for Bears," she said when he was done, and gave him a poke in the ribs. "I knew that was a good name for you!"

The old man had built up the fire, and they could see its beacon through the gathering dusk. Walter Landis had his wool gloves on and he had pulled his wool cap down over his ears. The wind was fanning sparks into the night; **5** the storm was close. The old man's face lit up as Cloyd walked into the clearing, with the grizzly woman right behind him.

Walter Landis was coughing worse than before, and wheezing too as he spoke. "Altitude," he said, "that's all it is. I'll be fine once I get down to the farm."

"Did you find it?" Cloyd had to know. "Did you find one of the caches?"

"Sure didn't," Walter Landis replied almost happily, and then he fetched four small rock samples out of his jacket pocket. "Actually, I quit on that metal detector and went back to prospecting, the way I first found the Pride of the West. Went looking for a vein."

"Did you find one?"

"Sure didn't," the old man said just as happily

as before. "But I found some promising float."[3] He held out four glittering samples, blue-gray minerals bedded in quartz, and Cloyd took them in his hand.

"This is high-grade galena ore,[4] Cloyd. I found these pieces of float this afternoon, on the ridge up above us here, where the mine is supposed to be."

7 The old man's eyes sparkled with conviction. "My guess is that they've drifted down the slope from the mine entrance itself. From *la Mina Perdida de la Ventana*."

"Maybe we could find the mine tomorrow," Cloyd said.

The old man started coughing. "One day more, and then the morning after that it's time to go home. But now, tell me about the bears. Find any grizzes?"

Cloyd told his story. When he told of the game warden sending for the helicopter, Walter Landis shook his head and said, "The government works in mysterious ways. I saw a grizzly at the Denver Zoo once. It made a sad sight, the grandest animal you'll ever see all fenced in by concrete walls. I'll never forget how clever he was with his claws—just sat there peeling a peach as delicate as you please."

8 By morning the storm had come and gone, and the day had dawned clear. There were several inches of slushy snow on the tents and on the world of East Ute Creek.

To Cloyd's surprise, Walter Landis announced that he didn't want to spend this day looking for the lost mine. "No," he said, "I've thought about it, and these blue skies are my answer. That mine has eluded discovery for going on two hundred and fifty years now. I might find it, but then again there's at least a chance I might not. I still believe in that legend,

Cloyd. Someone, some day, will rediscover the mine and prove the story true. And somewhere in these mountains, there's that room of solid gold I dreamed about my whole life…but I have an even better dream today. I'd like to ride up to the Window itself with my Ute guide, if he can arrange it. I haven't even had a peek at it yet!"

Cloyd didn't know what to say. Walter Landis had his heart set on the Window, but the Window was high, maybe too high for him. Cloyd told him so.

"Been looking at it on the map," the old man said. "Twelve thousand eight hundred and fifty-seven feet. I really want to stand in that spot with you, Cloyd."

And so they saddled their horses, Blueboy and the sorrel mare, and they rode up East Ute Creek and onto the Divide, with the Pyramid dominating the sky to the northeast. Everywhere they looked, the new snow lingered on the slopes that lay in the shade.

"How do you feel this morning?" Cloyd asked the old man.

"Full of wrath and cabbage," Walter Landis replied. "Lead on."

Cloyd led the way on the trail that angled high above the timberline across the grassy slope of a mountain that gave them a view down into the headwaters of East Ute Creek. They could see their sheepherder tent there and the grizzly woman's squat mountaineering tent. They could even make out the grizzly woman by the dark braid down her back as she sat on the log by the campfire and made her notes. Ursa had said she wanted to write down everything that had happened in the last week, while she could still remember exactly the way it had happened.

The trail passed through a swale[5] in the Divide, and now they were looking down the

---

3. **float:** loose ore that becomes deposited at a distance from its source.
4. **galena** (gə-lē′nə) **ore:** a gray mineral that often contains lead and sometimes silver.

5. **swale** (swāl): a marshy area of land.

---

6 Drawing Conclusions
What does Walter's attitude suggest about float? That it is valuable.

7
Metaphor. Compares Walter's eyes to gem or other sparkling mineral to emphasize his excitement.

8
Coming of snow signals start of new season.

9
Summarizing
Why might Window be too high for Walter? His health is not good, and air may be too thin for him to breathe.

10
Walter means that he feels strong and good.

11
As a scientist, Ursa must keep accurate records of her observations.

Pacific side into the headwaters of the Rincon La Vaca, where the red-haired man had first seen the grizzly and her cubs in May. Cloyd pointed out the broad green meadows of the Pine miles away at the foot of the Rincon La Vaca. "That's the way I came up here last year," he said. "Snowslide Canyon and the Pride of the West are only about five miles down the Pine from that big meadow."

Cloyd saw the Window first, but he said nothing.

A moment later, the old man cried "*La Ventana*!" when he spied the massive notch. As they rode onto the broad, green tundra bench below it, that landmark gap in the long ridge at the Pyramid's shoulder opened wider and wider until they were directly beneath it.

Cloyd could count only one cloud in all the world, and it was clinging to the foot of the San Juan Range so far to the east and south that it was probably down in New Mexico.

The old man's eyes were studying the thread of an elk trail that angled up the slope toward the Window.

"You can't get a horse up there," Cloyd said. "Or at least, you shouldn't. There's no place to turn around."

"Let's leave our horses here by this melt pond."

"You aren't going to try to go up there, are you?"

"Not without your company."

Walter counted the contour lines[6] on the map. "Only five hundred-some foot of climb. That'd be about like climbing the stairs at home fifty times."

Though he was afraid, Cloyd said no more. The old man had his mind made up.

Across the tundra, through the mountain willow, up across the scree slope of fine rock,

6. **contour lines:** On a map a contour line connects places that have the same elevation.

Cloyd led the way. Walter was limping badly, breathing hard, wheezing, but each time he stopped for a rest he got his breath back, and each time the wide Window looming above pulled him on.

With a hundred yards to go, the old man had a coughing attack that turned his face red, then purple. The coughing wouldn't quit, and Cloyd was scared. Walter motioned for Cloyd's water bottle, and a few sips slowed down the attack. Finally it quit.

"Let's turn back," Cloyd said. "We don't have to get up there."

"Doesn't matter if I fail," Walter replied. "As long as I try my best. I'll be all right now, Cloyd. The spirit is willing...."

Step by step, the old man advanced up the steep slope, and Cloyd followed right behind. They were going to make it after all! At the "Windowsill," he helped Walter up, and then they were both standing in the Window. All the hundred jagged peaks of the Needles and the Grenadiers were spiking into the sky on this new horizon, with the wide Ute Lakes Basin and the three forks of Ute Creek filling up the world in between.

"And here we are," the old man said quietly. "Gosh all fishhooks, what a view."

It seemed so much like a dream, almost like he was dreaming that he had come here with the old man.

It seemed even more like an image from a dream when Walter reached into his pocket and produced the bearstone. It was there on the palm of his hand, that small turquoise grizzly fashioned so long ago by the Ancient Ones. Cloyd didn't know that Walter had brought the bearstone into the mountains.

With his free hand Walter motioned all around him, to the Rio Grande Pyramid, so close and so imposing, to the faraway mesas of New Mexico and Arizona, to the fourteen-thousand-foot peaks of the Needles, to the banded cliffs

---

12 Analyzing
Why does Cloyd say nothing about seeing Window? He does not want to ruin surprise for Walter.

13
Exaggeration. Cloyd can see only one cloud. Narrator exaggerates by calling it one cloud in world to emphasize how clear sky is.

14
Metaphor. Compares trail to thread to indicate how narrow it is.

15 Summarizing
Why does Cloyd not say anything? He knows he cannot dissuade Walter from going to top.

16
Personification. Window has human ability to pull Walter on. This means Walter's desire to reach Window motivates him to continue.

17
Walter's unfinished sentence probably ends, "but the flesh is weak," meaning he wants to go on but may not be physically able to do so.

18
Metaphor. Equates part of world they can see to whole world.

19 Drawing Conclusions
Why does it seem like dream to Cloyd? Answers will vary. Place where they are is far removed from world they are used to, as though it were a dream.

of the Rio Grande country. "I've been looking for the time and the place to return this," he said, holding up his hand as Cloyd tried to speak. "This is the time, and this is the place."

Cloyd felt the bearstone in his own hand, smooth and blue and powerful, and he felt the old man's hand closing his fingers on it. "I'm much obliged," Walter Landis was saying.

He knew he couldn't refuse the old man this moment, and so he said, "Thank you."

"I won't be back here," the old man said.

With a quick smile, Cloyd said, "You never know for sure."

"No, I know. I'm just lucky I got away with this trip.... *You'll* be back here, though. You'll remember this day, whenever you come. You'll remember me."

I *will* come back, Cloyd vowed to himself. "I'll remember," he said.

"Dreams aren't practical things," the old man said quietly. "Not when they first get started. I had a dream of going back to the mountains.... It seemed like a crazy idea, but here I am."

Cloyd slipped the bearstone into his pocket. It felt good, having the bearstone in his pocket again. It made him feel strong.

Walter Landis asked, "When did you first dream of coming up here, up this high, where you could look out over it all?"

"That's easy," Cloyd said. "My first day at the farm—it was that day I found the bearstone in the cave way up on the mountain above the farm. I could see a few of the peaks sticking up."

"You can dream, Cloyd. You climbed this mountain here; you must've had to work awful hard to get to the top of that old Rio Grande Pyramid. My gosh, it takes my breath away just looking at it. Your dream now, it's about the bears, isn't it?"

"I want those two cubs to live."

The old man acknowledged Cloyd's determination with a simple nod.

They stayed in the Window a long while, as the sun rode toward the Needles and the Grenadiers. At last they both knew it was time to go.

They were just about to start down when the old man took one last look around. "There's something I always wanted to do," he said. Then he spat down toward East Ute Creek. "That's my contribution to the great Atlantic Ocean," he said with a grin. "And here's my contribution to the great Pacific Ocean," he declared, hawking[7] toward the Rincon La Vaca.

They came off the mountain laughing.

*   *   *

It might not have happened if the bearstone weren't in his pocket and the Tlingit grizzly song in his head. The grizzly woman and the old man were both asleep that last night in the camp on East Ute Creek. But Cloyd couldn't sleep, and he found himself wandering away from the embers of the fire into the chill of the night. The moon was just about to rise; meteors were falling every minute, more meteors than he'd ever seen. His heart was full of thankfulness, for the old man, for the grizzly woman, for the mountains.

It was because of the bears that he couldn't sleep.

Softly, barely moving, he began to do the bear dance, forward and back. Where were those cubs tonight? Still alive?

He was the one who had opened their cages. This night they might be starving to death.

He began to chant the Tlingit song the grizzly woman had taught him:

> "*Whu! Bear!*
> *Whu Whu!*
> *So you say*
> *Whu Whu Whu!*
> *You come.*"

7. **hawking:** clearing the throat.

20
Walter feels that time and place are sacred or special in some way.

21 Analyzing
Why does Walter thank Cloyd? Like Cloyd, Walter apparently thinks bearstone, along with Cloyd's attentive care, have made him fit enough to climb mountain after his accident.

22 Analyzing
What does Walter mean by saying dreams are not practical? Answers will vary. People imagine themselves doing things that do not make sense to others or that have no concrete value.

23
Cloyd associates bearstone with climbing to Window.

24
Exaggeration. Looking at Pyramid does not literally take Walter's breath away. He says that to emphasize how great a task climbing it is.

25
Point of View. Narrator reports on what Cloyd later thinks about what happened.

26
Cloyd worries about safety and well-being of cubs.

27 Drawing Conclusions
Why does Cloyd connect his opening of cage to cubs starving to death? Cloyd feels responsible for what might happen to cubs.

PORTFOLIO ASSESSMENT
Human interest articles in newspapers and magazines often tell stories of individuals embarking on dangerous quests. Students may want to write such an article about Cloyd's bravery and determination as he sets out on his

quest. Suggest that they invent quotations from Cloyd and Walter about the purpose of the quest and the danger involved. Remind students to be sure to maintain the characterization Hobbs developed. Consult with students individually to agree on how their articles will be as-

sessed. A computer word processor may be used for final drafts and to make headlines and newspaper columns. (See *Portfolio Assessment and Professional Support Materials,* especially the section entitled **Suggestions for Portfolio Projects.**)

28
Cloyd wants to take place of cubs' parents, perhaps of their father, who might be his spirit helper.

29
Personification. Bears' noses have power to act independently of bears.

30 Making Inferences
Why does Cloyd take Ursa's pack? It contains everything he will need to survive alone.

31 Drawing Conclusions
Who are three people whose strength he carries? Walter, Ursa, and Cloyd.

Chapter 16

1
Atmosphere. Narrator creates picture of place undisturbed by human beings.

2 Making Inferences
Why does Cloyd sniff wind? Perhaps to try to get scent of bear cubs.

3
Metaphor. Compares surface of lake to dome in a building high above heads of people inside.

4
Cloyd apparently has to reason with himself about why he is killing fish.

It came to him as he was singing and dancing, something he could do for those cubs. He had a rod and a reel, and he was good at catching fish. It was something he could do for them that might make a difference.

28 In the morning, the old man and the grizzly woman heard him out. He would return to the Roell Creek Basin, and he would try to feed the cubs for a little while. He could leave fish around for them. He had no doubt he could accomplish this.

Walter Landis wasn't speaking. Walter had seen his determination. Now the old man was thinking hard.

"It's not a bad idea," the grizzly woman said with a glance toward the old man. "Those cubs would be wild as the wind, and you couldn't get **29** near them, but their noses would pick up dead fish, that's for certain. But you'd be all alone, Cloyd. It's always risky to be alone in the mountains."

"I know," he said. "I'll be careful, like you."

The old man didn't speak for a long time, until he said finally, "The bearstone's back in your pocket. Dreams aren't practical, but we can't live without them."

Cloyd was saying good-bye to his horse. He was telling Blueboy that it wouldn't be long before they'd be back at the farm together. He told the blue roan that Ursa would ride him out of the mountains, that it would be an honor to carry the grizzly woman out of the mountains.

It was strange waving good-bye as the old man and the grizzly woman led their strings of **30** horses up the meadow toward the Divide. He shouldered the grizzly woman's pack. It was going to be heavy. The riders were both looking back and waving, and now he gave them a stronger wave. He wondered if he was crazy, if he should yell to them and run toward them up the meadow.

But he had dreamed he could do something

for these bears, and he was the one who had turned them loose. No one else was going to try to help. It was up to him.

Cloyd turned and started up into the forest. **31** Inside him, he didn't feel so alone. He was carrying the strength of three people.

16

1 Lost Lake deserved its name. Most summers, no hikers visited Lost Lake. No human beings saw the deer and the elk come up out of the forest on the shadowy mountainside to graze the short grass around the lake, and no one saw the occasional mountain goats on the slides of scree rock across the canyon of Roell Creek. No one saw the black bears, frequent visitors to this wild basin where they could feast on the berries that grew thick along the lush and narrow canyon bottom.

No one saw a Ute boy proceeding slowly down Roell Creek from above, from somewhere high above. No one saw how often he **2** stopped to search with his dark eyes or to sniff the wind. No one heard how silently he moved as he picked his way through tangles of deadfall timber up to Lost Lake, and no one heard the splash of his lure again and again on the surface of the lake, or the splashing of trout as he brought them to shore.

He gave no shout of excitement, but his heart was singing. These cutthroats were larger and fatter than any he'd caught before. They were **3** all in a frenzy for his little metal spinner on the **4** dome of their world. It was for a good reason they were dying, Cloyd thought, as he was cutting their heads open across their spinal cords to stop their thrashing in the grass. The meat was bright red, and it was firm. These fish were giving up their lives to keep two grizzly cubs and the hope of grizzlies alive.

Were those cubs near enough still to smell

Lost Lake, Weminuche Wilderness, San Juan Mountains in southwestern Colorado.

Courtesy, Will Hobbs

these trout? Had they left this basin? Were they even still alive?

On the slope below the lake, in the trees, Cloyd left four fish each at two places a mile from one another. He could only hope that the strong scent of the fish would bring in those bears. The sun had set behind the Needles. He hurried back to his camp at the lake to fix the trout he had saved for himself.

Late the next morning he checked where he had left the fish. At the first place, the trout *5* were gone. He was hopeful, though he couldn't make out tracks. Here he left three more fish.

Still at a distance from the second site, he could hear the magpies squawking. Then he *6* could see those black-and-white pirates at the foot of the boulder field that spilled from the peaks separating Lost Lake and Hidden Lake. He sneaked closer and closer until he had a good view. His four trout were gone. Had the

magpies flown off with the fish? It didn't seem likely. Had the cubs come as well? Coyotes maybe? Raccoons?

Next time he wanted to see who was taking *7* his cutthroats. He planted more fish in the dark, then went to see what he could see at first light. He hoped he wasn't too late.

Once again, the first batch was gone.

The magpies were just descending on the second site, the one where the boulder field met the woods. This time he had placed the fish on a spruce that had been felled not so long before *8* by rumbling boulders—its needles were only now beginning to yellow. It was easy to see the silvery fish against that red log.

The birds had jostled two cutthroats to the ground in their commotion, and the third was still in place when he saw a small paw reach for it. Then he saw the blond, doglike face of the brown cub. Brownie! he thought. Now Cocoa's

Beardance **571**

5 Drawing Conclusions
Why is Cloyd concerned about identifying tracks? Some animal other than bears could have eaten fish. Bear tracks would let him know for sure that cubs were getting fish.

6
Narrator calls magpies "pirates" to suggest they steal from other animals.

7
Figurative Language. Cloyd does not literally plant fish as he would a seed. He sets out fish hoping to be able to tell whether bears are getting them.

8
Boulders rolling down mountain knock over trees.

571

9 Summarizing
What had Cocoa learned about porcupines? To not disturb them in order not to get stuck by their quills.

10
Metaphor. Compares black bear knocking over Cocoa to bowling ball knocking down pins.

11 Making Inferences
Why does black bear keep Cloyd from being of help? Black bear eats fish intended for cubs.

12
Ursa said spirit helper would come in dream.

13
Cloyd interprets bear's motioning with eagle feather as its desire to kill Cloyd, as bear in previous dream had wanted.

14
Metaphor. Compares dream to person dressed in disguise.

15 Analyzing
What are other possible interpretations of Cloyd's dream? Answers will vary. One interpretation is that bear in dream is motioning for Cloyd to join him and to become a bear—or at least to dress like one.

face suddenly appeared. He couldn't quite make out what was wrong, but it looked as if the cocoa cub had sprouted bristles all around the mouth.

9 Then he knew. Cocoa had learned about porcupines the hard way.

It wasn't but a minute before a black bear appeared, a very large black bear, with its narrow face and a streak of white under its neck. Cloyd was astonished as the bear rushed the cubs and bowled them over with a swipe, growling and baring its fangs.

The cubs scampered away faster than he would have thought possible. With the big black bear in hot pursuit, they fled along the edge of **10** the boulders. The black bear bowled over Cocoa, who was in the rear, and bit hard. Cocoa disappeared, yelping, into the trees as the black bear hesitated, distracted by the squawking of the magpies behind. Then the big bear turned back for the fish.

Cloyd fretted through the afternoon and the evening, but he could come up with no good **11** answers. With that black bear around, he was going to be of no help to the cubs. Over and over, he tried to recall exactly what the cubs had looked like in the morning. They were skinny, too skinny, too weak and too small to defend themselves from animals like that black bear. And Cocoa had a snoutful of porcupine quills. Wouldn't they keep her from eating? Both looked like they were starving.

If only he could talk to the grizzly woman, and ask her what to do. Ursa was probably back in Montana by now. If only she knew he'd found the cubs! If only she could tell him what to do next!

12 It didn't come to him by thinking. It came to him in a dream, after he'd given up thinking and had given in to his exhaustion. At first he'd thought it was a bad dream. He was back at the Bear Dance, only this time he had fallen in the endurance dance at the very end.

In his dream, all the growler sticks stopped as a result of his fall, and all the dancing stopped. Suddenly a huge bear appeared, motioning toward him with an eagle feather. The bear had an arrow through its neck and one in its heart. He was terrified of this bloody bear, and he couldn't get up. Someone was saying, "It's bad luck to fall. The Bear Dance is over." The growler sticks remained silent, and he glanced over to the big resonating drum. The eight men who'd been chanting and making the thunder were bears also; or were they men who'd sewn the skins of bears closed around them?

He was squinting and trying to tell whether the singers were men or bears when he woke from his dream. He reached for his water bottle. The frightful dream had awakened him. He realized he'd dreamed again of the bear that he had betrayed to Rusty the summer before, the one Rusty had killed, the one the **13** grizzly woman had said might be his spirit helper. He remembered what this bear wanted from him. It wanted his blood and the meat from his bones.

Cloyd drank from his water bottle. Dream-dancing, he thought, raised as much thirst as real dancing. He reached out to the little tent pocket where he kept his tiny flashlight and the bearstone, and he felt for the bearstone in the dark with his fingers.

That's when it came to him, what he could do, what he could try. The singers in his dream **14** had been dressed in the skins of bears. Maybe this was a good dream in disguise.

Hadn't the grizzly woman said that the shamans whose spirit helpers were bears used to wear the skins of bears?

He wasn't a shaman, he knew that. He didn't even have a spirit helper. The grizzly woman had said you could only dream a spirit helper, and the only spirit helper he seemed to dream **15** wanted his life.

He would have to keep going on his own, without a spirit helper.

When Cloyd made his climb he found the big grizzly undisturbed. She was buried in the scree slide, in the shadows beneath the towering north face of Mt. Oso, undisturbed by scavengers or even the spoiling effects of the sun. Working tirelessly, he tore at the scree, throwing the rocks aside until she was free. In the shade of Mt. Oso, the September cold at 12,500 feet had kept her from starting to stink.

All he had was his pocketknife. It would have to be good enough. Fortunately, it was sharp.

16 He was good at skinning. He had slaughtered many of his grandmother's sheep and goats over the years, and he always fleshed out the hides for her. She tanned them the old way, with the brains, not with battery acid like some people were using.

This skinning was much harder. When the flesh turns cold, it isn't so easy to separate the hide from it. He worked carefully, separating the face of the bear from her skull. Around the paws was the hardest. His knife was dulling ter- **17** ribly. He wished there'd been a whetstone in one of the pockets of the grizzly woman's pack.

But at last, after nearly a day's work, he was done. The cubs' mother looked hideous now, stripped of her fur, a mass of red muscles. His grandmother had told him about this, and now he could see it was true: a bear stripped of its hide looks like a human being.

One last task remained. With his dull knife, he had to sever her skull from her neck bones. He would need the brains.

Covering the grizzly's headless body with rocks, he thanked her for the gift of her skin **18** and skull. The sun was setting as he started down the mountain with the heavy fur over his shoulder and the skull under one arm.

It was going to take time to flesh this hide as best he could, stake it out, then tan it with the

brains from the skull. He'd better get started this night. There was no telling how long the cubs would last. Were they males or females? he wondered. One of each?

He would use the biggest of the aluminum pots and mash the brains until they made a paste. Her brains would make just the right **19** amount for tanning her hide. His grandmother had said that it was an example of the fittingness of things: a mouse's brain was just the right amount for tanning a mouse, and the same went for a sheep or a goat.

Or a bear, Cloyd thought.

17

1 With the days growing shorter and the nights longer and colder, the bears of the Weminuche Wilderness were heeding the call from within to feed all they might, to lay in fat against the time of their long sleep. The big male black bear who counted as part of his territory the wild and remote basin of Roell Creek was partial to this high, hanging canyon above all his other haunts. It was small and confining **2** enough for him to patrol against other bears, yet large enough to provide him with more than he could eat during a month's stay in the **3** fattest time of the year.

The summer's monsoons, sweeping up from Mexico in July and August, had brought even more rain than usual to the high country, and more forage than usual. The black bear was making his rounds, gorging first on the cur- **4** rants and wild raspberries thick along Roell Creek, gooseberries and serviceberries[1] too. Along the lush stream bottom he grazed on watercress, and the thick-stemmed grasses flanking the edge of the bogs he found just as delectable. Then he started working his way up

1. **serviceberries:** berries of the shadbush or service tree, also called Juneberry tree.

16
"Flesh out the hides" means separate hides from animals' flesh.

17 Drawing Conclusions
What would Cloyd do with a whetstone? He would use it to sharpen his knife.

18
Description. Cloyd's appearance must be terrifying.

19
Cloyd uses traditional tanning method his grandmother taught him.

Chapter 17

1 Finding Cause and Effect
How does length of daylight affect bears? They apparently respond to changes in amount of daylight that correspond to changes of seasons.

2
Black bear is able to keep other bears out of his territory.

3
Figurative Language. Refers to time of year when bears must put on fat for winter. Also refers to time of year when end of summer harvest is available for bears to eat.

4
Black bear enjoys a variety of foods in his diet, not just meat and fish.

5

Imagery. Narrator uses images that appeal to sense of smell.

6

Point of View. Narrator reports bear's thoughts, as well as thoughts of people.

7 Drawing Conclusions
Why will black bear kill cubs?
They represent a threat to his territory and food supply.

8

Black bear responds instinctively to presence of what he thinks is a grizzly.

9 Summarizing
How does Cloyd make himself "tall . . . with his arms"? He raises his bearskin-covered arms over his head to make grizzly appear taller than Cloyd's height alone.

10

Bearskin Cloyd is wearing contains mother bear's scent.

the hillsides, where the forest floor offered countless rotting mushrooms.

Still the bear was hungry, and so he kept along the paths that he followed every day. For several days now, there'd been no fish at the two places where he had found them before. But the memory of the fish was strong, and the smell of them was still promising in his memory. He included them in his rounds just in **5** case. At the place by the creek he found no fish, only the lingering smell of fish. Nearing the second place, at the foot of the rockslide, he grew hopeful. The fish smell was strong. But there was another scent too, and it wasn't the human scent he'd first smelled around these fish.

6 This was bear scent, and it made him irritable. The black bear suspected the cubs that weren't his kind, the grizzly cubs who had appeared in the basin without their mother. He **7** would kill them now if he got the chance.

The fish were there as before, five of them lying on the log, and he began to feed on them, alertly sniffing the wind. The bear scent was still here, still strong. When he was done with the last of the fish, he would look around for those cubs.

As the black bear was starting on the third fish, a big silvertip grizzly appeared suddenly in the boulder field. The grizzly stood to its full height atop a boulder and pawed the air, then woofed threateningly.

Cloyd spread his arms wide and high, showing the claws that weren't his. What do I do now? he thought. The black bear had dropped the fish in his mouth, but had taken a few steps closer, squinting for a better look and growling. **10** **8** The hairs along its spine were standing on end, and now the black bear was standing on two legs and woofing back at him.

What if he charges me? thought Cloyd. I have nothing to fight with. This is a big bear, this black bear, and he's bristling up for a fight.

"Bears are great bluffers," he remembered

Ursa saying, and so he put all his faith in the grizzly woman. If his cubs were to have a chance, he had to run off this black bear.

He's going to charge any second, Cloyd thought. I have to do something first.

Cloyd sprang from the boulder and leaped onto the elk trail at the edge of the boulder field, not thirty feet away from the black bear. **9** From all fours he stood up and made himself tall with his height and his arms. From deep in his throat he brought out a roar that surprised him, hearing it come from inside himself. For a moment he even felt ferocious, growling and displaying his grizzly claws.

The black bear squinted for a better look and saw that this was not only a grizzly, it was one with a human face in addition to its own. The bear turned and ran from the natural superiority of the grizzly and the terrifying oddness of the two faces.

With a look over his shoulder, the black bear glanced back to see the grizzly in pursuit, running on two legs only. The black bear was fast and soon covered the mile down to the lip of the hanging basin where the creek spilled in waterfalls on its plunge to the valley of Vallecito Creek far below. Still in full flight, the black bear picked up the elk trail that led down the mountainside, and in an hour's time was miles away and three thousand feet below.

Two pairs of highly interested eyes and ears had witnessed Cloyd's performance. It was their sense of smell that had brought the cubs to this place. Once again, they had smelled fish. **10** But this time they had also smelled their mother.

They edged closer. The black bear had fled, and the bear that was their mother and yet hadn't sounded or moved like their mother saw them approaching, and took one of the fish in its mouth.

For a long time they watched and waited, and

then their hunger and their loneliness drove them close, where their mother's scent was strong and tinged with the suggestion of death.

11   Cloyd saw them coming in like puppies begging for care yet fearful of a whipping. Their round little ears were forward at one moment, then laid back on their heads the next. Brownie led and Cocoa followed with a muzzle all stuck with quills. Cloyd let them come closer, whimpering. They backed away, came closer yet, backed away again. They were so close now, he could almost reach out and touch them. Their eyes could see he wasn't their mother, yet their noses told them he was. He held out the fish with his claw-covered hand and he began to talk to them soothingly. "C'mon Brownie, c'mon Cocoa...."

Brownie was standing just an arm's length away, swiping at the air with one paw.

"That's right, that's right...."

Cocoa's eyes were forlorn behind the noseful of quills.

Brownie was sitting now, but seemed reluctant to accept the fish from Cloyd's outstretched

12 fingers. Cloyd took the fish again by his teeth, shook it back and forth a few times, then stuck his face out with it toward the little bear's face.

Brownie's eyes and Cloyd's met as slowly,

13 slowly, the cub brought its face close, its dark eyes locked on Cloyd's. The fur on the cub's muzzle was blond, almost gold. Slowly and gingerly, Brownie took the big fish.

Cloyd spent the day with them, right there, with the cubs crawling all over him and mouthing him with their needle-sharp front

14 teeth. Girl bears, he saw, that's what they were. When Brownie broke the skin on his hand once, Cloyd gave her a swat the way her mother would have done and sent her tumbling. After that she didn't bite so hard. Grizzlies had excellent memories, he was discovering. They learned everything fast.

He liked the way they walked flat on their feet, like people. They would stand like little people to play with his hair or to box each other, with one forepaw shielding their faces and the other flailing away. They played with the button on his flannel shirt that was showing

15 between the rawhide boot lacings that brought the bearskin together down his middle. Cocoa let him pry open her mouth; the stub of a quill was lodged in the pink of her jaw. He should pull it, along with the others, before her mouth got infected. His fingers couldn't get a good enough grip, and she bit him. Her back teeth, he noticed, were flat for grinding, like his.

As the sun was dropping behind the Needle Mountains in the west, he began to climb to his camp at Lost Lake. The cubs followed the bear that almost always walked on two legs, that was not their mother and yet was. At the lake, they sat on their haunches and watched the bear with two faces cast something magical out onto the surface of the lake and bring in fish after fish for them. These fish were alive and needed to be subdued.

16   Cloyd ate enough of the grizzly woman's trail mix to take the edge off his hunger. Then he crawled in under the low branches on the side of a dwarf spruce thicket away from the wind. The cubs came in and curled up with him. The grizzly's hide would be his sleeping bag this night.

In the morning he would pull the quills from Cocoa's face, and the one inside her mouth,

17 with the tweezers in Ursa's first aid kit.

The trees sheltered him from the wind and the night air, but the cold from the ground was reaching him even through the grizzly's thick fur. Tomorrow he would make a bed of spruce needles under a low-ceilinged overhang he'd seen among the ledges on the steep slope below the lake. Under that roof he'd stay dry if night rains came.

18   He had to start living like a bear.

11
Simile. Compares cubs to puppies to emphasize cubs are playful and inexperienced.

12
Drawing Conclusions
Why does Cloyd put fish in his mouth? To show cubs it is something to eat.

13
Connotation. "Lock" suggests eyes are fixed and cannot move.

14   Drawing Conclusions
What is significant about fact that both cubs are female? In a few years they can both produce cubs to speed up process of restoring grizzly population of Colorado.

15
Cloyd keeps bear skin on all day as he gets to know cubs.

16   Analyzing
Why does Cloyd not eat fish? He would have to cook it, and cooking might scare off cubs.

17
Cloyd waits to pull quills because he wants cubs to be thoroughly used to him before he causes pain that pulling quills will bring.

18
Plot. Starting to live like a bear will be a major turning point for Cloyd.

19

Imagery. Narrator's words appeal to senses of smell, touch, and hearing.

20

Cloyd can feel vibrations of thunder in ground.

The cubs tucked themselves in close as he lay **19** on his side. They had a strong animal smell, like wet dogs, only muskier. His body warmed as it gained heat from the bears. The fast beating of Cocoa's heart slowed as the cub fell asleep, and then it came loud and soothing like the beating of a drum.

The wind rustled the branches of the dwarf spruce, and before long there was thunder crashing over the peaks. It rained, and it rained hard. He should have found a better place to bed down, but if he tried to move the cubs in the storm, he might become separated from them.

The hide was thick, but the rain ran in under the dwarf spruces and found his head, his neck, his legs. The <u>searing</u> white bolts were striking the peaks directly above the lake now, and the **20** thunder was rumbling the ground underneath him. The cubs slept through the storm, but it scared him to be alone and so far away from the farm. What would he do tomorrow, and the next day?

© Stephen J. Krasemann/DRK Photo

18

Cloyd let Cocoa and Brownie maul him and pummel him and crawl all over him, just as their mother had let them. He talked to them with words and a stream of noises he could make with his lips. The bears learned fast that the skin on his hands was not as tough as his fur-covered body and that he didn't like it if they were too rough with their needle-sharp teeth. Soon they knew his moods and his warnings and his commands from the tone of his voice. They could tell when he was playing and when he wasn't. They couldn't touch his face with tooth or claw, but if he turned sideways, it was a signal he would allow a quick lick with the tongue.

After the first night the three of them sheltered under the rock overhang on the steep, forested slope below the lake. Besides a good sleeping place, Cloyd had found a perfect arrowhead there, two inches long, surely a Ute arrowhead. It was the Weminuche Utes—his own band—who had hunted in the summers in these mountains. It made him feel good to know that even the wildest places had been familiar to them.

Cloyd was marking the days with a tiny notepad and the stub of a pencil that Ursa had left in her pack. It was dry under his stone roof during three nights of hard rains, as the spruces swayed and creaked in the wind, and the lightning and thunder attacked at intervals all through the night. He was warm in the grizzly skin on a bed of boughs and needles, and the two cubs nestled against him added more warmth still.

Cloyd had made six marks on the notepad, and still he was reluctant to climb out of their mother's fur. He didn't want to break the spell. Each day, all day, he foraged with them. This was the time, while food was abundant, when they needed to be eating all they could. Every day was a ceaseless quest for food. He overturned rotten logs for them and watched approvingly as they went along licking up the ants and grubs with their quick tongues. He ate berries alongside them, and watercress along the creek, but he didn't try the mushrooms they relished. They seemed to know which ones to avoid, but still, the mushrooms were beyond their prime and swarming with tiny, translucent larvae.[1]

Each morning, a new sheet of clear ice covered Lost Lake, but the ice would break up by noon. Cloyd kept fishing for himself and the cubs. He thought about drying some of the fish, but the sun only appeared above the peaks for three or four hours each day, and the peaks drew clouds. This basin was a cold, cold place, and he began making plans to leave. He wouldn't want to get caught here by a big snow.

It would be up to the cubs whether or not they wanted to follow him out of this basin. It was time for him to be heading back to the old man and the farm on the Piedra. And school, he thought. He hadn't been thinking about it, but school had already started. School seemed as vague and faraway as it had back in the years he used to take his grandmother's sheep and goats out into the canyons. When he got back to school, Mr. Pendleton was going to teach him the secret of making fire with the bow drill.

On the bench by the shore of Lost Lake, he unlaced the bearskin and rolled it into a tight bundle, then tied it off. All the time, he had his eyes on the cubs. They were busy playing hide-and-seek, one of their favorite games. From their mother's skull, he took one of the molars for luck, to go along with the bearstone and the Ute arrowhead. As he was placing their mother's skull in a safe place up in a tree, the cubs were having one of their wrestling and

1. **larvae** (lär′vē): wormlike forms of insects before they develop into adults.

Chapter 18

1
Bear cubs adapt quickly to relationship with Cloyd.

2
Symbol. Arrowhead represents Cloyd's heritage to him.

3
Metaphor. Compares lightning and thunder to war planes or artillery that attack his fortified position.

4 Making Inferences
Why does Cloyd not want to break spell? Answers will vary. Maybe he is afraid cubs will run away. Maybe he is enjoying living like a bear and does not want to stop.

5
Cloyd does things he had observed mother bear doing.

6 Drawing Conclusions
What does ice on lake indicate? Weather is getting colder as winter gets closer.

7 Making Inferences
What is advantage of drying fish? Drying preserves fish so Cloyd and cubs can eat it after lake freezes over.

8 Expressing an Opinion
Why does Cloyd put skull in tree? Answers will vary. Perhaps as a gesture of respect for grizzly.

boxing matches, striking each other, dodging, clinching, biting, bristling up and growling in mock battle.

He tied the bundled grizzly skin onto his backpack.

When the moment came, and he called to the cubs to come along, they showed no surprise that he'd shed his grizzly skin. Everything was the same, nothing was different. He turned to go, and they followed.

For them, Cloyd realized, he was a bear.

They were seeing a bear.

He recalled his grandmother's words from when he was little. In the very earliest time, she'd said, a person could become an animal if he wanted to and an animal could become a person. Sometimes they were animals and sometimes people, and it made no difference.

9 Climbing into the sky, climbing for that narrow ledge high above the lake of robin's-egg
10 blue that sat at the deadly foot of Mt. Oso, he glanced over his shoulder and saw the two cubs following close behind, the brown and the cocoa. It felt like he was living with these cubs in the very earliest time.

Cloyd led the cubs across the Ute Lakes Basin, but he stayed miles away from the trail. If these cubs were going to have a future, he had to think like their mother.

The meadows down on Middle Ute Creek had turned gold from the frosts. He could see a
11 big patch of white down there, slightly moving. Sixto Loco's big flock. Cloyd could see a long, long way into the Rio Grande country. Below
12 the dark spruce forests, the aspens blanketing the mountainsides were beginning to turn gold.

As he crossed the wide tundra fields, the cubs dug furiously in the runs of countless voles, and succeeded in capturing several. Cloyd was content to chew on his own dwindling food supply.

The cubs were also eating the frosted tops and the roots of certain wildflowers. As they grazed at the edge of a parsnip patch, an almost full-grown family of ptarmigans, more white than brown now with fall advancing,
13 exploded into flight immediately in front of them. Cocoa and Brownie looked at each other in surprise, then gave chase. The cubs put on a burst of speed, but the low-flying ptarmigans were fast, and quickly left them behind.

Cloyd was on his way back to East Ute Creek, to a small food cache that Walter and the grizzly woman had left for him, when he glimpsed a rider far below on the trail bound for the Divide. The man had a string of packhorses behind him. Tony Archuleta, Cloyd realized, on
14 his way home after resupplying Sixto Loco. He recognized Tony's hat, the chaps.

Here was a way to get a message to Walter. He could stay longer with the cubs if he could tell Walter. Cloyd scratched out a note on the little notepad. If he hurried, he could leave the note on the trail for Tony Archuleta to find.

Cloyd told the cubs to stay. He didn't want them near a trail that people used. He sat them down and pushed their noses down and told them to wait there beside his pack.

At first, when he turned away, they started to follow. Once more he told them, and this time he struck each of their muzzles with a sharp tap as he spoke.

This time they did as he said. They watched him go. He realized as he raced away into the
15 forest that it wasn't his doing. It was something their mother had already taught them.

At the place where Cloyd intercepted the trail, he knew he had to work fast. He pegged his note to the center of the trail with a sharp stick. Just to make sure Tony couldn't miss it, he hastily gathered rocks and shaped them into a large arrow, right in the trail, pointing at the note. Then he fled up the slope, into the trees, to watch.

It wasn't long before Tony Archuleta came along the trail, leading his pack string. Cloyd saw the man with the dark mustache get off his horse, pick up the note, read it, and look all around. But Cloyd wouldn't let himself be seen. Tony smiled broadly as he tucked the note into his shirt pocket, then kicked all the little rocks free of the trail.

Cloyd returned with the cubs to the camp on East Ute Creek and found it quiet and bare, full of good memories. He wouldn't stay long. He only wanted to pick up the food left for him and to cache the heavy bearskin. He might return for it; it made a good blanket. Cloyd removed a long, amber claw from a forepaw to add to the tooth, bearstone, and arrowhead.

He followed the stream down into the aspen forests, where the days were warmer and the nights not as cold. If he could stay with the cubs awhile longer, a week maybe, it would increase their chances. The longer he could stay with them, the better.

As he had guessed, there was still plenty of food lower down. The grass remained green in places, and the cubs found good grazing in the grass and weeds. Brownie and Cocoa slapped at grasshoppers in the air and pounced on the ones on the ground; they even ate moths. Cottontail rabbits were not much trouble for them to catch. They ate the bark from the aspens, they ate rotten mushrooms, they ate willow roots and willow bark. Every day the cubs raked countless chokecherries into their mouths. Cloyd ate just a few. Very many chokecherries would sour his stomach.

The days of mid-September were passing as Cloyd dropped farther still into the tall pine forest, where the cubs robbed squirrels' caches by the dozens. The pine nuts were bigger and oilier than spruce nuts, and Cloyd began to eat them as well, stashing plenty away in his pack. The cubs were amazingly strong. Mostly they were turning over their own rocks and logs now, often working as a team. Their noses led them to the carcass of a deer. Brownie and Cocoa liked that smelly old carcass.

Brownie and Cocoa were thriving. Cloyd could see that they were putting on weight. He thought they might have gained ten or fifteen pounds apiece since he and the grizzly woman had first seen them. What did they weigh now, maybe sixty-five pounds? The fur around their necks and chests was growing extra long and coarse into a ruff, and just behind their necks that trademark hump that grizzlies have above their shoulders was starting to show.

The cubs found acorns plentiful in the scrub oak, and here and there the creek banks were splashed red with wild roses thick with rose hips.[2] Cloyd had chewed on rose hips in the desert, but the fruits of these mountain roses grew fatter and larger and sweeter.

More and more as the days went by, he was grazing alongside the bears, eating the sweet stems of grasses that they ate, trying out the roots they dug up. He swam with them in icy beaver ponds and fished alongside them in the streams. Lying on his belly where the banks overhung the creeks, he practiced at feeling under the banks for trout that hid in the shadows behind dangling roots. He caught four fish that way, onehanded, under the banks.

One day he was sure his hands were feeling the scales of a big fish. It felt a little funny, but he closed on it and pulled it out anyway. Waiting attentively on the bank, Brownie and Cocoa were just as surprised as he was to discover he had a half-grown beaver by the tail. In midair, the beaver was turning around and trying to bite him. Cloyd cried out and threw the beaver up in the air, trying to get it away from him.

The beaver landed on the bank, where the grizzly cubs pounced on it. The beaver was trying to get back into the water, but the cubs

2. **rose hips:** the red fruit of the rose plant, used in jelly or tea.

16 Drawing Conclusions
Why would Cloyd not let Tony see him? Tony would probably want to talk, and Cloyd wants to keep cubs as far away from humans as possible.

17
Metaphor. Compares old camp to container and memories to objects in container.

18
Cloyd's presence with cubs will give them chance to put on fat they need to survive winter.

19
Personification. Noses have power to lead cubs as though noses are people.

20
Metaphor. Compares red of roses to bright red paint splashed onto rose bushes.

21
Cloyd takes on more and more habits of bears.

22 Summarizing
Why are cubs waiting? They expect Cloyd to catch fish for them.

23 Making Generalizations
What does cubs' attack on beaver suggest about their maturity? Cubs are getting close to point where they will be able to take care of themselves.

580

24
Cloyd intends to wear symbols of his identity.

25
Weight of cubs must be hard for Cloyd to manage, especially at angle.

26
Irony. Man wears camouflage to avoid being seen, but cubs and Cloyd see him first.

27 Analyzing
What might man think when he sees Cloyd and cubs? Answers will vary. He is probably startled and surprised. He might also be confused by what he sees.

28 Drawing Conclusions
Why would this experience help cubs live longer? They will do everything they can to stay away from humans in future.

29
Cloyd hears guns because autumn hunting season has started.

30
Figurative Language. Bears stop all movement, as though they were frozen.

knew how to block its escape route. They took turns attacking the beaver, trying for a hold. The beaver stood and faced. Its teeth and claws seemed like <u>formidable</u> weapons to Cloyd, but Cocoa, with a lunge, caught the beaver by the back of its neck. After a few strong shakes, the **26** beaver was dead.

Cloyd kept a piece of the skin and scraped the fur from it. He would soften the skin and sew it into a small pouch with the big needle in **27** the grizzly woman's sewing kit, then hang it from his neck by a rawhide bootlace. In this **24** medicine bundle he would keep the grizzly claw, the grizzly tooth, the arrowhead, and the bearstone.

One day Cloyd was surprised to see Cocoa snap her jaws shut on a bee buzzing by at high speed. With a gulp, she'd swallowed the bee. There were other bees close by, honeybees, and the cubs were curious. They soon discovered a **28** cottonwood with a hive in the cavity where a big branch had broken out. The only trouble was, the bees' nest was about six feet off the ground.

Cloyd wondered how his bears might get at that hive. All he could think of was to offer **29** himself as a ladder. He stood a couple feet away from the tree, then leaned against it. The cubs were quick thinkers. Brownie ran right up his **25** back, with Cocoa barely behind. One stood on his head, one on his shoulder. There was much commotion up there, with all the stirred-up bees and the excited whining of the cubs as they jockeyed for position on his head and shoulders.

Cloyd was stung once on his hand and once on his arm, but he gritted his teeth and held on. With a glance up, he saw Brownie fish out a big piece of honeycomb, and he saw both cubs chewing on the sticky stuff, swallowing honeycomb and bees and all.

He would have liked to stay longer in the lower country. He was keeping track in the grizzly woman's notepad: it was September the

19th, as close as he could tell, the day the cubs came rushing to him, terrified, and froze behind his legs. His instincts weren't as good as theirs. Instead of retreating, he advanced, wondering what had spooked them. Cloyd, and then the cubs too, looked down the slope. He saw a man stalking in a crouch, wearing camouflage clothes and holding a huge compound bow at the ready, the kind Rusty had used. "What the hell," the man swore under his breath when he saw Cloyd and the two cubs at his side.

Cloyd fled, just as terrified as the cubs. He ran as fast as he could. The man chased for a while, and then he quit.

Afterward, Cloyd thought some good had come from this. The cubs had seen a human being, and they had been terrified. Their mother had taught them well. This was good. They would live a lot longer this way.

Cloyd had roamed far from East Ute Creek, up and down the flanks of the mountains above the Rio Grande. Now he started to make his way back to the high country, where it would be **29** safer. At his back he heard the guns of autumn.[3] It was a good lesson for the bears to be fleeing those sounds. He would have to avoid anywhere men could reach on horseback, anywhere hunters might reach from their camps on foot.

Up the steep slopes he led the cubs toward East Ute Creek, through the deadfall timber and across the rockslides and the grassy avalanche chutes. East Ute Creek, where he had said good-bye to Walter and Ursa, seemed like the closest thing to home. But when he was almost back to the old campsite, watching the meadow from the forested slopes above, a party of hunters came riding up the trail, right up the **30** meadows of East Ute Creek. Brownie and Cocoa froze in place and watched the riders

---

3. **guns of autumn:** a reference to the fall hunting season.

TRANSPARENCY 38	TRANSPARENCY 41
Fine Art Theme: *Learning to Appreciate Heritage* – features artwork that shows appreciation of the legacy of previous generations.	**Reader Response** *Dark Shadows* – invites students to identify internal and external conflict experienced by a literary character.

pass by far below. Cloyd wished he could stay on East Ute Creek again and fish the stream with his rod and reel. But he would have to lead the bears to safer places.

When the meadow was clear again, he crossed the creek and disappeared with the bears into the timber, heading for the back side of the ridge where there were no trails.

He should've stopped for the night earlier, but it was all steep slopes, nothing that looked hospitable. It was dusk. Then, with no warning, **31** Brownie was gone. The earth had swallowed her up. One second she was investigating some small hole on the slope, the next she was gone.

He should have held on to Cocoa: the two of them were thick as thieves. Now Cocoa was gone down the hole too.

His tiny flashlight with its nearly dead batteries couldn't penetrate the blackness. But he could hear them whimpering, far below.

Reading Check

1. What makes up the main portion of a grizzly's diet?
2. According to Ursa, why do bears slide down snowbanks?
3. Why does Cloyd open the cages and release the cubs?
4. How does Cloyd get the idea to use the bearskin to help the cubs?
5. Why is it necessary for the cubs to gain weight?

For Study and Discussion

Analyzing and Interpreting the Novel

1. What do you think causes Ursa to tell the game wardens about the orphaned cubs?

2. On page 563, the game warden says "we have to protect these *particular* grizzlies, not the *idea* of grizzlies. That's our responsibility." **a.** How do you interpret the game warden's statement? **b.** Do you agree with the game warden? Why or why not?

3a. How do you feel about Cloyd's decision to free the bears? **b.** What would you have done in a similar situation?

4. Ursa claims that people who visit the wilderness don't want it to be totally safe. Do you agree with her statement? Why or why not?

5a. What do you think Cloyd's dream means? **b.** Do you think the dream is a good omen or a bad one?

6. Why do you think Cloyd refuses to let Tony Archeluta see him?

Literary Elements

Understanding the Novel

Plot

1. The most important element of plot is **conflict.** Conflict usually occurs when a character must face one or many obstacles that stand in the way of his or her desires. There are two types of major conflict: **internal** and **external.** External conflict can take place between two characters, between a character and natural forces, or between opposing views held by separate characters or groups of characters. Internal conflict occurs in the thoughts and emotions of a character. Find one example of internal conflict and examples of each type of external conflict in the novel.

READING CHECK
1. Three-fourths of diet is vegetable material (p. 553).
2. To have fun (p. 556).
3. He thinks leaving them to their chances of surviving in wilderness is better than sending them to zoo (p. 565).
4. He dreams about people dressed in bearskins at Ute Bear Dance (p. 572).
5. To put on fat to sustain them during their hibernation in winter (pp. 573, 577).

FOR STUDY AND DISCUSSION
1. Answers will vary. One possibility is she hopes they will help cubs survive winter in wilderness. 2a. Allowing cubs to remain in wilderness might work toward restoring grizzly population, but it might not. They know they can save cubs by taking them to zoo, so they feel they must do so. 2b. Students should support their opinions with logical reasons.
3a. and b. Answers will vary. Students should have logical reasons for their responses to both questions.
4. Some students may disagree and point out that hikers are out for sport, not to be hurt. Those who agree may feel that a wilderness is not really a wilderness unless there is some danger. 5a. Possible interpretation is that bear's eating Cloyd is symbolic of Cloyd becoming one with bear. 5b. Some who interpret dream as bad omen may think it means Cloyd will be killed by bear. Some who think dream is good omen may point out that Cloyd got idea for using bearskin in dream.
6. If Tony sees Cloyd, he may approach him to talk. Cloyd does not want cubs to have any further contact with humans.

CLOSURE
Divide the class into two groups. Let each member of the first group make up a question about events in this section of the novel. Then play a game requiring students in the second group to answer the first group's questions.

EXTENSION AND ENRICHMENT
Ask students to look through copies of newspapers, magazines, or other sources for stories about conflicts involving the protection of an endangered species. In most cases people on both sides of the conflict have valid concerns.

Ask several students to debate the issues involved in one such conflict, and then let the class discuss the conflict and how it might be resolved.

LITERARY ELEMENTS

1. One internal conflict is guilt Cloyd feels for having betrayed grizzly by telling Rusty where it was; another is Cloyd's doubts after freeing cubs. One external conflict between characters is that between Ursa and Haverford. An external conflict with nature occurs when Cloyd has to endure cold and rough terrain. An external conflict involving opposing views is one between wardens and Ursa and Cloyd about saving cubs versus saving potential grizzly population in Colorado.

2. Following examples are representative of methods students may find. **Physical description:** "She was carrying a big pack, but she wasn't bent under it. Her legs were sinewy and strong, and she came striding toward him . . ." (p. 538). **Dialogue:** "'You're young,' she said. 'Cloyd, you could be one who fights for bears'" (p. 554). **Reactions:** "Cloyd watched the confusion in the grizzly woman's face and the regret clouding the face of the younger man" (p. 561). **Actions:** Cloyd's action of freeing cubs (p. 565). **Thoughts:** Cloyd doubts whether he has a spirit helper. "He hadn't done anything for bears. One had died because of his careless words" (p. 554).

3. Representative examples follow. **a.** "For a long time they watched and waited, and then their hunger and their loneliness drove them close . . ."(pp. 574–575). **b.** Cloyd says goodbye to Walter and Ursa, and to a comfortable life at Walter's farm, to stay in wilderness to help bears. **c.** Cloyd makes decision to free cubs and not to involve Ursa so she cannot be blamed for it.

Character

2. Characters in a novel or story are revealed in a number of ways. We learn who they are through their actions, their dialogue, the reactions of other characters, and the author's descriptions. In many cases, we can also listen in on the character's thoughts. It is possible that we will learn more about a character in a novel than we do about our friends in real life, whose minds we can never read. Find examples in the novel of the following methods for revealing character.

> Physical description
> Dialogue
> Reactions of another character
> Actions
> Internal thoughts

Theme

3. A **theme** is the central idea about life expressed in a literary work. Plot, characterization, figurative language, and setting all contribute to the thematic development. While you will discover that *Beardance* has one major theme, it also has a number of subordinate themes. Some themes explored in *Beardance* are listed below. For each theme, find an example in the novel that supports it.

a. Animals and humans are alike in some ways.

b. We sometimes have to make sacrifices to get what we want.

c. Making difficult decisions is part of growing up.

Language and Vocabulary

Using Active Verbs

To make the action in a book vivid and immediate, writers choose strong, active verbs. For example, instead of using the word *walk*, an author might choose *stroll, amble, meander,* or *stalk.* Each of these words indicates a **specific** action, rather than a **general** one. We know exactly what the author wants us to see.

Many words in English can function as different parts of speech. For example, the word *belly,* which is commonly used as a noun, is used as a verb in the phrase "they *bellied* up to the gap" (page 558). We can infer the meaning of the word to be "crawled on their bellies." Similarly, Hobbs uses *glass* as a verb in this sentence: "*Glass* the outlet" (page 558). In this context the word *glass* means "scan" or "look at."

1 Find five examples of active verbs in *Beardance* and use each one in a complete sentence.

2 Use each of the following words as a verb in a complete sentence: *closet, snake, mother, wall, parade.*

Writing About Literature

Recognizing Dynamic Characters

A **dynamic** character is one that is capable of growth and change. A **static** character does not grow or change. Cloyd changes in several significant ways in the second section of the novel. At first he is consumed with doubt about his own abilities. He doesn't believe he is capable of having a spirit helper and still feels guilt over the death of the male grizzly. He looks to Ursa for guidance and wishes he knew as much as she does. As the novel progresses, however, Cloyd's faith in himself grows. He risks his own safety to help the orphaned cubs and proves himself to be a leader who can take on responsibility. In a short essay explain how Cloyd's character has changed so far in the novel. Using your own words, tell why you think Cloyd is a dynamic character.

The Weminuche Wilderness

The geography of southwestern Colorado, where *Beardance* takes place, includes mountains, vast wilderness areas, forests, and rivers. The Continental Divide, the mountainous ridge which runs through it, is the largest watershed in the United States. Water on the western side of the Divide runs to the Pacific, while water on the eastern side runs to the Atlantic. During his journey, Cloyd travels back and forth over this great dividing line between west and east.

San Juan Mountains, Colorado.

Making Connections: Activities

Copy or draw your own version of the map on pages 518–519. Using a highlighter or colored marker, draw arrows to follow the action of the novel on your map. (You don't have to be completely accurate.) Mark key points where Cloyd and Ursa observe bears or where significant moments in the plot occur. You can design a key for any symbols you use or draw pictures to show the action. Exhibit your maps.

©Larry Ulrich/DRK Photo

LANGUAGE AND VOCABULARY

1. Possibilities include *glassed* (Cloyd glassed the canyon to look for the bears); *hurled* (the bear hurled a fish at the cubs); *inched* (Cloyd inched his way through the brush); *flicked* (the mother bear flicked mice to the cubs); *angle* (Cloyd angled his way up the trail).

2. Following sentences illustrate sense in which words should be used. The cubs would *closet* themselves in their den for the winter. The Pine River *snaked* through the mountains. Dressed in the bearskin, Cloyd *mothered* the cubs. Cloyd *walled* up the mouth of a cave. The cubs *paraded* through the forest.

WRITING ABOUT LITERATURE

Essays could focus on Cloyd's change from someone who did not believe his grandmother's stories about bears to someone who is actually living those stories. They could also deal with Cloyd's growing sense of responsibility for the cubs.

LITERATURE AND GEOGRAPHY

You might want to have students work on maps in groups, with each member of the group responsible for movement and events in one or more chapters. Maps do not have to be completely accurate, but they should reflect general locations of events.

OBJECTIVES
The overall aim is for students to analyze the plot of the **novel** by considering the **turning point, crisis,** and **climax** of the story. For a complete list of objectives, see the **Teacher's Notes.**

VOCABULARY
The underlined words are in the Glossary. You can call students' attention to the vocabulary words given in the footnotes. Encourage students to make lists of unfamiliar words and to look up these words in a dictionary.

FOCUS / MOTIVATION
Ask students to imagine that they are in danger of dying. How would they feel? What would they think about? Then ask students to imagine their rescue. What would come to mind?

Chapter 19

1 Making Inferences
Why does Cloyd want to avoid sheep? Answers will vary. Maybe he is worried about dogs attacking him. Maybe he is worried Sixto will think sheep are in danger and shoot him.

2
Fire suggests Sixto is near by.

3
Inference. Cloyd, an experienced camper, draws conclusion based on clues.

4
Figurative Language. Fear of Sixto makes skin on Cloyd's neck tense, which feels like something is crawling on him.

5
Cloyd's fear makes him imagine Sixto to be a fierce creature.

6
Simile. Compares beard to tangled moss hanging from trees.

7 Analyzing
What does narrator mean by Sixto's "weathering"? Skin is wrinkled and deeply tanned from being in sun and harsh weather.

8
Sixto's greeting is much friendlier than Cloyd expected.

584

19

1 He'd taken great pains to skirt the flock and the six sheepdogs guarding the flock.

Where was Sixto Loco?

Cloyd had to get a rope. Only a long rope could possibly save those cubs. He didn't know exactly what he was going to do with it, but he knew he might have to try to squeeze down that hole.

The shadows were growing long, and the flock was moving gradually down the meadow of Middle Ute Creek, headed by habit back to its bedding grounds by the camp.

He could see no movement in the shepherd's camp by the creek. Where was Sixto Loco?

2 Cloyd watched from the trees as long as he could. Finally he crept in close to the fire. There was a covered pail on the coals, and the coffeepot was sitting on a flat rock next to the coals. No smoke issued from the little metal chimney sticking out of the tent; the front of the weather-beaten canvas tent was shut and tied in three places. The tent should be empty.

3 If Sixto Loco was sleeping inside that tent, it wouldn't be closed from the outside.

4 He felt like he was being watched. Even the thought of this man called *la Sombra* made the skin on the back of his neck crawl. Keeping low to the ground, he pulled up two pegs at the back of the tent, then poked his head inside.

The floor was covered with woolly sheepskins. A rifle stood in a front corner against a tall pair of snowshoes. At least Sixto Loco couldn't shoot him with his rifle. Behind the little sheepherder stove, on top of some bags of rock salt,[1] there was the coil of rope he needed. . . .

As he was about to shimmy forward for the rope, he found himself shooting backward on

---
1. **rock salt:** Salt is a necessary nutrient for sheep, deer, and other plant-eating animals.

---

his belly. Something had him by the foot and was dragging him outside.

Cloyd flipped himself over and found the spidery form of the grizzled sheepherder standing over him, the proud *pastor,*[2] the last of the sheepherders of the San Juan Mountains. Somehow the man had slipped a noose over Cloyd's foot without Cloyd even feeling it.

Cloyd's heart jumped. The man looked like an old billy goat, and he seemed to breathe fire.

5 The eyes were reddened and bloodshot, and they gave the sheepherder a fearful look. Dark and lined and leathery, his face showed no hint **6** of mercy. The gray-black beard grew long and unkempt, like Spanish moss from a tree.

7 Sixto Archuleta might have been close to seventy years old, but his weathering made it impossible to tell. He could have been younger. His plaid shirt was patched in several places. His waist was wrapped with a curious, braided sash attached to a worn piece of leather. On his hip the man wore a bone-handled knife, and there was a blood smear on his jeans.

In a hesitating tone, low and broken as if the man were unused to speech, Sixto Loco said two words in Spanish: *"Yuta coyote."*

Cloyd was too stunned by the man's appearance, too afraid to speak.

"I caught the Yuta coyote," Sixto Archuleta repeated, this time in accented English, with the trace of a smile crossing his broken, yellowed teeth. The man bent down and undid the noose from Cloyd's ankle.

8 "Can you talk? You hungry? Don't just sit there! Throw some wood on the fire!"

Cloyd got up cautiously and then did what the man said. He started breaking branches from the pile near the fire. He was looking for the best line if he chose to run. "Sheepmen hate grizzlies," Ursa had said. "Don't let Sixto see

---
2. *pastor:* In Spanish a *pastor* is a shepherd.

MOTIVATIONAL SUMMARY
Cloyd, with the help of Sixto Loco, rescues the cubs from the Lost Mine of the Window, but only after he promises never to reveal the mine's location. The boy and the bears then meet a party of men headed by Rusty, and Cloyd nar- rowly escapes death in an avalanche. Although he and the cubs are still alive, they have to strug- gle to find food and to avoid freezing to death. Eventually, Cloyd helps the cubs establish a den, but the cubs, without the example of their mother to lead them, are reluctant to hibernate.

PRESENTATION
Events happen fast in this part of the novel, and students may be tempted to read ahead to find out what happens next. You might want to take this into consideration in making reading assign- ments. Chapters 19 and 20 form a logical unit,

your picks and shovels," Tony Archuleta had warned.

As Sixto Loco was adding grounds and water **12** to the big black coffeepot, he asked with a trace **9** of a grin, "Did that old man you were with find any gold?"

Cloyd blew on the coals and determined they were still alive. He was slow to answer as he began to lay wood on the fire. "A nugget in the creek," he answered guardedly.

10 "My nephew was right about you, Cloyd **11** Atcitty. You're a coyote, a Ute coyote. I see you coming and going around these mountains like a shadow yourself."

What did Sixto Loco know? Cloyd wondered. Did he know about the bears?

The shepherd grinned, showing his broken teeth. His shaggy eyebrows, silver and black, rose as he asked a question. "You and Walter Landis were trying to find *la Mina Perdida de la Ventana,* no?"

"Walter would've liked to find it," Cloyd said **14** truthfully, "but he didn't."

Cloyd could hear bells now, the bells on the goats that were on the leading edge of the big sheep flock. They were returning to their bed- ding grounds.

Sixto had melted two spoonfuls of lard. The man was always in motion. From inside his tent he brought out a sack of flour, and he rolled the edges of the sack down far enough to expose the flour. Into the sack he poured the melted lard and a cup of water. Cloyd couldn't tell what he was doing. "What about you?" Sixto asked gruffly. "You didn't want to find the mine?"

"I don't like mines," Cloyd said. "I worked in Walter's mine last summer in Snowslide Canyon. It's dark in there, freezing cold...."

"How come you stayed up here by yourself? Are you crazy?"

"I . . . I like it up here."

Cloyd began to hope that he could borrow the rope, as long as he made no mention of the **16**

bears. He had to think of an excuse for why he needed it.

Cloyd could see that those baleful eyes didn't believe his reason for staying on in the high country alone. The old shepherd pointed with a gnarled finger up above them to the west. "See where the sun's going down on that ridge, right behind the big tree? Yesterday it set in that little notch between that big tree and the dead one. From this campsite, the sun sets right there on a special day. Yesterday was exactly halfway between the longest day and the shortest day of the year. You know what that means, Coyote? **13** Up here, winter's coming soon. I have to take the sheep down pretty quick. After this, you have to be crazier than me to stay up here."

All the while, the spidery man was at work, yet he never seemed hurried. Sixto had five lit- tle cakes like thick tortillas frying in the skillet. *"Gordas,"* he said gruffly, pointing with his lips as his hands flattened out five more. " 'Fat ones.' "

The flock had drawn close. It was all familiar to Cloyd, the bleating of the sheep from down in their throats, the quicker, higher blats of the goats.

Suddenly three of the sheepdogs appeared as if from nowhere, and they proceeded to sniff Cloyd cautiously, with their long tails slung low on the ground. The dogs were long-haired, of mixed colors, half wild. He could see the hack- les rising on their necks and along their backs.

"They smell something on you," Sixto Archuleta observed as he was pulling the big pail off the coals. The bloodshot eyes fell on **15** Cloyd. "Maybe some kind of animal," the crazy man said with a knowing smile.

Cloyd was so taken aback that he said noth- ing. He wasn't even sure what Sixto Loco had said.

Now the rest of the dogs were coming around and sniffing him. With a harsh word from Sixto, they scattered.

16 Cloyd's eyes were devouring those fat tor-

9 Drawing Conclusions
What does Sixto's question suggest about how much he knows about Walter? It sug- gests he was aware of what Wal- ter was doing in mountains.

10
Sixto obviously knows who Cloyd is.

11
Simile. Compares Cloyd's cau- tious, silent movement in moun- tain to shadow.

12
Personification. Eyes have human ability to believe. Narra- tor intends to say Sixto's facial ex- pression shows he does not believe Cloyd.

13
Sixto warns Cloyd of approach- ing winter.

14 Finding Details
Why is this scene familiar to Cloyd? He looked after his grandmother's sheep when he was younger.

15 Making Inferences
What does Sixto's smile suggest? That he might know about bears.

16
Personification. Eyes have human ability to eat, meaning Cloyd's hunger is evident from his facial expression.

Chapters 21 and 22 can each be assigned separately, and Chapters 23 and 24 go together to form the conclusion.

Sixto Loco and Rusty reappear in this part of the story. You may want to ask students to recall these men and to discuss briefly their impressions of them. You can point out that literature often deals with the difference between how things seem to be and how they really are, and you can ask students to keep this idea in mind when they read about Sixto and Rusty in the remaining chapters. The questions in **For Study and Discussion** will help students clarify how they feel about these two men.

The **Literary Elements** exercise focuses on **plot**. Before students begin reading, ask them to look for an event that serves as the **turning point** of the novel. You can also ask them to

---

17 Drawing Conclusions
What does Sixto's statement indicate? That he definitely knows about the bears.

18
Goats nursed dogs as though dogs were goats. This creates special bond between goats and dogs.

19
Personification. Fingers have ability to remember, as though they have separate existence.

20 Summarizing
Why had Cloyd's stomach ached other nights? He had not had enough to eat.

21
Sixto seems genuinely to care about Cloyd.

22
Sixto seems to identify with bears just as Cloyd does.

23
Irony. Sixto calls old people "young and stupid" to mean they did not understand balance and harmony of nature. Use to answer **study question 1**, p. 610.

24 Drawing Conclusions
What does Sixto imply by this statement? He was afraid to tell anyone about seeing grizzlies for fear others would hunt and kill them.

---

tillas. He was about to reach when the shepherd **20** signaled him to wait, and pried the lid off the pail. The delicious aroma of beans and mutton wafted Cloyd's way. Sixto handed him a ladle. "Spread it on the fat ones," he explained.

Two of the goats had come right up to the campfire and were blatting impatiently. Cloyd could see they needed to be milked. Sixto grabbed one nanny goat by the hind leg and **17** started to milk her. "It's been thirty years since I lost a sheep to a bear," he said proudly, and **21** then he watched for Cloyd's reaction.

Cloyd allowed no emotion to show, and the man continued. "I sleep with one eye open, but **18** really it's the dogs. All six of my dogs, I put them on one of these nanny goats before they even opened their eyes. When they're suckled to a nanny, they grow up thinking they're part goat. They love these animals and they take care of them. They watch out for the sheep too, even though they don't respect them, for often the sheep are stupid snivelers."

"I used to have a flock of sheep and goats," Cloyd said. "A small one." He wanted to milk the second goat himself. The man might offer him some milk. He grabbed her by the leg, as Sixto Archuleta had done. The grizzled shepherd handed him the pail.

19 It had been a long time, but his fingers could remember.

Sixto strained the milk and passed it to Cloyd. It tasted warm and good. "Now let's eat," the shepherd said.

Cloyd had thought all the eating was done. Maybe Sixto could tell he was still hungry. The **23** shepherd picked out a lamb from the flock and slaughtered it exactly the way Cloyd had learned from his grandmother, and he skinned it exactly the same way too. Sixto fried the blood they had caught, and then he made a **24** stew with carrots and onions and potatoes and plenty of meat.

This night wouldn't be like the others, with his stomach aching when he went to sleep.

Even the lamb's head was set to cook in the coals, a delicacy for the morning. Sixto was like an Indian, Cloyd thought, using every part.

It was the man's eyes that made him look so mean, Cloyd thought, all red and bloodshot. The campfire smoke had made his eyes look that way. It wasn't him. It was all the time he'd spent squatting by campfires.

More *gordas* on the skillet. Sixto was throwing scraps of meat to the dogs. "We have a lot of eating to do, Coyote. You don't have any fat on your ribs, I think."

The dogs were back sniffing his legs again, this time four of them. Their snouts were wrinkled with suspicion, and their tails were down on the ground like the tails of coyotes.

To Cloyd's amazement, Sixto said, "They smell those bears on you. Now tell me what happened to my she-bear and the cub that was almost black. Tell me who the woman was who was with you, who was part Indian but not Ute. Tell me how you come to be with those two cubs, and tell me where they are now."

Cloyd couldn't mask his surprise. "You knew about that mother grizzly and you didn't kill her?"

The old shepherd heaved a sigh and said, "I used to see her boyfriend too once in a while, **22** the one that was killed last summer. Why should I kill them? They're old coyotes like me…like you. We're the last of the breed."

Cloyd was trying to take this all in.

"When I was young I killed too many bears," Sixto said. "I was a *tonto*, a stupid. Everyone was young and stupid back then, even the old people."

"You've seen grizzlies up here, and never told anybody?"

"There's still a lot of *tontos* out there."

It was starting to get dark. The shepherd put out a flashing beacon where the flock had bed-look for the **climax** of the story, or the point of greatest emotional intensity. If you have found it useful to discuss the events of the chapters after students have read them, you will probably want to continue that practice until the end of the novel.

ded down, and he filled a hollowed-out log with rock salt. Afterward, by the campfire, Cloyd told his story, from first seeing the cubs to the death of their mother to losing Brownie and Cocoa down a deep hole on that ridge facing Middle Ute Creek.

"Ayeee," Sixto Archuleta whistled, on hearing what had happened to the cubs.

Cloyd could see the dread in the proud shepherd's face. Something had spooked him, and it wasn't the cubs' predicament. At last Sixto said, "This is bad. I know that place. This is really bad."

25 The shepherd would say no more. Cloyd wondered if Sixto would help after all. He had to get help to those cubs soon.

Above the Rio Grande Pyramid, clouds were scudding across the crescent moon. "Look at that," Sixto cried, pointing a crooked finger.

26 "The horns of the moon can't hold any water."

"What does that mean?"

"Weather coming."

20

Cloyd slept warm with the little sheepherder stove only a few feet away. He hadn't slept so warm since he'd left the farm. In the middle of the night the fire nearly burned out, but Sixto got up and stoked it. The wind was giving the

1 wall tent a bad buffeting, but this tent was so well staked out, it felt strong as a house.

In the morning, the woolly backs of the sheep were covered with an inch or two of snow. The day dawned crisp and clear with five hundred animals all exhaling vapor clouds into the morning air, all huddled close for warmth and protection.

Cloyd was sitting on a log, sharpening his pocketknife with Sixto's whetstone. There was something about the bears that he'd been thinking about for a long time; Sixto Archuleta

2 might know something about this. "Have you

ever seen a grizzly's den? Is it very deep?"

He hoped a den wouldn't be very deep. He didn't know how deep his cubs could dig, or if they would dig a den at all.

"'Course it's deep," Sixto answered. "I've seen a couple. They tunnel six, eight feet, then make a sleeping room about six feet across.

3 Both of the ones I saw were dug under tree roots. You know what . . . you'd think they'd dig their dens on the slopes facing the sun, where it would be warmer, but they are smart and that would be stupid. They'd be waking up all winter if they did that. The earth keeps them warm

4 enough. They den in the shadows, where the sun won't disturb them until it's spring."

5 Just then a light plane appeared and buzzed the camp. Its wings were white underneath and red on top. The plane came in so low on the meadow that Cloyd could almost see the pilot. All of a sudden, the sheep were running, scattering, bleating hysterically. Lambs were getting separated from their mothers. It was hard to tell if the lambs or the ewes were more panicked.

6 Sixto Archuleta's eyes were on fire. Cloyd found out about the narrow sash around the shepherd's waist: after the airplane's second pass, Sixto started picking up stones, and he unleashed the sash from his waist and fitted a stone to it. A sling! Whirling the weapon around and around, Sixto was ready when the plane came back the third time, and he let the stone fly with terrific velocity.

The pilot must have wanted an especially good look, because he was flying even lower than before. The sheep were running recklessly in all directions.

Cloyd couldn't follow the flight of the stone, but he saw the plane coming right toward them,

7 and he saw its windshield suddenly spiderweb all over with cracks as the stone struck.

The boy turned with awe to the shepherd. "Was that a lucky shot?"

25 Making Inferences
Why will Sixto not say any more? Answers will vary. Perhaps he does not want to alarm Cloyd until it is time to do something for cubs.

26
Two ends of crescent moon look like horns of cow or other animal.

Chapter 20

1
Sixto is used to camping in bad weather, and his tent is put up well to withstand storms.

2 Summarizing
Why is Cloyd concerned about den? Cubs will need one soon, and Cloyd feels responsible for helping them establish one.

3
Sixto draws conclusion about habits of grizzlies on basis of only two examples.

4 Making Inferences
What other reason might cause bears to den where they do? Digging into rocky slope would be much harder than digging into soil.

5
Figurative Language. Refers to buzzing sound of plane that is louder because plane is so low.

6
Metaphor. Compares anger in Sixto's expression to fire to show his emotion is intense.

7
Figurative Language. Crack in windshield resembles pattern of spiderweb.

23
Imagery. Words appeal to sense of smell.

24
Cloyd tries to convince himself leaving is all right.

25 Drawing Conclusions
Where does sound of breaking glass come from? Lantern. Cloyd apparently lands on it, and it shatters.

26
Now Cloyd is in darkness like cubs.

27
Cloyd feels confident of his ability to continue his search.

28
Atmosphere. Narrator describes mine as frightening, inhospitable place.

29
Metaphor. Compares three tunnels to spokes coming from central hub of a wheel.

30
Exaggeration. Cloyd's heart is beating so fast and hard it feels as if it is jumping.

31
When Cloyd hears Sixto, he realizes cubs must be nearby.

foot ladder joined this level to the one below. He tested the first rung of the ladder with his foot. It crumbled with only a little pressure.

Cloyd returned to the main tunnel, but it soon played out. The only way to continue was **28** down the twenty-foot ladder. He went back and stood above the drop a long time, paralyzed. **23** His throat felt like it was stuffed with wool. His fright had a smell to it, an ominous sour smell suddenly coming out of his skin. He turned and fled.

Outside the mine, clouds had covered up the Window. The wind was blowing hard and cold. Winter was on its way. He told himself it was **24** okay to give up. It was time to start back for the farm.

No matter which way he turned it over in his mind, he just couldn't. He couldn't leave the **29** bears behind. He hated that mine and he could sense his own death, but the bears were still inside it, lost in the pitch dark. He'd gone down ropes before, he told himself; he'd climbed up ropes. He had to try.

Cloyd turned and started inside again. This time when he came to the drop and the ladder, **30** he didn't hesitate. Tying off the rope to a boulder, he eased the lantern to the bottom of the drop. With the rope passed behind his back, he started down the slope, bracing with his feet. Toward the bottom he slipped and came down hard. In a heartbeat, the mine was filled with **25** the sound of breaking glass and with utter **26** darkness.

Panicky, he reached for the flashlight and flicked it on. Its light seemed strong enough, but its beam was flickering. These batteries were playing out. How long would they last? His heart gradually stopped racing. He told himself to try to stay calm. The beam would hold **27** for a while. He was going to keep going. Nothing could stop him now unless he was buried with rock.

Farther and farther into the mountain he **31**

continued, passing side tunnels that went nowhere. One was closed by a cave-in. He wondered if this was the place where Sixto's brother had met his death.

For a long time, he waded through water halfway to his knees. He was shaking with cold. Water was dripping out of the ceilings and running down the walls. He knew that if he touched anything here, it all might come down.

After Cloyd passed through a series of rooms, the tunnel began to climb. He stopped every few minutes to listen for the bears or for Sixto, but there was no sound but the dripping of water. The tunnel narrowed and climbed. He eased on all fours through an opening braced by rotten timbers. More rooms, more side tunnels that led nowhere, nothing anymore that he could call the main tunnel. The one he was following spoked off into three directions, each leading into rooms where ore had been removed, each climbing and narrowing.

The second tunnel led to a room where the flashlight's beam, flickering from strong to weak and back, fell on another skeleton. His heart jumped in his chest, yet he crept closer. A rusted sword lay close by the bones. Next to the sword lay a rawhide bag chewed apart by rats. He knelt to discover…gold coins, perhaps fifty pieces of Spanish gold, each a little bigger than a quarter. Had no one discovered this place before, not even Sixto and his brother?

He would take only one of the coins. . . .

Cloyd backtracked to the third tunnel. A hundred feet into it, he heard something. Not the bears, not the whimpering of the cubs. He listened again. It was Sixto Loco calling, *"Coy-o-te! Yu-ta coy-o-te!"*

He kept moving forward; the echoing voice stopped. Several minutes later Sixto called again, and this time his voice was much stronger. Cloyd yelled back, "Here I am, Sixto, here I am! Where are you, Brownie? Cocoa,

Groups of three or four students may be interested in conducting a panel discussion to evaluate Cloyd's decision to return to the bear cubs. Suggest that they investigate such things as fall temperatures and snowfall levels in the Colorado mountains before they present their discussion. One panel member should be thoroughly versed in the plot, one in the characters, and one in the Colorado elements. Consult with panel members individually to agree on how their participation will be assessed. Audiotapes of panel discussions may be included in student portfolios. (See *Portfolio Assessment and Professional Support Materials,* especially the section entitled **Suggestions for Portfolio Projects.**)

---

hey Cocoa! I'm coming for you!" He made the smacking noise with his lips that he'd used so often to talk to them.

In less than a minute the bears appeared in the shadows at the edge of the light. Then they raced toward him. He got down on the floor of the tunnel with them, and he let them whimper and whine and lick his face and claw him up and down in their excitement.

"Sixto!" he called. "Can you hear me?"

32 The old sheepherder replied joyously, "I can hear you! I can hear you!"

"They're okay, they're fine. When I come out, though, we can't be around people. I don't want them to be around people."

There was silence, and then Sixto's voice came again. "I understand. You turn them loose, Coyote, then come back to my camp. We'll come out of the mountains together. It's time to come out of the mountains."

33 Cloyd didn't respond. He hadn't been making plans, he'd only been going from day to day. There was so much he had to think about. "What is it?" the shepherd called.

"I'm...I'm not sure I can," Cloyd said tentatively. "I might have to stay with them."

"How long?" Sixto called.

34 "I don't know...until I think they're safe."

"You're crazy! Bad weather's coming. It's too high up here, too cold! You might stay a little while, but if you stay too long..."

"I'll just stay a little while."

35 "I tell you what, Coyote, I'll leave my tent right where it is. It's a strong tent. It can stand there all winter I bet. I'll leave the food I've got left. I'll leave the stove, I'll leave some other stuff. I have a pair of snowshoes, and a pair of winter boots. You'll need those things if a big snow comes!"

"Thank you," he called. "Thank you!"

At the place where Cloyd was standing, a side room bulged from a narrow opening in the tunnel.

36 His light followed one of the bears inside, and at first he doubted his eyes. He shone the light all around. There was nothing wrong with his eyes. This was the room, at the end of the Spaniards' tunneling, that Walter Landis had dreamed of his whole life. A natural pocket, its walls were made of gleaming, crystalline gold. This was the freak of nature,

37 the chamber of solid gold that Walter liked to paint with word pictures down on the farm. "The heart of the mountain," Walter called it.

The Spanish hadn't removed this gold when the end came. They'd only just discovered this room.

But he would never tell the old man that he'd been in this mine. And not because of any

38 ghosts. Because Sixto Loco had helped him, and Sixto had asked him to keep a promise.

He turned with the cubs for daylight. When

39 they got to the ledge and the open air, it was snowing.

21

1 Far below, the aspen forest was turning quickly toward its prime. The bears were watching with him. Several days before September ran out, the colors reached their vivid peak, and the flanks of the mountains were all wrapped in blankets of gold sprinkled here and there with patches red like fire.

No wind was arriving to shake the leaves pre-

2 maturely from the trees. Skies of the deepest blue marked each day as fall hung suspended in its glory. It almost seemed this was the way it always was in the mountains, as if the lightning bolts and the thunder, the drenching rains, the sudden hailstorms, and the early snows were made-up memories.

Sixto Archuleta and his flock had disappeared over the Divide, and the sheepherder too, like the grizzly woman and the old man, had become a memory.

Cloyd was glad he had stayed to see all this, to

---

32 Drawing Conclusions
Why is Sixto's reply joyous? He is as excited as Cloyd that cubs are all right.

33 Analyzing
What does Cloyd's lack of response suggest? That he may not be ready to leave cubs.

34 Making Inferences
When will Cloyd think cubs are safe? Answers will vary. Probably when they have settled into their winter den.

35
Sixto wants to cooperate any way he can.

36
Personification. Light given human ability to move on its own.

37
Metaphor. Compares Walter's verbal description of room to a vivid painting.

38
Cloyd respects Sixto too much to reveal his secret even to Walter.

39 Drawing Conclusions
What does snow signify for bears? Winter will soon arrive in low country, and it is time for bears to hibernate.

Chapter 21

1
Description. Narrator describes brilliant color of leaves at their peak to indicate season is fall.

2
Metaphor. Compares fall season to ornament suspended by a string to suggest that no force in nature disturbs season's beauty.

592

3
Cubs cannot find as much food as they had before.

4 Drawing Conclusions
What happened to beaver? It was cutting down a tree for its dam, and tree fell on beaver, killing it.

5
Cloyd does not want cubs to go near sheep for fear sheepherders will kill them.

6 Expressing an Opinion
Why has Sixto been so kind to Cloyd and cubs? Answers will vary. Maybe he has been misjudged all these years. Maybe he realizes Cloyd is doing something important and wants to help.

7 Drawing Conclusions
Why did Sixto leave food strung in tree? So animals cannot get it.

8
Cloyd needs food, but he is limited in how much he can take because of mountains ahead of him.

9
Setting. Narrator begins new section by indicating time has passed.

10 Summarizing
Why should Cloyd have frozen? Pilot might not notice him standing still, but motion of running might catch pilot's eye.

see it from up high looking down. In the shadows behind the peaks, the new snow lingered. 3 Everywhere else it had burned off. The cubs weren't finding their table as crowded as before. They were depending more and more on roots and nuts. Their claws had grown longer and they'd become more powerful diggers since he first spied them.

Every day Brownie and Cocoa would catch a few mice scurrying between runs in the grass. With a thrown stick, Cloyd struck a grouse that 4 had flown to a low branch. And the cubs smelled out a big beaver that had felled a tree on itself.

A few days after Sixto's flock disappeared over the Divide, Cloyd started for the shepherd's camp on Middle Ute Creek. The ammonia smell of sheep urine was still strong on the 5 meadow. He wanted the bears to continue to avoid the scent of sheep, as their mother had taught them. In the deep timber high above the meadow, he spoke to them and knocked his finger sharply across their muzzles. He told them to stay behind and wait for him.

6 The sheepherder who was supposed to be so fierce had left his tent pitched for Cloyd, as he had said he would. Inside, Cloyd found all manner of gear that might be useful to him. The first thing Cloyd noticed was the shepherd's sling, which he had worn around his waist, and a note on it that said, *"Bienvenidos,*[1] *Yuta coyote.* The sling is yours. You could be a good shot too if you practiced. Eat the food, use what you like, *'Mi casa es su casa.'*[2] Good luck with your purpose."

The flashlight remained, the axe, the snowboots Sixto had talked about, the long snowshoes with wood frames and rawhide webbing, a big box of matches, the whetstone, lard cans

1. **Bienvenidos** (byĕn-bē-nē′*th*ōs): Spanish for "safe arrival," or "welcome."
2. **Mi casa es su casa** (mē kä′sä ĕs sū kä′sä): Spanish for "my house is your house."

for cooking, two blankets, even the sheepskins 7 on the floor. Most important of all, Sixto had left food strung in a tree. Cloyd lowered the food down and inventoried it. He'd never guessed Sixto would leave this much for him. The sack of flour was here, with the baking powder and salt already mixed in. He could make all the "fat ones" he wanted. Sixto had left cornmeal too, lard, a sack of beans, coffee, even sugar. Cloyd counted four dozen assorted canned goods, including tuna, chicken, pork, peaches, plums, cherries.

8 He packed all he could carry. Cloyd worked quickly, wanting to return to the bears as soon as he could. He had room for only half the food. He tucked the whetstone into his pack and tied on the big snowboots. When he'd lashed the long snowshoes to the pack, he was done.

9 It was several days later, as Cloyd was bringing the cubs across the Divide, over the grassy slopes high above the tree line, that he heard the plane. He was heading for the drainages of the Pine River that felt like home and would eventually lead him back to Walter Landis. He'd always hurried the cubs to cover when planes approached, but this time there was nowhere to hide. Cloyd began to run, with his heavy pack bouncing from side to side on his back. It was much heavier than it used to be. The cubs could have run much faster if he wasn't holding them back.

The plane passed over the Divide, a thousand feet above him perhaps. He hoped wildly that the pilot hadn't been looking his way. Now he realized that he should have searched out a rugged spot to cross the Divide, one with plenty 10 of hiding places. At any rate, he shouldn't have run. He should have frozen, made a tent of himself and the leaning backpack that he could have hidden the cubs under.

Too late now. The plane banked and

THE NOVEL

returned, this time flying low. Cloyd huddled with the bears next to a rock sticking out of the tundra, but it was no use. The damage was done. It was that same plane, white under the wings, red on top, only with a new windshield. It buzzed him so closely that he even got a **11** glimpse of the pilot, in a gray shirt, with hair that looked like it had been cut by a helicopter flying upside down.

What did it matter? Cloyd kept telling himself. They couldn't catch him and take the cubs. Now he was down in the timber, now he was on his guard.

12 Every day the game warden came looking, buzzing all around the mountains like an angry insect. For six days Cloyd kept on the move, visiting basins high above the Pine River that had no trails up them. The Dog Rincon. The Grouse Rincon. Basins with no names. At last he'd come to a deep pond at the head of the rugged Cañon Paso, where he felt secure. The pond hadn't completely iced over yet, and he was catching fish out of it.

The leaves were off the aspens now, blown off by two days of high winds. The first week of October was ending, and the skies were turning gray. He was wearing many layers of clothes now, even his wool gloves and his wool cap in the daytime. Sixto Archuleta's snowboots, rubber on the outside with leather uppers, insulating felt on the inside, were keeping his feet warm and dry. And he had the snowshoes in case he would need them.

There was cover at one edge of the pond, a dense spruce forest. No trail led up the Cañon Paso toward him; there was only the kind of hard going that he and the bears had managed as they sought out the most rugged and pro- **17** tected places. That game warden, Haverford, **13** would never find him. It made his heart go fast—being hunted, being an outlaw. It made him feel like a grizzly himself.

Every day he was practicing with the sling. One time out of six he could hit a piece of granite no bigger than a basketball, across the pond.

He would have felt better if he hadn't lost the bearstone. It happened when they'd first come to this pond. He'd been showing the bearstone to the cubs, telling them about it. Brownie's **14** tongue had quickly flashed, and she'd swallowed the bearstone right before his eyes.

He hoped losing the bearstone wasn't a bad sign. He still hoped he could find the bearstone in one of Brownie's scats.

Maybe the game warden had given up and wasn't hunting him and the bears after all, Cloyd thought. But he knew better. He had a bad feeling.

15 At least Walter Landis would know by now that he was okay. Walter would have been told about him being spotted by the airplane. Walter would have been told that he was with the cubs, that he was okay.

The old man would be pleased. Walter would like the idea of Cloyd hiding out from that game warden who wanted to bring in the last grizzlies.

By now the game warden must have a pretty good idea, Cloyd realized, about how those two cubs got out of those cages. It must have made him mad.

It was hard to understand the government. **16** The grizzly woman had said that some of the government people had spent the whole summer trying to find grizzlies in Colorado so they could protect them and bring more. Then there were other government people, like the game warden, who'd like it better if the last grizzly bears were in the zoo.

These cubs were still living wild. He'd been **17** careful not to feed them his food. It was okay for him to graze along with them, but it couldn't work the other way around.

They'd said there wasn't even much chance of one cub surviving. So far they were both

11
Cloyd recognizes uniform and haircut of game warden.

12
Simile. Compares noise of plane to noise of insect to reinforce idea that plane and its pilot are pests.

13
Thoughts of being hunted and being an outlaw cause emotional reaction in Cloyd.

14
Symbol. Bearstone is symbol of Cloyd's identity, and it is now inside bear. Symbolically, Cloyd has become one with bear.

15 Making Inferences
Why would warden speak to Walter about Cloyd? Answers will vary. Perhaps to report sighting; perhaps to question Walter about Cloyd's plans.

16
Irony. It is ironic that government agencies work for opposite results.

17 Summarizing
Why does Cloyd not feed cubs his food? Answers will vary. Cubs need to behave as wild animals to be able to survive after Cloyd leaves.

18
Cloyd's instincts prove correct once again.

19 Drawing Conclusions
Why is Cloyd careful to step only on rocks? So he will not leave footprints hunters can follow.

20
Metaphor. Compares Rusty to medieval lord who owns large amounts of land and controls all people living on it.

21
Personification. Lungs have human ability to scream for air, meaning they badly need oxygen.

22 Synthesizing
How might the unfinished sentence be completed?
". . . the men must not be near them."

doing okay. Why wouldn't the game warden just leave him alone to help them beat the odds?

He hadn't thought that anyone could track **21** him to this place at the head of the Cañon Paso. All the same, he had a bad feeling, and he was keeping sentry now on the bald spot far below.

18 His fears and his waiting had been justified. Down the mountain, three men were moving across the bald spot. Cloyd recognized the big man in the lead by his bright shock of red hair and the full red beard.

Cloyd's heart was suddenly in his throat. There, right down there, was the man he hated, coming hard and fast after him. Rusty Owens, who'd gone to Alaska. Rusty, the red-haired man, the man who killed the bear. Now **22** Rusty was entering the trees, leading two others up the faint game trail.

Cloyd knew there was only one man who could have tracked him here—the best hunter, trapper, and tracker in the San Juan Mountains. Rusty wasn't in Alaska any longer.

All the men had snowshoes strapped to their backpacks.

The cubs had seen the men too, or smelled them, and they were just as alarmed as Cloyd.

No need to strike his tent; it was rolled up in his pack. He only kept it for an emergency. He hadn't used it since the day he'd met those cubs and fed them fish and they had followed him up to Lost Lake.

19 Up and out of the Cañon Paso he climbed, careful to step only on rocks. Brownie and Cocoa seemed to know too. They knew they were being hunted and they seemed to be aware that their tracks would give them away.

Cloyd was determined. *Rusty Owens wouldn't catch him.* He couldn't allow that to happen. Rusty Owens was a proud man. Rusty thought **20** he could do anything. Rusty Owens thought he was the lord of the mountains. But Rusty Owens wouldn't catch him and these cubs.

He climbed up and over, into the basin of the Rincon La Osa, without the men catching sight of him. All the while his lungs were screaming for air. He had climbed more than a thousand feet above the timberline, almost straight up, without ever stopping to slow his heart or catch his breath.

Deeper and deeper into the mountains Cloyd withdrew, zigzagging in a route he judged would be impossible to follow. He kept going through the dusk, finding a place to ball up with the cubs only when he couldn't possibly continue. Before dawn he was up and moving. Brownie and Cocoa understood his urgency. They often stopped to look and listen. Nothing. If the bears, with their senses, couldn't hear or **22** smell those men . . . He was beginning to feel safe.

A view of the San Juan Mountains, Weminuche Wilderness, Colorado.

Now that he was so close to the Divide, he determined to cross back over to the Rio Grande side. At the head of the Pine River, he skirted the low meadows of Weminuche Pass. In the trees high above the pass, he began to work his way west toward the Ute Creeks by way of the northern slopes of the Rio Grande Pyramid. No trails could be found on that northern side of the Pyramid. It was wild and it was rugged. When it was safe again, he could visit Sixto's camp on Middle Ute Creek and resupply with the food there.

The wind blew hard all night the second night, and the snow began to fall on the third day. Daytime arrived dark and never turned brighter. The snow fell silently hour after hour in flakes big as half-dollars. The wind was gone, it was uncannily quiet. He sheltered with the cubs in a dense cluster of spruce where almost no snow was reaching the ground.

The snow began to fall even more heavily at night. Cloyd had seen snow fall this fast, this long only once the previous winter at the farm down on the Piedra.

The following day the storm raged on, this time with powerful gusts of wind that blew the snow from the trees. Cloyd stayed put. He had the snowshoes but it would be crazy to travel in this storm. He was sure that he'd shaken the men behind him. Even if he hadn't, the snow had come along to cover his tracks.

After two days, the storm had mostly cleared. Squalls were still dropping heavy snow here and there, but the sun was beginning to shine through now and again.

In the openings among the trees, four feet of snow covered the ground.

It was bitterly cold in the wake of the storm. Moving would warm him up. He was wearing all his layers, from his thermal underwear to his bright-red mountaineering shell, and still he was cold. It was time to be moving again. He started out on the snowshoes.

The cubs followed in the trail that Cloyd broke as he headed in the direction of the Ute Creeks. This was an altogether different world from the mountains he'd known two days before. Everything was softer, rounder, quieter. With the white of the snow and the dark green of the spruce timber, the world had only two colors now.

To his surprise, the cubs started looking back, as if they were being followed. They kept looking back, when there was nothing to be seen back there. They yawned with anxiety as Cloyd had seen dogs yawn.

Cloyd trusted the cubs' senses. He shoed faster. If those men were back there, they were using his packed trail, while he had to break the snow.

He was about five hundred feet below the

© Tom Till/DRK Photo

23
Heavy cloud cover makes day darker than usual, but it is not as dark as night.

24
This snowstorm is unusually heavy.

25 Analyzing
In what ways is it a different world? Snow has changed look of place, but statement suggests change is more profound than this.

26
Figurative Language. Cloyd walks faster, wearing snowshoes.

27 Drawing Conclusions
What does this fact imply? Men are able to move faster on packed snow.

5
Cloyd puts spruce branches down on ground to lie on.

6
Metaphor. Compares his mood to bird flying high.

7
Metaphor. Compares sunlight reflecting off snow to ball or other object bouncing off hard surface.

8 Analyzing
Why does Cloyd stop running?
He realizes there has been an attack of some kind, and he wants to approach tent cautiously.

9
Cloyd explains why bears cannot be allowed to eat human food.

10
Exaggeration. Compares Cloyd's sorrow and disappointment to mourning for dead person.

11 Making Inferences
Why does Cloyd feel responsible for what has happened?
Answers will vary. Maybe he thinks camp was attacked by someone looking for him.

It was a strange feeling, knowing that for all the world he was dead now. Walter would hear that he was dead, his grandmother and his sister would hear that he was dead. Yet his heart was pounding in his chest, strong with the will to live.

As it was getting dark, Cloyd kicked out a well in the snow down to ground level, and then he cut enough spruce branches to make a bed six inches thick. The worst cold always seemed to come right up through the ground. His shelter had no roof, but the snow walls cut the wind. There was nothing to do but lie down and pull the bears close against him. He maneuvered his arms back through the sleeves of his thermal underwear, his flannel shirt, his sweatshirt, his pile jacket, and his rain shell. He had to keep his hands close against his body, or his fingers would freeze.

The bears huddled close. Exhausted, he fell asleep with one bear against his belly and chest, and the other wrapped around his head.

*   *   *

Cloyd came off the mountain at the place where East and Middle Ute Creeks flowed together, and he turned up the middle branch. The cubs were gnawing the willows along the stream, finding the bark to their liking. Cloyd carried the one snowshoe under his arm as he followed the line of trees along the edge of the meadow. There was little snow under the trees, and only a foot and a half had fallen on the meadow. Not nearly so much had fallen down on the Ute Creeks as above on the slopes of the Pyramid.

Sixto's tent would be waiting for him only a few miles up the meadow. His spirits were soaring. The bears were finding the white world to their liking. They were striking the snow with their forepaws, rolling in it, biting it, chasing their shadows. As Cloyd walked the edge of the trees, Brownie and Cocoa stayed out in the

meadow, clawing here and there through the snow for grass and roots.

At first glance Cloyd couldn't tell what was wrong. But magpies meant mischief, and he could hear magpies squawking up there around the campsite. Usually they congregated around a carcass. Cloyd was squinting into the bright sunlight bouncing off the snow, and he could see just enough to know something was wrong with the tent. He started to run. The tent was all out of shape, barely standing. The storm?

Once Cloyd saw the gashes in the canvas, he stopped running. As he walked up on the scene, his eyes took in the devastation. Everything was ripped and strewn and destroyed. The canned goods had been set up along a log and then exploded with shots from a high-powered rifle. Brownie and Cocoa were lapping at the remains of their contents. "No!" he shouted, and lunged at them, striking one and bowling the other over. "Get out of there!" he raged. "Leave this garbage alone! You have to be wild! You get around garbage, there'll be people there! Some of them will be afraid of you! They'll kill you!"

The cubs kept away and watched, all abashed and intimidated, as he picked up the shredded remains of a can of stew. The cubs had never seen him all mad like this. Good, he thought.

Cloyd snatched up an empty feed sack and began picking up the mess. When he was done he tossed the sack into the branches of a tree, and then he turned to the mutilated tent. Only one pole was holding it up. Even the guy lines to the pegs had been cut. All around the campsite there were pieces of destruction, some showing and others hidden under the snow.

He went around picking things up, turning the objects over in his hands, mourning for everything that had been lost. He was sorry for himself, but he felt even worse for Sixto. The old sheepherder had left him his whole camp, all his valuable possessions. What would he ever say to Sixto, how would he make up for it?

Who would do this? Why? Why would anyone do this?

Then his eye fell on something these people had brought and left here—a big, empty whiskey bottle. Now he could see what had happened. Whoever it was, they'd gotten drunk and done all this for no reason at all, only to amuse themselves with their own meanness.

The sheepherder stove had been broken into pieces, the chimney had been flattened, the food bag had been cut down out of the tree and all its contents slashed and scattered. The flashlight Sixto had retrieved from the entrance of the mine had been smashed. Inside the tent, Cloyd found the pots and pans crushed, the blankets tossed around. Where was the box of big kitchen matches? Seven matches, soaked under the snow that had fallen in through the wide gashes in the canvas, were all he could find.

12 Seven matches.

He wanted to get away from this place, to lead the cubs away as quickly as he could. But first he had to collect everything that might be useful: the matches, a skillet, one dented cooking pot, a big spoon, the remains of the bag of flour, a little lard, a can of peaches and one of apricots that the marksmen had missed, the beans the magpies hadn't already carried away, all the parachute cord[1] and rope he could salvage, pieces of canvas, the two blankets that hadn't been damaged at all, and the small folding army shovel the vandals had also overlooked. With a strip from one of the blankets, he could make a headband to save his ears from the cold. He bundled all this salvage into the largest piece of canvas, and he slung it over his shoulder and walked off.

The snow on the meadows was melting. Not **13** fast, but it was melting. The sun was out, and his wool gloves were drying. He was angry, and he was hurt, but he felt himself lifting with **14** determination. He wasn't going to let this drive him out of the mountains.

Cloyd made his camp where he had camped with the old man, at the second site along East Ute Creek. He made a low-ceilinged lean-to of cut branches for a shelter. He retrieved the bearskin from the tree where he had cached it, and used it for a third blanket at night. Storms could blow through the Window high above **15** and around the Pyramid. He resolved to carry through what he had started. Now he wanted to see the cubs safely into winter.

The problem was denning. The grizzly woman and the game warden who had cared about bears had agreed that denning was the problem. The cubs might not dig a den from instinct. If they did, they might only scratch out an approximation of one, which wouldn't take **16** them through the winter. They would freeze to death in a den that wasn't good enough.

Maybe how to dig the den was something they would have learned from their mother.

He could dig the den for them. He had the folding camp shovel. But he knew they wouldn't den for a while yet. If he could find any food to add to the meager supplies he'd brought from the ruins of Sixto's camp, he could stay with them awhile. There were snowshoe hares[2] around; he'd seen one or two, almost completely turned white. Every day he practiced long hours with the sling, with smooth round rocks he fished out of the creek.

Cloyd was putting off using the seven matches. The sun had dried them out and they looked serviceable, but he had to save them. He ate the can of apricots first, and then, after a few days, the can of peaches. He savored each **17** bite, and he drank the juice slowly. Hunger was

---

1. **parachute cord:** a thin, sturdy, smooth type of rope.

2. **snowshoe hares:** large rabbits that turn brown in the summer and white in the winter.

---

12 Analyzing
Why does narrator repeat this phrase and set it up as a separate paragraph? To emphasize that Cloyd would have to get by with far less than he thought he would have.

13
Despite setback, Cloyd has some reason to feel good about things.

14
Personification. Events at Sixto's camp have power to drive Cloyd away, but he will not let them do so.

15
Despite hardships he has already experienced, Cloyd is determined to make sure cubs survive.

16 Finding Cause and Effect
Why is a good den essential to keep from freezing to death? A good den will protect cubs from snow and bitter cold that will come.

17
Personification. Hunger has human or animal ability to chew at Cloyd's insides.

gnawing at him, but it was a pain he could tolerate if he kept his mind off it. He was good at doing without things; that was something that went way back with him.

18   There was another idea in the back of his mind. He realized this idea had been planted when he'd first found the arrowhead. All the deer and all the elk hadn't dropped to lower elevations when the snowstorm had come. There was a big bull elk he was seeing every day on the meadow, digging up the grass. If he **21** could make an arrow for his arrowhead, and a bow for the arrow, and if he could sneak up **19** extremely close...

It took three of his matches to start a fire. He was hungry, and he cooked up a few *gordas*. He had half a dozen arrows ready that he'd fashioned from dead willow. He hardened the points of five in the fire. It might be possible to **20** take small game without an arrowhead.

It was easy to come by the feathers. With bits of his *gordas* he lured the gray jays in close, then baited the spot under the deadfall trap[3] he'd constructed. A tug on a piece of cord, and the log would sometimes drop on the bird. Brownie and Cocoa watched his technique with admiration. The cubs could eat as many jays as he could provide.

His bow, when he was done with it, looked **22** barely sturdy enough. It might work if he was lucky. Parachute cord would have to do for a bowstring. With thread he'd taken from the seams in the canvas, he tied the feathers to the arrow shaft and hafted the arrowhead to the arrow.

The days of mid-October Cloyd spent hunt- **23** ing, mostly for that solitary bull elk that was still too stubborn to abandon the high country. Cloyd stalked it in the twilight, in the cold, gray

hours on either side of the ever-shortening days. Despite his gloves and snowboots, his fingers and toes always ached with cold. During the day he would lie shivering in wait beside the elk trails, waiting for his prey to walk by at close range.

He'd heard stories of animals that would offer themselves to the hunter, simply show themselves up close and allow the hunter to take their lives as a gift. The big bull elk knew Cloyd was hunting him, but this elk hadn't grown so old by being generous. Cloyd could remember times when deer had walked right into his and Walter's camp on this very meadow. One morning while they were eating breakfast, three spike bucks[4] had walked into camp, big-eyed, curious, to within fifteen feet of them as Cloyd and Walter stood there sipping cocoa and just watching.

But those curious young deer were gone. There was only this one enormous, cautious elk with antlers three feet high and just as wide.

When he wasn't hunting the elk, Cloyd was practicing with the sling. There was a scree slope that came down to the meadow on the other side of the creek, and there was a big marmot who taunted him from those rocks. He'd let many a stone fly at that whistle pig, and he'd come within a whisker several times.

The days were coming so clear, bright, and blue, one after the next, that it was an afterthought when he realized he needed to make another snowshoe. Winter could come back at any time. He knew he wasn't thinking well. He should have made the snowshoe even before the bow and arrow.

For two days he worked on the snowshoe, until he knew it was strong enough. He fashioned the frame from green willow branches, and he wove canvas strips and smaller branches

---

3. **deadfall trap:** a trap constructed by balancing logs or weights so that when they are disturbed, the animal is pinned beneath.

4. **spike bucks:** male deer with antlers that have no branches.

to make the webbing. Canvas strips served for the binding to hold his boot.

24 All the time he was keeping track of the days, marking them on a stick with his knife. The day of the slide had been the eleventh of October. Ten days had passed since then. The days were growing ominously short, and his hunger was hurting him all the time. He used two more matches to start a fire to make his last pot of beans, his last *gordas*.

▶ It had to be time, he thought, for making the den. The beans and *gordas* gave him the strength he needed. He took the cubs and ranged the mountainside up above the meadow, up in the spruce trees. Between the meadow and the barren heights above the tree line, a dense forest of spruce swathed the steep slopes at the foot of the Continental Divide. It was the kind of site Sixto had described, a north-facing slope that would lie in the shadows all winter, out of the path of the sun. All winter long the Divide's towering ridge, which included the Window, would block the sun. In the shadows, the snows would accumulate deep **25** and undisturbed to shelter the den over the entire span of deep winter.

At last Cloyd found a place he liked, a steep bank under a massive spruce, whose roots would hold the ceiling and keep it from collapsing. ◀

The ground was frozen and made for hard digging at first. It was slow work with the tiny shovel. But it was a good tool and sturdy. He could use it as a shovel or adjust the blade at right angles and use it as a pick.

The cubs showed little interest until the morning of the second day, when he broke **26** through into unfrozen dirt. They began digging beside him. He kept the entrance small, only big enough for him to crawl through.

Cloyd tunneled back eight feet before he **27** started making the sleeping chamber. As he chipped out dirt and rock and pushed it behind

him, the cubs pushed it out the rest of the way. All the while he talked to them. "This is where you're going to make your big sleep. Any day now. You go in here and fall asleep real soon, Cocoa. You got that, Brownie?"

Without food he couldn't work, and so he used up the last of it and the last of his matches.

Late the third day the work was done. The den extended fourteen feet into the mountain. Strong roots in the ceiling convinced Cloyd he'd made a den that couldn't collapse on the cubs. The sleeping chamber was round, six feet across and four feet high.

28 Every day after that, he visited the den. He would go inside the den each day with the bears, bringing soft branches with him, hoping they would lie down on the branches and go to sleep for the winter. They joined him in lining the den with more spruce boughs, but they showed no interest in staying inside the den. They would soon go outside to play on the slope, while he would try to call them back into the den.

Somehow they knew. For some reason, the time wasn't right.

Or else they didn't have the idea at all.

He was so hungry, he'd often stumble from lightheadedness. But he was so close now, he couldn't turn and leave. Any day now, the cubs should den up.

The day came when he had his chance at the solitary elk. He was kneeling behind a bush when the elk appeared in the little clearing along one of the paths it had been using. Cloyd had been daydreaming that he was standing in a hot shower and letting the steaming water **29** pour over and over him. Suddenly he saw, like an apparition, the immense antlers, the great head, the dark ruff around the neck. With a few more steps, the elk was standing in full view, not twenty feet away. Then the bull began to dig in the snow with a front hoof. Cloyd bent the bow back, trying to get enough force

24
Setting. Narrator reveals date to readers.

25 Summarizing
How will snow shelter den? By piling up in front of opening, snow will keep wind out of den.

26
Dirt deeper in hole is not frozen because cold air has not penetrated to it.

27
Cloyd and cubs work as team.

28 Summarizing
Why does Cloyd visit den? He wants to encourage cubs to hibernate.

29
Simile. Compares sighting elk to seeing supernatural vision.

SOCIAL STUDIES LINK
Students interested in the history of the Spanish conquistadors or those interested in coins might want to research Spanish gold pieces to find out how they were mined and minted in the Americas. You might suggest that some students research the coins and others research the conquests and explorations of the Spanish. Both groups of students could then present the information they collect.

30 Analyzing
Why would Cloyd thank animal for its life? Cloyd feels kinship with all nature and sees animal as helper in keeping him alive.

31
In cold weather in past, Cloyd could go inside house or sit by campfire to get warm. Now he can do neither.

32
Personification. Cold has human power to seek vulnerable parts of Cloyd.

33
Metaphor. Compares Cloyd's body to predator that attacks itself to keep itself alive.

34
No matter how badly Cloyd wants bears to hibernate, he cannot force them to do so until their instincts tell them to.

Chapter 23

1
Cloyd has more important things on his mind, like finding food to keep from starving.

2 Analyzing
What does narrator mean by saying nights are long? There is less daylight, but narrator means nights seem longer to Cloyd than they really are because he cannot sleep well.

3
Figurative Language. Mountain is higher than clouds, and its peak seems to be set on clouds.

4
Simile. Compares voices to music to suggest they sound good to Cloyd.

5
Ditch is used to irrigate farm, and valve and gate allow Walter to regulate amount of water he uses.

602

---

behind this one piece of stone to find the animal's heart. . . .

Before he was quite ready, the bow made a cracking sound. He let the arrow fly anyway. The elk was gone.

30 At once he realized that he had forgotten to thank the animal for its life. Even when he slaughtered goats and sheep, he had always done that.

Cloyd didn't see the elk after that. In the night it snowed again, and even the last stubborn solitary bull elk in the high country knew it was time to leave.

It wasn't a big snow, only six inches. But four or five days in a row, these snows came. When he could venture out, he gnawed on willow bark alongside the bears, and once they led him to a thicket of serviceberries where the berries had dried in place rather than dropped to the ground.

It turned much colder, and the wind blew
31 until he thought the spruces might break. This cold was worse than any he had known before. He was wearing the bearskin again. He laced it tight with parachute cord around his limbs and
32 up his belly and chest. The cold still found his bones, but it couldn't kill him. Every day he led the cubs to the den, and went into the den with them and begged them to stay.

Their stomachs were shrinking, he knew. The grizzly woman had said that for a week or so before hibernation, they ate almost nothing and didn't need food.
33 But he did. He was starving. His body had turned on him some time before and had been eating its own fat and then his muscles. He had his chance at a snowshoe hare with the sling, but it was white against the snow, and his stone barely missed. "Sleep, bears," he pleaded,
34 "while I still have a chance to go home."

23

1 It was November now, Cloyd guessed, but he'd forgotten some time before to make the notches in the stick and so he'd lost track. The temperatures were dropping below zero, how far below he couldn't guess. The creek was iced over except for pockets here and there. As he walked about, the snow crunched loudly under his boots. The nights were so much longer than the days. He slept in the den with the cubs now. He should have thought of it sooner, but he hadn't been thinking well. It was so much warmer inside the earth and out of the wind. The air in the confines of the den was warmed by the breathing of the bears, and his own breath. Inside the earth, with his clothes and the bearskin and the two blankets, he wasn't cold.

2 The nights were long. Cloyd's sleep was starved and restless. He'd lie awake remembering White Mesa, the aromatic sagebrush, the smell of juniper wood burning. He'd drift into sleep seeing the shapes of the mesas and the
3 slickrock rims of the hidden canyons. Above the mesas and the canyons, Blue Mountain
4 would be riding on a cloud. He could hear his grandmother's and his sister's voices, like music. They were gathering piñon[1] nuts. He was calling to them, but they couldn't hear him. He could hear a raven thrashing by, but he couldn't see it. The moon was rising over a sheer red wall. A goat was blatting, and water was trickling over a pour-off.

Twice in the den, he dreamed of the farm. The first time, it was raining and raining and would never quit. The cottonwood trees, bare except for a few golden leaves, were collapsing into the raging river. The old man was stand-
5 ing there, watching the river eat away at the headgate, where the big valve in the concrete

---

1. **piñon** (pǐn′yŏn′): a small pine tree with edible seeds.

---

gate let the water into his ditch. Every minute huge chunks of dark earth were tearing loose and collapsing into the river. "There's nothing we can do!" the old man cried, and he threw up his hands. Then the river broke through and it went tearing down the pasture in a <u>surging</u> flood. The house and the barn were immediately stranded on an island, with the river raging by around both sides. Before he woke, Cloyd saw the water all gone, but so was the big barn, and there was nothing but boulders where there used to be hayfields and pastures and an orchard.

The second time he dreamed of the farm, he'd just gotten off the bus from school where it dropped him on the highway. He walked that mile to the farm all night in his dreams, knowing somehow that he would find the old **6** man dead inside the house when he eventually got there.

It wasn't only in the den that Cloyd dreamed. He dreamed in the daytime too, in the sunshine or in the shadows or with the snow falling **7** on his hair. There was nothing to do now but wait, wait for the cubs to den or for his own body to eat itself up from the inside.

There hadn't been one certain day that had come along when he'd made this decision to stay until the end. It was all the days passing, one day after the other, as he'd grown accustomed to his hunger and accepted it. He knew now that he would die here. He would never have the strength to leave. It was a strange fate for him, that he would choose this death, that he would die for these two bears. Yet it was a death that belonged to him, and he could accept it.

Next summer the grizzly woman would return, and she would find these bears alive.

Every day now, Cloyd stood in place for long **8** periods of time, doing the steps of the bear dance in place. Barely moving his feet, he danced the three steps forward, three steps back. He was dancing himself into the dream

Painting of bears dancing. Ute.
Photo courtesy of the Colorado Historical Society

6 Expressing an Opinion
What might these dreams mean? Answers will vary. Maybe they symbolize that Cloyd will never return to farm. Maybe they have no special meaning but are result of Cloyd's hunger.

7
Cloyd has put himself completely at mercy of nature in form of bears.

8 Making Inferences
Why does Cloyd turn now to Bear Dance? Answers will vary. Perhaps he hopes to receive help and guidance from his spirit helper.

that had started when he'd found the bear-stone, maybe even before that, when he was little and first heard the thunder coming off the big resonating drum, the scratching and growling of bears.

As he danced himself into a trance every day, his traveling soul would leave his body, as it had left his body the time he had risen above the Bear Dance and seen the dancing from above. His traveling soul soared above East Ute Creek, and he could see three bear forms down there—two cubs and the grizzly with a human face standing upright, barely shuffling its feet, three steps forward, three steps back.

His traveling soul lifted up, up, until it was soaring over the Divide, above the Window, above the Rio Grande Pyramid. All the world was cloaked with snow, all the thousand peaks were softened and all the valleys softened, and it was a world more silent and restful than any he had ever known.

When the light turned down every day, he led the cubs back up the steep slope to the den.

He began making notches in the stick again, but his mind no longer turned the notches into meaning. He no longer differentiated between the dreams of his denning sleep and his waking dreams on the meadow. It was all a dream that he was living inside of now, a dream not far from death.

Yet his body was stubborn and had reserves greater than he would have known. He was still standing, still doing the bear dance.

His traveling soul was out of his body and up on the Divide. The sun was high in the sky; the berries were ripe; he was eating sweet berries in a thicket high on the Divide. With no warning came a terrible roar, and he fell back onto the ground. An enormous bear with brown fur tipped with silver was standing over him, and it had an arrow in its neck and one in its chest. Blood was streaming from the bear's wounds and from its mouth, and it was shaking its head

back and forth and roaring horribly.

"What do you want with me?" he said to the bear.

"Who are you?" the bear roared.

"I'm a Weminuche Ute," he answered. He knew that he owed this bear for something and that his time had come to give back. "I know why you have come," he told the bear. "I give you permission now."

He watched from outside as the great bear tore the flesh from his bones and left them scattered and gleaming on the ground.

Now the bear reappeared with no arrows and no blood streaming from his wounds.

He didn't know where the song came from, but he knew there was a song he was supposed to sing to this bear, and he knew the words to the song. He sang,

> "Whu! Bear!
> Whu Whu!
> So you say
> Whu Whu Whu!
> You come.
> You're a fine young man
> You Grizzly Bear
> You crawl out of your fur.
> You come
> I say Whu Whu Whu!
> I throw grease in the fire.
> For you
> Grizzly Bear
> We are the same person!"

The bear was pleased with his song. "Here, I will help you," the bear said, and together they began reassembling his bones. When his skeleton was fully reassembled, the bear touched each of his bones and called them by name, and new flesh grew on his bones.

He was himself again.

Now the bear had the head of a bear and the body of a human being. "Who are you?" Cloyd asked.

"I'm the keeper of the animals," the bear-man replied. "Listen carefully. There is one animal, white as the snow, that stays among the peaks even in winter. Take your best weapon **15** and climb high until you find this animal. You have my permission to take him to sustain your own life."

16 When Cloyd's feet came to rest, he remembered every detail of his dream.

17 The following morning he shed the bearskin and told the cubs to stay behind. They watched him go. He could still see them down there on the snowbound meadow, far below, when he had cleared the tree line and was inching toward the Divide.

He wasn't wearing the snowshoes. These slopes had already shed their snow once, and the snow didn't lie deep enough as yet to slide again. He couldn't climb but two or three steps at a time before he ran out of air and out of strength. He barely had the strength to lift his legs, but he kept climbing.

With a glance over his shoulder he noticed **18** his tracks, and, it was curious to note, he was leaving the tracks of a bear.

He was living inside the spirit world now.

After a time the Window came into view high above him. Toward the Window he climbed, the center point of his spirit world. Vaguely he knew he'd been there before, that it was important to him, this towering gap in the sky. He'd been there more than once. But he couldn't remember when or how, or what had happened there.

And so the Window drew him on and up. When he'd nearly reached it, and the towering **21** rockwalls on either side seemed to take up all the world except the gap of sky between them, he sat down and looked back the way he'd come. There were peaks strung all along the horizon, jagged snowbound peaks that seemed familiar, but he couldn't remember their **19** names. He wondered why he had come here.

He wondered what he was doing on the top of the world, when it was all cloaked in winter.

He sat there a long time. He couldn't think of a reason to go up or to go down. After a time something odd caught his eyes, something on the slope not so far away. Two strips of black in the snow, curling away from each other. Raven **20** feathers? Now they were moving as if they were alive, and moving in unison. He blinked and looked closer. An animal was moving toward him from across the slope.

A mountain goat, he realized. The "feathers" were the black horns of a mountain goat. Then he remembered who he was and why he had climbed this mountain. Slowly, he took the sling from his waist and fitted a stone to it, keeping another ready in his left hand.

The white goat kept coming on, along the trace of a goat path, walking right toward him. Now he could see that there were two more goats following at some distance.

The leader was a yearling, filled with curiosity. Its winter coat had grown out long and shaggy, and all Cloyd could see to aim at were the horns and the eyes and the nose.

When the goat was thirty feet away from him, it stopped and stood still, nibbled the lichens on a rock, then turned its head sideways as if to give him a better target. Cloyd thanked the goat as he had thanked the many goats he had slaughtered when he was growing up with his grandmother, and then he whirled the sling.

The stone sank into the soft spot behind the goat's eye. The goat stood for a second, and then all four legs collapsed. Cloyd went to it and bled the goat with his knife. The animal's quivering ceased.

The liver was warm, and he chewed it slowly. At first it came back up, but then his stomach began to accept it.

Slowly, slowly, he carried the goat down the mountain on his shoulder, dragging it when he

---

15
Keeper of animals gives Cloyd advice about how to obtain food.

16
Personification. Cloyd's feet seem to operate on their own, as though they have life apart from him.

17 Drawing Conclusions
Why does Cloyd shed bearskin before he leaves? It is heavy and will be a burden to him as he climbs mountain.

18 Analyzing
Does Cloyd really leave tracks of bear? No, but in his mind's eye he sees bear tracks where there are really human tracks.

19
Cloyd does not remember his dream or permission of animal keeper.

20
Personification. Black strips have power to move.

21
Cloyd puts his experience slaughtering goats to good use.

22 Drawing Conclusions
Why is Cloyd interested in starting fire using bow drill?
He no longer has any matches, and he needs fire to cook goat.

23 Analyzing
Is Cloyd really out of hope?
Probably not. He has been in much worse situations before, and he has never given up. There is no reason to think he will give up now.

24
Cloyd begins to doubt he has done everything he can to make bow drill work.

25
Metaphor. Compares wad of tinder to bird's nest because it resembles one.

26
Figurative Language. Narrator describes high-pitched whine of bow as singing.

27
Cloyd has a hot meal for first time in weeks.

28
As Ursa has told Cloyd, refusal to eat is one sign hibernation is near.

29 Drawing Conclusions
Why do heart beat and breathing slow down? Bears have entered deep sleep of hibernation.

fell under its weight. As soon as he got down, he would skin it. He could make a hat out of that shaggy fur, a hat big enough to pull down over his ears.

The cubs were not as interested in food as he had thought they would be. They ate the heart and a few scraps of fat, but that was all.

When he denned with the cubs that night, he didn't dream. He was filled with purpose. All **22** he could think about were the components of the bow drill. He'd come very close to making fire on the blacktop behind the school that next-to-last day of the school year. He'd made plenty of smoke, almost fire.

The next day he worked all day long at mak-**27** ing a bow drill. The bow itself was only a third of the size of his failed hunting bow. Parachute cord was fine for the string, his teacher had said. His best arrow, cut short, would make a good drill. One end of the drill would turn in the brace he was carving for his palm. The other, sharper end would turn in the tiny **28** socket he dug out in the soft board he'd shaped from a dry piece of spruce.

He worked hard on his tinder, shredding bark and mixing it with needles and the finest of twigs.

The hard part had always been transferring his coals from the board to his tinder. That's when his coals had always gone out.

Seven times, the same thing happened. He'd worked all afternoon making tinder and work-**23** ing the bow. The daylight was going, and he was all out of hope.

"I don't mind failing," the old man had said, **29** "as long as I tried my best."

24 Haven't I tried my best? Cloyd thought. What else can I do?

Just then, he had an idea of his own. It was a simple idea, maybe a good one.

This time he dug a little depression in the **25** ground, and he placed his nest of tinder in the depression. When his kindling was ready, he

began to work the bow back and forth, faster and faster, as the cubs sat attentively and watched.

He was making plenty of smoke, and the fine coals that were being produced in the soft spruce were falling out of the socket and into the **26** nest of tinder. He kept making that bow sing. More and more coals were falling into the nest, without the need of being transferred from the board, and the tinder itself was smoking.

When the moment was right, he blew on the nest of tinder.

And it exploded into flame. He could see in the cubs' eyes, they thought he'd made magic.

He went to sleep with a warm belly. He'd made plenty of coals and then smothered them so they would burn slowly all night. But even if they weren't still alive in the morning, he could make fire again with the bow drill as the old Utes had.

The next four days, the cubs wouldn't eat any meat at all. They went in and out of the den, sniffing the wind, pacing. Cloyd could tell a big storm was coming in. Maybe this storm was what the cubs were waiting for.

The snow started to fall in the evening and fell hard all night. This was powder snow, the kind he remembered from midwinter at the farm. It fell for three days, and the cubs watched one evening from the tunnel as it covered up all their tracks into the den.

Apparently they were satisfied. No enemies would track them to their den. When they went to sleep that night, Cloyd heard their hearts slow down, beating more slowly than he had ever heard before. Their breath came much less often. In the morning, their hearts were beating even slower. He said good-bye to them, each one aloud by name. They didn't stir. He knew he could leave them now.

"Good-bye, Cocoa," he said again. "Good-bye, Brownie."

30 He squeezed quietly through the tunnel toward the soft light, and they didn't follow. Before he started down the slope, he watched a long time. The snow was beginning to pile up around the entrance, and it was quickly covering his tracks.

This was the big storm that was the proof of winter, the storm the bears had been waiting for. There'd be no melting here on these shadowy slopes until spring.

31 He knew what he had to do. He would cook up all the goat meat he could carry, he would fashion a pack out of canvas and rope, and he would start over the Divide. At its shortest, the route down the Pine River was twenty-five miles long. But he would travel far out of his way to avoid the avalanche chutes.

He waited three days after the storm. He could hear the snow sliding off the peaks, and he could wait until it had settled down.

32 Then he started out. If anyone had seen him, they would have thought they'd seen a snowshoeing grizzly.

But no one was in the backcountry, no one at all. No one marked his slow and painful progress, in a week's time, over the Divide and down the valley of the Pine.

No one saw him until he walked through the door of the Cowboy Bar, four miles beyond the Pine River trailhead, at the end of the plowed road around the northern tip of Vallecito Reservoir. The men and the women there didn't see the bearskin when he came to the door; it was rolled up in his pack with the blan-**33** kets. They saw a dark-skinned Ute boy with long, shaggy black hair under a strange peaked cap of white fur that was streaked with blood. His lips were blackened, cracked, and bleeding. He was wearing a red mountaineering shell, top and trousers, smeared with dried blood. They could see that he was unused to speaking. **36** They could see that he'd suffered much. None of the men and women there was saying a

word; they only stared. He said, "Would somebody drive me to Walter Landis's place on the Piedra River?"

*   *   *

He asked the man to drop him at the highway. He didn't want to drive in. He'd come all this way, he could walk a mile more.

It was just turning dark when he reached the orchard and caught sight of the old farmhouse **34** in the spruce trees. There was no smoke coming out of the chimney, and he was filled with dread. Walter Landis was dead, his heart was telling him. Walter is dead, I've come too late.

He went into the mudroom without knocking, and he didn't take off any of his clothes or his boots. He opened the next door and stood between the kitchen and the parlor. The house was cold. No lights were on.

He switched on the parlor light, and a figure stirred there in the far corner, in the easy chair. The old man was blinking to try to adjust to the light, and he was trying to understand who it was he was seeing there at the entrance of the parlor.

"It's me," Cloyd said. "It's me."

35 The old man looked, and looked again, and wiped his hands over his eyes, and stared.

"It's really me," Cloyd said, and then he walked over to the old man and put a hand on his shoulder.

"Lord, lord," the old man said, still uncertain. "Rusty said you were dead."

"It's cold in here," Cloyd said disapprovingly. "You forgot to make a fire."

Ashen-faced, Walter was struggling to his feet. "You're alive," he said. "You're not dead." The old man reached with both hands and placed them on Cloyd's shoulders. He was looking Cloyd up and down in wonder. "I'll bet **36** you've got a story to tell. . . . You look like something the cat spit out."

Cloyd took his medicine bundle from around

30
Connotation. Word "squeezed" suggests physical difficulty Cloyd has getting out of den.

31
Cloyd wastes no time getting ready to leave for home.

32 Drawing Conclusions
Why does Cloyd look like a grizzly in snowshoes? He is wearing bearskin to keep warm.

33
Description. Cloyd's appearance shows something of hardships he has endured.

34 Drawing Conclusions
Why does lack of smoke fill Cloyd with dread? In cold weather, Walter probably needs fire to keep warm. If there is no fire, there may be no Walter.

35
Walter is still groggy from sleep and does not recognize Cloyd at first.

36
Simile. Compares Cloyd to something cat spit out to indicate Cloyd's bedraggled appearance.

37

Cloyd cannot break his promise to Sixto not to tell anyone about mine.

38

Metaphor. Compares Walter's coming to life to someone returning from dead.

39 Making Inferences

Why does Rusty return bearstone to Walter? He knows it meant a lot to Cloyd, and he wants Walter to have it to remember Cloyd by.

40

Irony. Because Rusty killed what he thought was last grizzly in Colorado, it is ironic he starts rebuilding grizzly population.

Chapter 24

1

Personification. Sun has human ability to climb.

2

Cloyd does Bear Dance to help cubs awaken from hibernation.

3

Gift he wants is ability to see invisible things.

his neck and brought out the coin for Walter. It was hard to work the fingers on his right hand. The index finger was numb and useless from frostbite. But he brought out the coin for Walter between his thumb and his middle finger.

The old man reached for his reading glasses on the end table and put them on. "Spanish gold piece," he marveled. "Where'd you find it?"

37 "In the mountains," Cloyd said with a grin. It was as specific as he was ever going to get.

38 The old man was coming to life now. He grinned back. His skin was glowing red instead of pale white. "We've got to get a fire started...I nodded off...I was going to when I woke up. Say, have I got something for you...." The old man disappeared into his room, then quickly returned with a huge smile on his face and a small turquoise carving of a bear held out on **39** his palm. "Guess what Rusty found smack in a fresh bear scat back in the mountains."

Cloyd took it between his thumb and middle finger. Yes, it really was the bearstone.

"They can't take those cubs out of the mountains now," Cloyd said.

"No, they won't, and Rusty'll be awful happy to hear they're alive. It was you he was after rather than those bears....I sent him, Cloyd. I knew if anyone could find you, he could. Rusty was going to help bring you out and let you know they decided to leave those bears alone."

"Good," Cloyd said. He was so weary. "That's good," he said.

"Let me tell you a secret that will never go beyond the three of us. You know how Rusty's always been one to take the law into his own **40** hands....You'll never guess what he brought back from Alaska and let go in the Weminuche Wilderness in September: a yearling grizzly! Caught it in a culvert trap[2] and drove it back to

---

2. **culvert trap:** a trap made of a large metal pipe sealed shut at one end. When an animal steps inside the trap, it triggers a door to fall shut behind it.

Colorado. He said it had to be a male, to make up for the one he killed. He was hoping at least one of yours turned out to be a female."

Cloyd closed his fingers on the bearstone. "They both are."

24

1 The sun was climbing higher in the sky, and each day it cleared the Divide for a few more minutes. Each day the sun shone a few minutes longer on the steep slope below the Window and above East Ute Creek. All winter long, this slope had lain in the shadows in the grip of extreme cold. But the sun had arrived, and winter was giving way to spring even at 11,600 feet on the shady side of the Divide.

At 7,000 feet, on a farm at the edge of the wilderness, a Ute boy was doing the bear dance, even though it was early March and the Bear Dance wouldn't be held until nearly the end of **2** May. It was a tradition he had learned, that the people helped the bears to awaken after their long sleep.

He had selected a special place to perform his bear dance. He'd climbed high above the farm to the place where he had found the ancient blue stone carved in the image of a grizzly. He'd walked the ledge and now stood on the chalky floor of the cave high above the farm.

He hoped to dance until he could see things **3** that otherwise would be invisible. For a gift, he knew he should give something in return. He'd shinnied behind the slab that had fallen from the roof of the cave, and he had replaced the bearstone in the pottery jar where he had found it. To the remains of the infant buried there, wrapped in a robe of rabbit fur and turkey feathers, he'd whispered "Thank you." He didn't need to carry the bearstone any longer. The strength of the bear was inside him.

As he faced the snow-clad tips of the moun-

PORTFOLIO ASSESSMENT
A sequel tells what happens to literary characters after a work ends. Does Ursa return in the summer? Do she and Cloyd look for the bear cubs? Do the wardens return? Do the bear cubs survive? Does Walter survive the winter? What happens to Sixto, Rusty, and Tony? These are some of the questions a sequel might answer. Some students may be interested in writing a sequel or giving an oral presentation about what happens. Suggest that students plan their sequels carefully, showing growth and change in the characters while still complying with Hobbs's development of his characters. Consult with students to agree on how their sequels will be assessed. (See *Portfolio Assessment and Professional Support Materials*, especially the section entitled **Suggestions for Portfolio Projects**.)

tains showing above the canyon of the Piedra, his dancing deepened, until it carried him above the forests and even above the Divide. He **4** could see all over. On the slopes facing the sun, the first flowers were blooming and the first patches of grass greening. Water was trickling at the edges of the snowbanks, rivulets were rushing from underneath them, and marmots were whistling from the rockslides.

He saw the place he was looking for, a small hole in the snow beneath an immense spruce tree, on a slope he well remembered. There was a bit of water dripping from an icicle suspended above the hole.

A sharp nose was poking its way out, and now **5** a broad face, bright and curious, was looking out on the world all shining and new. A second face appeared, and two bears, one brown and one the shade of cocoa, pushed through the snow and sat in front of their den, sniffing the spring wind and the scent of growing things newly come to life.

6   He had found his dream.

He saw them tumble and slide down the slope with their old playfulness, and he saw them lope across the crusted white meadow in that shuffling gait of the grizzly, with their heads carried close to the ground.

They were going to grow wild and large and powerful, and go about their ancient ways. If he ever came across them again, they might stand **7** and pause and wonder. But then they would turn and go. They had known him in a bear's dream, and he had known them in his.

© Stephen J. Krasemann/DRK Photo

4
Description. Narrator describes sights of spring.

5
Figurative Language. World called shining and new because earth is renewed in spring.

6   Expressing an Opinion
What might Cloyd feel at this moment? Answers will vary. Happiness, joy, a sense of accomplishment, and hope for future are possibilities.

7
Cloyd does not expect bears to truly recognize him in future.

READING CHECK

1. He will not dig, touch walls, or tell anyone about mine (p. 588).
2. So cubs will not be attracted to sheep later and risk being shot (p. 592).
3. Camp has been destroyed (p. 598).
4. Heartbeats and breathing slow down more than in ordinary sleep (p. 606).
5. Cloyd returns it to where he had found it (p. 608).

FOR STUDY AND DISCUSSION

1. That people did not understand harmony that should exist between nature and humans.
2. Answers will vary. **a.** Sixto is much friendlier and more helpful than his reputation indicated he would be. **b.** Some students may express surprise, others approval, and others disapproval. Sixto knows why game wardens are out, and he feels justified throwing rock at them because he feels that their policies are wrong.
3. Most students will probably believe he would keep his promise. Cloyd is type of person who follows through on his commitments.
4a. He thinks Rusty is trying to hunt cubs. 4b. Most students will find it ironic that Rusty, who killed what was thought to be last grizzly in Colorado, has brought Alaskan grizzly to help reestablish grizzly population.
5a. Hunter who thanks animal shows respect for nature and connection to it. Hunter who takes and gives nothing does not see connection between nature and people. 5b. When Cloyd does not thank the elk, he fails to kill it; when he thanks the goat, he is successful.

Reading Check

1. What promise does Cloyd make to Sixto Loco?
2. Why is it necessary for Cloyd and the cubs to avoid the sheep?
3. What does Cloyd discover when he returns to Sixto's tent?
4. How does Cloyd know when the bear cubs are ready to den?
5. What happens to the bearstone at the end of the novel?

For Study and Discussion

Analyzing and Interpreting the Novel

1. On page 586 Sixto Loco tells Cloyd that "everyone was young and stupid back then, even the old people." What does he mean by this?

2a. Compare your impression of Sixto Loco with what you learned about him earlier in the novel. Is he what you expected or is he different? **b.** How do you feel about Sixto when he slings a rock at the airplane?

3. Did you believe Cloyd would keep his promise to Sixto? What about his character made you think so?

4a. Why doesn't Cloyd tell Rusty and the other men that he survived the avalanche? **b.** Do you find the end ironic—that is, not what you expected?

5a. Explain the difference between the hunter who thanks the animal for the gift of its life and "the hunter who only takes and gives nothing in return." **b.** How is this difference shown in the novel?

Literary Elements

Understanding the Novel
Theme

1. A **theme** is a central idea or insight about life or human nature expressed in a literary work. The main theme of *Beardance* might be expressed as follows: "Cloyd's relationship with bears and the natural world is part of a spiritual journey, in which he resolves to take responsibility and make a personal sacrifice to help others. Through his efforts he achieves a new spiritual understanding and becomes a wiser, stronger person." Or the theme might be summed up more simply, as in Cloyd's grandmother's saying: "Live in a good way. Give something back." Cite episodes or passages from the novel that illustrate this theme.

Crisis

2. The crisis can be considered the **turning point** of a story. It involves the actions or the decisions the major characters make to resolve the conflict. There may be more than one crisis leading up to the final outcome or resolution. The crisis comes before the climax of events in the story. **a.** Describe the major crisis that occurs in *Beardance*. **b.** List the significant events that lead up to this crisis.

Climax

3. The **climax** of a story marks the peak of greatest emotional intensity, interest, action, or suspense. The events leading up to this point reach their fullest development, and the sequence of events following the climax becomes inescapable. In which part of *Beardance* does the climax occur?

Resolution

4. The actions that bring a story to its conclusion form the **resolution.** The resolution in a novel follows the climax. How is the major conflict in *Beardance* resolved?

Writing About Literature

Analyzing the Quest

The story told in *Beardance* is a type of **quest** story. In a quest story a character is often on a personal search for enlightenment. Cloyd's quest is to come to a new level of spiritual understanding.

By the end of *Beardance*, Cloyd has succeeded in his quest. He now has hope that grizzlies will survive in Colorado. Along the way he has turned into a skillful hunter who can survive by using only what nature provides. He succeeds in making fire with the bow drill, and he learns to use a bow and arrow to get a food supply. Beyond these practical skills, he has matured emotionally. At the end of the novel, we see that he is at peace with himself and nature.

Using examples from the novel, write a short essay addressing Cloyd's coming-of-age. Find places in the novel that show evidence of Cloyd's growing strength and responsibility. How does he resolve the problems he faces at the beginning of the novel? What has he learned in the process? How has the completion of the quest changed him?

Focus on Writing a Letter

Writing a Business Letter

A **business letter** is a letter written to an individual or an organization for a specific purpose. The purpose of this kind of letter may be to request or order an item, to make a complaint, to express appreciation, or to request information. There are many other possible purposes for a business letter. Business letters use standard English and a formal tone.

A business letter consists of six parts: heading, inside address, salutation, body, closing, and signature. These parts are usually arranged on the page in **block form,** as shown in the sample below.

Your Address   (heading)
Today's Date

Name of the Person or   (inside address)
Company You Are Writing

Dear _____ :   (salutation)
_____ (body)
_____
_____
_____

Sincerely yours,   (closing)
_____   (your signed name)
_____   (your typed or printed name)

Ursa tells Cloyd that state and federal agencies might bring some grizzly bears to the San Juan Mountains from Yellowstone National Park (see page 554). Suppose that you want to find out more about the grizzlies of Yellowstone: for example, the size of the population, the bears' habits, and the official policy on moving, or translocation, of the animals. Write a business letter to the park administration requesting information on these or similar topics. Use the following address for your letter:

The Superintendent
Yellowstone National Park, WY 82190

Save your writing.

(see page 554)

LITERARY ELEMENTS

1. Possible examples: Cloyd begins his mission to save cubs out of guilt he feels for betraying dead grizzly. He sacrifices comfort to stay with cubs after their mother's death, and he endures great hardship to see them safely denned. By giving back to nature for what he thinks is his betrayal, Cloyd lives a good life.

2. Answers will vary. **a.** Major crisis is capture of cubs by game wardens. Once Cloyd realizes cubs will not be left alone to make it on their own, he feels need to take action. **b.** Most significant event leading up to crisis is death of mother grizzly. Also important is meeting Ursa and learning importance of bear to Native Americans.

3. One possible climax occurs when Cloyd rescues bears from mine. At that point he decides not to leave mountains as long as bears need him, and rest of novel stems from that. Another possible climax occurs when Cloyd is caught in avalanche. After that he thinks hunters are out for cubs, so he must redouble his efforts to help cubs.

4. Major conflict is resolved when bears fall asleep for their period of hibernation. At that point Cloyd has done all he can to help them.

WRITING ABOUT LITERATURE

Here are some examples students might use in their essays: Cloyd's decision to look for grizzlies after he hears about them from Rusty; his decision to free cubs; his decision to try to rescue cubs from mine; his decision to stay with them until they are safe.

FOCUS ON WRITING A LETTER

Students' letters should follow the business letter form. They should keep audience and purpose in mind as they clearly state their message.

What got me started writing *Bearstone,* my first novel, was the surprising news that a grizzly had been killed in the San Juan Mountains; not far from where we were living, in 1979. The bear was killed by an outfitter who said he didn't realize it was a grizzly. The idea I began my story with was that of a Ute boy meeting the last grizzly in Colorado. This being fiction, I got to make up how it would all happen. The boy became Cloyd, with Walter and Rusty soon joining the story.

After the 1979 incident, the experts once again agreed that the grizzlies were all gone. They were extinct in Colorado. I would never have had the heart to invent the idea for *Beardance* if there hadn't been reason to hope that there might still be some left after all. It was a 1990 sighting of a mother grizzly and three cubs by a rancher on horseback that gave me that hope. In the summers following the sighting, bear biologists tested hair samples and other evidence found in the area, and now believe that these remote mountains of southwestern Colorado may indeed be home to a few surviving grizzlies.

Now I could begin to imagine Cloyd returning to the mountains and meeting the mate and the cubs of the bear that had been killed in *Bearstone.* After reading for months, learning all I could about grizzlies and the traditions of native people all across the continent regarding bears, I began work on the novel. I found myself struggling with my early chapters, trying to get the story to come to life, so I decided to take a break from my desk and hike back up to the Window, that spectacular notch in the Continental Divide which I saw as the geographic focus of the story.

Standing in the Window, I could imagine I saw Cloyd and Walter camping down on East Ute Creek far below. I could almost see the entrance to the lost gold mine on the ridge above the creek. And I could imagine Cloyd with the two grizzly cubs, Brownie and Cocoa, as the snow was starting to fall. I practically ran home, my head bursting with ideas for my story. I poured all of my love of the mountains and of bears into the writing, as well as my deep respect for native traditions.

I found my fingers flying all day and into the night. In writing, as in reading, you're imagining what it's like to be someone else, and I was fully imagining being Cloyd Atcitty, at 11,800 feet with winter coming on, risking his life for those grizzly cubs. I completed the novel in a sort of trance, much like his, in a little less than a month. It was a wonderful experience, and I don't know if one like it will ever come again.

OBJECTIVES
The overall aim is for students to demonstrate the ability to draw inferences from their reading.

PRESENTATION
Discuss with students the process of drawing inferences, giving as many examples as necessary for them to understand fully. Then read the passage from *Beardance* to students. Have them respond to the questions individually or in small groups.

FOCUS ON *Reading and Critical Thinking*

DRAWING INFERENCES

*I*n *Beardance,* Will Hobbs usually describes scenes directly, leaving little for the reader to guess about. Occasionally, however, you must draw **inferences,** or conclusions, about aspects of the plot, the setting, or the motivation of the characters.

For example, at the moment in Chapter 2 when Cloyd and Walter see the first of the Pine's upper meadows, Walter reverently quotes a line from Psalm 23: "He maketh me to lie down in green pastures" (see page 527). What inference does the author intend for you to draw about Walter at this point?

Reread the following passage about Cloyd from the beginning of Chapter 4. On a separate sheet of paper, answer the questions that follow the passage.

He hated feeling sorry for himself. It reminded him of that year in the group home in Durango when he was angry all the time, when he failed all his classes on purpose, when he bullied kids out of dimes and quarters.

He used to be like that.

He used to be like that before he found the bearstone in the cave high above the old man's farm, before he dreamed of visiting the wilderness named after his own band of Utes. Before he'd worked for Walter, and before Walter had taken him into the mountains.

The loneliness and anger was still inside him, like a poisonous desert plant waiting for a big rain. He could keep it from growing if he didn't feed it. Taking care of the old man and the farm hadn't left any time for feeling sorry for himself. He'd driven the tractor in winter and summer, plowed snow and cut hay. He'd hand-shoveled the deep snow from the walks around the old farmhouse. Every day in winter, he'd taken the axe and chopped the ice to keep the hole in the pond open for Blueboy and the other horses to drink. He'd brought in the firewood all winter and irrigated the fields in the summer and done a hundred other chores. It was a good feeling, to work that hard for someone you cared about.

Drawing Inferences

1. What inferences can you draw about how Cloyd has changed?

2. What clues in the passage point to the reasons for this change in Cloyd?

3. Why is being in the wilderness important to Cloyd?

DRAWING INFERENCES
Students have been drawing inferences about people and situations throughout their lives. It is such a natural thinking process that it becomes difficult to isolate and define. Give students concrete examples from everyday life. For example, describe the following encounter: You meet a good friend in the hall between classes and he or she walks past you without saying "Hi." Ask students what they might think after such an encounter. If they answer that they might think their friend is upset with them, is having a bad day, or is just tired, tell them that they have just drawn inferences about their friend based on his or her behavior.

Answers
Answers will vary.
1. Cloyd is a better person when he has someone to care about. He changed from an angry bully to a willing, helpful worker.
2. That "He used to be like that" before Walter took him to his farm; that "It was a good feeling, to work that hard for someone you cared about."
3. His group of Utes had lived in the wilderness, and Cloyd is proud of his heritage.

The overall aim is for students to learn how to write a personal letter or a business letter. For a complete list of objectives, see the **Teacher's Notes.**

HOLT WRITER'S WORKSHOP

This computer program provides help for all types of writing through guided instruction for each step of the writing process. (Program available separately.)

See *Elements of Writing, Second Course,* Chapter 34, for more instruction on writing letters.

WRITING A LETTER

Much of the history of civilization is preserved in the form of letters, especially information about the day-to-day lives of ordinary people. You might want to make some collections of letters available to students in the classroom. These might include the collected letters of famous authors or historical figures, or letters that have similar themes, such as collections of love letters.

Prewriting

Encourage students to be as specific as possible in selecting a purpose for their letters. If a student decides to write a thank-you note, for example, he or she should narrow that purpose further. For example, the student should plan to write a thank-you note for a videogame received as a birthday present. In writing a business letter, students should identify by name the business they are writing to and should tell precisely what they want to accomplish by writing.

Writing

Before students begin writing, discuss the polite, respectful tone appropriate to business letters and the more informal, conversational one appropriate to personal letters. Give examples as necessary. Remind students writing personal letters that their tone may vary widely, depending upon their intended audience. For example, the tone of a letter

PRESENTATION

You might want to begin by asking students to consider potential audiences for their letters (record these on the chalkboard). Students might select their audiences based on interest level or on which of the two types of letters they need more practice with. Next, you can ask students to work individually or in small groups to think about specific purposes for writing to their audiences. Then have students select specific purposes appropriate for the audiences they choose.

FOCUS ON *Writing*

WRITING A LETTER

There are many purposes for writing a letter: to thank a friend for a favor, to issue or decline an invitation, to give a relative an update on events in your life, or to request information. Telephones and computers have changed the ways people communicate, but letters are still an important part of our lives. In this assignment you will have the chance to write a letter of your own.

Prewriting

1. Decide on the **purpose** and **audience** for your letter. The style and form of a letter depend on whether it is a personal or business letter. In a **personal letter,** your purpose is to convey your ideas, express your feelings, or tell some news. Personal letters may also include thank-you notes, invitations, or letters of regret. This type of letter has an informal style and tone, and it is usually written by hand.

In a **business letter,** your purpose may be to request information, order a product, complain about a product or service, or express praise or appreciation. A business letter uses standard English, a formal tone, and a specific format. It is usually typewritten.

[See **Focus** assignments on pp. 548 and 611.]

2. Jot down in a sentence or two the **main idea** of your letter: for example, to request more information about bears in a national park or to tell your cousin about getting your new bike.

Writing

1. You may find these guidelines helpful as you draft a business letter:

- State the reason for your letter in the first paragraph.
- Use a polite, respectful tone.
- Include all necessary information: be sure your reader can understand why you are writing and what you are asking.
- Use standard English: avoid slang, contractions, and abbreviations.

2. The six parts of a business letter are the following:

- heading
- inside address
- salutation
- body
- closing
- signature

Be sure to arrange these parts correctly on the page. Follow the **block form** shown here.

Your Address
Today's Date

Name of the Person or
Company You Are Writing

Dear _____ :

_____
_____
_____
_____

Sincerely yours,

_____ (your signed name)
_____ (your typed or printed name)

At this point, you may want to divide the class into a personal letters group and a business letters group. Have each group work through the writing process as outlined in the textbook.

To close, ask students to comment on any aspect of the assignment that caused problems for them. You can ask other students to suggest ways of solving those problems, and you can review any aspect of the process that seems problematic.

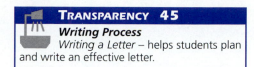

3. Personal letters have a more flexible format. In a personal letter, remember to show some interest in the person to whom you are writing. You can, for example, ask questions about his or her activities, as well as give news about your own.

Evaluating and Revising

1. When you have finished your letter, look it over to make sure that you have clearly said what you wanted to say. For example, if you have written a personal letter of invitation, be sure you have included specific information about the occasion, the time and place, and any other details your guest might need to know. If you have written a business letter of complaint, be sure you have mentioned specifics: why you were unhappy with the product or service, how you were affected, and what you believe should be done to correct the problem.

2. You may find the following checklist helpful as you revise your letter.

Checklist for Evaluation and Revision

✓ Have I stated my message clearly?
✓ Have I used the proper format for a personal or business letter?
✓ Have I included all the necessary information?

   Here is how one writer revised part of the body of a business letter.

Writer's Model

Please send me ~~the~~ <u>one</u> scratching post for #30618B
cats, ~~an~~ item in your catalogue. I
enclose a money order ~~for~~ <u>in</u> the amount
$35.50 for of the scratching post, ~~together with~~ plus shipping and
handling, ~~other costs.~~ I appreciate your Please send it ~~quick~~
prompt attention to this order. ~~because the cat is wrecking the furni-~~
~~ture.~~

Proofreading and Publishing

1. Proofread your letter and correct any errors you find in grammar, usage, and mechanics. (Here you may find it helpful to refer to the **Handbook for Revision** on pages 712–755.) Then prepare a final version of your letter by making a clean copy.

2. Publish your writing by addressing an envelope, adding postage, and mailing your letter!

Portfolio If your teacher approves, you may wish to keep a copy of your work in your writing folder or portfolio.

to a peer might be different from that used in a letter to a grandparent.

Evaluating and Revising
Have students work in small groups according to the types of letters they have written. Students can then use the **Checklist for Evaluation and Revision** to edit one another's letters. Groups might also want to develop additional questions pertinent to the specific types of letters they will be working with. For example, a group might add the question, "Have I used the appropriate tone?"

Proofreading and Publishing
Emphasize the importance of correct spelling of proper nouns. Also review the correct use of titles and abbreviations. Students who wrote personal letters may enjoy decorating and personalizing their letters and envelopes.

PORTFOLIO ASSESSMENT
Suggest that students keep reader's journals for this unit to help them make connections among the epics as they read. Journals could take the form of web maps or charts that show graphically the common elements and recurrent patterns and themes that students discovered. Consult with them individually to agree on how their journals will be assessed. Journals may be included in student portfolios. (For more information on student portfolios, see the *Portfolio Assessment and Professional Support Materials* booklet in your teaching resources.)

PART III

LITERARY HERITAGE

Unit Nine   THE EPIC

Selections from

THE ILIAD
624

BEOWULF
645

SUNDIATA
656

619

THE EPIC

OVERVIEW OF THE UNIT

The epic unit presents students with a blend of timeless myths, legends, folk tales, and historical events. Through the study of epics, students will learn about the magnificent feats of classic heroes, the strange magic of monsters, and the customs and values of people of different cultures and past ages.

The unit opens with excerpts from the *Iliad,* which will familiarize students with Homeric style, Greek mythology, and the Trojan War. *Beowulf,* an epic poem written in Anglo-Saxon, or Old English, is filled with the excitement of monarchs, warriors, and monsters. The unit concludes with the Malian epic *Sundiata,* in which a griot, or storyteller, narrates the history of Sundiata, a great ruler.

OBJECTIVES OF THE UNIT

The aims of the unit are for the student:

- To identify types of folk and literary epics and to determine their differences
- To apply a set of guidelines for reading an epic to the study of the *Iliad, Beowulf,* and *Sundiata*
- To identify the characteristics and conventions of an epic and to apply these conventions to the selections in this unit
- To analyze selected characters, their heroic characteristics, and their relationships with other characters in selected epics in this unit
- To evaluate the plots, conflicts, outcome of events, and conclusions of the selections in this unit
- To interpret the intended meaning of the symbolism within an epic
- To infer from an epic the values and beliefs of the culture that produced it
- To write a comparison/contrast essay
- To make connections between literature and cultures

CONCEPTS AND SKILLS

The following concepts and skills are treated in this unit:

CLOSE READING

LITERARY ELEMENTS/TERMS AND TECHNIQUES

OPPORTUNITIES FOR WRITING

Writing About Literature

Focus on Comparison and Contrast

CONNECTIONS

FOCUS ON READING AND CRITICAL THINKING

FOCUS ON WRITING

TRANSPARENCIES

The following unit support materials with specific correlations to literature selections are available in the **Fine Art and Instructional Transparencies with Teacher's Notes and Blackline Masters** section of your *Audiovisual Resources Binder.*

FINE ART TRANSPARENCIES

Theme: Waiting for a Hero
46 *Frederick Douglass Series No. 21,* Jacob Lawrence
47 *My Hero,* Ilisha Helfman

READER RESPONSE

48 Coming Attractions
49 Test of Strength
50 Send a Message

LITERARY ELEMENTS

51 Analyzing an Epic
52 The Epic Hero

WRITING PROCESS

53 Writing a Comparison/Contrast Essay

INTRODUCING THE UNIT

Because this unit addresses such exciting topics as heroes and gods, many different approaches can be considered. You might introduce the broad theme of the unit by initiating the following activities.

1. Ask students to compile a list of well-known people, both past and present, who, through their actions, might be considered heroic. Encourage students to find photographs, newspaper clippings, and literary sources that feature these personalities. Have students share their choices in an informal presentation, telling why these heroes are significant and what qualities make them extraordinary individuals.

2. Offer your students a hands-on activity. Have them make small cartoon sketches of a mythical beast or hero. Students should feel free to doodle and search out the shapes that define their imagined characters. Ask them to cut out their creations and then assemble them together on one large sheet of colored paper.

FOR UNIT PLANNING

- Transparencies 46–53: *Audiovisual Resources Binder*
- *Portfolio Assessment: Professional Support Materials*
- Test Generator

- Mastery Tests: Teaching Resources F, pp. 120, 122
- Analogy Test: Teaching Resources F, p. 127
- Composition Test: Teaching Resources F, p. 128

SELECTION (Pupil's Page)	TEACHING RESOURCES F (page numbers shown below)							AV BINDER
	Teacher's Notes	Reading Check	Study Guide	Language Skills	Building Vocabulary	Selection Vocab. Test	Selection Test	Audio-cassette
THE EPIC *Introduction* (p. 610)	55							
Homer retold by Barbara Leonie Picard *from The Iliad* (p. 628)	56	62	63, 66	70	74, 76	77, 79	80, 82	
translated by Ian Serraillier *from Beowulf* (p. 646)	84	88	89	92	96, 98	99, 100	101	TAPE 3 SIDE B
D. T. Niane Translated by G. D. Pickett *from Sundiata* (p. 656)	103	106	108	111	114	116, 117	119	TAPE 3 SIDE B

3. Ask students to consider actions of their own that might be considered great or even heroic. Have they ever rescued an animal? Have they ever assisted a person in a dangerous situation? Ask students to write brief summaries of the event and how it made them feel about themselves. You might remind students that heroic deeds are not always deeds that save lives but are actions that help others or touch their lives in a meaningful way. After students have edited their work, you might ask for volunteers to share their polished efforts with the class.

PORTFOLIO ASSESSMENT

Suggestions for use of portfolios as support for this unit are described in the *Portfolio Assessment and Professional Support Materials* booklet accompanying this program. Specific suggestions are provided for a variety of student projects that may be suitable for inclusion in a portfolio. In addition, copying masters are provided for guides that may be used for evaluation and assessment of student projects.

Student Learning Options

THE EPIC

1. Writing an Original Epic
Ask students to use their knowledge of the epic to write part of an original epic poem. Students could focus on the hero's final battle with evil, as in the excerpts in the unit. Students might also include "Names and Places" guides for their epics.

2. Creating a Relief Sculpture
Students can bring the action of an epic poem or familiar story to life by sculpting a hero out of clay to make a relief. Students should adorn heroes with identifying clothing and objects. Students can create their own "museum" by displaying reliefs and making small note cards explaining their work.

3. Role-Playing Gods
Have students work in small groups to write dialogue that might have taken place among the gods as they intervened in the lives of warriors. Groups can then stage the scenes they have written, using costumes, props, and sound effects if desired.

4. Identifying Legend and Fact
Ask students to research both the legendary King Arthur and the real king, who lived during the sixth century, on whom the legend may have been based. After students have finished their research, ask them to identify aspects of the legend that correspond with the history of the real king and aspects of the legend that seem to be purely fictional. Students should be prepared to defend their opinions.

Exploring the Subject

Legends about heroic figures have provided material for writers and artists through the centuries. Beautifully illustrated manuscripts from the Middle Ages add to the present notion of traditional stories.

About the Artwork

The Trojan War is depicted; soldiers engage in hand-to-hand combat, and many have already fallen in battle. The soldiers are depicted with the clothing and equipment of the artist's day, rather than in attire appropriate to the time of Homer. Above the battle, one can see some of the gods and goddesses. The early Greeks believed these deities had human emotions and chose sides in wartime.

THE EPIC

When the illustration shown on these pages was created more than fifteen hundred years ago, the *Iliad* was already a very old poem. According to some scholars, the epic was composed between 900 and 700 B.C. Its subject matter, the Trojan War, deals with an event that had occurred centuries earlier, around 1200 B.C. For a story to last that long and to continue to be read and enjoyed, it must be exceptional.

Working with a partner or in a small group, draw up a list of stories or books you have read that you think will still be read a thousand years from now. Tell why you think these works are ageless. Compare your lists with those of other students and see if you agree on any titles.

Greeks and Trojans in battle from *The Ambrosiana Iliad*. Illustrated manuscript (third to fifth centuries A.D.).
Biblioteca Ambrosiana, Milan

TEACHING RESOURCES F
Teacher's Notes, p. 55

THE EPIC

You might introduce this unit by asking students to examine the illustration and to read the first paragraph of the introductory material on p. 622. Ask students to identify other epics they have read or seen adapted on TV or in a movie and to tell the class what they remember about them.

Each **epic** in this unit is a product of a different culture, yet all are thematically related. Each poem has its **hero,** struggling to attain an ideal. The hero, as a representation of his culture, is cast in unique settings and circumstances. His actions proclaim his heroic character; moreover, his circumstances and his responses to them reveal universal aspects of the human condition. He embodies the qualities of human greatness, but his weaknesses, however few, may lead to **tragedy.**

Questions and activities in the unit guide students to a recognition of the traditions of various cultures, the major themes in an epic, and the literary techniques used in works of this genre. Reading activities strengthen students' understanding of **characterization, plot, theme,** and **setting.** Writing activities direct students to compare characters, to analyze the values and beliefs that governed the lives of ancient Africans, and to apply prewriting strategies for a comparison/ contrast essay.

Focus on Reading and Critical Thinking increases understanding of methods of comparison and contrast. **Focus on Writing** leads students through the writing process for a comparison/contrast essay.

Ask students to discuss their concepts of **myths,** **legends,** and **folk tales.** Have them give examples of each. Ask them to speculate on historical events that might have influenced development of these stories.

PRESENTATION

The material in this introduction focuses on the different types of **epics** and their origins. Before students read the selections in this unit, you may want to discuss the historical background of each. In addition, you might ask students to fa-miliarize themselves with the **Guidelines for Close Reading.** Stop after each guideline to discuss its importance. These guidelines will help students recognize some of the major characteristics and conventions of an epic poem.

INTRODUCTION TO THE EPIC

1

Usually told in episodes, developing the history of a nation.

2

Some disagreement exists concerning attribution of authorship of these "known" writers. For example, the *Iliad* and *Odyssey* are attributed to Homer, but the events described took place about four hundred years before the poems were composed.

3

Found in fragments and pieced together to form what we know now as *The Epic of Gilgamesh.*

4

The Divine Comedy reveals the transformation of its protagonist from a state of sin to one of divine grace.

5

Christian poem about man's creation and his fall from divine grace; largely concerns itself with the struggle between good and evil.

6

While **hero** may have special supernatural powers, he is subject to death and suffering as are all mortals.

1 An *epic* is a long narrative work, usually in verse, about heroic people and events. The characters in epics are depicted as larger than life and possessing great strength and dignity. Because of these qualities, the word *epic,* in our day, has come to stand for something that is grand or colossal in size.

There are two general types of epics. One is the *folk epic,* which develops out of an oral tradition of songs and legends, and which does not have a known author. The other type is the *literary epic,* which is *2* written by a known author and which imitates the characteristics of the folk epic.

3 The earliest of the ancient epics is *Gilgamesh* (gĭl′gə-mĕsh), composed in the Near East more than four thousand years ago. There are three outstanding epics from classical antiquity. The *Iliad* (ĭl′ē-əd) and the *Odyssey* (ŏdə-sē), attributed to the Greek poet Homer, were composed about the eighth century B.C. The *Aeneid* (ĭ-nē′ĭd) was composed by the Roman poet Virgil in the first century B.C. It is called a literary epic because it was written in imitation of the Homeric poems. The longest poem in the world is the *Mahabharata* (mə-hä′bä′rə-tə), an ancient Indian epic, which consists of eighteen volumes. It is fifteen times as long as the Bible.

The Middle Ages produced several great epics, including *Beowulf* (bā′ə-wo͝olf′), set down in Old English, or Anglo-Saxon; *The Song of Roland,* the national epic of France; *The Poem of the Cid* (sĭd), the *4* national epic of Spain; and *The Divine Comedy,* by the Italian poet Dante, considered by some readers to be the greatest poem ever writ-*5* ten. The most celebrated epic in the English language is John Milton's *Paradise Lost,* written in the seventeenth century. Some readers believe that Milton's work is the last great epic in world literature.

In addition to those reading skills that you bring to any literary work, reading an epic requires that you understand certain characteristics of the form. For example, it is customary for an epic to be written in a dignified style. When you read an ancient epic that has been translated into Modern English, you will find that the language of the modern version is often formal and stately, to convey the flavor of the original.

An epic tends to draw upon many sources: myths, legends, folk tales, and historical events. Whereas Sundiata (so͞on-dyä′tə) was a real figure, the events recounted in the epic *Sundiata* are largely the accumulation of many stories told over several centuries.

6 Although the characters in epics experience very much the same emotions that we do, their actions are extraordinary, superhuman, or fantastic. Beowulf, for instance, can wage an underwater battle against a monster while wearing a suit of armor.

The hero of an epic is often a *demigod*; that is, one of his parents is divine. Thus, in the *Iliad*, Achilles is the son of Thetis, a sea goddess, and a mortal father. It is also common for the gods and goddesses to intervene in the lives of human characters and to take sides.

7 In some epics it is customary for the narrative to open in the middle of the action. This is the case in the Homeric epics and in the *Aeneid*.

An epic generally reflects the values of the society from which it originates. Thus, we are able to understand a great deal about the ideals of medieval Germanic society by reading the epic of *Beowulf*.

In this unit you will be introduced to some of the greatest epics in world literature. Here are some guidelines to assist you in reading these works.

Guidelines for Close Reading

1 1. **Read for pleasure and understanding.** Read actively, asking questions as you read. Try to anticipate what will happen next.

2 2. **Become familiar with the names of characters and places.** The names in these epics may seem strange at first. Refer to the list provided at the opening of each selection as often as is necessary. The individual entries identify the people and places mentioned in the epic.

3 3. **Take note of the heroic characteristics of the central figure or figures.** The qualities attributed to the hero reveal the underlying beliefs and values of the society that produced the epic. Ask yourself if these ideals still appeal to modern readers.

4 4. **Determine the role played by gods, goddesses, and other supernatural agents.** In particular, consider their responsibility for the destiny of human beings.

5. **Look for common elements in different epics.** For example, in many epics the hero undertakes a perilous journey or is involved in *5* dangerous adventures. Watch for recurrent patterns and themes.

7
In medias res: meaning "in the middle of things"; commonly used convention in **epics**. Story opens in middle of action.

GUIDELINES FOR CLOSE READING

1
Reading is often more pleasurable if readers can identify personally with the story and characters. However, for a deeper understanding of an epic's significance, readers must respond to clues by drawing **inferences** from them.

2
Readers should become familiar with pronunciations of names as well as their spellings. Spellings may vary among translations.

3
Hero embodies these characteristics: bravery, strength, prowess, virtue, loyalty to an ideal or nation.

4
Supernatural forces often intervene, causing unexpected shifts in **plot**.

5
Possible recurring elements: struggle against fate, quests, hero aided by friend of heroic but lesser abilities, battle against hostile forces and insurmountable odds.

This version of *The Judgment of Paris* was painted during the Renaissance. Artists and writers of this period were influenced by classical styles, taking their subjects from legends and myths of earlier centuries. Cecchino Da-Verona was part of a movement which began in Italy during the fourteenth century, spread throughout Europe, and lasted until the seventeenth century. This was a time of rebirth or renewal. Emphasis was placed on reviving the "best" of earlier civilizations, especially Greek and Roman works of art and literature.

INTRODUCTION TO THE ILIAD

1

Poems were part of an oral tradition. Homer's *Iliad* and *Odyssey* were recited by minstrels and only later written down.

2

Although Trojan War lasted ten years, the *Iliad* only deals with fifty-one days during last year of the war.

3

In ancient Greek times, audiences were familiar with the war's historical background; Homer did not need to supply these details.

4

In Homer's **epics**, gods and goddesses play an important role in human affairs. They have favorites, are vengeful, and are often in **conflict** with one another.

The Judgment of Paris by Cecchino Da Verona (fifteenth century).
Museo Nazionale del Bargello, Florence

THE ILIAD

Two great classical epics, the *Iliad* and the *Odyssey*, are attributed to **1** Homer. According to tradition, he was a blind poet who lived around the eighth century B.C. The events recounted in both epics were legendary even in Homer's time. The background for both poems was **2** the Trojan War, a long conflict between Greeks and Trojans, which had taken place around 1200 B.C.

Historians believe that the reasons for the Trojan War were eco-**3** nomic. However, according to legend, the war began over a woman, who became known as Helen of Troy. The story goes that all the gods and goddesses were invited to the wedding of Peleus and Thetis **4** except Eris, the goddess of discord. She was determined to be revenged for this insult. She threw a golden apple among the wedding guests, which was inscribed "For the Fairest." The apple was immediately claimed by three goddesses: Hera, queen of the gods; Athena, goddess of wisdom and the arts; and Aphrodite, queen of love and beauty. Zeus, the king of the gods, left the judgment of the contest to a mortal named Paris, who was a Trojan prince. Each of the goddesses attempted to bribe Paris. Hera promised him wealth and power; Athena assured him of great glory in war; Aphrodite offered him the most beautiful woman in the world as his wife. Paris gave the apple to Aphrodite, a decision which infuriated the other goddesses.

In the kingdom of Sparta, in Greece, lived King Menelaus and his
5 beautiful wife, Helen. Helen had been much sought after as a bride,
and before she chose a husband, all her suitors took an oath to defend
her if it ever became necessary. Paris sailed to Sparta, and with the
assistance of Aphrodite, persuaded Helen to elope with him. He took
6 her to Troy, a great fortified city across the Aegean Sea. Menelaus
called together the Greek chieftains who had pledged to protect
Helen. After two years of preparation, the Greek armies sailed to
Troy to recover Helen.

Thus began the Trojan War, which lasted for ten years. In the end,
7 the Greeks won and Helen was returned to her husband. One of the
Greek soldiers who fought in the war was Odysseus, whose adventures
are the subject of Homer's *Odyssey*.

8   The *Iliad* is named for Ilium, or Troy, which is the setting of the first
epic. It opens in the last year of the Trojan War. Things have not been
going well in the Greek camp. Then, a quarrel erupts between
Achilles, the greatest of the Greek warriors, and Agamemnon, leader
of the Greek forces. Ironically, this quarrel, too, is over a woman.

*The Abduction of Helen by
Paris* by a follower of
Fra Angelico (fifteenth
century). Wood, irregular
octagon, painted surface.
The National Gallery, London

5
Helen the Fair, daughter of Zeus,
was hatched from a swan's egg;
she was considered to be the
most beautiful woman in the
world.

6
Paris was also known for his physical beauty and masculine prowess.

7
Menelaus planned to kill Helen
but instead takes her back home
to disgrace her.

8
It means "The Tale of Troy," so
titled because of war's effects on
Troy.

VISUAL CONNECTIONS
About the Artwork
One of the major artists of the fifteenth century was Fra Angelico,
an Italian painter and a Domini-
can friar. In keeping with his position as a brother in a religious
order, he painted only religious
subjects, intending his paintings
to instruct and inspire viewers.
His style influenced that of his
pupils and admirers. However,
some of his followers chose classical subjects, as in this octagonal
painting which borrows its subject from the *Iliad*. The painting is
a fairly early example of using lin-
ear perspective, with background
features drawn smaller than
those in the foreground.

NAMES AND PLACES IN THE *ILIAD*

Greeks

9

9 **Achaian** (ə-kī′ən, ə-kā′ən): a Greek.

Achilles (ə-kĭl′ēz): leader of the Myrmidons and hero of the *Iliad*.

Agamemnon (ăg′ə-mĕm′nŏn′): king of Mycenae (mī-sēn′nē) and leader of the Greeks.

Automedon (ô-tŏm′ə-dŏn): Achilles' charioteer.

Calchas (kăl′kəs): a soothsayer, or prophet, in the Greek camp.

Helen: the wife of Menelaus, abducted by Paris.

Menelaus (mĕn′ə-lā′əs): king of Sparta, husband of Helen, and brother of Agamemnon.

Myrmidon (mûr′mə-dŏn′, dən): a warrior from Thessaly; a follower of Achilles.

Nestor (nĕs′tər, tôr′): a wise old man, counselor to the Greeks.

Odysseus (ō-dĭs′yōōs′, ō-dĭs′ē-əs): king of Ithaca and shrewdest of the Greeks.

Patroclus (pə-trō′kləs): the close friend of Achilles.

Menelaus
Vatican Museums

Six Myrmidons. Attic, black-figured amphora (vase) (575–550 B.C.) by the Camtar Painter

J. M. Rodocanachi Fund, Courtesy, Museum of Fine Arts, Boston

TRANSPARENCIES 46 & 47

Fine Art
Waiting for a Hero – features artwork showing heroes or heroic ideals from diverse cultural traditions.

10 Trojans

Andromache (ăn-drŏm′ə-kē): Hector's wife.

Astyanax (ə-stī′ə-năks′): son of Hector and Andromache.

11 **Cassandra** (kə-săn′drə): a daughter of King Priam, who has the gift of prophecy.

Hector (hĕk′tər): a Trojan prince and greatest warrior in Troy.

Hecuba (hĕk′yoŏ-bə): queen of Troy.

Idaeus (ī-dē′-əs): the herald of the Trojans.

Paris (păr′ĭs): a Trojan prince who abducted Helen.

Pergamus (pəŭr′gə-məs, -mŏs′): the citadel, or fortress, of Troy.

Priam (prī′əm): king of Troy.

Scaean (sē′ăn) **Gate:** the gateway to the city of Troy.

12 Gods and Goddesses

Aphrodite (ăf′rə-dī′tē): goddess of love and beauty. She sides with the Trojans.

Apollo (ə-pŏl′ō): god of youth, music, prophecy, archery, and the sun. He is called **Phoebus** (fē′bəs) **Apollo,** from the Greek word for "shining." He helps the Trojans.

Ares (âr′ēz): god of war. He takes sides with Aphrodite.

Artemis (är′tə-mĭs): goddess of hunting, wild animals, and the moon. She helps the Trojans.

Athena (ə-thē′nə): goddess of wisdom, arts, crafts, and war. She is called **Pallas** (păl′əs) **Athena.** She sides with the Greeks.

Hades (hā′dēz): god of the underworld.

Hephaestus (hĭ-fĕs′təs): god of fire and metalworking.

Hera (hîr′ə): goddess of marriage, Zeus's wife, and queen of the gods. She sides with the Greeks.

Hermes (hûr′mēz): god of travelers, thieves, and messenger of the gods.

Olympus (ō-lĭm′pəs): the highest mountain in Greece, the home of the gods and goddesses.

Poseidon (pō-sī′dən): god of the sea. He favors the Greeks, who are a seafaring people.

Thetis (thē′tĭs): a sea goddess, the mother of Achilles.

Zeus (zoōs): god of the sky and weather, and king of the gods. He favors the Trojans but has to be neutral in order to pacify Hera, his wife.

Bronze statue (c. 465 B.C.) identified as Poseidon or Zeus.
National Archaeological Museum, Athens

10
Historians for centuries believed that the city Troy and the Trojan people were legendary creations of Homer and the Bronze Age Greeks. However, the discovery of the ruins of Troy in the 1870s by the archaeologist Heinrich Schliemann led to the conclusion that a historical city and people of Troy had existed. The city was probably founded in the third millenium B.C. and went through several phases of destruction and rebuilding before being inhabited by the Trojans described in Homer's *Iliad.* Troy was a significant town in ancient times because of its strategic position as a crossroads between Europe and the East. The ruins of Troy are located near the Dardanelles in present-day Turkey.

11
Cassandra received the gift of prophecy from Apollo but later he condemned her to the fate of never being taken seriously.

12
Gods and goddesses were very much like humans except for their immortality. They were all subjects of Zeus, but even Zeus sometimes deferred to fate. The gods, used as explanations for both events and natural phenomena, were also sources of guidance, protection, and assistance.

VISUAL CONNECTIONS
About the Artwork
A mystery that has puzzled archaeologists is the identity of this bronze statue. Both arms of the statue are extended. (Only one raised arm can be seen in this photograph.) The statue depicts a god in the act of throwing, but the object being thrown is missing. If it is a trident, a three-pronged spear, the statue must be Poseidon, the sea god. If a thunderbolt, the statue must be Zeus, king of gods.

OBJECTIVES
The overall aim is for the students to recognize important events, actions, and characters in the *Iliad* and to analyze the characters of Hector and Achilles. For a complete list of objectives, see the **Teacher's Notes**.

VOCABULARY
The underlined words are in the Glossary. The **Vocabulary Activity** in the **Teacher's Notes** reviews common prefixes and discusses how they often reverse the meanings of root words.

FOCUS / MOTIVATION
In myths, gods and goddesses intervene in the lives of **heroes**, often changing the course of events. Ask students how a hierarchy of gods, playing favorites, might affect their own lives.

TEACHING RESOURCES F

Teacher's Notes, p. 56
Reading Check, p. 62
Study Guide, pp. 63, 66
Language Skills, p. 70
Building Vocabulary, pp. 74, 76
Selection Vocabulary Test, pp. 77, 79
Selection Test, pp. 80, 82

PREREADING FOCUS
The headnote focuses on **conflict** and the **theme** of fighting and anger. Ask students to keep in mind the basic conflicts among characters as they read the *Iliad*.

The Iliad

1
Though Agamemnon, as commander-in-chief and king of Mycenae, has higher rank, Achilles has power as the Greeks' best fighter, their favorite, and champion.

2 Making Generalizations
What does the opening speech suggest about Achilles' character? He is decisive, strong-willed, and unafraid to express his views.

3
Calchas had gained favorable reputation before the war as a prophet and had predicted when Achilles was nine that Troy could not be taken without him.

4
Foreshadowing. Achilles' comment about the king and prophet's fear of Agamemnon hint at ensuing quarrel.

5
Conflict. Agamemnon has refused to heed assembly's prior request or priest's pleas to accept ransom. Example of gods' intervention in lives of characters.

FROM

The Iliad

Retold by
BARBARA LEONIE PICARD

The Quarrel

Chryses,[1] a priest of Apollo, comes to the Greek camp to ransom his daughter, Chryseïs,[2] who is a captive. When Agamemnon refuses to release the girl, Apollo sends a pestilence to punish the Greeks. For nine days he rains his arrows on the Greeks. Then Achilles calls a conference, which leads to a bitter quarrel.

For nine days did the plague rage, and on the tenth day, Achilles from Phthia,[3] who was the youngest of all the kings and princes of the Greeks, called the other leaders to an assembly. When they were all gathered together, he stood up and spoke. "My friends, without a doubt one of the gods is angry with us, else would this plague not have come upon us. Let us with no more delay ask a priest, or one who is skilled in such matters, to tell us which of the gods we have displeased by our neglect, that we may speedily offer sacrifices to appease his wrath. For otherwise, or so it seems to me, we shall never live to take Troy. We shall all of us die here, on the shore, and the theft of Helen will go unavenged."

Achilles sat down, and immediately Calchas the prophet arose. "Lord Achilles, son of King Peleus, I can tell you which of the gods is angered with us, and why. But first, swear to me that you will protect me, whatever I may say, for I fear that my words will displease one amongst us, who is the best of all the Greeks. Promise me your protection, and I will speak."

"Have no fear, Calchas," replied Achilles, "but speak the truth to us, for while I live no man of all the Greeks shall harm you." He paused a moment and glanced across to where Agamemnon sat, before adding, "Not even great King Agamemnon himself, whom I have often heard declare himself to be the best of all the Greeks, shall do you ill, I promise it."

"Then," said Calchas, reassured, "I will tell you why this plague has come upon us. It comes from immortal Apollo, and not because we have forgotten to sacrifice to him, but because King Agamemnon would not heed the pleas of old Chryses, who is Apollo's priest. Until the maiden Chryseïs is given back to her father, freely and unransomed, the god will not lift his wrath from us."

Agamemnon frowned at his words, and, when Calchas had done, the great king sat silent, glowering, knowing that the eyes of everyone were upon him. Then he rose. "Your words always make ill hearing, Calchas. Never

1. **Chryses** (krī'sēz).
2. **Chryseïs** (krī-sē'ĭs).
3. **Phthia** (thī'ə): a town in Thessaly, a section of Greece on the Aegean Sea.

memnon. Agamemnon retorts that he would be better off without Achilles' assistance but that first he will take a woman Achilles won. Achilles is about to draw his sword when he feels an invisible hand holding him by the hair.

6 have I heard you prophesy good fortune or the favor of the gods, but warnings and bad omens come always easily to your tongue. Now you choose to blame me for Apollo's wrath and this plague, and say that in my hands alone lies the remedy." He paused, remembering how all the other kings and princes had been for accepting the ransom and restoring Chryseïs to her father. He flung out his arm in an angry gesture. "Very well, the priest shall have his daughter back. I do not want to let her go, but I would rather lose her than be the death of all the Greeks. Odysseus shall make ready a ship and take the girl to Thebe."

7 There was a murmur of approval from the assembled Greeks, but Agamemnon looked about him sullenly. He had been at fault and he had been set down before them all, and he was not minded to be the only one to suffer. He caught sight of Achilles, with his friend Patroclus sitting at his side. They were smiling at each other, now that it seemed likely that Apollo's wrath would soon be ended. Agamemnon thought how it was young Achilles who had called the assembly, and so caused his discomfiture. Suddenly he shouted out, "I am the leader of you all, and the greatest king amongst you. It is not fitting that I alone should be without my chosen spoils. I **8** shall send away Chryseïs because I must, but I will have instead a share of the booty of some other man—yours, perhaps, Achilles."

9 Achilles sprang to his feet, his eyes blazing. "You are our leader, King Agamemnon, but in this you presume too much. I have no quarrel with the Trojans. They have never stolen my father's cattle or his horses, nor have they harvested our fields of grain in Phthia. The mountains are too high and the sea too wide that lie between Troy and my father's land. No, I have led the Myrmidons to battle against the Trojans for the sake of your brother's quarrel, that he might win back his wife; though, since I was

Achilles. Detail from Attic, red-figured amphora (c. 450–440 B.C.).
Vatican Museums

never a suitor for Helen's hand—being too young by far—I was bound by no oath to do so. Remember that, before you talk shamelessly of

6 Agamemnon resents prophecies of Calchas because seer once suggested that the king's boasts had angered goddess Artemis, causing trouble for the Greek fleet.

7 Summarizing
How is Agamemnon portrayed here? He is shown to be proud and spiteful.

8 In ancient Greek culture, women who were taken as spoils of war represented marks of honor. Giving up Chryseïs lowers Agamemnon's status.

9 Characterization. Achilles exhibits his fiery temper. He uncharacteristically disputes words of his commander.

VISUAL CONNECTIONS
About the Artwork
Painters of Grecian vases produced both red-figured and black-figured designs. For the red-figured vase, the figure was very finely sketched, and then detailing and background were painted in black. Achilles is shown wearing side curls, which usually are seen on very youthful figures. Apparently these were used to make clear that he was younger than his friend Patroclus.

tions reveal their attitudes and motives. You might tell students to pay particular attention to the role of gods and goddesses in the story.

You might want to discuss the importance of Homeric style. The *Iliad* and the *Odyssey* are written in heroic dimensions; the narrative style is elevated, and the events are presented in grand proportion. Many poets have emulated Homer's style, thus contributing to the conventions associated with the **epic** genre. Inform students that works written after the *Illiad* and the *Odyssey* that have similar characteristics are said to contain Homeric features. Depending upon your class, you may wish to introduce the concepts of the *Homeric epithet* and *Homeric simile.*

10

Conflict. Achilles, who has no consequential quarrel with the Trojans, feels he has not received adequate remuneration for his participation in the fighting.

11

Conflict. Agamemnon attempts to dishonor Achilles and reestablish his superiority by taking Briseïs.

12 Drawing Conclusions
Why does Achilles follow Athene's advice? Out of respect for gods; ignoring her would bring him into disfavor.

13

Patroclus was sent to Troy by his father as an advisor. Second in command to Achilles, he is also his closest friend.

14

Nestor, oldest of the Greek leaders, intervenes. He is voice of wisdom and speaks from experience.

sharing my booty." He paused for a moment, and then went on hotly, "And what is my share of the booty compared with all that you have taken from the towns that we have sacked? **10** Because I am accounted a good warrior, and because my father's men are brave, to me falls more than my fair share of the fighting, so long as the battle lasts. But when the fighting is over, do I get a like share of the spoils? No. After you, King Agamemnon, have taken your pick, I get some small thing of little worth from whatever is left over, and I have to be content with that. What have I gained from this war with Troy? A little gold and silver and a few slaves—not many, since, unlike you, I am always ready to take a ransom for my captives." He paused again, and then said, "By all the gods, it would be better if I were to set sail with my father's men and return to Phthia, rather than stay here, slighted, to win more wealth for you to carry home to Mycenae."

Agamemnon laughed. "Go if you will," he sneered. "We shall do well enough without you. You may be brave, and a fine warrior, but of all the kings and princes of the Greeks, you, with your arrogance and your hot temper that you have not yet learned to curb, you are the one whom I could best do without. Go home. Take your ships and your Myrmidons. Lord it over your own men, show your temper to your friends and rail at them and not at me. Go home; but part, at least, of your booty you shall leave behind. When we sacked the city of Lyrnessus, you chose as your share of the spoils **11** the girl Briseïs,[4] to be your slave. I must give up Chryseïs to her father, since it is the will of Apollo; but you shall give up Briseïs to me, since that is my will." He laughed again, shortly. "And when she is gone from your hut and dwells in mine, perhaps you will have learned at last that I am indeed the leader of all the Greeks, and a greater king than your father Peleus."

For a moment Achilles was too angry to speak or even move, and then he laid his hand upon the silver hilt of his sword, for in his rage he would have leaped upon Agamemnon and killed him there, in sight of all the other Greeks; but before even Patroclus could **12** restrain him, prudent Athene, goddess of wisdom, who had been watching from high Olympus, came swiftly down amongst them, unseen of any, and standing behind Achilles, she took hold of his long yellow hair. He looked round and knew at once that it was one of the immortal gods who held him back, and he thrust his sword again into its scabbard, and immediately Athene left him.

Achilles, furious, but obedient to the divine injunction,[5] said, "Your wits must be befuddled with wine, Agamemnon, that you speak so to one who is braver than yourself. One day you will regret those words which have cost you my help and the help of my father's men, for neither I nor they, nor the friends who came with me to Troy, will fight any longer against the Trojans for your sake." He sat down, flushed **13** and still angry, beside Patroclus.

Agamemnon would have scoffed further at him, but old Nestor rose. He was the king of Pylos,[6] and had come with ninety ships to fight against the Trojans with Antilochus[7] his son, who had been one of Helen's suitors. He was the oldest of all the kings and princes of the Greeks, and his counsel was valued amongst them and his words were always heard with respect.

14 "Shame upon you both!" he exclaimed. "How King Priam and his sons would rejoice to hear you now. I can chide you both, since I am older by far than either of you. In my time

4. **Briseïs** (brĭ-sē'ĭs).

5. **injunction:** command.
6. **Pylos** (pī'lŏs).
7. **Antilochus** (ăn-tĭl'ə-kəs).

630

I have known greater warriors than any here today, and called them my comrades in battle. I fought beside Peirithoüs[8] and great Theseus[9] himself, against the Centaurs[10] who dwelt in the mountain caves. No such grim fighting as that shall we see before the walls of Troy, yet we destroyed the Centaurs utterly. Even Theseus did not scorn my counsel, so why should you? Cease your quarreling, my friends. Let Achilles keep the girl he won, King Agamemnon, she is his by right. And, as you have said yourself, he is a fine warrior, and the Trojans fear him. As for you, Achilles, you are yet very young; you should show more respect to a great king whose lands are far wider than any you will ever rule."

"What you say is true, good Nestor," said Agamemnon, "but I am weary of Achilles' arrogance, his flouting of my authority, and his quick temper, which we see far too often."

Before he could speak further, Achilles broke in, "Your authority, King Agamemnon, do I no longer acknowledge. If you will, come and take the girl from me. I shall not prevent you. For I chose her by your favor: and what a man has given, that may he take away. Yet I warn you, lay but a finger on any of the goods I brought with me from Phthia, and it will not be Trojan blood which will be red upon my sword." He rose abruptly, flung his cloak about him, and gestured to his friend. "Come, Patroclus." And without another glance at Agamemnon, he left the assembly, and Patroclus went with him.

Achilles withdraws to his tent and refuses to fight. The war rages on. The Trojans are led by Hector, son

8. **Peirithoüs** (pī-rĭth′ō-əs): At his wedding, a quarrel erupted between his people, the Lapiths, and the Centaurs.
9. **Theseus** (thē′sē-əs): a hero who killed the Minotaur, a monster half man and half bull.
10. **Centaurs** (sĕn′tôrz′): monsters that were half man and half horse.

of King Priam and the greatest warrior in Troy. He returns home from battle to spend a few moments with his wife, Andromache, and their child, Astyanax.

Hector and Andromache

Hector turned and hurried from his house, down the broad street from the Pergamus towards the Scaean Gate; and as he neared the gateway, Andromache saw him and came running to him from the watchtower beside the gate, followed by the nurse who carried Astyanax.

Hector smiled when he saw the child, but Andromache was weeping. She took hold of his hand. "Your courage will be the end of you, dear husband. Must you go again to battle? Think of me, if you will not consider yourself. My mother is dead, my father died when the town of Thebe was taken, and my seven brothers Achilles slew. I have no one left but you, Hector. To me you are not only husband, but father and mother and brother as well. If I lose you, what have I left? Have pity on me, Hector, and on our son. Stay with me on the wall today. Call the Trojans together and let them take their stand by the wild fig tree. For opposite the old fig tree the wall is weakest, and three times today have I watched the Greeks attack it at that place." She held his hand in both of hers and clasped it close to her.

He put his other arm about her. "My dearest wife, if I stayed with you and kept from battle, how could I face our people ever again? Indeed, I think that I could not keep from the fighting even if I would; for, all my life, I have learned only to be valiant and first in danger, to lead other men where they should follow, and to earn honor for my father and myself." He sighed. "I think that we cannot win this

22
Characterization. Hector portrayed as sympathetic character, a loving husband concerned about fate of his people as well as that of his wife and son. He is a great warrior with a civilized nature.

23
She is eventually awarded as a slave to Neoptolemus, Achilles' son, to whom she bears three sons.

24
Helmet was given to him by Apollo and is his most characteristic piece of armor. His title is "Bright Helmeted Hector."

war, Andromache, and that there must come a **22** day when Troy will fall to the Greeks. My heart is torn when I think of all who will suffer then, my mother, my father, my brothers and sisters, our people; but for none of them do I grieve as I grieve for you, my wife, whom some Greek will take as the spoils of battle. Then, far away over the sea, in Greece, in the house of a harsh master, someone, someday, will see you weeping as you work at the loom or fetch water from the spring, and he will say, "She was the wife of Hector, the greatest warrior among the Trojans." And, hearing, your tears will flow yet faster for the husband who was not able to save you." He paused and then broke out, "Oh, may **23** I be dead and the earth heaped high above me, before I hear your cries as they carry you off into slavery."

Andromache wept; and Hector turned from her and, leaning forward, stretched out his hands to take Astyanax from the nurse. But the child was afraid of the great horsehair **24** crest on his father's helmet, and shrank back into his nurse's arms, so that Hector and Andromache, for all their grief, had to smile, and even laugh a little, as Hector took off his helmet and laid it on the ground, and Astyanax, reassured, came willingly into his arms.

Hector's Farewell (c. 1815) Drawing by Felice Giani (1758–1823).
Cooper-Hewitt Museum, the Smithsonian's National Museum of Design

VISUAL CONNECTIONS
About the Artwork
In the nineteenth century, when this drawing was produced, there was a revival of interest in classical art forms, as had also been true during the Renaissance. The difference was that nineteenth-century artists had the benefit of recent archaeological finds, and they tried to be as faithful as possible to these ancient models.

Ideas for Writing
Students might compare the drawing of Hector's farewell to the fifteenth-century paintings on pp. 624–625. Which one is more authentic? Students might research some aspect of dress during the two different periods.

Then Hector kissed his son, and holding him, prayed for him. "Great Zeus and all you immortal gods, grant that my child shall be brave and prove to be, even as I am, the greatest warrior amongst the Trojans, and grant
25 that he shall rule mightily, here in Troy. And let there be a day, when, coming back from battle, it will be said of him, 'He is a far better man than his father,' so that he may gladden his mother's heart."

He put Astyanax in Andromache's arms, and she smiled at him through her tears. He held her and the child close to him, and said,
26 "Do not torment yourself too much, dearest wife, for no man can send me down to the land of Hades before the time allotted by the immortal gods. Now go home and busy yourself with the household tasks, that you may forget to fret for me. War is not for women, but for men. And of the men in Troy, for me above all others, who should one day rule here."

27 He kissed her, and put on his helmet, while she went up the street towards the Pergamus, turning back time after time to see him, though her eyes were all but blinded by her tears.

Achilles' close friend, Patroclus, asks to borrow Achilles' armor and to lead his men, the Myrmidons, into battle. Patroclus is slain by Hector, who then strips Achilles' armor from his body. Grief for his dead friend rouses Achilles' desire for vengeance. Wearing new armor forged by the god Hephaestus, Achilles mounts his chariot and rides to battle. He pursues Hector to the gates of Troy.

The Vengeance

King Priam came upon the walls of Troy, and from the watchtower beside the Scaean Gate, **28** he saw his people driven in rout before the spears of the Greeks and he called down to the

Francis Bartlett Fund, Courtesy, Museum of Fine Arts, Boston

Thetis watching Hephaestus as he makes the armor of Achilles. Attic, red-figured amphora (c. 460–450 B.C.) by the Dutuit Painter.

gatekeepers, bidding them fling wide the gates, that the fleeing Trojans might win through to safety.

Through the Scaean Gate the Trojans poured, with the Greeks coming after them across the plain. But their fear gave them speed, and of those Trojans who had lived to cross the river all passed safely through the gates. All save Hector. He stood before the gateway, watching the oncoming Greeks, and wondering what it were best to do: to save his

25
To prevent him from avenging his father's death, Astyanax is eventually murdered by either Odysseus or Neoptolemus.

26
Epic. Deterministic view of death. Chance plays no part in epic. Fate determines time of death.

27 Drawing Conclusions
Why does Andromache turn back "time after time" to see her husband? She fears she will never see him again.

28
Plot. Hector's indecision will soon cost him his life.

VISUAL CONNECTIONS
Exploring the Subject
In the painting on this vase, Thetis, mother of Achilles, is watching Hephaestus in his toils. In Greek mythology, Hephaestus was the god of metalworking and fire. He was a master artisan, making weapons, dwellings, and furnishings for the gods. Generally described as a kindly, peace-loving god, he was popular with both mortals and immortals. He and Athene were patrons of handicrafts, he the protector of blacksmiths and she the protector of weavers.

29
Characteristic Greek scene— parting of father and son. Hec- tor's imminent death is closely associated with fate of Troy.

30
Summarizing
Making Inferences
What does Priam fear has hap- pened to his sons? Do you think Hector will listen to Priam's pleas? Priam believes they have been slain. Hector has shown himself to be a man of honor; he will not retreat.

31
Later, Achilles' son Neoptolemus does murder Priam.

32
Hector's dilemma is between up- holding heroic code of honor and heeding supplications of his fam- ily.

33
Irony. Hector's pride in his abili- ties as warrior and leader ironi- cally lead to his death and downfall of Troy.

34
Characterization. Implies that Hector not only desires peace but that he realizes Achilles seeks to avenge his friend's death. He is a very human character.

35
Drawing Conclusions
What does Hector's gesture of shrugging his shoulders imply? Shows that Hector is resigned to his fate; he knows he has no alternative but to stand and face Achilles.

life and live to fight again, or to stay and face Achilles.

▶ It was Priam, from the watchtower, who first **32** saw Achilles as he drew near, his god-given armor shining in the afternoon sun, and in **29** fear the old king called down to Hector, "My son, I beg of you, come within the walls. Do not stay to meet with Achilles. Many of my people has he slain since he first came against Troy, and many sons have I lost to his pitiless spear. Today Lycaon[11] went forth and, against my **30** will, young Polydorus,[12] and I have not seen either return. Oh, my dearest and my best and eldest son, who should be king in my place **33** when I am gone, do not let me have to mourn the death of a third son in a single day." ◀

Hector looked up at him, and his heart was filled with pity, but he shook his head and set his heavy shield against the wall, and remained where he was, before the gates, alone.

King Priam tore his gray hair and pleaded **34** with his son, and, while he spoke, those who stood near him on the wall moved aside to let Queen Hecuba come by. When she came to the watchtower, to her husband's side, and looked down and saw Hector standing there alone, she gave a great cry.

"If you are slain, my son," said Priam, "who will be left to guard the men and women of Troy? For you are our strong shield and our safety, and if you are killed we shall be left **31** defenseless. Troy will fall to Achilles and the Greeks, and I, your old father, shall be slain, my naked body left for the dogs and the vul- tures, as though I had not been a king."

So Priam spoke with tears, yet he could not **35** persuade his son. Nor could Hecuba prevail with him, though she, too, wept and said, "Have pity on me, my child, if on no other. I gave you life: must I now see that life taken from you with my own eyes?"

But Hector, torn between two duties, stood where he was until he, too, could see Achilles coming, in the forefront of the Greeks. Then he almost turned and fled in through the gates, but checked himself, thinking, "If I go within the walls to safety now, I must face Poly- damas,[13] who gave me such good counsel, bid- ding me order the Trojans back to the city when he knew that Achilles was to fight again: and I would not hear him. He will reproach me, that by my folly so many men have died who did not need to die. How can I go into the city now, to hear some wretch of no account say of me, 'Hector, in his pride, has brought ruin on his people'? No, I would rather stay and meet Achilles and either kill him or die glori- ously."

Then he thought how, perhaps for the Greeks as well as for the Trojans, the war had lasted long enough. "What if I were to lay down my weapons and strip off my armor and go all unarmed to meet Achilles, offer him Helen for Menelaus, and half of the great wealth of Troy, that the war between us might be over and our two peoples be at peace?" For a moment he was eager and hopeful; and then he remembered that it was he who had killed Patroclus, and that there could be no mercy for him from Achilles, though he offered him the whole of Troy and all its riches, for himself alone. "He would kill me as I stood unarmed before him. For between Achilles and myself there can be no pretty speeches, such as loving youths and maidens toss lightly to one another—fool that I was to think it." He shrugged his shoulders and took up his shield again.

Moving forward from the Scaean Gate, he saw Achilles running towards him, brandish-

11. **Lycaon** (lī-kā′ŏn).
12. **Polydorus** (pŏl-ĭ-dō′rəs): Priam's youngest son.

13. **Polydamas** (pō-lĭd′ə-məs): Hector's brother-in-law.

634

▶Reading Skills Objective: Identifying Cause-and-Effect Relationships

Hector prepares for battle.
Franco–Flemish wool and silk
tapestry (1472–1474).
(*Above*) Hector being armed,
surrounded by Andromache,
Astyanax, Hecuba, Helen,
and Polyxene. (*Below*) Hector
detained by Priam.

VISUAL CONNECTIONS

About the Artwork

Throughout the Renaissance, tapestry-making was a high art form. In Flanders (ruled at the time by the French) the fifteenth and sixteenth centuries produced particularly fine tapestries. Royalty, as well as wealthy clergymen, feudal nobles, and rich merchants, owned huge collections of the hangings.

They were used as interior wall hangings and as decorations for holiday celebrations and battle tents. Favorite subjects included myths, chivalrous and romantic adventures, and pastoral (romanticized rural) scenes.

Ideas for Writing

In this tapestry, various details give an impression of bustling activity. Students might write essays in which they discuss their observations about the various details. For example, what is Hector's attitude toward the coming battle? What are the attitudes of the other people in the scene toward Hector? How do the costumes add to the mood of the depicted scene?

Hector asks Achilles to exchange an oath ensuring that "the victor will respect the other's body." Explain to students that proper burial rites were all-important to the ancient Greeks.

According to their religious beliefs, one whose body was not buried could not cross over the River Styx into Hades, the land of the dead.

36

Characterization. Hector's fear and retreat was probably intended to shock Homer's audience. Perhaps seems more understandable to modern readers. Hector is a **hero,** but his opponent is superhuman.

37 Comparing/Contrasting
What is contrasted to the description of Hector's flight around the walls of Troy? Images of former peacetime are evoked, contrasting with present conflict.

38

Hector is alone, outside city walls, and removed from help of the gods. His only defense is flight.

39

Hector is deceived by gods and stops to engage Achilles, believing he will be helped. He has actually been abandoned by gods.

40

This was a normal request between opponents. To respect the corpse was a point of honor. Achilles refuses.

41

Metaphor. Analogy identifies Achilles as wolf and Hector as sheep. Again, hot-tempered Achilles refuses to listen to reasonable request.

42

Athene intervenes, influencing events of battle.

ing his father's long spear, and knew that the time was very close when Patroclus might be avenged.

36 Then suddenly he thought, "By all the immortal gods, I do not want to die," and a great fear came upon him, and he turned and fled along the walls; and with a shout, Achilles was after him, signing to his men to keep away, for Hector was for him alone.

Past the watchtower Hector fled, and by the old figtree, and on to the smoother surface of the wagon track, a short distance from the walls, where the going was easier; and close after him came Achilles. They reached, and passed, the two springs and the washing **37** troughs of stone, where, in the days of peace, before the Greek ships had come, the wives and women of Troy had brought their clothes to wash. On, on, they ran, as though it were a race that they were running, and for a prize. A prize there was indeed, and it was Hector's life.

Right around the city they ran; and ever Hector sought to run close in beneath the walls, so that the watchers might drop stones and weapons down on Achilles. But Achilles saw his intention, and always contrived to keep between him and the walls, to prevent him. **38** Three times about the city they ran, and each time, as they passed the Scaean Gate, Hector tried to turn aside to escape within; and each time Achilles was there to intercept him and drive him back again on to the track.

But when they came for the fourth time to the springs and the washing troughs, the immortal gods, beguiling him—for he was doomed—sent Hector's fear from him, and he stood and turned to face Achilles. And in that **39** moment, bright Apollo, till then his constant protector, abandoned him, leaving him, at last, to stand alone.

Breathlessly Hector called out to Achilles, "I will fly from you no longer, son of Peleus. Here let one of us make an end of the other. But first let us take an oath together that whichever is **40** the victor will respect the other's body. I swear to you, Achilles, that if the gods are with me today and let me take your life, your armor I shall keep for myself, but your body I shall give to the Greeks, that they may burn it as befits the son of a king. Give me your oath to do likewise for me."

Achilles stood a short way off and leaned upon his spear, his breast heaving underneath **41** the shining armor. When he had breath enough to speak, he said, "You must be mad to talk to me of oaths. There are no oaths made between men and beasts of prey. Wolves do not swear oaths with the sheep within the fold. There can be no oaths between us, Hector." He straightened up and moved his hand along the spear shaft. "Now show if you have courage, son of Priam, or whether all your great fame is undeserved, for the time has come for you to pay me for the death of Patroclus." He raised his spear and flung it; but Hector, watching carefully, crouched down, so that it passed over him and lodged, transfixed and quivering, in the ground behind him.

"Your aim was poor, Achilles. Now may the gods speed my spear and may it find its mark, for all Troy's enemies, you are the one most to be feared." Hector cast his spear and his aim was true, for the bronze head struck, ringing, full upon Achilles' shield; but the shield made by immortal Hephaestus held and was not pierced, and the spear fell harmlessly to the ground.

Hector stood dismayed, for he had no second spear; then he drew his sword and stepped aside, ready to fall upon Achilles, who leaped forward to snatch up once again his father's **42** spear: and Athene herself, unseen, put it into his hand. And so the two of them stood close and faced each other, Achilles in the armor which a god had made for him, and Hector in Achilles' armor which the gods had given to

Peleus; and each watched the other warily to see where he should strike, for on that next blow would hang the outcome of the combat.

43 But Achilles knew the weak place in his own armor that he had brought from his father's house and worn so many times: a gap between the breastplate and the cheekpiece of the helmet. And there he thrust his spear, into Hector's neck, and Hector fell to the ground, gasping out his life.

Achilles laughed to see him. "Fool that you were, Hector. You forgot me when you killed Patroclus. Did you think that I would not remember you?"

44 Weakly, with fast ebbing breath, Hector whispered, "I beg of you, Achilles, accept a ransom for my body, that my people may burn it fittingly. Do not leave me for the vultures."

Angrily and bitterly Achilles answered him,

Achilles Kills Hector by Peter Paul Rubens (1577–1640). Museum Boymans–Van Beuningen, Rotterdam

45 "Ask me no favors, Hector. Was it not you who would have set the head of Patroclus upon the walls of Troy? By all the gods, I wish that in my hatred I might tear and devour your flesh myself, for the grief that you have brought to me. There does not live the man who could pay me ransom enough for your body. Let your father offer your weight in gold. He shall never look upon your face again, nor shall your mother lay you on a bier and weep for you."

The blood dripped from the wound in Hector's neck, and his voice was no more than a **46** murmur. "Your heart is hard as iron, Achilles, how could I have hoped to move you?" His voice rattled in his throat, his head sank down, and he was dead.

Exulting, Achilles raised the triumph cry and bent to strip his armor from Hector's body; and the Greeks ran forward, rejoicing

43
With help of the gods, Achilles partly satisfies his desire for vengeance by slaying Hector. Thus, **climax** of **conflict**.

44
Foreshadowing. Priam will eventually attempt to ransom his son's body.

45
Hector had intended to cut off Patroclus' head and give it to the dogs.

Finding Details
46 Analyzing
What simile is used to describe Achilles? What does Hector mean? "Your heart is as hard as iron." Achilles is unyielding and pitiless; he will not be dissuaded by Hector's pleas.

VISUAL CONNECTIONS
About the Artist
Peter Paul Rubens was one of the greatest Renaissance artists, known for his large-scale, colorful, baroque paintings. Originally from Siegen, Germany, Rubens studied art in Italy. He maintained a studio in Antwerp and traveled to Spain, Italy, France, and England to do paintings commissioned by royalty. He became Brussels' court painter in 1609. Many of his paintings deal with mythological, classical, and Biblical themes. Rubens also produced sculpture, tapestries, architectural designs, and illustrations for books. In addition to his artistic pursuits, he was noted for his diplomatic abilities. He was involved in peace negotiations between England and Spain and was knighted by England's King Charles I.

About the Artwork

"Attic," when applied to pottery or other artwork, refers to the work produced on the plain of Attica, the area where the city of Athens is located. According to legend, Athens, the principal city in Greece, is named for the goddess Athene because she gave the people the gift of the olive tree.

In this painting, the woman at the right is using a shuttle to weave the crosswise thread (weft) through the lengthwise thread (warp) while the woman on the left is pressing the already woven weft threads together to make a compact fabric. At the bottom of the painting, the warp threads are tied to loom weights to stretch and secure them while the weaving is done. Archaeologists have found loom weights by the hundreds in excavations of sites dating to the ancient world. Some of these were made of stone, but most were ceramic.

47

Hector's body is defiled by Greeks. Patroclus' death is further avenged by mutilating Hector's body.

48

Having lost their strongest warrior, Trojans equate fate of their city with Hector's defeat.

49

Characterization. Andromache skillfully and caringly runs the household. Her relationship with Hector is characterized by love and concern.

The Metropolitan Museum of Art, Fletcher Fund, 1931

Women working wool on loom. Attic, black-figured lekythos (vase), sixth century B.C. (31.11.10)

that the Trojans had lost their greatest warrior. And there were many, seeing Hector lying **47** there defenseless, thrust their sharp spears into his body, who would not have dared to face him while he lived.

48 Watching, helplessly and with horror, from the walls, the Trojans cried aloud and lamented that their best protection against the enemy was lost. Queen Hecuba shrieked and tore her veil; and it was all that they could do to hold back old Priam, who would have run out through the Scaean Gate in frenzy to reach his son.

Hector's wife, Andromache, was in her husband's house, working at her loom on a strip of purple cloth, adorning it with flowers of every **49** color. She had just called to her women to set the great tripod and cauldron upon the fire, so that there should be hot water ready for a bath for Hector when he came from the battlefield, for it was nearing evening.

They were hastening to do her bidding at that very moment when she heard the sounds of lamentation from the walls. Her cheeks grew pale and her hand shook, so that the shuttle fell to the floor, and she ran out from the house and through the streets to the wall, and the people made way for her. She looked down upon the plain, gave one cry, and fell senseless into the arms of those about her.

50 When she came to herself again, she wept and exclaimed, "To what an ill fate were we born, you and I, Hector. And to what an ill fate has our little son been born, that he is left fatherless while yet a babe." And so she wept, and her women wept with her.

51 There were some amongst the triumphant Greeks who were for attacking the city at that very moment, sure that it would fall easily to them while the Trojans were all confounded by the calamity that they had seen and crushed by their great loss.

52 And though at first Achilles agreed with them, he then said, "Let Troy be. I have done what I came out to do. Let us return to the ships, for we have had a great victory today. Shall Patroclus lie longer unburied, unmourned and forgotten? I shall not forget him so long as I still live; and even if, in the land of Hades, men forget their dead, yet I shall remember Patroclus, even there. Come, let us go."

And Achilles, in his hatred, pierced the sinews[14] of Hector's feet from heel to ankle and bound them together with a thong, and made fast the body to the back rail of his chariot, so that the head lay along the ground. He flung in Hector's weapons and his own armor, then leaped himself into the chariot, and snatching the reins and the whip from Automedon, he turned the horses' heads for the shore. He lashed them to a gallop, and Xanthus and Balius[15] went like the West Wind, who was their 53 sire; and so Hector's body was dragged behind the chariot all across the Trojan plain, with his dark hair trailing in the dust.

14. **sinews** (sĭn′yōoz): tendons.
15. **Xanthus:** (zăn′thəs); **Balius** (bā′lĭ-əs): twin horses.

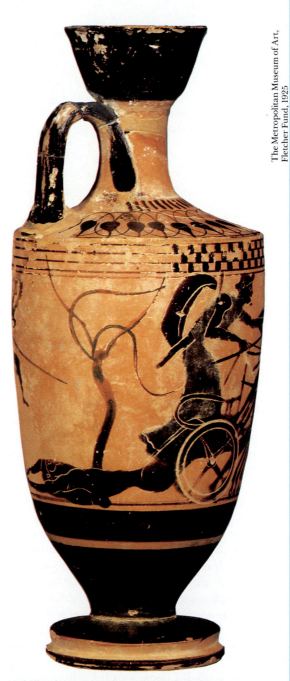

The Metropolitan Museum of Art, Fletcher Fund, 1925

Achilles dragging Hector's body. Attic, black–figured lekythos (early fifth century B.C.). Attributed to the Diosphos Painter.

VISUAL CONNECTIONS
About the Artist
The Diosphos Painter—his actual name is unknown—is considered to be among the most prominent of Attic ceramic artists. The names of a number of artists of the ancient world are known to archaeologists, but in the case of unsigned work, scientists can sometimes still deduce that several pieces were produced by the same hand because of similarities in details of style, workmanship, and materials. In such a case, a name is assigned, usually referring to one characteristic about the artist's work.

50

Foreshadowing. Their fates are more bleak than Andromache's statement reveals. Her son will be murdered as well.

51 Summarizing
How do the Greeks, other than Achilles, view Hector's death?
Other Greeks view Hector's death in terms of its effect on the war.

52
Achilles, involved on a more personal level, gives command to return so that Patroclus can be buried.

53
Hector's death and public defilement of his body fulfills Achilles' desire for vengeance.

The Iliad **639**

54

To honor a dead hero, athletic contests called funeral games were staged.

55

During Trojan War, Idaeus was official herald of Trojan forces.

56

Automedon, Achilles' charioteer, drove immortal horses for Achilles and Patroclus.

57 Expressing an Opinion
Is Priam behaving wisely? Answers will vary. He sacrifices his pride and puts his life in danger in attempt to have his son's body returned to him.

58

Irony. Achilles will not live to see his father again. He, like Hector, will be slain in Trojan War.

59

It was believed that ghost of deceased could not enter Hades unless cremated or buried.

60

Thetis already advised Achilles to return Hector's body.

61

Foreshadowing. Later in war, Paris kills Achilles with arrow by shooting him in the heel, only vulnerable place on his body.

62 Analyzing
To whom is Achilles referring? Patroclus.

54 *The Greeks hold a funeral feast and games to honor the memory of Patroclus. After twelve days, King Priam goes to Achilles to ransom the body of his son,* **59** *Hector. Achilles, who is moved by the old man's grief, relents and returns Hector's body so that he can be mourned by the people of Troy. The poem ends when the remains of Hector's body are laid to rest in a* **60** *burial mound.*

The Ransom

Priam came down from his chariot, and leaving
55 Idaeus to hold the horses and the mules, he went alone into the hut of Achilles.

Achilles, having at that moment finished his meal, was sitting, unsmiling, apart from his
56 companions, and only Automedon was near him, to pour more wine for him, or fetch more meat, should he demand it. Straight to Achilles old Priam went, unhesitatingly; and before he
57 could be prevented, knelt in front of him and clasped his knees in supplication, and kissed the hands which had slain his son.

Achilles looked at him with amazement; whilst all his companions in the hut fell silent, watching the stranger who had come amongst them, and wondering who he might be.

"Great Achilles, I beseech your mercy in the name of King Peleus, your father, whose years equal mine, and who, even as I, stands now on
58 the sad threshold of old age. Yet, unlike me, he lives with hope, hope that one day soon he will see his dear son return to him, victorious after many battles. But I, I have no hope to lighten my remaining days. The dearest and the best of all my sons is gone, and I shall never speak with
62 him or hear his voice again. Nor will he ever return victorious to his father's house. Yet one little grain of comfort would it bring to me, in my last years, if I might look upon his face once more and touch him with my hands; and a great solace would it be to me if, in the sad and

lonely, unprotected days which yet remain to me, I could remember how his body had been
59 burnt with all honor as befitted the son of a king, and if I could look upon the burial mound which his mourning comrades had raised for him. In the name of your own father
60 and in the name of immortal Thetis,[16] your mother, have mercy, great Achilles, and give back to Priam, that most wretched king, the body of Hector, his son. A great ransom have I brought you for him; do not refuse it." The tears streamed down his cheeks and he could hardly speak for weeping. He clasped Achilles' hands and said, "I implore you, have pity on an old man who must humble himself and kneel to one who has slain so many of his sons."

Achilles, much moved, gently loosed the old king's clasp and put him from him. His eyes were filled with tears and he turned his head away, thinking how his father Peleus would wait
61 in vain for his homecoming. "I shall never see my father or my own land again," he thought. Then he thought how he would never again see Patroclus, a far greater grief than any other, and the tears would not be denied. And so they wept together: Achilles for his father and his friend, with the old king crouched at his feet, weeping for his son.

But at last, as Achilles' tears grew less, he was once again aware of Priam, and immediately he stood and raised the old man kindly, saying, "Your courage is indeed great, King Priam, that you ventured alone amongst your enemies to seek me out. But, come, sit here upon this seat and let us put aside our sorrowing. For of what avail are tears? They cannot bring back the
62 dead. That is a thing which I have learnt." And he led him to a chair.

But Priam shook his head sternly. "Should I sit and take my ease, son of Peleus, while Hector lies in the dust amongst his enemies? No. Give

---

16. **Thetis** (thē′tĭs).

TRANSPARENCY 49

Reader Response
Test of Strength — asks students to identify heroic characteristics and evaluate a literary character according to this criteria.

him back to me and let me see him. Take the ransom I have brought you, it is a fitting price for the son of a great king."

For a moment Achilles frowned, then with an effort he forced down his rising anger and **63** answered, "Do not provoke me with ill-chosen words, good king. I shall give you Hector's body, as you ask, for I think that you came here today by the will of the gods, else could you not have reached my hut unharmed." He signed to Automedon to follow him, and quickly left the hut.

Outside, he called Idaeus, bidding him go in to his master and rest himself; then he ordered Automedon to unharness the mules and the horses from the wagon and the chariot, and to carry the ransom into his hut. "But leave a tunic and two cloaks to wrap the body in," he said, "lest Priam, seeing his son's wounds, should reproach me, and I should grow angry at his **64** words and do what I would afterwards regret. For I would not dishonor the gods by mistreating a suppliant, and he a gray-haired king."

He bade the captive women take Hector's body from where it lay, and, in some place apart, where Priam could not see them, to wash it and anoint it with oil and wrap it in the tunic **65** and the cloaks. And when all had been done as he commanded, he himself helped to lay Hector's body on the wagon; and as he did so, in his heart he cried out, "Do not be angry, Patroclus, if, even in the land of Hades, you hear that I have given Hector's body to the father who loved him. Do not be angry with me, but understand why I have done it, even as you would have understood while you yet lived."

Then Achilles returned once more into his hut. "I have done as you asked, King Priam. Your son lies on your wagon. Tomorrow you shall bear him back to Troy. But now you shall eat and drink with me, and for tonight you shall lie safely beneath my roof."

Priam sat, and Achilles gave him roasted **66** meat upon a platter, and Automedon brought bread to him in a basket; and in silence they ate and drank together peaceably, the old king and the young warrior who had slain his son.

When the meal was finished, it had grown dark, and a slave set torches on the walls, and Priam, rested and refreshed, looked well for the first time at Achilles, all golden in the flaring torchlight, and saw how all that he had heard of his peerless beauty was true, and he **67** thought, "Truly, rumor has not lied. He is like one of the immortal gods to look upon."

Achilles, watching, marked how Priam gazed at him, but he said nothing; and it was Priam who broke their silence.

68 "This is the first time in twelve long days," he said, "that I have sat to eat and drink with other men, for I have cared nothing for food or wine since Hector died. As little as I have tasted, so little have I slept for grief. But this evening, son of Peleus, I have eaten and drunk with you, and now I am weary and would sleep."

At once Achilles ordered beds to be prepared for Priam and Idaeus in the outer porch. "For- **69** give it, good king," he said, "that I put an honored guest to sleep outside. But if any leader of the Greeks should come here through the darkness to speak with me tonight—as well might be—he would see you, should you be lying near the hearth, and know you for the king of Troy. And if word reached Agamemnon that you were here, no doubt, to spite me, he would try to make it difficult for you to take with you the body of your son, which I have given you leave to take. But now, before we part tonight, tell me, how many days do you need to celebrate the funeral rites of Hector? For I doubt, with matters as they are, that the Greeks will go out to fight unless I go with them; and I shall keep from battle for as many days as you need."

Priam, touched by his offer, said "I am grateful for your kindness, son of Peleus. May the gods reward you for it. You must know that it is

63
Characterization. Tension rises as Achilles tries to control his anger. His volatile character is suggested by his warning.

64
Use to answer **study question 1c,** p. 643.

65 Summarizing
Analyzing
What does Achilles do after giving orders to the women? Why does Achilles do this? He helps with Hector's body. He probably wants to show that his intentions are honorable and that he has not lost his respect for the dead.

66
Irony. The two share a meal together, each suffering a loss caused by the other.

67
Hero. Achilles is of semi-divine birth and bears godlike qualities. Priam can see that Achilles is extraordinary.

68
Return to eating and sleeping symbolizes resolution of **conflict.**

69 Analyzing
How is Achilles' character further developed by these actions? He shows kindness and respect; he is protective of Priam; he endangers his allegiance to Greeks by allowing Priam to stay.

TRANSPARENCY 48
Reader Response
Coming Attractions – asks students to portray the highlights of a literary character's performance.

TRANSPARENCY 52
Literary Elements
The Epic Hero – explores the nature of an epic hero as a special type of character.

CLOSURE
Ask students to recall the events that lead to the main **conflict**. Have students identify the conflict, the characters involved, and its resolution. Ask them also to compare and contrast the heroes, Achilles and Hector.

70
No funeral games will be held because of time; Hector's funeral will not be as elaborate as that of Patroclus or other heroes due to brevity of truce.

71 Finding Details
What two factors make Priam's journey successful? Kindness of Achilles, assistance of Hermes.

72
Cassandra has prophetic powers; possibly these powers enable her to see arrival first.

73
The Pergamus is the citadel, or fortress, of Troy.

74
Foreshadowing. She clearly implies ultimate fate of her son as well as of Troy.

75
Characterization. Hecuba's eulogy epitomizes sentiments of a warrior's mother.

76
Helen's lament concerns itself with Hector's kindness. He was one of her few protectors and had not judged her.

70 not easy for us, pent up in our city as we are, to venture far from the walls to fetch wood. Give us eleven days, good Achilles. Nine days to mourn for Hector and to gather the wood we shall need for his pyre; on the tenth day we shall burn him and keep his funeral feast, and on the eleventh we shall raise the burial mound above him." He paused, then added, "On the twelfth day, if need be, we shall fight again."

Achilles smiled a little. "You shall have your twelve days' truce, King Priam, I give you my word on it." He laid his hand for a moment upon the old king's arm in reassurance, saying to him, "Now lie down and sleep, you and your <u>herald</u>, and have no fear, for you will be safe beneath my roof."

71 And so, amongst his enemies, Priam slept calmly and in peace; but long before dawn Hermes, once again in the likeness of a Greek youth, woke him, saying, "You came to Achilles as a suppliant, and as a guest he has received you. Him you can trust, for you sleep beneath his roof; yet you can trust no other amongst the Greeks. Do not delay here, close by the ships. A great ransom you have given for your son, but it would be a ransom three times as great that the people of Troy would need to pay to buy your freedom, once Agamemnon knew that you were here."

Hastily, and in fear, Priam roused Idaeus, and they hurried from Achilles' hut, while Hermes himself harnessed the mules and the horses and, once again, led them safely past the ships across the plain. At the ford of the Scamander[17] he left them and returned to high Olympus.

72 As the sun was rising, the wagon and the chariot came slowly along the track towards the Scaean Gate. Cassandra, Hector's sister, watching from the walls, beheld, in the first light of day, her father and Idaeus, and saw that they

17. **Scamander** (skă-măn′dər): river of Troy.

had returned with him whom they had gone to fetch, and with a loud cry she roused all the people. "Come, all you men and women of Troy. If ever you welcomed back Hector, living, from the battle, come now and welcome him, dead. For he died to save our city and us all."

Out from their houses and out from Priam's palace came the people of Troy, crowding about the gates as Priam brought home his son, and with tears and wailing they welcomed him, **73** following the wagon up the wide street to the Pergamus.

In the palace Hector was laid upon a bier, and about him stood the singers to sing his <u>dirge</u>; and one by one the noble women of the household made lament for him.

74 First spoke Andromache, his wife, with her arms clasped about her husband's head. "Oh, Hector, ill-fated are we whom you have left defenseless, and ill-fated is your little son, but most ill-fated of all am I, your unlucky wife; for you did not stretch out your arms to me when you were dying, nor speak to me in words which I might have remembered with tears and treasured in my heart for all my life."

75 Beside her stood Queen Hecuba. "You were the eldest and the dearest to me of all my children, Hector," she said. "And while you lived divine Apollo, the Bright One, cared well for you. Yet even in your death the immortal gods did not utterly forsake you; for, though I dared not hope to do so, I have seen your dear face once again, and in all honor do you lie in your father's house, and in all honor shall we celebrate your funeral." But, after that, she could say no more for weeping.

76 Then Helen came to them, and the women drew aside as she passed and would not look at her, walking slowly until she stood beside the bier, looking down on Hector. "Kind Hector," she said quietly, "of all the brothers of Paris, you alone never reproached me for the trouble that I brought on Troy, and always would you

642

642 THE EPIC

Some students may enjoy writing sketches of one or more of the characters in the *Iliad*. They should include information given about the characters from the selection as well as their own **inferences** based upon what they have read.

Encourage students to read accounts of the legend of Helen of Troy and her rescue from the Trojans. Some research indicates that some of the people and places described in the *Iliad* actually existed. Other students might research the history of Troy and either write an essay or report

their findings to the class. Students might enjoy reading Jean Giraudoux's play *Tiger at the Gates* to get a closer look behind the walls of Troy.

---

defend me against the harsh words of others. Now that you are gone, in all Troy I have no man to speak for me, save your father, who, with you, alone was kind." And she drew her veil across her face to hide her tears.

77 For nine days was Hector mourned; and on the tenth day, when dawn was come, they laid him on a tall pyre and fired it. All day it burnt, and through the night the ashes smoldered; but on the morning of the eleventh day they poured wine upon the ashes and gathered up the dead man's bones and laid them in a golden urn and set upon it stones and earth, raising a high burial mound.

And so, by the compassion of Achilles, was Hector buried, who had slain Patroclus and brought Achilles so much grief.

Reading Check

1. Why does Calchas ask for Achilles' protection?
2. How has Agamemnon angered the god Apollo?
3. How does Agamemnon make an enemy of Achilles?
4. Why is Patroclus mistaken for Achilles during battle?
5. What prevents the Greeks from attacking Troy?
6. What oath does Hector ask Achilles to swear before their combat?
7. How does Achilles know which is the weakest place in the armor Hector is wearing?
8. What is Hector's dying request?
9. Why does Priam go to Achilles' hut?
10. What truce do Achilles and Priam agree upon?

For Study and Discussion

Analyzing and Interpreting the Epic

1. Achilles, the greatest of the Greek warriors, is the hero of the *Iliad*. He is depicted as having intense emotions. **a.** How does he show that he is quick to anger in his quarrel with Agamemnon? **b.** How is his anger shown later in the story? **c.** Where does he admit that he cannot control his rages? **d.** How does this human failing make Achilles a more believable figure?

2. Hector is the greatest warrior among the Trojans. **a.** What impression do you receive of him in the scene with his family? **b.** How does Homer evoke sympathy for him in the combat with Achilles? **c.** Do you find him more or less admirable than Achilles? Explain.

3. In the *Iliad* the outcome of battles is often decided by the Olympian gods and goddesses. Where else do they intervene to affect the action?

4. **a.** What aspect of Achilles' nature is revealed in the scene with Priam? **b.** How does this scene make a nobler figure of Achilles?

5. Women play an important role in this epic. Identify each of these figures and explain her role in the events: Helen, Hecuba, Andromache, Cassandra.

Writing About Literature

▶ Comparing Heroic Figures

Write an essay comparing Achilles and Hector. What do you learn about each hero from his words, his actions, and his thoughts, as well as from the reactions of others? How are they alike and how are they different?

▶Before students begin this writing assignment, you may want to refer them to the **Writing About Literature** section on p. 672.

77
Hector's funeral, brought about, ironically, by Achilles' compassion, is relatively quiet.

READING CHECK
1. He is afraid of Agamemnon (p. 628).
2. Captures Chryses' daughter; refuses to give her back (p. 628).
3. Insults him; wants part of his booty (p. 629).
4. Wears Achilles' armor (p. 633).
5. The walls (p. 631).
6. To respect the other's body after death (p. 636).
7. It is his armor (p. 636).
8. To accept ransom for his body (p. 637).
9. To ask for son's body (p. 640).
10. Eleven-day truce (p. 642).

FOR STUDY AND DISCUSSION
1a. Springs to his feet with blazing eyes; becomes "too angry to speak or even move." 1b. Seeks revenge; tells Hector he "could tear and devour his flesh himself"; gets angry with Priam. 1c. Says if Priam reproaches him, he will become angry and do something he will regret. 1d. Humanized by inability to control emotions.
2a. Loving husband and father, courageous and responsible. 2b. Worries about family's grief and begs Achilles to return his body. 2c. Answers may vary. Hector seems more compassionate.
3. Athene stops Achilles from attacking Agamemnon. Hermes wakens Priam.
4a. Compassion. 4b. He shows empathy.
5. Helen and Paris are cause of Trojan war; Hecuba, Hector's mother, pleads to him not to fight Achilles; Andromache, Hector's wife, begs him to stop fighting; Cassandra, Hector's sister, alerts Troy to arrival of Priam and Hector's body.

Exploring the Subject

Scandinavian Vikings (Norsemen or Northmen) raided the coasts of continental Europe from about the fourth to the eleventh century. They carried the story of Beowulf with them into some of these other lands, including England.

In the harsh northern lands—Denmark, Sweden, and Norway—each farmer had to be not only a stock-breeder but also a fisherman and boat-builder. These Northmen were brave, fiercely independent, often cruel, and faithful to the death. When overpopulation forced them to look for new land and livelihoods, they set sail, fighting if they were opposed. They settled in various countries, including those we now call Italy, France, and Spain. Except in Anglo-Saxon England, they failed to have a great influence on their adopted lands. Instead, they were assimilated by the existing populations. Vikings were called Danes in England, Varangians in Russia.

The man who led the Varangian invasion of Russia was Rurik. According to legend, he and his troops were asked by the people of Novgorod, Russia, to come there and found a just, orderly government for them. Historians do not accept this version, however. They believe he seized a small coastal town, made it his stronghold, and then proceeded inland to capture Novgorod. Rurik is believed to be the founder of the Rurikid dynasty, which ruled Russia until 1598.

MEETING INDIVIDUAL NEEDS

ESL/LEP •The fact that *Beowulf* is written in one continuous block of text makes it difficult to read. Keeping this in mind, you may want to focus on a few short segments, reading them aloud, then asking the class to paraphrase. Also, with the help of a reference librarian, you may want to find artistic reproductions from various *Beowulf* editions that depict the main characters and their dramatic interactions. Make copies of these and share them with the class, using the pictures as departure points for discussion of the poem. Complementing the text with visual references will stimulate interest and facilitate comprehension.

BEOWULF

1 Although *Beowulf* was composed around the eighth century, its legendary adventures are much older and were probably known for centuries before the poem was written. The poem reveals a great deal

2 about the customs and values of the Germanic people who invaded

3 the British Isles and established settlements there in the Middle Ages.

4 Important in this society was the relationship of the lord and his thanes, or followers. In return for loyalty and military service, the lord rewarded his followers with treasure and feasts.

5 The poem focuses on the adventures of Beowulf, a great warrior with superhuman powers. In his youth, Beowulf battles with two terrible monsters, Grendel and Grendel's mother. In his old age, he

6 fights his last battle against a fire dragon. The only surviving manuscript of the poem is in Anglo-Saxon, or Old English. The excerpts you will read are from a verse translation in Modern English by Ian Serraillier.

Names and Places in *Beowulf*

Beowulf (bā′ə-wo͞olf′): hero of the epic. He is from the land of the Geats, in Sweden.

Breca (brĕk′ə): Beowulf's opponent in a swimming match.

Geats (yă′əts, yā′əts): a people in Sweden. Beowulf becomes their king and rules them for fifty years.

Grendel (grĕn′dəl): a troll-like monster who lives in the fens and attacks the warriors of Hrothgar's court.

7 **Heorot** (hā′ō-rŏt): the mead hall built by King Hrothgar to feast his followers.

Hrothgar (hrŏth′gär): the Danish king who builds Heorot.

Unferth (ŭn′fârth): a jealous noble who attacks Beowulf as a braggart.

Wulfgar (wo͞olf′gär): herald of King Hrothgar.

Statue of Rurik, a Viking chief who settled in Russia in A.D. 862.

INTRODUCTION TO BEOWULF

1
Beowulf, based on earlier Germanic tales, was composed by Anglo-Saxons. Source for modern translations is one surviving manuscript from about A.D. 1000, probably a copy of an earlier one.

2
Pagan and Christian ideas are expressed in the poem. Beowulf himself is a blend of history and myth.

3
Events described in *Beowulf* may have occurred as early as the fifth century; one datable event is Hygelac's raid on Franks, which occurred in A.D. 520.

4
Relationship crucial to warrior society; ideal thane gave unquestioning loyalty.

5
Beowulf is the embodiment of Anglo-Saxon ideals: courageous, unfailingly loyal, and always willing to test himself against fate (Wyrd).

6
Its complete version is characterized by majestic language, **rhythm,** and a somber mood.

7
Setting in which the episode takes place.

F R O M

Beowulf the Warrior

Translated by
IAN SERRAILLIER°

The Battle with Grendel

1 Hrothgar, King of the Danes, glorious in battle,
Built him a huge hall—its gleaming roof
Towering high to heaven—strong to withstand
The buffet of war. He called it Heorot

2 And lived there with his Queen. At time of feasting 5
He gave to his followers rings and ornaments
And bracelets of bright gold, cunningly wrought,°

3 Graved with runes° and deeds of dead heroes.
Here they enjoyed feasts and high fellowship,
Story and song and the pride of armed peace. 10
But away in the treacherous fens, beyond the moor,

4 A hideous monster lurked, fiend from hell,
Misbegotten son of a foul mother,
Grendel his name, hating the sound of the harp,
The minstrel's song, the bold merriment of men 15
In whose distorted likeness he was shaped
Twice six feet tall, with arms of hairy gorilla
And red ferocious eyes and ravening jaws.
He, one night, when the warriors of Hrothgar lay
Slumbering after banquet, came to Heorot, 20
Broke down the door, seized in his fell grip
A score and more of the sleeping sons of men
And carried them home for meat. At break of day
The hall of Heorot rang loud and long
With woe of warriors and grief of the great King. 25
Thereafter, from dark lake and dripping caves
Night after night over the misty moor
Came Grendel, gross and grim, famished for flesh.
Empty the beds, no man dared sleep at Heorot,

Silver arm ring from Hornelund, Denmark (tenth century).
National Museum, Denmark

Three–ringed gold collar with filigree and carved figures from Gotland, Sweden (sixth century A.D.). This is an example of fine Viking craftsmanship.
Statens Historiska Museet, Stockholm

°**Serraillier** (sə-rāl′yər). 7. **cunningly wrought:** skillfully made. 8. **runes:** characters in an ancient alphabet.

In *Beowulf,* a superhuman hero battles hideous monsters in order to save the Danes. After students read the text, invite them to think of stories from their own cultures in which heroes and monsters clash. Examples may be taken from a wide variety of sources—from comic books to bedtime stories. Do these stories have anything in common with *Beowulf?* In what ways are they different? What kinds of weapons are used? Who is the enemy? What is the enemy's objective? What role, if any, do women play? Who wins in the end? By what means?

5 But Grendel smelt them out of their hiding place,   30
And many a meal he made of warriors.
For twelve years he waged war with Hrothgar,
Piling grief upon grief. For twelve years
He haunted great Heorot.

5
Grendel is established as an implacable force against which warriors are powerless.

VISUAL CONNECTIONS
Exploring the Subject
The ship pictured here is seventy-two feet long with a draft of only three feet and planks less than one inch thick. Demonstrating its seaworthiness, a replica built in 1893 successfully sailed across the Atlantic. The Vikings were the best sailors and shipbuilders of their time, sailing as far east as Constantinople (Istanbul) and as far west as the New World. The Viking war ship, the *drakkar* (with a prow shaped like a dragon), was for many years the terror of European coasts.

Vikings were bold, imaginative raiders. They sometimes transported stolen horses in their narrow ships. If the need arose, in moving from one place of plunder to another, they could transport their vessels over land.

Relating Expression Skills
Some students might like to do further research on Viking ships and make presentations to the class on the designs of the ships. They should note any design elements that have been adapted by modern ship builders. Other students researching Viking ships might enjoy making diagrams or drawings of the ships or even making models out of balsa or cardboard.

University Museum of National Antiquities, Oslo, Norway

A Viking ship discovered in Gokstad, Norway, in 1880.

MEETING INDIVIDUAL NEEDS

ESL/LEP • Lines 44–47 may be difficult to understand because the referent *he* is used in a confusing way. Beginning with "Aged Hrothgar ...," read these four lines aloud and explain that *he* in line 47 ("Boldly *he* strode forth till *he*

stood at his feet") refers to Beowulf, not Hrothgar. "*His* feet" refers to Hrothgar's feet.

6 Analyzing
How does the poet help the listener to visualize the scene? By providing realistic details.

7
Description. Hrothgar, once a great warrior, is now broken old man, and the great hall is somber. In contrast, Beowulf depicted as young and vigorous.

8
"Giver of treasure" and "Lord of the rousing war song" are **kennings,** an Anglo-Saxon literary device that describes a person or thing in a metaphorical way.

9
Use to answer **study question 3,** p. 654.

10
Even though Hrothgar is now old and cannot defeat Grendel, Beowulf will not intrude in Hrothgar's sovereign territory without permission.

11 Summarizing
How does Hrothgar greet Beowulf? As an old family friend, almost as a son.

12
Use to answer **study question 4a,** p. 654.

When Beowulf, the young Swedish warrior, heard of Hrothgar's plight, he was determined to help him. With fourteen of his bravest men he sailed away over the Baltic Sea to Denmark. They left their boat at anchor and climbed up the white cliff.

Thus came the warriors   35
To Heorot and, heavy with weariness, halted by the door.
6 They propped their spears by a pillar; from blistered hands
Their shields slid clattering to the floor. Then Wulfgar,
Herald of the King, having demanded their errand,
Ran to his royal master and quick returning   40
Urged them within. The long hall lay before them,
The floor paved with stone, the roof high-raftered.
In mournful state upon his throne sat brooding
7 Aged Hrothgar, gray-haired and bowed with grief.
Slowly he raised his eyes, leaden, lusterless,   45
And gazed upon the youth as with ringing step
Boldly he strode forth till he stood at his feet.
8   "O noble Hrothgar, giver of treasure,
Lord of the rousing war song, we bring you greeting.
Because we grieve deep for your desolation,   50
Over the long paths of the ocean have we labored,
I and my warriors, to rid you of the brute
That nightly robs you of rest. I am no weakling.
9 With my trusty blade I have slain a monster brood
And blindly at night many a foul sea-beast   55
That writhed and twisted in the bounding wave.
10 I beg you to grant my wish. I shall not fail."
    Then Hrothgar stretched out his arms in welcome
And took him by the hand and said, "Beowulf,
I knew you as a child, and who has not exulted   60
11 In your fame as a fighter? It is a triumph song
That ocean thunders to her farthest shore,
It is a whisper in the frailest seashell.
Now, like your princely father long ago,
In the brimming kindness of your heart you have come   65
To deliver us."
                    But Unferth bristled at these words—
Unferth, who sat always at the feet of Hrothgar,
A groveling, jealous man who could not bear
That anyone should win more fame than he.
12   "Braggart!" he cried. "Are you not that Beowulf   70
Who failed against Breca in the swimming match?

Viking ship with sea monster. Ms. Ashmole 1511, f.86v (late twelfth century).
Bodleian Library, Oxford

Have students locate the Scandinavian countries Denmark, Norway, and Sweden—the home of the ancient Vikings—on a world map. Then have them locate the British Isles, the countries of northern Europe, and northern Russia. Interested students may want to map out the path the Viking invaders took through these countries. Point out that with the Vikings came their tales of Beowulf.

About the Artwork
Painted in Romanesque style, the figures are boldly outlined shapes filled with bright color. The effect is one of overlapping planes rather than three-dimensional figures. Dragons and sea serpents, fearsome symbols to Vikings, are often a focus of their artwork.

Exploring the Subject
In the mythology of early Scandinavian people, there are land monsters, such as Grendel, and sea monsters to threaten Norsemen. The tales depict a universe consisting of the heavens, the earth, and the world below. At the center, supporting all three with its roots, is the world tree. Coiled around the earth is a serpent, its tail caught in its own mouth—a major threat to seamen. In the world below, a dragon gnaws at the root of the world tree and threatens universal destruction.

Relating Expression Skills
Students might bring pictures to class of modern conceptions of monsters in folklore, fiction, and movies and compare these with descriptions of monsters in *Beowulf*. What qualities make each fearsome? Are current-day conceptions of monsters more frightening to us? Why or why not?

13

Unferth desires to undermine Beowulf's claims to being a great fighter.

14

Use to answer **study question 4b,** p. 654.

15 Drawing Conclusions

To what does "northeaster" refer? Storm; in Northern Europe, harsh weather tends to arrive from the northeast.

16

Beowulf sarcastically calls Unferth "brave." He humiliates Unferth by remarking that a truly brave man would have killed Grendel.

17

Alliteration. Repetition of words beginning with *m* and *d* calls attention to grim **atmosphere** associated with Grendel. *Beowulf* contains many examples of alliteration.

18

Poet uses kennings to emphasize that Grendel personifies evil.

19

Suspense. Grendel possesses superhuman strength. Most mortal men would find it impossible to overcome such an enemy.

13 Seven nights you <u>wallowed</u> in the wintry sea—
Some sport that was!—sport for jeering waves
That jollied you like spindrift° from crest to crest
Till, sick with cold, you shrieked for mercy. Who heard?   75
Not Breca, who long since had battled to land,
But the sea, tired at last of its <u>puny</u> plaything,
<u>Spewed</u> you ashore."

                        Angrily Beowulf answered:
14 "That's a drunkard's tale! True, Breca was first
Ashore, but I could have raced him had I wished.   80
We were boys then, with our full share of folly,
Plunging—sword in hand—giddily to battle
With monster whales, when a storm came sweeping down
And gruesome waves ground and trampled us under.
It was Breca that cried for help—I fought to save him,   85
15 But a fierce northeaster whipped us apart
And I saw him no more. In the dark and bitter cold,
The icy brine° was heaving <u>murkily</u> with monsters.
Glad was I of my sword and mailcoat—for a serpent
Had wound his <u>sinewy</u> coils about my waist,   90
And squeezing, dragged me below. But before he could break me,
I slew him—nine others too before the raging floodtide
Rolled me to land. . . . .
16 I am not aware that you, brave Unferth, can boast
Such a record. If you be as bold as you <u>proclaim</u>,   95
Tell me, how comes it that Grendel is still alive?
Ha, I know a coward when I see one! Soon,
If the King be willing, I shall <u>grapple</u> with Grendel
And show you what courage means." . . . .

17   Over the misty moor   100
From the dark and dripping caves of his grim <u>lair</u>,
Grendel with fierce ravenous stride came stepping.
A shadow under the pale moon he moved,
18 That fiend from hell, foul enemy of God,
Toward Heorot. He beheld it from afar, the gleaming roof   105
19 Towering high to heaven. His tremendous hands
Struck the studded door, wrenched it from the hinges
Till the wood splintered and the bolts burst apart.
Angrily he prowled over the polished floor,

74. **spindrift:** spray from the waves. 88. **brine** (brīn): ocean.

A terrible light in his eyes—a torch flaming!   110
As he scanned the warriors, deep-drugged in sleep,
Loud loud he laughed, and pouncing on the nearest
Tore him limb from limb and swallowed him whole,
20 Sucking the blood in streams, crunching the bones.
Half-gorged, his gross appetite still unslaked,°   115
Greedily he reached his hand for the next—little reckoning
21 For Beowulf. The youth clutched it and firmly grappled.

Such torture as this the fiend had never known.
In mortal fear, he was minded to flee to his lair,
22 But Beowulf prisoned him fast. Spilling the benches,   120
They tugged and heaved, from wall to wall they hurtled.
And the roof rang to their shouting, the huge hall
Rocked, the strong foundations groaned and trembled.
Then Grendel wailed from his wound, his shriek of pain
Roused the Danes in their hiding and shivered to the stars.   125
The warriors in the hall spun reeling from their couches,
In dull stupor they fumbled for their swords, forgetting
No man-made weapon might avail. Alone, Beowulf
Tore Grendel's arm from his shoulder asunder,°
23 Wrenched it from the root while the tough sinews cracked.   130
And the monster roared in anguish, well knowing
That deadly was the wound and his mortal days ended.
Wildly lamenting, away into the darkness he limped,
24 Over the misty moor to his gloomy home.
But the hero rejoiced in his triumph and wildly waved   135
In the air his blood-soaked trophy.

           And the sun,
God's beacon of brightness, banishing night,
Made glad the sky of morning. From near and far
The Danes came flocking to Heorot to behold
25 The grisly trophy—Grendel's giant arm   140
Nailed to the wall, the fingertips outspread,
With nails of sharpened steel and murderous spikes
Clawing the roof. Having drunk their fill of wonder,
Eagerly they followed his track to the lake, and there
Spellbound they stared at the water welling with blood,   145
Still smoking hot where down to the joyless deep

115. **unslaked:** unsatisfied. 129. **asunder:** apart.

20
Hero. Before he battles Grendel, Beowulf sees full horror of Grendel's appetite; only a true hero would test fate by grappling with such a monster (example of the **epic hero**).

21 Finding Details
What part of Grendel's body does Beowulf clutch? Grendel's hand.

22
Imagery. Descriptive details provide vivid images of the force of fight between Grendel and Beowulf.

23
Beowulf fights Grendel on equal terms—with his bare hands. Grendel is protected against weapons by a magic spell and can be killed only by this method.

24 Drawing Conclusions
What can the reader assume happens to Grendel? Grendel bleeds to death as did his many victims.

25
Description. Poet creates a vivid picture of Grendel's severed arm. It is a trophy establishing Beowulf as the greatest of heroes.

26 Summarizing
How do the people want to honor Beowulf? They believe he should be king.

27
With Grendel's defeat, custom and order are restored.

28
Beowulf's mother is seen as privileged to have borne such a son. In a warrior society, a woman's status was determined by that of her husband and male relatives.

29
Epic. Queen predicts that Beowulf will be rewarded with his society's greatest honor—poets everywhere will sing of his exploits. He will become immortal in song.

VISUAL CONNECTIONS
Exploring the Subject
Helmets and swords were often beautifully ornamented, reflecting the status of their owners and the importance of weapons in a warrior culture. Ornamental helmets such as this one found in the Swedish boat grave at Vendel were made of iron overlaid with silver and gilded bronze. The helmet was made shortly before *Beowulf* was composed (eighth century).

The Vikings valued good swords and believed they possessed magical properties. Swords were prized by their owners and often personalized with names. They were so valued that they were rarely included with other articles placed in graves. To have one's sword buried with one was a sign of great esteem.

He had dived, downward to death. And they praised Beowulf
And swore that of all men under the sun, beyond measure
26 Mightiest was he and fittest to govern his people.

Meanwhile, in the hall at Heorot the grateful King,   150
All glooming gone, his countenance clear and cloudless
As the sky in open radiance of the climbing sun,
Gave thanks to God for deliverance. "Beowulf," he said,
"Bravest of men, I shall love you now as my son.
All I have is yours for the asking. Take   155
What treasure you will. But first let us feast and be merry."

Straightway they washed the blood from the floor, propped up
The battered door; the drooping walls they draped
With embroidery, bright hangings of woven gold.
27 There was drinking and feasting again, revelry of heroes,   160
And the jeweled goblets clashed. At last the King,
Aged Hrothgar, gray-haired giver of treasure,
Ordered gifts to be brought. To Beowulf he gave
A sword and mailcoat and banner of gleaming gold;
A plated helmet so tough no steel might cleave it;   165
Eight prancing horses with golden harness
And bridles of silver, the proudest saddled with his own
Battle-seat, all set with splendid jewels,
Most cunningly inlaid; to each of the warriors
A sword and bountiful recompense of gold   170
For their friend that Grendel slew.
                    Then the minstrel sang
Of rousing deeds of old. Like flames in the firelight
The heart leapt to hear them. And when he had done
And the harp lay silent, the Queen of the Danes spoke out:
"Beowulf, dearest youth, son of most favored   175
28 And fortunate of mothers, this your deed is matchless.
29 Greater than all these. In the farthest corners
Of the earth your name shall be known. Wherever the ocean
Laps the windy shore and the wave-worn headland,
Your praise shall be sung."
                    And now the feast was ended.   180
With final clarion of trumpets they left the hall,
Hrothgar and his gracious Queen, leading Beowulf
To a stately chamber to rest. But the Danes remained.
Clearing the banquet, they brought couches spread
With pillows and warm coverlets, and lay down,   185

Helmet from Vendel,
Sweden (seventh century).
Statens Historiska Museet,
Stockholm

Viking sword from
Steinsvik, Lodingen,
Nordland [Norway]
(tenth century).

University Museum of National Antiquities,
Oslo, Norway

TRANSPARENCIES 46 & 47	
Fine Art	
Waiting for a Hero – features artwork showing heroes or heroic ideals from diverse cultural traditions.	

TRANSPARENCY 48
Reader Response
Coming Attractions – asks students to portray the highlights of a literary character's performance.

TRANSPARENCY 49
Reader Response
Test of Strength – asks students to identify heroic characteristics and evaluate a literary character according to this criteria.

30 Each with his broad shield at his head, his mailcoat,
His spear and shining helmet—as was the custom
Long ere Grendel came. Now fearless of monster,
Their minds were at ease, quiet as the summer sea,
The sparkling water, unmurmuring and serene   190
Under the moon. In comfort of spirit, in blessed
31 Trust and tranquillity they sank to rest.

32 *Grendel's mother, a she-monster as horrible as her son, comes out of her lair to avenge the death of Grendel. She snatches up one of the Danes and carries him off, along with Grendel's arm and claw. Beowulf follows her to her den and plunges into the lake in full armor. There is a fierce struggle. Finally, Beowulf finds a magic sword and kills the monster.*

Beowulf becomes king of the Geats and rules over them for fifty years. Then
33 *a dragon begins to ravage the land, and Beowulf goes out to fight his final battle. He overcomes the dragon, but receives his death wound. His final request is that his followers raise a funeral pyre and build a mound upon his ashes, to serve as a beacon to sailors.*

Beowulf's final battle with the dragon. Illustrated by Rockwell Kent (1882–1971) for *Beowulf* (1932).
Rare Books and Manuscripts Division, The New York Public Library, Astor, Lenox and Tilden Foundations

30
Even in sleep, Danes are warriors ready to spring into action; battle is a dominant **theme** in this **epic.**

31   Making Generalizations
What mood is evoked at the end of this section of Beowulf*?*
Episode with Grendel is resolved; mood is one of well-being, peace, and tranquility.

32
Viking custom required avenging death of kinsmen or exacting *wergild,* compensatory payment. Grendel's mother is acting in accordance with custom, but the Danes, unaware of her existence, are taken by surprise.

33
Beowulf, now old, continues to test himself against fate—a quality Norsemen considered heroic. While he succeeds in slaying dragon, Wyrd (fate) ends Beowulf's life.

VISUAL CONNECTIONS
About the Artist
Rockwell Kent was an American painter, illustrator, and writer. He also was a wanderer and adventurer who lived at various times in Maine, Newfoundland, and Alaska. Two of the books that he illustrated, now much admired, are editions of *Moby Dick* and *Beowulf.*

TRANSPARENCY 51

Literary Elements
Analyzing an Epic – prompts students to identify and evaluate basic elements of an epic.

READING CHECK
1. Grendel (p. 647).
2. To slay Grendel (p. 648).
3. Unferth (p. 648).
4. Returns to the lake (p. 651).
5. Sword, mailcoat, gold banner, helmet, eight horses and gold harness, silver bridles, king's own jeweled battle-seat (p. 652).

FOR STUDY AND DISCUSSION
1a. Castle built to withstand attack. 1b. Food, entertainment, jewelry.
2a. Hates men's laughter and music; resents his likeness to men. 2b. Grendel is too strong and cannot be killed with weapons.
3. Has slain monsters and sea beasts.
4a. Says Beowulf lost swimming contest and shrieked for mercy. 4b. Says it is drunkard's tale; tells true story.
5a. Grips Grendel's hand, rips arm off, showing superhuman strength. 5b. Tells Hrothgar he has slain monsters and sea serpents (ll. 54–56, 60–63, 90–95).
6. Drinking, feasting, and singing.
7a. Bravery, loyalty, fame, glory.
7b. Heroes are loyal to lords and men; gain glory and fame by bravery, good deeds.

LITERARY ELEMENTS
1. Examples of alliteration: "Built him a huge hall" (l. 2), "Came Grendel, gross and grim, famished for flesh" (l. 28), "Towering high to heaven. His tremendous hands" (l. 106), "He had dived, downward to death" (l. 147).
2. Kennings: "giver of treasure" (ll. 48 and 162), "Lord of the rousing war song" (l. 49).

Reading Check

1. Who wages war against Hrothgar for twelve years?
2. Why does Beowulf make the journey to Heorot?
3. Who accuses Beowulf of boasting?
4. Where does Grendel go after he is fatally wounded?
5. How does King Hrothgar reward Beowulf?

For Study and Discussion

Analyzing and Interpreting the Epic

1a. What indications are there in the opening lines that this poem is about a warrior society? **b.** How are Hrothgar's followers rewarded in times of "armed peace"?

2a. What motives for Grendel's savagery are given in lines 11–18? **b.** Why are Hrothgar and his warriors powerless to stop Grendel?

3. Why does Beowulf believe that he can destroy Grendel? See lines 53–57.

4a. How does Unferth attempt to cast doubt on Beowulf's reputation as a fighter? **b.** How does Beowulf defend himself against Unferth's charge?

5. Beowulf defeats Grendel in hand-to-hand combat, without the help of any weapons. **a.** How does this episode emphasize the hero's superhuman prowess? **b.** Where else in the selection are we told that Beowulf has performed extraordinary feats?

6. What customs are restored at Heorot after Grendel's death?

7a. What heroic characteristics are celebrated in the epic of Beowulf? **b.** What is the importance of such qualities as loyalty, fame, and glory?

Literary Elements

Recognizing Characteristics of Old English Poetry

Old English poems like *Beowulf* were memorized and recited at banquets in the halls of kings and rulers by wandering poets (see lines 171–180). Eventually the poems came to be written down.

The translation in your textbook retains certain features of the oral tradition of Old English poetry. One important characteristic of this verse was **alliteration,** the repetition of similar consonant sounds, usually at the beginning of words. In Old English poetry, alliteration usually occurs on three or more accented syllables in a line. Ian Serraillier creates a similar effect in line 36:

> To *H*eorot and, *h*eavy with weariness, *h*alted by the door

1 Find at least two places in the poem where alliteration is used for emphasis.

Another characteristic in Old English poetry is the use of a descriptive phrase as an indirect way of identifying a person or thing. The term for this device is **kenning.** The sun, for example, is called "God's beacon of brightness" in 2 line 137. What kennings are used for Hrothgar?

CLOSURE
Ask students to cite the values that Beowulf embodies and to identify passages that convey the values of a warrior society.

EXTENSION AND ENRICHMENT
Students might enjoy drawing or painting scenes from *Beowulf,* depicting the hall, the monster and **hero** in battle, or the warriors feasting in the great hall. Students' efforts might be displayed on a bulletin board.

Other students might write essays telling the story of Beowulf from Grendel's point of view. They might enjoy speculating on Grendel's life before Hrothgar built his mead-hall.

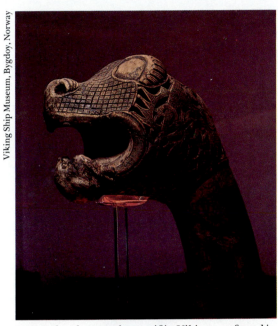

Viking Ship Museum, Bygdøy, Norway

Dragon head, a popular motif in Viking art, found in a burial ship discovered in Oseberg, Norway, in 1904.

Focus on Comparison and Contrast

Identifying a Main Idea

In a comparison/contrast essay, you can focus on the similarities of your subjects, on their differences, or on both. You will help your readers to follow your essay better if you clearly state your focus or **main idea** in the introduction.

For example, for a comparison/contrast essay on Achilles and Beowulf, you might state your main idea this way: "Both Beowulf and Achilles are heroic in their quest for fame and glory, but each hero has a different idea of loyalty." An essay beginning with this statement will probably focus on both similarities and differences.

Choose a pair of subjects for comparison and contrast: for example, football/baseball or cats/dogs as pets. List their similarities and differences. Then write one or two sentences to state the main idea for a comparison/contrast essay on your subjects. Save your notes.

About the Translator

Ian Serraillier (1912–)

A poet, translator, and novelist, Ian Serraillier often retells famous literary works for young readers. He has published more than thirty-five books, including *The Enchanted Island* (1964), stories adapted from Shakespeare's most famous works; *The Challenge of the Green Knight* (1967), a poem about Sir Gawain and the Green Knight; and *Robin in the Greenwood* (1968), a collection of ballads.

When asked about the pronunciation of his name, he responded with the following limerick and note:

If in Doubt
Just call me Ian SerRAILlier
Of Sussex, U.K. (not Australia).
This is not my best verse
But I have written worse
So it's neither a hit nor a failure.

The Christian name is easy—just ignore the first nine letters in antediluvIAN.

Connecting Cultures

Famous Monsters

In many heroic stories the enemy is as repulsive as the hero is admirable. Like Grendel, the monsters often live in darkness and hate light. Often they are cannibals.

Making Connections: Activities

Using an encyclopedia or a mythology book, write a brief description of each of the following famous monsters: Cyclops, Medusa, and the Minotaur. How does each one compare with Grendel?

VISUAL CONNECTIONS
About the Artwork
Carved in wood, this dragon head is covered with an elaborate interlace pattern. This pattern, derived from metalwork motifs, is typically found in Viking and Anglo-Saxon artwork. The purpose of sculptured posts such as this one is unknown.

FOCUS ON COMPARISON AND CONTRAST
Students might brainstorm lists of comparable subjects from this unit or from their personal experience to use for this activity. To help students list similarities and differences, you might suggest they use a graphic aid such as a Venn diagram. Encourage students to be thorough in their lists in order to draw sound conclusions for their main ideas.

ABOUT THE TRANSLATOR
As a child, Serraillier had a classical education, reading and writing verse primarily in Greek and Latin. After his first year at Oxford, he changed from the study of classics to English. He has written a number of modern versions of classical myths, such as *The Gorgon's Head* and *Heracles the Strong.* In contrast, his novels, *The Silver Sword* and *There's No Escape,* are stories that take place during World War II.

CONNECTING CULTURES
1. *Cyclops:* Greek mythology, member of race of one-eyed cannibal giants, loyal to family unit.
Medusa: Greek mythology, one of the Gorgons, winged sisters; hair made of snakes; Medusa was only mortal Gorgon.
Minotaur: Greek mythology, monster in Crete having the body of a man and head of a bull. Like Grendel, these monsters have distorted human characteristics, magic powers, superhuman strength or size. Also share cannibalistic eating habits and intense family loyalty.

Students may be interested to know that the Islamic word for god, *Allah,* originated in the Hebrew language. The Hebrew word for god is *eloah.* Like Judaism and Christianity, Islam is a monotheistic religion; that is, the worshippers believe in only one god. In the story, Sundiata is determined to destroy the people of Sosso (along with their king Soumaoro) because they are pagans; that is, they do not believe in a single god.

INTRODUCTION TO SUNDIATA: AN EPIC OF OLD MALI

1
Although it is centuries old, *Sundiata: An Epic of Old Mali* is a relatively recent **epic.** Nonetheless, it includes many of the conventions established in earlier epics.

2
Names for storytellers in other societies include Anglo-Saxon *scop,* English *bard,* French *minstrel* and *troubadour.*

3
During this time, Timbuktu (which became known as the "meeting point of camel and canoe") was one of the richest commercial cities of Africa, and one of its schools became a center of scholarship in history, law, and Islamic religion.

SUNDIATA: AN EPIC OF OLD MALI

1 Like other epics that were preserved by oral tradition before they were written down, the story of Sundiata was passed down over the centuries by professional storytellers. In ancient Africa these storytellers,
2 known as *griots* (grē′ō), were oral historians who memorized the history of their people. Today griots are often entertainers as well as poets and historians.

Sundiata was a thirteenth-century leader who founded the Empire of Mali. The empire, which flourished from 1235 to 1500, was an area in West Africa that included most of present-day Gambia, Guinea,
3 Senegal, and Mali. The city of Timbuktu became a great center of learning.

The epic of Sundiata exists in many versions. The version of the epic that you will read here is told by Djeli Mamadou Kouyaté, a griot of the Keita clan. It is translated from Malinke, the language of the Mandingo people of Senegal and Gambia.

A rider on horseback, eleventh–fifteenth centuries A.D. Terra cotta found near Jenné, Inland Niger Delta region, Mali.

Private Collection

Names and Places in *Sundiata*

Balla Fasséké (bäl-ä fäs-ā′kā): son of Gnankouman Doua. He becomes Sundiata's personal griot.

Dankaran Touman (dän-kä′rän to͞o-män): son of Sassouma Bérété and Naré Maghan. He becomes king of Mali after his father's death.

Dayala (dä-yä′lä): a village in the valley of the Niger where Sundiata and his army make camp before the decisive battle against Soumaoro.

Djeli Mamadou Kouyaté (djä-lē mä-mä′do͞o ko͞o-yä′tä): griot who narrates the history of Mali.

Farakourou (fä′rä-ko͞o′ro͞o): master smith of the forge in Mali.

Gnankouman Doua (gnän-ko͞o′män do͞o-ä): Naré Maghan's personal griot and father of Balla Fasséké.

Kolonkan and Djamarou (kŏ-lŏn′kän; djä-mä′ro͞o): Sogolon's daughters.

Krina (krē-nä): Soumaoro's place of encampment. This is where the final great battle between Soumaoro and Sundiata is waged.

Mali (mä-lē): Old Mali, an empire in West Africa.

Manding Bory (män-dēng bŏ-rē): Sundiata's brother, son of Naré Maghan and his third wife, Namandjé.

Mandingoes (män-dēng′gōs): inhabitants of Mali.

Mema (mā-mä): Sundiata finds refuge at Mema during his exile.

Moussa Tounkara (mo͞os-sä to͞on-kä′rä): king of Mema. He trains Sundiata to become a great warrior.

Naré Maghan Kon Fatta (nä-rä mä-khän kŏn fät-tä): king of Mali; father of Sundiata, Dankaran Touman, and Manding Bory.

Niani (nē-ä-nē): a village, the first capital of Mali.

Noumounkeba (no͞o-mo͞on-kä′bä): tribal chief in charge of Sosso's defense.

Sassouma Bérété (säs-so͞o-mä bĕ-rä-tä): first wife of Naré Maghan and mother of Dankaran Touman. She is jealous of Sogolon and wins the Mali throne for her son through intrigue.

Sofas (sō-fäs): infantrymen.

Sogolon Kedjou (sō-gō-lōn kä-djo͞o): second wife of Naré Maghan and mother of Sundiata.

Sosso (sōs-sō): Sumaoro's capital, a great city with eighty-eight fortresses.

Soumaoro Kanté (so͞o-mä-ō′rō kän-tä): evil sorcerer king of Sosso.

Sundiata Keita (so͞on-djä′tä kä-ē′tä): hero of the epic. Also known as **Mari Djata** (mä-rē djä-tä), **Sogolon Djata** (sō-gō′lōn djä-tä), **Naré Maghan Djata** (nä-rä mä-khän djä-tä).

Wagadou (wä-gä-do͞o): a name for Old Ghana.

OBJECTIVES
The overall aim is for students to identify and analyze characteristics of the **epic** and of an **epic hero** in *Sundiata: An Epic of Old Mali*. For a complete list of objectives, see the **Teacher's Notes**.

VOCABULARY
Draw students' attention to the words explained in the footnotes. Encourage students to keep lists of any other unfamiliar words and their definitions. Students might then compile a class glossary of definitions and pronunciations for this and other epics in the unit.

PREREADING FOCUS
The first two segments chronicle Sundiata's difficult childhood. Suggest that students try to get a visual picture of how Sundiata might have looked and explain why everyone treated him with derision.

Sundiata

1
Selection begins with a ritualized opening that is characteristic of many epics.

2
Metaphor. Compares Sundiata to sun, which rises in east and sets in west.

3 Analyzing
What effect does narrator's mention of sorcery have? It builds suspense by foreshadowing conflict with sorcerer.

F R O M
Sundiata
An Epic of Old Mali
Translated by
D. T. NIANE

Werner Forman/Art Resource, NY

The Words of the Griot°
Mamadou Kouyaté

1 Listen to my word, you who want to know; by my mouth you will learn the history of Mali.

By my mouth you will get to know the story of the ancestor of great Mali, the story of him who, by his <u>exploits</u>, <u>surpassed</u> even Alexander **2** the Great;[1] he who, from the East, shed his rays upon all the countries of the West.

Listen to the story of the son of the Buffalo, the son of the Lion. I am going to tell you of Maghan Sundiata, of Mari-Djata, of Sogolon Djata, of Naré Maghan Djata; the man of many **3** names[2] against whom sorcery could avail nothing.

On the night that Sundiata is born, a flash of lightning lights up the sky. This is taken as a sign that he is destined to become a great warrior and king. Like heroes in other epics, however, Sundiata must overcome many obstacles before he can fulfill his destiny.

°**Griot** (grē'ō): a French term for an expert storyteller. In ancient Africa, griots were historians and preservers of tradition. **Mamadou Kouyaté** (mä'mōō-dōō kōō-yä'tā).
1. **Alexander the Great:** Alexander of Macedon (356–323 B.C.). He conquered Greece, the Persian Empire, and Egypt. His empire extended from the Mediterranean to India.
2. **the man of many names:** His names include the name of his father, Naré Maghan, and his mother, Sogolon. Through his mother, Sundiata is son of the Buffalo, and through his father, he is son of the Lion.

An altar iron from Mali, showing a dancing figure. These altar irons were placed in family shrines.

You might invite students to give their definitions of the word *destiny* and to identify fictional characters who have struggled to fulfill their destinies. Tell students that Sundiata must overcome not only other people but also his own infirmities in order to fulfill his destiny.

MOTIVATIONAL SUMMARY
Maghan Sundiata's birth is marked by a sign that he is destined to become a great warrior and king. However, his childhood is difficult, and he is banished, despite his promised destiny. During his exile, Sundiata trains as a hunter and

Childhood

God has his mysteries which none can fathom. You, perhaps, will be a king. You can do nothing about it. You, on the other hand, will be unlucky, but you can do nothing about that either. Each man finds his way already marked out for him and he can change nothing of it.

Sogolon's son had a slow and difficult childhood. At the age of three he still crawled along on all-fours while children of the same age were already walking. He had nothing of the great beauty of his father Naré Maghan. He had a head so big that he seemed unable to support it; he also had large eyes which would open wide whenever anyone entered his mother's house. He was taciturn and used to spend the whole day just sitting in the middle of the house. Whenever his mother went out he would crawl on all fours to rummage about in the calabashes[3] in search of food, for he was very greedy.

Malicious tongues began to blab. What three-year-old has not yet taken his first steps? What three-year-old is not the despair of his parents through his whims and shifts of mood? What three-year-old is not the joy of his circle through his backwardness in talking? Sogolon Djata (for it was thus that they called him, prefixing his mother's name to his), Sogolon Djata, then, was very different from others of his own age. He spoke little and his severe face never relaxed into a smile. You would have thought that he was already thinking, and what amused children of his age bored him. Often Sogolon would make some of them come to him to keep him company. These children were already walking and she hoped that Djata, seeing his companions walking, would be tempted to do likewise. But nothing came of it. Besides,

Sogolon Djata would brain the poor little things with his already strong arms and none of them would come near him any more.

The king's first wife was the first to rejoice at Sogolon Djata's infirmity. Her own son, Dankaran Touman, was already eleven. He was a fine and lively boy, who spent the day running about the village with those of his own age. He had even begun his initiation[4] in the bush. The king had had a bow made for him and he used to go behind the town to practise archery with his companions. Sassouma was quite happy and snapped her fingers at Sogolon, whose child was still crawling on the ground. Whenever the latter happened to pass by her house, she would say, "Come, my son, walk, jump, leap about. The jinn[5] didn't promise you anything out of the ordinary, but I prefer a son who walks on his two legs to a lion that crawls on the ground." She spoke thus whenever Sogolon went by her door. The innuendo would go straight home and then she would burst into laughter, that diabolical laughter which a jealous woman knows how to use so well.

Her son's infirmity weighed heavily upon Sogolon Kedjou; she had resorted to all her talent as a sorceress to give strength to her son's legs, but the rarest herbs had been useless. The king himself lost hope.

When Sundiata is seven years old, the king, Naré Maghan, names him successor to the throne. He then appoints Balla Fasséké to be the young prince's griot. Although Sundiata is the rightful heir to the throne of Mali, he has a powerful enemy in his father's first wife, Sassouma Bérété, who seeks the kingdom for her own son, Dankaran Touman.

3. **calabashes** (kăl′ə-băsh′əz): hollow shells of a gourdlike fruit, used as household utensils or bowls for holding food or drink.

4. **initiation** (ĭ-nĭsh′ē-ā′shən): a period of instruction, in which a young warrior would receive training and undergo tests of his skill.

5. **jinn** (jĭn): *n. pl.* of *jinni*. In Muslim legend, the jinn are supernatural beings who inhabit the earth. They can take human or animal form and can affect the lives of human beings.

4
Style. Author addresses audience. Creates impression that story is being told orally, as epics were for centuries.

5
Description of Sundiata as a child is a departure from many epics, which describe heroes as god-like.

6
Hyperbole. Narrator exaggerates size of child's head to create a comic effect.

7
Figurative Language. Narrator personifies tongues.

8
People gossiped about Sogolon's son.

9
Although Djata seems delayed physically for his age, he seems advanced mentally.

10
Style. Narrator uses informal language for comic effect.

11
In some societies men, especially kings, have more than one wife at a time. King married Sogolon after he already had one wife.

12 Drawing Conclusions
Why does Dankaran Touman practice archery? Men of community are expected to develop archery skill for hunting and war.

13
Sassouma snaps her fingers at Sogolon as a sign of ridicule and disrespect.

14 Drawing Conclusions
What is implied by Sassouma's statement about jinn? A jinn promised Sogolon's son would be special.

PRESENTATION

You might want to read the first two sections aloud so that students can get a sense of the storyteller's style. Then, as students read the rest of the epic for themselves, suggest that they pay particular attention to the role of the storyteller, clues to the values and beliefs of Malian culture, and the characterization of Sundiata as an epic hero. Students might also consider how this African epic compares in style to the *Iliad* and *Beowulf*.

15
Metaphor. Comparison suggests Djata will one day show courage and power of lion.

16
A member of council of elders who feels responsibility to speak up on behalf of dead king's wishes.

17
Dankaran Touman becomes king when he is fifteen years old.

18 Analyzing
Why does narrator refer to short memories of people? The king had named Djata successor to the throne. People seem to have forgotten this fact.

19 Making Inferences
What does this sentence imply about Djata? That he still has not learned to walk.

20
In epics, supernatural beings often play a role in determining the destiny of the hero.

21 Finding Details
Where does Sassouma's power come from? From fact that she is current king's mother, not from her position as wife of former king.

22
A *calabash* is a large, hard-shelled gourd often used as a utensil.

23
Figurative Language. Term "son of misfortune" can mean that he is source of misfortune, that he suffers misfortune, or that she is unfortunate.

The Lion's Awakening

15 A short while after this interview between Naré Maghan and his son the king died. Sogolon's son was no more than seven years old. The council of elders[6] met in the king's palace. It **16** was no use Doua's[7] defending the king's will which reserved the throne for Mari Djata, for the council took no account of Naré Maghan's wish. With the help of Sassouma Bérété's **17** intrigues, Dankaran Touman was proclaimed king and a regency council[8] was formed in which the queen mother was all-powerful. A short time after, Doua died.

18 As men have short memories, Sogolon's son was spoken of with nothing but irony and **19** scorn. People had seen one-eyed kings, one-armed kings, and lame kings, but a stiff-legged king had never been heard tell of. No matter how great the destiny promised for Mari Djata might be, the throne could not be given to someone who had no power in his legs; if the **20** jinn loved him, let them begin by giving him the use of his legs. Such were the remarks that Sogolon heard every day. The queen mother, Sassouma Bérété, was the source of all this gossip.

21 Having become all-powerful, Sassouma Bérété persecuted Sogolon because the late Naré Maghan had preferred her. She banished Sogolon and her son to a back yard of the palace. Mari Djata's mother now occupied an old hut which had served as a lumber-room of Sassouma's.

The wicked queen mother allowed free passage to all those inquisitive people who wanted to see the child that still crawled at the age of seven. Nearly all the inhabitants of Niani filed into the palace and the poor Sogolon wept to see herself thus given over to public ridicule. Mari Djata took on a ferocious look in front of the crowd of sightseers. Sogolon found a little consolation only in the love of her eldest daughter, Kolonkan. She was four and she could walk. She seemed to understand all her mother's miseries and already she helped her with the housework. Sometimes, when Sogolon was attending to the chores, it was she who stayed beside her sister Djamarou, quite small as yet.

Sogolon Kedjou and her children lived on the queen mother's left-overs, but she kept a little garden in the open ground behind the village. It was there that she passed her brightest moments looking after her onions and gnougous.[9] One day she happened to be short of condiments and went to the queen mother to beg a little baobab leaf.[10]

"Look you," said the malicious Sassouma, "I **22** have a calabash full. Help yourself, you poor woman. As for me, my son knew how to walk at seven and it was he who went and picked these baobab leaves. Take them then, since your son is unequal to mine." Then she laughed derisively with that fierce laughter which cuts through your flesh and penetrates right to the bone.

Sogolon Kedjou was dumbfounded. She had never imagined that hate could be so strong in a human being. With a lump in her throat she left Sassouma's. Outside her hut Mari Djata, sitting on his useless legs, was blandly eating out of a calabash. Unable to contain herself any longer, Sogolon burst into sobs and seizing a piece of wood, hit her son.

23 "Oh son of misfortune, will you never walk? Through your fault I have just suffered the greatest affront of my life! What have I done, God, for you to punish me in this way?"

Mari Djata seized the piece of wood and,

---

6. **council of elders:** a powerful group of advisers who could override the king's wishes.
7. **Doua:** Gnankouman Doua, the griot of Naré Maghan.
8. **regency council:** a group to govern until the king would be old enough to assume the throne.

9. **gnougous** (noo′goos): root vegetables.
10. **baobab** (bā′ō-băb′) **leaf:** The hard-shelled fleshy fruit is known as "monkey bread." The leaves are used in seasoning food.

24 looking at his mother, said, "Mother, what's the matter?"

"Shut up, nothing can ever wash me clean of this insult."

"But what then?"

"Sassouma has just humiliated me over a matter of a baobab leaf. At your age her own son could walk and used to bring his mother baobab leaves."

"Cheer up, Mother, cheer up."

"No. It's too much. I can't."

25 "Very well then, I am going to walk today,"
26 said Mari Djata. "Go and tell my father's smiths to make me the heaviest possible iron rod. Mother, do you want just the leaves of the baobab or would you rather I brought you the whole tree?"

Benin aquamanile in the shape of a leopard.
Brass. British Museum, London, Great Britain.

"Ah, my son, to wipe out this insult I want the tree and its roots at my feet outside my hut."

Balla Fasséké,[11] who was present, ran to the master smith, Farakourou, to order an iron rod.

Sogolon had sat down in front of her hut. She was weeping softly and holding her head between her two hands. Mari Djata went calmly back to his calabash of rice and began eating again as if nothing had happened. From time to time he looked up discreetly at his mother who was murmuring in a low voice, "I want the whole tree, in front of my hut, the whole tree."

All of a sudden a voice burst into laughter behind the hut. It was the wicked Sassouma telling one of her serving women about the

11. **Balla Fasséké:** the son of Doua. He was a powerful singer and would become Sundiata's griot.

Bridgeman/Art Resource, NY

GEOGRAPHY LINK
Have students locate the country of Mali and the Niger River on a map of the African continent. Encourage students to use an encyclopedia or other reference sources to learn more about contemporary Mali. Students could research its capital city, population, terrain, crops, language, and culture. Have students record what they learn in their journals or learning logs.

27
Farakourou's question suggests that he knew Djata would walk sooner or later.

28
Farakourou's father must have foreseen need for it.

29
Balla Fasséké's statement has the quality of a saying and suggests that insults are seen as very grave and powerful in that society. Interesting contrast to saying "Sticks and stones may break my bones, but words can never hurt me."

30
Metaphor. Balla Fasséké compares Djata to a young lion, suggesting he thinks boy will grow up to exhibit courage and strength of a lion.

31
Personification. Balla Fasséké speaks of bush as though it had human capability to understand.

32
Iron bar is so heavy it took six men to carry it from blacksmith shop, yet Djata is able to pick it up with one hand.

33 Drawing Conclusions
Why do Djata's legs tremble?
Answers will vary. Perhaps leg muscles are poorly developed from lack of use, and holding himself up strains them.

34
Spontaneous hymn suggests society values song as a means of expression.

35
Referring to Allah indicates people practice religion of Islam.

36
Metaphor. Drops of sweat are compared to beads.

---

scene of humiliation and she was laughing loudly so that Sogolon could hear. Sogolon fled **30** into the hut and hid her face under the blankets **31** so as not to have before her eyes this heedless boy, who was more preoccupied with eating than with anything else. With her head buried in the bed-clothes Sogolon wept and her body shook violently. Her daughter, Sogolon **32** Djamarou, had come and sat down beside her and she said, "Mother, Mother, don't cry. Why are you crying?"

Mari Djata had finished eating and, dragging himself along on his legs, he came and sat under the wall of the hut for the sun was scorching. What was he thinking about? He alone knew.

The royal forges were situated outside the **33** walls and over a hundred smiths worked there. The bows, spears, arrows and shields of Niani's warriors came from there. When Balla Faséké came to order the iron rod, Farakourou said to **27** him, "The great day has arrived then?"

"Yes. Today is a day like any other, but it will see what no other day has seen."

The master of the forges, Farakourou, was the son of the old Nounfaïri, and he was a **34**
28 soothsayer[12] like his father. In his workshops there was an enormous iron bar wrought by his father Nounfaïri. Everybody wondered what this bar was destined to be used for. Farakourou called six of his apprentices and told them to carry the iron bar to Sogolon's house.

When the smiths put the gigantic iron bar down in front of the hut the noise was so frightening that Sogolon, who was lying down, jumped up with a start. Then Balla Fasséké, son **35** of Gnankouman Doua, spoke.

29 "Here is the great day, Mari Djata. I am speaking to you, Maghan, son of Sogolon. The waters of the Niger can efface the stain from

12. **soothsayer** (sooth′sā′ər): a seer, one who predicts the future.

the body, but they cannot wipe out an insult. **30** Arise, young lion, roar, and may the bush know **31** that from henceforth it has a master."

The apprentice smiths were still there, Sogolon had come out and everyone was watching Mari Djata. He crept on all-fours and came to the iron bar. Supporting himself on his knees and one hand, with the other hand he picked up the iron bar without any effort and stood it up vertically. Now he was resting on nothing but his knees and held the bar with both his hands. A deathly silence had gripped all those present. Sogolon Djata closed his eyes, held tight, the muscles in his arms tensed. With a violent jerk he threw his weight on to it and his knees left the ground. Sogolon Kedjou was all eyes and watched her son's legs which were trembling as though from an electric shock. Djata was sweating and the sweat ran from his brow. In a great effort he straightened up and was on his feet at one go—but the great bar of iron was twisted and had taken the form of a bow!

Then Balla Fasséké sang out the "Hymn to the Bow," striking up with his powerful voice:

"Take your bow, Simbon,
Take your bow and let us go.
Take your bow, Sogolon Djata."

When Sogolon saw her son standing she stood dumb for a moment, then suddenly she sang these words of thanks to God who had given her son the use of his legs:

"Oh day, what a beautiful day,
Oh day, day of joy;
Allah Almighty, you never created
    a finer day.
So my son is going to walk!"

Standing in the position of a soldier at ease, Sogolon Djata, supported by his enormous rod, **36** was sweating great beads of sweat. Balla

Fasséké's song had alerted the whole palace and people came running from all over to see what had happened, and each stood bewildered before Sogolon's son. The queen mother had rushed there and when she saw Mari Djata standing up she trembled from head to foot. After recovering his breath Sogolon's son dropped the bar and the crowd stood to one

37 side. His first steps were those of a giant. Balla Fasséké fell into step and pointing his finger at Djata, he cried:

"Room, room, make room!
38 The lion has walked;
Hide antelopes,
Get out of his way."

Behind Niani there was a young baobab tree, and it was there that the children of the town

39 came to pick leaves for their mothers. With all his might the son of Sogolon tore up the tree and put it on his shoulders and went back to his mother. He threw the tree in front of the hut and said, "Mother, here are some baobab leaves for you. From henceforth it will be outside your hut that the women of Niani will come to stock up."

Sogolon Djata walked. From that day forward the queen mother had no more peace of mind.
40 But what can one do against destiny? Nothing.

Sundiata is forced into exile. He and his family eventually find shelter at the court of Moussa Tounkara. Sundiata soon astonishes everyone with his strength and intelligence. His mother, Sogolon, prepares him to fulfill his destiny and claim the kingdom of Mali.

FROM
Exile

It was at the court of Mema that Sundiata and Manding Bory went on their first campaign. Moussa Tounkara was a great warrior and therefore he admired strength. When Sundiata was fifteen the king took him with him on campaign. Sundiata astonished the whole army with his strength and with his dash in the charge. In the course of a skirmish against the mountaineers he hurled himself on the enemy with such vehemence that the king feared for his life, but Mansa Tounkara admired bravery too much to stop the son of Sogolon. He followed him closely to protect him and he saw

41 with rapture how the youth sowed panic among the enemy. He had remarkable presence of mind, struck right and left and opened up for himself a glorious path. When the enemy had

42 fled the old "sofas"[13] said, "There's one that'll make a good king." Moussa Tounkara took the son of Sogolon in his arms and said, "It is destiny that has sent you to Mema. I will make a great warrior out of you."

From that day Sundiata did not leave the king

43 any more. He eclipsed all the young princes and was the friend of the whole army. They spoke about nothing but him in the camp. Men

44 were even more surprised by the lucidity of his mind. In the camp he had an answer to everything and the most puzzling situations resolved themselves in his presence.

Soon it was in Mema itself that people began to talk about Sundiata. Was it not Providence which had sent this boy at a time when Mema had no heir? People already averred that Sundiata would extend his dominion from Mema to Mali. He went on all the campaigns. The enemy's incursions became rarer and rarer

45 and the reputation of Sogolon's son spread beyond the river.

After three years the king appointed Sundiata Kan-Koro-Sigui, his Viceroy,[14] and in the king's absence it was he who governed. Djata had now seen eighteen winters and at that time he

13. **sofas:** infantrymen.
14. **Viceroy** (vīs′roi′): a governor who rules as the representative of a sovereign.

37
Characterization. Now Djata has become the typical larger-than-life epic hero.

38
Metaphor. Compares Djata to a lion able to chase down swift antelopes.

39
Exaggeration. Epic heroes are often able to perform incredible feats of strength.

40
Narrator's repeated remarks about inexorable nature of destiny probably reflect a social belief.

41
Metaphor. Panic is compared to seed and Sundiata to the farmer who sows it on the battlefield.

42
Older men realize Sundiata's potential for greatness.

43
Metaphor. Sundiata compared to a heavenly body that moves in front of another, causing it to disappear.

44 Synthesizing
Why is Sundiata's clearness of mind important? A king must be intelligent, as well as brave and fierce in battle, in order to be a good ruler.

45
Figurative Language. Expression "beyond the river" means his reputation has spread far and wide.

was a tall young man with a fat neck and a powerful chest. Nobody else could bend his bow. Everyone bowed before him and he was greatly loved. Those who did not love him feared him and his voice carried authority.

The king's choice was approved of both by **46** the army and the people; the people love all who assert themselves over them. The soothsayers of Mema revealed the extraordinary destiny of Djata. It was said that he was the successor of Alexander the Great and that he would be even greater; the soldiers already had a thousand dreams of conquest. What was impossible with such a gallant chief? Sundiata **49** inspired confidence in the sofas by his example, for the sofa loves to see his chief share the hardship of battle.

Djata was now a man, for time had marched on since the exodus from Niani and his destiny was now to be fulfilled. Sogolon knew that the time had arrived and she had performed her **50** task. She had nurtured the son for whom the world was waiting and she knew that now her mission was accomplished, while that of Djata was about to begin. One day she said to her son, "Do not deceive yourself. Your destiny lies not here but in Mali. The moment has come. I have finished my task and it is yours that is going to begin, my son. But you must be able to wait. Everything in its own good time."

Soumaoro Kanté, an evil sorcerer who is the king of Sosso, has invaded Mali. He defeats Dankaran Touman and proclaims himself king of Mali by right of conquest. When Sundiata learns of this, he makes plans to return to Mali and claim the kingdom of his fathers.

History

We are now coming to the great moments in the **47** life of Sundiata. The exile will end and another sun will arise. It is the sun of Sundiata. Griots know the history of kings and kingdoms and that is why they are the best counsellors of kings. Every king wants to have a singer to perpetuate his memory, for it is the griot who rescues the memories of kings from oblivion,[15] as men have short memories.

Kings have prescribed destinies just like men, and seers who probe the future know it. They have knowledge of the future, whereas we griots are depositories[16] of the knowledge of the past. But whoever knows the history of a country can read its future.

Other peoples use writing to record the past, but this invention has killed the faculty of memory among them. They do not feel the past any more, for writing lacks the warmth of the human voice. With them everybody thinks he knows, whereas learning should be a secret.[17] The prophets did not write and their words have been all the more vivid as a result. What paltry learning is that which is congealed in dumb books!

I, Djeli Mamadou Kouyaté, am the result of a long tradition. For generations we have passed on the history of kings from father to son. The narrative was passed on to me without alteration and I deliver it without alteration, for I received it free from all untruth.

Listen now to the story of Sundiata, the Na'Kamma, the man who had a mission to accomplish.

At the time when Sundiata was preparing to assert his claim over the kingdom of his fathers, Soumaoro was the king of kings, the most pow-

15. **oblivion** (ə-blĭv′ē-ən): the state of being totally and completely forgotten.
16. **depositories** (dĭ-pŏz′ĭ-tôr′ēz): places where things are put for safekeeping. Here, griots are being described as preservers of knowledge and history for future generations.
17. **learning . . . secret:** Traditional griots believe that something is lost when knowledge is shared widely through books and writings. They believe knowledge should be carefully guarded and passed down from one griot to another by word of mouth.

51 erful king in all the lands of the setting sun.
52 The fortified town of Sosso was the bulwark of fetishism[18] against the word of Allah.[19] For a long time Soumaoro defied the whole world.
53 Since his accession to the throne of Sosso he had defeated nine kings whose heads served him as fetishes in his macabre chamber. Their skins served as seats and he cut his footwear from human skin. Soumaoro was not like other men, for the jinn had revealed themselves to him and his power was beyond measure. So his countless sofas were very brave since they believed their king to be invincible. But Soumaoro was an evil demon and his reign had produced nothing but bloodshed. Nothing was taboo for him. His greatest pleasure was publicly to flog venerable old men. He had defiled every family and everywhere in his vast empire there were villages populated by girls whom he had forcibly abducted from their families without marrying them.
54 The tree that the tempest will throw down does not see the storm building up on the horizon. Its proud head braves the winds even when it is near its end. Soumaoro had come to despise everyone. Oh! how power can pervert a man.

In the climax of the epic, Sundiata battles Soumaoro. Before the last encounter, however, there is a battle of words, conducted through sorcery.

Krina

Sundiata went and pitched camp at Dayala in the valley of the Niger. Now it was he who was blocking Soumaoro's road to the south. Up till that time, Sundiata and Soumaoro had fought each other without a declaration of war. One does not wage war without saying why it is being waged. Those fighting should make a declaration of their grievances to begin with.
55 Just as a sorcerer ought not to attack someone without taking him to task for some evil deed, so a king should not wage war without saying why he is taking up arms.

Soumaoro advanced as far as Krina, near the village of Dayala on the Niger and decided to assert his rights before joining battle. Soumaoro knew that Sundiata also was a sor-
56 cerer, so, instead of sending an embassy, he committed his words to one of his owls. The night bird came and perched on the roof of Djata's tent and spoke. The son of Sogolon in his turn sent his owl to Soumaoro. Here is the dialogue of the sorcerer kings:

"Stop, young man. Henceforth I am the king of Mali. If you want peace, return to where you came from," said Soumaoro.

"I am coming back, Soumaoro, to recapture my kingdom. If you want peace you will make amends to my allies and return to Sosso where you are the king."

"I am king of Mali by force of arms. My rights have been established by conquest."

"Then I will take Mali from you by force of arms and chase you from my kingdom."
57 "Know, then, that I am the wild yam of the rocks; nothing will make me leave Mali."

"Know, also, that I have in my camp seven master smiths who will shatter the rocks. Then, yam, I will eat you."

"I am the poisonous mushroom that makes the fearless vomit."

"As for me, I am the ravenous cock, the poison does not matter to me."

"Behave yourself, little boy, or you will burn your foot, for I am the red-hot cinder."

"But me, I am the rain that extinguishes the cinder; I am the boisterous torrent that will carry you off."

"I am the mighty silk-cotton tree that looks from on high on the tops of other trees."

18. **fetishism** (fĕt′ĭ-shĭz′əm): the worship of *fetishes*, objects believed to have magical power.
19. **Allah** (ăl′ə, ä′lə): the supreme being in the Muslim religion.

51
Figurative Language. "Lands of the setting sun" refers to lands of west because sun sets in west.

52
Sundiata's campaign against Sosso is to be a religious war against pagans.

53
Characterization. Narrator characterizes Soumaoro as a monster. In addition to endowing heroes with superhuman goodness, epics often endow enemies of heroes with fantastically evil natures.

54
Foreshadowing. Narrator uses metaphorical language to foreshadow Soumaoro's downfall.

55
Analogy. Behavior of sorcerers and kings compared. Such analogies are characteristic of epics.

56
Fact that both men are sorcerers adds a supernatural dimension to their conflict.

57
Metaphor. Conversation between Sundiata and Soumaoro takes form of a string of metaphors. Soumaoro first declares himself to be a wild yam which cannot be dislodged from its growing place in the rocks. Sundiata says he has men who can crush rocks so he can eat yam. Soumaoro then says he is a poisonous mushroom; Sundiata responds that he is a cock that can eat poisonous mushrooms. For each of Soumaoro's assertions to prove his superiority, Sundiata has an assertion of his own. Conversation characterizes both men as not only brave, but intelligent and quick-witted, and shows importance of language in this culture.

	TRANSPARENCY 46 & 47
	Fine Art
	Theme: *Waiting for a Hero* – features artwork showing heroes or heroic ideals from diverse cultural traditions.

	TRANSPARENCY 49
	Reader Response
	Test of Strength – asks students to identify heroic characteristics and evaluate a literary character according to this criteria.

	TRANSPARENCY 50
	Reader Response
	Send a Message – invites students to write a "fan letter" to an epic hero telling him or her the characteristics they most admire.

58
In some societies, king sits on an animal skin as a sign of his authority.

59
Metaphor. Narrator compares argument between two men to war.

60 Drawing Conclusions
Why would ironworkers, or blacksmiths, be called "sons of fire"? They work with red-hot iron. Fire is an essential tool of their trade.

61
Symbol. Setting sun is a symbol of the imminent end of Soumaoro's reign.

"And I, I am the strangling creeper that climbs to the top of the forest giant."

"Enough of this argument. You shall not have Mali."

58 "Know that there is not room for two kings on the same skin, Soumaoro; you will let me have your place."

"Very well, since you want war I will wage war against you, but I would have you know that I have killed nine kings whose heads adorn my room. What a pity, indeed, that your head should take its place beside those of your fellow madcaps."[20]

"Prepare yourself, Soumaoro, for it will be long before the calamity that is going to crash down upon you and yours comes to an end."

Thus Sundiata and Soumaoro spoke **59** together. After the war of mouths, swords had to decide the issue.

Soumaoro is killed in battle. Sundiata attacks the fortress of Sosso and gains entrance to Soumaoro's magic chamber. He releases the sorcerer's prisoners and then destroys the city of Sosso.

Sosso was a magnificent city. In the open plain her triple rampart with awe-inspiring towers reached into the sky. The city comprised a hundred and eighty-eight fortresses and the palace of Soumaoro loomed above the whole city like a gigantic tower. Sosso had but one gate; colossal **60** and made of iron, the work of the sons of fire. Noumounkeba[21] hoped to tie Sundiata down outside of Sosso, for he had enough provisions to hold out for a year.

61 The sun was beginning to set when Sogolon Djata appeared before Sosso the Magnificent. From the top of a hill, Djata and his general staff gazed upon the fearsome city of the sorcerer king. The army encamped in the plain opposite the great gate of the city and fires were

Collection of Xenobia Bailey. Photograph Tom Jenkins
©1989 Dallas Museum of Art. All Rights Reserved.

Mali Formal Crown (1989). A head adornment made of yarn, multicolored beads, and mirrors.

lit in the camp. Djata resolved to take Sosso in the course of a morning. He fed his men a double ration and the tam-tams[22] beat all night to stir up the victors of Krina.

At daybreak the towers of the ramparts were black with sofas. Others were positioned on the ramparts themselves. They were the archers. The Mandingoes were masters in the art of storming a town. In the front line Sundiata placed the sofas of Mali, while those who held the ladders were in the second line protected by the shields of the spearmen. The main body of the army was to attack the city gate. When all was ready, Djata gave the order to attack. The drums resounded, the horns blared and like a tide the Mandingo front line moved off, giving mighty shouts. With their shields raised above their heads the Mandingoes advanced up to the foot of the wall, then the Sossos began to rain large stones down on the assailants. From the rear, the bowmen of Wagadou shot arrows at the ramparts. The attack spread and the town was assaulted at all points. Sundiata had a murderous reserve; they were the bowmen whom the king of the Bobos had sent shortly before

20. **madcaps:** rash or impulsive people.
21. **Noumounkeba:** a tribal chief who is in charge of defending Sosso.

22. **tam-tams:** war drums used to stir warriors on toward victory and to communicate messages.

TRANSPARENCY 51	TRANSPARENCY 52
Literary Elements	**Literary Elements**
Analyzing an Epic – prompts students to identify and evaluate basic elements of an epic.	*The Epic Hero* – explores the nature of an epic hero as a special type of character.

Krina. The archers of Bobo are the best in the world. On one knee the archers fired flaming arrows over the ramparts. Within the walls the thatched huts took fire and the smoke swirled **62** up. The ladders stood against the curtain wall and the first Mandingo sofas were already at the top. Seized by panic through seeing the town on fire, the Sossos hesitated a moment. The huge tower surmounting the gate surrendered, for Fakoli's smiths had made themselves masters of it. They got into the city where the screams of women and children brought the Sossos' panic to a head. They opened the gates to the main body of the army.

Then began the massacre. Women and children in the midst of fleeing Sossos implored mercy of the victors. Djata and his cavalry were now in front of the awesome tower palace of **63** Soumaoro. Noumounkeba, conscious that he was lost, came out to fight. With his sword held aloft he bore down on Djata, but the latter dodged him and, catching hold of the Sosso's braced arm, forced him to his knees whilst the sword dropped to the ground. He did not kill him but delivered him into the hands of Manding Bory.

Soumaoro's palace was now at Sundiata's mercy. While everywhere the Sossos were begging for quarter,[23] Sundiata, preceded by Balla Fasséké, entered Soumaoro's tower. The griot knew every nook and cranny of the palace from his captivity[24] and he led Sundiata to Soumaoro's magic chamber.

When Balla Fasséké opened the door to the room it was found to have changed its appear-**64** ance since Soumaoro had been touched by the fatal arrow. The inmates of the chamber had lost their power. The snake in the pitcher was in the throes of death, the owls from the perch were flapping pitifully about on the ground.

Everything was dying in the sorcerer's abode. It was all up with the power of Soumaoro. Sundiata had all Soumaoro's fetishes taken down and before the palace were gathered together all Soumaoro's wives, all princesses taken from their families by force. The prisoners, their hands tied behind their backs, were **65** already herded together. Just as he had wished, Sundiata had taken Sosso in the course of a morning. When everything was outside of the town and all that there was to take had been taken out, Sundiata gave the order to complete its destruction. The last houses were set fire to and prisoners were employed in the razing of **66** the walls. Thus, as Djata intended, Sosso was destroyed to its very foundations.

Yes, Sosso was razed to the ground. It has disappeared, the proud city of Soumaoro. A ghastly wilderness extends over the places where kings came and humbled themselves before the sorcerer king. All traces of the houses have vanished and of Soumaoro's seven-storey palace there remains nothing more. A field of desolation, Sosso is now a spot where guinea fowl and young partridges come to take their dust baths.

Many years have rolled by and many times the moon has traversed the heaven since these **67** places lost their inhabitants. The bourein,[25] the tree of desolation, spreads out its thorny undergrowth and insolently grows in Soumaoro's **68** capital. Sosso the Proud is nothing but a memory in the mouths of griots. The hyenas come to wail there at night, the hare and the hind come and feed on the site of the palace of Soumaoro, the king who wore robes of human skin.

Sosso vanished from the earth and it was Sundiata, the son of the buffalo, who gave these places over to solitude. After the destruction of Soumaoro's capital the world knew no other master but Sundiata.

23. **begging for quarter:** pleading for their lives.
24. **from his captivity:** Balla Fasséké had been held prisoner in the palace of Soumaoro.

25. **bourein:** a dwarf shrub.

62
The curtain wall is outermost wall of city.

63
Climax. Two leaders face each other in hand-to-hand combat.

64
Soumaoro has apparently been killed by an arrow. His sorcerer's power ends with his death.

65
Irony. Soumaoro thought he could outlast Sundiata a year, but he is defeated in a morning.

66 Expressing an Opinion
Why does Sundiata destroy city? Answers will vary. Some possibilities include to punish people for their pagan ways and to keep them from rebuilding.

67
Symbol. "Tree of desolation" represents complete defeat of Soumaoro and Sossos.

68
Tone. Narrator's tone is contemptuous.

READING CHECK
1. Seven (pp. 659–660).
2. To be king of Mali (p. 664).
3. By the oral tradition perpetuated by griots (p. 664).
4. The city is destroyed to its very foundations and becomes a field of desolation (p. 667).

FOR STUDY AND DISCUSSION
1. The griot calls upon the reader to listen and then introduces the epic hero and the struggle he will encounter.
2. Answers will vary. Sundiata is different from other children in his slow physical development and distorted body. People make fun of him, and he speaks little, never smiles, and seems thoughtful and serious.
3. Answers may vary. After the king dies, his first wife, Sassouma, becomes very powerful through intrigue and influences the regency council to name her son as king.
4. He develops the combative skills of a warrior and also learns to use his wits.
5a. Soumaoro had used evil sorcery.
5b. Yes; for example, Sundiata's mother uses her talents to try to heal her son.
6a. The climax occurs when Sundiata defeats Soumaoro in battle.
6b. Answers will vary. Students might say that the storyteller adds great detail to create suspense and to intensify the mood of excitement.
7. Answers will vary. Some possibilities include to punish people for their evil ways and to keep them from rebuilding.
8. Answers will vary. **a.** Writing threatens the place the griots hold in their society. **b.** Students who agree might say that people become too dependent on looking up information rather than committing it to memory. Those who disagree might suggest that writing has improved memory because less information is lost.

668

Reading Check

1. How old was Sogolon's son before he began to walk?
2. According to Sundiata's mother, what is his destiny?
3. How was the history of Sundiata preserved?
4. What happens to the city of Sosso after Sundiata's victory?

For Study and Discussion

Analyzing and Interpreting the Epic

1. How does the griot prepare you for the story of Sundiata?

2. What is unusual about Sundiata's childhood?

3. Although Sundiata is named successor to the throne of Mali, the king's wishes are not carried out. Why not?

4. Sundiata grows to manhood while he is in exile. What skills does he learn at the court of Mema?

5a. We are told that Soumaoro had become "the king of kings." By what means had he gained this power?   **b.** Does the epic imply that there is good sorcery as well as evil sorcery?

6a. What is the climax of the epic?   **b.** Why do you think the griot goes into such great detail at this point?

7. Why do you think Sundiata decides to destroy the magnificent city of Sosso rather than have it occupied?

8. The griot believes that the power of the storyteller resides in memory.   **a.** Why does the griot distrust writing?   **b.** Do you agree that dependence on writing has ruined the faculty of memory? Give reasons for your answer.

Writing About Literature

Analyzing Values and Beliefs

Using the selection in your textbook, what conclusions can you draw about the values and beliefs of the culture that produced *Sundiata?* What importance is given to courage, skill in combat, honorable behavior, and faith? Write an essay in which you discuss your conclusions. For assistance, see *Writing About Literature,* which begins on page 672.

Focus on Comparison and Contrast

Organizing Details

You can choose either of two methods to organize the details in a comparison/contrast essay.

In the **block method** you present all the details about the first subject and then all the corresponding details about the second subject.

In the **point-by-point method** you discuss one point or feature at a time as it relates to both your subjects.

The chart below shows how each method might work for an essay comparing the trumpet with the clarinet. S = Subject; P = Point

Block	Point-by-Point
S1: Trumpet	P1: Structure
P1: Structure	S1: Trumpet
P2: Sound	S2: Clarinet
P3: Range	P2: Sound
S2: Clarinet	S1: Trumpet
P1: Structure	S2: Clarinet
P2: Sound	P3: Range
P3: Range	S1: Trumpet
	S2: Clarinet

Use one of these methods to write an outline for a comparison/contrast essay on a topic of your choice. Save your notes.

► Before students begin this writing assignment, you may want to refer them to the **Writing About Literature** section on p. 672.

OBJECTIVES
The overall aim is for students to analyze the attitudes of characters in passages from the *Iliad* and to compare and contrast them.

PRESENTATION
Students might benefit from hearing the lines spoken by Andromache and Hector read aloud by a female and male student respectively. Then students can work in small groups to answer the questions. You might want to create a Venn diagram on the chalkboard and have group members come up to list their findings in the appropriate columns. Students should support their responses to question 4 with specific details from the text.

FOCUS ON *Reading and Critical Thinking*

USING METHODS OF COMPARISON AND CONTRAST

*T*o **compare** is to look for ways in which things are alike. To **contrast** is to look for ways in which they are different. You can often gain insight into a particular work by comparing or contrasting some aspect of it with another, similar work. You can also compare and contrast different elements within the same work. In the following excerpts from the *Iliad*, Hector and Andromache address the same question: will Hector go out to fight Achilles? Compare and contrast Hector's reasons for wanting to fight with Andromache's argument for having him remain with her.

Andromache: "Your courage will be the end of you, dear husband. Must you go again to battle? Think of me, if you will not consider yourself. My mother is dead, my father died when the town of Thebe was taken, and my seven brothers Achilles slew. I have no one left but you, Hector. To me you are not only husband, but father and mother and brother as well. If I lose you, what have I left? Have pity on me, Hector, and on our son. Stay with me on the wall today. . . . "

Hector: "My dearest wife, if I stayed with you and kept from battle, how could I face our people ever again? Indeed, I think that I could not keep from the fighting even if I would; for, all my life, I have learned only to be valiant and first in danger, to lead other men where they should follow, and to earn honor for my father and myself. . . . I think that we cannot win this war, Andromache, and that there must come a day when Troy will fall to the Greeks. My heart is torn when I think of all who will suffer then, my mother, my father, my brothers and sisters, our people; but for none of them do I grieve as I grieve for you, my wife, whom some Greek will take as the spoils of battle. . . . Oh, may I be dead and the earth heaped high above me, before I hear your cries as they carry you off into slavery."

Using Methods of Comparison and Contrast

On a sheet of paper, address the following questions:

1. What goals do Hector and Andromache share?

2. In what ways are Hector and Andromache thinking of themselves?

3. How do they each feel about revenge? courage? and sacrifice?

4. Which argument do you feel is more persuasive?

USING METHODS OF COMPARISON AND CONTRAST
One way to gain insight into characters in a story or play is through comparison and contrast. Students should note that characters can have the same goals or general attitudes but can differ in their approach to those goals or in their behaviors.

Answers
Answers will vary.
1. Hector and Andromache are concerned with each other's welfare and safety.
2. Andromache does not want her husband to die, and she does not want to be alone. Hector thinks of his honor and duty to country, yet he worries about Andromache's fate when Troy falls.
3. Andromache seems to think that getting revenge is not worth losing Hector. She says that Hector's courage will get him killed, and she feels she has sacrificed enough. Hector feels duty- and honor-bound to avenge the deaths of his countrymen. He has learned to be courageous all his life and sees no other alternative. He grieves for many people and their sacrifices. He is willing to sacrifice his life.
4. Students may feel that Hector's argument is more persuasive because of the emotional appeal of his argument. As a soldier, he is obligated to place his country before his own life and family. Other students may feel that Andromache's argument is more persuasive. The emotional appeal of her argument—that she and their son need Hector—is also very compelling. Student responses may depend on which of Hector's duties they see as more important—his duties as a soldier, or his duties as a husband and father.

The overall aim is for students to write a comparison/contrast essay.

You might help students list topics for their comparison/contrast essays. Ask each student to think of at least five general subjects such as cats, dogs, food, vacations, and so forth. Then each student can write his or her list on the chalkboard, being careful not to repeat topics already on the board. Then you might model how to find subcategories of these general subjects that would be suitable to compare and contrast. Refer students to the Venn diagram that compares two types of cats. Encourage

HOLT WRITER'S WORKSHOP

This computer program provides help for all types of writing through guided instruction for each step of the writing process. (Program available separately.)

See *Elements of Writing, Second Course,* Chapter 9, for more instruction on comparing and contrasting.

WRITING A COMPARISON/CONTRAST ESSAY

Because people make decisions every day based on comparison, students will be familiar with the thought processes necessary to write this type of essay. They may have difficulty with the necessary methods of organization.

Prewriting

Remind students that they cannot just tell but must *show* that differences and similarities exist for their subjects. Encourage students to support their assertions with vivid details, pertinent examples, and relevant descriptions. For example, rather than simply stating that lions are more social than leopards, students should describe the social habits of lions and the solitary habits of leopards.

Writing

You might want to have students write one draft of the body of their essays using the block method and another draft using the point-by-point method. Students can then evaluate which method is more appropriate to their subjects, supporting details, and main ideas. Students might also experiment with several different openers to find the best one.

FOCUS ON *Writing*

WRITING A COMPARISON/CONTRAST ESSAY

A comparison/contrast essay examines the patterns or relationships of two subjects. In this kind of essay, you can focus on similarities between the subjects, on differences, or on both.

Prewriting

1. When you choose a pair of subjects for a comparison/contrast essay, make sure that the subjects have some significant differences as well as some points in common. You may want to list similarities and differences on a Venn diagram. The sample diagram below shows similarities and differences for an essay about lions and tigers:

Lions	(shared)	Tigers
■ social	■ largest cats	■ solitary
■ Africa	■ carnivorous	■ Asia
■ open habitat	■ stalk prey and rely on short bursts of speed	■ jungle habitat

[See **Focus** assignment on page 655.]

2. Think about your **purpose** and **audience.** Your purpose in this kind of essay is usually to inform your readers. Therefore, consider what they may already know about the topic. Also think about what background they may need in order to understand your essay.

3. Identify your **main idea** and state it in one or two sentences. For example, you might state the main idea for a comparison/contrast essay on lions and tigers this way: "Although both lions and tigers share many

features, each species of big cat has a distinctive habitat and way of life." [See **Focus** assignment on page 655.]

Writing

1. Try to capture your reader's attention in the **introduction** of your essay. You might use one of the following openers:

- ■ a question
- ■ a quotation
- ■ a brief anecdote
- ■ a striking fact

Remember to state your main idea in the introduction of your essay.

2. Use one of the two methods outlined below to arrange the details in the **body** of your essay.

Block Method	Point-by-Point Method
Subject 1: _____	Point 1: _____
Point 1: _____	Subject 1: _____
Point 2: _____	Subject 2: _____
Point 3: _____	Point 2: _____
Subject 2: _____	Subject 1: _____
Point 1: _____	Subject 2: _____
Point 2: _____	Point 3: _____
Point 3: _____	Subject 1: _____
	Subject 2: _____

[See **Focus** assignment on page 668.]

3. Restate your main idea in the **conclusion** of your essay. You may want to add a comment or evaluation in your final paragraph.

4. Use **transitional words and phrases** to help your reader follow the connections of ideas in your essay. Here are some helpful transitions for comparison and contrast:

Comparison		Contrast	
also	likewise	although	however
and	similarly	but	instead
another	too	despite	yet

Evaluating and Revising

1. Exchange papers with a partner. Offer each other comments and suggestions. Be sure you have not omitted any important information about your subjects. Here is one paragraph from an essay about lions and tigers.

Writer's Model

Although
Both lions and tigers share many

features. Each species of big cat has a
                                    a
distinctive habitet and way of life.
                       exclusively
Both species are almost ~~exceptionally~~

carnivorous. Preying on antelope, deer,
                     boar ⊙ *Lions and tigers*
zebra, and wild ~~bore. They~~ also use

similar hunting techniques: they care-

fully stalk their prey, relying on a sud-
     after a brief chase from ambush ⊙
den burst of speed to bring it down.

2. You may find the following checklist helpful as you revise your essay.

Checklist for Evaluation and Revision

✓ Have I clearly identified the pair of subjects for my essay?

✓ Do I state my main idea in the introduction?

✓ Do I use either the block method or the point-by-point method to organize my essay?

✓ Does my essay include all the important information about the subjects?

✓ Do I use transitions to make my writing clear and coherent?

✓ Do I end with a strong conclusion?

Proofreading and Publishing

1. Proofread your essay and correct any errors you find in grammar, usage, and mechanics. (Here you may find it helpful to refer to the **Handbook for Revision** on pages 712–755.) Then prepare a final version of your essay by making a clean copy.

2. Consider some of the following publication methods for your essay:

- submit your essay to the school newspaper or magazine

- present your essay as an oral report to the class

- join with other students who have explored similar topics and organize a round-table discussion

Portfolio If your teacher approves, you may wish to keep a copy of your work in your writing folder or portfolio.

with some of the terms in this unit, you might have them look them up in the **Literary Terms and Techniques** (p. 696).

When presenting **The Writing Process,** you may want to stress the evaluating and revising stages of the process. Point out that writers must

evaluate a draft, identifying its strengths and weaknesses before they can make improvements; they can *revise* a draft by adding, cutting, reordering, and replacing words, phrases, and sentences. You may also want to point out that revising and proofreading differ in intent—revis-

WRITING ABOUT LITERATURE

Developing Skills in Critical Thinking

Many of the compositions you will be asked to write in English class will be about the literature you read. The writing may be in response to an examination question, a homework assignment, or a research *1* project. At times you may be assigned a topic to work on; at other times you may be instructed to choose your own subject.

In writing about literature, you generally focus on some aspect of a work or group of works. For example, you may compare two characters in a story; you may discuss the conflict that is developed in a play; *2* you may analyze the imagery in a poem. Such writing assignments are an important part of literary study, which aims at greater understanding and appreciation of the works you read.

Writing about a literary work brings you closer to it. Before you write a composition about a story, a poem, or a play, you must read *3* and reread the selection carefully. You must sort out your thoughts and reach conclusions. In putting your thoughts down on paper, you become more fully involved with the work.

Throughout your studies you will become familiar with a great *4* many elements that are useful in analyzing literary works. When you refer to the techniques a writer uses to create suspense, for instance, you may use the term *foreshadowing*. In discussing the attitude a writer takes toward a subject, you may concern yourself with *tone*. In examining the musical effects of a poem, you may point to patterns of *rhyme*

ing focuses on substantive changes while proof-reading concentrates on surface errors.

Answering Examination Questions treats nine common methods of developing essays. The list is not exhaustive, and you may wish to expand it. Tell students that methods frequently overlap and that a combination of methods often effectively supports an argument.

When discussing **Writing on a Topic of Your Own,** you may introduce students to other strategies for choosing and limiting topics, including brainstorming, looping, cubing, clustering, and asking *5W-How* questions.

and *rhythm*. These words are part of a common vocabulary used in writing about literature. You can assume that your readers will understand what you mean when you write about such elements. (See the *Guide to Literary Terms and Techniques,* page 696.)

The material on the following pages offers help in planning and writing papers about literature. Here you will find suggestions for answering examination questions, choosing topics, gathering evidence, organizing essays, and writing, evaluating, and revising papers. Also included are several model essays.

The Writing Process

1 We often refer to writing an essay as a *process*, which consists of six key stages: **prewriting, writing, evaluating, revising, proofreading,** and **making a final copy.** In this process, much of the important work—the thinking and planning—comes before writing the first draft.

2   In the **prewriting** stage, the writer must decide what to say and how
3 to say it. Prewriting includes choosing a topic, gathering ideas and or-
4 ganizing them into a plan, and developing a *thesis*—the main idea for the paper. In the **writing** stage, the writer uses the plan to write a first draft of the essay. In the **evaluating** stage, the writer judges the first draft to identify strengths and weaknesses in content, organization,
5 and style. **Revising,** the fourth stage, involves making changes to improve the weaknesses in the draft. The writer can revise by adding, cutting, reordering, or replacing words. In the **proofreading** stage, the writer reads the draft to locate and correct any mistakes in gram-
6 mar, usage, and mechanics. The last stage, **making a final copy,** involves preparing a clean copy and then proofreading it to catch any mistakes made in copying.

The stages of the writing process are related. For this reason, there is usually a "back and forth" movement among the stages. Few writers finish one stage completely before they move on to the next one. At the same time, few writers move in a straight line from one stage to the next. For example, the writer might think up new ideas as he or she is writing a first draft. This would probably require going "back"
7 to prewriting to restate the thesis or to locate new supporting evidence. This movement among the stages of the writing process is a natural part of writing—for all writers.

The amount of time devoted to each stage will vary with individual assignments. During a classroom examination, you will have limited

1
Writing is a process because a series of steps is involved, as in other processes such as cooking, sewing, and building a house.

2
Skipping the prewriting stage usually wastes time because writing becomes disorganized, unfocused.

3
Prewriting strategies may include asking and answering questions about the topic.

4
Plan might be formal outline or simple list.

5
Revising: "reseeing"; involves rethinking, reconsidering.

6
Clean copy is indication writer cares about essay and reader.

7   Synthesizing
What constitutes evidence when writing about literature? Responses will vary. Possible answers: direct quotation, summary of episode, and reference to specific detail, imagery, or character's speech.

1

Taking careful notes while reading, recalling class discussion, and developing answers to kinds of questions likely to be asked are good ways to prepare for essay exams.

2

To be relevant, answer must directly relate to question. Purpose of answering question is to prove understanding of concept.

3

Expert test-takers ask themselves "Why do I say this?" and then provide answer for person evaluating test.

4

Usually, at least two pieces of evidence should be given to support each main point.

5

When answering essay questions, many writers find asking themselves additional questions is a good prewriting strategy for answering essay questions. The verb in the test question determines what questions to ask.

time to plan your essay and to proofread your paper. For a term paper, you may have weeks or months to prepare your essay.

On the following pages the steps in this process are illustrated through the development of several model essays.

Answering Examination Questions

1 Often you may be asked to show your understanding of a literary work or topic by writing a short essay in class. Usually, your teacher will give you a specific question to answer. How well you do will depend not only on how carefully you have read and mastered the material, but on how carefully you read and interpret the essay question.

2 Before you begin to write, be sure you understand what the question calls for. If a question requires that you give *three* reasons for a character's actions, your answer will be incomplete if you supply only *two* reasons. If a question specifies that you deal with the *theme* of a work, take care not to give a summary of action or your answer will be unacceptable. Always take some time to read the essay question carefully in order to determine how it should be answered.

3 Remember that you are expected to demonstrate specific knowledge of the literature. Any general statement should be supported by evidence. If you wish to show that a character changes, for example, you should refer to specific actions, dialogue, thoughts and feelings, or direct comments by the author, in order to illustrate your point. If you are allowed to use your textbook during the examination, you may occasionally quote short passages or refer to a specific page in order to provide supporting evidence.

4 At the start, it may be helpful to jot down some notes to guide you in writing your essay. If you have four main points to make, you may then decide what the most effective order of presentation will be. You might build up to your strongest point, or you might present your points to develop a striking contrast. Aim for a logical organization.

Remember that length alone is not satisfactory. Your answer must be clearly related to the question, and it must be presented in acceptable, correct English. Always take some time to proofread your paper, checking for mistakes in spelling, punctuation, and usage.

5 Let us look briefly at some common instructions used in examinations.

ANALYSIS

6 A question may ask you to *analyze* some aspect of a literary work. When you analyze something, you take it apart to see how each part works. In literary analysis you generally focus on some limited aspect of a work in order to better understand and appreciate the work as a whole. For example, you might analyze the technique of suspense in "The Sea Devil" (page 30); you might analyze O. Henry's use of irony in "A Retrieved Reformation" (page 210); you might analyze Twain's tone in "Cub Pilot on the Mississippi" (page 428).

COMPARISON CONTRAST

7 A question may ask that you *compare* (or *contrast*) two characters, two settings, two ideas. When you *compare*, you point out likenesses; when you *contrast*, you point out differences. Sometimes you will be asked to *compare and contrast*. In that event, you will be expected to deal with similarities and differences. You might, for instance, compare and contrast the two fathers in "A Cap for Steve" (page 78); you might compare the characters of the folk heroes in "Paul Bunyan's Been There" (page 175) and "John Henry" (page 183). Sometimes the word *compare* is used to include both comparison and contrast. Always check with your teacher to make sure that you understand what the question calls for.

DEFINITION

8 A question may ask you to *define* a literary term—to answer the question "What is it?" To define a term first assign it to a general class or large group. Then discuss the features or characteristics that make it different from other members of the same class or group. You should also provide a specific example to illustrate the term. For example, if asked to define the term *metaphor,* you would first say it is a figure of speech (large group) in which two unlike things are compared (feature). You might use Emily Dickinson's poem, "I Like to See It Lap the Miles" (page 468) as an example of metaphor. Here the metaphor compares a train to a horse.

DESCRIPTION

9 If a question asks you to *describe* a setting or a character, you are expected to give a picture in words. In describing a setting, remember to include not only features of the physical locale, but those features that establish the historical period or evoke a mood. In describing a character, you should deal with both direct characterization and indirect characterization (see page 234). You might describe the setting in "The Parachutist" (page 235); you might describe the hawk in the same story.

DISCUSSION

10 The word *discuss* in a question is much more general than the other words we've looked at. When you are asked to discuss something, you

---

6 First answering the question "What are the parts?" is helpful in planning an answer to an analysis question.

7 When planning an answer to a comparison/contrast question, ask "How are these things alike?" and "How are they different?"

8 Specific examples should be given to illustrate features that make the term different from other members of its class.

9 When answering questions that call for **description**, test-takers should keep in mind the purpose for describing. Purpose is usually to convey dominant impression created by **setting** or character. Question might be "What dominant impression is created?"

10 A good way to plan an answer to a discussion question is to ask "What major points could I make about this topic?" and "How are these points related?"

are expected to examine it in detail. If you are asked to discuss the images in a poem, for example, you must deal with all major images; if asked to discuss the use of dialect in a story or poem, you must be sure to cover all significant examples. You might be asked to discuss humorous elements in a group of poems (pages 500–506).

EVALUATION 11 If a question asks you to *evaluate* a literary work or some aspect of one or more works, you are expected to determine whether an author has achieved his or her purpose. To evaluate, you must apply standards of judgment that may relate to both literary content and form. For example, you might be asked to evaluate the use of rhyme to reveal the speaker's state of mind in "The Raven" (page 474). You might be asked to evaluate O. Henry's use of the surprise ending in "A Retrieved Reformation" (page 210).

EXPLANATION 12 A question may ask you to *explain* something. When you explain, you give the reasons for something being the way it is. You make clear a character's actions, or you show how something has come about. For example, you might explain what the talents are of "The No-Talent Kid"(page 10); you might explain the mystery of identity in "The Rule of Names" (page 220); you might explain how the author gives the appearance of authenticity to the story of "The Man Without a Country" (page 142).

ILLUSTRATION 13 The word *illustration, demonstrate,* or *show* asks that you provide examples to support a point. You might be asked for examples of Harriet Tubman's courage illustrated in "They Called Her Moses" (page 419). You might be asked to demonstrate exaggerated characteristics of heroes in the American folk tales about Paul Bunyan and John Henry (pages 175–183).

INTERPRETATION 14 The word *interpret* in a question asks that you give the meaning or significance of something. You might, for example, be asked to interpret "The Road Not Taken" (page 471), a poem that is famous for its symbolism.

At times it will be useful to combine approaches. In discussing a subject, you may draw upon illustration, explanation, or analysis. In comparing or contrasting two works, you may rely on description or interpretation. However, an examination question generally will have a central purpose, and you should focus on this purpose in preparing your answer.

11
To plan an evaluative answer, test-taker must first ask "What are the criteria for making a judgment?"

12
Before beginning an answer to a question calling for explanation, test-taker might ask "How many applicable reasons can I think of?"

13
Illustration requires test-takers to plan an answer by recalling as many examples as they can.

14
Test-taker must ask "What is the meaning of this work?" or "What is the meaning of this element in the work?"

Using the Writing Process to Answer an Essay Question

Even if you are well prepared for an examination, you may not develop your essay effectively unless you manage your time well. Although you may have to work quickly, you should nevertheless devote some time to each stage of the writing process. The following suggestions indicate how you can use the writing process to develop an answer to an essay question. Once you become familiar with this pattern, you will have a plan that enables you to work quickly and efficiently.

PREWRITING

1 In an essay examination, the question itself gives a narrow topic. Its key verb also suggests a way to answer the question. Several prewriting steps remain:

2 **1.** *Write a thesis statement.* A thesis statement gives the main idea of your essay. It should appear at the beginning of your essay.

3 **2.** *Develop points to support, or explain, the thesis.* The main idea should be supported by at least two main points. In a short essay all the points may be discussed in a single paragraph. In a longer essay each point may be discussed in a separate paragraph. Each point must clearly support the main idea of the essay.

4 **3.** *Locate supporting evidence from the literary work(s).* Evidence can include specific details, direct quotations, incidents, or images. This evidence should support or explain each main point you are discussing.

5 **4.** *Organize the main points and evidence.* You should arrange your ideas and details into a logical order—one that your reader can follow easily. By arranging your ideas, you will develop a plan that you can use to write your essay. This plan should include an introduction, a body, and a conclusion for your essay.

WRITING A FIRST DRAFT

6 Write your essay, following the plan you made in prewriting. In the introduction, state the title of the literary work and your thesis. In the body, present the main points and the supporting evidence. In the conclusion, state your thesis again or summarize your main points. Be sure to use language that is serious enough for your purpose (to convey ideas) and for your audience (your teacher, in most *7* cases). Also use transitional expressions (words or phrases that connect ideas, such as *first, then,* and *finally*) to make it clear how ideas are related.

8

This process is easier if the writer has double-spaced to provide room for revising.

9

One effective method of proofreading is to begin with the last sentence and read in reverse; then reread in normal order. This method helps writers to avoid seeing what they think they wrote instead of what is actually on the page.

SAMPLE EXAMINATION QUESTIONS AND ANSWERS

1

The question asks the writer to tell what the **conflict** is about and to give reasons.

2

Notes are timesaving device. Writer can discover evidence and formulate plan for answering.

3

In a single-paragraph essay, thesis is almost always the first sentence.

EVALUATING AND REVISING

Quickly evaluate, or judge, your essay by answering the following questions:

Purpose	1. Have I answered the specific question given?
Introduction	2. Have I included a thesis statement that expresses the main idea of my essay?
Body	3. Have I included at least two main points that support the thesis statement?
	4. Have I included evidence from the literary work to support each main point?
	5. Is the order of ideas clear and logical?
Conclusion	6. Have I included a conclusion that states the main idea again or that summarizes the main points?

PROOFREADING AND PUBLISHING

8 Using your evaluation, improve your essay by *adding, cutting, reordering,* or *replacing* words.

9 Read your essay to locate and correct any mistakes in grammar, usage, and mechanics. You can make a clean copy of your essay if your teacher says you have time to do so. If so, proofread again to catch any mistakes made in copying.

Sample Examination Questions and Answers

On the following pages you will find some sample examination questions and answers for study and discussion. Note that the assignments (shown in italics) may be phrased as direct questions or as essay topics.

QUESTION 1 *In* Beardance *(page 520), Cloyd faces a difficult decision after the grizzly cubs are captured by the game wardens. In a single paragraph, explain his conflict.*

DEVELOPING AN ANSWER 2 Before writing, jot down some prewriting notes to guide you:
Cloyd believes these cubs may be the last grizzlies in Colorado.
Cloyd wants the bear cubs to be free so that they can grow up in the wild.
Cloyd learns that the cubs will be taken to a zoo, where they will spend the rest of their lives.
If Cloyd frees the cubs, he will be breaking the law.
Once free, the cubs might not survive in the wilderness.

3 In the opening sentence of your answer, state your *thesis,* your main point, wording it in such a way that you restate the key words of the question.

Here is a model answer based on the writer's notes.

Main Idea *4*   **Cloyd knows that if he frees the cubs, he will not only be breaking the law but also putting the cubs at risk.** He believes that these bears are the last grizzlies in Colorado. According to the law, the cubs must

Supporting Statements *5* be taken to a zoo, where they will spend the rest of their lives. If Cloyd frees the cubs, they may not be able to survive on their own. He would then be guilty of causing their deaths.

Length: 79 words

4
Main idea is a general statement about the **conflict.**

5
Supporting statements are facts, details that validate the main ideas.

II

QUESTION *6* *Discuss the clues that point to the true identity of Mr. Underhill in "The Rule of Names" (page 220). Refer to your textbook.*

**DEVELOPING
AN ANSWER**

Before writing, go through the story and jot down all the clues that point to Mr. Underhill's identity. Use these prewriting notes to guide your writing.

**WRITING AN
ANSWER**

Here is a model answer for the question.

Main Idea   **Mr. Underhill, in "The Rule of Names," is really a powerful dragon named Yevaud that has come to Sattins Island in disguise.** Through the story there are clues that indicate Mr. Underhill is not what he seems to be. When he first appears in the story he is breathing

Clue 1 *7* hard. The breath comes out of his nostrils "as a double puff of steam"

8 (page 220). According to legend, dragons are fire-breathing. Mr.

Clue 2   Underhill has come to Sattins Island as a wizard, but he is not a great success. His magic remedies are weak, and his enchantments are a failure. Whenever a strange ship comes to the island, Mr. Underhill

Clue 3   stays out of sight. Another indication that he has something to hide is that he does not allow people to visit his cave. Dragons keep their

Clue 4   treasures in caves. When the boys try to pry open the door, they are

Clue 5   greeted by a terrific roar and a "cloud of purple steam" (page 221), a further clue to the wizard's true identity. We learn that Mr. Underhill

Clue 6   has an enormous appetite. After visiting Palani, the schoolteacher, and the children, he becomes very hungry. Dragons are known for

Conclusion *9* devouring maidens. When we put these clues together, we are prepared for Mr. Underhill's transformation into a dragon.

Length: 213 words

6
Writer will not only have to list clues but will also have to explain them.

7
Writer names clues and then explains them.

8 Drawing Conclusions
Why is a page number mentioned? Writer is quoting directly from text.

9 Expressing an Opinion
Is Mr. Underhill's name a clue? Responses will vary. Dragons frequently reside under hills and mountains.

III

10
Writer has two alternatives—either is "correct." Writer will be evaluated on how effectively argument is supported.

11 Finding Details
How would you support the view that the narrator is sane? Responses will vary.

12
Although phrases are acceptable when taking notes, many writers use complete sentences; this helps them clarify ideas.

13 Synthesizing
What other pattern of organization might the writer choose? Responses will vary. Might organize evidence around behavior before and after the murder.

14 Analyzing
How does point 1 relate to the main idea? Narrator's claims about hearing are fantasies, hallucinations.

QUESTION 10 *Is the narrator of Poe's "The Tell-Tale Heart" (page 273) mad or sane? Give your interpretation, referring to specific details in the story. You may use your textbook.*

DEVELOPING AN ANSWER 11 Begin by deciding whether the narrator in the story is mad or sane. Then list details from the story that support your viewpoint. The following set of notes supports the opinion that the narrator is mad.

12 Notes
The narrator is mad.
He claims to hear sounds in hell, the insects in the wall, the dead man's heart beating.
He is nervous; his broken speech shows he is in a state of excitement.
He has no rational motive for killing the old man.
He is obsessed by the old man's eye, which he calls the Evil Eye.
He has contradictory emotions: he pities the old man, but chuckles at the thought of murder; after he kills the old man, he smiles gaily.
He is unable to control himself, working himself up to an hysterical pitch in the presence of the police.
He keeps insisting on his sanity.

13 There is a considerable amount of information to organize here. You might try grouping the notes so that you can present the evidence under a few categories, perhaps 1) his sense of hearing; 2) his lack of motive for the murder; 3) his inability to control his emotions.

WRITING AN ANSWER Here is a model essay that uses the writer's notes.

Main Idea *The narrator in Poe's "The Tell-Tale Heart" is incapable of distinguishing between reality and fantasy.* Although he tries to convince his audience that he is sane, pointing to examples of his cleverness and cunning, his behavior throughout the story reveals a diseased mind.

Point 1 14 **One significant piece of evidence is his claim that his sense of hearing is acute.** In his very first speech, he says that he can hear "many things in hell' (page 273). A little later he says he has been in the habit of listening to the deathwatches in the wall (page 274). Before he suffocates the old man, he claims to hear the man's heart beating, and again, after the old man has been murdered and his body dismembered, the narrator claims to hear the heart beating in ever-increasing loudness.

Supporting Statements

Point 2 *15*   **Another indication of his insanity is his admission that he has no rational motive for killing the old man.** In fact, he loves the old man,

Supporting Statements   but he is obsessed by the old man's blue eye, an "Evil Eye" which vexes him. For eight nights he postpones the murder, until the sight of the eye incites him to fury.

Point 3   **Furthermore, the narrator is unable to control his emotions, and he seems to be constantly on the verge of hysteria.** He admits to

16 being "very dreadfully nervous" (page 273); his speech is broken, showing his state of excitement and tension. His emotions also are

Supporting Statements   contradictory. He pities the old man, yet chuckles inwardly (page 274). After he smothers the old man, he smiles gaily (page 275). His behavior after murdering the old man also shows that he is emotionally unbalanced. He brings the police officers into the room where he has buried the body and places his own chair on the very spot where the dismembered corpse is concealed. He soon works himself up into a frenzy, foaming at the mouth, raving, swearing, and scraping his chair upon the boards. His confession is brought on by his delusion that the police actually know of the crime and hear the heart beating, but deliberately wish to mock him.

Length: 357 words

15
Writer rephrases part of thesis statement—one definition of insanity is inability to distinguish between reality and fantasy.

16
Here, evidence (supporting statements) includes direct quotations, summary of incident, and reference to detail.

CHOOSING A TOPIC

1

If students have read a work together, writer might choose topic from issues raised in class discussion. Questions at end of selection may also suggest topic.

2

To choose topics, writers might ask themselves questions about different elements of work. Possible questions include the following: What kind of person is a particular character? What changes occur in a particular character? What is the function of setting in the work? How should the work be interpreted—what does it mean? What is the relationship between two elements in the work? How is the work similar to (or different from) another work?

3

Writer might brainstorm or list ideas and then consider time and space required to develop each topic. If broad topic is particularly interesting, writer could narrow by choosing one aspect.

4 Comparing/Contrasting
How does the topic differ from the thesis? Topic is subject of paper; thesis includes claim made about subject that must be supported by evidence.

Choosing a Topic

1 At times you may be asked to choose a topic of your own. Often it will be necessary to read a work more than once before a suitable topic presents itself.

2 A topic may focus on one element or technique in a work. If you are writing about fiction, you might concentrate on some aspect of a plot, such as conflict. Or you might concentrate on a character, setting, or theme. If you are writing about poetry, you might choose to analyze imagery or figurative language. A topic may deal with more than one aspect of a work. You might, for example, discuss several elements of a short story in order to show how an idea or theme is developed.

3 Above all, be sure to limit a broad subject to a manageable topic—one that is sufficiently narrow. A narrow topic is one you can discuss in the time and space you have for the essay. Once you have a topic in mind, your object is to form it into a *thesis*, a controlling idea that represents the conclusion of your findings. You would then need to present the evidence supporting your position. It may be necessary to read a work several times before you can formulate a thesis. Here are some examples:

The Diary of Anne Frank (page 334)

Topic Analyzing the character of Anne
Thesis *4* During the months that Anne and her family are in hiding, she develops into a serious, considerate, and courageous person.

Beowulf (page 646) and *Sundiata* (page 658)

Topic Comparing characters of Beowulf and Sundiata
Thesis Both characters, who have superhuman attributes, value courage and honor above all else.

"Flowers for Algernon" (page 240)

Topic Explaining the effect of increasing intelligence on Charlie's life
Thesis As Charlie becomes more intelligent, he finds himself becoming more isolated from other people.

"The Dog That Bit People" (page 413)

Topic Describing Muggs
Thesis Muggs was a big, irritable, moody dog, who intimidated everyone with whom he came into contact.

"The Road Not Taken" (page 471)

Topic Explaining significance of title
Thesis The speaker emphasizes the choice he made in life by not taking the easier and more conventional path.

"The Raven" (page 474)

Topic Discussing the responses of the speaker to the raven
Thesis The speaker, at first seemingly assured, becomes increasingly distracted and loses emotional control.

"The Land and the Water" (page 265)

Topic Interpreting the theme of the story
Thesis When some of her neighbors are lost at sea, a young girl learns for the first time that death can touch young people like her.

Gathering Evidence/ Developing Major Points

1 It is a good idea to take notes as you read, even if you do not yet have a topic in mind. Later on, when you have settled on a topic, you can discard any notes that are not relevant. Some people prefer a worksheet, others index cards. In the beginning, you should record all your reactions. A topic may emerge during this early stage. As you continue to read, you will shape your topic into a rough thesis.

2 When you take notes, make an effort to state ideas in your own words. If a specific phrase or line is so important that it deserves to be quoted directly, be sure to enclose the words in quotation marks. When you transfer your notes to your final paper, be sure to copy quotations exactly.

In working with a short poem, you may cite phrases and lines without identifying the quotations by line numbers. If you cite lines in a long poem, you should enclose the line numbers in parentheses following the quotation. The following note, which is for "Casey at the Bat" (page 503), shows you how to do this:

> When the narrator describes the final pitch, he says: "And now the pitcher holds the ball, and now he lets it go,/And now the air is shat-
3 tered by the force of Casey's blow" (lines 47–48).

4 The slash (/) shows the reader where line 47 ends and line 48 begins.

1
One Reader's Response notes in **Close Reading** (pp. 4–6, 206–209, 287–298, 404–406) provide examples of kinds of notes to take during first-reading. On second reading, notes can be expanded.

2
Important step—putting ideas in own words helps writer clarify thoughts.

3
Page number(s) from which quote is taken should be enclosed in parentheses.

4
And is capitalized after the slash as it is in poem.

If you cite three or more lines, you should separate the quotation from your own text. The following note, which is for "Paul Revere's Ride" (page 136), shows you how to do this:

After he climbs the North Church tower, Revere's friend looks into the distance and sees the British crossing by water:

5 Where the river widens to meet the bay–
A line of black that bends and floats
On the rising tide, like a bridge of boats.
(lines 54–56)

Let us suppose that you have chosen to contrast the characters of the narrator and his Uncle Wash in the following story.

Thanksgiving Hunter

JESSE STUART

"Hold your rifle like this," Uncle Wash said, changing the position of my rifle. "When I throw this marble into the air, follow it with your bead;[1] at the right time gently squeeze the trigger!"

6 Uncle Wash threw the marble high into the air and I lined my sights with the tiny moving marble, gently squeezing the trigger, timing the speed of my object until it slowed in the air ready to drop to earth again. Just as it reached its height, my rifle cracked and the marble was broken into tiny pieces.

7 Uncle Wash was a tall man with a hard leathery face, dark discolored teeth and blue eyes that had a faraway look in them. He hunted
8 the year round; he violated all the hunting laws. He knew every path, creek, river and rock cliff within a radius of ten miles. Since he was a
9 great hunter, he wanted to make a great hunter out of me. And tomorrow, Thanksgiving Day, would be the day for Uncle Wash to take me on my first hunt.

Uncle Wash woke me long before daylight.

"Oil your double-barrel," he said. "Oil it just like I've showed you."

I had to clean the barrel with an oily rag tied to a long string with a knot in the end. I dropped the heavy knot down the barrel and

1. **bead:** the sight at the muzzle end of a gun barrel.

5
Separating quotation from body of paper makes the lines easier to read.

6
Characterization. Narrator is excellent shot.

7
Leathery face may come from spending much time outdoors.

8 Making Generalizations
What does Wash's willingness to violate hunting laws indicate? Responses will vary. He does not respect law; believes hunting to be his right.

9
Wanting to pass on his skill may indicate Wash's affection for narrator.

pulled the oily rag through the barrel. I did this many times to each barrel. Then I rubbed a meat-rind over both barrels and shined them with a dry rag. After this was done I polished the gunstock.

10 "Love the feel of your gun," Uncle Wash had often told me. "There's nothing like the feel of a gun. Know how far it will shoot. Know your gun better than you know your own self; know it and love it."

Before the sun had melted the frost from the multicolored trees and from the fields of stubble and dead grasses, we had cleaned our guns, had eaten our breakfasts and were on our way. Uncle Wash, Dave Pratt, Steve Blevins walked ahead of me along the path and talked about the great hunts they had taken and the game they had **11** killed. And while they talked, words that Uncle Wash had told me about loving the feel of a gun kept going through my head. Maybe it is because Uncle Wash speaks of a gun like it was a living person is why he is such a good marksman, I thought.

12 "This is the dove country," Uncle Wash said soon as we had reached the cattle barn on the west side of our farm. "Doves are feeding here. They nest in these pines and feed around this barn fall and winter. Plenty of wheat grains, rye grains, and timothy seed here for doves."

13 Uncle Wash is right about the doves, I thought. I had seen them fly in pairs all summer long into the pine grove that covered the knoll east of our barn. I had heard their mournful songs. I had seen them in early April carrying straws in their bills to build their nests; I had seen them flying through the blue spring air after each other; I had seen them in the summer carrying food in their bills for their tiny young. I had heard their young ones crying for more food from the nests among the pines when the winds didn't sough[2] among the pine boughs to drown their sounds. And when the leaves started turning brown I had seen whole flocks of doves, young and old ones, fly down from the tall pines to our barnyard to pick up the wasted grain. I had seen them often and been so close to them that they were no longer afraid of me.

"Doves are fat now," Uncle Wash said to Dave Pratt.

14 "Doves are wonderful to eat," Dave said.

And then I remembered when I had watched them in the spring **15** and summer, I had never thought about killing and eating them. I had thought of them as birds that lived in the tops of pine trees and that hunted their food from the earth. I remembered their mournful songs that often made me feel lonely when I worked in the cornfield near the barn. I had thought of them as flying over the deep hollows

2. **sough** (sŭf, sou): make a murmuring sound; sigh.

10
Characterization. Speech indicates depth of Wash's feelings for guns.

11
Uncle's speech has had strong effect on narrator.

12
Characterization. Wash has observed doves closely; focuses on habitat and food supply, thinking of them as game.

13
Narrator has also observed doves closely but thinks of them almost as companions.

14
Pratt and Wash share similar attitude toward doves.

15 Analyzing
How does this paragraph underscore differences between Wash and the narrator? Responses will vary. Narrator has never thought of doves as food. He is conscious of their beauty, aware of them as fellow creatures.

16
Characterization. Wash is proud of his skill.

17
Doves will come when they hear other doves call; hunters learn to imitate sound.

18
Narrator and others follow Wash's orders; perhaps Wash is good leader.

19
Tone. Passage indicates narrator's sympathy for birds.

20 Analyzing
What does this passage reveal about the narrator? He does not choose to join others; kicking shoe against needles may indicate frustration, doubt; narrator may be having second thoughts about hunting trip.

in pairs in the bright sunlight air chasing each other as they flew toward their nests in pines.

"Now we must get good shooting into this flock of doves," Uncle Wash said to us, "before they get wild. They've not been shot among this season."

16 Then Uncle Wash, to show his skill in hunting, sent us in different directions so that when the doves flew up from our barn lot, they would have to fly over one of our guns. He gave us orders to close in toward the barn, and when the doves saw us, they would take to the air and we would do our shooting.

17 "And if they get away," Uncle Wash said, "follow them up and talk to them in their own language."

18 Each of us went his separate way. I walked toward the pine grove, carrying my gun just as Uncle Wash had instructed me. I was ready to start shooting as soon as I heard the flutter of dove wings. I walked over the frosted white grass and the wheat stubble until I came to the fringe of pine woods. And when I walked slowly over the needles of pines that covered the autumn earth, I heard the flutter of many wings and the barking of guns. The doves didn't come my way. I saw many fall from the bright autumn air to the brown crab-grass-colored earth.

19 I saw these hunters pick up the doves they had killed and cram their limp, lifeless, bleeding bodies with tousled feathers into their brown hunting coats. They picked them up as fast as they could, trying to watch the way the doves went.

"Which way did they go, Wash?" Dave asked as soon as he had picked up his kill.

"That way," Uncle Wash pointed to the low hill on the west.

"Let's be after 'em, men," Steve said.

20 The seasoned hunters hurried after their prey while I stood under a tall pine and kicked the toe of my brogan[3] shoe against the brown pine needles that had carpeted the ground. I saw these men hurry over the hill, cross the ravine and climb the hill over which the doves had flown.

I watched them reach the summit of the hill, stop and call to the doves in tones not unlike the doves' own calling. I saw them with guns poised against the sky. Soon they had disappeared the way the doves had gone.

I sat down on the edge of a lichened[4] rock that emerged from the rugged hill. I laid my double-barrel down beside me, and sunlight fin-

3. **brogan** (brō′gən): a heavy work shoe, fitting ankle-high.
4. **lichened** (lī′kənd): covered with lichen, a type of plant that grows in colored patches on wood or rock.

gered through the pine boughs above me in pencil-sized streaks of
21 light. And when one of these shifting pencil-sized streaks of light
touched my gun barrels, they shone brightly in the light. My gun was
cleaned and oiled and the little pine needles stuck to its meat-rind-
22 greased barrels. Over my head the wind soughed lonely among the
pine needles. And from under these pines I could see the vast open
fields where the corn stubble stood knee-high, where the wheat stubble would have shown plainly had it not been for the great growth of
crab grass after we had cut the wheat; crab grass that had been
blighted by autumn frost and shone brilliantly brown in the sun.

23 Even the air was cool to breathe into the lungs; I could feel it deep
down when I breathed and it tasted of the green pine boughs that flavored it as it seethed through their thick tops. This was a clean cool
24 autumn earth that both men and birds loved. And as I sat on the
lichened rock with pine needles at my feet, with the soughing pine
boughs above me, I thought the doves had chosen a fine place to find
food, to nest and raise their young. But while I sat looking at the earth
about me, I heard the thunder of the seasoned hunters' guns beyond
the low ridge. I knew that they had talked to the doves until they had
got close enough to shoot again.

As I sat on the rock, listening to the guns in the distance, I thought
Uncle Wash might be right after all. It was better to shoot and kill
with a gun than to kill with one's hands or with a club. I remembered
the time I went over the hill to see how our young corn was growing
after we had plowed it the last time. And while I stood looking over
25 the corn whose long ears were in tender blisters, I watched a groundhog come from the edge of the woods, ride down a stalk of corn, and
start eating a blister-ear. I found a dead sassafras[5] stick near me, tip-
toed quietly behind the groundhog and hit him over the head. I
didn't finish him with that lick. It took many licks.

When I left the cornfield, I left the groundhog dead beside his ear
26 of corn. I couldn't forget killing the groundhog over an ear of corn
and leaving him dead, his gray-furred clean body to waste on the
lonely hill.

27 I can't disappoint Uncle Wash, I thought. He has trained me to
shoot. He says that I will make a great hunter. He wants me to hunt
like my father, cousins and uncles. He says that I will be the greatest
marksman among them.

I thought about the way my people had hunted and how they had
loved their guns. I thought about how Uncle Wash had taken care of
his gun, how he had treated it like a living thing and how he had told

---

5. **sassafras** (săs′ə-frăs′): a type of tree having a fragrant bark.

21
Imagery. Descriptive details appeal to sight; show that narrator is observant, takes notice of surrounding world.

22
Soughed: making murmuring or rustling sound; appeals to sense of hearing.

23
Use of **imagery** in this paragraph appeals to all five senses and reinforces depiction of narrator as observant.

24
Narrator recognizes bond between men and birds.

25
"Tender blisters" are young kernels of corn.

26 Making Generalizations
What does the inability to forget the incident reveal about the narrator? Responses will vary. Narrator deeply regrets action.

27
Characterization. Narrator feels sense of duty and loyalty to Wash, rest of family, tradition.

28

Narrator's thoughts indicate that he does not feel same about guns as Wash does.

29

Characterization. Wash values guns more than clothing, home.

30

Conflict. Narrator wants to please Wash but does not want to kill.

31

Figurative language. Narrator's use of **metaphor** ("they were waving clouds of green") and **personification** ("sad world"), coupled with earlier use of **imagery,** suggests narrator has poetic nature.

32

Characterization. Narrator values life.

33

Gun is becoming distasteful.

28 me to love the feel of it. And now my gun lay beside me with pine needles sticking to it. If Uncle Wash were near he would make me pick the gun up, brush away the pine needles and wipe the gun barrels with my handkerchief. If I had lost my handkerchief as I had seen Uncle Wash often do, he would make me pull out my shirttail to wipe **29** my gun with it. Uncle Wash didn't object to wearing dirty clothes or to wiping his face with a dirty bandanna; he didn't mind living in a dirty house—but never, never would he allow a speck of rust or dirt on his gun.

It was comfortable to sit on the rock since the sun was directly above me. It warmed with a glow of autumn. I felt the sun's rays against my face and the sun was good to feel. But the good fresh autumn air was no longer cool as the frost that covered the autumn grass that morning, nor could I feel it go deep into my lungs; the autumn air was warmer and it was flavored more with the scent of pines.

Now that the shooting had long been over near our cattle barn, I heard the lazy murmur of the woodcock in the pine woods nearby. Uncle Wash said that the woodcocks were game birds and he killed them wherever he found them. Once I thought I would follow the **30** sound and kill the woodcock. I picked up my gun but laid it aside again. I wanted to kill something to show Uncle Wash. I didn't want him to be disappointed in me.

Instead of trying to find a rabbit sitting behind a broom-sedge[6] cluster or in a briar thicket as Uncle Wash had trained me to do, I felt relaxed and lazy in the autumn sun that had now penetrated the pine boughs from directly overhead. I looked over the brown, vast autumn earth about me where I had worked when everything was green and growing, where birds sang in the spring air as they built their nests. I **31** looked at the tops of barren trees and thought how a few months ago they were waving clouds of green. And now it was a sad world, a dying world. There was so much death in the world that I had known: flowers were dead, leaves were dead, and the frosted grass was lifeless in the wind. Everything was dead and dying but a few wild birds and rabbits. I had almost grown into the rock where I sat but I didn't want **32** to stir. I wanted to glimpse the life about me before it was covered with winter snows. I hated to think of killing in this autumn world. **33** When I picked up my gun, I didn't see life in it—I felt death.

I didn't hear the old hunters' guns now but I knew that wherever they were, they were hunting for something to shoot. I thought they would return to the barn if the doves came back, as they surely would, for the pine grove where I sat was one place in this autumn world that

6. **broom sedge:** a type of beard grass, also known as broom grass.

was a home to the doves. And while I sat on the rock, I thought I would practice the dove whistle that Uncle Wash had taught me. I **34** thought a dove would come close and I would shoot the dove so that I could go home with something in my hunting coat.

As I sat whistling a dove call, I heard the distant thunder of their guns beyond the low ridge. Then I knew they were coming back toward the cattle barn.

And, as I sat whistling my dove call, I heard a dove answer me. I called gently to the dove. Again it answered. This time it was closer to me. I picked up my gun from the rock and gently brushed the pine **35** needles from its stock and barrels. And as I did this, I called pensively **36** to the dove, and it answered plaintively.

I aimed my gun soon as I saw the dove walking toward me. When it walked toward my gun so unafraid, I thought it was a pet dove. I lowered my gun; laid it across my lap. Never had a dove come this close to me. When I called again, it answered at my feet. Then it fanned its wings and flew upon the rock beside me trying to reach the sound of my voice. It called, but I didn't answer. I looked at the dove **37** when it turned its head to one side to try to see me. Its eye was gone, with the mark of a shot across its face. Then it turned the other side of its head toward me to try to see. The other eye was gone.

As I looked at the dove the shooting grew louder; the hunters were getting closer. I heard the fanning of dove wings above the pines. And I heard doves batting their wings against the pine boughs. And the dove beside me called to them. It knew the sounds of their wings. Maybe it knows each dove by the sound of his wings, I thought. And **38** then the dove spoke beside me. I was afraid to answer. I could have reached out my hand and picked this dove up from the rock. Though **39** it was blind, I couldn't kill it, and yet I knew it would have a hard time to live.

When the dove beside me called again, I heard an answer from a pine bough nearby. The dove beside me spoke, and the dove in the **40** pine bough answered. Soon they were talking to each other as the guns grew louder. Suddenly, the blind dove fluttered through the treetops, chirruping its plaintive melancholy notes, toward the sound of its mate's voice. I heard its wings batting the wind-shaken pine boughs as it ascended, struggling, toward the beckoning voice.

34
Although narrator does not want to kill, pleasing Wash appears to be more important.

35
Pensively: thoughtfully; has **connotation** of sadness.

36
Plaintively: sadly; has **connotation** of suffering.

37
Dove has been blinded by a hunter.

38   Making Generalizations
What does the blind dove symbolize? Responses will vary. Nature abused by man; helplessness of small creatures; power of life.

39
By allowing dove to live, narrator is abandoning Wash's code, choosing to live by his own values.

40
Tone. Sad call of doves is contrasted with sound of guns; doves are depicted as loving, gentle creatures.

What are values that Wash and the narrator do not share? Responses will vary. Respect for law; attitudes toward guns, life; sympathy for creatures; love of nature's beauty.

42

Chart is important prewriting step that helps writer impose order on material. Further reorganization may be necessary, but charting evidence helps writer see patterns, form thesis.

Contrast, as you recall, focuses on differences. However, you must be selective about the differences you choose to point out. There wouldn't be much point, for example, in noting that Uncle Wash is older than the narrator, since age is not an essential feature in the story. If you have read the story carefully, you have no doubt concluded that the story points out a difference in attitudes toward hunt-
41 ing and killing. In other words, the story makes you, the reader, look closely at different *values*.
42 You might work out a chart of this kind for taking notes:

Uncle Wash

He is described as a "tall man with a hard leathery face." He is a seasoned sportsman, used to the outdoors.

He is a "great hunter" and wants his nephew to follow in his footsteps.

He takes better care of his gun than of his person or home. He never allows his gun to be dirty or rusty. He tells the narrator to know and love his gun. He speaks of his weapon "like it was a living person."

He has no respect for hunting laws. He hunts all year round. He has no attachment to the things he kills. He talks about the doves being fat and making "good shooting."

He likes to show his skill as a hunter. He teaches his nephew how to shoot. He shows others how to close in around the doves, how to follow them, and how to call to them.

The Narrator

He is a beginner. This is to be his first hunt.

He doesn't want to disappoint his uncle. He has never openly questioned his uncle's ideas. He has followed his uncle's advice in cleaning his rifle, in shooting at targets.

He has a sensitivity to nature that the others lack. He has observed the doves all summer. He talks about their "mournful songs." He has watched them building nests and feeding their young. They are not afraid of him. He had never thought about killing and eating them.

He loves the feel of the cool autumn earth. He prefers enjoying nature to joining the hunt.

He once killed a groundhog, and the memory of the killing has haunted him.

There is so much death in the autumn world that he hates the thought of killing.

The dove, blinded by a hunter, becomes a symbol for nature misused by people. The narrator's decision not to kill the bird shows that he has rejected the code of the hunters.

You might find at this point that a thesis statement has begun to emerge: *Uncle Wash views nature as a challenge to the hunter's skill, while the narrator feels protective toward the natural world and its creatures.* You would continue to study the story, gathering additional evidence and refining your ideas. The next step is organizing your ideas.

Organizing Ideas

Before you begin writing, organize your main ideas to provide for an introduction, a body, and a conclusion. The introduction should identify the author (or authors, if you are dealing with two or more works), the work (or works), or the problem that is under study. It should contain a statement of your thesis as well. The body of your paper should present the evidence supporting your thesis. The conclusion should bring together your main ideas.

1 This is one kind of plan you might use for a short paper. It indicates the main idea of each paragraph.

INTRODUCTION

Paragraph 1 *2* *Thesis* Uncle Wash views nature as a challenge to the hunter's skill, while the narrator feels protective toward the natural world and its creatures.

BODY

Paragraph 2 *3* Uncle Wash, whose skill as a hunter is greatly admired, has no qualms about hunting and killing wildlife.

Paragraph 3 The narrator, who is sensitive to the mystery and beauty of nature, finds hunting and killing distasteful.

CONCLUSION

Paragraph 4 In making the decision not to kill the blind dove, in fact—not to kill any of the creatures in the woods, the narrator resists the pressures of the hunters and listens to his own, inner sense of right and wrong.

Writing the Essay

1 As you write your essay, you should use language that is serious enough for your purpose and audience. Remember that your purpose is to convey ideas clearly, and that you are writing for your
2 teacher or, occasionally, for your classmates. Use transitional expressions (words like *then, second,* and *therefore*) to make the order of ideas clear.

ORGANIZING IDEAS

1
Plan is example of informal outline. Only main ideas are included. Writer will develop each point using evidence from story.

2
Thesis statement indicates writer will prove two major points.

3
Although phrases are acceptable in informal outlines, writer chooses complete sentences to clarify ideas.

WRITING THE ESSAY

1
Language should be clear and precise. Slang and colloquialisms are inappropriate; however, writer should be careful to sound thoughtful, not pompous.

2 Finding Details
What are some other examples of transitional expressions? Responses will vary. Examples: *after, before, however, in addition.*

Here is a model essay based on the prewriting plan. Notice how the essay follows the writer's plan.

3

Title of short story is enclosed in quotation marks.

4

Thesis statement can occur at any point in introduction; most often it is last sentence in introductory paragraph. Model demonstrates, however, that thesis statement may appropriately appear elsewhere.

5 Analyzing

How does the topic sentence relate to the thesis statement? Topic sentence is restatement of idea in first clause of thesis.

6

Supporting evidence includes direct quotations, details, summary of incident.

7

Conclusion explains significance of conflicting attitudes stated in thesis.

TITLE
INTRODUCTION *3*
Identify the selection and the subject.
Thesis *4*

BODY *5*
Topic Sentence

Supporting Evidence *6*

Topic Sentence

Show evidence of close reading.

CONCLUSION *7*

CONTRASTING ATTITUDES TOWARD NATURE IN
"THANKSGIVING HUNTER"

In Jesse Stuart's "Thanksgiving Hunter," the two main characters, Uncle Wash and the narrator, represent contrasting attitudes toward nature. *Uncle Wash views nature as a challenge to the hunter's skill, while the narrator feels protective toward the natural world and its creatures.* The situation that the story presents, the narrator's first hunt, brings these two attitudes into conflict.

Uncle Wash, whose skill as a hunter is greatly admired, has no qualms about hunting and killing wildlife. His "hard leathery face" shows that he is a seasoned sportsman, used to the outdoors. He does not allow anything to interfere with his pleasure in hunting. He has no respect for hunting laws and violates them by hunting out of season. To him, doves are not gentle creatures but fat birds that make "good shooting." He enjoys hunting and enjoys teaching others how to close in around the doves and how to call to them. He considers his weapon to be a living thing and tells the narrator to know and love his gun.

The narrator, by contrast, is sensitive to the mystery and beauty of nature, and finds hunting and killing distasteful. This Thanksgiving hunt is an important occasion. It is his first hunt, and a great deal is expected of him. Although he doesn't want to disappoint his uncle, he cannot bring himself to use his gun to inflict pain and death. There is so much death in autumn that he hates the thought of killing. He has observed the doves all summer; he has listened to their songs and watched them building their nests and feeding their young. He feels he cannot betray their trust. Moreover, he remembers killing a groundhog once, and the memory of that killing has haunted him.

Stuart presents these characters without drawing moral judgments about them. The resolution of the conflict, however, seems to say that Stuart's sympathies lie with the narrator. The dove that has been blinded by a hunter becomes a symbol for nature misused by people. In its innocence the dove answers the narrator's call. He knows that the dove will have a hard time trying to survive, yet he cannot kill it. His decision not to kill—to face Uncle Wash with his hunting coat empty—shows that the narrator has resisted the pressures of the hunters and has trust in his own sense of right and wrong.

Length: 397 words

Evaluating and Revising Papers

When you write an essay in class, you have a limited amount of time to plan and develop your essay. Nevertheless, you should save a few minutes to read over your work and make necessary corrections.

1   When an essay is assigned as homework, you have more time to prepare it carefully. Get into the habit of revising your work. A first draft of an essay should be treated as a rough copy of your manuscript. Chances are that reworking your first draft will result in a clearer and stronger paper.

2   To evaluate an essay, you judge its content, organization, and style. Your aim is to decide what the strong points and weak points are in your essay. Knowing this, you will be able to revise, or make the

3   changes that will improve your essay. To evaluate your essay, answer the following questions:

Guidelines for Evaluating a Paper

Introduction   1. Have I included an introduction that identifies the title and author of the literary work(s)?
   2. Have I included a thesis statement that gives the main idea of the essay?
Body   3. Have I included at least two main points that support the thesis statement?
   4. Have I included evidence from the literary work to support each main point?
Conclusion   5. Have I included a conclusion that brings together the main points?
Coherence   6. Does the order of ideas make sense?
Style   7. Do the sentences differ in length and in the way they begin?
Word Choice   8. Is the language serious enough for the purpose and audience?
   9. Have I defined unfamiliar words for the audience?
   10. Have I used vivid and specific words?

Using your evaluation, you can revise your essay. Writers revise by using four basic techniques: *adding, cutting, reordering,* or *replacing.* For example, if the order of ideas is not clear, you can *add* words like *first, second,* and *finally.* If your language is not serious enough, you can *replace* slang and contractions with formal language. You can *cut* evidence that does not explain a main point, and you can *reorder* ideas

4   that are difficult to follow.

On the following pages you will find a revised draft of the essay that appears on page 692. The notes in the margin show which revision technique the writer used. Study the two versions of the essay. As you do so, notice how the writer has revised for greater clarity, accuracy,

5   and conciseness.

EVALUATING AND REVISING PAPERS

1
Professional writers evaluate and rewrite constantly. If experienced writers use this process to achieve good writing, then, logically, so should inexperienced writers.

2
One step in the process might be to share the draft with other writers and ask for feedback.

3
Participating in peer-group evaluation can help writers learn to evaluate their own work more effectively. By answering these questions about someone else's work, writers can learn to apply guidelines to themselves.

4
Writers can also add evidence, cut unnecessary words from sentences, replace unclear ideas with clear ones, and reorder words in sentences for clarity.

5
Conciseness: absence of superfluous ideas, details, or words.

6
Combining of first two sentences makes more concise statement.

7
Added information clarifies relationship of the hunt to story and to thesis statement.

8
Cutting unnecessary words makes sentence more concise.

9
Addition to sentence makes statement more accurate.

10
Cutting sentence improves conciseness.

11
Combining sentences creates more concise statement. Addition of "To him" changes inaccurate generalization to accurate statement.

12
Additions create parallelism.

13
Moving sentence improves logical order of paragraph, sums up information, and provides lead into next paragraph.

14   Analyzing
Why did the writer add the phrase "by contrast"? Transitional phrase clarifies relationship between paragraphs.

15
Addition of specific detail clearly identifies which hunt the writer is discussing.

694

---

cut; reorder   6   In Jesse Stuart's ~~short story~~ "Thanksgiving Hunter," Uncle Wash

cut; add; cut   and the narrator ~~are the~~ *two* main characters. ~~They~~ represent contrasting

attitudes toward nature. Uncle Wash views nature as a challenge to

the hunter's skill, while the narrator feels protective toward the

add; cut   7   natural world and its creatures. *The situation that the story presents, the narrator's first hunt, brings* These two attitudes ~~are brought~~

cut   into conflict ~~during the hunt.~~

Uncle Wash, whose skill as a hunter is greatly admired, has no

cut   8   qualms about hunting and killing wildlife. ~~We are told that he has~~

replace; cut   *His* ~~"a~~ hard leathery face," ~~which~~ shows that he is a seasoned sportsman,

replace; cut   9   used to the outdoors. *He does not allow anything to* ~~Nothing~~ interferes with his pleasure in hunting.

cut   10   ~~He is a "great hunter" and wants his nephew to follow in his footsteps.~~

He considers his weapon to be a living thing and tells the narrator

add; cut   to know and love his gun. He has no respect for hunting laws, *and* ~~He~~

replace; add   11   violates ~~the laws~~ *them* by hunting out of season. *To him,* Doves are not gentle

creatures but fat birds that make "good shooting." He enjoys hunting

add; replace   12   and teach*es* *enjoys* *ing* others how to close in around the doves and how to call

reorder   13   to them.

replace   14   The narrator, ~~who~~ *by contrast,* is sensitive to the mystery and beauty of

add; add   15   nature, finds hunting *and* and killing distasteful. This *Thanksgiving* hunt is an

694   WRITING ABOUT LITERATURE

important occasion. It is his first hunt, and a great deal is

<table>
<tr><td>add; replace 16</td><td>expected of him. *Although* He doesn't want to disappoint his uncle. He has *he cannot bring himself*</td></tr>
<tr><td>replace</td><td>*to use his gun to inflict pain and death.* never openly questioned his uncle's ideas. There is so much death in</td></tr>
<tr><td>replace 17</td><td>autumn that he hates the thought of killing. He has observed the birds *doves* *he has listened to their songs and watched them building their nests and feeding their young.*</td></tr>
<tr><td>add; cut</td><td>all summer, and he feels he cannot betray their trust. He once killed</td></tr>
<tr><td>add; add</td><td>*Moreover, he remembers killing* *once* a groundhog, and the memory of that killing has haunted him.</td></tr>
<tr><td>cut 18</td><td>Stuart presents these characters in the story without drawing</td></tr>
<tr><td>replace 19</td><td>moral judgments about them. The *resolution of the conflict, however,* end of the story seems to say that</td></tr>
<tr><td>cut; add</td><td>Stuart's sympathies lie with the narrator. The blind dove becomes a *that has been blinded by a hunter*</td></tr>
<tr><td>add; cut 20</td><td>symbol for nature misused by people. *In its innocence* The dove innocently answers the</td></tr>
<tr><td></td><td>narrator's call. He knows that the dove will have a hard time trying</td></tr>
<tr><td>replace 21</td><td>to survive, yet he cannot kill it. In making the *His* decision not to</td></tr>
<tr><td>replace; add; replace</td><td>kill any of the creatures in the woods, *to face Uncle Wash with his hunting coat empty — shows that* the narrator resists the *has ed*</td></tr>
<tr><td>replace; cut</td><td>pressures of the hunters and listens to *has trust in* his own inner sense of right</td></tr>
</table>

and wrong.

Proofreading and Publishing

1 Proofread your essay to correct any mistakes in grammar, usage, and mechanics. Pay special attention to the correct capitalization and punctuation of any quotations you use as supporting evidence. Make a final copy of your essay by using correct manuscript form or your teacher's instructions. After writing this clean copy, proofread again to catch mistakes made in copying. Then share your work.

16
Changes add to clarity and conciseness; unnecessary details are cut, and another clause is added to explain what narrator experiences that will lead to his uncle's disappointment.

17
Addition of details improves clarity and accuracy.

18
Cutting unnecessary phrase improves readability.

19
Again, addition of details to sentences improves both clarity and accuracy.

20
Change is for accuracy; adverb modifying "answers" has been cut because it gives incorrect meaning to sentence.

21
Changes are for conciseness and accuracy; decision to face Uncle Wash is the crucial one that shows the narrator has resisted hunters' pressures.

PROOFREADING AND PUBLISHING

1
To proofread, some writers begin by placing their left index finger by the first word of the first sentence and the right index finger on the punctuation mark that ends sentence. They then read the sentence to check for coherence, clarity, and correctness, repeating this process with every sentence in the essay.

LITERARY ELEMENTS TRANSPARENCIES

In the *Audiovisual Resources Binder,* you will find **Literary Elements** transparencies with accompanying **Teacher's Notes** and student activity pages. You may want to use these audiovisual materials when discussing the specific literary elements identified on the following pages.

Alliteration: See Sound Effects in Poetry, Transparency 36.

Literary Terms AND Techniques

ALLITERATION *The repetition of a sound in a group of words.* Alliteration is used in many common expressions: "safe and sound," "over and out," "do or die." Most alliteration occurs at the beginning of words, but sometimes we also find alliteration in the middle or at the end of words, as in "tickled pink" and "dribs and drabs."

Two uses of alliteration seem to be to gain emphasis and to aid our memory. This is why many advertising jingles depend on alliteration and why so many products are given names that are alliterated.

Politicians often use alliteration. When we are asked to put up with hardship, we are asked to "tighten our belts" or to "bite the bullet." A famous political slogan during a presidential campaign went "Tippecanoe and Tyler too!"

Poets use alliteration to the most obvious and memorable effect. Here are some examples of alliteration in poetry:

> Mere prattle, without practice,
> Is all his soldiership.
> > William Shakespeare
> > *Othello*

> Open here I flung the shutter, when, with
>   many a flirt and flutter,
> In there stepped a stately Raven of the
>   saintly days of yore.
> > Edgar Allan Poe
> > "The Raven"

> I like to see it lap the miles,
> And lick the valleys up,
> > Emily Dickinson

Sometimes alliteration is used simply for the fun of it. One poet, Algernon Charles Swinburne, wrote a poem that made fun of his own style. He had been criticized for using too much alliteration. So he composed "Nephelidia" (little clouds), which is complicated and funny nonsense. It starts this way:

> From the depth of the dreamy decline of the
>   dawn through a notable nimbus of nebulous
>   noonshine,
> Pallid and pink as the palm of the flagflower that
>   flickers with fear of the flies as they float,

Swinburne makes the amusing point that heavily alliterated poetry can seem to mean more than it does.

Prose writers use alliteration, too, but they have to be careful not to sound too artificial. Mary O'Hara's story "My Friend Flicka" uses alliteration in its title. Some of the most memorable expressions from the King James translation of the Bible are alliterated: "Let there be light: and there was light" (Genesis), and "There is no new thing under the sun" (Ecclesiastes).

See pages 474, 480, 654.

ALLUSION *A reference to a work of literature or to an actual event, person, or place, which the speaker expects the audience to recognize.* Allusions are used in everyday conversation, as well as in prose and poetry. The great danger with an allusion is that the reader or listener won't understand it. People can seem snobbish if they allude to very obscure works or events.

Writers often allude to other works of literature. In titling one of his plays *The Ugly Duckling,* A. A. Milne alludes to the fairy tale by Hans Christian Andersen.

Literature contains many allusions to the Bible. Emily Dickinson expects us to recognize her allusion to a thunderous speaker in the New Testament when she says that a train "roared like Boanerges." The title of a section of a biography about Harriet Tubman is "They Called Her Moses," which alludes to the Biblical leader Moses. In that case, we are expected to make the connection between Moses and Harriet Tubman, both deliverers of their people.

Allusions to the myths of ancient Greece and Rome are also common in literature. The great writers used to be carefully trained to read both Latin and Greek. We do not study these languages as intensely nowadays, so we miss many of the allusions that writers like William Shakespeare, John Milton, William Wordsworth, and Alfred, Lord Tennyson took for granted. When the speaker in Edgar Allan Poe's poem "The Raven" thinks that the Raven came from "Night's Plutonian shore," he expects us to know that he is alluding to the shore of the underworld ruled by Pluto, a Roman god identified with night and darkness.

Allusions to the media are growing more and more common, though these are not as lasting as allusions to the Bible and classical literature. Squeaky, in the story "Raymond's Run" by Toni Cade Bambara, de-

696

scribes an encounter with some unfriendly girls as "one of those Dodge City scenes." This is an allusion to the television series "Gunsmoke," a Western that was popular in the l950s and l960s.

See page 481.

ANECDOTE *A very short story which is told to make a point.* Many anecdotes are funny; some are jokes. Originally, anecdotes were little-known, entertaining facts about a person or about a historical event. Anecdotes are used in nearly all kinds of literature. Mark Twain uses several anecdotes in his tale "The Celebrated Jumping Frog of Calaveras County." Twain tells this anecdote to prove that a man named Jim Smiley would bet on *anything*:

> Why, it never made no difference to *him*—he'd bet on *anything*—the dangdest feller. Parson Walker's wife laid very sick once, for a good while, and it seemed as if they warn't going to save her; but one morning he come in, and Smiley up and asked him how she was, and he said she was considerable better—thank the Lord for his inf'nite mercy—and coming on so smart that with the blessing of Prov'dence she'd get well yet; and Smiley, before he thought, says, "Well, I'll resk two and a half she don't anyway."

See pages 417, 436, 447, 448, 449.

ATMOSPHERE *The general mood or feeling established in a piece of literature.* Atmosphere can be gloomy, peaceful, frightful, tense, etc. Atmosphere is usually achieved through description. Landscapes, such as dark, dank moors that ooze a steaming mist, often lend themselves to creating atmosphere. Poe is famous for the creation of gloomy atmospheres, as in this opening passage of his story "The Fall of the House of Usher." Notice how the italicized words make us sense the atmosphere:

> During the whole of a *dull, dark* and soundless day in the *autumn* of the year, when the clouds *hung oppressively low* in the heavens, I had been passing alone, on horseback, through a singularly *dreary* tract of country, and at length found myself, as the *shades of the evening* drew on, within view of the *melancholy* House of Usher.

Atmosphere doesn't always have to be spooky and frightening. Notice how the italicized words create an atmosphere of comfort and well-being in this passage from Washington Irving's "The Legend of Sleepy Hollow":

> His stronghold was situated on the banks of the Hudson, in one of those *green, sheltered, fertile nooks* in which the Dutch farmers are so fond of *nestling.* A great elm tree spread its broad branches over it. At the foot of the tree *bubbled* up a *spring* of the *softest* and *sweetest water,* in a little well formed of a barrel. The spring then stole *sparkling* away through the *grass* to a neighboring *brook* that *bubbled* along among alders and dwarf willows. Close by the farmhouse was a vast barn, which might have served for a church, every window and crevice of which seemed *bursting* forth with the *treasures* of the farm.

See page 278.

BALLAD *A storytelling poem that uses regular patterns of rhythm and strong rhymes.* Most ballads are meant to be sung. **Folk ballads**, in fact, are sung long before they are written down. Others, the so-called **"literary" ballads,** are composed by writers and are not specifically intended for singing. Most ballads are full of adventure, action, and romance, such as you find in Sir Walter Scott's rousing "Lochinvar." Many ballads tell stories of famous villains, like Jesse James and Billy the Kid. One very famous folk ballad, "John Henry," celebrates the heroic railroad worker who raced a machine. There are often several versions of folk ballads, since they change a bit as people sing them and pass them on.

See page 185.

BIOGRAPHY *The life story of a person written by someone else.* When a person writes his or her own biography, it is called an *autobiography.* Ann Petry wrote a biography called *Harriet Tubman: Conductor on the Underground Railroad.* Richard Wright wrote his own life story in an autobiography called *Black Boy.* Biography and autobiography are two of the most popular forms of nonfiction, and most libraries have a section set aside for them. Almost every famous person has been the subject of a biography. Some famous people have had three or four biographies written about them, by different people.

CHARACTERIZATION *The methods used to present the personality of a character in a narrative.* A writer can create a character by: (1) giving a physical description of the character; (2) showing the character's actions and letting the character speak; (3) revealing the character's thoughts; (4) revealing what others think of the character; and (5) commenting directly on the character. Characterization can be sketchy, particularly if the character does not take an important role in a story. Or, characterization can be extraordinarily full, as when the character is the main focus of a story.

Literary Terms and Techniques

Conflict: See Transparency 43. See also Evaluating a Play, Transparency 26. For conflict in the novel, see Transparency 44. See also Elements of the Short Story, Transparency 21.

Literary Terms and Techniques

Washington Irving describes Ichabod Crane in "The Legend of Sleepy Hollow" in many ways to reveal his character. Here is a physical description:

> The name of Crane was not inapplicable to his person. He was tall, but exceedingly lank, with narrow shoulders, long arms and legs, hands that dangled a mile out of his sleeves, feet that might have served for shovels, and his whole frame most loosely hung together.

Here Irving tells about Ichabod's thoughts and fears:

> How often did he shrink with curdling awe at the sound of his own steps on the frosty crust beneath his feet, and dread to look over his shoulder, lest he should behold some uncouth being tramping close behind him!

Here he reveals what others think of Ichabod:

> He was, moreover, esteemed by the women as a man of great learning, for he had read several books quite through. . . .

And here Irving gives his own evaluation of his hero:

> He was, in fact, an odd mixture of small shrewdness and simple credulity.

Sometimes animals can be characterized, using the same techniques. Rudyard Kipling's famous story "Rikki-tikki-tavi" has as its hero a little mongoose, who is characterized as if he were a person.

See pages 28, 86, 234, 317, 394.

COMEDY *A literary work with a generally happy ending. A comedy can be funny and, sometimes, rather serious under it all.* Any narrative can be a comedy—a short story, novel, play, or narrative poem, though the term is most often applied to plays. One of the typical plots of comedies is the one involving young lovers who almost don't get together. The plot of such a comedy always ends happily, often with a marriage, and the theme usually has something to do with the power of love. A comedy that has these characteristics is A. A. Milne's play *The Ugly Duckling.* Many movies and novels are also based on this kind of plot.

Television features a great many situation comedies—weekly episodes about funny complications that take place in the lives of the same group of characters. Slapstick comedy, with a lot of rough-housing and knockabout humor, was popular in early movies. The films of Abbott and Costello, Lau-

rel and Hardy, and the Three Stooges are examples.

See page 317.

CONFLICT *The struggle that takes place between two opposing forces.* A conflict can take place between a character and a natural force, like a bear or a hurricane; between two characters; or between opposing views held by separate characters or groups of characters. Such conflicts are **external** conflicts. Conflict can also be **internal**—it can exist within the mind of a character who must make a difficult decision or overcome a fear.

Usually, a conflict arises when a character's wishes or desires are blocked. In Sir Walter Scott's poem "Lochinvar," Ellen's father is marrying her to someone else, and so Lochinvar is blocked from wedding the maiden he loves. Lochinvar resolves this conflict by stealing Ellen away from her own bridal feast. We might expect this to produce new conflict, but as the poem tells us, Lochinvar and Ellen escape and are never seen again.

In Arthur Gordon's story "The Sea Devil," a man struggles with a manta ray which nearly drowns him. In Dorothy Canfield's story "The Apprentice," a girl's views on how she should behave clash with her parents' views. In Langston Hughes's story "Thank You, M'am," the character Roger has an internal conflict: he must decide whether to respect someone's trust in him, or do the easy thing and run away.

In many types of literature, especially in novels and dramas, there are two or more kinds of conflict. In the play *The Diary of Anne Frank,* for example, there is the conflict between the "family" in hiding and the hostile outside world which seeks to destroy them; there is the conflict of views between Anne and the adults; there is also the internal conflict within Anne's mind, between her feelings of love for her parents and her desire to please them, and her need to grow up and be herself.

See **Plot.**
See also page 218.

CONNOTATION *All the emotions and associations that a word or phrase arouses.* Connotation is different from **denotation,** which is the strict literal (or "dictionary") definition of a word. For example, the word *springtime* literally means "the season of the year between the vernal equinox and the summer solstice." But *springtime* usually makes most people think of love, rebirth, youth, and romance.

Drama: See Evaluating a Play, Transparency 26.

Poets are especially sensitive to the connotations of words. For example, Poe uses the word *midnight* in "The Raven." *Midnight* literally means "the middle of the night." But the word *midnight* has certain connotations associated with death, remorse, and gloom that help create the poem's atmosphere of foreboding. You can imagine how different the poem would be if you were to substitute the phrase "high noon" for *midnight*.

See pages 219, 461.

DESCRIPTION *The kind of writing that creates pictures of persons, places, things, or actions. Description may also tell how something sounds, smells, tastes, or feels.* Washington Irving, a master of description, gives us this picture of Ichabod Crane's route homeward. Notice how he uses words like *barking, crowing, chirp,* and *twang,* which help us hear certain sounds.

The hour was as dismal as himself. Far below him, the Tappan Zee spread its dusky and indistinct waste of waters, with here and there the tall mast of a sloop riding quietly at anchor under the land. In the dead hush of midnight he could even hear the barking of the watchdog from the opposite shore of the Hudson, but it was so vague and faint as only to give an idea of his distance from this faithful companion of man. Now and then, too, the long-drawn crowing of a cock, accidentally awakened, would sound far, far off, from some farmhouse away among the hills—but it was like a dreaming sound in his ear. No signs of life occurred near him, but occasionally the melancholy chirp of a cricket or, perhaps, the guttural twang of a bullfrog from a neighboring marsh, as if sleeping uncomfortably and turning suddenly in his bed.

See **Atmosphere, Imagery.**
See also pages 20, 67.

DIALECT *A representation of the speech patterns of a particular region or social group.* Dialect is often used to make a character or place seem authentic. Some of the regional dialects in the United States are the Down-East dialect of Maine, the Cajun dialect of Louisiana, and the dialects of the South and West.

Hosea Bigelow was one of the great American humorists who used dialect simply for the fun of it—and sometimes to make a point. Here is a letter he wrote to the editor of a Down-East newspaper about a debate in the United States Senate:

To Mr. Buckenam.
  Mr. Editer, As i wuz kinder prunin round, in a little nussry sot out a year or 2 a go, the Dbait in the sennit cum inter my mine. An so i took & Sot it to wut I call a nussry rime. I hev made sum onnable Gentlemun speak that dident speak in a Kin uv Poetikul lie sense the seeson is dreffle backerd up This way.
  ewers as ushul
  Hosea Bigelow.

DIALOGUE *Talk or conversation between two or more characters.* Dialogue usually attempts to present the speech of characters in a realistic fashion. It is used in almost all literary forms: biography, essays, fiction and nonfiction, poetry, and drama. Dialogue is especially important in drama, where it forwards *all* the action of the play. Dialogue must move the plot of a play, reveal the characters, and even help establish some of the mood. When dialogue appears in a play, there are no quotation marks to set it apart, since—besides stage directions—a play is nothing but dialogue.

When dialogue appears in a prose work, or in a poem, it is usually set apart with quotation marks. Since actual life is conducted almost entirely in dialogue, a short story that uses a lot of dialogue will not only move fast, but it will also seem realistic.

See **Dialect.**
See also pages 70, 182, 394.

DRAMA *A story written to be acted out on a stage, with actors and actresses taking the parts of specific characters.* The word *drama* comes from a Greek word meaning "act," so it is important to stress the idea of action in a drama. While reading a drama, we have to try to imagine real people playing the parts on stage.

We usually think of two main kinds of drama. **Tragedies** are serious plays in which a hero or heroine suffers defeat or death. William Shakespeare's *Hamlet* and *Macbeth* are tragedies, as is *The Diary of Anne Frank.* **Comedies** are lighter plays, which usually end happily and are often funny. A. A. Milne's play *The Ugly Duckling* is a comedy.

Drama involves the use of **plot,** the series of related events that make up the story.

Conflict, the most important element in the plot, pits the characters in a play against one another, or against forces that are powerful and sometimes greater than they are. The characters carry forward the plot of a play by means of **dialogue.**

Most playwrights include **stage directions,** which tell the actors and actresses what to do or what feelings to project when certain lines are spoken. The

Literary Terms and Techniques

Literary Terms and Techniques   **699**

Epic: See Analyzing an Epic, Transparency 51. See also The Epic Hero, Transparency 52.

Essay: See Distinguishing Between Facts and Opinions, Transparency 31.

Exposition: See Distinguishing Between Facts and Opinions, Transparency 31.

Literary Terms and Techniques

stage directions are useful to the director, who must help the actors and actresses interpret their lines. The director decides things like the timing of a line, the speed of delivery, the way the actors and actresses stand or move when speaking their lines, and what they do when they are not speaking their lines. The director really interprets the way the whole play should go. In many productions, the director is as important as the author of the play.

Most plays are presented on stages with **sets.** The set is a representation of the room, landscape, or other locale in which the play takes place. **Props** are important items used in the drama, such as a telephone, a sword, a book, a glass of water, or any other item that figures in the action. **Lighting** helps to establish the desired moods, or the time of day or the season.

Each act of a play is usually composed of several scenes. The end of each act often includes a **climax,** which is an emotional or suspenseful moment, designed to keep the audience interested so it will come back after the intermission. The final act of the drama usually builds to a final climax or **crisis,** which is greater than any that went before. The end of the drama involves the **resolution** of the conflict: usually by death in a tragedy, or by marriage in a comedy.

See **Dialogue.**
See also pages 317, 394.

ELEGY *A mournful poem or lament, usually a meditation on the death of someone famous or of someone important to the writer.* Elegies may also be laments on the nature of death itself, or on the loss of youth and beauty. The most famous elegy is probably "Elegy Written in a Country Churchyard," by the English poet Thomas Gray. One of its frequently quoted stanzas is

The boast of heraldry, the pomp of power,
And all that beauty, all that wealth e'er gave,
Awaits alike the inevitable hour.
The paths of glory lead but to the grave.

Walt Whitman's poem "O Captain! My Captain!" is one of several elegies he wrote mourning the death of Abraham Lincoln.

EPIC *A long narrative poem that relates the deeds of a hero.* Epics incorporate myth, legend, folk tale, and history, and usually reflect the values of the societies from which they originate. The tone is generally grand, and the heroes and their adventures appear larger than life.

Many epics were drawn from an oral tradition and are known as **primary epics.** These were transmitted by song and recitation before they were written down. Two of the most famous primary epics of Western civilization are Homer's *Iliad* and *Odyssey.* Another primary epic is one of the earliest works in history, the *Epic of Gilgamesh,* from ancient Mesopotamia.

A second type of epic is the **literary** or **secondary epic.** These were written down from the start. Examples include the *Aeneid,* Rome's national epic written by the poet Virgil to give the ancient Romans a sense of their own destiny; the *Divine Comedy,* the great epic of the Middle Ages written by the Italian poet Dante; and *Paradise Lost* and *Paradise Regained,* two great epics written by the seventeenth-century English poet John Milton.

See **Narrative Poetry.**
See also pages 622, 624, 645, 656.

ESSAY *A short piece of prose writing which discusses a subject in a limited way and which usually expresses a particular point of view.* The word *essay* means "an evaluation or consideration of something." Most essays tend to be thoughtful considerations about a subject of interest to the writer. Most essays are *expository* in nature, which simply means that they do not tell a story, but explain or give information about a situation, an event, or a process.

See **Exposition.**

EXPOSITION *The kind of writing that explains something or gives information about something.* Exposition can be used in fiction and nonfiction, but its most familiar form is the **essay.** A typical example of exposition is this passage from Henry David Thoreau's *Walden,* in which Thoreau explains why he decided to spend some time alone in a cabin in the woods:

I went to the woods because I wished to live deliberately, to front only the essential facts of life, and see if I could not learn what it had to teach, and not, when I came to die, discover that I had not lived. I did not wish to live what was not life, living is so dear; nor did I wish to practice resignation, unless it was quite necessary. I wanted to live deep and suck out all the marrow of life, to live so sturdily and Spartan-like as to put to rout all that was not life. . . .

Exposition is also that part of a play or other narrative that helps the reader understand important background information. For example, in *The Diary of Anne Frank* the authors provide background information, or exposition, in the first scene. Here the audience is told how the Frank family and others were forced to go into hiding in a warehouse in Amsterdam, to escape the Nazis.

See **Essay.**
See also pages 197, 397.

FABLE *A brief story with a moral, written in either prose or poetry.* The characters in fables are often animals who speak and act like human beings. The most famous fables are those of Aesop, who was said to be a Greek slave living in the sixth century B.C. Almost as famous are the fables of the seventeenth-century French writer, La Fontaine.

A typical fable is Aesop's "Belling the Cat," the story of the mice who decided to put a bell around a cat's neck so they'd hear it coming. It was a wonderful solution that every mouse applauded. Then came the obvious problem: Who would actually put the bell on the cat? Their solution had merely gotten them another problem. The moral of the story is "It is easy to propose impossible remedies."

FICTION *A prose account which is invented and not a record of things as they actually happened.* Much fiction is based on real personal experience, but it almost always involves invented characters, or invented actions or settings, or other details which are made up for the sake of the story itself. Fiction can be brief, as a fable or short story is, or it can be book length, as a novel is.

FIGURATIVE LANGUAGE *Any language that is not intended to be interpreted in a strict literal sense.*

When we call a car a "lemon," we use figurative language. We do not mean that the car is really a citrus fruit, but that its performance is "sour"—it will cause its owner to lose money. When we refer to someone as a lamb, or a peach, or a rock, or an angel, we know that the person is none of those things. Instead, we mean simply that the person shares some quality with those other things.

The main form of figurative language used in literature is **metaphor.** Metaphor makes a comparison between two different things. The father in Mary O'Hara's story "My Friend Flicka" uses metaphors when he says that the mares are hellions and the stallions outlaws. He is comparing the mares to ghastly creatures from hell. They are not *really* from hell, as we know, but the comparison makes us realize how troublesome they can be. To say the stallions are outlaws is also a metaphor, because it compares the horses to human outlaws. Horses do not have legal institutions: that's reserved for humankind. By comparing the stallions to human outlaws, this speaker shows how bad they are and how hard they are to control.

These metaphors are stated clearly: "The mares *are* hellions." But sometimes a metaphor does not state the comparison so directly. We also use a metaphor when we say something like: "Kate's sunny smile enchanted us." We are actually comparing her smile to the brightness and the welcoming warmth of the sun.

Similes are another form of figurative language. Similes are easy to recognize because they always use special words to state their comparisons. When the poet Robert Burns says "My luve is like a red, red rose," he uses a simile. It is a comparison and it is, indeed, like a metaphor. But it's different because it uses a special word to state the comparison. That word is *like.* Other words and phrases used in similes are *as, as if, than, such as,* and *resembles*—all of which state a comparison directly. Just as with metaphor, the simile does not use *all* the points of comparison for its force. It uses only some. For instance, the comparison of "my luve" to "a rose" does not necessarily mean that the loved one is thorny, nor that she lives in a garden, nor that she has a green neck. Rather, it means that "my luve" is delicate, fragrant, rare, and beautiful, as the flower is.

Emily Dickinson uses a simile in "I Like to See It Lap the Miles" when she says that the train is "punctual as a star." But she also uses a metaphor in this poem, since she makes other comparisons between the train and an animal, which seems to be a horse. The verbs in particular suggest this metaphor: she tells us that the train *laps, licks, feeds itself, steps, peers, crawls, chases,* and *neighs at its own stable door.* All of these verbs describe actions that we know a train cannot perform, but an animal can.

Similes in everyday language are common. "He was madder than a hornet." "She roared like a bull." "Louie laughed like a hyena." "Float like a butterfly, sting like a bee." "Be as firm as Gibraltar and as cool as a cucumber." "She resembles Wonder Woman."

See **Metaphor, Simile, Symbol.**
See also pages 50, 178, 468.

FLASHBACK *An interruption of the action in a story to tell about something that happened earlier in time.* The usual plot moves in chronological order: it starts at a given moment, progresses through time, and ends at some later moment. A flashback interrupts that flow by suddenly shifting to past time and narrating important incidents that make the present action

Fiction: See Elements of the Short Story, Transparency 21, for work with basic elements of fiction. For Analyzing and Evaluating a Novel, see Transparency 44.

Literary Terms and Techniques

Literary Terms and Techniques

more understandable. Usually there is a signal to indicate the flashback, but occasionally a writer will leave out the signal. The reader must pay very close attention to find the point where the narrative picks up the action again.

The play *The Diary of Anne Frank* is almost entirely a flashback. In the opening scene, when Mr. Frank enters the warehouse, it is 1945. The play then flashes back to 1942, and not until the final scene are we brought back to 1945 again.

See page 394.

FOLK TALE *A story that was not originally written down, but was passed on orally from one storyteller to another.* Folk tales often exist in several forms because they are carried by storytellers to different parts of the world. Over the years, and according to changing local customs, the same tale can take on slightly different qualities. Many fairy tales, such as the story of Cinderella and the story of Jack and the Beanstalk, are folk tales that originated in Europe, and versions of them later appeared in the Appalachian Mountains of the New World. Folk tales often involve unreal creatures, like dragons, cannibalistic giants, and chatty animals.

In the United States, folk tales have grown up about such figures as the frontiersman Davy Crockett, the steel-drivin' man John Henry, and the original cowhand Pecos Bill.

See **Tall Tale.**
See also pages 178, 180, 182, 185.

FORESHADOWING *The use of hints or clues in a narrative to suggest action that is to come.* Foreshadowing helps to build suspense in a story because it alerts the reader to what is about to happen. It also helps the reader enjoy all the details of the buildup. Lewis Carroll uses a bit of foreshadowing in his poem "Jabberwocky" when he has the old man warn: "Beware the Jabberwock, my son! / The jaws that bite, the claws that catch!" But foreshadowing is more common in short stories, longer fiction, and drama. It is often said that if a loaded gun is presented in Act One of a play, it should go off before Act Five. In other words, the gun in the first act usually foreshadows some danger to come.

See page 229.

HERO/HEROINE *The chief character in a story or drama.* In older heroic stories, the heroes and heroines often embody qualities that their society thought were best and most desirable. The heroines and heroes in such stories are often of noble blood and are usually physically strong, courageous, and intelligent, characteristics that are shown by the epic hero Sundiata. Often the conflict involves the hero or heroine with a monster or with a force that threatens the entire social group. For example, Beowulf must kill the monster Grendel, who has nearly destroyed the Danes. Folk heroes like Daniel Boone and John Henry, and the heroes of tall tales, like Paul Bunyan, share most of these heroic qualities with their counterparts in myth.

Nowadays, we use the term **hero** or **heroine** to mean the main character in any narrative. At times, this person might be admirable, as in "Thank You, M'am" by Langston Hughes, in which Mrs. Jones rewards a boy with kindness instead of punishment. At times, however, the hero or heroine in modern stories is not entirely admirable. Some of them might even show ordinary human weaknesses, such as fear or poor judgment. For example, in Mary O'Hara's story "My Friend Flicka," the hero, Kennie, seems to be a failure in everything but his devotion to his horse. In some stories, the hero or heroine might even be "unheroic" and not admirable at all. In Washington Irving's "The Legend of Sleepy Hollow," the hero, Ichabod, is cowardly and superstitious, just the opposite of the noble, strong, intelligent heroes of old.

IMAGERY *Words and phrases that describe something in a way that creates pictures, or images, that appeal to the reader's senses.* Most images tend to be visual, though many times a writer will also use words that suggest the way things sound, smell, taste, or feel to the touch. Images appear in all kinds of writing: poetry, nonfiction, fiction, and drama. Not all writers use imagery extensively. But those who do, use it in an effort to make an experience in literature more intense for us. Because good images involve our sensory awareness, they help us to be more responsive readers.

Washington Irving, in "The Legend of Sleepy Hollow," describes something (a phantom?) as if it were a wind that could be felt and heard: "some rushing blast, howling among the trees." Katrina Van Tassel is described in images that appeal to our sense of taste: "a blooming lass of fresh eighteen, plump as a partridge, ripe and melting and rosy cheeked as one of her father's peaches." The Van Tassel barnyard is described in visual images that also make our mouths water: "he pictured to himself every roasting-pig running about with an apple in his mouth. The pigeons were snugly put to bed in a

Inference: For information on fact and opinion in nonfiction, see Transparency 31.

comfortable pie, and tucked in with a coverlet of crust; the geese were swimming in their own gravy."

See **Description.**
See also pages 465, 467.

INFERENCE *A reasonable conclusion made about something based on certain clues or facts.* Often the writer of a piece of literature will not tell us everything there is to tell. At times, we have the pleasure of drawing an inference about a scene, a character, or an action. The process of drawing an inference is pleasurable, because we are actually making a discovery on our own.

In her poem "I Like to See It Lap the Miles," Emily Dickinson never tells us that she is describing a train. Yet readers have inferred that she is talking about a train from clues given in the poem: it speeds over the miles, goes around mountains and through passages hewn out of rocks, hoots and makes other noises, "chases itself" downhill, and when it stops, it is quiet.

In "Casey at the Bat," Ernest Lawrence Thayer never tells us directly that Casey is a fellow who is very sure of himself. He lets us infer that his character is enormously confident—perhaps even overconfident—when Casey lets a perfectly good ball go by and says, "That ain't my style." By that point in the poem, we also infer that Casey's pride and confidence are going to do him in.

See page 615.

INVERSION *A reversal of the normal order of words in a sentence, usually for some kind of emphasis.* The normal word order in an English sentence is subject-verb-complement. When writers and speakers invert, or reverse, this pattern, the word or phrase that is placed out of order usually receives more emphasis. The device often appears in poetry, but it occurs in prose and in speech as well. In poetry, inversion is often used to make a line's rhythm beat out in a certain way, or to achieve a certain end-rhyme.

Edgar Allan Poe used inversion in many of his poems. In these lines from "The Raven," we find inversion in the clause in the second line. Poe probably used inversion here so that he could get a word to rhyme with *nevermore:*

But the Raven, sitting lonely on the placid bust, spoke only
That one word, as if his soul in that one word he did outpour.

The normal word order of the last clause would be:

. . . as if he did outpour his soul in that one word.

At times, inversion can make a passage sound too literary or poetical, or even old-fashioned. Its use must be cautious, since too much inversion makes a passage seem artificial.

See page 485.

IRONY *A contrast between what is stated and what is really meant, or between what is expected to happen and what actually does happen.* Irony is used in everyday conversation. When we say, "It's not at all warm here," when we're standing in the desert in July, we are using irony.

There are three kinds of irony used in literature: (1) **Verbal irony** occurs when a writer or speaker says one thing and means something entirely different; (2) **Irony of situation** occurs when a situation turns out to be completely different from what we expect; (3) **Dramatic irony** occurs when a reader or an audience knows something that a character in a play or story does not know. Irony is used in literature for all kinds of effects, from humor to serious comments on the unpredictable nature of life.

A humorous example of *verbal irony* is found in this short verse by Lewis Carroll:

The Crocodile

How doth the little crocodile
　Improve his shining tail,
And pour the waters of the Nile
　On every shining scale!

How cheerfully he seems to grin,
　How neatly spread his claws
And welcomes little fishes in
　With gently smiling jaws!

This speaker says one thing but really means something else. He says that the crocodile "welcomes" little fish into his "gently" smiling jaws. He really means that the crocodile is eating the fish and that his massive, toothy jaws are anything but gentle.

One of the most famous examples of *irony of situation* is the ending of William Shakespeare's tragedy *King Lear.* After a terrible struggle and a mighty battle, King Lear is saved by his faithful daughter, Cordelia. We expect her to be able to enjoy her victory, but just the reverse happens: she is executed after the battle is won. She lies dead in Lear's arms, and, instead of enjoying his new-found freedom and safety, Lear dies too. This unpleasant ending is so ironic that throughout the eighteenth century, people insisted that the play be performed with a happy ending.

A good example of *dramatic irony* is found in the play *The Diary of Anne Frank*. We, the audience, are told at the beginning of the play that no one but Mr. Frank survives the Nazi prison camps. Thus, we watch the play knowing what the main characters themselves don't know: that only one of them will survive the war.

See page 218.

LEGEND   *A story handed down from the past. Legends seem to have some basis in history.* A legend usually centers on some historical incident, such as a battle or a journey in search of a treasure or the founding of a city or nation. A legend usually features a great hero or heroine who struggles against some powerful force to achieve the desired goal. Most legends were passed on orally long before they were written down, so the characters became larger than life, and their actions became fantastic and unbelievable. An example of a famous legend is the story of the Trojan War, which figures in three classical epics.

See page 624.

LIMERICK   *A comic poem written in five lines, rhymed in the pattern a a b b a, and having a definite pattern of rhythm.* Writing limericks is a great popular pastime. Much of the fun comes in finding rhymes to match the name of a person or place. A typical limerick begins like this: "There was a young girl from St. Paul." What comes later is up to the writer.

Sometimes writers of limericks twist the spellings of the rhyming words to build more humor. The following limerick plays on the Irish spelling of a town south of Dublin, *Dun Laoghaire*, pronounced "dun leery."

An ancient old man of Dun Laoghaire
Said, "Of pleasure and joy I've grown
    waoghaire.
  The life that is pure,
  Will suit me I'm sure,
It's healthy and noble though draghaire."

You can see that the pattern of rhythm for lines 1, 2, and 5 is the same and that the pattern for lines 3 and 4 is the same.

See page 500.

LYRIC POEM   *A brief poem which expresses an emotion and which usually represents the poet as "I."* (A lyric poem does *not* tell a story. A poem that tells a story is called a **narrative poem.**) The word *lyric* is derived from the word *lyre*, a musical instrument. The lyre is a stringed instrument remotely related to our guitar. It was struck in chords by the ancient Greek lyric poets, who sang their poems in a chant-like fashion. The lyre was used to help build up the emotional effects and to help the listener respond to the poem. Today we do not necessarily associate the lyric poem with music, although we do call the words to songs "lyrics."

English poet Leigh Hunt expresses a number of emotions in this lyric poem:

Jenny Kissed Me

Jenny kissed me when we met,
  Jumping from the chair she sat in;
Time, you thief, who love to get
  Sweets into your list, put that in!
Say I'm weary, say I'm sad,
  Say that health and wealth have missed
    me,
Say I'm growing old, but add,
  Jenny kissed me.

See page 492.

METAMORPHOSIS   *In literature, a fantastic change, mainly of shape or form.* Myths often use metamorphosis to suggest a close relationship among gods, humans, and the world of nature. The Greek goddess Aphrodite, for instance, sprang from the foam of the sea. The goddess Athena appeared to the Greek hero Odysseus in the form of a mist. She also assumed the form of an owl when it suited her. Such metamorphoses reflected the ancient Greeks' wonder about the nature of the world, by suggesting that the shapes of things were not necessarily true indications of what the things really were. If an owl could be a goddess, then it was only wise for a Greek to be cautious of the owl and to respect it.

In A.D. 8, a Roman poet named Ovid collected the Greek and Roman myths of shape-changing into a book called *The Metamorphoses*. One of the famous stories from Ovid's collection is "Midas," in which a king is given the power to change everything he touches into gold. *The Metamorphoses* influenced many later writers to introduce sudden changes of form or shape into their works. Metamorphoses are found in many popular European folk tales, in which handsome princes are often reduced to ugly and repellent creatures. In "The Princess and the Frog," a frog is transformed back into a beautiful prince, and in "Beauty and the Beast," a prince is transformed into a beast and then returned to his original form.

Metamorphoses are used in modern literature as well. In "Flowers for Algernon," Daniel Keyes writes about a scientifically induced metamorphosis, in which a retarded man is transformed into a mental giant as a result of a surgical procedure. In fact, metamorphoses are found in many works of science fiction.

METAPHOR   *A comparison made between two different things, as in the saying "Life is a dream," "You are my sunshine," or "He is a peach."* The intention of a metaphor is to give added meaning to one of the things being compared. A metaphor is one of the most important forms of **figurative language.** It is used in virtually all forms of language, including everyday speech, formal prose, and all forms of fiction and poetry.

If we say, "He was a gem to help me out," we use a metaphor, because we say a person is a gem. Gems are stones; they are hard; they glisten; they are often quite small. But these are *not* the qualities which the metaphor wants us to consider. We rely on our listener to understand that the metaphor is comparing the person's *value* to a gem's value.

If we say, "Misers have hearts of flint," we do not mean that their hearts are small dark stones that are bloodless and nonfunctioning. Rather, we mean that misers cannot show sympathy and kindness, just as the piece of stone cannot.

Metaphors are not always stated directly. In "Paul Revere's Ride" (page 136), Longfellow says that the spark struck out by Revere's horse "kindled the land into flame with its heat." Longfellow expects us to understand that the "fire" refers to the American Revolution.

A poet will sometimes **extend** a metaphor throughout a poem. Langston Hughes does this in his poem "Mother to Son." In the second line, the mother compares life to a stairway, and throughout the poem she talks of life as if it *were* a stairway. A metaphor is also extended throughout the following poem by Emily Dickinson. In the first line, the poet compares hope to a bird. Throughout the poem, she continues to describe hope as if it were a bird:

Hope is the thing with feathers
That perches in the soul,
And sings the tune without the words,
And never stops at all,

And sweetest in the gale is heard;
And sore must be the storm

That could abash the little bird
That kept so many warm.

I've heard it in the chillest land,
And on the strangest sea;
Yet, never, in extremity,
It asked a crumb of me.

> See **Figurative Language, Simile.**
> See also pages 468, 469.

MONOLOGUE   *A long speech spoken by one character.*
> See page 394.

MYTH   *A story, often about gods and goddesses, that attempts to give meaning to the world.* Almost every society has myths which explain the beginnings of the world, the beginnings of the human race, and the origins of evil. Myths tell people other things that they are concerned about: who their gods are, what their most sacred beliefs are, who their heroes are, and what their purpose in life is.

The term "classical mythology" refers to the myths told by the ancient Greeks and Romans. Most of the classical myths have to do with divinities who lived on Olympus, such as Zeus, Aphrodite, Apollo, Athena, and many others.

NARRATION   *The kind of writing or speaking that relates a story (a narrative).* Narration tells about a series of connected events, explaining what happened, when it happened, and to whom it happened. Narration can be fictional, or it can be based on actual events. Narration can take the form of prose or poetry. It can be as long as a novel, or it can be as brief as an anecdote, which may be only a paragraph. Short stories, narrative poems, myths, fables, and legends are all examples of narration.

> See **Point of View.**
> See also pages 123, 140.

NARRATIVE POETRY   *Poetry that tells a story.* A narrative poem is usually longer than a lyric poem, though it need not be extensive. For instance, Lewis Carroll's poem "Jabberwocky" tells a story about a young man who slays a monster, but the poem is only twenty-eight lines long. In "Casey at the Bat," Ernest Lawrence Thayer tells, in fifty-two lines, the entire saga of Mudville's hero and his humiliating strikeout.

In Edgar Allan Poe's "The Raven," a narrator uses 108 lines to tell the story of a strange bird that flew

Literary Terms and Techniques   **705**

Novel: See Analyzing and Evaluating a Novel, Transparency 44.

Onomatopoeia: See Sound Effects in Poetry, Transparency 36.

Literary Terms and Techniques

into his study, an event which seems to have driven him to madness. Other famous narrative poems are Henry Wadsworth Longfellow's "Paul Revere's Ride" and Sir Walter Scott's "Lochinvar."

See **Ballad, Narration, Point of View.**
See also pages 140, 486.

NONFICTION *Any prose account that tells about something that actually happened or that presents factual information about something.* Fiction is invented; nonfiction is *not* invented. One of the chief kinds of nonfiction is the history of someone's life. When a person writes his or her own personal life history, we call it **autobiography** (such as Richard Wright's *Black Boy*). When someone else writes a person's life history, we call it **biography** (such as Ann Petry's book called *Harriet Tubman: Conductor on the Underground Railroad*). Another kind of nonfiction is the **essay.**

Essays are among the most common forms of nonfiction, and they appear in most of the magazines we see on newsstands. Another kind of nonfiction is also found on newsstands: in the newspaper itself. News stories, editorials, letters to the editor, and features of all kinds are forms of nonfiction. Travel accounts, personal journals, and diaries are also forms of nonfiction.

See **Biography, Essay.**
See also page 402.

NOVEL *A fictional narrative in prose, generally longer than a short story.* The novel allows for greater complexity of character and plot development than the short story. The forms the novel may take cover a wide range. For example, there are the **historical novel,** in which historical characters, settings, and periods are drawn in detail; the **picaresque novel,** presenting the adventures of a rogue; and the **psychological novel,** which focuses on characters' emotions and thoughts. Other forms of the novel include the **detective story,** the **spy thriller,** the **Western,** and the **science-fiction novel.**

See pages 514, 547, 581, 610.

ONOMATOPOEIA *The use of a word whose sound in some degree imitates or suggests its meaning.* The names of some birds are onomatopoetic, imitating the cries of the birds named: *cuckoo, whippoorwill, owl, crow, towhee, bobwhite.* Some onomatopoetic words are *hiss, clang, rustle,* and *snap.* In these lines from Edgar Allan Poe's poem "The Bells," the word *tintinnabulation* is onomatopoetic:

Keeping time, time, time
In a sort of Runic rhyme,
To the *tintinnabulation* that so musically wells
From the bells, bells, bells, bells,
Bells, bells, bells—

See page 480.

PARAPHRASE *A summary or restatement of a piece of writing, which expresses its meaning in other words.* A paraphrase of Ernest Lawrence Thayer's poem "Casey at the Bat" might go this way:

The Mudville baseball team was behind in the last inning, and it looked as if Casey would not even get a chance at bat. But, when some batters before him actually got on base, everyone had high hopes that Casey could win the game with one of his famous home runs. But Casey showed off, did not swing at the first two good pitches, and struck out on the third one.

It is clear that such a paraphrase takes all the fun out of the original poem. The purpose of the paraphrase is to see that we understand just what really did happen in the poem.

See page 485.

PARODY *The humorous imitation of a serious piece of literature, or of some other art form, for the sake of amusement or ridicule.* In literature, a parody can be made of a character, a plot, a writer's style, or a theme.

Casey, in Ernest Lawrence Thayer's "Casey at the Bat," is a parody of the great heroes of old, like King Arthur, who never fail to come to the rescue of their people. The last and highest hopes of the home-team crowd are focused on Casey, their conquering hero. But all hopes die, and the hero fails the home team after all.

The following verse is a parody of the style of Edgar Allan Poe's "The Raven," a poem which has been often parodied over the years:

Once upon a midnight dreary, while I shivered eerie, bleary,
Full of teary leer-y, fear-y
Thinking of my lost Lenore, my lost Lenore. . . .
Lenore and nothing more!
Not the oaken door, the grocery store, the dreadful bore, the apple core, the golf fore, the marine corps, or the Lakers' score:
My lost Lenore and nothing more.
While I shivered nearly freezing, in my thin pajamas sneezing,

Who should wing right in a-breezing but a bristling Raven wheezing,
Wheezing, wheezing right above my chamber
door.

Such parodies are fun and harmless, even if they do
make us laugh a bit at some of the techniques used
by a respected poet like Poe.

See page 332.

PERSONIFICATION *A figure of speech in which
something nonhuman is given human qualities.* In these
lines from "Blow, Blow, Thou Winter Wind," William Shakespeare personifies the wind. He addresses it as if it were a person who could
consciously act with kindness or unkindness. He
also gives it teeth and breath.

Blow, blow, thou winter wind,
Thou art not so unkind
    As man's ingratitude.
Thy tooth is not so keen,
Because thou are not seen,
    Although thy breath be rude.

PLOT *The sequence of events that take place in a story.*
Short stories, novels, dramas, and narrative poems
all have plots.

The major element in a plot is a **conflict,** or a struggle of some kind that takes place between the characters and their environment, or between warring
desires in the characters' own minds. A plot will introduce the characters, reveal the nature of their
conflict, and show us how the conflict is resolved.

Many times, especially in novels and plays, there will
be more than one plot. In *The Diary of Anne Frank,*
the main plot tells what happens as the "family"
hides from their enemies; the **subplot** tells what
happens to Anne and her growing love for Peter.

See **Conflict.**
See also pages 218, 317, 394.

POETRY *Traditional poetry is language arranged in
lines, with a regular rhythm and often with a definite
rhyme scheme. Nontraditional poetry does away with regular rhythm and rhyme, though it usually is set up in lines.*
There is no satisfactory way of defining poetry, although most people have little trouble knowing
when they read it. Some definitions offered by those
concerned with poetry may help us. The English
poet William Wordsworth called it "the spontaneous
overflow of powerful feelings." Matthew Arnold, an

English writer and poet of the nineteenth century,
defined it in this way: "Poetry is simply the most
beautiful, impressive and widely effective mode of
saying things."

Poetry uses **figurative language** and **imagery** extensively. It is often divided into **stanzas.** Poetry often
uses **rhyme** in order to create a kind of music or to
emphasize certain moods or effects. Poetry depends
heavily on strong **rhythms,** even when the rhythms
are not regular. Techniques like **alliteration** and **inversion** are often considered especially poetic.

There are two general categories of poetry: **narrative poetry,** which tells a story, and **lyric poetry,**
which does not tell a story but expresses some personal emotion. Some of the well-known poetic
forms are the **ballad,** the **elegy,** and the **limerick.**

See **Figurative Language, Rhyme, Rhythm.**
See also pages 99, 140, 480, 502, 510.

POINT OF VIEW *The vantage point from which a
story is told.* Every story has to have a point of view,
since it has to be told to us by some "voice." Writers
may tell their stories from a third-person point of
view, or they may use a first-person point of view.

(1) The **third-person point of view** is one of the
most common in literature. In this point of view, a
story is told by someone not in the story at all. The
following paragraph is an example of the third-
person point of view. We are told here that a character, Hester Martin, has made a decision. She is
referred to in the third person ("she"), which is how
this point of view gets its name:

Hester Martin could let the insult get her down.
She could reply rudely or call for the manager
and make a formal complaint. But she decided
against both courses. Instead she took the man
aside and explained to him what it felt like to have
a total stranger say something cruel, even if the
man did not intend to be insulting. The man did
not intend to be insulting at all, and once Hester
told him how she felt, he changed his manner entirely. Hester had done the right thing. She had
educated someone.

This is an example of an **omniscient,** or **all-
knowing, third-person point of view.** The narrator
tells us things that Hester Martin does not directly
think or observe. The narrator tells us also that
Hester made the right decision.

A third-person point of view might *not* be all-
knowing. A **limited third-person point of view** tells
us what only one character sees, feels, and thinks.

Plot: See Transparency 9. For
plot in a novel, see Transparency
44. For plot in drama, see Transparency 26.

Poetry: See Sound Effects in Poetry, Transparency 36.

Point of View: See Elements of
the Short Story, Transparency 21.

Literary Terms and Techniques

Rhyme: See Sound Effects in Poetry, Transparency 36.

Literary Terms and Techniques

This same scene written from a limited third-person point of view might go this way:

> Hester Martin felt her face flush. Did he notice, too? Should she go to his manager? Should she insult him back? She took a moment to bring her emotions back under control, but when she collected herself she drew the man aside and lectured him carefully and patiently on the subject of insulting a patron. His apologies and his extraordinary politeness and caution gave her a small measure of satisfaction.

This limited third-person point of view tells the story from the point of view of one character only. The narrator does not tell us what other characters are thinking or feeling.

(2) The **first-person point of view** tells everything from the vantage point of a narrator who is usually a character in the story. We can be told only what this narrator knows and feels. We cannot be told what any other character thinks, except when the narrator may guess about that character's feelings or thoughts. The first-person is a very limited point of view, but its popularity is secure since we all identify with "I" in a story. The passage about Hester Martin's decision might be told like this by a first-person narrator:

> I felt my face burn with the insult. I wondered if he noticed it. Should I go to his manager? No, I thought. And I won't stoop to his level and return the comment. When I thought I could control myself, I took the man aside and I told him in no uncertain terms that I did not like being insulted by a stranger. The only satisfaction I got was watching him try to squirm out of it, telling me he didn't mean it as an insult. But at least I got him to admit he was wrong. Maybe he learned a lesson.

The first-person point of view is much like our own view of life. It is limited to what one person knows and is controlled by that one person's thoughts and feelings.

See page 262.

PROSE   *All literature which is not written as poetry.* Essays, short stories, novels, biographies, and most dramas are written in prose. Prose styles differ widely, from the simple and direct style of a story like Mary O'Hara's "My Friend Flicka," to the tense, nervous style of Poe's "The Tell-Tale Heart." One of the most remarkable pieces of prose is Abraham Lincoln's "Gettysburg Address," which was so short that very few people who were present when Lincoln spoke actually remembered hearing it.

REFRAIN   *A word, phrase, line, or group of lines that is repeated regularly in a poem or song, usually at the end of each stanza.* Refrains are sometimes used to emphasize a particularly important idea. In Poe's "The Raven," for example, the sentence "Quoth the Raven, 'Nevermore'" is a refrain. It helps to build up the mood of despair, and it reminds us continually of the sound of the name of the dead Lenore.

Sometimes the refrain in a poem or song is repeated exactly the same way, and sometimes it is varied slightly for effect. One of the delights in refrains is in anticipating their return.

RHYME   *The repetition of sounds in words that appear close to each other in a poem.* One of the primary uses of rhyme seems to be as an aid to memory. You may have used some of the simpler rhymes for this purpose yourself, such as the one about months, beginning: "Thirty days hath September, April, June, and November." A rhyme that might help you remember a spelling rule is the one beginning: "*I* before *e* except after *c*."

The most familiar form of rhyme is **end rhyme.** This simply means that the rhymes come at the ends of the lines. The following lines are from a long poem on music, by the English poet Alexander Pope. In this part of the poem, Pope is trying to recreate the sounds of the underworld when Orpheus sings there in an attempt to rescue his beloved Eurydice:

> What sounds are heard,
> What scenes appeared,
>   O'er all the dreary coasts!
>   Dreadful gleams,
>   Dismal screams,
>   Fires that glow,
>   Shrieks of woe,
>   Sullen moans,
>   Hollow groans,
> And cries of tortured ghosts!

Each of these rhymes is an exact rhyme, although we would now pronounce *heard* differently from *appeared.*

Rhyme that occurs within a line is called **internal rhyme.** One of the masters of internal rhyme is Edgar Allan Poe, who uses it in the first line of "The Raven": "Once upon a midnight *dreary,* while I pondered, weak and *weary.*" One of Poe's clever internal rhymes is "lattice" and "thereat is" (lines 33–34).

Rhythm: See Sound Effects in Poetry, Transparency 36.

Setting: For setting in the short story, see Transparency 21. For setting in a novel, see Transparency 44.

Clearly, in poetry, rhymes are used for more than an aid to memory. Rhymes in the works of Pope or Poe, or any other careful poet, serve many purposes. One is to increase the musicality of the poem. (Songwriters also do this.) Another purpose of rhyme is to give delight by rewarding our anticipation of a returning sound, as in Pope's "coasts"/ "ghosts" rhyme. Rhyme is also used for humor. *Limericks,* for instance, would not be half so funny if they did not rhyme. The English poet George Gordon, Lord Byron invented one of the funniest rhymes in English when he rhymed "intellectual" with "hen-pecked you all."

See **Poetry.**
See also pages 474, 480, 501.

RHYTHM *The pattern of stressed and unstressed sounds in a line of poetry.* All language has rhythm of some sort or another, but rhythm is most important in poetry, where it is carefully controlled for effect.

There are several effects of rhythm in poetry. Rhythm lends poetry a musical quality, which gives the reader or listener pleasure. Rhythm can also be used to imitate the action being described in a poem. For example, in Robert Browning's poem "How They Brought the Good News from Ghent to Aix," the rhythm actually imitates the galloping rhythm of horses' hoofs.

And there was my Roland to bear the whole
weight
Of the news which alone could save Aix from her
fate,
With his nostrils like pits full of blood to the
brim,
And with circles of red for his eye sockets' rim.

One thing to remember is that good poets usually put the stress on the most important words in the line. If you say a line to yourself in a natural voice, you will hear that the most important words demand stress.

In addition to using a pattern of stressed and unstressed syllables, a poet has another powerful means of building rhythm. This is by the use of **repetition.** In this passage from "The Bells," Edgar Allan Poe repeats the word *bells* eighteen times. He echoes the word three more times with the repetition of the rhyming word *knells.* He also repeats the word *time* six times, and echoes it twice more with the rhyming word *rhyme.* All of this repetition builds up a kind of pounding rhythm, which might remind us of the repeated ringing of bells themselves.

Keeping time, time, time,
In a sort of runic rhyme,
  To the throbbing of the bells,
Of the bells, bells, bells—
  To the sobbing of the bells;
Keeping time, time, time,
  As he knells, knells, knells,
In a happy runic rhyme,
  To the rolling of the bells,
Of the bells, bells, bells:
  To the tolling of the bells,
Of the bells, bells, bells, bells,
  Bells, bells, bells—
To the moaning and the groaning of the
bells.

See **Alliteration, Rhyme.**
See also pages 462, 482, 484, 491.

SETTING *The time and place in which the events of a story take place.* In short stories, novels, poems, and nonfiction, setting is established by **description.** In dramas, setting is usually established by **stage directions,** but since dramas normally have **sets** which appear before the audience, elaborate descriptions of setting are unnecessary.

In some stories, setting is not important at all, but in other stories setting is very significant. Washington Irving's story "The Legend of Sleepy Hollow," for example, could happen in only one setting—a "spellbound" region, where people believe in ghosts:

A drowsy, dreamy influence seems to hang over the land. The whole neighborhood abounds with local tales, haunted spots, and twilight superstitions; and the nightmare seems to make it the favorite scene of her gambols.

Setting can serve simply as the physical background of a story, or it can be used to establish atmosphere. In his poem "The Raven," Edgar Allan Poe uses setting to establish an atmosphere of gloom and mystery. He does this by telling us what time it is (a "midnight dreary"), what month it is ("bleak December"), what the study looks like ("each separate dying ember wrought its ghost upon the floor"), and what sounds are heard ("the silken, sad, uncertain rustling of each purple curtain").

See **Atmosphere.**
See also page 239.

Literary Terms and Techniques

Suspense: See Transparency 42.

Theme: For theme in the short story, see Transparency 21. For theme in a novel, see Transparency 44.

SIMILE *A comparison made between two different things, using a word such as* like *or* as. Similes are *figures of speech* and are common in everyday language and in most forms of literature. We use similes when we say, "He fought like a tiger"; "He was as mild as a dove"; "She was as cool as a cucumber." A more poetic use of simile is this, from George Gordon, Lord Byron's "Stanzas for Music":

> There will be none of Beauty's daughters
> With a magic like thee;
> And like music on the waters
> Is thy sweet voice to me.

See **Figurative Language.**
See also pages 468, 499.

STANZA *A group of lines forming a unit in a poem.* Some poems, such as limericks, consist of a single stanza. "Lochinvar" by Sir Walter Scott is divided into eight stanzas, each of which has six lines and the same rhyme scheme.

See **Poetry.**

SUSPENSE *That quality in a literary work that makes the reader or audience uncertain or tense about what is to come next.* Suspense is a kind of "suspending" of our emotions. We know something is about to happen, and the longer the writer can keep us guessing, the greater the suspense. Suspense is popular in any kind of literature that involves **plot,** whether it be nonfiction, drama, short stories, novels, or narrative poems.

Every reader of Ernest Lawrence Thayer's "Casey at the Bat," for example, wants to find out if the hero of the poem will come to the rescue of the Mudville Nine. Holding the reader off for as long as possible is part of the poet's strategy of building suspense.

Suspense is possible even when the reader *knows* what to expect. Even though we know in Edward Everett Hale's "The Man Without a Country" that Philip Nolan has died in exile, we want to keep on reading to find out what his life at sea was like. We also are kept in suspense over Nolan's feelings; we want to know if he changed his mind about his country during his exile.

See **Foreshadowing, Plot.**
See also page 229.

SYMBOL *Any person, place, or thing which has meaning in itself but which is made to represent, or stand for, something else as well.* A symbol can be an object, a person, an action, a place, or a situation. Writers sometimes rely on commonly used symbols: most people know, for example, that an old man with a scythe usually is a symbol for time, that a dove is a symbol for peace, that a snake is often a symbol for evil, that ice is often a symbol for hatred, and that red is often a symbol for passion. But often we have to be on our toes in order to understand what something in literature is supposed to symbolize.

Symbols are often personal. In Robert Frost's poem "The Road Not Taken," we know that the road symbolizes a choice, but we do not know exactly what choice the poet has in mind. Frost purposely leaves its full meaning indefinite, so that the road can take on any number of symbolic meanings. For Frost, it may have symbolized a choice of careers—should he be a schoolteacher or a poet, for example. For us, it may symbolize other choices. Frost's road works well as a symbol because everybody has choices to make and nobody can make all of them. There has to be "a road not taken" in everyone's life.

A symbol is like a rock thrown in a pond: we see the splash right away, but then we notice that the ripples go much farther that we expected. As we reflect on a symbol, its suggested meanings move out like the ripples, slowly and ever more widely.

See page 472.

TALL TALE *A highly improbable, humorous story that stretches facts beyond any hope of belief.* Tall tales feature things like people as high as mountains, pancake griddles two city blocks wide, and lakes used for boiling vegetables. Tall tales seem to have been extremely popular in the American West, where even nature seemed to assume gigantic proportions. The tales of Mike Fink, John Henry, and Paul Bunyan were the delight of the evening campfire. "The Notorious Jumping Frog of Calaveras County," by Mark Twain, is a celebrated example of the tall tale in American literature.

See pages 178, 180, 182, 185.

THEME *The main idean expressed in a literary work.* Many stories, such as some murder mysteries and sports stories, seem to have little to say about life or about human nature. Such stories are told chiefly for entertainment, and theme is of little or no importance in them. But other stories do try to make a comment on the human condition, and in those stories, theme is of great importance.

Because themes are rarely expressed directly, they are not always obvious to the reader. Theme is one of those qualities which must be dug out and thought about. One of the rewards of reading is the pleasure of coming upon the theme of a literary work on our own.

Usually, however, careful writers plan their stories so that readers can pick out sentences or events that point toward the theme. Such "key passages" are recognizable because they seem to speak directly to us as readers. They make direct, thoughtful statements, discussing the meaning of an action or a lesson the characters may have learned.

For example, Dorothy Canfield's story "The Apprentice" is a story with a strong theme. Its theme has to do with a young person's coming-of-age, or achieving adult status. A key passage in this story explicitly tells us that when the young heroine realizes what unendurable tragedy is, she becomes a mature adult.

Often the title of a story will also help us arrive at its theme. This is the case with "The Apprentice." The title reminds us of the old custom of apprenticeship, where young people learn a particular skill that prepares them to earn their living as adults.

Some simple themes can be stated in a single sentence. But sometimes a literary work is so rich and complex that a paragraph or essay is needed to state the theme satisfactorily.

See pages 38, 96, 271, 317, 394, 610.

TONE *The attitude the writer takes toward his or her subject.* A writer may approach a subject with absolute seriousness, as Abraham Lincoln approached the subject of the war dead in his speech "The Gettysburg Address." Or, a writer can approach a subject with humor and mockery, as Ernest Lawrence Thayer approaches Casey in "Casey at the Bat." We get the feeling that Thayer is mocking Casey because he presents him as a proud and vain hero whose overconfidence prevents him from winning the ball game.

Tone is present in all kinds of writing. It is very important for a reader to recognize the tone of a biography. A biographer who loves his or her subject may not be completely objective or truthful. The same is true of a biographer who does *not* think well of his or her subject. In poetry, tone can sometimes change our entire view of a subject. Arthur Guiterman has written a poem called "The Vanity of Earthly Greatness," which is a very serious topic. But Guiterman only pretends to be solemn about this "deep" subject. His tone makes us laugh at something that most people treat very seriously. On

the other hand, Edgar Allan Poe's "The Raven" is totally serious in tone. If we make fun of the poem (see the example under **Parody**), we can see how tone can change our entire view of a situation.

See pages 103, 435.

TRAGEDY *A serious literary work which portrays a heroic, dignified, or courageous character who comes to a terrible end, such as death or exile.* Any narrative can be a tragedy—short stories, novels, narrative poems, and plays, though the term is most often applied to plays. Some famous tragedies are the dramas of ancient Greece, such as *Agamemnon, Oedipus Rex,* and *Antigone.* The tragedies written by William Shakespeare are also famous. They include such plays as *Romeo and Juliet, Julius Caesar, Hamlet,* and *Macbeth.* All of these titles are the names of people, and this is appropriate, since tragedies usually tell of the downfall of one person. In older tragedies (such as the Greek tragedies and Shakespeare's tragedies), this person is usually a noble character, perhaps a king, queen, prince, or princess. This tragic hero or heroine often falls because of a defect in character, which gives way under the stress of events. Or, a tragic hero or heroine might fall because a series of outside events just cannot be controlled. The outcome of the action in a tragedy is always terrible. Tragedies are not usually depressing, however, because they show us how human dignity and courage can be maintained, even in the face of defeat.

See page 393.

YARN *An exaggerated story that seems to go on and on, like a ball of yarn.* A yarn is a story told in the tradition of the **folk tale,** often handed down orally from teller to listener. A yarn seems to be built out of many episodes, which gradually are added on to the central core of a story. The origins of the yarn are connected to the sea and to stories told by sailors.

HANDBOOK FOR *Revision*

Contents

Part 1: Model Essays

■ Persuasive Essay   ■ Informative Essay

The essays on the following pages are shown in two versions: a rough draft and a final copy. In the draft, the writer has evaluated and revised the essay for logic, clarity, style, and specific support. The writer has also proofread the essay for errors in grammar, usage, punctuation, spelling, and capitalization. The corrections are shown on the draft. The reasons for many of the revisions and corrections are shown in the margin.

Handbook for Revision

Symbols for Revising and Proofreading

Symbol	Example	Meaning of Symbol
≡	Elm street	Capitalize a lowercase letter.
/	Chang's Father	Lowercase a capital letter.
/	a͡gile footwork	Change a letter.
∧	the libary	Insert a word, letter, or punctuation mark.
ℓ	Are we we home?	Delete a word, letter, or punctuation mark.
ℓ	Where is my hat?	Delete and close up.
ⓣⓡ	Please take my friend to the station and me.	Transfer the circled material.
⑭	"Hi," she cried.	Begin a new paragraph.
⊙	Shut the door	Add a period.
∧	Yes that's true.	Add a comma.
∨	Pablos coat	Add an apostrophe.
⊙	as follows	Add a colon.
∧	Sam Leon, Jr. Lisa Gray, Ph.D.	Add a semicolon.

WRITING PROCESS TRANSPARENCIES

In the *Audiovisual Resources Binder,* you will find **Writing Process** transparencies with accompanying **Teacher's Notes** and student activity pages. You may want to use these audiovisual materials when discussing specific aspects of the writing process or of particular types of writing, such as the transparencies listed below.

Writing an Informative Essay: See Transparency 27.

Writing a Persuasive Essay: See Transparency 17.

MODEL 1: A PERSUASIVE ESSAY
Rough Draft

FUTURE HOMEMAKERS

Capitalization

home economics is a subject that goes by some new names these

Commas in series

days: Life-Management Education Work and Family Studies or

Family and Consumer Sciences. It is not only the names that are

Run-on sentence

changing, there are some new attitudes toward home economics,

as well.

All across the country, in high school and junior high,

Combine sentences

more and more boys are enrolling in these courses. *which* They have

Spelling

traditionaly been regarded as the domain of girls. In 1993, for

example, over 40 percent of home economics students in Grades

Subject-verb agreement

7–12 *were* was boys; in 1968, the figure was less than 5 percent. This

Sentence fragment

trend is likely to continue. Because boys are recognizing that

these subjects are interesting and valuable. Our school should

offer a variety of home economics courses and should encurage

Pronoun-antecedent agreement

both boys and girls to enroll in *them* it.

The most *important* serious reason for expanding our curriculum in

this area is that everyone, both male and female, will be a

MODEL 1: A PERSUASIVE ESSAY
Final Copy

FUTURE HOMEMAKERS

Home economics is a subject that goes by some new names these days: Life-Management Education, Work and Family Studies, or Family and Consumer Sciences. It is not only the names that are changing. There are some new attitudes toward home economics, as well.

All across the country, in high school and junior high, more and more boys are enrolling in these courses, which have traditionally been regarded as the domain of girls. In 1993, for example, over 40 percent of home economics students in Grades 7–12 were boys; in 1968, the figure was less than 5 percent. This trend is likely to continue, because boys are recognizing that these subjects are interesting and valuable. Our school should offer a variety of home economics courses and should encourage both boys and girls to enroll in them.

The most important reason for expanding our curriculum in this area is that everyone, both male and female, will be a

Title

Introduction

Body

Background

Opinion statement

Supporting evidence

Commas with appositive phrase

homemaker in the future. As Nick Rhoton the 1993 president of the Future Homemakers of America has said, "Home economics isn't just a class; it shows how to live in your society. Social

Repetition

trends and economic trends make it increasingly likely that both partners in a marriage will hold jobs and will participate in

Pronoun usage

running the home. If and when *we* ~~you~~ become parents, we will all appreciate the chance we had in school to take courses in child care, nutrition, family finances, and communications skills.

Word choice

Single people with no partner to help them will depend *even more* ~~the most~~ ~~clearly~~ on knowing the basics of home management.

Transition

Another ^ A reason to support this change is that it will educate both boys and girls about possible career opportunities. *For example,* Knowing

Subject-verb agreement

how to fix lunch for a group of toddlers *is* ~~are~~ a step toward finding a job in day care. A course in child development might spark a

Spelling

student's ambition for a career in psychology.

Finally, knowing more about home economics subjects can

Apostrophe

make student's everyday lives fuller and more fun. Consider, for

Spelling

example, some of the aplications of basic design principles.

homemaker in the future. As Nick Rhoton, the 1993 president of the Future Homemakers of America, has said, "Home economics isn't just a class; it shows how to live in your society." Social and economic trends make it increasingly likely that both partners in a marriage will hold jobs and will participate in running the home. If and when we become parents, we will all appreciate the chance we had in school to take courses in child care, nutrition, family finances, and communications skills. Single people with no partner to help them will depend even more on knowing the basics of home management.

Another reason to support this change is that it will educate both boys and girls about possible career opportunities. For example, knowing how to fix lunch for a group of toddlers is a step toward finding a job in day care. A course in child development might spark a student's ambition for a career in psychology.

Finally, knowing more about home economics subjects can make students' everyday lives fuller and more fun. Consider, for example, some of the applications of basic design principles.

Logical appeal

Logical appeal

Emotional appeal

Handbook for Revision

Usage

Spelling

Learning just a little about color combinations can help students to coordinate their rooms, as well as their wardrobes.

It's time to let go of the stereotypes. Expanding the curriculum in home economics is in everyone's interest, both in the short and the long term. Write the school board to day *today* to express your support for learning how to be a future homemaker.

Learning just a little about color combinations can help students to coordinate their rooms, as well as their wardrobes.

It's time to let go of the stereotypes. Expanding the curriculum in home economics is in everyone's interest, both in the short and the long term. Write the school board today to express your support for learning how to be a future homemaker.

Conclusion

MODEL 2: AN INFORMATIVE ESSAY
Rough Draft

THE DANCES OF THE HONEYBEES

Capitalization/ Usage

Spelling

Commas with interrupter

Combine sentences

Repetition

Sentence fragment/Spelling

Colon

Can animals think? not so long ago, most scientists would of answered that question with a firm "No." Experts on animal behavior believed that instinct, not inteligence, was the ruling force in the animal kingdom.

An astonishing series of experiments by the Austrian scientist Karl von Frisch however has provided evidence. Some animals can not only think but also communicate. These experiments earned von Frisch a Nobel Prize in 1973. These experiments focused on the dances of honeybees inside their hives.

Von Frisch showed that these dances communicate important information. About food sources such as necter and pollen. He divided the dances into two categories round dances and tail-wagging dances.

MODEL 2: AN INFORMATIVE ESSAY
Final Copy

THE DANCES OF THE HONEYBEES

Can animals think? Not so long ago, most scientists would have answered that question with a firm "No." Experts on animal behavior believed that instinct, not intelligence, was the ruling force in the animal kingdom.

An astonishing series of experiments by the Austrian scientist Karl von Frisch, however, has provided evidence that some animals can not only think but also communicate. These experiments, which earned von Frisch a Nobel Prize in 1973, focused on the dances of honeybees inside their hives.

Von Frisch showed that these dances communicate important information about food sources such as nectar and pollen. He divided the dances into two categories: round dances and tail-wagging dances.

Title

Introduction

Main idea

Body

Handbook for Revision

Round Dance

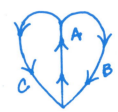

Tail-Wagging Dance

Subject-verb agreement

The bees uses round dances to announce the existence of a food source located relatively close to the hive—nearer than about 100 yards. Round dances convey specific information about

Run-on sentence/ Double comparison

distance and direction dances are more slower and shorter for distant food sources, more agitated and longer for closer ones. The dancing bee shows her fellow workers the direction to the food by the point at which she reverses the circle in a round dance.

Honeybees switch to the tail-wagging dance to share news about food sources located more than 100 yards or so from the hive. In the tail-wagging dance, the bees' movements signal the location of the food source. The liveliness of the dance

Subject-verb agreement

communicate additional information: the more excited the dancer, the richer and more desirable the food is likely to be.

Round Dance

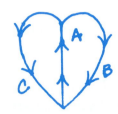

Tail-Wagging Dance

Diagram

The bees use round dances to announce the existence of a food source located relatively close to the hive—nearer than about 100 yards. Round dances convey specific information about distance and direction. Dances are slower and shorter for distant food sources, more agitated and longer for closer ones. The dancing bee shows her fellow workers the direction to the food by the point at which she reverses the circle in a round dance.

Explanation of process

Honeybees switch to the tail-wagging dance to share news about food sources located more than 100 yards or so from the hive. In the tail-wagging dance, the bees' movements signal the location of the food source. The liveliness of the dance communicates additional information: the more excited the dancer, the richer and more desirable the food is likely to be.

Additional details

Perhaps the most remarkable feature of the honeybees'

Subject-verb agreement

dances ~~are~~ is what scientists call "displacement." The dances are

removed from the immediate situation in the hive and relate to a

Pronoun usage

food source ~~who~~ that may be several miles away. The dancers have

Pronoun-antecedent agreement

apparently stored information about the food while ~~it~~ they returns to

the hive; they then use a symbolic language to express the

information.

Some important mysteries about these dances continue to

Transition

puzzle scientists. For example, How do the other bees in the dancers'

"audience" receive the information about distance, direction, and

Spelling

desireability in a pitch-dark hive? The most likely explanation

seems to be some kind of acoustical signaling. Ingenious

experiments continue to probe the honeybees' amazing art of

communication. In the meantime, Karl von Frisch's landmark

Adjective needed

discoveries are enough to show that a tiny creature possesses startling

abilities.

Perhaps the most remarkable feature of the honeybees' dances is what scientists call "displacement." The dances are removed from the immediate situation in the hive and relate to a food source that may be several miles away. The dancers have apparently stored information about the food while they return to the hive; they then use a symbolic language to express the information.

Some important mysteries about these dances continue to puzzle scientists. For example, how do the other bees in the dancers' "audience" receive the information about distance, direction, and desirability in a pitch-dark hive? The most likely explanation seems to be some kind of acoustical signaling. Ingenious experiments continue to probe the honeybees' amazing art of communication. In the meantime, Karl Von Frisch's landmark discoveries are enough to show that a tiny creature possesses startling abilities.

Interpretation and comment

Conclusion

Handbook for Revision

Handbook for Revision

For definitions of grammatical terms, see the **Grammar Reference Guide** on pages 745–748.

Part 2: Sentence Structure

- Sentence Fragments
- Run-on Sentences
- Comparisons

SENTENCE FRAGMENTS

A **sentence** is a group of words that expresses a complete thought. A sentence has a subject and a predicate. A group of words that looks like a sentence but that doesn't make sense by itself is a **sentence fragment.**

1. Correct a fragment by adding the necessary sentence parts. Usually you will need to add a verb, a subject, or both.

Fragment

A group of climbers, including Nace and Osborn. [verb missing: what about the group of climbers, or what did they do?]

Sentence

A group of climbers, including Nace and Osborn, **started** their journey up the side of the mountain.

Fragment

Enjoys the fascinating behavior of scorpions. [subject missing: who or what enjoys?]

Sentence

Gerald enjoys the fascinating behavior of scorpions.

Fragment

One spring day, near a lake in northern Michigan. [subject and verb missing]

Sentence

One spring day, near a lake in northern Michigan, the **men worked** in a swamp.

2. Correct a subordinate-clause fragment by connecting it to an independent clause.

Fragment

If Mary doesn't die after eating the mushroom. The children will know that it isn't poisonous.

Sentence

If Mary doesn't die after eating the mushroom, **the children** will know that it isn't poisonous.

RUN-ON SENTENCES

A **run-on sentence** consists of two complete sentences run together as if they were one sentence. Most run-ons are *comma splices*—or two complete thoughts separated only by a comma. Other run-ons are *fused sentences*—two complete thoughts separated by no punctuation.

1. Correct a run-on sentence by using a period to form two complete sentences.

Run-on

During World War I, Dorothy Canfield and her children joined her husband in France, she spent three years doing war work there.

Corrected

During World War I, Dorothy Canfield and her children joined her husband in France. **She** spent three years doing war work there.

2. Correct a run-on by using a comma and a coordinating conjunction (such as *and, but,* or *yet*) to create a compound sentence.

Run-on

The narrator loses his self-control he finally confesses to the crime.

Corrected

The narrator loses his self-control, **and** he finally confesses to the crime.

3. Correct a run-on by using a semicolon to form a compound sentence.

Run-on

A simile uses *like* or *as* in a comparison, a metaphor compares two different things directly.

Corrected

A simile uses *like* or *as* in a comparison; a metaphor compares two different things directly.

4. Correct a run-on by using a semicolon plus a conjunctive adverb (such as *however*, *moreover*, or *nevertheless*) to form a compound sentence.

Run-on

Daniel Keyes's story "Flowers for Algernon" has won several awards it has been translated into many languages.

Corrected

Daniel Keyes's story "Flowers for Algernon" has won several awards; **moreover,** it has been translated into many languages.

COMPARISONS

1. Be sure that a comparison contains items of the same or a similar kind. Add any words that may be necessary to clarify your meaning.

Nonstandard

The heroic ideals of the ancient Greeks were different from the Anglo-Saxons.

Standard

The heroic ideals of the ancient Greeks were different from **those** of the Anglo-Saxons.

2. Include the word *other* or *else* when comparing one member of a group with the rest of the members.

Nonstandard

Katrina liked "The Tell-Tale Heart" more than any story in our anthology.

Standard

Katrina liked "The Tell-Tale Heart" more than any **other** story in our anthology.

Nonstandard

More than anyone at Lincoln High School, Walter Plummer wanted to join the A Band.

Standard

More than anyone **else** at Lincoln High School, Walter Plummer wanted to join the A Band.

3. Avoid double comparisons.

Nonstandard

In James Ramsey Ullman's "Top Man," Nace showed that he was **more braver** than Osborn.

Standard

In James Ramsey Ullman's "Top Man," Nace showed that he was **braver** than Osborn.

Nonstandard

Kalpurtha is one of the **most highest** peaks in the Himalayas.

Standard

Kalpurtha is one of the **highest** peaks in the Himalayas.

Handbook for Revision

Case Forms of Personal Pronouns: For review, see Pronouns, *Teaching Resources C,* page 15. See Possessive Case, *Teaching Resources C,* page 161.

Handbook for Revision

Part 3: Pronouns

- Pronoun-Antecedent Agreement
- Case Forms of Personal Pronouns

PRONOUN-ANTECEDENT AGREEMENT

The noun or pronoun to which a pronoun refers is called its **antecedent.**

1. A pronoun must agree with its antecedent in number and in gender.

> **Example**
> Peg loves **Rollie,** and she becomes worried when she cannot find **him.**

2. Use a singular pronoun to refer to an antecedent that is a singular indefinite pronoun. Use a plural pronoun to refer to an antecedent that is a plural indefinite pronoun.

> **Nonstandard**
> **Each** of these women poets has **their** own style.
>
> **Standard**
> **Each** of these women poets has **her** own style.
>
> **Example**
> **Many** of the writers we read used humor in **their** essays.

3. When the antecedent may be either masculine or feminine, rephrase the sentence to avoid an awkward construction, or use both the masculine and the feminine forms.

> **Standard**
> In *The Diary of Anne Frank,* **all** the characters in hiding have **their** hopes and dreams.
>
> **Standard**
> In *The Diary of Anne Frank,* **each** of the characters in hiding has **his or her** hopes and dreams.

4. Use a plural pronoun to refer to two or more antecedents joined by *and.*

> **Nonstandard**
> **Sir Walter Scott** and **Henry Wadsworth Longfellow** wrote **his** poems in the nineteenth century.
>
> **Standard**
> **Sir Walter Scott** and **Henry Wadsworth Longfellow** wrote **their** poems in the nineteenth century.

5. Use a singular pronoun to refer to two or more singular antecedents joined by *or* **or** *nor.*

> **Nonstandard**
> In the opening section of the *Iliad,* neither **Agamemnon** nor **Achilles** holds **their** temper.
>
> **Standard**
> In the opening section of the *Iliad,* neither **Agamemnon** nor **Achilles** holds **his** temper.

Sentences of this type can sound awkward if the antecedents are of different genders. If a sentence sounds awkward, revise it.

> **Awkward**
> **Each** of my friends is preparing **his or her** oral interpretation of Edgar Allan Poe's "The Raven."
>
> **Revised**
> **All** my friends are preparing **their** oral interpretations of Edgar Allan Poe's "The Raven."

CASE FORMS OF PERSONAL PRONOUNS

1. Be sure to use the correct case for personal pronouns that are part of compound constructions.

> **Nonstandard**
> In "The Rule of Names" by Ursula K. Le Guin, the fisherman Birt is in love with Palani, the

schoolteacher; at the end of the story, Birt and **her** run away. [object form used for subject]

Standard

In "The Rule of Names" by Ursula K. Le Guin, the fisherman Birt is in love with Palani, the schoolteacher; at the end of the story, Birt and **she** run away.

Nonstandard

Did Mr. Lonergan encourage you and **she** to prepare a report on Cathy Song? [subject form used for object]

Standard

Did Mr. Lonergan encourage you and **her** to prepare a report on Cathy Song?

Nonstandard

Between you and **I,** how long did you study for the test? [subject form used for object of preposition]

Standard

Between you and **me,** how long did you study for the test?

2. Use the possessive case of a personal pronoun before a gerund. Use the objective case of a personal pronoun before a participle.

Nonstandard

Tigers will usually not let anything disturb **them** feeding.

Standard

Tigers will usually not let anything disturb **their** feeding.

Nonstandard

At the end of "Raymond's Run," when Squeaky catches sight of Raymond, she laughs when she sees **his** jumping down from the fence.

Standard

At the end of "Raymond's Run," when Squeaky catches sight of Raymond, she laughs when she sees **him** jumping down from the fence.

Verbs: For review, see Parts of Speech, *Teaching Resources A,* page 16. See Action Verbs and Linking Verbs, *Teaching Resources B,* page 35. See also Vivid, Precise Verbs, *Teaching Resources B,* page 178.

Handbook for Revision

Part 4: Verbs

- Missing or Incorrect Verb Endings
- Subject-Verb Agreement
- Sequence of Tenses

MISSING OR INCORRECT VERB ENDINGS

1. A *regular verb* forms the past and past participle by adding *-d* or *-ed* to the infinitive form. Don't make the mistake of leaving off or doubling the *-d* or *-ed* ending.

Nonstandard

When he left prison, Jimmy Valentine was **suppose** to lead a law-abiding life.

Standard

When he left prison, Jimmy Valentine was **supposed** to lead a law-abiding life.

Nonstandard

When he went fishing, the man in "The Sea Devil" nearly **drownded.**

Standard

When he went fishing, the man in "The Sea Devil" nearly **drowned.**

2. An *irregular verb* forms the past and past participle by

- changing a vowel
- changing consonants
- adding *-en*
- making no change at all

Subject-Verb Agreement: See Agreement of Subject and Verb, *Teaching Resources B,* page 165. See also Agreement, *Teaching Resources C,* page 50.

Handbook for Revision

Examples

Infinitive	Past	Past Participle
buy	bought	(have) bought
draw	drew	(have) drawn
take	took	(have) taken
cost	cost	(have) cost

When you proofread your writing, check your sentences to determine which form—past or past participle—is called for. Remember that many nonstandard verb forms sound quite natural. Keep a dictionary handy to check any verb forms you're not sure about.

Nonstandard
Jared **has went** to rehearsal already.

Standard
Jared **has gone** to rehearsal already.

Nonstandard
Ted **seen** several movies based on stories by Poe.

Standard
Ted **has seen** several movies based on stories by Poe.

Nonstandard
The escape of the scorpions **throwed** Durrell's whole family into confusion.

Standard
The escape of the scorpions **threw** Durrell's whole family into confusion.

SUBJECT-VERB AGREEMENT

1. A verb must agree with its subject in number—either singular or plural. The number of a subject is not changed by a phrase or clause intervening between the subject and the verb.

Nonstandard
The chapters of that novel **is** short.

Standard
The chapters of that novel **are** short.

2. Use a singular verb to agree with the following singular indefinite pronouns: *anybody, anyone, each, either, everybody, everyone, everything, neither, nobody, no one, one, somebody,* and *someone.*

Nonstandard
Everyone in *The Diary of Anne Frank* **are** afraid of the Nazi storm troopers.

Standard
Everyone in *The Diary of Anne Frank* **is** afraid of the Nazi storm troopers.

Nonstandard
These poems are good to read aloud, since **each** of them **include** humor.

Standard
These poems are good to read aloud, since **each** of them **includes** humor.

3. Use a plural verb to agree with the following plural indefinite pronouns: *both, few, many,* and *several.*

Nonstandard
Many of Edgar Allan Poe's stories **has** an unusual narrator.

Standard
Many of Edgar Allan Poe's stories **have** an unusual narrator.

Nonstandard
Few of the students in our class **has** read any poetry by Walt Whitman.

Standard
Few of the students in our class **have** read any poetry by Walt Whitman.

4. The following indefinite pronouns are singular when they refer to singular words and plural when they refer to plural words: *all, any, most, none,* and *some.*

Nonstandard
Some of the meal **are** ready.

Standard
Some of the meal **is** ready.

Nonstandard
Some of the books you need **is** in the library.

Standard
Some of the books you need **are** in the library.

5. Subjects joined by *and* usually take a plural verb.

Nonstandard
In "Too Soon a Woman," the **children** and **Mary** nearly **starves** to death.

Standard
In "Too Soon a Woman," the **children** and **Mary** nearly **starve** to death.

When the elements of a compound subject joined by ***and*** may be considered a single item or refer to the same thing, the compound subject takes a singular verb.

Nonstandard
The crowd thinks that their **hope** and **salvation are** Casey.

Standard
The crowd thinks that their **hope** and **salvation is** Casey. [*Hope* and *salvation* refer to the same thing.]

6. Singular subjects joined by *or* or *nor* take a singular verb.

Nonstandard
Neither **Henry Wadsworth Longfellow** nor **O. Henry are** a contemporary writer.

Standard
Neither **Henry Wadsworth Longfellow** nor **O. Henry is** a contemporary writer.

7. When a singular subject and a plural subject are joined by *or* or *nor*, the verb agrees with the subject nearer the verb.

Nonstandard
Neither **Larry** nor the other family **members seems** to like scorpions very much.

Standard
Neither **Larry** nor the other family **members seem** to like scorpions very much.

8. When the subject follows the verb, as in questions and in sentences beginning with *here* and *there*, identify the subject and make sure that the verb agrees with it.

Nonstandard
Here **are** a **list** of some articles about Harriet Tubman.

Standard
Here **is** a **list** of some articles about Harriet Tubman.

Nonstandard
Where **is** the **Garhwal Himalayas** on this map?

Standard
Where **are** the **Garhwal Himalayas** on this map?

9. A collective noun takes a singular verb when the noun refers to the group as a unit. A collective noun takes a plural verb when the noun refers to the individual parts or members of the group.

Examples
At the end of the story, the **family was** overjoyed that Ken and Flicka were both recovering.

The **committee were** still undecided, and the members continued to discuss three different proposals.

10. A verb should always agree with its subject, not with its predicate nominative.

Nonstandard
Abraham Lincoln's **words** in "The Gettysburg Address" **was** a landmark in the history of American public speaking.

Standard
Abraham Lincoln's **words** in "The Gettysburg Address" **were** a landmark in the history of American public speaking.

11. The contractions *don't* and *doesn't* must agree with their subjects.

Verbs **731**

Sequence of Tenses: For information on past and past perfect tenses, see *Teaching Resources B,* page 127.

Misplaced Modifiers: See Careful Placement of Modifiers, *Teaching Resources D,* page 48.

Handbook for Revision

Examples

In *Pyramus and Thisby,* the **actors don't** pronounce some of their words correctly.

At the end of "The Oklahoma Land Run," the **girl** with the injured horse **doesn't** hesitate to stake her claim ahead of Yancey.

SEQUENCE OF TENSES

1. **Changing verb tense in mid-sentence or from sentence to sentence without good reason creates awkwardness and confusion. Be sure that the verb tenses in a single sentence or in a group of related sentences are consistent.**

Awkward

Squeaky **confesses** that she **thought** that Cynthia Procter **is** a phony.

Better

Squeaky **confesses** that she **thinks** that Cynthia Procter **is** a phony.

2. **The past perfect tense with *had* is used to express an action that was completed before another action in the past.**

Nonstandard

Old Don Anselmo **lived** in Río en Medio, where his ancestors **settled** hundreds of years ago.

Standard

Old Don Anselmo **lived** in Río en Medio, where his ancestors **had settled** hundreds of years ago.

Part 5: Word Order

■ Misplaced Modifiers   ■ Dangling Modifiers

MISPLACED MODIFIERS

Avoid a *misplaced modifier,* which is a modifying phrase or clause that is placed too far from the word it sensibly modifies.

Misplaced

This book describes Harriet Tubman's struggle to lead slaves to freedom on the Underground Railroad **by Ann Petry.**

Clear

This book **by Ann Petry** describes Harriet Tubman's struggle to lead slaves to freedom on the Underground Railroad.

Misplaced

Old Walter Landis stroked **without answering** the white bristles of his beard.

Clear

Without answering, old Walter Landis stroked the white bristles of his beard.

DANGLING MODIFIERS

Avoid *dangling modifiers,* which are phrases or clauses that do not sensibly modify any word or group of words in the sentence.

Dangling

Prepared for the challenge, the rough seas were no problem.

Clear

Prepared for the challenge, we had no problem with the rough seas.

Comma Usage: For review, see Punctuation Marks, *Teaching Resources C,* page 17. See also Punctuating Interrupters in Sentences, *Teaching Resources C,* page 127. For practice with punctuation in quotations, see *Teaching Resources C,* page 37.

Part 6: Comma Usage

- Compound Structure
- Items in a Series
- Two or More Adjectives
- Nonessential Elements
- Introductory Elements
- Interrupters

COMPOUND STRUCTURE

Use a comma before a coordinating conjunction (*and, but, or, nor, for, so,* and *yet*) that joins two independent clauses. If the clauses are very short, you may omit the comma.

Examples

Mr. Helmholtz didn't know any of the people involved**, and** he yawned and turned to the funnies.

— Vonnegut, "The No-Talent Kid" (p. 15)

He tried to claw the slipknot off his wrist**, but** there was no time.

— Gordon, "The Sea Devil" (p. 33)

We kept a fire going under a hole in the roof**, so** it was full of blinding smoke**, but** we had to keep the fire so as to dry out the wood.

— Johnson, "Too Soon a Woman" (p. 163)

ITEMS IN A SERIES

Use commas to separate words, phrases, and clauses in a series.

Examples

Mama **dances, laughs, dances.** [series of verbs]

— Cisneros, "Chanclas" (p. 69)

She **drew a deep breath, snipped her thread, laid down the sock, and again looked across at her husband.** . . . [series of predicates]

— O'Hara, "My Friend Flicka" (p. 109)

No mess liked to have him permanently, because his presence cut off all talk **of home or of the prospect of return, of politics or letters, of peace or war.** . . . [series of phrases]

— Hale, "The Man Without a Country" (p. 146)

It has eluded you, it has eluded me, it has eluded everybody who has seen her. [series of clauses]

— Milne, *The Ugly Duckling* (p. 302)

TWO OR MORE ADJECTIVES

Use a comma to separate two or more adjectives preceding a noun. However, do not use a comma before the final adjective in a series if the adjective is thought of as being part of a noun. Determine if the adjective and noun form a unit by inserting the word *and* between the adjectives. If *and* fits sensibly, use a comma.

Example

Two bull elk with **wide, branching** antlers, all in velvet, came out of the woods and approached the pond. [wide *and* branching; comma needed]

— Hobbs, *Beardance* (p. 528)

NONESSENTIAL ELEMENTS

A *nonessential* (or *nonrestrictive*) clause or participial phrase contains information that is not necessary to the meaning of the sentence. Use commas to set off nonessential clauses and nonessential participial phrases. An *essential* (or *restrictive*) clause or participial phrase is not set off by commas, because it contains information that is necessary to the meaning of the sentence.

Nonessential Clause

That novel**, which you recommended,** was on sale. [The clause can be omitted without changing the main idea.]

Handbook for Revision

Comma Usage **733**

Interrupters: See Appositives, *Teaching Resources C,* page 180.

Essential Clause

The novel **that you recommended** was on sale. [The clause is necessary to identify which novel is meant.]

Nonessential Phrase

That tale**, written by Edgar Allan Poe,** is a suspenseful story.

Essential Phrase

The stories **written by Edgar Allan Poe** are among her favorite tales.

INTRODUCTORY ELEMENTS

Use a comma after *yes, no,* or any mild exclamation such as *well* or *why* at the beginning of a sentence. Also use a comma after an introductory participial or infinitive phrase, after two or more introductory prepositional phrases, and after an introductory adverb clause.

Examples

"No, you keep it," Steve said, and then there was nothing to say.

— Callaghan, "A Cap for Steve" (p. 84)

Well, he finds that you own more than eight acres.

— Sedillo, "Gentleman of Río en Medio" (p. 100)

Riding higher and higher on the wind, the hawk went west by the dam like a button of silver far below. [introductory participial phrase]

— Niland, "The Parachutist" (p. 237)

After their supper in the bunkhouse, Gus and Tim walked down to the brook. [introductory prepositional phrases]

— O'Hara, "My Friend Flicka" (p. 119)

When I was a boy, there was but one permanent ambition among my comrades in our village on the west bank of the Mississippi River. [introductory adverb clause]

— Twain, "Cub Pilot on the Mississippi" (p. 428)

INTERRUPTERS

1. Appositives and appositive phrases are usually set off by commas.

Examples

Nick Bottom, **a weaver,** takes the part of the lover Pyramus.

"It's for my name, **Ursa."**

— Hobbs, *Beardance* (p. 539)

2. Words used in direct address are set off by commas.

Examples

"Very good, **Suba. Popi,** don't shout."

— Le Guin, "The Rule of Names" (p. 222)

Well, **son,** I'll tell you:
Life for me ain't been no crystal stair.

— Hughes, "Mother to Son" (p. 461)

"Then, **Roger,** you go to that sink and wash your face," said the woman, whereupon she turned him loose—at last.

— Hughes, "Thank You, M'am" (p. 232)

3. Use commas to set off parenthetical expressions.

Examples

It was that same night, **I think,** that I awoke to find Nace sitting up in his blanket and staring at the mountain.

— Ullman, "Top Man" (p. 55)

A tangled rope, **he knew,** would spoil any cast.

— Gordon, "The Sea Devil" (p. 32)

I thought, **however,** that after seven days adrift I would become accustomed to the sea, to my anxious way of life, without having to spur my imagination in order to survive.

— García Márquez, "Fighting Off the Sharks for a Fish" (p. 41)

But the Airedale, **as I have said,** was the worst of all my dogs.

— Thurber, "The Dog That Bit People" (p. 413)

Sentence Variety: See Types of Sentences, *Teaching Resources B,* page 137.

Part 7: Style

- Sentence Variety
- Creative Use of Synonyms
- Stringy Sentences
- Vivid Words
- Overwriting
- Clichés
- Levels of Language

SENTENCE VARIETY

1. Create sentence variety in length and rhythm by using different kinds of clauses, as well as simple sentences.

Little Variation

In "Flowers for Algernon" by Daniel Keyes, Charlie Gordon is a mentally handicapped janitor. Charlie enrolls in night school. He wants to be smart. Charlie has surgery. The surgery increases his intelligence. Charlie becomes extremely learned. Then he has trouble communicating with people. The mouse Algernon starts to regress, however. Charlie is disturbed. He conducts experiments to find out the reason.

More Variation

In "Flowers for Algernon" by Daniel Keyes, Charlie Gordon, who is a mentally handicapped janitor, enrolls in night school because he wants to be smart. He undergoes surgery, and his intelligence increases. Charlie becomes extremely learned, only to find that he has trouble communicating with people. When the mouse Algernon starts to regress, however, Charlie is disturbed, and he conducts experiments to find out the reason.

2. Expand short, choppy sentences by adding details.

Choppy

Kurt Vonnegut was born in Indianapolis. He studied biochemistry. He was drafted into the army and was captured. He used his experiences during the war as the basis for one of his novels.

More Detailed

The writer Kurt Vonnegut was born in Indianapolis, Indiana, in 1922. He studied biochemistry at Cornell University. During World War II, he was drafted into the army and was captured by the Germans. His experiences working in a slaughterhouse in the German city of Dresden became the basis for one of his best-known novels, *Slaughterhouse-Five.*

3. Vary sentence openers by using appositives, single-word modifiers, phrase modifiers, clause modifiers, and transitional words.

Little Variation

Mr. Helmholtz mentions the need for a drum to Walter Plummer. Walter realizes that he knows where to find one. He rushes off to buy it. Mr. Helmholtz sees a newspaper ad. He finds out that the Knights of Kandahar are selling their bass drum. The Knights of Kandahar are a local organization. He decides to buy the drum with his own money. He dials the Knights repeatedly. He gets only a busy signal each time.

More Variation

When Mr. Helmholtz mentions the need for a drum to Walter Plummer, Walter realizes that he knows where to find one, and he rushes off to buy it. **Meanwhile,** Mr. Helmholtz sees a newspaper ad. **In the ad,** he reads that the Knights of Kandahar, **a local organization,** are selling their bass drum. **Deciding to buy the drum with his own money,** he dials the Knights. **However,** he gets only a busy signal each time.

Vivid Words: See Vivid, Precise Nouns, *Teaching Resources C,* page 65. See Vivid, Precise Verbs, *Teaching Resources B,* page 178.

Handbook for Revision

4. Simplify long, rambling sentences by breaking them up and regrouping ideas.

Rambling

In "The Glorious Bird," which is an essay by Gerald Carson, the author explores what American patriotism is by combining the legendary exploits of a bald eagle named Old Abe, who was the mascot for Company C of the Eighth Wisconsin Volunteer Infantry of the Union forces, with historical facts about the Civil War.

Better

In his essay "The Glorious Bird," Gerald Carson explores the theme of American patriotism by combining an eagle's legendary exploits with historical facts about the Civil War. Old Abe, a bald eagle, was the mascot of Company C of the Eighth Wisconsin Volunteer Infantry of the Union forces.

STRINGY SENTENCES

Simplify stringy sentences by writing as concisely as you can. Pare down your use of prepositional phrases. Reduce clauses to phrases, if possible. If you can, reduce clauses and phrases to single words.

Stringy

As a child, Mark Twain cherished the ambition of becoming the pilot of a steamboat. When Twain was an apprentice for steamboat piloting, however, he had an experience that was not so good with a cranky pilot whose name was Brown. This man lashed out at Twain's brother, whose name was Henry, and the cub pilot committed a bad offense against the code of discipline by striking Brown in return.

Better

Young Mark Twain cherished an ambition to become a steamboat pilot. As an apprentice, however, Twain had a bad experience with a cranky pilot named Brown. When Brown lashed out at Twain's brother Henry, the cub pilot committed a bad offense by striking Brown in return.

OVERWRITING

1. Eliminate unnecessary words.

Wordy

"Mother to Son" uses an extended **metaphor and comparison** for life as a stairway.

Better

"Mother to Son" uses an extended **metaphor** for life as a stairway.

2. Avoid pretentious, complicated words where plain, simple ones will do.

Pretentious

In "I Like to See It Lap the Miles," Emily Dickinson **utilizes** imagery to **endow** the train with the **profile** of an animal.

Simpler

In "I Like to See It Lap the Miles," Emily Dickinson **uses** imagery to **give** the train the **qualities** of an animal.

CREATIVE USE OF SYNONYMS

Avoid repetition by using synonyms creatively.

Awkward

The **atmosphere** of the last scene of Act One is joyful at first, but then a crash from below abruptly changes the **atmosphere.**

Better

The **atmosphere** of the last scene of Act One is joyful at first, but then a crash from below abruptly changes the **mood.**

VIVID WORDS

1. Replace vague words with specific ones.

Vague

The man was able to stabilize himself again, and he saw the old posts in the channel.

Specific

And once more the man was able to get his feet on the bottom and his head above water, and he saw ahead of him the pair of ancient stakes that marked the approach to the channel.

—Gordon, "The Sea Devil" (p. 35)

2. Replace abstract words with vivid, concrete words that appeal to the senses.

Abstract

The bird hovered high in the sky. The kitten sensed the change in the flight pattern and became fearful.

Concrete/Sensory

Now there at two thousand feet the bird hovered. The kitten was alarmingly aware of the change, blinking at the pulsations of beaten air as the wings flapped, hearing only that sound.

—Niland, "The Parachutist" (p. 237)

CLICHÉS

A *cliché* is a tired expression. Replace clichés in your writing with fresh, vivid expressions.

Cliché

She was **cool as a cucumber.**

Vivid

On the Arkansas summer days it seemed she had a private breeze which swirled around, cooling her.

—Angelou, "I Know Why the Caged Bird Sings" (p. 439)

LEVELS OF LANGUAGE

Depending on your purpose, audience, and form of writing, you should use an appropriate level of language. For example, *formal English* is appropriate for serious essays, reports, and speeches on solemn occasions. *Informal English* is suitable for personal letters, journal entries, and many articles. The following chart gives an outline of formal and informal levels of language.

	Formal	Informal
WORDS	longer, rare, specialized	shorter, colloquial
SPELLING	in full	contractions
GRAMMAR	complex, complete	compound, fragmentary

Formal English usually creates a serious tone. Informal English tends to have a friendlier, more personal tone.

Formal

While they were thus engaged, Ben Price sauntered in and leaned on his elbow, looking casually inside between the railings. He told the teller that he didn't want anything; he was just waiting for a man he knew.

—O. Henry, "A Retrieved Reformation" (p. 215)

Informal

"You signing up for the May Day races?" smiles Mary Louise, only it's not a smile at all. A dumb question like that doesn't deserve an answer. Besides, there's just me and Gretchen standing there really, so no use wasting my breath talking to shadows.

—Bambara, "Raymond's Run" (p. 23)

Handbook for Revision

Part 8: Glossary of Usage

a, an Use the indefinite article *a* before words beginning with a consonant sound. Use the indefinite article *an* before words beginning with a vowel sound.

Examples

Cloyd paused for *a* moment.

"The Rule of Names" takes place on *an* island.

accept, except *Accept* is a verb meaning "to receive." *Except* may be used as either a verb or a preposition. As a verb, *except* means "to leave out." As a preposition, *except* means "excluding."

Examples

Osborn does not *accept* Nace's cautious advice.

All the family *except* Mr. Frank perished in concentration camps. [preposition]

None of the Trojans was *excepted* from Achilles' revenge. [verb]

adapt, adopt *Adapt* means "to change or adjust something in order to make it fit or to make it suitable." *Adopt* means "to take something and make it one's own."

Examples

Has Hobbs's novel *Beardance* been *adapted* into a movie?

On the night of April 18, 1775, Paul Revere and his friend *adopted* a simple system of signals: one if by land, and two if by sea.

affect, effect *Affect* is a verb meaning "to influence." As a verb, *effect* means "to bring about" or "to accomplish." As a noun, *effect* means "the result of an action."

Examples

How do you think the story of Sundiata *affected* the griot's listeners?

In "A Cap for Steve," the experience with the cap *effected* a change in Dave Diamond's attitude toward money. [verb]

In "The Land and the Water," the death of the young people had a powerful *effect* on the narrator. [noun]

all, all of The word *of* can usually be omitted, except before some pronouns.

Examples

All my classmates liked reading "My Friend Flicka" by Mary O'Hara. [preferable to *All of*]

All of us saw the television production of *The Diary of Anne Frank.* [*Of* is necessary.]

among, between Use *between* when you are referring to two things at a time, or to more than two when an item is being compared individually with each of the others.

Examples

Kim couldn't decide *between* Gabriel García Márquez and Kurt Vonnegut as the subject for her report.

Tracy's report explored differences *between* essays, biographical sketches, and autobiographical memoirs.

Use *among* when you are referring to more than two items.

Example

Among the epics we have read, which was Diana's favorite?

amount, number Use *amount* to refer to a singular word. Use *number* to refer to a plural word.

Examples

In "Too Soon a Woman," it took a great *amount* of courage for Mary to test the mushroom by eating it.

O. Henry includes a *number* of ironic situations in "A Retrieved Reformation."

anxious, eager *Anxious* means "worried" or "uneasy." *Eager* means "feeling keen desire or strong interest."

Examples

In *Sundiata,* Sogolon Kedjou is *anxious* about her little son's failure to walk.

Lonnie is *eager* to read more stories by Edgar Allan Poe.

as, like *Like* is a preposition. In formal situations, do not use *like* for the conjunction *as* to introduce a subordinate clause.

Examples

Humorous rhymes were a favorite device for poets *like* Ogden Nash.

Did the *Iliad* end *as* you expected it would?

assure, ensure *Assure* means "to give confidence to" or "promise." *Ensure* means "to make sure" or "to guarantee."

Examples

Rob *assures* Kennie that he can have any colt he wants.

To *ensure* the families' safety, Mr. Frank warns them against making any noise while the workers are in the building.

awhile, a while   *Awhile* is an adverb meaning "for a short time." *A while* is made up of an article and a noun and means "a period or space of time."

Examples

Dennis and Mark stayed *awhile* after class to talk with Mr. Ortiz.

James Ramsey Ullman worked for *a while* as a reporter.

bad, badly   *Bad* is an adjective. *Badly* is an adverb. In standard English, only the adjective form should follow a sense verb, such as *feel, see, hear, taste, look,* or other linking verb.

Examples

In "Mother to Son," the speaker uses several metaphors to refer to her *bad* experiences in life.

In "The Apprentice," Peg thinks at first that her mother has treated her *badly.*

Charlie feels *bad* about the death of Algernon.

because   In formal situations, do not use the construction *reason . . . because.* Instead, use *reason . . . that.*

Informal

In Gerald Durrell's story, the *reason* for the family's confusion was *because* the scorpions had escaped from the matchbox.

Formal

In Gerald Durrell's story, the *reason* for the family's confusion was *that* the scorpions had escaped from the matchbox.

beside, besides   *Beside* is a preposition meaning "by the side of" or "next to." *Besides* may be used as either a preposition or an adverb. As a preposition, *besides* means "in addition to" or "also." As an adverb, *besides* means "moreover."

Examples

Did Tony sit *beside* you at lunch today?

Besides May Swenson, which other poets did you enjoy reading? [preposition]

Lewis Carroll was a famous writer; he was a gifted mathematician, *besides.* [adverb]

between   See **among, between.**

bring, take   *Bring* means "to come carrying something." *Take* means "to go carrying something."

Examples

Please *bring* copies of "The Raven" to class tomorrow.

Please *take* this copy of the newsletter to Ms. Trujillo in Room 224.

compare to, compare with   Use *compare to* when you want to stress either the similarities or the differences between two things. Use *compare with* when you wish to stress both similarities and differences.

Examples

Many people *compared* Harriet Tubman *to* Moses in the Old Testament.

Stan's report *compared* the *Iliad with Beowulf.*

connote, denote   *Connote* means "to suggest or imply." *Denote* means "to indicate or signify explicitly."

Examples

In "A Retrieved Reformation," the phrase "thinly gilded" *connotes* "out of style."

The title "A Retrieved Reformation" *denotes* "a restored change for the better."

Glossary of Usage   **739**

convince, persuade *Convince* means "to win someone over through argument." *Convince* is usually followed by *that* and a subordinate clause. *Persuade* means to move someone to act in a certain way. *Persuade* is often followed by *to*.

Examples

In a famous essay, Edgar Allan Poe tried to *convince* his readers *that* the details in a short story should all contribute to a single effect.

Mrs. Flowers *persuaded* young Maya *to* read literary passages aloud.

could of Do not write *of* with the helping verb *could*. Write *could have*. Also avoid *had of, ought to of, should of, would of, might of,* and *must of*.

Example

No one except Paul Bunyan *could have* [not *of*] solved the mosquito problem.

different from, different than Use *different from*, not *different than*.

Example

A legend is *different from* a myth because a legend usually has some basis in history.

doesn't, don't *Doesn't* is the contraction of *does not*. *Don't* is the contraction of *do not*. Use *doesn't*, not *don't*, with *he, she, it, this, that,* and singular nouns.

Examples

Walter Plummer *doesn't* [not *don't*] play the clarinet very well.

At the end of "Casey at the Bat," the Mudville players *don't* [not *doesn't*] win the game.

due to the fact that Replace this wordy phrase with *because*.

Wordy

Due to the fact that the actors in *Pyramus and Thisby* can hardly read or write, they have trouble figuring out the meaning of their lines.

Better

Because the actors in *Pyramus and Thisby* can hardly read or write, they have trouble figuring out the meaning of their lines.

eager See **anxious, eager.**

effect See **affect, effect.**

emigrate, immigrate *Emigrate* means "to leave a country or a region to settle elsewhere." *Immigrate* means "to come into a country or region to settle there." *Emigrate* is used with *from; immigrate* is used with *to*.

Examples

In the nineteenth century, millions of people *immigrated to* the United States from Europe.

More recently, America has received many new settlers who have *emigrated from* Asian countries.

ensure See **assure, ensure.**

everyday, every day *Everyday* is an adjective meaning "daily" or "common." *Every day* is an adverbial phrase meaning "each day."

Examples

Have you ever wondered what *everyday* life was like in colonial America?

Every day he was in Japan, Lincoln Mendoza saw or learned something new.

everyone, every one *Everyone* is an indefinite pronoun. *Every one* consists of an adjective and a pronoun and means "every person or thing of those named."

Examples

Everyone laughed when Gloria read "Jabberwocky" aloud in class.

Sam has read *every one* of O. Henry's short stories.

except See **accept, except.**

farther, further *Farther* refers to geographical distance. *Further* means "in addition to" or "to a greater degree."

Examples

Osborn wanted to go *farther* up the mountain, but Nace was cautious.

In "The Deer Thief," the judge was convinced when he questioned the hunter *further*.

fewer, less Use *fewer*, which tells "how many," to modify a plural noun. Use *less,* which tells "how much," to modify a singular noun.

Examples

There were no *fewer* than 48,000 casualties at the Battle of Gettysburg.

Jimmy Valentine's romance caused him to have *less* interest in his career as a safecracker.

good, well *Good* is an adjective. *Well* may be used as an adjective or an adverb. The expressions *feel good* and *feel well* mean different things. *Feel good* means "to feel happy or pleased." *Feel well* means "to feel healthy."

Examples

At the end of the story, Steve feels *good* about his father.

Russ had to go home early because he did not feel *well*.

Avoid using *good* to modify an action verb. Instead, use *well* as an adverb meaning "capably" or "satisfactorily."

Nonstandard

Arthur Gordon uses suspense *good* in "The Sea Devil."

Standard

Arthur Gordon uses suspense *well* in "The Sea Devil."

had of See **could of.**

hardly, scarcely The words *hardly* and *scarcely* convey negative meanings. They should never be used with another negative word.

Examples

Kennie *can* [not *can't*] *hardly* lift Flicka's head out of the water.

In "Too Soon a Woman," the children *had* [not *hadn't*] *scarcely* enough food to survive.

he, she, they Do not use an unnecessary pronoun after the subject of a clause or a sentence. This error is called the *double subject*.

Nonstandard

In "The Rule of Names," Mr. Underhill *he* turns out to be a dragon in disguise.

Standard

In "The Rule of Names," Mr. Underhill turns out to be a dragon in disguise.

historic, historical *Historic* means "crucial" or "especially important." *Historical* means "concerned or connected with history."

Examples

April 19, 1775, was a *historic day* because it marked the beginning of the American Revolution.

The legend of Sundiata is rooted in *historical* facts.

how come In informal situations, *how come* is often used instead of *why*. In formal situations, *why* should always be used.

Informal

I don't know *how come* they left the room.

Formal

I don't know *why* they left the room.

imply, infer *Imply* means "to suggest something indirectly." *Infer* means "to interpret" or "to get a certain meaning from a remark or an action."

Examples

Several episodes of Will Hobbs's novel *imply* that a young person must undergo tests and trials in order to achieve maturity.

Do you *infer* from the narrator's words in "The Tell-Tale Heart" that he is insane?

in, into, in to *In* means "within." *Into* means "from the outside to the inside." *In to* refers to motion with a purpose.

Examples

Will Hobbs's novel takes place *in* the West.

Ben Price walked *into* the Elmore Bank to arrest Jimmy Valentine.

During math class, Pam came *in to* deliver a message.

its, it's *Its* is a possessive pronoun. *It's* is the contraction for *it is* or *it has.*

Examples

Todd's favorite poem was *The Cremation of Sam McGee;* he especially liked *its* rhythm.

It's clear from Cathy Song's poem that she cherishes memories of her grandfather.

kind(s), sort(s), type(s) With the singular form of each of these nouns, use *this* or *that.* With the plural form, use *these* or *those.*

Examples

Are you familiar with *this type* of poem?

It is not easy to adapt *those kinds* of stories to the screen.

lay, lie The verb *lay* means "to put (something) in a place." *Lay* usually takes an object. The past tense of *lay* is *laid.* The verb *lie* means "to rest" or "to stay, to recline, or to remain in a certain state or position." *Lie* never takes an object. The past tense of *lie* is *lay.*

Examples

Please *lay* those books on the desk. [present tense of *lay*]

At the end of Morley Callaghan's story, Steve's father talks to him as the boy *lies* in bed. [present tense of *lie*]

leave, let *Leave* means "to go away." *Let* means "to permit" or "to allow." Avoid using *leave* for *let.*

Nonstandard
Leave us alone!

Standard
Let us alone!

Standard
The flight was scheduled to *leave* at 2:35.

less See **fewer, less.**

might of, must of See **could of.**

number See **amount, number.**

on, onto, on to *On* refers to position and means "upon," "in contact with," or "supported by." *Onto* implies motion and means "to a position on." Do not confuse *onto* with *on to.*

Examples

May Swenson's poem describes cars *on* a freeway.

The mother scorpion scuttled *onto* the back of Larry's hand.

Robert Frost moved to England in 1912; he went *on to* publish his first two volumes of poems.

or, nor Use *or* with *either.* Use *nor* with *neither.*

Examples

Pilar will write her report *either* on Emily Dickinson *or* on Aurora Levins Morales.

Neither Sir Walter Scott *nor* Robert Browning was an American poet.

ought to of See **could of.**

principal, principle *Principal* is an adjective meaning "first" or "main." It can also be a noun meaning the head of a school. *Principle* is a noun meaning "rule of conduct" or "a fact or general truth."

Examples
The *principal* characters in Will Hobbs's tale are Cloyd and Walter.

In "Gentleman of Río en Medio," Don Anselmo sticks to his *principles*.

real In informal situations, *real* is often used as an adverb meaning "very" or "extremely." In formal situations, *very* or *extremely* is preferred.

Informal
The man in "The Sea Devil" came *real* close to being drowned.

Formal
The man in "The Sea Devil" came *very* close to being drowned.

relation, relationship *Relation* refers to a person connected to another by kinship. *Relationship* refers to a connection between thoughts or meanings.

Examples
Do your friends and *relations* enjoy detective stories?

What is the *relationship* between a simile and a metaphor?

respectfully, respectively *Respectfully* means "with respect" or "full of respect." *Respectively* means "each in the order indicated."

Examples
Stories like "Top Man" and "The Land and the Water" have taught me to regard the power of nature *respectfully*.

Gerald Carson and James Thurber are the authors of "The Glorious Bird" and "The Dog That Bit People," *respectively*.

rise, raise *Rise* means "to go up" or "to get up." *Rise* never takes an object. The past tense of *rise* is *rose*. *Raise* means "to cause (something) to rise" or "to lift up." *Raise* usually takes an object. The past tense of *raise* is *raised*.

Examples
Sogolon Djata *rises* and takes the steps of a giant.

Raise your hand if you would like to be in the cast of the class play.

scarcely, hardly See **hardly, scarcely.**

should of See **could of.**

sit, set *Sit* means "to rest in an upright, seated position." *Sit* seldom takes an object. The past tense of *sit* is *sat*. *Set* means "to put (something) in a place." *Set* usually takes an object. The past tense of *set* is *set*.

Examples
Philip Nolan often *sat* alone in his cabin.

The hawk was forced to *set* the kitten down.

some, somewhat In writing, do not use *some* for *somewhat* as an adverb.

Nonstandard
Uncle Horatio was surprised *some* at the behavior of Muggs.

Standard
Uncle Horatio was surprised *somewhat* at the behavior of Muggs.

than, then *Than* is a conjunction used in comparisons. *Then* is an adverb telling *when*.

Examples
Squeaky could run faster *than* any of her classmates.

First Sundiata slays Soumaoro, *then* he destroys the city of Sosso.

that See **who, which, that.**

this here, that there   The words *here* and *there* are unnecessary after *this* and *that*.

Example
This [not *this here*] selection is a lyric poem, but *that* [not *that there*] poem is an epic.

try and   In informal situations, *try and* is often used instead of *try to*. In formal situations, *try to* should be used.

Informal
Try and be on time for rehearsal.

Formal
Try to be on time for rehearsal.

use to, used to   Be sure to add the *d* to *use*.

Example
Mr. Rescigno *used to* [not *use to*] require his social studies students to memorize "The Gettysburg Address."

well   See **good, well**.

when, where   Do not use *when* or *where* to begin a definition.

Nonstandard
An inference is *when* you make a reasonable conclusion about something based on certain clues or facts.

Standard
An inference is a reasonable conclusion about something based on certain clues or facts.

Nonstandard
Irony is *where* there is a contrast between what is stated and what is really meant.

Standard
Irony is a contrast between what is stated and what is really meant.

where   Do not use *where* for *that*.

Nonstandard
Ray read *where* Henry Wadsworth Longfellow wrote a literary epic about Hiawatha.

Standard
Ray read *that* Henry Wadsworth Longfellow wrote a literary epic about Hiawatha.

who, which, that   *Who* refers to persons only. *Which* refers to things only. *That* may refer to either persons or things.

Examples
The poet *who* wrote "Speaking" was Simon J. Ortiz.

The Battle of Gettysburg, *which* took place in the summer of 1863, was a turning point of the Civil War.

A writer *that* Lucille liked a lot was Richard Wright.

One story *that* most readers remember vividly is "The Tell-Tale Heart."

who, whom   *Who* is used as the subject of a verb or as a predicate nominative. *Whom* is used as an object of a verb or as an object of a preposition. The use of *who* or *whom* in a subordinate clause depends on how the pronoun functions within the clause.

Examples
In *Pyramus and Thisby, who* is the wife of Duke Theseus?

Margot, *who* is Anne's sister, is quiet and patient.

The writer *whom* Tom liked best was Daniel Keyes.

To *whom* do the characters turn for help when little Agatha is trapped in the safe?

whose, who's   *Whose* is the possessive form of *who*. *Who's* is a contraction for *who is* or *who has*.

Examples
Maya Angelou, *whose* writings have made her a celebrated author, read a poem entitled "On the Pulse of Morning" at the inauguration of President Clinton.

Who's prepared to read a stanza of "The Raven" aloud?

without, unless Do not use the preposition *without* in place of the conjunction *unless*.

Example

The man realizes that he will drown *unless* [not *without*] he can get the rope to break.

would of See **could of.**

your, you're *Your* is the possessive form of *you.* *You're* is the contraction of *you are.*

Examples

Your book is on the table.

You're trying out for the play, aren't you?

Subject-Verb Agreement: See Agreement of Subject and Verb, *Teaching Resources B,* page 165.

Nouns: For review of parts of speech, see *Teaching Resources A,* page 16. See Proper Nouns and Common Nouns, *Teaching Resources C,* page 34. See also Vivid, Precise Nouns, *Teaching Resources C,* page 65, and Noun Clauses, *Teaching Resources A,* page 111.

Pronouns: See *Teaching Resources C,* page 15.

Handbook for Revision

Part 9: Grammar Reference Guide

SUBJECT-VERB AGREEMENT

A verb should agree with its subject in number—singular or plural.

Dave and **Steve were** left alone in the corridor, knowing that the other **boy was** preparing his father for the encounter.

> —Callaghan, "A Cap for Steve" (p. 82)

At each end **were clusters** of golden arrows, and underneath the crossbar, a **shield** with painted stars and stripes **was** attached.

> —Carson, "The Glorious Bird" (p. 409)

What he had the most of **was** time.

> —Sedillo, "Gentleman of Rió en Medio" (p. 100)

NOUNS

A **noun** is a word used to name a person, place, thing, or idea. Nouns can function in sentences as subjects, direct objects, indirect objects, objects of prepositions, predicate nominatives, and appositives.

Jimmy slid back a **panel** in the **wall** and dragged out a dust-covered **suitcase.**

> —O. Henry, "A Retrieved Reformation" (p. 211)

Mr. Underhill had decided that since his **true-name** was no longer a **secret,** he might as well drop his **disguise.**

> —Le Guin, "The Rule of Names" (p. 228)

Quince, the **director,** gives each **player** a **script.**

PRONOUNS

A **pronoun** is a word used in place of a noun or of more than one noun. **Personal pronouns** refer to the person speaking (first person), the person spoken to (second person), or the person, place, or thing spoken about (third person).

	Singular		
	Subject Form	Object Form	Possessive Form
First Person	I	me	my, mine
Second Person	you	you	your, yours
Third Person	he	him	his
	she	her	her, hers
	it	it	its

	Plural		
	Subject Form	Object Form	Possessive Form
First Person	we	us	our, ours
Second Person	you	you	your, yours
Third Person	they	them	their, theirs

Verbs: See Vivid, Precise Verbs, *Teaching Resources B,* page 178. See also Action Verbs and Linking Verbs, *Teaching Resources B,* page 35. For information on verb phrases, see *Teaching Resources B,* page 62.

Adjectives: For exercises on adjective clauses, see *Teaching Resources A,* page 56. See Careful Placement of Modifiers, *Teaching Resources D,* page 48.

Handbook for Revision

A **reflexive pronoun** ends in *-self* or *-selves* and refers back to the subject of a verb.

> I wedged **myself** into a cleft in the wall and let out the rope which extended between us.
>
> —Ullman, "Top Man" (p. 65)

> The great ray settled to the bottom and braced its wings against the mud and hurled **itself** forward and upward.
>
> —Gordon, "The Sea Devil" (p. 35)

An **intensive pronoun** ends in *-self* or *-selves* and adds emphasis to a noun or pronoun in the same sentence.

> In "Raymond's Run," Squeaky **herself** narrates the story.

A **relative pronoun** is used to introduce adjective and noun clauses.

> The brave men, living and dead, **who** struggled here, have consecrated it far above our poor power to add or detract.
>
> —Lincoln, "The Gettysburg Address" (p. 158)

> In our country, we have an animal to **which** we have given the name "dog," or, in the local dialect of the more mountainous districts, "doggie."
>
> —Milne, *The Ugly Duckling* (p. 313)

> She was a large woman with a large purse **that** had everything in it but hammer and nails.
>
> —Hughes, "Thank You, M'am" (p. 230)

An **interrogative pronoun** is used to begin questions.

> "**What** do you reckon it's like," she said, "being on the bottom in the eelgrass?"
>
> —Grau, "The Land and the Water" (p. 270)

A **demonstrative pronoun** is used to point out a specific person or thing.

> "**This** is the first island I've seen that had no wizard," said Blackbeard one evening to Goody Guld. . . .
>
> —Le Guin, "The Rule of Names" (p. 223)

An **indefinite pronoun** is used to refer to people or things in general.

> But I couldn't help thinking it was **something** else.
>
> —Grau, "The Land and the Water" (p. 271)

VERBS

A **verb** is a word that expresses action or a state of being. An **action verb** tells what action someone or something is performing.

> A rabbit **sprang** twenty yards like a bobbing wheel, and the sight **drew** the hawk like a plummet, but the rabbit **vanished** in a hollow log. . . .
>
> —Niland, "The Parachutist" (p. 236)

A **linking verb** helps to make a statement by serving as a link between two words (for example, subject with predicate nominative or predicate adjective). The most commonly used linking verbs are forms of the verb *be.*

> The Americanization of Mexican me **was** no smooth matter.
>
> —Galarza, *Barrio Boy* (p. 191)

> I **feel** sick inside.
>
> —Keyes, "Flowers for Algernon" (p. 248)

A **helping verb** is a verb that can be added to another verb to make a verb phrase.

> Perhaps he **had** sneaked upstairs to lie on her bed where he **was** not supposed to go—not that *she* **would have** minded!
>
> —Canfield, "The Apprentice" (p. 89)

ADJECTIVES

An **adjective** is a word used to modify a noun or pronoun. Adjectives tell *what kind, which one,* or *how many.*

> And the **silken, sad, uncertain** rustling of **each purple** curtain/ Thrilled me—filled me with **fantastic** terrors never felt before.
>
> —Poe, "The Raven" (p. 475)

The articles *the, a,* and *an* are adjectives. *An* is used before a word beginning with a vowel sound or with an unsounded *h.*

ADVERBS

An **adverb** is a word used to modify a verb, an adjective, or another adverb. Adverbs tell *how, when, where,* and *to what extent.*

> Alongside the grizzly woman, he inched **forward** on his belly into a cluster of rocks that would shield them from view. When the moment came, he found the mother grizzly digging as **vigorously** as **ever.**
> —Hobbs, *Beardance* (p. 552)

> I shall be telling this with a sigh
> **Somewhere** ages and ages **hence:**
> Two roads diverged in a wood, and I—
> I took the one **less** traveled by,
> And that has made all the difference.
> —Frost, "The Road Not Taken" (p. 471)

PREPOSITIONS

A **preposition** is a word that shows the relationship of a noun or a pronoun to some other word in the sentence. Prepositions are almost always followed by nouns or pronouns. A group of words that begins with a preposition and ends with a noun or pronoun is called a **prepositional phrase.**

> One spring day, the men were working **in a swamp, near a lake in northern Michigan,** when they heard a droning noise. [three prepositional phrases]
> —Dolbier, "Paul Bunyan's Been There" (p. 175)

CONJUNCTIONS

A **conjunction** is a word used to join words or groups of words. **Coordinating conjunctions** join equal parts of a sentence or similar groups of words.

> It was very cold, **but** the wind had fallen **and** the mountain seemed to hang suspended in a vast stillness.
> —Ullman, "Top Man" (p. 63)

Correlative conjunctions are used in pairs to join similar words or groups of words.

> **Both** Abraham Lincoln **and** Martin Luther King, Jr., were remarkable orators.

A **subordinating conjunction** is used to introduce a clause that has less importance than the main clause in a sentence.

> **If** you still think me mad, you will think so no longer **when** I describe the wise precautions I took for the concealment of the body.
> —Poe, "The Tell-Tale Heart" (p. 275)

A **conjunctive adverb** is an adverb used as a conjunction to connect ideas.

> All the workingmen in *Pyramus and Thisby* are uneducated; **nevertheless,** they manage to amuse Theseus and Hippolyta.

INTERJECTIONS

An **interjection** is a word that expresses emotion and has no grammatical relation to other words in the sentence.

> **Oh,** young Lochinvar is come out of the west.
> —Scott, "Lochinvar" (p. 482)

> "**H'm'm? Oh—well,** so you do."
> —Vonnegut, "The No-Talent Kid" (p. 13)

PHRASES

A **phrase** is a group of words that does not contain a subject and a verb.

A **prepositional phrase** is a group of words that begins with a preposition and ends with a noun or pronoun.

> **inside** the house   **with** them
> **across** the lake   **after** dinner

An **appositive** is a noun or pronoun placed beside another noun or pronoun to identify or explain it. An **appositive phrase** is made up of an appositive and its modifiers.

> Dave Diamond, **a poor man, a carpenter's assistant,** was a small, wiry, quick-tempered individual who had learned how to make every dollar count in his home.
> —Callaghan, "A Cap for Steve" (p. 78)

Adverbs: See *Teaching Resources D,* page 31. For exercises on Adverb Phrases, *Teaching Resources D,* page 81. See also Adverb Clauses, *Teaching Resources A,* page 89.

Phrases: See *Teaching Resources A,* page 126. For exercises on phrases and clauses, see *Teaching Resources A,* page 13. See Appositives, *Teaching Resources C,* page 180. For practice changing clauses into phrases, see *Teaching Resources B,* page 20.

Handbook for Revision

Clauses: See Phrases and Clauses, *Teaching Resources A,* page 13. For practice with clauses, see Noun Clauses, *Teaching Resources A,* page 111. See also Adjective Clauses, *Teaching Resources A,* page 56, and Adverb Clauses, *Teaching Resources A,* page 89.

Handbook for Revision

A **participial phrase** consists of a participle and its complements or modifiers. The entire participial phrase acts as an adjective.

> Larry**, feeling the movement of her claws,** glanced down to see what it was, and from that moment things got increasingly confused.
>
> —Durrell, *My Family and Other Animals* (p. 105)

An **infinitive phrase** consists of an infinitive together with its modifiers and complements. The entire phrase can be used as a noun, an adjective, or an adverb.

> With this faith we will be able **to hew out of the mountains of despair a stone of hope.** [infinitive phrase used as an adverb modifying *able*]
>
> —King, "I Have a Dream" (p. 195)

CLAUSES

A **clause** is a group of words that has a subject and a verb. An **independent clause** expresses a complete thought and can stand by itself as a sentence.

> Then Hrothgar stretched out his arms in welcome.
>
> —*Beowulf* (p. 648)

A **subordinate clause** does not express a complete thought and cannot stand alone.

> She had never imagined **that hate could be so strong in a human being.**
>
> —*Sundiata* (p. 660)

Part 10: Mechanics

■ Capitalization ■ Punctuation

CAPITALIZATION

1. FIRST WORDS

■ **Capitalize the first word of every sentence.**

Example

All that was nearly fifty years ago. If Nolan was thirty then, he must have been near eighty when he died.

> —Hale, "The Man Without a Country" (p. 151)

■ **Capitalize the first word of a direct quotation when the word begins with a capital letter in the original. If the original writer has not used a capital letter, do not capitalize the first word of the quotation.**

Examples

"**N**o," she said. "**G**o now! If you come back into this house without those groceries, I'll whip you!"

> —Wright, *Black Boy* (p. 49)

"**A**ll right! All right, you dope," shouted the owner, "**d**on't just stand there! Get the broom and sweep that mess up."

> —Keyes, "Flowers for Algernon" (p. 254)

■ **Traditionally, the first word in a line of poetry is capitalized, although some writers do not follow this rule for reasons of style.**

Examples

There was a young man from Bengal
Who went to a fancy-dress ball.
   He went just for fun
   Dressed up as a bun,
And a dog ate him up in the hall.

> —Anonymous Limericks (p. 504)

One eats
the moon in a tortilla
Eat frijoles
and you eat the earth

> —Valle, "Food" (p. 470)

2. THE PRONOUN *I* AND THE INTERJECTION *O*

■ **Capitalize the pronoun *I* and the interjection *O*.**

748   HANDBOOK FOR REVISION

Examples

Now **I** maintain to this day that the female scorpion meant no harm.

—Durrell, "My Family and Other Animals" (p. 105)

O Captain! my Captain! our fearful trip is done.

—Whitman, "O Captain! My Captain!" (p. 160)

3. PROPER NOUNS AND PROPER ADJECTIVES

A *proper noun* names a particular person, place, or thing. A *proper adjective* is formed from a proper noun. Capitalize proper nouns and proper adjectives.

Examples

Brazil	Africa	China	Greece
Brazilian	African	Chinese	Greek

▌ In proper nouns consisting of two or more words, do *not* capitalize articles (*a, an, the*), short prepositions (those with fewer than five letters, such as *at, of, for, with*), and coordinating conjunctions (*and, but, for, nor, or, so, yet*).

Examples

Nobel Prize	Mayor Reyes	President Truman
San Diego	Isle of Wight	Molokai

If you are not sure whether to capitalize a word, check in an up-to-date dictionary.

4. NAMES OF PEOPLE

▌ Capitalize the names of people. Note that some names may contain more than one capital letter.

Examples

Toni Cade Bambara	Mary O'Hara
Simon J. Ortiz	D'Arcy Niland

5. GEOGRAPHICAL NAMES

▌ Capitalize geographical names, such as towns, cities, counties, townships, states, regions, countries, continents, islands, mountains, bodies of water, parks, roads, highways, and streets.

Examples

New Orleans	Kentucky	Dade County
Australia	Tampa Bay	Third Avenue
Central Park	Lake Huron	Nova Scotia
Catalina Island	Route 495	Oak Street

▌ Note that words such as *south, east,* and *northwest* are *not* capitalized when they indicate direction.

Examples

west of the Rockies   north of town

6. ORGANIZATIONS

▌ Capitalize the names of organizations, teams, businesses, institutions, buildings, and government bodies.

Examples

National Football League
Mayo Clinic
Chicago Bulls
University of Nebraska
Sears Tower
Treasury Department

7. HISTORICAL EVENTS

▌ Capitalize the names of historical events and periods, special events, and calendar items.

Examples

Wars of the Roses	the Renaissance
Vietnam War	Flag Day
Kansas State Fair	Olympic Games
Saturday	World Series

8. NATIONALITIES, RACES, AND RELIGIONS

▌ Capitalize the names of nationalities, races, and peoples.

Handbook for Revision

Examples

Pakistani	African American	Trinidadian
Inca	Filipino	Cherokee
Inuit	Korean	Puerto Rican

▌ Capitalize the names of religions and their followers, holy days, sacred writings, and specific deities.

Examples

Taoism	Passover	Holy Spirit
Presbyterian	Ash Wednesday	God
Islam	Vedas	Lent
Pentecost	Allah	the Talmud

9. BRAND NAMES

▌ Capitalize the brand names of business products. Do *not* capitalize the noun that often follows a brand name.

Examples

Ford cars	Timex watches
Planters peanuts	Uncle Ben's rice

10. PARTICULAR PLACES, THINGS, AND EVENTS

▌ Capitalize the names of ships, trains, airplanes, spacecraft, monuments, buildings, awards, planets, and any other particular places, things, or events.

Examples

Santa Maria	*Silver Meteor*	*Air Force One*
Mercury	Eiffel Tower	*Columbia*
Room 406	Golden Globe Award	World Trade Center

11. SPECIFIC COURSES, LANGUAGES

▌ Do *not* capitalize the names of school subjects, except for languages and for course names followed by a number.

Examples

chemistry	sociology	biology
Spanish	German	Biology 101

12. TITLES OF PEOPLE

▌ Capitalize a title belonging to a particular person when it comes before the person's name.

Examples

President Clinton	Professor Rodriguez
General Summers	Miss Delano

▌ Do *not* capitalize a title used alone or following a person's name, especially if the title is preceded by *a* or *the*.

Examples

Patricia Gruber, mayor of Denver
the senator's office
a duke's title

▌ Capitalize a word showing a family relationship when the word is used with a person's name but *not* when it is preceded by a possessive.

Examples

Aunt Ruth	Uncle Merle	my uncle Merle

13. TITLES OF LITERARY AND OTHER CREATIVE WORKS

▌ Capitalize the first and last words and all important words in titles of books, magazines, newspapers, short poems, stories, historical documents, movies, television programs, works of art, and musical compositions.

Unimportant words within titles are articles (*a, an, the*), short prepositions (fewer than five letters, such as *at, of, for, to, from, with*) and coordinating conjunctions (*and, but, for, nor, or, so, yet*).

Examples

Beardance	*Barrio Boy*
"Flowers for Algernon"	*Travel and Leisure*
"My Friend Flicka"	*Indian Council*
The Diary of Anne Frank	*Mrs. Doubtfire*

Punctuation: See *Teaching Resources C,* page 17. For practice with punctuation in quotations, see *Teaching Resources C,* page 37. See also Punctuating Interrupters in Sentences, *Teaching Resources C,* page 127. For exercises on semicolons, see *Teaching Resources E,* page 60.

▮ The word *the, a,* or *an* written before a title is capitalized only when it is the first word of a title.

Examples

"**T**he Land and the Water"

"**A** Cap for Steve"

PUNCTUATION

1. END MARKS

▮ End marks—*periods, question marks,* and *exclamation points*—are used to indicate the purpose of a sentence.

Use a period to end a statement (or declarative sentence).

Example

I grew very fond of these scorpions.

—Durrell, *My Family and Other Animals* (p. 104)

▮ A question (or interrogative sentence) is followed by a question mark. Note that a direct question may have the same word order as a declarative sentence. Since it is a question, however, it is followed by a question mark.

Examples

"Who brings food into the house?" my mother asked me.

—Wright, *Black Boy* (p. 47)

"The bus leaves at noon?" he asked.

▮ Use an exclamation point to end an exclamation.

Examples

"Look out! Look out! They're coming!" screamed Margo.

—Durrell, *My Family and Other Animals* (p. 105)

"Oh! This horse needs a blanket, that is the trouble," said Coyote.

—"Coyote Shows How He Can Lie" (p. 181)

Then I heard Nace shout, "Jump!"

—Ullman, "Top Man" (p. 59)

How she still loved it!

—O'Hara, "My Friend Flicka" (p. 109)

▮ An imperative sentence may be followed by either a period or an exclamation point.

Examples

Just do the best you can with the girls.

—Johnson, "Too Soon a Woman" (p. 165)

"Come back!" he called. "Come off the snow!"

—Ullman, "Top Man" (p. 64)

▮ Use a period after an abbreviation.

Examples

Personal Names: Juan A. A. Sedillo

Titles Used with Names: Dr., Ms., Mrs., Mr., Rev., Capt.

States: N.M., S.D., Conn.

Time of Day: A.M., P.M.

Years: B.C., A.D.

Addresses: St., Ave., Blvd.

Organizations and Companies: Inc., Co., Corp.

Units of Measure: lb., oz., in., ft., yd., mi.

▮ No periods are used in abbreviations with states when the zip code is included: MD 20678

▮ Abbreviations in the metric system are often written without periods: for example, km for kilometer, kg for kilogram, ml for milliliter. Abbreviations for government agencies and international organizations and some other frequently used abbreviations are written without periods: for example, FBI, UNESCO, and PBS.

2. COMMAS: CONVENTIONAL USES

▮ Use a comma to separate items in dates and addresses.

Examples

I wrote to Frances on March 21, 1995.

I sent the letter to 42 Maple St., Norcross, GA 30310.

Handbook for Revision

Semicolons: See *Teaching Resources E,* page 60.

▮ **Notice that a comma also separates the final item in a date and in an address from the words that follow it. A comma does *not* separate the month from the day, the house number from the street name, or the state name from the ZIP code.**

▮ **Use a comma after the salutation of a friendly letter and after the closing of any letter.**

Examples

Dear Ms. McDermott,	My dear Keith,
Sincerely yours,	Yours truly,

For other uses of commas, see **Part 6** (pp. 733–734).

3. SEMICOLONS

▮ **Use a semicolon between independent clauses that are closely related in thought and that are not joined by *and, but, or, nor, for, so,* or *yet.***

Example

After that night they knew that Steve didn't go to the park to play ball; he went to look for the cap.

—Callaghan, "A Cap for Steve" (p. 81)

▮ **Use a semicolon between independent clauses joined by a conjunctive adverb or a transitional expression.**

Example

It was rather unfortunate that just as I entered the door lunch should be served**; however,** I placed the matchbox carefully on the mantelpiece in the drawing room, so that the scorpions should get plenty of air. . . .

—Durrell, *My Family and Other Animals* (p. 105)

▮ **Use a semicolon (rather than a comma) before a coordinating conjunction to join independent clauses that contain commas.**

Example

Its heart bursting with the strain, its eyes dilated wild and yellow, it came down until the earth skimmed under it; and the kitten cried at the silver glare of the roofs not far off, and the expanding earth, and the brush of the grass.

—Niland, "The Parachutist" (p. 238)

4. COLONS

▮ **Use a colon before a list of items, especially after expressions like *as follows* and *the following.***

Example

Jon's favorite writers were the following**:** Morley Callaghan, Will Hobbs, O. Henry, and Maya Angelou.

▮ **Use a colon before a statement that explains or clarifies a preceding statement.**

Example

Suddenly, with four pounds of fish within my grasp, I felt uncontrollable terror**:** driven wild by the scent of blood, the sharks hurled themselves with all their strength against the bottom of the raft.

—García Márquez, "Fighting Off the Sharks for a Fish" (p. 42)

▮ **Use a colon in certain conventional situations: between the hour and the minute, between chapter and verse in a Biblical citation, and after the salutation of a business letter.**

Examples

8:15 P.M.	Matthew 3:2	Dear Dr. Stern:

5. ITALICS

▮ **When writing or typing, indicate italics by underlining. Use italics for titles of books, plays, periodicals, works of art, films, television programs, record albums, long musical compositions, ships, trains, aircraft, and spacecraft.**

Quotation Marks: See Punctuation Marks, *Teaching Resources C,* page 17. For practice with punctuation in quotations, see *Teaching Resources C,* page 37.

Examples

BOOK: *The Call of the Wild*

PLAY: *A Midsummer Night's Dream*

PERIODICAL: *TV Guide*

WORK OF ART: *The Jolly Flatboatmen*

FILM: *Sleepless in Seattle*

TELEVISION PROGRAM: *Safari*

RECORD ALBUM: *Unforgettable*

LONG MUSICAL COMPOSITION: *A Sea Symphony*

SHIP: *Pequod*

TRAIN: *Orient Express*

AIRCRAFT: *Spruce Goose*

SPACECRAFT: *Sputnik II*

■ **Use italics for words, letters, and figures referred to as such.**

Examples

Principal may be a noun or an adjective.

When you form the past tense of that verb, change the *y* to *i* and add *ed.*

My lucky number is *29.*

6. QUOTATION MARKS

■ **Use quotation marks to enclose a direct quotation—a person's exact words.**

Example

She said, **"Go on with us or die."**
> —Petry, "They Called Her Moses" (p. 424)

■ **Do *not* use quotation marks to enclose an indirect quotation.**

Example

Dr. Nemur says I'm trying to cram a lifetime of research and thought into a few weeks.
> —Keyes, "Flowers for Algernon" (p. 256)

■ **Begin a direct quotation with a capital letter.**

Example

Gus said, **"I**t's de fever. It burns up her flesh. If you could stop de fever she might get vell."
> —O'Hara, "My Friend Flicka" (p. 117)

■ **When an expression identifying the speaker interrupts a quoted sentence, the second part of the quotation begins with a small letter.**

Example

"If you are slain, my son," said Priam, **"w**ho will be left to guard the men and women of Troy?"
> —Homer, The *Iliad* (p. 634)

■ **A direct quotation is set off from the rest of the sentence by commas or by a question mark or an exclamation point.**

Examples

"Rub it in**,**" said Plummer, bitterly.
> —Vonnegut, "The No-Talent Kid" (p. 128)

"Did you get there**?**" I asked dully.
> —Ullman, "Top Man" (p. 66)

She said when they got him back to Savannah, got him in prison there, they whipped him until a doctor who was standing by watching said, "You will kill him if you strike him again**!**"
> —Petry, "They Called Her Moses" (p. 424)

■ **Commas and periods are always placed inside closing quotation marks.**

Examples

"I won't be back here**,**" the old man said.
> —Hobbs, *Beardance* (p. 569)

"I followed his tracks and I found yellow hair where the dog passed beneath low branches**.**"
> —"The Deer Thief" (p. 179)

■ **Question marks and exclamation points are placed inside closing quotation marks if the quotation is a question or an exclamation. Otherwise, they are placed outside.**

Examples

"What's the matter?" Dave asked quickly.
> —Callaghan, "A Cap for Steve" (p. 80)

"Oh, *Mom!*" she shouted in ecstasy.
> —Canfield, "The Apprentice" (p. 96)

Have you read Robert Frost's poem "Birches"?

Let's all sing "Jingle Bells"!

Handbook for Revision

Apostrophes: See Punctuation Marks, *Teaching Resources C,* page 17. For practice with contractions, see *Teaching Resources E,* page 11.

■ **When both the sentence and the quotation at the end of the sentence are questions (or exclamations), only one question mark (or exclamation point) is used. It is placed inside the closing quotation marks.**

Example

Are you familiar with Alice Walker's essay "The Civil Rights Movement: How Good Was It?"

■ **When you write dialogue, begin a new paragraph every time the speaker changes, and enclose each speaker's words in quotation marks.**

Example

"Well," said Coyote, "I had to pay a big price for that power. I learned it from my enemy."

"What did you pay?"

"One horse. But it was my best buffalo horse, with a fine bridle."

"Is that all?"

"Yes."

—"Coyote Shows How He Can Lie" (p. 181)

■ **When a quotation consists of several sentences, place quotation marks at the beginning and at the end of the whole quotation.**

Example

She said, without turning her head, to me, "I hear you're doing very good schoolwork, Marguerite, but that it's all written. The teachers report that they have trouble getting you to talk in class."

—Angelou, "I Know Why the Caged Bird Sings" (p. 439)

■ **Use single quotation marks to enclose a quotation within a quotation.**

Example

"The only thing to do is what we all have to do now and then: smile, shrug, and say, 'Well, that's just one of those things that's not for me.' "

—Vonnegut, "The No-Talent Kid" (p. 18)

■ **Use quotation marks to enclose titles of short works, such as short stories, short poems,** articles, songs, episodes of television programs, and chapters and other parts of books.

Examples

SHORT STORY: "The Apprentice"
SHORT POEM: "Calling in the Cat"
ARTICLE: "Sacred Pieces from Sardinia"
SONG: "Rock of Ages"
TV EPISODE: "Heart of a Champion"
CHAPTER: "Learning About Amphibians"

7. APOSTROPHES

POSSESSIVE CASE

■ **To form the possessive of a singular noun, add an apostrophe and an *s.* Add only the apostrophe to a proper name ending in an *s* sound if the addition of *'s* would make the name awkward to pronounce.**

Examples

a **book's** pages   Mr. **Rodriguez'** office
the **child's** toys   **Hercules'** labors

■ **To form the possessive of a plural noun ending in *s,* add only the apostrophe.**

Examples

the **workers'** votes   the **students'** grades

■ **Do *not* use an apostrophe with possessive personal pronouns or with the possessive pronoun *whose.***

Incorrect

She thought that this pen was **your's.**

Correct

She thought that this pen was **yours.**

Incorrect

Who's desk is this?

Correct

Whose desk is this?

■ **To form the possessive of an indefinite pronoun, add an apostrophe and an *s.***

Examples

Somebody's umbrella is in the hall.
Everyone's opinion is important.

CONTRACTIONS

▌ **Use an apostrophe to show where letters, numbers, or words have been omitted in a contraction.**

Examples

I'm home. (I am)   **We've** found it. (We have)
Let's go. (Let us)   **Where'll** you be? (Where will)

in the **'90s** (1990s)   two **o'clock** (of the clock)

PLURALS

▌ **Use an apostrophe and an *s* to form the plurals of letters, numerals, signs, and of words referred to as words.**

Examples

That word has three *s'*s.
Write your *t'*s more clearly.
You can use *&'*s to save space.
I suggest cutting some of the *and'*s in the first paragraph.

8. HYPHENS

▌ **Use a hyphen to divide a word at the end of a line.**

Example

The writer Ursula K. Le Guin was born in California in 1929.

▌ **Do *not* divide a one-syllable word.**

Incorrect

A humorous imitation of a literary work is called a parody.

Correct

A humorous imitation of a literary work is **called** a parody.

▌ **Divide an already hyphenated word only at a hyphen.**

Incorrect

The puzzled tourist describes some strange-looking creatures made of metal and glass.

Correct

The puzzled tourist describes some **strange-looking** creatures made of metal and glass.

▌ **Do *not* divide a word so that one letter stands alone.**

Incorrect

The men didn't know if the filly was dead or a-live.

Correct

The men didn't know if the filly was dead or **alive.**

▌ **Use a hyphen with compound numbers from *twenty-one* to *ninety-nine* and with fractions used as adjectives.**

Examples

   fifty-two cards   a **two-thirds** majority

9. DASHES

▌ **Use a dash to indicate an abrupt break in thought or speech.**

Example

When you've been hanging by the arms for ten minutes over a very deep moat, wondering if it's too late to learn how to swim—(*He puts her down.*) What I meant was that I should *like* to hold you forever.

                            —Milne, *The Ugly Duckling* (p. 310)

10. PARENTHESES

▌ **Use parentheses to enclose material that is added to a sentence but is not considered of major importance.**

Example

Early in the century, Momma (we soon stopped calling her Grandmother) sold lunches to the sawmen in the lumberyard (east Stamps) and the seedmen at the cotton gin (west Stamps).

                  —Angelou, "I Know Why the Caged Bird Sings"
                            (p. 438)

Handbook for Revision

Glossary

The words listed in the glossary in the following pages are found in the selections in this textbook. You can use this glossary to look up words that are unfamiliar to you. Strictly speaking, the word *glossary* means a collection of technical, obscure, or foreign words found in a certain field of work. Of course, the words in this glossary are not "technical, obscure, or foreign," but are those that might present difficulty as you read the selections in this textbook.

Many words in the English language have several meanings. This glossary does not give all the meanings of a word. The meanings given here are the ones that apply to the words as they are used in the selections in the textbook. Words closely related in form and meaning are frequently listed together in one entry (**afflict** and **afflicted**), and the definition is given for the first form. Regular adverbs (ending in *-ly*) are defined in their adjective form, with the adverb form shown at the end of the definition.

The following abbreviations are used:

adj., adjective	*n.*, noun
adv., adverb	*v.*, verb

For more information about the words in this glossary, consult a dictionary.

A

abash (ə-băsh′) *v.* To make ill at ease or embarrassed.

abate (ə-bāt′) *v.* To lessen.

abdominal (ăb-dŏm′ə-nəl) *adj.* In the abdomen, the part of the body between the chest and the hips.

abduct (ăb-dŭkt′) *v.* To kidnap; take away by force.

abode (ə-bōd′) *n.* Home; dwelling place.

abominable (ə-bŏm′ə-nə-bəl) *adj.* Hateful.

abound (ə-bound′) *v.* To have a plentiful supply of.

abrupt (ə-brŭpt′) *adj.* Sudden.—**abruptly** *adv.*—**abruptness** *n.*

absorption (ăb-sôrp′shən, ăb-zôrp′-) *n.* The passing of matter into the bloodstream.

abundance (ə-bŭn′dəns) *n.* A great supply.—**abundant** *adj.*

abyss (ə-bĭs′) *n.* Any great depth or void.

accelerate (ăk-sĕl′ə-rāt′) *v.* To make something happen more quickly than usual.

accentuation (ăk-sĕn′chōō-ā′shən) *n.* Stress; emphasis.

access (ăk′sĕs′) *n.* **1.** A way of approaching or getting something. **2.** An outburst.

accession (ăk-sĕsh′ən) *n.* The attainment of power or rank.

acclaim (ə-klām′) *n.* General approval.

acclimate (ə-klī′mĭt, ăk′lə-māt′) *v.* To become accustomed to a foreign climate or to a new environment.

accommodate (ə-kŏm′ə-dāt′) *v.* To oblige.

account (ə-kount′) *v.* To consider.

acknowledge (ăk-nŏl′ĭj) *v.* To accept the validity of.

acute (ə-kyōōt′) *adj.* Severe.

adequate (ăd′i-kwĭt) *adj.* Sufficient; good enough.

adhere (ăd-hîr′) *v.* To stick to; stay attached.

adjacent (ə-jā′sənt) *adj.* Next to.

adjourn (ə-jûrn′) *v.* To end a meeting.

adversary (ăd′vər-sĕr′ē) *n.* An enemy.

adobe (ə-dō′bē) *n.* Sun-dried brick.

adorn (ə-dôrn′) *v.* To decorate; add ornaments.

adrift (ə-drĭft′) *adj.* and *adv.* Without direction or purpose.

aesthetic (ĕs-thĕt′ĭk) *adj.* Relating to principles of beauty.—**aesthetically** *adv.*

affable (ăf′ə-bəl) *adj.* Friendly; agreeable.

affect (ə-fĕkt′) *v.* To pretend.

affinity (ə-fĭn′ə-tē) *n.* **1.** A close relationship. **2.** An attraction.

affirm (ə-fûrm′) *v.* To declare something to be true.

afflict (ə-flĭkt′) *v.* To cause to suffer.—**afflicted** *adj.*

affront (ə-frŭnt′) *n.* Insult; offense to one's dignity.

aggravate (ăg′rə-vāt′) *v.* To annoy; irritate.—**aggravating** *adj.*

aggressive (ə-grĕs′ĭv) *adj.* **1.** Hostile. **2.** Bold.

aghast (ə-găst′, ə-gäst′) *adj.* Shocked.

agility (ə-jĭl′ĭ-tē) *n.* Nimbleness; quickness.

agitated (aj′ə-tāt′əd) *adj.* Upset; disturbed.—**agitation** *n.*

agony (ăg′ə-nē) *n.* Intense suffering.

alert (ə-lûrt′) *v.* To warn of danger.

alien (ā′lē-ən, āl′yən) *adj.* **1.** Foreign. **2.** Strange and unfriendly.

alight (ə-līt′) *v.* To settle; come down.

align (ə-līn′) *v.* To ally with; to line up with.

allot (ə-lŏt′) *v.* To give out; assign.

allure (ə-loor′) *v.* To tempt; attract.

allusion (ə-loo′zhən) *n.* A reference; mention.

aloft (ə-lôft′, ə-lŏft′) *adv.* High above the ground.

aloof (ə-loof′) *adv.* Apart; separate.

alpine (ăl′pīn′) *adj.* Growing above the timberline in high mountains.

altitude (ăl′tə-tood′, -tyood′) *n.* Height above sea level.

amber (ăm′bər) *adj.* Brownish-yellow in color.

amble (ăm′bəl) *v.* To walk in a slow, relaxed way.

amends (ə-mĕndz′) *n.* Something done or paid to make up for a loss or injury.

amiable (ā′mē-ə-bəl) *adj.* Friendly.—**amiably** *adv.*

amnesia (ăm-nē′zhə) *n.* A loss of memory.

ample (ăm′pəl) *adj.* Plentiful.

amplify (ăm′plə-fī) *v.* To increase or make louder.

amputate (ăm′pyoo-tāt′) *v.* To cut off.—**amputation** *n.*

anatomical (ăn′ə-tŏm′ĭ-kəl) *adj.* Referring to the structure of the body.

anatomy (ə-năt′ə-mē) *n.* The study of the shape and structure of animals and plants.

anecdote (ăn′ĭk-dōt′) *n.* A brief story.

anguish (ăng′gwĭsh) *n.* Great suffering.

animated (ăn′ə-mā′tĭd) *adj.* Lively.

annals (ăn′əlz) *n. pl.* Records; history.

antagonist (ăn-tăg′ə-nĭst) *n.* Enemy; opponent; adversary.

ante (ăn′tē) *n.* **1.** An amount of money that a player in a card game must put in the pot. **2.** The amount a person pays as his or her share.

anteroom (ăn′tĭ-room′, -room′) *n.* A small room that leads into a larger room.

anticipation (ăn-tĭs′ə-pā′shən) *n.* An expectation.

apologetic (ə-pŏl′ə-jĕt′ĭk) *adj.* Showing or expressing regret for a wrong.—**apologetically** *adv.*

appall (ə-pôl′) *v.* To shock; horrify.—**appalling** *adj.*

apparatus (ăp′ə-rā′təs, -răt′əs) *n.* Equipment.

apparition (ăp′ə-rĭsh′ən) *n.* A ghostly shape or figure.

appease (ə-pēz′) *v.* To satisfy; soothe.

appendix (ə-pĕn′dĭks) *n.* Additional material at the end of a book or article.

appraise (ə-prāz′) *v.* To judge the quality or value of.—**appraisingly** *adv.*

apprehensive (ăp′rĭ-hĕn′sĭv) *adj.* Fearful.—**apprehensively** *adv.*

appropriation (ə-prō′prē-ā′shən) *n.* Money given for a certain purpose.

apt (ăpt) *adj.* Suitable.—**aptly** *adv.*

ardent (är′dənt) *adj.* Passionate.—**ardently** *adv.*

arduous (är′joo-əs) *adj.* Difficult; laborious.

arid (ăr′ĭd) *adj.* Very dry.

aromatic (ăr′ə-măt′ĭk) *adj.* Having a pleasant aroma, either sweet, spicy, or pungent.

arrogance (ăr′ə-gəns) *n.* Overbearing pride.—**arrogant** *adj.*

ascend (ə-sĕnd′) *v.* To move upward.—**ascending** *adj.*

ascent (ə-sĕnt′) *n.* Upward climb.

askew (ə-skyoo′) *adv.* Crookedly.

aspect (ăs′pĕkt′) *n.* Appearance.

assailant (ə-sā′lənt) *n.* A person who attacks another.

assassin (ə-săs′ĭn) *n.* Murderer.

assault (ə-sôlt′) *n.* An attack.

assent (ə-sĕnt′) *v.* To agree.

assert (ə-sûrt′) *v.* To defend or maintain one's right or claim over something.

assess (ə-sĕs′) *v.* To judge the importance or value of.

asset (ăs′ĕt′) *n.* An advantage.

assiduous (ə-sĭj′oo-əs) *adj.* Hardworking.—**assiduously** *adv.*

attire (ə-tīr′) *n.* Clothing.

atypical (ā-tĭp′ĭ-kəl) *adj.* Unusual.

audacious (ô-dā′shəs) *adj.* Showing no fear; daring; bold.

auspicious (ô-spĭsh′əs) *adj.* Favorable.

authoritative (ə-thôr′ə-tā′tĭv, ə-thŏr′-) *adj.* Official; reliable.

avail (ə-vāl′) *v.* To make use of.

avenge (ə-vĕnj′) *v.* To get revenge for.

aver (ə-vûr′) *v.* To declare the truth of something.

avert (ə-vûrt′) *v.* To turn away.

awed (ôd) *adj.* Filled with respect and wonder.

awesome (ô′səm) *adj.* Inspiring wonder and dread.

B

badger (băj′ər) *v.* To nag.—**badgering** *n.*

baffle (băf′əl) *v.* To puzzle or confuse.

ă pat/ā pay/âr care/ä father/b bib/ch church/d deed/ĕ pet/ē be/f fife/g gag/h hat/hw which/ĭ pit/ī pie/îr pier/j judge/k kick/ l lid, needle/m mum/n no, sudden/ng thing/ŏ pot/ō toe/ô paw, for/oi noise/ou out/oo took/oo boot/p pop/r roar/s sauce/ sh ship, dish/t tight/th thin, path/th this, bathe/ŭ cut/ûr urge/v valve/w with/y yes/z zebra, size/zh vision/ə about, item, edible, gallop, circus/à *Fr.* ami/œ *Fr.* feu, *Ger.* schön/ü *Fr.* tu, *Ger.* über/ KH *Ger.* ich, *Scot.* loch/N *Fr.* bon.

baleful (bāl′fəl) *adj.* Threatening harm.

balk (bôk) *v.* To refuse.

banner (băn′ər) *adj.* Outstanding.

banter (băn′tər) *v.* To tease; make gentle fun of.

bar (bär) *v.* To prevent.

barometer (bə-rŏm′ə-tər) *n.* An instrument that measures air pressure and is used to predict change in the weather.

barren (băr′ən) *adj.* **1.** Empty. **2.** Without plant life.

barter (băr′tər) *v.* To trade.

bayou (bī′ōō, bī′ō) *n.* A swamp.

beacon (bē′kən) *n.* **1.** A warning signal. **2.** A light, such as a fire, used as a guide.

bearing (bâr′ĭng) *n.* A determination of someone's or something's position.

befit (bĭ-fĭt′) *v.* To be suitable.

befuddle (bĭ-fŭd′l) *v.* To confuse.

beguile (bĭ-gīl′) *v.* To charm or amuse.

behoove (bĭ-hōōv′) *v.* To be necessary or right for.

belfrey (bĕl′frē) *n.* A tower in which a bell is hung.

belligerent (bə-lĭj′ər-ənt) *adj.* Ready to fight.—**belligerently** *adv.*

benignant (bĭ-nĭg′nənt) *adj.* Kind.

bereft (bĭ-rĕft′) *adj.* Deprived of something.

beseech (bĭ-sēch′) *v.* To beg.

besiege (bĭ-sēj′) *v.* To surround in order to attack and capture.—**besieged** *adj.*

betray (bĭ-trā′) *v.* **1.** To be disloyal to. **2.** To reveal.—**betraying** *adj.*

bevy (bĕv′ē) *n.* A large group.

bier (bîr) *n.* A stand for holding a body or coffin.

bilk (bĭlk) *v.* To cheat.

billow (bĭl′ō) *v.* To cause to swell out.

blackjack (blăk′jăk′) *n.* A kind of oak tree with a black bark.

bland (blănd) *adj.* Calm; peaceful.—**blandly** *adv.*

blat (blăt) *n.* The bleating noise made by a sheep.—*v.* To bleat.

bleak (blēk) *adj.* Barren.

blunder (blŭn′dər) *v.* To move clumsily or carelessly into harm's way.

blunt (blŭnt) *adj.* Abrupt.—**bluntly** *adv.*

blurt (blûrt) *v.* To speak suddenly without thought.

bluster (blŭs′tər) *n.* **1.** Empty threats. **2.** Loud, noisy talk.

bog (bôg, bŏg) *n.* An area of soft, spongy, water-soaked ground.

boisterous (boi′stər-əs, -strəs) *adj.* Unruly; rough; violent.

bolt (bōlt) *v.* To run away.

booty (bōō′tē) *n.* Prey or plunder taken in war.

brace (brās) *v.* To prop up or support.

breach (brēch) *n.* An opening.

brimful (brĭm′fōōl′) *adj.* Completely full.

bristle (brĭs′əl) *v.* To show anger.

broach (brōch) *v.* To bring up a topic for discussion.

brocade (brō-kād′) *n.* A rich cloth with a raised design woven into it.

brood (brōōd) *v.* To hover.

buffet (bŭf′ĭt) *v.* To strike repeatedly; knock about.

bulrush (bōōl′rŭsh′) *n.* A cattail.

buoyant (boi′ənt, bōō′yənt) *adj.* **1.** Having buoyancy, the ability to keep afloat. **2.** Cheery.

burnish (bûr′nĭsh) *v.* To make shiny.—**burnished** *adj.*

C

cache (kăsh) *n.* A hiding place or storage place; also the things stored.

cajole (kə-jōl′) *v.* To coax.

calamity (kə-lăm′ĭ-tē) *n.* Extreme misfortune.

caliber (kăl′ə-bər) *n.* Degree of quality.

camouflage (kăm′ə-flazh′, -fläj′) *adj.* Merging with the background.

candid (kăn′dĭd) *adj.* Honest.

canker (kăng′kər) *v.* To become infected.

canopy (kăn′ə-pē) *n.* A cloth that serves as a roof or cover.

caper (kā′pər) *v.* To jump about playfully.

capitulate (kə-pĭch′ōō-lāt′) *v.* To give up.

captor (kăp′tər, -tôr′) *n.* Someone or something that holds a person or animal prisoner.

carillon (kăr′ə-lŏn′, kə-rĭl′yən) *n.* A set of bells that can be played from a keyboard.

carp (kärp) *n.* A kind of fish.

cascade (kăs-kād′) *v.* To fall in great amounts.

causeway (kôz′wā′) *n.* A raised road, often above water.

cavernous (kăv′ər-nəs) *adj.* **1.** Like a cave. **2.** Empty; hollow.

cavort (kə-vôrt′) *v.* To run and jump in a playful manner.

ceaseless (sēs′lĭs) *adj.* Continual; never-ending.

celebrity (sə-lĕb′rə-tē) *n.* A famous figure.

centennial (sĕn-tĕn′ē-əl) *n.* One-hundredth anniversary celebration.

chaos (kā′ŏs′) *n.* Complete disorder.

charger (chär′jər) *n.* A horse trained for battle.

chasm (kăz′əm) *n.* A deep crack in the earth's surface.

chastise (chăs-tīz′) *v.* To punish.—**chastisement** *n.*

chide (chīd) *v.* To scold.

chortle (chôrt′l) *n.* A laugh, midway between a chuckle and a snort.

chronicle (krŏn′ĭ-kəl) *v.* To record; list.

churn (chûrn) *v.* To stir up.

cicada (sĭ-kā′də, -kä′-) *n.* A family of large, flylike insects with transparent wings.

circumference (sər-kŭm′fər-əns) *n.* The measurement of the outer edge of a circular object.

clarion (klăr′ē-ən) *n.* Sound of a trumpet.

cleave (klēv) *v.* To split.

clemency (klĕm′ən-sē) *n.* Mercy.

clientele (klī′ən-tĕl′) *n.* Customers.

cloddish (klŏd′dĭsh) *adj.* Ignorant; dull; stupid.

coax (kōks) *v.* To persuade by using soothing words and an agreeable manner.

colossal (kə-lŏs′əl) *adj.* Gigantic.

commemorate (kə-mĕm′ə-rāt′) *v.* To honor the memory of someone or some event.

commend (kə-mĕnd′) *v.* To recommend.

commission (kə-mĭsh′ən) *v.* To give someone a job to do.—*n.* A fee or percentage paid to another for doing something.

common (kŏm′ən) *n.* A public park in a village or town.

commotion (kə-mō′shən) *n.* A noisy bustling about.

commute (kə-myōōt′) *v.* To travel back and forth regularly, as from one city to another.

compacted (kəm-păkt′ĭd) *adj.* Dense and packed down.

compassion (kəm-păsh′ən) *n.* Pity.

compensate (kŏm′pən-sāt′) *v.* To reimburse.

competent (kŏm′pə-tənt) *adj.* Able; capable.

compliance (kəm-plī′əns) *n.* The act of following a request.

component (kəm-pō′nənt) *n.* One of the main parts of something.

compressor (kəm-pres′ər) *n.* A machine for increasing the pressure of gases.

comprise (kəm-prīz′) *v.* To include; consist of.

compromise (kŏm′prə-mīz′) *v.* **1.** To settle by concessions from both sides. **2.** To put someone's good reputation in danger.

compulsory (kəm-pŭl′sə-rē) *adj.* Required.

con (kŏn) *v.* To study.

conceive (kən-sēv′) *v.* To think of.

condense (kən-dĕns′) *v.* To put in a briefer form.

condescend (kŏn′dĭ-sĕnd′) *v.* **1.** To lower oneself willingly. **2.** To deal with others in a proud or overbearing way.

condiment (kŏn′də-mənt) *n.* A seasoning for food, such as various spices.

confines (kən-fīns′) *n.* The limits or restrictions of a space.

confront (kən-frŭnt′) *v.* To stand or to put face to face with; to oppose.

congeal (kən-jēl′) *v.* To solidify.

congregate (kŏng′grĭ-gāt′) *v.* To gather into a flock or group.

conical (kŏn′ĭ-kəl) *adj.* Shaped like a cone.

conjure (kŏn′jər, kən-jōōr′) *v.* To summon or call upon.—**conjure up** To evoke or call to mind.

conscientious (kŏn′shē-ĕn′shəs) *adj.* Careful; painstaking.

consciousness (kŏn′shəs-nĭs) *n.* An awareness of one's thoughts, feelings, and sensory impressions.

consecrate (kŏn′sə-krāt′) *v.* To dedicate as something sacred.

consolation (kŏn′sə-lā′shən) *n.* Comfort.

consolidate (kən-sŏl′ə-dāt′) *v.* To strengthen; establish firmly.

conspicuous (kən-spĭk′yōō-əs) *adj.* Easily seen; noticeable.

constancy (kŏn′stən-sē) *n.* Steadfastness; firmness of purpose.

constitution (kŏn′stə-tōō′shən, -tyōō′shən) *n.* One's state of health.

constrained (kən-strānd′) *adj.* Forced; unnatural.

constraint (kən-strānt′) *n.* Lack of ease; unnaturalness in manner.

consul (kŏn′səl) *n.* An official representative of a government.

consume (kən-sōōm′, -syōōm′) *v.* To use up.

contagion (kən-tā′jən) *n.* A tendency to spread by contact.

contemplate (kŏn′təm-plāt′) *v.* **1.** To look at thoughtfully. **2.** To think about intently.

contend (kən-tĕnd′) *v.* **1.** To compete. **2.** To hold to be a fact.

contort (kən-tôrt′) *v.* To twist into unusual shapes.—**contorted** *adj.*

Glossary

ă pat/ā pay/âr care/ä father/b bib/ch church/d deed/ě pet/ē be/f fife/g gag/h hat/hw which/ĭ pit/ī pie/îr pier/j judge/k kick/ l lid, needle/m mum/n no, sudden/ng thing/ŏ pot/ō toe/ô paw, for/oi noise/ou out/ŏŏ took/ōō boot/p pop/r roar/s sauce/ sh ship, dish/t tight/th thin, path/*th* this, bathe/ŭ cut/ûr urge/v valve/w with/y yes/z zebra, size/zh vision/ə about, item, edible, gallop, circus/ä *Fr.* ami/œ *Fr.* feu, *Ger.* schön/ü *Fr.* tu, *Ger.* über/ΚΗ *Ger.* ich, *Scot.* loch/Ν *Fr.* bon.

contrite (kən-trīt′, kŏn′trīt′) *adj.* Repentant.

convene (kən-vēn′) *v.* To come together, as for a meeting.—**convened** *adj.*

converge (kən-vûrj′) *v.* To come together at a point; meet.

convey (kən-vā′) *v.* **1.** To carry from one place to another. **2.** To make known.

conviction (kən-vĭk′shən) *n.* A strong belief or certainty.

convoy (kŏn′voi′, kən-voi′) *v.* To accompany in order to protect.

convulsion (kən-vŭl′shən) *n.* A violent muscle spasm; a fit.

convulsive (kən-vŭl′sĭv) *adj.* Like a convulsion.—**convulsively** *adv.*

coordination (kō-ôr′də-nā′shən) *n.* The ability of the muscles to act together and result in a smooth action.—**coordinate** *adj.* Having all parts working together harmoniously.

countenance (koun′tə-nəns) *n.* A face.

counteract (koun′tər-ăkt′) *v.* To act against.

courtier (kôr′tē-ər, kōr′-, -tyər) *n.* One who serves a king or queen at court.

cove (kōv) *n.* A bay.

covet (kŭv′ĭt) *v.* **1.** To long for with envy. **2.** To want excessively.

covey (kŭv′ē) *n.* A small group.

cower (kou′ər) *v.* To shrink back, as in fear.

crag (krăg) *n.* A projecting rock.

cranium (krā′nē-əm) *n.* The skull.

cranny (krăn′ē) *n.* A crevice or small opening.

craven (krā′vən) *adj.* Cowardly.—**cravenly** *adv.*

credible (krĕd′ə-bəl) *adj.* Believable.

creed (krēd) *n.* A statement of belief.

crescent (krĕs′ənt) *n.* The moon in its first or last quarter, when its shape is thin and not rounded.—*adj.* Shaped like a crescent moon.

crest (krĕst) *n.* **1.** A crownlike growth on the head of some birds. **2.** Summit.

crystallize (krĭs′tə-līz′) *v.* To take definite shape.—**crystallized** *adj.*

cudgel (kŭj′əl) *v.* To strike, as with a club.

cunning (kŭn′ĭng) *adj.* Clever in a tricky way. *n.* Cleverness; trickery.—**cunningly** *adv.*

curative (kyoo′-ə-tĭv) *adj.* Something that cures; a remedy.

curator (kyoo-rā′tər, kyoor′ə-tər) *n.* A person in charge of a museum, library, or exhibit.

curb (kûrb) *v.* To control or hold back.

curry (kûr′ē) *v.* To groom a horse.

curt (kûrt) *adj.* Rude and abrupt.—**curtly** *adv.*

curvaceous (kûr-vā′shəs) *adj.* Pleasingly curved.

D

dauntless (dônt′lĭs, dänt′-) *adj.* Fearless; courageous.

dawdle (dôd′l) *v.* To spend time aimlessly.

daybed (dā′bĕd′) *n.* A couch that can also be used as a bed.

decade (dĕk′ād′, dĕ-kād′) *n.* A period of ten years.

decorum (dĭ-kôr′əm, dĭ-kōr′əm) *n.* Proper appearance.

decree (dĭ-krē′) *v.* To establish or decide.

deem (dēm) *v.* To judge.

default (dĭ-fôlt′) *n.* Failure to do something.

defile (dĭ-fīl′) *v.* To violate; insult; make unclean.

deft (dĕft) *adj.* Skillful.

degenerate (dĭ-jĕn′ə-rāt′) *v.* To deteriorate; become morally debased.

deign (dān) *v.* To stoop to do something beneath one's dignity.

dejection (dĭ-jĕk′shən) *n.* Sadness.

delectable (dĭ-lĕk′tə-bəl) *adj.* Delicious.

delete (dĭ-lēt′) *v.* To take out; omit.

delve (dĕlv) *v.* To study something deeply.

denizen (dĕn′ə-zən) *n.* One who lives in a certain place.

depression (dĭ-prĕsh′ən) *n.* A shallow hole.

deprive (dĭ-prīv′) *v.* To take something away from; dispossess.

depute (dĭ-pyoot′) *v.* To assign.

derelict (dĕr′ə-lĭkt) *adj.* Something or someone abandoned or deserted.

derisive (dĭ-rī′sĭv, -zĭv, -rĭs′iv, -rĭz′) *adj.* Mocking, ridiculing.—**derisively** *adv.*

descend (dĭ-sĕnd′) *v.* To go down.

desolation (dĕs′ə-lā′shən) *n.* **1.** Wretchedness. **2.** Wasteland; ruin.

deteriorate (dĭ-tîr′ē-ə-rāt′) *v.* To become worse.—**deterioration** *n.*

detract (dĭ-trăkt′) *v.* To take away; subtract.

devastation (dĕv-əs-tā′shən) *n.* Destruction; ruin.

devise (dĭ-vīz′) *v.* To plan.

devoid (dĭ-void′) *adj.* Completely lacking in; without.

devotee (dev′ə-tē′, -tā′) *n.* An adherent or devoted believer in someone or something.

dexterity (dĕk-stĕr′ə-tē) *n.* Skill.

diabolical (dī′ə-bŏl′ĭ-kəl) *adj.* Very cruel; fiendish.

diadem (dī′ə-dĕm′) *n.* Crown.

diameter (dī-ăm′ə-tər) *n.* Width; the distance across the center of a circular object.

differentiate (dĭf′ə-rĕn′shē-āt′) *v.* To see or understand the difference between, as sleeping or waking.

dilapidated (dĭ-lăp′ə-dā′tĭd) *adj.* In very bad condition.

dilate (dī-lāt′, dī′lāt′, dĭ-lāt′) *v.* To expand.

diligent (dĭl′-ə-jənt) *adj.* Careful.

din (dĭn) *v.* To stun with deafening noise.

dinghy (dĭng′ē) *n.* A small rowboat.

direful (dīr′fəl) *adj.* Fearful; terrible.

dirge (dûrj) *n.* **1.** A funeral song. **2.** Any sad piece of music.

discard (dĭs-kärd′) *v.* To remove from use.—**discarded** *adj.*

discern (dĭ-sûrn′, -zûrn′) *v.* To perceive or recognize.

discernable (dĭ-sûr′nə-bel, dĭ-zûr′-) *adj.* Capable of being seen or detected.

discerning (dĭ-sûr′nĭng, dĭ-zûr′-) *adj.* Keen; showing good understanding.

disciple (dĭ-sī′pəl) *n.* A pupil.

discomfiture (dĭs-kŭm′fĭ-chŏŏr) *n.* Discomfort.

disconcert (dĭs′kən-sûrt′) *v.* To confuse; upset.—**disconcerted** *adj.*

disconsolate (dĭs-kŏn′sə-lĭt) *adj.* Very sad.

discord (dĭs′kôrd′) *n.* **1.** A disagreement. **2.** In music, a lack of harmony.

discourse (dĭs′kôrs′, -kōrs′) *v.* To speak.

discreet (dĭ-skrēt′) *adj.* Careful; prudent.—**discreetly** *adv.*

discrimination (dĭs-krĭm′ə-nā′shən) *n.* Prejudice.

disdain (dĭs-dān′) *n.* Scorn.—**disdainful** *adj.*

disheveled (dĭ-shĕv′əld) *adj.* Disorderly in appearance.

dislodge (dĭs-lŏj′) *v.* To force from a position.

dismay (dĭs-mā′) *v.* To trouble; fill with fear.

dismember (dĭs-mĕm′bər) *v.* To cut the arms and legs off.

dispassionate (dĭs-păsh′ən-ĭt) *adj.* Fair; not partial.

dispel (dĭs-pĕl′) *v.* To get rid of.

dispirit (dĭs-pĭr′ĭt) *v.* To make unhappy; depress.—**dispirited** *adj.*

displace (dĭs-plās′) *v.* To take the place of.

display (dĭs-plā′) *v.* To show.

dispose (dĭs-pōz′) *v.* To arrange.—**dispose of** To get rid of.

disposition (dĭs′pə-zĭsh′ən) *n.* Management.

dispute (dĭs-pyōōt′) *n.* An argument.

dissemble (dĭ-sĕm′bəl) *v.* To pretend; feign.

dissolution (dĭs′-ə-lōō′shən) *n.* The process of dissolving into nothingness.

distort (dĭs-tôrt′) *v.* To twist out of shape.

distracted (di-străk′tĭd) *adj.* Confused.—**distraction** *n.*

divine (dĭ-vīn′) *v.* To guess; figure out.

docile (dōs′əl) *adj.* Tame; easily handled.

doff (dôf, dŏf) *v.* To take off.

dogged (dô′gĭd, dŏg′ĭd) *adj.* Persistent; stubborn.—**doggedly** *adv.*

doleful (dōl′fəl) *adj.* Sad.

dominance (dŏm′ə-nəns) *n.* Right; authority or control over.

dominion (də-mĭn′yən) *n.* Territory of control.

dosage (dō′sĭj) *n.* A specified amount of a medication.

drab (drăb) *adj.* Dull; colorless.

dread (drĕd) *adj.* Terrifying.

drone (drōn) *n.* **1.** A lazy person. **2.** A low, continuing sound.—*v.* To make a low, continuing sound.—**droning** *adj.*

drudgery (drŭj′ə-rē) *n.* Hard work.

dwindle (dwĭn′dl) *v.* To shrink; become smaller and smaller.

E

ebb (ĕb) *v.* **1.** To become less. **2.** To recede; flow back.

ebony (ĕb′ə-nē) *adj.* Black.

eclipse (ĭ-klĭps′) *v.* To reduce in importance.

ecstasy (ĕk′stə-sē) *n.* Great joy.

eddy (ĕd′ē) *n.* Circular motion.

efface (ĭ-fās′) *v.* To erase; wipe out.

ejaculation (ĭ-jăk′yə-lā′shən) *n.* A sudden shout.

elation (ĭ-lā′shən) *n.* Great joy.

elemental (ĕl′ə-mĕnt′l) *adj.* Basic; fundamental.

eloquence (ĕl′ə-kwəns) *n.* Forceful and graceful speech.

elude (ĭ-lōōd′) *v.* To escape from being noticed.

elusive (ĭ-lōō′sĭv) *adj.* Hard to find or catch.

emancipate (ĭ-măn′sə-pāt′) *v.* To free someone.—**emancipation** *n.*—**emancipated** *adj.*

emerge (ĭ-mûrj′) *v.* To come out.

Glossary

ă pat/ā pay/âr care/ä father/b bib/ch church/d deed/ĕ pet/ē be/f fife/g gag/h hat/hw which/ĭ pit/ī pie/îr pier/j judge/k kick/ l lid, needle/m mum/n no, sudden/ng thing/ŏ pot/ō toe/ô paw, for/oi noise/ou out/ŏŏ took/ōō boot/p pop/r roar/s sauce/ sh ship, dish/t tight/th thin, path/th this, bathe/ŭ cut/ûr urge/v valve/w with/y yes/z zebra, size/zh vision/ə about, item, edible, gallop, circus/ä *Fr.* ami/œ *Fr.* feu, *Ger.* schön/ü *Fr.* tu, *Ger.* über/KH *Ger.* ich, *Scot.* loch/N *Fr.* bon.

emigrate (ĕm′ĭ-grāt′) *v.* To leave one's country to live elsewhere.—**emigration** *n.*

eminent (ĕm′ə-nənt) *adj.* Outstanding.

employ (ĕm-ploi′) *v.* To use.

encompass (ĕn-kŭm′pəs, ĭn-) *v.* To include.

encumber (ĕn-kŭm′bər) *v.* To weigh down or burden.

endeavor (ĕn-dĕv′ər) *v.* To try.

engulf (ĕn-gŭlf′, ĭn-) *v.* To cover completely.

enmesh (ĕn-mĕsh′) *v.* To entangle, as in a net.

enrapture (ĕn-răp′chər, ĭn-) *v.* To fill with joy.—**enraptured** *adj.*

enterprising (ĕn′tər-prī′zĭng) *adj.* Ambitious and imaginative.

entrails (ĕn′trālz′, trəlz) *n.* The inner parts of a thing.

entrance (ĕn-trăns′, -träns′, ĭn-) *v.* To fill with delight.—**entranced** *adj.*

entreat (ĕn-trēt′, ĭn-) *v.* To plead; beg.

enumerate (ĭ-nōō′mə-rāt′, ĭ-nyōō′-) *v.* To list.

envelop (ĕn-vĕl′əp, ĭn-) *v.* To cover completely.

envision (ĕn-vĭzh′ən) *v.* To picture in the imagination.

epilogue (ĕp′ə-lôg′) *n.* A short portion added to a work of literature to complete or conclude the story.

epitaph (ĕp′ə-tăf, -täf′) *n.* The writing on a tombstone.

era (îr′ə, ĕr′ə) *n.* An important period of time.

erratic (ĭ-răt′ĭk) *adj.* Straying; wandering.

escort (ĕs′kôrt′) *v.* To accompany.

esteem (ĕ-stēm′, ĭ-stēm′) *v.* To hold in high regard.—**esteem** *n.*

etch (ĕch) *v.* **1.** To draw; outline. **2.** To make a clear impression.

etiquette (ĕt′ə-kĕt′, -kĭt) *n.* Proper social or official behavior.

evoke (ĭ-vōk′) *v.* To call forth; draw out.

evolve (ĭ-vŏlv′) *v.* To develop.

exact (ĕg-zăkt′, ĭg-) *v.* To demand.

exalt (ĕg-zôlt′, ĭg-) *v.* To raise in importance.—**exalted** *adj.*

exasperate (ĕg-zăs′pə-rāt′, ĭg-) *v.* to annoy greatly.—**exasperating** *adj.*

exasperation (ĕg-zăs′pə-rā′shən, ĭg-) *n.* A feeling of great annoyance.

excavate (ĕk′skə-vāt′) *v.* To make a hole by hollowing out.

exertion (ĕg-zûr′shən, ĭg-) *n.* Effort.

exhilaration (ĕg-zĭl′ə-rā′shən, ĭg-) *n.* Excitement.

exodus (ĕk′sə-dəs) *n.* The departure of a large number of people.

exotic (ĕg-zŏt′ĭk, ĭg-) *adj.* **1.** Interestingly different. **2.** Foreign.

expire (ĕk-spīr′, ĭk-) *v.* To die.

exploit (ĕk′sploit′, ĭk-sploit′) *n.* A bold or heroic deed.

exposition (ĕk′spə-zĭsh′ən) *n.* Public exhibition.

exquisite (ĕks′kwĭ-zĭt) *adj.* Of great beauty.

extinguish (ĕk-stĭng′gwĭsh, ĭk-) *v.* To put out.

extract (ĕk-străkt′, ĭk-) *v.* To draw out or pull out.

exult (ĕg-zŭlt′, ĭg-) *v.* To rejoice.

F

fabulous (făb′yə-ləs) *adj.* Astonishing; hard to believe.

faculty (făk′əl-tē) *n.* The ability or power to perform some function.

fan (făn) *v.* To blow on.

fanatical (fə-năt′ĭ-kəl) *adj.* Enthusiastic beyond reason.

farce (färs) *n.* Something ridiculous and laughable.

fastidious (fă-stĭd′ē-əs, fə-) *adj.* Fussy; not easily pleased.

fathom (făth′əm) *v.* To understand; get to the bottom of.

felicitous (fĭ-lĭs′ə-təs) *adj.* Fit; well-chosen.

fell (fĕl) *v.* To cut down.—*adj.* Cruel.

fen (fĕn) *n.* Swamp; marsh.

ferment (fər′mĕnt′) *v.* To undergo a chemical reaction that changes sugar into other compounds.—**fermented** *adj.*

ferocity (fə-rŏs′ə-tē) *n.* Fierceness; cruelty.

fervent (fûr′vənt) *adj.* Showing great warmth of feeling; intense.—**fervently** *adv.*

fervor (fûr′vər) *n.* Intense feeling.

fester (fĕs′tər) *v.* To produce pus.—**festering** *adj.*

festoon (fĕs-tōōn′) *n.* A wreath.—*v.* To decorate with wreathes of flowers or leaves.

fetch (fĕch) *v.* To get or bring.

finesse (fĭ-nĕs′) *n.* Subtlety or artfulness.

finicky (fĭn′ĭ-kē) *adj.* Hard to please.

fissure (fĭsh′ər) *n.* A deep, narrow crack.

flail (flāl) *v.* To strike out vigorously but erratically.

flank (flăngk) *n.* Side. *v.* To be at the side of.

flaunt (flônt) *v.* To wave with pride.

flay (flā) *v.* To beat wildly, without aim.

fleck (flĕk) *n.* A tiny mark or spot.

flinch (flĭnch) *v.* To draw back or make a face, as if in pain.

flog (flŏg, flôg) *v.* To whip.—**flogger** *n.*

florid (flôr′ĭd) *adj.* Red-faced; ruddy.

flotsam (flŏt′səm) *n.* Wreckage.

flounder (floun′dər) *v.* To move clumsily.—**flounder-ing** *adj.*

flout (flout) *v.* To be scornful.

fluent (floo′ənt) *adj.* Flowing easily.—**fluently** *adv.*

forage (fôr′ĭj, fŏr′-) *n.* Food for animals.

forbidding (fər-bĭd′ĭng, fôr-) *adj.* Having a danger-ous or threatening appearance.

foray (fôr′ā′) *n.* A raid.

forefront (fôr′frŭnt′) *n.* The very front.

ford (fôrd, fōrd) *n.* A place in a river that is shallow enough to be crossed on foot.

forfeit (fôr′fĭt) *v.* To surrender.

forlorn (fôr-lôrn′, fər-) *adj.* Wretched; pitiful.

formidable (fôr′mə-də-bəl) *adj.* **1.** Causing fear or wonder. **2.** Commanding respect and admira-tion.

formula (fôr′myə-lə) *n.* A statement expressed in symbols and numbers.

fortify (fôr′tə-fī′) *v.* To build up strength.—**fortified** *adj.*

frantic (frăn′tĭk) *adj.* Wild with fear or pain; desper-ate.—**frantically** *adv.*

fraternity (frə-tûr′nə-tē) *n.* Fellowship.

frenzied (frĕn′zēd) *adj.* Frantic.

frenzy (frĕn′zē) *n.* Wild excitement.

fretful (frĕt′fəl) *adj.* Peevish; plaintive.

front (frŭnt) *v.* To face.

fruitless (froot′lĭs) *adj.* Unsuccessful.

fumigate (fyoo′mĭ-gāt′) *v.* To disinfect.—**fumigated** *adj.*

functional (fŭngk′shən-əl) *adj.* Practical; usable.

furrow (fûr′ō) *n.* A groove.

G

gait (gāt) *n.* Step; way of walking.

gallant (gə-lănt′, -länt′, găl′ənt) *n.* An attentive, cour-teous man.

gape (gāp, găp) *v.* To be wide open.—**gaping** *adj.*

gaunt (gônt) *adj.* Thin; underfed-looking.—**gauntly** *adv.*

genial (jēn′yəl, jē′nē-əl) *adj.* Friendly.—**genially** *adv.*

gesticulate (jĕ-stĭk′yə-lāt′) *v.* To make gestures; use motions with or instead of speech.

ghastly (găst′lē, gäst′-) *adj.* **1.** Like a ghost. **2.** Horrible.

giddy (gĭd′ē) *adj.* Dizzy; dazed.—**giddily** *adv.*

gilt (gĭlt) *n.* Gold applied in a thin layer.

gingerly (jĭn′jər-lē) *adv.* Very carefully; cautiously.

girth (gûrth) *n.* The measurement around some-thing.

glacial (glā′shəl) *adj.* Produced by glaciers—huge masses of ice and snow.

gland (glănd) *n.* One of many organs, cells, or groups of cells that produce a secretion.

glandular (glăn′jə-lər) *adj.* Referring to the activity of the glands.

glare (glâr) *v.* To stare angrily.

glaze (glāz) *v.* To apply a shiny coating.—**glazing** *n.*

glean (glēn) *v.* To find out bit by bit.

glib (glĭb) *adj.* Speaking easily and smoothly, often in a way that is not convincing.—**glibly** *adv.*

gloat (glōt) *v.* To take great pleasure in.

glower (glou′ər) *v.* To stare angrily.

glut (glŭt) *v.* To supply or fill to excess.

gluttonous (glŭt′n-əs) *adj.* Given to eating greedily and excessively.

gorge (gôrj) *n.* A deep, narrow passage with steep rocky sides and enclosed between mountains. *v.* To stuff with food.

gourmet (goor-mā′) *n.* One who is a fine judge of food and drink.

grapple (grăp′əl) *v.* To struggle.

grate (grāt) *v.* To rub something noisily against another object.

grave (grāv) *adj.* Serious; dignified.—**gravely** *adv.*

grenadier (grĕn′ə-dîr′) *n.* Originally, a soldier trained to use grenades.

grille (grĭl) *n.* A metal grating.

grimace (grĭm′ĭs, grĭ-mās′) *n.* A twisting or distor-tion of the face to express pain or disgust.

grisly (grĭz′lē) *adj.* Horrifying.

grope (grōp) *v.* To search in an uncertain way.

gross (grōs) *adj.* Referring to total income before deductions are made.

grotesque (grō-tĕsk′) *adj.* Strangely misshapen.—**grotesquely** *adv.*

grovel (grŭv′əl, grŏv′-) *v.* To assume a humble posi-tion; cringe.

Glossary

grueling (grōō′ə-ling) *adj.* Exhausting; causing extreme fatigue.

gruff (grŭf) *adj.* Surly; harsh.—**gruffly** *adv.*

gullible (gŭl′ə-bəl) *adj.* Easily fooled or cheated.

gully (gŭl′lē) *n.* A deep ditch.—*v.* To cut a deep ditch in the earth.

gutter (gŭt′ər) *v.* To melt quickly and run off in a stream as the wax of a burning candle does.

guttural (gŭt′ər-əl) *adj.* Coming from the throat.

gyrate (jī′rāt′) *v.* To circle.

H

haggard (hăg′ərd) *adj.* Worn-out looking; exhausted.

hallow (hăl′ō) *v.* To make holy.

hamlet (hăm′lĭt) *n.* A small village.

hardy (här′dē) *adj.* Strong and healthy.

harken (här′kən) *v.* To listen carefully.

harass (hăr′əs, hə-răs′) *v.* To worry; trouble.— **harassed** *adj.*

harry (hăr′ē) *v.* To torment.

hassock (hăs′ək) *n.* A large, padded footstool.

haughty (hô′tē) *adj.* Proud.

haunch (hônch, hänch) *n.* The hip and upper thigh.

haunt (hônt, hänt) *n.* A favorite place.

heathen (hē′*th*ən) *adj.* Unbelieving; pagan.

heed (hēd) *v.* To pay attention to.

heedless (hēd′lĭs) *adj.* Unmindful; thoughtless.

herald (hĕr′əld) *n.* Messenger.

herculean (hûr′kyə-le′ən, -kyōō′lē-ən) *adj.* Very difficult.

hew (hyōō) *v.* To carve or shape.

hoist (hoist) *v.* To lift; raise.

homestead (hōm′stĕd′) *n.* Farm property.

horde (hôrd, hōrd) *n.* A large, disorderly group.

hospitable (hŏs′pĭ-tə-bəl, hŏ-spĭt′ə-bəl) *adj.* Welcoming; friendly toward guests.

host (hōst) *n.* An army.

hostile (hŏs′təl) *adj.* Unfriendly.

hover (hŭv′ər, hŏv′) *v.* To stay suspended in one place.

hoyden (hoid′n) *n.* A tomboy.

hull (hŭl) *n.* The frame of a ship.

hussy (hŭz′ē, hŭs′ē) *n.* A bold, immoral woman.

hybrid (hī′brĭd) *adj.* Produced from a mixture of parent plants.

hypocrite (hĭp′ə-krĭt′) *n.* One who pretends to have qualities he or she does not have.—**hypocritical** *adj.*

hypodermic syringe (hī′pə-dûr′mĭk sə-rĭnj′, sîr′ĭnj) *n.* A glass tube with attached needle, used for giving injections.

hypothesis (hī-pŏth′ə-sĭs) *n.* A theory; a possible explanation.

I

illiteracy (ĭ-lĭt′ər-ə-sē) *n.* The inability to read and write.

immanent (ĭm′ə-nənt) *adj.* Existing or remaining within; inherent.

immemorial (ĭm′ə-môr′ē-l, -mōr′ē-əl) *adj.* Extending beyond recorded history.

immense (ĭ-mĕns′) *adj.* Huge; enormous.

imminent (ĭm′ə-nənt) *adj.* About to happen.

immortal (ĭ-môrt′l) *adj.* One who lives forever.

impact (ĭm′păkt′) *n.* Force.

impair (ĭm-pâr′) *v.* To weaken; damage.

impartial (ĭm-pär′shəl) *adj.* Not prejudiced; even-handed.

impassioned (ĭm-păsh′ənd) *adj.* Very emotional.

impede (ĭm-pēd′) *v.* To interfere with.

impend (ĭm-pĕnd′) *v.* To be about to happen.— **impending** *adj.*

impenetrable (ĭm-pĕn′ĭ-trə-bəl) *adj.* Incapable of being passed through or broken into.

imperceptible (ĭm′pər-sĕp′tə-bəl) *adj.* Barely noticeable.—**imperceptibly** *adv.*

imperial (ĭm-pîr′ē-əl) *adj.* Referring to an emperor.

imperious (ĭm-pîr′ē-əs) *adj.* Domineering; arrogant (like an emperor).

impersonation (ĭm-pûr′sə-nā′shən) *n.* The embodiment or representation in physical form of some idea.

impetuous (ĭm-pĕch′ōō-əs) *adj.* Eager to act; impatient.

implement (ĭm′plə-mənt) *n.* A tool.

implicit (ĭm-plĭs′ĭt) *adj.* without doubt; absolute.— **implicitly** *adv.*

implore (ĭm-plôr′, -plōr′) *v.* To beg; ask.—**imploring** *adj.*—**imploringly** *adv.*

imply (ĭm-plī′) *v.* To suggest; hint.

imposing (ĭm-pō′zĭng) *adj.* Impressive because of its size.

inanimate (ĭn-ăn′ə-mĭt) *adj.* Lifeless.

inarticulate (ĭn′är-tĭk′yə-lĭt) *adj.* **1.** Unable to speak. **2.** Not clearly spoken.

inaudible (ĭn-ô′də-bəl) *adj.* Not able to be heard.

incentive (ĭn-sĕn′tĭv) *n.* Something that stimulates one to action.

incision (ĭn-sĭzh′ən) *n.* A cut.

incisor (ĭn-sī′zər) *n.* A tooth shaped for cutting—the middle four upper and middle four lower teeth.

Glossary

inclination (ĭn′klə-nā′shən) *n.* A desire to do something.

incompetent (ĭn-kŏm′pə-tənt) *adj.* Not capable.

incomprehensible (ĭn′kŏm-prĭ-hĕn′sə-bəl) *adj.* Not able to be understood.

incredible (ĭn-krĕd′ə-bəl) *adj.* Unbelievable.

incursion (ĭn-kûr′zhən) *n.* A sudden invasion or raid into hostile territory.

indecorous (ĭn-dĕk′ər-əs) *adj.* Not proper.

indelible (ĭn-dĕl′ə-bəl) *adj.* Not able to be erased.

indifferent (ĭn-dĭf′ər-ənt, ĭn-dĭf′rənt) *adj.* Uninterested; not caring one way or the other.

indignant (ĭn-dĭg′nənt) *adj.* Very angry.—**indignantly** *adv.*

indignation (ĭn′dĭg-nā′shən) *n.* Great anger; outrage.

indispensable (ĭn′dĭs-pĕn′sə-bəl) *adj.* Necessary.

indistinct (ĭn′dĭs-tĭngkt′) *adj.* Not clear.

indomitable (ĭn-dŏm′ə-tə-bəl) *adj.* Not easily defeated or discouraged.

indubitable (ĭn-dōō′bə-tə-bəl, ĭn-dyōō′-) *adj.* Definite; without a doubt.—**indubitably** *adv.*

induce (ĭn-dōōs′, -dyōōs′) *v.* To persuade.

indulgent (ĭn-dŭl′jənt) *adj.* Overly considerate or generous.—**indulgently** *adv.*—**indulge** *v.*

inert (ĭn-ûrt′) *adj.* Without power to move; inactive.

inevitable (ĭn-ĕv′ə-tə-bəl) *adj.* Sure to happen.—**inevitability** *n.*

infallible (ĭn-făl′ə-bəl) *adj.* Never wrong.—**infallibly** *adv.*

infamous (ĭn′fə-məs) *adj.* Having a bad reputation.

infectious (ĭn-fĕk′shəs) *adj.* Catching.

infernal (ĭn-fûr′nəl) *adj.* Evil.

infinite (ĭn′fə-nĭt) *adj.* Limitless; endless (like infinity).

infirmity (ĭn-fûr′mĭ-tē) *n.* Disability; defect.

inflexible (ĭn-flĕk′sə-bəl) *adj.* Unchanging; firm.

inflict (ĭn-flĭkt′) *v.* To force something unpleasant on someone.—**inflicted** *adj.*

infuse (ĭn-fyōōz′) *v.* To fill with.

ingenious (ĭn-jēn′yəs) *adj.* Very clever.

inherent (ĭn-hîr′ənt, hĕr′ənt) *adj.* Essential.

inimitable (ĭn-ĭm′ĭ-tə-bəl) *adj.* Not able to be imitated; matchless.

innate (ĭ-nāt′, ĭn′āt′) *adj.* Natural; inborn.

innuendo (ĭn′yōō-ĕn′dō) *n.* An indirect, derogatory remark; insinuation.

inquest (ĭn′kwĕst′) *n.* An investigation.

inquisitive (ĭn-kwĭz′ə-tĭv) *adj.* Overly curious; prying.

insignia (ĭn-sĭg′nē-ə) *n.* A badge; emblem.

insinuate (ĭn-sĭn′yōō-āt′) *v.* To hint at or suggest something in an indirect way.—**insinuating** *adj.*

insistent (ĭn-sĭs′tənt) *adj.* Demanding.

insolent (ĭn′sə-lənt) *adj.* Disrespectful.—**insolently** *adv.*

instinctive (ĭn-stĭngk′tĭv) *adj.* Inborn; not learned.

insufferable (ĭn-sŭf′ər-ə-bəl) *adj.* Impossible to put up with.

insulate (ĭn′sə-lāt′, ĭns′yə-) *v.* To prevent the loss of heat or electricity by covering with a nonconducting material.

insuperable (ĭn-sōō′pər-ə-bəl) *adj.* Not to be surmounted or overcome.

insupportable (ĭn′sə-pôr′tə-bəl, -pōr′) *adj.* Not capable of giving support.

intangible (ĭn-tăn′jə-bəl) *adj.* Not capable of being precisely identified.

intercept (ĭn′tər-sĕpt′) *v.* To stop or cut off.

intercourse (ĭn′tər-kôrs′, -kōrs′) *n.* Association with others, as in conversation.

interlude (ĭn′tər-lōōd′) *n.* An intervening period of time.

interminable (ĭn-tûr′mə-nə-bəl) *adj.* Endless.

intervene (ĭn′tər-vēn′) *v.* **1.** To interfere. **2.** To be located between.

intimate (ĭn′tə-mĭt) *adj.* **1.** Close in affection; very friendly. **2.** Essential; innermost.—**intimately** *adv.*

intimate (ĭn′tə-māt′) *v.* To hint.—**intimation** *n.*

intimidate (ĭn-tĭm′ĭ-dāt′) *v.* To frighten through threats of violence.

intolerable (ĭn-tŏl′ər-ə-bəl) *adj.* Unbearable.

intolerant (ĭn-tŏl′ər-ənt) *adj.* Unwilling to put up with.

intricate (ĭn′trĭ-kĭt) *adj.* Elaborately detailed.

intrigue (ĭn′trēg′, ĭn-trēg′) *n.* A secret plot.

introspective (ĭn′trə-spĕk′tĭv) *adj.* Given to private thought; contemplative.

invariable (ĭn-vâr′ē-ə-bəl) *adj.* Unchanging; constant.—**invariably** *adv.*

inventory (ĭn′vən-tôr′ē, -tōr′ē) *n.* A list of supplies on hand. *v.* To make an itemized list of.

Glossary

invincible (ĭn-vĭn′sə-bəl) *adj*. Unbeatable.

involuntary (ĭn-vŏl′ən-tĕr′ē) *adj*. Done without conscious thought.

invulnerable (ĭn-vŭl′nər-ə-bəl) *adj*. Not able to be harmed.

irk (ûrk) *v*. To annoy or tire; vex.

ironic (ī-rŏn′ĭk) *adj*. Opposite to what might be expected.—**ironically** *adv*.

irresistible (ĭr′ĭ-zĭs′tə-bəl) *adj*. Strongly appealing.

irresolute (ĭ-rĕz′ə-lo͞ot′) *adj*. Undecided; uncertain.

isolate (ī′sə-lāt, ĭs′ə-) *v*. To separate; set apart.

itinerant (ī-tĭn′ər-ənt, ĭ-tĭn′-) *adj*. Going from place to place in order to work.

J

jaunt (jônt, jänt) *n*. A short trip.

jest (jĕst) *v*. To joke.—**jestingly** *adv*.

jolt (jōlt) *v*. To jar or shake up.

jostle (jŏs′əl) *v*. To push and shove.

jovial (jō′vē-əl) *adj*. Good-humored.—**jovially** *adv*.

jubilation (jo͞o′bə-lā′shən) *n*. Rejoicing.

judicious (jo͞o-dĭsh′əs) *adj*. Wise (like a judge).

jut (jŭt) *v*. To stick out.

K

kiln (kĭl, kĭln) *n*. An oven for baking or firing substances.

kindle (kĭnd′l) *v*. To start (a fire).

kindling (kĭnd′lĭng) *n*. Bits of dry wood or other dry material used to start a fire.

knoll (nōl) *n*. A small hill.

L

lacerate (lăs′ə-rāt′) *v*. To tear, or cut jaggedly.—**lacerated** *adj*.

lagoon (lə-go͞on′) *n*. Shallow pool of water.

lair (lâr) *n*. A wild animal's den.

lament (lə-mĕnt′) *v*. **1.** To grieve; mourn. **2.** To regret deeply.—*n*. An expression of grief.

lamentation (lăm′ən-tā′shən) *n*. An expression of grief.

lank (lăngk) *adj*. Tall and thin.

lateral (lăt′ər-əl) *adj*. Sideways.

lattice (lăt′ĭs) *adj*. Woven like a screen.

leaden (lĕd′n) *adj*. Burdened; depressed.

league (lēg) *n*. A distance of about three miles.

leer (lîr) *v*. To look at slyly or evilly.

legacy (lĕg′ə-sē) *n*. Something handed down from an ancestor.

legend (lĕj′ənd) *n*. A caption or inscription.

legion (lē′jən) *n*. A large group; band.

lethargy (lĕth′ər-jē) *n*. A state of dullness or inaction; stupor; apathy.—**lethargic** *adj*.

liability (lī′ə-bĭl′ə-tē) *n*. A disadvantage.

liberality (lĭb′ə-răl′ə-tē) *n*. Generosity.

limber (lĭm′bər) *v*. To loosen up by exercise.—*adj*. Supple; lithe.

listless (lĭst′lĭs) *adj*. Showing a lack of energy or interest.—**listlessly** *adv*.

literate (lĭt′ər-ĭt) *adj*. Able to read and write.

lithe (līth) *adj*. Supple; nimble.

loathe (lōth) *v*. To hate intensely.

lob (lŏb) *v*. To move clumsily.

loll (lŏl) *v*. **1.** To lounge about in a relaxed way. **2.** To hang out loosely.

loom (lo͞om) *v*. **1.** To appear dimly or indistinctly, as through a mist. **2.** To appear to the mind as large or threatening.

lope (lōp) *v*. To run with a long stride.

low (lō) *v*. Moo.—**lowing** *n*.

lucidity (lo͞o-sĭd′ĭ-tē) *n*. Clearness; intelligence.

ludicrous (lo͞o′dĭ-krəs) *adj*. Ridiculous; laughable.

lumber (lŭm′bər) *v*. To move slowly and clumsily.

luminous (lo͞o′mə-nəs) *adj*. **1.** Able to shine in the dark; glowing. **2.** Filled with light.

lurid (loor′ĭd) *adj*. Glowing or glaring through a haze.

lurk (lûrk) *v*. To wait in ambush; remain concealed.

lusterless (lŭs′tər-lĭs) *adj*. Dull.

lusty (lŭs′tē) *adj*. Vigorous; strong.

M

macabre (mə-kä′brə, -bər) *adj*. Gruesome; horrible.

majestic (mə-jĕs′tĭk) *adj*. Grand; dignified.

makeshift (māk′shĭft′) *adj*. Made quickly and used as a substitute.

malice (măl′ĭs) *n*. A desire to hurt others.—**malicious** *adj*.

malignant (mə-lĭg′nənt) *adj*. Harmful; malicious.

manacle (măn′ə-kəl) *n*. **1.** A shackle or restraint. **2.** Something that prevents or impedes action.

maneuver (mə-no͞o′vər, -nyo͞o′-) *v*. To move.

manifest (măn′ə-fĕst′) *adv*. Plain; apparent; evident; obvious.—**manifestly** *adv*.

manifold (măn′ə-fōld) *adj*. Many and different.

mantle (măn′təl) *n*. **1.** A sleeveless cape or cloak. **2.** A thick covering, as of snow.

massive (măs′ĭv) *adj*. Unusually large.

mast (măst, mäst) *n*. A pole used to support the sails and rigging of a ship.

mastodon (măs′tə-dŏn′) *n.* An extinct animal that resembled an elephant.

matron (mā′trən) *n.* A married woman, one mature in age and appearance.—**matronly** *adv.*

matted (măt′ĭd) *adj.* Tangled.

maul (môl) *v.* To beat or tear at roughly.

meager (mē′gər) *adj.* Scanty; insufficient.

melancholy (mĕl′ən-kŏl′ē) *n.* Great sadness.—*adj.* Very sad.

mellow (mĕl′ō) *adj.* Rich.—**mellowness** *n.*

menace (mĕn′ĭs) *n.* A threat.

mercurial (mər-kyŏŏr′ē-əl) *adj.* Changing quickly (like mercury).

merge (mûrj) *v.* To blend in.

mesa (mā′sə) *n.* A hill or plateau having steep sides and a flat top, common in the southwestern United States.

meticulous (mə-tĭk′yə-ləs) *adj.* Extremely precise about minor details; fussy.

midwifery (mĭd′wĭf′rē, -wī′fər-ē) *n.* The practice of assisting in childbirth.

minstrel (mĭn′strəl) *n.* Poet-musician.

misbegotten (mĭs′bĭ-gŏt′n) *adj.* **1.** Abnormally conceived. **2.** Wretched.

mishap (mĭs′hăp′, mĭs-hăp′) *n.* An unfortunate accident.

mobile (mō′bəl, -bēl′, -bīl′) *adj.* Movable.—**mobility** *n.*

mobilize (mō′bə-līz′) *v.* To move into action.

molest (mə-lĕst′) *v.* To bother or to harm.

momentarily (mō′mən-târ′ə-lē) *adv.* For a short time.

momentum (mō-mĕn′təm) *n.* The driving force of a moving object.

monotony (mə-nŏt′n-ē) *n.* Sameness.

monsoon (mŏn-sōōn′) *n.* A condition of high wind and heavy rain.

moor (mōōr) *n.* Wasteland.

mooring (mōōr′ĭng) *n.* The place where a boat is tied up.

morass (mə-răs′, mô-) *n.* A swamp.

mortal (môrt′l) *n.* A human being.

mottled (mŏt′ld) *adj.* Covered with spots of different colors and shapes.

murky (mûr′kē) *adj.* Dark and gloomy.—**murkily** *adv.*

muster (mŭs′tər) *v.* To assemble; gather together.

mutilate (myōōt′l-āt′) *v.* To cut off or otherwise destroy a part of the body.—**mutilated** *adj.*

mutinous (myōōt′n-əs) *adj.* Rebellious.

N

naiveté (nä′ēv-tā′) *n.* Simplicity; lack of worldliness.

nettle (nĕt′l) *n.* A stinging or prickly plant.

neurosurgeon (nōōr′ō-sûr′jən, nyōō′-) *n.* A doctor who specializes in surgery involving the nervous system.

nock (nŏk) *v.* To fit an arrow into a bow.

nonchalant (nŏn′shə-länt′) *adj.* Unconcerned; casual.—**nonchalantly** *adv.*—**nonchalance** *n.*

nondescript (nŏn′dĭ-skrĭpt′) *adj.* Commonplace; uninteresting.

nontransferable (nŏn-trăns-fûr′ə-bəl) *adj.* Not usable by anyone else.

nostalgia (nŏ-stăl′jə, nə-) *adj.* A longing for something in the past or far away.

novelty (nŏv′əl-tē) *n.* Something new or unusual.

O

oasis (ō-ā′sĭs) *n.* An area of peace and welcome.

oblique (ō-blēk′) *adj.* Slanting; sloping.

oblivious (ə-blĭv′ē-əs) *adj.* Not aware.

obnoxious (ŏb-nŏk′shəs, əb-) *adj.* Highly unlikable; hateful.

obscure (ŏb-skyōōr′, əb-) *adj.* Little known.

obsession (əb-sĕsh′ən, ŏb-) *n.* An idea or thought that is impossible to get rid of.

obstinate (ŏb′stə-nĭt) *adj.* Stubborn.—**obstinately** *adv.*

omen (ō′mən) *n.* A sign of something to come.

ominous (ŏm′ə-nəs) *adj.* Warning; threatening.—**ominously** *adv.*

onslaught (ŏn′slôt′, ôn′-) *n.* An attack.

opportunist (ŏp′ər-tōō′nĭst, -tyōō′nĭst) *n.* One who takes unfair advantage of another or of a situation.

oppression (ə-prĕsh′ən) *n.* Power used to crush or to persecute.

orbit (ôr′bĭt) *n.* Path someone moves in.

ordeal (ôr-dēl′) *n.* A very unpleasant experience.

ornate (ôr-nāt′) *adj.* Very fancy.

orthodontist (ôr′thə-dŏn′tĭst) *n.* A dentist who specializes in straightening teeth.

Glossary

ă pat/ā pay/âr care/ä father/b bib/ch church/d deed/ĕ pet/ē be/f fife/g gag/h hat/hw which/ĭ pit/ī pie/îr pier/j judge/k kick/ l lid, needle/m mum/n no, sudden/ng thing/ŏ pot/ō toe/ô paw, for/oi noise/ou out/ŏŏ took/ōō boot/p pop/r roar/s sauce/ sh ship, dish/t tight/th thin, path/*th* this, bathe/ŭ cut/ûr urge/v valve/w with/y yes/z zebra, size/zh vision/ə about, item, edi- ble, gallop, circus/à *Fr.* ami/œ *Fr.* feu, *Ger.* schön/ü *Fr.* tu, *Ger.* über/ᴋʜ *Ger.* ich, *Scot.* loch/ɴ *Fr.* bon.

Glossary **767**

767

ostentatious (ŏs′tĕn-tā′shəs, ŏs′tən-) *adj.* Showy.—**ostentatiously** *adv.*

overwhelming (o′vər-hwĕl′mĭng) *adj.* Overpowering.

P

pagan (pā′gən) *n.* **1.** A heathen. **2.** A non-Christian.

palatable (păl′ə-tə-bəl) *adj.* Fit to be eaten; pleasant to the taste.

paltry (pôl′trē) *adj.* Insignificant; worthless.

pandemonium (păn′də-mō′nē-əm) *n.* Noisy confusion.

paroxysm (păr′ək-sĭz′əm) *n.* A sudden outburst.

passionate (păsh′ən-ĭt) *adj.* Intense.—**passionately** *adv.*

paternal (pə-tûr′nəl) *adj.* Referring to a father.

patron (pā′trən) *n.* **1.** A customer. **2.** A person who supports an artist or musician.

peer (pîr) *n.* **1.** Nobleman. **2.** Equal.

peerless (pîr′lĭs) *adj.* Unmatched.

peeve (pēv) *v.* To annoy.

pelt (pĕlt) *n.* The skin of an animal, with the fur or hair still on it.

penetrate (pĕn′ĭ-trāt′) *v.* To force a way into; pierce.

pensive (pĕn′sĭv) *adj.* Thoughtful.

pent (pĕnt) *adj.* Shut in.

perception (pər-sĕp′shən) *n.* Sensation; realization; knowledge.

percussion (pər-kŭsh′ən) *n.* A musical instrument, such as a drum, that is played by striking.

perilous (pĕr′əl-əs) *adj.* Risky.

perimeter (pə-rĭm′ə-tər) *n.* The outer boundary of something.

periscope (pĕr′ə-skōp′) *n.* A tubelike instrument with lenses and mirrors that enables one to see an area otherwise not viewable.

permeate (pûr′mē-āt′) *v.* To spread through.—**permeated** *adj.*

perpendicular (pûr′pən-dĭk′yə-lər) *adj.* At a right angle.—**perpendicularly** *adv.*

perpetuate (pər-pĕch′ōō-āt′) *v.* To preserve the memory of someone or something.

perpetuity (pûr′pə-tōō′ə-tē, -tyōō′ə-tē) *n.* Eternity; an unlimited time.

perplexity (pər-plĕk′sə-tē) *n.* Confusion.

persistent (pər-sĭs′tənt) *adj.* Repeated; continued.—**persistently** *adv.*

perverse (pər-vûrs′) *adj.* Stubbornly difficult.

pervert (pər-vûrt′) *v.* To lead astray; corrupt.

petition (pə-tĭsh′ən) *n.* A formal request signed by a number of people.

pewter (pyōō′tər) *n.* Objects made from pewter, a mixture of tin and other metals.

phobia (fō′bē-ə) *n.* An exaggerated fear.

phonetic (fə-nĕt′ĭk) *adj.* Referring to the sounds of language.

photostat (fō′tə-stăt′) *v.* To make a copy of something using a certain kind of machine.

piety (pī′ə-tē) *n.* Reverence; religious devotion.

pinion (pĭn′yən) *v.* To tie or bind.—**pinioned** *adj.*

pinnacle (pĭn′ə-kəl) *n.* The highest point; summit; peak.

piston (pĭs′tən) *n.* A disk or cylinder fitted into a tube and moved back and forth by pressure, as in an engine.

placid (plăs′ĭd) *adj.* Quiet; peaceful.

plague (plāg) *adj.* A pestilence or epidemic disease.

pliable (plī′ə-bəl) *adj.* Flexible.—**pliability** *n.*

pliant (plī′ənt) *adj.* Easily bent; flexible.

pluck (plŭk) *n.* Courage.

plumage (plōō′mĭj) *n.* Feathers of a bird.

plume (plōōm) *n.* A large feather or cluster of feathers worn as decoration.

plummet (plŭm′ĭt) *n.* Something that drops straight down.

plunder (plŭn′dər) *v.* To rob.

poise (poiz) *v.* To be balanced in a certain position.—**poised** *adj.*

ponder (pŏn′dər) *v.* To think deeply about.

pore (pôr, pōr) *v.* To study or read with care; with *over.*

portal (pôrt′l, pōrt′l) *n.* An entrance; door.

posterity (pŏ-stĕr′ə-tē) *n.* All those yet to be born.

potent (pōt′nt) *adj.* Powerful; strong.—**potency** *n.*

potentiality (pə-tĕn′shē-ăl′ə-tē) *n.* A possible ability.—**potential** *adj.*

pounce (pouns) *v.* To spring at and seize.

preamble (prē′ăm′bəl) *n.* An introductory statement.

precinct (prē′sĭngkt) *n.* District or area.

precipice (prĕs′ə-pĭs) *n.* A high vertical or overhanging face of rock; the brink of a cliff.

precipitous (prĭ-sĭp′ə-təs) *adj.* Extremely steep.

predator (prĕd′ə-tər, -tôr′) *n.* An animal that lives by catching and feeding on other animals.

predecessor (prĕd′ə-sĕs′ər, prē′də-) *n.* One who comes before another, as in a job or a political office.

predicament (prĭ-dĭk′ə-mənt) *n.* A difficult situation.

predominant (prĭ-dŏm′ə-nənt) *adj.* Most important.—**predominantly** *adv.*

preeminence (prē-ĕm′ə-nəns) *n.* The condition of holding first place in a particular grouping.—**preeminently** *adv.*

prefix (prē-fĭks′, prē′fĭks′) *v.* To add to the beginning of, or put before, a word.

preliminary (prĭ-lĭm′ə-nĕr′ē) *n.* Something that comes before or introduces something else.

premature (prē′mə-tyŏŏr′, -tŏŏr′, chŏŏr′) *adj.* Unexpectedly early; before the correct time for.—**prematurely** *adv.*

preoccupy (prē-ŏk′yə-pī) *v.* To absorb; engross the thoughts of.

prescribe (prĭ-skrīb′) *v.* To order or ordain beforehand.

prestige (prĕ-stēzh′, -stēj) *n.* High standing in the eyes of others.

presume (prĭ-zŏŏm′) *v.* To dare.

presumption (prĭ-zŭmp′shən) *n.* The act of taking something for granted.

pretext (prē′tĕkst′) *n.* An excuse.

prevail (prĭ′vāl′) *v.* To win out.

prevailing (prĭ-vā′lĭng) *adj.* Predominant; widespread.

prevalence (prĕv′ə-ləns) *n.* The state of being widespread.—**prevalent** *adj.*

prim (prĭm) *adj.* Formal; stiff.—**primly** *adv.*

prime (prīm) *adj.* Excellent; of finest quality.—*v.* To prepare.—*n.* The peak of perfection.

proclaim (prō-klām′, prə-) *v.* To announce or declare.

prodigious (prə-dĭj′əs) *adj.* **1.** Amazing. **2.** Huge.

prodigy (prŏd′ə-jē) *n.* An unusually gifted child.

profound (prə-found′, prō) *adj.* **1.** Deep. **2.** Wise.—**profoundly** *adv.*

profusion (prə-fyŏŏ′zhən, prō-) *n.* Abundance.

progressive (prə-grĕs′ĭv) *adj.* Ever-increasing.

prophesy (prŏf′ə-sī′) *v.* To predict.

proposition (prŏp′ə-zĭsh′ən) *n.* **1.** A statement that something is true. **2.** Proposal or plan.

propound (prə-pound′) *v.* To offer for consideration.

prostrate (prŏs′trāt′) *adj.* Stretched out.

protrude (prō-trŏŏd′) *v.* To jut out.

providential (prŏv′ə-dĕn′shəl) *adj.* Of or resulting from divine intervention.—**providentially** *adv.*

provocation (prŏv′ə-kā′shən) *n.* An action that annoys or irritates.

provoke (prə-vōk′) *v.* To make angry.

prowess (prou′ĭs) *n.* Superior strength or courage.

prudent (prŏŏd′ənt) *adj.* Cautious.

prune (prŏŏn) *v.* To cut off dead or live parts of a plant in order to improve growth or shape.

pry (prī) *v.* To examine in a nosy way.

pulsation (pŭl-sā′shən) *n.* Throbbing or rhythmical beating.—**pulsate** *v.*

pummel (pŭm′əl) *v.* To strike at repeatedly.

pungent (pŭn′jənt) *adj.* Sharp-smelling.

puny (pyŏŏ′nē) *adj.* Weak.

Q

quarry (kwôr′ē, kwŏr′ē) *n.* **1.** A mine from which marble and other kinds of stone are taken. **2.** A hunted object or person.

quash (kwŏsh) *v.* To suppress or put down.

quaver (kwā′vər) *v.* To shake; tremble.—*n.* A vibration.—**quavering** *adj.*

quicksilver (kwĭk′sĭl′vər) *n.* Mercury, a metal that moves very quickly in its liquid form.

quizzical (kwĭz′ĭ-kəl) *adj.* Puzzled; questioning.—**quizzically** *adv.*

R

radius (rā′dē-əs) *n.* A measure of circular area or extent.

rail (rāl) *v.* To scold; abuse.

rampart (răm′pärt) *n.* A defense.

rapacious (rə-pā′shəs) *adj.* Greedy; plundering.—**rapaciously** *adv.*

raptor (răp′tər) *n.* Bird of prey.

rash (răsh) *adj.* Unthinking; reckless.—**rashly** *adv.*

rasp (răsp, räsp) *v.* To scrape with a harsh sound.

rational (răsh′ən-əl) *adj.* Reasonable; able to think clearly.

ravage (răv′ĭj) *v.* To destroy.

rave (rāv) *v.* To talk like an insane person.

ravening (răv′ən-ĭng) *adj.* Greedy.

ravenous (răv′ən-əs) *adj.* Extremely hungry.

ravine (rə-vēn′) *n.* A deep, narrow valley.

raze (rāz) *v.* To demolish; destroy completely.

realm (rĕlm) *n.* A kingdom.

ă pat/ā pay/âr care/ä father/b bib/ch church/d deed/ĕ pet/ē be/f fife/g gag/h hat/hw which/ĭ pit/ī pie/îr pier/j judge/k kick/ l lid, needle/m mum/n no, sudden/ng thing/ŏ pot/ō toe/ô paw, for/oi noise/ou out/ŏŏ took/ŏŏ boot/p pop/r roar/s sauce/ sh ship, dish/t tight/th thin, path/*th* this, bathe/ŭ cut/ûr urge/v valve/w with/y yes/z zebra, size/zh vision/ə about, item, edible, gallop, circus/ā *Fr.* ami/œ *Fr.* feu, *Ger.* schön/ü *Fr.* tu, *Ger.* über/KH *Ger.* ich, *Scot.* loch/N *Fr.* bon.

rear (rîr) *v.* To bring up (a child).

rebound (rē′bound′, rĭ-) *v.* To spring back.

rebuke (rĭ-byo͞ok′) *v.* To show disapproval.

recede (rĭ-sēd′) *v.* To become farther away; withdraw.

reckless (rĕk′lĭs) *adj.* Heedless; without regard for consequences.—**recklessly** *adv.*

reclaim (rĭ-klām′) *v.* To take back.

recoil (rĭ-koil′) *v.* To spring back.

recommence (rē′kə-mĕns′) *v.* To begin again.

recompense (rĕk′əm-pĕns′) *v.* To reward.

reconnaissance (rĭ-kŏn′ə-səns, zəns) *n.* An advance study made by exploring and surveying.

recurrent (rĭ-kûr′ənt) *adj.* Happening repeatedly.

redemptive (rĭ-dĕmp′tĭv) *adj.* Serving to make amends for.

reformation (rĕf′ər-mā′shən) *n.* A change to a better way of behaving.

refrain (rĭ-frān′) *v.* To keep someone from doing something.

regal (rē′gəl) *adj.* Kingly.

regression (rĭ-grĕsh′ən) *n.* A return to an earlier, less-advanced state.

rehabilitate (rē′hə-bĭl′ə-tāt′) *v.* To return someone or something to a useful condition.

relent (rĭ-lĕnt′) *v.* To become less firm or strict about something.—**relenting** *adj.*

relentless (rĭ-lĕnt′lĭs) *adj.* **1.** Continuous. **2.** Pitiless; unmerciful; unfeeling.

relevant (rĕl′ə-vənt) *adj.* To the point.—**relevancy** *n.*

relic (rĕl′ĭk) *n.* A fragment of something that no longer exists.

relish (rĕl′ĭsh) *v.* To enjoy the flavor of.

reluctance (rĭ-lŭk′təns) *n.* Unwillingness.—**reluctant** *adj.*—**reluctantly** *adv.*

reminiscence (rĕm′ə-nĭs′əns) *n.* A memory.

remorse (rĭ-môrs′) *n.* Strong regret over something.

remote (rĭ-mōt′) *adj.* Aloof; cold; indifferent.

render (rĕn′dər) *v.* **1.** To give or hand over. **2.** To make.

rendezvous (rän′dā-vo͞o′, rän′də-) *n.* A meeting place.

renown (rĭ-noun′) *n.* Fame.

repast (rĭ-păst′, -päst′) *n.* A feast; meal.

repercussion (rē′pər-kŭsh′ən) *n.* A result, often an unpleasant one.

repose (rĭ-pōz′) *v.* To lie at rest.

reproach (rĭ-prōch′) *v.* To blame; scold.—**reproachfully** *adv.*

repugnant (rĭ-pŭg′nənt) *adj.* Disagreeable; arousing disgust.

resigned (rĭ-zīnd′) *adj.* Giving in; accepting without complaint.—**resignedly** *adv.*—**resign** *v.*—**resignation** *n.*

resolute (rĕz′ə-lo͞ot) *adj.* Firm; determined.—**resolutely** *adv.*

resolution (rĕz′ə-lo͞o′shən) *n.* Firmness; determination.

resolve (rĭ-zŏlv′) *n.* Intention; determination.—*v.* To decide or make a decision about.

resonant (rĕz′ə-nənt) *adj.* Rich-sounding.

resonate (rĕz′ə-nāt′) *v.* To make a prolonged, repeated, echoing sound.—**resonating** *adj.*

resort (rĭ′zôrt′) *v.* To turn to for help.

resound (rĭ-zound′) *v.* To sound loudly.

resource (rē′sôrs′) *n.* A source of support or help.

resourceful (rĭ-sôrs′fəl, rĭ-sōrs′-, rĭ-zôrs′-, rĭ-zōrs′-) *adj.* Able to deal effectively with a situation.

respirator (rĕs′pə-rā′tər) *n.* **1.** A mask worn to keep substances in the air from being breathed in. **2.** A machine that gives artificial respiration.

respite (rĕs′pĭt) *n.* Period of rest or relief.

resplendent (rĭ-splĕn′dənt) *adj.* Shining.

restrain (rĭ-strān′) *v.* To control; limit.

restriction (rĭ-strĭk′shən) *n.* A limit.

resurrect (rĕz′ə-rĕkt′) *v.* To bring back into life or into use.

retaliate (rĭ-tăl′ē-āt′) *v.* To strike back.

retard (rĭ-tärd′) *v.* To slow down.

retrieve (rĭ-trēv′) *v.* To find or regain.

revel (rĕv′əl) *n.* A celebration.

revelry (rĕv′əl-rē) *n.* A noisy celebration.

reverberate (rĭ-vûr′bə-rāt′) *v.* To re-echo.

revere (rĭ-vîr′) *v.* To respect.

reverent (rĕv′ər-ənt) *adj.* Showing respect, as for something sacred.—**reverently** *adv.*

righteous (rī-chəs) *adj.* Virtuous; just.—**righteousness** *n.*

rigid (rĭ′jĭd) *adj.* Not moving.

ritual (rĭch′o͞o-əl) *n.* A set routine or procedure.

roan (rōn) *n.* A horse with a dark brown coat sprinkled with white hairs.

rosette (rō-zĕt′) *n.* A decorative ornament resembling a rose, made of ribbon or silk.

rouse (rouz) *v.* To awaken.

rousing (rou′zĭng) *adj.* Stirring; exciting.

rout (rout) *v.* To defeat.

rucksack (rŭk′săk′, ro͞ok′-) *n.* A backpack; knapsack.

ruffle (rŭf′əl) *v.* To make feathers stand out.

rummage (rŭm′ĭj) *v.* To search thoroughly; ransack.

rupture (rŭp′chər) *n.* Bursting.

ruthless (rōōth′lĭs) *adj.* Cruel.

S

sack (săk) *v.* To loot or plunder.

sacrilege (săk′rə-lĭj) *n.* A lack of respect for a sacred person or object.

sage (sāj) *adj.* Wise.—**sagely** *adv.*

sallow (săl′ō) *adj.* Of a pale, sickly color.

sally (săl′ē) *v.* To come out.

salutary (săl′yə-tĕr′ē) *adj.* Doing good; wholesome; beneficial.

salvage (săl′vĭj) *v.* To rescue or save something left after a disaster for further use.—*n.* Things saved from destruction after a disaster.

sarcastic (sär-kăs′tĭk) *adj.* Given to sharp, biting humor.—**sarcastically** *adv.*

saunter (sôn′tər) *v.* To walk in a leisurely way.

savor (să′vər) *v.* To enjoy.

scabbard (skăb′ərd) *n.* A sheath for a sword or other weapon.—*v.* To cover or sheathe a weapon.

scamper (skăm′pər) *v.* To hurry away.

scan (skăn) *v.* To look at carefully.

scant (skănt) *adj.* Meager; inadequate.

scat (skăt) *n.* Animal excrement.

scavenger (skăv′ən-jər) *n.* An animal that feeds on dead or decaying matter.

scoff (skôf, skŏf) *v.* To jeer at.

score (skôr, skōr) *n.* Twenty of anything.

scour (skour) *v.* To search thoroughly.

scowl (skoul) *v.* To frown; show disapproval.

scrutinize (skrōōt′n-īz′) *v.* To inspect carefully.

scud (skŭd) *v.* To be driven before a wind.

scuttle (skŭt′l) *v.* To run off in haste; hurry.

scythe (sī*th*) *n.* A long-handled blade used to cut grass.

sear (sîr) *v.* To burn.

securities (sĭ-kyōōr′ə-tēz) *n.* Stock certificates or bonds.

sedate (sĭ-dāt′) *v.* To induce calm or sleep.

self-assurance (sĕlf′ə-shōōr′əns) *n.* Confidence.

semantic (sə-măn′tĭk) *adj.* Referring to the relationships between words and meanings.

senility (sĭ-nĭl′ə-tē) *n.* A condition, usually occurring in old people, in which the mental powers are weakened.

sensibility (sĕn′sə-bĭl′ə-tē) *n.* The ability to respond emotionally.

shake (shāk) *n.* A rough shingle.

shallow (shăl′ō) *adj.* Not deep.

shamble (shăm′bəl) *v.* To walk in an awkward way.

shearing (shîr′ĭng) *adj.* Breaking apart as a result of stress exerted in two directions at once.

sheath (shēth) *n.* A case or covering, as for a sword.

sheen (shēn) *n.* Glossy brightness.

sheepish (shē′pĭsh) *adj.* Bashful; embarrassed.—**sheepishly** *adv.*

sheer (shîr) *adj.* Nearly perpendicular; steep.

shimmer (shĭm′ər) *v.* To shine.—**shimmering** *adj.*

shirk (shûrk) *v.* To avoid doing something that should be done.—**shirker** *n.*

shrew (shrōō) *n.* A woman who scolds a lot.

sidle (sīd′l) *v.* To move sideways, often in a sneaky way.

siege (sēj) *n.* An organized attack.

simultaneous (sī′məl-tā′nē-əs) *adj.* Happening at the same time.—**simultaneously** *adv.*

sinew (sĭn′yōō) *n.* A tendon.

sinewy (sĭn′yōō-ē) *adj.* Strong; tough; muscular.

singular (sĭng′gyə-lər) *adj.* Unusual; peculiar.—**singularly** *adv.*

sinister (sĭn′ĭ-stər) *adj.* Evil-seeming.

skiff (skĭf) *n.* A small boat.

skirmish (skûr′mĭsh) *n.* A minor conflict or battle.

skirt (skûrt) *v.* To move along the edge or border of.

skulk (skŭlk) *v.* To move stealthily.

slacken (slăk′ən) *v.* To slow up.

slack (slăk) *n.* Looseness.

slake (slāke) *v.* To satisfy thirst.

slight (slīt) *v.* To treat rudely or scornfully.

smite (smīt) *v.* **1.** To hit. **2.** To attack.

smolder (smōl′dər) *v.* To burn without a flame.—**smoldering** *adj.*

sneer (snîr) *v.* To show contempt.

sodden (sŏd′n) *adj.* Thoroughly wet.

sojourn (sō′jûrn, sō-jûrn′) *v.* To stay for a short time.

solace (sŏl′ĭs) *n.* Comfort.

solicitous (sə-lĭs′ə-təs) *adj.* Attentive.

solicitude (sə-lĭs′ə-tōōd′, -tyōōd′) *n.* Care; concern.

solitude (sŏl′ə-tōōd′, -tyōōd′) *n.* Aloneness.

sorrel (sôr′əl, sŏr′-) *adj.* Light reddish brown.

Glossary

ă pat/ā pay/âr care/ä father/b **bib**/ch **church**/d **deed**/ĕ pet/ē be/f **fife**/g **gag**/h **hat**/hw **which**/ĭ **pit**/ī **pie**/îr **pier**/j **judge**/k **kick**/ l **lid**, need**le**/m **mum**/n **no**, sud**den**/ng **thing**/ŏ pot/ō **toe**/ô **paw**, **for**/oi **noise**/ou **out**/ŏŏ **took**/ōō **boot**/p **pop**/r **roar**/s **sauce**/ sh **ship**, di**sh**/t **tight**/th **thin**, **path**/*th* **this**, ba**the**/ŭ **cut**/ûr **urge**/v **valve**/w **with**/y **yes**/z **zebra**, **size**/zh vi**si**on/ə **about**, **item**, edi**ble**, gal**lop**, cir**cus**/à *Fr.* **ami**/œ *Fr.* **feu**, *Ger.* **schön**/ü *Fr.* **tu**, *Ger.* **über**/KH *Ger.* **ich**, *Scot.* lo**ch**/N *Fr.* **bon**.

sovereignty (sŏv′ər-ən-tē) *n.* Independence.

span (spăn) *v.* To stretch completely across, as a bridge spans a body of water.—*n.* A period of time.

spar (spär) *n.* A pole used to support a ship's rigging.

sparing (spâr′ĭng) *adj.* Careful; restrained.

spasm (spăz′əm) *n.* A sudden, short-lived burst of activity or energy.

specter (spĕk′tər) *n.* **1.** A ghost. **2.** Something that causes fear or terror.

spectral (spĕk′trəl) *adj.* Ghost-like.

speculation (spĕk′yə-lā′shən) *n.* An unproved explanation; thought; guess.—**speculate** *v.*

spell (spĕl) *n.* A short period of time.

spew (spyōō) *v.* To cast out.

spontaneous (spŏn-tā′nē-əs) *adj.* Not planned.

spout (spout) *v.* To gush out forcefully.

spraddle (sprăd′l) *v.* To sprawl.—*n.* Sprawl.

sprout (sprout) *v.* To develop shoots, like a plant.

spume (spyōōm) *n.* The foamy part of a wave.

squall (skwôl) *n.* A sudden, brief, violent storm.

squat (skwŏt) *adj.* Short and thick.

stabilize (stā′bə-līz′) *v.* To become steady.

stalk (stôk) *v.* To pursue in a furtive or stealthy manner.

staple (stā′pəl) *n.* A basic food, such as flour, sugar, or salt.

stark (stärk) *adj.* Unrelieved; complete.

starveling (stärv′lĭng) *adj.* Starving.

stately (stāt′lē) *adj.* Dignified.

stethoscope (stĕth′ə-skōp′) *n.* An instrument used to listen to pulse beats.

stifle (stī′fəl) *v.* **1.** To smother. **2.** To hold back.—**stifled** *adj.*

still (stĭl) *v.* To quiet; calm.

stilted (stĭl′tĭd) *adj.* Stiff; formal.

stimulant (stĭm′yə-lənt) *n.* A substance that speeds up bodily activity.

stipulate (stĭp′yə-lāt′) *v.* To state the conditions of an agreement.—**stipulated** *adj.*

stoical (stō-ĭ-kəl) *adj.* Not caring about either pain or pleasure.

stolid (stŏl′ĭd) *adj.* Dull; lacking in imagination.—**stolidly** *adv.*

stout (stout) *adj.* **1.** Brave. **2.** Thick.—**stoutly** *adv.*

strew (strōō) *v.* To scatter.

stride (strīd) *v.* To walk with long, rapid steps.

stupendous (stōō-pĕn′dəs, styōō-) *adj.* **1.** Amazing. **2.** Huge.

stupor (stōō′pər, styōō′-) *n.* Daze.

subdue (səb-dōō′, -dyōō′) *v.* To control or conquer.

subside (səb-sīd′) *v.* To sink or settle.

succeed (sək-sēd′) *v.* **1.** To come after; follow. **2.** To have success.

succession (sək-sesh′ən) *n.* A series.

successor (sək-sĕs′ər) *n.* One who comes after another, as in a job or a political office.

sufferance (sŭf′ər-əns, sŭf′rəns) *n.* Tolerance; permission.

suite (swēt) *n.* A group of attendants.

sullen (sŭl′ən) *adj.* Glum; ill-humored.—**sullenly** *adv.*

sumptuous (sŭmp′chōō-əs) *adj.* Magnificent.

sup (sŭp) *v.* To eat.

suppliant (sŭp′lĭ-ənt) *n.* Someone who begs humbly.

supplication (sŭp′lĭ-kā′shən) *n.* Petition; humble request.

supposition (sŭp′ə-zĭsh′ən) *n.* Something that is supposed, or considered to be true.

surge (sûrj) *v.* To swell and roll violently in waves.

surly (sûr′lē) *adj.* Rude; ill-natured.

surmise (sər-mīz′) *v.* To guess; suppose.

surmount (sər-mount′) *n.* **1.** To overcome. **2.** To be on top of.

surpass (sər-păs′) *v.* To outdo; exceed.

surreptitious (sûr′əp-tĭsh′əs) *adj.* Secret.—**surreptitiously** *adv.*

suspend (sə-spĕnd′) *v.* To hang supported, as from a chain.

sustain (sə-stān′) *v.* **1.** To keep up; keep in effect. **2.** To experience; undergo.—**sustained** *adj.*

swagger (swăg′ər) *v.* To walk in a proud, self-important way.

swath (swŏth, swôth) *n.* A long strip.

sweltering (swĕl′tər-ĭng) *adj.* Oppressively hot and humid.

symmetrical (sĭ-mĕt′rĭ-kəl) *adj.* Regular; wellproportioned; with corresponding parts; possessing balance and beauty of form.

syndrome (sĭn′drōm′) *n.* A group of symptoms that occur together in a particular illness.

T

taboo (tə-bōō′, tă-) *adj.* Forbidden; prohibited.

taciturn (tăs′ĭ-tûrn′) *adj.* Untalkative.

tactful (tăkt′fəl) *adj.* Considerate of another's feelings.—**tactfully** *adv.*

talon (tăl′ən) *n.* A sharp claw.

tangible (tăn′jə-bəl) *adj.* Real; definite.

tantalization (tăn′tə-lĭ-zā′shən) *n.* Teasing or torment.

tarry (tăr′ē) *v.* To stay longer than planned; linger.

taunt (tônt) *v.* To make fun of; mock.

taut (tôt) *adj.* **1.** Tight. **2.** Tense.

tawny (tô′nē) *adj.* Golden brown in color.

taxidermy (tăk′sə-dûr′mē) *n.* The art of stuffing and mounting the skins of dead animals to make them seem lifelike.

tedious (tē′dē-əs) *adj.* Boring.

teem (tēm) *v.* To be crowded or full of.—**teeming** *adj.*

teeter (tē′tər) *v.* To move unsteadily.

temper (tĕm′pər) *v.* To treat steel to make it hard and flexible.—**tempered** *adj.*

tempest (tĕm′pĭst) *n.* A severe storm.

tenacious (tə-nā′shəs) *adj.* **1.** Hard to get rid of. **2.** Stubborn.—**tenaciously** *adv.*

tend (tĕnd) *v.* To look after.

tentative (tĕn′tə-tĭv) *adj.* Not definite, uncertain.—**tentatively** *adv.*

terse (tûrs) *adj.* Brief and to the point.

theory (thē′ə-rē, thîr′ē) *n.* An idea offered to explain a happening.

thermal (thûr′məl) *adj.* Designed to retain body heat.

thrash (thrăsh) *v.* To move about wildly.

threshold (thrĕsh′ōld′, thrĕsh′hōld′) *n.* A doorway.

thrive (thrīv) *v.* To flourish; prosper.

tiller (tĭl′ər) *n.* A part of a boat used in steering.

tinge (tĭnj) *v.* To give a slight hint of.

titanic (tī-tăn′ĭk) *adj.* Large and powerful.

tolerable (tŏl′ər-ə-bəl) *adj.* Fairly good.—**tolerably** *adv.*

tolerate (tŏl′ə-rāt′) *v.* To endure; bear.

torrent (tôr′ənt, tŏr′-) *n.* A violent, swift rush of water.

totem (tō′təm) *n.* Image or emblem that serves as the symbol of a family or clan.

totter (tŏt′ər) *v.* To be unsteady; rock or shake.—**tottering** *adj.*

tourniquet (tŏŏr′nĭ-kĭt, -kā′, tûr′-) *n.* Any device tied around a part of the body (over an artery) to stop bleeding.

tousle (tou′zəl) *v.* To make untidy.—**tousled** *adj.*

towering (tou′ər-ĭng) *adj.* Of great height.

tranquil (trăn′kwəl) *adj.* Peaceful.—**tranquility** *n.*—**tranquilize** *v.* To calm.

transfix (trăns-fĭks′) *v.* **1.** To make motionless, as with amazement or awe. **2.** To pierce through.

transfusion (trăns-fyōō′zhən) *n.* The injection of large amounts of blood into the body.

transgression (trăns-grĕsh′ən, trănz-) *n.* The breaking of a law.

translucent (trăns-lōō′sənt, trănz-) *adj.* Almost transparent.

transparent (trăns-pâr′ənt, -păr′ənt) *adj.* Clear; able to be seen through.

traverse (trăv′ərs, trə-vûrs′) *v.* To cross; travel.

tread (trĕd) *n.* Step; to walk on.

tresses (trĕs-əz) *n.* Hair.

tribulation (trĭb′yə-lā′shən) *n.* Something that causes suffering or distress.

tribute (trĭb′yōōt) *n.* Money paid (out of fear) by one nation to another.

troubadour (trōō′bə-dôr′, -dōr′, -dōōr′) *n.* A traveling poet-musician.

trough (trôf, trŏf) *n.* **1.** A long narrow container used for water or feed for animals. **2.** Any similarly shaped container.

tumbler (tŭm′blər) *n.* **1.** An acrobat. **2.** A drinking glass. **3.** A part of a lock.

tumult (tōō′məlt, tyōō′-) *n.* A noisy disturbance.

tyranny (tĭr′ə-nē) *n.* Power that is used cruelly or unjustly.

U

ultimate (ŭl′tə-mĭt) *adj.* Final.

unabashed (ŭn′ə-băsht′) *adj.* Not embarrassed.

unapproachable (ŭn-ə-prō′chə-bəl) *adj.* Distant; not friendly.

unassuming (ŭn′ə-sōō′mĭng) *adj.* Humble; modest.

uncanny (ŭn′kăn′ē) *adj.* Strange; weird.—**uncannily** *adv.*

uncouth (ŭn′kōōth′) *adj.* **1.** *Archaic* Unfamiliar. **2.** Not refined; crude.

undaunted (ŭn′dôn′tĭd) *adj.* Not discouraged; not giving up.

ă pat/ā **pay**/âr **c**are/ä father/b **bib**/ch **church**/d **deed**/ĕ pet/ē be/f **fife**/g **gag**/h **h**at/hw **wh**ich/ĭ **p**it/ī **pie**/îr **pier**/j **judge**/k **kick**/
l lid, needle/m **mum**/n **no**, sudde**n**/ng thi**ng**/ŏ pot/ō toe/ô paw, for/oi n**oi**se/ou **out**/ŏŏ took/ōō boot/p **pop**/r **roar**/s **sauce**/
sh **ship**, di**sh**/t tight/th **thin**, pa**th**/*th* **th**is, ba**th**e/ŭ cut/ûr **urge**/v **valve**/w **with**/y **yes**/z **zebra**, si**ze**/zh vi**s**ion/ə **a**bout, it**e**m, edible, gallop, circus/à *Fr.* **a**mi/œ *Fr.* f**eu**, *Ger.* sch**ö**n/ü *Fr.* t**u**, *Ger.* **ü**ber/KH *Ger.* i**ch**, *Scot.* lo**ch**/N *Fr.* bo**n.**

understate (ŭn′dər-stāt′) *v.* To express in a restrained way.—**understated** *adj.*

ungainly (ŭn′gān′lē) *adj.* Awkward; clumsy.

unhygienic (ŭn′hī′jē-ĕn′īk) *adj.* Not healthful.

unkempt (ŭn-kĕmpt′) *adj.* Uncombed; messy.

unperceived (ŭn′pər-sēvd′) *adj.* Unseen; not noticed.

unwavering (ŭn′wā′vər-ĭng) *adj.* Steady; sure.

uproot (ŭp-rōot′, -rōot′) *v.* To remove completely.

urchin (ûr′chĭn) *n.* a mischievous youngster.

urn (ûrn) *n.* A vase containing the ashes of a cremated body.

V

vacuous (văk′yōo-əs) *adj.* **1.** Empty. **2.** Showing lack of intelligence or interest. **3.** Meaningless.

vagabond (văg′ə-bŏnd′) *n.* A tramp.

vain (vān) *adj.* Not successful.—**in vain.** To no use.

valiant (văl′yənt) *adj.* Brave.

valid (văl′ĭd) *adj.* True.

validate (văl′ə-dāt′) *v.* To declare something legal.

vandal (văn′dl) *n.* Someone who destroys or spoils someone else's property.

vanity (văn′ə-tē) *n.* **1.** The state of being overly proud and concerned about oneself. **2.** Uselessness.

variant (vâr′ē-ənt) *adj.* Differing.

vault (vôlt) *v.* To leap.

vaulted (vôlt′əd) *adj.* Having an arched ceiling.

veer (vîr) *v.* To turn.

vehement (vē′ə-mənt) *adj.* Very emotional; intense.—**vehemently** *adv.*—**vehemence** *n.*

venerable (věn′ər-ə-bəl) *adj.* Old and respected.

venture (věn′chər) *v.* **1.** To say at the risk of another's disapproval. **2.** To dare.—*n.* An undertaking which involves risk.

verify (věr′ə-fī) *v.* To prove that something is true.

verse (vûrs) *v.* To make familiar with.

vex (věks) *v.* To annoy.

vibrant (vī′brənt) *adj.* Full of life.

vigilant (vĭj′ə-lənt) *adj.* Watchful.—**vigilance** *n.*

virtuosity (vûr′chōo-ŏs′ə-tē) *n.* Skill.

visage (vĭz′ĭj) *n.* The face.

vocation (vō-kā′shən) *n.* A type of work.

vogue (vōg) *n.* Fashion.

void (void) *adj.* Not usable. *n.* Total emptiness; nothingness.

voracious (vô-rā′shəs, vō-, və-) *adj.* Greedy; ravenous.—**voraciously** *adv.*

W

wallop (wŏl′əp) *v.* To hit with a hard blow.

wallow (wŏl′ō) *v.* To flounder.

wampum (wŏm′pəm) *n.* Beads made from polished shells.

wane (wān) *v.* To dwindle.

wanton (wŏn′tən) *adj.* Without cause; reckless.—**wantonly** *adv.*

warrant (wôr′ənt, wŏr′-) *v.* To state; declare.

wary (wâr′ē) *adj.* Cautious.—**warily** *adv.*

waver (wā′vər) *v.* To become unsteady.

wayward (wā′wərd) *adj.* **1.** Not able to be controlled. **2.** Headstrong; willful.—**waywardness** *n.*

wean (wēn) *v.* To accustom a baby or young animal to food other than mother's milk.

wearisome (wîr′ē-səm) *adj.* Causing fatigue.

weathered (wěth-ərd) *adj.* Worn, as if by exposure to harsh conditions.

wedge (wěj) *n.* Anything that separates people or things.

well (wěl) *v.* To pour forth.

wigwam (wĭg′wŏm′) *n.* An American Indian dwelling, usually having an arched framework covered with hides or bark.

wily (wī′lē) *adj.* Tricky.

wince (wĭns) *v.* To shrink back or make a face, as if in pain.

windbreak (wĭnd′brāk′) *n.* A row of trees planted as a shelter from the wind.

winsome (wĭn′səm) *adj.* Pleasing; attractive.

wiry (wīr′ē) *adj.* Lean and strong.

wistful (wĭst′fəl) *adj.* Sad with longing.—**wistfully** *adv.*

wont (wônt, wōnt, wŭnt) *adj.* Used; accustomed.

woolgathering (wool′gă*th*′ər-ĭng) *n.* Daydreaming.

wrangle (răng′gəl) *v.* To argue.

wrath (răth, räth) *n.* Great anger.

writhe (rī*th*) *v.* To squirm.—**writhing** *adj.*

wrought (rôt) *v.* Formed.

wry (rī) *adj.* Ironic.

Outline OF *Concepts* AND *Skills*

Page numbers in italics refer to entries in Literary Terms and Techniques

READING/LITERARY SKILLS

Outline of Concepts and Skills

Outline of Concepts and Skills

Outline of Concepts and Skills

Index OF *Contents* BY *Types*

INDEX OF FINE ART TRANSPARENCIES BY TYPE

In the *Audiovisual Resources Binder,* you will find **Fine Art** transparencies that relate thematically to the literary units in the textbook. Each **Fine Art** transparency is accompanied by **Teacher's Notes** and student activity pages. Although these **Fine Art** transparencies are arranged in unit order, you may want to relate them to a variety of selections by genre, such as those listed below.

Folklore, Epics: For examples of people who overcome or persevere under challenging circumstances, see Transparencies 1, 28, 29, 46, and 47.

Short Stories: For family gatherings and multicultural celebrations, see Transparencies 6, 7, and 19.

Nonfiction: See Transparencies 2, 6, 7, 18, 19, 47 for activities and accomplishments of ordinary and extraordinary people.

Novel: For view of Native American heritage and belief, see Transparencies 38 and 39.

Plays: For public performances, audiences, and community, see Transparencies 23 and 24.

Poetry: For various human situations and conditions including separateness, generations, heritage, and heroism, see Transparencies 6, 7, 28, 33.

Index of Contents by Types

Index OF *Fine Art* AND *Illustrations*

Photo Credits

Index OF *Authors* AND *Titles*

The page numbers in italics indicate where a brief biography of the author is located.

Index of Authors and Titles